EXPLORING CORPORATE STRATEGY

Fifth edition

EXPLORING CORPORATE STRATEGY

Fifth edition

GERRY JOHNSON
Cranfield School of Management

KEVAN SCHOLES
Sheffield Business School

PRENTICE HALL EUROPE

London New York Toronto Sydney Tokyo Singapore
Madrid Mexico City Munich Paris

First published 1984
This fifth edition published 1999 by
Prentice Hall Europe
Campus 400, Maylands Avenue
Hemel Hempstead
Hertfordshire, HP2 7EZ
A division of
Simon & Schuster International Group

Typeset in 10/12pt Caslon 224 Book
by Mathematical Composition Setters Ltd, Salisbury, UK

Library of Congress Cataloging-in-Publication Data

Available from the publisher

British Library Cataloguing in Publication Data

A catalogue record for this book is available from the British Library

ISBN 0-13-080739-7 (text only)
ISBN 0-13-080740-0 (text & cases)

1 2 3 4 5 03 02 01 00 99

CONTENTS

Case Studies 547

N = New; U = Updated

STRATEGY IN ACTION: ILLUSTRATIONS

PREFACE

It has been many years since the first edition of *Exploring Corporate Strategy*. There have been many interesting and important developments in the subject of corporate strategy during that time. Equally important has been the vastly increased recognition of the importance of the subject to practising managers in both the public and the private sectors. This has been reflected in the widespread inclusion of corporate strategy in educational programmes at undergraduate, postgraduate and professional levels, as well as its adoption in short courses and consultancy assignments. It is now accepted that an understanding of the principles and practice of strategic issues is not just the concern of top managers, but essential for most levels of management – though clearly emphases within the subject will vary. We have consistently argued the importance of this wider 'uptake', so these are changes which we welcome.

The combined sales of our first four editions have exceeded 400,000. This fifth edition is being published only two years after the fourth edition. The overall structure of the book, of course, remains the same; and most of the content within this structure is substantially the same as for the fourth edition. There is, however, more attention given to the development of material to do with core competences, knowledge, learning and innovation and the linkages between these. A number of other concepts and approaches, for example corporate parenting, have been updated and revised. These changes are in response to requests and observations by readers and adopters of the book; and we are most grateful for these. A more substantial revision of content will of course follow for the 6th edition.

However, there are other changes to this 5th edition which are important. The design and layout has been changed substantially to improve readability. For example, each chapter has clear learning outcomes and a summary. Important 'definitions' are highlighted in the margins and there has been particular attention given to illustrations and case studies. All the 81 illustrations now have questions. This allows them to be used as mini-cases by tutors and for students to check out their own progress on understanding the text. We have also taken the opportunity to up-date and change many of the illustrations. A new feature of the book is case examples at the end of each chapter. We have also revised some of the case studies in the case collection and added 9 relatively brief additional case studies, again in response to requests from users of the book. *A guide to how to get the most from all the features and learning materials in/with* Exploring Corporate Strategy *follows this preface*.

Our aim has been to develop both the content and style of the book and we hope you will be pleased with the results of our efforts.

Exploring Corporate Strategy is not a book of corporate planning techniques, but rather builds on the practice of strategic management, as researchers and practitioners in the area understand it. It is a book primarily intended for students of strategy on undergraduate, diploma and master's courses in universities and colleges; students on courses with titles such as Corporate Strategy, Business Policy, Strategic Management, Organisational Policy and Corporate Policy. However, we know that many such students are already managers who are undertaking part-time study: so this book is written with the manager and the potential manager in mind.

The style of the book reflects our personal experience as active teachers and consultants for more than twenty years. It is the blending of theory with practice which is at the heart of good strategic management and the study of the subject should reflect that experiential learning, such as case studies is of great benefit in the study of strategy, for it allows students both to apply concepts and theories, and, just as improtantly, to build their own. However, it is also the case that the growing body of research and theory can be of great help in stimulating a deep understanding of strategic problems and strategic management. Our approach builds in substantial parts of such research and theory, and encourages readers to refer to more; but we also assume that readers will have the opportunity to deal with strategic problems through such means as case study work or projects, or, if they are practising managers, through their involvement in their own organisations. Our view in this respect is exactly the same as the writers of a medical or engineering text, and we encourage readers to take the same view. It is that good theory helps good practice, but that and understanding of the theory without an understanding of the practice is very dangerous particularly if you are treating a patient, building a bridge or, as with this book, dealing with organisations.

The text develops the theme that strategy and the management of strategy can be thought of in at least two rather different ways. First, it can be seen as analysis and planning. Second, it can be seen as a matter of *decision making* within a *political and cultural context*. Both these aspects of strategic management are relevant to the study of strategy, and the text incorporates both. For example, one of the themes running through the book is the importance of a clear analysis of the strategic situation facing the organisation and a rational assessment of the future options available to it. In considering such issues, the book includes, for example, discussion of the value of environmental audits, structural and strategic group analysis of competitive environments, value chain analysis, life cycle models of strategic analysis and choice, and the findings of those researchers who have tried to understand the relationship between strategic positioning of organisations and financial performance. The recent interest in resource-led strategies and the core competences of organisations is now given a much fuller treatment. In short, one of the themes is that the employment of rational models of analysis and choice in organisations is important to strategic management.

However, the book also draws on the growing research and literature on decision-making processes within a political and cultural context, considers explicitly how such influences can be understood and what mechanisms exist for managing strategic change within such systems. The book also recognises that strategic management is as relevant to the public sector and to not-for-profit organisations as it is to the private sector of industry and commerce. Indeed, the period since the first edition was published has seen unprecedented changes in the recognition of strategic management in the pubic sector against the background of significant changes in their role and method of operation. This 'new era' is reflected in discussions and examples throughout the book. We also have a good many references, examples and illustrations of the application of strategic management concepts to the public sector. Many of these changes in the public sector are also mirrored in the larger private sector organisations, and our coverage of the importance of organisation design and processes of resource allocation and control reflect these changes.

The structure of the book is explained in some detail in Chapter 1. However, it might be useful to give a brief outline here. The book is in four parts.

Part I comprises an introduction to corporate strategy, first in terms of its characteristics and the elements of strategic management (Chapter 1), and then in terms of how strategic decisions actually come about in organisations (Chapter 2), and also examines the relationship between organisational strategy and culture.

Part II is concerned with strategic analysis. Chapter 3 is concerned with organisations' position within their 'business' environment. This includes an analysis of organisations' competitive position. Chapter 4 analyses the factors underpinning strategic capability – particularly issues of analysing and understanding core competences. Chapter 5 is concerned with analysing and understanding organisational purposes. It is centred around the question of whom the organisation is there to serve and includes a discussion of corporate governance – with international comparisons.

Part III deals with strategic choice. Chapter 6 is concerned with analysing and establishing the broad bases of strategic choices. This includes positioning, generic product/market strategies, strategic intent, ownership, scope of activities and corporate parenting. Chapter 7 deals with choices of both strategic direction and method, including discussions of how core competences might provide directions for development and of strategic alliances. Chapter 8 is devoted to strategy evaluation and selection.

The final part – Part IV – is about strategy implementation. It picks up strongly the recent literature on strategic architecture. Chapter 9 is about organisation design through three levels of detail: structures, centralisation/devolution, and organisational configurations. Chapter 10 combines resource allocation and control in a way which reflects important new themes and changes: the importance of information technology, business process re- engineering, internal market mechanisms and the importance of shaping the context as well as the content of strategy. Chapter 11 considers approaches to and methods of managing change and provides important links back to Chapters 2 and 5.

Many people have helped us with the development of this new edition. First and foremost have been the adopters of the current edition – many of whom we have had the pleasure of meeting at our annual seminars. Many of you have provided us with constructive criticism and thoughts for the new edition – we hope you are happy with the results! Also, our students and clients at Sheffield and Cranfield are a constant source of ideas and challenge. It would be impossible to write a book of this type without this direct feedback. Our own work and contacts have expanded considerably as a result of our book and we now both have important links across the world who have been a source of stimulation to us. Our contacts in Ireland, Holland, Denmark, Sweden, France, Australia, New Zealand and Singapore are especially valued.

We would like to thank those who have contributed directly to the book by providing case studies, and those organisations which have been brave enough to be written up as case studies. The growing popularity of *Exploring Corporate Strategy* has often presented these case study companies with practical problems in coping with direct enquiries from tutors and students. We hope that those using the book will respect the wishes of the case study companies and not contact them directly for further information. *Sheffield Theatres Trust has made this a proviso of releasing the case study for inclusion*. Raje Jagden and Tony Clayton of PIMS Associates have been helpful in commenting on Chapters 7 and 8, as have Tony Grundy and David Pitt-Watson on Chapter 5 and 8 and Phyl Johnson on Chapters 2 and 3. Andrew Campbell of Ashridge Strategic Management Centre has also been especially helpful in revising and updating chapter 6. Special thanks are due to all those who provided and helped develop illustrations, their assistance is acknowledged at the foot of those illustrations – thank you to all these contributors. Special thanks are due to the library staff at Cranfield and Sheffield for their valuable assistance with references. Our thanks are also due to those who have had a part in preparing the manuscript for the book, particularly Claire Parkin at Sheffield and Alison Southgate at Cranfield.

Gerry Johnson
Kevan Scholes

November 1998

GETTING THE MOST FROM EXPLORING CORPORATE STRATEGY

Through the various editions of *Exploring Corporate Strategy* we have tried to respond to the continuing demand for more material while keeping the size of the text manageable for readers. These demands have included more depth in topics, more coverage of particular sectors or simply more examples and tasks for students. We have already produced additional materials and publications and now – in this fifth edition – we have changed the design and layout to assist readers in working through the text. We have also improved the cross-referencing to other material where it is relevant to a particular section of the text. This Guide gives practical advice on how you can get the best from the new learning features and the wide and varied range of materials which support the book.

USING EXPLORING CORPORATE STRATEGY

To get the most from *Exploring Corporate Strategy* and related materials the broad advice to students and managers is to ensure that you have achieved three things:

- you understand the concepts
- you can apply these concepts to practical situations – if you are a manager it is particularly important to apply the concepts to your own work context
- you read more widely than ECS.

FEATURES OF THE TEXT

- *Learning outcomes* are included at the beginning of each chapter which show what you should have achieved on completing the chapter. Check that you have understood all of these.
- *Key terms* are highlighted in the text and explained in the margins.
- *Strategy in Action: Illustration* boxes appear throughout the chapter and include questions so they can be used as 'mini' cases. Make sure that you read and answer these to check that you understand the theory/practice connection. If you are a manager, always ask yourself an additional question: 'what are the lessons for me and my

organisation from this example?'. Do this for the Case Examples and Case Studies too, if you can. The best strategic managers are those who can transfer learning from one situation to another.

- *Chapter summaries* help you to recap and review the main points of the chapter.
- *Recommended Key Readings* are listed at the end of each chapter. Make sure that you are familiar with those which are relevant to your course of study.
- *Work Assignments*, are now organised in two levels of difficulty. Your tutors may have set some of these as course tests. In any case, you should treat these in the way you would previous examination papers – as a means of testing your own learning of both concepts and applications. If you are a manager, take the opportunity to work through these assignments for your own organisation and involve other members of your team if you can.
- *Case Examples*, which are a new feature for this edition, are included at the end of each chapter to help you consolidate your learning of the major themes. Answer the questions at the end of the example.
- If you are using the *Case Studies* edition try to read the cases relevant to the topics on your course – even if they are not set as class work or assessments. The *Guide to Using Case Studies* on page 549 indicates the main focus of each case and the relevant chapter. Case Study introductions highlight which key learning points are covered by the case.

Check the Prentice Hall Website (see p. xxiv) regularly for updates and additional material and ask if your tutor has a copy of the *Exploring Corporate Strategy* video (see purchasing details on p. xxiv).

Part opening pages provide a brief explanation of the topics covered in the following chapters.

II

STRATEGIC ANALYSIS

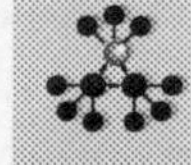

3

ANALYSING THE ENVIRONMENT

Learning Outcomes list what you should have achieved or understood by the end of each chapter.

Strategy in Action: illustrations appear throughout the text to illustrate the theory/practice connection.

Key terms are highlighted in the text with an explanation in the margin to emphasise some of the most important learning points.

36 • INTRODUCTION

themselves as managers at all. As a partner in a major accountancy firm put it: 'We see ourselves as the largest network of sole traders in the world.' The problems of developing and implementing strategy within such a context are, therefore, heavily linked to the management of internal political influences (see Chapter 5) and the ability to take account of, and where necessary to change, organisational culture (see Chapters 2 and 11). Another factor is the pressure those in the professions find themselves under to be more 'commercial' in their approach. Such pressure may come from government, as in the case of doctors; or it may be a function of size, as has been found in the growing accountancy firms. This has meant that such organisations have had to be concerned with competitive strategy (see Chapter 6).

SUMMARY

- Strategy is concerned with the long-term direction and development of an organisation, so all organisations are faced with the challenge of managing strategy.
- Strategy is the direction and scope of an organisation over the long term, which achieves advantage for the organisation through its configuration of resources within a changing environment, to meet the needs of markets and to fulfil stakeholder expectations.
- Strategic decisions may be about a search for strategic 'fit', by which is meant trying to find ways to match the organisation's activities to the environment in which it operates. Strategic decisions could also be based on trying to 'stretch' the resources and competences of the organisation to create new opportunities, even new markets.
- Strategies will also be influenced by the values and expectations of stakeholders in and around the organisation, and the extent of the power they exert. The culture within which the organisation exists and the culture of the organisation itself will also influence its strategy.
- Strategic decisions are made at a number of levels in organisations. Corporate-level strategy is concerned with an organisation's overall purpose and scope; business unit (or competitive) strategy with how to compete successfully in a market; and operational strategies with how resources, processes and people can effectively deliver corporate- and business-level strategies.
- The formulation of business-level strategies is best thought of in terms of strategic business units which are parts of organisations for which there are distinct external markets for goods or services. These may not represent formal structural divisions in an organisation, however.
- Strategic management is distinguished from day-to-day operational management by the complexity of influences on decisions, the fundamental, organisation-wide implications that strategic decisions

CORPORATE STRATEGY: AN INTRODUCTION • 37

have for the organisation, and their long-term implications. It can be problematic for managers not least because their strategic horizons are likely to be limited by their experience and organisational culture and most of their training may have been in operational management.
- Strategic management can be conceived of in terms of strategic analysis, strategic choice and strategy implementation. Strategic analysis is the process of trying to understand the strategic position of the organisation in terms of its external environment, internal resources and competences, and the expectations and influence of stakeholders. Strategic choice involves understanding the underlying bases guiding future strategy, generating strategic options for evaluation and selecting from among them. Strategy implementation is concerned with the translation of strategy into organisational activity through organisational structure and design, resource planning and the management of strategic change.
- There are different explanations of how strategy is actually managed in organisations, varying from those which emphasise high degrees of managerial choice and control to those which argue that managers actually have much less influence than they think.
- Different organisations in different contexts are likely to emphasise different aspects of the strategic management process. For some the major challenge will be developing competitive strategy; for yet others it will be building organisational structures capable of integrating complex global operations; for yet others it will be understanding their competences so as to focus on what they are especially good at; and for still others it will be developing a culture of innovation. Strategic priorities need to be understood in terms of the particular context of an organisation.

RECOMMENDED KEY READINGS

It is useful to read about how strategies are managed in practice and some of the lessons which can be drawn from this which inform key themes in this book. For example:

- For readings on the concepts of strategy in organisations, John Kay's book, *Foundations for Corporate Success: How business strategies add value*, Oxford University Press, 1993, is a helpful explanation from an economics point of view. For a wider theoretical perspective, see R. Whittington, *What is Strategy and Does it Matter?*, Routledge, 1993.
- It is also useful to read accounts of where the management of strategy in organisations has made an impact on organisational performance. Reference is also often made in this book to G. Hamel and C.K. Prahalad, *Competing for the Future*, Harvard Business School Press, 1994, which draws extensively on examples of successful strategies in organisations.
- For a discussion of strategy in different types of organisations, see H. Mintzberg, J. Quinn and S. Ghoshal (eds), *The Strategy Process: Concepts, contexts and cases*, 4th edition, Prentice Hall, 1998.

Recommended key readings provide sources for additional study on particular topics or concepts

Summaries recap and review the main points of the chapter

90 • INTRODUCTION

WORK ASSIGNMENTS

2.1. Read the annual report of a company with which you are familiar as a customer (for example a retailer or transport company). Identify the main characteristics of the *intended* strategy as explained in the annual report; and the characteristics of the *realised* strategy as you perceive it as a customer.

2.2 Using the categories explained in sections 2.3 to 2.6, characterise how strategies have developed in different organisations (e.g. New Town,* Castle Press,* Iona,* KPMG*).

2.3 ● Planning systems exist in many different organisations. What role should planning play in the National Health Service (see Illustration 2.2), a multinational corporation such as IKEA (see Illustration 1.1), Nokia* or The News Corporation.*

2.4 With reference to the explanations of incremental strategy development in Illustration 2.3, what are the main advantages and disadvantages in trying to develop strategies incrementally?

2.5 ● What is the difference between 'logical incrementalism', 'muddling through' and 'intuitive management'? (References 12, 13, 16 and 28 will be helpful here.)

2.6 ● Incremental patterns of strategy development are common in organisations, and managers see advantages in this. However, there are also risks of strategic drift. How might such drift be avoided while retaining the benefits of incremental strategy development? (Reference to the recommended readings by Quinn, Miller and Senge could be useful here.)

* refers to a case study in the Text and Cases edition.
● denotes more advanced work assignments.

STRATEGIC MANAGEMENT IN PRACTICE • 91

CASE EXAMPLE

*KPMG (A): Strategy Development in a Partnership**

By 1997 KPMG had grown to be the largest professional services firm in the world with over 78,000 staff in 153 countries. Although parts of the enterprise had been incorporated, KPMG remained a partnership or, to be more precise, a federation of many partnerships spread across the world. Over the years the firm had grown, prospered and amalgamated with others to become the huge enterprise it was. It was undeniably a success story; yet this was a business facing an increasingly competitive environment on a global basis. There was a need to develop strategies appropriate to these changing conditions.

The Partnership Heritage

From 1993 to 1997 Colin Sharman had been the UK senior partner of KPMG. In March 1997 he also took over as international chairman. Sharman had been responsible for the review of strategy that had taken place in KPMG in the UK in the 1990s and was acutely aware of what it meant to manage strategy in a partnership. He emphasised that in the UK, for example, where there were 600 partners, they were 'owners who also work in the business. It's rather like a large family company in which the owners come to work in it every day'. As a matter of law, these partners had to be consulted on certain matters, for example taking leases on new properties.

In common with many partnerships, the legacy was an emphasis on powerful, influential individual partners, skilled in their areas of professional expertise and with strong personal relations at senior level with clients. Such a partner would typically have been a chartered accountant who had spent ten to fifteen years in the firm working his or her way up to a senior client management position in a specialist area such as audit or tax. Given a successful record in developing business with clients and providing first class professional services, the appointment to partner might take place, providing existing partners were in agreement. Thereafter the new partner would seek to further a reputation for winning new clients, building relationships with existing clients and ensuring excellence of service by cultivating a network of trusted managers and other partners with whom he or she would co-operate.

Attempts to formalise strategic planning in such a context were difficult. In the past in KPMG, committees had been set up to do it or partners given special responsibility for it; but whilst planning procedures or plans themselves might be evident, they did little to change the way in which the firm developed. The successful growth of the past had come about on the basis of excellence of professional advice given to clients and through longstanding relationships built by experienced partners. The strategic direction emerged from this. Where there were problems or disagreements, these were resolved between the partners themselves.

The Situation in 1992

The review of KPMG's strategy began in 1992, when Colin Sharman took over responsibility for KPMG's largest UK region (the south east), with 300 of the UK partners. He described what he inherited:

> In many respects the way we did things had its benefits. It was based on a network of very bright people, professionally trained and dedicated to providing quality advice to their clients. But

* This case can be used in conjunction with case studies B and C describing subsequent developments in KPMG in the Text and Cases version of this book.

Case examples at the end of each chapter help consolidate your learning of the major themes.

Work Assignments, now organised into two levels of difficulty, can be used as a means of testing your learning of theory and concepts.

TEACHING AND LEARNING RESOURCES

Prentice Hall Website (www.prenhall.co.uk)

Material for students and tutors is added and updated on a regular basis including:

- topical material which relates to themes in the book
- updates/cross-references to case studies
- work assignments
- tutor support material

Exploring Corporate Strategy – the Video

Designed to assist tutors, the video is modular in format and lasts for a total of 75 minutes. Coverage:

- strategy in different contexts
- the Cultural Web
- Four of the case studies from the 5th edition
  - Brewery Group Denmark – development and management of international strategy
  - KPMG – the management of strategic change
  - Burmah Castrol Chemicals Group – corporate parenting, portfolio management and corporate structure in an international context
  - Iona Community – mission and stakeholder analysis

The video can be purchased through Sheffield Hallam University Press, Sheffield S1 1WB.

The Exploring Strategic Management Series

This new series from Prentice Hall builds on readers' knowledge of *Exploring Corporate Strategy* and provides more depth by topic or sector. All these books have been written in conjunction with Gerry Johnson and Kevan Scholes. Books available are:

- V Ambrosini with G Johnson and K Scholes *Exploring Techniques of Analysis and Evaluation in Strategic Management*; ISBN: 0-13-570680-7
- T Grundy with G Johnson and K Scholes *Exploring Strategic Financial Management*; ISBN: 0-13-570102-3
- J Balogun and V Hope-Hailey with G Johnson and K Scholes *Exploring Strategic Change*; ISBN: 0-13-263856-8

A NOTE FOR TUTORS

Instructor's Manual

A comprehensive set of supporting material for tutors including:

- how to plan programmes using the text
- using the case studies
- Teaching notes for case studies
- tutor briefs for chapter end work assignments and questions linked to illustrations

Since the first publication of the book we have always been concerned that good quality practical support and advice to tutors is provided. This has been one of the driving forces behind the growth of the support material. The advice above for students and managers is also likely to be relevant to tutors.

Since 1989 we have run annual one-day workshops for tutors (also in Scotland since 1995). These have proved to be very popular with both experienced tutors and those who are new to the subject.

We now hope that the exploitation of our website will make this support more comprehensive, more universal in coverage and more consistent in terms of the support tutors can expect, irrespective of their location.

We are always happy to receive feedback from users of the book. Contact us at KScholes@scholes.u-net.com or G.Johnson@cranfield.ac.uk

THE AUTHORS

Gerry Johnson BA PhD (left) is Professor of Strategic Management at Cranfield School of Management. He is author of numerous books and papers on Strategic Management, is a member of the editorial board of the Strategic Management Journal and referees for many European and US academic journals. His research work is primarily concerned with processes of strategy development and change in organisations. He is a regular visitor to universities throughout Europe, the USA and Australasia; and he works extensively as a consultant at a senior level on issues of strategy formulation and strategic change with many UK and international firms.

Kevan Scholes MA, PhD, DMS, CIMgt, FRSA (right) is Principal Partner of Scholes Associates – a consultancy specialising in strategic management. He is also Visiting Professor of Strategic Management and formerly Director of Sheffield Business School, UK. He has extensive lecturing and consultancy experience of both public and private sector organisations. This includes a wide range of on-going international work in Ireland, Australia, New Zealand and Singapore. He has a special interest in the strategic management of Professional Service Organisations. He has also been an advisor on management development to a number of national bodies and is a Companion of the Institute of Management.

I
INTRODUCTION

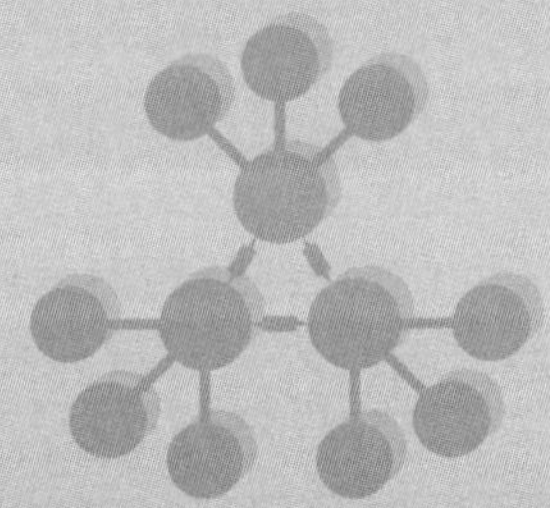

THIS PART EXPLAINS:

- The concepts and some of the main terms necessary to understand the field of strategy and strategic management.
- The structure of this book: in particular what is meant by strategic analysis, strategic choice and strategy implementation, how these relate to each other and how they may differ by organisational context.
- Different explanations about how strategies develop in organisations and evidence as to how these, again, differ by organisational context.

Chapter 1 explains why the study of strategic management is important, how it differs from other aspects of management and explains some of the main concepts and terms used throughout the rest of the book. It also provides a framework for thinking about strategic management in terms of ways of understanding strategic issues (strategic analysis), bases and means of deciding on strategies to be followed (strategic choice) and the main issues that need to be tackled in making strategies happen (strategy implementation). It goes on to show that different aspects of strategic management are likely to be important in different contexts; the small business context is, for example, very different from the multi-national business; public sector organisations and not-for-profit organisations will also be different.

The framework introduced in Chapter 1 is useful for thinking about the problems of strategic management. However, strategies followed by organisations do not come about solely as a result of managers thinking about strategic issues. Chapter 2 introduces a second major theme of the book; namely that we also need to understand the practice of strategic management as it actually occurs in organisations. This chapter shows how strategies develop over time in organisations and explores in more detail different explanations and research evidence about how strategic decisions come about. It reaches the conclusion that, whilst the framework explained in Chapter 1 is, indeed, useful for thinking about the problems and issues of strategic management, the way strategies come about is related to the cultural and political processes at work in organisations. Exploring the topic of strategic management therefore also requires that these organisational processes are taken into account.

The challenge of strategic management is to be able to think through complex issues facing organisations about their long-term direction, formulate clear views as to what direction should be followed in the future and manage this within the day-to-day realities of how the organisation functions. These two chapters in Part I set out how this book can help readers address this challenge.

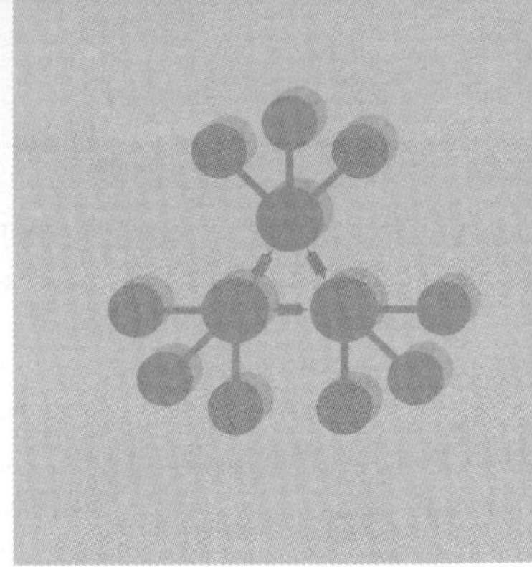

1
CORPORATE STRATEGY: AN INTRODUCTION

LEARNING OUTCOMES

After reading this chapter you should be able to:

- Describe the characteristics of strategic decisions.
- Define what is meant by strategy and strategic management.
- Identify strategic business units (SBUs) in organisations.
- Explain how strategic priorities vary by level: corporate, business and operational.
- Understand the vocabulary of strategy.
- Explain the elements of the *Johnson and Scholes* strategic management model (see Exhibits 1.3 and 1.4).
- Explain the difference between strategy as 'fit' and 'stretch'.
- Understand what distinguishes strategic management from operational management.
- Understand which elements of the strategy model are likely to be most important in different contexts.

By 1998 Ingvar Kamprad had seen IKEA transformed from the mail-order furniture business he set up in Sweden in 1949 into a £3 billion plus retail furnishing empire with 139 stores in 28 countries. Retail commentators and business analysts saw the firm as a major success story; success based on the unique benefits it offered to customers and its consistent implementation of a clear long-term strategy. The issue that faced Ingvar Kamprad, the founder, and Anders Moberg, the chief executive of IKEA, was how to continue the success of the past. Illustration 1.1 gives an overview of the developments of IKEA.

The approach IKEA had taken to meeting customer needs and developing its business had followed a consistent pattern over many years. However, the changes that had taken place, albeit incrementally, had substantially changed the direction of the business in that time: they were changes which were long-term in nature and had far-ranging implications for organisational structure and control and the logistics of the operation.

They also raised challenges for the future. In short, they were major *strategic* developments.

All organisations are faced with the need to manage strategic development: some from a position of strength, like IKEA; some needing to overcome significant problems. This book deals with why reviews of strategic direction take place in organisations, why they are important, how such decisions are taken, and some of the tools and techniques that managers can use to take strategic decisions. This chapter is an introduction and explanation of this theme, and deals with the questions of what is meant by 'strategy' and 'strategic management', why they are so important and what distinguishes them from other organisational tasks and decisions. In discussing these it will become clearer how the book deals with the subject area as a whole. The chapter draws on IKEA's development for the purposes of discussion; and as the book progresses, other such illustrative 'strategies in action' are used to help develop discussion.

One other point should be made before proceeding. The term 'corporate strategy' is used here for two main reasons. First, because the book is concerned with strategy and strategic decisions in all types of organisation – small and large commercial enterprises as well as public services – and the word 'corporate' embraces them all. Second, because, as the term is used in this book (discussed more fully in section 1.1.2), 'corporate strategy' denotes the most general level of strategy in an organisation and in this sense embraces other levels of strategy. Readers will undoubtedly come across other terms, such as 'strategic management', 'business policy' and 'organisational strategy', all of which are used to describe the same general topic.

1.1 THE NATURE OF STRATEGY AND STRATEGIC DECISIONS

Why are the issues facing IKEA described as 'strategic'? What types of decisions are strategic decisions, and what distinguishes these from other decisions no doubt being taken in the company?

1.1.1 The Characteristics of Strategic Decisions

The characteristics usually associated with the words 'strategy' and 'strategic decisions' are these.

- Strategic decisions are likely to be concerned with or affect the *long-term direction* of an organisation. IKEA set out along a path which was difficult to reverse. In the 1950s and 1960s the company could have been defined, essentially, as a Scandinavian furnishing retailer. By the late 1990s the whole thrust of its strategy had shifted to a global scale and IKEA was facing the challenge of how to develop into the twenty-first century. In so doing it had to consider other key issues.

- Strategic decisions are normally about trying to achieve some *advantage* for the organisation, for example over competition. IKEA had been successful not because it was the same as all other furniture retailers, but because it was different and offered particular benefits which distinguished it from other retailers. Similarly, strategic advantage could be thought of as providing higher quality value-for-money services than other providers in the public sector, thus attracting support and funding from government. Strategic decisions are sometimes conceived of, therefore, as the search for effective *positioning* in relation to competitors so as to achieve advantage in a market or in relation to suppliers.
- Strategic decisions are likely to be concerned with the *scope of an organisation's activities*: does (and should) the organisation concentrate on one area of activity, or should it have many? For example, for years IKEA had defined the *boundaries* of its business in terms of the type of product ('furnishing items of good design and function') and mode of service (large retail outlets and mail order). While not owning its manufacturing, it did have an in-house design capability which specified and controlled what manufacturers supplied to the company. There were signs by the late 1990s, however, that IKEA was extending its product scope from furnishings into other product areas, as with its experiments with housing. Over the years it had also substantially widened its geographical scope to become one of the few truly multinational retailers in the world.

  The issue of scope of activity is fundamental to strategic decisions because it concerns the way in which those responsible for managing the organisation conceive the organisation's boundaries. It is to do with what they want the organisation to be like and to be about.
- Strategy can be seen as the *matching of the activities of an organisation to the environment* in which it operates. This is sometimes known as the search for *strategic fit*.[1] While the market for furnishings was mature, with little prospect of overall growth, the management of IKEA had seen that the retail provision of furnishing in most countries did not meet the expectations of customers. Customers frequently had to wait for delivery of items which were highly priced. The market provided another opportunity. Customer tastes were relatively common in different countries except in specialised segments of the market: buyers wanted everyday furniture which was well designed and looked good, but which was reasonably priced.

IKEA also knew that it faced significant differences in its markets. By the 1990s the number of countries in which IKEA was represented was a great deal larger than in the company's early days. This meant that IKEA had to understand buying habits and preferences from a much wider base, from markets close to its Swedish home, to the USA, and even to the Far East and eastern Europe.

STRATEGY IN ACTION
Illustration 1.1

IKEA

Managing strategy requires the consideration of a wide range of factors to develop a coherent long-term direction for an organisation.

In 1953, just four years after Ingvar Kamprad had produced his first mail order catalogue featuring locally produced furniture, he opened his first store in Almhult, Sweden. Since then, he and his successors have created a global network of stores in 28 countries. Initially stores were opened only in Scandinavia, but as greater levels of success were experienced, stores were built in countries further afield where the rewards, but also the risks of failure, were much higher. In all these countries the retailing concept of Ingvar Kamprad remained the same: 'to offer a wide range of furnishing items of good design and function at prices so low that the majority of people can afford to buy them'.

In the 1980s, Anders Moberg became the chief executive. However, the influence of Ingvar Kamprad could still be found. IKEA had always been frugal in its approach. In its early years it had relocated to Denmark to escape Swedish taxation. Echoes of the same philosophy and style could be seen in Anders Moberg. He would arrive at the office in the company Nissan Primera, dressed in informal clothes, and clock in just as other employees did. When abroad he travelled on economy class air tickets and stayed in modest hotels. He expected his executives to do likewise. Such prudence was extended to the company whose shares were held in trust by a Dutch charitable foundation and not traded. Furthermore, IKEA's expansion plans envisaged only internal funding with 15 per cent of turnover being reinvested.

The 1980s saw rapid growth. IKEA benefited from changing customer attitudes, from status and designer labels to functionality, encouraged by an economic recession. It also developed a number of unique elements which came to make up IKEA's winning business formula: simple, high quality Scandinavian design, global sourcing of components, knock-down furniture kits that customers transported and assembled themselves, huge suburban stores with plenty of parking and amenities such as cafés, restaurants, wheelchairs and even supervised child-care facilities. A key feature of IKEA's concept was universal customer appeal crossing national boundaries, with both the products and shopping experience designed to support this appeal. Customers came from different lifestyles: from new homeowners to business executives needing more office capacity. They all expected well styled, high quality home furnishings, reasonably priced and readily available. IKEA met this expectation by encouraging customers to create value for themselves by taking on certain tasks traditionally done by the manufacturer and retailer, for example the assembly and delivery of products to their homes.

IKEA made sure that every aspect of its business system was designed to make it easy for customers to adapt to their new role. For example, information to assist customers make their purchase decisions was provided in a 200-page glossy catalogue; during their visit to the store customers were supplied with tape measures, pens and notepaper to reduce the number of sales staff required; furniture was displayed in 100 model rooms; and sales staff were expected to involve themselves with customers only when asked.

To deliver low-cost yet high-quality products consistently, IKEA also had 30 buying offices around the world whose prime purpose was to identify potential suppliers. Designers at headquarters then reviewed these to decide which would provide what for each of the products, their overall aim being to design for low cost and ease of manufacture. The most economical suppliers were always chosen over traditional suppliers, so a shirt manufacturer might be employed to produce seat covers. Although the process through which acceptance to become an IKEA supplier was not easy, it was highly coveted, for, once part of the IKEA system, suppliers gained access to global markets, and received technical assistance, leased equipment, and advice on how to bring production up to world quality standards. By the mid 1990s IKEA was offering a range of 12,000 items, from 1,800 suppliers in 45 countries at prices 20–40 per cent lower than for comparable goods. However, by 1998 the means of achieving low cost was receiving some critical attention. It was reported that IKEA was sourcing its goods from suppliers in eastern Europe which paid its workers poverty level wages (see Illustration 5.5).

Having to cope with widely dispersed sources of components and high-volume orders, made it imperative for IKEA to have an efficient system for ordering its supplies, integrating them into products and delivering them to the stores. This was achieved through a world network of fourteen warehouses. These provided storage but also acted as logistical control points, consolidation centres and transit hubs, and aided the integration of supply and demand, reducing the need to store production runs for long periods, holding down unit costs by minimising the costs of inventory and helping stores to anticipate needs and eliminate shortages.

By the end of the 1990s IKEA was turning its attention to new opportunities for growth. It had opened stores in eastern Europe and the one-time Soviet republics, believing these represented great future potential. In 1997 it announced its plan to open twelve new stores a year internationally in cities such as Frankfurt, Shanghai, Chicago, and Roclab in Poland and to double manufacturing capacity by building up to twenty factories in eastern Europe by 2002. There were also plans to develop new areas of business. In partnership with a building contractor, IKEA was market testing in Sweden 'flat packed' housing which could be assembled by two men and a crane in a week at prices about 30 per cent less than the going rate. It was also developing new sources of supply, entering into an agreement with a timber company to develop new wood material for furniture. However, the company was also facing problems. IKEA was experiencing growing competition on an international front. It had decided to implement a programme of cost savings, rationalising its supply chain and product range in order to cut purchasing costs by an overall average of 10 per cent. The company had stated the intention of cutting what had become 2,400 suppliers by one-quarter and focusing on increased volumes with a smaller range of products and fewer suppliers.

In 1996, Ingvar Kamprad announced that IKEA would be split into three, comprising the retailing operations, an organisation holding the franchise and trademarks, and a third arm involved mainly in finance and banking. The first two would form the core of the group, controlled at arm's length by trust-like organisations; the latter's shares would be jointly owned by Kamprad's three sons. The structure was devised in an effort to ensure that the privately held organisation should not be broken up or sold off in a succession battle after Ingvar Kamprad retired. He also wanted to ensure that it would not be put under the sorts of external pressures for continual growth often faced by publicly quoted companies. Internally, IKEA's strategy was managed at different levels. A committee of senior executive at headquarters in Denmark was responsible for overseeing investment in new markets and stores; responsibility for product development and purchasing lay with IKEA of Sweden; and country managers tailored the presentation and marketing of products to home territories.

Questions

1. Using the characteristics discussed in section 1.1.1 write out a statement of strategy for IKEA.
2. With reference to section 1.2.5 in particular, note down the characteristics of IKEA's strategy which could be explained by the notions of:
   (a) strategic management as 'environmental fit'
   (b) strategic management as the 'stretching' of capabilities.

Sources R. Norman and R. Ramirez, 'From value chain to value constellation: designing interactive strategy', *Harvard Business Review*, vol. 71, no. 4(1993), pp. 65–77, company data and newspaper articles.

IKEA could no longer assume that its knowledge of earlier markets would necessarily apply: for example, it had found that shopping habits in the USA differed substantially from those in Europe, and this had required a change in the way it serviced the market. Therefore, while the principles of IKEA's business idea were adhered to around the world to produce a consistent product quality and shopping experience, store management had been given a greater degree of freedom to adapt to local market needs.

IKEA's management had, however, decided that there were some markets, attractive though they were, where it did not make sense to try to control IKEA's operations directly. Here the company recognised that local knowledge in fine-tuning the business to local needs was vital; or the problems of long-distance control were too great to manage the operation effectively on this basis. It had, therefore, established local joint ventures through franchise arrangements.

There were wider environmental issues which affected IKEA's fortunes; for example, IKEA was less susceptible to economic downturn than many of its competitors. This may have been because its prices were often lower; but it was also because, when a customer took a purchasing decision at IKEA, he or she walked away with the goods. In other stores, since delivery was often delayed, purchase decisions were also often delayed. Economic conditions in the different countries in which IKEA operated did, however, affect its success: for example, the growth in car ownership, particularly in less highly developed countries, determined the percentage of the population which could shop at an IKEA store.

Taking a *strategic fit* approach to strategy development means, as in the case of IKEA, trying to identify the opportunities which exist in the environment and tailoring the future strategy of the firm to capitalise on these, for example by locating in particularly favourable markets or seeking to appeal to attractive market segments.

- However, strategy can also be seen as *building on or 'stretching' an organisation's resources and competences* to create opportunities or to capitalise on them.[2] This does not just mean trying to ensure that resources are available, or can be made available, to take advantage of some new opportunity in the market place. Rather, it means identifying existing resources and competences which might be a basis for creating new opportunities in the market place. IKEA illustrates this well.

The product range IKEA had designed and developed was not only low cost but unique, not only because of its kit form but also in its style and image. Moreover, IKEA benefited from years of design experience dedicated to its operation and markets. Product range was further enhanced by the design of the stores, even down to the food served in them. The logistics of the operation, from sourcing of products to control of stock and the immediate supply of the product to take away, had been learned over many years and provided not only a quite distinct way of operating, but a service greatly appreciated by customers. In short, both the physical aspects of resources and the experience built up over the years had been consciously developed to service the evident opportunity in the market place. However, all of this experience had been employed, in effect 'stretched', to create a different market opportunity and way of doing business from that which had previously existed in the furniture market. IKEA's approach had been described as follows:

> IKEA set out systematically to reinvent value and the business system that delivers it for an entire cast of economic actors. The work-sharing, co-productive arrangements the company offers to customers and suppliers alike force both to think about value in a new way – one in which customers are also suppliers. Suppliers are also customers and IKEA itself is not so much a retailer as the central star in a constellation of services, goods, design, management, support and even entertainment.[3]

Of course, in practice, organisations develop strategies on the bases of both environmental 'fit' and 'stretch'. IKEA's experiment with housing in the late 1990s was, presumably, the result of identifying a possible market opportunity; but it was also an attempt to capitalise on its skills in developing kit-form products at low cost.

- Strategies may require *major resource* changes for an organisation. For example, the decision that IKEA took to develop its operations internationally had significant implications in terms of its need to obtain properties for development and access to funds by which to do this, sometimes for projects which might be seen as high risk – for example, entering new markets in times of recession. The size of the operation in terms of numbers of people working in it, property and physical stock held had to rise significantly. The need to control a multinational enterprise, as opposed to a national operation, also began to require skills and control systems of a different sort. It was a problem which many retailers had found difficulty coping with. A major reason has been that retailers underestimate the extent to which their resource commitments rise and how the need to control them takes on quite different proportions. Strategies, then, need to be considered not only in terms of the extent to which the existing resource capability of the organisation is suited to opportunities, but also in terms of the extent to which resources can be obtained and controlled to develop a strategy for the future.
- Strategic decisions are therefore likely to *affect operational decisions*: for example, the internationalisation of IKEA required a whole series of decisions at operational level. Management and control structures to deal with the geographical spread of the firm had to change. The way in which suppliers were controlled and the methods of developing and distributing stock required revision to deal with the extended distribution logistics. Marketing and advertising policies needed to be reviewed by country to ensure their suitability to different customer behaviours and tastes. Personnel policies and practices had to be reviewed. Store operations needed to change too: for example, in the

USA, IKEA saw the need to add to the core product range from local suppliers, install serviced loading bays, and erect bollards to stop the shopping trolleys being taken to all parts of the car parks, which are very large in the USA.

This link between overall strategy and operational aspects of the organisation is important for two other reasons. First, if the operational aspects of the organisation are not in line with the strategy, then, no matter how well considered the strategy is, it will not succeed. Second, it is at the operational level that real strategic advantage can be achieved. IKEA has been successful not only because of a good strategic concept, but also because the detail of how the concept is put into effect – the *strategic architecture* – in terms of its logistics of buying and servicing, shop layout and merchandising to supplier and customer relations, all developed over many years, is difficult to imitate.[4]

- The strategy of an organisation is affected not only by environmental forces and resource availability, but also by the *values and expectations* of those who have *power* in and around the organisation. In some respects, strategy can be thought of as a reflection of the attitudes and beliefs of those who have most influence on the organisation. Whether a company is expansionist or more concerned with consolidation, and where the boundaries are drawn for a company's activities, may say much about the values and attitudes of those who influence strategy – the *stakeholders* of the organisation. In IKEA the insistence on internal financing influenced long-term development and the direction of the company: the influences of the founder and chief executive remained pronounced. The emphasis on frugality and simplicity clearly influenced the way the company operated. Indeed, critics pointed to what they saw as a disregard for the well-being and welfare of the low-paid workers of suppliers in the name of keeping down costs (see Illustration 5.5).

  There are, of course, other stakeholders who have influence: in many companies, shareholders or financial institutions; certainly management and the workforce, buyers and perhaps suppliers; and the local community. The beliefs and values of these stakeholders will have a more or less direct influence on the strategy development of an organisation.

strategy *is the direction and scope of an organisation over the long term: which achieves advantage for the organisation through its configuration of resources within a changing environment, to meet the needs of markets and to fulfil stakeholder expectations*

Overall, if a *definition* of a strategy is required, the most basic is that it is the long-term direction of an organisation. However, these characteristics can provide a basis for a more complete definition:

> **Strategy** is the *direction* and *scope* of an organisation over the *long term*: which achieves *advantage* for the organisation through its configuration of *resources* within a changing *environment*, to meet the needs of *markets* and to fulfil *stakeholder* expectations.

A consequence of these characteristics of strategic decisions is that they are likely to be *complex in nature*. This is especially so in organisations with wide geographical scope, such as multinational firms, or wide ranges of products or services. However, there are other significant problems in developing effective strategies. Strategic decisions may also have to be made in situations of *uncertainty*: they may involve taking decisions on views of the future which it is impossible for managers to be sure about. Strategic decisions are also likely to demand an *integrated* approach to managing the organisation. Unlike functional problems, there is no one area of expertise, or one perspective, that can define or resolve the problems. Managers, therefore, have to cross functional and operational boundaries to deal with strategic problems and come to agreements with other managers who, inevitably, have different interests and perhaps different priorities. They also have to manage and perhaps change relationships and networks outside the organisation, for example with suppliers, distributors and customers.[5] Strategic decisions may also involve *change* in organisations. Not only is it problematic to decide upon and plan those changes, it is even more problematic to implement them if the organisation has been used to operating in ways, perhaps developed over years, which are not in line with the desired future strategy.

1.1.2 Levels of Strategy

Strategies exist at a number of levels in an organisation. Individuals may say they have a strategy – to do with their career, for example. This may be relevant when considering influences on strategies adopted by organisations, but it is not the subject of this book. Taking IKEA as an example, it is possible to distinguish at least three different levels of organisational strategy. **Corporate strategy** is concerned with the overall purpose and scope of the organisation to meet the expectations of owners or major stakeholders and add value to the different parts (often individual businesses) of the enterprise.

corporate strategy *is concerned with the overall purpose and scope of the organisation to meet the expectations of owners or major stakeholders and add value to the different parts of the enterprise*

For example, for IKEA, as for many corporate headquarters, a significant issue was how broad the organisation should be in terms of its types of businesses and geographical coverage. Clearly the decision has been taken to become multinational, but just which geographical regions and locations should this include? There was also consideration by the end of the 1990s about the types of product or service that should be offered; the move into housing is an example here. Decisions also have to be taken at the corporate centre about the basis of allocation of resources to the different IKEA operations across the world. In so doing the corporate centre should be asking just how it adds value to the operating businesses within the group. It might argue, for example, that the provision of services from the centre and the overall direction of a coherent strategy across the world does so. Corporate-level strategy is also likely to be concerned with the expectations of owners. In the case of IKEA this took form in the way in which the firm was structured to maintain its independence according to the wishes of its founder.

In other publicly quoted businesses, corporate-level strategy is heavily influenced by the expectations of shareholders and the stock market. Being clear about this corporate level of strategy can be important; it is a *basis* of other strategic decisions. It may well take form in an explicit or implicit statement of 'mission' which reflects such expectations.

business unit strategy *is about how to compete successfully in a particular market*

The second level can be thought of in terms of **business unit strategy**. Here strategy is about how to compete successfully in a particular market: the concerns are therefore about how advantage over competitors can be achieved; what new opportunities can be identified or created in markets; which products or services should be developed in which markets; and the extent to which these meet customer needs in such a way as to achieve the objectives of the organisation – perhaps long-term profitability, market growth or measures of efficiency. So, whereas corporate strategy involves decisions about the organisation as a whole, strategic decisions here need to be related to a **strategic business unit** (SBU).[6] A SBU is a part of the organisation for which there is a distinct external market for goods or services (i.e. distinct from another SBU). In public sector organisations a corresponding definition of a SBU might be a part of the organisation or service for which there is a distinct client group. At this level of strategy, the basis of strategic decisions is how customer or client needs can best be met, usually to achieve some sort of competitive advantage for the organisation. It is therefore very important that there is clarity about the needs of customers (or clients) and who competitors are for a particular SBU. Confusion can often arise here because a SBU may not be defined in terms of an organisational structure. IKEA has to decide the level at which business unit strategy should be formulated. Since the company wishes to ensure its image, ranges and style are consistent with its overall purpose and identity throughout the world, there is a corporate-level influence on business strategy. Within this, however, strategies need to be tailored to meet the needs of particular markets. Notionally, at least, each store has a distinct market and in that sense is a different SBU; but more realistically it may be that strategies need to differ, by broader geographical markets. The market in western Europe may be different from that in eastern Europe or the Far East for example. If IKEA does enter the market for housing, then it needs to develop a separate competitive strategy in the housing market; and in this sense housing would be a different SBU.

a **strategic business unit** *(SBU) is a part of the organisation for which there is a distinct external market for goods and services*

This example also emphasises the difference between a SBU and a division of an organisation. A SBU is a unit of an organisation for strategy-making purposes. It may or may not be a separate structural part of the organisation. ICI has a paints business which sells paints to various sorts of customers including industrial buyers and retail buyers. ICI Paints might choose to organise itself with an industrial division and a retail division. However, within those structural divisions there will be a need for different strategies according to different markets. Retailers could include huge multiple chain stores buying direct from ICI and small retailers buying through distributors. These are distinct markets which require different strategies, and are therefore different SBUs.

The third level of strategy is at the operating end of the organisation. Here there are **operational strategies** which are concerned with how the component parts of the organisation in terms of resources, processes, people and their skills effectively deliver the corporate- and business-level strategic direction. For example, in IKEA it was of crucial importance that design, store operations and sourcing operations dovetailed into higher-level decisions about product range and market entry. Indeed, in most businesses, successful business strategies depend to a large extent on decisions which are taken, or activities which occur, at the operational level. The integration of operational decisions and strategy is therefore of great importance.

operational strategies *are concerned with how the component parts of the organisation in terms of resources, processes, people and their skills effectively deliver the corporate- and business-level strategic direction*

1.1.3 The Vocabulary of Strategy

At the end of section 1.1.1, a definition of strategy was given. It can be dangerous to offer a definition, because lengthy semantic discussions can follow about whether or not it is precise enough, and whether everyone would agree with it. In fact, there are different definitions according to different authors.[7] There are also a variety of terms used in relation to strategy, so it is worth devoting a little space to clarifying some of these.

Exhibit 1.1 and Illustration 1.2 employ some of the terms that readers will come across in this and other books on strategy. Exhibit 1.1 explains these in relation to a personal strategy we may have followed ourselves – becoming fit. Illustration 1.2 shows how these relate to an organisation – in this case, British Airways. Not all these terms are always used in organisations or in strategy books: indeed, in this book the word 'goal' is rarely used. Moreover, it may or may not be that mission, goals, objectives, strategies and so on are written down precisely. In some organisations this is done very formally; in others it is not. As is shown in Chapter 2, a mission or strategy might sometimes more sensibly be conceived of as that which is implicit or can be deduced about an organisation from what it is doing. However, as a general guideline the following terms are often used.

A *mission* is a general expression of the overall purpose of the organisation, which, ideally, is in line with the values and expectations of major stakeholders and concerned with the scope and boundaries of the organisation. It is sometimes referred to in terms of the apparently simple, but actually challenging question: '*What business are we in?*'

A *vision* or *strategic intent* is the desired future state of the organisation. It is an aspiration around which a strategist, perhaps a chief executive, might seek to focus the attention and energies of members of the organisation.

If the word *goal* is used, it usually means a general aim in line with the mission. It may well be qualitative in nature. On the other hand, an *objective* is more likely to be quantified, or at least to be a more precise aim in line with the goal. However, in this book the word 'objective' is used whether or not there is quantification.

Exhibit 1.1 The vocabulary of strategy

TERM	DEFINITION	A PERSONAL EXAMPLE
Mission	Overriding purpose in line with the values or expectations of stakeholders	Be healthy and fit
Vision or strategic intent	Desired future state: the aspiration of the organisation	To run the London Marathon
Goal	General statement of aim or purpose	Lose weight and strengthen muscles
Objective	Quantification (if possible) or more precise statement of the goal	Lose 10 pounds by 1 September and run the Marathon next year
Core competences	Resources, processes or skills which provide 'competitive advantage'	Proximity to a fitness centre, supportive family and friends and past experience of successful diet
Strategies	Long-term direction	Associate with a collaborative network (e.g. join running club), exercise regularly, compete in marathons locally, stick to appropriate diet
Strategic architecture	Combination of resources, processes and competences to put strategy into effect	Specific exercise and diet regime, appropriate training facilities, etc.
Control	The monitoring of action steps to: • assess effectiveness of strategies and actions • modify strategies and/or actions as necessary	Monitor weight, miles run and measure times: if progress satisfactory, do nothing; if not, consider other strategies and actions

Core *competences* are the bases upon which an organisation achieves strategic advantage in terms of activities, skills or know-how which distinguish it from competitors and provide value to customers or clients.

The concept of *strategy* has already been defined. It is the long-term direction of the organisation. It is likely to be expressed in fairly broad statements of the direction that the organisation should be taking and the types of action required to achieve objectives: for example, in terms of market entry, new products or services, or ways of operating.

Strategic architecture, as used in this book, means the combination of organisational processes, resources, and competences to put the strategy into effect. This in turn will need to be translated into specific *actions* and *tasks* which link broad direction to specific operational issues and individuals.

STRATEGY IN ACTION Illustration 1.2

British Airways and the Vocabulary of Strategy

The annual reports and public statements of companies often contain elements of the vocabulary of strategy used in this book. The following examples are taken from British Airways' annual reports for 1993/94 and 1994/95.

Mission

'To be the best and most successful company in the airline business.'

'To build profitably the world's premier global alliance, with a presence in all major world markets.'

Vision/Strategic Intent

'To ensure that British Airways is the customer's first choice through the delivery of an unbeatable travel experience.'

Goals*

'To be a good neighbour, concerned for the community and the environment.'

'To provide overall superior service and good value for money in every market segment in which we compete.'

'To excel in anticipating and quickly responding to customer needs and competitor activity.'

Core Competence

'Anyone can fly airplanes, but few organisations can excel in serving people. Because it's a competence that's hard to build, it's also hard for competitors to copy or match.'

Strategies

'To maintain our position in the forefront of the globalisation of the airline industry ... By the turn of the century almost eighty per cent of the world air travel will be based on 6 major markets in the world ... British Airways' strategy is geared to securing a significant presence in these markets.'

'Continuing emphasis on consistent quality of customer service and the delivery to the marketplace of value for money.'

Strategic Architecture

'Arranging all the elements of our service so that they collectively generate a particular experience: to orchestrate the service.'

'Franchising is proving to be a successful way of expanding the British Airways network, benefiting from British Airways' infrastructure support and the franchisees' low operating costs, at minimal financial risk to British Airways.'

Controls

'The marketplace performance unit tracks some 350 measures of performance, including aircraft cleanliness, punctuality, technical defects on aircraft, customers' opinions on check-in performance and the time it takes for a customer to get through when telephoning a reservations agent.'

'The Board has established a system of internal financial control which includes manuals of policies and procedures and a Code of Business Conduct to provide guidance and assistance to all employees in their dealing with customers and suppliers.'

*Many organisations make public broad goals rather than specific objectives, as the latter can give competitors valuable insights into the company's strategy.

Question

Using this illustration as an example and referring to Exhibit 1.1, note down and explain examples of the vocabulary of strategy in the annual report of a company or public service organisation of your choice.

Sources Company annual reports.

Prepared by Sara Martin, Cranfield School of Management and Tony Jacobs, Bristol Business School.

It is, then, important to exercise some degree of *strategic control* so as to monitor the extent to which the action is achieving the objectives and goals.

1.2 STRATEGIC MANAGEMENT

What, then, is *strategic management*? It is not enough to say that it is the management of the process of strategic decision making. This fails to take into account a number of points important both in the management of an organisation and in the area of study with which this book is concerned.

The nature of strategic management is different from other aspects of management. Exhibit 1.2 summarises some of these differences. An individual manager is most often required to deal with problems of operational control, such as the efficient production of goods, the management of a salesforce, the monitoring of financial performance or the design of some new system that will improve the efficiency of the operation. These are all very important tasks, but they are essentially concerned with effectively managing resources already deployed, often in a limited part of the organisation within the context and guidance of an existing strategy. Operational control is what managers are involved in for most of their time. It is vital to the effective implementation of strategy, but it is not the same as strategic management.

The scope of strategic management is greater than that of any one area of operational management. Strategic management is concerned with complexity arising out of ambiguous and non-routine situations with organisation-wide rather than operation-specific implications. This is a major challenge for managers who are used to managing on a day-to-day basis the resources they control. It can be a particular problem because of the background of managers who may typically have been trained, perhaps over many years, to undertake operational tasks and to take operational responsibility. Accountants find that they still tend to see problems in financial terms, marketing managers in marketing terms, and so on. Each aspect in itself is important, of course, but none is adequate alone. The manager who aspires to manage, or influence, strategy needs to develop a capability to take an overview, to conceive of the whole rather than just the parts of the situation facing an organisation. Because strategic management is characterised by its complexity, it is also necessary to make decisions and judgements based on the *conceptualisation* of difficult issues. Yet the early training of managers is often about taking action, or about detailed *planning* or *analysis*. This book explains analytical approaches to strategy, and it is concerned too with action related to the management of strategy. There is also, however, an emphasis on developing concepts of relevance to the complexity of strategy which informs this analysis and action.

Exhibit 1.2 Characteristics of strategic management and operational management

STRATEGIC MANAGEMENT	OPERATIONAL MANAGEMENT
● Ambiguous	● Routinised
● Complex	
● Organisation-wide	● Operationally specific
● Fundamental	
● Long-term implications	● Short-term implications

Nor is strategic management concerned only with taking decisions about major issues facing the organisation. It is also concerned with ensuring that the strategy is put into effect. It can be thought of as having three main elements within it, and it is these that provide the framework for the book. **Strategic management** includes *strategic analysis*, in which the strategist seeks to understand the strategic position of the organisation, *strategic choice*, which is to do with the formulation of possible courses of action, their evaluation and the choice between them, and *strategy implementation*, which is concerned with both planning how the choice of strategy can be put into effect, and managing the changes required.

strategic management *includes strategic analysis, strategic choice and strategy implementation*

Before discussing these elements it is useful to make clear how they relate to each other and, therefore, why Exhibit 1.3 is shown in the form it is. The figure could have been shown in a linear form – strategic analysis preceding strategic choice, which in turn precedes strategy implementation. Indeed, many texts on the subject do just this. However, in practice, the elements of strategic management do not take this linear form: they are interlinked. One way of evaluating a strategy is to begin to implement it, so strategic choice and strategy implementation may overlap. Since strategic analysis should be an ongoing activity, it will overlap with the implementation of strategy. It is for structural convenience only that the process has been divided into sections in this book; it is not meant to suggest that the process of strategic management must follow a neat and tidy path. Indeed, the evidence provided in Chapter 2 on how strategic management occurs in practice suggests that it usually does not.

1.2.1 Strategic Analysis

strategic analysis *is concerned with understanding the strategic position of the organisation in terms of its external environment, internal resources and competences, and the expectations and influence of stakeholders*

Strategic analysis is concerned with understanding the strategic position of the organisation in terms of its external environment, internal resources and competences, and the expectations and influence of stakeholders. The

Exhibit 1.3 **A basic model of the strategic management process**

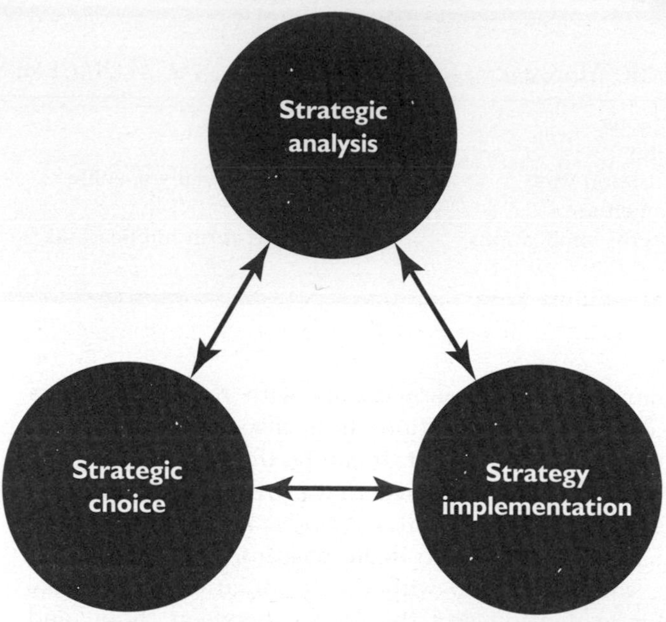

sorts of questions this raises are central to deciding future strategy. What changes are going on in the environment, and how will they affect the organisation and its activities? What are the resources and competences of the organisation and can these provide special advantages or yield new opportunities? What is it that those people and groups associated with the organisation – managers, shareholders or owners, unions and others who are stakeholders in the organisation – aspire to, and how do these affect what is expected for the future development of the organisation?

The history of IKEA suggests that a great deal of care was taken by those planning the development of the business in analysing different strategic moves. Decisions to enter new geographical markets required careful consideration about the economy in those countries, current and future demand in the market for furnishings, the historical and likely future activities of competitors, the most attractive locations in terms of demographic profiles of potential customers, and so on. An equally important issue was how the particular and special competences of the firm might be configured to provide competitive advantage. This was done by reconceiving how value might be provided to customers. 'Upstream' value was provided by careful design and sourcing of a wide range of merchandise. However, uniquely, the added value of IKEA was also provided by the management's design of the operation 'downstream' so that customers could add value themselves in their selection, transportation and assembly of the furniture.

The aim of *strategic analysis* is, then, to form a view of the key influences on the present and future well-being of the organisation, and what opportunities are afforded by the environment and the competences of the organisation. These are discussed briefly below.

- The *environment*. The organisation exists in the context of a complex commercial, economic, political, technological, cultural and social world. This environment changes and is more complex for some organisations than for others. How this affects the organisation could include an understanding of historical and environmental effects, as well as expected or potential changes in environmental variables. Many of those variables will give rise to *opportunities* and others will exert *threats* on the organisation. A problem that has to be faced is that the range of variables is likely to be so great that it may not be possible or realistic to identify and analyse each one; and therefore it is useful to distil out of this complexity a view of the key environmental impacts on the organisation. Chapter 3 examines how this might be possible.
- The *resources and competences* of the organisation which make up its *strategic capability*. Just as there are outside influences on the organisation and its choice of strategies, so there are internal influences. One way of thinking about the strategic capability of an organisation is to consider its *strengths* and *weaknesses* (what it is good or not so good at doing, or where it is at a competitive advantage or disadvantage, for example). These strengths and weaknesses might be identified by considering the resource areas of a business, such as its physical plant, its management, its financial structure and its products. Here, then, the aim is to form a view of the internal influences – and constraints – on strategic choice.

  However, it is also important to consider the particular competences of the organisation and the way in which they may yield opportunities. On occasions, specific resources – for example, the particular location of an organisation – could provide it with competitive advantage. However, competences which provide real advantage – in this book we refer to them as *core competences* – are more likely to be activities, know-how and skills which *in combination* provide advantages for that organisation which others find difficult to imitate. In IKEA, it was not one resource or activity that was of particular importance but the combination of many and the experience in managing them that provided the company with its competitive advantage. An understanding of what these are may also lead to the identification of new opportunities. Here, then, resources and competences are seen as aspects of the organisation not so much to be 'fitted' into environmental opportunities or demands; but rather to be 'stretched' to create new opportunities. Chapter 4 examines resource and competence analysis in detail.
- There are a number of influences on and manifestations of an organisation's *purpose*; Chapter 5 explores these. Formally, the issue of

corporate governance is important. Here the question is: which stakeholder group *should* the organisation primarily serve and how should managers be held responsible for this? The *expectations* of different *stakeholders* affect purpose and what will be seen as acceptable in terms of strategies advocated by management. Which views prevail will depend on which group has the greatest *power*, and understanding this can be of great importance in recognising why an organisation follows the strategy it does. *Cultural influences* from within the organisation and from the world around it also influence the strategy an organisation follows, not least because the environmental and resource influences on the organisation are likely to be interpreted in terms of the assumptions inherent in that culture. Chapter 5 builds on the discussion in Chapter 2 to show how cultural influences on strategy can be examined. All of this raises *ethical* issues about what managers and organisations do and why. This array of influences also takes form in statements of *objectives*. These are also discussed in Chapter 5.

Together, a consideration of the *environment*, *strategic capability*, the *expectations* and the *purposes* within the *cultural* and *political* framework of the organisation provides a basis for the strategic analysis of an organisation. Such an understanding needs to take the future into account. Is the current strategy capable of dealing with the changes taking place in the organisation's environment? Is it likely to deliver the results expected by influential stakeholders? If so, in what respects, and if not, why not? It is unlikely that there will be a complete match between current strategy and the picture which emerges from the strategic analysis. The extent to which there is a mismatch is the extent of the strategic problem facing the strategist. It may be that the adjustment that is required is marginal, or it may be that there is a need for a fundamental realignment of strategy. Assessing the magnitude of strategic change required and the ability of the organisation to effect such changes is another important aspect of strategic analysis. Chapter 2 provides an understanding of why problems of strategic change exist.

1.2.2 Strategic Choice

strategic choice *involves understanding the underlying bases guiding future strategy, generating strategic options for evaluation and selecting from among them*

An understanding of the influences of the environment, the competences of the organisation and the influence of stakeholders and culture provides a basis for strategic choice. **Strategic choice** involves understanding the underlying bases guiding future strategy, generating strategic options for evaluation and selecting from among them.

- *Identifying bases of strategic choice*. There are a number of fundamental issues which need to be addressed in generating and considering strategic options open to the organisation. Some of these *bases of strategic choice* arise from an understanding of stakeholder expectations and influence; and it may be important to reflect these in statements of *strategic mission* and *intent* which provide overall guidance about the nature or aspirations of the organisation: for example, in terms of product, market and geographical *scope* or matters as fundamental as *ownership* of the organisation. There are also bases of strategic choice in terms of how the organisation seeks to compete at SBU level. This requires an identification of *bases of competitive advantage* arising from an understanding of both markets and customers, and special competences that the organisation has to offer which contribute to its *generic* strategy. IKEA had achieved a basis of retailing which was quite unique – or *differentiated* from other furniture retailers – and sought to build future strategy on that distinctive strategy. A corporate body with many business units also faces challenges to do with the balancing of its *portfolio* of SBUs, its overall *financial strategy* and the extent to which it can reconcile the bases of strategy at the corporate level with those at the business unit level. This is an issue of *parenting*. It is less of a problem for an organisation like IKEA which seeks to offer a similar service throughout the world; but for the organisation that comprises different types of business, finding ways in which the centre adds value, rather than diminishes value, for the businesses is a significant parenting challenge.

- *Generation of strategic options*. There may be several possible courses of action that an organisation could follow. In the 1970s and 1980s, IKEA had faced a decision about the extent to which it was to become a truly multinational firm. By the 1990s the international scope of its operations posed the organisation other choices of *strategic direction*. Which areas of the world was it now most important to concentrate on? Could the existing experience and competences of IKEA be used as bases for entering new markets or providing new services or products? Within these, what *methods* of strategic development direction were most appropriate? Should the company attempt to follow these strategies by its own internal development or by joint venture activity – as, for example, IKEA did with its suppliers and, on occasions, through franchising its store operations?

All of these considerations are important and need careful consideration: indeed, in developing strategies, a potential danger is that managers do not consider any but the most obvious course of action – and the most obvious is not necessarily the best. A helpful step in *strategic choice* can therefore be to generate *strategic options*.

- *Evaluation and selection of strategic options*. Strategic options can be examined in the context of the strategic analysis to assess their relative merits. In deciding between options open to them, IKEA management might have asked a series of questions. First, which of these options built upon strengths, overcame weaknesses and took advantage of opportunities, while minimising or circumventing the threats that the business faced? This is an assessment of the *suitability* of the strategy. It can be thought of as evaluating if there is a 'fit' between the resource capability of the organisation and its environment; or if resource capability can be developed, or 'stretched', to yield new opportunities. However, a second set of questions is important. To what extent could a strategic option be put into effect? Can required finance be raised, sufficient stock be made available at the right time and in the right place, staff be recruited and trained to reflect the sort of image IKEA was trying to project? These are questions of *feasibility*. Even if these criteria could be met, would the choice be *acceptable* to the stakeholders? For example, suppose, in reviewing strategic options, IKEA management could see logic in substantial variation by country in product range and store design. Would this be acceptable to the corporate centre, and perhaps ultimately to the heritage established by Ingvar Kamprad? It might also be regarded as too risky because it could dilute the overall image of IKEA worldwide: acceptable risk is an important criterion.

Useful though such criteria of evaluation are, there is unlikely to be a clear-cut 'right' or 'wrong' choice because any strategy must inevitably have some dangers or disadvantages. So in the end, choice is likely to be a matter of management judgement. The *selection* process cannot always be viewed or understood as a purely objective, logical act. It is strongly influenced by the values of managers and other groups with interest in the organisation, and ultimately may very much reflect the power structure in the organisation.

Strategic choice is dealt with in Part III of the book. Chapter 6 deals with questions concerning the identification of bases of strategy both in terms of overall corporate mission and parenting, and in terms of competitive advantage at the business unit level, especially in terms of how it positions itself with regard to competition. Chapter 7 discusses strategic options in more detail, particularly in terms of the direction that an organisation might take in terms of product or market development; how resources and competences can be stretched to achieve this; and what methods of strategy development, such as internal development, joint ventures or acquisition, might be appropriate. Chapter 8 goes on to consider criteria of evaluation and the bases of choice of strategies.

strategy implementation *is concerned with the translation of strategy into organisational action through organisational structure and design, resource planning and the management of strategic change*

1.2.3 Strategy Implementation

Strategy implementation is concerned with the translation of strategy into organisational action through organisational structure and design, resource planning and the management of strategic change. Successful implementation of strategy is likely to be dependent on the extent to which these various components are effectively integrated to provide, in themselves, competences which other organisations find it difficult to match. The sorts of question that are likely to be important in planning strategy implementation might, therefore, include the following.

Who is to be responsible for carrying through the strategy? What changes in *organisational structure* and design are needed to carry through the strategy? There may also be a need to adapt the *systems* used to manage the organisation. What will different departments be held responsible for? What sort of information systems are needed to monitor progress? Implementation will also involve *resource planning*, including the logistics of implementation. What are the *key tasks* needing to be carried out? What changes need to be made in the resource mix of the organisation? Is there a need for new people or the retraining of the workforce?

The implementation of strategy also requires the managing of *strategic change*; and this requires action on the part of managers in terms of the way they manage change processes, and the mechanisms they use for it. These mechanisms are likely to be concerned not only with organisational redesign, but also with changing day-to-day routines and cultural aspects of the organisation, and overcoming political blockages to change.

Part IV of the book deals with strategy implementation. Issues of organisation structure and design are dealt with in Chapter 9, resource allocation and control are discussed in Chapter 10, and issues of managing strategic change are discussed in Chapter 11.

The influences on, and elements of, strategic management discussed in sections 1.2.1 to 1.2.3 are summarised in Exhibit 1.4 and form the structure of the remainder of the book.

1.2.4 Strategic Management as 'Fit' or 'Stretch'[8]

These discussions of strategic management raise an issue which was touched upon earlier (section 1.1.1). This concerns the extent to which the emphasis is on developing strategy on the basis of 'fit' with the environment as management understands it, or 'stretching' the organisation on the basis of resources and competences which can create opportunities for strategy development.

The notion of **strategic fit** sees managers trying to develop strategy by identifying opportunities arising from an understanding of the environmental forces acting upon the organisation, and adapting resources so as to take advantage of these. Here it would be seen as important to achieve the correct *positioning* of the organisation, for example in terms of the extent to which it meets clearly identified market needs. This might take the form of a small business trying to find a particular niche in a market, or a multinational corporation seeking to place most of its investments in businesses which have found successful market positions or have identified attractive markets.

strategic fit *sees managers trying to develop strategy by identifying opportunities arising from an understanding of the environmental forces acting upon the organisation, and adapting resources so as to take advantage of these*

However, there is little evidence to suggest that firms competing in markets which appear to offer attractive opportunities necessarily perform

Exhibit 1.4 A summary model of the elements of strategic management

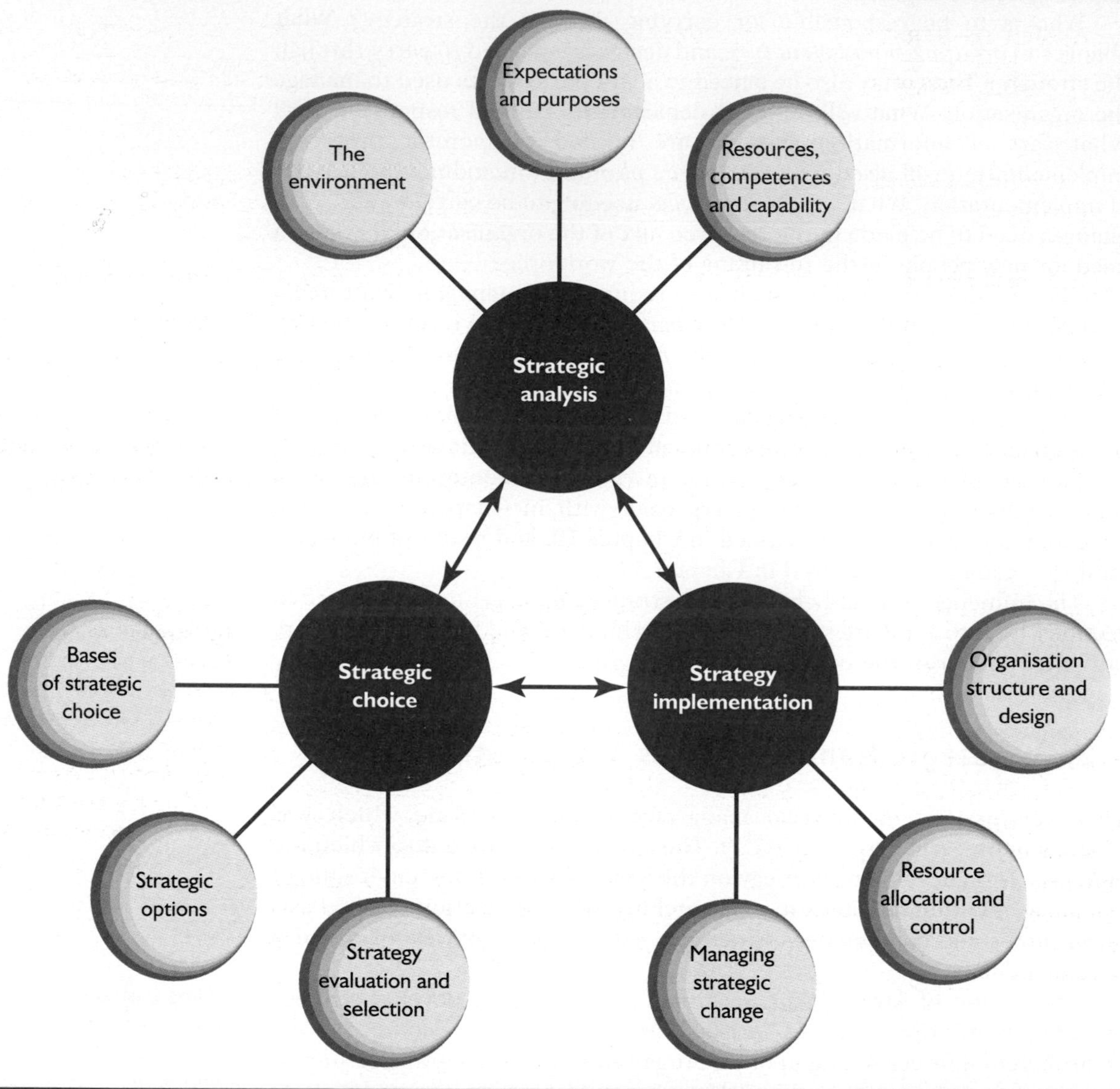

better than organisations that compete in markets which seem less attractive.[9] A study of businesses in mature markets[10] concluded that success could not be explained by the conditions of markets or the general state of the industry. Success was the result of managers' abilities in identifying strategies for growth on the basis of 'stretching' competences unique to the organisation to provide advantages over competition or

Exhibit 1.5 The leading edge of strategy: fit or stretch

Aspect of Strategy	Environment-led 'Fit'	Resource-led 'Stretch'
Underlying basis of strategy	Strategic fit between market opportunities and organisation's resources	Leverage of resources to improve value for money
Competitive advantage through ...	'Correct' positioning Differentiation directed by market need	Differentiation based on competences suited to or creating market need
How small players survive ...	Find and defend a niche	Change the 'rules of the game'
Risk reduction through ...	Portfolio of products/businesses	Portfolio of competences
Corporate centre invests in ...	Strategies of divisions or subsidiaries	Core competences

Source Adapted from G. Hamel and C.K. Prahalad, *Competing for the Future*, Harvard Business School Press, 1994.

create new opportunities. **Strategy development by 'stretch'** is the identification and leverage of the resources and competences of the organisation which yield new opportunities or provide competitive advantage. In this sense, 'stretch' is about innovating on the basis of current strengths. For example, the innovating organisation may have the ability to create a culture which encourages its people to experiment. A small business might try to change the 'rules of the game' in its market to suit its own competences. A large multinational corporation may be concerned less with trying to identify businesses which have achieved historic success in terms of market position, than with trying to identify businesses with particular competences which it can help develop to give competitive advantage or create new opportunities. These differences are summarised in Exhibit 1.5.

strategy development by 'stretch' *is the identification and leverage of the resources and competences of the organisation which yield new opportunities or provide competitive advantage*

1.2.5 Explaining Strategic Management Processes

There is a danger of thinking of the process of strategic management as an orderly sequence of steps. It is quite likely that readers will not find the elements described here clearly evident in practice, and might therefore conclude that strategic management in their organisation does not take place. It is important to repeat that the model used in this book, and summarised in this chapter and in Exhibit 1.4, is a useful device for the structuring of the book and a means by which managers and students of strategy can *think through* strategic issues and explore the domain of 'corporate strategy' – it is not, however, an attempt to describe how the processes of strategic management always or necessarily take place in the social, political and cultural arenas of organisations. There are different ways in which the process of strategic management can be explained. These are reviewed more fully in Chapter 2, but it is useful to outline some of the differences here. These are summarised in Exhibit 1.6.

One view of strategic management is, indeed, that strategy can and should be managed through *rational planning* processes in the form of a sequence of steps involving setting objectives, the analysis of environmental trends and resource capabilities, continuing through the evaluation of different options, and ending with the careful planning of the strategy's implementation. Here, then, the underlying principle is that strategies are the outcome of careful objective analyses and planning,[11] and in this way managers are able to make decisions which establish the future direction of their organisation. Many organisations do have formal planning systems, and find that they contribute usefully to the development of the strategy of their organisation. However, not all organisations have them, and even when they do, it would be a mistake to assume that the strategies of organisations necessarily come about through them.

The management of the strategy can also be thought of as a process of *crafting*.[12] Here strategic management is seen, not as a formal planning process, but rather in terms of processes by which strategies develop in organisations on the basis of managers' experience, their sensitivity to changes in their environment and what they learn from operating in their market. This does not mean that managers are not thinking about the strategic position of their organisation, or the choices it faces, but that it may not be taking place in a highly formalised way such as through planning systems.

Third, *complexity and chaos theory*[13] argue that the world in which organisations exist is highly complex and unpredictable. It is inconceivable that managers can know all there is to know about this complexity, let alone predict its effects specifically. However, it is possible that people's experience within a particular context can help them become sensitive to the complexity and uncertainty around them. They do this by becoming familiar with patterns in the complexity and uncertainty. When there are deviations from these patterns they are able to sense them intuitively. Strategic management should therefore be seen as more to do with building the capacity to be intuitive, and taking action based on that.

A fourth view is that, on the whole, managers think that they have more choice in developing strategies than they really do. Institutional theorists[14] argue that organisations exist in relation to other similar organisations: accountancy firms are similar, universities are similar, publishing firms are similar and so. Over time, similarities develop in terms of the way people in those organisation see their organisations and the environment in which the organisation operates, including the nature of customers, suppliers, competitors and so on. They also have ways of

Exhibit 1.6 Different explanations of processes of strategic management

Managerial choice and control according to different theories

High ←——————————————————————————————→ Low

RATIONAL PLANNING	CRAFTING OR LOGICAL INCREMENTALISM	CHAOS/ COMPLEXITY	CULTURAL/ INSTITUTIONAL	ECOLOGICAL/ NATURAL SELECTION
Managers' rational decisions direct the future of the organisation through formal planning systems	Strategy is managed on the basis of experience and learning	Managers are sensitive to patterns in a complex world and may respond to deviations from such patterns	Managers are 'captured' by institutionalised assumptions and ways of doing things (culture); strategic development is constrained by these	Organisational cultures constrain strategies; success depends on the extent to which these fit environmental conditions

doing things which tend to be similar. These ways of seeing the world and ways of doing things can be so taken for granted, so *institutionalised*, it is difficult for people to question or change them. Indeed, they can come to be seen as *the* legitimate way to behave within an industry or profession, so organisational strategies tend to develop within institutionally similar cultural parameters.

A view still further removed from the idea that managers control the destiny of their organisation is that of the *population ecologists*.[15] They agree that organisations build up ways of doing things, whether within institutional frameworks or not. They argue that the success of organisations depends on the extent to which these ways of doing things coincide with the needs of the environment. If they do coincide, the organisation prospers; if they do not, the organisation suffers or maybe even dies. It is like *natural selection*. Some organisations' cultures are well suited to the environments in which they operate; others are less so. The extent to which managers affect this is overstated.

It might be assumed that, as a result of a rational planning approach, managers could make major changes in strategy; the implication of the other explanations is that this is unlikely. Most of them suggest that strategies are likely to develop incrementally in organisations. Strategies are likely to develop by adapting or building on existing strategies. 'Crafting' suggests that this may be done proactively – indeed, as Chapter 2 explains, the notion of 'logical incrementalism' has developed. The institutional view suggests, on the other hand, that incremental strategy development is less proactive and more the result of strategies being constrained by institutional cultures. The argument of the ecologists is that incremental development is inevitable and will in time lead to the decline, even demise, of most organisations. Chapter 2 examines more fully different patterns of strategy development.

It is important to understand these different explanations because they all provide insights into the challenges that managers face. To cope with the variety and range of factors in considering strategy, managers have to operate by means of a simplification process. They reduce the 'infinite' to a manageable frame of reference on the basis of their personal experience or their organisation's past experience embedded in its culture. However, this experience can be a significant restraint on change. The ability to stand apart from and question the assumptions within such experience and culture is therefore especially important. In so far as the strategic tools and techniques explained in the book are concerned, they are more to do with being able to question and challenge than they are to do with formalised procedures of planning.

However, the discussion in the book continually returns to the processes by which strategy actually develops in organisations, and therefore to the explanations which emphasise managerial experience and cultural constraints. It is the task of the reader to judge to what extent, and how, the concepts discussed in the book and the techniques of analysis described can contribute to the sorts of questioning and challenge that are required to manage strategy.

1.3 STRATEGIC MANAGEMENT IN DIFFERENT CONTEXTS

The retail development of IKEA has been used in this chapter to illustrate different aspects of strategic management. To a greater or lesser extent, all these aspects are relevant for most organisations. However, it is likely that different aspects will be more important in some contexts and in some organisations than in others. For example, IKEA is a retail business, and, in retailing, the need to understand customer needs and values and to consider these in relation to product and customer service is crucially important; more so than it would be in a firm supplying commodity raw materials in an industrial setting, for example. However, in IKEA itself, the strategic emphases have changed over time. Its multinational scope meant that structural and control issues became much more important in the 1980s and 1990s than they had been when it was more geographically limited in the 1960s. It would, then, be wrong to assume that all aspects of strategic management are equally important in all circumstances. This section reviews some of the ways in which aspects differ in different contexts. Differences are also shown in Illustration 1.3.

1.3.1 The Small Business Context[16]

Small businesses are likely to be operating in a single market or a limited number of markets, probably with a limited range of products or services. The scope of the operation is therefore likely to be less of a strategic issue than it is in larger organisations. It is unlikely that small businesses will have central service departments to undertake complex analysis and market research; rather, it may be senior managers themselves, perhaps even the founder of the firm, who has direct contact with the market place and whose experience is therefore very influential. Indeed, in small firms the values and expectations of senior executives, who may themselves be in an ownership position, are likely to be very important, and even when current management are not owners, it may be that the values and expectations of the founders persist. It is also likely that, unless the firm is specialising in some particular market segment – and identifying a market niche of some sort may make a lot of sense – it will be subject to significant competitive pressures; so issues of competitive strategy are likely to be especially important for the small firm. However, decisions on competitive strategies are likely to be strongly influenced by the experience of those running the business, so the questions and challenges posed on the nature of competition in Chapter 3 and bases of competitive strategy in Chapter 6 are likely to be especially relevant.

Small firms are also likely to be private companies. This significantly affects their ability to raise capital. Combined with the legacy of the founder's influence on choice of product and market, this may mean that choices of strategy are limited. The firm may see its role as consolidating its position within a particular market. If it does not, and is seeking growth, then the raising of finance for the development of strategic relationships with funding bodies such as banks becomes a key strategic issue.

1.3.2 The Multinational Corporation[17]

The key strategic issues facing multinationals are substantially different from those facing the small business. Here the firm is likely to be diverse in terms of both products and geographical markets. It may be that the firm is in a range of different types of business in the form of subsidiary companies within a holding company structure, or divisions within a multidivisional structure. Therefore, issues of structure and control at the corporate level (see Chapter 9), and relationships between businesses and the corporate centre, are usually a major strategic issue for multinational firms. Indeed, a central concern is the extent to which the corporate centre adds to or detracts from the value of its businesses (see Chapters 6 and 9). At the business unit level, many of the competitive strategic issues will, perhaps, be similar to those faced by smaller firms – though the strength of the multinational within a given geographical area may be greater than for any small firm. However, for the multinational parent company a significant issue will be how corporate business units

STRATEGY IN ACTION Illustration 1.3

Strategic Issues in Different Contexts

The strategic issues faced by managers in different organisations depend on their business context.

Multinational Corporation

'Any big multinational corporation is intrinsically complex. It has multiple layers of managers, and in most cases, multiple businesses – it develops products, manufactures and sells them, and services them in multiple countries ... A choice [of strategy] in principle ... has to be embedded in a complex industrial and managerial structure so that the myriad choices made daily within the organisation fall in line with the chosen strategic orientation.'

Y. Doz, *Introduction to Strategic Management in Multinational Companies*, Pergamon, 1986, pp. 6–7

A Business within a Conglomerate

'We are, of course, constrained to some extent by the wishes of our parent organisation. Keeping them happy is important. But our real focus needs to be on how we keep ahead of competition in our markets. We try to ensure that all our managers – whatever their functional responsibility – ask how they can ensure we simultaneously meet the needs of our customers, and do so in ways that our competitors can't match.'

CEO of a consumer goods company, part of a multinational conglomerate

Professional Partnership

'In recent years, "professional partnerships" like accountants have become huge organisations with sales in excess of $5 billion. Yet they still tend to be organised to serve national or regional markets, with partners being responsible for all aspects of service delivery to clients, with which they may personally identify. You also need to remember that partnerships are not hierarchies: you can't easily tell partners what to do. However, clients are beginning to require international service delivery. This cuts across the traditional structure and culture of partnerships: for example, in the way it requires team-working across national boundaries, and therefore planned integration of resources. It is not always easy to get partners to go along with this. As one of my colleagues said: a great deal of management of a professional service

should be allocated resources given their different, and often competing, demands for them; and how this is to be co-ordinated. Indeed, the co-ordination of operational logistics across different business units and different countries may become especially important. For example, a multinational manufacturing company such as Toyota or General Motors has to decide on the most sensible configuration of plants for the manufacture of cars. Most have moved from manufacturing a particular car at a particular location, and now manufacture different parts of cars in different locations, bringing together such components for the assembly of a given model in a given location. The logistics problems of co-ordinating such operations are immense, requiring sophisticated control systems and management skills far organisation has to do with "keeping the fleas in the bucket".'

David Pitt-Watson, past director of Braxton Associates

Charity Sector

'If your mission is, say, to eliminate poverty or save the planet, then almost anything you do can be justified. If management is weak and without legitimacy (which is too often the case), this means staff often set their own personal agendas. To a greater extent than most private organisations, there are also multiple stakeholders. This is at its most extreme in membership organisations. Senior managers can find themselves buffeted by warring factions both outside and inside the organisation. Commitment is also a two-edged sword. Young staff in particular often join with a view that they are going to change the world, and find out that many jobs are pretty routine. There is a great danger that they then invest their energy in trying to create their vision of the world within the organisation. Many not-for-profit organisations have had terrible problems with in-fighting. Some become unmanageable and implode.'

Sheila McKechnie,
Chief Executive, Consumers' Association;
director of Shelter until 1995

Public Sector

'In highly developed societies such as ours, the consumer/the citizen increasingly demands greater choice in the services and goods provided. Such choice can only be developed and enhanced in an environment of competition and so far no other mechanism for guaranteeing this choice has been found to exist. It is inevitable that public services, such as local government, will be subject to even greater competition, in the broadest sense, and the way in which its services are both funded and provided will therefore radically change. Even if free market models of provision are found wanting, competition in the provision of public services is here to stay because consumers demand it.'

Rob Hughes, President of the Society of Local Authority Chief Executives. Public lecture at Sheffield Business School in May 1995 entitled 'The power of choice'.

Question

Refer to Exhibit 1.4 and answer the following question separately *in relation to each of the contexts*:

Which element of the strategy model is being emphasised? Why?

removed from those in the smaller firm. An important choice that a major multinational has to make is the extent to which it controls such logistics centrally, or devolves autonomy to operating units. It is, again, an issue of structure and control, the subject of Chapters 9 and 10 of this book.

1.3.3 Manufacturing and Service Organisations

While differences exist between organisations providing services and those providing products, there is also an increasing awareness of similarities. Competitive strategy for a service firm is concerned less with a product itself and more with wider aspects of the organisations that make up that service, whereas Ford's ability to compete effectively with Japanese manufacturers depends to a greater extent on the physical product which gives it advantages over Japanese producers at a price which is also competitive – factors which are likely to be linked back into the production process. For a firm which competes on the basis of the services it provides – for example, insurance, management consultancy and professional services – there is no physical product. Here competitive advantage is likely to be much more related to the extent to which customers value less tangible aspects of the firm. This could be, for example, the soundness of advice given, the attitude of staff, the ambience of offices, the swiftness of service and so on. Senior management in manufacturing organisations may therefore believe they exercise more direct control over competitive strategy than can be exercised in a service firm. However, most have come to understand that, since physical products are often perceived by customers as very similar, other features such as service or brand image are just as important in achieving competitive advantage. Bases of competitive advantage related to physical products, resources, organisational competences and value to customers are discussed in Chapters 4, 6 and 10 in particular.

1.3.4 The Innovatory Organisation[18]

There are an increasing number of organisations that claim to depend substantially on innovation for their strategic success, and still others which argue the importance of becoming more innovatory. Certainly businesses in the field of high technology products or those dependent on research and development, for example in the pharmaceutical industry, have long experienced the extent to which innovation is important. Innovation is seen as the ability to 'change the rules of the game'. The successful innovatory organisation is likely to be one which is acutely aware of, but likely to challenge, its traditional competences so as to be able to 'stretch' these into new opportunities. In such circumstances it is unlikely to be the formal procedures of organisations that matter so much as the type and quality of the people, the sources of knowledge in the organisation and the extent to which the prevailing culture encourages the transfer of knowledge and the questioning of what is taken for granted perhaps on the basis of the diversity of past experience. Innovation will also be influenced by how people are managed and how they interact. For example, organisational structures which encourage interaction and integration, rather than formal divisions of responsibility, may encourage innovation.

1.3.5 Strategy in the Public Sector[19]

The concepts of strategy and strategic management are just as important in the public sector as in commercial firms. However, like the private sector, the public sector is diverse, as some examples show.

- *Nationalised companies* may be similar in many respects to commercial organisations; the differences are associated with the nature of ownership and control. There is likely to be a good deal of direct or indirect control or influence exercised from outside the organisation, by government in particular. A commercial enterprise that is state controlled may find not only planning horizons determined more by political than market conditions, but also constraints on investment capital and therefore on bases of financing, and on the latitude that managers have to change strategies. The latter may be influenced by a requirement for top management to control their organisation more centrally for reporting purposes – for example, to government ministers. Understanding the power of different stakeholders (see Chapter 5) and constraints on change (see Chapter 2) may be especially important here.
- A *government agency* has a labour market, and a money market of sorts; it also has suppliers and users or customers. However, at its heart lies a political market which approves budgets, and provides subsidies. It is the explicit nature of this political dimension which managers – or officers – have to cope with which particularly distinguishes government bodies, be they national or local, from commercial enterprises. This may in turn change the horizons of decisions, since they may be heavily influenced by political considerations, and may mean that analysis of strategies requires the norms of political dogma to be considered explicitly. However, although the magnitude of the political dimension is greater, the model of strategic management discussed here still holds. What is different is that certain aspects of strategic analysis and choice, notably those to do with political influences (see Chapter 5), are more important.
- *Public service* organisations – for example, health services and many of the amenities run by local government – face difficulties from a strategic point of view because they may not be allowed to specialise, and may not be able to generate surpluses from their services to invest in development. This can lead to a mediocrity of service where strategic decisions mainly take the form of striving for more and more efficiency so as to retain or improve services on limited budgets. Careful analyses of resources (see Chapter 4) and allocation of those resources become very important (see Chapter 10).
- In the public sector, the notion of competition is usually concerned with competition for *resource inputs*, typically within a political arena. The need to demonstrate *value for money* in outputs has become increasingly important. Many of the developments in management practices in the public sector, such as changes to internal markets, performance indicators, competitive tendering and so on, are attempts to introduce elements of competition in order to encourage improvements in value for money.

- Overall, the role of ideology in the development of strategy in the public sector is probably greater than that in commercial organisations. Putting it in the terminology of this book, the criterion of *acceptability to stakeholders* in strategic choice is probably of greater significance in the public sector than in the commercial sector.

1.3.6 Privatised Utilities

Increasingly, organisations that were once within the public sector have been privatised. This change in status has typically been made because government sees benefits in requiring such organisations to become more sharply focused on markets and, specifically, on customer requirements and competitive pressures. Managers in such organisations therefore find themselves more explicitly having to face an understanding of the dynamics of competition (see Chapter 3) and the formulation of clear competitive strategies (see Chapter 6). This is important internally for the clarification of strategy, but also because these organisations may also be answerable to government regulators, acting as a surrogate for a real competitive market, or there to create a competitive market (as in the electricity supply industry in the UK) by progressive deregulation. Indeed, it may be that formalised planning systems (see Chapter 2) are important not only for internal purposes, but also as a way of ensuring visible public accountability.

1.3.7 The Voluntary and Not-for-profit Sectors[20]

In the voluntary sector it is likely that underlying values and ideology will be of central strategic significance. The values and expectations of different stakeholder groups in organisations play an important part in the development of strategy. This is particularly the case where the *raison d'être* of the organisation is rooted in such values, as is the case with organisations providing services traditionally not for profit, such as charities.

In not-for-profit organisations such as charities, churches, private schools, foundations and so on, the sources of funds may be diverse and are quite likely not to be direct beneficiaries of the services offered. Moreover, they may provide funds in advance of the services being offered – in the form of grants, for example. There are several implications. Influence from funding bodies may be high in terms of the formulation of organisational strategies. Competition may be high for funds from such bodies; but the principles of competitive strategy (see Chapter 6) nonetheless hold. However, since such organisations might be dependent on funds which emanate not from users but from sponsors, there is a danger that they may become concerned more with resource efficiency than with service effectiveness (see Chapter 4). The multiple sources of funding likely to exist, linked to the different objectives and expectations of the funding

Exhibit 1.7 Some characteristics of strategic management in not-for-profit organisations

CHARACTERISTICS	LIKELY EFFECTS
Objectives and expectations	
• May be multiple service objectives and expectations • May be multiple influences on policy • Expectations of funding bodies very influential	• Complicates strategic planning • High incidence of political lobbying • Difficulties in delegating/decentralising responsibilities and decision making
Market and users	
• Beneficiaries of service not necessarily contributors of revenue/resources	• Service satisfaction not measured readily in financial terms
Resources	
• High proportion from government, or sponsors • Received in advance of services • May be multiple sources of funding	• Influence from funding bodies may be high • May be emphasis on financial or resource efficiency rather than service effectiveness • Strategies may be addressed to sponsors as much as clients

bodies, might also lead to a high incidence of political lobbying, difficulties in clear strategic planning, and a requirement to hold decision making and responsibility at the centre, where it is answerable to external influences, rather than delegate it within the organisation. The characteristics and difficulties of strategic management in not-for-profit organisations are summarised in Exhibit 1.7.

1.3.8 Professional Service Organisations

Traditionally based values are often of particular importance in professional service organisations where professional advice has traditionally been seen as more important than revenue-earning capability. To a large extent this was the case in medicine, accountancy, law and other professions.

Private sector professional firms may also have a partnership structure. Partners may be owners and perhaps bear legal responsibility for advice and opinion offered by the firm; they may therefore carry considerable power; and there may be many of them – each of the top four accountancy firms now aspires to global strategies, but each may have thousands of partners. Traditionally, although interacting with clients and exercising actual or potential control over resources, these partners may not have regarded themselves as managers at all. As a partner in a major accountancy firm put it: 'We see ourselves as the largest network of sole traders in the world.' The problems of developing and implementing strategy within such a context are, therefore, heavily linked to the management of internal political influences (see Chapter 5) and the ability to take account of, and where necessary to change, organisational culture (see Chapters 2 and 11). Another factor is the pressure those in the professions find themselves under to be more 'commercial' in their approach. Such pressure may come from government, as in the case of doctors; or it may be a function of size, as has been found in the growing accountancy firms. This has meant that such organisations have had to be concerned with competitive strategy (see Chapter 6).

SUMMARY

- Strategy is concerned with the long-term direction and development of an organisation, so all organisations are faced with the challenge of managing strategy.
- Strategy is the direction and scope of an organisation over the long term, which achieves advantage for the organisation through its configuration of resources within a changing environment, to meet the needs of markets and to fulfil stakeholder expectations.
- Strategic decisions may be about a search for strategic 'fit', by which is meant trying to find ways to match the organisation's activities to the environment in which it operates. Strategic decisions could also be based on trying to 'stretch' the resources and competences of the organisation to create new opportunities, even new markets.
- Strategies will also be influenced by the values and expectations of stakeholders in and around the organisation, and the extent of the power they exert. The culture within which the organisation exists and the culture of the organisation itself will also influence its strategy.
- Strategic decisions are made at a number of levels in organisations. Corporate-level strategy is concerned with an organisation's overall purpose and scope; business unit (or competitive) strategy with how to compete successfully in a market; and operational strategies with how resources, processes and people can effectively deliver corporate- and business-level strategies.
- The formulation of business-level strategies is best thought of in terms of strategic business units which are parts of organisations for which there are distinct external markets for goods or services. These may not represent formal structural divisions in an organisation, however.
- Strategic management is distinguished from day-to-day operational management by the complexity of influences on decisions, the fundamental, organisation-wide implications that strategic decisions

have for the organisation, and their long-term implications. It can be problematic for managers not least because their strategic horizons are likely to be limited by their experience and organisational culture and most of their training may have been in operational management.

- Strategic management can be conceived of in terms of strategic analysis, strategic choice and strategy implementation. Strategic analysis is the process of trying to understand the strategic position of the organisation in terms of its external environment, internal resources and competences, and the expectations and influence of stakeholders. Strategic choice involves understanding the underlying bases guiding future strategy, generating strategic options for evaluation and selecting from among them. Strategy implementation is concerned with the translation of strategy into organisational activity through organisational structure and design, resource planning and the management of strategic change.
- There are different explanations of how strategy is actually managed in organisations, varying from those which emphasise high degrees of managerial choice and control to those which argue that managers actually have much less influence than they think.
- Different organisations in different contexts are likely to emphasise different aspects of the strategic management process. For some the major challenge will be developing competitive strategy; for yet others it will be building organisational structures capable of integrating complex global operations; for yet others it will be understanding their competences so as to focus on what they are especially good at; and for still others it will be developing a culture of innovation. Strategic priorities need to be understood in terms of the particular context of an organisation.

RECOMMENDED KEY READINGS

It is useful to read about how strategies are managed in practice and some of the lessons which can be drawn from this which inform key themes in this book. For example:

- For readings on the concepts of strategy in organisations, John Kay's book, *Foundations for Corporate Success: How business strategies add value*, Oxford University Press, 1993, is a helpful explanation from an economics point of view. For a wider theoretical perspective, see R. Whittington, *What is Strategy and Does it Matter?*, Routledge, 1993.
- It is also useful to read accounts of where the management of strategy in organisations has made an impact on organisational performance. Reference is also often made in this book to G. Hamel and C.K. Prahalad, *Competing for the Future*, Harvard Business School Press, 1994, which draws extensively on examples of successful strategies in organisations.
- For a discussion of strategy in different types of organisations, see H. Mintzberg, J. Quinn and S. Ghoshal (eds), *The Strategy Process: Concepts, contexts and cases*, 4th edition, Prentice Hall, 1998.

REFERENCES

1. In the 1980s much of the writing and practice of strategic management was influenced by the writings of industrial organisations economists. One of the most influential books was Michael Porter, *Competitive Strategy*, Free Press, first published 1980. In essence, the book describes means of analysing the competitive nature of industries so that managers might be able to select among attractive and less attractive industries and choose strategies most suited to the organisation in terms of these forces. This approach, which assumes the dominant influence of industry forces and the overriding need to tailor strategies to address those forces, has become known as a 'fit' view of strategy.
2. The notion of strategy as 'stretch' is perhaps best explained in G. Hamel and C.K. Prahalad, *Competing for the Future*, Harvard Business School Press, 1994.
3. R. Norman and R. Ramirez, 'From value chain to value constellation: designing interactive strategy', *Harvard Business Review*, vol. 71, no. 4 (1993), pp. 65–77.
4. Strategic architecture is discussed by various authors in different ways. Hamel and Prahalad (see reference 2 above) devote a chapter to it and John Kay uses the term extensively in *Foundations of Corporate Success*, Oxford University Press, 1993.
5. There are many books and papers which discuss the concept of networks and relationships in and between organisations. For example, see J.C. Jarillo, *Strategic Networks: Creating the borderless organisation*, Butterworth/Heinemann, 1993, for networks between organisations; and M.S. Granovetter, 'The strength of weak ties', *American Journal of Sociology*, vol. 78, no. 6 (1993), pp. 1360–80, for networks within organisations.
6. The term 'SBU' can be traced back to the development of corporate-level strategic planning in General Electric in the USA in the early 1970s. For an early account of its uses, see W.K. Hall, 'SBUs: hot, new topic in the management of diversification', *Business Horizons*, vol. 21, no. 1 (1978), pp. 17–25.
7. For a discussion of alternative definitions, see C.W. Hofer and D. Schendel, *Strategy Formulation: Analytical concepts*, West, 1978, pp. 16–20.
8. See reference 2 above.
9. Richard Rumelt has shown that firm strategy had a greater impact on performance than the nature of the industry in which the firm was operating ('How much does industry matter?', *Strategic Management Journal*, vol. 12, no. 3 (1991), pp. 167–85).
10. See C. Baden-Fuller and J.M. Stopford, *Rejuvenating the Mature Business: The competitive challenge*, Routledge, 1992.
11. There were many books that took a formalised strategic 'planning approach' in the 1970s. These are less common now, but there remain texts which take a similar approach (e.g. G. Greenley, *Strategic Management*, Prentice Hall, 1989) and others which take an explicitly analytical approach, largely excluding social, political and cultural aspects of strategic management (e.g. R. Grant, *Contemporary Strategy Analysis*, 2nd edition, Blackwell, 1995).
12. See H. Mintzberg, 'Crafting strategy', *Harvard Business Review*, vol. 65, no. 4 (1987), pp. 66–75.
13. Ralph Stacy's paper 'Strategy as order emerging from chaos', *Long Range Planning*, vol. 26, no. 1 (1993), pp. 10–17, is a good example of the managerial implications of complexity and chaos theory.
14. A good review of work on institutional theory is provided by Richard Scott in his book *Institutions and Organisations*, Sage, 1995.
15. Michael Hannan and John Freeman have written extensively about population ecology. See, for example, *Organizational Ecology*, Harvard University Press, 1989.
16. For strategy development in small businesses, see C. Barrow, R. Brown and L. Clarke, *The Business Growth Handbook*, Kogan Page, 1995.
17. There are now many books on managing strategy in multinationals. In this book we will refer often to C. Bartlett and S. Ghoshall, *Managing Across Borders: The transnational solution*, Harvard Business School Press, 1989; and G. Yip, *Total Global Strategy*, Prentice Hall, 1995.
18. A good review of aspects of innovation and their organisational implications can be found in J. Tidd, J. Bessant and K. Pavitt, *Managing Innovations: Integrating technological, marketing and organisational change*, Wiley, 1997.
19. D. McKevitt and A. Lawton, *Public Sector Management: Theory, critique and practice*, Sage, 1994.
20. See J.M. Bryson, *Strategic Planning for Public and Nonprofit Organizations*, Prentice Hall, 1995.

WORK ASSIGNMENTS

1.1 Using the characteristics discussed in section 1.1.1, write out a statement of strategy for British Steel* or an organisation with which you are familiar.

1.2 Using Exhibit 1.1 and Illustration 1.2 as a guide, note down and explain examples of the vocabulary of strategy used in the annual report of a company of your choosing.

1.3 ● Using annual reports and press articles, write a brief case study (similar to the IKEA illustration or the British Steel* case) which shows the strategic development and current strategic position of an organisation.

1.4 Using Exhibit 1.4 as a guide, note down the elements of strategic management discernible in the British Steel* case or an organisation of your choice.

1.5 ● With particular reference to section 1.2.4, note down the characteristics of strategy development in IKEA or Microsoft/Netscape which would be explained by the notion of (a) strategic management as 'environmental fit', and (b) strategic management as the 'stretching' of capabilities.

1.6 ● Using Exhibit 1.4 as a guide, show how the different elements of strategic management differ in:
(a) a multinational business (e.g. Burmah Castrol*)
(b) a professional services firm (e.g. KPMG*)
(c) a public sector organisation (e.g. Royal Alexandra Hospital*)
(d) a small business
(e) a high technology business (e.g. Microsoft or Netscape).

---

* refers to a case study in the Text and Cases edition.
● denotes more advanced work assignments.

CASE EXAMPLE

Microsoft and Netscape

Four years ago (1994), with great fanfare, Marc Andreesen, a 24 year old Silicon Valley *wunderkind*, launched a new way to search and retrieve information from the World Wide Web. His company was Netscape. His invention was the Navigator Internet browser. The world's press hailed the arrival of a cyber-genius, and predicted he would create a new computer standard that could make him as powerful as Microsoft's Bill Gates. For a moment Andreesen seemed to have the world in his pocket. Netscape grabbed 80 per cent of the booming browser market. It began building intranets, providing systems for companies to create their own Web-like networks. It became the platform and promoter of Sun Microsystem's Java, a new software language that challenged the foundation of Gates' own fortune, the DOS and Windows operating systems for personal computers (PCs). When Netscape was listed on the stock market in August 1995 its shares took off like a rocket. Before the company had made a net profit it was valued at $2.7 bn (£1.7 bn). Andreesen, a chubby, good-looking youth who lived on junk food and had just bought his first suit, found his share was worth $55m. Jim Clark, the venture capitalist who put up the money for Netscape, was worth nearly £1 bn.

Gates initially dismissed the Internet and Netscape as unimportant, but Netscape's surging sales, and the phenomenal growth and popularity of the Net, quickly forced him to change his tune. Marshalling the vast resources of Microsoft, and spending hundreds of millions of dollars on research and development, he had 2,000 of his best programmers rush out a browser of his own, the Explorer, and then bombarded the public with free copies. Microsoft's share of the browser market soared from 2.9 per cent at the end of 1995 to more than 40 per cent today, while Netscape's share has fallen to 54 per cent.

Last week Netscape shocked analysts when it announced that it expected to lose $85m–$89m in its fourth quarter. It said it planned to take a $35m charge to cover layoffs and other restructuring moves.

As the stock plunged 21 per cent (to $18.56), Netscape suddenly looked mortal. Some analysts believe the company may be in terminal decline and may not be able to survive – at least as an independent company.

For the past few months Netscape has been looking for help from the US Justice Department, which last October charged Microsoft with using its monopolistic 90 per cent control of all PC operating systems to force computer manufacturers to install its browser on their machines. On 11 December, Judge Thomas Jackson issued a preliminary injunction to force Microsoft to make available two versions of Windows to PC manufacturers, one including the browser and one without. The Justice Department also wants Microsoft to remove the Explorer icon that automatically appears on the computer screen when a user starts the Windows program. Microsoft denies that it uses unfair business practices, and claims it is simply exercising its right to enhance its operating system. It says an Internet browser is an integral part of its Windows software.

The stakes that Gates is playing for are much bigger than those publicly admitted. In May 1995, Gates wrote: 'The Internet is the most important single development to come along since the IBM PC was introduced in 1981. It has enough users that it is benefiting from the positive feedback loop of the more users it gets, the more content it gets; and the more content it gets, the more users it gets.' He went on to say that it presented a huge threat to Microsoft, because rival companies such as Netscape and Sun were trying to use it to 'commoditise the underlying operating system.' David Rosenfield of Value Line says: 'Many believe that Microsoft's actions [in developing its own browser] reflect its fear that Netscape might gain control of the desktop [computer] and its browser would evolve into an alternative platform to Windows.' Netscape's stunning loss, the first on operations since it went public in 1995, makes that improbable now. Microsoft seems increasingly likely to dictate technology standards on the Internet.

Netscape officials insist that losing the browser war is not a death blow. They point out that less than 10 per cent of the company's profits now come from browser sales, and nearly 80 per cent come from the more complex and lucrative 'enterprise' software it designs for corporate clients. Netscape is expected to announce within the next two weeks that it will offer its browser free to corporate clients. Chris Selland, director of Internet computer strategies at the Yankee Group, believes that this could achieve more than just stemming its loss of market share. 'If you sell something, you have to support it,' says Selland. 'For that, you require a lot of people. It is not cheap. But if you give it away you can tell users: "You are on your own." Microsoft, on the other hand, has to support Explorer because it claims it is part of Windows 95, and people have paid for that.'

More worrying for Netscape is the marked decline in revenues from enterprise sales. Jim Barksdale, Netscape's president, blamed the losses on troubled economic conditions in Asia as well as increasing competition in America. Some analysts point out that Netscape has made the situation worse by frequently chopping and changing its strategies. Don DiPalmer, of Forrester Research in Boston, says: 'Netscape has had a rocky 1997, and some real problems with software and frequent releases of new versions of its software. Buyers of technology are not willing to commit themselves to the numerous revision cycles that these people are asking them to accept. And they are getting worried about Netscape. With Microsoft and Oracle they have no doubts that they can deliver on their promises.' Netscape's sales, which were $150m in the third quarter, sank to $125–$130m in the last quarter. For the full year the company expects a loss of $113m–$117m on sales of $450m; in 1996 it made a profit of $21m on sales of $346m.

Although Microsoft's critics have been accusing it of using anti-competitive tactics ever since it introduced the MS-DOS operating system for the first IBM PC in 1981, no case has been upheld against it. Critics claim this has as much to do with prevailing political and economic theories as lack of evidence, and that the Justice Department has only recently accepted the argument that free-market forces do not necessarily guarantee the success of the best product in high technology fields, as they usually do in other areas of commerce.

Brian Arthur, the Santa Fe Institute economics professor who has been advising the Justice Department, says: 'I was met with an enormous degree of hostility from other economists when I first suggested in 1984 that capitalism doesn't work in high technology. Whenever a company gets ahead [in high technology] it has an increasing advantage over its rivals, makes increasing returns, and is able to lever its position to dominate other markets. What I was saying was unacceptable because it was during the cold war and I was suggesting there was a fundamental flaw in capitalism.' Arthur names a series of 'inferior products' that have outdone superior ones, such as the VHS video beating Betamax and DOS beating Apple's operating system.

The concept of what most economists call 'network externalities' has now been more widely embraced. It means that the more that people use a given technology, the more likely that technology is to beat its competitors. In the computer industry the first company to establish an industry standard and a large installed base of products invariably dominates its market, as Microsoft dominates PC operating systems. Moreover, it puts it in a position to expand into other markets and dominate them in the same way.

'When Microsoft tried to buy Intuit [which makes software for electronic finance] in 1995 there was a fear that it would lever itself from there into banking, and we would soon have a Microsoft Bank,' says Arthur. The Justice Department challenged the acquisition in court, and Microsoft dropped its bid.

Microsoft is dismissive of such theories. It is bitterly contesting Judge Jackson's appointment of Lawrence Lessig, a Harvard Law School professor, to review the legal aspects of the antitrust charges. It claims the judge has delegated excessively broad powers to Lessig, who is to deliver a report to the court by the end of May. Microsoft says Lessig is biased against it, and has sought to prove this by giving the court copies of his electronic mail.

Brad Smith, a Microsoft lawyer, says: 'The network externalities theory misses the realities in our industry. The first thing you have to do in our industry if you develop a good product is to develop a second product that is better, or someone else is going to develop one that is going to make yours obsolete.

'The premise of network externalities is that if you have such a strong base you don't have to spend time and energy to protect yourself but can expand into other areas. I don't think the premise is a sound one. All the great successes that became failures, such as Word Perfect, dBase, Lotus 1-2-3, were people who took their eye off the ball. People here at Microsoft are constantly worrying about how to make our products better before someone else does.'

While Arthur and his fellow economists are aware of the danger of heavy-handed government intervention creating a greater problem than the one it seeks to solve, they are afraid that without intervention the incentives for innovation will be destroyed.

'What is at stake here is going to decide what the rules are going to be for the next 20, 30 and 50 years,' he says. 'In an ideal world, Netscape could not have been easily challenged by Microsoft. The fear now is that nobody will have the incentive to become the next Netscape. Gates is like a bully in a schoolyard. Someone has to stop him.'

Questions

1. Refer to section 1.1 and explain why the issues facing Netscape and Microsoft are strategic.
2. List (separately for Netscape and Microsoft) the main factors which you would identify from a strategic analysis of the situation under the three headings of environment, resources and expectations.
3. Think about the strategic choices for the future for each company in relation to the issues raised in section 1.2.2.
4. This case concerns global competition in an innovative industry. Refer to section 1.3 and decide how this particular context 'shapes' the relative importance of the elements of strategy (as shown in Exhibit 1.4).

Source *Sunday Times*, January 1998. Reproduced with permission.

2
STRATEGIC MANAGEMENT IN PRACTICE

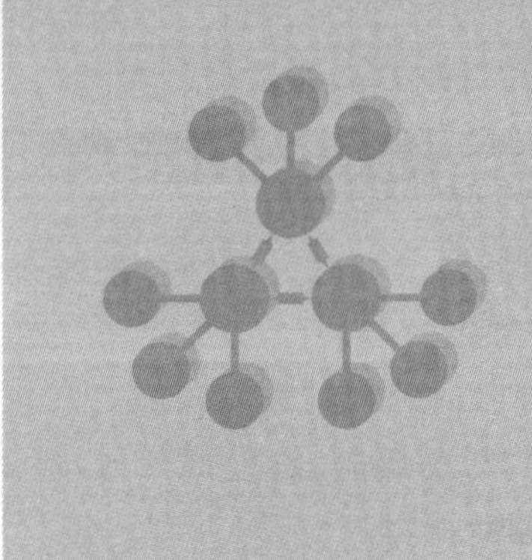

LEARNING OUTCOMES

After reading this chapter you should be able to:

- Describe different strategy development processes.
- Explain the benefits and problems of strategic planning systems.
- Explain the difference between intended and realised strategies.
- Understand the different 'routes' by which realised strategies occur.
- Explain the influence of cultural and political processes on strategy development.
- Explain organisational culture and describe the cultural web.
- Explain the reasons for strategic drift.
- Understand what is meant by a learning organisation.

2.1 INTRODUCTION

In Chapter 1 strategy was defined, as were the elements of strategic management – strategic analysis, strategic choice and strategy implementation. These elements provide a framework to help readers *think* about strategic problems and formulate strategy. It is important to understand, however, that this framework does not describe how organisational strategies *actually* come about. So before going on to examine the elements of the framework in more detail in Parts II, III and IV, it is useful to have a clearer understanding of how strategies come about in practice. This chapter provides a basis for that understanding.

The chapter has three parts (see Exhibit 2.1). The first part looks at *patterns of strategy development*: that is, the ways in which strategies are observed to develop over time in organisations. The conclusion reached is that strategic changes may take different forms, but they do not usually occur as major, one-off changes in direction; rather, they are more gradual, incremental developments, with only occasional, more 'transformational' change.

Exhibit 2.1 A framework for understanding strategic management in practice

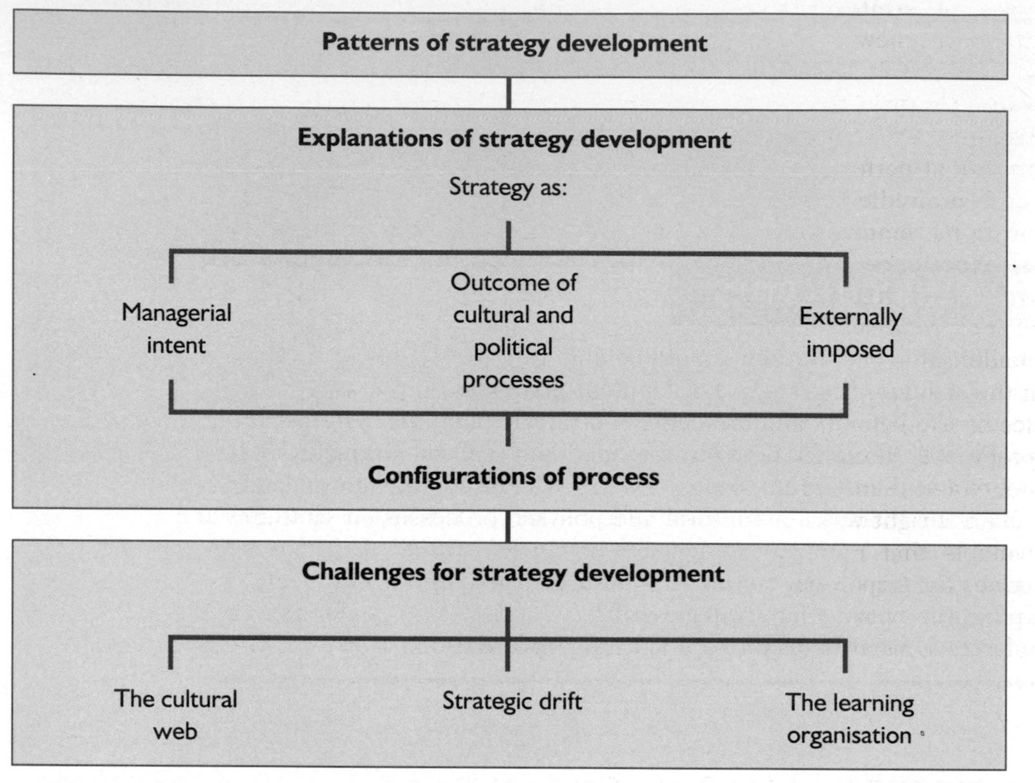

The second and main part of the chapter discusses three general *explanations of strategy development* in organisations which build on the discussion of different theories of strategy introduced in section 1.2.5 of Chapter 1. First, that strategies develop as a result of deliberate *managerial intent*; second, that strategies can be better explained as the *outcome of cultural and political processes* in and around organisations; and third, that strategy development is *imposed* on organisations. These three explanations are discussed in some detail not only because they provide different insights into how strategies come about, but also because they are important when it comes to considering how, in practice, managers might influence strategic decisions and implement strategic change. However, it is rare to find organisations in which singular explanations are adequate to explain strategic decision making and strategy development. Different types of organisation have different *configurations of strategy processes* in which the different explanations provided in this part of the chapter are more or less in evidence. Some typical configurations are reviewed and examples given.

The final part of the chapter builds on this review of processes to raise some *challenges for strategy development*. Since cultural and political processes of strategy development are important, the first section describes a framework – the *cultural web* – by which such influences can be explored. It is a framework which is subsequently used throughout the book. There is then a discussion as to why there is a tendency in organisations for *strategic drift*, in which strategies fail to change and organisational performance declines. Third, given an increasingly turbulent and unpredictable world and the importance of innovation in organisations, managers need to find ways of challenging their own and others' experience; the notion of a *learning organisation* is therefore discussed. Here organisations are seen as being reliant less on analysis and formalised processes of planning, and more on debate, experimentation and challenge.

In the *summary* at the end of the chapter, lessons are drawn from the practice of strategic decision making in terms of *implications for the study of strategy* and the content of this book. It is, however, important to sound a warning: because managers behave in particular ways does not mean that these are the right ways or the most sensible ways. The approach taken in this book is that readers will be able to assess a good deal better for themselves the importance and relevance of different approaches, concepts and techniques covered in the rest of the book if they understand the management of strategy as it happens in practice: and that is the role of this chapter.

2.2 PATTERNS OF STRATEGY DEVELOPMENT

Since strategy is about the long-term direction of an organisation, it is typically thought of in terms of major decisions about the future. However, it is a mistake to conceive of organisational strategy as necessarily developing through one-off major changes. The strategic development of organisations is better described and understood typically in terms of continuity, or 'momentum' of strategy:[1] once an organisation has adopted a particular strategy, it tends to develop from and within that strategy, rather than fundamentally changing direction.

2.2.1 Punctuated Equilibrium

Historical studies of organisations have shown that there are usually long periods of relative *continuity* during which established strategy remains unchanged or changes *incrementally*, and there are also periods of *flux* in which strategies change but in no very clear direction. *Transformational*

Exhibit 2.2 **Patterns of strategy development**

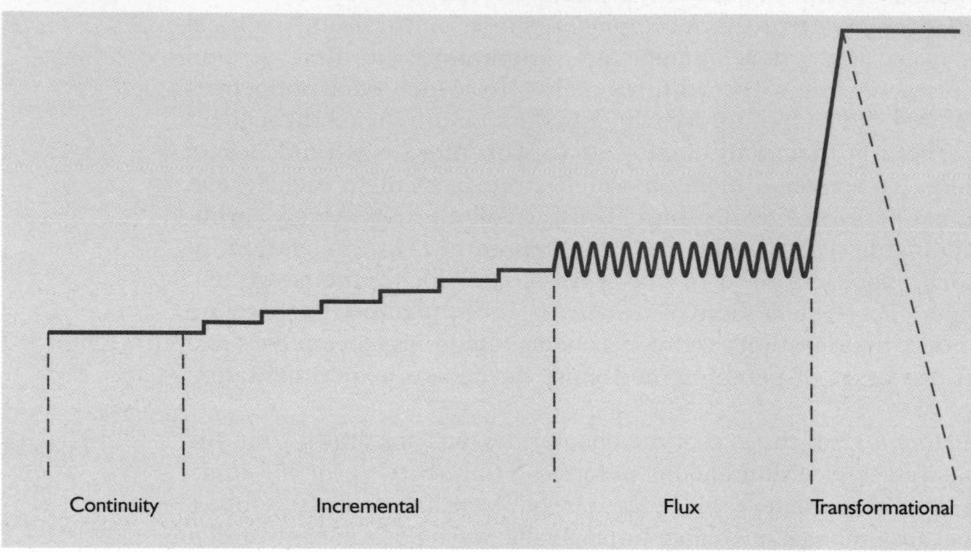

punctuated equilibrium *is the tendency of strategies to develop incrementally with periodic transformational change*

change, in which there is a fundamental change in strategic direction, does take place but is infrequent. This pattern has become known as **punctuated equilibrium**[2] – the tendency of strategies to develop incrementally with periodic transformational change – and is illustrated in Exhibit 2.2 and Illustration 2.1.

A specific strategic move – perhaps a product launch, or a significant investment decision – establishes a strategic direction which, itself, guides decisions on the next strategic move – an acquisition perhaps. This in turn helps consolidate the strategic direction, and over time the overall strategic approach of the organisation becomes more established. As time goes on, each decision taken is by this *emerging* strategy and, in turn, reinforces it. Exhibit 2.3 shows this. This process could, of course, lead to a quite significant shift in strategy, but incrementally.

In many respects, such gradual change makes a lot of sense. No organisation could function effectively if it were to undergo major revisions of strategy frequently; and, in any case, it is unlikely that the environment will change so rapidly that this would be necessary. Incremental change might therefore be seen as an adaptive process to a continually changing environment; and in this sense it corresponds to what was referred to in Chapter 1 as the 'fit' concept of strategic management. There are, however, dangers. Environmental change may not always be gradual enough for incremental change to keep pace: if such incremental strategic change lags behind environmental change, the organisation may get out of line with its

STRATEGY IN ACTION
Illustration 2.1

Punctuated Equilibrium: The Burton Group

Organisations experience long periods of stability during which established strategies change gradually. They undergo transformational change on an infrequent basis.

The Family Era, 1901–70: 'Consistent Momentum'

Prior to 1970, Burton was a manufacturer of men's made-to-measure suits which were sold through its retail outlets. The company was family controlled with a paternalistic and centralised view of management. By the late 1960s, the rise in demand for ready-to-wear suits by younger, fashion-conscious men and increased competition from fashion boutiques led the family to appoint Ladislas Rice as CEO to realign the company's strategy.

The Rice Era, 1970–76: 'Attempted Transformation and Flux'

Rice attempted the radical reorganisation of changing focus from manufacturing to retailing, with an emphasis on ready-to-wear fashion clothes, and embarked on a strategy of diversification into different types of retailing to utilise Burton's strong capital base and extensive property portfolio. The retail businesses were organised as divisions and encouraged to make annual plans for profitable development.

The Spencer Era, 1977–81: 'Consolidation'

Continued poor performance led to a strategy of consolidation of existing units rather than continued broadening of Burton's retail base. A boardroom struggle was resolved with Rice resigning as chief executive. The aim of his successor, Spencer, was 'to eliminate loss-making businesses' and modernise retail outlets.

The Halpern Era, 1981–90: 'Successful Transformation and Flux'

Ralph Halpern sought to refocus the business on fashion retailing. He closed down manufacturing, disposed of non-fashion retail chains and invested heavily in 'lifestyle' retailing – different fashion retail concepts for different market segments. This transformed Burton's retail presence and its performance. However, following the takeover of Debenhams in 1985, there was concern that the company had lost the clear direction and success of the early 1980s. Declining performance and overinvestment in property led to Halpern's resignation in 1990.

Burton in the 1990s: 'Back to Basics and Beyond'

The appointment of John Hoerner as CEO in 1992 saw the company enter a period of consolidation. Cost reduction involved extensive restructuring to achieve better integration and communication and led to the loss of 2,000 jobs. Supplier relationships were overhauled and a refocused target market strategy for the different brands resulted in better profit margins. However, 1997 saw the announcement that Debenhams would be demerged from the other 'multiples' businesses, which became Arcadia. The intent was to bring greater clarity and focus to what had become recognised as different retailing approaches.

Questions

Drawing on Chapter 2 in general, and section 2.2.1 in particular:

1. Explain why you think Burton has gone through cycles of 'punctuated equilibrium'.
2. Do you think the pattern of 'punctuated equilibrium' is inevitable? Can managers have an influence over this? How?

Prepared by Tony Jacobs, Bristol Business School.

Exhibit 2.3 **Strategic evolution and consolidation**

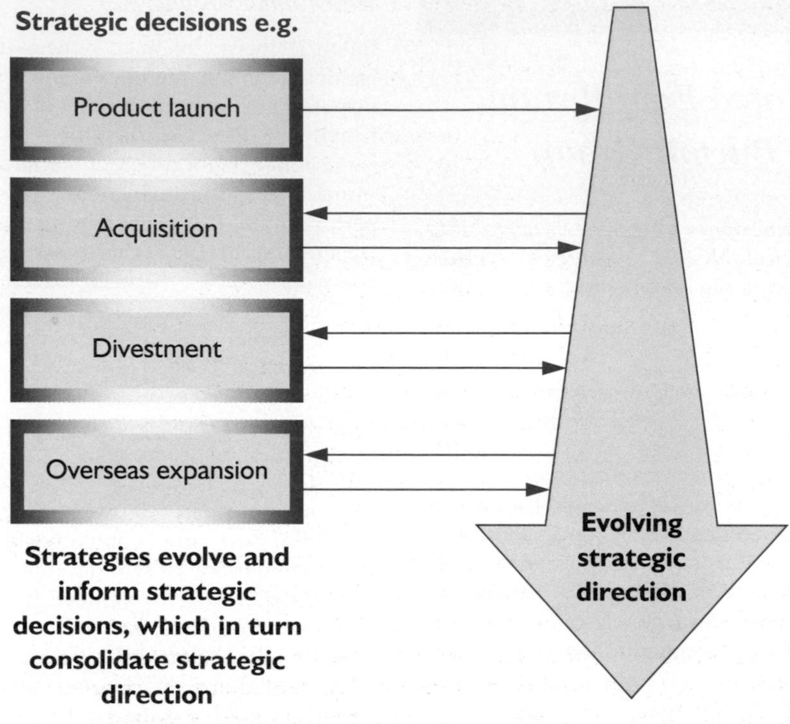

environment and, in time, need more fundamental, or transformational, change. Indeed, transformational change tends to occur at times when performance has declined significantly. There is another danger: that organisations become merely reactive to their environment and fail to question or challenge what is happening around them or to innovate to create new opportunities; in short, they become complacent. Some of these dangers can be seen as inherent in the descriptions of strategic management which follow.

Such dangers are also the concern of those who advocate a *stretch* view of strategic management, who argue that it is not sufficient just to be responsive to the environment; that the strategist should be more innovatory, proactively trying to *create* new markets, or new opportunities. For example, companies that develop entirely new products or services may be creating customer needs and expectations that did not previously exist, and in this way be creating new markets. It can, of course, be risky to do so because the innovations may not be accepted in the market (see section 2.8.2); but if they are, this is another way in which transformational change can occur.

2.2.2 Intended and Realised Strategies

Conceiving of organisations' strategies in terms of such patterns of change means that it is important to be careful about just what is meant by 'strategy' and how it comes about. This can be explained in different ways.

- Typically, strategy has been written about as though it is developed by managers in an *intended*, planned fashion. **Intended strategy** is an expression of desired strategic direction deliberately formulated or planned by managers. It may be that the implementation of this intended strategy is also planned in terms of resource allocation, structure and so on. Strategy is here conceived of as a deliberate, systematic planned process of development and implementation (see route 1 in Exhibit 2.4).[3] As explained in Chapter 1, it is broadly the framework adopted in this book because it is a convenient way of thinking through the issues relating to strategy. However, it does not necessarily explain how strategies actually come about, or are 'realised'. **Realised strategy** is the strategy actually being followed in practice.

intended strategy *is an expression of desired strategic direction deliberately formulated or planned by managers*

realised strategy *is the strategy actually being followed in practice*

- In many organisations which attempt to formulate strategies in such systematic ways, the intended strategies do not become realised; or only part of what is intended comes about. Much of what is intended follows route 2 in Exhibit 2.4 and is *unrealised*; it does not come about in practice. There may be all sorts of reasons for this, and the rest of the chapter helps explain some of these. It may also be the case, of course, that managers decide that a strategy, as planned, should not be put into effect: for example, if circumstances facing the organisation change.
- Strategy could also be *imposed* on an organisation (route 3 in Exhibit 2.4). It could be imposed by an external agency such as government, as has occurred in the deregulation of industries in many countries; or by a parent company on a subsidiary. It could be that environmental conditions severely limit the choices that managers can make or the strategies they can follow. For example, the cutting of costs may be forced by recession or conditions in a commodity market, and may mean that there is little opportunity to follow strategies substantially different from those of other businesses in that market.
- If strategy is regarded as the long-term direction of the organisation, which develops over time, then it can also be seen as the *outcome of cultural and political processes* (route 4 in Exhibit 2.4).[4] The management of organisations depends a great deal on the knowledge and experience of those involved. This experience and ways of doing things are built up over years, often taken for granted (or tacit) and applied in managing the strategy of organisations. In organisations, managers typically reconcile different views, based on experience,

Exhibit 2.4 **Strategy development routes**

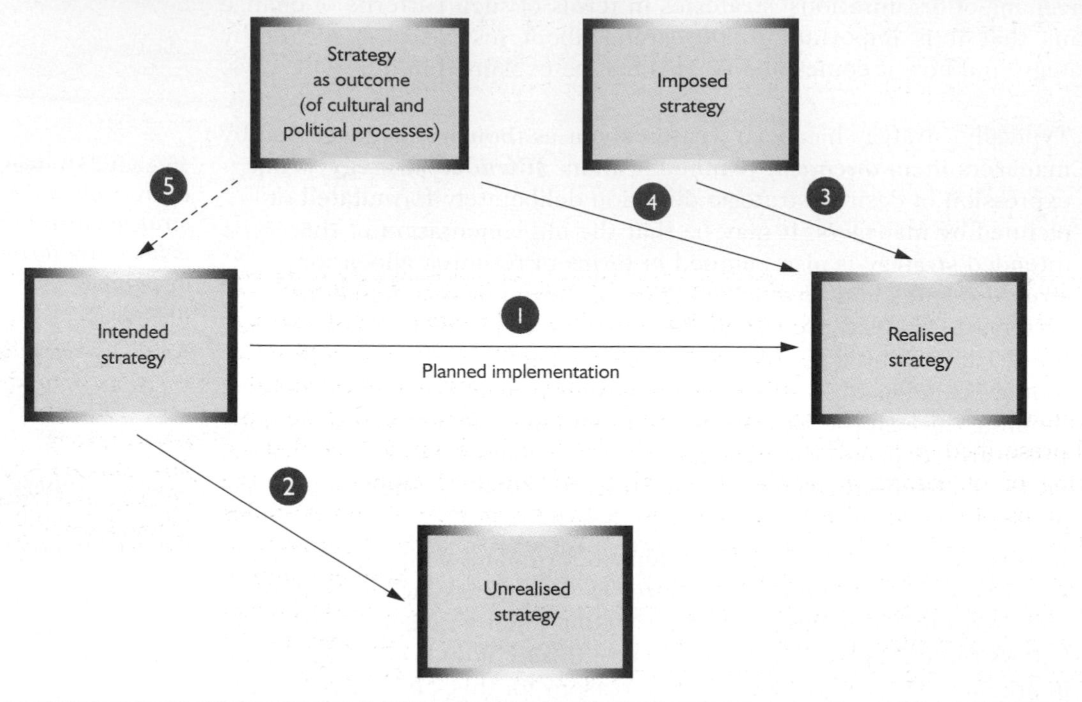

through *negotiation* or the exercise of *power*; and this occurs within established ways of doing things, or *routines*, that make up the culture of the organisation. Strategy can be seen as the outcome of such processes. If plans exist, they may perform the role of monitoring the progress or efficiency of a strategy which emerges as the outcome of such experience and ways of doing things. Or they may do little more than pull together the views and 'wisdom' built up over time in the organisation. Indeed, it is often a complaint of chief executives that the planning systems in their organisation have degenerated into little more than post-rationalisations of where the organisation has come from. This is route 5 in Exhibit 2.4. It can be dangerous because the organisation appears to be taking a proactive, systematic approach to strategy development when it is not.

These different explanations of how strategies and their implications are developed are now explored in more detail. However, it is important to stress that it is most unlikely that any one of the explanations given here accounts entirely for the processes at work in an organisation; strategy development needs to be understood in terms of a mix of processes, and this is demonstrated in section 2.7.

2.3 STRATEGY DEVELOPMENT AS MANAGERIAL INTENT

The idea that strategy comes about in organisations through deliberate managerial intent can, itself, be explained in different ways. Here the *planning* view, a *command* view and the notion of *logical incrementalism* are discussed.

2.3.1 The Planning View[5]

In the 1960s and 1970s, books were written about strategy which took the view that strategy not only could but that it should come about through formalised **strategic planning**, a sequence of analytical and evaluative procedures to formulate an intended strategy and the means of implementing it. Such books advocated the setting up of corporate planning departments and prescribed tools and techniques that should be used. These included the setting of objectives or goals; the analysis of the environment and the resources of the organisations, so as to match environmental opportunities and threats with resource-based strengths and weaknesses; the generation of strategic options and their evaluation; and the planning of implementation through resource allocation processes, the structuring of the organisation and the design of control systems – all to be done in a prescribed way in the organisation. An example of such a system is given as Illustration 2.2.

strategic planning *is a sequence of analytical and evaluative procedures to formulate an intended strategy and the means of implementing it*

While many of the steps described in such a planning system are similar to those adopted in this book, the difference is that proponents of such a planning view tend to argue that a highly systematic approach is *the* rational approach to strategy formulation. The evidence of the extent to which the formalised pursuit of such a systemised approach results in organisations performing better than others is, however, equivocal[6] – not least because it is difficult to isolate formal planning as the dominant or determining effect on performance. Formalised planning can, however, be useful in various ways:

- It can provide a structured means of *analysis and thinking* about complex strategic problems, requiring managers to *question and challenge* what they take for granted.
- It can be used as a way of involving people in strategy development, therefore helping to create *ownership* of the strategy.
- Strategic planning may also help to *communicate* intended strategy.
- It can be used as a means of *control* by regularly reviewing performance and progress against agreed objectives or previously agreed strategic direction.
- It can be a useful means of *co-ordination*, for example by bringing together the various SBU strategies within an overall corporate strategy, or ensuring that resources within a business are co-ordinated to put strategy into effect.

STRATEGY IN ACTION
Illustration 2.2

National Health Service Business Planning Cycle 1995/96

Strategic planning aims to analyse and evaluate strategic options and to co-ordinate activity.
NHS Trusts in England formulate annual strategic plans to meet the specific health needs of their local populations in line with national health policy, baseline requirements and medium-term (3–5 year) objectives. They have to meet set deadlines for business plans.

	ORGANISATION	SEPTEMBER	OCTOBER	NOVEMBER	DECEMBER	JANUARY	MARCH
NATIONAL	**NHS Executive**	• Issue availability of revenue		• Issue common information requirements	• Issue revenue allocation to health authorities • Review plans • Announce initial capital allocations		
REGIONAL	**NHS Executive Regional Offices**		• Review Trust draft strategic direction of service providers		• Joint agreement on capital investment (by 23/12)	• Review Trust draft business plans and notify external finance limits	• Arbitrate • Sign off corporate contracts with RHA/DHAs
REGIONAL	**Regional health authorities** (RHA)		• Review contracting intentions of purchasers of services			• Notify health authorities of capital cash limits	
LOCAL	**District health authorities** (DHA) (purchasers of services)	• Publish initial purchasing plans and contracting intentions (by 15/09)		• Submit draft outline of corporate contract to Regional Office		• Issue finalised contracting intentions (by 20/01) • Submit final local corporate contract to Regional Office	• Agree and sign all contracts (by 15/03) • Make purchasing plans public
LOCAL	**NHS trusts** (service providers)	• Submit draft strategic direction (if appropriate) • Inform purchasers of major changes to pricing structure	• Submit business plans for capital investment	• Publish initial first cut prices • Submit draft business plans based on analysis of needs		• Provide finalised prices to purchasers of services	• Agree and sign all contracts (by 15/03) • Publish strategic direction

Source Philip Davies, Cranfield School of Management.

- It can encourage a *longer-term view* of strategy than might otherwise occur. Planning horizons vary, of course. In a fast-moving consumer goods company, 3–5 year plans may be appropriate. In companies which have to take very long term views on capital investment, such as those in the oil industry, planning horizons can be as long as 14 years (in Exxon) or 20 years (in Shell).

There may, however, be dangers in the formalisation of strategic planning. They include the following:[7]

- Strategies are more or less successfully implemented through people. Their behaviour will not be determined by plans. So the *cultural and political dimensions* of organisations have to be taken into account. Planning processes are not typically designed to do this.
- The strategy resulting from deliberations of a corporate planning department, or a senior management team, may not be *owned* more widely in the organisation. In one extreme instance, a colleague was discussing the strategy of a company with its planning director. He was told that a strategic plan existed, but found that it was locked in the drawer of the executive's desk. Only the planner, and a few other senior executives, were permitted to see it.
- The managers responsible for the implementation of strategies, usually line managers, may be so busy with the day-to-day operations of the business that they cede responsibility for strategic issues to specialists. However, the specialists do not have power in the organisation to make things happen. The result can be that strategic planning becomes an *intellectual exercise* removed from the reality of operation. As General William Sherman said in 1869 in the context of the American Civil War: 'I know there exist many good men who honestly believe that one may, by the aid of modern science, sit in comfort and ease in his office chair and, with figures and algebraic symbols, master the great game of war. I think this is an insidious and most dangerous mistake.'[8]
- The process of strategic planning may be so cumbersome that individuals or groups in the firm might contribute to only part of it and *not understand the whole*. This is particularly problematic in very large firms. One executive, on taking over as marketing manager in a large multinational consumer goods firm, was told by his superior: 'we do corporate planning in the first two weeks of April, then we get back to our jobs.'
- There is a danger that strategy becomes thought of as *the plan*. Managers may see themselves as managing strategy because they are going through the processes of planning. Strategy is, of course, not the same as 'the plan': strategy is the long-term direction that the organisation is following, not a written document on an executive's shelf. Here we get back to the difference between *intended* and *realised* strategies.

- Strategic planning can become over-detailed in its approach, concentrating on extensive analysis which, while sound in itself, may miss the major strategic issues facing the organisation. For example, it is not unusual to find companies with huge amounts of information on their markets, but with little clarity about the strategic importance of that information. The result can be *information overload* with no clear outcome.
- Planning can become obsessed with the search for absolute determinants of performance – a set of economic indicators, for example – or a definitively *right strategy*. In the first place, it is unlikely that a 'right' strategy will somehow naturally fall out of the planning process. It might be more important to establish a more generalised strategic direction within which there is flexibility. As Mintzberg puts it: 'If you have no vision, but only formal plans, then every unpredicted change in the environment makes you feel your sky is falling in.'[9]

Certainly there has been a decline in the use of formal corporate planning departments. For example, a study of corporate planning in the oil industry found that, between 1990 and 1996, corporate planning staff had declined from 48 to 3 in BP, 60 to 17 in Exxon, 38 to 12 in Mobil and 54 to 17 in Shell.[10]

2.3.2 The Command View

a **command view** *is where strategy develops through the direction of an individual or group*

If planning has to do with managerial intent, so too does a second explanation of how strategies develop in organisations: a **command view**. Here strategy develops through the direction of an individual or group, but not necessarily through formal planning.

At the extreme, strategy could be seen as the product of an autocratic leader who brooks no argument and sees other managers as there to implement his or her decisions. More common, perhaps, is the situation where a dominant leader has become personally associated with strategy development of the organisation. It could be that this individual turned round the business in times of difficulty and, as such, personifies the success of the organisation. Charismatic leaders are also often seen as central to the strategy of their organisation:[11] their personality or reputation may be seen as a positive force, and other managers may willingly defer to such an individual and see strategy as his or her province. In some organisations an individual is central because he or she is its owner or founder; this is often the case in small businesses. Others in the organisation may see strategic direction of the organisation as inevitably and properly associated with that individual.

In public sector organisations, officials or civil servants are meant to work to the direction of their political masters, which at least in theory is the command or 'will of the people', perhaps through a process of mandate and elections. Indeed, political leaders often call upon such mandated authority to justify their assertion of an overall economic or social strategy.

2.3.3 The Logical Incremental View

Given the complexity of organisations and the environments in which they operate, managers cannot consider all possible strategic options in terms of all possible futures and evaluate these against preset, unambiguous objectives, especially in an organisational context in which there are conflicting views, values and power bases. So the idea that strategies can be preset on a grand scale through neat, logical, sequential planning mechanisms is unrealistic. Rather, strategy building takes place through 'successive limited comparisons'.[12]

In a study of major multinational businesses, Quinn[13] concluded that the management process could best be described as *logical incrementalism*. Managers have a view of where they want the organisation to be in years to come and try to move towards this position in an evolutionary way. They do this by attempting to ensure the success and development of a strong, secure, but flexible core business, building on the experience gained in that business to inform decisions about the development of the business and perhaps experimenting with 'side bet' ventures. There may be recognition that such experiments cannot be expected to be the sole responsibility of top management – that they should be encouraged to emerge from lower levels, or 'subsystems' in the organisation. Effective managers realise that they cannot do away with the uncertainty of their environment by trying to 'know' about how it will change. Rather, they try to be sensitive to environmental signals through constant scanning and by testing changes in strategy in small-scale steps. Commitment to strategic options may therefore be tentative in the early stages of strategy development. There is also a reluctance to specify precise objectives too early, as this might stifle ideas and prevent experimentation. Objectives may therefore be fairly general in nature. Overall, **logical incrementalism** can be thought of as the deliberate development of strategy by 'learning through doing'. In this sense it resembles the 'crafting' explanation[14] of strategy development given in section 1.2.5 of Chapter 1.

logical incrementalism *is the deliberate development of strategy by 'learning through doing'*

Such a process is seen by managers to have benefits. Continual testing and gradual strategy implementation provides improved quality of information for decision making, and enables the better sequencing of the elements of major decisions. Since change will be gradual, the possibility of creating and developing a commitment to change throughout the organisation is increased. Because the different parts, or 'subsystems', of the organisation are in a continual state of interplay, the managers of each can learn from each other about the feasibility of a course of action. Such processes also take account of the political nature of organisational life, since smaller changes are less likely to face the same degree of resistance as major changes. Moreover, the formulation of strategy in this way means that the implications of the strategy are continually being tested out. This continual readjustment

Exhibit 2.5 **Incremental change**

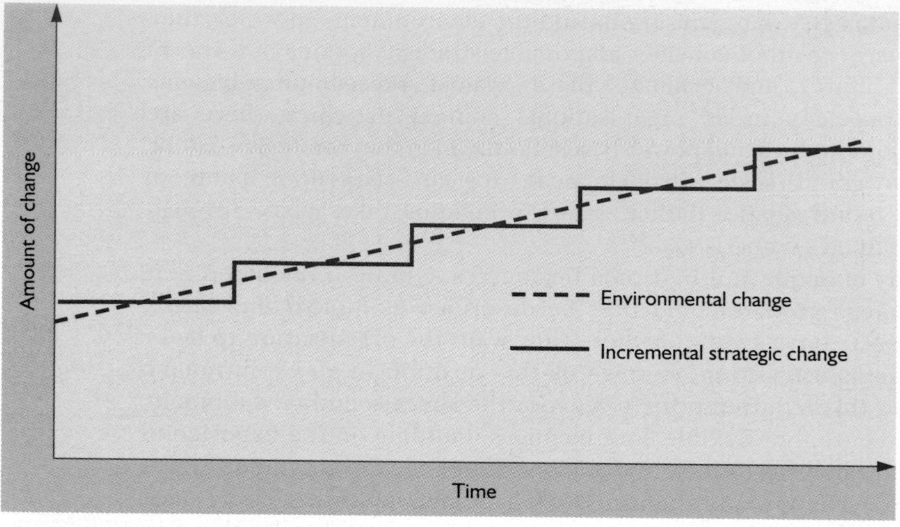

makes sense if the environment is considered as a continually changing influence on the organisation. It is a process through which the organisation keeps itself in line with such change, as shown diagrammatically in Exhibit 2.5.

Logical incrementalism does not, then, see strategic management in terms of a neat sequential model. The idea that the implementation of strategy somehow follows a choice, which in turn has followed analysis, does not hold. Rather, strategy is seen to be worked through in action.

This view of strategy making is similar to the descriptions that managers themselves often give of how strategies come about in their organisation. Illustration 2.3 provides some examples of managers explaining the strategy development process in their organisation. They see their job as 'strategists' as continually, proactively pursuing a strategic goal, countering competitive moves and adapting to their environment, while not 'rocking the boat' too much, so as to maintain efficiency and performance. Quinn himself argues that 'properly managed, it is a conscious, purposeful, pro-active, executive practice'.[15]

There is, however, another explanation of incremental strategy development: that it is an inevitable outcome of the cultural and political processes of organisations: that problems are dealt with by applying taken-for-granted experience and ways of doing things, and by negotiation to make decisions.[16] Strategy develops as an accumulation of such decisions over time. This is a view which is now discussed in more detail.

STRATEGY IN ACTION
Illustration 2.3

An Incrementalist View of Strategic Management

Managers often see their job as managing adaptively; continually changing strategy to keep in line with the environment, while maintaining efficiency and keeping stakeholders happy.

- 'You know there is a simple analogy you can make. To move forward when you walk, you create an imbalance, you lean forward and you don't know what is going to happen. Fortunately, you put a foot ahead of you and you recover your balance. Well, that's what we're doing all the time, so it is never comfortable.'[1]
- 'The environment is very fast changing. You can set a strategic direction one day and something is almost certain to happen the next. We do not have a planning process which occurs every two years because the environment is stable, but a very dynamic process which needs to respond to the unexpected.'[1]
- 'I begin wide-ranging discussions with people inside and outside the corporation. From these a pattern eventually emerges. It's like fitting together a jigsaw puzzle. At first the vague outline of an approach appears like the sail of a ship in a puzzle. Then suddenly the rest of the puzzle becomes quite clear. You wonder why you didn't see it all along.'[2]
- 'The real strength of the company is to be able to follow these peripheral excursions into whatever ... one has to keep thrusting in these directions; they are little tentacles going out, testing the water.'[3]
- 'We haven't stood still in the past and I can't see with our present set-up that we shall stand still in the future; but what I really mean is that it is a path of evolution rather than revolution. Some companies get a successful formula and stick to that rigidly because that is what they know – for example, [Company X] did not really adapt to change, so they had to take what was a revolution. We hopefully have changed gradually and that's what I think we should do. We are always looking for fresh openings without going off at a tangent.'[3]
- 'The analogy of a chess game is useful in this context. The objective of chess is clear: to gain victory by capturing your opponent's king. Most players begin with a strategic move, that assumes a countermove by the opponent. If the countermove materialises, then the next move follows automatically, based on a previous winning strategy. However, the beauty of chess is the unpredictability of one's opponent's moves. To attempt to predict the outcome of chess is impossible, and therefore players limit themselves to working on possibilities and probabilities of moves that are not too far ahead.'[4]

Questions

1. With reference to these explanations of strategy development, what are the main advantages of developing strategies incrementally?
2. Is incremental strategy development bound to result in strategic drift? How might this be avoided?

Sources

1. Quotes from interviews conducted by A. Bailey as part of a research project sponsored by the Economic and Social Research Council (Grant No.: R000235100).
2. Extract from J.B. Quinn, *Strategies for Change*, Irwin, 1980.
3. Extracts from G. Johnson, *Strategic Change and the Management Process*, Blackwell, 1987.
4. From a manager on a MBA course.

2.4 STRATEGY DEVELOPMENT AS THE OUTCOME OF CULTURAL AND POLITICAL PROCESSES

This part of the chapter explains how the development of strategies can be explained in cultural terms (section 2.4.1) and as a political or networking process (section 2.4.2). It then brings these explanations together and shows their relevance in the context of how strategic decisions are made in organisations (section 2.4.3).

2.4.1 The Cultural View

Organisational culture is the 'deeper level of basic *assumptions and beliefs* that are shared by members of an organisation, that operate unconsciously and define in a basic taken-for-granted fashion an organisation's view of itself and its environment'.[17] Management cannot be conceived of just in terms of the manipulation of techniques or tools of analysis; it is also about the application of experience built up over years often within the same organisation or industry. This is rooted not only in individual experience, but also in group and organisational experience reflected in organisational routines accumulated over time. It is therefore important to recognise the significance of organisational culture in strategy development. The **cultural view** takes the position that strategies can be seen as the outcome of the taken-for-granted assumptions and routines of organisations.

cultural view *strategies are the outcome of the taken-for-granted assumptions and routines of organisations*

This taken-for-grantedness is likely to be handed down over time within a group. That group might be, for example, a managerial function such as marketing or finance; a professional grouping, such as accountants; an organisation as a whole; and more widely an industry sector, or even a national culture. There are, then, many cultural frames of reference which influence managers: Exhibit 2.6 shows this graphically and Illustration 2.4 gives examples of 'taken-for-grantedness' at the regional and industry levels (sometimes called an *industry recipe*).[18] Such taken-for-granted assumptions are also likely to exist at the organisational level – the organisational *paradigm*[19] – and can be especially important as an influence on the development of organisational strategy. Although the term 'paradigm' is not commonly used by institutional theorists,[20] they argue in much the same way: that it is important to recognise the way in which organisations operating in similar environments or industries come to resemble each other in terms of cultural norms and in the strategies they employ (see page 27 and Exhibit 1.6).

An organisation's paradigm can be traced to different influences:

- An organisation with a relatively stable management, and a long-term *momentum of strategy*, is likely to have a more homogeneous paradigm than one in which there has been rapid turnover of management and significant change forced upon it.

Exhibit 2.6 Cultural frames of reference

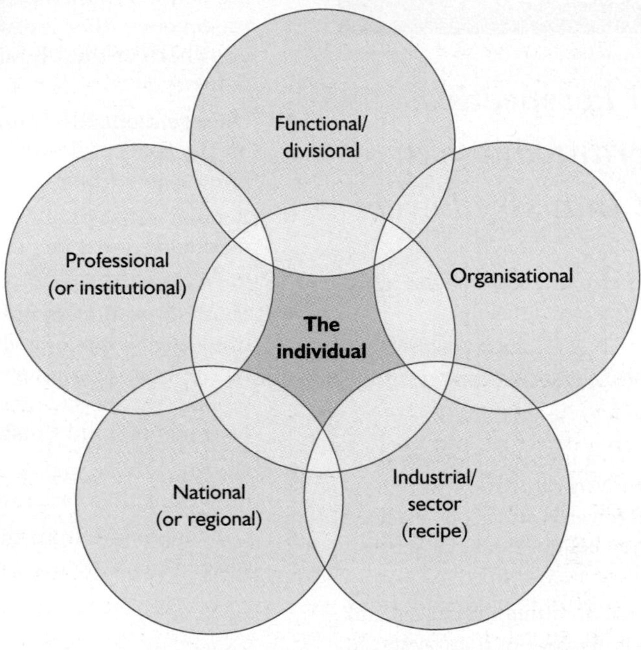

- Organisations with a dominant *professional influence*, perhaps an accountancy firm, are likely to demonstrate a homogeneous paradigm.
- *Industry influences* may be particularly strong if the transfer of staff between firms tends to be limited to that industry, as it often is in engineering, banking and many parts of the public sector, for example.

In this book the word '**paradigm**' is frequently employed to mean the set of assumptions held relatively in common and taken for granted in an organisation. Because they are taken for granted (or tacit), they are unlikely to be talked about as problematic. They are also likely to evolve gradually rather than change rapidly. For an organisation to operate effectively there has to be such a generally accepted set of assumptions; in effect, it represents *collective experience* without which people would have to 'reinvent their world' for different circumstances that they face. The paradigm allows the experience gathered over years to be applied to a given situation to make sense of it, to conceive of a likely course of action and the likelihood of success of that course of action. The paradigm is not, then, the same as the explicit *values* of an organisation, though these may be informed by the paradigm; nor is it the same as the *strategy* of an organisation, though that too will be informed by the paradigm.

a **paradigm** *is the set of assumptions held relatively in common and taken for granted in an organisation*

STRATEGY IN ACTION
Illustration 2.4

A Cultural Perspective: Taken-for-grantedness at Regional and Industry Levels

Shared assumptions help to explain the way business is done and strategy develops.

At Regional Level: The Overseas Chinese in East Asia[1]

- The Chinese work hard not only because they have been brought up to value hard work, associated material rewards and social esteem, but also because they believe financial success brings honour to their ancestors.
- A high value is placed on human relations and trust, built on social obligation. If an overseas Chinese fails to demonstrate trustworthiness to members of the business community, credits and financial help will not be extended and exclusion from the overseas Chinese network locally and internationally is likely.
- Harmony and reciprocity are emphasised, with avoidance of confrontation and business relationships dictated by legality. To initiate business relationships, Chinese entrepreneurs never approach one another directly, but rather use a mutual acquaintance, who acts as the matchmaker. Relationships begin with minor transactions with little risk involved and little trust required. Gradually, larger exchanges involving more risks and greater mutual trust are transacted.
- Mythological influences affect business: for example, that the Japanese race had its origins in China, explaining why so much business is done with the Japanese.

At Industry Sector Level: Producers in the Scottish Knitwear Industry[2]

Managers in the industry assume:

- Scottish firms are not good at designing high-fashion garments.
- The competitive boundaries of the industry are defined to include only Scottish producers. Other knitwear producers, even elsewhere in the UK, are in a different industry.
- Only gentlemanly competition is permitted on the basis of design, service and quality. Price competition is frowned upon.
- Retailer satisfaction, achieved through producing small lots of customised garments, is the key to success.
- Scottish producers only ever buy dyed yarn from local suppliers which are considered to be the best. Machinery will never fully replace the labour-intensive, highly skilled methods of hand finishing.
- Design, service and quality are more important than price to the consumer.
- Consumers are from the top 5 per cent of wage earners, so demand is price inelastic.

Questions

For both the Chinese and Scottish knitwear examples:

1. Suggest ways in which taken-for-grantedness might
   (a) provide benefits
   (b) be problematic in managing in that context.
2. If you were appointed CEO of a Scottish knitwear firm and wanted to see rapid growth in terms of sales volume, what difficulties might you face?

Sources

1. D.C.L. Ch'ng, *The Overseas Chinese Entrepreneurs in East Asia*, Committee for Economic Development of Australia, December 1993.
2. J.F. Porac, H. Thomas and C. Baden-Fuller, 'Competitive groups as cognitive communities: the case of Scottish knitwear manufacturers', *Journal of Management Studies*, vol. 26, no. 4 (1989) pp. 397–416.

Prepared by Sara Martin, Cranfield School of Management.

The relationship between the paradigm and organisational strategy needs to be made clear. Exhibit 2.7 helps to do this. Environmental forces and organisational capabilities do not in themselves create strategy; people create strategy. The forces at work in the environment, and the organisation's capabilities in coping with these, are made sense of in terms of the experience[21] of managers and the collective assumptions within the paradigm. However, environmental forces and organisational capabilities, while having this indirect influence on strategy formulation, nonetheless impact on organisational performance more directly. For example, many consumer goods companies which were very powerful in the 1970s lost significant market share in the 1980s and 1990s as grocery retail chains became bigger and buying power became more centralised. Initially, many failed to recognise the impact such changes would have on them. Their view about market structure assumed direct influence by them over consumer buying behaviour; the retailer was seen just as a distributor. It took many years for some to come to terms with the fact that the retailers had become of major strategic importance as customers in their own right. The consumer goods companies' strategies continued to be driven by their long-established paradigms, while the behaviour of the retailers – for example, in moving to other suppliers – directly affected their performance, for many resulting in substantial loss of market share and profits. The potential difference between the actual influences and managerial perceptions of the influences on the organisation can give rise to significant problems – and is an issue returned to later.

The taken-for-grantedness in organisations or industries is, then, one of the major problems in trying to develop innovative strategies in organisations. The influence of the paradigm is, in essence, conservative. Innovation is likely to mean questioning, even challenging, basic assumptions, which can be uncomfortable for those who attempt it and threatening for those who do not welcome it. This is the more so since, at the organisational level at least, the paradigm is likely to be linked to other aspects of organisational culture, such as organisational *rituals*, *stories* and the everyday *routines* of organisational life. Section 2.8.1 of this chapter considers further how these wider cultural aspects of organisations are linked to other aspects of strategic management.

2.4.2 Organisational Politics and Networks

a **political view** *is that strategies develop as the outcome of processes of bargaining and negotiation among powerful internal or external interest groups (or stakeholders)*

The **political view**[22] of strategy development is that strategies develop as the outcome of processes of bargaining and negotiation among powerful internal or external interest groups (or stakeholders). Different interest groups (or *stakeholders*) may have different expectations and may even be in conflict; there may be differences between groups of managers, between managers and shareholders, or between powerful individuals. These differences are resolved through processes of *bargaining*, *negotiation* or perhaps *edict*.

Exhibit 2.7 The role of the paradigm in strategy formulation

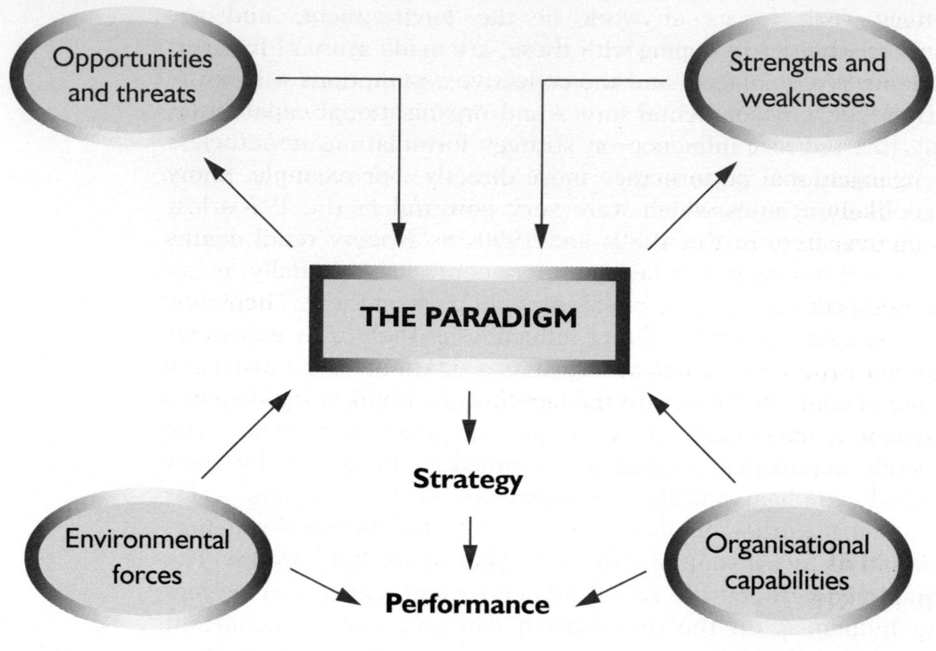

Powerful individuals or groups may also influence the sort of *information* that is seen to be important. Information is not politically neutral, but rather can be a source of power for those who control what is seen to be important; so the withholding of information, or the influences of one manager over another because that manager controls sources of information, can be important. Powerful individuals and groups may also strongly influence the *identification of key issues*, the *objectives* of the organisation and even the strategies eventually selected. Differing views may be pursued not only on the basis of the extent to which they reflect environmental or competitive pressures, for example, but also because they have implications for the status or influence of different stakeholders.

Even if an organisation is not overtly political in such ways, it is important to understand the extent to which the relationships between individuals, perhaps built up over many years, may be important. There are those who explain organisational working on the basis of *social networks*.[23] Here organisations are not depicted as hierarchies or power groupings so much as different interest groups or operations which need to co-operate with each other, negotiate what should be done and find ways of accommodating different views. For example, in professional services firms such as accountants or lawyers, partners may not be organised hierarchically, but will have co-operated and found ways of working with each other over many years. Those managers who work for them may, similarly, have worked for many years in the firm and have become trusted by the partners. In such circumstances, it is likely that decisions will come about as a result of the discussions and, again, bargaining that goes on within the social interaction and networks that exist between such individuals. Similarly, a multinational firm working on a global scale is unlikely to be solely reliant on formal structural processes to make things happen. It is likely that it will be dependent on the network of contacts that builds up over time between different parts of the organisation across the world.

Such a perspective on decision making, whether seen as explicitly political or more to do with networks, therefore suggests that strategies may emerge through processes of bargaining and negotiation (see Illustration 2.5). Understanding the influence of such processes is important; Chapter 5 returns to this in more detail.

2.4.3 Cultural and Political Processes in Strategic Decision Making

Studies which have traced how particular strategic decisions are made in organisations[24] show how cultural and political processes play a part in strategy development. These processes are represented in Exhibit 2.8.

The *awareness* of strategic issues in organisations is not necessarily an analytical process; rather, people get a 'gut feeling' based on their previous experience or received wisdom. These people may not be managers; they may be those in most direct contact with whatever stimulates this awareness, such as sales staff dealing with customers. This awareness 'incubates' as various stimuli help build up a picture of the extent to which circumstances deviate from what is normally to be expected, perhaps in terms of internal performance measures such as turnover or profit performance; or perhaps customer reaction to the quality and price of service or products. This accumulation of stimuli eventually reaches a point where the presence of a problem cannot be ignored. Typically, a *triggering point* is reached when the formal information systems of the organisation highlight the problem; a variance against budget may become undeniable or a number of sales areas may consistently report dropping sales. At this stage, however, issues may still be ill-defined.

Issue formulation involves a number of processes. Information gathering takes place, but not always in a highly structured, objective manner. Information is likely to be sought and gathered on a verbal and informal basis, though this may be supplemented through more formal analysis. However, the rationalisation of information so as to clarify the

STRATEGY IN ACTION Illustration 2.5

Negotiation, Networking and Political Activity

Managers explain how strategies may come about through processes of negotiation, networking or political activity.

Bargaining and Negotiation

'There is negotiation in the sense that strategy is generated by the management team trying to work out amongst themselves who gets what in what way. Then it is a political process, the top management team negotiating amongst themselves where they should be.'

'There is always some sort of jockeying for position, but it is a fairly equal balance in terms of power, I suppose. We tend to be reasonably open about bidding for power in terms of developing strategy and bidding for resources for those strategies.'

Networking

'It's very, very baronial: it's very much strategy development on the informal network, which, as an outsider, is difficult. I found this one of the hardest companies to get into because of the informal networks. Things are done through a "my mates will sort it out for me" approach.'

'Some partners are perhaps less influential, but bring other partners along with them. Clearly they will have a certain amount of success because they will have backing. And if you have got a clear strategic thinker, but he doesn't have the backing of the partnership, then clearly that is going to be a barrier to making progress.'

Political Activity

'The politics of what he [the leader] wants and the senior executives want will pervade strategy as, at the lower level, will the individual strategies of individual managers . . . I wouldn't view it negatively; I would say in terms of our organisation that whilst people have agendas, those agendas are up front, rather than hidden – although common sense and experience tells me that this isn't always the case.'

'It's partly to do with the fact that we are structured in directorates and the directorate tend to try and fight their own corner, and there are times when one directorate will quite clearly be more powerful than another one. It's partly been based on the individuals concerned; powerful individuals who have been around for a long time.'

Questions

Consider this illustration in relation to the explanation of cultural and political processes in section 2.4.

1. To what extent do you think these processes are
   (a) inevitable,
   (b) problematic
   (c) beneficial?
2. How do planning (see section 2.3.1), command (section 2.3.2) or logical incremental (section 2.3.3) approaches to strategy development deal with the bargaining, networking and political activity in organisations?

Source Quotes from interviews conducted by A. Bailey as part of a research project at Cranfield School of Management sponsored by the Economic and Social Research Council (Grant No.: R000235100).

Exhibit 2.8 Phases of strategic decision making

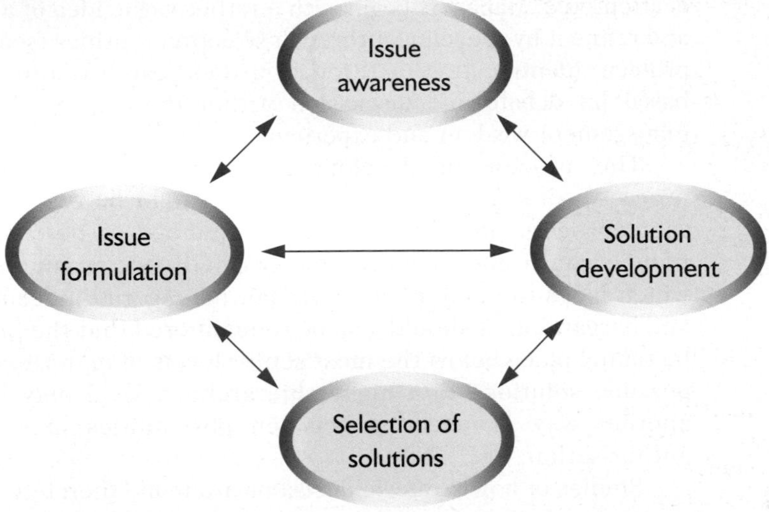

situation draws heavily on *managerial experience* and the assumptions encapsulated in the paradigm. The role of information generated from more formalised analysis is often to post-rationalise or legitimise managers' emerging views of the situation.

Through *debate and discussion* there may be an attempt to reach an organisational view on the problem to be tackled. The emerging view therefore takes shape in terms of both individual and collective experience, with different views resolved through political processes or by drawing on social networks. It may also be that these processes of issue formulation trigger a different problem; or it may be that no consensus is reached and the issue may re-enter an information-gathering phase. So the process tends to be interactive.

It is worth noting that there is an underlying assumption in much management literature that *consensus* is a 'good thing' because it facilitates collective action and a clear understanding about strategy. However, the evidence on this is equivocal.[25] It can be argued that a lack of consensus encourages challenge, questioning and experimentation. It may be that consensus is beneficial in some circumstances, perhaps when the organisation is facing crisis or needs to make changes quickly; but that in circumstances where the organisation has time to develop strategies and to 'play with ideas' so as to develop innovatory solutions, a lack of consensus may be of benefit given the sorts of iterative process described here, because innovation requires the challenging and questioning of taken-for-granted assumptions.

In *developing solutions*, managers typically 'search' for known, existing or tried solutions; or wait for possible solutions to emerge, drawing on their experience before design of a solution custom-built to address the problem is attempted. Managers begin with a rather vague idea of a possible solution and refine it by recycling it through selection routines (see below) back into problem identification or through further search routines. The process is based on debate and discussion within the organisation and collective management wisdom and experience.

The process of developing solutions may, then, overlap with processes of *selecting solutions*. They might be regarded as part of the same process, in which a limited number of potential solutions get reduced until one or more emerges. It is not so much formal analysis which plays the major role here, but managerial judgement, negotiation and bargaining. It should also be remembered that the process might well be taking place below the most senior levels of management, so referring possible solutions to a higher hierarchical level may be required, and another way of selecting between possibilities may be to seek this authorisation.

Studies of how strategic decisions are made therefore suggest that they emerge as the *outcome* of managerial experience within a social, political and cultural context, even if formal planning procedures exist.

In some respects, this is reflected in the different ways in which many organisations now set about the development of strategy. For example, in the past decade there has been a substantial growth of *strategy workshops*, typically for groups of senior managers, perhaps the board of an organisation. Other organisations have recognised that such workshops might beneficially involve a wider community, including managers from different levels and, for example, operatives experienced in dealing with customers, suppliers and so on. The participants remove themselves from day-to-day responsibilities to tackle strategic issues facing their organisation. Such events may well use the sorts of techniques of analysis and planning described in this book. However, rather than just relying on these to throw up strategic solutions, a successful workshop process works through issues in face-to-face debate and discussion, drawing on and surfacing different experiences, interests and views.

2.5 IMPOSED STRATEGY DEVELOPMENT

2.5.1 Enforced Choice

an **enforced choice** *is the imposition of strategy by agencies or forces external to the organisation*

There may be situations in which managers face **enforced choice** of strategy; by this is meant the imposition of strategy by agencies or forces external to the organisation. Government may dictate a particular strategic course or direction – for example, in the public sector, or where it exercises extensive regulation over an industry – or choose to deregulate or privatise an organisation previously in the public sector. In the 1980s and early 1990s in many countries, governments decided to privatise public utilities and deregulate state-controlled enterprises. In the privatisation plans for British Rail in the 1990s, it was the government which laid down the overall industry structure. This included setting up Railtrack as a free-standing business controlling tracks and many of the stations, such that newly established rail-operating businesses running the trains would be required to become customers of Railtrack. This was not a choice of the managers, it was the intent of government. Businesses in the private sector may also be subject to such enforced direction, or significant constraints. The multinational corporation seeking to develop businesses in some parts of the world may be subject to governmental requirements to do this in certain ways, perhaps through joint ventures or local alliances. An operating business within a multidivisional organisation may regard the overall corporate strategic direction of its parent as akin to enforced choice; or a subsidiary may have strategies imposed on it from corporate head office.

2.5.2 The Environment as Constraint

In some organisations, managers see their scope of strategic choice as severely limited. For example, in the oil industry, senior executives argue that they have to manage strategy for a commodity in a market dominated by raw material prices and availability, and that all they can do is to keep costs down, learn to be as good as possible at forecasting changes in that environment and respond as rapidly as possible to such changes.

In Chapter 1 (section 1.2.5), reference was made to 'population ecologists'. These are writers and researchers on organisations who argue that the strategic choice available to an organisation is relatively limited;[26] that the environment is such a dominant influence that most organisations, perhaps other than those that are very large, are unable to influence their operating environments – they merely buffer themselves from, or respond to, changes in that environment. Such strategy development as exists occurs through a process similar to that of *natural selection*. Variations occur within the sorts of organisational processes, structures and systems described in section 2.4 above. These variations may be more or less relevant to the environmental pressures that the organisation faces, and therefore may result in one organisation performing better, or worse, than another. Those organisations that perform better may then be able to retain, duplicate or reduce such positive variations, and so improve their standing in relation to other organisations.

There are, then, different ways in which the world external to an organisation, in the form of its environment, the government or its parent body, may exercise significant influence such that degrees of managerial latitude are severely reduced. Illustration 2.6 gives examples of this and also shows how managers are likely to deal with such constraint in political ways. It is the view in this book that, while such constraint can indeed exist for managers in some organisations, it is not so for all; and that, even where such pressures are severe, it is the job of managers to develop the skills and strategies to cope with the situation. This is the point made by Baden-Fuller and Stopford[27] in their study of businesses in mature, often unattractive, industry environments. It was the firms with managers who could develop strategies to overcome such apparently constraining environments which performed well.

2.6 A NOTE ON STRATEGIC VISION

The idea of strategic *vision* was introduced in Chapter 1. How such a vision might emerge demonstrates that no one explanation given above is likely to provide a complete explanation of how strategies develop. For example, a strategic vision might be deliberately formulated as part of the planning process in an organisation. Or it might be associated more personally with the founder of a business and perhaps have become embedded in the history and culture of the organisation. This seems to be the case for IKEA, where the original vision of Ingvar Kamprad to provide good-value furniture at a price all could afford has become part of the paradigm.

Vision might also be associated with an external agency's imposition of strategy. Those public sector organisations subject to the privatisation and deregulation policies of the UK government of Mrs Thatcher in the 1980s, or the rapid movement towards the free market in the Czech Republic after 1989, have been affected by the 'vision' of governments.

Vision could also be thought of as related to intuition. Some writers suggest that strategic management has so consistently emphasised the importance of analysis – as in the planning view – that the role of intuition has been neglected.[28] They argue that setting up new businesses, new ventures, turnaround and new strategies are the products of creative, innovatory management rather than detailed planning. This may be associated with executives of especially high intuitive capacity, who see what other managers do not see and espouse new ways of working. However, the extent to which such intuition has an effect on strategy is likely to depend on the power or influence of the intuitive manager. So the outcome of the intuition may be seen as a 'vision' associated with the 'command' of a leader, or a political process of influence if the manager is in a more junior position.

STRATEGY IN ACTION
Illustration 2.6

Externally Dependent Strategy Development

Strategy may be imposed by external agencies and coporate parents.

Managers often explain that their strategic choices are constrained, or imposed, by external forces. These forces can take the form of regulative pressures from the government or requirements from a parent organisation. Political influences also impinge as groups or individuals dominate the strategy development process, negotiating and bargaining between departments or SBUs for limited resources. 'Externally dependent' is a configuration commonly found in public sector organisations and subsidiaries of conglomerates. Here managers describe their experience in both cases.

Public Sector: Local Government

> 'Whatever the government says, in terms of how it approaches local authorities, has a massive effect on where we go.'
>
> 'There is obviously the overlay of the party political situation and that has a lot of impact in terms of whether we can, or how we can, go forward in a particular way.'
>
> 'I think it's intensely political; we are structured in directorates, directorates tend to try and fight their own corners and it's partly based on the actual individuals concerned. There are the big directorates – Housing and Environment – which always have an awful lot of power in the sense of getting things done and not getting things done.'

Subsidiaries

> 'We are restricted certainly by the availability of funds, we have restrictions on our headcount and we are restricted by the amount of cash we can keep here. All our money is taken back to France. There are other limiting factors in that people in the centre might say "We don't like the way you are doing that, so don't do it".'
>
> 'The parent shows you the field you're allowed to play on and we have two major constraints in terms of putting in the UK distribution system – I was not allowed to acquire vehicles and I wasn't allowed to acquire people to drive them or run the warehouses.'
>
> 'The truth is that there is bargaining between divisions and sometimes if someone believes that a particular course or direction is the right way to go but can't get agreement from their peers they will start off on that track anyway by getting support from their team.'

Questions

1. Why have these configurations emerged as dominant in each case, bearing in mind the organisational contexts? In both cases suppose a new CEO wanted to introduce more formalised planning systems. What problems would he or she face? How effective might such systems be in achieving a change in strategic direction for such an organisation?
2. What is the role of planning likely to be where externally dependent strategy development processes are evident?
3. What skills do effective strategists need to develop in such circumstances?

Source Quotes from interviews conducted as part of ESRC funded research project (Grant No. R000235100).

Prepared by Clare Avery, Cranfield School of Management.

2.7 CONFIGURATIONS OF STRATEGY DEVELOPMENT PROCESSES

What has been provided in sections 2.3 to 2.6 are different explanations of how strategies develop. However, it is likely that elements of these will be found in all organisations to a greater or lesser extent. Different processes account for the development of strategy; and the mix of such processes is likely to differ by organisation or organisational context, forming *configurations of strategy development*. Exhibit 2.9 shows some of these configurations and summarises the dominant characteristics of each as managers see them, as well as the organisational contexts of each. Although it is not suggested that these configurations define precisely how strategy develops across all organisations, they represent typical general tendencies of strategy development. Illustration 2.3 gives an example of the logical incremental configuration and Illustration 2.6 an example of the externally dependent configuration.

A number of observations can be made about these configurations which help our understanding of strategy development processes.

- Unidimensional processes of strategy development are not common in practice. For example, elements of planning are often evident but in conjunction with other processes of strategy development.
- There seem to be two overarching explanations given by the managers about strategy development. Exhibit 2.9(a) and (b) represent views of strategy development which are in essence proactive, planning, rational views of the process. Exhibit 2.9(c) and (d) emphasise more cultural and political processes in organisations. If the command dimension is considered too, it further emphasises the importance of managerial experience, since individuals who take a lead in strategy development are likely to do so on the basis of their experience not just analytical procedures.
- There is evidence that these two overall views may arise because of the experience of how strategies develop at different levels in the organisation. The more rational, planning view of strategy tends to be seen most by senior executives, particularly chief executives. The cultural and political processes tend to be seen most by managers below the level of the board. This is, perhaps, not surprising, since it may be the chief executives who have put into place planning procedures, whereas the managers are operating daily within the culture of the organisation.
- The notion of incrementalism can be explained in two ways: first, as represented by Exhibit 2.9(a), which describes it as an essentially logical incremental process; and second, as represented by Exhibit 2.9(c), which acknowledges that strategy changes incrementally, but sees this as the outcome of cultural and political processes. It could be that in the same

Exhibit 2.9 Configurations of strategy development processes

Profile with Dominant Dimensions	Characteristics	Rather Than	Typical Organisational Contexts	Managerial Example
(a) Logical incremental *Planning* *Incrementalism*	Standardised planning procedures Systematic data collection and analyses Constant environmental scanning Ongoing adjustment of strategy Tentative commitment to strategy Step-by-step, small-scale change	Intrusive external environment Dominant individuals Political processes Power groups	Manufacturing and service sector organisations Stable or growing markets Mature markets Benign environments	'What I'm always engaged in is an ongoing process of developing, of scanning the horizon for market developments that are likely to affect my business and then devising and changing strategic responses.' (see Illustration 2.3)
(b) Rational command *Planning* *Command*	Senior figure or group determines and directs strategy Strong vision or mission Definite and precise objectives Rigorous analysis of environment Clear plans	Pronounced political influences Traditional 'ways of doing things' External forces determine strategy	Large manufacturing and financial services businesses Growing and stable markets Competitive environment	'The CEO is the dominant character really. He drives and sets the vision, and he certainly modifies the strategy. I would say that he has the strongest influence.'
(c) Muddling through *Cultural* *Political* *Incremental*	Bargaining, negotiation and compromise accommodate conflicting interests of groups Groups with control over critical resources more likely to influence strategy Standardised 'ways of doing things' Routines and procedures embedded in organisational history Gradual adjustments to strategy	Analytical, evaluative rationality Deliberate, intentional, process Managers in control of organisation's destiny Well defined procedures Analytical evaluation and planning Externally driven strategy Deliberate managerial intent	Professional service firms (e.g. consultancy or law firms) Unstable, turbulent environment New and growing markets	'Sometimes we have to make concessions to partners if we favour a certain direction or option, in order to encourage them to accept the idea.'
(d) Externally dependent *Enforced choice* *Political*	Strategy is imposed by external forces (e.g. legislation, parent organisation) Freedom of choice severely restricted Groups dealing with the environment have greater influence over strategy Political activity likely within organisation and between external agencies	Strategy determined within the organisation Planning systems impact on strategy development Managers influence strategic direction	Public sector organisations, larger manufacturing and financial service subsidiaries Threatening, declining, unstable and hostile environments	'We feel severely constrained by the policies of central government and the community influence is also quite strong – sometimes vociferously articulated by interest groups who lobby members.' (see Illustration 2.6)

Prepared by Clare Avery, Cranfield School of Management.

organisation it is evident that strategies do change incrementally; but explanations of this given by the chief executive, for example, might differ from those given by other managers in the organisation.

- Different configurations are associated with different contexts. The *logical incremental* (Exhibit 2.9(a)) account of strategy development is most commonly to be found among managers in organisations in relatively stable or benign environments. The *rational command* (Exhibit 2.9(b)) dimension, on the other hand, tends to be most evident in hostile or competitive organisational environments. *Muddling through* (Exhibit 2.9(c)) is commonly found in professional service type businesses, where there may be many influential partners and professionals and long-established traditions. Not surprisingly, the *externally dependent* (Exhibit 2.9(d)) account is found in public sector organisations or subsidiaries of conglomerates where there is a likelihood of strategy being imposed from outside the organisation.
- It is difficult to relate these configurations to organisational performance. The suggestion that one particular configuration is better than another is problematic because what might be best for a small, independent manufacturing company might be inappropriate for an accountancy or law partnership. Such evidence as does exist suggests that organisations which change incrementally seem to perform better than those that do not. However, this could be because incremental change tends to take place in environments which are relatively benign or stable; so it may not be the processes of incrementalism which account for the success, but the nature of the environment they are in.

The overall lesson is that there is no one way in which strategies develop. It matters that those who are seeking to influence strategy development in organisations are aware of, and can take account of, the processes actually at work in the organisations. For example, in an organisation strongly dominated by a commanding figure, or by the cultural and political processes of the organisation, it may be a mistake to assume that the introduction of formal planning procedures will necessarily lead to more effective strategy formulation. Quite possibly, such procedures will be seen as peripheral or bureaucratic.

2.8 CHALLENGES FOR STRATEGY DEVELOPMENT

So far this chapter has concentrated on explaining how strategies develop in organisations. In this section, implications arising from these explanations are raised which form some of the challenges in trying to manage the process. There are two key issues underlying these challenges. The first is the evident influence of managerial experience within a political and cultural organisational context. A clear understanding of how such influences come about and their impact is important. A framework – the *cultural web* – which provides this understanding is introduced; the implications are then discussed in terms of the risk of *strategic drift* in organisations.

The second key issue is the difficulty that organisations face in developing strategies in complex, changing environments, and the possibility that traditional mechanistic ways of doing so are inadequate especially in organisations which seek to innovate. The notion of the *learning organisation* is therefore discussed.

2.8.1 The Cultural Web[29]

Trying to understand the culture of an organisation is clearly important, but it is not straightforward. A strategy and the values of an organisation may be written down, but the underlying assumptions which make up the paradigm are usually evident only in the day-to-day conversation or discussions of people, or may be so taken for granted that they can be observed only in what people actually do. To understand the taken-for-grantedness may, then, mean being very sensitive to what is signified by the more physical manifestations of culture evident in an organisation. Indeed, it is especially important to understand these wider aspects because not only do they give clues about the paradigm, but they are also likely to reinforce the assumptions within that paradigm. In effect, they are the representation in organisational action of what is taken for granted. The **cultural web** is a representation of the taken-for-granted assumptions, or paradigm, of an organisation and the physical manifestations of organisational culture (see Exhibit 2.10). It is now described using Illustration 2.7 as a basis for discussing its relevance.

The **cultural web** *is a representation of the taken-for-granted assumptions, or paradigm, of an organisation and the physical manifestations of organisational culture*

All organisations must develop a degree of coherence in their culture for them to be able to function effectively. Indeed, at its best, a cultural system in which the various parts of the organisation are all working to a common end can provide advantage. It will be shown in Chapters 4 and 10 that it can be the very basis of *competitive advantage* in markets because it may prove so difficult to imitate. However, it may also be very difficult to change. Institutional theorists and population ecologists[30] (see section 1.2.5 in Chapter 1 and sections 2.4.1 and 2.5.2 in this chapter) argue that organisations are captured by their own cultures, which are the product of history, or the product of institutional forces that exist across organisations: that professional service firms all tend to behave in the same way; that organisations in the public sector have common cultures; that engineering firms tend to be similar and so on. Certainly, the evidence is that organisational cultures are not easy to change, and that therefore they can impair the development of organisational strategies. This is an issue returned to particularly in Chapter 11.

Illustration 2.7 shows a cultural web drawn up by trust managers in the National Health Service in the UK in 1994, shortly after trusts were established. It is now used as a basis for explaining the cultural web. (It

Exhibit 2.10 The cultural web

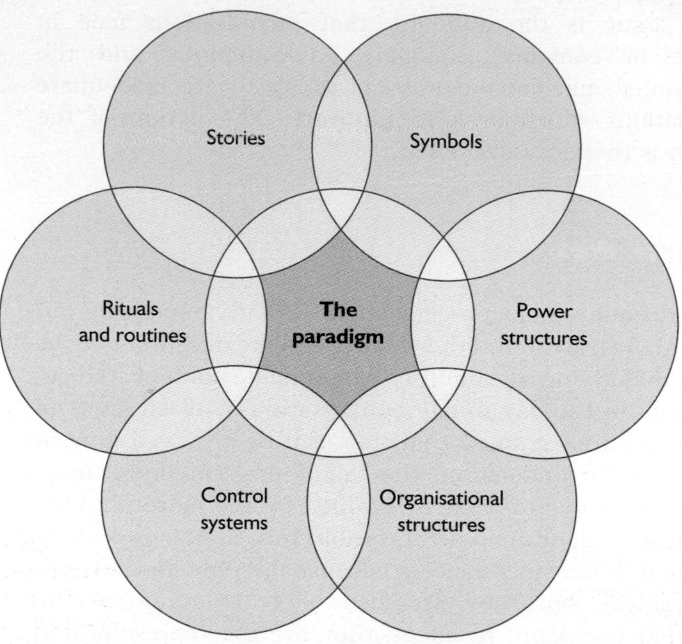

should, however, be borne in mind that this is the view of managers; clinicians might well have quite different views.)

The assumptions which constitute the *paradigm* reflect the common public perception in the UK that the NHS is a 'good thing'; a public service which should be provided equally, free of charge. However, it is medical values that are central and, in general, those providing them who know best. This is an organisation about the provision of medical care for those who are ill, subtly different from an organisation to serve the needs of those who are ill, and quite different from serving the needs of those who are not ill – for example, pregnancy is not an illness, but pregnant women often argue that hospitals treat them as though they are ill. Overall, the NHS is seen as 'belonging' to those who provide the services; and it is the acute sector within hospitals which is central to the service rather than, for example, care in the community.

The other elements of the cultural web include the following:

- The *routine* ways that members of the organisation behave towards each other, and towards those outside the organisation, make up 'the way we do things around here'. At its best, this lubricates the working of the organisation, and may provide a distinctive and beneficial organisational competence.[31] However, it can also represent a taken-for-grantedness about how things should happen which is extremely difficult to change and protective of core assumptions in the

STRATEGY IN ACTION
Illustration 2.7

A Cultural Web of the UK National Health Service in the Early 1990s

The cultural web is a representation of taken-for-granted aspects of an organisation.

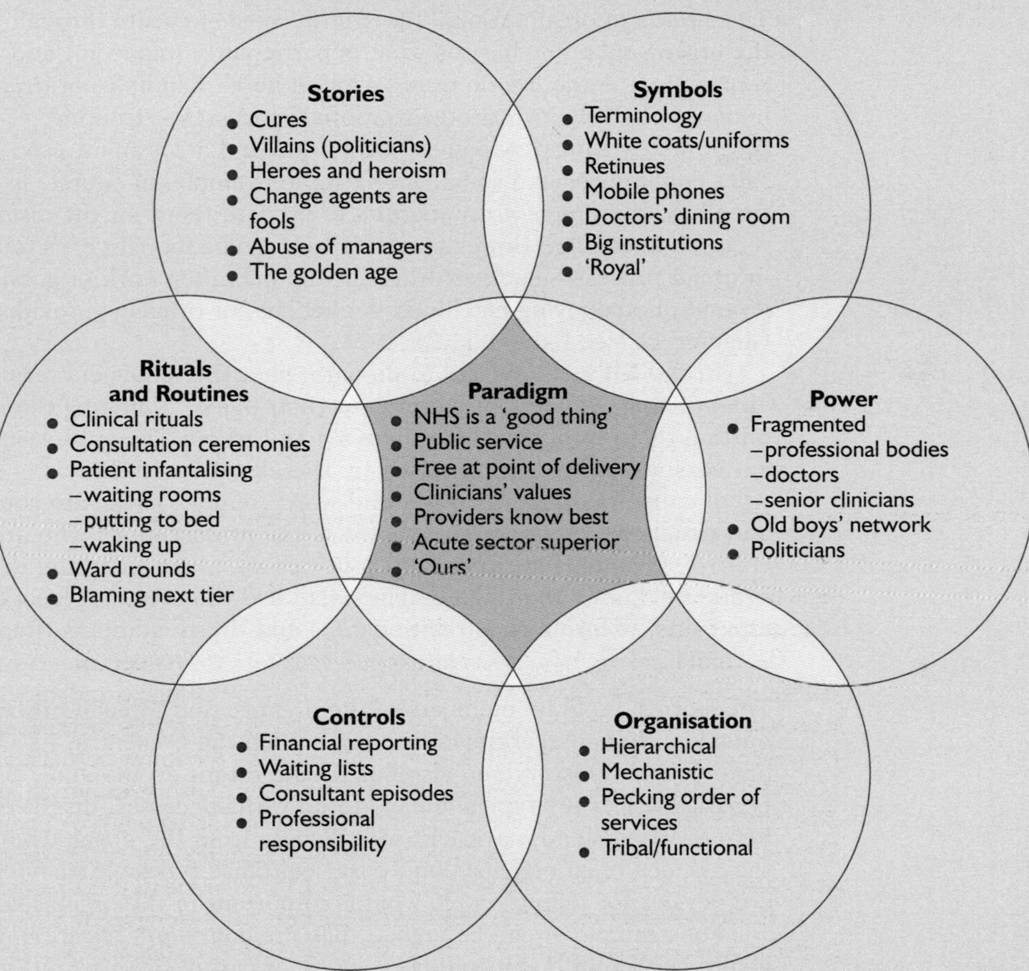

Questions

1. Read through section 2.8.1 of the text and ensure that you understand what are the elements of the cultural web (using the NHS managers example).
2. From all the detail in this web, develop up to four statements which together you feel would encapsulate the culture of the NHS at that time.
3. What are the implications of this analysis in terms of the ease or difficulty with which new strategies might be developed?

paradigm. For most of its history, doctors and nurses in the NHS, indeed patients too, took for granted that the doctor or nurse knew best. This took form, for example, in routines of consultation and of prescribing drugs. A hospital might espouse 'patient care', but staff would find it unusual, even uncomfortable, if patients exercised this in terms of questioning and challenging the wisdom of a doctor or a course of medication.

- The *rituals* of organisational life are the special events through which the organisation emphasises what is particularly important and reinforces 'the way we do things around here'. Examples of ritual can include relatively formal organisational processes – training programmes, interview panels, promotion and assessment procedures, sales conferences and so on. An extreme example, of course, is the ritualistic training of army recruits to prepare them for the discipline required in conflict. However, rituals can also be thought of as relatively informal processes such as drinks in the pub after work or gossiping around photocopying machines. A checklist of rituals is provided in Chapter 11 (see Exhibit 11.7).

  In the NHS, rituals had to do with what the managers termed 'infantilising', which 'put patients in their place' – making them wait, putting them to bed, waking them up and so on. The subservience of patients was further emphasised by the elevation of clinicians with ritual consultation ceremonies and ward rounds. These are routines and rituals which emphasise that it is the professionals who are in control. Overall, the rituals and routines are about ensuring that everyone 'knows their place'. They also had the effect, at least for the clinicians, of formalising relationships and thus distancing them from patients.

- The *stories*[32] told by members of the organisation to each other, to outsiders, to new recruits and so on, embed the present in its organisational history and also flag up important events and personalities. They typically have to do with successes, disasters, heroes, villains and mavericks who deviate from the norm. They distil the essence of an organisation's past, legitimise types of behaviour and are devices for telling people what is important in the organisation.

  For example, it can be argued that the dominant culture of the health service in many countries is one of curing sickness rather than promoting health; and most of the stories within health services concern developments in curing – particularly terminal illnesses. The heroes of the health service are in curing, not so much in caring. In 1994, many in the NHS regarded the system as under attack by government changes, so it is perhaps not surprising that there were also stories about villainous politicians trying to change the system, the failure of those who try to make changes, and tales about their mistakes and of heroic acts by those defending the system (often well known medical figures).

- *Symbols*,[33] such as logos, offices, cars and titles, or the type of language and terminology commonly used, become a short-hand representation of the nature of the organisation. For example, in long-established or conservative organisations it is likely that there will be many symbols of hierarchy or deference to do with formal office layout, differences in privileges between levels of management, the way in which people address each other and so on. In turn this formalisation may reflect difficulties in changing strategies within a hierarchical or deferential system. The form of language used in an organisation can also be particularly revealing, especially with regard to customers or clients. For example, the head of a consumer protection agency in Australia described his clients as 'complainers', and in a major teaching hospital in the UK, consultants described patients as 'clinical material'. While such examples might be amusing, they reveal an underlying assumption about customers (or patients) which might play a significant role in influencing the strategy of an organisation. The sort of distancing from the emotional side of patient care in a hospital inherent in such terminology is likely to be reflected in behaviour and therefore in realised strategy.

  Other symbols in the NHS reflected the various institutions within the organisation, with uniforms for clinical and nursing staff, distinct symbols for clinicians, such as their staff retinues, and status symbols such as mobile phones and dining rooms. The importance of the size and status of physical buildings was reflected, not least, in the designation of 'Royal' in the name of a hospital, seen as a key means of ensuring that it might withstand the threat of closure.

  Although symbols are shown separately in the cultural web, it should be remembered that many elements of the web are symbolic, in the sense that they convey messages beyond their functional purpose. Routines, control and reward systems and structures are symbolic in so far as they signal the type of behaviour valued in an organisation.

- *Power structures* are also likely to be associated with the key assumptions of the paradigm. The paradigm is, in some respects, the 'formula for success', which is taken for granted and likely to have grown up over years. The most powerful managerial groupings within the organisation are likely to be closely associated with this set of core assumptions and beliefs.[34]

  For example, accountancy firms may now offer a whole range of services, but typically the most powerful individuals or groups have been qualified chartered accountants with a set of assumptions about the business and its market rooted in the audit practice. Power may not be based just on seniority. In some organisations, power could be lodged within other levels or functions: for example, with technical experts in a hi-tech firm. In the NHS, the power structure was fragmented between, for example, clinicians, nursing and management in the organisation, each of which had its own symbolic distinctions. However, historically, senior clinicians were the most powerful and managers had hitherto been seen as 'administration'. As with many other organisations, there was also a strong informal network of individuals and groups which coalesced around specific issues to promote or resist a particular view.

- The *control systems*, measurements and reward systems emphasise what it is important to monitor in the organisation, and to focus attention and activity upon. For example, public service organisations have often been accused of being concerned more with stewardship of funds than with quality of service; and in their procedures, more with accounting for spending than with regard for outputs. This was reflected in the NHS with an emphasis on financial controls and reporting. Reward systems are important influences on behaviours, but can also prove to be a barrier to success of new strategies. For example, an organisation with individually based bonus schemes related to volume could find it difficult to promote strategies requiring teamwork and an emphasis on quality rather than volume.
- *Organisational structure* is likely to reflect power structures and, again, delineate important relationships and emphasise what is important in the organisation. Both structural and control aspects of the NHS were formal: formal hierarchical, mechanistic structures with a lot of reporting of a financial nature, but also monitoring of waiting lists and the time taken by consultants to see patients, reflecting assumptions about what patient care involved. However, underlying formal structures and controls were the less formal systems, described as 'tribal', relating to the professional constraints and norms that exercised control over individuals; and the 'old boys' network', which allowed the organisation to come together, particularly under threat. Moreover, participants pointed out that, when it came to organisation and control, the formal systems had been largely imposed on them: 'it is not what the NHS is all about; they are just the measures placed upon people'.

The overall picture of the NHS was of a system fundamentally about medical practice, fragmented in its power bases historically, with a division between clinical aspects of the organisation and its management; indeed, a system in which management had traditionally been seen as relatively trivial. As one executive put it: 'there is an arrogance of clinicians, but it is a justifiable arrogance; after all, it is they who deliver on the shopfloor, not management'. The managers were not finding strategy development and strategic change easy to manage.

The cultural web is, then, a useful tool for understanding the underlying assumptions, linked to political, symbolic and structural aspects, of an organisation. How the web can be used analytically is discussed in section 5.5.6 of Chapter 5; and as a vehicle for considering strategic change in section 11.3 of Chapter 11.

2.8.2 The Risk of Strategic Drift[35]

The influence of the paradigm and 'the way we do things around here' is likely to have important implications for the development of strategy in organisations.

Faced with pressures for change, managers typically try to minimise the extent to which they are faced with ambiguity and uncertainty, by looking for that which is familiar. This raises difficulties when managing strategic change because it may be that the action required is outside the scope of the paradigm and the constraints of the cultural web, and that members of the organisation would therefore be required to change substantially their core assumptions and routines. Desirable as this may be, the evidence is that it does not occur easily, as Illustration 2.8 shows. Managers are more likely to attempt to deal with the situation by searching for what they can understand and cope with in terms of the existing paradigm. Exhibit 2.11 shows how this might occur.[36] Faced with a stimulus for action – in this case, declining performance – managers first seek means of improving the implementation of existing strategy. This could be through tightening controls and improving the accepted way of operating. If this is not effective, a change of strategy may occur, but a change which is in line with the existing paradigm and ways of doing things. For example, managers may seek to extend the market for their business, but assume that it will be similar to their existing market, and therefore set about managing the new venture in much the same way as they have been used to. Alternatively, as shown in Illustration 2.8, even where managers know intellectually that they need to change, indeed know technologically how to do so, they find themselves constrained by organisational routines, assumptions or political processes. What is occurring is the predominant application of the familiar and the attempt to avoid or reduce uncertainty or ambiguity. This is likely to continue until there is, perhaps dramatic, evidence of the redundancy of the paradigm and it associated routines.

This is an alternative explanation of incremental strategy development. Indeed, it could be that changing the strategy within the paradigm makes sense: after all, it does encapsulate the experience of those in the organisation, and permits change to take place within what is familiar and understood. However, the outcome of processes of this kind may not be an adaptive approach which keeps strategy in line with environmental change, as shown in Exhibit 2.5. Rather, it may be adaptation in line with the experience enshrined in the organisational culture. Nonetheless, the forces in the environment will have an effect on performance. Over time this may well give rise to the sort of **strategic drift** shown in Exhibit 2.12 (phase 1) in which the organisation's strategy gradually moves away from relevance to the forces at work in its environment. As Illustration 2.8 shows, even the most successful companies may drift in this way. Indeed, Danny Miller argues that there is a tendency – he calls it the Icarus Paradox – for businesses to become victims of the very success of their past.[37]

strategic drift *occurs when the organisation's strategy gradually moves away from relevance to the forces at work in its environment*

STRATEGY IN ACTION
Illustration 2.8

Technological Change and Organisational Inertia in the Computer Industry

An organisation's 'Achilles heel' can often be found in its past bases of success.

In a fast-moving, technologically complex and innovative industry dominated by small firms with well developed communication and technology transfer, one firm's inability to keep pace with innovations in manufacturing processes forced it out of business.

Kasper Instruments produced photolithographic alignment equipment, used to manufacture semiconductor devices. Their manufacture required the transfer of small, intricate patterns onto the surface of a wafer of semiconductor material such as silicon. This transfer process called lithography required only certain areas of the wafer to be exposed to light, with masks used to provide the appropriate shield.

Contact aligners were the first form of mask to be used commercially and, as the name suggests, these made contact with the wafers. Kasper Instruments had earned its position as industry leader because of its expertise in the contact alignment technique. However, as technology became more advanced, proximity masks were able to be used. These did not come into contact with the wafer, so the risk of damage was reduced. Technology within the industry continued to develop incrementally until a quite different process of electron beam alignment was developed in which a focused beam wrote directly onto the wafer. Yet, in each stage of innovation the industry leader was unable to make the technological transition. It was in the switch from contact to proximity aligners that Kasper Instruments lost its position of industry leader to Canon and was ultimately forced to leave the industry.

The technological change needed for Kasper to keep pace with Canon and introduce the more efficient proximity alignment technique was, in technological terms, relatively minor; and the top team at Kasper were keenly aware of the need to change. However, they seemed unable to rise to Canon's challenge, refusing to accept the obsolescence of their own expert knowledge in the contact technique. While Kasper continually held onto the past, trying to modify its own production technique to include some elements of Canon's innovative procedures, with no success, its market share slipped away. When the engineers at Kasper were given a Canon proximity aligner to take apart with a view to producing their own model, they dismissed it as a mere copy of their own (very different) contact aligner and in doing so cost the company the opportunity to imitate, re-innovate and regain their place at the cutting edge of competition.

What seemed to be a small incremental development in technology required Kasper to totally rethink the way it did business, from its production processes to its sales and marketing strategies. In its failure to translate its technical understanding of the need for change by changing the routinised processes existing in the organisation, it was not alone. Throughout the history of technological change within this industry, each innovation has been a harbinger of doom for the market leader. Kasper Instruments was just one of many firms that found it just could not meet the challenge of change.

Questions

1. Which processes of strategic management described in this chapter might have helped to avoid Kasper's problems?
2. Would these processes be suited to organisations facing less innovatory or changing environments?

Source R. Henderson and K. Clark, 'Architectural innovation: the reconfiguration of existing product technology and the failure of established firms', *Administrative Science Quarterly*, vol. 35 (1990), pp. 9–30.

Prepared by Phyl Johnson, Cranfield School of Management.

Exhibit 2.11 The dynamics of paradigm change

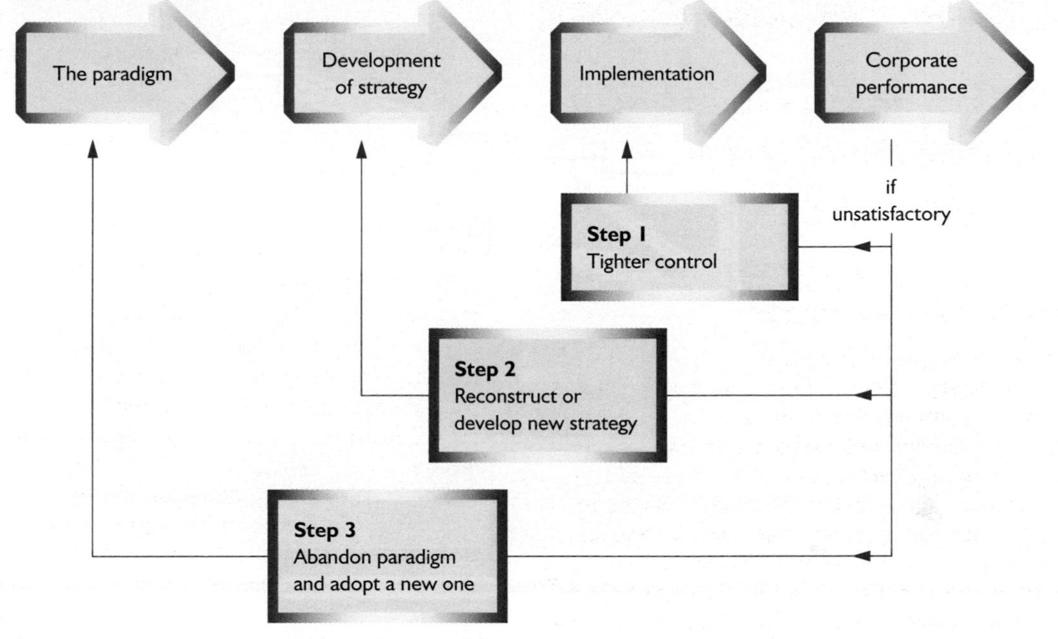

Source Adapted from P. Grinyer and J-C. Spender, *Turnaround: Managerial recipes for strategic success*, Associated Business Press, 1979, p. 203.

This pattern of drift is made more difficult to detect and reverse because, not only are changes being made in strategy (albeit within the parameters of the organisation's culture), but, since such changes are the application of the familiar, they may achieve some short-term improvement in performance, thus tending to legitimise the action taken.

However, in time, either the drift becomes apparent or environmental change increases, and performance is affected (phase 2 in Exhibit 2.12). Strategy development is then likely to go into a state of flux, with no clear direction (phase 3), further damaging performance. Eventually, more transformational change is likely, if the demise of the organisation is to be avoided (phase 4).

In positive terms, organisational culture can be thought of as encapsulating distinctive competences; more dangerously, it can also be a conservative influence, likely to prevent change, stifle innovation and result in a momentum of strategy which can lead to strategic drift. Identifying when an organisation is at risk of, or in a state of, strategic drift is a challenge to the manager of strategy. There is a fine dividing line between the organisation which is running smoothly and effectively, building on

Exhibit 2.12 The risk of strategic drift

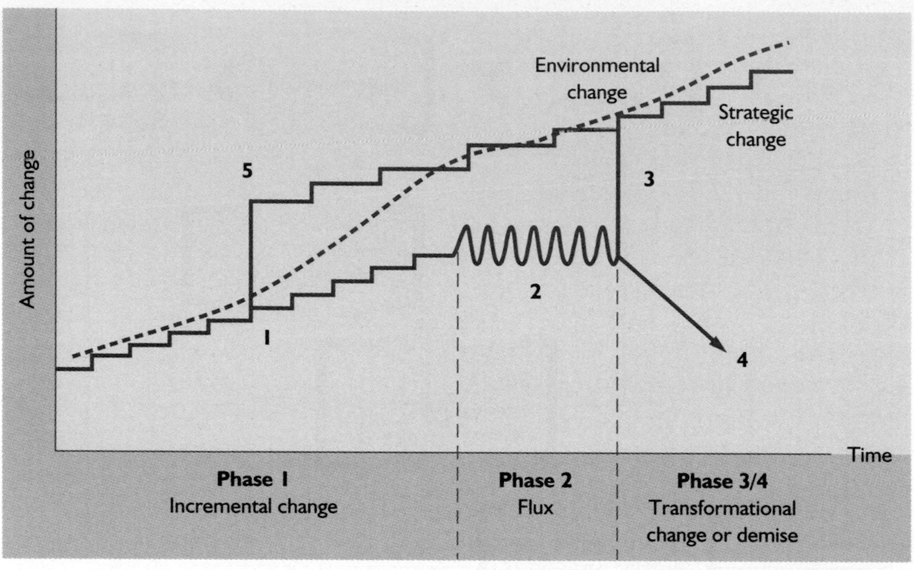

competences embedded in its culture, and an organisation which is at risk of drift. Some guidelines on symptoms of strategic drift are given as part of the discussion of the management of strategic change in Chapter 11 (see section 11.3.1).

This description of strategic drift conforms to the notion of a *lack of fit* with the environment. However, it is worth noting a different problem that organisations can face. Those organisations that seek to *stretch* what they regard as their core competences to create new opportunities could also find problems. In section 2.2.1, it was noted that transformational change might be attempted through the development of entirely new products or services which seek to create new customer needs and expectations not previously in existence. This could succeed and in so doing create a shift in the market in line with the intended strategy. However, there is the risk that such an organisation could find itself 'ahead' of its environment (represented by phase 5 in Exhibit 2.12). In the graph, the strategy and the environment eventually realign, but in reality this might not happen and the lag in time before such realignment could cause significant problems, not least in performance.

All this goes to emphasise the delicate balance that an organisation faces in developing its strategy. It has internal cultural pressures which tend to constrain strategy development, and environmental forces, not least in terms of its markets, which it must cope with. How it might do so is the central theme of this book.

2.8.3 Uncertainty and the Learning Organisation

The speed of electronic communications across the world in the late 1990s could not have been conceived of by managers 20 or 30 years ago; major changes in global political structures, such as the breaking up of the Soviet bloc in 1989, surprised even informed commentators; the extent to which scientific innovations will achieve medical breakthroughs, and when, is difficult to predict.

Chaos theorists[38] who write about management argue that the organisational world appears to be so turbulent and chaotic that it is not possible to predict what will happen or when, so traditional approaches to strategic management are simply not appropriate. There is no point in formalised planning approaches with predetermined fixed objectives and analysis that may take weeks or months to work through. The idea that top managers can formulate strategies implemented by others becomes redundant because top managers are less in touch with such a complex and turbulent world than those in the organisation. The notion that there needs to be agreement and consensus around the issues facing the organisation is also questionable: the environment is too complex and rapidly changing for this to be likely or even desirable.

Writers on innovation make similar points. Traditional ways of conceiving of management are likely to stifle rather than encourage innovations.[39] The need is to build on a recognition of the innate ability of managers to draw on their experience, but to develop the capacity for this to be used more flexibly and in a questioning, *learning organisation*.[40] Rather than regarding experience as something which is fixed and a constraint on development, managers need to develop organisations in which they continually *challenge* such experience from the world around them and from the different experiences of their colleagues. To do this they need to develop organisations which are *pluralistic*, in which different, even conflicting ideas and views are welcomed; in which such differences are surfaced and become the basis of debate; in which experimentation is the norm. This is more likely to take place where *informality* of working relationships is found. New ideas emerge more through *networks* of working relationships than through hierarchies; more through dialogue, even storytelling, than through formal analysis. The job of top management is to create this sort of organisation by building teams and networks that can work in such ways; by allowing enough *organisational slack* that there is time for debate and challenge; and by releasing control rather than holding onto it. This may be done, for example, through the development of different types of organisational structure (see Chapter 9) and through the development of the everyday behaviour and culture of the organisation (see Chapters 10 and 11). The **learning organisation** is, then, one capable of benefiting from the variety of knowledge, experience and skills of individuals through a culture which encourages mutual questioning and challenge around a shared purpose or vision.

the **learning organisation** *is capable of benefiting from the variety of knowledge, experience and skills of individuals through a culture which encourages mutual questioning and challenge around a shared purpose or vision*

Exhibit 2.13 Different approaches to strategic management

	Unpredictable environment	Predictable environment
Central direction possible	Strategic intent	Strategic planning
Central direction impossible or undesirable	Encouraging 'intrapreneurship'	Incremental strategy development

Source Developed by R. Harrison, Strategy and Board Secretariat, Department of Education and Employment. Reproduced with permission.

Certainly, there is increasing recognition that the formal systems of management, so much the orthodoxy of the past, need to be questioned, not least in the management of strategy. For example, so much has been recognised within the Department for Education and Employment, a central government body in the UK. It has developed a framework for explaining the need for different approaches to strategic management given the recognition that it faces environments with different degrees of uncertainty, and can exercise more or less central control on strategy developments (see Exhibit 2.13). In situations where changes in the environment are relatively predictable and central control is possible, then formal planning systems may make sense. Where the environment is increasingly uncertain, but central control remains possible, then a more incremental approach to strategy development may be sensible. If the environment is more uncertain but central control desirable, then it has to be recognised this cannot be done through detailed planning, but the development of a clear 'strategic intent' or vision by the centre may be more important. However, in situations where there is high uncertainty in the environment and the centre cannot or should not exert control – and this might be the case where creative thinking and innovation are necessary – then it is intrapreneurship that should be encouraged, by which is meant the encouragement of individuals to question, challenge and take personal responsibility for influencing strategy development.

Similar arguments are put forward consistently throughout this book: that different structures and approaches to strategic management are appropriate in different circumstances. Nonetheless, the view taken here is that this does not mean that the techniques of analysis dealt with in this book are inappropriate or redundant; rather that their role is more to do with the challenging and questioning of received wisdom and taken-for-granted assumptions – a role which is becoming increasingly necessary in a changing world.

SUMMARY AND IMPLICATIONS FOR THE STUDY OF STRATEGY

This chapter has dealt with the processes of strategic management as they are to be found in organisations: it has therefore been descriptive rather than prescriptive. However, it is important to understand the reality of strategy development in organisations, not least because those who seek to influence the strategy of organisations must do so within that reality. Moreover, it is this book's intention that the subject should be approached in such a way that it builds upon this understanding of that reality.

Some of the lessons of this chapter are now summarised and related to what follows in the rest of the book.

- It is important to distinguish between the *intended* strategy of managers – that which they say the organisation should follow – and the *realised* strategy of an organisation – that which it is actually following. This is particularly important when considering how relevant current strategy is to a changing environment: it is likely to be more useful to consider the relevance of realised strategy than that of intended strategy.
- Strategy usually evolves *incrementally*: strategic change tends to occur as a continual process of relatively small adjustments to existing strategy, through activity within the subsystems of an organisation. However, there is likely to be an overall strategic direction, a strategic *momentum*, which is persistent over time. The result tends to be a pattern of *punctuated equilibrium* in which long periods of incremented strategy development are interrupted by periodic transformational change.

There are different explanations of how strategies develop in different ways in organisations.

- Strategies might develop through *managerial intent* as a result of *planning systems*, *command* or direction by individuals or groups, or through *logical incremental* crafting of strategy.
- Strategies might also develop as the outcome of cultural processes, in which strategy is informed by the taken-for-granted assumptions and routines of organisations, or be the result of political processes of bargaining and negotiation.

- Incremental change in organisations could, therefore, be explained in terms of both *cultural and political processes*, and managers experimenting and *learning by doing*.
- Strategies might also be imposed on organisations either by external agencies of forces (*enforced choice*) or because the environment acts to constrain the strategic decisions available to the organisations.
- It is unlikely that any one of these explanations sufficiently describes the strategy development processes in an organisation. Rather, it is likely that a mixture, or *configuration of processes*, accounts for how strategies develop.
- The *cultural web* of an organisation – its political structures, routines, and rituals and symbols – is likely to exert a preserving and legitimising influence on the core beliefs and assumptions that comprise the paradigm, thereby making strategic change more difficult to achieve.
- Over time the organisation may become out of line with a changing environment (*strategic drift*), eventually reaching a point of crisis. At this time, more fundamental or transformational change may occur.
- As environments become more unpredictable, and the need for innovation increases the reliance on managerial experience, but within more flexible, *learning organisations*, becomes especially important. In such organisations, the surfacing of assumptions, explicit debate about them and a diversity of views are encouraged.

The approach taken in this book has been influenced by this understanding of how strategies develop in organisations. First, as has been said in Chapter 1, the idea of a purely sequential model of strategic management has been rejected. The headings of strategic analysis, choice and implementation are a useful structure for the book, and for thinking about the problems of strategy, but readers are urged to regard these aspects of strategic management as interdependent and an influence on one another; and just as likely to occur in terms of social, political and cultural processes as through formal planning systems.

Indeed, this chapter has also highlighted the substantial influences of the beliefs and assumptions of the managers within a cultural setting. For this reason, emphasis is also placed in this book on the importance of understanding the nature of core assumptions (the paradigm) in an organisation, and the cultural and political context in which they exist. This chapter has provided a framework (the cultural web) by which such influences can be understood, and this framework is used elsewhere in the book. In Chapter 4 it is related to an analysis of core competences of organisations; and these are in turn considered in the development of competitive strategy, discussed in Chapters 6 and 10. In Chapter 5 the cultural web is used as a tool or checklist for analysing the relationship between strategy and culture. In Chapter 11 it is recognised that such aspects of the organisation provide a major stumbling block to the implementation of strategic change. The chapter therefore returns to the processes of strategic management with a view to examining how strategy and strategic change can be managed.

While the reality of judgement and the prevalence of bargaining processes in organisations are accepted, the book also contains examples of, and references to, many techniques of quantitative and qualitative analysis. The value of such analytical approaches is not to be diminished. Not only do they provide an essential tool for managers to think through strategic problems and analyse possible solutions, but they also provide means whereby the taken-for-granted wisdom of the organisation and assumed courses of action can be questioned and challenged.

The overall aim is, then, to provide a framework for strategy and strategic management which usefully combines the rigour of analysis with the reality of the processes of management.

RECOMMENDED KEY READINGS

- On incremental strategic change, see J.B. Quinn, *Strategies for Change: Logical incrementalism*, Irwin, 1980; also summarised in H. Mintzberg, J.B. Quinn and S. Ghoshal (eds), *The Strategy Process*, 4th edition, Prentice Hall, 1998. Compare this with G. Johnson, 'Rethinking incrementalism', *Strategic Management Journal*, vol. 9, no. 1 (1988), pp. 75–91, and D. Miller, *The Icarus Paradox*, Harper Business, 1990.
- V. Ambrosini with G. Johnson and K. Scholes, *Exploring Techniques of Analysis and Evaluation in Strategic Management*, Prentice Hall, 1998, contains a paper by A. Bailey and C. Avery entitled 'Discovering and defining the process of strategy development' which provides a means of analysing processes of strategy development in organisations.
- A debate between Henry Mintzberg and Igor Ansoff on the merits of different approaches to strategic management appeared in the *Strategic Management Journal* in 1990 and 1991. These papers were 'The design school: reconsidering the basic processes of strategic management' by H. Mintzberg (vol. 11, no. 3, 1990), a critique of this by I. Ansoff (vol. 12, no. 6, 1991) and a riposte by Mintzberg entitled 'Learning 1, Planning 0' in the same volume.
- For explanations of organisational culture, see E. Schein, *Organisational Culture and Leadership*, Jossey-Bass, 1992; and for a discussion of the importance of organisational culture on strategy developments, see G. Johnson, 'Managing strategic change: strategy, culture and action', *Long Range Planning*, vol. 25, no. 1 (1992), pp. 28–36.
- Good discussions of the relevance of chaos theory to strategic management are in R. Stacey, *Dynamic Business Strategies in an Unpredictable World*, Kogan Page, 1992, and 'Strategy as order emerging from chaos', *Long Range Planning*, vol. 26, no. 1 (1993) pp. 10–17.
- The concept of the learning organisation is explained in P. Senge, *The Fifth Discipline: The art and practice of the learning organisation*, Doubleday/Century, 1990.
- Managing strategy in innovatory organisations is discussed by J. Tidd, J. Bessant and K. Pavitt in *Managing Innovation: Integrating technological, market and organizational change*, Wiley, 1997.

REFERENCES

1. The idea of strategy 'momentum' is explained more fully in D. Miller and P. Friesen, 'Momentum and revolution in organisational adaptation', *Academy of Management Journal*, vol. 23, no. 4 (1980), pp. 591–614.
2. The concept of punctuated equilibrium is explained in E. Romanelli and M.L. Tushman, 'Organisational transformation as punctuated equilibrium: an empirical test', *Academy of Management Journal*, vol. 37, no. 5 (1994), pp. 1141–61.

3. The framework used here is, in part, derived from the discussion by H. Mintzberg and J.A. Waters, 'Of strategies, deliberate and emergent', *Strategic Management Journal*, vol. 6, no. 3 (1985), pp. 257–72.
4. There are now numerous books and papers which show the significance of cultural and political processes: for example, the books published by researchers at the Centre for Corporate Strategy and Change at Warwick Business School, including A. Pettigrew, *The Awakening Giant*, Blackwell, 1985; and A. Pettigrew, E. Ferlie and L. McKee, *Shaping Strategic Change*, Sage, 1992. See also G. Johnson, *Strategic Change and the Management Process*, Blackwell, 1987. Institutional theorists also emphasise the extent to which managers are 'captured' by their institutional culture; see W.R. Scott, *Institutions and Organizations: Foundations for organizational science*, Sage, 1995.
5. For books with an avowedly planning approach to strategy, see the books by John Argenti, especially *Practical Corporate Planning*, George Allen and Unwin, 1980. For a text based on a similar approach, see A.J. Rowe, K.E. Dickel, R.O. Mason and N.H. Snyder, *Strategic Management: A methodological approach*, 4th edition, Addison-Wesley, 1994.
6. L.C. Rhyne, 'The relationship of strategic planning to financial performance', *Strategic Management Journal*, vol. 7, no. 5 (1986), pp. 423–36, indicates that, while most research on the subject does show some benefits from financial planning, other studies give contrary or non-conclusive findings on the relationship between formal planning and performance. P. McKiernan and C. Morris, 'Strategic planning and financial performance in the UK SMEs: does formality matter?', *Journal of Management*, vol. 5 (1994), pp. S31–S42, also conclude that there is little evidence of direct links between formal planning and performance.
7. These conclusions are drawn from H. Mintzberg, *The Rise and Fall of Strategic Planning*, Prentice Hall, 1994.
8. Sherman's quote is taken from B.G. James, *Business Wargames*, Penguin, 1985, p. 190.
9. Also from *The Rise and Fall of Strategic Planning* (see reference 7).
10. Strategic planning among the oil and gas majors is a study carried out by Rob Grant and his findings were presented at the Strategic Management Conference in Barcelona, Spain, in 1997.
11. Much of what writers such as Tom Peters set out to show is the central role of corporate leaders in the formulation and change of strategy: for example, see T. Peters and R.H. Waterman, *In Search of Excellence*, Harper and Row, 1982; and T. Peters and N.K. Austin, *A Passion for Excellence: The leadership difference*, Random House, 1988.
12. Lindblom's paper, 'The science of muddling through', *Public Administration Review*, vol. 19 (Spring 1959), pp. 79–88, is one of the earliest which criticises an over-rational view of strategy formation and argues for an incremental perspective within a social and political context.
13. J.B. Quinn's research involved the examination of strategic change in companies and was published in *Strategies for Change*, Irwin, 1980. See also J.B. Quinn, 'Strategic change: logical incrementalism', in H. Mintzberg, J.B. Quinn and S. Ghoshal (eds), *The Strategy Process* (European edition), Prentice Hall, 1995.
14. See H. Mintzberg, 'Crafting strategy', *Harvard Business Review*, vol. 65, no. 4 (1987), pp. 66–75.
15. See *Strategies for Change* (reference 13), p. 58.
16. This alternative explanation is given in G. Johnson, 'Rethinking incrementalism', *Strategic Management Journal*, vol. 9, no. 1 (1988), pp. 75–91.
17. This definition is taken from E. Schein, *Organisational Culture and Leadership*, Jossey-Bass, 1985, p. 6.
18. The term 'industry recipes' originates in the work of J-C. Spender: see P. Grinyer and J-C. Spender, *Turnaround: Managerial recipes for strategic success*, Associated Business Press, 1979, and *Industry Recipes: The nature and sources of management judgement*, Blackwell, 1989.
19. 'Paradigm' is a term used by a number of writers: see, for example, J. Pfeffer, 'Management as symbolic action: the creation and maintenance of organisational paradigms', in L.L. Cummings and B.M. Staw (eds), *Research in Organisational Behaviour*, JAI Press, 1981, vol. 3, pp. 1–15, and G. Johnson, *Strategic Change and the Management Process*, Blackwell, 1987.
20. For a good summary of institutional theory, see W.R. Scott, *Institutions and Organizations*, Sage, 1995.
21. Here the term 'experience' is used. Studies which have examined this at the individual level are often referred to as research in managerial cognition. For an explanation and examples of such work, see A. Huff, *Mapping Strategic Thought*, Wiley, 1990; and for a summary of work in the field, see J.P. Walsh, 'Managerial and organizational cognition: notes from a trip down memory lane', *Organization Science*, vol. 6, no. 3 (1995), pp. 280–321.
22. There has been relatively little published which has examined strategic management explicitly from a political perspective, but it is a central theme of D. Buchanan and D. Boddy, *The Expertise of the Change Agent: Public performance and backstage activity*, Prentice Hall, 1992.
23. The concept of the organisation as a set of social networks is discussed by, for example, M.S. Granovetter, 'The strength of weak ties', *American Journal of Sociology*, vol. 78, no. 6 (1973), pp. 1360–80, and G.R. Carroll and A.C. Teo, 'On the social networks of managers', *Academy of Management Journal*, vol. 39, no. 2 (1996), pp. 421–40.
24. This section brings together the work of a number of researchers. For a thorough discussion of the problem of awareness and diagnosis stages of the decision-

making process, see M.A. Lyles, 'Formulating strategic problems: empirical analysis and model development', *Strategic Management Journal*, vol. 2, no. 1 (1981), pp. 61–75; H. Mintzberg, O. Raisinghani and A. Theoret, 'The structure of unstructured decision processes', *Administrative Science Quarterly*, vol. 21, no. 2 (1976), pp. 246–75; and L.M. Fahey, 'On strategic management decision processes', *Strategic Management Journal*, vol. 2, no. 1 (1981), pp. 43–60.

25. Evidence on the importance of consensus in organisations can be found in G. Dess and N. Origer, 'Environment, structure and consensus in strategy formulation: a conceptual integration', *Academy of Management Review*, vol. 12, no. 2 (1987), pp. 313–30, and G. Dess and R. Priem, 'Consensus-performance research: theoretical and empirical extensions', *Journal of Management Studies*, vol. 32, no. 4 (1995), pp. 401–17.
26. For example, see H.E. Aldrich, *Organisations and Environments*, Prentice Hall, 1979, and B. McKelvey and H. Aldrich, 'Populations, natural selection and applied organisational science', *Administrative Science Quarterly*, vol. 28, no. 1 (1983), pp. 101–28.
27. See C. Baden-Fuller and J.M. Stopford, *Rejuvenating the Mature Business: The competitive challenge*, Routledge, 1992.
28. For a discussion of the intuitive role of strategic management, see D.K. Hurst, J.C. Rush and R.E. White, 'Top management teams and organisational renewal', *Strategic Management Journal*, vol. 10, (1989), pp. 87–105. This is also a theme developed by R. Stacey, *Managing Chaos: Dynamic business strategies in an unpredictable world*, Kogan Page, 1992.
29. A fuller explanation of the cultural web can be found in G. Johnson, 'Managing strategic change: strategy, culture and action', *Long Range Planning*, vol. 25, no. 1 (1992), pp. 28–36.
30. See reference 20 on institutional theory and reference 26 on population ecology.
31. The organisational benefits of routines are discussed by economists such as R.R. Nelson and S.G. Winter, *An Evolutionary Theory of Economic Change*, Harvard University Press, 1982. In Chapter 4 of this book, the importance of routines is also shown as potentially underlying the core competences of organisations. In this sense, routines at their most valuable can be thought of as what G. Hamel and C.K. Prahalad refer to as 'bundles' of skills and 'the integration of a variety of individual skills': *Competing for the Future*, Harvard Business School Press, 1994.
32. The significance of organisational stories is explained in A.L. Wilkins, 'Organisational stories as symbols which control the organisation', in L.R. Pondy, P.J. Frost, G. Morgan and T.C. Dandridge (eds), *Organisational Symbolism*, JAI Press, 1983, and in J. Martin, M. Feldman, M. Hatch and S. Sitkin, 'The uniqueness paradox in organisational stories', *Administrative Science Quarterly*, vol. 28, no. 3 (1983), pp. 438–53.
33. The significance of organisational symbolism is explained in G. Johnson, 'Managing strategic change: the role of symbolic action', *British Journal of Management*, vol. 1, no. 4 (1990), pp. 183–200.
34. A number of writers and researchers have pointed to the links between the locus of power in organisations and the perceived ability of such powerful individuals or groups to 'reduce uncertainty': see D.J. Hickson *et al.*, 'A strategic contingencies theory of intra-organisational power', *Administrative Science Quarterly*, vol. 16, no. 2 (1971), pp. 216–29; D.C. Hambrick, 'Environment, strategy and power within top management teams', *Administrative Science Quarterly*, vol. 26, no. 2 (1981), pp. 253–76. Since the paradigm is, in effect, the 'perceived wisdom' of how to operate successfully, it is likely that those most associated with it will be the most powerful in the organisation.
35. For a fuller discussion of strategic drift, see G. Johnson, 'Rethinking incrementalism', *Strategic Management Journal*, vol. 9, no. 1 (1988), pp. 75–91.
36. This figure is based on that shown in P. Grinyer and J-C. Spender, *Turnaround*, p.203 (see reference 18).
37. See D. Miller, *The Icarus Paradox*, Harper Business, 1990.
38. The reference of chaos theory to management is explained by R. Stacey in *Managing Chaos* (see reference 28 above) and a summary paper, 'Strategy as order emerging from chaos', *Long Range Planning*, vol. 26, no. 1 (1993), pp. 10–17.
39. See, for example, J. Tidd, J. Bessant and K. Pavitt, *Managing Innovation: Integrating technological, market and organizational change*, Wiley, 1997, and J. Seely-Brown and P. Duguid, 'Organizational learning and communities of practice: toward a unified view of working, learning and innovation', *Organization Science*, vol. 2, no. 1 (1991), pp. 40–57.
40. See P. Senge, *The Fifth Discipline: The art and practice of the learning organisation*, Doubleday/Century, 1990.

WORK ASSIGNMENTS

2.1. Read the annual report of a company with which you are familiar as a customer (for example a retailer or transport company). Identify the main characteristics of the *intended* strategy as explained in the annual report; and the characteristics of the *realised* strategy as you perceive it as a customer.

2.2 Using the categories explained in sections 2.3 to 2.6, characterise how strategies have developed in different organisations (e.g. New Town,* Castle Press,* Iona,* KPMG A and KPMG C*).

2.3 ● Planning systems exist in many different organisations. What role should planning play in the National Health Service (see Illustration 2.2), a multinational corporation such as IKEA (see Illustration 1.1), Nokia* or The News Corporation.*

2.4 With reference to the explanations of incremental strategy development in Illustration 2.3, what are the main advantages and disadvantages in trying to develop strategies incrementally?

2.5 ● What is the difference between 'logical incrementalism', 'muddling through' and 'intuitive management'? (References 12, 13, 16 and 28 will be helpful here.)

2.6 ● Incremental patterns of strategy development are common in organisations, and managers see advantages in this. However, there are also risks of strategic drift. How might such drift be avoided while retaining the benefits of incremental strategy development? (Reference to the recommended readings by Quinn, Miller and Senge could be useful here.)

---

* refers to a case study in the Text and Cases edition.
● denotes more advanced work assignments.

CASE EXAMPLE

*KPMG (A): Strategy Development in a Partnership**

By 1997 KPMG had grown to be the largest professional services firm in the world with over 78,000 staff in 153 countries. Although parts of the enterprise had been incorporated, KPMG remained a partnership or, to be more precise, a federation of many partnerships spread across the world. Over the years the firm had grown, prospered and amalgamated with others to become the huge enterprise it was. It was undeniably a success story; yet this was a business facing an increasingly competitive environment on a global basis. There was a need to develop strategies appropriate to these changing conditions.

The Partnership Heritage

From 1993 to 1997 Colin Sharman had been the UK senior partner of KPMG. In March 1997 he also took over as international chairman. Sharman had been responsible for the review of strategy that had taken place in KPMG in the UK in the 1990s and was acutely aware of what it meant to manage strategy in a partnership. He emphasised that in the UK, for example, where there were 600 partners, they were 'owners who also work in the business. It's rather like a large family company in which the owners come to work in it every day'. As a matter of law, these partners had to be consulted on certain matters, for example taking leases on new properties.

In common with many partnerships, the legacy was an emphasis on powerful, influential individual partners, skilled in their areas of professional expertise and with strong personal relations at senior level with clients. Such a partner would typically have been a chartered accountant who had spent ten to fifteen years in the firm working his or her way up to a senior client management position in a specialist area such as audit or tax. Given a successful record in developing business with clients and providing first class professional services, the appointment to partner might take place, providing existing partners were in agreement. Thereafter the new partner would seek to further a reputation for winning new clients, building relationships with existing clients and ensuring excellence of service by cultivating a network of trusted managers and other partners with whom he or she would co-operate.

Attempts to formalise strategic planning in such a context were difficult. In the past in KPMG, committees had been set up to do it or partners given special responsibility for it; but whilst planning procedures or plans themselves might be evident, they did little to change the way in which the firm developed. The successful growth of the past had come about on the basis of excellence of professional advice given to clients and through longstanding relationships built by experienced partners. The strategic direction emerged from this. Where there were problems or disagreements, these were resolved between the partners themselves.

The Situation in 1992

The review of KPMG's strategy began in 1992, when Colin Sharman took over responsibility for KPMG's largest UK region (the south east), with 300 of the UK partners. He described what he inherited:

> In many respects the way we did things had its benefits. It was based on a network of very bright people, professionally trained and dedicated to providing quality advice to their clients. But

* This case can be used in conjunction with case studies B and C describing subsequent developments in KPMG in the Text and Cases version of this book.

there were problems, especially if we remember that our primary purpose is to provide services to our clients; and I emphasise here the needs of our clients, which may not always coincide with the skills, experience and interests of the partner who has dealt with that client historically.

We have a matrix structure like many other professional service organisations. We have a delivery structure for services along discipline lines. We have different practice units for audit, for tax, for management consultants and for corporate recovery [see figure below]. Separately we focus on our market sectors through firm-wide multidisciplinary groups that are industry based, focusing on banking, insurance, manufacturing and so on. But the dominant axis remains the discipline-based practice units, and that is the primary interface to the market.

Our mission involves providing the highest quality of services to our individual clients but our practice units are discipline based. The only way that we focus across disciplines is through our market sector groups, but they merely co-ordinate and do not run the business. Hence there is a conflict between our stated goals and our structure.

KPMG can be characterised as professional, highly conservative and sometimes complacent. There is also an attitude that our partners can – and will – 'do anything', different from a 'do well' culture. And also a belief from right across the firm that being a generalist, rather than a specialist, is the most desirable state. Partners believe they should have a say in decision making. It is not always seen like that from within the organisation and there is a belief that the senior partners in the organisation actually operate on the principle of management by edict. So we have partners who are struggling to keep the power to themselves and senior partners trying to manage but sounding like dictating. Either way, it does not help effective management.

There is a widespread network of committees – the answer for most things in the organisation is to set up a committee, a retreat into collectivism at the drop of a hat. Alongside that, the responsibilities of individuals within the organisation are so ill defined that it makes

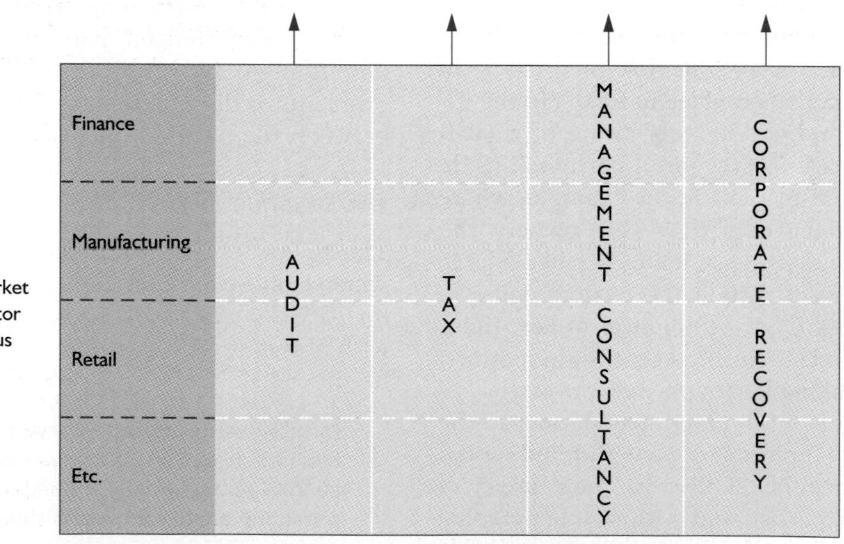

Delivery structure for services in 1992

achieving change very difficult. Our control systems are full of paradoxes. At lower levels our staff see controls as bureaucratic, taking time away from the real business of being a professional services firm. That may be true, but at the higher levels there is a belief that we have poor controls and poor management information to run the business. Both of those are probably right – we spend a lot of time collecting and controlling the things that don't help us to run the business. Alongside that we have too much poor discipline – a lack of rigour and not caring about doing it right the first time. That is not surprising if we are asking people to spend a lot of their time on data that are never used to manage the business. But poor discipline, endemic through an organisation, is a major barrier to new ways of working. For example, there is too little value placed on managing carefully to timescales. It is regarded as much better to whirl around in frenzied activity at the last minute. That applies whether we are serving clients or whether we are trying to do something that contributes towards managing the business. You will hear people bragging about the extremely long hours that they work, doubtless to reinforce the air of crisis that they are managing (though never creating!).

The 'mystique of partnership' doesn't always help. Promotion to partner is seen as the summit of a KPMG person's career with virtually no second prizes for those who do not make it – we have a culture of 'up or out'. Partners, once created, are quite distinct and elevated people within the organisation. There are also problems with the discipline structure of audit, tax, consultancy and so on being dominant; problems illustrated, for example, by the tales people tell about how awful one of the other disciplines is. Nor is the 'cult of the individual' always helpful. The kinds of people who are lionised are mavericks – people out of the mould; people who have broken the mould; people who don't conform, who are entirely individuals – there are lots of stories about individuals. You can imagine the way some of this expresses itself, especially when it comes to 'them and us' – partners and the rest or, at lower levels, senior managers and the rest. For example, in our London office we have three levels of dining room and partners get their tea brought to their desks in china pots on silver trays.

The Challenge of Strategy Development

The challenge Colin Sharman faced in 1992 in the south east region, in 1993 for the UK as a whole and, again in 1997 as he took worldwide responsibility, was how to manage the development of strategy in one of the largest partnerships in the world. He described the challenge as follows:

> In practice, of course, we have moved a long way from the Victorian notion of partnership and we run ourselves increasingly on corporate lines. I am the senior partner, the managing director, and I have a management team who make many of the operational decisions of an executive board. But the partners have to be consulted and have to agree – or at least not disagree – with any change.
>
> But it is not just about partnership. Over 70 per cent of our total workforce are graduates, a highly intelligent group of people who, quite rightly, need to be convinced we are following the right strategy. This is not just an issue of drawing up some sort of plan and communicating it well through the organisation, but also of winning hearts and minds.

Questions

1. Drawing on the explanations in sections 2.3–2.6 of Chapter 2, explain how strategy develops in a partnership such as KPMG.
2. What are the advantages and disadvantages of this approach to strategy development?
3. Use the cultural web to identify the elements of KPMG's culture as described by Colin Sharman.
4. Why might formalised strategic planning not be especially effective in such a culture?

II
STRATEGIC ANALYSIS

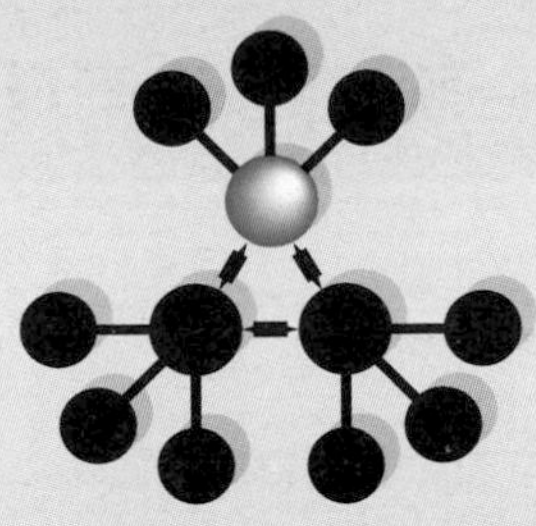

In Chapters 1 and 2 it was explained that there are different explanations of how strategies develop in organisations. There are those who argue that managers have little choice about the strategies they follow because the impact of their environment is so great as to force strategies upon them or constrain them with regard to strategic choice. Others argue that for commercial organisations the forces at work in an industry are the most important influence on performance: for example, that industries in more attractive environments will perform better that those in less attractive environments. This is disputed by others, who provide evidence that the resources, competences and strategies of particular organisations explain differences in performance. There is, then, a debate between those who argue that it is the environment and environmental influences that are the most important consideration when analysing the strategic position of an organisation and those who argue that it is organisation-specific resources and competences that are the most important consideration.

This in turn relates to the difference between a 'fit' view of strategic management and a 'stretch' view of strategic management, as explained in Chapter 1. A 'fit' approach is about identifying opportunities in the environment and building strategy by matching resource capabilities to those opportunities. A 'stretch' view argues that strategies should be built on the unique competences and resources of an organisation, by seeking out markets in which such competences have special value or by trying to create new markets on the basis of such competences.

There are other considerations too. Cultural similarities across industries or within, for example, professions may give rise to organisations having similar purposes and strategies and responding to environmental forces in similar ways. There is, however, evidence that different organisations have different cultures which are associated with their being more or less proactive in their markets, with more or less aggressive strategies. The implication is that culture will affect strategy and performance.

Strategic analysis is concerned with understanding the relationship between the different forces affecting the organisation and its choice of strategies. It may be that the environment exercises severe constraints or yields potential opportunities, and this needs to be understood. It may be that the firm has particular competences on which it can build, or that it needs to develop these. It may be that the expectations and

THIS PART EXPLAINS:

- The impact of the environment, organisational capability and expectations on strategy.
- How to assess an organisation's standing in the environment.
- The determinants of strategic capability – resources, competences and linkages.
- The factors which shape organisational purposes – governance, stakeholder expectations, business ethics and the cultural context.

objectives of stakeholders who influence the organisation or the culture of the organisation play an important role in determining the strategy.

- Chapter 3 is concerned with the environment of an organisation in terms of macro influences, future scenarios and specific forces affecting competition. The challenge is to make sense of this so as to understand the key variables affecting the performance of the organisation and how the organisation is positioned in terms of such influences.
- Chapter 4 is concerned with analysing and understanding an organisation's strategic capability and how it underpins the competitive advantage of the organisation or sustains excellence in providing value-for-money products or services. This is done in relation to three issues: the resource base of the organisation; how these resources are deployed and controlled to create organisational competences; and how activities are linked together, both inside the organisation and in the 'supply' and 'distribution' chains, to provide more generic competences. Core competences are also explained as those which underpin the competitive edge of the organisation and are difficult to imitate.
- Chapter 5 looks at organisational purposes and how they arise. It is concerned with understanding whom the organisation is there to serve. This is divided into four themes: corporate governance; stakeholder analysis; business ethics; and cultural analysis. Together they provide an assessment of the cultural and political context in which strategies are developed and pursued.

Although this part of the book is divided into three chapters, it should be stressed that there are strong links between these different influences on strategy. Environmental pressures for change will be constrained by the resources available to make changes, or by an organisational culture which may lead to resistance to change; and capabilities yielding apparent opportunities will be valuable only if opportunities in the environment can be found. The relative importance of the various influences will change over time and may show marked differences from one organisation to another.

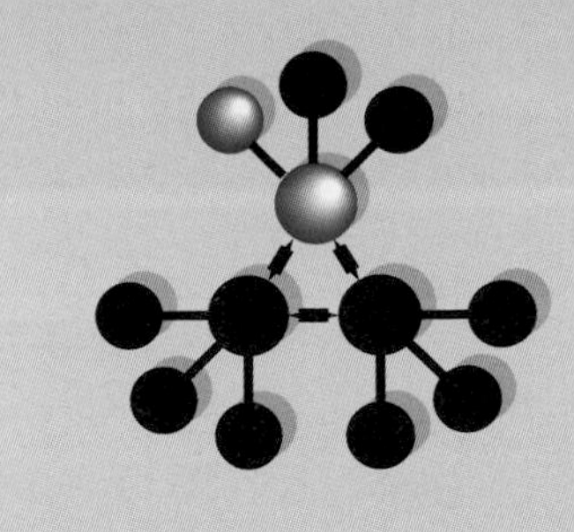

3
ANALYSING THE ENVIRONMENT

LEARNING OUTCOMES

After reading this chapter you should be able to:

- Describe the determinants of environmental uncertainty.
- Undertake a PEST analysis, identify key environmental drivers of change and the differential impact of change.
- Use the Porter diamond to analyse bases of competitive advantage within nations.
- Develop scenarios and explain their implications.
- Undertake a five forces analysis for an organisation.
- Undertake a strategic group analysis for an industry or a public service.
- Analyse the segments within a market and explain the implications to providers of products/services.
- Use a directional policy matrix to consider the portfolio of a business.
- Undertake a competitor analysis exercise.

3.1 INTRODUCTION

Managers face difficulties in trying to understand the environment. First, 'the environment' encapsulates many different influences; the difficulty is making sense of this diversity in a way which can contribute to strategic decision making. Identifying very many environmental influences may be possible, but it may not be much use because no overall picture emerges of really important influences on the organisation.

The second difficulty is that of uncertainty. Managers typically claim that the pace of technological change and the speed of global communications mean more and faster change now than ever before. Whether or not change is in fact faster now,[1] and whether or not the changes are more unpredictable, it remains the case that, while it is important to try to understand future external influences on an organisation, it is very difficult to do so.

Third, it must be realised that managers are no different from other individuals in the way they cope with complexity. They tend to simplify such complexity by focusing on aspects of the environment which, perhaps, have been historically important, or confirm prior views (see section 3.6).[2] This is not perverse managerial behaviour; it is the natural behaviour of everyone faced with complexity. One of the tasks of the strategic manager is to find ways in which he or she and their colleagues can break out of the tendency towards oversimplification while still achieving useful and usable analysis.

In this chapter, frameworks for understanding the environment of organisations are provided with the aim of trying to identify key issues, find ways of coping with complexity and also challenging managerial thinking. These frameworks are provided in a series of steps briefly introduced here and summarised in Exhibit 3.1.

- As a first step, it is useful to take an initial view of the *nature of the organisation's environment* in terms of how uncertain it is. Is it relatively static or does it show signs of change, and in what ways? Is it simple or complex to understand? This helps in deciding what focus the rest of the analysis is to take.
- A second step might be an *audit of environmental influences*. Here the aim is to identify which macro environmental influences are likely to affect the organisation's development or performance. This can be done by considering the way in which *political, economic, social and technological* influences impinge on organisations. It is increasingly useful to relate such influences to growing trends towards *globalisation* of industries. It may also be helpful to construct pictures – or *scenarios* – of possible futures, to consider the extent to which strategies might need to change.
- The third step moves the focus towards an explicit consideration of the immediate environment of the organisation – for example, the competitive arena in which the organisation operates. *Five forces analysis* aims to identify the key forces at work in the immediate or competitive environment and why they are significant.

From these steps should emerge a view of the really important developments taking place around the organisation. It may be that there are relatively few of outstanding significance; or it could be that there are many interconnected developments.

- The fourth step is to analyse the organisation's *competitive position*, that is, how it stands in relation to other organisations competing for the same resources, or customers, as itself. This may be done in a number of ways, but this chapter concentrates on: (a) *strategic group analysis*, which maps organisations in terms of similarities and dissimilarities in the strategies they follow; (b) the analysis of *market*

Exhibit 3.1 **Steps in environmental analysis**

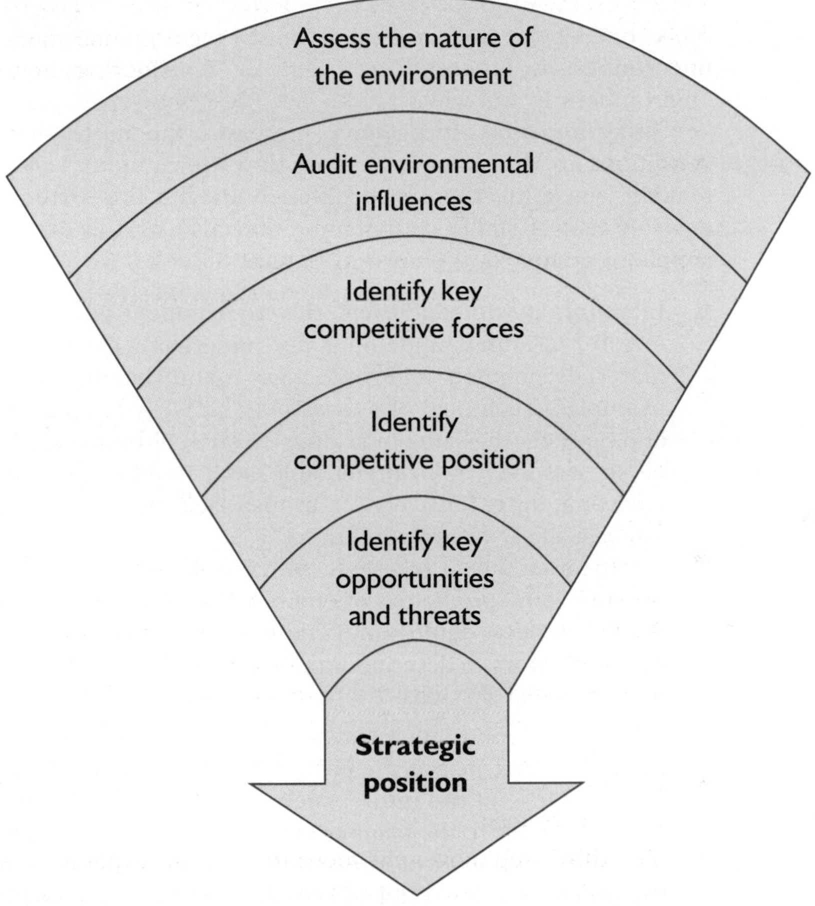

segments, which seeks to establish the segments of markets which might be most attractive; (c) *competitor analysis*; and (d) *attractiveness analysis*, which maps the organisation's competitive position in relation to the attractiveness of the market(s) in which it operates.

The aim of such analyses is to develop an understanding of *opportunities* which can be built upon and *threats* which have to be overcome or circumvented: an understanding which needs to be considered in terms of the resource base and competences of the organisation (Chapter 4) and which will contribute to strategic choice (Part III).

3.2 UNDERSTANDING THE NATURE OF THE ENVIRONMENT

environmental uncertainty *increases the more that environmental conditions are dynamic or the more they are complex*

Since one of the main problems of strategic management is coping with uncertainty, it is useful to begin by considering how uncertain the environment is and why.

Environmental uncertainty increases the more that environmental conditions are dynamic or the more they are complex;[3] and the approach to making sense of this may differ both by the extent to which the environment is stable or dynamic, and also by the extent to which it is simple or complex, as shown in Exhibit 3.2.

- In *simple/static* conditions, the environment is relatively straightforward to understand and is not undergoing significant change. Raw materials suppliers and some mass manufacturing companies are examples. Technical processes may be fairly simple, and competition and markets the same over time. In such circumstances, if change does occur, it is likely to be predictable, so it could make sense to analyse the environment extensively on an historical basis as a means of trying to forecast likely future conditions.

  In situations of relatively low complexity, it may also be possible to identify some predictors of environmental influences. For example, in public services, demographic data such as birth rates might be used as lead indicators to determine the required provision of schooling, health care or social services.
- In *dynamic* conditions, managers need to consider the environment of the future, not just of the past. They may employ structured ways of making sense of the future, such as *scenario planning*, which is discussed later in the chapter (see section 3.3.3), or they may rely more on building the sort of innovative, learning organisation described in Chapter 1 (section 1.3.4), Chapter 2 (section 2.8.3) and Chapter 9 (section 9.2.7). Here the emphasis is on creating the organisational conditions necessary to encourage individuals and groups to be intuitive and challenging in their thinking about possible futures.
- Organisations in *complex* situations face an environment difficult to comprehend. They may, of course, face dynamic conditions too. With more and more sophisticated technology, there is an increasing move towards this condition of greatest uncertainty. The electronics industry is in this situation. A multinational firm, or a major public service such as a local government authority with many services, may also be in a complex condition because of its diversity, while different operating companies within it face varying degrees of complexity and dynamism.

  It is difficult to handle complexity by relying primarily on analysis. Complexity as a result of diversity might be dealt with by ensuring that different parts of the organisation responsible for different aspects of diversity are separate, and given the resources and authority to handle

Exhibit 3.2 Approaches to making sense of the environment

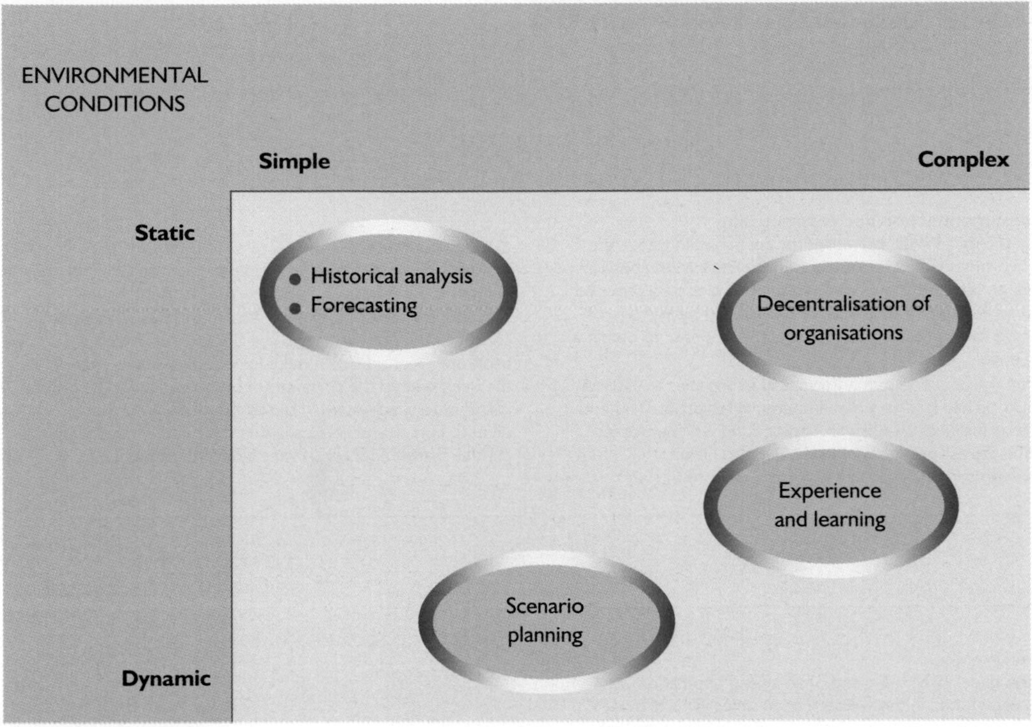

their own part of the environment. So organisational *structure* is important (see Chapter 9). Or it may be that an organisation has *learned* to cope with complexity especially well, and this strategic competence based on *experience* may provide competitive advantage (see Chapter 4).

3.3 AUDITING ENVIRONMENTAL INFLUENCES

Illustration 3.1 shows some of the macroenvironmental influences important to organisations. It is not intended to provide an exhaustive list, but it does give examples of ways in which strategies are affected by such influences and some of the ways in which organisations seek to handle aspects of their environment.[4]

Environmental forces which are especially important for one organisation may not be the same for another; and, over time, their importance may change. A multinational corporation might be especially concerned with government relations and understanding the policies of local governments,

STRATEGY IN ACTION
Illustration 3.1

Examples of Environmental Influences

A wide variety of environmental influences can affect organisational strategy and performance.

Government action and restructuring

- By the mid 1990s, pressures for cost containment from governments had become a priority issue within public health services around the world. This pressure required pharmaceutical companies to ensure that new drugs were safe, efficient and cost effective in order to obtain a licence.
- The introduction of market-based economies in eastern Europe had lead to a new imperative for profit. This and the transfer of western technology and work practices led to great productivity gains, but also higher unemployment and job insecurity.

Capital markets

During 1996, Eurotunnel, the operator of the Channel Tunnel, was negotiating to restructure its debt, having suspended interest payments in autumn 1995. The bank consortium – not wishing to see Eurotunnel declared bankrupt – considered a debt-for-equity swap as part of the deal to keep the company in business. However, other shareholders did not wish to see their equity further diluted. Eurotunnel was caught in the middle, needing to placate shareholders with very different interests.

Demographics

By the mid 1990s, the trend of an ageing population was well established in the western economies. This provided many companies with an easily identifiable target market for their goods/services.

Other markets, such as Asia, however, were experiencing a population explosion and a resulting reduction in the average age of their population, giving these markets their own particular needs and opportunities.

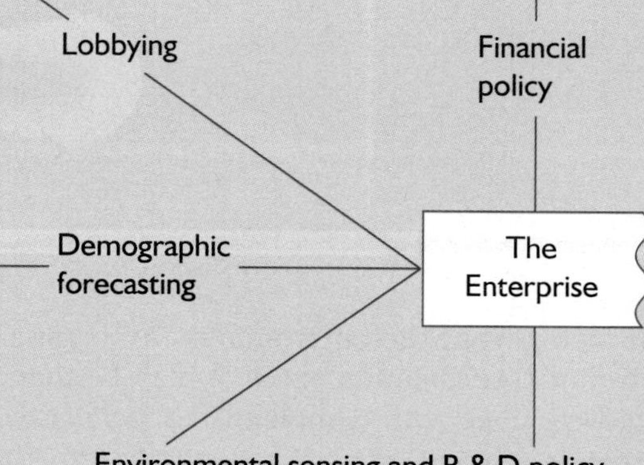

Sociocultural

Growing health consciousness, sophisticated and social pressures on smokers in western countries has affected the sales of tobacco products in these markets. This situation led to controversial advertising campaigns by tobacco companies such as Philip Morris, which attempted to play down the risks of passive smoking in an attempt to protect their market, and a switch by the tobacco companies into concentrating their efforts on the developing world.

Technology

- The high costs of R&D, the long lead times and the critical need for new products to treat *antibiotic-resistant drugs* led Glaxo Wellcome and SmithKline Beecham to announce their first scientific collaboration in 1996.
- The development of 3D graphic accelerator chips has enabled computer games companies to create PC-based games which match those found in arcades in terms of graphics quality and realistic 3D effects, leading to increased sales of computer games.

Questions

1. Using this illustration and Exhibit 3.3 as a guide, draw up an audit for an 'industry' environment of your choice.
2. Which of the influences you identified are likely to be the main 'drivers for change' in the future? Why?

Prepared by Tony Jacobs, Bristol Business School.

Labour market
In the 1990s, high levels of unemployment combined with continued 'downsizing' of workforces and the automation of many processes changed the face of the UK labour market.

The labour force had to become more flexible as there was an increasingly high demand for labour on short-term contracts and for part-time working – especially in the service sector.

In addition, the traditional power of the trade unions diminished.

Competition
Deregulation of the UK financial services sector led to intense competition in the industry. Building societies began to compete directly with domestic banks in the early 1980s. In the 1990s, many shed their mutual ownership status and converted to public companies.

In response, many banks merged or acquired other financial service providers to obtain the critical mass required to be successful in an increasingly competitive industry.

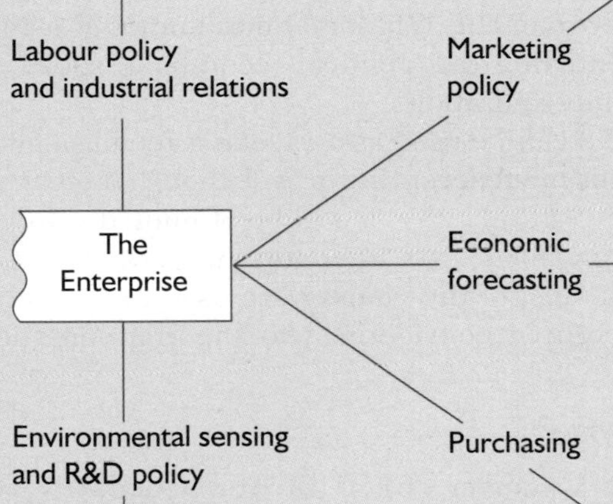

Economic conditions
By 1996, Japan had witnessed four years of economic stagnation, exchange rate pressure, financial crisis and political upheaval. This forced many Japanese companies to restructure, shifting production overseas and reducing their workforce in Japan.

The change in corporate fortunes enabled Ford to take management control of Mazda, and News Corporation to buy a stake in a Japanese television station – both unprecedented investments which would have been unthinkable before the recession.

Ecology
Widespread concern and anger caused by the failure of UK water companies to plug water leaks – in some cases as high as 30 per cent – while introducing bans on the use of water helped companies which produced hazard detection and measurement equipment to increase their sales as the water companies were forced by Ofwat, the industry's regulator, to address the problem and reduce leakage rates.

Suppliers
- Brazil is the world's largest coffee producer. In 1994, severe frosts cut the yield of the 1995 coffee bean harvest to less than half that predicted. This disruption to supplies forced Brazil's coffee-roasting industry to import coffee for domestic consumption for the first time ever.
- In mid 1996 the price of platinum surged on the world's markets as threatened strike action led to concerns over the metal's availability.

since it may be operating plants or subsidiaries within many different countries with different political systems. It is also likely to be concerned with labour costs and exchange rates, which will affect its ability to compete with multinational rivals. A retailer, on the other hand, may be primarily concerned with local customer tastes and behaviour. A computer manufacturer is likely to be concerned with its technical environment which leads to product innovation and perhaps obsolescence. Public sector managers and civil servants are likely to be especially concerned with public policy issues, public funding levels and demographic changes. However, none of these forces will remain constant, and managers need to be aware of their changing impact.

3.3.1 PEST Analysis

As a starting point, it is useful to consider what environmental influences have been particularly important in the past, and the extent to which there are changes occurring which may make any of these more or less significant in the future for the organisation and its competitors. Exhibit 3.3 is designed to help by providing a summary of some of the questions to ask about key forces at work in the macroenvironment. It is sometimes known as a **PEST analysis**, which involves identifying the political, economic, social and technological influences on an organisation.

PEST analysis *involves identifying the political, economic, social and technological influences on an organisation*

The headings in Exhibit 3.3 can be used as a *checklist* to consider and prompt analysis of the different influences. However, although a great deal of information can be generated in this way, it will be of limited value if it remains merely a listing of influences. It is, therefore, important that the sorts of model discussed in the rest of the chapter are used to inform and guide analysis. It is useful to begin by considering two important questions.

What are Key Drivers of Change?

environmental drivers of change *are forces likely to affect the structure of an industry or market*

It may be possible to identify a number of key **environmental drivers of change**, that is forces likely to affect the structure of an industry or market. A good example is the forces which are increasing the globalisation of some markets (see also Exhibit 3.4):[5]

- There is an increasing *convergence of markets* worldwide for a variety of reasons. In some markets, customer needs and preferences are becoming more similar. For example, there is increasing homogeneity of consumer tastes in goods such as soft drinks, jeans, electrical items (e.g. audio equipment) and personal computers. The opening of McDonald's in Moscow signalled similar tendencies in fast food. As some markets globalise, those operating in such markets become *global customers* and may search for suppliers who can operate on a global basis. For example, the global clients of the major accountancy firms may expect the accountancy firms to provide global services. In turn

Exhibit 3.3 A PEST analysis of environmental influences

1. What environmental factors are affecting the organisation?
2. Which of these are the most important at the present time? In the next few years?

Political/legal
- Monopolies legislation
- Environmental protection laws
- Taxation policy
- Foreign trade regulations
- Employment law
- Government stability

Sociocultural factors
- Population demographics
- Income distribution
- Social mobility
- Lifestyle changes
- Attitudes to work and leisure
- Consumerism
- Levels of education

Economic factors
- Business cycles
- GNP trends
- Interest rates
- Money supply
- Inflation
- Unemployment
- Disposable income
- Energy availability and cost

Technological
- Government spending on research
- Government and industry focus on technological effort
- New discoveries/development
- Speed of technology transfer
- Rates of obsolescence

this may provide opportunities for *transference of marketing* across countries. Marketing policies, brand names and identities, and advertising may all be developed globally. This further generates global demand and expectations from customers, and may also provide marketing cost advantages for global operators.

- There may, then, be *cost advantages* of global operations. This is especially the case in industries in which large volume, standardised production is required for optimum *economies of scale*, as in some components to the electronics industry. Other cost advantages might be achieved by central *sourcing efficiencies* from lowest-cost suppliers across the world. *Country-specific costs*, such as labour or exchange rates, encourage businesses to search globally for low cost in these respects as ways of matching the costs of competitors which have such advantages because of their location. For example, given increased reliability of communication and cost differentials of labour, some software companies base their customer service departments in India, where there is highly skilled but low-cost staff. A telephone enquiry from Holland could well be routed to Bombay. Other businesses face high *costs of product development* and may see advantages in operating globally with fewer products rather than incurring the costs of wide ranges of products on a more limited geographical scale.

Exhibit 3.4 Drivers of globalisation

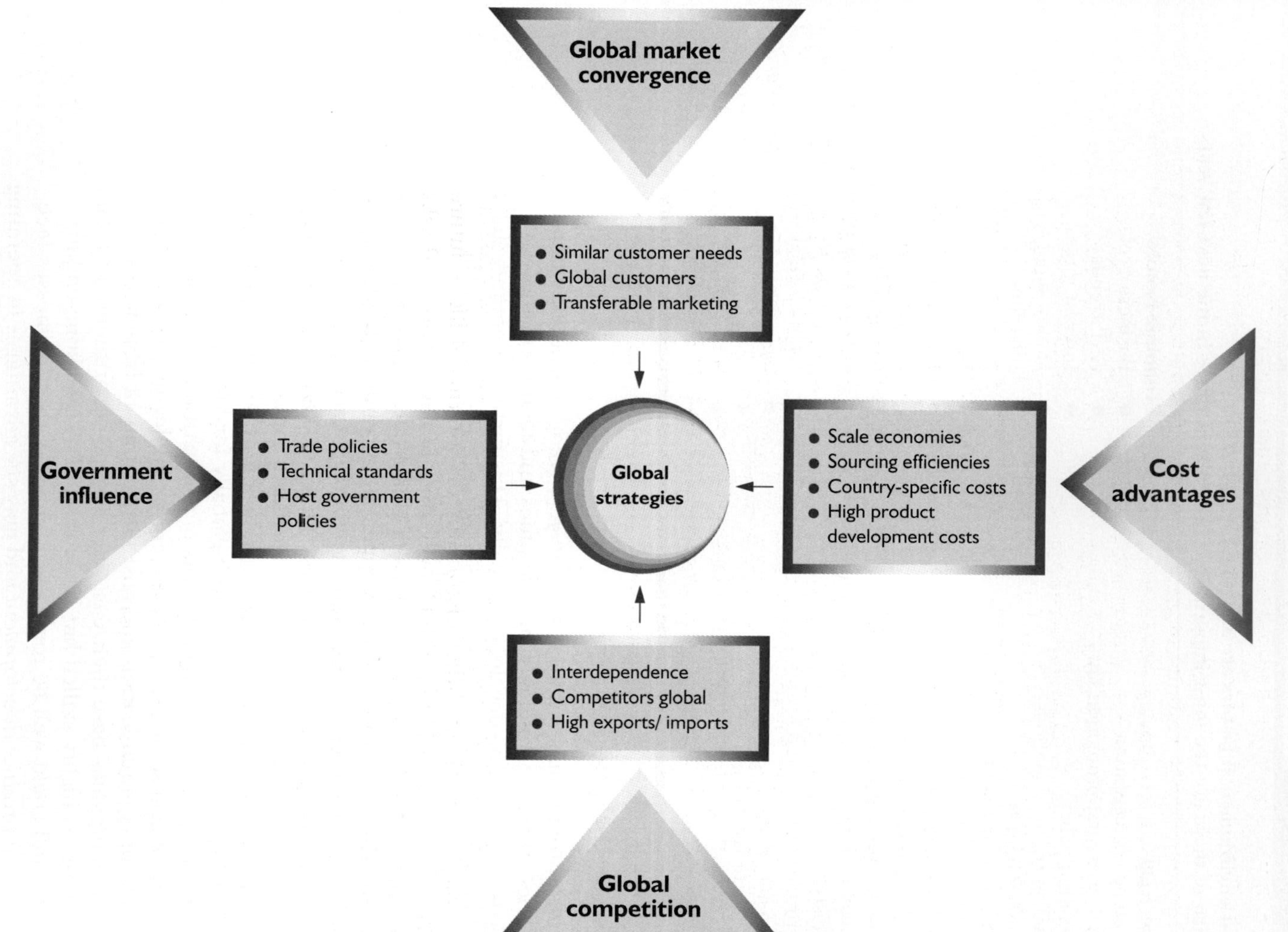

Source Based on G. Yip, *Total Global Strategy*, Prentice Hall, 1995, chapter 2.

- The activities and policies of *governments* have also tended to drive the globalisation of industry. Political changes in the 1990s meant that almost all trading nations function with market-based economies, and their *trade policies* have tended to encourage free markets between nations. This has been further encouraged by *technical standardisation* between countries of many products, such as in the airline industry. However, it is worth noting that in many industries country-specific regulations still persist and reduce the extent to which global strategies are possible. It may also be that particular *host governments* actively seek to encourage global operators to base themselves in their countries. The Conservative government in the UK in the 1980s and 1990s regarded the country's move to a lower-wage economy as a benefit in attracting investment from such companies.
- *Global competition* is therefore becoming increasingly evident, and as it does, it encourages further globalisation. If the levels of *exports and imports* between countries are high, it increases interaction between competitors on a more global scale. If a business is competing globally, it also tends to place globalisation pressures on competitors, especially if customers are also operating on a global basis. It may also be that the *interdependence* of a company's operations across the world encourages the globalisation of its competitors. For example, if a company has sought out low-cost production sites in different countries, these low costs may be used to subsidise competitive activity in high-cost areas against local competitors, thus encouraging them to follow similar strategies.

What are the Differential Impacts of Key Environmental Influences?

PEST analysis may also help examine the *differential impact* of external influences on organisations, either historically or in terms of likely future impact. This approach builds on the identification of key drivers, and asks to what extent such influences will affect different organisations or industries differently. As Illustration 3.2 shows, the automobile industry has more potential for global development than over-the-counter (OTC) pharmaceuticals; ethical pharmaceuticals, however, show increasing signs of globalisation.

Here the illustration focuses on industry drivers for globalisation. However, the same sort of exercise can be undertaken by managers in a particular organisation to consider the differential impact of key drivers in the environment on competitors or the strategic options they are considering (see, for example, the competitor analysis shown in Illustration 3.8).

3.3.2 Porter's Diamond

An example of important environmental influences particularly relevant in the context of global competition is provided by Michael Porter in his book,

STRATEGY IN ACTION
Illustration 3.2

Industry Globalisation Drivers

Identifying drivers for change in industries can help to explain their development.

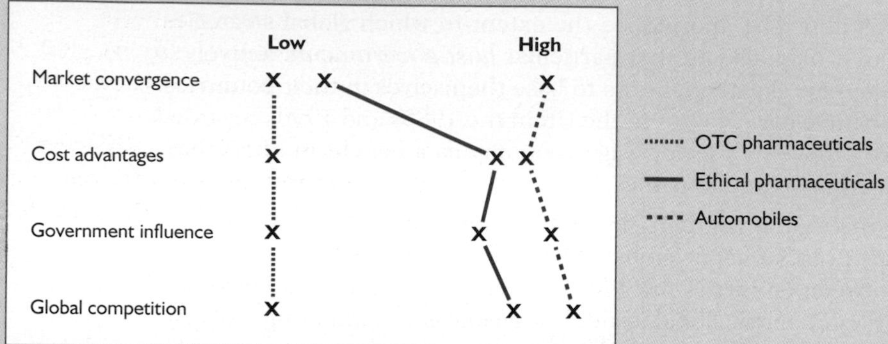

Market Convergence

Higher. Japanese automobile companies were successful at exploiting common customer needs when they first entered markets. Focusing on fundamental needs common to all countries, such as reliability and economy, their standardised products became acceptable in most countries. Subsequently, other car companies followed this approach.

Lower. Over-the-counter (OTC) pharmaceuticals are different in most major markets: for example, in the brand names used for products. Differences also remain between markets for ethical (prescription) pharmaceuticals because medical treatment differs across the world.

Cost Advantages

Higher. Ford's 'centres of excellence' aim to reduce the duplication of R&D efforts and exploit the differing expertise around the world. One example was the Ford Mondeo, introduced in 1993 as Ford's first global car. In

Porter's diamond *suggests that there are inherent reasons why some nations are more competitive than others, and why some industries within nations are more competitive than others*

The Competitive Advantage of Nations.[6] What has become known as **Porter's diamond** suggests that there are inherent reasons why some nations are more competitive than others, and why some industries within nations are more competitive than others. (See Exhibit 3.5.)

Porter suggests that the national home base of an organisation plays an important role in shaping the extent to which it is likely to achieve advantage on a global scale. This home base provides basic factors which organisations are able to build on and extend to provide such advantage.

- There may be specific *factor conditions* which help explain the basis of advantage on a national level. These provide initial advantages which the case of ethical pharmaceuticals, the high cost of R&D provides an incentive for globalisation to achieve economies of scale.

Lower. The marketing budgets of OTC pharmaceuticals are geared up for national brand names, leaving little scope for global economies of scale.

Government Influence

Higher. US government action and threats of tariffs, quotas and protectionist measures have encouraged Japanese automobile companies to open manufacturing plants in the USA and to use production facilities in the UK and other countries as a springboard into mainland Europe.

In the case of ethical pharmaceuticals, governments are adopting policies of cost containment in health care. These and the harmonisation of clinical standards are facilitating more globalised approaches to markets.

Lower. There are legislative standards on OTC pharmaceuticals, such as maximum allowed dosage, but these vary from country to country. This incompatibility means that there is little scope for globalisation.

Global Competition

High. Automotive companies trade across countries and across continents. Companies with largely regional bases (e.g. BMW, Peugeot) face competitive pressures to develop globally. Similarly, the advent of global companies in ethical pharmaceuticals is itself a spur to globalisation in the industry.

Low. Because of the different legislation governing the use of OTC pharmaceuticals, competition is only at the local level rather than global.

Questions

1. Choose another industry with which you are familiar (or the brewing industry case study from the case section of this book) and map the drivers for globalisation in that industry.
2. Ensure that you can justify this by describing the reasons for the plots for each of the four parameters.

Source Adapted from G. Yip, *Total Global Strategy*, Business School edition, Prentice Hall, 1995, chapter 2.

Prepared by Tony Jacobs, Bristol Business School.

are subsequently built upon to yield more advanced factors of competition. For example, in countries such as Sweden and Japan, in which either legislation or custom means that it is difficult to lay off labour, there has been a greater impetus towards automation of industries; and the linguistic ability of the Swiss has provided a significant advantage to its banking industry.

- Home *demand conditions* provide the basis upon which the characteristics of the advantage of an organisation are shaped. For example, Japanese customers' high expectations of electrical and electronic equipment have provided an impetus for those industries in

Exhibit 3.5 **The determinants of national advantage (Porter's diamond)**

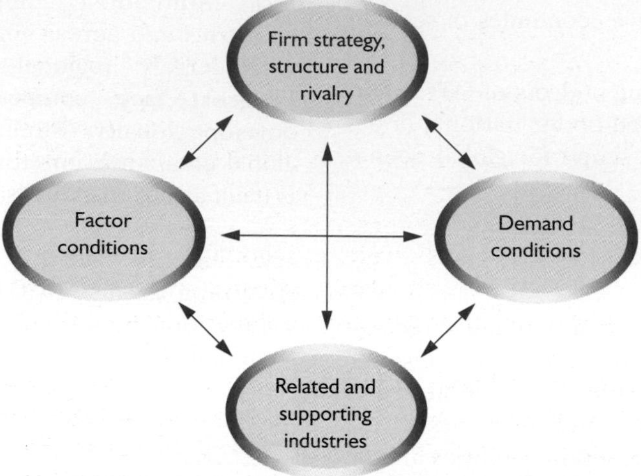

Japan. The remoteness of Sweden's power plants from centres of population and the existence of energy-intensive paper and steel industries have placed extensive home demand on high-voltage electrical distribution equipment suppliers, and historically helped to create advantage for that industry.

- One successful industry may lead to advantage in *related and supporting industries*. In Italy, for example, the leather footwear industry, the leather working machinery industry and the design services which underpin them benefit from one another. In Denmark, the successes in dairy products, brewing and industrial enzymes industries are interrelated; and in Singapore, port services and ship repair industries are mutually advantageous.
- The context of characteristics of *firm strategy, structure and rivalry* in different countries also helps explain bases of advantage. In Germany, the propensity for systematic, often hierarchical processes of management has been particularly successful in providing reliability and technical excellence in engineering industries. Domestic rivalry and the search for competitive advantages within a nation can help provide organisations with bases for achieving such advantage on a more global scale. Japanese electrical and automobile industries are good examples of this. Especially important is the extent of domestic rivalry within a nation. Porter argues that one of the main reasons for success in Japan is the extent of domestic rivalry within many of its industries. Germany is successful in the chemical industry in part because of the competition between its domestic

chemicals companies; and pharmaceuticals in Switzerland are successful because of competition between local competitors in that industry.

Porter's diamond has been used in various ways. At a national level it has been employed by governments to consider the policies that they should follow to encourage the competitive advantage of their industry. Since the argument is, in essence, that domestic characteristics of competition should yield advantages on a wider basis, the implication is that competition should be encouraged at home, rather than industries being protected from overseas competition. However, governments can also act to foster such advantage by, for example, ensuring high expectations of product performance, safety or environmental standards; or encouraging vertical co-operation between suppliers and buyers on a domestic level, which could lead to innovation.

Organisations have also used Porter's diamond as a way of trying to identify the extent to which they can build on home-based advantages to create competitive advantage in relation to others on a global front. For example, British Steel and British Telecom in the UK might argue that their experience of privatisation before similar businesses in other countries should provide a basis for their achieving advantage in global competition. Benetton, the Italian clothing company, has achieved global success by using its experience of working through a network of largely independent, often family-owned manufacturers to build its network of franchised retailers using advanced information systems.

3.3.3 The Use of Scenarios[7]

The identification of major environmental influences and drivers can also usefully be built into the construction of scenarios as a way of considering environmental influences. Scenario planning is especially useful in circumstances where it is important to take a *long-term view* of strategy, probably a minimum of five years; where there are a *limited number of key factors* influencing the success of that strategy; but where there is a *high level of uncertainty* about such influences. For example, in the oil industry there is a need for views of the business environment of up to 20 years; and while a whole host of environmental issues are of relevance, a number of these, such as raw material availability, price and demand, are of crucial importance. Obviously, it is not possible to forecast precisely such factors over a 20-year time horizon, but it can be valuable to have different views of possible futures.

scenario planning *builds plausible views of different possible futures for an organisation based on groupings of key environmental influences and drivers of change about which there is a high level of uncertainty*

Scenario planning is not just based on a hunch, then, but builds plausible views of different possible futures for an organisation based on groupings of key environmental influences and drivers of change about which there is a high level of uncertainty. The result is a limited number of logically consistent, but different scenarios which can be considered alongside each

STRATEGY IN ACTION
Illustration 3.3

Building Scenarios

The book publishing industry and oil industry both face changing environments which are hard to predict on the basis of experience or historical analysis.

(a) The Book Publishing Industry: Scenarios from Configurations of Factors

Step 1: Identify High Impact, High Uncertainty Factors in the Environment

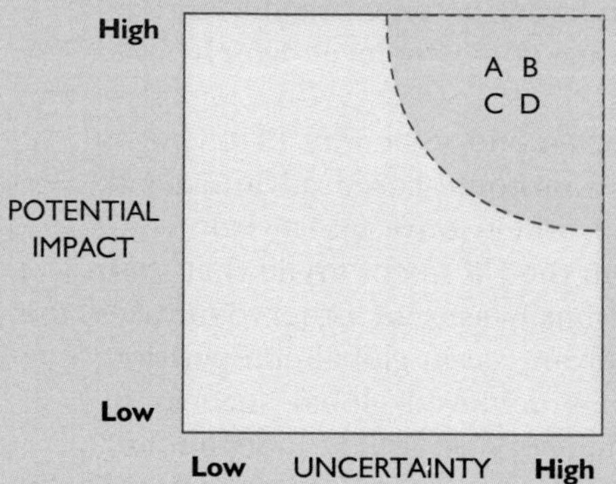

A: Development of electronic communications market

B: Consumer perceptions of books compared with electronic substitutes

C: Costs of paper and other raw materials

D: Government spending and regulation

Step 2: Identify Different Possible Futures by Factor

A: (i) Rapid change
   (ii) Measured change
B: (i) Favourable
   (ii) Unfavourable
C: (i) High and increasing
   (ii) Stabilising
D: (i) In support of books
   (ii) In support of electronic media

Step 3: Build Scenarios of Plausible Configurations of Factors

Scenario 1: no great change Favourable consumer perceptions of books compared with electronic substitutes (B(i)) are supported by government spending and regulation (D(i)). There is measured change in the development of electronic communications markets (A(ii)) and stable costs of paper and other raw materials (C(ii)).

Scenario 2: electronic chaos Rapid change in the development of the electronic communications market (A(i)) is encouraged by government spending and regulation in support of electronic media (D(ii)). Furthermore, unfavourable consumer perceptions of books compared with electronic substitutes (B(ii)) are combined with high and increasing costs of paper and other raw materials (C(i)).

Scenario 3: information society Stable consumer perceptions of books compared with electronic substitutes (B(ii)), measured change in the development of electronic communications markets (A(ii)) and government spending and regulation in support of books are favourable (D(i)). However, there is concern over the high and rising cost of paper and other raw materials (C(i)).

(b) Thematic Scenarios at Shell

The oil industry faces an ever-changing environment which is hard to predict on the basis of past experience

In an attempt to develop strategies for the 25 years between 1995 and 2020, the companies of the Royal Dutch/Shell Group developed two global scenarios. While at an initial reading these scenarios might appear as 'favourable' and 'unfavourable', they can be seen as more complex in their implications.

New Frontiers

In this scenario, economic and political liberalisation increase wealth creation in the societies which adopt them. However, enormous upheavals are also experienced as longstanding barriers are dismantled and poor countries assert themselves, claiming a larger role on the world's economic and political stage. While rapid economic growth of 5–6 per cent is sustained in these developing countries, there is slow erosion of the comparative wealth of the developed world, which produces problems as new priorities and lifestyles are gradually established. Big companies find themselves increasingly challenged, as cheaper capital and fewer international barriers lead to an environment of relentless competition and innovation. This creates a high level of energy demand, and substantial new resource development and improvements in efficiency are required to fuel this growth and prevent demand outstripping supply.

Barricades

In this scenario, liberalisation is resisted and restricted because people fear they might lose what they value most – jobs, power, autonomy, religious traditions, cultural identity. This creates a world of regional, economic, cultural and religious division, and conflict in which international business cannot operate easily. Markets are constricted and difficult for outsiders to enter, as reforms are structured to help insiders. Oil prices are depressed because of instability, followed by a huge rise as trouble flares in the Middle East. There is increasing divergence between rich and poor economies as many poor countries become marginalised, partly due to a lack of foreign investment. In the developed world, coalitions of 'green' and other political interests increasingly cause energy to be regarded as something bad, other than for its tax-raising potential. The unfavourable investment climate which this produces is reinforced by the deep divides around the world. Widespread poverty and environmental problems are experienced in poorer countries, while in richer nations, a shrinking labour force and ageing population are causes for concern.

Question

Choose another industry with which you are familiar (or the brewing industry from the Cases section of this book) and construct two or three scenarios for the future using one or both of the approaches in this illustration.

Sources *Long Range Planning*, vol. 28, no. 6 (1995), pp. 38–47; *Accountancy*, March 1995, pp. 54–5.

Prepared by Sara Martin, Cranfield School of Management, and Tony Jacobs, Bristol Business School.

other. There are two main benefits of such an exercise. The first is that managers can examine strategic options against the scenarios and ask: 'what should we do if ... ?', or 'what would be the effect of ... ?' In effect, the scenarios can be used for sensitivity testing of possible strategies (see Chapter 8). The second benefit is that the implications of scenarios can be used to challenge the taken-for-granted assumptions about the environment in which managers operate; in this way scenarios can promote more innovative thinking and approaches to strategy development. This may be particularly important where change is unpredictable and the future uncertain, or where there are long time horizons, because operating managers may be so concerned with the short term that they neglect to consider the long term. Two examples of scenarios are shown in Illustration 3.3.

The main steps in drawing up scenarios are as follows.

1. First it is necessary to identify the key assumptions, or forces, that are to be included. This may build on the sort of PEST analysis described in section 3.3.1. These assumptions should be restricted to environmental forces, rather than including the strategic action of the organisation or of competitors. It is also important that the number of assumptions is kept to just a few since the complexity in drawing up scenarios rises dramatically in proportion to the number of assumptions included. This can be done in two ways:
   - By using the forces which historically have had the greatest impact on the organisation, although the danger here is that this does not take into account the uncertainty of future change.
   - By focusing on the factors which (i) have high potential impact – perhaps the drivers of change identified in the PEST analysis – and (ii) are uncertain, as with the factors identified in step 1 in Illustration 3.3(a) on the book publishing industry.
2. Scenarios may be built in two ways:
   - The first is to construct scenarios from the particular factors identified. This is a sensible approach if the number of factors is low, such as the four in Illustration 3.3(a). Different but consistent configurations of these factors might be systematically examined to build three, or perhaps four, scenarios, as shown in steps 2 and 3 of Illustration 3.3(a).
   - If the number of factors being considered is large, it may not be feasible to undertake this 'building up' process. Instead, the 'tone' of scenarios is set – for example, (i) an optimistic future and a pessimistic future, or (ii) according to dominant themes, as in Shell (Illustration 3.3(b)). In either case, the proponents of scenario planning argue that the allocation of probabilities to factors should be avoided; it endows the scenarios with spurious accuracy, which can be unhelpful given the purpose of the scenarios.
3. If factors with both high impact and high uncertainty have been used then the scenarios must represent possible futures worthy of building into the process of strategic choice: section 8.2.2 in Chapter 8 discusses this.

3.4 THE COMPETITIVE ENVIRONMENT: FIVE FORCES ANALYSIS

So far the concern has been with understanding broad aspects of the environment. However, inherent within the notion of strategy is the search for the opportunity to identify bases of advantage. In business, this might be advantage over competitors; in the public sector, it might be advantage in the procurement of resources. The aim is to identify if there are factors in the environment which influence the capability of an organisation to position itself to such advantage.

There has already been some discussion of this in terms of factors at the national and supranational level which are likely to affect an organisation's – or indeed a nation's – ability to compete effectively (section 3.3.2 above). This section draws on the 'five forces' approach that Porter[8] proposes as a means of examining the competitive environment at the level of the strategic business unit or SBU (see Chapter 1, section 1.1.2). **Five forces analysis** is a means of identifying the forces which affect the level of competition in an industry, and which might thus help managers to identify bases of competitive strategy (see Exhibit 3.6). Although designed primarily with businesses in mind, it is of value to most organisations.

five forces analysis *is a means of identifying the forces which affect the level of competition in an industry*

It is important to emphasise that, to be of most value, a five forces analysis needs to be carried out by examining the influences on the immediate, or competitive, environment of individual SBUs. If the analysis is attempted at a more generalised level, the variety of influences in the environment will be so great as to reduce the value of the analysis. The five forces employed in the analysis will now be discussed in detail.

3.4.1 The Threat of Entry

Threat of entry to an industry will depend on the extent to which there are *barriers to entry*, which most typically are as follows:

- *Economies of scale*. In some industries, economies of scale are extremely important: for example, in the production of electrical components, in distribution (e.g. brewing) or in sales and marketing (e.g. fast-moving consumer goods industries).
- *The capital requirement of entry*. The capital cost of entry will vary according to technology and scale. The cost of setting up a retail clothing business with leased premises and stock from wholesalers is minimal when compared with the cost of, for example, entering capital-intensive industries such as chemicals, power or mining.
- *Access to distribution channels*. For decades brewing companies, in Germany, the UK and France, have invested in the financing of bars and pubs, which has guaranteed the distribution of their products and made it difficult for competitors to break into their markets.

Exhibit 3.6 Five forces analysis

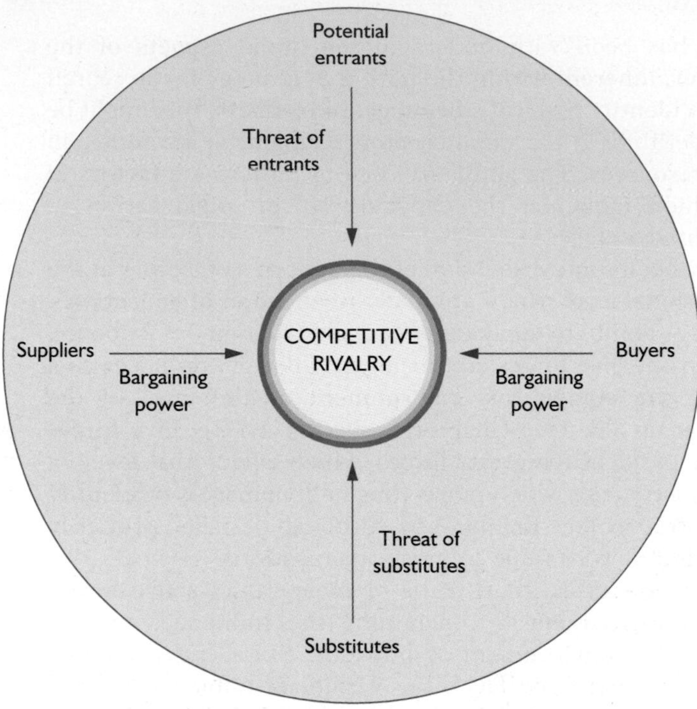

Source Adapted from M.E. Porter, *Competitive Strategy*, Free Press, 1980, p. 4. Copyright by The Free Press, a division of Macmillan Publishing Co., Inc. Reproduced with permission.

- *Cost advantages independent of size*. To a large extent these are to do with early entries into the market and the experience so gained. It is difficult for a competitor to break into a market if there is an established operator which knows that market well, has good relationships with the key buyers and suppliers, and knows how to overcome market and operating problems. However, the increasing globalisation of markets is facilitating market entry to one part of the world from another. A company may have gained experience and built a reputation in its home market which it can transfer to another. This phenomenon is related to the 'experience curve' and is dealt with in more detail in Chapter 4 (section 4.3.3).
- *Expected retaliation*. If a competitor considering entering a market believes that the retaliation of an existing firm will be so great as to prevent entry, or mean that entry would be too costly, this is also a barrier. Entering the breakfast cereal market to compete with Kellogg's would be unwise unless very careful attention was paid to a strategy to avoid retaliation.

- *Legislation or government action*. Legal restraints on competition vary from patent protection, to regulation to control markets (e.g. over-the-counter pharmaceuticals and insurance), through to direct government action. In 1995, the US government threatened the Japanese government with trade sanctions because, it argued, the Japanese government promoted restrictions to the access of foreign competition. Of course, managers in hitherto protected environments might face the pressures of competition for the first time if governments remove such protection. For example, in the late 1980s and 1990s many public services such as health services or rail systems, traditionally operated as state monopolies, increasingly faced deregulation and privatisation.
- *Differentiation*. By differentiation is meant the provision of a product or service regarded by the user as different from and of higher value than the competition; its importance will be discussed more fully in Chapter 6. However, here it is important to point out that organisations able to achieve strategies of differentiation provide for themselves real barriers to competitive entry. For example, Marks and Spencer in the UK has an image for reliability and quality underpinned by staff training, product and quality specification and control at supplier level, and strong corporate values supportive of the quality image. Nor is the idea of differentiation peculiar to the private sector. For example, in universities and hospitals, research excellence may serve to differentiate the services offered.

Barriers to entry differ by industry and by product/market, so it is impossible to generalise about which are more important than others (see Illustration 3.4). What is important to establish are: (a) which barriers, if any, exist; (b) to what extent they are likely to prevent entry in the particular environment concerned; and (c) the organisation's position in all this – is it trying to prevent the competition of entrants, or is it attempting to gain entry, and how?

3.4.2 The Power of Buyers and Suppliers

The next two forces can be considered together because they are linked. All organisations have to obtain resources and provide goods or services; this is what has become known as the supply chain, value chain or value system of an organisation (see Chapter 4, section 4.3.1). Moreover, the relationship of buyers and sellers can have similar effects in constraining the strategic freedom of an organisation and in influencing the margins of that organisation.

Buyer power is likely to be high when:

- There is a concentration of buyers, particularly if the volume purchases of the buyers are high. This is the case in grocery retailing in France and the UK, where just a few retailers dominate the market.

STRATEGY IN ACTION
Illustration 3.4

Barriers to Market Entry

Entry barriers vary from industry to industry and by product/market.

The Pharmaceutical Industry

The pharmaceutical industry's barriers to entry were historically high R&D costs and long lead times which required access to large amounts of capital. Other barriers included varying clinical standards and regulations across different markets, which increased development costs by duplicating the regulatory approval process.

More recently, governments have sought cost containment. As a result, drugs companies have to show that the benefits of new branded drugs are clinically desirable and quantifiable, and that they perform better than existing drugs, to ensure that they appear on 'approved prescribing' lists.

The Luxury Car Market

With few exceptions (the Lexus being one), car manufacturers have found it difficult to break into the luxury end of the car market. The major barrier to entry here has been brand name and recognition, but there are others. Clear differentiation both from more standard car models and from other luxury car manufacturers is needed. Also, increasingly, a network of suppliers is required to source the specialist components required for a luxury car. This network takes time and experience to build and suppliers may be reluctant to commit to it for a manufacturer not already established in the market place.

The UK Supermarket Grocery Retail Industry

Within this industry, the main barrier has been planning restrictions on out-of-town developments. New site availability has been limited, pushing up land and building costs. There is also a high initial investment cost in the technology required for point-of-sale scanning and stock control systems.

There are economies of scale to be gained in purchasing and distribution which a new entrant would not have immediate access to. The profitable area of selling own-brand goods would also not be available to a new entrant until it could buy in a volume that would interest manufacturers.

Competition among existing retailers is intense, with the top five retailers having over 50 per cent of the market, making entry more difficult and requiring a disproportionate amount to be spent on marketing to gain market presence.

The Football Industry

Professional football clubs in the lower divisions in England have found it increasingly difficult to break into and sustain a position at the higher levels. A major reason for this has been a marked increase in the level of finances required to obtain top players and invest in ground facilities necessary to compete effectively in the Premier League.

Questions

1. Identify the barriers to entry for another industry.
2. Suggest how environmental or market changes might change the barriers to entry identified in the illustration and your additional example.

Prepared by Tony Jacobs, Bristol Business School.

This power will be further increased when:

- The supplying industry comprises a large number of small operators.
- There are alternative sources of supply, perhaps because the product required is undifferentiated between suppliers or, as for many public sector operations in the 1980s and 1990s, when the deregulation of markets spawned new competitors.
- The component or material cost is a high percentage of total cost, since buyers will be likely to 'shop around' to get the best price and therefore 'squeeze' suppliers.
- The cost of switching a supplier is low or involves little risk.
- There is a threat of backward integration by the buyer (e.g. by acquiring a supplier) if satisfactory prices or quality from suppliers cannot be obtained.

Supplier power is likely to be high when:

- There is a concentration of suppliers rather than a fragmented source of supply. This is usually the case in the provision of finance by central government to public corporations such as the National Health Service or the BBC in the UK.
- The 'switching costs' from one supplier to another are high, perhaps because a manufacturer's processes are dependent on the specialist products of a supplier, as in the aerospace industry, or a product is clearly differentiated. (Switching costs may be the actual cost of changing suppliers, for example because machines or systems would have to be changed, or an unacceptably high risk of change, for example if a low-cost item is nonetheless of critical importance to a buyer.)
- If the brand of the supplier is powerful. This links to switching costs because, as might be the case for some consumer goods, a retailer might not be able to do without a particular brand.
- There is the possibility of the supplier integrating forwards if it does not obtain the prices, and hence the margins, it seeks.
- The supplier's customers are highly fragmented, so their bargaining power is low.

Some organisations may rely on supplies other than tangible goods. For example, for professional services, such as management consultancy, corporate tax advice or teaching, the availability of skilled staff is crucial. However, while this may be a significant constraint, the suppliers may not be organised to exert power. In other cases, most obviously if trade union power is strong, labour supply may not only be important, but also exercise power.

A significant problem in constructing strategies is therefore the extent to which power can be enhanced, or mutual interest accommodated, in the supplier–buyer channel. For example, many manufacturers, faced with competitive demands for higher productivity at lower cost, have reduced the number of suppliers of components significantly. The suppliers remaining gained in volume orders, but have had to prove themselves against strict criteria of quality and delivery. Of course, it might be possible for a supplier to seek out market segments with less powerful buyers, or to differentiate products so that buyers become more dependent on that product. It might also be possible to build mutually advantageous links with suppliers and buyers – a point discussed below and also in Chapter 4 in the context of an organisation's value chain.

3.4.3 The Threat of Substitutes

The threat of substitution may take different forms:

- There could be *product-for-product substitution* – the fax for the postal service and then e-mail for the fax are examples.
- There may be *substitution of need* by a new product or service rendering an existing product or service superfluous; for example, if more precise casting means that engine blocks are cast to a finer specification, then demand for cutting tools may be reduced.
- *Generic substitution* occurs where products or services compete for need; for example, furniture manufacturers and retailers compete for available household expenditure with suppliers of televisions, videos, cookers, cars and holidays.
- *Doing without* can also be thought of as a substitute; certainly for the tobacco industry this is so.

The availability of substitutes can place a ceiling on prices for a company's products, or make inroads into the market and so reduce its attractiveness. The key questions that need to be addressed are: (a) whether or not a substitute poses the threat of obsolescence to a firm's product or service, or provides a higher perceived benefit or value; (b) the ease with which buyers can switch to substitutes, usually determined by the one-time costs facing the buyer making such a change; and (c) to what extent the risk of substitution can be reduced by building in switching costs, perhaps through added product or service benefits meeting buyer needs.

3.4.4 Competitive Rivalry

Organisations need to be concerned with the extent of direct rivalry between themselves and competitors. What is it based upon? Is it likely to increase or decrease in intensity? How can it be influenced?

The most competitive conditions will be those in which *entry* is likely, *substitutes* threaten and *buyers* or *suppliers* exercise control; previously

Exhibit 3.7 The life cycle model

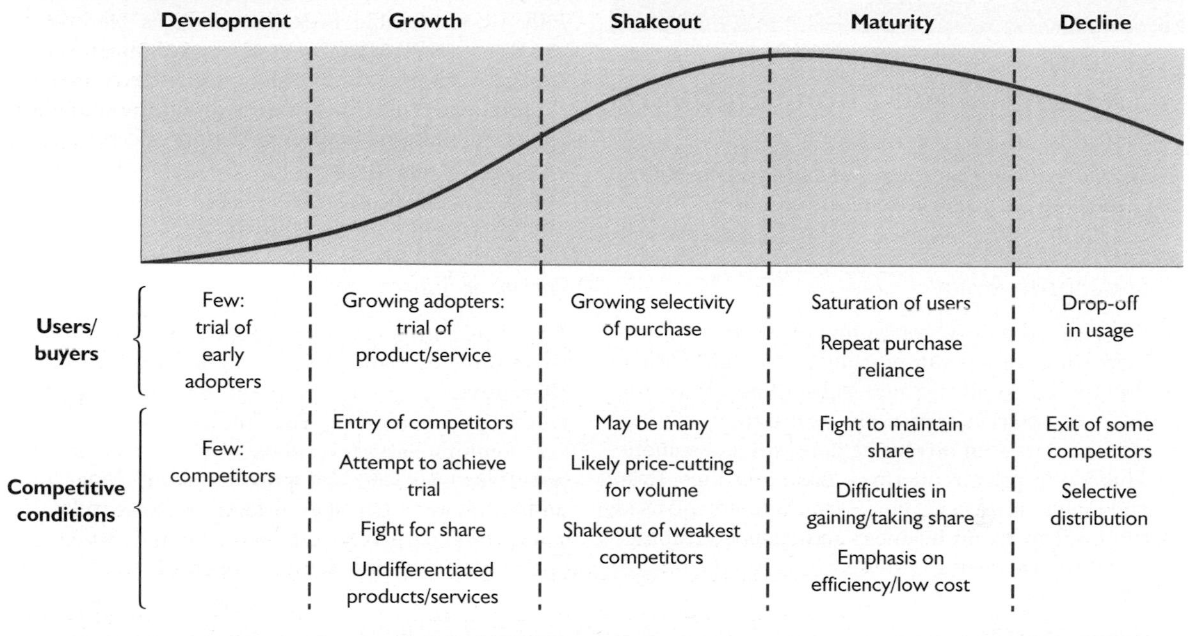

discussed forces are relevant here. However, there are likely to be other forces which affect competitive rivalry:

- The extent to which competitors are *in balance*. Where competitors are of roughly equal size, there is the danger of intense competition as one competitor attempts to gain dominance over another. Conversely, the less competitive markets tend to be those with dominant organisations within them.
- Market *growth rates* may affect rivalry. The idea of the life cycle[9] suggests that conditions in markets, primarily between growth stages and maturity, are important, not least in terms of competitive behaviour. For example, in situations of market growth, an organisation might expect to achieve its own growth through the growth in the market place; whereas when markets are mature, this has to be achieved by taking market share from competitors. Exhibit 3.7 summarises some of the conditions that can be expected at different stages in the life cycle.
- The existence or development of *global customers* may increase competition among suppliers as they try to win their business on a global scale.

STRATEGY IN ACTION
Illustration 3.5

The UK Mobile Phone Industry

Five forces analysis provides an understanding of the competitive nature of an industry.

Competitive Rivalry

By 1996 the level of competitive rivalry was increasing as operators sought to differentiate themselves to attract new subscribers. With the executive market approaching saturation, emphasis was placed on attracting domestic consumers. This led to price reductions, customer incentives and higher advertising costs. Operators recognised the need to retain business and reduce customer switching between networks.

Buying Power

Buying power varied. With dealers it was low. As operators paid bonuses for new subscribers, dealers could give away handsets and still make a profit on each sale. The power of the *service providers* was greater. Although their statutory monopoly position was removed in 1993, a small number of businesses were responsible for 80 per cent of the mobile phone subscriber base by 1994. Unlike Vodafone and Cellnet, both Mercury one2one and Orange had largely avoided the service provider route, preferring to develop their own direct dealer relationships and customer support structures. Although fragmented, the power of the *consumer* was high, with operators vying for their business.

Power of Suppliers

The power of suppliers was dependent on the supplier. The design and price of a handset could play a significant part in attracting new subscribers to a network operator, particularly where service features and tariffs were similar. However, there were at least seven *equipment manufacturers* competing for market share. Manufacturers with a considerable presence, such as Motorola and Ericsson, posed a threat of forward integration into network operations. The *government* played a prominent role in the growth of the mobile phone market by issuing operators' licences to increase competition. The government maintained an active interest in the industry and intervened when it felt justified.

Threat of Substitutes

The threat of substitutes existed as high tariffs could drive consumers back to cheaper *fixed line* alternatives or discourage them from entering the mobile phone market. The *Internet*, *pagers* and *fax* communication systems were increasing in popularity, but did not pose a major threat to mobile phones. Cheaper pricing of these substitutes, however, reduced the use and revenue potential of the mobile phone operators.

Threat of Entrants

The threat of entrants was low. Obtaining an operator's licence was the principal barrier to entry, although the high cost of entry was a deterrent to many potential entrants. This position could, however, change as the long-term profitability of the mobile phone industry becomes more fully established.

Questions

1. Viewing this industry through the eyes of a network operator (such as Cellnet):
   (a) Which would you regard as the three most important threats to your business?
   (b) How could you respond to each of these to lessen its impact?
2. What are the main benefits and limitations of five forces analysis?

Prepared by Sara Martin, Cranfield School of Management, and Tony Jacobs, Bristol Business School.

- *High fixed costs* in an industry, perhaps through high capital intensity or high costs of storage, are likely to result in competitors cutting prices to obtain the turnover required. This can result in price wars and very low-margin operations.
- If the addition of *extra capacity is in large increments*, the competitor making such an addition is likely to create at least short-term overcapacity and increased competition.
- Again, *differentiation* is important. In a commodity market, where products or services are not differentiated, there is little to stop customers switching between competitors.
- If the *acquisition of weaker companies* by stronger companies results in the provision of funds to improve the competitive standing of such firms, their ability to compete more effectively may be enhanced.
- Where there are *high exit barriers* to an industry, there is again likely to be the persistence of excess capacity and, consequently, increased competition. Exit barriers might be high for a variety of reasons: they may vary from a high investment in non-transferable fixed assets such as specialist plant, to the cost of redundancy, to the reliance on one product in order to be credible within a market sector even if the product itself makes losses.

Illustration 3.5 shows an analysis of the forces faced in the competitive environment of the UK mobile phone industry.

3.4.5 Competition and Collaboration[10]

Much of the discussion so far has emphasised the notion of competition and the competitive nature of an industry or market. However, advantage may not always be achieved by competing. It is possible that collaboration between organisations may be a more sensible route to achieving advantage, that organisations may seek to compete in some markets and collaborate in others, or in other markets be competing and collaborating simultaneously. Identifying opportunities for collaboration nonetheless requires an understanding of the structure of industries, and the frameworks explained above can be used for this purpose too.

Collaboration between potential competitors or between buyers and sellers is likely to be advantageous when the combined costs of buying and transactions (such as negotiating and contracting) are less through collaboration than the internal cost that would be incurred by the organisation operating alone: for example,

- When the result of collaboration gives greater added value to an organisation than operating singly.
- When the collaboration allows the organisation to concentrate on its own core competences (see Chapter 4) and avoid peripheral, wasteful activities.

Some examples of this can be seen by using the five forces framework.

- *Buyer–seller collaboration*. A manufacturer of automobile components faces daunting competition to secure orders from one of the major car manufacturers if the basis of competition is the product alone. However, a number of component manufacturers have sought to build close links with car manufacturers so as to reduce lead times for delivery, to help in research and development activities, to build joint information systems and reduce stock, and even to take part in planning teams to design new models. The collaborative relationships which are then built up have the effect of raising switching costs for the manufacturers.
- *Collaboration to increase buying power*. In setting up the structure of the National Health Service in the UK, the Conservative government of the early 1990s may have been trying to foster a spirit of healthy competition between hospitals. However, doctors may place more emphasis on competition for resources from government. They may seek to collaborate within professional bodies to try to exert influence on the government, as a supplier, for increases in resources. The Labour government which came to power in 1997 argued that collaboration and co-operation were more effective in the NHS than competition.
- *Collaboration to build barriers to entry or avoid substitution*. Faced with threatened entry or substitute products, organisations in an industry may collaborate to invest in research and development or marketing. For example, marketing boards in agriculture have been set up to promote the joint interests of producers; trade bodies have been established to promote an industry's generic features such as safety standards or technical specifications in order to speed up innovation and pre-empt the possibility of substitution. In effect, both are collaborative means of promoting differentiation.
- *Collaboration to gain entry and competitive power*. An organisation that seeks to develop its operations outside its traditional boundaries could find that collaboration is needed through either informal networking or formal alliances (see Chapter 7). Illustration 3.6 shows how collaboration in the pharmaceutical industry has helped to improve the competitive position of different companies. The only way of gaining local market knowledge may be to collaborate with local operators. Indeed, in some parts of the world, governments require entrants to collaborate in such ways. Collaboration may also be advantageous for purposes of developing required infrastructure such as distribution channels, information systems or research and development activities. It may also be needed for cultural reasons: buyers may prefer to do business with local rather than expatriate managers.

STRATEGY IN ACTION
Illustration 3.6

Collaborative Ventures in the Pharmaceutical Industry

Collaboration between potential competitors and with buyers may help improve competitive positioning.

In the pharmaceutical industry, companies are faced with rapid scientific and technological change, high cost of research and development, high risk of failure and increasing buying power. Collaboration through a variety of different alliances has become common.

Collaboration between Potential Competitors ...

... to Enter Markets

Japanese pharmaceutical companies, lacking historical presence in the UK, entered into collaborative sales and marketing agreements with existing strong industry players in order to gain entry. Astra, a Swedish company with a strong position in the UK, took the lead in a co-promotion to market Takeda's *candesartan* (trade name Amias) in the UK, for the treatment of hypertension. Takeda and Astra would normally be competitors with brands Zoton and Losec in the gastrointestinal market. However, the collaborative arrangement on Amias allowed Astra to strengthen its position with cardiovascular products. In turn, Takeda gained market entry knowledge, allowing it to establish a credible UK market position from which to launch new products, the first of which was for diabetes, an area in which neither Astra nor Takeda had a strong position.

... to Reduce the Threat of Competition

In the UK, Ashbourne Pharmaceuticals had a strong position in the dispensing doctor segment of the market. Ashbourne specialised in providing alternative brands to the market leader but also entered into arrangements with other companies to consolidate its own market position and provide them with increased revenues and avoid head-on competition. For example, Eli Lilly, a minor player in the gastrointestinal ulcer market, co-operated with Ashbourne to launch Lilly's *nizatidine* under Ashbourne's brand, Zinga. This allowed Eli Lilly's molecule to compete successfully and displace Glaxo's Zantac within the dispensing doctor segment – something which Eli Lilly had been unable to achieve itself.

... for Innovation

The Human Genome Project (HGP) is an international 15-year effort to discover the key 60,000–80,000 human genes and make them accessible for further biological study. The huge cost of this programme was borne by means of collaboration between pharmaceutical companies and academia, thus allowing more effective targeting of their research and development efforts.

Collaboration between Suppliers and Buyers ...

... to Gain Entry and Share Risk

Roche produced a high priced product, Pulmozyme, for treating cystic fibrosis. Whilst effective in many cases, the treatment did not work for all patients. Roche entered into agreements with health authorities to share the risk of the treatment, thus gaining wider distribution; whilst health authorities, increasingly subject to budget restrictions, could purchase against the achievement of agreed outcome criteria in the treatment of patients.

... to Reduce Cost

In the developing area of disease management, pharmaceutical companies and health providers, such as hospitals, agreed to share savings resulting from the optimal management of a defined medical condition. Salick, owned largely by Zeneca, did this for cancer treatment and Eli Lilly for diabetes programmes.

Question

For each of the collaborative ventures, list the potential benefits and potential risks for the parties involved.

Prepared by Graham Leask, Cranfield School of Management.

3.4.6 Key Questions Arising from Five Forces Analysis

Five forces analysis can be used to gain insights into the forces at work in the industry environment of a SBU which need particular attention in the development of strategy. The following questions help focus the analysis.

- What are the *key forces* at work in the competitive environment? These will differ by type of industry. For example, for grocery manufacturers the power of retail buyers is likely to be of extreme importance, whereas for computer manufacturers the growing power of chip manufacturers and growth in competitive intensity might be regarded as most crucial. For a deregulated public service, new entrants with more commercial experience might be the central issue.
- Are there *underlying forces* – perhaps identified from the PEST analysis or from an analysis of global forces – which are driving competitive forces? For example, the competitive strength of lower-cost high technology manufacturers in the Asia Pacific region is an underlying and persistent threat to European and US automobile producers.
- Is it likely that the forces will *change*, and if so, how? For example, pharmaceutical businesses built strong market positions on their expertise in marketing branded drugs to a highly fragmented set of buyers – the doctors. However, government action in many countries, such as the promotion of generic drugs and the introduction of new treatment protocols, buying procedures and price regulation, has had the effect of significantly increasing competitive pressures on such firms and forcing them to reconsider their competitive strategies.
- How do particular competitors stand in relation to these competitive forces? What are their strengths and weaknesses in relation to the key forces at work? The issues of *competitive standing* and *competitive positioning* are therefore important and are dealt with next.
- What can management do to *influence* the competitive forces affecting a SBU? Can barriers to entry be built, power over suppliers or buyers increased, or ways found to diminish competitive rivalry? These are the fundamental questions relating to *competitive strategy* and will be a major concern of Chapter 6.
- Are some industries more *attractive* than others? It can be argued that some industries are intrinsically more profitable than others because, for example, entry is more difficult, or buyers and suppliers are less powerful. In theory, then, the corporate strategist might use industry analysis as a means of identifying which industries are more or less attractive than others (see section 3.5.4). However, it is dangerous to assume that the forces identified in such an analysis are deterministic of business success. For example, why would the Koreans wish to enter what appear to be highly unattractive markets such as chemicals, tanker building or automobiles? The answer may be that they believe

that they can achieve competitive advantage which others cannot achieve: that competitive success depends more on their particular competences, which give them competitive advantage, than on the characteristics of the industry. This theme is returned to in Chapters 4 and 6.

3.5 IDENTIFYING THE ORGANISATION'S COMPETITIVE POSITION

Arguably, all organisations – public or private – are in a competitive position in relation to each other, in so far as they are competing either for customers or, notably in the public services, for resources. It is therefore important that they understand their relative positioning and its implications in strategic terms. The auditing of environmental influences outlined in section 3.3 and the structural analysis in section 3.4 provide indications of key factors which will affect positioning, but there are some useful ways of pulling these together to help analysis. This section reviews different ways of doing this.

3.5.1 Strategic Group Analysis[11]

One problem in analysing competition is that the idea of the 'industry' is not always helpful because its boundaries can be unclear and are not likely to provide a sufficiently precise delineation of competition. For example, Guinness and Albani, the Danish brewer, are presumably in the same industry – brewing – but are they competitors? The former is a publicly quoted multinational drinks business; the latter is owned by a foundation and concentrates on a local market in Denmark. In a given industry there may be many companies each of which has different interests and which compete on different bases. There is a need for some intermediate basis of understanding the relative position of organisations between the level of the individual firm and the industry. One such level is the market segment, and this is taken up in section 3.5.2 below; another is the strategic group.

Strategic group analysis aims to identify organisations with similar strategic characteristics, following similar strategies or competing on similar bases. Such groups can usually be identified using two, or perhaps three, sets of key characteristics as a basis of competition. The sorts of characteristics which distinguish between organisations and help identify strategic groupings are summarised in Exhibit 3.8.[12] Which of these characteristics are especially relevant in terms of a given organisation or industry needs to be understood in terms of the history and development of that industry, the identification of the forces at work in the environment, the strategies of the organisations

strategic group analysis *aims to identify organisations with similar strategic characteristics, following similar strategies or competing on similar bases*

Exhibit 3.8 Some characteristics for identifying strategic groups

It is useful to consider the extent to which organisations *differ* in terms of **characteristics** such as:

- Extent of **product (or service) diversity**
- Extent of **geographical coverage**
- Number of **market segments served**
- **Distribution channels used**
- Extent (number) of **branding**
- **Marketing effort** (e.g. advertising spread, size of salesforce)
- **Extent of vertical integration**
- Product or service **quality**
- **Technological leadership** (a leader or follower)
- **R&D capability** (extent of innovation in product or process)
- **Cost position** (e.g. extent of investment in cost reduction)
- **Utilisation of capacity**
- **Pricing policy**
- Level of **gearing**
- **Ownership structure** (separate company or relationship with parent)
- Relationship to **influence groups** (e.g. government, the City)
- **Size of organisation**

Source Adapted from M.E. Porter, *Competitive Strategy*, Free Press, 1980; and J. McGee and H. Thomas, 'Strategic groups: theory, research and taxonomy', *Strategic Management Journal*, vol. 7, no. 2 (1986), pp. 141–60.

being considered and so on. The aim is to establish which characteristics most differentiate one group of organisations from another.

For example, in Illustration 3.7, diagram (a) shows a strategic group map of the European food manufacturing industry in the 1980s.[13] Here the key characteristics of geographical coverage of Europe and marketing intensity are used, showing clear distinctions between four groupings at the time. A1 are multinational companies operating across the world with strong brands. A3 are national companies with major brands and high levels of marketing support, although for a more limited range than A1 companies. B2 companies operate nationally, but are typically not market leaders. C3 are companies specialising in own-label supplies and focusing on low-cost production.

This sort of analysis is useful in several ways:

- It helps identify who the most direct competitors are, on what basis competitive rivalry is likely to take place within strategic groups, and how this is different from rivalry within other groups. For example, the multinationals were competing on the basis of marketing (and especially branding) and the control of manufacturing resources across countries. The own-label suppliers were especially concerned with keeping down costs.

- It raises the question of how likely or possible it is for an organisation to move from one strategic group to another. Mobility between groups is, of course, a matter of considering the extent to which there are barriers to entry between one group and another. In Illustration 3.7, diagram (b) shows the sorts of mobility barrier for the groupings identified in the industry. These may be substantial, particularly for a business trying to enter the multinational group; the minor national brands are, perhaps, less secure in their position, being susceptible to both major brand and low-price competition.
- Strategic group mapping might also be used to identify opportunities. For example, in Illustration 3.7, diagram (c) suggests there were vacant 'spaces' in the European food industry at the end of the 1980s which could provide opportunities for new strategies and new strategic groups. It is interesting to see that by the mid 1990s some of these spaces were, indeed, becoming occupied. For example, B1 (pan-European branders) was an attractive space, since it offered economies of scale across a market which was developing its logistics network, harmonising legislation and showing signs of converging consumer tastes in some product areas. In the 1990s it became clear that Unilever, Nestlé and Mars were beginning to focus on just such a strategy.
- Strategic group mapping can also help identify significant strategic problems. As suggested above, minor national brands were identified as occupying an insecure position, without marketing support or manufacturing economies. It was not surprising when Colman's, one of the firms identified in diagram (a), was acquired by Unilever in 1995. Unilever then began to use its own marketing resources to build the Colman's brand.

3.5.2 Market Segmentation

Strategic group analysis is about analysing differences between organisations which are potential or actual competitors. **Market segmentation analysis** seeks to identify similarities and differences between groups of customers or users. This is important because not all users are the same: they have different characteristics and needs, behave differently, and so on. Markets are therefore most usefully thought of in terms of market segments, and identifying which organisations are competing in which market segments is, in itself, a useful and important exercise.[14]

market segmentation analysis *seeks to identify similarities and differences between groups of customers or users*

In undertaking a market segmentation analysis, the following should be considered.

- There are many bases of market segmentation: Exhibit 3.9 summarises some of these. It is important to consider which bases of segmentation are most important. For example, in industrial markets, segmentation is often thought of in terms of industrial classification of buyers – 'we sell to

STRATEGY IN ACTION Illustration 3.7

Strategic Groups and Strategic Space

Mapping of strategic groups can provide insights into the competitive structures of industries, and the opportunities and constraints for development.

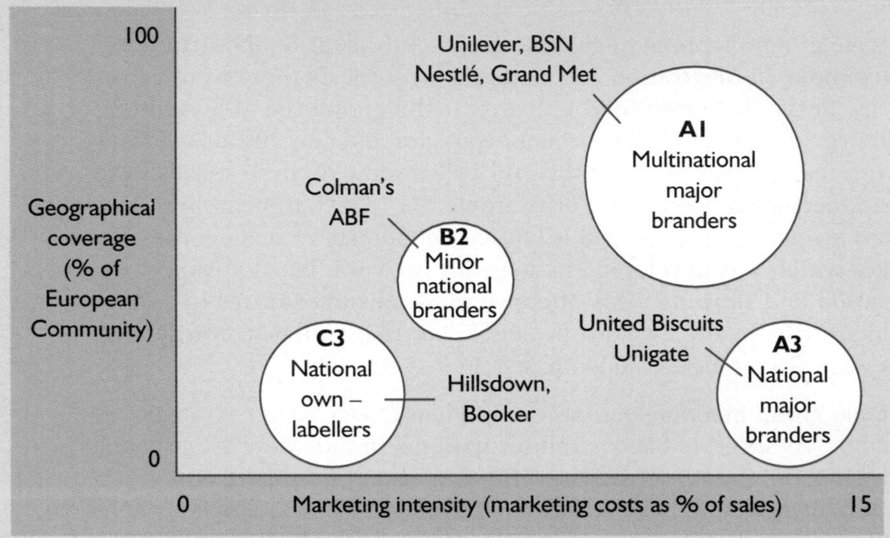

(a) Strategic groups: food industry in the 1980s

Questions

1. How might this analysis influence the next strategic moves of the following types of business?
   (a) A multinational major brander.
   (b) A national own-labeller.
   (c) A national major brander.
   (d) A minor national brander.
2. Undertake a strategic group analysis in an industry with which you are familiar (or the

the car industry', for example. However, it may be that this is not the most useful basis of segmentation when thinking of strategic development. Segmentation by buyer behaviour (for example, direct buying versus those users who buy through third parties such as contractors) or purchase value (for example, high-value bulk purchasers versus frequent low-value purchasers) might be more appropriate in some markets. Indeed, it is often useful to consider different bases of segmentation in the same market to help explain the dynamics of that market and suggest strategic opportunities for development.

Geographical coverage (% of EC)	Marketing intensity 0		15
100			Consumer brand identification Proprietary process knowledge R&D capability Economies of scale available Marketing and organisational skills
		Low production costs Low total costs Technologically advanced Some proprietary process	
0	Low-cost production Proprietary process Retailer switching costs Local knowledge and regulations		Manufacturing process knowledge Brand loyalty Marketing skills Local knowledge

Marketing intensity (marketing costs as % of sales)

(b) Summary of mobility barriers

Geographical coverage (% of EC)	Marketing intensity 0		15
100	Pan-European own-label suppliers	Pan-European branders	Multinational major branders
	Regional own-label suppliers	Regional weak/ minor branders and own-label suppliers	Regional major branders
0	National own-label suppliers	National minor branders	National major branders

Marketing intensity (marketing costs as % of sales)

(c) Strategic space analysis

brewing industry in the Cases section of this book). Go through the following steps:

(a) Identify strategic characteristics and plot groups.
(b) Assess mobility barriers.
(c) Identify any viable strategic spaces.

Source Adapted from J. McGee and S. Segal-Horn, 'Strategic space and industry dynamics', *Journal of Marketing Management*, vol. 6, no. 3 (1990). Copyright © Weston Publishers Ltd.

- It is also important to assess the attractiveness of different market segments. This can be done by applying the five forces analysis described in section 3.4 by market segment.
- Relative market share (i.e. share in relation to competitors) within market segments is an important consideration. There is an important relationship between market power and performance in commercial organisations.[15] This is not just because of scale benefits of size, but also because of 'experience curve' effects which are discussed more fully in the next chapter (see section 4.3.3 in Chapter 4). The firm which has

Exhibit 3.9 Some criteria for market segmentation

TYPE OF FACTOR	CONSUMER MARKETS	INDUSTRIAL/ ORGANISATIONAL MARKETS
Characteristics of people/organisations	Age, sex, race Income Family size Life cycle stage Location Lifestyle	Industry Location Size Technology Profitability Management
Purchase/use situation	Size of purchase Brand loyalty Purpose of use Purchasing behaviour Importance of purchase Choice criteria	Application Importance of purchase Volume Frequency of purchase Purchasing procedure Choice criteria Distribution channel
Users' needs and preferences for product characteristics	Product similarity Price preference Brand preferences Desired features Quality	Performance requirements Assistance from suppliers Brand preferences Desired features Quality Service requirements

built up most experience in servicing a particular market segment should not only have lower costs in so doing, but also have built relationships which may be difficult to break down. The earlier discussion on life cycles of markets (see section 3.4.4 above) suggests that it might be useful, for example, to distinguish segments which are growing and where there is no dominant share competitor, from mature segments, with little growth and a competitor with a dominant share. The opportunities, competitive dynamics and required strategies will be different in each.

- In the introduction to this part of the book and in the next chapter, the importance of identifying the strategic competences of the organisation is discussed (see section 4.3 in Chapter 4). The key point is that organisations are most likely to achieve competitive advantage by developing and building strategies upon their own unique competences. It may therefore be important for a business to try to identify market segments which are especially suited to its particular competences. This theme is further developed in the discussion in Chapter 7 of different strategic directions open to organisations.

Exhibit 3.10 **Perceived value by customers in the electrical engineering industry**

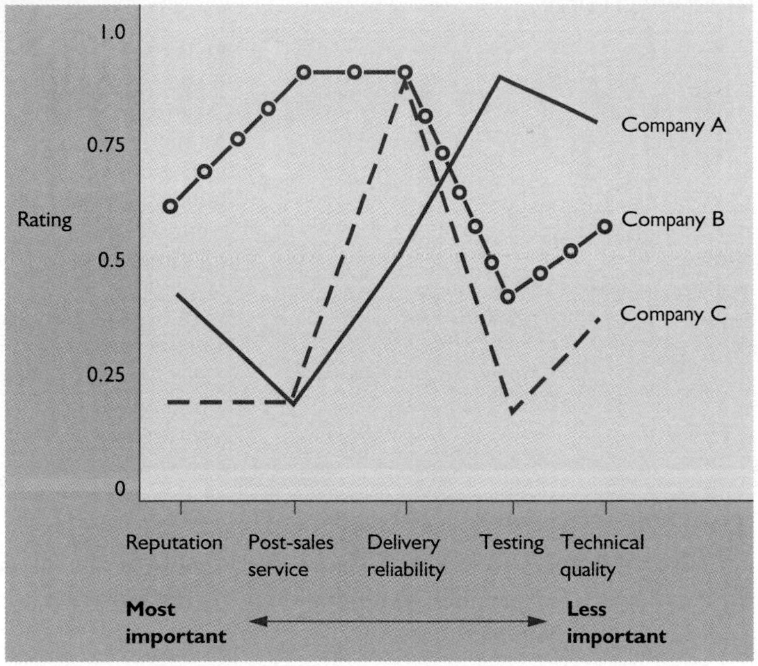

- It may therefore be beneficial to concentrate on a narrow, specialist focus in one or more segments, rather than to take a broad approach to a market. This issue of *focus* is a key issue relating to strategic choice and forms an important part of the discussion in Chapter 6 (see section 6.3.4).

3.5.3 Analysing Perceived Value by Customers

Chapter 6 shows that the development of competitive strategy needs to be based on a clear understanding of dimensions of strategy valued most by customers. This may be done as follows:[16]

- The first step is to identify relevant market segments within which customers and competitors can be identified. Exhibit 3.10 is based on a distinct segment comprising company-based buyers of electrical engineering equipment.
- The second step is to ask what characteristics of the product or service customers value most. This may be done by market research, for example. In the market segment for engineering products on which

Exhibit 3.11 Indicators of SBU strength and market attractiveness

Indicators of SBU Strength Compared with Competition	Indicators of Market Attractiveness
• Market share • Salesforce • Marketing • R&D • Manufacturing • Distribution • Financial resources • Managerial competence • Competitive position in terms of, e.g. image, breadth of product line, quality/reliability, customer service	• Market size • Market growth rate • Cyclicality • Competitive structure • Barriers to entry • Industry profitability • Technology • Inflation • Regulation • Workforce availability • Social issues • Environmental issues • Political issues • Legal issues

Exhibit 3.10 is based, the overall reputation of the competitors, post-sales service, delivery reliability, testing facilities and technical quality were seen as important.

- The third step is to rate how important these dimensions are to customers. In this instance, reputation and the need to provide good post-sales service and reliable delivery were especially valued.
- Different competitors can then be profiled against the dimensions which have been identified in order to consider the relative strengths of competitors. For example, in Exhibit 3.10 it is clear that the strengths which the products of company A possess are not the dimensions most valued by customers; whereas B's strengths appear to have a better match.
- This in turn raises important questions about the basis of an organisation's competitive strategy. Company A needs to consider if it should attempt to switch its resources to an emphasis on building customer service and delivery; try to shift buyers' perceptions of its service levels; attempt to persuade customers that, for example, technical quality is of greater importance than they currently think it is; or focus on a market niche in which customers already believe this to be so.

3.5.4 Market Attractiveness and Business Strength (The Directional Policy Matrix)

One way to consider the competitive position of a SBU is by means of what has become known as the *directional policy matrix*,[17] which is a form of

Exhibit 3.12 Market attractiveness/SBU strength matrix

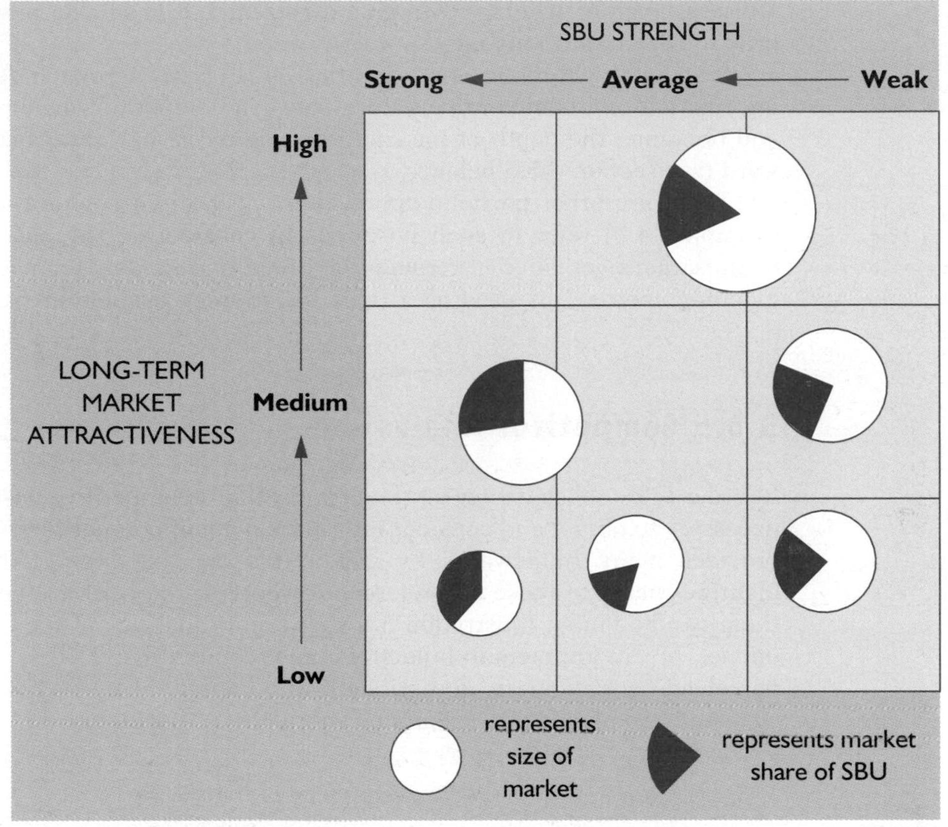

portfolio analysis used by some organisations. The **directional policy matrix** positions SBUs according to (a) how attractive the relevant market is in which they are operating, and (b) the competitive strength of the SBU in that market. Each SBU is positioned within the matrix according to a series of indicators of attractiveness and strength. The factors typically considered are set out in Exhibit 3.11. However, these should not be thought of as preordained. The factors should be those most relevant to the organisation and its market: for example, as identified by PEST or five forces analysis for attractiveness and through competitor analysis to identify SBU strength. Some analysts also choose to show graphically how large the market is for a given business unit's activity, and even the market share of that SBU. The resulting output might look something like Exhibit 3.12.

the **directional policy matrix** *positions SBUs according to (a) how attractive the relevant market is in which they are operating, and (b) the competitive strength of the SBU in that market*

This matrix provides a useful way of directing managers' attention to key forces in the environment, and raises questions about appropriate strategies for different business units and the portfolio as a whole. For example, managers in a firm with the portfolio shown in Exhibit 3.12 will be concerned that they have relatively low shares in the largest and most attractive market, whereas their greatest strength is in smaller markets with little long-term attractiveness.

It should be borne in mind that the value of this approach depends on information of a comparative nature between competitors being available; and obtaining the depth of information required is not always straightforward (see section 3.5.5 below).

There are other portfolio approaches. Chapters 4 (section 4.5) and 6 (section 6.4.1) refer to such portfolios in considering the balance of an organisation's activities in terms of its SBUs; and in Chapter 8 a life cycle mapping approach is used as a basis for strategy evaluation (see section 8.2.1).

3.5.5 Competitor Analysis

In order to establish a view on the organisation's competitive position, it is necessary to obtain and consider information about competitors. This book provides many frameworks by which this can be done. Exhibit 3.13 identifies many of these and references where in the book explanations of them can be found. Illustration 3.8 shows how analyses of the differential impact of environmental influences and competitive forces, the value perceived by customers, and strength of competitors by market segment were all employed to examine competitive positions for chartered surveyors.

3.6 ENVIRONMENTAL ANALYSIS IN PRACTICE

There is evidence that organisations which are good at sensing the environment perform better than those that are not.[18] However, a major problem is the difficulties that managers have in understanding the complexity of the environment of a modern organisation and relating signals in the environment to likely influences on the organisation. Research which has looked at how managers make sense of their environment emphasises a number of key points:[19]

- Managers have to simplify the complexity of the environment they face. It is not possible for them to operate in terms of 'perfect knowledge'. Understanding the effect of the *simplification processes* is important, not least because it shows how analysis using some of the frameworks in this chapter can be helpful.
- Given the complexity of the environment and its influences on organisations, even if a manager has a very rich understanding of that

Exhibit 3.13 Bases of competitor analysis

All the following bases for analysing competitors are discussed in the sections listed below:

Section	Basis
2.4.1	The core assumptions (paradigms) of competitors
2.8.1, 5.5	The culture of competitors
3.3.1, 3.3.2	Differential impacts of environmental influences/drivers
3.3.3	Impact of different scenarios on competitors
3.4	Differential impact of competitive forces on competitors
3.5.1	Identification of bases of competitive rivalry (strategic group analysis)
3.5.2	Which market segments are targeted by which competitors
3.5.3	How competitors rate against what customers most value
3.5.4	Relative strengths of competitors and market attractiveness
4.3.1	Value chain comparisons among competitors
4.3.2	Core competences of competitors
4.3.3	Relative cost efficiencies of competitors
4.3.4	Relative cost effectiveness of competitors
4.4	Comparative analysis and benchmarking against competitors
4.5	Comparative analysis of portfolios of competitors
4.6.1	SWOT analysis to identify relative strengths and weaknesses of competitors
4.6.2, 10.3.1	Critical success factors (CSF) to outperform competitors
5.3	Influence of competitors' stakeholders on their strategies
5.6.1, 6.2.2	The different missions of competitors
5.6.2, 5.6.3	The objectives of competitors
6.2.1	The different ownership structures of competitors and their implications
6.2.3, 6.4.1	The bases of relatedness of portfolios of competitors
6.2.3	Different bases of global competition between competitors
6.3	Bases of competitive advantage of competitors*
6.3.2	Different bases of differentiation of competitors* (* and the extent to which these are defensible)
6.4.2	The suitability of competitors' financial strategy to their portfolios
6.4.3	The parenting skills of corporate parents and the relationship of these to their portfolios
7.2	The strategic directions being followed by competitors
7.3	The methods of strategic development being followed by competitors
7.3.2	Mergers and acquisitions – could be *of* a competitor or between competitors
7.3.3	Strategic alliances – could be with competitors
8.3.2	The risk to competitors of the strategies they are following
8.3.3	Analysing acceptability – reaction of stakeholders of competitors to their strategies
10.2.5	How resource configuration influences competitive advantage

STRATEGY IN ACTION
Illustration 3.8

Competitor Analysis in Commercial Chartered Surveying

Techniques of analysis can reveal similarities and differences in the strategic positions of competitors.

Chartered surveyors provide real estate consultancy services to the business sector. They range from sole practitioners to multinational firms. A competitor analysis of firms employed a number of different techniques to understand competitive positions of rivals in the UK and Europe. The competitors were:

- **Firm A** (the focus of the study) – a multi-product private partnership with an annual turnover of just under £20m, headquarters in central London, a UK regional network of four offices and international operations through alliances in the USA and Europe.
- **Firm B** – the largest property consultancy in the world, with over 3,800 employees worldwide and a UK turnover of about £55m per annum.
- **Firm C** – a corporation with the most comprehensive network of UK offices and an extensive worldwide network of alliances. UK turnover approximately £65m per annum.
- **Firm D** – A radically modernised firm which had become incorporated in the 1990s. It had a diversified range of products in both the residential and agricultural sectors. UK turnover approximately £45m per annum.

Competitor Analysis in the UK Market

An analysis of buyers' perceived bases of added value revealed five key factors in the UK. However, the analysis of relative competitive positions against these factors did not show marked differences (see diagram (a)).

A similar analysis on an international scale identified different factors, flagged up more differences (see diagram (b)) and emphasised buyers' perceived links between a wide international coverage and international reputation.

- Firm B was the only firm with complete ownership of all of its 80 worldwide offices, whilst other competitors relied largely on alliances. The benefits of ownership over alliance were reflected in perceived reputation, co-ordination and consistent high quality.
- Firm A had a minor international influence and did not have the resources for major international investment. Its reputation and perceived level of international service thus suffered, although it was seen to be doing well in its co-ordination of alliances.

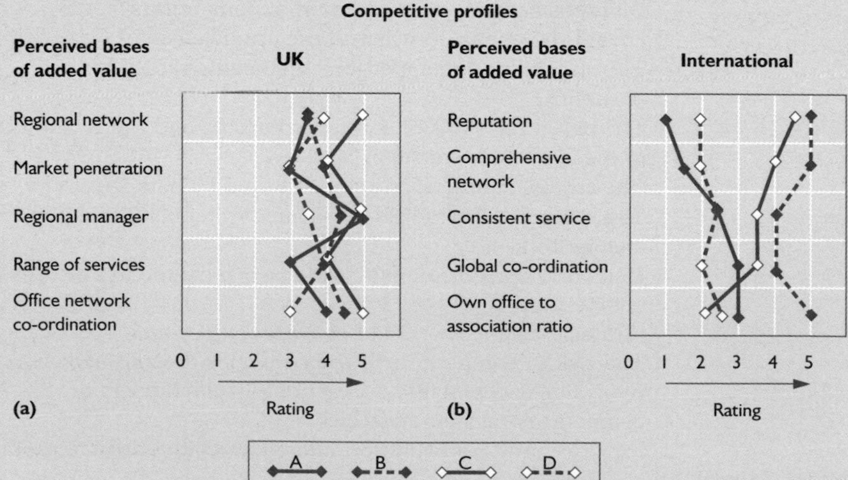

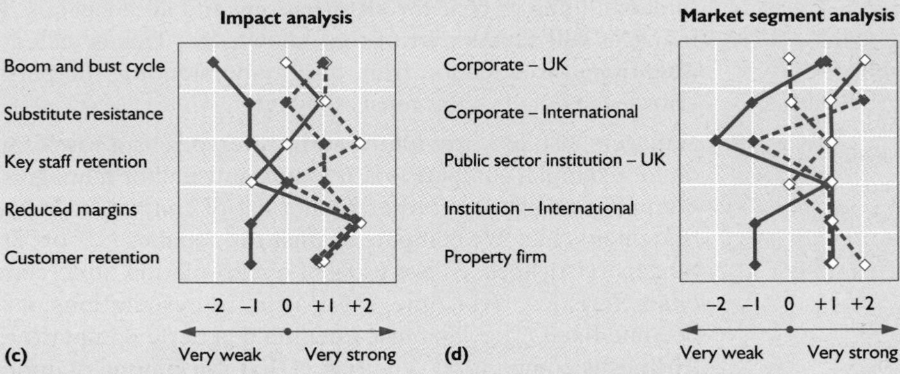

Impact and Market Segment Analysis

The analysis then assessed how the firms might be able to deal with changing factors within the UK market. It therefore combined analyses of strength by market segment and impact analysis (see page 107) based on PEST and five forces analyses.

Impact analysis Key environmental factors were identified and the variable impacts of these on the different firms assessed (see diagram (c)).

- The boom–bust nature of property cycles was a problem for firm A which operated predominantly in the UK and only in the commercial sector. Firm B was much more international, and D was diversified into non-commercial markets. Both were therefore less susceptible to UK economic cycles.
- Firm A suffered from the loss of key staff, of major concern in a professional service business. It also had a stable client base, but was experiencing increasing pressure on client retention from the larger firms and niche players.
- There was an increasing trend for major clients to seek a 'one-stop shop' complete portfolio of services from one firm throughout regions or the entire UK. Firm A was susceptible to this trend owing to its limited regional network and smaller range of services.

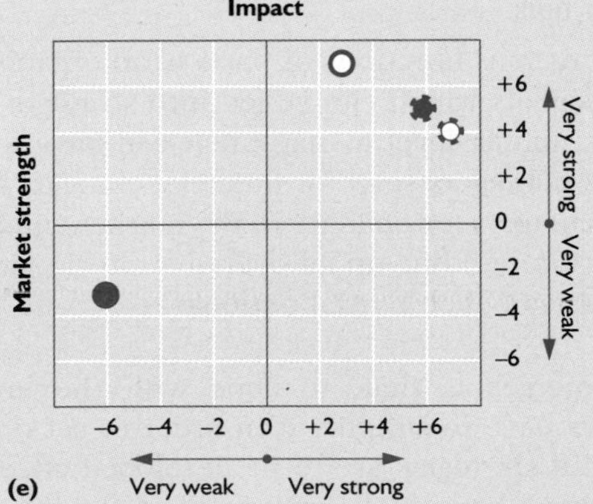

Market segment analysis (diagram (d))

- Firm A's major clients were predominantly UK corporations and institutions owing largely to its historically strong City of London representations. The client base was not evenly spread across the six segments and, since institutions were becoming less involved in commercial property, the client base could become even narrower.
- The international networks of companies possessed by B and C proved lucrative in times of slack domestic investment demand. This was particularly evident during the slump of the early 1990s when German institutions started investing in the UK.

The combined picture of strength by segment and against key impacts (see diagram (e)) emphasised the vulnerability of firm A's competitive position.

Questions

1. What other techniques of analysis could be used for the purpose of competitor analysis?
2. For what purpose would you use them?

Prepared by Robert Sloss, Cranfield School of Management.

environment it is unlikely that he or she will bring that complex understanding to bear for all situations and all decisions. Rather, the manager will access part of that knowledge. This is called **selective attention**: the selection from total understanding the parts of knowledge which seem most relevant.

selective attention *is the selection from total understanding the parts of knowledge which seem most relevant*

- Managers also use *exemplars* and *prototypes* as a way of making sense of, for example, competition. It is not unusual for managers to refer to a dominant competitor rather than a list of competitive characteristics. Statements like 'We compete against the Japanese ... ' or 'The service on Singapore Airlines ... ' are ways of encapsulating quite complex sets of characteristics. Over time, this partial representations of reality can become fixed. The Japanese become a generic competitor; Singapore Airlines *is* competition. The risk is that the 'chunk' of information most often used becomes the only information used. The danger is then that stimuli from the environment are selected out to fit these dominant representations of reality. Information which squares with Singapore Airlines being the main competitor is taken on board, while information counter to this is not. Sometimes this distortion can lead to severe errors as managers miss crucial indicators because they are, in effect, scanning the environment for issues and events that are familiar or readily recognisable.[20]
- Over time, managers' experience can build up and contribute to a collective know-how, which is taken for granted in the organisation and in Chapter 2 is referred to as a *paradigm*. As explained in Chapter 2, this can lead to both a filtering of information and, consequently, significant strategic inertia in organisations or the failure to see the potential for new ideas.
- Managers tend to be biased towards seeing *threats rather than opportunities*,[21] largely because forces which are perceived to have a potentially high impact on the organisation, but to be outside its control, are seen as threatening. Managers then become sensitive to information which confirms or reinforces such a bias, rather than to other information which counters it. There is therefore a need to find ways of challenging such a bias.
- Theoretically, at least, the various functions or parts of an organisation scan the environment for signals which can be fed into strategic decision making. However, middle-level management can have a very parochial outlook. Finance managers scan for financial changes in the environment; marketing managers for changes in the market and so on. So there may be difficulties in building up an overall strategic view of the environment on the basis of such partial outlooks.

The overall picture which emerges is that, to cope with the level of complexity they face, managers have to simplify it in order to get on with the job of managing. However, if strategies are to be developed effectively and innovation is to occur, there have to be means of questioning and challenging that which is taken for granted by managers. The major role of the frameworks of analysis described in this chapter is to do just this. In themselves they do not provide answers or categorical conclusions; their primary purpose is to question and challenge.

SUMMARY

- The ability to sense changes in the environment is important because perceived changes in environmental influences signal the possible need for changes in strategy: they throw up opportunities and warn of threats. These can be built into a SWOT (strengths, weaknesses, opportunities and threats) analysis, outlined at the end of Chapter 4.
- Clarifying the nature of the environment helps provide an initial view on appropriate ways of understanding the influences of that environment. In *simple, static* conditions, historical analysis and forecasting may be sensible. In more *dynamic* conditions, *scenario planning* may be important. As the environment becomes more *complex*, the design of organisation *structure* and development of a *learning culture* is important.
- Carrying out an initial audit of *environmental influences*, beginning at the macro level with an understanding of political, economic, social and technological influences can provide an overall view of the variety of forces at work. This can also help identify key influences and *drivers of change* and provide the basis of examining the extent to which these have differential impact on industries or organisations within industries.
- *Porter's diamond* can be useful in understanding how national differences can provide conditions giving inherent advantage to nations or enterprises within them.
- When there are long-term strategic horizons but uncertainty around relatively few key environmental forces, *scenario planning* can be a useful way of considering the implications of such influences on strategy and questioning taken-for-granted assumptions about the organisation's environment.
- *Five forces analysis* provides a means of identifying the forces which determine the nature of the competitive environment, especially in terms of barriers to entry, the power of buyers and suppliers, the threat of substitutes and other reasons for the extent of competitive intensity. It can also be used to examine the benefits of collaboration within industries.
- In considering the *positioning* of the organisation in relation to others with which it competes for customers or resources, it is necessary to

establish its relative strengths in its market by means of *strategic group analysis*, *market segmentation* and *attractiveness analysis* (by means of a directional policy matrix).

- The application of these and other techniques of analysis can also be useful in undertaking *competitor analysis*.

RECOMMENDED KEY READINGS

- L. Fahey and V.K. Narayanan, *Macro-environmental Analyses for Strategic Management*, West, 1986, is a structured approach to analysing the strategic effects of environmental influences on organisations.
- G. Yip, *Total Global Strategy*, Prentice Hall, 1995, chapter 2, explains in more detail the forces for globalisation in industries.
- M.E. Porter, *Competitive Strategy: Techniques for analysing industries and competitors*, Free Press, 1980, is essential reading for those who are faced with an analysis of an organisation's competitive environment.
- V. Ambrosini with G. Johnson and K. Scholes (eds), *Exploring Techniques of Analysis and Evaluation in Strategic Management*, Prentice Hall, 1998, contains relevant papers entitled 'Scenarios made easy' by D. Mercer, and 'Competitor analysis' by G. Johnson, C. Bowman and P. Rudd.

REFERENCES

1. Henry Mintzberg argues that environmental change is not now faster than it was: see *The Rise and Fall of Strategic Planning*, Prentice Hall, 1994, chapter 4.
2. References concerned with bias in managerial perception are given below (see reference 19), but readers should also refer back to the discussion in Chapter 2 on the influence of cultural aspects of organisations on environmental scanning (see section 2.4.1).
3. R. Duncan's research, on which this classification is based, can be found in 'Characteristics of organisational environments and perceived environmental uncertainty', *Administrative Science Quarterly*, vol. 17, no. 3 (1972), pp. 313–27.
4. Of the books which review environmental influences on organisations, L. Fahey and V.K. Narayanan, *Macroenvironmental Analyses for Strategic Management*, West, 1986, remains one of the best.
5. See G. Yip, *Total Global Strategy*, Prentice Hall, 1995, chapter 2.
6. See M.E. Porter, *Competitive Advantage of Nations*, Macmillan, 1990.
7. See P. Schwartz, *The Art of the Long View*, Century Business, 1991, and G. Price's chapter, 'The why and how of scenario planning' in V. Ambrosini with G. Johnson and K. Scholes (eds), *Exploring Techniques of Analysis and Evaluation in Strategic Management*, Prentice Hall, 1998.
8. See M.E. Porter, *Competitive Strategy: Techniques for analysing industries and competitors*, Free Press, 1980.
9. For a discussion of the value of life cycle models, see P. McKiernan, *Strategies of Growth*, Routledge, 1992.
10. The benefits and problems of collaborative strategies between organisations are discussed in F.J. Contractor and P. Lorange, 'Cooperative strategies in international business', and J.C. Jarillo and H.H. Stevenson, 'Cooperative strategies: the payoffs and pitfalls', *Long Range Planning*, vol. 24, no. 1 (1991), pp. 64–70.
11. For examples of different uses of strategic group analysis, see P. Lewes and H. Thomas, 'The linkage between strategy, strategic groups and performance in the UK retail grocery industry', *Strategic Management Journal*, vol. 11, no. 5 (1990), pp. 385–97; R. Reger and A. Huff, 'Strategic groups: a cognitive perspective', *Strategic Management Journal*, vol. 14, no. 2 (1993), pp. 103–24; and the paper by J. McGee and S. Segal-Horn in reference 13 below.

12. The characteristics listed in Exhibit 3.8 are based on those discussed by Porter (reference 6) and by J. McGee and H. Thomas, 'Strategic groups: theory, research and taxonomy', *Strategic Management Journal*, vol. 7, no. 2 (1986), pp. 141–60. This paper also provides a useful background to strategic group analysis.
13. This discussion on strategic group mapping and strategic space is based on the paper by J. McGee and S. Segal-Horn, 'Strategic space and industry dynamics', *Journal of Marketing Management*, vol. 6, no. 3 (1990) p. 175–93.
14. A useful discussion of segmentation in relation to competitive strategy is provided in M.E. Porter, *Competitive Advantage*, Free Press, 1985, chapter 7. See also the discussion on market segmentation in P. Kotler, *Marketing Management*, 8th edition, Prentice Hall, 1994.
15. A useful discussion of the relationship between market share and business performance is to be found in R.D. Buzzell and B.T. Gale, *The PIMS Principles: Linking strategy to performance*, Free Press, 1987, especially chapter 5.
16. This approach and the example shown in Exhibit 3.10 are dealt with more extensively in G. Johnson, C. Bowman and P. Rudd's chapter, 'Competitor analysis' in V. Ambrosini with G. Johnson and K. Scholes (eds), *Exploring Techniques of Analysis and Evaluation in Strategic Management*, Prentice Hall, 1998.
17. See A. Hax and N. Majluf, 'The use of the industry attractiveness–business strength matrix in strategic planning', in R. Dyson (ed.), *Strategic Planning: Models and analytical techniques*, Wiley, 1990.
18. D. Norburn's work supports this and is summarised in 'Directors without direction', *Journal of General Management*, vol. 1, no. 2 (1974) pp. 37–49. See also D. Miller and P. Friesen, 'Strategy making in context: ten empirical archetypes', *Journal of Management Studies*, vol. 14, no. 3 (1977), pp. 253–80, and A. Pettigrew and R. Whipp, *Managing Change for Competitive Success*, Blackwell, 1991.
19. For a review of many of these points, see the introduction to J. Dutton, E. Walton and E. Abrahamson, 'Important dimensions of strategic issues: separating the wheat from the chaff', *Journal of Management Studies*, vol. 26, no. 4 (1989), pp. 380–95.
20. See A. Tversky and D. Kahnemann, 'Judgements under uncertainty: heuristics and biases', *Science*, vol. 185 (1995), pp. 1124–31.
21. See J.E. Dutton and S.E. Jackson, 'Categorizing strategic issues: links to organizational action', *Academy of Management Review*, vol. 12, no. 1 (1987), pp. 76–90.

WORK ASSIGNMENTS

In the assignments which follow, the analysis of an industry is normally required. For this purpose, the European brewing industry,* the world automobile industry,* the pharmaceutical industry* or an industry of your choice could be useful.

3.1 Identify characteristics of stable, dynamic and complex industry environments. Using these characteristics, identify organisations which you think face stable, dynamic or complex environments.

3.2 Using Illustration 3.1 and Exhibit 3.3 as a guide, undertake an audit of an industry environment. What are the key environmental influences on firms in that industry? What are the main drivers of change?

3.3 Drawing on section 3.4, carry out a five forces analysis of an industry. What are the key competitive forces at work in that industry? Are there any changes that might occur which would significantly affect bases of competition in the industry?

3.4 Compare two industries in terms of the key environmental influences and competitive forces in them. Assess and compare the entry barriers, and the extent of competitive rivalry in the two industries.

3.5 ● Building on assignments 3.3 and 3.4, identify the main changes likely in an industry. Following the guidelines in section 3.3.3 and Illustration 3.3, construct scenarios for the industry for an appropriate time period.

3.6 ● Building on section 3.5.1 and Illustration 3.7:

(a) Identify the strategic characteristics which most distinguish organisations in an industry. Construct one or more strategic group maps on these bases.

(b) Assess the extent to which mobility between strategic groups is possible. (If you have constructed more than one map for the industry, do the mobility barriers you identify differ among them? What does this signify?)

(c) Identify any vacant strategic spaces in the maps. Do any represent viable strategic positions? What would be the characteristics of an organisation competing in such a space?

3.7 Assume you have just become personal assistant to the chief executive of a major pharmaceutical company. He knows you have recently undertaken a business management degree and asks if you would prepare a brief report summarising how scenario planning might be useful to a company in the pharmaceutical industry.

3.8 ● To what extent are the models discussed in this chapter appropriate in the analysis of the environment of a public sector or not-for-profit organisation?

3.9 ● Using the tools of analysis in this chapter, write a report for an organisation (e.g. PSA Peugeot Citroën,* BMW* or Kronenbourg*) which assesses its industry environment and its competitive position within that environment.

3.10 ● Using analytical approaches outlined in this chapter as a basis for your work, undertake a competitor analysis of an industry of your choice.

---

* refers to a case study in the Text and Cases edition.
● denotes more advanced work assignments.

CASE EXAMPLE

Irish Ports

John Mangan and James Cunningham

Introduction

The Republic of Ireland (ROI), a member of the European Union since 1973, is an island country located in the north west of Europe with a population of some 3.6 million. With the opening of the Channel Tunnel linking England with Continental Europe, Ireland became the only EU member without a land link to the rest of the EU and, thus, totally dependent on air and maritime transport modes for external access. In addition, Ireland has both a large economic dependence on external trade and is in a peripheral location *vis à vis* the economic centre of gravity of the EU. Consequently, ports are of special importance to the Irish economy. National transport policy in Ireland reflected these constraints (through subsidised targeted investment in infrastructure); nevertheless Ireland was still able to enjoy real GDP growth of some 7 per cent in 1996 and this positive trend looked as though it would continue. At market prices, GDP per capita in Ireland in 1996 stood at approximately IR£12,000 (IR£1 = US$1.50 approximately). Ports are critical nodes facilitating both trade flows and, to a lesser extent, tourism flows. Their operational efficiency and cost structures can thus have a considerable impact on the wider economy.

In the 1990s, the port industry, like many industries, was subject to increasing amounts of competition with implications for both national port policies and for port management. Competition for Irish ports came internally from individual ports such as Rosslare, Dublin and Cork and externally from ports outside the ROI, particularly the Northern Ireland ports (Belfast, Warrenpoint and Larne). In addition, ports faced competition from various airports and airlines operating to and from Ireland.

Government Policy and Ports

A significant EU-aided programme of investment was under way into port infrastructure in the Republic of Ireland. Between 1994 and 1999, a total co-financed investment of IR£163m was scheduled to be made at Irish ports – one of the aims of this investment was a reduction in combined port and shipping costs to users over the period 1994–1999 by a cumulative minimum of 15 per cent in real terms. Together with this investment programme was a substantial programme of reform concerning the management of Irish ports. Irish ports had been governed by relatively old legislation, namely the Harbours Acts 1946 to 1976. A government-appointed review group was established in 1991 to review the policy and legislation governing commercial ports in Ireland. The review group's report noted that 'Ireland's ports have been severely constrained in their ability to respond commercially because of the restricted legislation under which they operate.' Prior ministerial approval was, for example, required for setting rates and charges, borrowing money, carrying out harbour improvements, and acquiring and disposing of property. The review group considered four alternative structures for Irish ports in order to bring about greater commercialisation:

- Privatisation.
- Amalgamation/regionalisation of ports.
- A national sea ports company, on the model of *Aer Rianta* (the state-owned company operating Ireland's three main airports).
- Separate state companies to operate individual ports (i.e. the state remains the sole shareholder).

The review group recommended that commercial state companies should be set up to

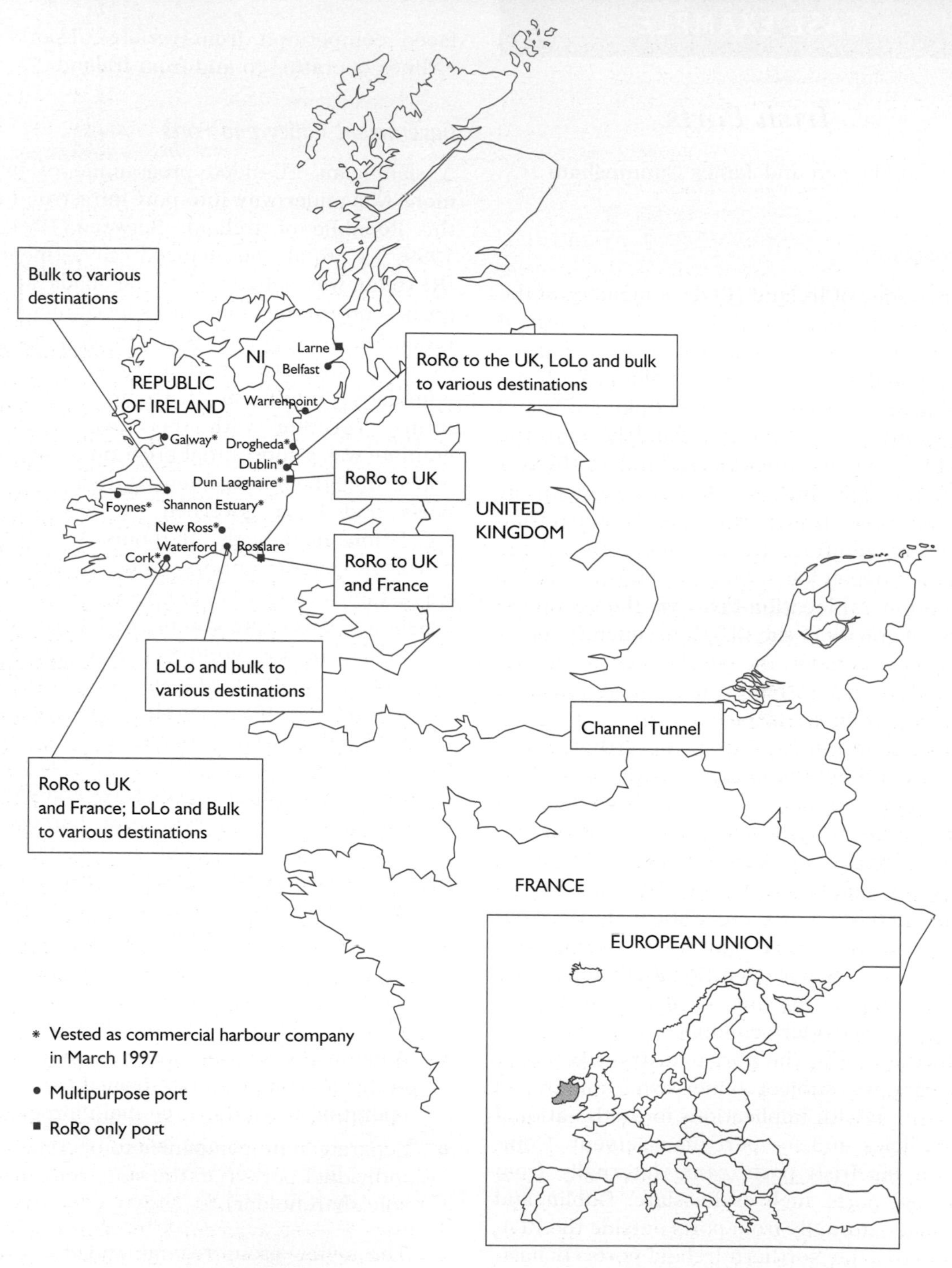
Bulk to various destinations
RoRo to the UK, LoLo and bulk to various destinations
RoRo to UK
RoRo to UK and France
LoLo and bulk to various destinations
RoRo to UK and France; LoLo and Bulk to various destinations
Channel Tunnel
REPUBLIC OF IRELAND
NI
Larne
Belfast
Warrenpoint
Galway*
Drogheda*
Dublin*
Dun Laoghaire*
Foynes*
Shannon Estuary*
New Ross*
Waterford
Rosslare
Cork*
UNITED KINGDOM
FRANCE
EUROPEAN UNION
* Vested as commercial harbour company in March 1997
● Multipurpose port
■ RoRo only port

manage twelve key (in effect the largest) Irish ports. Consequently the Harbours Act 1996 was passed with the purpose of 'freeing Ireland's key ports from direct departmental control and giving them the commercial freedom they need to be able to operate as modern, customer-oriented service industries'. In March 1997 the first eight ports (see map) out of a planned twelve ports were vested as commercial harbour companies (previously they were known as harbour authorities).

Industry Structure

Sea freight is generally divided into two categories, namely containerised freight (where freight is held in containers which are generally 20 feet or 40 feet long) and bulk freight (where the freight is not stored in containers e.g. oil, cattle.). Containers are either lift-on, lift-off (LoLo) or roll-on, roll-off (RoRo). Republic of Ireland ports handled nearly 34 million of freight tonnes in 1996. Dublin had the largest throughput at over 11 million tonnes, followed by Shannon Estuary, followed by Cork. RoRo comprised 17 per cent of all volumes, LoLo 13 per cent and bulk the remainder. In comparison, ports in Northern Ireland (NI) handled 19.9 million tonnes of goods in 1996. In addition, Northern Ireland ports handled 58 per cent of the whole island volume of RoRo traffic in 1996 which had decreased from a high of 71 per cent in 1994. The reason usually cited for NI's higher share was the higher frequency of cheaper, shorter sailings rendering ROI ports and their services less competitive. Fleet replacements and product revamps by the ferry companies were renewed efforts on their behalf to attract a greater share of the growing market.

Sea passengers used the RoRo ferry services from Dublin, Dun Laoghaire, Rosslare and Cork. Ferry services between Republic of Ireland and UK ports had improved dramatically with the introduction of new ferries on the Irish Sea passenger market by the two major ferry operators, Stena and Irish Ferries. Stena operated the HSS high speed ferry from Dun Laoghaire to Holyhead taking just 99 minutes, and the similarly fast Lynx service from Rosslare to Fishguard. The ports in Dun Laoghaire and Rosslare had been upgraded significantly to facilitate these fast ferry services. However, the ferries were much more susceptible to bad weather conditions than conventional passenger ferries. Irish Ferries had opted for increased capacity instead of speed on their routes to the UK from Dublin and Rosslare, with their new ferries able to carry up to 1,500 passengers. The company took delivery of these new ferries from 1995 to 1997. The journey time took over three hours but with significantly upgraded facilities on board. Sea passengers also had the choice of using the ports and ferry services in Northern Ireland, namely Larne and Belfast. Passengers could book their tickets directly from the ferry companies or through a travel agency. The ferry companies were facing increased competition from airlines as a result of the EU's open skies policy. In 1997, airfares on Ireland–UK routes were as low as IR£59 plus taxes and included a friend travelling free. In 1996, 3.9 million passengers used ferry services between the UK and Ireland (as opposed to 6.9 million by air) while only 318,000 passengers used the (seasonal) RoRo ferry services between Ireland and France (as opposed to 2.9 million by air). Indeed, despite the emphasis by the Irish government on enhancing the profitability of the Irish tourism sector, the ferry companies were not benefiting greatly from this growth because of the bias among tourists to use air transport in preference to sea travel.

Another issue of interest to both airlines and ferry companies was the intended abolition of duty free sales within the EU. The European Commission planned to outlaw duty free sales for intra-EU passengers in 1999. This would have a considerable effect, in terms of lost revenue, on both ports and ferry companies. Some operators also had duty free sales incorporated into the remuneration packages of employees. In some instances this comprised up to one-third of the total remuneration of such staff, so the elimination of duty free could ultimately lead to increases in operators' costs with a knock-on effect of increasing passenger fares.

In the passenger market, the ferry operators were constantly monitoring factors such as consumer price indices, booking patterns, level of disposable incomes, volume of retail sales, tourism statistics, long-term demand, the traffic mix carried on sailings, and exchange rate fluctuations. Shipping companies carrying sea freight focused on the market plans of large customers, customer product data (types of goods being carried), the overall state of the economy, global trading patterns, levels of imports and exports and the rate of multinational corporations (MNC) start-ups. The Irish government was pursuing a policy promoting regionalisation of MNC start-ups and this in turn affected traffic patterns. Shipping companies carrying sea freight needed to achieve a close match between supply and demand owing to market demands. The rates that shipping companies charged to the customer were flexible whereas the physical resources such as the provision of routes were not. Further constraints that both port and ferry operators faced were the types of handling facilities available at each port, lack of berths, water depth and port channel access and land access to sea ports. In addition, both ports and ferry operators were susceptible to changes that might occur in the transport industry in Ireland.

The Future

The competitiveness of Irish ports would come under greater scrutiny when European monetary union (EMU) began in 1999. Based on 1997 economic indicators Ireland was likely to be one of the first members. The UK government had said, however, that it would not join until at least 2002. This posed difficulties for Ireland. The Irish economy was export-led with a large, but decreasing, volume of exports going to the UK. Ireland was thus torn between following sterling or the Deutshmark and the other EMU currencies. If it chose the latter option by participating in EMU, then currency fluctuations between the ECU and sterling could adversely affect the levels of trade between Ireland and the UK, and thus the demand for freight transportation between both countries. The ports sector in Ireland was, then, subject to many influences, and operated in competitive, dynamic and diverse markets, with associated challenges for both policy-makers and individual port managers.

Questions

1. Building on Illustration 3.1 and Exhibit 3.3 in the chapter, identify the main environmental forces affecting Irish ports.
2. Which of these forces are the most significant drivers of change and why?
3. Undertake a five forces analysis from the perspective of a manager of a major Irish port. What are the main conclusions from this analysis?
4. Based on this analysis, identify any important environmental influences which are uncertain. Build different scenarios incorporating these factors. What are the implications of the different scenarios?

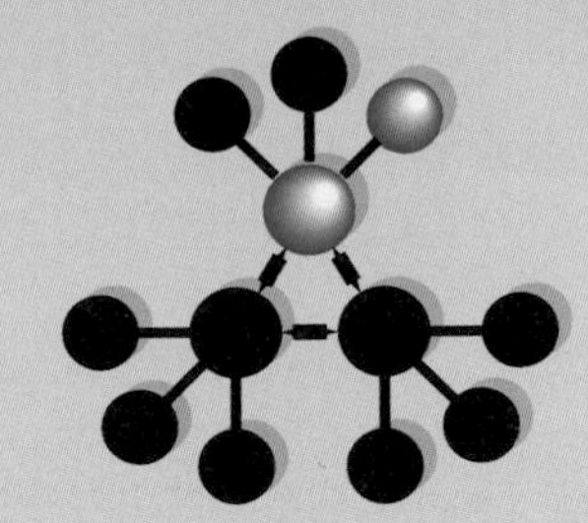

4
RESOURCES, COMPETENCES AND STRATEGIC CAPABILITY

LEARNING OUTCOMES

After reading this chapter you should be able to:

- Undertake a resource audit and explain the implications.
- Define unique resources and core competences.
- Identify the core competences of an organisation.
- Draw up a value chain for an organisation and the 'industry' in which it operates.
- Identify sources of cost efficiency and added value for an organisation.
- Explain different types of linkage and how they can underpin competitive advantage.
- Undertake a benchmarking exercise.
- Undertake a portfolio analysis.
- Undertake a SWOT analysis.

4.1 INTRODUCTION

Chapter 3 has underlined the importance of analysing and understanding the external environment in which an organisation is operating. This environment creates both opportunities for and threats to the organisation's strategic development. But successful strategies are also dependent on the organisation having the *strategic capability* to perform at the level which is required for success. This chapter is concerned with analysing the strategic capability of an organisation. It will be seen that strategic capability can be related to three main factors: the *resources* available to the organisation; the *competence* with which the activities of the organisation are undertaken; and the *balance* of resources, activities and business units in the organisation.

Analysing the strategic capability of an organisation is clearly important in terms of understanding whether the resources and competences *fit* the environment in which the organisation is operating, and the opportunities and threats which exist. Many of the issues of strategic development are concerned with changing strategic capability to fit a changing environment better. The major upheavals in many manufacturing industries during the 1980s were examples of such adjustments in strategic capability, involving major gains in labour productivity and the adoption of new technologies. However, understanding strategic capability is also important from another perspective. The organisation's capability may be the leading edge of strategic developments, in the sense that new opportunities may exist by *stretching* and exploiting the organisation's unique resources and competences either in ways which competitors find difficult to match or in genuinely new directions, or both.[1] This requires organisations to be more *innovative* in the way they develop and exploit their resources and competences.

This chapter will be concerned with analysing and understanding strategic capability with both the 'fit' and 'stretch' perspectives in mind. This will require an assessment of the resources and competences which have been built up through the delivery of the organisation's current and previous strategies. Herein lies a danger. It is possible that managers will favour new strategies which exploit these resources and competences, and may not see many of the opportunities and threats discussed in Chapter 3. This could lead to *strategic drift*, as discussed in Chapter 2. The resource management systems of the organisation will reinforce this tendency, since they are geared to the management of resources and processes to support current strategies. For example, plants are located in particular places, and communication systems have been set up in certain ways. In other words, strategy formulation is not occurring in a 'greenfield site' situation. This may not encourage managers to think innovatively about how resources and competences can be stretched to create new opportunities.

In order to understand strategic capability, it is necessary to consider organisations at various levels of detail. There are broad issues of capability which are relevant to the organisation as a whole. These are largely concerned with the *overall balance* of resources and *mix* of activities. At the detailed level there are assessments to be made of the quantity and quality of each *key resource area*, such as buildings, machines and people. However, a major theme of this chapter is that the central issue in understanding the strategic capability of an organisation is an assessment of the *competences* which exist to undertake the various separate activities of the business, such as design, production, marketing, delivery, and customer liaison and support. It is an understanding of the competence in performing these various *value activities* and managing the *linkages* between activities which is crucial when assessing strategic capability.

Before reviewing the range of analytical methods which can contribute to understanding an organisation's strategic capability, it is necessary to see how the various analyses will contribute to the overall assessment of this

Exhibit 4.1 Analysing strategic capability

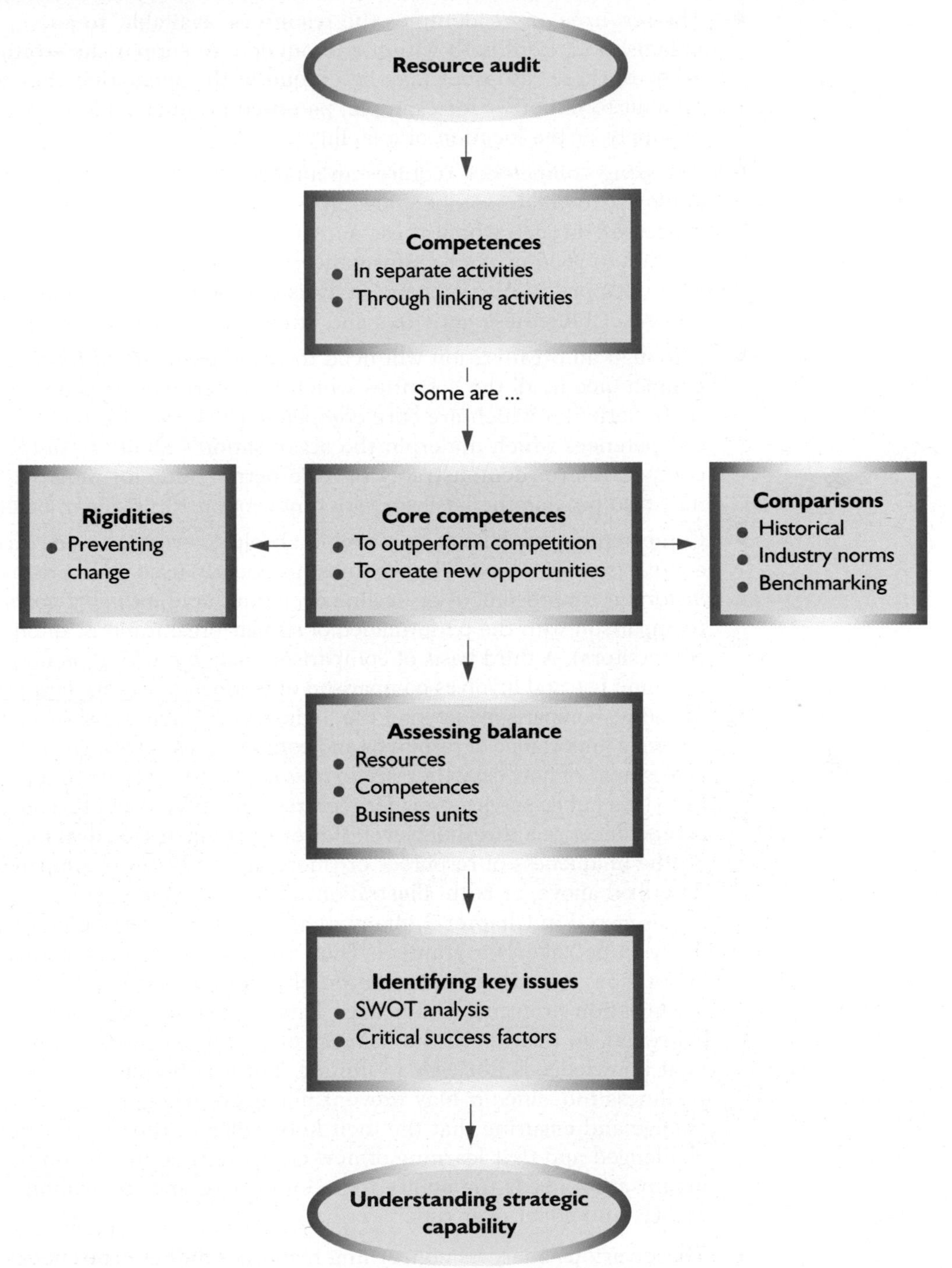

capability. Exhibit 4.1 provides a systematic way to move from an audit of resources to a deeper understanding of strategic capability.

- The *resource audit* identifies the resources 'available' to an organisation, from both within and outside, to support its strategies. Some of these resources may be unique in the sense that they are difficult to imitate – for example, patented products, a low-cost source of supply or the location of a facility.
- *Assessing competence* requires an analysis of how resources are being *deployed* to create competences in separate activities, and the processes through which these activities are linked together. Usually, the key to good or poor performance is found here rather than in the resources *per se*. Value chain analysis can be useful in understanding and describing these activities and linkages.
- Although an organisation will need to reach a *threshold level* of competence in all the activities which it undertakes, it is only some of these activities which are *core competences*. These are the competences which underpin the organisation's ability to outperform competition (or demonstrably provide better value for money). They may also provide the basis on which new opportunities can be created.
- Competences are difficult to assess in absolute terms, so some basis of *comparison* is needed. The two most frequently used comparisons are *historical* (improvement or decline over time) and *industry norms* (comparison with the performance of similar organisations, often competitors). A third basis of comparison, *benchmarking*, is now in common use and involves comparison of competences with *best practice*, including comparisons beyond the 'industry'. Exhibit 4.2 shows that the strategic importance of resources and competences is strongly linked to an assessment of how easy they are to *imitate*. So to compete in an industry or to be a public service provider requires a necessary set of resources and competences to a threshold level. However, competitive advantage is built on the uniqueness of resources or (more often) the core competences described above, or both. Illustration 4.1 shows some examples.
  As discussed in Chapter 2, many of an organisation's competences are likely to be 'taken for granted'. They are part of the tacit knowledge[2] about 'how you run an organisation like this', and are embedded in the organisation's routines and rituals. This is a two-edged sword: it is often a strength in relation to the delivery of current strategies, since this tacit knowledge is not easy to imitate; but it is potentially a major weakness too, since it may prevent managers recognising the need for change and ensuring that the tacit knowledge in the organisation is challenged and that learning of new competences occurs. So the organisation needs the ability to be innovative and the willingness to change and adapt over time.
- These various analyses concerning resources and competences usually relate to separate *strategic business units* in the way that was defined

Exhibit 4.2 Resources, competences and competitive advantage

	Same as competitors' or easy to imitate	Better than competitors' and difficult to imitate*
RESOURCES	Necessary resources	Unique resources
COMPETENCES	Threshold competences	Core competences

* Provides the basis to outperform competitors or demonstratably provide better value for money

and discussed in Chapter 1. An organisation's overall strategic capability will also be influenced by the extent to which its resources, competences and strategic business units are *balanced* as a whole. *Portfolio analyses* can be helpful in addressing issues of balance and will be important considerations at the corporate centre of an organisation.

- Resource analysis can often prove difficult or fruitless if attempts are made to list the key issues (such as *strengths and weaknesses*) before some of these other analyses have been undertaken. This *identification of key issues* is critical and is best undertaken as a means of summarising the key strategic insights which have emerged from other analyses.

4.2 RESOURCE AUDIT[3]

A **resource audit** identifies and classifies the resources that an organisation owns or can access to support its strategies. It should attempt to assess the quantity of resources available, the nature of those resources, and the extent to which the resources are unique. Typically, resources can be grouped under the following four headings:

a **resource audit** *identifies and classifies the resources that an organisation owns or can access to support its strategies*

- *Physical resources*. An assessment of an organisation's physical resources should stretch beyond a mere listing of the number of

STRATEGY IN ACTION
Illustration 4.1

Competitive Advantage through Resources and Competences

The examples below demonstrate how a variety of resources and competences have formed the bases of competitive advantage for their organisations. What is common to all is that the resources and competences in question are difficult to imitate.

Caterpillar

In the early 1940s, Caterpillar was one of several medium-sized firms in the heavy construction equipment industry struggling to survive intense competition. Just before the outbreak of the Second World War, the US Department of War announced that, in order to pursue a global war, it would need one worldwide supplier of heavy construction equipment to build roads, airstrips and army bases. After brief competition, Caterpillar was awarded the contract and, with the support of the Allies, was able to develop a worldwide service and supply network for heavy construction equipment at very low cost. By continuing to own and operate this network after the war had ended, Caterpillar was able to become the dominant firm in the heavy construction equipment industry. Furthermore, this valuable capability enables Caterpillar management still to advertise its ability to deliver any part, for any Caterpillar equipment, to any place in the world, in under two days. In fulfilling this promise, Caterpillar remains the market share leader in most categories of heavy construction equipment, despite economic recessions and labour strife. The high costs associated with duplicating its worldwide network prevent many firms from competing with Caterpillar even in the 1990s.

Mailbox Inc.

Mailbox Inc. is a very successful firm in the bulk mailing business in the Dallas–Fort Worth market, enjoying an enormous market share. However, just like other firms in the industry, Mailbox gathers mail from customers, sorts it by postal code, and then takes it to the post office to be mailed. Rather than its competitive advantage having been generated from any 'big decisions', its success depends on doing lots of little things right. For example, the way it manages accounting, finance, human resources and production separately is not exceptional. However, to manage all these functions so well, and so consistently over time, is exceptional. Thus, firms seeking to compete against Mailbox will not have to imitate just a few internal attributes, but thousands of such attributes – a seemingly daunting task.

Hewlett Packard

The powerful and enabling culture of Hewlett Packard is an organisation phenomenon which, like reputation, trust, friendship and teamwork, is not patentable, but is very difficult to imitate. One of the most important components of Hewlett Packard's culture is that it supports and encourages teamwork and co-operation even across divisional boundaries. Using this capability, Hewlett Packard has been able to enhance the compatibility of its numerous products, including printers, plotters, personal computers, mini computers and electronic instruments. By co-operating across these product categories, Hewlett Packard has been able almost to double its market value, without introducing any radical new products or technologies.

Questions

1. Referring to Exhibit 4.1 and using the three examples in this illustration to trigger your thinking, list further examples where competitive advantage could be achieved through:
   (a) owning unique resources
   (b) competence in separate activities
   (c) the management of linkages.
2. How easy would it be to imitate each of the factors?
3. What general conclusions might you draw from your answers to questions 1 and 2 about the relationship between resources, competences and competitive advantage?

Source J.B. Barney, 'Looking inside for competitive advantage', *Academy of Management Executive*, vol. 9, no. 4 (1995), pp. 49–61.

Prepared by Sara Martin, Cranfield School of Management.

machines, buildings or the production capacity. It should ask questions about the nature of these resources, such as the age, condition, capability and location of each resource, since these factors will determine the usefulness of the resources in gaining competitive advantage.

- *Human resources*. The analysis of human resources should examine a number of questions. An assessment of the number and types of different skills within an organisation is clearly important, but other factors, such as the adaptability of human resources, must not be overlooked. The innovative capability of people is of particular importance in 'fast-moving' situations.
- *Financial resources*. These include the sources and uses of money, such as obtaining capital, managing cash, the control of debtors and creditors, and the management of relationships with suppliers of money (shareholders, bankers, etc.).
- *Intangibles*.[4] A mistake which can be made in a resource analysis is to overlook the importance of intangible resources. There should be no doubt that these intangibles have a value, since when businesses are sold part of the businesses' value is 'goodwill'. In some businesses, such as professional services, retailing or the catering industry, goodwill could represent the major asset of the company and may result from brand names, good contacts, corporate image or the value attached to the innovative capability (such as patented processes).

If the resource audit is to be useful as a basis for further analyses, two important points need to be borne in mind:

- The audit should include all resources which the organisation can *access* to support its strategies, and should not be narrowly confined to the resources which it owns in a legal sense. Some strategically important resources may be outside the organisation's ownership, such as its network of contacts or customers.
- Unique resources should be identified within the wider list of resources necessary to pursue a strategy (see Exhibit 4.2). **Unique resources** are those which create competitive advantage and are difficult to imitate (for example, a patented product).

unique resources *are those which create competitive advantage and are difficult to imitate*

4.3 ANALYSING COMPETENCES AND CORE COMPETENCES

The difference in performance of different organisations in the same 'industry' is rarely fully explainable by differences in their resource base *per se*. Superior performance will also be determined by the way in which resources are *deployed* to create competences in the organisation's separate activities, and the processes of linking these activities together to sustain excellent performance. Although the organisation will need to achieve a threshold level of competence in all of its activities, only some will be core competences. These are the competences which underpin the organisation's ability to outperform competition – or demonstrably to provide better value for money. Core competences need to be difficult to imitate, otherwise they will not provide long-term advantage. They may also be the basis on which new opportunities are created (as discussed in Chapter 7).

This section of the chapter will consider how an organisation's competences can be understood and analysed in two 'steps' (see Exhibit 4.3):

- *Value chain analysis* will be used to describe the various activities which are necessary to undertake a particular business or public service, and how these separate activities link together (section 4.3.1). It will also be used to describe which of these many activities underpin the competitive advantage of the organisation – the core competences as discussed above (section 4.3.2).
- The latter part of the section will be concerned with analysing the *bases* on which an organisation's core competences can be built. The discussion will look at *cost efficiency* (section 4.3.3), *value added* (section 4.3.4), the management of *linkages* between activities (section 4.3.5) and the issue of the *robustness* of competences to imitation or competitive threat (section 4.3.6) and the innovative processes which help the organisation to stay ahead (section 4.3.7).

Together these discussions are designed to help readers understand the importance of analysing organisational competences and how these determine the overall strategic strength or weakness of the organisation (its strategic capability).

4.3.1 Value Chain Analysis[5]

value chain analysis *describes the activities within and around an organisation, and relates them to an analysis of the competitive strength of the organisation*

Value chain analysis describes the activities within and around an organisation, and relates them to an analysis of the competitive strength of the organisation (or its ability to provide value-for-money products or services). Value analysis[6] was originally introduced as an accounting analysis to shed light on the 'value added' by separate steps in complex manufacturing processes, in order to determine where cost improvements could be made or value creation improved, or both. These two basic steps of identifying *separate activities* and assessing the *value added* by each were linked to an analysis of an organisation's competitive advantage by Michael Porter.

One of the key aspects of value chain analysis is the recognition that organisations are much more than a random collection of machines, money and people. These resources are of no value unless deployed into activities and organised into routines and systems which ensure that products or

Exhibit 4.3 Analysing competences and core competences

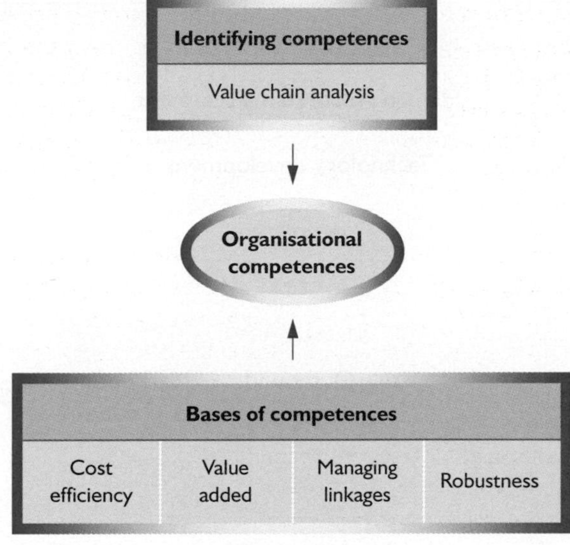

services are produced which are valued by the final consumer or user. In other words, it is these competences to perform particular activities and the ability to manage linkages between activities which are the source of competitive advantage for organisations. Porter argued that an understanding of strategic capability must start with an identification of these separate *value activities*. Exhibit 4.4 is a schematic representation of the value chain within an organisation. **Primary activities** are *directly* concerned with the creation or delivery of a product or service and can be grouped into five main areas: inbound logistics, operations, outbound logistics, marketing and sales, and service.

primary activities *are directly concerned with the creation or delivery of a product service*

- *Inbound logistics* are the activities concerned with receiving, storing and distributing the inputs to the product or service. They include materials handling, stock control, transport, etc.
- *Operations* transform these various inputs into the final product or service: machining, packaging, assembly, testing, etc.
- *Outbound logistics* collect, store and distribute the product to customers. For tangible products this would be warehousing, materials handling, transport, etc. In the case of services, they may be more concerned with arrangements for bringing customers to the service if it is a fixed location (e.g. sports events).
- *Marketing and sales* provide the means whereby consumers/users are made aware of the product or service and are able to purchase it. This

Exhibit 4.4 The value chain

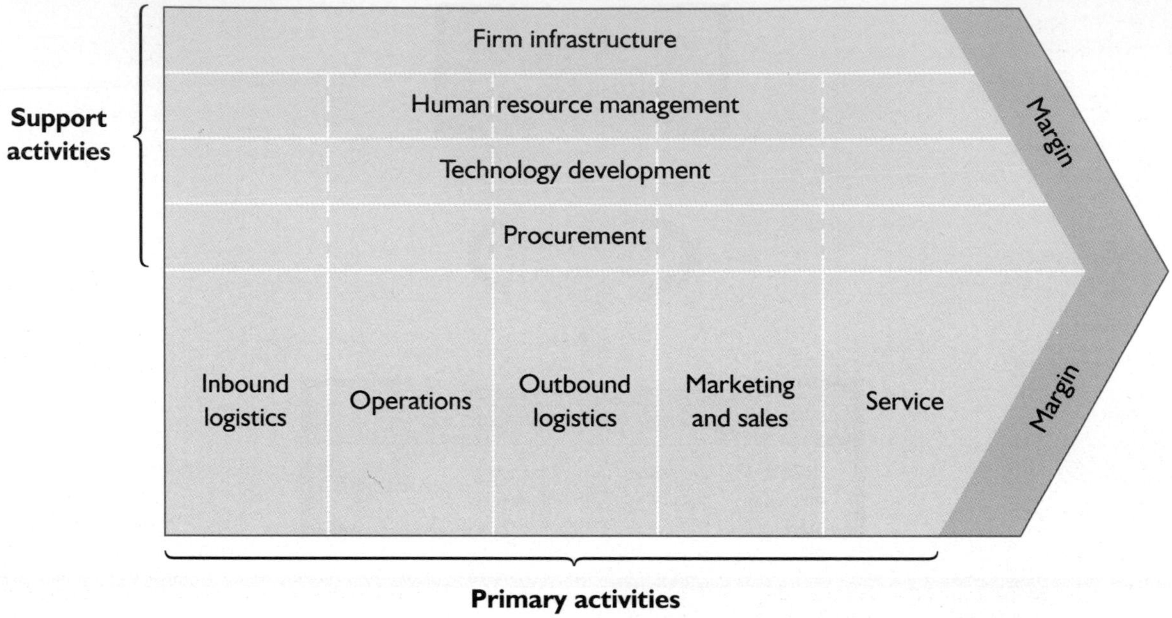

Support activities

Firm infrastructure					Margin
Human resource management					
Technology development					
Procurement					
Inbound logistics	Operations	Outbound logistics	Marketing and sales	Service	Margin

Primary activities

Source M.E. Porter, *Competitive Advantage*, Free Press, 1985. Used with permission of The Free Press, a division of Macmillan Inc. Copyright 1985 Michael E. Porter.

would include sales administration, advertising, selling and so on. In public services, communication networks which help users access a particular service are often important. For example, this became one key role for Passenger Transport Executive bodies following the deregulation of buses in the UK in the late 1980s.

- *Service* includes all those activities which enhance or maintain the value of a product or service, such as installation, repair, training and spares.

support activities *help to improve the effectiveness or efficiency of primary activities*

Each of these groups of primary activities is linked to support activities. **Support activities** help to improve the effectiveness or efficiency of primary activities. They can be divided into four areas:

- *Procurement*. This refers to the *processes* for acquiring the various resource inputs to the primary activities. As such, it occurs in many parts of the organisation.
- *Technology development*. All value activities have a 'technology', even if it is simply know-how. The key technologies may be concerned directly with the product (e.g. R&D product design) or with processes (e.g.

Exhibit 4.5 The value system

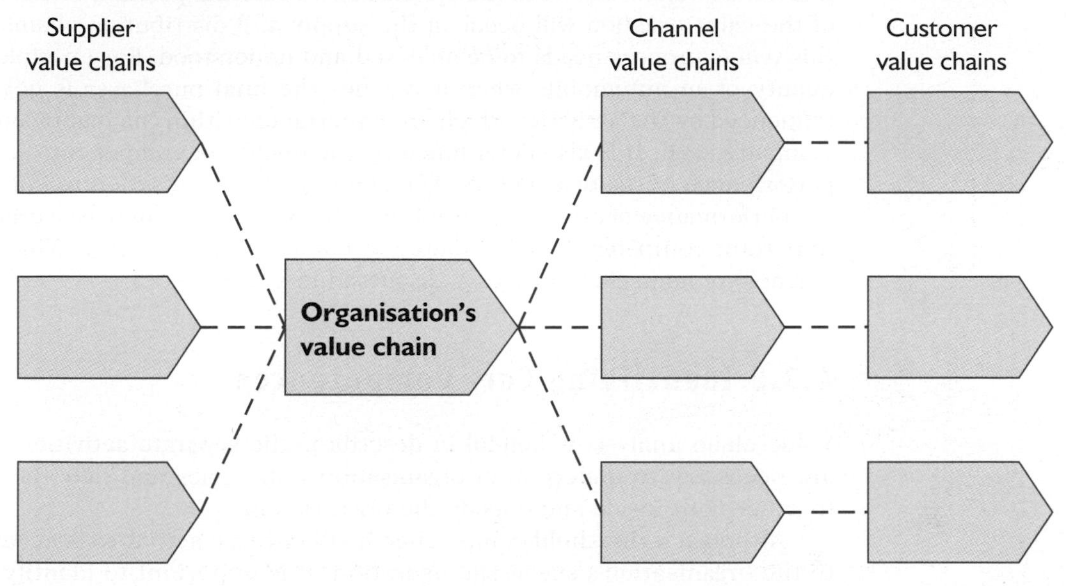

Source M.E. Porter, *Competitive Advantage*, Free Press, 1985. Used with permission of The Free Press, a division of Macmillan Inc. Copyright 1985 Michael E. Porter.

process development) or with a particular resource (e.g. raw materials improvements). This area is fundamental to the innovative capacity of the organisation.

- *Human resource management*. This is a particularly important area which transcends all primary activities. It is concerned with those activities involved in recruiting, managing, training, developing and rewarding people within the organisation. This, in turn, determines whether the organisation is rigid or innovative.
- *Infrastructure*. The systems of planning, finance, quality control, information management, etc. are crucially important to an organisation's performance in its primary activities. Infrastructure also consists of the structures and routines of the organisation which sustain its culture. Again, this determines the level of rigidity or innovation in the organisation.

In most industries it is very rare that a single organisation undertakes all of the value activities from the product design through to the delivery of the final product or service to the final consumer. There is usually specialisation of role and any one organisation is part of the wider *value system* which creates a product or service (see Exhibit 4.5). Indeed, it is this process of specialisation which often underpins excellence in creating value for money. In understanding the basis of an organisation's strategic capability, it is not sufficient to look at the organisation's internal position alone. Much of the value creation will occur in the supply and distribution chains, and this *whole process* needs to be analysed and understood. For example, the quality of an automobile when it reaches the final purchaser is not only influenced by the activities which are undertaken within the manufacturing company itself. It is also determined by the quality of components and the performance of the distributors. The ability of an organisation to influence the performance of other organisations in the value chain may be a crucially important competence and a source of competitive advantage. This is an example of managing linkages – discussed in section 4.3.5.

4.3.2 Identifying Core Competences[7]

Value chain analysis is helpful in describing the separate activities which are necessary to underpin an organisation's strategies and how they link together both inside and outside the organisation.

Although a threshold competence in all of these activities is necessary to the organisation's successful operation, it is important to identify core competences within this. **Core competences** are those competences which critically underpin the organisation's competitive advantage. Core competences will differ from one organisation to another depending on how the company is positioned and the strategies it is pursuing. For example, consider how small shops compete with supermarkets in grocery retailing. All shops need to have a threshold competence in the basic activities of purchasing, stocking, display, etc. However, the major supermarkets are pursuing strategies which provide lower prices to consumers through their core competences in merchandising, securing lower cost supplies and managing in-store activities more efficiently. This gives a supermarket competitive advantage over smaller shops. It is difficult for smaller shops to imitate these competences, since they are underpinned by key resources such as computerised stock ordering systems and own-brand labels. So a 'corner shop' grocery store gains competitive advantage over supermarkets by concentrating more on convenience and service through *different* core competences – personal service to customers, extended opening hours, informal credit, home deliveries, etc. The key resources for the successful corner shop are the style of the owner and the choice of location. These aspects of service are valued by some consumers and are difficult for the supermarkets to imitate without substantially increasing their costs.

core competences *are those competences which critically underpin the organisation's competitive advantage*

It is also important to understand that those unique resources and core competences which allow supermarkets to gain competitive advantage over corner shops are not unique resources or core competences in the competitive rivalry between supermarkets. They are necessary resources and threshold competences to survive as a supermarket (i.e. within this particular strategic group, as discussed in Chapter 3). The competitive rivalry between supermarkets is therefore achieved through other unique resources (perhaps a key site) or core competences (perhaps in the management of own-brand supply). However, industry experience shows that these tend to be easily imitated. Consequently, long-term competitive advantage needs to be secured by continually shifting the ground of competition. So a core competence could be the processes of innovation (in many aspects of the business, such as brand development, marketing, or financial services).

The development of global competition in the automobile industry[8] over recent decades also illustrates this issue well (see Exhibit 4.6). During the 1950s and 1960s, the US giants such as Ford and General Motors dominated the global market through the critical success factor of *market access* supported by core competences of establishing dealer networks and, later, overseas production plants. Meanwhile, Japanese manufacturers were developing competences in defect-free manufacture. By the mid 1970s they were significantly outperforming Ford on *quality and reliability* – which became critical success factors (see section 4.6.2 below) in allowing them to achieve global sales. By the mid 1980s, both Ford and the major Japanese companies had achieved similar competence in achieving these critical success factors. Although maintaining a global network was a critical success factor which continued to distinguish Ford and the Japanese from many European companies such as Peugeot, the production and supplier management activities underpinning quality (reliability) were becoming threshold competences. The competitive arena then switched to competences which would create some uniqueness of product in an increasingly 'commodity-like' industry. The new critical success factor became the ability to provide unique product designs and features at low volumes of manufacture – underpinned by core competences in 'lifestyle niche' marketing by companies like Mazda. This agility in design and manufacturing techniques also became a core competence in the global competition. This example of the automobile industry is provided to demonstrate the need for constant review and innovation. The impact of technological change can be profound in many industries, 'changing the rules of the game' and providing opportunities for new entrants to succeed as incumbent players fail to respond.

Most service industries are currently experiencing this need to innovate in relation to the impact of information technology. Innovative ways of redesigning services and their delivery abound, ranging from 'direct-line selling' to the exploitation of the Internet. IT is also a source of many new services previously impractical or too costly with older technologies.

It should be remembered from earlier discussions that it is important to identify an organisation's core competences not only for reasons of ensuring or continuing good 'fit' between these core competences and the changing nature of the markets or environment (as illustrated in this example), but because core competences may also be the basis on which the organisation stretches into new opportunities. So, in deciding which competences are

Exhibit 4.6 How core competences change over time: the world automobile industry

Source Based on G. Hamel and A. Heene (eds), *Competence-based Competition*, Wiley, 1994, pp. 16–18.

core, this ability to exploit the competence in more than one market or arena is another criterion which could be used. This ability will require a capacity for innovation and a willingness to change. The development of 'added-value' services and geographical spread of markets are two typical ways in which core competences can be exploited to maintain progress once traditional markets are mature or saturated. These issues will be discussed more fully in Chapter 7 when looking at how strategic choices relate to an organisation's core competences.

Value chain analysis is a reminder that the long-term competitive position of an organisation is concerned with its ability to sustain value-for-money products or services. It can be helpful in *identifying* those activities which the organisation must undertake at a threshold level of competence to stay in business. However, for the purpose of building a strategy to achieve competitive advantage, it is necessary to go beyond this, to identify which *core competences* exist to provide competitive advantage. This is difficult because such core competences must meet a number of challenging criteria. They must not only provide *value to the buyer*, but also be difficult for competitors to imitate, so they will be *rare*; *complex* (because they are not explained by one factor but by linked factors), or so embedded in organisational practice or knowledge as to be, in effect, *tacit*. So it may be necessary to identify aspects of the organisation that might not be the most visible. Indeed, if they were visible, it would be relatively easy for competitors to imitate them. So there has to be an 'unpacking' of competences. A useful way of doing this can follow a number of steps and is also shown in Illustration 4.2.

1. The first step is to identify SBUs that are clearly successful. In the example shown in Illustration 4.2 the chosen SBU manufactured and sold consumer goods to major UK retailers. It had won several major retail accounts and increased profits significantly.
2. The second step is to identify the bases of perceived value by the customers, in this case the retailers. The sort of exercise described in section 3.5.3 in Chapter 3 is useful here. These can be thought of as the *primary reasons* for success. In the case of the SBU in Illustration 4.2 they were to do with the reputation of its brand, the excellence of its service, its track record for delivery, and its product range and innovation associated with it. In particular, it is important to concentrate on primary reasons for success in which the SBU scores better than competition. In the case of this SBU, it was seen as particularly successful in terms of its level of service and its range.
3. It is then necessary to 'unpack' each of these bases of success. In Illustration 4.2 this is only shown for two of the primary reasons for success, but in reality it was done for all of them. The managers ask why the business is especially successful at providing good service, or an innovative range and so on. These can be regarded as the *secondary reasons for success*. This is likely to give rise to quite broad explanations. In this case the managers recognised that a good deal of their success was underpinned by their distribution and logistics systems, but that this could be matched by competitors. However, they also identified that their flexibility and rapid response seemed to be ahead of competitors'. They also commented that one of the important reasons for success was that they were able to find ways of solving the problems that buyers in the retailers might get themselves into, for example by getting the order mix wrong or by overordering.
4. The next step is more challenging. The requirement is to unpack each of the secondary reasons for success. Why is this SBU particularly flexible? How is it able to solve buyers' problems and so on? This is

STRATEGY IN ACTION Illustration 4.2

Core Competences for a Consumer Goods Business

Core competences underpinning competitive success can be embedded in linked organisational activities at an operational (or tertiary) level.

From 1996 to 1998 a consumer goods company had won several major retail accounts from competitors. In order to identify the core competences underpinning its competitive advantage it analysed how it uniquely met the retailers' criteria of supplier selection by 'unpacking' them in terms of its organisational processes as shown below.

Questions

1. Why would it be difficult for competitors to imitate the competences that the company identified?
2. Bearing in mind the description of the learning organisation in Chapter 2 (section 2.8.3), what competences at the secondary and tertiary levels might this company need to have in order to be seen as a successful innovator in consumer goods?

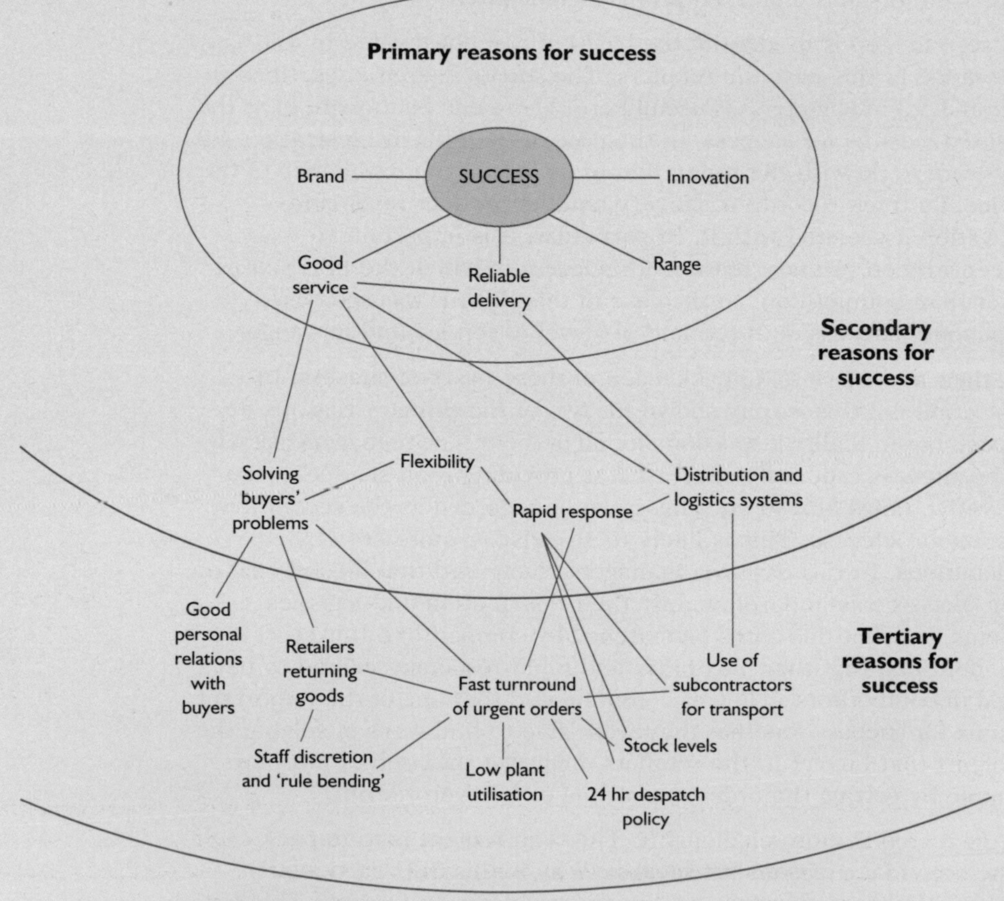

more difficult because it requires the managers to get down to *tertiary reasons for success* at operational levels of detail that may not be immediately obvious. Indeed, in this company some of the explanations that managers arrived at brought to the surface activities in the organisation that:

- 'bent the rules' – for example, taking back goods from major retailers when, strictly speaking, the systems of the business did not allow it;
- used 'organisational slack' that management was trying to do away with, such as under-utilised production lines;
- were taken for granted – for example, it was 'custom and practice' rather than company policy to prioritise the solving of problems of the buyers of the major retailers.

This exercise can lead to very extensive explanations about bases of success. Illustration 4.2 is very simplified. In reality, each of the primary reasons for success was traced through to tertiary reasons in detail resulting in hundreds of explanations.

5. The final step is to look for patterns of explanation. It is unlikely that any one factor explains a core competence. It is more likely that there are linked factors. Here what emerged was that the relationship between the sales personnel and the buyers encouraged them to 'ask the impossible' of the company when difficulties arose; and the combination of sound logistics, stock levels, spare capacity and staff discretion to the point of rule-bending resulted in competitive advantage. Moreover, much of this was embedded in operational levels of activity in the organisation which were not evident to competitors – indeed, had not been clear to the managers before undertaking the analysis.

The sections which follow look at different bases of organisational competences.

4.3.3 Analysing Cost Efficiency[9]

One contributor to the provision of value-for-money products or services is the efficiency with which the organisation undertakes its activities. **Cost efficiency** is a measure of the level of resources needed to create a given level of value. Cost efficiency is determined by a number of factors often called *cost drivers* (see Exhibit 4.7), and it is important to understand the competences associated with each of these factors and whether or not they are core competences (i.e. provide competitive advantage). Innovative ways of managing these cost drivers can create cost reductions and competitive advantage.

cost efficiency *is a measure of the level of resources needed to create a given level of value*

- *Economies of scale* are traditionally an important source of cost advantage in manufacturing organisations, since the high capital costs

Exhibit 4.7 Sources of cost efficiency

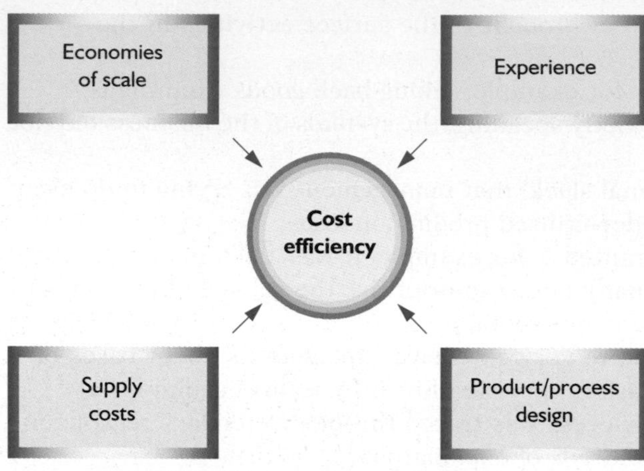

of plant need to be recovered over a high volume of output. In other industries, similar economies are sought in distribution or marketing costs. So organisations may sustain their competitive advantage through core competences in activities which maintain these scale advantages. This could include the ability to secure funding for large-scale investments, competence in mass-consumer advertising (to maintain volume) or the ability to develop and sustain global networks of partners or distributors.

- *Supply costs* clearly influence an organisation's overall cost position, and they are of particular importance to organisations which act as intermediaries where the value added through their own activities is low and the need to identify and manage input costs is critically important to success. Trading organisations sustain their competitive advantage in this way. The way in which supplier relationships are controlled is of major importance in sustaining this position and will be discussed in section 4.3.5 below. In commodity or currency trading, the key resource is information and hence competitive advantage can be gained through core competences which maintain higher-quality information than that of competitors. Traditionally, this was concerned with personal contacts and networks, but now the information technology (IT) capability of traders is critical to their success. There have been many innovations in how IT can 're-engineer' supply chains with vast reductions in cost.
- *Product/process design* also influences the cost position. Assessments of efficiency in production processes have been undertaken by many

organisations over a number of years through the monitoring of *capacity fill*, *labour productivity*, *yield* (from materials) or *working capital* utilisation. The important issue is to analyse which of these are the cost drivers that underpin the core competences of the organisation. For example, managing capacity fill has become a major competitive issue in many service industries, involving marketing special offers (while protecting the core business) and having the IT capability to analyse and optimise revenue. The highly complex pricing regimes in the airline industry are manifestations of this competitive activity. Illustration 4.3 shows that, in some industries, innovative thinking about the processes of product development may also improve efficiency.

In contrast, much less attention has been paid to how product *design* may contribute to the overall cost competitiveness of the company. Where it has been undertaken, it has tended to be limited to the production processes (e.g. ease of manufacture). However, product design will also influence costs in other parts of the value system – for example, in distribution or after-sales service. The ability to conceive of the design/cost relationship in this more holistic way and to gain the information needed for such an analysis requires successful organisations to have good contacts and relationships throughout their value chain (as discussed in section 4.3.5 below).

- *Experience*[10] is a key source of cost advantage and there have been many studies concerning the important relationship between the cumulative experience gained by an organisation and its unit costs – described as the *experience curve*. The premise of these findings is that, in any market segment of an industry, price levels tend to be very similar for similar products. Therefore, what makes one company more profitable than the next must be the level of its costs. The *experience curve* suggests that an organisation undertaking any activity learns to do it more efficiently over time, and hence develops core competences in this activity arising from its experience and producing cost advantage. Since companies with higher market share have more cumulative experience than others, it is clearly important to gain and hold market share, as discussed in Chapter 3. It is important to remember that it is the *relative market share* in definable market segments which matters. In highly fragmented industries it is quite possible to operate profitably without dominating a market. The objective is to have more experience than anyone else in that segment.

There are two important implications of the experience curve work which should influence organisations' thinking about their strategic position:

- Growth is not optional in many markets. If an organisation chooses to grow more slowly than the competition, it should expect the competitors to gain cost advantage in the longer term – through

STRATEGY IN ACTION
Illustration 4.3

Drivers of Cost Efficiency in Innovation: The Drug-testing Process

Improving cost efficiency requires identification of those factors where significant reductions in cost could be achieved.

Until recently, pharmaceutical companies have tended to operate inefficiently, largely because their success and ability to make money have not provided any incentive to become more efficient. However, a number of changes in the industry are now forcing companies to review their operations.

According to the UK Centre for Medicines Research, it takes $11\frac{1}{2}$ years for a typical drug to pass through basic research, clinical testing and regulatory approval. But the time taken up by both basic research and regulatory approval is reducing. This is due to a better understanding of the structure and functions of drug molecules at the basic research end of the continuum, and to pressure being applied by patient lobby groups forcing regulatory bodies to work more quickly. The net effect has been to increase the proportion of pre-product launch time taken up by clinical trials from 46 per cent in the 1970s to 55 per cent in the early 1990s. However, in an attempt to increase revenues, the larger pharmaceutical companies are now aiming to cut the time a drug spends in clinical trials from almost seven years to five. So competitive advantage is being sought through redesigning this trials process.

At the core of these efforts is information technology. It has been estimated that by collecting data electronically at hospitals and transferring it to a central location, analysis will be more rapid, such that the period between the end of a trial and the completion of statistical analysis can be cut from months to weeks. Pharmaceutical companies have also looked to reduce the number of different trials conducted, a factor encouraged by the increasing willingness of national regulators to accept results from trials held in foreign countries. Also, some companies have chosen to use contract research organisations (CROs) which specialise in running trials, to reduce the time taken up by this activity. While using CROs is not cheaper than in-house drug development, it is faster because the company does not need to recruit staff to run the trials.

Elsewhere, the basics of trial design are being questioned. For example, at the moment only responses to one size of dose are recorded. While it may be more difficult mechanically and statistically to test a range of doses in order to take account of differences in metabolism between individuals, it is argued that it may be more economical.

Questions

1. List the main contributing factors to speeding up the drug-testing process.
2. Give examples from other industries or public services where each of these factors might be equally relevant to reduction of cost in the 'value chain'.
3. Why does it often take the arrival of new entrants to the industry before such changes occur?

Source *Financial Times*, 11 January 1996.

Prepared by Sara Martin, Cranfield School of Management.

experience. The Japanese car manufacturers are an example of this phenomenon occurring on an international scale from the 1970s onwards. The core competences which helped an organisation establish itself in a market will be of little long-term competitive value in growing markets. They will be displaced by the need for new core competences – for example, in marketing and distribution to mass markets.

- Organisations should expect their real unit costs to decline year on year. In high-growth industries this will happen quickly, but even in mature industries this decline in costs should occur. Organisations which fail both to recognise and to have the innovative capability to respond to this are likely to suffer fierce competition. These cost reductions may relate to any of the activities of the organisation, including the management of linkages with the supply and distribution chain (section 4.3.5). Historically, one of the criticisms of public services was that their quasi-monopoly status had tended to shield them from the pressures to push down unit costs and provide better value for money.

4.3.4 Analysing Value Added (Effectiveness)[11]

Effectiveness is a measure of the level of value which can be created from a given level of resources. The assessment of effectiveness is essentially related to how well the organisation is matching its products or services to the identified needs of its chosen customers and the competences which underpin this effectiveness (or vice versa). Unlike cost analysis, the potential sources of value added or effectiveness are likely to be many and varied. Exhibit 4.8 summarises the kind of value-added features which may need to be provided to perform effectively. The key question is: what are the critically important features and the core competences which underpin these features? For example:

effectiveness *is a measure of the level of value which can be created from a given level of resources*

- How well matched are the product or service features to the requirements of customers? More importantly, is the added cost of providing unique features more than recovered through the value which customers place on this uniqueness (through better prices or improved budget allocation)? Are these features easily imitated by competitors? In organisations employing doctors, lawyers or teachers, the personal competence of individual professionals may be the key feature of the service from the customer viewpoint.
- Are the services which support the product matched with client expectations and, again, do these represent perceived value? For example, this could apply to systems of delivery or technical back-up.
- Are the systems for communicating with customers before, during and after purchase adding value to the relationship? For example, this could

Exhibit 4.8 Assessing effectiveness

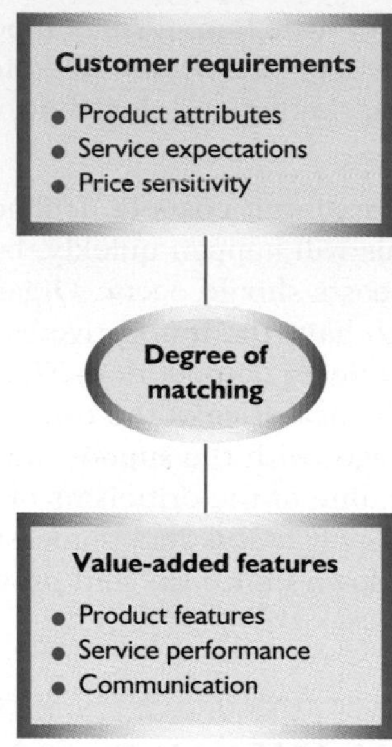

apply to the processes through which brand names or corporate image is built and communicated through the marketing literature or sales information. Any one of these could be a core competence.

If organisations are to compete on a value-added basis, it is important to remember that the detailed assessment of value added must be done from the viewpoint of the customer or user of the product or service. Although this may seem a self-evident statement, it may not be done by organisations for several reasons:

- Many manufacturers may be distanced from the final users by several intermediaries – other manufacturers and distributors. Although it is important to recognise the strategic role of intermediaries (as direct customers), there is a danger that an understanding of value to the final customer is filtered through or interpreted by these other parties rather than assessed directly. In other words, many manufacturers are out of touch with the realities of their markets. In the extreme, this could result in their product or component being substituted, for any of the reasons discussed in Chapter 3 (section 3.4.3).
- Value of the product or service is often conceived of by groups of professionals (such as designers, engineers, teachers or lawyers) and not tested out with customers or clients. This is an important criticism of many public service organisations. It can result in a false view of what

the core competences of the organisation are or need to be, as discussed in section 4.3.2 above. It will be seen in Chapter 10 that 'social controls' which operate within these professional groups may stifle innovation. The organisation needs the capability to break these rigidities.

- Customers' concept of value changes over time – either because they become more experienced (through repeat purchase) or because competitive offerings become available which offer better value for money. So value is a relative rather than an absolute measure. The automobile industry example in section 4.3.2 illustrated this point. In order to avoid some of these pitfalls it may be necessary to undertake research on customer perceived use value,[12] as discussed in Chapter 3 (see Illustration 3.8). Yet again this illustrates the point that organisations must be innovative – even in order just to stand still. An inability or unwillingness to innovate and change will take the organisation backwards.

4.3.5 Managing Linkages

Core competences in separate activities may provide competitive advantage for an organisation, but nevertheless over time may be imitated by competitors. Core competences are likely to be more robust and difficult to imitate if they relate to the management of *linkages* within the organisation's value chain and linkages into the supply and distribution chains. It is the management of these linkages which provides 'leverage' and levels of performance which are difficult to match (see Exhibit 4.9). **Leverage** is a measure of the improvement in performance achieved through the management of linkages between separate resources and activities. For example:

leverage *is a measure of the improvement in performance achieved through the management of linkages between separate resources and activities*

1. The ability to *co-ordinate* the activities of specialist teams or departments may create competitive advantage through improving value for money in the product or service. Specialisation of roles and responsibilities is common in most organisations and is one way in which high levels of competence in separate activities is achieved. However, it often results in a set of activities which are incompatible – different departments pulling in different directions – adding overall cost and diminishing value in the product or service.

   This management of internal linkages in the value chain could create competitive advantage in a number of ways:

   - There may be important linkages between the *primary activities*. For example, a decision to hold high levels of finished stock might ease production scheduling problems and provide for a faster response time to the customer. However, it will probably add to the overall cost of operations. An assessment needs to be made of whether the value added to the customer by this faster response through holding stocks is greater than the added cost.

Exhibit 4.9 Core competences through managing linkages

Type of Linkage	Type of Activity	Example
Internal linkage	Primary–primary	Interdepartmental co-ordination
	Primary–support	Computer-based operational systems
	Support–support	Managing innovation through people
External linkage	Vertical integration	Extend ownership of activities in supply/distribution chain
	Specification and checking	... of supplier/distributor performance
	Total quality management Merchandising activities	Working with suppliers/distributors to improve their performance
	Reconfigure value chain	... by deleting activities
	Strategic alliances	(see Chapter 7)

- It is easy to miss this issue of managing linkages between primary activities in an analysis if, for example, the organisation's competences in marketing activities and operations are assessed separately. The operations may look good because they are geared to high-volume, low-variety, low unit cost production. However, at the same time, the marketing team may be selling speed, flexibility and variety to the customers. So high levels of competence in separate activities are not enough if, as here, the competences are incompatible: that is, they are not related to the same view of what value for money means to the customer.
- The management of the linkages between a *primary activity* and a *support activity* may be the basis of a core competence. It may be key *investments in systems or infrastructure* or in the processes of innovation which provide the basis on which the company outperforms competition. Computer-based systems have been exploited in many different types of service organisation and have fundamentally transformed the customer experience. Travel bookings and hotel reservation systems are examples which other services would do well to emulate. They have created within these organisations the competence to provide both a better service and a service at reduced cost. They have allowed the organisations to create genuinely new services from these core competences or to expand rapidly into new markets.
- Linkages between different *support activities* may also be the basis of core competences. For example, the extent to which human resource development is in tune with new technologies has been a key feature in the implementation of new production and office

technologies. This is often concerned with how the processes of innovation are managed in an organisation. If innovation is to lead to competitive advantage, then this will rarely be achieved if innovation is not embraced by people within the organisation and other parts of the value chain. This will invariably require a reassessment of their roles and behaviours. In learning organisations (see Chapter 2, section 2.8.3), innovation and change become so embedded in the culture that they are a core competence of the organisation. They create competitive advantage as other organisations fail to break the rigidities which are stifling the innovative processes which are crucial to survival.

2. In addition to the management of internal linkage, competitive advantage may also be gained by the ability to *complement* or *co-ordinate* the organisation's own activities with those of suppliers, channels or customers.[13] Again, this could occur in a number of different ways:
   - *Vertical integration* attempts to improve performance through ownership of more parts of the value system, making more linkages internal to the organisation. However, the practical difficulties and costs of co-ordinating a wider range of internal activities can outweigh the theoretical benefits.
   - Within manufacturing industry the competence in *closely specifying* requirements and controlling the performance of suppliers (sometimes linked to quality checking and penalties for poor performance) can be critical to both quality enhancement and cost reduction.
   - A more recent philosophy has been *total quality management*,[14] which seeks to improve performance through closer working relationships between the various specialists within the value system. For example, many manufacturers will now involve their suppliers and distributors at the design stage of a product or project. In a sense this can be seen as pooling the innovative capability of the different players in the value chain. Not only does this prove to be more efficient but also it can result in a more holistic approach to innovation and the improvement of value for money.
   - The *merchandising* activities which manufacturers undertake with their distributors are now much improved and are an important means of increasing their control over distributor performance through training, incentives, joint promotions, in-store displays and so on. Again this can lead to much more innovative ways of bringing goods to market.
   - Performance may sometimes be improved by *reconfiguring* the value chain to reduce costs or increase effectiveness. This could mean deleting activities altogether. New entrants to industries might achieve entry in this way, since the incumbent organisations have 'taken for granted' that the value chain *must* be configured in the traditional way. For example, in the UK, Direct Line Insurance

revolutionised the household and motor insurance markets in the 1990s by cutting out the need for insurance brokers and going direct to individual householders. Many of the changes in the public services during the 1980s and 1990s (such as competitive tendering and internal markets) were attempts to improve performance through reconfiguring the value chain.

- There are often circumstances where the overall cost can be reduced (or value increased) by formal *collaborative arrangements* between different organisations in the value system. It will be seen in Chapter 7 that this is often the rationale behind joint ventures, such as the technology sharing in the international aerospace or telecommunications industries.

3. Most of these examples of improving performance through managing linkages emphasise the benefits which can arise through developing competences in various types of *co-ordination*. However, it needs to be remembered that in the best organisations these competences are not only concerned with systems and procedures, but found in the routines of the organisation and, as such, are embedded in the culture. So co-ordination occurs 'naturally' because people know their place in the wider picture or it is simply 'taken for granted' that activities are done in particular ways. Competences which are embedded within the culture are difficult to imitate and therefore are usually core competences.[15] The implication of this is that a critically important issue in sustaining value-for-money products and services is how the tacit knowledge and routines[16] within the organisation are maintained and developed in ways which match the intended strategies. This is discussed in the later sections of the book – particularly Chapter 10. The downside of culturally sustained core competences is that they can become *key rigidities*.[17] **Key rigidities** are activities which are deeply embedded and difficult to change.

key rigidities *are activities which are deeply embedded and difficult to change*

Illustration 4.4 shows how Levi Strauss attempted to improve its management of both internal and external linkages as a source of competitive advantage.

4.3.6 Robustness

It has already been noted that the strategic importance of an organisation's competences relates to how easy or difficult they are to imitate. This is why competences in managing linkages between activities tend to be more robust than simply competences in separate activities. But robustness also relates to the specific nature and 'ownership' of the organisation's competences.

- It depends on who *owns* the competence and whether it is easily transferable. For example, in professional service organisations, some services are built around the competence of specific *individuals* – such as the surgeon in 'leading edge' medicine. Clearly, the

STRATEGY IN ACTION
Illustration 4.4

Human Resources and the Value Chain at Levi Strauss

Being viewed as a good company can lead to favourable relationships with stakeholders, which, in turn, can result in competitive advantage. Each link in the value chain presents an opportunity to affect the development of reputation and needs to be managed with this in mind.

External Linkages

In response to dramatic price competition from countries with lower labour costs, Levi Strauss has sought to develop relationships with manufacturers in low-wage countries in such areas as Latin America and Southeast Asia. In the process of doing so, the company recognised that explicit and strict global sourcing guidelines, covering ethical policies to environmental requirements, would enable them to avoid relationships with firms whose practices could threaten their reputation. Application of the guidelines has led Levi to make some difficult decisions: for example, withdrawing from partnerships in the People's Republic of China owing to human rights problems.

However, it is much more common for the organisation to work with suppliers to help them comply. An example is a supplier factory in Bangladesh which was found to employ children under the age of 14. Rather than refusing to work with the organisation, Levi Strauss decided to pay for 25 under-age employees to go to school, while the contractors continued to pay them as if they were working and agreed to hire them back once they achieved legal working age. This example shows a strong commitment to the reputational effects of supplier relations within the value chain segment of inbound logistics.

Internal Linkages

Opportunities are seen to exist which enhance reputation through the way in which Levi Strauss utilises both human and physical resources in the manufacturing process. Given the labour intensity of production in the garment industry, the human resource management support function plays an especially important role. A reputation for fairness and progressive employee practices results in an exceptional labour pool and the foundation for an above-average company workforce. Several human resource initiatives within Levi Strauss have contributed to its overall firm reputation. The broadest example is its aspirations statement, which addresses issues like employee opportunities and empowerment, ethics, communication and the need to have fun in all endeavours.

Specifically, the operations benefit from this reputation as this aspirations statement is translated into everyday practice on the shopfloor. For example, Levi Strauss pursues empowerment by encouraging employees actively to develop their own abilities through company-sponsored training and development, and to accept as much authority and responsibility as is within their capabilities. Further, millions of dollars have been invested to convert assembly lines into team manufacturing processes. As well as enhancing the quality of life – including improving health and safety conditions, and reducing tedium – greater efficiencies have been achieved, such as a 70 per cent reduction in time taken to produce each item, reduced need for resewing, lower absenteeism, lower turnover and fewer days lost to injury.

Questions

1. Using the categories in Exhibit 4.9, identify the ways in which advantage was gained by Levi Strauss through managing linkages.
2. Repeat the processes for another organisation of your choice.

Source S. Preece, C. Fleisher and J. Toccacelli, 'Building a reputation along the value chain at Levi Strauss', *Long Range Planning*, vol. 28, no. 6 (1995), pp. 88–98.

Prepared by Sara Martin, Cranfield School of Management.

organisation is vulnerable to the loss of this individual's services. Other (routine) services are sustained through a *corporate* competence to organise and deliver the service – for example, in orthopaedic clinics. These are more robust competences as they are less dependent on one individual.

- Most organisations have difficult decisions to make about which activities (in the value chain) they should undertake themselves and which should be outsourced. Usually, it is advisable to ensure that core competences reside within the organisation, since they fundamentally underpin current strategies and may be the basis for new avenues of strategic development. The problem is that organisations may not have analysed adequately which of their competences are core and which are threshold, as mentioned above. Or, perhaps more frequently, they may not regard 'new' competences as core and hence may continue to access them from external sources, inhibiting the organisation's ability to learn and to develop these competences and increasing their vulnerability to these 'suppliers'.[18] The case example at the end of this chapter illustrates these issues of outsourcing. IT developments in organisations have been blighted by this problem, in the sense that managers in the organisation have failed properly to comprehend how IT investments can transform the way in which activities are performed. In turn, the external suppliers, or consultants, do not understand the business well enough to tailor their advice and ensure that it becomes properly embedded in the organisation.

4.3.7 Tacit and Explicit Knowledge

A key issue emphasised throughout this book is that many of the competences of an organisation are embedded in the tacit knowledge and routines of the organisation that can be difficult to identify and explain. This might, of course, give an organisation short-term competitive advantage as competitors find such embedded knowledge difficult to imitate. However, longer-term competitive advantage is more likely to be secured by organisations who are most competent at managing *knowledge creation*. Nonaka and Takeuchi provide a categorisation of knowledge creation processes which can be used as a checklist against which to assess how competent an organisation is at the process of innovation.[19] Based on their research with Japanese companies, they distinguish between two types of knowledge. *Explicit knowledge* is codified, 'objective' knowledge that is transmitted in formal systematic language. In contrast, *tacit knowledge* is personal, context-specific and therefore hard to formalise and communicate. Usually, competence requires both kinds of knowledge. For example, a driving instructor can drive a car through tacit knowledge, but to teach others requires explicit knowledge of the driving process.

Nonaka and Takeuchi argue that truly innovative companies are ones that can modify and enlarge the knowledge of individuals to create a 'spiral

Exhibit 4.10 Knowledge-creating processes

From \ To	Tacit knowledge	Explicit knowledge
Tacit knowledge	Socialisation (sympathised knowledge)	Externalisation (conceptual knowledge)
Explicit knowledge	Internalisation (operational knowledge)	Combination (systematic knowledge)

Source I. Nonaka and H. Takeuchi, *The Knowledge Creating Company*, Oxford University Press, 1995.

of interaction' between tacit and explicit knowledge through the four processes shown in Exhibit 4.10.

- *Socialisation* is a process of sharing experiences between individuals and thereby allowing them to acquire tacit knowledge from others without a formal system or the use of language. The apprenticeship model in craft industries is a good example.
- *Externalisation* is the process of articulating tacit knowledge into explicit concepts. This can be very difficult. It may require a combination of different methods such as model building, metaphors or analogies.
- *Combination* is the process of systematising concepts into a 'knowledge system', for example by linking separate bodies of explicit knowledge. Individuals achieve this through formal methods of meetings, documents or computer networks.
- *Internalisation* is the process of embodying explicit knowledge into tacit knowledge. It is closely related to 'learning by doing'.

Illustration 4.5 gives examples of all four processes.

STRATEGY IN ACTION
Illustration 4.5

Innovation and Knowledge Creation

Truly innovative companies have high levels of competence in managing the 'spiral of interaction' between tacit and explicit knowledge through the four processes shown in Exhibit 4.10.

Socialisation (Tacit to Tacit)

Honda Honda set up 'brainstorming camps' to solve problems in development projects. The meetings were usually away from the workplace and were open to every employee who was interested in the project; status and credentials were never challenged. Such camps were not just a forum for creative dialogue but also a medium for sharing experiences and enhancing mutual trust among participants. The camps reoriented the 'mental models' of all individuals but not in a forceful way.

Externalisation (Tacit to Explicit)

Canon The case of Canon's mini-copier is a good example of how an analogy was used effectively for product development. The major barrier to lowering costs was the internal drum. In the end a disposable drum was used. The origin of this idea came from Hiroshi Tanaka (team leader of the taskforce) who explored how the technology for manufacturing beer cans could be used for a copier drum.

Combination (Explicit to Explicit)

Kraft Kraft was a manufacturer of dairy and processed foods and utilised EPOS (electronic point of sale) data from retailers to create new sales systems and methods. Kraft developed an information-intensive marketing programme called 'micro-merchandising' which provided supermarkets with timely and detailed recommendations on the optimal merchandise mix supported by sales promotions based on the analyses of their EPOS data. Their analyses of data produced a unique classification of stores and shoppers and were capable of pinpointing who shopped where and how.

Internalisation (Explicit to Tacit)

General Electric Documents, manuals and oral stories help people internalise what they have experienced and also to transmit it to others. GE documented all customer enquiries and complaints (more than 14,000 per day) and then 'programmed' them into 1.5 million potential problems and their solutions. The system is equipped with an on-line diagnosis function which uses artificial intelligence technology to provide telephone operators with quick answers to enquiries. If solutions are not found, 12 full-time specialist repair experts produce solutions on the spot and these are then programmed into the database. Crucially, new product development staff regularly spend time with the telephone operators and 12 specialists to 're-experience' the customer problem-solution knowledge.

The Spiral of Knowledge Creation

New product development often occurs from a spiral through the four modes above. *Socialisation* processes (perhaps like the brainstorming camps in Honda) help define the broad 'field' or boundaries within which the product will sit. *Externalisation* will take this rich mix of tacit knowledge and convert it to a 'product concept'. This product concept is 'tested' and 'justified' against other bodies of explicit knowledge in the organisation such as market analysis, profit targets, production capability, i.e. the process of *combination*. Out of this comes the product prototype. The organisation's commercialisation of the new product now crucially depends on *internalisation* of this knowledge, perhaps through piloting.

Questions

1. Why is tacit knowledge important to competitive advantage?
2. What are the advantages and disadvantages of trying to make tacit knowledge explicit?
3. Does the spiral of knowledge have to start with 'socialisation'?

Source I. Nonaka and H. Takeuchi, *The Knowledge Creating Company*, Oxford University Press, 1995.

Organisations that can manage the interaction and linkages between these two types of knowledge (through the four processes) are likely to develop levels of competence in the process of innovation which are very difficult to imitate. So this can be a core competence of the organisation.

4.4 COMPARATIVE ANALYSIS AND BENCHMARKING

An organisation's strategic capability is ultimately assessed in *relative* terms. This section will look at a number of different *bases* for this comparative analysis or benchmarking of an organisation's capability.

The preceding sections have considered how analysing the resources and competences of an organisation can build up an understanding of the competitive position of the organisation in its industry. It is also valuable to assess how these resources and competences have changed and developed historically, since this gives insights into why the organisation has chosen, or been forced, to change.

This section discusses these two different bases of comparison, the *historical* and the *industry norm*, as valuable means of improving the understanding of an organisation's strategic capability. It will also be suggested that more valuable insights can be developed by comparing *best practice* beyond the industry in which the organisation currently operates. The role of financial analyses in assessing organisational competence will also be discussed (section 4.4.4).

4.4.1 Historical Analysis

Historical analysis looks at the deployment of the resources and the performance of an organisation by comparison with previous years in order to identify any significant changes. Typically, financial ratios such as sales/capital and sales/employees will be used, and any significant variations in the proportions of resources devoted to different activities will be identified. This can reveal trends which might not otherwise be apparent.

historical analysis *looks at the deployment of the resources and the performance of an organisation by comparison with previous years in order to identify any significant changes*

It is important that historical comparisons are made against a realistic set of expectations. For example, a requirement for innovation and *continuous improvement* means that historical performance is something to be improved upon not simply matched. This has been the subject of heated debate in many public services as performance indicators have been developed and continuous year-on-year efficiency gains have been demanded.

4.4.2 Comparison with Industry Norms

An historical analysis can be improved significantly by the additional comparison with similar factors analysed for the industry as a whole[20] or

STRATEGY IN ACTION
Illustration 4.6

Comparative Analyses using Local Authority League Tables

Council tax payers can judge the value for money provided by their council using annually produced league tables to compare authorities across England and Wales.

(a) Average council tax bills (£)

	Councils	1996/97	1995/96	% Increase
England		**541.51**	**511.60**	**5.80**
Conservative	19	525.48	525.65	−0.03
Independent	13	528.97	505.38	4.67
Labour	165	521.90	490.70	6.36
Lib Dem	52	569.60	561.27	1.48
Hung	109	562.07	521.61	7.76

(b) Total expenditure per head of population

Borough Council	£ per head
London Boroughs: average	911.00
Tower Hamlets	1,452.92
Richmond	584.88
County Councils: average	629.00
Powys	795.35
Dorset	547.81
Metropolitan Councils: average	761.00
Manchester	1,005.50
Solihull	606.20

(c) Averages for 15 worst-performing councils

	1993/94	1994/95	Improvement
Average time taken to relet council homes	14 wks	10 wks	29%
% of tenants in arrears of 13 weeks or more	20%	14%	30%
Rent collected as % of rent due	93%	96%	3%
% householder planning applications processed in 8 weeks	45%	60%	33%
% council tax benefit claims processed in 14 days	29%	61%	110%
% of council tax collected compared to amount budgeted to collect	84%	89%	6%
Average length of stay of homeless families in B&B accommodation	46 wks	26 wks	43%
% housing benefit claims processed in 14 days	35%	68%	94%
% student grants paid on time	54%	88%	63%
% pupils with special needs assessed in 6 months	2%	18%	Improved by a factor of 9

According to the Audit Commission, the league tables for 1994/95 (excerpts of which are set out below) illustrate that 'local authorities are remarkably complacent about the efficient delivery of basic services. While those councils which performed worst in 1993/94 improved, the overwhelming majority made little progress. Most councils provide a majority of services to a high average level, but there are still wide variations between the best and worst performances for similar services provided by comparable authorities. The figures further show that neither political control nor prosperity guarantees good performance.'

Sources *The Independent*, *The Times*, *Financial Times*, 21 March 1996.

Prepared by Sara Martin, Cranfield School of Management.

Questions

1. What conclusions might the chief executive of individual authorities and financial journalists draw from these data?
2. What are your conclusions about the benefits of performance indicators and comparative league tables of this type. Use other examples to support your case if you wish.

between similar public service providers. An **industry norm analysis** compares the relative performance of organisations in the same industry (or public service) against an agreed set of performance indicators. Illustration 4.6 shows that these comparisons (particularly in the public services) are often in the form of 'league tables'. Again, this helps to put the organisation's resources and performance into perspective and reflects the fact that it is the *relative* position of a company which matters in assessing its strategic capability. This analysis needs to be undertaken in relation to the organisation's separate activities and not just its overall product or market position.

an **industry norm analysis** *compares the relative performance of organisations in the same industry (or public service) against an agreed set of performance indicators*

One danger of industry norm analysis (whether it be in the private or public sector) is that the whole industry may be performing badly and losing out competitively to other industries that can satisfy customers' needs in different ways, or to different countries.

Therefore, if an industry comparison is performed, it is wise to make some assessment of how resources and competences compare not only with direct competitors, but also with those in other countries and industries. This can be done by looking at a few of the more important measures of resource utilisation, such as stock turnover and yield from raw materials.

The shortcomings of industry norm analysis have encouraged organisations to develop different approaches to inter-company comparisons. Rather than attempting to establish the 'norm', there is a search for *best practice* and the establishment of *benchmarks of performance* related to that best practice. For example, *competitor profiles*[21] are detailed dossiers about the resources and competences of competitors and their relative performance activity by activity and not just overall. The greatest value of this type of best-practice analysis is to be gained if comparisons are also made *beyond* the industry, as will now be discussed.

4.4.3 Benchmarking[22]

Benchmarking seeks to assess the competences of an organisation against 'best in class' wherever that is to be found. Benchmarking can start in simple ways – often revealing some startling differences. It has, however, been developed into a much more comprehensive audit of organisations' competences and critical success factors in both the public and private sectors.

benchmarking *seeks to assess the competences of an organisation against 'best in class' wherever that is to be found*

For example, ICI Paints, with over fifty manufacturing operations around the world, started by assembling metrics of key performance indicators and sending 'league tables' to the local managers on a quarterly basis. Soon the lower performers were seeking advice from the 'best in class' as to how their efficiency was achieved. Within a short period, requests for the publication of 'best practice' information were forthcoming. Perhaps surprisingly, not only the lower performers improved but also those in the middle and top echelons by, on average, similar amounts.

STRATEGY IN ACTION
Illustration 4.7

Benchmarking Innovation: DNA-based Technologies

For organisations dealing with 'state-of-the-art' innovation, benchmarking can be used to establish research, development and testing priorities.

DNA-based technologies are of central importance to the understanding, diagnosis and treatment of many diseases such as cancer and respiratory and cardiovascular diseases. There is a considerable amount of research spending in both academic and commercial laboratories into the development and application of these technologies. Despite the considerable commercial advantage that would accrue from any major breakthrough individual laboratories do need to ensure that they are deploying their research effort and money effectively. Benchmarking is one way in which organisations in the same field can share their expertise and wisdom whilst still operating independently.

One benchmarking study was conducted in the USA by an 'expert opinion benchmarking exchange' – a survey among leading scientists heading 45 DNA laboratories. It sought to establish the best views on a number of related issues ranging from which strands of DNA research were most likely to produce practical outcomes to the disease areas where DNA-diagnostics were most likely to prove successful. This peer review benchmarking also established a collective opinion on what were seen as the leading-edge organisations on the various aspects of DNA-diagnostic research and applications.

There were practical outcomes of the benchmarking exercise for the participants. They were able to use the results to review their own research priorities. From a commercial viewpoint it also provided them with a basis on which to decide potential joint ventures and partnerships and to assess potential companies for acquisition.

Questions

1. In general, what are the dangers in benchmarking by this expert opinion approach and how might these be avoided?
2. From the point of view of an individual laboratory, list the merits and demerits of participating in a 'peer review' benchmarking exercise of this type.

Source Best Practices Benchmarking & Consulting LLC website.

Skandia (see Illustration 10.1 in Chapter 10) also compared figures for similar processes in its different business units and then carried out a macrobenchmarking study across the insurance industry to identify critical areas and potentials. This consortium approach involved insurance companies across Scandinavia, the Netherlands and the UK. Having established 'the large numbers' Skandia then embarked on a series of microbenchmarking studies involving detailed process analysis and an understanding of the perceived best process. This was then implemented across its operations. Illustration 4.7 shows how benchmarking was undertaken by state-of-the-art DNA-based technologies.

The potential for change from benchmarking is enhanced by partnerships across industries. Hewlett Packard, the 1995 winner of the European Award, contrasted its phone handling on lease agreements with a major telephone banking operation. The UK Prison Services compared queuing problems during visiting periods with the Post Office Counters operations. Karolinska Hospital in Sweden has achieved significant improvements in the speed of handling patient admission and surgical procedures through a study of a major automotive plant, and British Airways improved aircraft maintenance and turnround time by studying the processes surrounding Grand Prix racing pit stops.[23]

Frequently it is the cultural factors that are most significant to the individuals involved in the study and prevent direct adoption of the processes studied. Thus, a French hotel chain compared themselves with the greeting of guests at a Dominican monastery. Although the provision of washing and refreshment facilities on reception was not considered to be appropriate for the hotels, the paradigm as to what was possible was broken and led to a reconceptualisation of the process over the medium term.

The UK Customs and Excise won the 1996 European Best Practice Benchmarking Award™ for an innovative adaptation of benchmarking in order to meet the requirements of a public sector organisation to market test the value of their activities. The concept, to which they gave the title 'hybrid benchmarking' involved carrying out a benchmarking exercise to compare efficiencies within the private sector for each of their processes. Any that could be performed better externally were contracted out, whilst improvements of more than 20 per cent overall were achieved through the scrutiny of those practices which continued within the organisation.

It has been argued in this chapter that the competitive advantage of an organisation is likely to be underpinned by a combination of (some) unique resources, core competences in the performance of separate activities, and core competences concerned with the management of linkages between activities. Benchmarking can be undertaken at each of these 'levels', as shown in Exhibit 4.11.

Base budget reviews[24] have been used to build benchmarking into a wider strategic review by some organisations in which historically the idea of external comparison has been ignored or even resisted. Such reviews are most effective where they are applied to strategic business units or service areas and four fundamental questions are asked. First, *why* are these products or services provided at all? Second, why are they provided in *that particular way*? Third, what are the examples of *best practice* elsewhere? Fourth, how should the activities be *reshaped* in the light of these comparisons? Although this process is at least partially subjective, there are many examples of its successful application.

4.4.4 Financial Analyses[25]

Financial information and analyses may be one way in which assessments of competence can be made. Many of the measures listed in Exhibit 4.11

Exhibit 4.11 Benchmarking – at three levels

Level of Benchmarking	Through	Examples of Measures
Resources	Resource audit	Quantity of resources, e.g. ● revenue/employee ● capital intensity Quality of resources, e.g. ● qualifications of employees ● age of machinery ● uniqueness (e.g. patents)
Competences in separate activities	Analysing activities	Sales calls per salesperson Output per employee Materials wastage
Competences through managing linkages	Analysing overall performances	Market share Profitability Productivity

would be expressed in financial terms. Inevitably, those inside the organisation (particularly managers) are likely to have access to considerably more information than other stakeholders. The first important issue to recognise is that there will not be a single agreed view on how to assess the financial performance of a company, since different stakeholders will have different expectations of the company. This concept of stakeholder expectations is covered more fully in Chapter 5, but for the current purpose it is important to distinguish between three different types of financial expectation which will influence the view taken on an organisation's competences and performance, and the type of financial information needed or used in such an assessment:

- *Shareholders* are essentially concerned with assessing the quality of their *investment* and the payoffs they can expect both in dividends and in capital growth (reflected in share price). Therefore, they will be mainly concerned with measures such as earnings per share, price/earnings (P/E) ratio and dividend yield. Comparisons across companies are a key measure of attractiveness to investors and a basis of their judgement on the overall competence of the organisation. Shareholder value analysis is discussed in more detail in Chapter 8 (section 8.3.1).
- *Bankers* and other providers of interest-bearing loans are concerned about the *risk* attached to their loans and the competence with

which this is managed. A consistently good track record could be regarded (in itself) as a core competence by bankers and a reason to invest further with some companies and not others. This might be assessed through looking at the capital structure of the company – particularly the gearing ratio (of debt to equity), which indicates how sensitive the solvency of the company is to changes in its profit position. Interest cover is a similar measure which relates interest payments to profit.

- *Suppliers* and *employees* are likely to be concerned with the *liquidity* of the company, which is a measure of its ability to meet short-term commitments to creditors and wages. Bankers will share this concern because a deteriorating liquidity position may require correction through loans and the increased risk profile discussed above. Again, a track record in this area could be a core competence – for example, in improving supplier relationships, resulting in discounts or improved credit.

The following issues need to be borne in mind when using financial analyses to assess organisational competences:

- Financial ratios (stock turnover, sales margin, etc.) are of no importance in themselves. It is the implications of these ratios which are important, and these may not emerge until some sensible basis of comparison is established (see above). Even then a word of warning is necessary. It may be that an organisation is successfully differentiating itself from its competitors by extra spending in selected areas (e.g. advertising). Provided this results in added value (possibly through price or market share), this may well be a defensible spending pattern.
- Financial analyses which relate to those activities which are core competences of the organisation will be particularly useful. For example, rate of stock turnover may be important to a high street store, unit profit margins to a market stallholder, and sales volume to a capital-intensive manufacturer. It is important to be selective in the use of ratios.
- It should be remembered that core competences may change over time and so should the key financial measures to monitor. For example, during the introduction of a new product, the key factor may be establishing *sales volume*; once established, *profit per unit* might be most important, whilst during decline, *cash flow* may be essential to support the introduction of the next generation of products.

A major concern about traditional financial analysis from a strategic perspective is that it has tended to exclude two key stakeholder groups:

- *Community* – who are concerned with the *social cost* of an organisation's activities, such as pollution or marketing. This is rarely accounted for in traditional financial analyses, but it is an issue of growing concern. Matters of business ethics will be discussed more fully in Chapter 5 (section 5.4). Failure to pay proper attention to these issues could be a source of strategic weakness.

- *Customers* – who are concerned about value for money in products or services. This assessment is rarely made in traditional financial analyses, the implication being that companies which survive profitably in a competitive environment *must* be providing value for money. Where competitive pressures have not existed, such as among many public services, there are now serious attempts to develop performance measures more related to value for money. Financial analysis can assist this process only if information is collected for that purpose. Many management information systems are not geared to such a detailed analysis of separate value activities, making this process difficult. In the UK in the early 1990s, political weight was put behind this process by the development of a *citizens' charter* for many public services. This defined what was expected of each public service in terms of client expectations and value-for-money performance standards (see, for example, Illustration 5.2).

4.5 ASSESSING THE BALANCE OF THE ORGANISATION

The previous sections have been concerned with analysing the competences of an organisation through looking in detail at the separate activities which are undertaken and also the way that linkages are managed between these separate activities and within the wider value system. Such an analysis should provide a useful analysis of an organisation's competences within its separate strategic business units. However, in many organisations the strategic capability of the organisation will also be determined by the extent to which the organisation's business units are *balanced as a whole*.

portfolio analysis *analyses the balance of an organisation's strategic business units*

Portfolio analysis[26] analyses the balance of an organisation's strategic business units. It is a key aspect of strategic capability to ensure that the portfolio is strong. Portfolio analysis can be used to describe the current range of SBUs and to assess the 'strength' of the mix both historically and against future scenarios. The Boston Consultancy Group (BCG) proposed one of the first ways of classifying business units – in relation to market growth and company relative market share. Exhibit 4.12 shows this original matrix together with a number of other matrices.

The growth per share matrix permits SBUs to be examined in relation to (a) market (segment) share and (b) the growth rate of that market. Market growth rate is important for a SBU seeking to dominate a market because it may be easier to gain dominance when a market is in its growth state. In a state of maturity, a market is likely to be stable, with customer loyalties fairly fixed, so it is more difficult to gain share. But if all competitors in the growth stage are trying to gain market share, competition will be very fierce: so it will be necessary to invest in that

Exhibit 4.12 Product portfolio matrices

Market share

Market growth		High	Low
	High	Stars	Question marks
	Low	Cash cows	Dogs

(a) The original Boston Consulting Group Matrix (BCG)

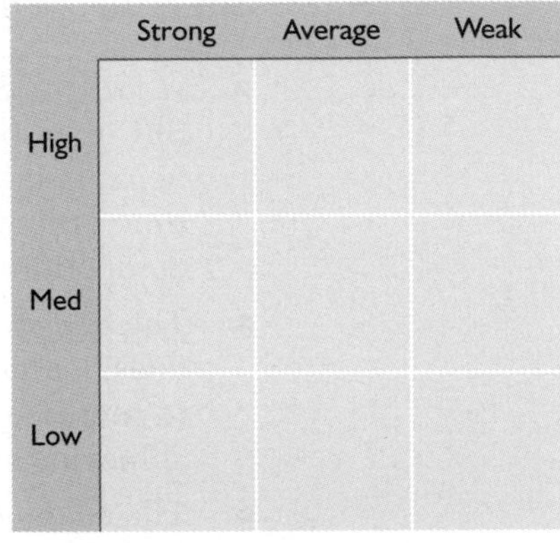

(b) Attractiveness matrix*

Competitive position

Stage of product / market evolution		Strong	Average	Weak
	Development			
	Growth			
	Shakeout			
	Maturity			
	Decline			

(c) Product / market evolution matrix

Public need and support + funding attractiveness		High	Low
	High	Public-sector star	Political hot box
	Low	Golden fleece	Back drawer issue

Ability to serve effectively

(d) Public sector portfolio matrix

*Also known as the 'directional policy matrix' (see section 3.5.4)

Sources Diagram (a) from research by the BCG. Diagram (b) adapted from C. Hofer and D. Schendel, *Strategy Formulation: Analytical concepts*. Reprinted by permission from p. 32; copyright 1979 by West Publishing Company. All rights reserved. Diagram (c) from C. Hofer, *Conceptual Constructs for Formulating Corporate and Business Strategies*, Intercollegiate Case Clearing House, Boston, no. 9-378-754, 1977, p. 3, and adapted by C. Hofer and D. Schendel, *Strategy Formulation: Analytical concepts*, p. 34. Diagram (d) from J.R. Montanari and J.S. Bracker, *Strategic Management Journal*, vol. 7, no. 3 (1986), reprinted by permission of John Wiley & Sons Ltd.

SBU in order to gain share and market dominance. Moreover, it is likely that such a SBU will need to price low or spend high amounts on advertising and selling, or both. This strategy is one of high risk unless this low-margin activity is financed by products earning higher profit levels. This leads to the idea of a balanced mix of SBUs.

- A *star* is a SBU which has a high market share in a growing market. The SBU may be spending heavily to gain that share, but experience curve benefits (see section 4.3.3) should mean that costs are reducing over time and, it is to be hoped, at a rate faster than that of the competition's.
- The *question mark* (or problem child) is also in a growing market, but does not have a high market share. It may be necessary to spend heavily to increase market share, but if so, it is unlikely that the SBU is achieving sufficient cost reduction benefits to offset such investments.
- The *cash cow* has a high market share in a mature market. Because growth is low and market conditions are more stable, the need for heavy marketing investment is less. But high relative market share means that the SBU should be able to maintain unit cost levels below those of competitors. The cash cow should then be a cash provider (e.g. to finance question marks).
- *Dogs* have low share in static or declining markets and are thus the worst of all combinations. They may be a cash drain and use up a disproportionate amount of company time and resources.

Although portfolio analyses can be useful in assessing how strategic business units contribute to the strategic capability of the organisation, some caution needs to be exercised in their use:

- There can be practical difficulties in deciding what exactly 'high' and 'low' (growth and share) can mean in a particular situation.
- The analysis should be applied to *strategic business units* (i.e. a *bundle* of products or services and the associated market *segments*) not to whole markets.
- Corporate management must develop the ability and devote time to reviewing the role of each strategic business unit in the overall mix of company activities. This is an important 'parenting' responsibility of the corporate centre in divisionalised organisations, and will be discussed in Chapters 6 and 9.
- Some authors are somewhat sceptical of whether the corporate headquarters really do add value to the company through these processes of buying, selling, developing or running down individual units to keep the portfolio balanced. They suggest that the free market might well allocate resources more effectively if the activities were separated and the corporate centre closed down. This issue will be discussed more fully in Chapter 10.

- The original BCG analysis concentrated on the needs of a business to plan its cash flow requirements across its portfolio. So *cash cows* will be used to create the funds needed for innovation and the development of *question marks* and *stars*. However, little is said about the behavioural implications of such a strategy. How does central management motivate the managers of *cash cows*, who see all their hard-earned surpluses being invested in other businesses? Indeed, perhaps the single factor which makes the creation and management of a balanced portfolio difficult in practice is the jealousy which can arise between the various strategic business units.
- In many organisations the critical resource to be planned and balanced will not be cash, but the innovative capacity, which consists of the time and creative energy of the organisation's managers, designers, engineers, etc. *Question marks* and *stars* are very demanding on these types of resource.
- The portfolio approach has also been used in the public sector,[27] as seen in Exhibit 4.12(d). Here the key judgements are concerned with the organisation's ability to provide perceived value for money with the resources which are likely to be available, and the political requirement to offer services. This latter point is often forgotten by public sector managers when reviewing their portfolio of activities for the future. A provider of public services will often be mandated to provide some statutory services, i.e. to keep a wider portfolio of services in order to satisfy the political objectives.
- The position of *dogs* is often misunderstood. Certainly, there may be some products which need immediate deletion – but even then there may be political difficulties if they are the brain-child of people with power within the organisation. However, other dogs may have a useful place in the portfolio. They may be necessary to complete the product range and provide a credible presence in the market. They may be held for defensive reasons – to keep competitors out. They may be capable of revitalisation.

Despite these concerns, however, portfolio analysis remains an important method of assessing the balance of an organisation and identifying strategic choices (see Chapter 6, section 6.4.1).

4.6 IDENTIFICATION OF KEY ISSUES

The last major aspect of resource analysis is the identification of the key issues arising from previous analyses. It is only at this stage of the analysis that a sensible assessment can be made of the major strengths and weaknesses of an organisation and their strategic importance. The analysis then starts to be useful as a basis against which to judge future courses of action.

4.6.1 SWOT Analysis[28]

a **SWOT analysis** *summarises the key issues from an analysis of the business environment and the strategic capability of an organisation*

A **SWOT analysis** summarises the key issues from an analysis of the business environment and the strategic capability of an organisation. So it brings together the main issues raised in this chapter and the previous one. The aim is to identify the extent to which the current strategy of an organisation and its more specific strengths and weaknesses are relevant to, and capable of, dealing with the changes taking place in the business environment. It can also be used to assess whether there are opportunities to exploit further the unique resources or core competences of the organisation. SWOT stands for strengths, weaknesses, opportunities and threats, but rather than just listing these in terms of managers' perceptions, the idea is to undertake a more structured analysis so as to yield findings which can contribute to the formulation of strategy. The procedure can be undertaken as follows:

- Identify the key changes in the organisation's environment following the analyses outlined in Chapter 3. While there is no fixed number which should be agreed upon, it is helpful if the list does not exceed seven or eight key points.
- The same process should then be undertaken in terms of the resource profile and competences of the organisation, following the analysis outlined in this chapter to identify the organisation's strengths and weaknesses. It is useful to keep the total list to no more than eight points. It is important to avoid overgeneralising this analysis and to keep to quite specific points: a statement such as 'poor management' means very little and could be interpreted in any number of ways. If it really means that senior managers have, historically, not been good at managing change in the organisation, that is a more specific and more useful point.

When this procedure is completed, the analysis should look something like the completed Illustration 4.8. This should provide some useful strategic insights. For example, Illustration 4.8 shows that the organisation already has many of the competences needed to meet the rising public expectations of health care. It also reveals that its good links with GPs were of particular benefit in meeting many of the key issues in the environment. Some issues (such as demographic trends – the ageing population) could be either opportunities or threats, depending on the extent to which the organisation can capitalise on its strengths in innovation and links with social services while coping with the redistribution of financial resources and the attitudes of providers (e.g. hospitals) to these changes. An analysis of perceived weaknesses should also recognise that their importance varies depending on the types of strategy the organisation is likely to pursue. For example, the concerns about the providers dominating the agenda would diminish if the health care provision became more market driven – an extreme example would be by providing citizens with vouchers to purchase their own health care from GPs and hospitals. In these circumstances, the health authority would be the key driver of demand for specific health care services by the

STRATEGY IN ACTION
Illustration 4.8

SWOT analysis

A SWOT analysis can be a useful way to summarise the relationship between key environmental influences, the strategic capability of the organisation and hence the agenda for developing new strategies.

The table below is from a SWOT analysis undertaken by a district health authority in the UK in 1996. The role of the health authorities at that time was to 'purchase' health care on behalf of their communities both directly from hospitals and indirectly through health care practitioners (GP fundholders). The organisation concluded that the most important areas of strength were the links with GPs and the capacity for innovation – and that these were core competences. Other areas needed development, such as information systems and performance assessments of different medical treatments.

Questions

1. Is the author correct in concluding that the items with the highest scores (either positive or negative) in the right-hand columns are the main strengths or weaknesses (respectively)?
2. She also concludes that the first two items are core competences? Could she have concluded this from this analysis alone?
3. What do the overall scores at the foot of the table tell you about the ability of the organisation to cope with the situation that it faces?
4. From your answers to questions 1–3 list the main benefits and limitations of SWOT analysis.

Source Debbie Sloan, MBA student. Reproduced with permission.

STRENGTHS AND WEAKNESSES	KEY ISSUES IN THE ENVIRONMENT							
	Politics/ legislation	Link between deprivation and health	New technologies (medical)	Rising public expectation	Demographic trends	Competitive market	+	–
Main strengths								
Capacity for innovation	+	+	+	++	+	++	8	0
Good GP links	+	++	+	+	+	+	7	0
Committed employees	+	+	+	+	0	+	5	0
Good joint working with social services	+	++	0	+	+	–	5	1
Main weaknesses								
Lack of outcome measures	–	– –	–	–	–	–	0	7
Information measurement systems	–	–	–	–	–	– –	0	7
Provider-dominated agenda	0	0	– –	– –	– –	++	2	6
Health authority is still defining its role and its membership	–	0	0	–	0	– –	0	4
No financial growth	+	–	–	–	–	+	2	4
+	5	6	3	5	3	7		
–	3	4	5	6	5	6		

way in which it chose to allocate vouchers to reflect (for example) the demographic characteristics of individuals (age, social deprivation or whatever). Providers would have to respond to this market demand.

4.6.2 Critical Success Factors[29]

Many organisations are now taking on board one of the key messages from this chapter: namely, that there is not a best and a worst set of resources and competences. Strength and weakness can be assessed only in relation to the types of strategy the organisation is pursuing or wishes to pursue. This is also a reminder that the separation of strategic analysis from strategic choice is somewhat artificial.

critical success factors *are those components of strategy in which the organisation must excel to outperform competition*

In Chapter 10 the idea of critical success factors (CSFs) will be used to map out the core competences needed to support specific strategies. Given this natural connection between analysis and choice, many organisations find the idea of CSFs a useful way of reflecting on the strategic messages which should come out of resource analysis. **Critical success factors** are those components of strategy in which the organisation must excel to outperform competition. They are underpinned by core competences in specific activities or in managing linkages between activities. For example, if 'speed to market' with new product launch is a CSF, it may be underpinned by core competences in the logistics of physical distribution and negotiating skills with key account retail outlets. The example in Exhibit 4.6, the world automobile industry, illustrates how the critical success factors changed over time from market access to quality/reliability to product features. This required the different core competences to gain competitive advantage as illustrated and previously discussed in section 4.3.2. CSF analysis underlines this important relationship among resources, competences and choice of strategies, which is also central to the idea of balanced scorecards for assessing performance. These will be discussed in Chapter 10 (section 10.4.3).

SUMMARY

- The choice of 'good' strategies by an organisation can only be partly guided by general principles of strategic 'fit' between the business environment and the resource base of organisations. Many competitors may achieve similar degrees of fit, yet some outperform others. This difference in performance results from the way in which resources are deployed to create competences in separate activities, how these are matched to the requirements for particular types of strategy and, crucially, the competence with which these activities are linked together to improve value for money in products or services.

- *Value chain analysis* can be a useful way of describing and analysing these important relationships between an organisation's resources, competences and strategies.
- An analysis also needs to identify which competences are core to the success of strategy and how these *core competences* can provide the basis of new opportunities.
- There can be a mismatch between the changing requirements from the business environment and the core competences of the organisation. This can be addressed in two broad ways: first, to acknowledge that new core competences need to be developed; or second, to find new opportunities where traditional core competences will provide competitive advantage.
- The competences of an organisation are likely to be 'taken for granted' as part of the tacit knowledge and routines within the organisation. This can give the organisation real competitive advantage if this tacit knowledge is valuable, rare (in the sense that competitors do not have it) and difficult to imitate. However, because this knowledge is tacit, managers often find it difficult to identify explicitly which are their core competences, to acknowledge the need for change and to develop new competences to address a changing situation. Therefore, there must be processes through which the tacit knowledge is surfaced and challenged, and new competences are learnt. Otherwise, the core competences become rigidities preventing change.
- The analysis of competences is useful for understanding an organisation at the level of the strategic business unit. In addition, a judgement needs to be made on the strength or weakness of the *portfolio* of strategic business units.
- Organisation performance can only really be judged in relative terms, either against *history* or in the context of the *norm* for the industry (i.e. against competition). Ideally, it should be judged against *best practice* wherever that may be found. *Benchmarking* analysis can provide such comparisons of the resources, competences in separate activities and overall competence of the organisation.
- Specific techniques for analysing resources and competences may provide only a partial picture. There is a need to pull these together to give an overall assessment of strategic capability. This may be done through a *SWOT analysis* or by assessing the extent to which the resources and competences relate to the *critical success factors*.

RECOMMENDED KEY READINGS

- A number of the chapters in V. Ambrosini with G. Johnson and K. Scholes (eds), *Exploring Techniques of Analysis and Evaluation in Strategic Management*, Prentice Hall, 1998, provide further discussion of approaches to analyses introduced in this chapter. Specifically: A. Shepherd on value chain analysis; M. Tampoe on core competences; G. Tomlinson on benchmarking; D. Faulkner on portfolio matrices; T. Jacobs, J. Shepherd and G. Johnson on SWOT analysis.
- A.N. Grundy with G. Johnson and K. Scholes, *Exploring Strategic Financial Management*, Prentice Hall, 1998, shows how a range of financial analyses can contribute to a strategic analysis.
- An extensive discussion of the value chain concept and its application can be found in M.E. Porter, *Competitive Advantage*, Free Press, 1985.
- J. Kay, *Foundations of Corporate Success*, Oxford University Press, 1993, discusses many aspects of the links between strategic capability and competitive success.
- An audit of innovatory capabilities in organisations is provided on pages 363–8 of J. Tidd, J. Bessant and K. Pavitt, *Managing Innovation: Integrating technological, market and organizational change*, Wiley, 1997.

REFERENCES

1. The concept of resource-based strategies was discussed by B. Wernerfelt, 'A resource-based view of the firm', *Strategic Management Journal*, vol. 5, no. 2 (1984), pp. 171–80. The idea of driving strategy development from the resources and competences of an organisation is discussed in G. Hamel and C.K. Prahalad, 'Strategic intent', *Harvard Business Review*, vol. 67, no. 3 (1989), pp. 63–76; G. Hamel and C.K. Prahalad, 'Strategy as stretch and leverage', *Harvard Business Review*, vol. 71, no. 2 (1993), pp. 75–84; G. Stalk, P. Evans and L.E. Shulman, 'Competing on capabilities: the new rules of corporate strategy', *Harvard Business Review*, vol. 70, no. 2 (1992), pp. 57–69; D. Collis and C. Montgomery, 'Competing on resources: strategy in the 1990s', *Harvard Business Review*, vol. 73, no. 4 (1995), pp. 118–28; and D.J. Teece, G. Pisano and A. Shuen, 'Dynamic capabilities and strategic management', Harvard Business School Working Paper, 1992.
2. The importance of analysing and understanding tacit knowledge is discussed in I. Nonaka and H. Takeuchi, *The Knowledge Creating Company*, Oxford University Press, 1995.
3. Resource audits are covered in V. Ambrosini with G. Johnson and K. Scholes (eds), *Exploring Techniques of Analysis and Evaluation in Strategic Management*, Prentice Hall, 1998. There are also a number of papers and standard texts which include traditional resource audits: for example, G.A. Steiner, *Strategic Planning: What every manager must know*, Free Press, 1979, chapter 8; R.M. Grant, *Contemporary Strategy Analysis*, 2nd edition, Blackwell, 1995, p. 122; and R.B. Buchelle, 'How to evaluate a firm', *California Management Review* (Fall 1962). The latter provides extensive checklists under functional areas. Readers who are unfamiliar with resource analysis in any functional area may wish to consult one of the following standard texts: P. Kotler, *Marketing Management: Analysis, planning, implementation and control*, 8th edition, Prentice Hall, 1993; N. Slack and S. Chambers, *Operations Management*, Pitman, 1995; R. Wild, *Production and Operations Management*, 5th edition, Nelson, 1995; M.W.E. Glautier and B. Underdown, *Accounting Theory and Practice*, 5th edition, Pitman, 1994; D. Torrington and L. Hall, *Personnel Management: A new approach*, 3rd edition, Prentice Hall, 1995; C. Fombrun, N. Tichy and M. Devanna, *Strategic Human Resource Management*, Wiley, 1990.
4. Intangible resources have become increasingly recognised as being of strategic importance: see R. Hall, 'The strategic analysis of intangible resources', *Strategic Management Journal*, vol. 13, no. 2 (1992), pp. 135–44, and 'A framework linking intangible resources and capabilities to sustainable competitive advantage', *Strategic Management Journal*, vol. 14, no. 8 (1993), pp. 607–18. J. Smythe, C. Dorwood and J. Reback, *Corporate Reputation: The new strategic asset*, Century Business, 1992, and J. Kay, *Foundations of Corporate Success*, Oxford University Press, 1993, chapter 6, look at one particular intangible asset – reputation.

5. An extensive discussion of the value chain concept and its application can be found in M.E. Porter, *Competitive Advantage*, Free Press, 1985. See also A. Shepherd's chapter, 'Understanding and using value chain analysis' in V. Ambrosini with G. Johnson and K. Scholes (see reference 3).
6. Value analysis was developed in the post-war period by Lawrence Miles. See, for example, L.D. Miles, *Techniques of Value Analysis and Engineering*, McGraw-Hill, 1961.
7. There are a number of recent books and articles about the importance of analysing and understanding core competences: G. Hamel and A. Heene (eds), *Competence-based Competition*, Wiley, 1994; M. Tampoe's chapter, 'Getting to know your organisation's core competences' in V. Ambrosini with G. Johnson and K. Scholes (see reference 3); G. Hamel and C.K. Prahalad, 'The core competence of the corporation', *Harvard Business Review*, vol. 68, no. 3 (1990), pp. 79–91; R.H. Hayes and G.P. Pisano, 'Beyond world class: the new manufacturing strategy', *Harvard Business Review*, vol. 72, no. 1 (1994), pp. 77–86; K. Gronhaug and O. Nordhaug, 'Strategy and competence in firms', *European Management Journal*, vol. 10, no. 4 (1992), pp. 438–44.
8. This example is from Hamel and Heene (reference 7 above), pp. 16–18.
9. Cost advantage is discussed by Grant (reference 3 above), chapter 7, and B. Karlof, *Strategic Precision*, Wiley, 1993, chapter 3.
10. P. Conley, *Experience Curves as a Planning Tool*, available as a pamphlet from the Boston Consulting Group. See also A.C. Hax and N.S. Majluf, in R.G. Dyson (ed.), *Strategic Planning: Models and analytical techniques*, Wiley, 1990.
11. A useful reference on adding value is Kay (reference 4 above), chapter 2.
12. Customer perceived use value analysis is discussed in D. Faulkner and C. Bowman, *The Essence of Competitive Strategy*, Prentice Hall, 1995, pp. 11–12.
13. The importance of managing vertical relationships has been stressed by Porter (reference 5 above) and Kay (reference 4 above), chapter 17.
14. See T. Powell, 'Total quality management as competitive advantage: a review and empirical study', *Strategic Management Journal*, vol. 16, no. 1 (1995), pp. 15–37; J.S. Oakland, *Total Quality Management*, 2nd edition, Butterworth/Heinemann, 1995.
15. J.B. Barney, 'Organisational culture: can it be a source of competitive advantage?', *Academy of Management Review*, vol. 11, no. 3 (1986), pp. 656–65.
16. See Nonaka and Takeuchi (reference 2 above) for a discussion of tacit knowledge.
17. D. Leonard-Barton, 'Core capabilities and core rigidities: a paradox in managing new product development', *Strategic Management Journal*, vol. 13 (Summer 1992), pp. 111–25.
18. The dangers of over-subcontracting are discussed in J.C. Jarillo, *Strategic Networks: Creating the borderless organisation*, Butterworth/Heinemann, 1993, chapter 4.
19. I. Nonaka and H. Takeuchi, *The Knowledge Creating Company*, Oxford University Press, 1995.
20. Inter-company comparisons are discussed in J. Ellis and D. Williams, *Corporate Strategy and Financial Analysis*, Pitman, 1993, chapter 7.
21. Competitor profiles are discussed in M.E. Porter, *Competitive Strategy*, Free Press, 1980, p.49.
22. G.H. Watson, *Strategic Benchmarking*, Wiley, 1993, and S. Codling, *Benchmarking Basics*, Gower, 1998, are a practical guide to benchmarking. See also G. Tomlinson's chapter, 'Comparative analysis: benchmarking' in V. Ambrosini with G. Johnson and K. Scholes (see reference 3). T. Clayton and B. Luchs, 'Strategic benchmarking at ICI Fibres', *Long Range Planning*, vol. 27, no. 3 (1994), pp. 54–63, is a useful case example. See also L.S. Pryor and S.J. Katz, 'How benchmarking goes wrong (and how to do it right)', *Planning Review* (USA), vol. 21, no. 1 (1993), pp. 7–11; G.H. Watson, 'How process benchmarking supports corporate strategy', *Planning Review* (USA), vol. 21, no. 1 (1993), pp. 12–15; D.L. Ransley, 'Training managers to benchmark', *Planning Review*, vol. 21, no. 1 (1993), pp. 32–6.
23. A. Murdoch, 'Lateral benchmarking, or what Formula One taught an airline', *Management Today*, November 1997, pp. 64–7.
24. Base budget reviews have been used by a number of public sector organisations in an attempt to take on board the philosophy of zero-based budgets in a way that could be worked in practice (see G. Roberts and K. Scholes, 'Policy and base budget reviews at Cheshire County Council', *Waves of Change Conference Proceedings*, Sheffield Business School, 1993).
25. A.N. Grundy with G. Johnson and K. Scholes, *Exploring Strategic Financial Management*, Prentice Hall, 1998, shows how a range of financial analyses can contribute to a strategic analysis. Also useful are J. Ellis and D. Williams, *Corporate Strategy and Financial Analysis*, Pitman, 1993; K. Ward, *Corporate Financial Strategy*, Butterworth/Heinemann, 1993.
26. A review of a range of portfolio analyses can be found in D. Faulkner's chapter, 'Portfolio matrices', in V. Ambrosini with G. Johnson and K. Scholes (see reference 3). The use of growth per share matrices is discussed by Hax and Majluf (reference 10 above). See also Karlof (reference 9 above), chapter 2. Some authors have warned of the need to use portfolio matrices with care: for example, S.P. Slatter, 'Common pitfalls in using the BCG portfolio matrix', *London Business School Journal* (Winter 1980).
27. J.R. Montanari and J.S. Bracker, 'The strategic management process at the public planning unit level', *Strategic Management Journal*, vol. 7, no. 3 (1986) pp. 251–65.

28. The idea of SWOT as a commonsense checklist has been used for many years: for example, S. Tilles, 'Making strategy explicit', in I. Ansoff (ed.), *Business Strategy*, Penguin, 1968. See also T. Jacobs, J. Shepherd and G. Johnson's chapter on SWOT analysis in V. Ambrosini with G. Johnson and K. Scholes (see reference 3).
29. See M. Hardaker and B.K. Ward, 'Getting things done', *Harvard Business Review*, vol. 65, no. 6 (1987), pp. 112–20.

WORK ASSIGNMENTS

4.1 Undertake a resource audit of an organisation with which you are familiar. Then identify which resources, if any, are unique in the sense that they are difficult to imitate (see Exhibit 4.2). Has the organisation gained competitive advantage as a result of this uniqueness? Why/why not? You can answer this in relation to Laura Ashley* if you so wish.

4.2 Use Exhibits 4.4 and 4.5 to map out the key value activities for Laura Ashley* or an organisation of your choice, both within the company and in the wider value system in which it operates.

4.3 By referring to Exhibit 4.3, explain how the organisation you have analysed in assignment 4.2 does or does not gain competitive advantage from:
(a) competence in the separate value activities
(b) managing linkages within the value chain.

4.4 ● Use Exhibits 4.7, 4.8 and 4.9 to explain how the control of relationships within the value chain could be changed to improve the efficiency or effectiveness, or both, of an organisation. Illustrate your answer by reference to an organisation of your choice, Laura Ashley,* Illustration 4.3 or Illustration 4.4.

4.5 Choose two organisations in the same industry and compare the configurations of their value chain. Explain how these relate to the organisation's competitive positioning.

4.6 Take any industry and public service and sketch out a map of how core competences have changed over time (use Exhibit 4.6 as an example). Why have these changes occurred? How did the relative strengths of different companies or service providers change over this period? Why?

4.7 Identify the strategic business units in an organisation of your choice. Use one of the portfolio matrices shown in Exhibit 4.12 to assess the extent to which these represent a well balanced portfolio. How would you strengthen this portfolio?

4.8 ● It has been said that the power of benchmarking is in understanding how value for money is created or lost in the separate activities of the organisation against the 'best in class' organisations for each activity. To what extent do you feel this is a universal prescription for improving competitive performance? Are there any dangers or pitfalls in this approach? Discuss.

4.9 Prepare a SWOT analysis for an organisation of your choice (see Illustration 4.8). Explain carefully why you have chosen each of the key items in your shortlists.

---

* refers to a case study in the Text and Cases edition.
● denotes more advanced work assignments.

CASE EXAMPLE

Outsourcing

From the late 1980s onwards, many organisations became aware of the impact on their performance of other companies in their supply and distribution chains. There was also a growing concern that companies were too stretched in terms of their spread of activities and were underperforming in some critical areas of their operations. By the mid 1990s, many organisations had turned their attention to reviewing 'in-house' performance on activities that could be outsourced. An article in *Management Today* in January 1997 outlined recent developments in outsourcing – as a means of improving the performance of companies.

When British Airways' chief executive Bob Ayling introduced the airline's millennium restructuring plan in autumn 1996 he suggested that some of the £1 billion savings BA needed to make over the next three years to retain its competitive edge might come from a modest amount of outsourcing. Activities such as baggage handling and refuelling would be scrutinised to see whether they were being done as well by BA staff as they could be by outside contractors. If they weren't, subcontracting would be considered. Some commentators, in provocative mood, thought Ayling much too tentative. He should go for broke, they suggested, and turn BA into a 'virtual airline', retaining its marketing function but outsourcing everything else up to and including flying the aircraft. The journalists were clearly exaggerating for effect but were nevertheless reflecting the currently popular belief that outsourcing (in which companies concentrate on the bits of their business that give them their competitive advantage and farm out the peripheral, non-core bits to others) is by and large a good thing.

Recent research suggests it may not be. The PA Consulting Group's report, *Strategic Sourcing*, provides, for the first time, quantitative evidence of a positive correlation between high levels of outsourcing and share price performance (demonstrating, says PA, that well-run companies, which usually perform well in the market, are likely to see effective outsourcing as part of good management practice). But it also makes very plain that the magic of outsourcing is not working for many (perhaps most) corporations. Only 5% of more than 300 companies and public sector organisations investigated by the PA researchers had found outsourcing high on benefits and low on drawbacks. For many of the rest, the outcome of such subcontracting was either mediocre or a total flop.

Traditionally, outsourcing has concentrated on activities which are remote from the heart or nerve centre of the company. Classical outsourcing theory says that a company should decide which of its functions give it competitive advantage (its core competences in management-speak) and which don't. Non-core functions can be farmed out to specialists if they conduct them more cheaply or better or both, but core functions never. To outsource core functions, say the theorists, is to hand over the things which made the company what it is – and which make its profits.

Increasingly, however, this rule is being questioned. It is now argued that there has been a confusion between core activities (things that are central to what one does) and core competences (the central things that one does well). Those who take this line now talk about outsourcing functions like customer care, an activity which most outsourcing theorists would consider so central to a company's success that only a lunatic would hand it over to a third party. If you cannot look after your customers, say the traditionalists, should you be in business at all? Aren't customers the *raison d'être* of every business?

Mark Astbury, sales and marketing director of Ventura, a company which handles customer service management for companies like Kingfisher, Cellnet and the Co-operative Bank, understands people's surprise that organisations should be prepared to entrust such sensitive work to outsiders, but the practice is not as odd as it first seems, he says. 'Cellnet, for instance, have said to themselves, "What are our core competences?" and they've come down firmly and said their core competence is in running a mobile phone network, that there are other things they don't regard as a core competences and one of those is customer service. Customer service is a core activity but they've decided to find a partner who can help them manage customers better than their competitors do and, crucially, better than they believe they can do themselves.'

Mike Webb, managing director of Mondial Assistance, which provides claims hotlines for a number of insurance companies, also argues for a redefinition of the concept of a core business. If you take an insurance company, he says, the instinctive thing to say is that a company that can't administer its own hotline can't be relied on to carry out its business effectively. 'But that's obviously nonsense. The company's responsibility is to assess the risk that customers represent and provide them with the most appropriate and cost-effective package of cover. It is also the company's responsibility to ensure that its spread of risk leaves it in a position to pay out claims where necessary. Investing in these skills is a cost-effective use of resources, but staffing the claims hotline is not.'

The outsourcing of areas of the business that are close to the customer raises the issue of what to do when a service provider underperforms. The thing about outsourcing is that to the customer, the whole operation is invisible. If the service provider does something that hurts the customer it isn't the provider who gets it in the neck it is the company which farmed out that part of its work. Several banks, including the Co-operative, are outsourcing cheque clearance, for example. It makes sense for the banks to outsource this particular process since the volume of cheques written is actually in steady decline, making it hard to justify spending time and money keeping the required technology up to date. For service providers, like Unisys, on the other hand, technology like image processing systems can be used across a range of businesses and a range of customers so it does not matter that the cheque processing business of the individual bank is declining.

It is not just what is being outsourced that is slowly changing, however, but also the way in which that outsourcing is conducted. Some pioneers are trying out variations, such as *co-sourcing*. For while traditional outsourcing may be perfectly suitable for low-risk peripheral activities such as cleaning or car fleet management, with higher risk strategic functions or processes, companies want to retain more of a say in the way in which work is done. With co-sourcing, the client company keeps responsibility for the management and strategic aspects of the outsourced activity, while the outside provider supplies consultancy services and often experienced personnel to help the business streamline the function or process. The financial group Société Generale has a co-sourcing arrangement with Arthur Andersen, under which an Andersen tax expert spends two days a week in the group's human resources office to advise senior management and expatriates on taxation issues.

Even assuming a certain corporate confidence in the ability to outsource well (quite an assumption), is there an irreducible core of activities which couldn't or shouldn't ever be subcontracted? One way is to identify which parts of the company constitute the 'corporate crown jewels'. But the definition of crown jewels may change over time, says Dr Chris Floyd, who runs consultant Arthur D. Little's technology and innovation management practice in the UK. 'In computers', he says, 'the crown jewel element was the hardware, so IBM outsourced the software, the operating system, to the little known Microsoft because they thought the operating system was a minor, peripheral technology. Then, over time, they found it was the operating system which became the crown jewels and what they were left with, the hardware, was the peripheral technology.'

The best companies, Little says, take a strategic, top-down approach to outsourcing – he terms it *strategic sourcing* – and are clear and disciplined in their decision-making and process management. Most outsourcing is done in a fairly piecemeal fashion, often for tactical reasons. Strategic sourcers, by contrast, outsource because they can see benefits for the wider organisation.

Questions

1. Choose an organisation with which you are familiar (perhaps IKEA from Chapter 1 or the Laura Ashley case study from the Cases section of this book). Refer to Exhibit 4.1 and identify the different ways in which outsourcing might improve the strategic capability of the organisation.
2. For the issue of *customer care* cited in the case example, draw up a table that compares the main potential benefits and pitfalls of:
   (a) in-house provision
   (b) outsourcing
   (c) co-sourcing.
   Remember to use 'improving value for money' as your yardstick (Exhibits 4.7 and 4.8 can be used as checklists).
3. From your answers to questions 1 and 2 draw up a list of questions which you think any organisation should ask before deciding to outsource a particular activity or business process.

Source Abridged from M. Brown, 'Outsourcing', *Management Today*, January 1997, pp. 56–60. With the kind permission of the copyright owner Haymarket Management Publications Ltd.

5
STAKEHOLDER EXPECTATIONS AND ORGANISATIONAL PURPOSES

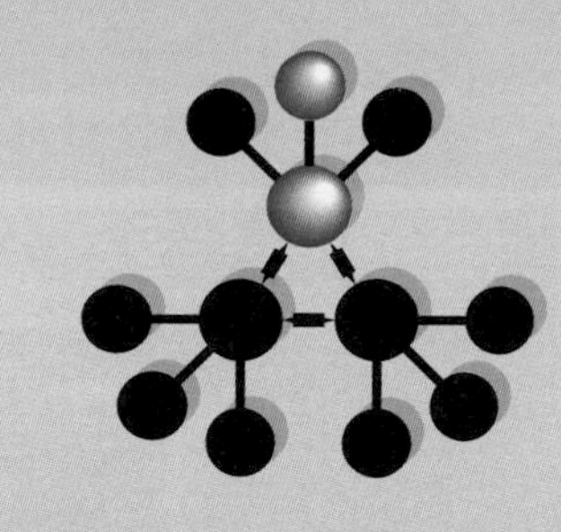

LEARNING OUTCOMES

After reading this chapter you should be able to:

- Explain the corporate governance arrangements in different countries.
- Define and list stakeholders of an organisation.
- Assess the power of stakeholders.
- Undertake a stakeholder mapping exercise.
- Describe different types of ethical stance and corporate social responsibility.
- Characterise the culture of an organisation.
- Define 'mission statements' and explain their use and limitations.
- Explain the different levels of objectives in organisations.

5.1 INTRODUCTION

There is a temptation to look for a neat and tidy way of formulating strategy. Such a method might, apparently, be achieved through the analysis of the organisation's environment (Chapter 3) and the extent to which the company's resources, or strategic capability (Chapter 4), are matched with or fit the environment, or vice versa. However, this strategic logic can fail to recognise the complex role which people play in the evolution of strategy, as introduced in Chapter 2. Strategy formulation is also about the *purposes* of the organisation and what people want the organisation to be like. This chapter is concerned with examining how the *political and cultural contexs* of an organisation can be analysed and understood as part of a strategic analysis. There has been a growing awareness of the central importance of these issues since the early 1980s.

Exhibit 5.1 Influences on organisational purposes

Exhibit 5.1 summarises how the theme will be progressed through the chapter by identifying four broad influences on an organisation's purposes. Although these will be discussed separately, it should be remembered that, in reality, they form part of a connected web of influences which *together* shape the purposes of an organisation at any given time:

- The fundamental questions are *whom should* the organisation be there to serve and *how should* the direction and purposes of an organisation be determined? This is the province of *corporate governance*. This relates not only to the power to influence purposes, but also the processes of supervising executive decisions and actions, and the issues of *accountability* and the *regulatory framework* within which organisations operate. There are significant differences in the approach to corporate governance in different countries and this will be reflected in the discussion.

- *Whom* the organisation *does actually* serve in practice is the second important issue. This will be addressed through the concept of *organisational stakeholders* and the extent to which they are interested in or able to influence the organisation's purposes. Stakeholders are those individuals or groups who depend on the organisation to fulfil their own goals, and on whom, in turn, the organisation depends. Typically, they include shareholders, customers, suppliers, banks, employees and the community at large. Understanding this requires an analysis or assessment of both the *power* and *interest* of different stakeholder groups.
- *Which purposes* an organisation should fulfil is influenced by *ethical* considerations. At the broadest level, these issues impinge on corporate governance – particularly in relation to the accountability of organisations. The ethical agenda is also strongly culturally driven and is concerned with *corporate social responsibility* to the various stakeholders – particularly those with little formal power (such as the community at large). It is also concerned with the ethical standards and behaviour of *individuals*.
- *Which purposes are actually* prioritised above others is also related to a variety of factors in the *cultural context* in which the organisation is operating. This relates back to the concept of the *cultural web*, introduced in Chapter 2 as a means of analysing an organisation's culture. This same approach can be used to understand how culture at several 'levels' might influence organisational purposes. This will include the broader issues of *national cultures* through important *reference groups* – such as professional bodies – to the *subcultures* within an organisation – perhaps at the business function level.

The chapter concludes with a discussion of the formal ways in which organisational purposes are expressed and communicated – particularly the role of *mission statements* and *objectives*.

Overall, this chapter is concerned with exploring how this set of influences can be analysed and understood as part of a strategic analysis. Managers may enter this analysis through any of the four main 'strands' in Exhibit 5.1, but it is important to understand the connections between these broad influences on an organisation's purposes.

5.2 CORPORATE GOVERNANCE[1]

the **governance framework** *determines whom the organisation is there to serve and how the purposes and priorities of the organisation should be decided*

The starting point in discussing an organisation's purposes will be the corporate governance framework within which the organisation is operating. The **governance framework** determines whom the organisation is there to serve and how the purposes and priorities of the organisation should be decided. It is concerned with both the functioning of the organisation and the distribution of power among different stakeholders. It will be seen that this is strongly culturally bound, resulting in different traditions and frameworks in different countries.[2]

The corporate governance agenda in most countries tends to be more implicit than explicit. This means that the legal and regulatory measures form only a part of the corporate governance.

5.2.1 The Governance Chain

The complexity of corporate governance has arisen for two main reasons. First, the practical need to separate *ownership* and *management control* of organisations is now the norm – except with very small businesses. The result has been that most organisations operate within a hierarchy or chain of governance. The *governance chain* identifies all those groups that have a legitimate influence on the organisation's purposes. Although the details of the chain will vary from one organisation to another, Exhibit 5.2 illustrates a typical chain of governance for a publicly quoted company in the UK. Second, there has been an increasing tendency to make organisations more visibly accountable not only to owners (e.g. shareholders), but also to other stakeholder groups. The rights of these various stakeholders will be discussed later.

Even in the simplified example of Exhibit 5.2 it can be seen that the managers who are driving strategy in the organisation may be very remote from the ultimate beneficiaries of the company's performance. The figure also highlights the information typically available to each 'player' in the chain to judge the performance of others. In the example, it is likely that many beneficiaries are either ignorant of or indifferent to the details of companies in which their money is invested. Many beneficiaries will have their interests 'guarded' by intermediaries – for example, asset managers for pension funds. Illustration 5.1 shows how powerful these intermediaries may be in determining the future of companies.

Given this degree of complexity in corporate governance, there are likely to be several *conflicts of interest* both between different stakeholder groups and for individual managers or directors as they try to balance these various interests. This is a particular issue for boards of directors and has resulted in important developments in both the role of the board and the disclosure of information. A very important question in large publicly quoted corporations is whether corporate managers should regard themselves as solely responsible to shareholders, or whether they have a wider responsibility as 'trustees of the assets of the corporation' on behalf of a wider range of stakeholders.[3]

5.2.2 Shareholders and the Role of the Governing Bodies

The primary statutory responsibility of the governing body of an organisation is to ensure that the organisation actually fulfils the wishes

Exhibit 5.2 **The chain of corporate governance: typical reporting structure**

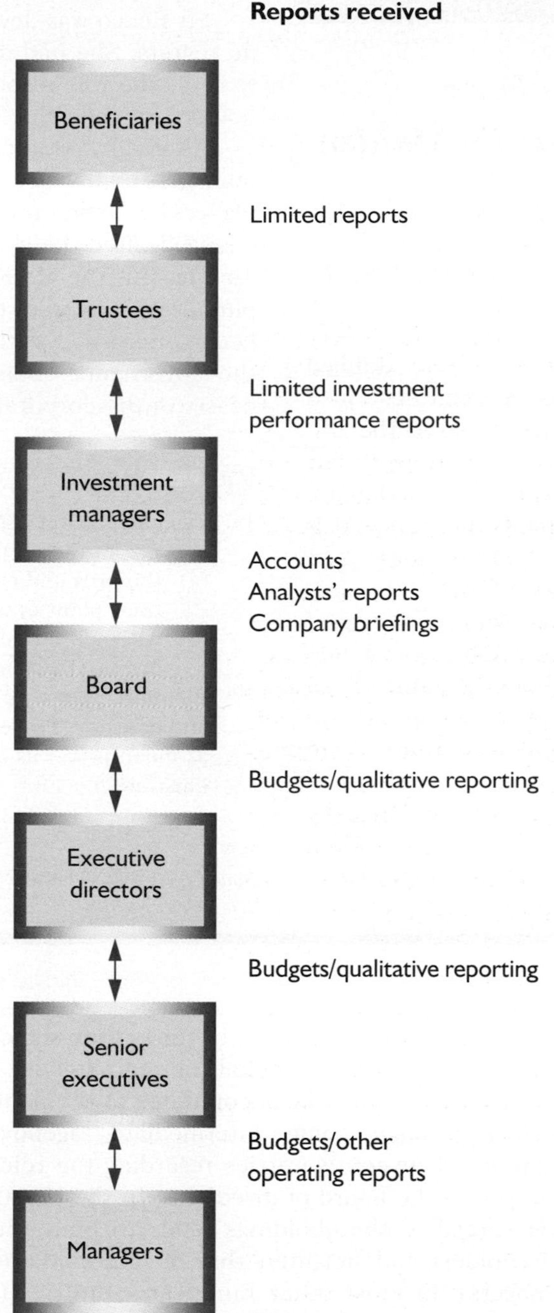

Source David Pitt-Watson, Braxton Associates. Reproduced with permission.

STRATEGY IN ACTION
Illustration 5.1

Sir Rocco Forte, Granada and the 'Ice Maiden'

Pension fund managers have become increasingly powerful players in determining the future of companies – sometimes shown dramatically during takeover bids.

The UK tabloid newspapers have dubbed Carol Galley the 'Ice Maiden' and described her as the most powerful woman in the UK. This will certainly strike a chord with Sir Rocco Forte, who lost his celebrated hotel chain partly because Galley and her associates no longer considered him the right man for the job. In 1996, Carol Galley was vice-chairman and fund manager of Mercury Asset Management (MAM), controlling over 900 pension funds throughout Britain. Even though Rocco Forte had a high profile in the business world, sentiment meant little to Galley who told him coolly that she had examined the £3.8 billion bid for Forte by Granada and considered it to be good. MAM voted its 14.6 per cent shareholding in Forte in favour of Granada. This action was seen as decisive by other shareholders.

Sir Rocco was devastated, but Galley had no regrets. She had done what she was paid to do – she was responsible to pension fund holders for the value of their stake in Forte.

Although, traditionally, pension fund managers had been discreet, barely visible players in the financial world, all this changed after the 'Big Bang' in the City of London in the 1980s. The pension fund plutocrats emerged from the shadows and became regarded as the key power players in the 'governance chain' and the most deadly beasts in the corporate jungle.

Questions

1. Refer to Exhibit 5.2 and list for each of the 'players' in the corporate governance chain:
   (a) the pros and cons of the takeover from their point of view
   (b) whether you feel they would have favoured or feared a takeover.
2. What are your own views about the benefits and dangers of investment managers having as much power as described in the illustration.

Source *Sunday Times*, 21 April 1996.

and purposes of the 'owners'. In the private sector, this would be the board of directors working on behalf of shareholders. In the public sector, the governing body would be accountable to the political arm of government – possibly through some intermediate 'agency'. There are important differences between countries regarding the role, composition and *modus operandi* of the board of directors.[4] In the UK, the USA and Australia, the wide spread of shareholdings tends to limit the power of the individual shareholders and heighten that of intermediaries (such as pension fund managers). In most other European countries (e.g. Belgium, the Netherlands and France), shareholding is more closely held and often minority led – perhaps by the founding family, financial institutions or other interests either acting together or using protective mechanisms such as preference shares. The board is strongly controlled by these particular shareholder interests. In Japan, the board tends to be viewed as just one part of a multilayered corporate decision-making process, and hence is usually dominated by corporate executives. Japanese banks tend to have shareholdings in organisations, as against simply providing loan capital. There is also likely to be a complex web of cross-shareholdings between companies. These latter two factors tend to reduce the pressure for short-term results[5] as against longer-term performance, in marked contrast to US/UK companies. In turn, this influences the approach to important aspects of strategy, such as investment.

These different traditions naturally bring with them different structures and compositions of the board. In the UK and USA, there is a single-tier board usually incorporating both executive and non-executive directors. The board supervises the activities and performance of managers to a greater or lesser extent. Many organisations have adopted a subcommittee structure which allows for a more detailed involvement of the board with the work of the managers of the organisation. Non-executive directors sometimes represent the interests of key stakeholders (e.g. institutional investors).

In many other European countries (notably Germany, the Netherlands and France), the *two-tier board* is either mandatory or prevalent. For example, in Germany, the 'upper-tier' or supervisory board oversees the work of the 'lower-tier' board, which is entrusted with the day-to-day management of the organisation. Importantly, the composition of this supervisory board is built around the principles of *co-determination* – half of the members being elected by shareholders, the other half by employees. However, the shareholders maintain the final say through the chairperson's casting vote.

The main potential benefit of the two-tier form of governance is the counterbalancing of the power of managers, which is often a feature of management-dominated unitary boards in the UK and USA – particularly where non-executive directors are weak or ineffective. There has been particular concern that managerial interests have dominated strategic decisions on issues such as diversification and acquisitions – decisions which have proved unsuccessful and not in the best interests of shareholders.[6] There has been much debate as to whether a legally prescribed balance of power is or is not beneficial. Proposals for industrial democracy were put forward in the UK in 1977 by the *Bullock Committee*,[7] but these were not acted on by government. In France, the two-tier system is optional.

In Japan, the composition of the board is heavily weighted towards executive members. However, as membership of the board is seen as a tier in the management hierarchy, the entry of executives onto the board is controlled by the chairperson, who will often take external advice (for example, from bankers) before a manager is promoted to director. In Japanese corporate culture, a prerequisite of a good director is someone who is able to continue to promote the interests of employees. So, in contrast to Germany, employees in Japan have power through cultural norms (trust and the implicit 'duties' of directors) rather than through the legal framework of governance.

The role of the board in nationalised industries is – in theory – very similar to the private sector, except that capital expenditure and borrowings are directly controlled by the minister responsible. In reality, the power of boards is often curtailed by political priorities and the involvement of ministers in management decisions (for example, prices, wages and plant closures). The desire to remove this conflict between political expediency and the need for longer-term strategic direction was an important reason behind the major privatisation programmes in many countries during the 1980s and 1990s.

The public services have a wide variety of arrangements for governing bodies, but there are some commonalities. There has been a move in many countries to increase the proportion of (so-called) independent members on governing bodies. These independent members are the nearest equivalent of the non-executive director in the private sector. Governing bodies are often factional, or representational, in practice even if not by regulation. This particularly applies to the place of employees and unions on governing bodies.

5.2.3 Rights of Creditors and Lenders

One of the reasons why the corporate governance situation varies so much from one country to another is the differing arrangements for corporate finance. There are the different 'traditions' regarding *equity/debt* ratios and the extent to which the *relationship* with bankers is regarded as one of partnership or simply 'contractual'. At one extreme, particularly in the USA and UK, equity is the dominant form of long-term finance and commercial banks provide debt capital; relationships with bankers are towards the contractual end of the spectrum. In contrast, in Japan (and to a lesser extent Germany), banks often have significant equity stakes and may be part of the same parent company, and the lead banks may organise the activities of other banks. The power of lenders in these two extremes is very different and exercised in different ways. UK and US banks may exercise their power through *exit* (i.e. withdrawing funds) even if this liquidates the company. Japanese banks are more concerned to steer the longer-term strategy of the organisation and to use their power to make their voice heard.

The trade creditor is the least protected stakeholder in the trading process and there is little in the corporate governance framework to redress this. So creditors need to mitigate their risk through prudence in their dealings.

5.2.4 Relationships with Customers and Clients

The legal framework of many countries enshrines the principle of *caveat emptor*, placing the burden of risk on the customer and giving the balance of power to the company. However, there have been some significant moves to temper this apparently harsh situation. Legislation to protect consumers' interests grew substantially from the 1960s onwards. In situations of natural monopolies, many governments created 'watchdog' bodies to represent the customers' interests. In the case of the privatised utilities in the UK and elsewhere, this has become enshrined in the office of the regulator (Oftel, Ofwat, etc.), whose powers of regulation set them up as a surrogate for the market (see Chapter 10, section 10.4.3) and who exert control over prices and services through a set of performance targets. This has important implications for how the companies construct their competitive strategies.

Even without the use of a legally binding framework, there have been other attempts to give more rights and voice to individual consumers. The *Citizen's Charter Initiative* in the UK public services was one such attempt. Each public service had to develop and publish a charter which stated the rights of clients and the performance standards which they could expect from the organisation (see Illustration 5.2). These performance standards raised the visibility to users of the organisation's performance, creating some measure of 'market pressure'.

5.2.5 Changes of Ownership: Mergers and Takeovers

The impact of corporate governance systems on strategy, and the differences between the USA and UK, and Continental European countries such as Germany, is shown most clearly in the area of takeovers (particularly hostile takeovers). In the USA and UK, the exposure of managers to the threat of takeover (i.e. a market pressure based system) is regarded as a primary means of ensuring the good performance of organisations. In contrast, in Germany the performance of companies is seen as being primarily controlled through institutional mechanisms such as equity ownership by banks, two-tier boards and co-determination. Therefore, the corporate governance issues around (hostile) takeovers are largely confined to those countries which have adopted the Anglo-Saxon market-based approach to governance. The specific issue has been the extent to which a free market in buying and selling shares and companies – over the head of the board of directors – should be constrained in law and codes of conduct, to produce a semi-regulated framework for takeovers. Equally important has been a concern with the *conflict of interest* which directors face in defending against a hostile bid, and the extent to which *defensive measures* should be regulated. Often, bids are regarded as hostile by boards of directors because they might jeopardise their *personal* position (as executives), whereas a takeover may actually be in the longer-term interests of the shareholders and positively beneficial to other stakeholders, such as employees or customers.

In the public services, similar questions have been asked about the role of managers and board members faced with privatisation or 'de-merger' of the organisation – as in the case of British Rail in the mid 1990s. Executive

STRATEGY IN ACTION Illustration 5.2

The Patient's Charter

There has been an increasing concern that the rights and voice of individual consumers should be enhanced. The public services have been attempting to do this.

In the early 1990s, many public services, in the UK and elsewhere, were keen to redress the balance of attention they were paying to their various stakeholders. In particular, the voice of the client was encouraged through various means, including, in the UK, what became known as the *Citizen's Charter*. This was prompted by the government, and major public services adopted their own charter.

In the case of the National Health Service, this was known as the *Patient's Charter* and was launched in 1991. The charter contained three main elements: a reaffirmation of seven existing rights of patients; the introduction of three new rights; and the publication of performance standards (both national and local). Standards were not rights, but helped clarify the expectations which government had of management in the health service in terms of quality of service.

Seven Existing Rights

- Health care on the basis of clinical need not ability to pay.
- Registration with a family doctor (GP).
- Emergency care at any time.
- Referral to a hospital consultant (through GP).
- Clarification of proposed treatment, including risks and alternatives.
- Access to health records.
- Freedom of whether to take part in medical research and training.

Three New Rights

- Detailed information on local health services, including quality standards and maximum waiting time.
- Guaranteed admission for treatment by a specific date no longer than two years after being placed on a waiting list.
- Any complaints to be fully and promptly investigated and a written reply sent by the chief executive or general manager.

Nine National Standards

- Respect for privacy, dignity, and religious and cultural beliefs.
- All people – including those with special needs – to be able to use services.
- Information to relatives and friends.
- Waiting time for ambulance (14 minutes maximum in urban areas).
- Waiting time for assessment in emergency (immediate assessment).
- Waiting time in outpatients (within 30 minutes of appointment time).
- Cancellation of operations (no cancellations on the day).
- A *named* nurse – or other professional – responsible for each patient.
- Discharge arrangements (follow-up needs).

In addition, local health authorities were required to develop a series of more detailed local standards for the guidance of patients.

Questions

1. Make your own critique of the benefit of the Patients's Charter as a means of increasing the power ('voice') of clients of the health service by asking what happens if:
   (a) my rights are not honoured (e.g. guaranteed admission for treatment)
   (b) the standards are not kept (e.g. ambulance times).
2. Are there ways in which you would improve the charter to meet the stated aims?

Source *Patient's Charter*, Department of Health, 1991.

board members may well diminish their personal career prospects through the privatisation and de-merger. This raises difficult ethical issues for managers, as will be discussed below (section 5.4.3).

5.2.6 Disclosure of Information

In understanding the political context within which organisations operate, it needs to be acknowledged that information is a key source of power. Therefore, it is an important aspect of corporate governance to establish a framework about *disclosure of information* to various stakeholder groups. This clearly has to be balanced with the commercial prerogative for confidentiality on certain aspects of an organisation's operation.

In the early 1990s in the UK, there was mounting criticism of the quality of financial reporting and the effectiveness of the independent auditing. This led to the establishment of the Cadbury Committee, which reported in late 1992 and again in 1996. The first report, which had the backing of the Bank of England, the London Stock Exchange and the accounting bodies, sought to establish a code of best practice on disclosure and audit arrangements. Companies listed on the Stock Exchange were required to make a statement in their annual report that they complied with the code of best practice. So this aspect of corporate governance was exercised not through statute but in a 'voluntary' way albeit with severe penalties (de-listing) for non-compliance.

It is interesting to note that the single issue which attracted most attention was the disclosure of *directors' pay*. This was the subject of a separate report in the UK – the Greenbury Report (see Illustration 5.3). Again, this indicated the need for corporate governance arrangements to address issues where there is potentially a conflict of interest. Of course, disclosure can be a costly and time-consuming business and is an important consideration for privately owned businesses when thinking about public flotation.

5.2.7 Conflicts of Expectations

The differing forms of corporate governance outlined above are intended to provide a framework within which the interests of different stakeholder groups are given formal power of decision within organisations. Although this may prove useful in smoothing the strategic decision-making process, it will not remove conflict of interests. Since the expectations of stakeholder groups will differ, it is quite normal for conflict to exist within organisations regarding the importance or desirability of many aspects of strategy. In most situations, a compromise will need to be reached between expectations which cannot all be achieved simultaneously.

STRATEGY IN ACTION
Illustration 5.3

The Greenbury Report on Directors' Pay in the UK

The Greenbury Report set down a number of proposals aimed at dealing with public and shareholder concerns about directors' remuneration. In the light of controversy over pay awards for directors, the report recommended that a number of changes were necessary if company accountability was to be strengthened.

In July 1995 the Greenbury Committee published the following proposed framework for executive pay. It recommended that all listed companies should comply with the code 'to the fullest extent practicable'.

- In determining directors' salaries, remuneration committees (RCs) should be sensitive to the wider scene – in particular, pay and employment conditions elsewhere in the company – so that their decisions are consistent and fair and are seen as such. Bonuses should not be allowed to become another guaranteed element of pay, and should normally be subject to an upper limit, such as a specified percentage of basic pay.
- RCs should be made up of non-executive directors who have no personal financial interest in the decisions taken. There should be no cross-directorships with executive directors, which could offer scope for 'mutual agreements to bid up each other's remuneration'. Non-executives should have a good knowledge and understanding of the company.
- Companies should detail all elements of remuneration for every individual director by name, including basic salary, the nature and value of benefits in kind, annual bonuses, pension entitlements and long-term incentive schemes, including share options.
- Grants of share options should be phased over time rather than issued as a block, and should never be offered at a discount. Full details of share options for each director should be disclosed.
- There is a strong case for setting directors' notice periods at, or reducing them to, one year or less.
- Directors of the recently privatised public utilities (gas, water, electricity) should command a greater pay premium where there is substantial competition and risk, where there is a wide diversity of activities or an international spread of operations, or where significant technological or structural change is under way.

The Greenbury Report also recommended that the government bring forward legal changes to tax share option gains as income rather than capital, and secondary legislation on small changes in company and pensions law on disclosure. The Stock Exchange should introduce continuing obligations for listed companies to enact the new code on executive pay. Investor institutions should use their power and influence to ensure the implementation of best practice on pay.

Questions

1. 'The Greenbury conclusions are a politically expedient overkill to the bad practice of a few companies.' Do you agree?
2. Why should disclosure be confined to directors. Why not senior managers, or all managers, or all employees?

Source *The Times*, 18 July 1995.

Prepared by Sara Martin, Cranfield School of Management.

Exhibit 5.3 **Some common conflicts of expectations**

- In order to grow, short-term profitability, cash flow and pay levels may need to be sacrificed.
- 'Short-termism' may suit managerial career aspirations but preclude investment in long-term projects.
- When family businesses grow, the owners may lose control if they need to appoint professional managers.
- New developments may require additional funding through share issue or loans. In either case, financial independence may be sacrificed.
- Public ownership of shares will require more openness and accountability from the management.
- Cost efficiency through capital investment can mean job losses.
- Extending into mass markets may require a decline in quality standards.
- In public services, a common conflict is between mass provision and specialist services (e.g. preventive dentistry or heart transplants).
- In public services, savings in one area (e.g. social security benefits) may result in increases elsewhere (e.g. school meals, medical care).

Exhibit 5.3 shows some of the typical stakeholder expectations that exist and how they might conflict. They include the conflicts between growth and profitability; growth and control/independence; cost efficiency and jobs; volume/mass provision and quality/specialisation; and the problems of suboptimisation, where the development of one part of an organisation may be at the expense of another. 'Short-termism' is often driven by the career aspirations of managers at the expense of the long-term health of the organisation. The different corporate governance traditions and frameworks tend to result in a different prioritisation of many of these items, as can be seen in the critique given in Exhibit 5.4.

5.3 STAKEHOLDER EXPECTATIONS[8]

The corporate governance framework of an organisation needs to be understood when analysing whom the organisation should be serving and how the purposes of the organisation should be determined. However, in reality this tends to provide no more than a broad framework for understanding the actual *political context* in which strategies are formulated and implemented within organisations. It is helpful to analyse and understand the expectations of different stakeholders in much more detail, and in particular to consider the extent to which they are likely to show an active interest in the strategic development of the organisation or seek to exercise an influence over its purpose and strategies. **Stakeholders** are those individuals or groups who depend on the organisation to fulfil their own goals and on whom, in turn, the organisation depends.

stakeholders *are those individuals or groups who depend on the organisation to fulfil their own goals and on whom, in turn, the organisation depends*

Exhibit 5.4 A critique of some different corporate governance systems

Anglo-Saxon Model (USA and UK)	
Strengths	**Weaknesses**
● Dynamic market orientation	● Volatile instability
● Fluid capital	● Short-termism
● Internationalisation possible	● Inadequate governance structures
European Model (Germany)	
Strengths	**Weaknesses**
● Long-term industrial strategy	● Internationalisation difficult
● Very stable capital	● Vulnerable to global market for companies
● Strong governance procedures	
Asian Model (Japan)	
Strengths	**Weaknesses**
● Long-term industrial strategy	● Growth of merger activity
● Stable capital	● Growth of institutional investor activism
● Overseas investments	● Growth of financial speculation
	● Secretive, sometimes corrupt, procedures

Source T. Clarke and E. Monkhouse (eds), *Rethinking the Company*, Financial Times/Pitman, 1994. Reproduced with permission.

Few individuals have sufficient power to determine unilaterally the strategy of an organisation. Influence is likely to occur only because individuals share expectations with others by being a part of a stakeholder group. Individuals need to identify themselves with the aims and ideals of these stakeholder groups, which may occur within departments, geographical locations, different levels in the hierarchy, etc. Also important are the external stakeholders of the organisation, who would typically include bankers, customers, suppliers, shareholders and unions. They may seek to influence company strategy through their links with internal stakeholders. For example, customers may pressurise sales managers to represent their interests within the company. Even if external stakeholders are passive, they may represent real constraints on the development of new strategies.

5.3.1 Identifying Stakeholders

When identifying stakeholders there is a danger of concentrating too heavily on the formal structure of an organisation as a basis for identification, since this can be the easiest place to look for the divisions in expectations mentioned previously. However, it is necessary to unearth the 'informal' stakeholder groups and assess their importance. Other problems in analysis are that individuals tend to belong to more than one group and also stakeholder groups will 'line up' differently depending on the issue or strategy in hand. For example, marketing and production departments could well be united in the face of proposals to drop certain product lines, while being in fierce opposition regarding plans to buy in new items to the product range. It is *specific events* which trigger off the formation of stakeholder groups. For these reasons, stakeholder analysis is most useful when related to an assessment of specific strategic developments, such as the introduction of a new product or extension into a new geographical area. In this sense it is also a tool for evaluating strategies, as will be seen in Chapter 8.

5.3.2 Stakeholder Mapping[9]

Stakeholder mapping identifies stakeholder expectations and power and helps in establishing political priorities. It consists of making judgements on two issues:

stakeholder mapping *identifies stakeholder expectations and power and helps in establishing political priorities*

- How *interested* each stakeholder group is to impress its expectations on the organisation's choice of strategies.
- Whether they have the means to do so. This is concerned with the *power* of stakeholder groups (see section 5.3.3).

Power/Interest Matrix

The power/interest matrix can be seen in Exhibit 5.5. This classifies stakeholders in relation to the power they hold and the extent to which they are likely to show interest in the organisation's strategies. The matrix indicates the type of relationship which the organisation needs to establish with each stakeholder group. As such, it is a useful analytical tool both in assessing the political ease or difficulty of particular strategies and also in planning the political dimension of strategic changes. Clearly, the acceptability of strategies to the *key players* (segment D) should be a major consideration during the formulation and evaluation of new strategies (see Chapter 8, section 8.3.3). Often the most difficult relationship to plan is with stakeholders in segment C (institutional shareholders often fall into this category). Although these stakeholders might, in general, be relatively passive, a disastrous situation can arise if their level of interest is underrated and they suddenly *reposition* to segment D and frustrate the adoption of a new strategy. A view might also be taken that it is a *responsibility* of strategists or managers to raise the level of interest of powerful stakeholders (such as institutional shareholders), so that they can better fulfil their expected role within the corporate governance framework. This could also be concerned with how non-executive directors are assisted in fulfilling their role, say, through good information and briefing.

Similarly, the needs of stakeholders in segment B need to be properly addressed – largely through information. They can be crucially important

Exhibit 5.5 Stakeholder mapping: the power/interest matrix

LEVEL OF INTEREST

POWER	Low	High
Low	**A** Minimal effort	**B** Keep informed
High	**C** Keep satisfied	**D** Key players

Source Adapted from A. Mendelow, *Proceedings of the Second International Conference on Information Systems*, Cambridge, MA, 1991.

'allies' in influencing the attitudes of more powerful stakeholders: for example, through *lobbying*. Again, it may be a key responsibility of managers to undertake this informing process with, for instance, representatives of community interests. The value of stakeholder mapping is in assessing the following:

- Whether the levels of interest and power of stakeholders properly reflect the corporate governance framework within which the organisation is operating, as in the examples above (non-executive directors, community groups).
- Whether strategies need to be pursued to *reposition* certain stakeholders. This could be to lessen the influence of a key player or, in certain instances, to ensure that there are more key players who will champion the strategy (this is often critical in the public sector context).
- Who are the key *blockers* and *facilitators* of change and how this will be responded to – for example, in terms of education or persuasion.
- The extent to which stakeholders will need to be assisted or encouraged to *maintain* their level of interest or power to ensure successful

implementation of strategies. For example, public 'endorsement' by powerful suppliers or customers may be critical to the success of a strategy. Equally, it may be necessary to discourage some stakeholders from repositioning themselves. This is what is meant by *keep satisfied* in relation to stakeholders in segment C, and to a lesser extent *keep informed* for those in segment B. The use of *side payments*[10] to stakeholders as a means of securing their acceptance of new strategies has traditionally been regarded as a key maintenance activity.

These questions, of course, raise some difficult ethical issues for managers in deciding the role they should play in the political activity surrounding strategic change. For example, are managers really the honest brokers who weigh the conflicting expectations of stakeholder groups? Or are they answerable to one stakeholder – such as shareholders – and hence is their role to ensure the acceptability of their strategies to other stakeholders? Or are they, as many authors suggest, the real power behind the throne, constructing strategies to suit their own purposes and managing stakeholder expectations to ensure acceptance of these strategies?

These are important issues for managers and other stakeholders to consider.[11] The corporate governance arrangements for the organisation will answer these questions only at the most general level. Against that backdrop, the balancing of the conflicting interests of different stakeholders is strongly determined by the ethical stance of the organisation and the individual managers. This will be discussed fully in section 5.4 below.

Illustration 5.4(a) shows how a stakeholder mapping exercise can assist in determining the political priorities involved in pursuing a new strategy, and some of the practical issues often encountered when undertaking such an analysis. The analysis relates to a German bank with headquarters in Frankfurt (Germany) and providing corporate banking services from head office and a regional office in Toulouse (France). It is considering the closure of its Toulouse office and providing all corporate banking services from Frankfurt. The analysis needs to address several issues.

1. It may be necessary to *subdivide* a stakeholder group into more than one group because there are important differences in expectations or power within that group. In the illustration, *customers* have been divided into those who are largely supportive of the strategy (customer X), those who are actively hostile (customer Y) and those who are indifferent (customer Z). In using stakeholder mapping, there is clearly a balance to be struck between describing stakeholders too generically – hence hiding important issues of diversity – and too much subdivision making the map confusing and difficult to interpret.
2. Most stakeholder groups consist of large numbers of individuals (such as customers or shareholders), and hence can be thought of largely independently of the expectations of individuals within that group. With some stakeholder groups this is not the case: they consist of a small number of individuals or even single individuals (e.g. the chairperson of

STRATEGY IN ACTION ILLLUSTRATION 5.4(a)

Stakeholder Mapping at Tallman GmbH

Stakeholder mapping can be a useful tool for determining the political priorities for specific strategic developments or changes.

Tallman GmbH was a German bank providing both retail and corporate banking services throughout Germany, Benelux and France. There were concerns about its loss in market share in the corporate sector which was serviced from two centres – Frankfurt (for Germany and Benelux) and Toulouse (for France). It was considering closing the Toulouse operation and servicing all corporate clients from Frankfurt. This would result in significant job losses in Toulouse, some of which would be replaced in Frankfurt alongside vastly improved IT systems.

Two power/interest maps were drawn up by the company officials to establish likely stakeholder reactions to the proposed closure of the Toulouse operation. Map A represents the likely situation and map B the preferred situation – where support for the proposal would be sufficient to proceed.

Referring to map A it can be seen that, with the exception of customer X and IT supplier A, the stakeholders in box B are currently opposed to the closure of the Toulouse operation. If Tallman was to have any chance of convincing these stakeholders to change their stance to a more supportive one, the company must address their questions and, where possible, alleviate their fears. If such fears were overcome, these people may become important allies in influencing the more powerful stakeholders in boxes C and D. The supportive attitude of customer X could be usefully harnessed in

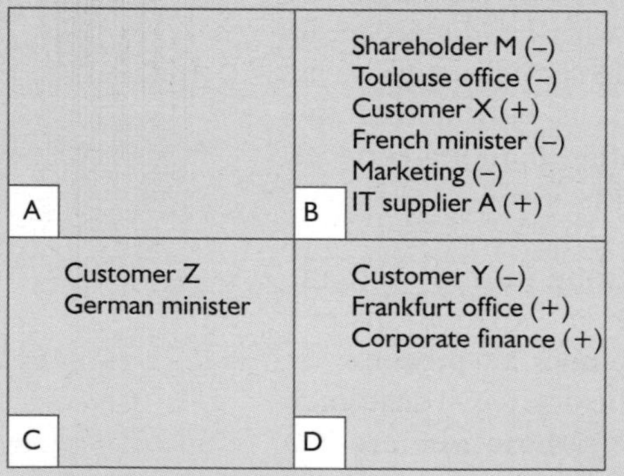

A	B: Shareholder M (–) Toulouse office (–) Customer X (+) French minister (–) Marketing (–) IT supplier A (+)
C: Customer Z German minister	D: Customer Y (–) Frankfurt office (+) Corporate finance (+)

Map A: The likely situation

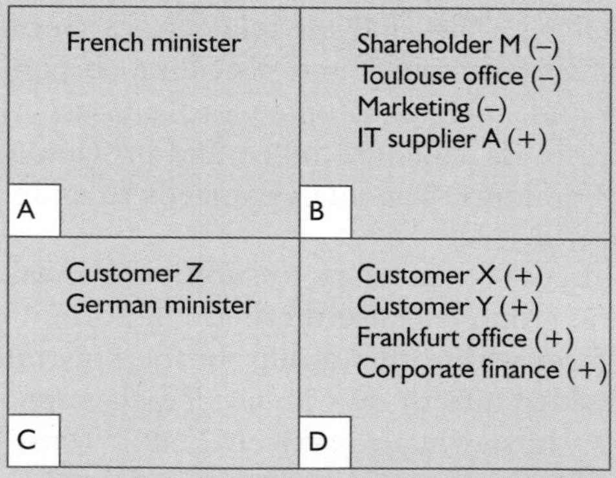

A: French minister	B: Shareholder M (–) Toulouse office (–) Marketing (–) IT supplier A (+)
C: Customer Z German minister	D: Customer X (+) Customer Y (+) Frankfurt office (+) Corporate finance (+)

Map B: The preferred situation

this quest. Customer X was a multinational with operations throughout Europe. They had shown dissatisfaction with the inconsistent treatment that they received from Frankfurt and Toulouse.

The relationships Tallman had with the stakeholders in box C were the most difficult to manage since, while they were considered to be relatively passive, largely owing to their indifference to the proposed strategy, a disastrous situation could arise if their level of interest was underrated. For example, if the German minister were replaced, her successor might be opposed to the strategy and actively seek to stop the changes. In this case they would shift to box D.

The acceptability of the proposed strategy to the current players in box D was a key consideration. Of particular concern was customer Y (a major French manufacturer who operated only in France – accounting for 20 per cent of Toulouse corporate banking income). Customer Y was opposed to the closure of the Toulouse operation and could have the power to prevent it from happening, for example by the withdrawal of its business. The company clearly needed to have open discussions with this stakeholder.

By comparing the position of stakeholders in map A and map B, and identifying any changes and mismatches, Tallman could establish a number of tactics to change the stance of certain stakeholders to a more positive one and to increase the power of certain stakeholders. For example, customer X could be encouraged to champion the proposed strategy and assist Tallman by providing media access, or even convincing customer Y that the change could be beneficial.

Tallman could also seek to dissuade or prevent powerful stakeholders from changing their stance to a negative one. For example, unless direct action were taken, lobbying from her French counterpart may well raise the German minister's level of interest. This has implications for how the company handles the situation in France. Time could be spent talking the strategy through with the French minister and also customer Y, so as to try to shift them away from opposition at least to neutrality, if not support.

Questions

To ensure that you are clear about how to undertake stakeholder mapping produce your own complete analysis for Tallman GmbH against a different strategy, i.e. *to service all corporate clients from Toulouse*. Ensure that you go through the following steps:

1. Plot the most likely situation (map A) – remembering to be careful to *reassess* interest and power for each stakeholder in relation to this *new* strategy.
2. Map the preferred situation (map B).
3. Identify the mismatches – and hence the political priorities. Remember to include the need to *maintain* a stakeholder in its 'opening' position (if relevant).
4. Finish off by listing the actions you would propose to take and give a final view of the degree of political risk in pursuing this new strategy.

the company or the minister of a government department). It is essential that the analysis properly acknowledges the extent to which the mapping of the *role* (e.g. chairperson) is concerned with that particular *individual*. It is useful to know if a new individual in that role would shift the positioning. Serious misjudgements can be made if proper care is not paid to this point.

In the example, it has been concluded that the German minister has been plotted in segment C on the grounds that she is largely indifferent to the new development – it is very low in her priorities. However, a change of minister might shift this situation overnight. Although it will be impossible to remove such uncertainties entirely, there are implications for the political priorities. For example, those permanent officials who are advising the minister need to be kept satisfied, since they will outlive individual ministers and provide a continuity which can diminish uncertainty. It is also possible, of course, that the German minister's level of interest will be raised by lobbying from her French counterpart. This has implications for how the company handles the situation in France.

3. Illustration 5.4(a) shows how the political priorities can be established from stakeholder mapping:
   - Plot a map showing how stakeholders would *line up* in relation to a new strategy (geographical rationalisation in the illustration).
   - Plot a second map showing how you would *like stakeholders to line up* if the strategy is to have the best chance of success.
   - By comparing these two maps and looking for the *mismatches*, the political priorities can be established. In the illustration, these are changing the interest of the French minister and customer Y away from opposition, and enfranchising customer X (to champion the strategy), perhaps by assisting with media access or in persuading customer Y.
   - It needs to be remembered that political priorities may also be concerned with *maintaining* stakeholders in their current positioning. In the illustration, this involves keeping the issue low in the priorities of the German minister (through efforts in France to discourage lobbying).

5.3.3 Assessing Power[12]

The previous section was concerned with analysing stakeholder expectations and highlighted the need to assess the power of the various stakeholders. Power is the mechanism by which expectations are able to influence strategies. It has been seen that in most organisations power will be unequally shared between the various stakeholders.

Before proceeding, it is necessary to understand what is meant here by 'power'. In particular, a distinction needs to be drawn between, on the one hand, the power that people or groups derive from their position within the organisation and through the formal corporate governance arrangements, and on the other, the power that they possess by other means. For the purposes of strategic analysis, **power** is best understood as the extent to which individuals or groups are able to persuade, induce or coerce others into following certain courses of action. This is the mechanism by which one set of expectations will dominate strategic development or seek compromise with others. Analysis of power must, therefore, begin with an assessment of the sources of power.

power *is the extent to which individuals or groups are able to persuade, induce or coerce others into following certain courses of action*

Exhibit 5.6 summarises the various sources of power for both internal and external stakeholders, and can be used as a checklist against which to make an assessment of how powerful each stakeholder is in influencing the strategic development under consideration. Since there are a variety of different sources of power, it is often useful to look for *indicators of power*, which are the visible signs that stakeholders have been able to exploit one or more of the sources of power listed in Exhibit 5.6. There are four useful indicators of power:

- The *status* of the individual or group. One measure of status might be position within the hierarchy, but others are equally important: for example, an individual's salary, or job grades of groups. Equally, the reputation that a group or individual holds with others will be very relevant.
- The *claim on resources* as measured by the size of a department's budget, or the number of employees within that group. In particular, trends in the proportion of resources claimed by that group may be a useful indicator of the extent to which its power is waxing or waning. A useful comparison can be made with similar groups in comparable organisations.
- *Representation* in powerful positions. This needs to be judged in relation to the corporate governance arrangements for the organisation. A good example of this is the composition of the board of directors and their particular specialisms. The weakness of the production function may result from lack of representation at board level. Within other organisations, representation on important committees could be a measure of power, although a simple headcount would overlook the extent to which the individuals are influential. Here individual status should be taken into consideration.
- *Symbols of power*. Internal division of power may be indicated in a variety of ways. Such physical symbols as the size and location of people's offices, and whether they have a secretary, carpets, or newspapers delivered each morning, are all important clues. Whether individuals are addressed by their first or second names, even the way they dress, may be symbols of power. In more bureaucratic organisations, the existence of 'distribution lists' for internal memoranda and other information can give useful clues to the power

Exhibit 5.6 Sources and indicators of power

Sources of Power

(a) Within organisations

- Hierarchy (formal power), e.g. autocratic decision making
- Influence (informal power), e.g. charismatic leadership
- Control of strategic resources, e.g. strategic products.
- Possession of knowledge and skills, e.g. computer specialists
- Control of the environment, e.g. negotiating skills
- Involvement in strategy implementation, e.g. by exercising discretion

(b) For external stakeholders

- Control of strategic resources, e.g. materials, labour, money
- Involvement in strategy implementation, e.g. distribution outlets, agents
- Possession of knowledge (skills), e.g. subcontractors
- Through internal links, e.g. informal influence

Indicators of Power

(a) Within organisations

- Status
- Claim on resources
- Representation
- Symbols

(b) For external stakeholders

- Status
- Resource dependence
- Negotiating arrangements
- Symbols

structure. These lists do not always neatly reflect the formal hierarchical structure and may provide pointers as to who is viewed as powerful within the organisation.

No single indicator is likely to uncover the structure of power within a company. However, by looking at all four indicators, it may be possible to identify which people or groups appear to have power by a number of these measures. More importantly, this assessment of power needs to be made *in relation to the particular strategy under consideration*. For example, the corporate finance function is likely to be more powerful in relation to developments requiring new capital or revenue commitments than in relation to ones which are largely self-financing or within the financial authority of separate divisions or subsidiaries. Illustration 5.4(b) shows how such an analysis was performed to assess the relative power of the corporate finance and marketing departments and the offices of the two-site corporate banking operations previously discussed. The corporate finance department was seen as powerful by all measures and the marketing department as universally weak. Equally, Frankfurt was particularly powerful in relation to Toulouse.

STRATEGY IN ACTION
Illustration 5.4(b)

Assessment of Power

Assessing the power of stakeholders is an important part of stakeholder mapping.

Internal stakeholders

INDICATORS OF POWER	CORPORATE FINANCE	MARKETING	FRANKFURT	TOULOUSE
Status				
Position in hierarchy (closeness to board)	H	L	H	M
Salary of top manager	H	L	H	L
Average grade of staff	H	M	H	L
Claim on resources				
Number of staff	M	H	M	M
Size of similar company	H	L	H	L
Budget as % of total	H	M	H	L
Representation				
Number of directors	H	None	M	None
Most influential directors	H	None	M	None
Symbols				
Quality of accommodation	H	L	M	M
Support services	H	L	H	L

External stakeholders

INDICATORS OF POWER	IT SUPPLIER A	CUSTOMER Y	SHAREHOLDER M
Status	M	H	L
Resource dependence	M	H	H
Negotiating arrangements	M	H	L
Symbols	H	H	L

H = high M = medium L = low

The corporate finance department is seen as powerful by all measures, and the marketing department universally weak. Equally, the Frankfurt operation is particularly powerful by comparison with Toulouse. This analysis provides important data in the process of stakeholder mapping, since the strategic importance of power is also related to whether individuals or groups are likely to exercise their power. This assessment thus helped in deciding where to locate the stakeholders on the power/interest maps.

Combining the results of this analysis with the stakeholder mapping exercise, it can be seen that Toulouse's only real hope is to encourage supplier A to reposition by convincing it of the increased IT opportunities which a two-centre operation would provide. Perhaps shareholder M could be helpful in this process through lobbying the supplier.

Prepared by Sara Martin, Cranfield School of Management.

Alongside this internal assessment of power, a similar analysis of the power held by external stakeholders needs to be carried out. The indicators of power here are slightly different:

- The *status* of an external party such as a supplier is usually indicated by the way that it is discussed among company employees, and whether the company responds quickly to the supplier's demands.
- *Resource dependence* can often be measured directly. For example, the relative size of shareholdings or loans, the proportion of a company's business tied up with any one customer, or a similar dependence on suppliers, can normally be easily measured. Perhaps the key indicator is the ease with which that supplier, financier or customer could switch or *be switched* at short notice. It might also be useful to examine the routines of the organisation – particularly the external linkages. These should indicate how dependency has been 'built in' to the organisational culture. This can be a problem for small businesses which are very dependent as tied suppliers on large manufacturers such as Ford, or large retailers such as Marks and Spencer.
- *Negotiating arrangements* include whether external parties are treated at arm's length or are actively involved in negotiations with the company. For example, a customer which is invited to negotiate over the price of a contract is in a more powerful position than a similar company which is given a fixed price on a take-it-or-leave-it basis.
- *Symbols* are also valuable clues: for example, whether the management team wines and dines a customer or supplier, or the level of person in the company who deals with a particular supplier. The care and attention paid to correspondence with outsiders will tend to differ from one party to another.

Again, no single measure will give a full understanding of the extent of the power held by external stakeholders, but the combined analysis will be very useful. Illustration 5.4(b) shows how an analysis of the power of external stakeholders can be performed. This analysis was used in the process of *stakeholder mapping* to make a political assessment of the strategy of closing down the Toulouse operation. It can be seen that Toulouse's only real hope of survival is to encourage supplier A to 'reposition' by convincing it of the increased IT opportunities that a two-centre operation would provide. Perhaps shareholder M could be helpful in this process through lobbying the supplier.

5.4 BUSINESS ETHICS[13]

The discussion in the previous sections has viewed organisational purposes as being concerned with the expectations of stakeholders – but particularly those who have formal 'rights' through the corporate governance framework and those stakeholders who are most interested and powerful in other ways.

However, there has been little discussion so far about the nature of stakeholder expectations: which purposes are regarded as more important than others and why? The answer to this question is concerned with two issues: first, the *ethical context* of the organisation, and second, the *cultural context* within which the organisation is operating. These issues are clearly related – for example, the very different attitudes to practices such as bribery in different countries. This and the subsequent section discuss these two related issues, commencing with business ethics.

Ethical issues concerning business and public sector organisations exist at three levels:

- At the *macro* level, there are issues about the role of business in the national and international organisation of society. This is largely concerned with assessing the relative virtues of different political and social systems, such as free enterprise and centrally planned economies, and the purposes which business enterprises are expected to fulfil. There are also important issues of international relationships and the role of business on an international scale. As mentioned in section 5.2, the differing corporate governance arrangements from country to country reflect differing emphases on these macro issues. So the first issue for individual organisations is the broad *ethical stance* which it takes in relation to the corporate governance framework within which it is operating.
- Within this macro framework, *corporate social responsibility* is concerned with the ethical issues facing corporate entities (private and public sector) when formulating and implementing strategies. This concerns the extent to which the organisation should move beyond the minimum obligations provided through corporate governance, and how the conflicting demands of different stakeholders can be reconciled.
- At the *individual* level, it concerns the behaviour and actions of individuals within organisations. This is clearly an important issue for the management of organisations, but it is discussed here only in so far as it affects strategy, and in particular the role of managers in the strategic management process.

5.4.1 The Ethical Stance

The corporate governance arrangements for an organisation determine the minimum obligations of an organisation towards its various stakeholders. Therefore, a key strategic issue within organisations is the *ethical stance* which is taken regarding obligations to stakeholders. The **ethical stance** is the extent to which an organisation will exceed its minimum obligations to stakeholders.

the **ethical stance** *is the extent to which an organisation will exceed its minimum obligations to stakeholders*

The key issue for managers is to understand and influence the ethical stance which the organisation is taking. Exhibit 5.7 outlines four *stereotypes* to illustrate the range of difference stances found in organisations:

- At one extreme there are organisations which have taken the view that the only responsibility of business is the short-term interests of shareholders.[14] Their ethical stance is that it is the domain of government to prescribe, through legislation, the constraints which society chooses to impose on businesses in their pursuit of economic efficiency (i.e. the arrangements for corporate governance). The organisation will meet these minimum obligations, but no more. Expecting companies to exercise other social duties can, in extreme cases, undermine the authority of government and give business organisations even more power: for example, multinationals operating in developing countries are often accused of usurping the legitimate roles of government.
- The ethical stance of category 2 is similar to the previous group, but it is tempered with a recognition of the *long-term benefit to the shareholder* of well managed relationships with other stakeholders. Many of the issues are therefore managed proactively and carefully as a matter of long-term self-interest. For example, external sponsorships or welfare provision might be regarded as sensible expenditures akin to any other form of investment or promotion expenditure. The avoidance of 'shady' marketing practices is necessary to prevent the need for yet more legislation in that area. It is argued that, if managers wish to maintain discretion in the long run over issues such as marketing practices, then they are wise to operate responsibly in the short term.
- The third category takes a different ethical stance. Their view is that stakeholder interests and expectations (wider than just shareholders) should be more *explicitly incorporated in the organisation's purposes* and strategies, and they will often go beyond the minimum obligations of corporate governance.[15] They also argue that the performance of the organisation should be measured in a much more pluralistic way than just through its bottom line. The Quaker companies of the nineteenth century are a good example: to a considerable extent, the attitudes of these companies have remained more socially progressive than others during the twentieth century. Companies in this category might argue that they would retain uneconomic units to preserve jobs, would avoid manufacturing or selling 'anti-social' products (see Illustration 5.5) and would be prepared to bear reductions in profitability for the social good. However, there are clearly important issues of balance. Many public sector organisations are, rightly, positioned within this group. They are subject to a wide diversity of expectations from their stakeholder groups, and unitary measures of performance are often inadequate in reflecting this diversity.

Exhibit 5.7 Four possible ethical stances

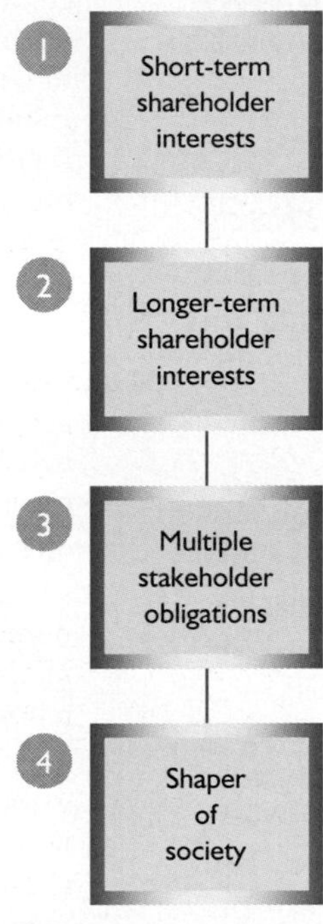

- The final group represents the *ideological* end of the spectrum. They have purposes which are concerned with *shaping society*, and the financial considerations are regarded as of secondary importance or a constraint. The extent to which this is a viable ethical stance clearly depends upon issues of corporate governance and accountability. Arguably, it is easier for a private, family-owned organisation to operate in this way, since it is not accountable to external shareholders. Some would argue that the achievements in public services have been largely because they have been mission driven in this way, and supported by the political framework in which they have operated. In many countries since the mid 1980s, there has been a major challenge to the legitimacy of this mission-driven stance within public services and a reassertion of the rights of citizens (as taxpayers) to expect demonstrable value for money from its public services. This has severely curtailed the ability of public services – particularly at the local level – to be proactive shapers of society.

  Charitable organisations face similar dilemmas – it is often fundamental to their existence that they have a zeal to protect and improve the interests of particular groups in society. But this has to be achieved within the corporate governance framework within which they operate. This can prove difficult given the inevitable political dimension

STRATEGY IN ACTION
Illustration 5.5

Corporate Responsibility: Good Words or Good Works?

Corporate responsibility must be judged by an organisation's actions not just by its aspirations.

Body Shop[1]

By 1996, Body Shop had become a symbol of how business success could be achieved while maintaining responsible – even missionary – attitudes to care for the environment and the rights of people in developing countries.

The company, which manufactures and sells skin and hair care products and cosmetics, was created and developed by Anita Roddick from her first shop in Brighton, UK, in 1976. The following are extracts from the second in a series of lectures which she gave in 1994, providing an insight into Body Shop's ethical stance and its practical approach to corporate social responsibility:

> 'I am no loony do-gooder, traipsing the world hugging trees and staring into crystals ... I am also not one of those people who is opposed to trade or change ... But I am concerned about *quality* in trade not just quantity.'
>
> 'We need trade that respects and supports communities and families ... safeguards the environment ... [and] encourages countries to educate their children, heal their sick, value the work of women and respect human rights. We need to measure progress by human development not gross product.'
>
> 'Business must not only avoid hideous evil, it must actively do good.'
>
> 'Our political postures must change – we have to stop endlessly whining for easier rules, lower costs and fewer restrictions ... we have to take longer-term views, invest in the communities and build long-lasting markets.'
>
> 'Inside Body Shop we are arguing whether we should follow Levi Strauss' example [and stop purchasing from China] ... many, including my husband Gordon, argue that we can make a positive difference [by trading with China].'
>
> 'Investing in Easterhouse, Glasgow, one of the worst examples of unemployment and housing in western Europe, was a moral choice. I would rather employ the unemployable than the already employed. The [products] are up to 30% more expensive and we are putting [25%] of the net profits back into the community. But it is better for the company. It is an example of what keeps the soul of the company alive.'
>
> 'We ... could not wait for the European Union to ratify environmental auditing; we did it ourselves.'
>
> 'I would rather be measured by how I treat

to their work. They also need to remain financially viable, which can bring problems with their image – sometimes seen as being overcommercial and spending too much on administration or promotional activities.

Whichever ethical stance an organisation takes, this stance should become an integral element of corporate strategy. Strategically, it helps a company to decide what kind of company it wishes to be – an important element in defining its organisational *purposes*. There is likely to be a strong relationship between the ethical stance and the character of the company.

weaker and frailer communities I trade with than by how great are my profits.'

IKEA[2]

IKEA, the Swedish furniture chain created by Ingvar Kamprad (and featured in Illustration 1.1), was the subject of a hard-hitting article in the *Sunday Times* in February 1998. The article concerned the working and living conditions in Romanian furniture factories. Although IKEA did not own any of the 25 factories which produced furniture for its stores, it had provided collateral for at least one factory to be bought from the state in 1992. In fact, there were allegations from the Federation of Wood Workers that the directors of the factory used money from IKEA and disregarded the law under which Romanian employees are entitled to be given the option of buying their own factory as a co-operative.

The article observed that the appalling conditions in Romania flew in the face of the politically correct image of IKEA fostered by Ingvar Kamprad who regularly wrote memos to staff which started with 'Dear IKEA family'.

The managing director of this factory admitted that he kept a competitive edge by paying employees an average of about 20p per hour (about one-fortieth of the pay levels in Sweden). IKEA's response to these issues was that it had no management responsibility for any Romanian factory. It accepted, however, that conditions were poor and that it had provided the collateral necessary for the purchase of one factory. It also restated its financial support for the Romanian furniture industry through credits which allowed new buildings with better working conditions. It believed that trade was better than aid and that it intended to continue to assist with financial and technical support and by expanding orders.

Questions

1. From the evidence you have in these extracts and referring to Exhibit 5.7, list the arguments and evidence for and against categorising the Body Shop and IKEA's ethical stance as one or more of the stereotypes in the exhibit.
2. Make *your* final decision of where, overall, you feel each company is placed. (Perhaps you could use a scale of 1–10 with 1–2 in short-term interests, 3–5 longer-term interests, 6–8 multiple stakeholders, and 9–10 shaper of society.)

Sources

1. 'Anita Roddick speaks out on corporate responsibility', Body Shop, 1994.
2. *Sunday Times*, 22 February 1998.

The ethical stance also helps to determine *how* the organisation will try to reach its goals and how it will relate to its various stakeholders.

5.4.2 Corporate Social Responsibility[16]

The previous section has identified the overall 'stance' which an organisation may take concerning its role in society, and the extent to which it will operate within or beyond its framework of corporate governance. This still leaves the need to identify the more detailed 'agenda' of issues which an

corporate social responsibility *is the detailed issues on which an organisation exceeds its minimum required obligations to stakeholders*

organisation may be taking into account when developing strategies, and the way in which the organisation will manage the agenda. **Corporate social responsibility** is the detailed issues on which an organisation exceeds its minimum required obligations to stakeholders. Exhibit 5.8 outlines a number of these issues, both internal and external to the organisation, and provides a checklist against which an organisation's actions on corporate social responsibility can be assessed.

One survey[17] showed several issues of concern in how organisations were addressing the various items listed in Exhibit 5.8. Although a large number of companies had produced guidelines on some or all of the issues, a significant number had no programme by which to put them into effect: 'the picture which emerges is one of good intentions often unfulfilled'. The authors concluded that companies in Britain had generally increased their awareness of and level of activity in some aspects of social responsibility, but they seemed to limit their involvement to a relatively narrow range of issues. They also indicated that most organisations failed to seek out best practice elsewhere, and this, they suggested, indicated that social responsibility considerations were not pursued as keenly as commercial activities.

5.4.3 The Role of Individuals and Managers

It should be clear from the preceding discussion that business ethics – as part of strategic management – raises some difficult issues for individuals and managers within organisations:

- What is the responsibility of an individual who believes that the strategy of his or her organisation – for example, its trading practices – is unethical or is not adequately representing the legitimate interests of one or more stakeholder groups? Should the individual report the organisation; or should he or she leave the company on the grounds of a mismatch of values? This has often been called *whistleblowing*.[18]
- Managers are usually in a powerful position within organisations to influence the expectations of other stakeholders. They have access to information and channels of influence which are not available to many other stakeholders. With this power comes an ethical responsibility to behave with *integrity*.

Given that strategy development can be an intensely political process, managers can often find real difficulties establishing and maintaining this position of integrity. As we have seen, there is a potential conflict for managers between what strategies are best for their own career and what strategies are in the longer-term interests of their organisation. Integrity is particularly threatened by the potential for insider-trading prior to acquisitions. The international business community was beset by a series of such cases in the 1980s.

Exhibit 5.8 **Some questions of corporate social responsibility**

Should organisations be responsible for ...

INTERNAL ASPECTS

Employee welfare
... providing medical care, assistance with mortgages, extended sickness leave, assistance for dependants, etc.?

Working conditions
... enhancing working surroundings, social and sporting clubs, above minimum safety standards, etc.?

Job design
... designing jobs to the increased satisfaction of workers rather than for economic efficiency?

EXTERNAL ASPECTS

Green issues
... reducing pollution below legal standards if competitors are not doing so?
... energy conservation?

Products
... danger arising from the careless use of product by consumers?

Markets and marketing
... deciding not to sell in some markets?
... advertising standards?

Suppliers
... 'fair' terms of trade?
... blacklisting suppliers?

Employment
... positive discrimination in favour of minorities?
... maintaining jobs?

Community activity
... sponsoring local events and supporting local good works?

Integrity is a key ingredient of professional management and is included in the code of conduct of professional bodies such as the Institute of Management.[19] Best practice is shared through the international links between these professional bodies.

5.5 THE CULTURAL CONTEXT

the **cultural web** *is a representation of the taken-for-granted assumptions, or paradigm, of an organisation and the physical manifestations of the organisation culture*

Chapter 2 introduced the concept of culture and its importance to strategic management, and provided an approach to analysing culture: the **cultural web** (see Exhibit 2.10) which, as explained in Chapter 2, is a representation of the taken-for-granted assumptions, or paradigm, of an organisation and the physical manifestations of the organisation culture. It was also acknowledged that there are a variety of cultural influences on individuals and stakeholders which shape their expectations. These were referred to as the *frames of reference* and are reproduced here as Exhibit 5.9. It is not the intention to repeat the introductory discussion of culture in this chapter, but to build on it in two ways:

- To identify the kinds of specific factors and issues which the strategist should be looking for in each of the cultural *frames of reference*, when building up a picture of how the cultural context will influence the prioritising of purposes by organisations.
- To show how organisational culture can be *characterised*, as a means of understanding the influences of culture on both current and future organisational purposes.

5.5.1 National and Regional Cultures[20]

It has already been noted that there are significant differences in the corporate governance frameworks between countries, and that the ethical stance and corporate social responsibility agenda will also differ. But the cultural context also influences the expectations of stakeholders directly.[21] For example, attitudes to work, authority, equality and a number of other important factors differ from one location to another.[22]

From the point of view of understanding organisational purposes, it is important to understand these influences for two reasons. First, values of society change and adjust over time, and therefore strategies which were acceptable and successful twenty years ago may not be so today. There has been an increasing trend within many countries for the activities of companies to be constrained by legislation, public opinion and the media. Second, companies which operate *internationally* have the added problem of coping with the very different standards and expectations of the various countries in which they operate. Illustration 5.6 shows how this can create issues and difficulties for stakeholders too in the case of Eurotunnel – a joint venture between the UK and France.

Although it is not shown separately in Exhibit 5.9 (for reasons of simplification), it may often be necessary to identify important *subnational* (usually regional) cultures. For example, attitudes to some aspects of employment, supplier relationships and, certainly, consumer preferences would differ significantly at a regional level even in a relatively small and cohesive country like the UK, and quite markedly elsewhere in Europe (e.g. between northern and southern Italy). In some respects there are also developing aspects of *supranational* culture beyond a single nation. For example, judgements on whether there is likely to be a move towards a 'Euro-consumer' with converging tastes and preferences are of crucial strategic importance to many organisations in planning their product and distribution strategies. Illustration 2.4 (Chapter 2) also showed an example of this issue in relation to Chinese culture.

Exhibit 5.9 **Cultural frames of reference**

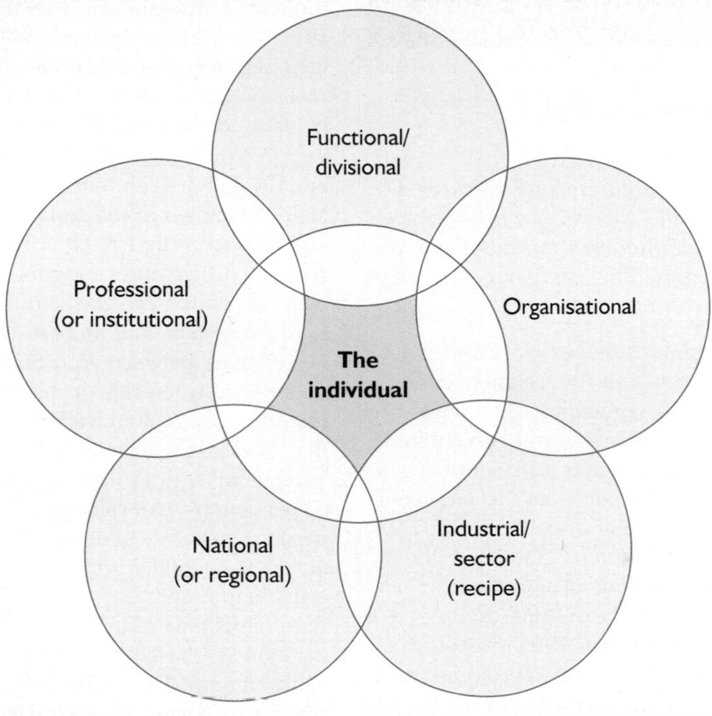

5.5.2 Professional and Institutional Cultures

Many individuals are members of a professional or institutional group whose values and beliefs are a powerful influence on that individual's expectations of the organisation and its purposes.[23] These allegiances may be highly institutionalised and directly related to the work situation, such as membership of a trade union or professional association. They may also be more informal and unrelated, such as membership of churches or political groups, but still very influential. An important trend in the 'post-industrial' economies has been the declining power of organised trade unions and the growing importance of professional groups as the number of 'knowledge workers' increases. Many organisations are now employing large numbers of professional staff from a number of different professions with very different professional values. So in health care the medical doctors, paramedics, nurses, and finance and managerial professionals may agree on purposes at one level (improving health), but there are key differences in expectations when purposes become specific through debates about priorities and resource allocation.

STRATEGY IN ACTION
Illustration 5.6

Eurotunnel

The different national traditions and cultures are reflected in the legal and governance frameworks too. This can cause difficulties for stakeholders, such as banks, when dealing with cross-country clients, such as Eurotunnel.

By the end of the summer season 1995, Eurotunnel, the Anglo-French operator of the Channel Tunnel, faced severe financial problems. Opening 18 months later than planned had cost it two summer seasons' revenue, which, together with a doubling of the £4.8 billion construction and development costs, meant that £7.8 billion of debt owed to 225 banks incurred a £700 million p.a. interest bill that dwarfed half-year turnover of £107 million or net cash inflow of £28 million (before interest).

Thus, on 14 September 1995, Eurotunnel simply announced that it would stop payment of interest for up to 18 months, allowed in the credit agreements, in order to review operations and the financing of the tunnel.

The banks had little option but to negotiate, but they were conscious that the management had grown traffic to 34 per cent of car cross-Channel traffic, 50 per cent of lorry cross-Channel traffic and 40 per cent of London to Paris/Brussels rail passengers. Therefore, replacing the management was unlikely to boost receipts. Also, the tunnel 'asset', while valued in the balance sheet at £9.4 billion, would realise a low sale value as a 'hole in the ground plus infrastructure'.

But the greatest problem (for the banks) was that Eurotunnel was actually two companies, Eurotunnel plc (UK) and Eurotunnel SA (France), co-chaired by the combative Sir Alastair Morton and the conciliatory Patrick Ponselle respectively, and subject to two contrasting commercial law systems. Under UK insolvency procedures, banks stand above most creditors. Thus, while most able to determine a company's behaviour and future, the banks also bear least risk via their 'secured creditor' status. French legal procedures are at the other end of the spectrum. Under *redressment judiciarie*, the interests of the enterprise and the employees rank above banks. French shareholders, who were 80 per cent of Eurotunnel's 721,000 shareholders, also had recourse under French law if a financial restructuring treated them unfairly as stakeholders.

In November 1995, Eurotunnel set up French and UK shareholders' committees with Mr Maurice le Maire appointed to the group board, novel in France and unique in the UK. On 12 February 1996, at the request of the group's auditors, the Paris commercial court appointed two mediators *mandataire ad hoc*, Lord Wakeham and Robert Badinter, to facilitate negotiations between Eurotunnel and its creditors over the restructuring of the debt, including unpaid interest since September 1995. The banks still had the power to terminate the interest standstill 'agreement' with Eurotunnel prior to March 1997, if 65 per cent by loan value voted to do so; nor did they need to co-operate in negotiation. But the prospect of at best the conflict progressing to the Paris commercial court, and at worst the precipitation of Eurotunnel into 'redressment' in France *and* administration in the UK, was likely to concentrate the banks' attention on achieving a negotiated restructuring that at least satisfied shareholders, employees and the company in addition to themselves. By 1996, the only completely satisfied stakeholder was the customer, enjoying a price war over cross-Channel travel provision and the price of duty-frees.

Questions

1. Do you feel that the rights of bankers as creditors should be high or low priority (as in the UK and France respectively)?
2. What might be the consequence to the development strategies of companies of changing the situation in the UK to align with French law?
3. How long can customers continue to benefit from the price-war and legal log-jam?

Sources Eurotunnel Prospectus, Reports and Accounts; *Financial Times*.

Prepared by Geoff Goddin, Thames Valley University, London.

5.5.3 Industry Recipes[24]

An **industry recipe** is a set of assumptions held in common within an industry or public service about organisational purposes and a 'shared wisdom' on how to manage organisations (see, for example, Scottish Knitwear in Illustration 2.4 of Chapter 2). It may prove difficult for individual firms to step out of line from this industry recipe without being dubbed as mavericks or cowboys. There is clearly an advantage to such cultural influences, in terms of maintaining standards and consistency between individual providers. Many industries have trade associations which also reinforce these norms, such as the Association of British Travel Agents (ABTA). Sometimes this occurs on an international scale, as with the Organisation of Petroleum Exporting Countries (OPEC).

an **industry recipe** *is a set of assumptions held in common within an industry or public service about organisational purposes and a 'shared wisdom' on how to manage organisations*

The danger is that managers may not look beyond their industry in thinking through strategies for the future. They become victims of industry 'groupthink' and do not see the lessons which can be learnt from outside their own industry. One of the advantages of *benchmarking*, as discussed in Chapter 4, is to challenge these taken-for-granted 'industry' assumptions by looking at best practice wherever it is found.

Because the dominant culture varies from one industry to another, the transition of managers between sectors can prove quite difficult. A number of private sector managers were encouraged to join public services during the 1980s in an attempt to inject new cultures and outlooks into the public sector. Many were surprised at the difficulties they experienced in adjusting their management style to the different tradition and expectations of their new organisation – for example, in issues like consensus building as part of the decision-making process.

5.5.4 Organisational Culture

It has been suggested that it is useful to conceive of the culture of an organisation as consisting of three layers[25] (see Exhibit 5.10):

- *Values* may be easy to identify in an organisation, and are often written down as statements about the organisation's mission, objectives or strategies. However, they tend to be vague, such as 'service to the community' or 'equal employment opportunities'.
- *Beliefs* are more specific, but again they are issues which people in the organisation can surface and talk about. They might include a belief that the company should not trade with Iraq, or that professional staff should not have their professional actions appraised by managers.
- *Taken-for-granted assumptions* are the real core of an organisation's culture. They are the aspects of organisational life which people find difficult to identify and explain, and are known as the organisational *paradigm*.

Exhibit 5.10 Culture in three layers

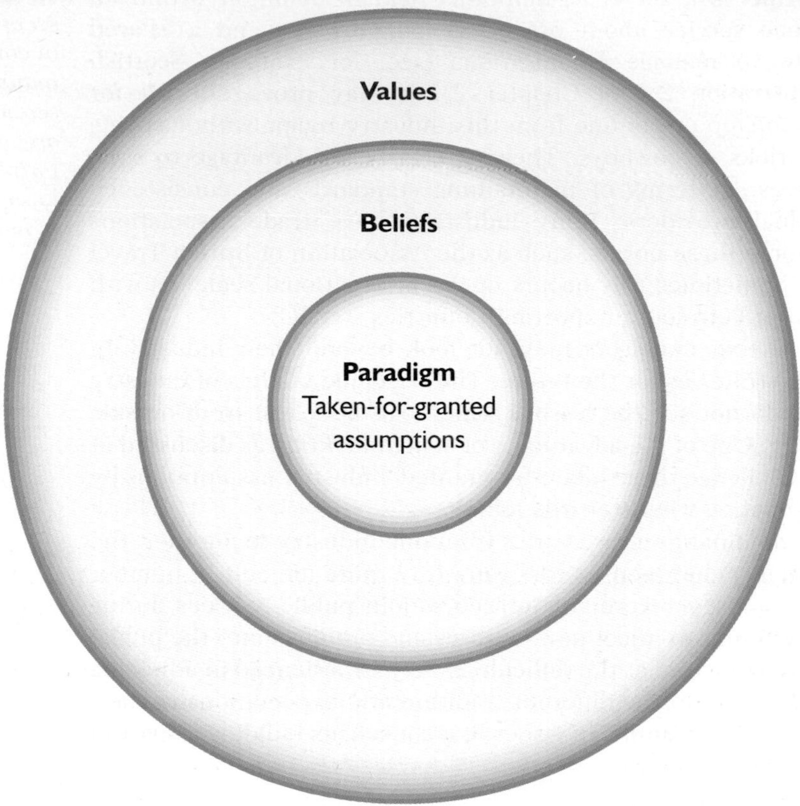

Source Adapted from E. Schein, *Organisation Culture and Leadership*, Jossey-Bass, 1985.

The existence of these three layers of culture presents an analytical dilemma. As organisations increasingly make visible their carefully considered public statements of their values, beliefs and purposes – for example, in annual reports, mission statements and business plans – there is a danger that these are seen as useful and accurate descriptions of the organisational paradigm. But they are likely to be at best only partially accurate, and at worst misleading, descriptions of the *real* organisational culture. This is not to suggest that there is any organised deception. It is simply that the statements of values and beliefs are often statements of aspiration or strategic intent of a particular stakeholder (such as the CEO) rather than accurate descriptions of the culture as it exists in the minds and hearts of people within and around the organisation. This 'real' culture is evidenced by the way the organisation actually operates: it is the taken-for-granted assumptions about 'how you run an organisation like this' and 'what really matters around here', as discussed in Chapter 2, and it may be a source of real competitive advantage.[26] For example, an outside observer of a police force might conclude from its public statements of purpose and priorities that it had a balanced approach to the various aspects of police work – catching criminals, crime prevention, community relations, etc. *However*, a deeper probing might quickly reveal that (in cultural terms) there is the 'real' police work (catching criminals) and the 'lesser work'.

5.5.5 Functional and Divisional Cultures

In seeking to describe, analyse and understand the relationship between culture and an organisation's strategies, it is not usually possible to characterise the whole organisation as one particular type of culture. There are usually important *subcultures* within organisations. These subcultures may arise in a number of ways – some of which are concerned with one or more of the external frames of reference already mentioned, such as unions or professions. The subcultures may also relate directly to the structure of the organisation. For example, the differences between geographical divisions in a multinational company, or between functional groups such as finance, marketing and operations, can be very powerful to the extent that they can be self-perpetuating (see section 5.5.6) and exclusive. In a divisional structure, different divisions may be *positioned* in different ways and pursue different generic strategies, as discussed in Chapter 3. These different positionings require or foster different cultures. Indeed, it will be seen later (Chapters 10 and 11) that matching strategic positioning and organisational culture is a critical feature of successful organisations.

5.5.6 Analysing the Cultural Web[27]

The cultural web can be used to describe and analyse culture at any of the levels discussed above. This can be done by observing the way in which the organisation (or industry or nation) actually operates – the cultural artefacts (the routines, rituals, stories, structures, systems, etc.). Out of these will also come the *clues* about the taken-for-granted assumptions. To use an analogy, it is like trying to describe an iceberg (which is mainly submerged). This is done by observing the parts of the iceberg which show and also (from these clues) inferring what the submerged part of the iceberg must look like.

Exhibit 5.11 outlines some of the questions which might be asked when analysing the cultural web. For example, a simple and effective way of gathering clues through organisational stories is to ask people to describe the most significant things that have happened to the company in the last two or three years. Observing which stories people *select* is an important clue to the taken-for-granted assumptions. Training programmes in an organisation can also be useful pointers to the paradigm. It can also be

Exhibit 5.11 Analysing the cultural web: some useful questions

Stories
- What core beliefs do stories reflect?
- How pervasive are these beliefs (through levels)?
- Do stories relate to:
  - strengths or weaknesses?
  - successes or failures?
  - conformity or mavericks?
- Who are the heroes and villains?
- What norms do the mavericks deviate from?

Routines and rituals
- Which routines are emphasised?
- Which would look odd if changed?
- What behaviour do routines encourage?
- What are the key rituals?
- What core beliefs do they reflect?
- What do training programmes emphasise?
- How easy are rituals/routines to change?

Organisational structure
- How mechanistic/organic are the structures?
- How flat/hierarchical are the structures?
- How formal/informal are the structures?
- Do structures encourage collaboration or competition?
- What types of power structure do they support?

Control systems
- What is most closely monitored/controlled?
- Is emphasis on reward or punishment?
- Are controls related to history or current strategies?
- Are there many/few controls?

Power structures
- What are the core beliefs of the leadership?
- How strongly held are these beliefs (idealists or pragmatists)?
- How is power distributed in the organisation?
- Where are the main blockages to change?

Symbols
- What language and jargon is used?
- How internal or accessible is it?
- What aspects of strategy are highlighted in publicity?
- What status symbols are there?
- Are there particular symbols which denote the organisation?

Overall
- What is the dominant culture (defender, prospector, analyser)?
- How easy is this to change?

useful to observe how hierarchical or informal are the structures and control systems. These are important clues to how new strategies might best be developed and implemented (as discussed in Chapters 9 and 10).

It must be remembered that it is not the separate answers and clues which matter, but the collective picture which they paint of the culture and subcultures. The important strategic issue is how these clues allow the strategist to characterise this culture, as discussed in the next section.

5.5.7 Characterising an Organisation's Culture

In understanding the influence of culture on organisational purposes, it is important to be able to characterise culture (at the various levels discussed above). In this section, the process of characterisation will be illustrated at the level of the organisation and its subcultures.

Miles and Snow[28] categorised organisations into three basic types in terms of how they behave strategically (Exhibit 5.12). When undertaking a strategic analysis, this provides a means of assessing the dominant culture of the organisation. By reviewing the clues from the cultural web analysis, it is possible to distinguish between a *defender* and a *prospector* organisation, and hence judge the extent to which new strategies might fit the current *paradigm*.

For example, defender cultures find change threatening and tend to favour strategies which provide continuity and 'security'. This is supported by a bureaucratic approach to management which may make the organisation averse to innovation. In contrast, a prospector culture thrives on change, favouring strategies of product and market development supported by a more creative and flexible management style. It is a culture in which innovation can prosper. However, the costs of innovation may not be justified (see below).

When characterising organisational cultures for the purposes of strategic analysis, it is important to remember several issues.

1. There is not a 'best' and 'worst' culture. The issue is how well the culture matches and supports the product or market positioning of the organisation (and vice versa). This needs to be linked to a parallel issue, which will be discussed in Chapter 10, about the match between positioning and organisational competences (see Exhibit 10.4).
   - A 'low-price' positioning – for example, a *commodity* product or service – is best supported by competences which emphasise cost improvement and perhaps a largely bureaucratic management regime. In turn, this is often well matched to a *defender* culture. The innovative nature of a prospector culture could make it difficult to contain costs within an acceptable level without demotivating people.
   - In contrast, a positioning of differentiation – perhaps through product features or service quality – requires more creative

Exhibit 5.12 Characterising culture

Organisation Type	Characteristics of Strategic Decision Making: Dominant Objectives	Preferred Strategies	Planning and Control Systems
Defender	Desire for a secure and stable niche in market	Specialisation; cost-efficient production; marketing emphasises price and service to defend current business; tendency to vertical integration	Centralised, detailed control; emphasis on cost efficiency; extensive use of formal planning
Prospector	Location and exploitation of new product and market opportunities	Growth through product and market development (often in spurts); constant monitoring of environmental change; multiple technologies	Emphasis on flexibility; decentralised control; use of *ad hoc* measurements
Analyser	Desire to match new ventures to present shape of business	Steady growth through market penetration; exploitation of applied research, followers in the market	Very complicated; co-ordinating roles between functions (e.g. product managers); intensive planning

Source Adapted from R.E. Miles and C.C. Snow, *Organizational Strategy, Structure and Process*, McGraw-Hill, 1978.

competences and a more flexible management regime. Innovation is the lifeblood of the organisation and this matches well with a *prospector* culture.

2. This matching of positioning, competences and dominant culture is likely to become embedded in successful organisations over a period of time. In other words, the key elements of the strategy become taken for granted and may represent core competences of the organisation, as mentioned in Chapter 4.

   Indeed, the relationship between strategy and dominant culture is usually *self-perpetuating*. So not only does a defender culture match well with a 'commodity' positioning, but it is likely to seek out those parts of the market which secure such a positioning. Moreover, the organisational routines – for example, *selection and recruitment* – are likely to perpetuate the dominant culture by not selecting individuals who will 'rock the boat'.

3. In many organisations, *cohesiveness* of culture is found at a level below the corporate entity, as discussed in section 5.5.5 above. Therefore, it is

important to decide whether this collection of subcultures is a strength or a weakness to the organisation. For example:

- A cohesive corporate culture can be characterised as one of *corporate clones*. Established routines are not deviated from; powerful symbols and stories exist which encourage a commitment to the strategies which the organisation has pursued *historically*; there is little tolerance of questioning and challenge, and so on. These are the circumstances where *strategic drift* is likely to occur, as discussed in Chapter 2.
- The opposite situation is equally worrying and could be described as *open (or covert) warfare*. Cultural cohesion is found only at the level of the sub-unit, and the ability to act corporately is very limited. The real 'enemy' or competitors are internal to the organisation. It has already been mentioned in section 5.5.5 that organisational design and control (for example, divisionalisation) can often create this situation and accidentally lose all the benefits for which the structures were put in place.
- Perhaps the most healthy situation is one of *constructive friction* – where a strong corporate culture is maintained, but where the core beliefs and assumptions are continuously subjected to critique from within the organisation. Challenge and debate, although not comfortable, are regarded as legitimate and signs of strength.

5.6 ORGANISATIONAL PURPOSES

The previous sections of this chapter have looked at the four main forces which will shape an organisation's purposes: *corporate governance*, *stakeholder expectations*, *business ethics* and the *cultural context*. This final section will look at ways in which organisations express and operationalise purposes at different levels of detail – through *mission*, *vision*, *intent* and *objectives*. Illustration 5.7 is an example for a police force.

5.6.1 Mission Statements

The **mission statement** is a generalised statement of the overriding purpose of the organisation. It can be thought of as an expression of its *raison d'être*. If there is substantial disagreement within the organisation or with extreme stakeholders as to its mission, it may well give rise to real problems in resolving the strategic direction of the organisation. If there is a mission statement and it is to be useful, it should address the following issues:[29]

the **mission statement** *is a generalised statement of the overriding purpose of the organisation*

- It should be *visionary*[30] and likely to persist for a significant period of time. This is important as a backcloth against which more detailed objectives and strategies can be developed, delivered and changed over

STRATEGY IN ACTION
Illustration 5.7

Organisational Purposes

Increasingly, organisations are finding it useful to 'publish' a statement of their purposes. This is usually done at several levels of detail, as the example of the Sussex Police shows.

The Sussex Police Standard

1. Purposes

The aims of the Sussex Police are to work with the community to:

- preserve a peaceful society
- prevent and detect offences
- protect life and property
- assist those in need

2. Values

- services to the public
- delivered to the highest quality
- openly and fairly
- and with value for money

As individuals we shall carry out our duties:

- with honesty and integrity
- courteously
- without fear or favour
- exercising responsible direction
- using the minimum necessary force

3. Objectives

The strategic focus for 1995/6 is preserving a peaceful society. We will therefore concentrate our efforts on:

1. The prevention and detection of crime.
2. Answering and attending calls from the public within the stated targets.

Crime objectives

- To increase the detection rate for violent crime to 70%.
- To achieve an overall burglary dwelling detection rate of 20%.
- To achieve a detection rate for total crime of 30%.

Administration of justice objectives

- Of those offences suitable for formal cautioning, to caution 50% by way of instant caution.
- 80% of Manual of Guidance files [paperwork completed following the arrest of crime offenders] to be without error on first submission.

Response to calls objectives

- 90% of 999 calls to the Sussex Police Control Room to be answered within 10 seconds.
- 90% of non-999 switchboard calls to be answered within 30 seconds.
- 90% of grade 1 calls to be responded to within the relevant target time (10 mins urban, 20 mins rural).
- All letters from the public to be answered within 10 working days (or an acknowledgement will be sent).

Public order and reassurance objectives

- To release 30 police officers for operational duty (by elimination of, or civilianisation of, non-operational police posts).
- To maintain the level of one Special Constable for every five divisional police officers.
- To reduce the number of working days lost through sickness by 5%.

Traffic objectives

- To reduce road accident casualties by one-third of the average of the 1981–5 figures by the year 2000.

Questions

1. How useful are these various statements of purpose to the shaping and implementation of the police force's strategy? In answering the question ensure that you give a critique of each of the various 'levels' of statement in order to establish:
   (a) what it is meant to achieve
   (b) whether you feel that it does so
   (c) any improvements you would suggest.
2. Comment on the extent to which these various levels of purpose are consistent with each other.

Source *A Policing Plan for Sussex, 1995/6.*

Prepared by Sara Martin, Cranfield School of Management.

time. In Chapter 1, the distinction was made between a *vision* as a 'desired future state of the organisation'; and *mission* as the 'overriding purpose of the organisation ... in line with the values and expectations of major stakeholders'. There is a great deal of difference between a mission statement which makes it clear that long-term profit growth is required, and a vision which is challenging, even exciting.

- The mission statement should clarify the main *intentions and aspirations* of the organisation and the reasons why the organisation exists. Hamel and Prahalad[31] prefer the term *strategic intent* to that of vision or mission; they see it as an 'animating dream'. It may be sensible to regard a statement of strategic intent as distinct from a mission statement: a mission statement should provide daily guidance. A powerful **strategic intent** is one that encapsulates the desired future state or aspiration of the organisation – the sense of discovery and destiny – that motivates managers and employees alike throughout the organisation. The challenge for corporate executives is that they can achieve this; the implications for business unit executives is that it will, in turn, strongly influence the strategic choices they make.

strategic intent *is the desired future state or aspiration of the organisation*

- The mission statement should describe the organisation's main activities and the position it wishes to attain in its industry.
- There should be a statement of the key *values* of the organisation, particularly regarding attitudes towards stakeholder groups and the ethical agenda discussed above.
- The organisation should have the intention and capability to *live up to* the mission statement, so, desirably, it should articulate expected behavioural standards.

Although mission statements have become much more widely adopted in the 1980s and 1990s, many critics regard them as bland and wide ranging. However, this may be necessary given the political nature of strategic management, since it is essential *at that level* to have statements to which most if not all stakeholders can subscribe.

The extent to which a mission statement is developed by wide involvement of stakeholders or communicated widely will be determined by many of the issues discussed in the previous sections on corporate governance, the ethical stance of the organisation and the relative power of external stakeholders. Mission statements can play very different roles in different circumstances (see Exhibit 5.13):

- If strategy is driven by managers who see other stakeholders and the corporate governance requirements largely as constraints, they may be *secretive* about organisational purposes and see little value in mission statements. When they do exist, they are simply paid lip-service and are not powerful influences on the strategic development of the organisation.
- In contrast, managers who have a missionary zeal for the organisation are likely to use the mission statement in an *evangelical* way to 'sell'

Exhibit 5.13 The role of mission statements

ETHICAL STANCE

DRIVERS OF STRATEGY		Legal minimum	Ideological
	Internal managers	Secretive	Evangelical
	External stakeholders	Regulations and procedures	Political

purposes to other stakeholders. The mission of the organisation is closely aligned to the *strategic intent* of these managers.

- Where strategy is dominated by powerful external stakeholders whose main concern is that the organisation *complies* with the corporate governance arrangements, the purposes are likely to become enshrined in the *regulations and procedures* of the organisation. The danger, of course, is that people lose sight of the mission and the *procedures become the purpose*, as with the classic faceless bureaucracy found in the centrally planned economies of eastern Europe prior to 1990.
- In contrast, if strategy is dominated by external stakeholder(s) with missionary zeal, the purposes of the organisation may become highly politicised. So the ability to produce a mission statement acceptable to all stakeholders can be difficult. This has remained one of the unresolved dilemmas of nationalised industries with government as a major stakeholder. The inability of national governments to sanction capacity reduction in basic industries such as steel (because of the social consequences) created major problems for the profitable management of steel companies in Europe throughout the 1970s, 1980s and early 1990s.

5.6.2 Corporate Objectives

Corporate objectives and unit objectives are distinguished in this chapter because there are different 'levels' of objectives with different characteristics. Corporate objectives are often expressed in financial terms. They could be the expression of desired sales or profit levels, rates of growth, dividend levels or share valuations. Increasingly, organisations use corporate objectives of a non-financial nature, such as employee welfare or technological advance, but it is rare for these to be unaccompanied by financial objectives. They are frequently formal statements of how the organisation intends to address stakeholder expectations. It is becoming increasingly recognised that there should be formal statements of objectives to be met on behalf of a variety of stakeholders, including customers, suppliers, employees and the community at large.

5.6.3 Unit Objectives

Unit objectives are here distinguished from corporate objectives in so far as they are likely to have the following characteristics:

- They relate to the individual units of the organisation. For example, they may be the objectives of a division or of one company within a holding company. In the case of public sector organisations, the unit could be a department of a local authority or a hospital.
- They may be financial objectives stated in much the same way as corporate objectives, but at a unit level. A corporate objective of a given growth in profit after tax might be translated into an objective for each business unit. They are likely to be more operational in nature than corporate objectives.
- Multiple objectives might well be more common at the unit level than at the corporate level. This is likely to be the case if objectives are conceived of in operational terms, since the operations of a business are multifaceted.

5.6.4 The Precision of Mission and Objectives

Many writers[32] have argued that objectives are not helpful unless they are capable of being measured and achieved, i.e. unless they are closed. This view is not taken here. Open statements may in fact be just as helpful as closed statements. For example, mission statements are very difficult to make in closed terms. Their role is to do with *focusing* strategy rather than deciding when it has been 'achieved'. In addition, there may be some objectives which are important, but which are difficult to quantify or express in measurable terms. An objective such as 'to be a leader in technology' may be highly relevant in today's technological environment, but it may become absurd if it has to be expressed in some measurable way. It is nonetheless valid as a statement of purpose and is an example of the importance of *flag-waving* in steering an organisation's strategy. So the aim of being a leader in technology is handed down not as a detailed blueprint or plan from the corporate centre, but as an indication of broad direction and focus, which then becomes a detailed reality as groups and individuals respond to this signal and progress it through their own priorities.

However, there are times when specific objectives are required. These are likely to be when urgent action is needed, such as in a crisis or at times of major transition, and it becomes essential for management to focus attention on a limited number of priority requirements. An extreme example would be in a *turnround* situation. If the choice is between going out of business and surviving, there is no room for latitude through vaguely stated requirements and control.

SUMMARY

- Organisational purposes are influenced by four main factors: corporate governance, stakeholder expectations, business ethics and culture. Together these factors shape the political and cultural context of an organisation's strategies.
- The *corporate governance* arrangements determine whom the organisation is there to serve and how the purposes and priorities should be decided. Corporate governance has become more complex for two main reasons. First, the separation of ownership and management control, and second, the increasing tendency to make organisations more visibly accountable to a range of stakeholders.
- Stakeholders differ in terms of the power that they hold and the extent to which they are actively interested in the strategies that the organisation is pursuing (or planning to pursue). Although they may be in agreement about the broad purposes of the organisation, at a more detailed level there are usually different expectations amongst different stakeholders. *Stakeholder mapping* is a method of analysing these differences and developing a 'political strategy'.
- *Business ethics* determine the broad 'stance' that an organisation takes about its purposes and relationships with the wider society within which it operates. This stance may vary from a narrow view that the short-term interests of shareholders should be paramount, through to some organisations that would see themselves as shapers of society. *Corporate social responsibility* is the detailed 'agenda' that is needed to support an organisation's stance.
- Purposes and priorities within organisations are strongly influenced by *culture* at various 'levels'. This ranges from the national culture, through organised groups (such as professions) to the organisation culture and subcultures.
- Culture can only be properly understood if the taken-for-granted assumptions can be unearthed. The *cultural web* is a useful tool for this purpose.

- It is important to identify and characterise the subcultures in an organisation in order to assess the ease or difficulty with which new strategies could be adopted. Strong cultures are not usually 'easy' – the secret is to achieve 'constructive friction' within an organisation.
- Purposes are formally expressed at different levels of detail, from overall mission statement through to detailed operational objectives for the various parts of the organisation.

RECOMMENDED KEY READINGS

- Useful general reference books on corporate governance are: D.D. Prentice and P.R.J. Holland, *Contemporary Issues in Governance*, Clarendon Press, 1993; T. Clarke and E. Monkhouse (eds), *Rethinking the Company*, Pitman, 1994.
- For more about the stakeholder concept, read I.I. Mitroff, *Stakeholders of the Organisational Mind*, Jossey-Bass, 1983, or R.E. Freeman, *Strategic Management: A stakeholder approach*, Pitman, 1984, or K. Scholes' chapter in V. Ambrosini with G. Johnson and K. Scholes (eds), *Exploring Techniques of Evaluation in Strategic Management*, Prentice Hall, 1998.
- Readers should be familiar with the political context of strategic decision making by reading either J. Pfeffer, *Managing with Power: Power and influence in organisations*, McGraw-Hill, 1994, or I.C. Macmillan and P.E. Jones, *Strategy Formulation: Power and politics*, 2nd edition, West Publishing, 1986.
- Readers can gain some useful insights into business ethics by reading G. Chryssides and J. Kaler, *Business Ethics*, Chapman and Hall, 1993; K. Smith and P. Johnson (eds), *Business Ethics and Business Behaviour*, Thomson Business Press, 1996.
- Useful books on corporate social responsibility are: W. Frederick, J. Post and K. Davis, *Business and Society: Management, public policy, ethics*, 7th edition, McGraw-Hill, 1992; T. Cannon, *Corporate Social Responsibility*, Pitman, 1992.
- E. Schein, *Organisation Culture and Leadership*, Jossey-Bass, 1985, is still useful in understanding the relationship between organisational culture and strategy. G. Johnson's chapter 'Mapping and re-mapping organisational culture' in V. Ambrosini with G. Johnson and K. Scholes, *Exploring Techniques of Analysis and Evaluation in Strategic Management*, Prentice Hall, 1998, shows how to carry out a cultural web exercise.
- A comprehensive coverage of the influence of national culture on strategy can be found in R. Mead, *International Management: Cross-cultural dimensions*, Blackwell, 1994.

REFERENCES

1. Useful general reference books on corporate governance are: D.D. Prentice and P.R.J. Holland, *Contemporary Issues in Governance*, Clarendon Press, 1993; T. Clarke and E. Monkhouse (eds), *Rethinking the Company*, Pitman, 1994; J. Charkham, *Keeping Good Company: A study of corporate governance in five countries*, Oxford University Press, 1994 (a précis of the findings can be found in J. Charkham, 'Corporate governance: lessons from abroad', in W. Nicoll, D. Norburn and R. Schoenberg (eds), *Perspectives on European Business*, Whurr Publishers, London, 1995); G. Mills, *Controlling Companies*, Unwin, 1988; and N. Bain and D. Band, *Winning Ways through Corporate Governance*, Macmillan, 1996. A special issue of *Human Relations*, vol. 48, no. 8 (1995) was also devoted to the topic.
2. These differences between countries are discussed in the general books (reference 1 above) and also in M. Yoshimori, 'Whose company is it? The concept of the corporation in Japan and the West', *Long Range Planning*, vol. 28, no. 4 (1995), pp. 33–44.
3. J. Kay and A. Silberston, 'Corporate governance', *National Institute Economic Review*, no. 153 (1995), pp. 84–96.

4. See T. Clarke and R. Bostock, 'International corporate governance', in Clarke and Monkhouse (reference 1 above).
5. Short-termism as an issue in the Anglo-American tradition is contrasted with the 'Rhine model' more typical of Germany, Switzerland, Benelux and northern European countries by M. Albert, 'The Rhine model of capitalism: an investigation', in Nicoll *et al.* (reference 1 above).
6. The influence of board composition on these issues of conflicts of interest is discussed in J. Goodstein, K. Gautam and W. Boeker, 'The effects of board size and diversity on strategic change', *Strategic Management Journal*, vol. 15, no. 3 (1994), pp. 241–50.
7. *Report of the Committee of Inquiry on Industrial Democracy*, Chairman: Lord Bullock, HMSO, 1977.
8. The early writing about stakeholders was concerned with 'coalitions' in organisations: for example, the seminal work by R.M. Cyert and J.G. March, *A Behavioural Theory of the Firm*, Prentice Hall, 1964. In recent years, stakeholder analysis has become central to strategic analysis: for example, I.I. Mitroff, *Stakeholder of the Organisational Mind*, Jossey-Bass, 1983; R.E. Freeman, *Strategic Management: A stakeholder approach*, Pitman, 1984; J. Harrison and H. Caron, *Strategic Management of Organisations and Stakeholders: Concepts*, West Publishing, 1993.
9. This approach to stakeholder mapping has been adapted from A. Mendelow, *Proceedings of 2nd International Conference on Information Systems*, Cambridge, MA, 1981. See also K. Scholes' chapter, 'Stakeholder analysis' in V. Ambrosini with G. Johnson and K. Scholes (eds), *Exploring Techniques of Analysis and Evaluation in Strategic Management*, Prentice Hall, 1998.
10. See Cyert and March (reference 8 above).
11. See Kay and Silberston (reference 3 above).
12. J. Pfeffer, *Managing with Power: Power and influence in organisations*, McGraw-Hill, 1994, and I.C. Macmillan and P.E. Jones, *Strategy Formulation: Power and politics*, 2nd edition, West Publishing, 1986, both provide a useful analysis of the relationship between power and strategy. C. Hardy (ed.), *Power and Politics in Organisations*, Ashgate, 1995, is also on this general theme.
13. There is a prolific flow of literature on business ethics. Readers can gain some useful insights into the field by reading the following: G. Chryssides and J. Kaler, *Business Ethics*, Chapman and Hall, 1993; J. Mahoney, 'An international look at business ethics: Britain', *Journal of Business Ethics*, vol. 9, no. 7 (1990) pp. 545–50; R. Johns, *Company Community Involvement in the UK*, R. Johns Associates, 1991; S. Hamilton, 'Cashing in on good works', *Business*, July 1991, p.99; K. Smith and P. Johnson (eds), *Business Ethics and Business Behaviour*, Thomson Business Press, 1996.
14. This position was argued strongly in the 1970s by M. Friedman, 'The social responsibility of business is to increase its profits', *New York Times Magazine*, 13 September 1970. He and others were concerned that business managers had been 'diverted' from their main role.
15. This is similar to what Kay and Silberston (reference 3 above) refer to as corporate managers being the 'trustees of the assets of the corporation'.
16. Useful books on corporate social responsibility are: W. Frederick, J. Post and K. Davis, *Business and Society: Management, public policy, ethics,* 7th edition, McGraw-Hill, 1992; and T. Cannon, *Corporate Social Responsibility*, Pitman, 1992.
17. D. Clutterbuck and D. Snow, *Working with the Community*, Weidenfeld and Nicolson, 1991.
18. R. Larmer, 'Whistleblowing and employee loyalty', *Journal of Business Ethics*, vol. 11, no. 2 (1992), pp. 125–8; M. Miceli and J. Near, *Blowing the Whistle: The organisational and legal implications for companies and employees*, Lexington Books, 1992.
19. S. Evers, *The Manager as a Professional*, Institute of Management, 1993. This is a document which checklists and expands upon the Code of Conduct and Guides to Professional Management Practice of the Institute of Management.
20. One of the earlier works on the influence of national culture was G. Hofstede, *Culture's Consequences*, Sage, 1980. A comprehensive coverage of this topic can be found in R. Mead, International Management: *Cross-cultural dimensions*, Blackwell, 1994.
21. See also C. Hampden-Turner and F. Trompenaars, *The Seven Cultures of Capitalism: Value systems for creating wealth in the United States, Britain, Japan, Germany, France, Sweden and the Netherlands*, Piatkus Business, 1994.
22. See S. Schneider, 'Strategy formulation: the impact of national culture', *Organization Studies*, vol. 10, no. 2 (1989) pp. 149–68; S. Schneider and A. Meyer, 'Interpreting and responding to strategic issues: the impact of national culture', *Strategic Management Journal*, vol. 12, no. 4 (1991) pp. 307–20; C. Randlesome *et al.*, *Business Cultures in Europe*, Heinemann, 1990; R.M. Kanter, 'In search of a single culture', *Business*, June 1991, pp. 58–66.
23. For a discussion of strategy in professional service organisations, see H. Mintzberg and J. Quinn, *The Strategy Process: Concepts, contexts and cases*, 3rd edition, Prentice Hall, 1995; K. Scholes, 'Strategic management in professional service organisations', Professorial Lecture, Sheffield Business School, 1994.
24. The term 'recipe' is used by J. Spender, Industry Recipes: *The nature and sources of management judgement*, Blackwell, 1989.
25. E. Schein, *Organisation Culture and Leadership*, Jossey-Bass, 1985.

26. J. Barney, 'Organisational culture: can it be a source of sustained competitive advantage?', *Academy of Management Review*, vol. 11, no. 3 (1986), pp. 656–65.
27. A detailed coverage of cultural web analysis can be found in G. Johnson, 'Mapping and re-mapping organisational culture', in V. Ambrosini with G. Johnson and K. Scholes (eds), *Exploring Techniques of Analysis and Evaluation in Strategic Management*, Prentice Hall, 1998.
28. R.E. Miles and C.C. Snow, *Organisational Strategy: Structure and process*, McGraw-Hill, 1978.
29. See A. Campbell and K. Tawadey, *Mission and Business Philosophy*, Butterworth/Heinemann, 1993; A. Campbell, M. Devine and D. Young, *A Sense of Mission*, Financial Times/Pitman, 1990; J. Abrahams, *The Mission Statement Book*, Ten Speed Press, 1995.
30. The importance of vision is discussed in I. Wilson, 'Realising the power of vision', *Long Range Planning*, vol. 25, no. 5 (1992), pp. 18–28; and R. Whittington, *What is Strategy and Does it Matter?*, Routledge, 1993, chapter 3.
31. See G. Hamel and C. Prahalad, 'Strategic intent', *Harvard Business Review*, vol. 67, no. 3 (1989), pp. 63–76.
32. For example, I. Ansoff, *Corporate Strategy*, Penguin, 1968, p. 44, argued that objectives should be precise and measurable.

WORK ASSIGNMENTS

5.1 ● For an organisation of your choice, map out a governance chain which clearly identifies all the key players through to the beneficiaries of the organisation's good (or poor) performance. To what extent do you think managers are:
(a) knowledgeable about the expectations of beneficiaries
(b) actively pursuing their interests
(c) keeping them informed?

How would you change any of these aspects of the organisation's operations? Why?

5.2 ● Critique the different traditions of corporate governance in the UK/USA, Germany and Japan in terms of your own views of their strengths and weaknesses. Is there a better system than any of these? Why?

5.3 Choose any organisation which does not operate a two-tier board (or the public sector equivalent).
(a) Would a two-tier board be a better form of governance? Why?
(b) What would you need to do to move to a two-tier system?
(c) Is this likely to be possible?

5.4 Discuss the reasons which led to the Greenbury Report on executive pay (Illustration 5.3). Do you agree with the proposals? Why/why not?

5.5 Using Illustration 5.4 as an example, identify and map out the stakeholders for Iona* or the Sheffield Theatres* or an organisation of your choice in relation to:
(a) current strategies
(b) a number of different future strategies of your choice.

What are the implications of your analysis for the management?

5.6 For The News Corporation* or an organisation of your choice, use Exhibit 5.7 to establish the *overall stance* of the organisation on ethical issues.

5.7 ● Identify the key corporate social responsibility issues which are of major concern in an industry or public service of your choice (refer to Exhibit 5.8). Compare the approach of two or more organisations in that industry, and explain how this relates to their competitive standing.

5.8 Use the questions in Exhibit 5.11 to plot out a tentative cultural web for Iona* or an organisation of your choice.

5.9 Use Exhibit 5.12 to identify organisations with which you are familiar which are close to the three Miles and Snow stereotypes. Justify your categorisation.

5.10 ● By using a number of the examples from above, critically appraise the assertion that 'culture can only really be usefully analysed by the symptoms displayed in the way the organisation operates'. Refer to Schein's book in the recommended key readings to assist you with this task.

---

* refers to a case study in the Text and Cases edition.
● denotes more advanced work assignments.

CASE EXAMPLE

Manchester United – Football Club or Global Brand?

On 8 September 1998 the board of Manchester United (MU) announced that they had received a takeover offer of £623.4m from BSkyB – the satellite broadcasting company (in which Rupert Murdoch's News International has a 40% stake). They were unanimously recommending that their shareholders accept the bid. When the news of these negotiations had leaked out two days earlier there was an uprising of indignation from fans and others who felt that the club should not fall into the hands of a media empire. There were concerns that media ownership would ruin the football industry as they had known and loved it for generations. In an open letter to fans Mark Booth, chief executive of BSkyB and Martin Edwards, chief executive of MU expressed BSkyB's appreciation that MU was not just another business but was 'part of the cultural fabric of Manchester and the nation'. The letter also said that the acquisition would create one of the great partnerships in sport.

The proud comments which opened the Chairman's report in October 1997 showed how successful MU had become both on and off the field since their flotation on the stock market in 1991:

> 1997 was an outstanding year for Manchester United plc and your Board is pleased to announce record profits and an increased dividend. Performance both on and off the field was excellent – the stadium operated at full capacity and MU won the Premier League Championship and reached the semi-finals of the European Champions Cup.

Turnover had grown by 350 per cent since 1993 to £88m and profits by 600 per cent to £19m – a record of which any business would be proud.

The 1990s had witnessed a transformation of the soccer industry in England with the creation of the Premier League of twenty clubs in 1992, a massive increase in television rights from £13m per annum in 1990 to £165m per annum by 1998, following the deal with Rupert Murdoch's B-Sky-B. There were several flotations in the stock market and the resultant major investments in ground improvements. Perhaps the most noticeable change was the ability and willingness of the major clubs – spear-headed by Manchester United – to exploit their popularity through merchandising at the ground, throughout the UK and (in the case of MU) worldwide. A new generation of fans was emerging who experienced football at a distance – through television coverage, publications and the purchase of merchandise, all of which were available worldwide.

The table shows how this shifting emphasis had changed the sources of income for Manchester United. Since 1990, television had risen from 8 per cent to 14 per cent; merchandising from 15 per cent to 33 per cent, whilst gate receipts represented 34 per cent of income in 1997 as against 55 per cent in 1990.

Breakdown of revenue by category

	1990	1997
Gate receipts	55%	34%
Merchandising and other	15%	33%
Television	8%	14%
Sponsorship and loyalties	15%	13%
Conferencing and catering	7%	6%
	100%	100%

Merchandising and related activities had expanded rapidly – with over 1,500 items in the on-site shop and hundreds of outlets throughout the world. There was also Manchester United mail order and in 1997 the club concluded a deal with BSkyB to launch a Manchester United satellite channel in 1998 broadcasting six hours per day. There was Manchester United Insurance credit card and you could have your wedding at the ground (but not your funeral – yet). The annual accounts in 1997 were proud to highlight that Manchester United was a genuinely international brand. Activities such as the pre-season Far East tour were strengthening that brand even more. Not all the fans were happy with this. As one of them remarked in the Channel 4 television programme *Without Walls* (1995):

> It's rather like prostitution really. Just because you *can* make money out of the club's name, doesn't mean that you *should*.

In 1996, Robin Launders who was then the finance director was interviewed in *Accountancy* magazine about the goals of Manchester United. He was keen to stress that he was not a football man – which proved no barrier to being recruited (as long as he didn't actually *dislike* football). His formula for success was expressed as follows:

> Running a football club is easy; all you've got to do is to make enough profit year after year to do three things: develop your team, develop your stadium and – if you're a quoted company – to pay a dividend. If you can do all these things, year on year, then life is good.

This prescription was not universally supported as comments from other interested parties showed:

> Football used to be about glory, romance, loyalty and the national game, and not about exploitation and multinational corporations. But that is exactly what Manchester United now is.
>
> *Journalist*

> They don't any more want 20-something working-class males chanting songs and generally having a good time. They want well behaved people who spend a lot of money – and that's what they've now got. A fan was recently evicted from the ground for standing up during the game.
>
> *A fan*

> Football clubs shouldn't be quoted on the stock market – that's about companies who have 1, 2 and 3 year plans. A football club has an 'audit' every Saturday afternoon [match day]. When Eric Cantona assaulted a Crystal Palace spectator, the shares dropped by 5p wiping £3m off the club's value.
>
> *Community leader*

> Getting in to watch a game is like a military campaign. A seat is like a commodity to be exploited. The 'added-value' package includes lunch (with an ex-player), a walk on the pitch and perhaps a word with a current team member. All for £200. Despite the fact that there are 63 corporate boxes there is still a waiting list of 100 companies. For individuals to get a match ticket you have to pay £10 a year to join a list – and no refund if you never get in. There are 100,000 on this list – so thats £1m up-front to start with.
>
> *A fan*

> Replica kit costs £65 and there have been 4 changes in 6 years. This is stealing from the public. When Dick Turpin [a famous highwayman] took your money – at least he wore a mask.
>
> *Tommy Docherty (former manager)*

This issue of constantly changing replica kit had caused some considerable resentment amongst parents of young fans. They felt pressurised by their children into spending these large amounts – and the club seemed indifferent to their concerns. In March 1998 two directors of Newcastle United Football Club resigned after a major public outcry following various remarks they had made – including boasting about how much money they were making on replica kit. A television programme revealed that the replica kit market in the UK was worth as much as £200m per annum in total, and that mark-up was as high as 200 per cent.

One reason for the change in 'spectator mix' referred to above was the rapid increase in ticket prices throughout the Premier League. In the first six years of operation the average ticket price rose by 144 per cent (more than four times the rate of general inflation). Ticket prices was one of the major issues to be investigated by a special committee set up by the new Labour government in 1997 to look at the future of the game. Inflation was also an issue with transfer prices and players wages – which by 1997 were rising at 20 per cent per annum. But the most spectacular inflation was to the benefit of original shareholders following the flotation of clubs. Martin Edwards, the chief executive of Manchester United, saw his original £600,000 shareholding grow in value to £55m – of which £33m was 'cashed in'. In 1997 this left him with about 15 per cent of the club's shares. (Collectively the directors held about 17 per cent of the shares.)

Chairmen of smaller clubs in the football league (which has 72 clubs) were dismayed by this growing rift between the top few clubs and the rest. As one chairman remarked:

> Matches can be rescheduled at short notice to suit satellite stations and their exclusive audiences. There is a disregard for the little clubs. The gap between the haves and the have-nots is too great. Manchester United is now marketed as the national team – which has taken it away from its roots and its local community. Football should be a love affair – otherwise you are just a business. The big clubs have forgotten their roots and are isolating themselves.

There were also some concerns that not enough money was recycled to schools and junior football – from where the next generation of players would come (although by 1997 many Premier League clubs had a considerable number of non-British players in their teams).

Rogan Taylor of the Football Research Unit at Liverpool University and the Football Supporters Association summed up his own feelings about the game:

> There is a huge difference in relationship between a football fan and their club as against a consumer and a product. No one is spreading the ashes of their grandfather down the aisles of Tesco. But everyday they do just that at football clubs throughout the land. It is more like a disciple going to a temple. Manchester United may have got a good middle class audience for 10 years or so – but others have supported them through the generations for 100 years.

The changing nature of the club's business and customer profile was also underlined in other ways. In 1995, there were 42 professional players and 31 coaching and ground staff at Old Trafford – but also 123 staff in merchandising and catering. A museum had just opened and there were plans to purchase adjacent land to extend the car parking available for corporate clients. The board had a number of non-executive directors who represented a range of business interests and expertise too, as shown in the following extract from the 1997 annual report:

> **Non-executive Directors 1997**
>
> **Professor Sir Roland Smith**, 69, (Non-Executive Chairman) has been a director of the company since 1991. He is Chancellor of The University of Manchester Institute of Science and Technology, a former director of the Bank of England, and chairman, director and consultant to other public and private companies.
> **Maurice Watkins**, 55, has been a director of the company since 1991 and a director of The Manchester United Football Club plc since June 1984. He is a partner in the Manchester firm of solicitors, James Chapman & Co., solicitors to the Group, and has provided legal advice to the Group over the last twenty years.
> **Amer AlMidani**, 40, has been a director of the company since 1991. He was a director of The Manchester United Football Club plc from February 1987 until January 1994. He has extensive interests in the hotel and leisure industries.

Greg Dyke, 50, is Chairman and Chief Executive of Pearson Television Limited, an executive director of Pearson PLC, and Chairman of Channel 5 Television Group. He is also a director of other media and leisure companies.

The pace of change in the sport, leisure and entertainment industries was frantic throughout many parts of the world in the late 1990s. Manchester United perhaps epitomised this change more than most. But had it got it right? How will they fare as part of BSkyB and the media industry?

Questions

1. Do you feel that the various aspects of corporate governance discussed in section 5.2 are appropriate for a football club? What changes in governance would you like to see?
2. Refer to section 5.3.2 and Exhibit 5.5 and undertake a stakeholder mapping exercise for any strategic development which is likely to be under consideration by the board (for example, 'The formation of a European superleague of major clubs'). How would you use this analysis if you were:
   (a) a board member wishing to support the strategy
   (b) an opponent of the strategy?
3. Refer to Exhibit 5.7 and decide which ethical stance you feel best describes Manchester United now and how you would wish to see the club. Justify your own position.
4. Refer to section 5.5.4 and decide what you feel were the key cultural characteristics of Manchester United in terms of values, beliefs and taken-for-granted assumptions: (a) pre-1990, and (b) in 1998 (post takeover).
   What are the implications of these changes to current and future strategies?
5. If you were allowed to write a short mission statement for Manchester United, what would it be? Does it properly reflect your answers to the questions above? Refer to Exhibit 5.13 for different types of mission statement.

Sources Annual reports; *Without Walls*, Channel 4, 1995; *Panorama*, BBC, December 1997.

III
STRATEGIC CHOICE

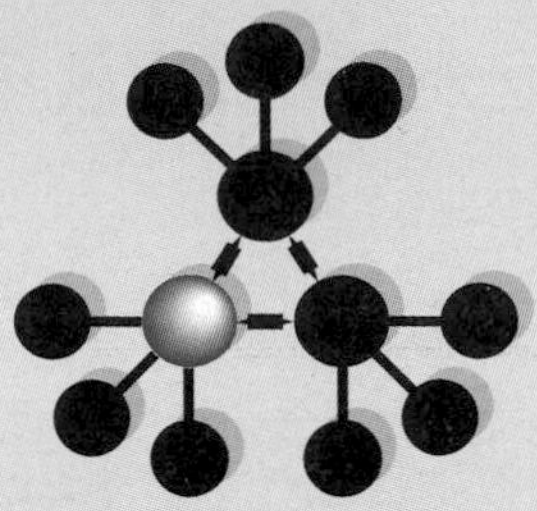

In many ways, strategic choice is the core of strategic management. It is concerned with decisions about an organisation's future and the way in which it needs to respond to the many pressures and influences identified in strategic analysis. In turn, the consideration of future strategies must be mindful of the realities of strategy implementation, which can be a significant constraint on strategic choice.

Chapter 2 showed that organisations are continually attempting to readjust to their environment, and one of the major criticisms which can be made of managers concerns their inability or unwillingness to consider the variety of strategic options open to the organisation. Rather, they tend to remain bound by their paradigm and resistant to change. It is for this reason that this part of the book presents a systematic way of looking at strategic choice. The steps outlined here help to promote a wider consideration of strategy and the appropriateness and consequences of options available to the organisation.

The discussion of strategic choice has been divided into three chapters to reflect the three elements of any development strategy. It is important that these elements are consistent with each other.

- Chapter 6 looks at some of the bases on which an organisation's strategies are built. These include issues which relate back to Chapter 5, such as the influence of organisational purposes or vision and the way in which ownership decisions affect strategic choice. The scope of the organisation in product/services and market terms is also considered, which also raises questions of international strategy. Bases of strategic choices at the SBU level are then considered by examining choices of generic competitive strategies (positioning). The chapter concludes by reviewing how corporate parents might or might not add value to the strategies of SBUs. This includes issues of portfolio management, financial strategy and corporate parenting.
- Chapter 7 deals with choices of both strategic direction and method. This includes considerations of how directions of strategic development can be built around market opportunities; developments of product; development of competences; and the various combinations of these three parameters. Development methods range from internal development, through strategic alliances to acquisitions and mergers.

THIS PART EXPLAINS:

- Corporate-level strategies – the importance of ownership, strategic intent, scope and diversity.
- The bases of SBU-level strategies – the strategy clock.
- Corporate parenting.
- Strategic options – the need to identify both the direction and method of development.
- Evaluating the suitability, acceptability and feasibility of strategies.
- How strategies are selected.

- Chapter 8 is concerned with strategy evaluation. This begins with a discussion of the evaluation criteria of suitability, feasibility and acceptability. Assessing the suitability of a strategy can be a useful means of 'screening' options before more detailed analyses. There are different techniques to undertake the screening, such as ranking options, decision trees and scenario planning. The assessment of acceptability is concerned with three things: the likely return should a strategy be adopted, the level of risk in a strategy, and the attitudes and reactions of stakeholders. Feasibility involves an assessment of whether the resources and competences are available to support a strategy. There are important links with discussions in Chapters 4 and 10. The chapter concludes with a brief review of how strategies are selected in organisations, with important links to the management of change (discussed in Chapter 11).

6

BASES OF STRATEGIC CHOICE

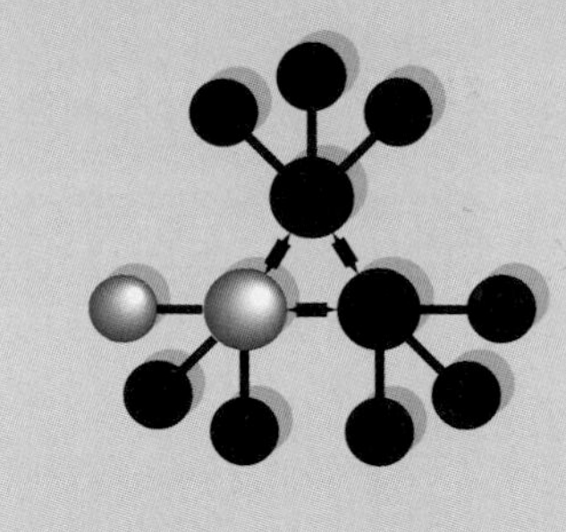

LEARNING OUTCOMES

After reading this chapter you should be able to:

- Explain the relationship between forms of ownership and strategic choice.
- Explain the importance of a clarity of mission or strategic intent on strategic choice.
- Explain the importance of determining 'what business we are in'.
- Explain different bases of achieving competitive advantage in terms of 'routes' on the strategy clock.
- Describe different ways in which a corporate parent might enhance SBU strategies.
- Explain the importance of the parenting matrix.

6.1 INTRODUCTION

Bases of strategic choice need to be considered both at the level of the SBU and at the level of the parent organisation; and the questions asked at these two different levels are likely to be mutually reinforcing. The strategic choices at SBU level can enhance the standing of a corporation (for example, with its investors) and the choices at the corporate level enhance those at the SBU level. This issue is addressed by considering *bases of strategic choice* at both the corporate and SBU levels, and links between these which can yield strategic advantage for an organisation. Exhibit 6.1 provides an outline of how this is discussed in the chapter.

1. The chapter begins with a discussion of *corporate-level* strategic issues in terms of *purposes and aspirations*. The issues raised here relate to some of the expectations which stakeholders have of the organisation (see Chapter 5).
   - For some organisations there may be issues of *ownership* to be addressed.

Exhibit 6.1 Bases of strategic choice

Corporate purpose and aspirations
- Ownership
- Mission and strategic intent
- Scope and diversity
- The global dimension

Bases of SBU strategy
- Achieving competitive advantage
- Price-based strategies
- Differentiation strategies
- Focus strategies

Enhancing SBU strategy: corporate parenting
- Portfolio management
- Financial strategy
- The role of the corporate parent
- The parenting matrix

- It is important for executives to make clear the overarching theme, *intent* or *mission* for the organisation: for example, in a commercial organisation in terms of type of business, levels of expected growth or dominance of markets.
- The *scope* of the organisation is important, in terms of the number of businesses or activities it chooses to be involved in, and the strategic logic behind this. This relates to the extent of *diversity* of the organisation. Decisions need to be made as to the extent of relatedness of the organisation's activities. If relatedness is important, this may facilitate the development of *synergies* between business activities or common *competences* at the corporate level.
- *Global dimensions* of such aspirations are considered specifically because they are increasingly raising fundamental challenges for organisations.

2. The chapter then moves to a discussion of generic *competitive strategies*. These are the fundamental bases on which a SBU seeks to achieve a lasting advantageous position in its environment by meeting the expectations of buyers, users or other stakeholders. They should in turn inform considerations discussed in Chapter 7 about the *directions* which business units may follow, such as developing new products or new markets, and the different *methods* by which these might be achieved, for example through internal development, acquisition or alliances.
3. The extent to which SBU strategies can be enhanced at the corporate level is then addressed. The issue here is how a parent body can add value to SBUs.
   - *Portfolio management* approaches are discussed here and elsewhere in the book as ways of trying to gain an understanding of the extent to which multiple SBUs make strategic sense in corporate terms.
   - There are implications here for the financial *strategy* of the corporate body.
   - The notion of corporate parenting is then explored in more detail, both in terms of *roles of corporate parents* and in terms of a *parenting matrix*, which is a further way of considering the portfolio of SBUs in the organisation.

In considering all this, it needs to be remembered that decisions at the corporate level and decisions on SBU generic competitive strategy, direction and method are not independent of each other. An organisation pursuing a *competitive strategy* of differentiation may also be pursuing a strategic *direction* of product or service development. Both these levels of strategic choice are likely to be influenced by the overall thrust of strategy at the *corporate level*; as is the *method* by which new developments are best achieved – through the organisation's own efforts, jointly with others, or by acquisition. This is summarised in Exhibit 6.2. The important point is that these various dimensions of strategic decisions need to be consistent with each other.

6.2 CORPORATE PURPOSE AND ASPIRATIONS

As shown in Chapter 5 (section 5.3), whatever the size or structure of an organisation, it has stakeholders who have greater or lesser interest in and power over what it does. These influences need to be taken into account in developing strategy. The management of the organisation – whether a multinational conglomerate or a family business, the managers of a charity or the senior executives of a public service – needs to consider strategic issues in this context.

Exhibit 6.2 **Development strategies**

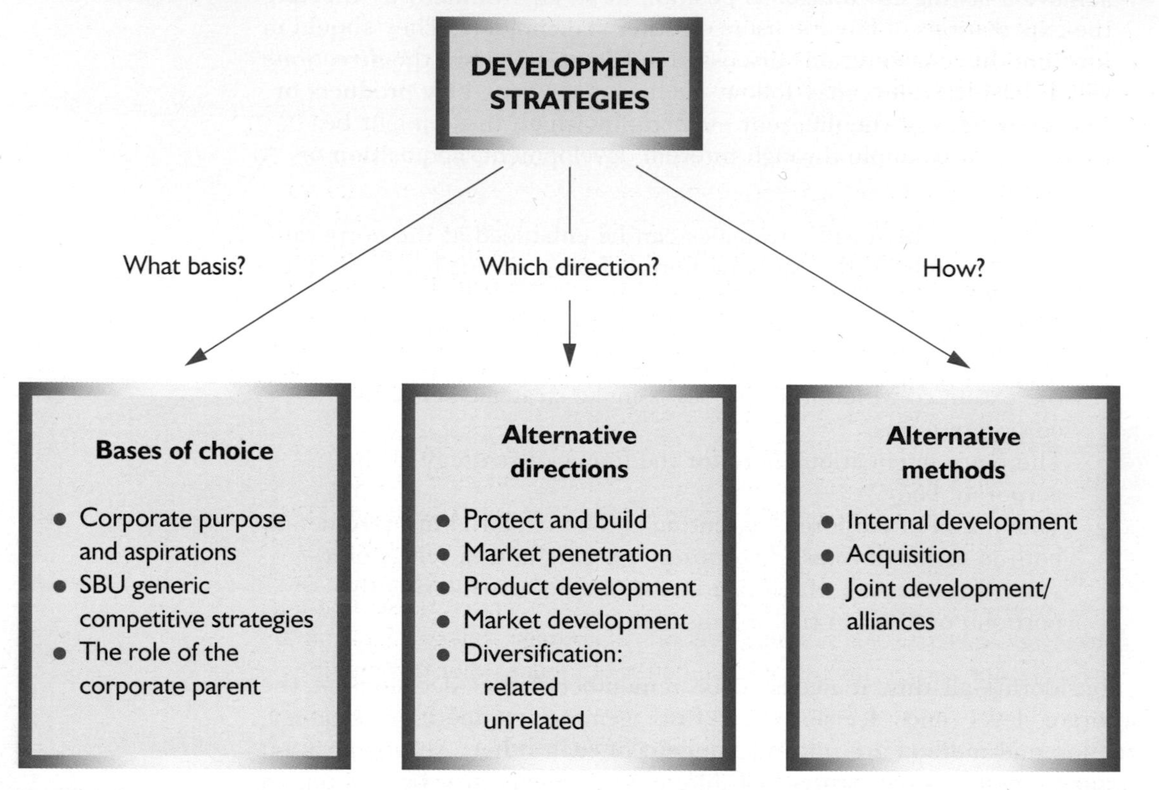

6.2.1 Ownership Structures

Executives may face issues concerned with changes in ownership which have a fundamental effect on the strategies to be followed. They may also have to consider if the current ownership structure is appropriate to the strategic needs of the organisation.

1. In the life cycle of many commercial organisations, a major strategic choice has to be made about whether it is appropriate to move from a *privately owned* organisation – a family business, for example – to a *publicly quoted* corporation. Such a decision might be made because the owners decide that increased equity is required to finance the growth of the business (see section 6.4.2). The decision is of major importance not least because the family members who own the business need to recognise that their role will change. They become answerable to a much wider group of shareholders and to institutions

acting for such shareholders. It therefore changes the stakeholder basis of the organisation and thus the influences and constraints on the development of organisational strategy. In Trent Buses (see Illustration 6.1) the decision was taken not to follow this route because of the potential for strategic choice to be strongly influenced by the requirements of investment analysts.[1]

2. The board of directors of a business has a responsibility to shareholders to provide them with a reasonable rate of return on their investment. It may be that the board arrives at the view that the sale to a different *corporate parent* may be to the advantage of a company or a business within the corporation. For example, a family-controlled firm might consider selling out to a corporation as a way of realising its assets. Or it may be that the board of a firm decides that it is not able to compete as an independent unit as well as it might within a corporate body, perhaps because it is trading nationally within increasingly global markets. The sale of the business might therefore make sense.

   Businesses also become the targets for acquisitions (see Chapter 7, section 7.3.2), and a board might decide that such an offer is more attractive to shareholders than the returns they can promise in the future. On occasions, businesses decide to merge, perhaps because the executives believe that the synergies resulting from coming together are greater than the businesses would achieve by operating independently. These decisions are, then, the outcome of considerations of strategy where a decision is reached that the business would be better off under other ownership.

3. Historically, most public sector bodies have been tightly controlled by the equivalent of their 'owners', the central or local government or government departments. However, latterly this has changed in a number of respects in many countries, notably by the *privatisation* of such public bodies.[2] In the UK, this process began in the 1980s with the government selling British Telecom and gas, water and electricity utilities. The effects were significant in terms of strategic choice. The government took such decisions in order to require organisations to face up to market forces, to become more aware of customer needs and competitive pressures. In turn, managers found more latitude in terms of strategic choice – what they could provide in terms of product or services; the ability to diversify, raise capital for expansion and so on. This is shown in Illustration 6.1 with regard to Trent Buses.

4. In both publicly quoted and state-owned companies, another example of changing ownership is when all or part of the organisation is sold to management – a *management buyout*.[3] This has happened, for example, in commercial organisations when managers of a business have been faced with a corporate decision to close or dispose of that business. Those who work in the organisation may have sufficient faith in its future to raise capital to buy the business themselves. In the public sector, too, buyouts have occurred: for example, when a public corporation has chosen to withdraw from a particular market or when

STRATEGY IN ACTION Illustration 6.1

Trent Buses

Forms of ownership are key strategic decisions and also affect strategic choice.

Founded in 1913, by the 1930s Trent Buses was a publicly quoted company, with the conglomerate BET holding 51 per cent of the shares. Trent retained its independence until it was nationalised in 1968. It remained in public ownership until 1986 when the Conservative government's Transport Act led to its privatisation and deregulation in the industry. Brian King, managing director of Trent Buses in 1997 and for a period during nationalisation, successfully mounted a management buyout in 1986 with three management colleagues.

> The change of ownership made a huge difference. We could see the inefficiencies. It was inward looking and bureaucratic rather than customer focused. We believed we could provide a better service at lower cost and set out to be the best UK bus company; and we were voted this by customers in 1996.
>
> We financed the buyout with a loan and a suspension of capital investment, using cash flow for repayment of the debt. We paid this back by 1990 and are now wholly owned by myself, four other senior managers and 150 employees. In 1988 we started to invest in a quality fleet of buses which, again, we paid for out of cash flow, and more recently we have bought Barton buses who are adjacent to us geographically. We would not have had this financial latitude when we were nationalised or, indeed, had we been part of a holding group.
>
> Our business is very locally focused. When we were nationalised we were seen as representatives of an 'absentee landlord'. We are now seen as the local bus company. We are very close to our market. All the directors spend time travelling on the buses with our customers. Under nationalisation I would have sat on committees rather than actually running the business. We are prepared to take risks more in setting up new routes and experimenting. I get actively involved with local businesses and local government. We 'punch above our weight' to influence the local arena in which we operate.
>
> Our success is clear enough. We have seen off cheaper competitors who have tried to enter our market. We buy replacement vehicles out of revenue. When we acquired the business it was turning over £16m and producing £200,000 profit before tax; by 1997 it is £27m with £3$\frac{1}{2}$ million profit.
>
> In the 1980s we were initially keen on flotation, but we realised that would mean too many people interfering with our business. We would have to keep growing to satisfy the City. Other bus companies have been driven into diversification, into acquiring train companies or overseas expansion. We want to be the best UK bus company; and we decided our current ownership structure is the most achievable way to do it.

Questions

1. What sorts of issues might Brian King and his colleagues have considered in deliberating about their management buyout?
2. For each of the ownership structures identified in this illustration (public ownership, private ownership and publicly quoted), suggest the sorts of strategic constraint on and opportunities for strategic choice that might exist for Trent Buses.

the government has sold off a nationalised enterprise such as the bus companies in the UK in 1986 (again see Illustration 6.1).

5. Even when a change in ownership has not been made, public sector organisations have been required to face questions of corporate purpose by other means.[4]
   - *Deregulation* has taken place in public sector monopolies such as broadcasting, public transport and airlines (especially in the USA), varying from completely opening access to private sector providers (creating a true market) to auctioning franchises to private sector bids (as with TV contracts in the UK and other countries).
   - *Compulsory competitive tendering (CCT)* and *market-testing* have required the separation of the roles of the *client*, who specifies the detail of the services required on behalf of 'customers', and the *provider*, who may previously have been in-house but is required to bid alongside other bidders. In central government departments in the UK the same process of splitting the client (policy-makers) and providers (government services) in the 1990s occurred through granting *agency status* to the service providers. For example, the UK Employment Services Group (providers of services relating to unemployment benefits and job seeking) was separated from the Department of Employment in this way.
   - *Quasi-markets* have also been created, driven by the view that value for money is not delivered by the 'natural' public sector monopolies, since there are fewer pressures to improve performance than in open markets. One type of quasi-market has been the appointment of *regulatory offices* (as with telecom, gas, water and electricity) as a substitute for a real market. Another approach has been the introduction of customer–supplier relationships *internal* to the organisation – so-called *internal markets* – health care in the UK and New Zealand are examples. (This is discussed further in Chapter 10, section 10.4, in terms of resource allocation and control.)

   These devices to reshape the product/market strategies of (previously) public sector enterprises have usually resulted in the need to revisit fundamentally issues of *positioning* and *competitive strategies*, discussed in section 6.3.

In all cases, these examples of the relationship between ownership and strategic choice make the point that choices of ownership are fundamental strategic decisions, which in turn require managers of those organisations to consider other bases of strategic choice and issues of direction and method. These are now considered.

6.2.2 Mission and Strategic Intent[5]

Managers need to be clear about what they see as the role of their organisation; this is often expressed in terms of a mission statement or a

The **mission statement** *is a generalised statement of the overriding purpose of the organisation*

strategic intent *is the desired future state or aspiration of the organisation*

statement of strategic intent. The **mission statement** is a generalised statement of the overriding purpose of the organisation; **strategic intent** is the desired future state or aspiration of the organisation (see Chapter 5, section 5.6.1). Such statements can be important because both external stakeholders and other managers in the organisation, not least in subsidiary parts of it, need to be clear about what the organisation is seeking to achieve and, in broad terms, how it expects to do so. At this level, strategy is not concerned with the details of SBU competitive strategy or the directions and methods the businesses might take to achieve competitive advantage (these are discussed later in this chapter and in Chapter 7). Rather, the concern here is overall strategic direction.

The importance of this can be seen when there is an absence of such clarity. For example, investors are often wary of investing in highly diversified firms because they are not clear about what the purpose of the organisation is. They are likely to question what is added by the corporation and could take the view that the different businesses would be more attractive for investment as independent entities. (Illustration 7.6 in the next chapter gives examples of businesses in which this has occurred.)

The managers of a subsidiary, charged with developing a strategy for that business, also need to be clear where they fit into the corporate whole. For example, is their business seen as central to corporate aspirations or peripheral? If they are not clear, it is unlikely that they will manage the business in ways to enhance the overall aspirations of the organisation. As Hamel and Prahalad[6] have highlighted, the importance of clear strategic intent can go much further: it can help galvanise motivation and enthusiasm throughout the organisation by providing what they call a sense of destiny and discovery. In the absence of this, there is a risk of the different parts of the organisation, different levels of management, indeed all members of the organisation, pulling in different directions.

Illustration 6.2 shows how mission or intent can encapsulate the basis of overall strategy for the benefit both of external stakeholders and, internally, of those who have to formulate and deliver SBU strategies. Some specific examples of this bridging role of mission and intent are now provided.

- Successful family businesses face difficult issues to do with family ownership. Part of the mission may be to retain ownership in the family. If this is so, not only does it potentially place constraints on the business, perhaps because of difficulties of financing the business for growth; it may also influence the strategies which are followed. For example, family businesses may seek to build on networks of family relationships, as is often the case in Chinese-controlled businesses in the Far East; or seek out market segments in which family heritage is seen as important, as is the case in some sections of merchant banking.
- Decisions on overall mission in a major corporation will exercise constraints elsewhere. Does the corporation aspire to short-term profits or long-term growth; to a focused set of highly related businesses or a more diversified set of businesses; to global coverage or the focus on

STRATEGY IN ACTION
Illustration 6.2

Komatsu's Mission to Encircle Caterpillar

Clarity of strategic intent can motivate an organisation to achieve its goals.

Komatsu is the second largest producer of earth-moving equipment after its arch rival, Caterpillar. However, this was not always so. In the 1950s it produced a limited range of low-quality products and, with a protected home market, had little or no incentive to improve. This position changed when Japan opened this market to foreign competition in the early 1960s.

In 1964, Kawai succeeded his father as chairman of Komatsu and announced the goal of 'Maru C': to 'encircle Caterpillar'. This statement of strategic intent – to concentrate all its efforts on surpassing Caterpillar – was to be the driving force of the company for more than two decades.

Initially, Komatsu focused on improving product quality to limit the loss of sales in its home market. Komatsu then signed licensing agreements with Caterpillar's competitors to gain access to the latest American technology. This move also enabled it to expand its product range, which made it more attractive to dealer networks – crucial if Komatsu was to build up sales volume. The next stage towards its goal was to enter secondary export markets such as China and eastern Europe, which helped build the critical mass required to challenge Caterpillar in the main markets of Europe and America.

By the 1980s, Komatsu was very successful: its growth from a regional producer of low-quality products to the second largest producer was impressive and was widely attributed to its goal of encircling Caterpillar. Yet Katada, Komatsu's third president, was beginning to question this strategy.

The goal that had served the company so well for over two decades was beginning to be overtaken by the changing business environment. Komatsu's sales began to fall as demand for heavy earth-moving equipment decreased and competition intensified; Komatsu was less focused on its markets' needs and more concerned with outdoing Caterpillar.

Katada changed the company's emphasis from providing construction equipment to being a 'total technology enterprise', and the new goal of 'Growth, Global, Groupwide' was adopted. In the three years since the new goal was introduced, Komatsu has reversed its sales decline and seen a 40 per cent growth in its non-construction equipment business.

Questions

1. What were the main benefits of a simple statement of purpose of 'encircling Caterpillar'?
2. What might Komtasu have done to avoid some of the downsides of 'encircling Caterpillar'?
3. Assess the power and impact of the new declared intent of being a 'total technology enterprise' pursuing a goal of 'growth, global, groupwide'.

Sources C.A. Bartlett and S. Ghoshal, 'Changing the role of top management', *Harvard Business Review*, vol. 73, no. 1 (1994), pp. 79–88; G. Hamel and C.K. Prahalad, *Competing for the Future*, Harvard Business School Press, 1994.

Prepared by Tony Jacobs, Bristol Business School.

selected countries; to investment in internal innovation and new products, or the acquisition of other businesses? These are, of course, all matters of strategic choice, but they are unlikely to change regularly. The overall stance of the corporation with regard to such matters may develop over many years, but by being made explicit the mission can help direct strategic choice.

- Mission or intent may be embodied in the founder of an organisation, or result from the arrival of a new leader; indeed, some would see this as the primary role of leaders.[7] Ingvar Kamprad's vision of the market opportunity and positioning of IKEA has played a fundamental role in guiding the successful strategy of that business over many decades. On taking over the leadership of the UK Labour Party, Tony Blair made it clear that he intended to transform the party from its socialist heritage and emphasis on state intervention to 'New Labour' with a continuing concern for the social good but an emphasis on incentives for individuals too. In both cases, a clarity of mission or intent provided a basis on which further strategic choice could be made.

6.2.3 What Business Are We In? The Issue of Scope and Diversity

strategic scope *is concerned with the boundaries that managers conceive for their organisation in terms of geography, product (or service) diversity or the way in which business is conducted*

The deceptively simple question 'What business are we in?' is important. It is about **strategic scope**, which is concerned with the boundaries that managers conceive for their organisation in terms of geography, product (or service) diversity or, indeed, the way in which business is conducted. This needs to be considered because such boundaries give guidance on the nature of the organisation. Indeed, many organisations try to address this, too, in their statements of mission or intent. When British Airways coined its stated intent to be 'the world's favourite airline' in the late 1980s, it was not just setting out an ambition; it was setting boundaries to the activities it would choose to get involved in and develop, and on what scale. When national and local governments started to describe themselves as 'enabling organisations' in the UK in the 1980s, it signalled a progressive withdrawal from the direct delivery of public services by government agencies, which had increased massively since 1945 in many countries.

Diversity or Relatedness

Most organisations begin their existence focused on a particular product or service. Some retain a focused approach with, perhaps, highly related SBUs; others become much more diversified. Decisions about the extent of diversity have received much attention from researchers who have tried to establish whether there is a relationship between the extent of relatedness of businesses within a corporation and financial performance at the corporate level.[8] It is important to understand that relatedness could exist in different ways.

- Different SBUs in a portfolio might seek to build on similar *technologies* or provide similar sorts of *products or services*. However, care should be taken here. For example, a manufacturer of paint might argue that the technology of paint manufacture is similar to the manufacture of nail varnish. Whilst technically this may be so, the skills associated with running a paints business are likely to be very different from those associated with running a fashion products business.
- SBUs might also be serving similar or different *markets*. Even if technology or products differ, it could be that customers are similar. The technologies underpinning frozen food, washing powders and margarine products may be very different, but all are sold through retail operations and Unilever operates in all these product fields.
- It may be especially useful to think of relatedness in terms of the *competences* on which the competive advantage of different SBUs is built. Unilever would argue that the marketing skills associated with the three product markets above are similar, for example.
- It could also be that relatedness is important not only between business units, but also between the business units and the skills or expertise of the parent or corporate centre. This issue is discussed more fully later in the chapter (see section 6.4.3 on corporate parenting).

Trying to pin down a direct relationship between relatedness and performance is therefore difficult because relatedness could mean many things. A corporate body may be able to manage many unrelated businesses if it chooses to follow a 'hands-off' relationship with those businesses. However, if it chooses to become involved in helping to form the strategic direction of those SBUs, it is likely that a much smaller number and more related set of businesses is appropriate and will give rise to better performance.[9] This issue is dealt with in more detail in Chapters 9 and 10, where the structure and control systems of organisations are discussed.

The questions posed at the corporate level are, first, whether the corporate body wishes to have a related set of SBUs or not; and if so, on what basis. This issue of relatedness in turn has direct implications for decisions about diversification (see Chapter 7, section 7.2.4).

The Global Dimension

The increasing globalisation of products and services was discussed in Chapter 3. An increasingly important issue is what geographical boundaries managers envisage for an organisation. Some organisations have chosen to retain a strong *domestic focus*, in the belief that their future is best served by concentrating on a distinct understanding of local markets. For example, German brewers see themselves as serving a consumer whose taste for their products will persist within what was historically a regulated environment,

STRATEGY IN ACTION
Illustration 6.3

Focused Global Strategies

Strategic focus on a global scale can give small to medium-sized businesses an opportunity for market leadership on a global scale.

German *Mittelstands* (small to medium-sized businesses) concentrate on a specific product or market and focus on areas that customers value most. By attempting to match their strengths with customers' needs, they are able to offer high-value products at premium prices, while globalisation increases sales to a level where R&D costs are covered. Examples include Hauni, with a 90 per cent market share in cigarette machines, SAP, producing business software, and Leybold, which focuses on coating and vacuum technology.

Successful Mittelstands identify the following qualities as being most valued by customers; their competitive advantage comes from focusing on, and differentiation along, these lines.

Innovative, Technological and Quality Products

Mittelstands focus on highly technical and innovative product/market niches and concentrate on perfecting products – 38 per cent cited quality as a source of competitive advantage. This focus on innovation and technological leadership creates differentiation and ensures self-reliance in R&D, which strengthens their product knowledge and prevents leaks of technical information. Mittelstands have a much higher level of patents per employee than larger companies.

Closeness to the Customer

By being close to their customers, Mittelstands receive invaluable information about product performance. This can then be used to strengthen their overall capabilities and ensure that developments have practical applications. Facilities are sometimes located close to customers to ensure that they do not lose touch with their market's needs.

Mittelstands also prefer to take full control of overseas operations, viewing the customer relationship as too important to delegate. They have on average 9.6 foreign subsidiaries – a high number for companies of their size. This commitment has paid off in terms of market share.

Quality of Employees

Continuity of staff ensures that long-term relationships with customers can develop, creating commitment on both sides to the business relationship. Contact between customers and technical staff ensures that new product developments have practical applications, tailored to customers' needs.

Service

By creating strong service networks and an emphasis on customer training in the handling and maintenance of products, Mittelstands have a method of ensuring customer satisfaction and differentiating their product from that of their competitors.

Questions

To what extent do the bases of the German Mittelstands' positioning described in the illustation provide:

1. the benefits of globalisation set out in Exhibit 6.3
2. the basis for lasting competitive advantage in their markets?

Sources A. Fisher, 'Hidden champions', *Financial Times*, 30 January 1996; H. Simon, 'Lessons from Germany's midsize giants', *Harvard Business Review*, vol. 70, no. 2 (1992), pp. 115–23.

Prepared by Tony Jacobs, Bristol Business School.

and one in which competitive entry remains difficult. In the public sector, geographical scope may be prescribed – for example, in local government. Other corporations, such as some of the commodity companies in oil and other raw materials, have long operated on a worldwide basis with very narrow product ranges. Other types of business, once traditionally domestic, are following strategies of geographic expansion. For example, Aldi and Netto are becoming Europe-wide grocery retailers.

Many organisations now consider the pursuit of *global strategies* as offering distinct benefits of cost reduction, improved quality, better ability to meet customer needs and increased competitive leverage. These are not always large corporations, as Illustration 6.3 shows. Indeed, there are lessons to be learned about global operations from the successes and failures of smaller businesses which have sought to operate on a global scale. A study of such start-ups on a global scale revealed that the key characteristics of success included the global vision by the founders of the start-up, the involvement of internationally experienced managers with international business networks, and the existence of some clear advantage in product or service terms capable of being exploited and sustained.[10] Such findings illustrate well the way in which the success of the strategy integrates clarity of corporate purpose and the exploitation of competitive advantage at the business unit level.

The benefits of global strategies are shown in Exhibit 6.3.[11] On the other hand, there are drawbacks to such strategies, such as the difficulty of penetrating certain markets, or the failure to meet local customer needs because of product standardisation or global marketing (also set out in Exhibit 6.3).

6.3 BASES OF SBU COMPETITIVE ADVANTAGE: THE 'STRATEGY CLOCK'

The previous section discussed some bases of strategic choice mainly at the corporate level. However, it also showed that there needs to be a compatibility between corporate-level strategy and the strategy of the SBUs. In some organisations, notably small businesses, these may be one and the same; but in most organisations there are a number of SBUs. In either event, it is important to be clear about the bases of strategic choice at this level.

Bases of strategic choice for organisations can usefully be considered in the context of the overall **competitive strategy**, the basis on which a SBU might achieve competitive advantage in its market. This section reviews these strategies, drawing on previous discussions concerning the competitive environment (Chapter 3), and competences and the value chain (Chapter 4); and looks forward to chapters which consider more specific strategic directions and methods (Chapter 7), the evaluation of strategies (Chapter 8) and the building of competences to sustain selected strategies (Chapter 10).

competitive strategy *is the basis on which a SBU might achieve competitive advantage in its market*

Exhibit 6.3 How global strategy levers achieve globalisation benefits

	Benefits				Major Drawbacks
Global Strategy Levers	Cost Reduction	Improved Quality	Enhanced Customer Preference	Competitive Leverage	All Levels Incur Co-ordination Costs, Plus
Global market participation	Increases volume for economies of scale	Via exposure to demanding customers and innovative competitors	Via global availability, global serviceability and global recognition	Advantage of early entry Provides more sites for attack and counter attack	Earlier or greater commitment to a market than warranted on own merits
Global products	Reduces duplication of development efforts Reduces purchasing, production and inventory costs	Focuses development and management resources	Allows consumers to use familiar product while abroad Allows organisations to use same product across country units	Basis for low-cost invasion of markets Offsets disadvantage of low market share	Less responsive to local needs
Global location of activities	Reduces duplication of activities Helps exploit economies of scale Exploits differences in country factor costs Allows flexibility versus currency changes and versus local bargaining power	Focuses effort Allows more consistent quality control		Allows maintenance of cost advantage independent of local conditions Provides flexibility on where to develop bases of competitive advantage	Distances activities from customer Increases risk of creating competitors More difficult to manage value chain
Others	Reduces design and production costs of marketing programmes	Focuses talent and resources Leverage of scarce, good ideas	Reinforces marketing messages by exposing customer to the same mix in different countries	Magnifies resources available to any country Provides more options and leverage in competitive attack and defence	Reduces adaptation to local customer behaviour and marketing environment Local competitiveness may be sacrificed

Source Based on G. Yip, *Total Global Strategy*, Prentice Hall, 1995, chapter 6.

For commercial organisations, the discussions in this section are concerned with establishing the bases on which a company can build and sustain competitive advantage. For public service organisations, the section is concerned with an equivalent issue: the bases on which the organisation chooses to sustain the quality of its services within agreed budgets; how it provides 'value for money'.

In 1980, Michael Porter's book *Competitive Strategy*[12] highlighted the importance and relevance of competitive strategies. Managers were provided with a 'language' for considering the bases of competitive advantage. Here Porter's arguments are developed in the light of their subsequent critique by others.[13] The approach is based on the principle that organisations achieve competitive advantage by providing their customers with what they want, or need, better or more effectively than competitors; and in ways which their competitors find difficult to imitate.

Assuming that the products or services of different businesses are more or less equally available, customers may choose to purchase from one source rather than another because either (a) the price of the product or service is lower than a competitor's or (b) the product or service is perceived by the customer to provide better 'added value' than that available elsewhere.[14] Although these are very broad generalisations, important implications which represent generic strategic options for achieving competitive advantage flow from them. These are shown in Exhibit 6.4 and portrayed in Illustration 6.4 in the context of Japanese car firms in the European car market. They are now discussed.

6.3.1 Price-based Strategies (Routes 1 and 2)

a **'no frills' strategy** *combines a low price, low perceived added value and a focus on a price-sensitive market segment*

Route 1 may seem unattractive, but there are successful organisations following it. It is the **'no frills' strategy** which combines a low price, low perceived added value and a focus on a price-sensitive market segment. It can be viable because there could exist a segment of the market which, while recognising that the quality of the product or service might be low, cannot or chooses not to afford to buy better-quality goods. This is Lada's position in the car market, and in Europe the grocery retail chains Aldi and Netto follow this strategy. Their stores are basic, their merchandise range is relatively limited with few speciality or luxury products, and their prices are very low. As Illustration 6.4 shows, a business may also seek to achieve market entry through route 1 and use this as a bridgehead to build volume before moving on to other strategies. The strategy may also be a viable means of competing in an industry in which major firms are following a different strategy, as shown in Illustration 6.5.

a **low price strategy** *seeks to achieve a lower price than competitors whilst trying to maintain similar value of product or service to that offered by competitors*

Route 2, the **low price strategy**, seeks to achieve a lower price than competitors whilst trying to maintain similar value of product or service to that offered by competitors. The problem here is that this is likely to be imitated by competitors which can also reduce price. The result is a reduction in margins in the industry as a whole, and an inability to reinvest

Exhibit 6.4 The strategy clock: Bowman's competitive strategy options

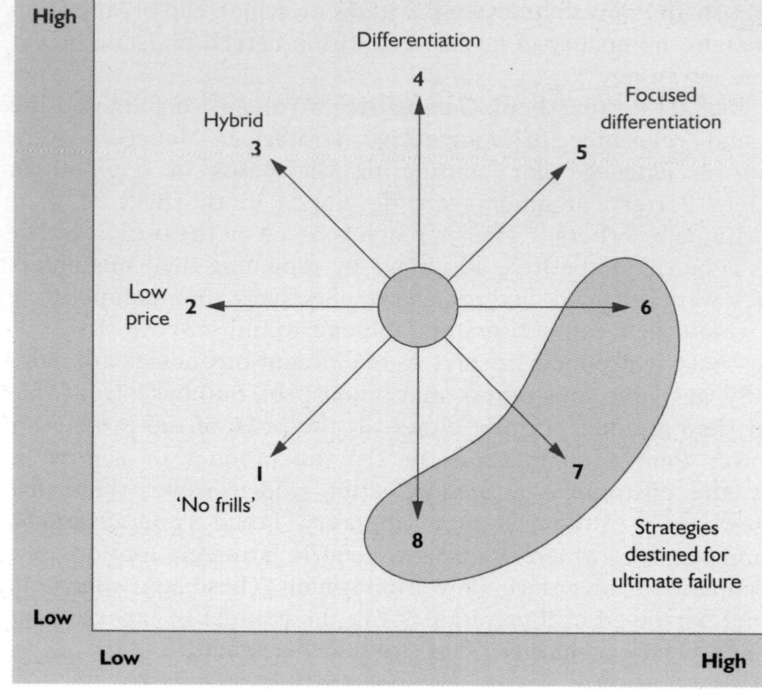

	Needs/risks	
1 'No frills'	Likely to be segment specific	
2 Low price	Risk of price war and low margins; need to be cost leader	
3 Hybrid	Low cost base and reinvestment in low price and differentiation	Differentiation
4 Differentiation		Differentiation
(a) Without price premium	Perceived added value by user, yielding market share benefits	Differentiation
(b) With price premium	Perceived added value sufficient to bear price premium	Differentiation
5 Focused differentiation	Perceived added value to a particular segment, warranting price premium	Differentiation
6 Increased price/standard value	Higher margins if competitors do not follow; risk of losing market share	Likely failure
7 Increased price/low value	Only feasible in monopoly situation	Likely failure
8 Low value/standard price	Loss of market share	Likely failure

Bowman uses the dimension 'Perceived Use Value'

STRATEGY IN ACTION
Illustration 6.4

Competitive Strategies of Japanese Car Firms in Europe

The strategy clock helps to explain how the strategies followed by Japanese car firms have developed in Europe since the 1960s.

Route 1

During the 1960s and early 1970s, the Japanese car manufacturers entered the European market by targeting the low-cost/low-added-value sector, which they believed would not be defended by European manufacturers. Their 'no frills' products were seen as cheap, and bought with few added value expectations. The sales volume that this produced and the experience gained from this market entry strategy allowed them to form a bridgehead into Europe and develop other, more profitable, strategies.

Route 2

By the late 1970s and early 1980s, the improved quality and reliability of their products changed the perception of their cars to that of being as good as their European competitors. However, the Japanese cars continued to be sold at a cheaper price than their rivals, which allowed them to increase sales volume further.

Route 3

Following their earlier success, the late 1980s saw the Japanese further advance their position by producing competitively priced cars that were more reliable and of better quality than their rivals. Competitors followed the Japanese and attempted to maintain their position by improving the quality and reducing the relative prices of their own cars.

Route 4

By the mid 1990s, the main Japanese manufacturers, in common with other car firms, were seeking ways to differentiate their products on the basis of providing extra features such as air-bags, air conditioning and longer-term warranties. However, the Japanese lead times for such innovations were less than most of their competitors'.

Route 5

Toyota's Lexus model – which stands alone from the rest of its range and does not use the Toyota name – is competing against manufacturers such as Jaguar and Mercedes in the luxury market segment. Because it is a new entrant, it does not have the 'pedigree' of its competitors; advertising campaigns aim to persuade buyers that they should be buying cars not on name, but on features.

Questions

1. Why do new entrants to industries often enter 'through' point 1 on the strategy clock?
2. Why did the incumbent market leaders not respond to the Japanese 'trading up' through positions 2 and 3 on the clock?
3. Would it be feasible to enter the market through route 5 and then move to other positions? Which other positions would be more or less difficult and why?

Prepared by Tony Jacobs, Bristol Business School.

STRATEGY IN ACTION
Illustration 6.5

EasyJet's 'No Frills' Strategy for Success

Concentrating on multiple bases for keeping costs down can provide a basis for a successful no frills strategy

EasyJet competes in the European market by offering a low-priced product. Words like brash, cheap, upstart and no frills have been used to describe this Luton-based airline which has begun to unsettle some of the airline industry's big players.

Haji-Ioannou, owner of easyJet, explained that its strategy is 'based on the belief that demand for short-haul air transport is price elastic – in simple English, if you reduce your price, more people will fly.' He went on to suggest that its low price strategy is successful in competition against the customer-service-laden premium pricing of other airlines. EasyJet forces the consumer to consider the wider implications of purchasing luxury: 'the question is not should I fly BA or easyJet, it's should I fly BA to Nice or buy another pair of jeans?' For easyJet's customer base this has proved to be a valid comparison.

Beneath the surface of easyJet's cosmetic cost savings of not offering in-flight food or different first, business and standard classes, is a philosophy of cost saving that permeates through the whole company, from its paperless office to its no-ticket flights. For example, easyJet has not entered the market for connecting flights and simply transports customers from A to B and back again. Consequently it is able to dispense with costly ticketing procedures along with the ticket vendors such as travel agents. EasyJet's customers simply ring the booking number emblazoned on the sides of its aircraft and book by credit card. As long as they identify themselves at the airport and present their booking reference number, they can then board their flight without a ticket. The absence of the need for connections to other flights has also allowed easyJet to operate out of the cheaper London Luton airport. These savings alone decrease the price of a flight by 25 per cent. EasyJet also makes the most of its favourable location at Luton by using the lack of competition for time slots to keep its flights off the tarmac and airborne, earning more hours of revenue per aircraft than the airlines operating out of busier airports can manage.

EasyJet would appear to have succeeded with its low-price strategy. However, in 1998 it attracted the unwelcome attention of BA whose own no frills European service, 'GO', was about to commence flights out of Stansted airport.

Questions

1. Read section 6.3.1 of the text and identify the bases of easyJet's no frills strategy.
2. How easy would it be to imitate easyJet's strategy?

Sources R. Rigby, 'Cheap and cheerful', *Management Today*, August 1997, pp. 52–3; F. Barrett, 'Just how low can they get', *Mail on Sunday*, 1 March 1998, p. 79.

Prepared by Phyl Johnson, Cranfield School of Management.

to develop the product or service for the long term. In the public sector, costs are, in effect, the 'price' of a service to government as the provider of funds. Here the expectation may, indeed, be that there will be year-on-year efficiency gains and that these will be achieved without loss of quality.

There are, however, ways in which a strategy of low price might be successful.

- The most ambitious is for the organisation to seek to sustain reduced prices over competition on the basis of having *the lowest* cost base such that competitors cannot hope to emulate it – of being a *cost leader* – and being prepared to sustain and win a price battle if necessary. However, cost leadership is very difficult to achieve. It has been argued that it can be achieved by means of substantial *relative market share advantage* because this provides a firm with cost advantages through economies of scale, market power (for example, buying power) and experience curve effects (see Chapter 4, section 4.3.3). However, it is not clear what 'substantial relative market share advantage' means.[15] In developing strategy, it is in any case dangerous to assume a direct link between relative market share advantage and sustainable advantage in the market because there is little evidence of sustainability; dominant firms lose market share and others overtake them. Moreover, if the idea of cost leadership is to be taken seriously as an industry-wide strategy, it is problematic for all but a very few firms – indeed, arguably in a given industry, for all but one firm. In its literal form, it is therefore not a basis for an industry-wide strategy.
- Porter actually defines[16] *cost leadership* as '*the* low-cost producer in its industry ... a low-cost producer must find and exploit all sources of cost advantage'. So the notion here is concerned with cost advantages through organisationally specific competences driving down cost throughout the value chain (see Chapter 4, section 4.3.3 and Exhibit 4.7). Cost advantages may reside in what is produced – for example, in terms of how a product is designed or in terms of its quality. But here the dangers are that the customer receives lower added value and an intended route 2 strategy slips to route 1 by default. Indeed, Porter observes that such 'low-cost producers typically sell a standard, or no-frills, product ... [Such a firm] will be an above-average performer in its industry provided it can command prices at or near the industry average'. It is therefore actually likely to be following a strategy which is somewhere between routes 1 and 2.
- An organisation may also be able to reduce cost by concentrating on aspects of its value chain which are especially valued by customers and outsourcing other activities (see Chapter 4, section 4.3.6) which can be carried out at less cost by others. There are, however, risks here too. Competitors may be able to do the same, so no advantage is gained. Or, still more problematic, the organisation may outsource activities which it has failed to recognise as actual or potential value-enhancing activities and are thus the basis of a differentiation strategy (see section 6.3.2 below).

- Cost advantage might also be achieved in terms of how a product is produced, perhaps because a business is able to obtain raw materials at lower prices than competitors, or able to produce more efficiently or benefit from economies of scale; or because it is located in an area where labour cost is low; or again because its distribution costs provide advantages. However, while all of these are potential advantages, if low cost is the basis of a strategy of low price, managers need to be sure that competitors cannot easily imitate or catch up with their cost advantages. This is problematic not least because most businesses have very little accurate information about the cost base of their competitors.
- It may be feasible to follow a strategy of low price to achieve competitive advantage within a market segment in which (a) low price is important; and (b) a business has cost advantage over competitors *operating in that segment*. An example here is the success of dedicated producers of own-brand grocery products for supermarkets. They are able to hold prices low because they can avoid the high overhead and marketing costs of major branded manufacturers. However, they can only do so provided they focus on that product or market segment.

It is important that the distinction between cost and price, and therefore cost leadership and low price, is clear. Competitive advantage is achieved in terms of customer needs through an organisation's output. Because a firm is trying to achieve cost leadership, or low cost, it does not necessarily mean that it will choose to price lower than competition. It may choose to invest surpluses from higher margins in research and development, or marketing – arguably, what Kellogg's and Mars do. In itself, low cost does not yield competitive advantage; it is how managers employ a low cost base that matters.

6.3.2 Added Value, or Differentiation Strategies (Route 4)

a **differentiation strategy** *seeks to provide products or services unique or different from those of competitors in terms of dimensions widely valued by buyers*

The next option is a broad **differentiation strategy** which seeks to provide products or services unique or different from those of competitors in terms of dimensions widely valued by buyers. The aim is to achieve higher market share than competitors (which in turn could yield cost benefits) by offering better products or services at the same price; or enhanced margins by pricing slightly higher. In public services, the equivalent is the achievement of a 'centre of excellence' status which could attract higher funding from government: for example, universities try to show that they are better at research or teaching than other universities. This strategy might be achieved through the following:

- Uniqueness or improvements in products: for example, by investment in R&D, design expertise or building on the innovatory capabilities in the organisation. This is often the basis upon which manufacturing firms such as those in the car industry seek to compete, by investing in technology or design to achieve greater reliability, product life or performance. However, it should be noted that such improvements are often not durable: competitors are able to catch up.

- Marketing-based approaches – in effect, demonstrating better than the competition how the product or service meets customer needs. Here the strategy is likely to be built on the power of the brand or by powerful promotional approaches – for example, Levis in clothing, or Heinz in food.
- Competence-based approaches in which an organisation tries to build differentiation as its core competences. If these really are competences which are peculiar to the organisation then it may well be very difficult for competitors to imitate them. However, identifying core competences as a basis for building a differentiation strategy is a challenging task (see Chapter 4, section 4.3.2).

The extent to which these approaches will be successful is likely to depend on a number of factors, some of which are demonstrated in Illustration 6.6 in relation to British Airways.

1. It is necessary to consider whether the organisation has clearly identified *who the customer is*. This is not always straightforward. For example, for a newspaper business, is the customer the reader of the newspaper, the advertiser, or both? They are likely to have different needs and values. If a strategy of differentiation is to be followed, which will it be based upon? Public sector organisations face a similar issue. It may be very important that they offer perceived added value; but to satisfy whom? There may be no market-based mechanisms for users to buy services. It may be that perceived added value is measured in terms of the extent to which pressure groups, institutions or politicians are satisfied.
2. The extent to which the organisation understands *what is valued by the customer*, user or perhaps a stakeholder group (such as a provider of funds in the public sector) can be dangerously taken for granted by managers. As explained in Chapters 2 and 4, managers may pursue strategies either on the basis of traditional ways of operating and taken-for-granted assumptions rooted in experience, or on the basis of resources and skills that the organisation has. Managers may therefore fail to address the most basic of questions: what does the customer value? A manager may conceive of a strategy of differentiation in technical terms: for example, as a better-engineered product. While the uniqueness may be real in technical terms, it is of no value in achieving competitive advantage unless it is of greater perceived value to the user than products or services of competitors. Indeed, a differentiating factor for an organisation may be the ability of the managers to be closer to the market than competitors, so that they can better sense and respond to customer needs.

STRATEGY IN ACTION
Illustration 6.6

British Airways' Bases for Differentiation

A value-added, differentiated service that customers want can provide a basis for premium prices.

In the highly competitive airline industry, BA's strategy is one of differentiation. It believes that by providing a high-quality service it is able to charge premium prices for all its services.

Sir Colin Marshall, BA's chairman, believes that 'orchestrating service to fill customers' value-driven needs' is a basis of differentiation. BA's processes are driven by customer service considerations, as it tries to make the experience of flying as effortless and pleasant as possible. Its recruitment policy ensures that only the 'right' people are employed; staff attend customer service training programmes and are given the freedom to react to individual circumstances to ensure customer satisfaction.

Marshall says that BA should 'excel in listening to its most valuable customers'. This has led to the continuous use of focus groups to establish what customers value and need; research is even conducted into why customers 'defect' to other airlines, and, where necessary, procedures are changed to improve service quality.

This process of differentiation has led to many changes: for example, BA's airport lounges are included as part of the total package, with everything they contain – from drinks to telephones – free to premium passengers; and fast-track check-in channels have been installed to enable premium passengers to move through immigration and customs with the minimum of delay.

In-flight, BA ensures that cabin crews are highly visible throughout the flight; research has shown that this creates a high level of customer satisfaction. BA's 'well-being in the air' programme provides healthy food options and demonstrates exercises that customers can perform to reduce the discomfort of long flights.

A sleeper service was also introduced for first-class customers on long-distance routes. Customers eat before boarding the flight, sleep onboard and use the arrivals lounge to shower, change and prepare themselves for the day ahead, while waiting for public transport or an office to open.

Marshall believes that, by arranging 'all the elements of [its] service so that they collectively generate a particular experience', BA has a good basis of differentiation. It appears to have worked. In an industry that lost billions, BA remained profitable. However, by the late 1990s other airlines were trying to compete in similar ways. BA faced the challenge of maintaining the bases of its differentiation strategy.

Questions

1. Read section 6.3.2 of the text and critique British Airways' differentiation strategy against the six factors discussed.
2. On the basis of your critique, suggest ways in which British Airways might further build its differentiation in the market.

Source S.E. Prokesch, 'Competing on customer service', *Harvard Business Review*, vol. 73, no. 6 (1995), pp. 100–16.

Prepared by Tony Jacobs, Bristol Business School.

3. It is important to be clear *who the competitors are*. For example, does the SBU see itself competing with a wide competitor base or with a much narrower base, perhaps within a particular market segment? In the latter case, a strategy of focused differentiation may be appropriate (see section 6.3.4 below). In the case of broad-based differentiation, it is likely that the SBU will have to concentrate on bases of differentiation commonly accepted across the industry or a market. For example, it is unlikely that a car manufacturer trying to compete in the broadly based saloon car market could achieve competitive advantage without recognising the buyers' concern with quality and reliability, which have become threshold requirements. The emphasis must, then, be on how to achieve an advantage in other ways, requiring a much more sophisticated understanding of customer needs and how these can be met by building on core competences.

4. Another problem in identifying relevant competitors occurs as markets globalise. For example, a company may find its bases of differentiation eroded by another company which it did not previously see as a competitor because it did not share common geographical markets. As the two competitors increase their geographical scope, they may become competitors. Or it could be that a competitor develops a basis of differentiation in one market and then enters another on the basis of this, thus challenging an established operator's strategic position.

5. The extent to which the basis of differentiation is *difficult to imitate* also needs to be considered. For example, a firm of accountants which carries out a relatively standardised audit procedure will find it difficult to differentiate its services based on variations of those procedures. Even if it can develop such variations, they may be copied rapidly by others. It is more likely that differentiation can be achieved on the basis of the extent to which those involved in the firm understand the needs of their clients, build relationships with individuals within the client base, and can ensure that their own services are integrated to meet the clients' needs.

   To take another example, an industrial goods company selling to contractors needs to recognise that the ability to provide assured delivery on time, up-to-date information on the progress of orders and rapid after-sales service may be of critical importance. How this is done will depend on different parts of the manufacturer's operations or value chain. So differentiation is based on a mix of activities, relationships and competences. This is likely to be an important basis of the sustainability of a strategy of differentiation. This was shown in Illustration 4.2 and is taken up again in Chapter 10 (see section 10.2.5).

6. The idea that competitive advantage through differentiation can be achieved on a static basis is questionable. There are two reasons for this. In many markets, customer needs change, and therefore *bases of differentiation may need to change*. However, even if relatively constant customer needs can be identified, over time competitors may

STRATEGY IN ACTION
Illustration 6.7

Crinkly Biscuits as Competitive Advantage?

In building a competitive strategy, executives need to be wary of spurious bases of competitive advantage.

Senior executives of an international food manufacturing company were taking part in a strategy workshop, discussing bases of competitive advantage for their strategic business units. The issues of competitive advantage based on perceived customer needs was raised, and one of the executives, the quality assurance manager for a biscuit business, commented as follows:

> I totally agree. In our business we know what customers want and we have invested to provide it. Our research shows that customers care a lot about the crinkles on the edges of their biscuits. They like neat regular crinkles. We have just invested £1 million in equipment that will deliver just that with very little wastage. We are the leader in this field.

In the discussion which followed, it became clear that there were at least three flaws in what the manager had said. First, his point of reference for considering his strategy was the end user, the consumer. In fact, the company referred to grocery retailers as 'competitors' because such retailers sold own-brand goods. Yet if the major retailers, which controlled 50 per cent of the distribution of biscuits, did not stock the product, it never reached the consumer. Whilst consumers were, of course, very important, the strategic customer was the retailer; but the business had no clear strategy for achieving competitive advantage with regard to retailers.

Second, it became clear that the identification of customer need was based on a survey which had pre-specified certain characteristics of biscuits, one of which was 'regular crinkles'. The quality assurance manager's colleagues were of the opinion that the fact that 'consumers had ticked a few boxes to do with ideas thought up by some guys in the R&D department' was a spurious basis upon which to build a strategy, let alone invest large amounts of capital.

Third, when challenged, the manager had to admit that there was nothing to stop a competitor buying similar equipment and achieving just the same quality of crinkles. If there was any competitive advantage – and this was dubious – it was easily imitable.

Questions

This example illustrates three common shortcomings in differentiation strategies:

(a) Value-for-money is incorrectly assessed by focusing on the wrong customer (or 'stakeholder').
(b) Inappropriate research to identify benefits
(c) Easy imitation of the supposed sources of differentiation.

Bearing in mind these shortcomings identified in the claim for differentiation made in the illustration:

1. Do the bases of differentiation espoused by British Airways in Illustration 6.6 overcome these shortcomings?
2. What *might have been* sustainable bases of differentiation for this biscuit business?

be able to imitate bases of differentiation. The implication is that a business following a differentiation strategy may have to review bases of differentiation continually, and keep changing, as is the case for those car manufacturers following strategies of broad differentiation. This was also the strategy so successfully followed by Microsoft with the rapid introduction of improvements in software features and shortening product life cycles, which made it difficult for competitors to keep pace. Again this stresses the potential importance of developing innovatory capabilities in organisations.

Some of these problems of identifying bases of differentiation are demonstrated in Illustration 6.7.

6.3.3 The Hybrid Strategy (Route 3)

a **hybrid strategy** *seeks simultaneously to achieve differentiation and a price lower than that of competitors*

A **hybrid strategy** seeks simultaneously to achieve differentiation and a price lower than that of competitors. Arguably, this is the strategy pursued by IKEA (see Illustration 1.1). Here the success of the strategy depends on the ability both to understand and to deliver enhanced value in terms of customer needs, while also having a cost base that permits low prices and is sufficient for reinvestment to maintain and develop bases of differentiation.[17] This should not be confused with just trying to keep costs down in general, while seeking to achieve differentiation; after all, presumably managers should always be trying to operate at the lowest cost commensurate with the strategy they are following.

It might be argued that, if differentiation can be achieved, there should be no need to have a lower price, since it should be possible to obtain prices at least equal to competition, if not higher. However, the hybrid strategy could be advantageous in the following circumstances:

- If much greater volumes than the competition can supply can be achieved, and margins still kept attractive because of a low cost base. This is what some Japanese car manufactures might claim.
- If it is possible to be clear about the core competences on which differentiation can be built, and then reduce costs on other activities. IKEA recognised that it could achieve a high standard of production, but at a low cost, whilst concentrating on building differentiation on the bases of its marketing, range, logistics and store operations (see Illustrations 1.1 and 5.5).
- If there is a market segment with particular needs which also facilitates a low-price approach. IKEA offers good quality but to a market segment that is prepared to build and transport its products.
- As an entry strategy in a market with established competitors. This is a strategic approach to new market development that Japanese firms sometimes use on a global basis. They search for the 'loose brick'[18] in

a competitor's portfolio of businesses – perhaps a poorly run operation in a geographical area of the world – then enter that market with a superior product and, if necessary, a lower price. The aim is to take share, divert the attention of the competitor, and establish a foothold from which they can move further. However, in following such a strategy it is important to ensure that (a) the overall cost base is such that low margins can be sustained, and (b) a clear follow-through strategy has been considered for when entry has been achieved.

6.3.4 Focused Differentiation (Route 5)

a **focused differentiation** *strategy seeks to provide high perceived value justifying a substantial price premium usually to a selected market segment*

A **focused differentiation** strategy seeks to provide high perceived value justifying a substantial price premium. However, if this strategy is followed, it is likely to mean that the business is competing in a particular market segment. In the market for saloon cars, Ford, Rover, Peugeot, Renault, Volkswagen and Japanese competitors are all competing within the one market, trying, often with some difficulty, to convince customers that their product is differentiated from their competitors'. A Lexus is also a saloon car, but it is not seeking to compete directly with these other manufacturers. It is offering a product with higher perceived value at a substantially higher price than in the saloon car market. It is therefore trying to attract different sorts of customers; a different market segment. However, this strategy raises some important issues:

- The choice may have to be made between broad differentiation across a market or a more focused strategy. Indeed, this may take on global proportions, as managers have to decide between a broad approach in increasingly global markets, or more selective focus strategies – as shown in Illustration 6.8.
- Because an organisation choosing to follow a focus strategy is likely to be targeting a particular market segment, it is important to realise that, within that segment itself, the strategy clock is just as relevant so managers face further choices. Lexus competes in the luxury car segment, but within that segment it is following a strategy quite distinct from other luxury car companies. Its competitors might be seen as top-of-the-range Mercedes and BMW. Against these competitors in this segment, Lexus is following a low-price or perhaps hybrid strategy. Its quality is just as good, but relative to those other models, its prices are lower.
- It is again important to be clear about which market segment (or segments) is being targeted, defined in terms of a coherent set of customer needs; and this needs to be translated into action which satisfies those customers. This may be difficult to do, if the organisation is attempting to compete in different market segments, with different needs. For example, department stores attempt to sell a wide range of products in one store. They may also attempt to appeal to different

STRATEGY IN ACTION
Illustration 6.8

Breadth or Focus in European Businesses?

It is important to consider the benefits of breadth or focus in international markets.

In the early 1990s, a study of European businesses showed that managers saw their strategies for the 1990s as increasingly dependent on the careful choice of breadth of markets, and on the linkage of market power and market segmentation.

> In the 1990s, for the big brewers, there will be more possibilities of up-scaling. I also strongly believe in the small niche breweries, either in a specific segment of the beer market, or in a specific area selling to bars. Medium-size breweries must make a choice. Either they must become big, or they must aim at some precise segment of the industry.
>
> *Dutch brewer*

> I do not think that the universal bank, such as BNP, will be more successful than specialised banks such as La Compagnie Bancaire ... I think there will be six to eight universal banks in Europe by the year 2000, three French banks, two British ones and a couple of German banks ... The other ones will have to specialise.
>
> *French retail banker*

> You have to divide the market into several segments ... Everybody knows that a high net worth individual in general is more profitable for a bank than just a blue collar worker in any factory. And the top of the market is an opportunity to become more international.
>
> *Dutch retail banker*

> Our target is to get within the top six companies because we think there are going to be six major players, and then a lot of minnows swimming around the edge. We think that is the place to be successful; the time of the middle ground has been and gone. There will be no middle ground players any more. You have either got to be investing heavily in major schemes, production and marketing, or you have to go for little niche markets.
>
> *British book publisher*

> If there is to be a European market in book publishing, it will be in the domain of heavy products (art books, encyclopaedias, etc.) or products having a high profitability threshold. On the other hand, in general literature, groups do not have any European strategy; it is a more risky and fragmented business where small firms can be effective.
>
> *French book publisher*

Questions

Have the trends forecast for each of the industries come about.

For each of the industries listed above, choose one company in that industry from your own country and answer the following questions.

1. How well positioned currently is your chosen company to survive these trends?
2. If it needs to reposition, what is its choices?
3. Compare the advantages and disadvantages of each choice?
4. Recommend what the company should do.

Source R. Calori and P. Lawrence (eds), *The Business of Europe: Managing change*, Sage, 1991, pp. 140–7.

customer types in so doing. But they run into problems because the store itself, the fixtures and fittings, the décor and store ambience, and the staff, may not be differentiated according to the different market segment needs.

- Focus strategies may conflict with stakeholder expectations. For example, a public library service could probably be run more cost efficiently if it were to pull out of low-demand market niches and put more resources into its popular branch libraries. It might also find that an extension of its services into audio and video tapes or new forms of public information service would prove popular. However, the extent to which these strategies would be regarded as within the library's remit might be hotly debated.
- New ventures often start in very focused ways – for example, new 'leading-edge' medical services in hospitals. It may, however, be difficult to find ways to grow such new ventures. Moving from route 5 to route 4 will mean a lowering of price and therefore cost, while maintaining differentiation features. On the other hand, maintaining a highly focused (route 5) approach may not be easy because users may not be prepared, or able, to pay the price or, as in the public sector, provide funding support to subsidise such projects.
- The advantages of the focused approach have to be carefully monitored because the market situation may change. Differences between segments may be eroded, leaving the organisation open to much wider competition. This was a concern for the manufacturers of luxury cars, such as Jaguar, as the top end of the executive car range came closer and closer to the style of luxury cars. Or the market may be further segmented by even more differentiated offerings from competitors.

6.3.5 Failure Strategies (Routes 6, 7 and 8)

The strategies suggested by routes 6, 7 and 8 are probably destined for failure. Route 6 suggests increasing price without increasing value to the customer. This is, of course, the very strategy that monopoly organisations are accused of following. However, unless the organisation is protected by legislation, or high economic barriers to entry, competition is likely to erode market share. Route 7 is an even more disastrous extension of route 6, involving the reduction in value of a product or service, while increasing relative price.

Route 8, reduction in value while maintaining price, is also dangerous, though firms have tried to follow it. There is a high risk that competitors will increase their share substantially.

Porter argues that there is another basis of failure, which is for a SBU to be unclear as to its fundamental generic strategy: he argues that too many end up being 'stuck in the middle'. They are following no clear generic strategy – a recipe for failure.

The strategy clock is, then, a market-based model of generic strategy options rooted in the question: what is of value in the product or service to the customer, user or provider of funding? It does not deny that the cost base of an organisation is crucially important, but it sees this as a means of developing generic strategies, and not as a basis for competitive advantage in itself.

6.3.6 The Management Challenge of Competitive Strategies

The various arguments made in this first part of the chapter pose significant challenges to managers in the development of strategy. To achieve real bases of sustainable advantage, it is important to do the following:

- Be clear which customers (or users) are the target for the strategy to be followed.
- Clearly identify customer needs and bases of added value in the market place, defined either broadly or, more likely, by market segment.
- Build sufficient knowledge of competitors' competences and cost structures to take an informed view about bases of competitive advantage.
- Given this understanding, consider and establish which of the competitive strategy routes is most appropriate for the organisation given its purpose and aspirations.
- Operationalise this strategy in such a way that customer needs are met by a mix of activities which is distinctly different from that of competitors and which is embedded in organisational competences (see Chapter 10, section 10.2).
- Ensure that the strategic directions and methods (see Chapter 7) of the organisation are in line with the generic strategy.

6.4 ENHANCING SBU STRATEGY: THE ROLE OF THE CORPORATE CENTRE

This chapter began with a discussion of how corporate purpose and aspirations are important elements of strategic choice. It made it clear that a significant question at the corporate level is to what extent SBU strategies are enhanced, or how they are managed, at the corporate level.

The relationship which different corporate bodies or divisions have with their SBUs varies considerably. Some see their role as aiding SBUs in the development of their strategy, by enhancing the basis of their competitive advantage. This might take the form of providing skills, knowledge or resources they would not have independently, encouraging useful linkages between businesses, facilitating the international development of those businesses and so on. Other corporate bodies see their role as primarily being answerable to external stakeholders – for example, financial institutions and shareholders – and letting the businesses get on with their own affairs. The form of this corporate control is discussed in Chapter 9 (section 9.4). What is discussed here is the role of the corporate centre in enhancing SBU strategies.

6.4.1 Managing Portfolios

A major issue is the extent to which the SBUs within a corporate portfolio mutually reinforce each other, are balanced, and are compatible with corporate skills and aspirations. Corporations with a portfolio of businesses face two corporate-level decisions: what businesses to include in the portfolio and how to interact with these businesses.

A number of tools have been developed for helping managers choose what businesses to have in the portfolio. Each tool gives more or less focus on one of two criteria: the attractiveness of the business, meaning how profitable it is and how fast it is growing; and the degree of 'fit' that the business has with the rest of the portfolio, meaning, are there synergies with other businesses and is this the sort of business the corporate parent will be good at looking after?

The *attractiveness* or *directional policy matrix*, discussed at the end of Chapter 3 (section 3.5.4) has been widely used to categorise businesses into those with good prospects and those with less good prospects. The implication is that the corporate parent should focus on the former and exit the latter. The *growth/share matrix*, discussed in section 4.5 of Chapter 4 (and also used in Exhibit 6.5) is a way of considering the balance and development of a portfolio. For example, if the corporate aspiration is high growth in income and the business is prepared to invest to gain that growth, then it may be prepared to support more *stars* and *question marks* than a parent which is concerned with stable cash generation and which may concentrate on preserving or building its *cash cows*. Other corporate bodies take the view that a balanced portfolio is desirable, with reliable cash cows providing surpluses which can be channelled into investments in growing market shares of fast-growing new SBUs, to turn them into stars and eventually cash cows. Managers need to exercise care here, however. They may neglect to think through the implications of decisions arising from such categorisation. For example, a *dog* could be written off without regard for the competitive consequences of pulling out of a market, and therefore handing a more dominant competitor even more market power and a stronger portfolio. Or, if cash cows are used to fund potential growth businesses, how will this affect the motivation of managers in the SBUs regarded as cash cows?

A different problem may arise for managers in public sector organisations. They may find it difficult to develop stars – services with real growth potential – or generate surpluses to be reinvested, because this may not be their brief from government. They may be expected to manage services which cannot make money, but which are public necessities. Further, if they seek to develop services which can grow and make money, these may be privatised or put out to private tender. It may be seen as legitimate for a local government leisure department to manage public parks and recreation grounds, but the development of indoor tennis and swimming pools with profit potential may be seen as an inappropriate activity. The definition of the appropriate portfolio of activities therefore requires a clarity of corporate purposes and aspirations.

The *Ashridge Portfolio Display*, described in section 6.4.4, addresses the question of fit. The implication is that corporate parents should focus on businesses they will be able to add a lot of value to. The *life cycle matrix*, used in Chapter 8 (section 8.2.1), is another way of categorising businesses. It can be used to assess attractiveness (mature businesses being less attractive) or fit (a company should have a balance of growth and mature businesses or a company should focus on one stage of the life cycle in order to get skilled at managing that stage).

The trend in management thinking has been to move away from focusing mainly on the attractiveness criterion towards focusing more on the fit criterion. Moreover, thinking about fit has been moving away from concepts of balance towards concepts of parenting added value. The reasons for these changes in thinking lie in two trends. First, many companies diversified in the 1970s and 1980s in order to get into more attractive businesses and balance their portfolios. Most of these initiatives failed and the late 1980s and early 1990s were periods of unbundling, break-ups, demergers and focus. The second trend has been the increasing sophistication of the capital markets. Shareholders no longer need companies to smooth earnings because they can smooth their returns by investing in a selection of companies with different earnings profiles. Moreover, shareholders can move money into attractive sectors, such as health care or emerging technologies, more easily than corporate parents can. The argument is that corporate parents should stop doing tasks that shareholders can more easily do for themselves (balance risk, smooth returns and find attractive sectors) and focus on creating additional value from the application of management expertise.

Thinking about fit has developed around two concepts – parenting and core competences. The parenting concept argues that corporations should seek to build portfolios that fit well with their corporate centre skills (parenting skills) and they should build parenting skills that are appropriate for their portfolio. By juggling these two principles, corporations should be able to move towards greater fit and hence greater success. The core competences idea is that corporations should build their portfolios around core competences shared across businesses and nurtured by the corporate centre. The core competence concept was addressed in Chapter 4 (section

4.3). The parenting concept is addressed in this chapter (section 6.4.4) and takes as its starting point the competences of the corporate centre.

The concept of fit has equal relevance in the public sector. The implication is that public sector managers should control directly only those services and activities that fit services and activities for which they have special managerial expertise. Other services should be outsourced or set up as independent agencies. Whilst the current trend towards outsourcing, privatising and setting up independent agencies is driven as much by political dogma as by corporate-level strategy analysis, the trend is in this direction.

6.4.2 Corporate Financial Strategy[19]

A basic issue which has to be faced is how an organisation is to be financed. Decisions on finance will be influenced by ownership – for example, whether the business is privately held or publicly quoted – and by the overall corporate intent of the organisation. For example, there will be a different financial need if a business is seeking rapid growth by acquisition or development of new products compared with if it is seeking to consolidate its past performance. Executives also need to recognise that the financial strategy they choose to follow could be helpful or could hinder strategies at SBU level. So financial strategy decisions are also linked to the added value that can be provided to SBU strategies. This section explains how this is so using the growth/share matrix as a basis of explanation (see Exhibit 6.5).

The financial strategy of an organisation needs to take into account the relationship between financial risk and financial return. The greater the risk, the greater the return required to investors. The growth/share matrix is a convenient way of considering the risk/return relationship among the various businesses that could exist in a corporation (see also Chapter 8, section 8.3.1 on return and section 8.3.2 on risk). The relationship between financial strategy, SBU strategy and the overall strategy of a corporation with a portfolio of SBUs is important, then, not only for shareholders, but also for those who seek to manage a portfolio effectively.

Question marks (or *problem children*) are clearly high risk. They are at the beginning of their life cycle and are not yet established in their markets; moreover, they are likely to require substantial investment. For those who wish to invest in them, therefore, there is a need to understand the nature of risk and a desire to seek high returns. A stand-alone business in this situation might, for example, seek to finance such growth from specialists in this kind of investment, such as venture capitalists who, themselves, seek to offset risk by having a portfolio of such investments.

The degree of risk remains high in high-growth situations even if relatively high market shares are being achieved – as is the case with *stars*. The market position here remains volatile and probably highly competitive. It could be that a business has been financed on the basis of venture capital initially, but as it grows and becomes established it needs to seek other

Exhibit 6.5 **Source of funding**

STARS	QUESTION MARKS
GROWTH PHASE	LAUNCH PHASE
Business risk high Financial risk low	Business risk very high Financial risk very low
Equity (growth investors)	**Equity** (venture capital)
CASH COWS	**DOGS**
MATURITY PHASE	DECLINE PHASE
Business risk medium Financial risk medium	Business risk low Financial risk high
Debt and equity (retained earnings)	**Debt**

Source Adapted from K. Ward, *Corporate Financial Strategy*, Butterworth/Heinemann, 1993, p. 32.

financing. Since the main attractions to investors here are the product or business concept and the prospect of future earnings, equity capital is likely to be appropriate; a business might seek to raise equity by public flotation.

Businesses which operate in mature markets with high shares (*cash cows*) should be generating regular and substantial surpluses. Here the risk is lower and the opportunity for retained earnings is high, and in the case of a portfolio of businesses, the corporation may be seeking to recycle such a surplus into its growth businesses. In these circumstances, it may make sense to raise finance through debt capital as well as equity, since reliable returns can be used to service such debt and, in any case, the return expected by lenders is likely to be less than those providing equity. (Since interest on debt has to be repaid, the risk for the business itself is higher than equity finance; so it is also reasonable for the business to expect the cost of debt to be lower than equity.) Provided increased debt (sometimes called *gearing* or *leverage*) does not lead to an unacceptable level of risk, this cheaper debt funding will in fact increase the residual profits achieved by a company in these circumstances. The danger is that the corporation overstretches itself, takes on too much debt, increases its risk by so doing, suffers a downturn in its markets and is unable to service its interest payments.

If a business is in decline, in effect a *dog*, then equity finance will be difficult to attract. However, borrowing may be possible if secured against residual assets in the business. At this stage, it is likely that the emphasis in the business will be on cost cutting, and it could well be that the cash flows from such businesses are quite strong. These businesses may provide relatively low-risk investment.

Conglomerates face a problem if they seek to develop a financial strategy for a portfolio of businesses where there is a mix of businesses more or less growing and in high- or low-share positions. What is the appropriate financial strategy? This cannot be answered in isolation from a consideration of overall corporate strategy. The corporation needs to consider its overall risk/return position. For example, if a corporation is seeking to follow a high-growth strategy by diversification and acquisition, then it may be perceived by the investing community as a high-risk business; as such, it may have difficulty raising debt capital, and those who provide equity may expect high return. Corporations which have sought high growth through an acquisitive diversification strategy have suffered because they have not had appropriate financial strategies. Either they have been either unable to attract equity investment or unwilling to do so, and have sought to finance growth out of borrowings, in effect relying on ever-growing cash growth to finance such borrowing. A decline in such growth means that debt cannot be serviced and could lead to bankruptcy.

The crucial point is that financial strategy should be driven by portfolio strategy. For example:

- A company focusing on a portfolio of high-growth, high-risk investments in emerging industries would need to have more equity and less debt, as is common with venture capital companies.
- A company focusing on a portfolio of mature cash cow businesses with reliable cash flows (like Hanson did) would need the opposite – more debt and less equity.
- A corporation seeking to develop new and innovative businesses on a regular basis might, in effect, be acting as its own venture capitalist, accepting high risk at the business level and seeking to offset such risk by encouraging new and innovative ideas. If it does so, it should consider if it has a role to play as those businesses mature, or if it needs to consider selling them on to other corporations, not least to raise capital for further investment.
- Innovative structures are also possible. KKR (Kohlberg, Kravis, Roberts), a leading leveraged buyout partnership, uses high levels of debt financing provided directly by institutions to the businesses. The equity element is managed through limited partnerships that have stakes in a number of investments.

corporate parenting *is the search for a fit between the skills of the corporate centre and the strategies of SBUs so as to add value to those SBUs*

6.4.3 Corporate Parenting: The Role of the Parent

A corporate parent has to take a view on how it will relate to and seek to enhance the strategies of SBUs. **Corporate parenting** is, then, the search for a fit between the skills of the corporate centre and the strategies of SBUs so as to add value to those SBUs. There are different approaches to this,[20] and some of these are shown in Exhibit 6.6. There are parents who seek to operate in a *portfolio management* style, with slim corporate head office staff seeking to balance investments in businesses by reviewing acquisition targets, buying wisely and divesting poor performers. However, there is limited evidence for the success of such an approach on its own.

A second role is as a *restructurer* of businesses, the role taken by the Hanson Group until the mid 1990s. It focused on acquisitions of businesses, certainly, but built these around its corporate-level skills in identifying restructuring and transformation opportunities. Its skills lay not just in an ability to buy and sell companies, but also in an ability to move executives, experienced in such restructuring, rapidly into organisations to improve performance.

A parent may also seek to add benefits to businesses by helping with the interrelationships between the businesses themselves. This is sometimes called *managing synergy* (see Chapter 8, section 8.2.1). The corporation may seek *to transfer skills and competences* from one business unit to another. These could be competences learned in the management of one value chain which are relevant to the value chain of another business. It could be that the marketing skills, highly developed in a consumer products business like Lever Brothers, part of Unilever, could be transferred into a less sophisticated business acquired by Unilever: for example, by moving experienced marketing executives. Unfortunately, in many cases this concept of synergy does not come to fruition. Skills are not always that easily identifiable or transferable because the businesses or their markets are dissimilar. It could also be that the corporate centre itself has special skills or expertise by which it is able to create value for the businesses by transferring these skills from the centre to the businesses. Rio Tinto, the mining conglomerate, has special expertise at managing risk and financing mine projects in high-risk locations. Canon has found that it is possible to create whole new businesses by combining optics, electronics and miniaturisation technologies. It has developed a highly sophisticated step-by-step approach that can take a new product idea from the laboratory to the creation of a whole new division.

Another approach is the *sharing of activities*. Marriott sought to share activities across its hotels, restaurants and airport facilities. Such shared activities included the ability to provide and learn from standardised hotel procedures and to benefit from shared procurement and distribution. They were supported by an organisational structure that encouraged integration and co-operation.

The four roles of the parent shown in Exhibit 6.6 can be expanded to include a fuller set of parenting skills and capabilities. These are discussed more fully in Chapter 9 (section 9.4.1), where issues of corporate structure and design are considered.

Exhibit 6.6 Roles of corporate parents

	Portfolio Managers	Restructurers	Skill Transferers	Activity Sharers
Strategic requirements	• Identifying and acquiring undervalued assets • Divesting low-performing SBUs quickly and good performers at a premium	• Identifying restructuring opportunities • Intervention in SBUs to transform performance • Sale of SBUs when restructuring complete or market conditions favourable	• Transferring skills to give competitive advantage in SBUs • Ongoing transfer of skills • Identification of appropriate skills to transfer	• Sharing activities to provide competitive advantage to SBUs • Identification of benefits of sharing which outweigh costs • Overcoming SBU resistance to sharing
Organisational requirements	• Autonomous SBUs • Small, low-cost corporate staff • Incentives based on SBU results	• Autonomous SBUs • Turnround skills of corporate staff • Incentives based on acquired SBU results	• Autonomous but collaborative SBUs • Corporate staff as integrators • Cross-SBU taskforces • Incentives based partly on corporate results	• SBUs encouraged to share • Strategic planning at different levels • Corporate staff as integrators • Incentives based on corporate results

Source Adapted from M.E. Porter, 'From competitive to corporate strategy', *Harvard Business Review*, May/June 1987.

6.4.4 The Parenting Matrix

In deciding on the appropriateness of the role of the parent and the mix of SBUs best suited to the parent, the *parenting matrix* can be useful. The Ashridge Portfolio Display[21] is a way of displaying this degree of 'fit' of a portfolio of businesses. Two dimensions of fit are assessed:

- Fit between the *critical success factors* of the SBUs (see section 4.6.2) and the skills, resources and characteristics of the parenting organisation.
- Fit between the *parenting opportunities* of SBUs (see below) and the skills, resources and characteristics of the parenting organisation.

The logic for using these two dimensions of fit is as follows. If the critical success factors of the business fit badly with the skills and characteristics of the parent organisation, then parent managers are likely to misunderstand the business and inadvertently do it harm. So the first measure of fit is about avoiding problems. For example, when BAT, a tobacco company, acquired Eagle Star, a financial services company, there was low *critical success factor fit*: the critical success factors of insurance did not fit well with the skills and characteristics of BAT managers. The result was problematic. BAT encouraged Eagle Star to gain market share (a normal strategy in tobacco) with the consequence that Eagle Star took on inappropriate insurance risks, incurring some big losses a few years later. The lack of fit was partly the cause of the subsequent losses. Fit between critical success factors of the business and the characteristics of the parent is therefore about downside risk. High fit means low risk of problems. Low fit means high risk of problems.

Fit between the parenting opportunities of the business and the characteristics of the parent is about opportunity. High fit means high potential for added value. Low fit means low potential. A 'parenting opportunity' is an opportunity for the business to improve that which can be better exploited with help from a parent organisation. For example, the business may need to cut costs and could be helped by a parent organisation with experience of doing this; the business may need to expand in Asia and would be helped by a parent with good Asian contacts; the business may need to improve its marketing skills and could be helped by a parent with strong marketing skills; and so on.

Exhibit 6.7 shows what a resulting portfolio might look like. *Heartland* businesses are ones which the parent can add value to without danger of doing harm. They should be at the core of future strategy. *Ballast* SBUs are ones the parent understands well but can do little for. They would probably be just as successful as independent companies. If they are part of a future strategy, they need to be managed with a light touch.

Value trap SBUs are dangerous. They appear attractive because there are opportunities for the parent to add value. But they are deceptively attractive, because there is a high danger that the parent's attentions will result in more harm than good. Value trap businesses should only be included in the future strategy if they can be moved into the heartland.

Exhibit 6.7 The parenting matrix: the Ashridge Portfolio Display

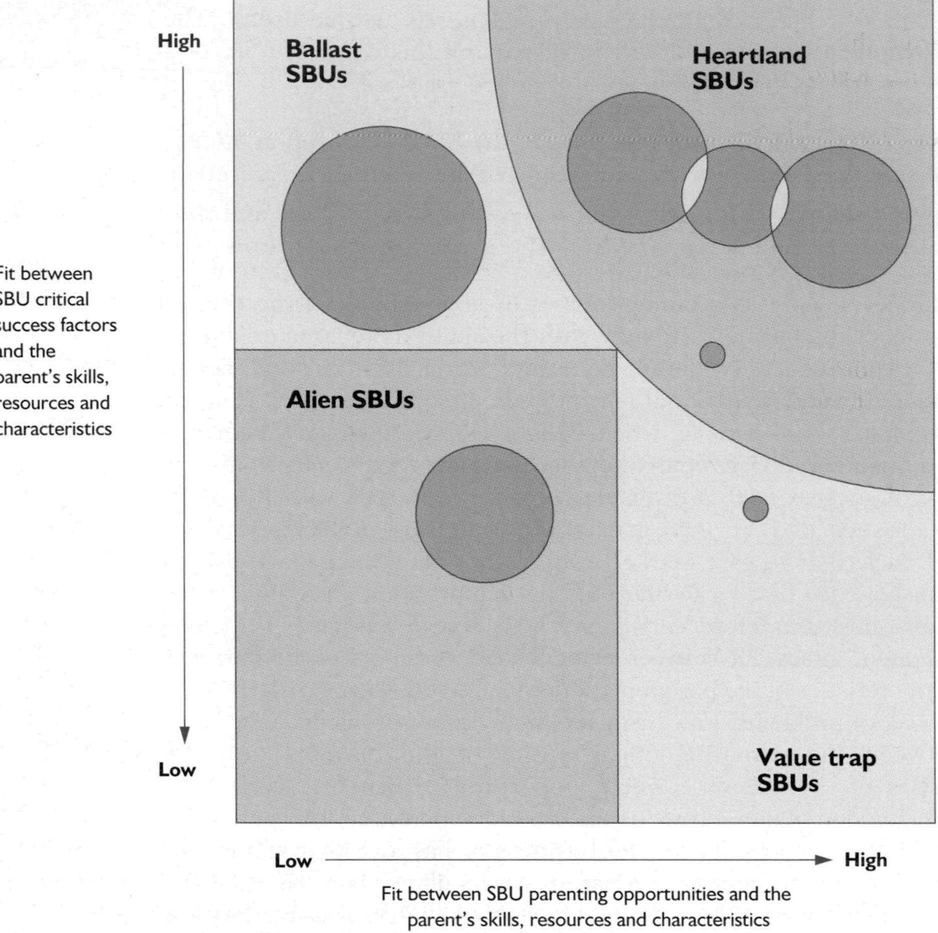

Source M. Goold, A. Campbell and M. Alexander, *Corporate Level Strategy*, Wiley 1994.

Some adjustments to the skills, resources or characteristics of the parent will probably be necessary. *Alien* SBUs are clear misfits. They offer little opportunity to add value and they rub awkwardly with the normal behaviour of the parent. Exit is the best strategy.

6.4.5 The Challenge of Parenting

Different corporate bodies will choose to exercise different roles in regard to parenting. However, whatever the role, it is important to ask a number of questions.

- If the parent is not enhancing the strategies of the SBUs, what is its role? A corporate body has a role to play with regard to purely corporate affairs, such as dealing with financial institutions and negotiating with governments. But if its role is limited to this, the cost of delivering these functions should be low to the SBU. A large and costly corporate headquarters which does little to enhance the strategies of its SBUs can be a great cost burden to SBUs, thus undermining potential market-based competitive advantage, and so reducing the overall returns for the parent.
- If the corporate body seeks to enhance the strategies of the SBUs, it must be very clear that there is a match between its skills in so doing and the help which the SBUs require to achieve competitive advantage. It must avoid undertaking roles which do not enhance strategies at the SBU level. For example, the corporate parent may impose cumbersome strategic planning more to do with providing information to the centre than with aiding the strategic development of the units; it may retain a large head office staff which duplicate the roles of executives in SBUs; or it may make demands on SBU strategy that are not sensible for that SBU.
- The corporate parent should also assess which SBUs should, most sensibly, be within its portfolio given these considerations. Illustration 6.9 shows how Unilever reviewed its role as a corporate parent and, in consequence, its portfolio.
- If the corporate parent does, indeed, seek to enhance SBU strategies, it needs to consider the extent to which there is a fit between the SBUs and the parent (see section 6.4.3 above), and the number of SBUs for which it can sensibly do so (see Chapter 9, section 9.4.1).
- Where, then, is greatest value to be added? An overall pattern has emerged in the last decade or so which suggests that organisations throughout the world are attempting to drive responsibility for strategic decisions nearer and nearer to markets. There is an attempt to ensure that SBU-specific competences are directed at developing successful competitive strategies. For example, the UK-based chemicals conglomerate ICI[22] chose to de-merge into two separate businesses, one based on its pharmaceutical operations, which it renamed Zeneca, and one based on its heavy chemicals business, for which the name ICI was retained. The strategic logic underlying this de-merger again reflects the belief that the corporate parent should enhance SBU strategy and, if it does not, can reduce the value of SBUs.

The trend towards deregulation and privatisation of public utilities and government authorities, increasing throughout the world, has a similar rationale underlying it. The aim is to give the responsibility for developing strategic capability and achieving competitive advantage in markets to the business unit level – to managers who are most closely in touch with their markets. The role of the parent has therefore been increasingly seen as one of facilitation or of taking a hands-off approach as far as possible.

STRATEGY IN ACTION
Illustration 6.9

Unilever's Parenting

The role of the parent is to add value to business units.

Unilever is a consumer products company, involved in food, detergents and personal products. Unilever has built particular skills, resources and characteristics which make it an effective parent of certain kinds of business, but a less effective parent of others. From 1985 onwards it undertook a review of its corporate portfolio.

Unilever had developed as a decentralised organisation, traditionally setting great store in the country or regional manager. It had a strong technology base and centralised corporate research laboratories. It also had a strong marketing focus, built round skills in product development and branding for mass market consumers. Finally, Unilever had an unusual human resource management process, monitoring the progress of 20,000 managers, a large portion of which were expatriates.

The skills, resources and characteristics of Unilever's corporate centre fitted well with the parenting opportunities and critical success factors of its businesses. Regionally focused consumer products businesses needed help to access product and market knowledge from across the globe. Consumer products businesses also benefited from the type of support Unilever provided in product marketing, basic technical research and new product development. For example, a typical mistake that consumer product companies make is to invest too little in new products. Because products have long lives, it is always tempting to prolong an existing product rather than take the risk of launching a replacement. Unilever found from long experience that continuous new product development was the right policy. The company therefore pressed its subsidiaries to push harder in this area than they would probably choose to do on their own.

Since the late 1980s, Unilever had disposed of businesses that were not heartland businesses (see diagram). The needs of a speciality chemical business were clearly different from the needs of a consumer products business and the critical success factors were different. For example, a speciality chemical business often operates from one site in serving a global market. Consumer goods businesses normally have many sites serving the slightly different needs of different regions. Tea plantations are also different. Unilever's skills in marketing, fat technology and new product development were of little relevance to a tea plantation.

On the diagram, Unilever's food businesses are identified as having the best fit because the combination of centralised skill management and decentralised decision making that Unilever was most comfortable with suits food businesses. The detergents businesses, for example, were becoming increasingly global, particularly in developed economies, and Unilever has been losing market share to companies more comfortable with a centralised management philosophy. The detergents businesses were therefore moving to the edge of Unilever's heartland (e.g. Procter & Gamble). The perfume and up-market cosmetics busi-

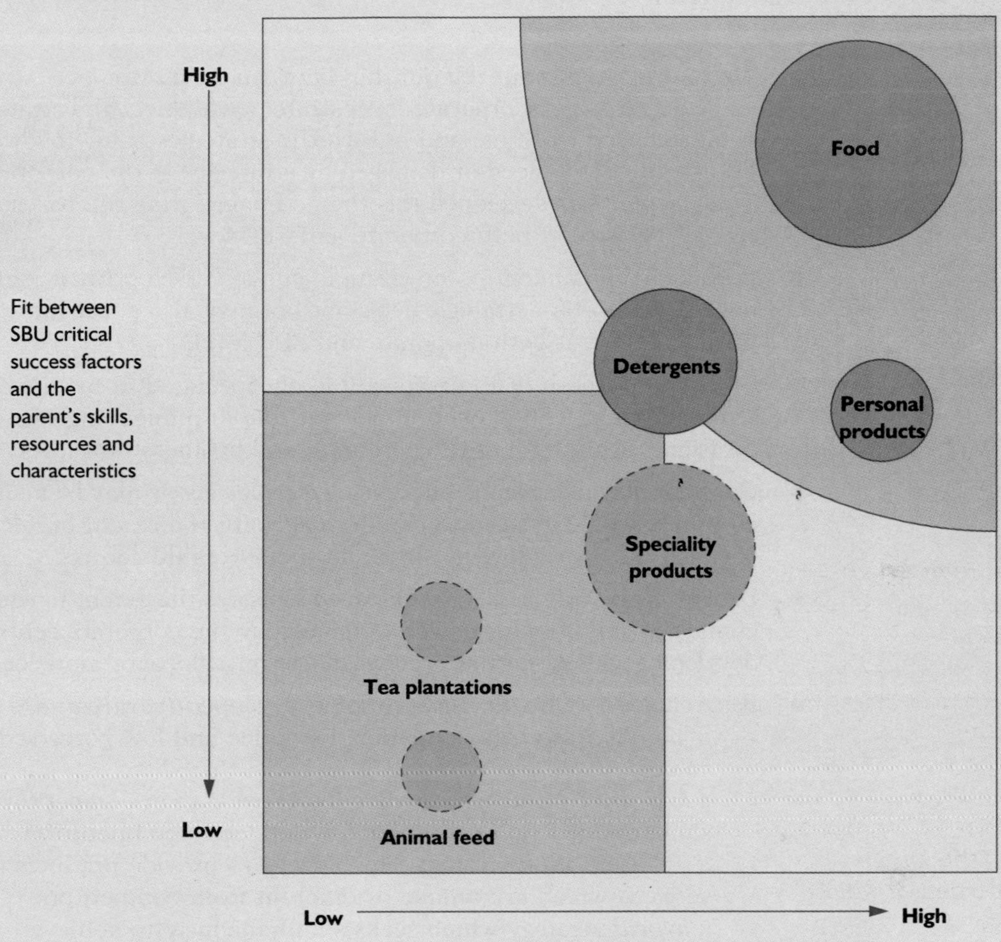

nesses, part of the personal products division, were also global, requiring a management approach that Unilever was less comfortable with. This led to the personal products businesses as a group being positioned differently from the food businesses.

Questions

1. How might the results of this parenting matrix exercise by Unilever differ from a portfolio exercise using the growth/share matrix?
2. How do the implications of this exercise relate to issues of organisational structure (see the case example on Unilever at the end of Chapter 9)?

Prepared by Andrew Campbell of Ashridge Strategic Management Centre.

SUMMARY

- There is an important relationship between *corporate-level strategy* and *SBU strategy*. Corporate-level strategy will affect the strategies being followed by SBUs; and in turn the strategies being followed by SBUs can be enhanced or damaged by strategies at the corporate level. This chapter has developed this theme by exploring the bases of strategic choice at both corporate and SBU level.
- Decisions on *ownership*, for example public versus private control, are not only important strategic decisions but may also affect the strategies being followed at both corporate and SBU level.
- Clarity of purpose of an organisation, encapsulated in its *mission* or *strategic intent* can play an important role in influencing strategic decisions, again both at the corporate and business unit level.
- Corporate level decisions on *product/service scope* may be made at the corporate level but need to take into account the extent of relatedness between SBUs or between SBUs and the corporate centre.
- Decisions on *geographical scope* need to assess the extent to which SBU competitive positioning can be enhanced by the corporate centre developing wide or narrow product ranges on a global or more local scale.
- Basic choices of SBU strategies to achieve *competitive advantage* include:
  - a '*no frills*' strategy combining low price and low perceived added value
  - a *low price* strategy providing lower price than competitors at similar added value of product or service to competitors
  - a *differentiation* strategy which seeks to provide products or services which are unique or different from competitors
  - a *hybrid* strategy which seeks simultaneously to achieve differentiation and prices lower than competitors
  - a *focused differentiation* strategy which seeks to provide high perceived value justifying a substantial price premium.
- The *role of the corporate centre* is to add value to the strategies of SBUs. It may do this in a number of ways, for example:
  - by choosing and managing a *portfolio* of businesses so as to maximise the potential of the SBUs within it
  - to develop a *corporate financial strategy* in line with the nature of the portfolio of SBUs
  - to provide *parenting skills and expertise* at the centre so as to enhance the value of SBU strategies.
- The *parenting matrix* is a useful way of assessing the extent to which the corporate centre can add such value in terms of the fit between the skills, resources and characteristics of the parent and (a) the critical success factors of the SBUs and (b) the parenting opportunities afforded by the SBUs.

In considering these bases of strategy of organisations, it should be evident that questions are raised which are pivotal in strategy development.

- Bases of strategic choice need to take account of the *environment* in which the organisation operates: for example, corporate aspirations or SBU competitive advantages may be eroded as technology changes or as new competitors enter markets.
- Similarly, the links to Chapter 4 should be clear in relation to the central importance of *core competences*. These relate both to the bases on which competitive advantage may be built – for example, in achieving and maintaining differentiation – and to the parenting skills exercised at the corporate level, which may, themselves, be core competences which can help achieve competitive advantage.
- Clearly, the expectations and influence of *stakeholders* also play a key role in determining the purpose and aspirations of an organisation, and these, in turn, can be seen to play an important role in determining the appropriate mix of SBUs in a portfolio.
- Little of the discussion so far has dealt with how the broad strategic choices discussed in this chapter might be put into effect. This raises questions about the *strategic direction* that an organisation might follow. Should it seek to develop new products or competences, enter new markets or diversify into different businesses, and by what *methods* should this be done? Should it be by internal development, alliances with other organisations or acquisitions? These issues are dealt with in Chapter 7.
- Reference has also been made throughout the chapter to the important links between decisions about the relationship between corporate-level strategies and SBU strategies, and the *structure and control* of organisations. These are the central issues of Chapters 9 and 10.

RECOMMENDED KEY READINGS

- The importance of a clarity of purpose and aspirations for an organisation is argued in G. Hamel and C.K. Prahalad, *Competing for the Future*, Harvard Business School Press, 1994, chapter 6, and in their paper 'Strategic intent', *Harvard Business Review*, vol. 67, no. 3 (1989), pp. 63–76.
- The strategic logic and benefits underlying global strategy development is provided in G. Yip, *Total Global Strategy*, Prentice Hall, 1995, chapter 6.
- M.E. Porter, *Competitive Advantage*, Free Press, 1985, chapter 2, provides a succinct review of his arguments on competitive strategies. For an extension of the discussion of the 'strategy clock' approach used here, see Cliff Bowman, *Strategy in Practice*, Prentice Hall, 1998, chapter 2.
- A summary of different portfolio analyses, their benefits and limitations is provided in David Faulkner's chapter, 'Portfolio analysis', in V. Ambrosini with G. Johnson and K. Scholes (eds), *Exploring Techniques of Analysis and Evaluation in Strategic Management*, Prentice Hall, 1998.
- The issue of parenting is discussed in detail in M. Goold, A. Campbell and M. Alexander, *Corporate Level Strategy*, Wiley, 1994.

REFERENCES

1. A discussion and examples of changes in ownership can be found in M. Vander Weyer, 'Only fools and masochists', *Management Today*, January 1996, pp. 26–30.
2. The privatisation of public utilities is discussed in P. Jackson and C. Price, *Privatisation and Regulation: A review of the issues*, Longman, 1994, chapter 3.
3. A useful paper on management buyouts is by M. Wright, B. Chiplin and S. Thompson, 'The market for corporate control: divestments and buy-outs', in M. Bishop and J. Kay (eds), *European Mergers and Merger Policy*, Oxford University Press, 1993.
4. See other chapters in *Privatisation and Regulation* (reference 2 above). M. Bishop, J. Kay and C. Mayer, *Privatisation and Economic Performance*, Oxford University Press, 1994, provides a number of in-depth case studies of deregulation.
5. For a discussion of the role of a clarity of mission, see A. Campbell, M. Devine and D. Young, *A Sense of Mission*, Hutchinson Business, 1990. However, G. Hamel and C.K. Prahalad argue in chapter 6 of their book, *Competing for the Future*, Harvard Business School Press, 1994, that mission statements have insufficient impact for the competence of a clarity of 'strategic intent'. This is more likely to be a brief but clear statement which focuses more on clarity of strategic direction (they use the word 'destiny') than on how that strategic direction will be achieved. See also Hamel and Prahalad on strategic intent in the *Harvard Business Review*, vol. 67, no. 3 (1989), pp. 63–76.
6. See reference 5 above.
7. This is the view of leadership taken by Hamel and Prahalad (see reference 5 above).
8. There is a very extensive literature on this topic. A review of the topic is provided in V. Ramanujam and P. Varadarajan, 'Research on corporate diversification: a synthesis', *Strategic Management Journal*, vol. 10, no. 6 (1989), pp. 523–52.
9. See R.M. Grant, A.P. Jammine and H. Thomas, 'Diversity, diversification and profitability among British manufacturing companies, 1972–84', *Academy of Management Journal*, vol. 31, no. 4 (1988), pp. 771–801.
10. See B.M. Oviatt and P.P. McDougall, 'Global startups: entrepreneurs on a world-wide stage', *Academy of Management Executive*, vol. 9, no. 2 (1995), pp. 30–45.
11. Exhibit 6.3 is based on the discussion in G. Yip, *Total Global Strategy*, Prentice Hall, 1995, chapter 6. The book provides a helpful overall discussion of global dimensions of strategy.
12. See M.E. Porter, *Competitive Strategy*, Free Press, 1980.
13. There are a number of papers which provide useful critiques of Porter's competitive strategies: M. Cronshaw, E. Davis and J. Kay, 'On being stuck in the middle or Good food costs less at Sainsburys', working paper, Centre for Business Strategy, London School of Business, 1990; C.W.L. Hill, 'Differentiation versus low cost or differentiation and low cost: a contingency framework', *Academy of Management Review*, vol. 13, no. 3 (1988), pp. 401–12; A. Karnani, 'Generic competitive strategies: an analytical approach', *Strategic Management Journal*, vol. 5, no. 4 (1984), pp. 367–80; S.S. Mathur, 'How firms compete: a new classification of generic strategies', *Journal of General Management*, vol. 14, no. 1 (1988), pp. 30–57, 'Generic strategies and performance: an empirical examination with American data. Part 1: Testing Porter', *Organisation Studies*, vol. 7, no. 1 (1986), pp. 37–55; D. Miller and P.H. Friesen, 'Porter's (1980) generic strategies and performance: an empirical examination with American data. Part 2: Performance implications', *Organisation Studies*, vol. 7, no. 3 (1986), pp. 255–61; R.E. White, 'Generic business strategies, organisational context and performance: an empirical investigation', *Strategic Management Journal*, vol. 7, no. 3 (1986), pp. 217–31; and D. Faulkner and C. Bowman, *The Essence of Competitive Strategy*, Prentice Hall, 1995.
14. Exhibit 6.3 is similar to the arguments and figures which Philip Kotler employs in discussing marketing-mix alternatives in his book *Marketing Management*, 8th edition, Prentice Hall, 1994. Section 6.3 is, however, based more specifically on the work of D. Faulkner and C. Bowman, *The Essence of Competitive Strategy*, Prentice Hall, 1995. But it should be noted that they use the term 'perceived use value' rather than 'perceived added value'.
15. The debate on the benefits of relative market share are complicated. There are perhaps three key points: (a) a firm with a high absolute market share may not have a high relative share because there may be a competitor which also has a comparable share; (b) arguments differ as to whether relative market share should be measured in terms of the nearest individual competitor, or the nearest two or three competitors; and (c) estimates of the relative market share necessary to achieve sustainable market power advantage vary between about 40 and 70 per cent. For discussion on this debate, see, for example, R.D. Buzzell and B.T. Gale, *The PIMS Principles*, Free Press, 1987, chapter 5. See also R.D. Buzzell, 'Are there natural market structures?', *Journal of Marketing*, vol. 45, no. 1 (1981), pp. 42–51.
16. These quotes concerning Porter's three competitive strategies are taken from his book *Competitive Advantage*, Free Press, 1985, pp. 12–15.

17. The researchers and writers who argue that cost-based strategies are not incompatible with differentiation include D. Miller, 'The generic strategy trap', *Journal of Business Strategy*, vol. 13, no. 1 (1992), pp. 37–42; and Hill (see reference 13 above). Their arguments are supported by the work of PIMS (see reference 15), who argue for the benefits of a 'virtuous circle' in strategy, by which they mean the search for low cost which provides surpluses to reinvest in differentiation and product advantages.
18. See G. Hamel and C.K. Prahalad, 'Do you really have a global strategy?', *Harvard Business Review*, vol. 63, no. 4 (1985), pp. 139–48.
19. For readers who wish to follow up the discussion in this section, see K. Ward, *Corporate Financial Strategy*, Butterworth/Heinemann, 1993, and T. Grundy and K. Ward (eds), *Developing Financial Strategies: A comprehensive model in strategic business finance*, Kogan Page, 1996.
20. The approaches described here are based on Michael Porter's article, 'From competitive to corporate strategy', *Harvard Business Review*, no. 65 (1987) pp. 43–59.
21. The discussion in this section draws on M. Goold, A. Campbell and M. Alexander, *Corporate Level Strategy*, Wiley, 1994, which provides an excellent basis for understanding issues of parenting.
22. See G. Owen and T. Harrison, 'Why ICI chose to demerge', *Harvard Business Review*, vol. 73 (1995), pp. 133–142.

WORK ASSIGNMENTS

6.1 ● Consider and compare (a) what the main aspirations of key stakeholders are, (b) how these affect corporate purpose, and (c) the implications on strategy for IKEA (Illustration 1.1), the NHS (Illustration 2.7), the Body Shop (Illustration 5.5) and a global corporation such as The News Corporation.*

6.2 ● Write a discussion paper explaining how privatisation of public services will or will not change the delivery of such services to the benefit of (a) taxpayers who finance the services and (b) the users of such services.

6.3 Choose a company with a wide geographical scope in its products or services (e.g. Burmah Castrol*). Using Exhibit 6.3 as a guideline, identify the benefits and drawbacks of such scope.

6.4 Using Exhibit 6.4, the strategy clock, identify examples of organisations following strategic routes 1 to 5. If you find it difficult to be clear about which route is being followed, note down the reasons for this, and consider if the organisations have a clear competitive strategy.

6.5 ● Michael Porter argues that a business must have a clear competitive strategy. Assess the extent to which any, or all, of the following have a clear competitive strategy:

(a) PSA Peugeot Citroën*
(b) Laura Ashley* (throughout its existence)
(c) an organisation of your choice.

6.6 You have been appointed personal assistant to the chief executive of a major manufacturing firm, who has asked you to explain what is meant by 'differentiation' and why it is important. Write a brief report addressing these questions.

6.7 ● Michael Porter argues that 'cost leadership' is a competitive strategy. Drawing on Porter's arguments, critiques cited in reference 13 and section 6.3 of this chapter, consider if this is appropriate.

6.8 ● How appropriate are bases of competitive advantage explained in section 6.3 for considering the strategies of public sector organisations? Illustrate your argument by reference to a public sector organisation of your choice.

6.9 ● Choose a number of companies with portfolios of SBUs (e.g. Burmah Castrol,* The News Corporation*). Using Exhibits 6.6 and 6.7 as a guide, identify and explain the role of the corporate parent. Explain how, if at all, the parent enhances or could enhance SBU strategies.

---

* refers to a case study in the Text and Cases edition.
● denotes more advanced work assignments.

CASE EXAMPLE

The Virgin Group

Virgin is a unique phenomenon. From financial services through to airlines and railways; from entertainment megastores, soft drinks and cinemas to clothes and even bridal salons, its name is instantly recognisable to the consumer. Research ranked Virgin among the top five brand names in the UK and among the top twenty-five in Europe, with the company associated with words such as 'fun', 'innovative', 'daring' and 'successful'. Richard Branson's personal image, his face and personality were high profile; for example, in British advertisements for Apple Computers, together with Einstein and Gandhi, he was featured as a shaper of the 20th century.

Origins and Ownerships

Virgin was founded in 1970 as a mail order record business and developed as a private company in music publishing and retailing. In 1986 the company was floated on the Stock Exchange with a turnover of £250 million. At the time there appeared to be obvious advantages. It allowed Branson to capitalise on the success of the company and gave the Group easier access to finance at a lower cost for its continued expansion whilst, arguably, attracting better management.

However, Branson tired of the public listing obligations. Compliance with the rules governing public limited companies and reporting to shareholders were both expensive and time consuming, and he resented making presentations in the City to people who, he believed, did not understand the business. The pressure to create short-term profit, especially as the share price began to fall, was the final straw: Branson decided to take the business back into private ownership and the shares were bought back at the original offer price, which valued the company at £240 million. Less than four years later, Virgin Music was sold to Thorn EMI for £510 million, according to Branson to support the cost of the battle then taking place between BA and Virgin Atlantic. By 1998, Branson's family trust owned the largest portion of the company, which was largely debt free. However, he was reported to be considering floating some of the businesses within his empire, the most ambitious being the possible flotation of the rail business. He had also toyed with the idea of selling off businesses gradually to managers.

The Virgin Group

The scope of the business portfolio of the Virgin Group, together with its ownership structure at the beginning of 1998, is shown in Exhibit 1. Some were wholly owned and Virgin held a share in many others. The extent of management integration across businesses was much less than in many other western corporations. For example, although some of the business units within the group targeted the same customer types and marketed to similar segments, there was no common customer database. It was rather like an Asian company such as Sony or Hyundai, built from the ground up, with the brand serving to bind them together. Like those firms, the array of businesses making up Virgin seemed to have little in common with each other except for a perceived emphasis on quality and the Virgin – and Branson – names and image.

Virgin had grown fast, becoming profitable and entering and claiming a significant share of new markets without the traditional trappings of the typical multinational. There was no head office, little sense of management hierarchy and there seemed to be a minimum of corporate bureaucracy. There was no 'group' as such: financial results were not consolidated either for external examination or, so Virgin claimed,

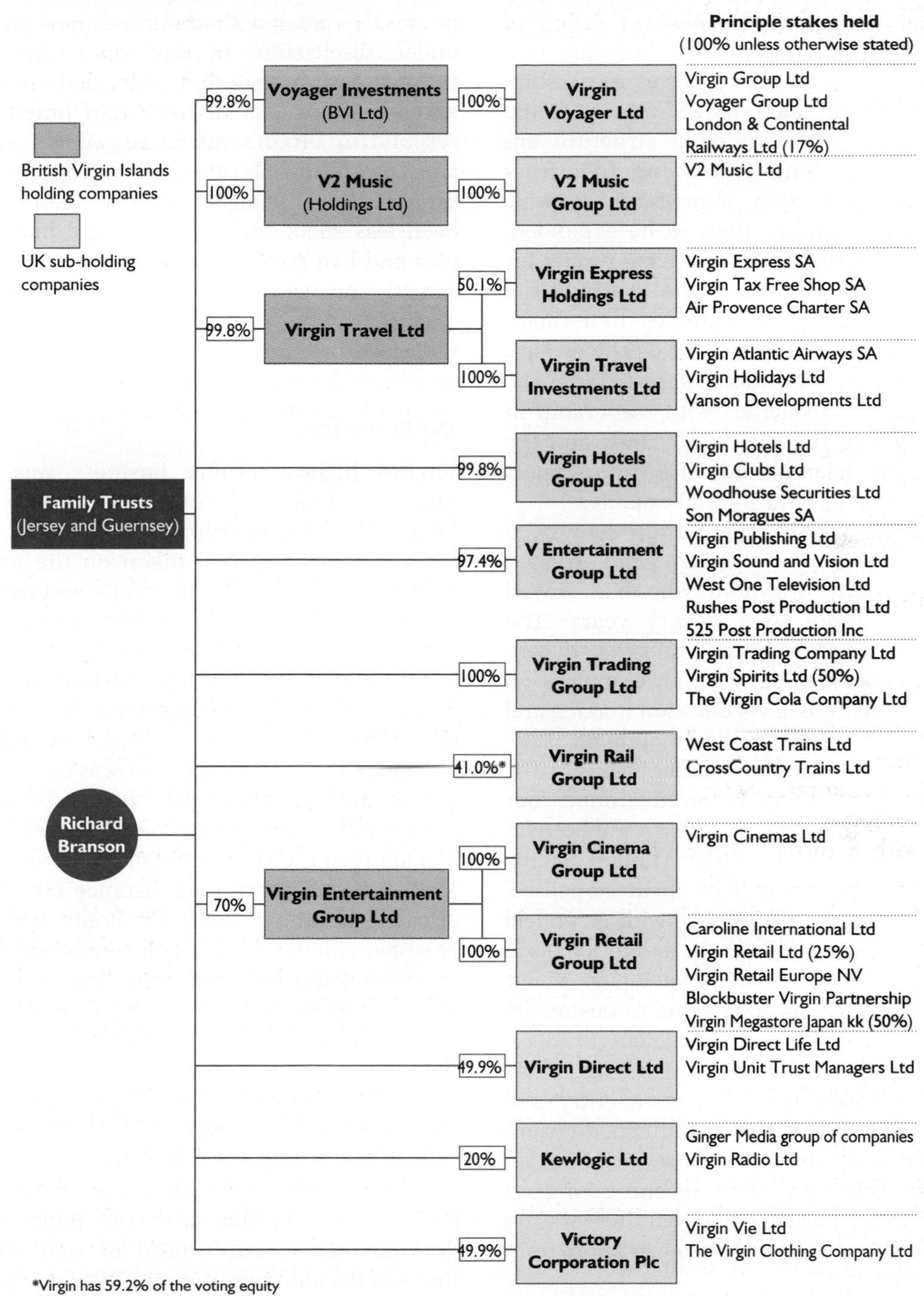

Exhibit 1 Branson's empire (January 1998)

for internal use. Each business or group of businesses ran its own affairs but was tied together through a degree of shared ownership, shared leadership and shared values. Some argued that Virgin's ownership structure enabled it to take long-term views free from investors' fixation with short-term returns. Indeed, Branson argued that, as he expanded, he would rather sacrifice short-term profits for long-term growth and the capital value of the various businesses. Others argued that financing, purely through, equity slowed the group's ability to expand. Still others suggested that the complex web of businesses with ownership in offshore trusts in the Channel Islands and the British Virgin Islands did little to support Branson's image of honesty and openness.

Historically, the Virgin Group had been controlled mainly by Branson and trusted lieutenants, many of whom who had stayed with him for more than twenty years. The approach to management was one that decentralised decision making, with an emphasis on autonomous business-level decision making and responsibility for their own development.

Branson's medicine for adding value to the businesses in the group revolved around four elements: the Virgin brand, Virgin's public relations and marketing skills, Virgin's understanding of the opportunity presented by 'institutionalised' markets, and Virgin's experience with greenfield start-ups. In Virgin language, an institutionalised market was a market dominated by a few competitors, not giving good value to customers because they had become inefficient or over-absorbed with each other. The Virgin brand made it possible to overcome barriers to entry and Virgin's low cost marketing skills helped ensure an excellent cost structure. However, Branson pointed out that this often meant taking on established market leaders, and that there was no expectation that this would result in short term profit gain.

Branson and his two-man business development team reviewed about fifty business proposals a week with about four new prospects under discussion at any one time. Good prospects were ones that addressed institutionalised markets, fitted the Virgin brand, could respond to Virgin's medicine, offered an enticing reward-to-risk ratio, and were represented by a capable management team. Branson had been less successful when he had had a good idea and had gone out to look for a manager to run it. The best proposals came to him from managers who wanted to run the business themselves.

The Businesses

Virgin's highest profile business was Virgin Atlantic, which had developed to be a major force in the international airline business. Over the years Branson had taken on the might of British Airways to obtain routes and develop a service which was rated highly amongst users. 'First class service at business class fares' was a selling point strongly emphasised by Virgin Atlantic. It was the first carrier to have a beauty therapist and a tailor on board as well as a chauffeur service to take business class passengers to and from the airport. It was also the first carrier to become non-smoking and even show a video trying to persuade smokers to stop. By 1997, passengers on long distance flights could also amuse themselves for hours with their personal videos packed with games and films.

Within the business units Branson adopted his own personal style of management. He prided himself on actively involving employees, seeking their ideas on ways of further adding value for his customers. Whilst critics commented that his levels of pay were often not as good as some competitors', they acknowledged the benefits of the involvement and enthusiasm of the staff in past success. In line with the philosophy of drawing on the enthusiasm of staff, in 1997 Branson decided to sell Virgin Radio to one of its presenters, Chris Evans. Virgin Radio had been attracting interest from Capital Radio, the largest

UK commercial radio company. Indeed, its bid of £87m had been agreed by Branson until a lesser offer of £85m came along from Evans. Branson, regarding Evans as a 'more sympathetic partner', agreed a deal whereby the presenter took 55 per cent of the equity, with support from a venture capital business. The aim was to build a nationwide commercial pop station and extend the appeal from the younger age group to a broader audience. Branson had decided that Evans was in a good position to do this. It was also in line with an approach to business development he had employed elsewhere: of taking or holding a share in a business, allowing the Virgin name to be used, but relying on others to put up the capital and manage things; in effect, a franchise arrangement.

However, by 1998 critics were pointing out that some of the business ventures were struggling; Virgin Cola had not proved especially successful and Virgin Vodka, launched in 1994, was to be found in just a few duty free shops and on Virgin Atlantic flights. But of most concern was the high profile acquisition of the UK West Coast rail line from the previously nationalised British Rail. It was cited as one of the most unpopular and inefficient train operators in Britain, according to a 1997 passenger survey, with complaints that the service was worse than it had been prior to privatisation. It was estimated that Virgin needed to double the number of passengers to be a success and spend £750 million on new rolling stock and service improvements. There were other costs too. Government subsidies would decline up to 2002 from around £77m in 1998 and it would be necessary for Virgin to pay the UK government annual franchise fees rising from £3.9m to £220m in 2012.

The Future

By 1998, Virgin had the popular image of a highly successful and exciting business. However in February 1998 an article in *The Economist* raised a number of concerns. It argued that Virgin was highly dependent on the profits of Virgin Atlantic; there were few other businesses making substantial profits and many seemed to be loss making. The airline industry was cyclical and facing increased competition as a result of deregulation. The Virgin brand, arguably its most precious asset, could become associated with major problems, even failure, related to its rail operations. This business was also extremely cash hungry; even its public share issue might leave Virgin facing the prospect of having to shed major parts of its empire – perhaps even Virgin Atlantic – to finance it. 'As with Virgin Music, Mr Branson would be selling his past in order to finance his future.'

Questions

1. What are (or could be) the advantages and disadvantages of public or private ownership for Virgin in its development?
2. What is the competitive strategy being followed by Virgin Atlantic? How does this differ from EasyJet (Illustration 6.5) and British Airways (Illustration 6.6).
3. Are there any relationships of a strategic nature between businesses within the Virgin portfolio?
4. Does the Virgin Group add value to its businesses? If so, how?

Note Exhibit 1 is, with permission, from *The Economist*, 21 February 1998. In the article from which it is taken it is explained that it is based on an attempt to 'assemble a picture ... by looking at 80 of [the] companies.'

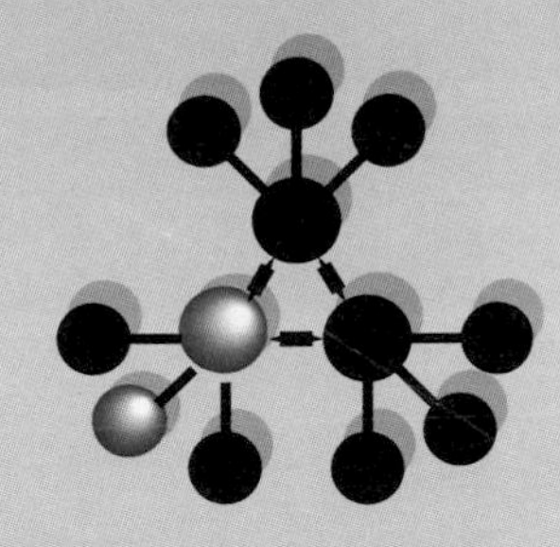

7
STRATEGIC OPTIONS: DIRECTIONS AND METHODS OF DEVELOPMENT

LEARNING OUTCOMES

After reading this chapter you should be able to:

- Explain how the three elements of a strategy (basis, direction and method) must complement each other.
- Identify the development direction options for an organisation.
- Explain how the PIMS database can be used.
- Compare three methods of development (internal, acquisition and alliances).
- Understand the different forms of strategic alliance.
- Describe the conditions for successful alliances.

7.1 INTRODUCTION

The previous chapter was concerned with the bases of strategic choice for organisations. Within this broad 'steer' for an organisation there are a number of specific options concerning both the *direction* and the *method* of developing the organisation's strategies, as previously indicated in Exhibit 6.2. This chapter will discuss these issues in the following way.

- Exhibit 7.1 is an adaptation of the traditional product/market matrix[1] often used for generating *directions* for strategic development. It considers the development directions 'available' to an organisation in terms of the *market coverage*, *products* and *competence base* of the organisation. This last dimension is an important extension of the traditional approach. Indeed, the figure is meant to emphasise that, in the long run, development in any of the boxes is likely to require the development of competences to cope with a changing situation. So, *innovation* is a key ingredient of strategic change.

Exhibit 7.1 **Directions for strategy development**

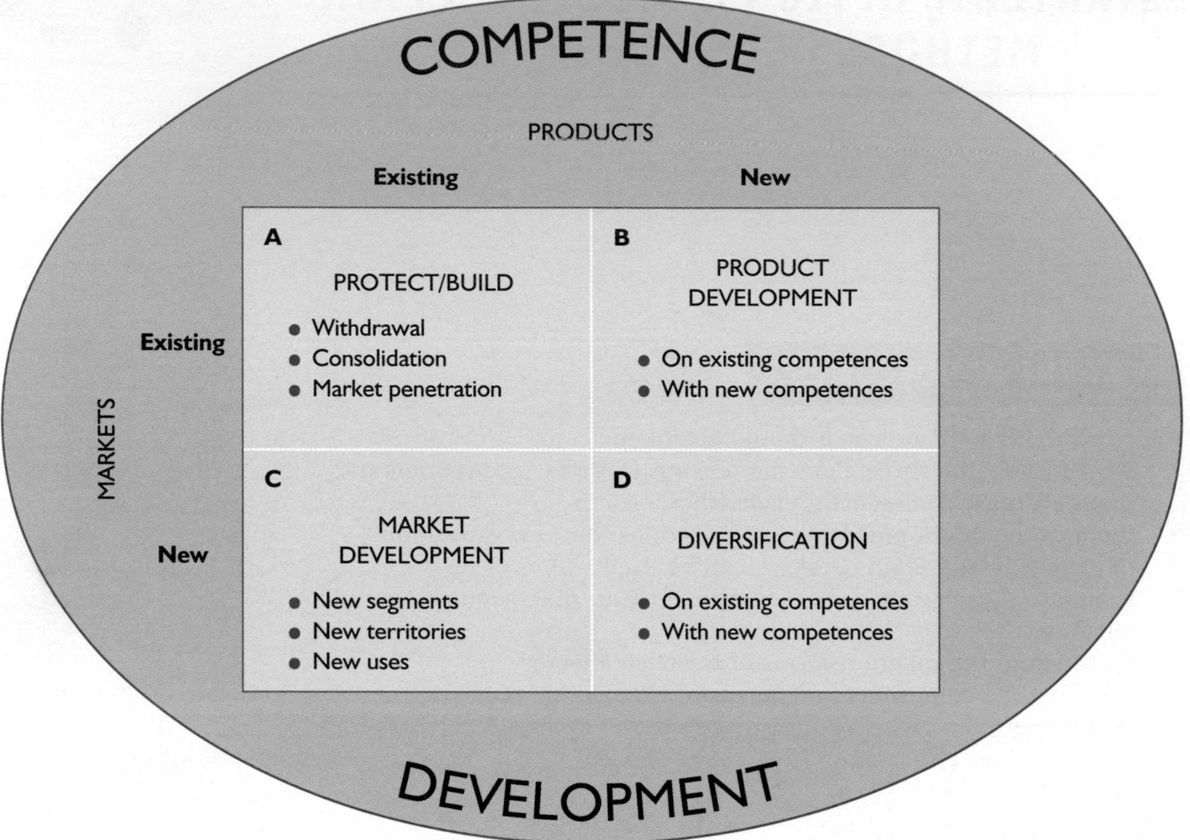

- Exhibit 7.1 outlines the broad types of development direction in terms of these three dimensions of markets, products and competences. These range from strategies concerned with protecting and building an organisation's position with its existing products and competences, through to major diversifications requiring development and change of both products and competences to enter or create new market opportunities. Each of the development directions shown in Exhibit 7.1 will be discussed in the next part of the chapter. Illustration 7.1 shows that, in reality, a combination of development directions is usually pursued.
- The later parts of the chapter consider the issue of development *methods*, which are an additional consideration whichever competitive strategies and specific directions an organisation might be pursuing. For example, an organisation may be pursuing a broad strategy of growth,

STRATEGY IN ACTION Illustration 7.1

Development Directions at Marks and Spencer

Successful organisations must not sit on their laurels – development usually requires a combination of the pure types of development direction discussed in this chapter.

In November 1997 Britain's top retailer – Marks and Spencer – announced an expansion programme costing £2bn over a three-year period. This was the biggest organic development programme ever announced by a British retailer. The major elements of the plan were:

- Adding 20 per cent more retail space to the 1 million square metres in its portfolio.
- Opening the 19 stores acquired from Littlewoods (another British retailer) in July 1997 as M&S outlets by summer 1998. The costs of conversion were expected to be about £100m.
- Development of more megastores (between 9,000 and 25,000 square metres) in regional out-of-town shopping centres.
- Launch of home shopping for its clothing merchandise – building on the existing mail order business which sold home furnishings, flowers, hampers and wine.
- Broadening its product range to provide a head-on challenge to supermarket chains beyond its traditional image of an additional supplier of premium or specialist foods.
- Re-equipping stores to cope with the planned European single currency.
- Expanding its operations in Continental Europe.
- Launching franchise operations in Poland and Australia.
- Opening two new M&S stores in Hong Kong.
- Linking up with Dickson Poon (the Hong Kong retailing tycoon who controls Harvey Nichols) to launch 20 franchised Brooks Brothers stores (the up-market US chain which M&S bought in 1988).
- Opening Brooks Brothers outlets in Europe.

All of this was a long way from the penny-bazaar foundations of the company in Leeds 100 years ago.

Questions

1. Refer to Exhibit 7.1 and classify the various development directions included in M&S's development plan.
2. List the arguments for and against each of these directions.
3. Is the package of developments self-consistent, or are there elements which might work against each other?

Source Sunday Times, 2 November 1997.

through positioning itself as the cheapest provider of 'regular' quality products (route 2 on the strategy clock in Exhibit 6.4). The development direction within this generic approach is one of *building* the organisation's competitive position by gaining market share (*market penetration*) through continued reduction of costs passed on to customers in price reductions. However, there are still choices as to the *method* by which this might be achieved. The cost improvements may be achieved *internally* by increasing the efficiency of current operations or through *strategic alliances* – perhaps to share distribution outlets with another (non-competing) company; or it may be achieved by *acquisition* of a competitor to gain market share and to benefit from the associated economies of scale.

7.2 ALTERNATIVE DIRECTIONS FOR STRATEGY DEVELOPMENT

This section reviews the different directions available to organisations in their development of strategies. The section is structured around the broad categories of development direction represented by the boxes in Exhibit 7.1 and introduced above.

7.2.1 Protect and Build on Current Position

Many strategic developments within organisations are concerned with developing the organisation from where it is currently, rather than being 'greenfield site' developments. Box A in Exhibit 7.1 represents development options which are concerned with protecting or building on the organisation's current position. These are options built around both the current products and competences of the organisation and how they can be *stretched* to improve the competitive position of the organisation in its current markets. Within this broad category there are a number of specific options which organisations might consider.

Withdrawal

It was emphasised in Chapter 6 that an important 'generic' consideration is the way in which the *scope* of an organisation's activities might change. Although this may be achieved through new strategies, it is also likely to require withdrawal from some current activities, particularly where the organisation lacks the competences to compete. There are many circumstances where complete or partial withdrawal would be the most sensible course of action. For example:

- Perhaps the most compelling reason for withdrawal from particular markets is that the organisation is unable to secure the resources or achieve the competence levels of the leaders in the market overall or the niches or segments of the market. The cost of repositioning or 'downsizing'[2] the organisation may be prohibitive, making withdrawal the most sensible course of action.

- In some markets, the *intrinsic value* of a company's products or assets is subject to changes over time, and a key issue may be the astute acquisition and disposal of these products, assets or businesses. This is particularly important for companies operating in markets which are subject to *speculation*, such as energy, metals, commodities, land or property.
- Since an organisation's unique resources and core competences are limited, there may need to be a review of the *priorities* for their deployment. So withdrawal from some activities releases resources and competences for others. The shift in a local authority's range of services over time is a good example of such a policy, as was Richard Branson's decision in 1992 to sell his original business, Virgin Records, to concentrate on the airline business. The key issue is which activities should be dropped and which should remain. This choice can be driven either by market opportunity or by a judgement on the degree to which particular strategies are likely to exploit the resources and core competences of the organisation.
- The expectations of dominant stakeholders may also be a reason for withdrawal. For example, the objective of a small entrepreneur may be to 'make a million' and then retire. So the expectations of the dominant stakeholder are largely short term, leading to a preference for strategies which make the company an attractive proposition to sell, rather than being guided by longer-term considerations of viability.
- It has already been mentioned in Chapters 5 and 6 that short-termism may also result from the expectations of the stock market putting pressure on managers to achieve short-term results or to divest activities (particularly in the USA and UK). So large, diverse companies may view their subsidiary companies as assets to be bought and sold as part of an overall corporate portfolio of investments.[3] Indeed, in some conglomerate companies, these activities of acquisition and disposal are the core competences of the corporate centre of the organisation and a key part of their parenting role (as discussed in Chapters 6 and 9).
- This lack of corporate concern for the longer-term viability and prospects of subsidiaries is one of the reasons why managers of subsidiaries look seriously at the possibility of a *buyout*[4] of the company from the parent. During the late 1980s and 1990s, buyouts (either complete or partial) by management or employees became common in the UK and to a lesser extent in France. Sometimes buyouts were triggered by the privatisation of companies in the public sector, where the management was able to bid for the company on sale (as with British Rail in 1995/96).

- Sometimes organisations will *partially* withdraw from a market by licensing the rights to other organisations. Whether this makes sense for the organisation is largely concerned with the relative competences of the organisation and the potential licensee in delivering value for money in that particular market. In turn, this will relate to the issues affecting the cost of operation and how the quality of product and service are maintained. Not surprisingly, the use of licence arrangements is common in overseas operations, as will be discussed below (section 7.3.3).
- Although hard-headed logic may point towards withdrawal as a sensible strategy, it is often culturally and politically difficult for organisations to swallow this pill. This is the reason why far too many organisations eventually have to withdraw from markets by voluntary or forced *liquidation*, where their position has become untenable.

Consolidation

consolidation *is concerned with protecting and strenghtening the organisation's position in its current markets through its current products*

Consolidation is concerned with protecting and strengthening the organisation's position in its current markets through its current products. Since this market situation is likely to be changing – for example, through improved performance of competitors or new entrants – consolidation does not mean standing still. Indeed, it may require considerable innovation to improve the value for money of the organisation's current products or services. It will require attention to the extent to which the organisation's resources and competences continue to fit the market need or how they should be adapted and developed to maintain the competitive position of the organisation.

Since consolidation is concerned with the maintenance of market share in existing markets, it is worth exploring *why* the maintenance of market share might be an important consideration to organisations when reviewing their strategic choices. In this context, the continuing work of the Strategic Planning Institute (SPI) through its PIMS (Profit Impact of Market Strategy) database is useful[5] (see Exhibit 7.2). This database contains the experiences of over 3,000 businesses (both products and services). Some of the more important PIMS findings, together with other research, are used in the various subsections of section 7.2. The link between performance and relative market share, which is also emphasised by the experience curve work (see Chapter 4, section 4.3.3), is supported by the findings of the PIMS database as shown in Exhibits 7.3 and 7.4. Return on investment rises steadily in line with relative market share.

A number of reasons are suggested as to why relative market share and return on investment (ROI) should be linked:

- The major factor seems to be *asset turnover*, with low-share businesses showing substantially higher investment/sales ratios than high-share businesses (sometimes nearly 25 per cent poorer). This can be attributed to scale economies in the use of fixed assets.

Exhibit 7.2 The PIMS framework for assessing strategic potential

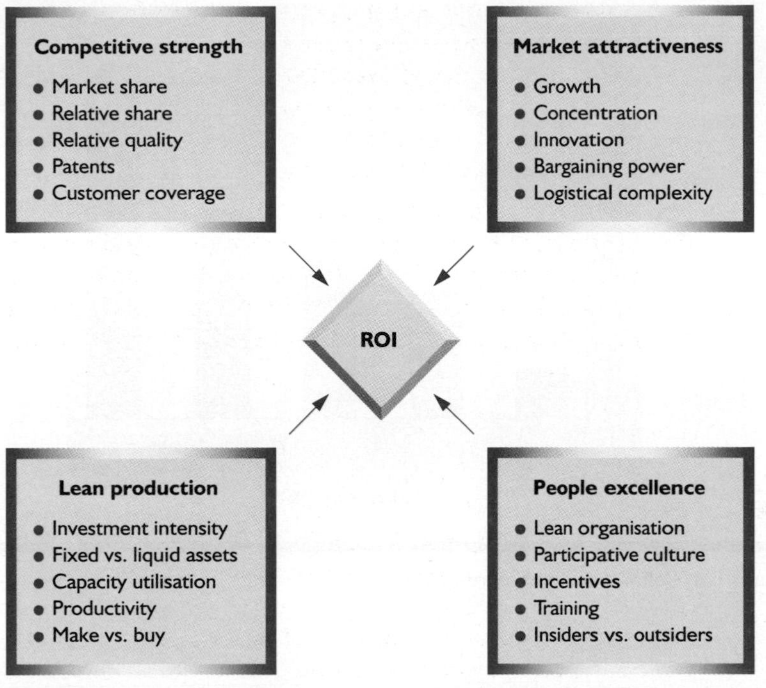

Source PIMS Associates Ltd. Reproduced with permission.

- The purchase/sales ratio differences between high- and low-market-share firms are also startling – high-market-share companies are able to buy more competitively or add more value to purchases. Economies of scale also show up in some other cost categories, such as marketing, but not in R&D. High-share businesses have higher R&D/sales ratios, largely because they are better placed to exploit innovation, as discussed below.
- A PIMS study of fast-moving consumer goods businesses[6] published in 1991 showed a strong interaction between *brand rank*, the *mix* of advertising and promotion activities, and profitability. The evidence showed that it is difficult to make profits unless the company has one of the leading three brands.

As well as underlining the importance of maintaining or improving market share, the PIMS database is useful in identifying those factors which help sustain a successful (profitable) strategy of consolidation:

- The indications are that high-market-share firms are more likely to develop strategies of higher price/higher quality than low-share

Exhibit 7.3 Market share drives profitability

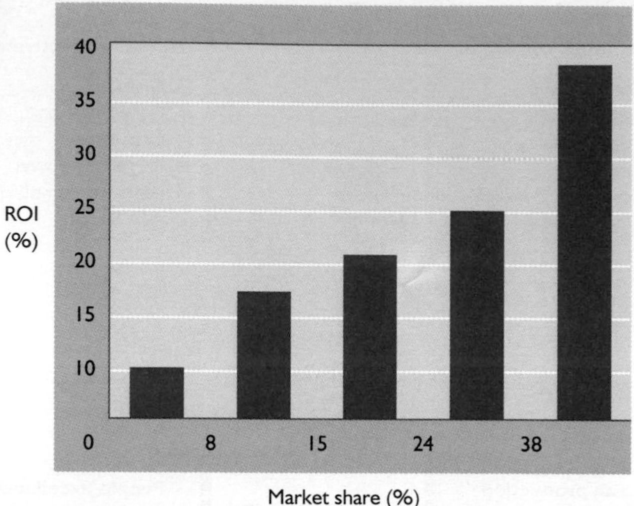

Source PIMS Associates Ltd. Reproduced with permission.

competitors. Longer-term PIMS evidence shows that this phenomenon may be self-sustaining. High-share firms tend to be more profitable, providing extra resources for R&D to improve and differentiate products, enhancing their market position and also justifying higher prices, which in turn increase profits. However, it must be remembered that high market share and size are not always the same. There are large firms which do not dominate the markets in which they operate; and there are small firms which dominate market segments.

- A PIMS study of competitiveness in Europe and North America[7] showed that key drivers of market share (whether maintenance of current share or share improvement, and value-added growth) were the organisation's competences to sustain *quality*, *innovation* and *intellectual property* (e.g. patents). All of these factors impact on the perceived value for money of the organisation's products or services, and can also act as barriers to entry for new competitors.
- The evidence shows that quality is important in the improvement of profit performance (Exhibit 7.5(a)). The best situation appears to be a combination of high share and high product/service quality, but even firms with low market shares demonstrate significantly higher profit performance if they have offerings of superior quality. (In this sense, quality can be a partial substitute for market share in sustaining advantage.)

Exhibit 7.4 **On average, market share has an important, positive influence on profits**

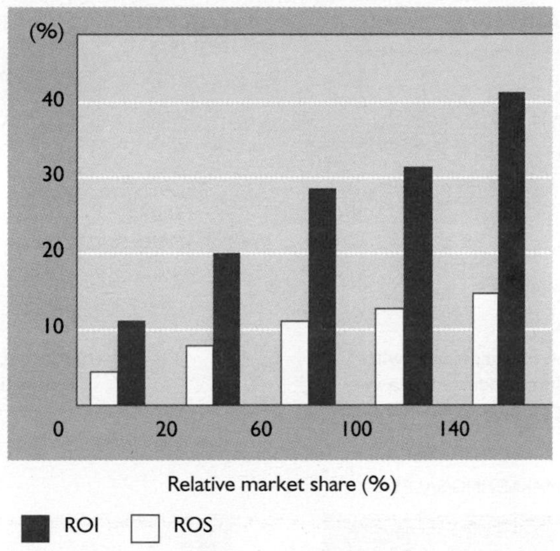

Note: 'Relative market share' is the company's share divided by the combined share of the three largest competitors. ROS is return on sales.

Source PIMS Associates Ltd. Reproduced with permission.

- Sometimes organisations try to defend or consolidate their position through increasing marketing expenditure. Exhibit 7.5(b) suggests that in itself this is unlikely to be effective. Heavy marketing expenditure (as a percentage of sales) is likely to damage ROI for organisations with low market share.
- The combined effect of marketing expenditure and product quality has also been studied. High marketing expenditure is not a substitute for quality: indeed, it appears that high marketing expenditure damages ROI most when quality is low (Exhibit 7.5(c)). It must be concluded that simply gearing up marketing expenditure as a means of consolidating a company's position is not sufficient.
- Another consolidation strategy is to seek improved productivity through *capital investment* – for example, by the mechanisation of routine tasks. However, there is evidence to suggest that increased capital intensity can damage return on investment, as shown in Exhibit 7.5(d), particularly for companies with weak market positions (see Exhibit 7.5(e)). The reasons for this are that capital intensity is also an exit barrier and provides real pressure to fill capacity. In this situation,

Exhibit 7.5 The PIMS findings relating to various types of consolidation strategy

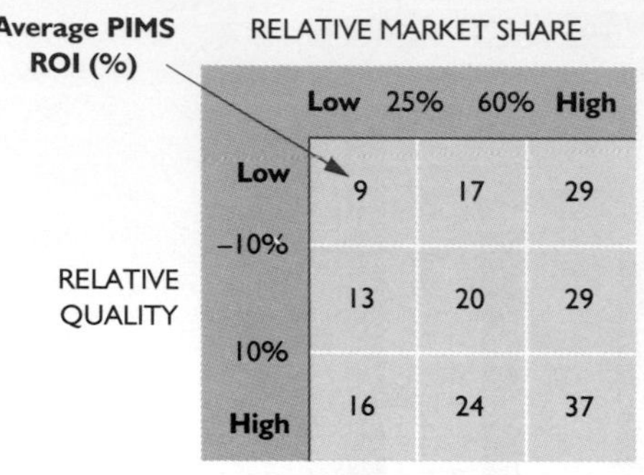

Average PIMS ROI (%) — RELATIVE MARKET SHARE (columns: Low, 25%, 60%, High) by RELATIVE QUALITY (rows: Low, −10%, 10%, High)

RELATIVE QUALITY \ RELATIVE MARKET SHARE	Low – 25%	25% – 60%	60% – High
Low – −10%	9	17	29
−10% – 10%	13	20	29
10% – High	16	24	37

(a) A market leader with premium products has a very strong competitive advantage

Average PIMS ROI (%) — MARKETING/SALES (columns: Low, 5%, 10%, High) by RELATIVE MARKET SHARE (rows: Low, 25%, 60%, High)

RELATIVE MARKET SHARE \ MARKETING/SALES	Low – 5%	5% – 10%	10% – High
Low – 25%	14	13	10
25% – 60%	21	20	21
60% – High	30	36	34

(b) Market share is critical when marketing intensity is high

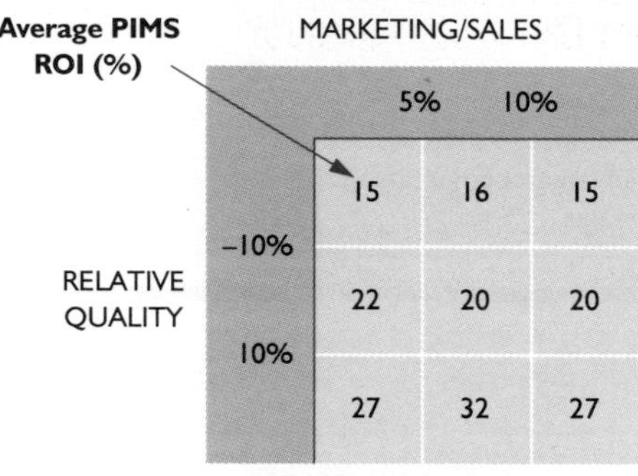

Average PIMS ROI (%) — MARKETING/SALES (columns: 5%, 10%) by RELATIVE QUALITY (rows: −10%, 10%)

RELATIVE QUALITY \ MARKETING/SALES	below 5%	5% – 10%	above 10%
below −10%	15	16	15
−10% – 10%	22	20	20
above 10%	27	32	27

(c) Heavy marketing is no substitute for quality

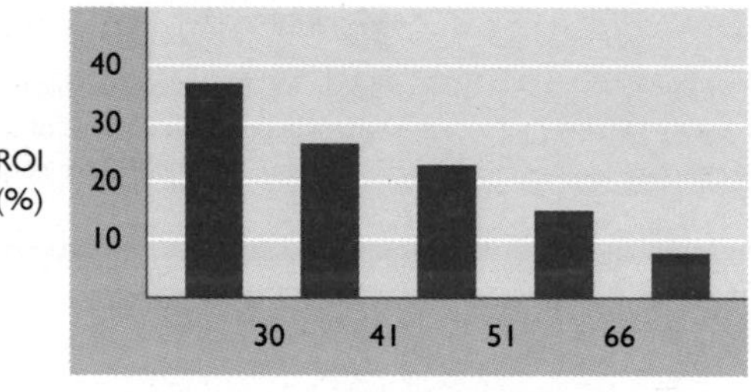

(d) High investment is a drag on ROI

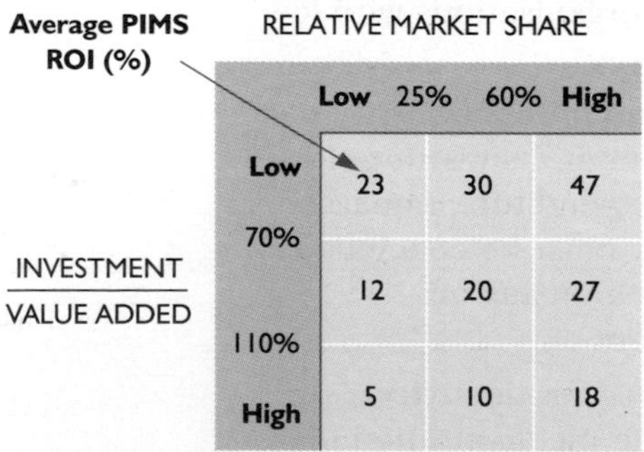

Average PIMS ROI (%) — RELATIVE MARKET SHARE (columns: Low, 25%, 60%, High) by INVESTMENT / VALUE ADDED (rows: Low, 70%, 110%, High)

INVESTMENT / VALUE ADDED \ RELATIVE MARKET SHARE	Low – 25%	25% – 60%	60% – High
Low – 70%	23	30	47
70% – 110%	12	20	27
110% – High	5	10	18

(e) The combination of weak market position and investment intensity is very damaging

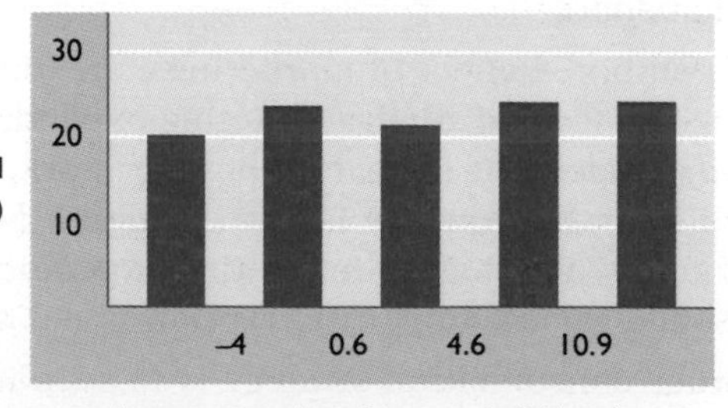

(f) Shrinking markets provide less opportunity for profitable performance

Source PIMS Associates Ltd. Reproduced with permission.

firms are likely to sacrifice margins to increase volume. Flexible manufacturing systems can partly relieve this pressure, as can the strategic use of subcontracting.

- During the transition from a mature to a declining market, an organisation may follow a strategy of harvesting: that is, gaining maximum payoff from its strong position. One of the most difficult strategic decisions is how long to remain in markets which are in decline, but where there is some hope of a market recovery. If turnround cannot be achieved fairly quickly, withdrawal from the market may well be necessary, since the extent to which organisations are likely to sustain a profitable position is dependent on the long-term real market growth (as shown in Exhibit 7.5(f)).

Market Penetration

Within the broad category of protecting and building the organisation's position, there may be opportunities to gain market share. This is known as *market penetration*. Much of the previous discussion is relevant to this option, since, for example, competences which sustain or improve quality or innovation or increasing marketing activity could all be means of achieving market penetration. So too are the arguments concerning the long-term desirability of obtaining a dominant market share. However, the ease with which an organisation can pursue a policy of market penetration will be dependent on the nature of the market and the organisation's resources and core competences, and the extent to which these can be developed:

- When the overall market is growing, or can be induced to grow, PIMS evidence shows that it is *relatively* easy for organisations with a small market share, or even new entrants, to gain share. This is because the absolute level of sales of the established organisations may still be growing, and in some instances those companies may be unable or unwilling to meet the new demand. Import penetration into some industries has occurred in this way.
- In contrast, market penetration in static *markets* can be much more difficult to achieve. The PIMS evidence on the cost of building market share is a reminder that it can be a costly process for weakly positioned businesses (see Exhibit 7.6(a)). Short-term profits are likely to be sacrificed, particularly when trying to build share from a low base.
- However, the complacency of market leaders may allow smaller-share competitors to catch up. Or a low-share competitor may build a reputation in a market segment of little interest to the market leader, from which it penetrates the wider market. Exhibit 7.6(b) shows that perceived quality (relative to competitors) is a key determinant for rapid market penetration by lower-market-share companies and helps high-share businesses resist this penetration. The PIMS database

Exhibit 7.6 **The PIMS findings concerning strategies of market penetration**

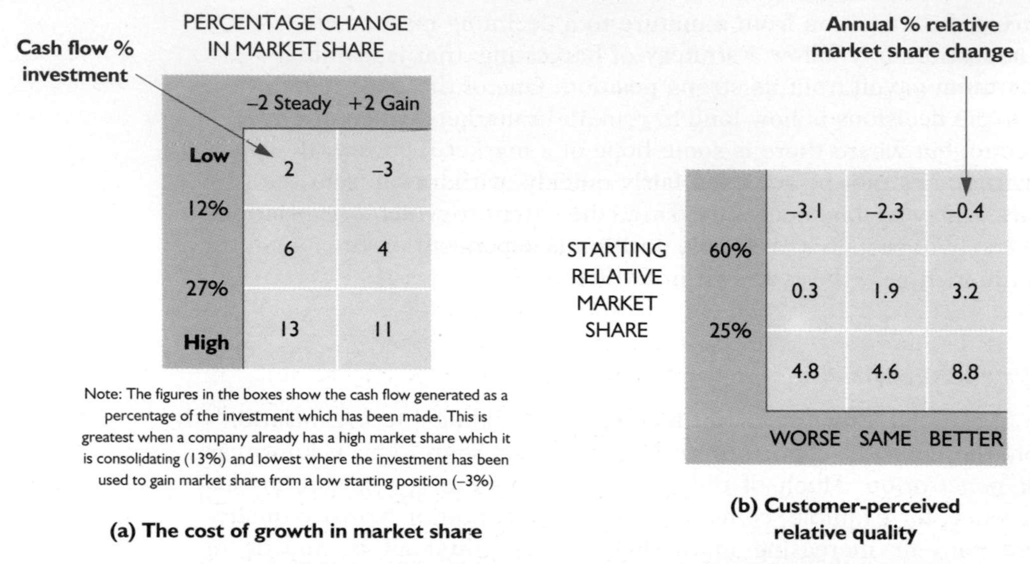

Note: The figures in the boxes show the cash flow generated as a percentage of the investment which has been made. This is greatest when a company already has a high market share which it is consolidating (13%) and lowest where the investment has been used to gain market share from a low starting position (–3%)

(a) The cost of growth in market share

(b) Customer-perceived relative quality

Source PIMS Associates Ltd. Reproduced with permission.

suggests that this relationship may have been strengthened recently either because markets have become more sensitive to quality, or because buyers and sellers are better at measuring it (including the emphasis on performance indicators in the public services).

7.2.2 Product Development

There are many reasons why companies might have a preference for product development. For example, retailers follow the changing needs of their customers by a continuing policy of introducing new product lines; and public services need to shift their pattern of services as needs change. In both these cases, a core competence for successful organisations is the ability to analyse and understand the changing needs of a particular group of customers or clients. Strategic development can be built around such a core competence. Similarly, product development may be preferred because the company has core competences related to R&D. When product life cycles are short – as with consumer electronics – product development becomes an essential requirement of an organisation's strategy, built around a core competence in R&D or the ability to acquire new products from elsewhere.

Despite the attractiveness of product development, it may often raise uncomfortable dilemmas for organisations. While new products may be vital to the future of the organisation, the process of creating a broad product line is expensive, risky and potentially unprofitable, because most new product ideas never reach the market; and of those that do, there are relatively few which succeed. Product development may require a commitment to high levels of spending on R&D. Exhibit 7.7(a) shows that, while high-market-share companies may benefit in profit terms from relatively high levels of R&D expenditure, companies in a weak market position with high expenditure may suffer.

Exhibit 7.7(b) also confirms that profitability can be depressed by overrapid rates of new product introductions, as organisations struggle to learn new competences needed to debug production, train salespeople, educate customers and establish new channels. The evidence shows that this is even more important for market followers, where more than moderate rates of innovation dramatically worsen profitability.

All of this evidence should encourage managers to ensure that the processes of innovation in the organisation are appropriate for the situation which they face. It is important to remember the following:

- Innovation can be driven in two broad ways – the processes of 'fit' and 'stretch' which have been discussed throughout the book. Fit-driven innovation requires high-quality information about changing customer needs and the creativity to know how to better provide for these needs. Stretch-driven innovation is concerned with assessing how the resources and competences of the organisation (particularly people, technologies and business processes) can be exploited to create new products and market opportunities.
- It is important to be clear about the current strength of the organisation's processes of innovation as discussed in section 4.3.7 of Chapter 4. There are choices on how new ideas and improvements might be fostered in the organisation in relation to the interplay between explicit and tacit knowledge. Illustration 4.5 showed how these processes can be combined to produce a 'spiral of knowledge creation' for successful product development.
- A further choice needs to be made about the *method* by which innovation will be secured. Whether it should be through the organisation's own internal efforts, by acquisition of innovations (e.g. products, processes or whole companies) or by alliances and partnerships (e.g. licensing). The relative merits of these different methods of strategy development will be discussed in section 7.3 below.

In the long term, product development is unlikely to be sustainable without the development or acquisition of new competences. For example, there may be a need to respond to a *change of emphasis* among customers concerning the importance of product/service features. This can occur because customers become more experienced in judging value for money – for example, through repeat purchase or because new choices become available in the market. One of the stated purposes behind the privatisation

Exhibit 7.7 The PIMS findings relating to product development

Average PIMS ROI (%)

RELATIVE MARKET SHARE \ R&D / SALES	Low – 0.5%	0.5% – 2.1%	2.1% – High
Low – 26%	13	13	10
26% – 60%	23	22	15
60% – High	32	35	33

(a) Dominant-share businesses are not hurt by heavy research and development

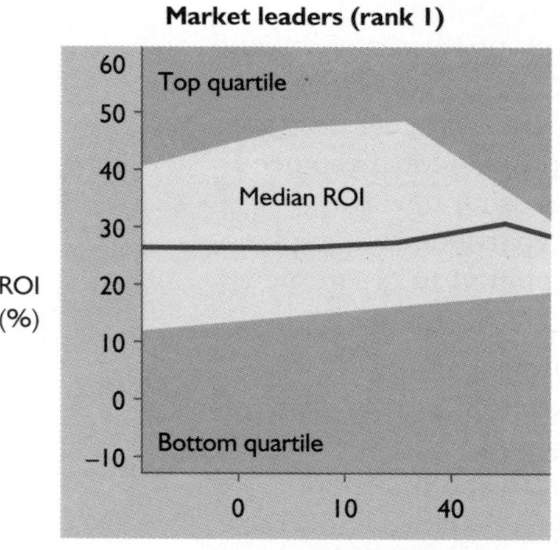

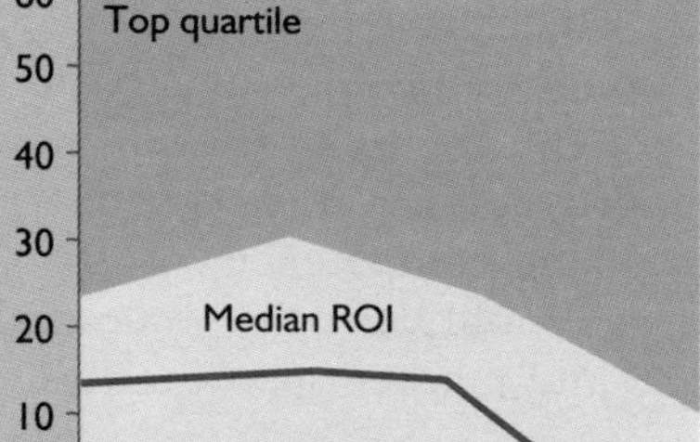

(b) High innovation hurts lower-ranking competitors

Source PIMS Associates Ltd. Reproduced with permission.

measures in the public services (described in Chapters 6 and 10) was to empower customers in this way – through increasing choice and raising consumers' awareness and expectations about value for money from public services.[8]

These shifts at the customer end require responses from the organisation. These may be concerned not with the basic features of the product or service, but with the need to improve other aspects of the customer experience: for example, the quality of information provided to clients, the clarity of billing, the ease of payment methods and so on. So the organisation needs *complementary competences* in aspects of the business which have been regarded as peripheral. As mentioned in Chapters 4 and 5, even the recognition that this is necessary can prove difficult, since the dominant culture and distribution of power are not attuned to such radical thinking.

As mentioned above, competence development may not only be concerned with ensuring a continued 'fit' with the changing needs of the existing markets (box B in Exhibit 7.1). It may be possible – or necessary – to stretch the organisation's resources and competences to enter new markets (box D). This will be discussed more fully in section 7.2.4 below.

The need to develop competences or products even to survive in existing markets is underlined by the consequences of not doing so. It is likely that the performance may become so poor in relation to that of competitors or other providers that the organisation becomes a target for acquisition, particularly by organisations which have core competences in *corporate turnaround*.[9]

7.2.3 Market Development

Most organisations have developed in ways which have resulted in *limited* coverage of the market by their products. It was emphasised in Chapter 6 that careful thought needs to be given to the way in which an organisation *positions* its products in markets – which inevitably means selectivity of market coverage. However, if the organisation's aspirations outstrip the opportunities in existing markets, it is natural to look for opportunities to exploit the current products in other markets. Three common ways of doing this are as follows.

1. *Extension* into market segments which are not currently served – although this might require some modification of the product to suit it to new segments. For example, a manufacturer of branded grocery products for the premium market may enter the mainstream market through 'own-brand' sales to supermarkets. This will require the development of new competences in (for example) key account selling.
2. Development of *new uses* for existing products. For example, manufacturers of stainless steel have progressively found new applications for the products which were originally used for cutlery and tableware. Nowadays, the uses include aerospace, automobile exhausts, beer barrels and many applications in the chemical manufacturing industry. Again, innovation within the organisation required competences in analysing each potential market and assessing the particular requirements of the product.
3. *Geographical* spread either nationally or internationally into new markets. Again, this may require some adjustment to product features or marketing methods. For example, it may be necessary to use agents for these new territories while sales volumes are low. It will also require

Exhibit 7.8 Three elements of a globalisation strategy

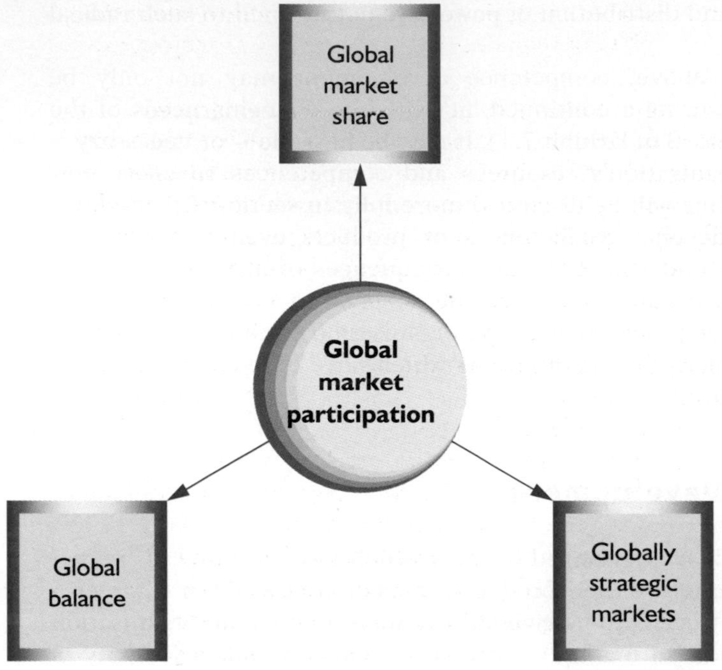

Source Based on G. Yip, *Total Global Strategy*, Prentice Hall, 1995, chapter 3.

other competences, for example in market analysis and language and cultural awareness. Chapter 3 discussed how in many industries there are increasing pressures for globalisation and that companies need to know how to respond and have the resources and competences to do so. Increased global market participation – as against simply selling more goods into a few new countries – requires the organisation to consider three main elements[10] (see Exhibit 7.8):

- The benefits of high market share (in a single country) have already been discussed in section 7.2.1 and illustrated in Exhibits 7.3 to 7.6. These benefits of global market share can be even more important in global markets – for example, by concentrating manufacturing on a small number of locations, both cost and quality benefits may result.
- High global market share is important, but not sufficient for global market participation. There also needs to be a *global balance* of revenues within the global market. This is one feature which has tended to distinguish Japanese companies in global markets from their competitors. For example, in the automobile industry,

companies like Toyota and Nissan have a significant presence in all three of the major 'arenas' (North America, Europe and Asia Pacific). In contrast, the major American companies (Ford and GM) are strong in two arenas (North America and Europe), while the major European players (e.g. Peugeot) tend to be strong only in Europe.

- There is also a need to be participating in *globally strategic markets*. These are countries which are important beyond their stand-alone attractiveness. This could occur for a number of reasons. For example, to be involved in at least one *large* market may be essential to get the cost structure or experience which is to be exploited elsewhere; it may be necessary to have a presence in the *home market of global customers* to gain access to, or credibility with, their global divisions or subsidiaries; in order to gain advantage over competitors there may be a need to operate in *competitors' home countries* or the countries where *competitors have a major presence*. Finally, a market may be strategically important because it is a source of industry innovation – for example, the USA for computer software, Germany for industrial control equipment, or the UK for popular music.

There are clearly important practical implications for organisations planning to increase their global participation, including the need to reassess the way in which the organisation's structure, design and control will need to change. These issues will be discussed in Chapters 9 and 10.

Illustration 7.2 shows how McDonald's expanded internationally by identifying new types of location as well as new countries. This continued, profitable growth also required competences in reducing opening costs of new outlets.

7.2.4 Diversification

Types of Diversification

diversification *involves directions of development which take the organisation away from its present markets and its present products at the same time*

Diversification is a term used in many different ways. In this chapter, **diversification** involves directions of development which take the organisation away from its present markets and its present products at the same time (i.e. box D in Exhibit 7.1). Diversification is traditionally considered under two broad headings: related and unrelated diversification.

related diversification *is development beyond the present product and market, but still within the broad confines of the 'industry'*

1. **Related diversification** is development beyond the present product and market, but still within the broad confines of the 'industry' (i.e. value chain) in which the company operates. For example, Unilever is a diversified corporation, but virtually all of its interests are in the fast-moving consumer goods industry. Related diversification may take several forms (see Exhibit 7.9).

STRATEGY IN ACTION
Illustration 7.2

McDonald's into New Markets

International growth may require the identification of new market segments as well as new countries.

In March 1996, McDonald's announced plans to accelerate its rate of expansion to a record high, adding between 2,500 and 3,200 restaurants to the 1995 total of 18,380. Although McDonald's still has more restaurants in the USA than abroad, the overseas side is growing more quickly, and in 1995 international operating profits exceeded US operating profits for the first time. International growth appears to be changing the company's shape, with the opening of markets in eastern Europe, India and China reportedly producing a wave of enthusiasm.

The international market is attractive for a number of reasons. First, international sales are more profitable than those at home owing to the lower level of competition. McDonald's is able to get more customers through its doors and charge higher prices. Another attraction is that growth has seemingly limitless potential. On any given day, McDonald's still serves barely half a per cent of the world's population. Its vision is to put everyone within easy reach of a Big Mac.

One reason why McDonald's has the potential to do this is that since 1990 it has slashed the cost of opening a typical restaurant by 30 per cent through the use of more efficient building designs, standardised equipment packages and global sourcing. This means that it can now open restaurants in locations that would have been hopelessly uneconomical five years ago. There are now McDonald's restaurants in more than 30 hospitals worldwide; in Wal-Mart discount stores across the USA; in the National Museum of Natural Science in Taichung, Taiwan; on the MS Silja Europa, a Swedish cruise ferry; in airports, schools and military bases; and on trains in Germany and Switzerland.

A new market development became operational in April 1996 when the first airborne McDonald's, dubbed McPlane, took off from Switzerland. The experimental project is a joint venture of McDonald's Switzerland, the Swiss tour operator Hotelplan, and Crossair, the charter subsidiary of the Swiss national airline, Swissair. Hotelplan uses the Crossair-operated aircraft as part of its programme of package tours taking holidaymakers from Swiss airports to Disneyland Paris and Mediterranean resorts.

Also, in spring 1996, McDonald's announced its biggest international acquisition with an agreement to buy the 80-strong chain of Burghy restaurants in Italy. The move was considered unusual for McDonald's because the company had only previously expanded by building its own restaurants. However, a company spokesman said the Burghy acquisition represented a 'unique opportunity' to treble its size in Italy.

Questions

1. Classify each of the development directions mentioned in the illustration into the categories in Exhibit 7.1.
2. Do you think the mix of the various development directions and methods is correct?

Source *Financial Times*, 11, 18 and 22 March 1996.

Prepared by Sara Martin, Cranfield School of Management.

Exhibit 7.9 Related diversification options for a manufacturer

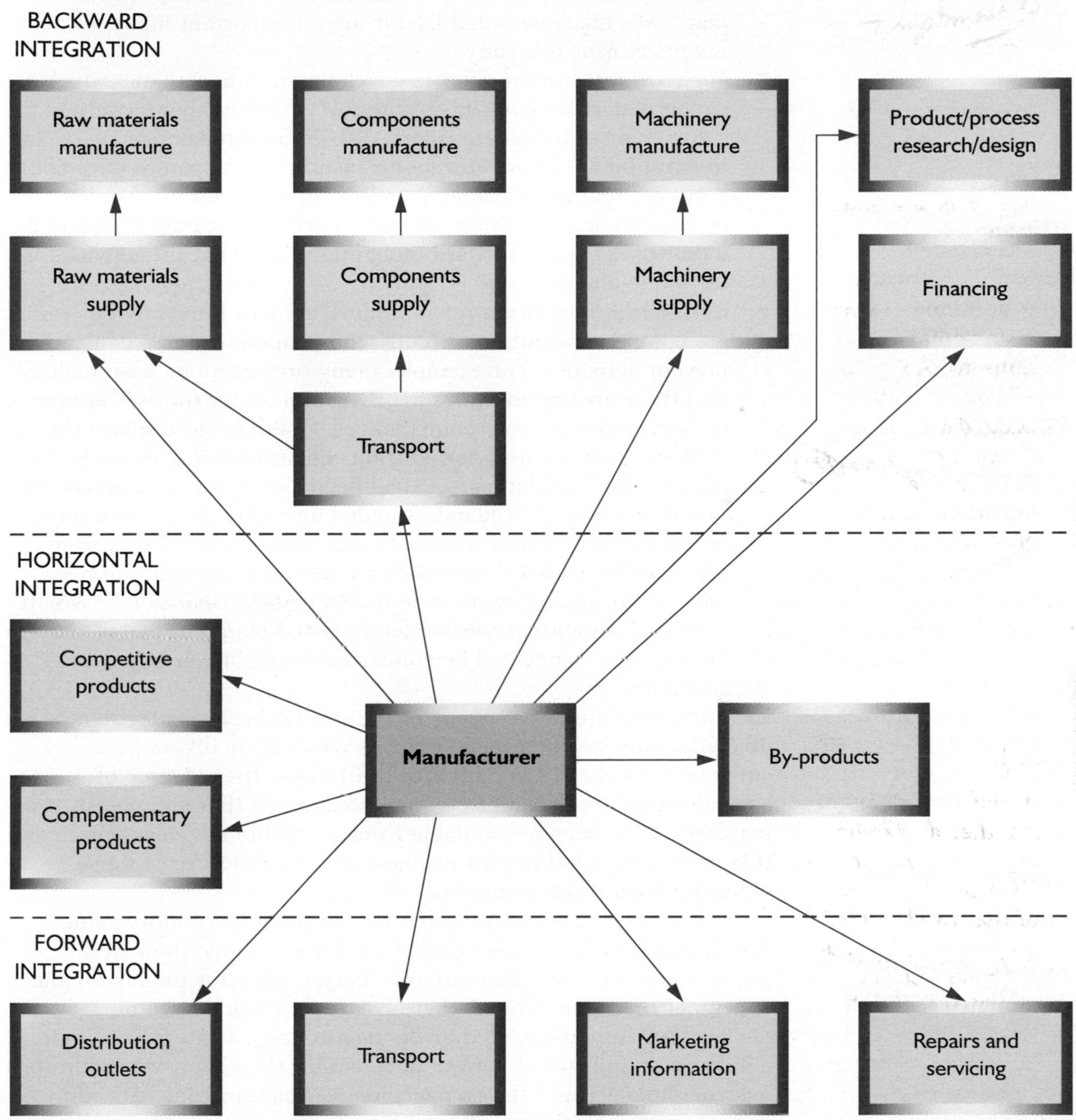

Note: Some companies will manufacture components or semi-finished items. In those cases there will be additional integration opportunities into assembly or finished product manufacture.

- *Backward integration* refers to development into activities which are concerned with the inputs into the company's current business (i.e. are further back in the value chain). For example, raw materials, machinery and labour are all important inputs into a manufacturing company.
- *Forward integration* refers to development into activities which are concerned with a company's outputs (i.e. are further forward in the value chain), such as transport, distribution, repairs and servicing. Illustration 7.3 shows how motor insurance companies were taking a more direct involvement in motor repairs – either through ownership or a 'licensing' scheme. **Vertical integration** describes either backward or forward integration into adjacent activities in the value chain.

vertical integration *describes either backward or forward integration into adjacent activities in the value chain*

- *Horizontal integration* refers to development into activities which are competitive with, or directly complementary to, a company's present activities. For example, many organisations have realised that there are opportunities in other markets for the *exploitation* of the organisation's core competences – perhaps to displace the current providers as a new entrant. Illustration 7.4 shows how the Automobile Association (AA) had been founded as a members' club for motorists in the UK and extended into providing rescue services for breakdowns. As this market came under fierce attack from specialist breakdown organisations, the AA extended into new markets by exploiting its expertise in *rapid response to crisis*. It launched a home service for electrical and plumbing emergencies, a development pioneered by similar motoring organisations in Australia.

Exhibit 7.10 summarises some of the detailed reasons for related diversification or, in reverse, reasons why highly diversified companies might divest activities to increase their degree of specialisation. For example, it may be decided that supplies of raw materials have become available from a reliable low-cost source and this provides a good reason to cease the manufacture of those materials within the company.

It needs to be recognised that the 'ownership' of more value activities within the value chain does not guarantee improved performance for the organisation or better value for money for the consumer or client. Indeed, there has been some degree of disillusionment with related diversification as a strategy, and more emphasis on improving performance within the value system through external linkages and the management of relationships with the various parties in the supply and distribution chains. The ability to achieve this could be a core competence. It would include the need to ensure that innovation and improvement of value for money are occurring within the other organisations (i.e. suppliers and distributors).

STRATEGY IN ACTION Illustration 7.3

Forward Integration: The British Insurance Industry

Sometimes, reconfiguring the value chain, perhaps through forward integration or licensing arrangements, is essential to improving value for money.

In a bid to reduce premiums and improve customer service, in 1995 insurance companies were establishing their own chains of motor-repair centres. In a similar approach to that taken by Direct Line, which cut out insurance brokers by dealing direct with the public, insurers were hoping to bypass garage owners and repair damaged vehicles themselves. While in essence each of the insurance companies was attempting the same thing, they were going about it in various ways.

Churchill Insurance

Churchill Insurance, one of Britain's largest telephone-based insurers, had opened a wholly owned repair centre in Rotherham, South Yorkshire. When fully operational it would be able to repair up to 60 cars a week using the latest technology. Vehicles belonging to customers who had accidents within a 50 mile radius of the centre would be picked up and taken in for repair. Owners were given a courtesy car to use until their vehicle was returned. All repairs were guaranteed for five years and there was no charge for the service, which the company said paid for itself. Customers avoided the nuisance of having to pay and claim back the cost of the repair, as this was done automatically.

Direct Line

Direct Line had taken a slightly different tack. It was intending to set up a limited number of wholly owned 'repair and development' centres. These would eventually represent centres of excellence, and would be supported by a much larger network of recommended, but independently owned garages. As the network grew, franchised garages bearing the Direct Line name would also be established.

Prospero Direct

Prospero Direct, another telephone-based insurer, already had a network of approved repair centres, but it had no plans to set up its own garages. Rather, it had chosen to control costs and thus offer lower premiums by installing video cameras throughout the network that were directly linked to Prospero's claims centre. Using this live link, the company claims that experts could more accurately assess damage and repairs and so ensure that the garages were not overcharging.

In all three instances, the customer benefited from reduced costs and an improved level of service.

Questions

1. Refer to Exhibit 7.10 and explain the logic behind the various forms of vertical integration described in the illustration.
2. What are the dangers in the strategy of each company?
3. Compare and contrast their approach to control of quality and cost of repairs by garages to decide which approach you feel has most chance of success.

Source *Sunday Times*, 25 June 1995.

Prepared by Sara Martin, Cranfield School of Management.

STRATEGY IN ACTION
Illustration 7.4

Exploiting Core Competences: The Automobile Association – The 4th Emergency Service

Organisations can best identify opportunities for strategic development if they are clear about their core competences.

The Automobile Association was founded in 1905 as a members' club for motorists, soon afterwards extending into the provision of rescue services in the event of breakdown. By 1995 it had become a multimillion-pound organisation, with its membership standing at 8 million. The array of services offered had become so diverse as to include the provision of both motor insurance and horse insurance. Despite this, the AA's market share of its traditional vehicle rescue service was falling as aggressive specialist competitors such as Green Flag and National Breakdown established themselves.

To reverse this trend, the AA restructured and actively sought to improve its general level of service. Furthermore, it attempted to differentiate itself from the competition and to extend into new markets by exploiting its new image as the 4th emergency service. The launch of AA Homeline was one example of these efforts. A subscription to this new home assistance service gives members the assurance of finding help with a range of common household problems, including plumbing, electrics, roofing, glazing, general building and household appliance repairs. In the event of an emergency, the member simply phones the hotline and is given the name of a recommended firm and a specific rate for the job. Once the job has been completed, the AA collects the money from the member and pays the firm. The customer is asked to complete a job satisfaction sheet which enables the AA to monitor each job and ensure the same level of quality service again and again.

In providing this service, the AA staked its reputation on its ability to vet firms and individuals thoroughly enough to keep the 'cowboys' off the list. However, by using its experience and competence in call handling, resource management and problem solving, the AA could ensure that each member received a quality service. Indeed, for a firm to be accepted onto the list, it must show sufficient public liability insurance, satisfactory credit checks and six recent customer references.

The AA denied that this new service was a move away from the travel and financial services offered in recent years, stating that it simply extended the AA's expertise in delivering and monitoring quality emergency services, and controlling costs for the benefit of members.

Question

Argue the case for and against the view that 'AA Homeline is an unrelated diversification which is likely to take important resources and management attention away from its core business'. Use Exhibits 7.10 and 7.11 to help with your analysis.

Source Excerpts from the national press and the *AA Handbook*.

Prepared by Sara Martin, Cranfield School of Management.

Exhibit 7.10 Some reasons for related diversification

POSSIBLE ADVANTAGES	EXAMPLES/COMMENTS
• Control of supplies	
Quantity	Tea processors own plantations to secure continuity of supply.
Quality	Components for motor cars may need to be manufactured by the company.
Price	Printing facility can be cheaper if in-house.
• Control of markets	UK shoe manufacturers own retail outlets to gain guaranteed distribution.
• Access to information	Shoe manufacturers are involved in machinery companies to keep abreast of developments.
• Cost savings	Fully integrated steel plants save costs of reheating and transport.
• Building on:	
Core competences	Firm of accountants moving into tax advice or corporate recovery.
Technology	Precision engineering equipment manufacturer in one market entering another with similar technical requirements.
• Spreading risk	Avoids over-reliance on one product or market, but builds on related experience.
• Resource utilisation	Manufacturer acquiring company for compatible products to fill capacity.

Another example of the need to assess these issues of diversification and specialisation is the locational decisions for the separate activities of international companies, and the extent to which separate locations should specialise or diversify their activities. The logic of gaining competitive advantage through building competences in separate activities suggests that the separate activities of design, component production, assembly and marketing may be optimally located in different countries. For example, in consumer electronics, component design and manufacture tend to be located in more advanced economies (e.g. Japan), while assembly is carried out in lower-wage economies (Korea, Taiwan, etc.).

Gaining advantage through specialisation needs to be balanced against the need for well managed linkages between these separate activities, which proves more difficult the more geographically dispersed are the separate activities. The most successful international companies are those which can develop organisational arrangements to exploit the advantages of specialisation and dispersion while managing linkages successfully. These issues were introduced in Chapter 6 and will be discussed more fully in Chapter 9.

unrelated diversification *is where the organisation moves beyond the confines of its current industry*

2. **Unrelated diversification** is where the organisation moves beyond the confines of its current industry. Historically, the literature on diversification has been dominated by an environment-led perspective of strategic options. So relatedness has tended to be defined in somewhat narrow terms: that is, opportunities beyond the current product and market base of the organisation and outside the current industry (i.e. value chain). However, as discussions in previous sections have revealed, this narrow definition tends to hide important differences in the degree of relatedness of diversification opportunities. Again, this is where the resource-led perspective is so important. Unrelated diversification really needs to be divided into three categories:
   - It may involve extension into new markets and new products by *exploiting* the current core competences of the organisation. For example, the global development of conglomerate businesses is more likely to work if these subsidiaries are similar or related – in the sense that they are conducive to the management (parenting) 'formula' from the centre (as discussed in Chapter 6). This is often crucial, since the core competences may be linked to the tacit knowledge and routines of the organisation (as discussed in Chapters 4 and 5) and hence difficult to imitate. So some conglomerates are good at buying lame ducks, turning them around and selling them on as going concerns. They would not be good at managing a diversified empire which did not share these common characteristics. These issues about the roles and relationships between the corporate centre and the divisions or subsidiaries of the organisation are concerned with parenting, have previously been raised in Chapter 6 and will be discussed fully in Chapter 9 (section 9.4).
   - Diversification by the exploitation of core competences may go beyond simply moving into markets which already exist: it may involve the *creation* of genuinely new markets. This is an example of the fit-led innovation mentioned in section 7.2.2. It requires very good market knowledge and the creativity to better provide for market needs. There are some elements of this in Illustration 7.4, in the sense that it was the absence of an efficient and reliable means for individual households to access the fragmented suppliers of electrical and plumbing services which created the AA's opportunity. Another example is the way in which research and development based on microelectronics technology has progressively spawned whole new markets which did not exist even twenty years ago (personal electronic organisers, interactive video games and so on).
   - The most extreme form of unrelated diversification is where *new competences* are developed for new market opportunities. Not surprisingly, this extreme end of the diversification spectrum is less common. In fact, if an entirely pedantic definition of unrelatedness were taken, it might never be observed at all – it usually proves

Exhibit 7.11 Some reasons for unrelated diversification

POSSIBLE ADVANTAGES	EXAMPLES/COMMENTS
● Need to use excess cash or safeguard profits	Buying a tax loss situation.
● Personal values or objectives of powerful figures	Personal image locally or nationally may be a strong motive.
● Exploiting underutilised resources and competences	Farmers use fields for camp sites. Local authorities use plastic waste for new materials.
● Escape from present business	A company's products may be in decline and unrelated diversification presents the only possible 'escape'.
● Spreading risk	Some companies believe that it is good sense not to have all their 'eggs in one basket' and so diversify into unrelated areas.
● Even out cyclical effects in a given sector	Toy manufacturers make subcontract plastic moulded products for industry.
● Benefit from synergistic effects	See text.

possible to identify some degree of relatedness in the market or resources or competences in any development opportunity. So this issue is really about *degrees of relatedness*, and the discussions which follow should be seen in that light. Exhibit 7.11 summarises some of the detailed reasons for unrelated diversification. Perhaps one of the reasons why diversification strategies run into difficulties is that organisations misjudge the degree of relatedness involved. This is a clear danger in vertical integration, which moves the organisation into activities that are adjacent in the value chain (e.g. supply or distribution), but which are entirely unrelated to the organisation's current competences.

Synergy[11] is a commonly cited reason for both *related* and *unrelated diversification*. Potentially, **synergy** can occur in situations where two or more activities or processes complement each other, to the extent that their combined effect is greater than the sum of the parts. Exhibit 7.12 outlines the conditions that need to be satisfied if strategies based on exploiting synergy are to be successful. This provides a useful link between the logic of synergy (opportunity to improve and the appropriateness of synergy) and

synergy *can occur in situations where two or more activities or processes complement each other, to the extent that their combined effect is greater than the sum of the parts*

Exhibit 7.12 Conditions for synergy

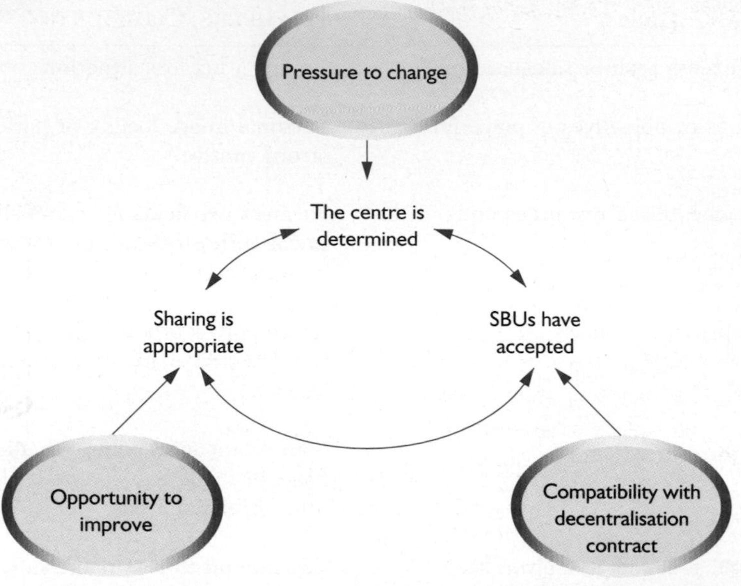

Source A. Campbell, 'Synergy and decentralisation', unpublished, 1991 (sponsored by McKinsey). Reproduced with permission.

the practical realities of adopting such a strategy (determination, acceptance and compatibility with the systems and culture of the organisation). This latter agenda is concerned with the issues of parenting which were discussed in Chapter 6.

Illustration 7.5 shows how Benetton claimed that there were synergies resulting from its diversification, while acknowledging that diversification may simply be *necessary* to achieve continuing growth once saturation occurs in current markets.

Diversification and Performance

Diversification has been one of the most frequently researched areas of business. Much of this research has been undertaken within the 'disciplines' adjacent to strategic management (e.g. economics, finance, law and marketing). There have also been a number of research studies which specifically attempt to investigate the relationship between the choice of diversification as a strategy and the performance of the organisation in financial terms.[12] Overall, it needs to be said that the various attempts to demonstrate the effects of diversification on performance are inconclusive. Early research[13] suggested that firms which developed through *related diversification* out-

STRATEGY IN ACTION
Illustration 7.5

Synergy from Diversification? The Benetton Empire

When traditional markets become saturated, organisations need to consider how best to develop. Synergy is often a justification for diversification.

By 1995 the Benettons had amassed an empire with aggregate sales of £4 billion, making it one of the five biggest companies in Italy. However, 30 years after the first knitwear shop was opened, growth in the group's traditional clothing core had peaked, and the family was attempting to fuel growth by finding new frontiers in old markets, but also by diversifying into completely new markets. 1994/95 was a big year for acquisitions, and the family now controls a company that spans Formula 1 racing, roadside restaurants, hypermarkets, merchant banking and big-name sporting goods such as Nordica, Prince and Rollerblade.

Despite the diversity of these acquisitions, Luciano Benetton explained that synergy existed between them. In the case of the original shops, the supermarkets and the hypermarkets, the synergy occurred in the consumers who buy from all three. As a contrast, there are unique production and operational synergies that have been maximised within the group's sports activities by the creation of the Benetton Sportsystem umbrella. For example, Nordica ski boots and Rollerblade in-line skates are both made from the same plastic composite material. Furthermore, at the Nordica production plant in Italy, the same machines that make Nordica boots can easily switch components to manufacture Rollerblade skate shells. Synergies also existed at the distribution end of both the food and sports businesses.

Gilberto Benetton explained that the group wanted to expand, but existing operations promised only 'normal' rate growth. The only solution, therefore, was to diversify.

Questions

1. Refer to Exhibit 7.10 and decide which of the factors you feel influenced the choice of development directions at Benetton.
2. Why is it so important for Benetton (and other companies) to argue that unrelated diversification is justified for reasons of synergy?
3. What risks was Benetton taking with these new directions of development?

Prepared by Sara Martin, Cranfield School of Management.

performed both those that remained specialised and those which developed through *unrelated diversification*. These findings were later questioned.[14] The sum total of all of the research work linking patterns of diversification to financial performance is unclear apart from one important message: successful diversification is difficult to achieve in practice. Some of the specific findings of the various research studies are as follows:

- The concept of diversity should not be interpreted too narrowly as relatedness in product terms. Diversity is also an issue on other dimensions, such as market spread or competence, as mentioned above. As stated in Chapter 6, there is some evidence[15] that profitability does increase with diversity, but only up to the *limit of complexity*, beyond which this relationship reverses. This raises the issue of whether managers can cope with large, diverse organisations – an issue which was raised in Chapter 6 and will be discussed further in Chapter 9. The PIMS database also supports the view that complexity, as measured by customer numbers or communication costs, reduces profit potential. The evidence on this is particularly stark for service-based businesses.[16]

- The theoretical benefits of synergy through diversification are often difficult to achieve in practice. This is particularly supported in the research on diversification through acquisition. For example, a study[17] of 33 major corporations between 1950 and 1986 concluded that more acquisitions were subsequently divested than retained, and that the net result was usually a dissipation of shareholder value and the company left vulnerable to corporate raiders. Other research suggests that the management of the process of diversification[18] may be a more important influence on performance than the type or mode of diversification itself. Illustration 7.6 shows that in the mid 1990s many large diversified organisations were choosing to split into separate companies, each with a much more clearly defined core business or market focus.
- An important conclusion of many research studies is that a universal prescription of the benefits of diversification is unlikely to be found. The likely success of diversification is extremely dependent on the circumstances of an organisation, such as the level of industry growth, market structures and the firm's size. Some studies[19] have also demonstrated that the relationship between performance and diversity will vary with the period of time studied (e.g. the point in the business cycle). For example, related diversification might be more suited to firms when there are opportunities for expansion in a growing economy. On the other hand, in times of little or no growth, a concentration on mainline products or seeking more market diversity might make more sense.
- Other studies[20] argue that a key factor is the resource situation of the organisation – particularly the area of underutilised resources. Underutilisation of physical resources or intangible resources (brand name, etc.) is likely to encourage related developments, whereas excess financial resources may well be used to underwrite unrelated developments (e.g. through acquisition), particularly if the other resources and competences are difficult to develop or grow quickly. This raises the question of whether successful performance is a *result* of choosing diversification or if the relationship is, in fact, the reverse. Perhaps successful organisations *choose* diversification because opportunities in their current product or market domain look limited.

STRATEGY IN ACTION
Illustration 7.6

Back to Basics: Splitting Up Diversified Companies

In the mid 1990s, many large, diversified organisations were choosing to split into separate companies, each with a much more clearly defined core business or market focus.

The UK Building Industry

In 1996, two of the most vertically integrated companies, Wimpey and Tarmac, swapped some of their businesses to each reduce their diversification. Wimpey took over Tarmac's house-building business in exchange for the latter's quarries and contracting. A major spur for these moves was the fact that the diversified companies were significantly outperformed by specialist builders in the 1990s' recession.

Hanson Splits into Four Companies

Once the epitome of the successful conglomerate, Hanson plc decided in 1996 to split into four separate companies, specialising in energy, tobacco, chemicals and building materials. One of the cited reasons for this change was the issue of succession to Lord Hanson. Although he was seen as possessing the skills to create and hold together a diversified empire, his potential successors were seen as 'operating people' who lacked these 'parenting' skills.

Lonrho De-merger

In December 1995, Dieter Bock, the CEO of Lonrho, embarked on a process of convincing investors that shareholders would benefit from an end to Lonrho's conglomerate status. The plan was to split the company into two separate, stock market quoted companies: a mining business and a business dealing with Lonrho's African trading and agricultural interests.

Thorn EMI De-merger

In February 1996, Sir Colin Southgate, the chairman of Thorn EMI, announced plans to split the company into EMI Music – one of the world's largest recording companies – and Thorn Rental Businesses. The company hoped that the rental business would benefit from the de-merger in terms of its public profile, which had long been overshadowed by the glamorous music division.

Questions

1. All of the 'empires' described in the illustration would have been created with strong arguments about the benefits of diversification. Why were these benefits not realised? (There may be several reasons.)
2. Will 'back to basics' also have its problems? Is it an over-reaction to the era of the conglomerate?

7.3 ALTERNATIVE METHODS OF STRATEGY DEVELOPMENT

The previous chapter was concerned with strategic choices at the broad or generic level – the *basis* on which the more detailed strategies are constructed. The previous section of this chapter reviewed the *alternative directions* in which organisations might develop. However, for any of these directions there are different potential *methods of development*. These methods can be divided into three types: internal development, acquisition (or disposal) and joint development (or alliances).

7.3.1 Internal Development

internal development *is where strategies are developed by building up the organisation's own resource base and competences*

Internal development is where strategies are developed by building up the organisation's own resource base and competences. For many organisations, internal development (sometimes known as 'organic development') has been the primary method of strategy development, and there are some compelling reasons why this should be so. Particularly with products which are highly technical in design or method of manufacture, businesses will choose to develop new products themselves, since the process of development is seen as the best way of acquiring the necessary core competences to compete successfully in the market place. Indeed, it has been seen above that these core competences may also spawn further new products and create new market opportunities.

A similar argument applies to the development of new markets by direct involvement. For example, many manufacturers still choose to forgo the use of agents, since they feel that the direct involvement gained from having their own salesforce is of advantage in gaining a full understanding of the market. This market knowledge may be a core competence in the sense that it creates competitive advantage over other organisations which are more distant from their customers.

The implications of these comments to the management of innovation in the organisation should be clear. Whatever strategic directions of development are being pursued, the organisation must have high levels of competence in the management of innovation, as discussed in Chapter 4 (section 4.3.7) and in section 7.2.2 above. The processes might relate to fit-led innovation – requiring good market knowledge – or stretch-led innovation where the leading edge is the further exploitation of resources and competences to create new market opportunities. If these competences in the management of innovation are not present in the organisation then further consideration should be given as to whether internal development is the best choice of development method. Perhaps the necessary competences in innovation should be acquired – either by acquisition of, or an alliance with another organisation (see below).

Although the final cost of developing new activities internally may be greater than that of acquiring other companies, the spread of cost may be more favourable and realistic. This is a strong argument in favour of internal development for small companies or many public services which may not have the resources available for major investment. The slower rate of change which internal development brings may also minimise the disruption to other activities.

An organisation may, of course, have no choice about how new ventures are developed. Those breaking new ground may not be in a position to develop by acquisition or joint development, since they are the only ones in the field. But this problem is not confined to such extreme situations. Organisations which would prefer to develop by acquisition may not be able to find a suitable target for that acquisition. For example, this is a particular difficulty for foreign companies attempting to enter Japan. Internal development also avoids the often traumatic behavioural and cultural problems arising from post-acquisition integration and coping with the different traditions and incompatibilities of the two organisations.

7.3.2 Mergers and Acquisitions[21]

acquisition *is where an organisation develops its resources and competences by taking over another organisation*

Acquisition is where an organisation develops its resources and competences by taking over another organisation. Development by acquisition tends to go in waves (for example, 1898–1900, 1926–29, 1967–73, 1985–87 and the early 1990s in the UK). It also tends to be selective in terms of industry sector. For example, in the UK, the 1960s activity was particularly important in electrical engineering and textiles, whereas between 1985 and 1987, high street retailing takeovers were common. The early 1990s saw a wave of mergers in professional service organisations, such as solicitors, property services, accountancy firms and financial services. International developments through acquisition have been critically important in some industries, such as newspapers and media, food and drink, and many sectors of the leisure industries.

A compelling reason to develop by acquisition is the speed with which it allows the company to enter new product or market areas. In some cases the product or market is changing so rapidly that this becomes the only way of successfully entering the market, since the process of internal development is too slow. Another reason for acquisition is the lack of resources or competence to develop a strategy internally. The necessary innovations cannot be put in place quickly enough – they must be acquired. For example, a company may be acquired for its R&D expertise, or its knowledge of a particular type of production system or business processes or of market needs. International developments are often pursued through acquisition (or joint development) for this reason of market knowledge. Illustration 7.7 shows that, in rapidly changing global industries in the 1990s, a combination of these factors led to a rapid growth in acquisition activity.

The competitive situation may influence a company to choose acquisition. In markets which are static and where market shares of companies are reasonably steady, it can be a difficult proposition for a new company to enter the market, since its presence may create excess capacity. If, however, the new company chooses to enter by acquisition, the risk of competitive reaction is reduced. The same arguments also apply when an established supplier in an industry acquires a competitor either for the latter's order book to gain market share, or in some cases to shut down

STRATEGY IN ACTION
Illustration 7.7

Mergers and Acquisitions in Global Industries

Survival in globalising industries may require reduction in unit costs, improvement in products or services and adequate market coverage. Mergers and acquisitions may be a way of achieving these things.

IT Industry

In 1995, almost 3,000 deals were tracked by Broadway Associates – a US consultancy – some 57 per cent higher than 1994. The total value of deals was US$134 billion. The telecommunications sector saw the largest deals with 98 transactions worth over US$20 billion. This included the acquisition of 49.99 per cent of Belgacom (Belgian) by a consortium of Ameritech, Singapore Telecom and Tele Denmark, and the alliance between Cable and Wireless of the UK and Veba of Germany.

The most active sector was software and services with 356 deals. A significant proportion of these acquisitions were of 'national champions' being purchased from abroad by companies looking for critical mass to operate globally. For example, ADP – a US payroll systems specialist – bought GSI, its French equivalent, while Ceridian – number two in payroll – bought Centrefile from the Natwest Bank in the UK.

Many acquisitions were driven by the pace of technological change. Companies with expertise in the Internet or ISDN (transmission technology) were prime targets for takeover, with more than ten European specialists being acquired by US companies seeking their expertise.

Kvaerner

By 1997 Kvaerner was an international engineering and construction group with a Norwegian parent and a London-based international headquarters. This position had been created following the acquisition of the British company Trafalgar House in 1996. The 1996 annual report explained the strategic importance of this merger as follows:

- To meet the changes in markets and technology.
- To provide a more comprehensive service to clients (including project financing).
- To be present in the most important markets to justify large investments in R&D.
- To run global operations from a location close to international market players (i.e. London not Oslo).
- To improve efficiency and quality.

Post-merger activities were important to achieving those benefits, in particular the creation of six new divisions from the merged Kvaerner/Trafalgar activities and the disposal of businesses outside these non-core areas.

Questions

1. Viewing each of the above acquisitions through the eyes of the acquirer (and remembering that improving competitive advantage is about the ability to provide better-value-for-money products or services), argue the case for each acquisition.
2. Remembering that many (even most) acquisitions do not deliver their promise, are there any of the above about which you would have doubts? Why?

Sources IT industry, *Financial Times*; Kvaerner annual report.

its capacity to help restore a situation where supply and demand are more balanced and trading conditions are more favourable.

There are also financial motives for acquisitions. If the share value or price/earnings (P/E) ratio of a company is high, then a firm with a low share value or P/E ratio may be a tempting target. Indeed, this is one of the major stimuli for the more aggressively acquisitive companies. An extreme example is asset stripping, where the main motive for the acquisition is short-term gain by buying up undervalued assets and disposing of them piecemeal.

Sometimes there are reasons of cost efficiency which make acquisition look favourable. This cost efficiency could arise from the fact that an established company may already be a long way down the experience curve and have achieved efficiencies which would be difficult to match quickly by internal development. The necessary innovation and organisational learning would be too slow. In public services, cost efficiency is usually the stated reason for merging units or rationalising provision (often by cutting out duplication or by gaining scale advantages).

Many of the problems associated with acquisition have been hinted at in the discussion of internal development. The overriding problem with acquisition lies in the ability to integrate the new company into the activities of the old. This often centres around problems of cultural fit. Where acquisition is being used to acquire new competences, this 'clash of cultures' may simply arise because the organisational routines are so different in each organisation. For example, a company which has grown and succeeded by dominating a particular segment of the market may feel the need to extend into the 'mainstream' and decide to do this by acquisition. It is likely that most of the routines of these two organisations will be very different: in manufacture, continuous flow versus batch production; in customer communications, advertising versus personal selling; in distribution, the use of intermediaries versus direct delivery, and so on.

Reasons for mergers may be similar to those for acquisitions. However, mergers are more typically the result of organisations coming together voluntarily. This is likely to be because they are actively seeking synergistic benefits, perhaps as a result of the common impact of a changing environment in terms either of opportunities or threats or of the excessive costs of innovation and change.

The research evidence on the financial consequences of acquisitions is again inconclusive, in a similar way to the research on diversification (of course, diversification is often achieved through acquisition). However, some of the findings do act as a reminder that acquisition is not an easy or guaranteed route to improving financial performance. It may take the acquiring company some considerable time to gain any financial benefit from acquisitions.[22] Some studies confirm the importance of non-economic factors such as previous experience of acquisitions;[23] decisions on whether to remove or retain executives of the acquired company;[24] and the management of post-acquisition cultural issues.[25]

7.3.3 Joint Developments and Strategic Alliances[26]

a **joint development** *is where two or more organisations share resources and activities to pursue a strategy*

A **joint development** is where two or more organisations share resources and activities to pursue a strategy. Joint development of new strategies has become increasingly popular particularly since the early 1980s.[27] This is because organisations cannot always cope with increasingly complex environments (such as globalisation) from internal resources and competences alone. They may see the need to obtain materials, skills, innovation, finance or access to markets, and recognise that these may be as readily available through co-operation as through ownership.

There are a variety of arrangements for joint developments and alliances. Some may be very formalised interorganisational relationships; at the other extreme, there can be very loose arrangements of co-operation and informal networking between organisations, with no shareholding or ownership involved. The reasons why these different forms of alliance might occur are varied, but they are likely to be concerned with the assets involved in the alliance. (It should be remembered here that the assets may not just be financial or physical, but could also include access to market, skills and intellectual property.) The form of the alliance is likely, therefore, to be influenced by the following:

- Asset *management*: the extent to which assets do or do not need to be managed jointly.
- Asset *separability*: the extent to which it is possible to separate the assets between the parties involved.
- Asset *appropriability*: the extent to which there is a risk of one or other of the parties involved appropriating the assets for itself.

Exhibit 7.13 summarises the different forms of alliance that exist and how different factors might influence the form of the alliance. In addition, the chart shows how the same factors might also affect the decision to acquire or merge, rather than to create an alliance.

Joint ventures are typically thought of as arrangements where organisations remain independent, but set up a newly created organisation jointly owned by the parents. The joint venture was a favoured means of beginning collaborative adventures between eastern and western European firms in the early 1990s, with eastern European firms providing labour, entry to markets and sometimes plant; and western companies providing expertise and finance.

Consortia may well involve two or more organisations in a joint venture arrangement, and will typically be more focused on a particular venture or project. Examples include large civil engineering projects, such as the Channel Tunnel, or major aerospace undertakings, such as the European Airbus. They might also exist between public sector organisations: for example, following the dissolution of the UK metropolitan county councils in 1986, functions such as public transport were taken over by co-ordinating consortia often involving both private and public sector organisations.

Exhibit 7.13 Types of and motives for strategic alliances

	Loose (market) relationships	Contractual relationships	Formalised ownership/ relationships	Formal integration
FORMS OF ALLIANCE	Networks Opportunistic alliances	Subcontracting Licences and franchises	Consortia Joint ventures	Acquisitions and mergers
INFLUENCES				
Asset management	Assets do not need joint management	Asset management can be isolated	Assets need to be jointly managed	
Asset separability	Assets cannot be separated	Assets/skills can be separated		Assets cannot be separated
Asset appropriability	High risk of assets being appropriated	Low risk of assets being appropriated		High risk of asset appropriation

Source Based on A. Gupta and H. Singh, 'The governance of synergy: inter-SBU co-ordination versus external strategic alliances', Academy of Management Annual Conference, Miami, FL, 1991.

Joint ventures or consortia usually involve formalised interorganisational relationships in the form either of shareholding or of agreements specifying asset sharing and distribution of profits. Such formalised arrangements are likely to occur when the following conditions hold:

- The assets involved need to be jointly managed: for example, as with the setting up of a production unit.
- However, the assets can be separated from the parent companies without damaging knock-on effects on those companies: for example, expertise can be specifically devoted to the joint venture without its removal harming the parents.
- At least in theory, there is a low risk that the assets could be appropriated by one or other party involved. Having said this, it has been argued that some firms enter joint ventures specifically to obtain know-how and expertise for their own internal development.

At the other extreme, **networks**[28] are arrangements whereby two or more organisations work in collaboration without formal relationships, but through a mechanism of mutual advantage and trust. Such networks can be enduring and provide considerable mutual benefit to the organisations involved. Network organisations are discussed more fully in Chapter 9 (section 9.2.7). Networks have been created in the airline industry by 'code-

networks *are arrangements whereby two or more organisations work in collaboration without formal relationships* sharing' arrangements, allowing passengers to use several 'partner' airlines while travelling on a single ticket. *Opportunistic alliances* might also arise focused around particular ventures or projects, but again may not be highly formalised. In this sense, these arrangements are much nearer to market relationships than to contractual relationships. They may exist for a number of reasons:

- Assets do not need joint management – capital, expertise, know-how and so on can come together more informally.
- Assets cannot be separated easily from the firms involved, or without harm being done: for example, it may be that one partner is providing access to distribution channels which are part of the company's operation as a whole.
- If the assets involved were split off into a separate organisation, there would be a high risk of their being appropriated by another party. This would be particularly the case for the know-how and skills of the different parties involved.

Many intermediate arrangements exist. One such is *franchising*, perhaps the best-known examples of which are Coca-Cola and McDonald's. Here the franchise holder undertakes specific activities such as manufacturing, distribution or selling, but the franchiser is responsible for the brand name, marketing and probably training. *Licensing* is common in science-based industries, where, for example, the right to manufacture a patented product is granted for a fee. With *subcontracting*, a company chooses to subcontract particular services or part of a process: for example, increasingly in public services responsibility for waste removal, cleaning and so on may be subcontracted to private companies.

All these intermediate arrangements are likely to be contractual in nature, but are unlikely to involve ownership. They typically arise for two reasons:

- Particular assets can be isolated for the purposes of management: for example, manufacturing under licence.
- These assets can be separated from the parent firm to their advantage: for example, by setting up distribution or manufacturing in a country in which it would find difficulty operating. Illustration 7.8 shows how the Public Finance Initiative was established to allow public sector organisations to gain advantage through partnerships with the private sector in the development and maintenance of capital items (particularly buildings).

Licensing or franchising is likely to take place, however, where there is a low risk of the assets involved being appropriated: for example, patent protection would prevent such appropriation for a licence holder. A less durable arrangement may be more appropriate if there is a risk of appropriation, as with a subcontracting arrangement, where the subcontractor may already be operating in the sphere of activity involved.

STRATEGY IN ACTION
Illustration 7.8

Public/Private Sector Alliances: the Public Finance Initiative

Strategic alliances are often justified through the improved value for money that they create in some or all of an organisation's activities.

As the public sector grew in importance in many countries during the thirty years or so after the Second World War, it was common practice for organisations to take on directly more and more activities. This included responsibility for the development of public assets (such as buildings) where the norm became that the public sector would, itself, design, construct, own and maintain the assets.

The changing circumstances of the public sector in the 1980s and 1990s (both financially and politically) in many countries inevitably left many public assets badly maintained and lacking in modern amenities. There were also political concerns that the public sector procurement model was inefficient and represented very poor value for money for the taxpayer. There were a number of notorious 'schemes' where architects, contractors and trade unions had clearly acted in their own self-interests – resulting in excessive costs and project overruns. Public sector short-termism often meant 'corner-cutting' on capital projects – storing up excessive maintenance costs in later years.

The Public Finance Initiative (PFI) was designed to address these strategic issues by assisting public/private sector alliances for the development and maintenance of public assets. Under a PFI deal the public sector organisation no longer bought an *asset* (e.g. a building) but a *service* (a maintained and managed building) for the payment of a fixed annual charge for an agreed period. This arrangement was meant to 'pressurise' contractors to finish projects on time and to have an overall view of costs (capital, running and maintenance costs).

In practice these new-style alliances have had some teething problems, in particular cultural clashes between public and private sector attitudes and procedures. Private sector capital often proved more expensive. However, one outcome was that public sector departments in areas such as design and construction started to reappraise their methods of working and improved their performance. Since they did not have a profit element, the 'in-house' service provider became a tough competitor for the potential private sector partner. Like many of the changes in the public services in the 'new era', perhaps the real power of the public/private sector partnerships was one of benchmarking best practice.

Questions

Argue the case for and against the following propositions.

1. 'Public/private sector partnerships bring the best aspects of the two sectors together.'
2. 'Partnerships like PFI are short-term political expedients.'
3. 'Public/private sector partnerships have no long-term future.'

In passing, it is worth noting that reasons for taking on full ownership in the form of acquisitions and mergers can also be explained in similar ways. Acquisitions and mergers are likely to take place where: (a) assets need joint management; (b) assets cannot be separated readily from either firm involved; and (c) there is a high risk of asset appropriation. Indeed, arguably the last two reasons are why an acquisition might be more attractive than a joint venture.

One research study of international strategic alliances[29] confirmed that the primary motivation to form alliances was the need for specific resources and competences to survive and succeed in globalising markets – particularly where technologies were changing too. Partners were chosen with these issues in mind. However, the success of alliances tended to be more dependent on how they were managed and the way in which the partners fostered the evolution of the partnership. For example, the following were found to be important:

- Proactive attitudes to commitment, trust and cultural sensitivity. An example would be the relationships between family companies based on long-standing business and social relationships between the families.
- Clear organisational arrangements – particularly concerning activities which crossed or connected the partners.
- The desire of all partners to achieve organisational learning from the alliance rather than to use partners to substitute for their lack of competences – so the processes of innovation in the organisation are enhanced by the partnership, not 'bypassed'.
- Allowing the alliance to evolve and change rather than prescribing it too parochially at the outset.
- Efforts by partners to achieve strong interpersonal relationships, including bonding and flexibility to changing circumstances.

SUMMARY

- A development strategy for the future has three elements: the broad *basis* of the strategy (already discussed in Chapter 6), the *direction* of development and the *method* of development. These three elements must be compatible with each other.
- Development directions can be identified by assessing the various 'combinations' of products and markets leading to four broad categories; *protect* and *build* (current products in current markets); *product development* (for existing markets); *market development* (with existing products), and *diversification* (away from existing products and markets).

- A key determinant in choosing new directions is the organisation's competences. Core competences provide a basis on which to develop and exploit new market opportunities.
- The PIMS database can be useful in understanding the experience of many other organisations in pursuing different strategies. The data can guide (but not dictate) choices of direction.
- For any development direction a further choice is needed – that of the method of development. There are three broad choices: *internal* development, *acquisition*, or *joint* development.
- Internal development has the major benefit of building organisational competences through learning. However, it can result in overstretched resources and the failure to take advantage of specialisation.
- Mergers and acquisitions are a common method of development, largely because of speed and the ability to acquire competences not already held 'in-house'. However, the track record of acquisitions is not good, largely owing to cultural differences and a failure of the 'parent' to understand (and influence) the businesses it has acquired.
- Strategic alliances have many different forms and are increasingly popular methods of development. The most successful alliances appear to be those where partners have positive attitudes to managing and developing the partnership and are concerned to use the alliance to develop their own competences, rather than simply using the partner to substitute for competences which they lack.

RECOMMENDED KEY READINGS

- M.E. Porter, *Competitive Advantage*, Free Press, 1985, discusses the logic of how strategies can be chosen dependent on the situation of the organisation.
- The work of the PIMS project and many of the findings are summarised in R.D. Buzzell and B.T. Gale, *The PIMS Principles*, Free Press, 1987.
- A good discussion of the reasons for, and problems with, mergers and acquisitions can be found in D. Jemison and P. Haspeslagh, *Managing Acquisitions: Creating value through corporate renewal*, Free Press, 1991, and A. Grundy, *Breakthrough Strategies for Growth*, Pitman, 1995.
- A useful book on strategic alliances is D. Faulkner, *Strategic Alliances: Cooperating to compete*, McGraw-Hill, 1995.
- Networks are discussed fully in J.C. Jarillo, *Strategic Networks: Creating the borderless organisation*, Butterworth/Heinemann, 1993.

REFERENCES

1. This figure is an extension of the product/market matrix: see H. Ansoff, *Corporate Strategy*, Penguin, 1988, chapter 6.
2. Downsizing can be difficult to achieve for a variety of reasons, as discussed in W. Cascio, 'Downsizing: What do we know? What have we learnt?', *Academy of Management Executive*, vol. 7, no. 1 (1993), pp. 95–104.
3. Divestment has been of concern in an international context for some considerable time. See J. Coyne and

M. Wright (eds), *Divestment and Strategic Change*, Philip Allan, 1986; M. McDermott, *Multinationals: Foreign divestment and disclosure*, McGraw-Hill, 1989.
4. M. Wright, B. Chiplin and S. Thompson, 'The market for corporate control: divestments and buy-outs', in M. Bishop and J. Kay (eds), *European Mergers and Merger Policy*, Oxford University Press, 1993.
5. The PIMS data are collected from organisations which subscribe to the services offered by the Strategic Planning Institute. The data shown here are aggregate data, but subscribers are able to access data more specific to their industry sector. More details of the PIMS methodology can be found in R.D. Buzzell and B.T. Gale, *The PIMS Principles*, Free Press, 1987.
6. PIMS, 'Marketing: in pursuit of the perfect mix', *Marketing*, 31 October 1991.
7. A. Clayton and C. Carroll, 'Building business for Europe', *Panorama of EU Industry*, 1995. This was a study of competitiveness undertaken jointly by PIMS Associates and the Irish Management Institute for the European Commission.
8. For a review of the effect of these changes in the public sector, see P. Jackson and C. Price, *Privatisation and Regulation: A review of the issues*, Longman, 1994.
9. Turnaround is discussed in S. Slatter, *Corporate Recovery*, Penguin, 1984. An approach to reshaping capabilities to achieve turnround is provided by C. Baden-Fuller and J. Stopford, *Rejuvenating the Mature Business: The competitive challenge*, 2nd edition, Routledge, 1995.
10. For a full discussion of building global market participation, see G. Yip, *Total Global Strategy*, Prentice Hall, 1995, chapter 3.
11. See A. Campbell and K. Luchs, *Strategic Synergy*, Butterworth/Heinemann, 1992.
12. V. Ramanujam and P. Varadarajan, 'Research on corporate diversification: a synthesis', *Strategic Management Journal*, vol. 10, no. 6 (1989), pp. 523–51, is a comprehensive review article on this topic.
13. R.P. Rumelt, *Strategy, Structure and Economic Performance*, Harvard University Press, 1974.
14. C.A. Montgomery, 'The measurement of firm diversification: some new empirical evidence', *Academy of Management Journal*, vol. 25, no. 2 (1982), pp. 299–307.
15. R.M. Grant, A.P. Jammine and H. Thomas, 'Diversity, diversification and profitability among British manufacturing companies, 1972–84', *Academy of Management Journal*, vol. 31, no. 4 (1988), pp. 771–801.
16. See T. Clayton, 'Services in focus', *PIMSletter no. 49*, PIMS Europe Ltd, 1992.
17. M.E. Porter, 'From competitive advantage to competitive strategy', *Harvard Business Review*, vol. 65, no. 3 (1987), pp. 43–59.
18. P. Varadarajan and V. Ramanujam, 'Diversification and performance: a re-examination using a new two-dimensional conceptualisation of diversity in firms', *Academy of Management Journal*, vol. 30, no. 2 (1987), pp. 380–93.
19. See A. Campbell and K. Luchs, 'Towards some new propositions on synergy', Ashridge Strategic Management Centre, 1990, for a summary of findings.
20. S. Chatterjee and B. Wernerfelt, 'The link between resources and type of diversification', *Strategic Management Journal*, vol. 12, no. 1 (1991), pp. 33–48.
21. Good discussions of the reasons for, and problems with, mergers and acquisitions can be found in D. Jemison and P. Haspeslagh, *Managing Acquisitions: Creating value through corporate renewal*, Free Press, 1991; J. McTaggart, P. Kontes and M. Mankins, *The Value Imperative*, Free Press, 1994; and J. Kay, *Foundations of Corporate Success*, Oxford University Press, 1993, chapter 10. A number of useful case studies are included in A. Grundy, *Breakthrough Strategies for Growth*, Pitman, 1995.
22. C. Loderer and K. Martin, 'Postacquisition performance of acquiring firms', *Financial Management*, vol. 21, no. 3 (1992), pp. 69–79.
23. G. Bruton, B. Oviatt and M. White, 'Performance of acquisition of distressed firms', *Academy of Management Journal*, vol. 37, no. 4 (1994), pp. 972–89.
24. A. Cannella and D. Hambrick, 'Effects of executive departures on the performance of acquired firms', *Strategic Management Journal*, vol. 14 (Summer 1993), pp. 137–52.
25. H. Ingham, I. Kran and A. Lovestam, 'Mergers and profitability: a managerial success story?', *Journal of Management Studies*, vol. 29, no. 2 (1992), pp. 195–208.
26. Two useful books on strategic alliances are: D. Faulkner, *Strategic Alliances: Co-operating to compete*, McGraw-Hill, 1995; and P. Lorange and J. Roos, *Strategic Alliances: Formation, implementation and evolution*, Blackwell, 1992.
27. K. Glaister and P. Buckley, 'UK international joint ventures: an analysis of patterns of activity and distribution', *British Journal of Management*, vol. 5, no. 1 (1994), pp. 33–51.
28. Networks are discussed fully in J.C. Jarillo, *Strategic Networks: Creating the borderless organisation*, Butterworth/Heinemann, 1993.
29. See Faulkner (reference 26 above), chapter 16.

WORK ASSIGNMENTS

7.1 Referring back to Exhibit 6.2 in Chapter 6, identify possible development strategies in terms of their combination of *direction* and *method* of development in one of the following:
(a) Brewery Group Denmark*
(b) Coopers Creek*
(c) an organisation of your choice.

7.2 ● Given incursions by Japanese firms in the automobile industry (or an industry of your choice), evaluate the strategic positioning of two competing western firms (e.g. PSA Peugeot Citroën* and Rover/Honda*).

7.3 In the case of Kronenbourg,* Laura Ashley* or an organisation of your choice, write a brief for the management explaining how the PIMS findings should influence their choice of strategies.

7.4 ● Illustration 7.3 shows organisations which are committed to vertical integration within their industry. Make a critical appraisal of the advantages and disadvantages of vertical integration and explain the circumstances in which it is most likely to succeed or fail.

7.5 With reference to Exhibit 7.9, map the development direction of the diversified interests of The News Corporation,* Laura Ashley* or an organisation of your choice in terms of backward, forward or horizontal integration. Explain how and why these have been changed over time.

7.6 ● It has been argued that diversification in many companies has not led to better performance. Indeed, as seen in Illustration 7.6, many organisations are now restructuring or divesting in order to create more focused companies or business units. Discuss the potential benefits and dangers of diversification and refocusing by drawing on these examples and others with which you are familiar.

7.7 ● Referring to Illustration 7.3 and using additional examples of your own, criticise the argument that 'synergy is a sound basis for acquisition'. Refer to P.C. Haspeslagh and D.M. Jemison, *Managing Acquisitions*, Macmillan, 1991, to assist with this assignment.

7.8 In the light of your analysis and discussion in assignment 7.6, write a short (one paragraph) statement to a chief executive who has asked you to advise whether or not the company should diversify. Write a similar statement to the chief executive of a hospital.

7.9 Referring to section 7.3 and Exhibit 7.13 in particular, examine the reasons for the following:
(a) the mergers and acquisitions in the IT and engineering industries (Illustration 7.7)
(b) the Public Finance Initiative (Illustration 7.8)
(c) the Rover/Honda alliance*
(d) two acquisitions or alliances of your choice.

7.10 ● 'Strategic alliances will not survive in the long term if they are simply seen as ways of "blocking gaps" in an organisation's resource base or competences.' Discuss this in relation to any alliances with which you are familiar, or Rover/Honda.*

---

* refers to a case study in the Text and Cases edition.
● denotes more advanced work assignments.

CASE EXAMPLE

Lonely Planet Publications – Personal Passion to Business Success

By 1998 Lonely Planet had come a long way from the husband and wife operation working on a kitchen table in 1972. The company produced 350 titles (some of which were in their ninth edition), covering some of the most inaccessible regions in the world. It employed over 250 staff in four offices in three continents, though the largest proportion (around 60 per cent) were employed in Melbourne, Australia, where the company continued to undertake the production of most of its English language books. Titles covering the Americas, Caribbean, Micronesia and Antarctica were produced in the US office. Lonely Planet also had 100 contracted authors and an annual turnover of A$34 m.

The financial performance of Lonely Planet was impressive by almost any measure. During the early 1990s the company enjoyed rapid growth and high profitability. For example, in 1998 sales were up 22 per cent over the previous year's A$27 million. Ninety-three per cent of sales came from guidebooks (Shoestrings and Travel Survival Kits), the remainder coming from its newer lines such as city guides and phrase books, diving guides, atlases and travel literature.

In spite of the change in the nature of the organisation as it grew, the books retained their chatty style and practical format, with much material being sent in from backpackers on the road.

Early Days

A newly married English couple, Tony and Maureen Wheeler, had founded the company after walking, hitching and backpacking their way to Australia in 1972. Soon the numerous 'how did you do it?' enquiries inspired them to write down their travel experiences and produce a 'cut and paste' publication called *Across Asia on the Cheap*. It was an instant success, which encouraged them to postpone their return to England and return to their first love of being 'on the road'. Tony Wheeler reflected on the early successes:

> Now I can look back and think that was a really clever idea, but at the time I didn't realise it. It was just a nice thing to do. As soon as we saw how well the first book went, we thought 'Lets do another'. We grew very slowly at first. It took us five years to get to ten titles.

Jim Hart: a New Partner

The year 1980 was an important one for Lonely Planet. Jim Hart, a friend of the Wheelers, with a mixture of travel and publishing experience, joined Lonely Planet from a major publishing house in Adelaide, South Australia. With Jim's involvement, the Wheelers' shoestring operation gradually took on more permanence, allowing them more time to travel and to undertake the intensive year-long research effort necessary for the production of an India guide. When the first edition of *India: A Travel Survival Kit* came out in 1981, it marked a major turning point for Lonely Planet. Previously, books priced at A$3.95 had sold up to 30,000 copies: by 1981 books priced at A$14.95 sold 100,000 copies. The India guidebook provided the steady income desperately needed for the company to finance its operations.

By the time Jim joined, Tony and Maureen had already established the Lonely Planet name and set up the beginning of an international distribution system. With Jim's involvement and with the publication of the India guide, Tony and Maureen could look forward to a period of stability.

In 1984/85 they set up a US office, which proved to be both difficult and costly. Nonetheless, it eventually worked, and in 1991 they were ready for further international expansion. The UK was the natural choice given the English language and its proximity to Continental European markets too.

This expansion into Europe was another major test for the company. Lonely Planet, had created a name for itself by publishing guidebooks to the world's more out-of-the-way places, and did not have an image as a provider of travel information about the industrialised countries of the West. Lonely Planet expected to meet fierce competition in the European market, which was dominated by the big American-produced guides.

In 1993, heartened by its UK experience, Lonely Planet set up an office in France. The French office marked a significant development for the company in that, unlike its other overseas offices, its role was not limited to promotion and distribution but included production of French translations. It also marked the company's first attempt to diversify into non-English-speaking markets and to control the content, presentation and marketing of its products and brand in those markets. Until this time, Lonely Planet had considered itself to be exclusively an English-language publisher. Foreign publishers had undertaken the translation of its books into other languages under various licensing arrangements.

On the Road Again: the Wheelers in the 1990s

While continuing to run the business, much of the Wheelers' time was still spent on the road – researching, which they described as 'dawn to dusk hard work and not without some annoyances'. Typically they travelled overseas half-a-dozen times a year, investigating new places, double-checking facts from one of their books, or simply enjoying life on the road. In 1997 and early 1998, for example, they went on safari in Zimbabwe and 'road-tested' the Antarctica guide, as well as visiting Tahiti, Guatemala and Belize.

The primary passion of the Wheelers was always to produce good travel information. Profit was important, but mainly because it was the means to grow and do more for travellers.

Publishing Industry Changes

The move towards global consolidation of publishing interests appeared to be part of the large players' corporate strategies. Control of newspapers, printing works, film libraries and production, databases, book retailing and publishing, radio and television broadcasting, satellite television and magazines began to converge in the expectation of massive economies of scale.

These global companies were also at the forefront of the implementation of new technologies that offered the possibility of increasing audience size and, hence, further levering the returns from their information stores. In this climate, smaller publishers survived by catering for specialist markets, which the large corporates could not service economically.

There were also important changes in distribution channels. In the late 1980s, the owner-operators of independent bookstores dominated the market numerically. In Australia, for instance, 75–80 per cent of bookstores were owner-operated stores or were small chains with two to five stores. The majority of these were not commercially aggressive and books were generally sold at the publisher's recommended retail price. This pricing structure was supported by a 100 year old international publishing cartel. Book retailers competed on the basis of convenience and service rather than price.

By the early 1990s, however, bookstore chains and large department stores were becoming increasingly dominant in the book retailing segment throughout the world. Book superstores had emerged in the USA to compete with discount stores – Wal-Mart alone had 18 per cent of the US book retail market. These stores were very commercially oriented. They offered a wide selection of books, and their size and buying power allowed them to negotiate large margins with publishers, who often had no choice but to comply or be denied access to their readers. Lower prices were in part passed on to consumers through heavy discounting of many titles.

Technology was changing too. The basic concept of presenting prepackaged information via the printed page in book form, the primary method of communicating information since the invention of the printing press, was being challenged. Publishers of travel information were frantically trying to assess the implications of new technologies. Further, the Internet allowed virtually free access to information from anywhere in the world and, significantly for Lonely Planet with its two-year recycle time, allowed users to gain instant access to current information – for example on current train timetables and weather patterns.

Lonely Planet went its own way in developing applications in response to these rapid developments in technology. In 1994 it had gathered a small group of editors and cartographers to develop applications for a Lonely Planet Internet site. In a few months, this group of half-a-dozen 'experimenters' had developed what became one the largest Internet sites in Australia. Although it was fun, they could not see anybody using anything but books on their travels well into the future. By early 1998 the Website was receiving 6 million hits per month and Lonely Planet was also providing travel information to other major sites such as Yahoo!, Travelocity and AOL.

Initially, Tony Wheeler, it was said, could not get himself excited about multimedia and sometimes wished the new technology would 'go away.' The younger staff did not share this sentiment. By 1998, however, he had been won over by the success of the Website.

Products

Lonely Planet attributed its success to a large range of titles, brand loyalty and the best form of advertising that accompanied that loyalty – word of mouth. Lonely Planet guidebooks were thoroughly revised every two to three years on average. By contrast, most of the company's competitors updated only small sections of their books, some on a yearly basis. Each Lonely Planet book was in a constant state of revision.

Most printing and binding of finished books was done in Hong Kong and Singapore. Apart from cost considerations and delivery time to major overseas markets, printers had to be able to 'section sew' books. This type of binding, which prevents pages from falling out and book spines from being broken, guaranteed that Lonely Planet books stood up to the hard treatment that they receive on the road.

Bulk distribution was decentralised through regional warehouses located in Melbourne, San Francisco, London and Singapore. From these locations, books were supplied to wholesale distributors in each country except Australia and the USA where sales and distribution to retailers were done directly by Lonely Planet.

A Valuable Asset

Lonely Plant also attracted the attention of the corporate giants of the publishing industry. During the late 1980s the Wheelers began to receive lucrative buyout offers from a number of large organisations including the software giant Microsoft, whose activity in multimedia led it to an approach about joint development of multimedia travel publications. Although flattered by Microsoft's interest, Tony, Maureen and Jim declined the offer, feeling that an association with such a large and powerful organisation could compromise Lonely Planet's independence. As Tony said, 'It really felt like we would be going to bed with an elephant and if it rolled over we would be crushed'. When asked why they didn't 'take the money and run,' Maureen said:

> I don't know if I'd like to travel without a reason, and I really, really like the books we do. I always did, right from the very first book. On a day-to-day basis, I really like all the people who work here, and who still enjoy working here. I suppose I just love the books.

Questions

1. Refer to Exhibit 7.1 and section 7.2 and describe in chronological order the development directions taken by Lonely Planet between 1972 and 1998.
2. Why were other directions *not* pursued?
3. Repeat the analysis in relation to methods of development (refer to section 7.3).
4. What are the choices on direction and method of development for the period ahead? Which would you recommend? Why?

Source Adapted from 'Lonely Planet Publications' in G. Lewis, A. Morkel and G. Hubbard, *Australian and New Zealand Strategic Management: Concepts, context and cases*, Prentice Hall, 1998. Thanks are due to Geoff Lewis for the provision of updated material.

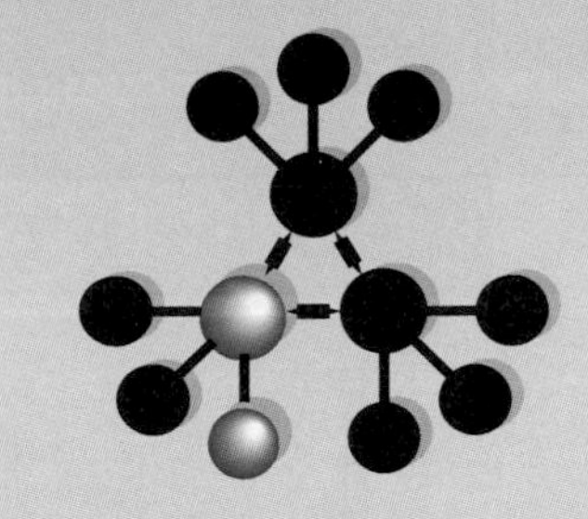

8
STRATEGY EVALUATION AND SELECTION

LEARNING OUTCOMES

After reading this chapter you should be able to:

- Define suitability, acceptability and feasibility.
- Understand how suitability can be tested.
- Explain the strengths and limitations of various methods of screening options.
- Explain the different approaches to assessing acceptability.
- Undertake a stakeholder mapping exercise.
- Undertake an assessment of feasibility of a strategy.
- Understand the different processes of strategy selection.

8.1 INTRODUCTION AND EVALUATION CRITERIA

The previous two chapters have discussed the strategic options available to organisations. This chapter will discuss how strategic options can be evaluated and the processes by which organisations might select strategies for the future. It is not the intention of the chapter to describe in detail a whole plethora of analytical techniques. Rather, the aim is to help readers understand the contribution that different types of technique can make in evaluating and selecting strategies.[1]

In assessing strategies – whether by formal or informal processes – there are three types of *evaluation criterion* which can be used:

- *Suitability* is a broad assessment of whether the strategy addresses the circumstances in which the organisation is operating (perhaps identified in a strategic analysis): for example, the extent to which new strategies would *fit* with the future trends and changes in the environment; or how the strategy might exploit the core competences of the organisation. This can often be the basis of a *qualitative* assessment concerned with testing out the *rationale* of a strategy and, as such, can be useful for *screening* options, as seen below.

Exhibit 8.1 A framework for the evaluation and selection of strategies

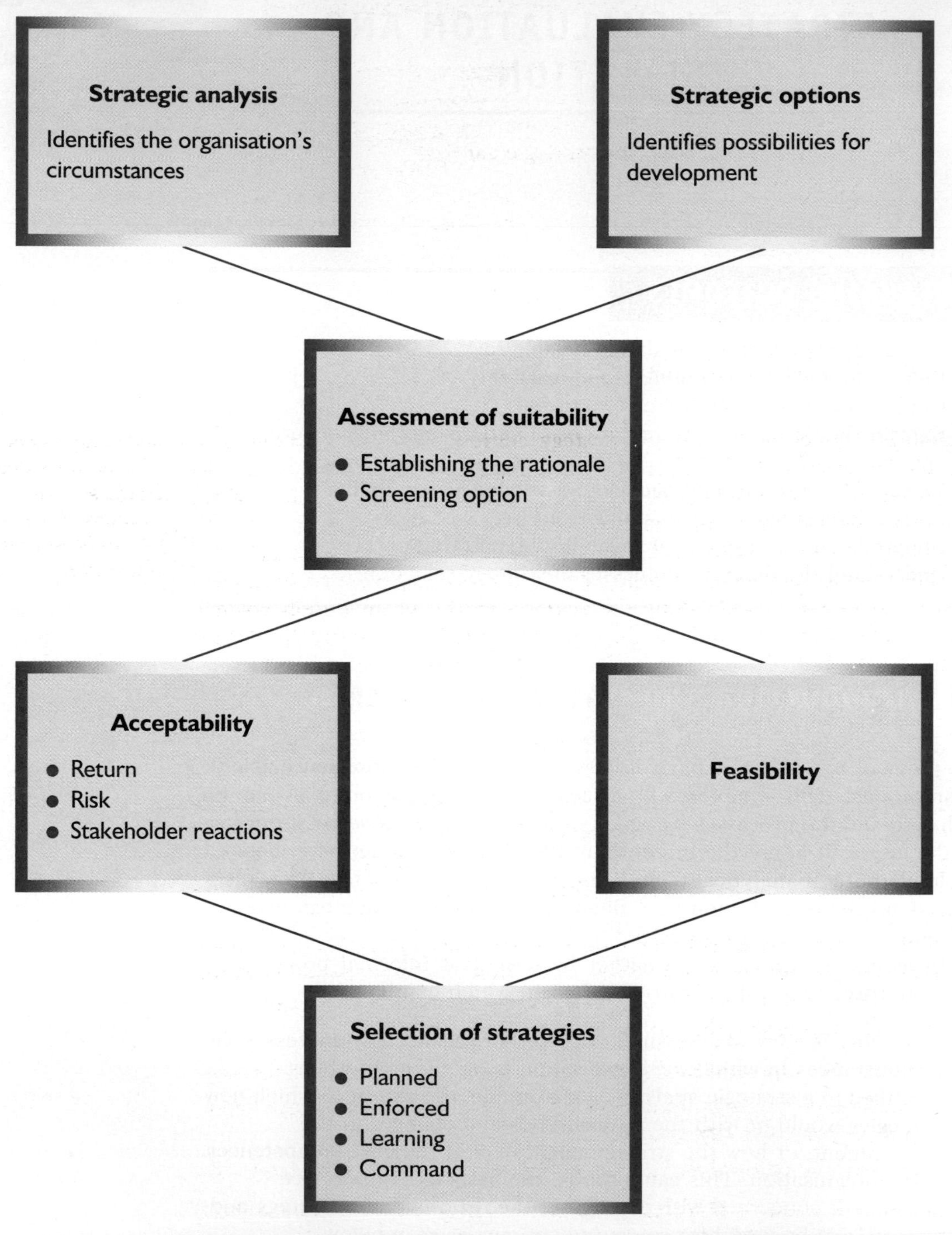

- *Acceptability* is concerned with the expected *performance outcomes* (such as the *return* or *risk*) if the strategy were implemented, and the extent to which these would be in line with the *expectations of stakeholders*.
- *Feasibility* is concerned with whether the strategy could be made to work in practice. Assessing the feasibility of a strategy requires an emphasis on more detailed – often *quantitative* – assessment of the practicalities of *resourcing* and strategic capability.

Exhibit 8.1 shows how these various aspects of evaluation and selection can be fitted together, and builds on the issues previously discussed concerning strategic analysis and strategic options.

8.2 ASSESSING SUITABILITY

Suitability concerns whether a strategy addresses the circumstances in which the organisation is operating. Assessing the suitability of strategic options can be a useful basis on which to screen options before more detailed analyses are undertaken concerning the acceptability and feasibility of those options. This process can consist of two stages: first, establishing the rationale/strategic logic for each strategic option *in its own right*; and second, establishing the *relative* merits of an option when a number of choices are available through processes for *screening* options for further evaluation. This section looks at each of these aspects of evaluation.

suitability *concerns whether a strategy addresses the circumstances in which the organisation is operating*

8.2.1 Establishing the Rationale

The assessment of suitability of a particular strategy is concerned with whether it addresses the circumstances in which the organisation is operating or wishes to operate. It can be a useful discipline to ask the 'champions' of new strategies to describe, clearly and succinctly, *why is this a good idea?*

This clearly relates back to the discussions in Part II of this book, since the main purpose of strategic analysis is to establish an understanding of the basis on which the suitability of strategies can be judged. For example, it will consist of assessing the extent to which a strategy:

- exploits the *opportunities* in the environment and avoids the *threats*;
- capitalises on the organisation's *strengths* and *core competences* and avoids or remedies the *weaknesses*;
- addresses the cultural and political context (as discussed in Chapter 5).

Exhibit 8.2 summarises different categories of analytical technique and the main contribution which they make to assessing the suitability of strategies.

Exhibit 8.2 Testing suitability

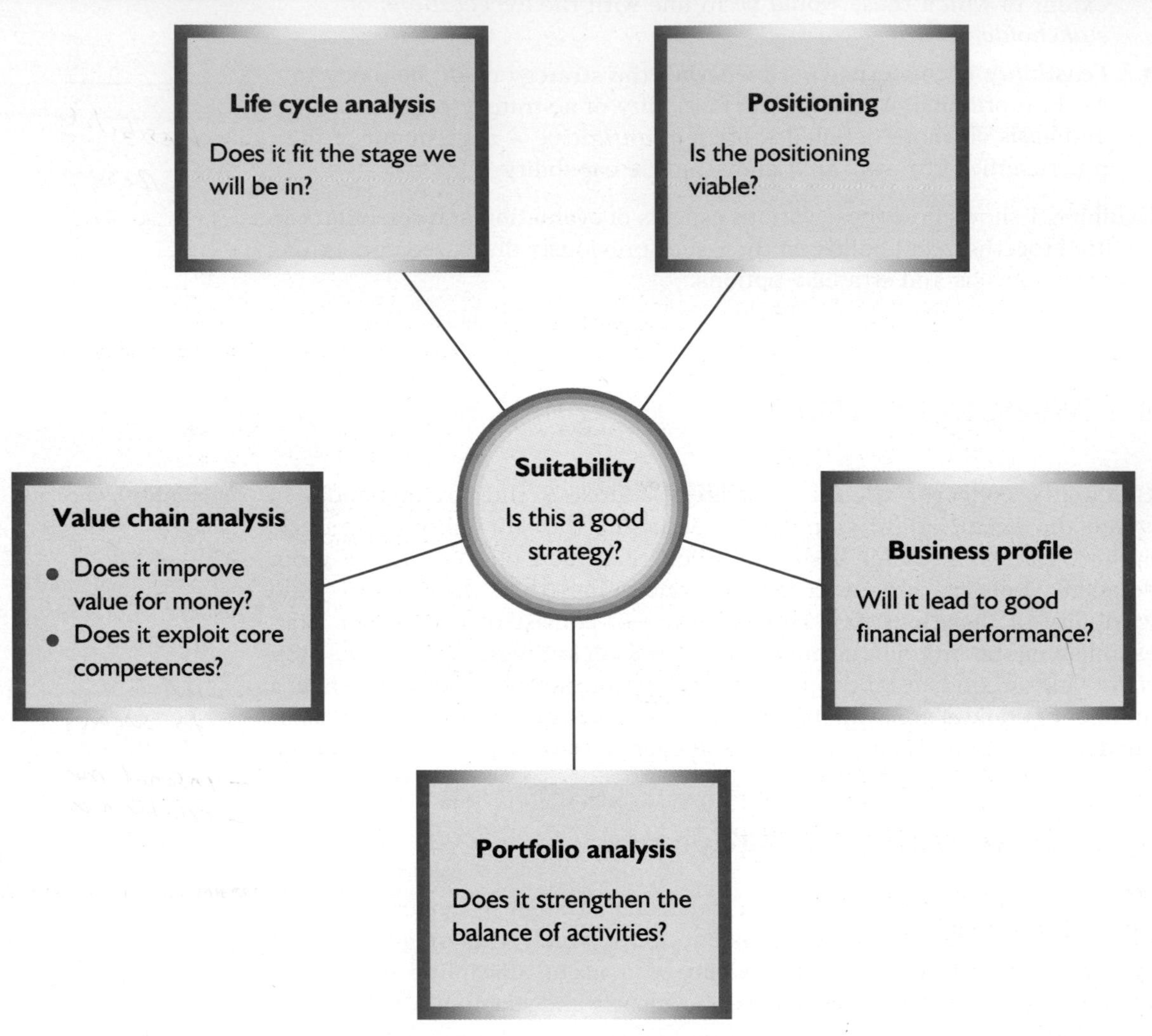

Life Cycle Analysis[2]

a **life cycle analysis** *assesses whether a strategy is likely to be appropriate given the stage of the product life cycle*

A **life cycle analysis** assesses whether a strategy is likely to be appropriate given the stage of the product life cycle. Some analyses combine this with the relative strength or weakness of the organisation in its market to produce a *life cycle/portfolio matrix* (see Exhibit 8.3). The life cycle/portfolio matrix consists of two dimensions. The *market situation* is described in four stages ranging from embryonic to ageing; the *competitive position* in five categories ranging from weak to dominant.

Exhibit 8.3 The life cycle/portfolio matrix

STAGES OF INDUSTRY MATURITY

COMPETITIVE POSITION	Embryonic	Growth	Mature	Ageing
Dominant	Fast grow Start up	Fast grow Attain cost leadership Renew Defend position	Defend position Attain cost leadership Renew Fast grow	Defend position Focus Renew Grow with industry
Strong	Start up Differentiate Fast grow	Fast grow Catch up Attain cost leadership Differentiate	Attain cost leadership Renew, focus Differentiate Grow with industry	Find niche Hold niche Hang in Grow with industry Harvest
Favourable	Start up Differentiate Focus Fast grow	Differentiate, focus Catch up Grow with industry	Harvest, hang in Find niche, hold niche Renew, turnaround Differentiate, focus Grow with industry	Retrench Turnaround
Tenable	Start up Grow with industry Focus	Harvest, catch up Hold niche, hang in Find niche Turnaround Focus Grow with industry	Harvest Turnaround Find niche Retrench	Divest Retrench
Weak	Find niche Catch up Grow with industry	Turnaround Retrench	Withdraw Divest	Withdraw

Source Arthur D. Little.

The purpose of the matrix is to establish the appropriateness of particular strategies in relation to these two dimensions. The crucial issue is establishing where an organisation is currently positioned on the matrix, and therefore what types of strategy are most likely to be suitable:

- The *position within the life cycle* can be determined in relation to eight external factors or descriptors of the evolutionary stage of the industry. These are: market growth rate, growth potential, breadth of product lines, number of competitors, spread of market share between these competitors, customer loyalty, entry barriers and technology. It is the balance of these factors which determines the life cycle stage. For example, an embryonic industry is characterised by rapid growth, changes in technology, fragmented market shares and pursuit of new customers. In contrast, ageing industries are best described by falling demand, declining number of competitors and, often, a narrow product line.

- The *competitive position* of the organisation within its industry can also be established by looking at the characteristics of each category in Exhibit 8.3. A *dominant* position is rare in the private sector and usually results from a quasi-monopoly. In the public sector, this may be a legalised monopoly status (e.g. public utilities). *Strong* organisations are those that can follow strategies of their own choice without too much concern for competition. A *favourable* position is where no single competitor stands out, but the leaders are better placed (as in grocery retailing in France or the UK). A *tenable* position is that which can be maintained by specialisation or focus. *Weak* competitors are ones which are too small to survive independently in the long run.

The danger is that such a detailed matrix can suggest that strategic choice is a simplistic affair; it is not, and so the A.D. Little matrix can only be helpful in guiding strategic choice.

Positioning

Positioning is a key test of suitability and was discussed in Chapter 6. The choice of generic product and market strategies forms the basis or framework within which the more detailed directions and methods of development are constructed. So assessing whether current and future positionings are viable can be done by asking whether *demand* is likely to grow or decline. For example, in mature markets, the size of the core market is often reduced by the development of a number of smaller viable 'niches'; the degree of *competitive rivalry* which exists; and the *relative competence* of the organisation in facing these competitive rivals with a particular product or market positioning. For example, the extent to which the organisation's unit costs are better than those of competitive rivals will determine the long-term viability of a low-price positioning. The uniqueness of the competences which underpin the value-added features of a product or service will determine the suitability of a positioning of differentiation. The extent to which an organisation is capable of supporting a particular positioning in its markets can be examined as follows:

1. The first step in assessing the suitability of a particular strategy is to list key resources and competences underpinning the strategy (column A in Exhibit 8.4). These might be identified by means of the type of competence analysis explained in Chapter 4 (section 4.3.2) and Illustration 4.2.
2. Second, these are examined in terms of the different bases of the product or market strategy. Column B1 (cost reduction) is particularly important for route 2 or 3 in the strategy clock discussed in Chapter 6

Exhibit 8.4 Assessing the suitability of a product/market strategy

A	B1	B2	C			
Resources and competences underpinning strategy	**Which of these resources/competences are likely to contribute to:**		**Which will be sustainable/ difficult to imitate**			
	Cost reduction	**Added value in terms of needs perceived by customers**	Valued	Rare	Complex	Tacit

(Exhibit 6.4). Column B2 (perceived added value) is particularly important for positionings on the strategy clock of 3, 4 or 5. So the question is asked: would this particular resource or competence underpin cost reduction (B1) or add to perceived value (B2)? For example, a competence in bulk purchasing may score highly in B1, but quite low in B2. In contrast, in-house R&D activities, although costly, may be essential processes of innovation and the source of unique product features which are highly valued by customers.

3. Finally, each of these resources and competences is revisited to establish whether it is sustainable or difficult to imitate: in other words, whether it is a genuinely unique resource or core competence (as seen in Exhibit 4.2) and hence provides competitive advantage to the organisation. The criteria used to judge this were also introduced in section 4.3.2 in Chapter 4. These criteria require an assessment of the extent to which competences are:
   - *valuable* to buyers
   - *rare* (i.e. not easily obtained by competitors)

- *complex* (e.g. made up of several organisational processes)
- embedded in the *tacit* knowledge or routines.

Analysis may well reveal that very few resources and competences are difficult to imitate on their own. Rather, it is likely to be the ability to manage linkages between separate activities and the tacit knowledge of the organisation that provides competitive advantage, as shown in Illustration 4.2 and highlighted in Chapter 6.

4. Assessing the relationship between the generic product/market strategy and the strategic capability of the organisation (resources and competences) will also be useful in a more detailed assessment of the feasibility of one or more strategies. This is often called *resource deployment analysis* and is discussed below (section 8.4.3). It is also a central consideration in preparing resource plans for implementing strategies, and *critical success factors analysis* is designed to ensure that the key resources and core competences will actually be in place to match the product/market positioning. This is part of establishing and maintaining the appropriate strategic architecture for an organisation, and is discussed in section 10.3.1 of Chapter 10.

Value Chain Analysis

value chain analysis *describes the activities within and around an organisation and relates them to an analysis of the competitive strength of the organisation*

/ reconfiguring linkages
- effect on value chain
- synergy

Value chain analysis describes the activities within and around an organisation and relates them to an analysis of the competitive strength of the organisation. Chapter 4 emphasised that understanding how cost was controlled and value created within the value system is very important when assessing the strategic capability of an organisation. It has also been mentioned above that an assessment of the type shown in Exhibit 8.4 usually reveals that the key to sustainable success can be found in the way the value system is *configured* – that the *linkages* between value activities are just as important as the competence in the separate activities. Therefore, the suitability of strategic developments may *also* be tested by the extent to which the strategy will reconfigure the value chain in a way which improves value for money and the competitive position of the organisation, as shown in Illustration 8.1.

The concept of *synergy*[3] is concerned with assessing how much extra benefit (value for money) can be created from reconfiguring the linkages in the value chain. Synergy can be sought in several circumstances, as is illustrated by the three strategies under consideration for the grocery retailer in Illustration 8.1:

- *Market development* (buying more shops) may improve performance in the value system, since it provides a further opportunity to exploit a good corporate image, and hence 'launch costs' are minimised compared with a new entrant. Buying power should also increase.
- *Product development* (into alcoholic drinks) would improve the use of a key resource (floor space), and cash is available to fund initial stock.

STRATEGY IN ACTION
Illustration 8.1

Value Chain Analysis: A Worked Example

Value chain analysis can be used to assess what extra synergistic benefits can be obtained from different strategies by changing linkages in the value system.

Owing to recent success, a grocery retailer has a large cash reserve and is considering expanding his operations. However, he is unsure whether he should buy more shops, expand into the alcoholic drinks market, or open a cash-and-carry wholesaler.

Questions

1. On the basis of this analysis, which strategy would you choose?
2. Are there any considerations not included in the analysis that might make you change your mind? Explain why.

DEGREE OF SYNERGY WITH PRESENT ACTIVITIES	STRATEGY 1: BUY MORE SHOPS	STRATEGY 2: EXPAND INTO ALCOHOLIC DRINKS	STRATEGY 3: OPEN CASH-AND-CARRY WHOLESALER
Use of cash	Produces profit from idle cash	Produces profit from idle cash	Produces profit from idle cash
Use of premises	None	More turnover/floor space	None
Use of stock	Perhaps small gains from moving stock between shops	None	Reduction of stock in shops as quick delivery guaranteed
Purchasing	Possible discounts for bulk	None	Reduced prices to shops
Market image	Good name helps launch (i.e. cost of launch reduced)	None	Little

- *Backward integration* (into wholesaling) may well produce cost advantage if better stock planning can be achieved between the wholesale and retail partners.

Synergy could arise through many different types of link or interrelationship: for example, in the market (by exploiting brand name, sharing outlets or pooling selling or promotional activities); in the company's operations (by shared purchasing, facilities, maintenance, quality control, etc.); and in product/process development (by sharing information and know-how).

Synergy is often used as a justification for product or market *diversification*, particularly through acquisition or merger.

Portfolio Analysis[4]

portfolio analysis *analyses the balance of an organisation's strategic business units*

Portfolio analysis analyses the balance of an organisation's strategic business units. Chapter 6 discussed how portfolio analysis can be used to establish the basis for an organisation's approach to diversity. Therefore, when evaluating *specific options* for the future, they can be plotted onto a matrix (see, for example, Exhibit 4.12) and the long-term rationale of business development can be highlighted. For example, if the original BCG matrix were used, the following questions could be asked:

- Will the strategy move the company to a dominant position in its markets? Which strategies are most likely to ensure a move from *question marks* through to *stars* and eventually to *cash cows*? Question marks require a sufficient level of innovative capability. If this is not present then perhaps the organisation should 'side-step' question marks via its acquisition strategy (see below).
- Since question marks and stars generally require an investment of funds, will there be sufficient cash cows to provide this necessary investment? A major reason for company bankruptcies is that a firm may invest heavily in the promotion and stocking policy for products in rapid growth, without profitable and well established products from which it can fund these new ventures.
- The matrix can also help in thinking about *acquisition* strategy. Companies that embark on acquisition programmes may forget that the most likely targets for acquisition programmes are not the stars and cash cows of the business world, but the question marks or dogs. There may be nothing wrong with acquiring a question mark, provided the resources and competences are there to move it towards stardom, bearing in mind the need for parenting skills as discussed in Chapter 6, and the real costs and difficulties of acquisition as pointed out in Chapter 7.

Business Profile Analysis

a **business profile analysis** *shows the extent to which a strategy matches the favourable performance parameters from PIMS analyses*

A **business profile analysis** shows the extent to which a strategy matches the favourable performance parameters from PIMS analyses. The PIMS database discussed in Chapter 7 can be used to profile the strategy of a strategic business unit against the parameters which PIMS has researched in relation to the strategy/performance match.[5] Illustration 8.2 shows how this profiling is done.

- The current strategic position of the frozen food business is 'scored' against the eleven parameters in Illustration 8.2(a). Evidence from the PIMS database shows that there are several factors associated

STRATEGY IN ACTION
Illustration 8.2

Profiling an Acquisition

The PIMS database can be used to profile the strategy of an SBU against the parameters which PIMS research in relation to the strategy/performance match. Sometimes it can suggest that a particular strategy, such as an acquisition, would weaken the business profile (of the combined company).

Questions

Read the narrative in the text, which relates to this illustration and then answer the following questions.

1. Refer to Exhibit 8.2 and decide if other methods of analysis would necessarily have concluded that the merger was an unattractive option.
2. List the strengths and weaknesses of business profiling as a technique for making strategic decisions.

Source PIMS Associates Ltd. Reproduced with permission.

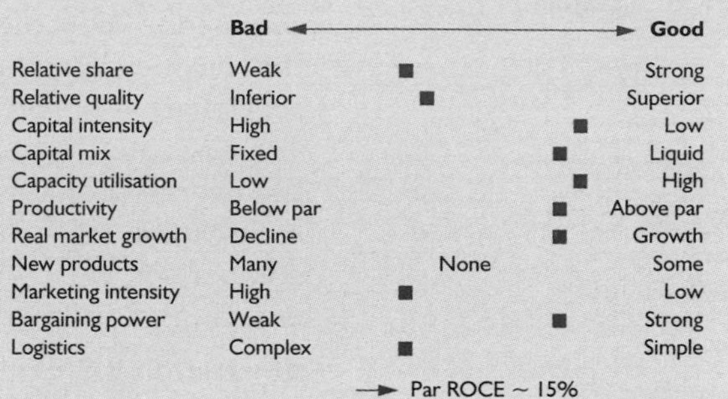

(a) A frozen food marketing business, considering buying its supplier

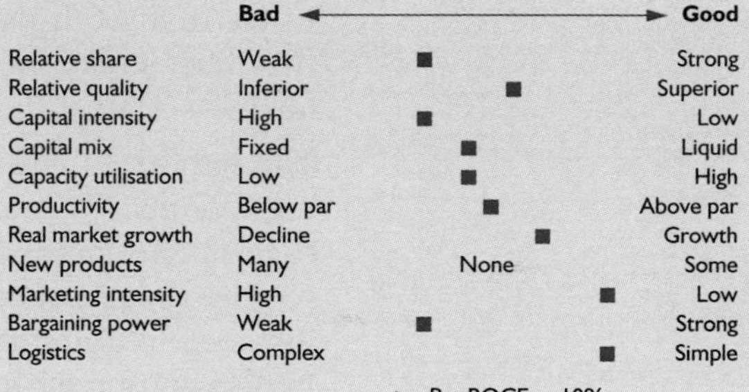

(b) The freezing business

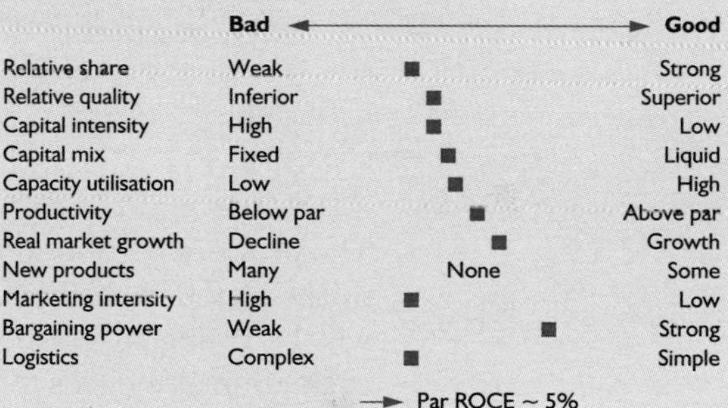

(c) The combined business

with this business which serve to lower its expected financial performance, such as weak relative market share, poor relative quality position, high marketing intensity and complex logistics. Some parameters, on the other hand, are more positive, such as asset flexibility, low capital intensity, high capacity utilisation and strong bargaining power with suppliers. This results in an above-average position overall and a likelihood of this business being able to cover its cost of capital.

- The company is considering backward integration through the acquisition of its major supplier of frozen food. The strategic position of this business is profiled separately (see Illustration 8.2(b)). It can be seen that, although there are some parameters which may give the business some strength (low marketing intensity and simple logistics), the overall profile is relatively weak, largely owing to a combination of high capital intensity and low share. A business like this, based on comparison with others, would normally earn returns below the cost of capital, but still better than break-even.
- Illustration 8.2(c) shows how the combined businesses would look after an acquisition which merged the activities into a single integrated company. The result is a business with no real strengths and the weak characteristics of both businesses. Its expected performance would be worse than both its component parts – not a surprising conclusion in this case, since the managers were planning to pit the newly integrated business against the might of Unilever. A clear case of negative synergy.
- The important issue, however, is that these drivers of profitability are interconnected, and building a strong business profile is more difficult than might appear. For example, a gain in relative market share may require the use of new outlets, and gaining these outlets may, in the first instance, require higher marketing intensity and increased complexity in distribution logistics. Hence any strengthening of one parameter may well weaken others and therefore not necessarily improve the business profile overall. These interrelationships need to be taken into account when evaluating the suitability of business strategies.

8.2.2 Screening Options

screening *is the process of comparing the relative merits of different strategies*

The previous section summarised ways in which the merits of specific strategies might be established against the *suitability* criterion. Typically, an organisation will be trying to make choices between a number of different strategies. So evaluation also needs to be concerned with how the *relative* merits of strategies can be assessed. This can be important in screening options before a more detailed assessment of acceptability and feasibility is undertaken. **Screening** is the process of comparing the relative merits of different strategies.

This is not to suggest that options eliminated at this stage of evaluation should be excluded from further consideration, since the process tends to be iterative in practice. This section begins by reviewing the basis on which specific strategies can be assessed – whether options are to be judged on an absolute basis, against each other, or against the 'do nothing' situation.

The section outlines three contrasting approaches to the screening of options (see Exhibit 8.5):

- *Ranking* options against a set of predetermined factors concerning the organisation's strategic situation. The extent to which specific options fit these criteria determines their position in this 'league table'.

Exhibit 8.5 Screening strategic options

The relative suitability of strategic options can be assessed by:

METHOD	APPROACH
Ranking	• Options are assessed against key factors in the environment, resources and stakeholder expectations • A score (and ranking) is established for each option
Decision trees	• Options are progressively 'eliminated' by introducing further criteria
Scenario planning	• Options are matched to different future scenarios • Contingency plans are prepared

- *Decision trees*, which also assess specific options against a list of key strategic factors. However, options are ranked by progressively eliminating others.
- *Scenarios*, which attempt to match specific options with a range of possible future outcomes and are particularly useful where a high degree of uncertainty exists (say, in the environment, as discussed in Chapter 3). Scenarios provide a means of keeping many more options under consideration.

Bases for Comparison

Chapter 4 has already discussed the importance of establishing an appropriate basis for comparison when assessing strategic capability. This is also needed during evaluation. If strategies are assessed only in absolute terms or against industry norms, this does not address a central issue in strategy evaluation: namely, the need to identify the *incentive to change* from the present strategy to a new strategy. It may therefore be helpful to use the 'do nothing' situation to assess the organisation's incentive to change.

The **'do nothing' situation** represents the likely outcome if the organisation were to continue with current strategies, disregarding any changes occurring in the environment or the resource position of the organisation. The easiest way to incorporate this situation into an evaluation is by including it as a strategic option to be evaluated alongside others. However, it must be remembered that 'do nothing' is not usually an option *per se* since failure to innovate and change usually takes an organisation backwards. However, the 'do nothing' situation provides a valuable base line against which to assess the incentive to change.

the **'do nothing' situation** *represents the likely outcome if the organisation were to continue with current strategies, disregarding any changes occurring in the environment or the resource position of the organisation*

A useful technique which incorporates this approach is *gap analysis*, which can be used to identify the extent to which existing strategies will fail to meet the performance objectives in the future.

Exhibit 8.6 Gap analysis

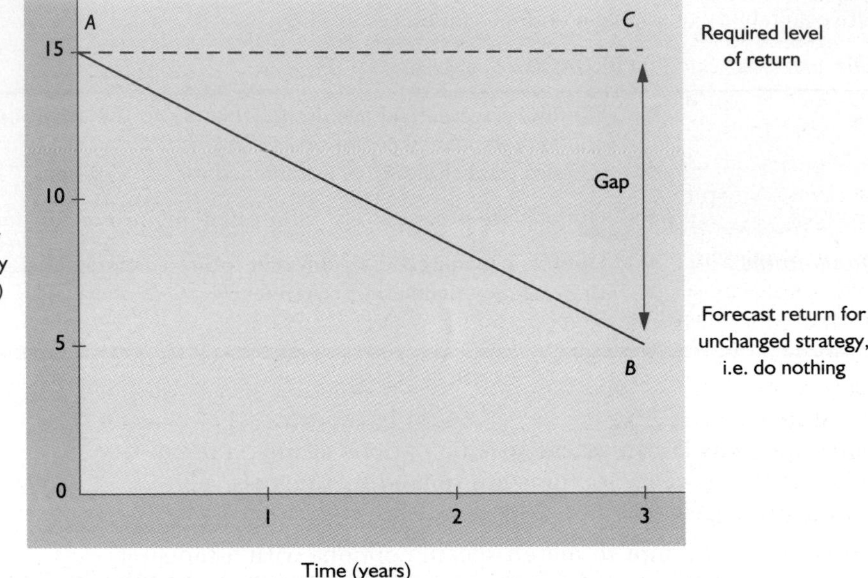

Note: The company is currently operating at 15% return on capital and wishes to maintain that level. Increased competition, escalating labour costs and deteriorating machinery underlie the forecast of declining profitability unless current strategies are revised. *BC* represents the gap which is likely to exist in three years' time between required performance and actual performance. The gap needs to be 'filled' by new strategies.

Exhibit 8.6 outlines the analysis for a single product/single market situation. This is a simplified example which illustrates the general approach. The analysis follows several steps:

- First, decide on key *performance criteria* – in this case, company profitability (ROC).
- Second, agree the required performance year-on-year into the future – in this case, 15 per cent ROC.
- Third, forecast the likely performance if strategies are unchanged – in this case, a steadily declining ROC because of increasing labour costs, deteriorating equipment and reductions in real prices resulting from innovations made by competitors.
- Finally, establish the *gap* between the forecast and required performance levels – this has to be 'filled' by new strategies.

Readers need to bear in mind that, like other forecasting techniques, gap analysis can be a difficult and time-consuming process. It is also usually necessary to apply measures other than profitability. Some of these may be easily quantifiable, such as productivity or volume of sales, whereas others may be more subjective but nonetheless very important, such as levels of quality or service.

Gap analysis is also used extensively in public sector planning.[6] Here the strategic problem is often concerned with whether the future demands on a public service are likely to change to such an extent that the current resource provision will prove wholly inadequate. This is particularly important when considering the statutory obligations of many public services, such as hospitals, education and social services. Demographic information is often of central importance in attempting to assess the likely future gaps in provision: for example, whether hospitals or social services can cope with an ageing population. In undertaking such an analysis it is essential to include ambitious targets about the gains that can be achieved by innovation in service design and delivery. It is not acceptable simply to 'pro rata' future resource requirements as a function of forecast demand. This has been a source of considerable friction between the political and executive arms of many public services.

Ranking

Ranking is a systematic way of analysing specific options for their suitability or fit with the factors arising from strategic analysis. As seen in Illustration 8.3, each option is assessed against a number of key factors which the strategic analysis identified in the organisation's environment, resources and expectations. One of the major benefits of ranking is that it helps the analyst to think through mismatches between a company's present position and the implications of the various strategic options. More sophisticated approaches to ranking assign weightings to each factor, in recognition that some will be of more importance in the evaluation than others.

ranking *is a systematic way of analysing specific options for their suitability or fit with the factors arising from strategic analysis*

Decision Trees[7]

Although decision trees have been widely used in operational decision making, their use in strategy formulation has not, in general, received a great deal of attention. A typical strategic decision tree is shown in Illustration 8.4. It can be seen that the end-point of the tree is a number of discrete development opportunities, as discussed in Chapter 7. Whereas ranking assumes that all options have equal merit (in the first instance), a **decision tree** ranks options by progressively eliminating others. This elimination process is achieved by identifying a few key elements or criteria which future developments are intended to incorporate, such as growth, investment and diversification. For example, in the illustration, choosing growth as an important aspect of future strategies would automatically rank options 1–4 more highly than 5–8. At the second step, the need for low-investment strategies would rank options 3 and 4 above 1 and 2, and so on.

a **decision tree** *ranks options by progressively eliminating others*

STRATEGY IN ACTION
Illustration 8.3

Ranking Options: Churchill Pottery

Ranking can usefully build on a SWOT analysis by comparing strategic options against the key strategic factors from the SWOT analysis.

In 1990 Churchill Pottery, based in Stoke-on-Trent, UK, was one of the subjects of a BBC series entitled *Troubleshooter*, where the management teams of a number of companies were invited to discuss their organisation's strategic development with Sir John Harvey-Jones (ex-Chairman of ICI). Like many traditional manufacturing companies at the time, Churchill found itself under increasing pressure from cheaper imports in its traditional markets, and was considering whether to move 'up market' by launching a new range aimed at the design-conscious end of the market. The ranking exercise below was done by a group of participants on a management programme having seen the Churchill Pottery video.

The results of the ranking are interesting. First, they highlight the need to do *something*. Second, the radical departures in strategy – such as moves into retailing or diversification – are regarded as unsuitable. They do not address the problems of the core business, do not fit the capabilities of Churchill and would not fit culturally. This leaves related developments as the front runners – as might be expected in a traditional manufacturing firm like Churchill. The choice boils down to significant investments in cost reduction to support an essentially 'commodity' approach to the market (options 2 and 5) or an 'added value' attack on the growing 'up-market' segments. The company chose the latter and with some success – presumably helped by their wide television exposure through the *Troubleshooter* series.

Questions

1. Has option 4 been ranked above the others because:
   (a) it has the most ticks
   (b) it has the least crosses
   (c) a combination of these
   (d) other reasons?
   Justify your answer.
2. List the main strengths and limitations of ranking analysis.

Source Based on the *Troubleshooter* series, BBC, 1990, 1993.

	Key Strategic Factors						
Strategic Options	Family Ownership	Investment Funds	Low Price Imports	Lack of Marketing/ Design Skills	Automation Low	Consumer Taste (Design)	Ranking
1. Do nothing	✓	?	✗	?	✗	✗	C
2. Consolidate in current segments (investment/ automation)	✓	✗	✓	?	✓	?	B
3. Expand overseas sales (Europe)	✗	✗	✗	✗	✗	?	C
4. Launch 'up-market' range	✓	✓	✓	✗	?	✓	A
5. Expand 'own-label' production (to hotel/catering industry	✓	✓	✓	?	✗	?	B
6. Open retail outlets	✗	✗	?	✗	?	?	C
7. Diversify	✗	✗	?	?	?	✓	C

✓ = favourable; ✗ = unfavourable; ? = uncertain or irrelevant.
A = most suitable; B = possible; C = unsuitable.

STRATEGY IN ACTION
Illustration 8.4

A Strategic Decision Tree for a Law Firm

Decision trees evaluate future options by progressively eliminating others as additional criteria are introduced to the evaluation.

A law firm had most of its work related to house conveyancing where profits had been significantly squeezed. Therefore, it wanted to consider a range of new strategies for the future. Using a strategic decision tree it was able to eliminate certain options by identifying a few key criteria which future developments would incorporate, such as growth, investment (in premises, IT systems or acquisitions), and diversification (for example, into matrimonial law which, in turn, often brings house conveyancing work as families 'reshape').

Analysis of the decision tree reveals that if the partners of the firm wish growth to be an important aspect of future strategies, options 1–4 are ranked more highly than options 5–8. At the second step, the need for low investment strategies would rank options 3 and 4 above 1 and 2, and so on.

The partners were aware that this technique has limitations in that the choice at each branch of the tree can tend to be simplistic. Answering 'yes' or 'no' to diversification does not allow for the wide variety of alternatives which might exist between these two extremes, for example *adapting the 'style' of its conveyancing service* (this could be an important variant of options 6 or 8). Nevertheless, as a starting point for evaluation, the decision tree provides a useful framework.

Questions

1. Try reversing the sequence of the three parameters (to diversification, investment and growth) and redraw the decision tree. Do the same eight options still emerge?
2. Add a fourth parameter to the decision tree. This new parameter is development by *internal methods* or by *acquisition*. List your sixteen options in the right-hand column.

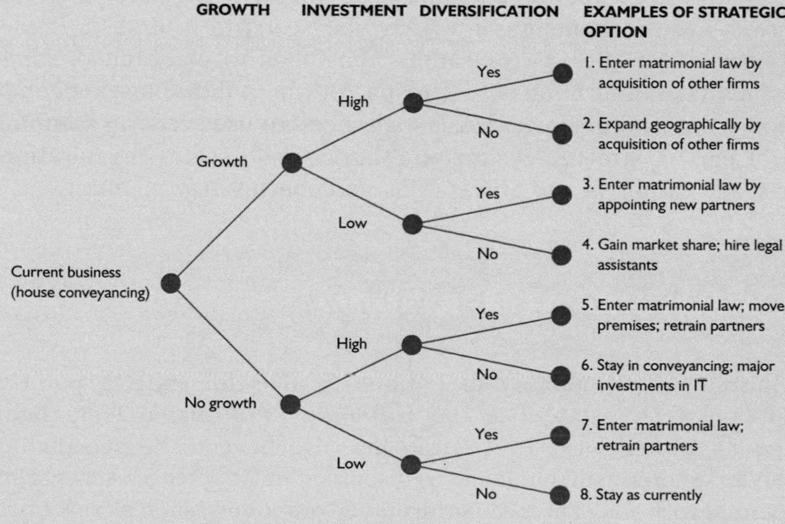

Decision trees combine the identification of options with a simultaneous ranking of those options.

Perhaps the greatest limitation of decision tree analysis is that the choice at each branch on the tree can tend to be simplistic. For example, answering 'yes' or 'no' to diversification does not allow for the wide variety of options which might exist between these two extremes (see Chapter 7). Nevertheless, as a starting point for evaluation, decision trees can often provide a useful framework.

Scenario Planning[8]

Ranking evaluates options against a specific list of items or criteria derived from a strategic analysis; decision trees achieve the same outcome by eliminating options through progressively introducing additional criteria to be satisfied. A third approach to screening is that of *scenario planning*, which was explained in Chapter 3 (see Illustration 3.3) as an important tool for assessing an organisation's environment in conditions of high uncertainty. Strategic options can be screened by matching them to the possible future scenarios.

The outcome of this process is likely to be not a single prioritised list of options (as with ranking and decision trees), but a series of *contingency plans* which identify the preferred option for each possible future scenario. For example, a company planning international expansion may be uncertain about a number of key economic factors, such as exchange rates or tariff barriers. One scenario might be relatively stable exchange rates and reducing tariff barriers. In these circumstances, the company might choose to develop by manufacturing in the UK and exporting. In contrast, a scenario of a strengthening pound and increasing barriers would make a strategy of overseas-based manufacture more favourable.

Equally important is the organisation's ability to monitor the onset (or otherwise) of the elements of a particular scenario in time to implement appropriate strategies. Organisations that need to make major long-term investments in innovation (e.g. aerospace), where future market conditions are uncertain and financial risk is high, need to use scenario planning as a central part of strategy evaluation. Many public sector organisations too have made extensive use of scenarios and contingency planning.

8.3 ANALYSING ACCEPTABILITY

acceptability *is concerned with the expected performance outcomes, such as risk or return, if a strategy is implemented*

Establishing the suitability of options is a useful starting point to an evaluation as it establishes the *rationale* or *strategic logic* behind a particular strategy. However, strategies also have to be acceptable to a variety of different stakeholders, as discussed in Chapter 5. **Acceptability** is concerned with the expected performance outcomes, such as risk or return, if a strategy is implemented.

Exhibit 8.7 **Assessing the acceptability of strategies**

APPROACH	USED TO ASSESS	EXAMPLES	LIMITATIONS
Analysing return			
Profitability analyses	Financial return of investments	Return on capital Payback period Discounted cash flow (DCF)	Apply to discrete projects Only tangible costs/benefits
Cost–benefit analysis	Wider costs/benefits (including intangibles)	Major infrastructure projects	Difficulties of quantification
Shareholder value analysis (SVA)	Impact of new strategies on shareholder value	Mergers/takeovers	Technical detail often difficult
Analysing risk			
Financial ratio projections	Robustness of strategy	Break-even analysis Impact on gearing and liquidity	
Sensitivity analysis	Test assumptions/robustness	'What if?' analysis	Tests factors separately
Simulation modelling	Aggregate impact on many factors	Comprehensive models Risk analysis	Quality of data on causal relationships
Stakeholder reactions	Political dimension of strategy	Stakeholder mapping Game theory	Largely qualitative

The acceptability of strategies can be assessed in three broad ways: *return*, *risk* and *stakeholder reactions*. Exhibit 8.7 summarises some of the approaches to assessing acceptability together with some of the limitations of particular analytical techniques. The general advice is to use more than one approach or technique in building up a picture of the acceptability of a particular strategy.

8.3.1 Analysing Return

An assessment of the returns likely to accrue from specific options is a key measure of the acceptability of an option. However, there are a number of different approaches to the analysis of return. This section looks briefly at three different assessments.

Profitability Analyses[9]

Traditional financial analyses have been used extensively in the evaluation of the acceptability of strategies. Three of the more commonly used approaches are as follows (see Exhibit 8.8):

- Forecasting the *return on capital employed* (ROCE) a specific time after a new strategy is implemented (e.g. the new strategy will result in a return on capital of 15 per cent by year 3). This is shown in Exhibit 8.8(a).
- *Payback period* has been used where a significant capital injection is needed to support a new venture. In Exhibit 8.8(b), the payback period is calculated by finding the time at which the cumulative net cash flow becomes zero – in the example, three and a half years.

  The judgement is then whether this is regarded as an adequate outcome and if the organisation is prepared to wait that long for a return. This will vary from one industry to another. Major public sector ventures such as bridge building may well be assessed on a payback period of up to 60 years.
- *Discounted cash flow* (DCF) analysis is perhaps the most widely used investment appraisal technique, and is essentially an extension of the payback period analysis. Once the net cash flows have been assessed for each of the years (see Exhibit 8.8(c)), they are discounted progressively to reflect the fact that funds generated early are of more real value than those in later periods (years). In the example, the discounting rate of 10 per cent reflects the value placed on money tied up in the venture. So the projected net cash flow of £2m in year 2 is discounted to £1.82m and so on. The net present value (NPV) of the venture is then calculated by adding all the discounted annual cash flows (after taxation) over the anticipated life of the project. DCF analysis is particularly useful for comparing the financial merits of strategies which have very different patterns of expenditure and return.

Exhibit 8.8 Some measures of profitability for strategy evaluation

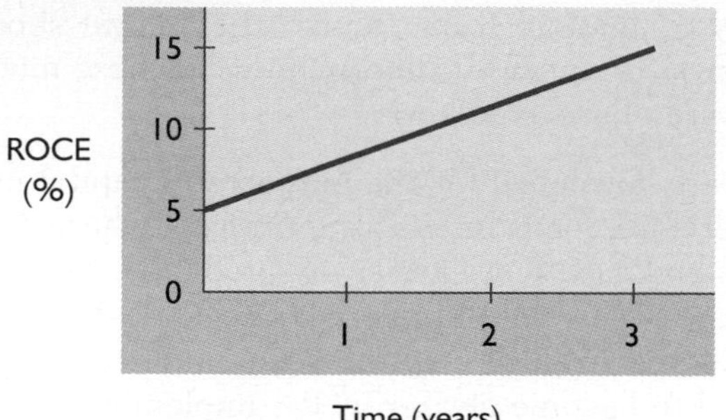

(a) Return on capital employed

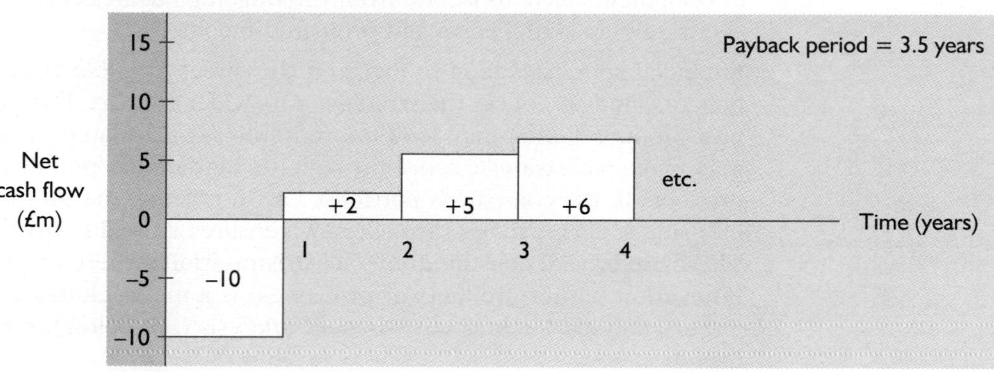

(b) Payback period

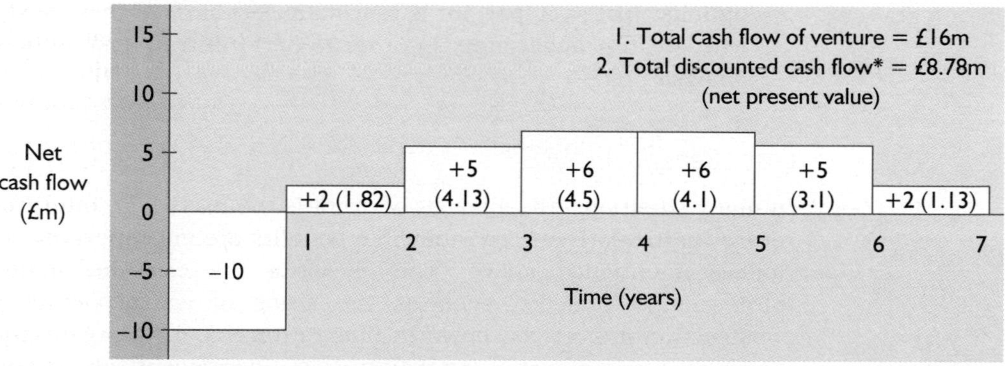

(c) Discounted cash flow (DCF)

* Using a discounting rate of 10%.
Figures in brackets are discounted by 10% annually.

Although the evaluation of strategies may be assisted by the use of one or more of these financial techniques, it is important to recognise some of the implicit assumptions which inevitably limit their use as comprehensive techniques of strategy evaluation. In particular, the analyst should not be misguided by the tidiness or apparent thoroughness of these methods. The major issues to be aware of are as follows:

- These methods were developed for the purposes of capital investment appraisal and, therefore, focus on discrete *projects* where the incremental costs and cash flows are easily predicted. Neither of these assumptions is necessarily valid in many strategic developments. The precise way in which a strategy might develop, and the costs and income flows, tend to become clearer as the implementation proceeds rather than at the outset. Also, there are often significant time lags between *revenue* expenditures and income benefits. Nor are strategic developments easy to isolate from the ongoing business activities in accurately assessing costs and projected income.
- Financial appraisals tend to focus on the direct *tangible* costs and benefits, and do not set the strategy in its wider context. For example, a new product launch may look unprofitable as an isolated project, but may make real strategic sense through the market acceptability of other products in the company's portfolio. Or, in reverse, the intangible cost of losing *strategic focus* through new ventures is readily overlooked. These are crucial considerations for organisations where investment in innovation (either products or processes) is a major element of cost. Other analyses, such as cost–benefit analysis (see below), may be useful.
- Overall, it is advisable to use a number of financial techniques in order to build up a picture of the financial attractiveness of various strategic options. Just as important is that managers surface those assumptions with greatest uncertainty in order to perform truly testing sensitivity analysis.

Cost–Benefit Analysis[10]

In many situations, the analysis of profit is too narrow an interpretation of return, particularly where intangible benefits are an important consideration as mentioned above. This is often the case for major public infrastructure projects, such as the siting of an airport or a sewer construction project, as shown in Illustration 8.5, or in organisations with long-term programmes of innovation (e.g. pharmaceuticals or aerospace). *Cost–benefit analysis* attempts to put a money value on all the costs and benefits of a strategic option, including tangible and intangible returns to people and organisations other than the one 'sponsoring' the project or strategy.

Although monetary valuation is often difficult, it can be done, and, despite difficulties, cost–benefit analysis is an approach which is valuable if

STRATEGY IN ACTION
Illustration 8.5

Sewerage Construction Project

Investment in items of infrastructure – such as sewers – often requires a careful consideration of the wider costs and benefits of the project.

In the early 1990s, Britain's recently privatised water companies were monopolies supplying water and disposing of sewage. They needed to invest in new sewerage systems to meet the increasing standards required by law. They often used cost–benefit analysis to assess projects. The figures below are from an actual analysis carried out in 1991.

Benefits

Benefits result mainly from reduced use of rivers as overflow sewers. There are also economic benefits resulting from construction. The following benefits are quantified in the table:

- The multiplier benefit to the local economy of increased spending by those employed on the project.
- The linkage benefit to the local economy of purchases from local firms, including the multiplier effect of such spending.
- Reduced risk of flooding from overflows or old sewers collapsing – flood probabilities can be quantified using historical records, and the cost of flood damage by detailed assessment of the property vulnerable to damage.
- Reduced traffic disruption from flooding and road closures for repairs to old sewers – statistics on the costs of delays to users, traffic flows on roads affected and past closure frequency can be used to quantify savings.
- Increased amenity value of rivers (e.g. for boating and fishing) can be measured by surveys asking visitors what the value is to them or by looking at the effect on demand of charges imposed elsewhere.
- Increased rental values and take-up of space can be measured by consultation with developers and observed effects elsewhere.

COST/BENEFIT	£m	£m
Benefits		
Multiplier/linkage benefits		0.9
Flood prevention		2.5
Reduced traffic disruption		7.2
Amenity benefits		4.6
Investment benefit		23.6
Encouragement of visitors		4.0
Total benefits		42.8
Costs		
Construction cost	18.2	
Less: Unskilled labour cost	(4.7)	
Opportunity cost of construction		(13.5)
Present value of net benefits (NPV)		29.3
Real internal rate of return (IRR)		15%

Note: Figures discounted at a *real* discount rate of 5% over 40 years.

- Increased visitor numbers to riverside facilities resulting from reduced pollution.

Construction Cost

This is net of the cost of unskilled labour. Use of unskilled labour is not a burden on the economy, and its cost must be deducted to arrive at opportunity cost.

Net Benefits

Once the difficult task of quantifying costs and benefits is complete, standard discounting techniques can be used to calculate net present value and internal rate of return, and analysis can then proceed as for conventional projects.

Questions

1. What do you feel about the appropriateness of the listed benefits?
2. How easy or difficult is it to assign money values to these benefits?

Source G. Owen, Policy Research Centre, Sheffield Business School.

its limitations are understood. Its major benefit is in forcing people to be explicit about the various factors which should influence strategic choice. So, even if people disagree on the value which should be assigned to particular costs or benefits, at least they are able to argue their case on common ground and decision-makers can compare the merits of the various arguments.

Shareholder Value Analysis[11]

During the 1980s, attempts were made to address many of the limitations and criticisms of traditional financial analyses. At the same time, renewed attention was paid to the primary legal responsibility of company directors: namely, the creation of value and benefits for the shareholders. The takeover boom of the 1980s caused both corporate raiders and victims alike to look at how corporate development strategies were, or were not, generating shareholder value.

Together, these factors spawned *shareholder value analysis* (SVA). Applying this within the strategic management process requires a new mindset which is called *value management*:

- It emphasises that discounted cash flow analysis should concentrate on evaluating strategies at the strategic business unit level and not just separate investment projects. Because of complex interdependencies, it may not be sensible to evaluate a project separately using incremental cash flow analysis. For example, BP's 'Project 1990' for culture change was inseparable from many other strategic initiatives and it was not feasible to evaluate the project financially in isolation.
- The financial analysis must be driven by an understanding of the value creation process and the competitive advantage which the organisation derives from this process. In particular, it is critical to identify the key cash generators of the business, which are called the *value drivers*. One very important *external* value driver is competitive rivalry, which has a direct impact on margins. Ultimately, the net present value (NPV) of a strategy or strategic decision is likely to be critically dependent on a relatively small number of these factors. Value management's big contribution is to emphasise how important managing value drivers is to making strategic decisions, and in implementation and control.
- Value management involves a mastery of a complex system of value drivers (the value system) with many interdependencies. For example, quality of service in a supermarket may allow price premiums to be maintained. But this service level is dependent on and sustained by a number of other factors and investments – for example, staff training and checkout systems. This is needed right down to the level of having supermarket trolleys which run straight.
- Increasing customer value does not necessarily mean that value (to the company) is added. Increased quality of service may simply *protect*

> existing cash flow streams and avoid loss in value to the company. However, superior value to the customer may result in higher margins or capturing market share ('value capture'). So managers need to make many judgements on how value may be created, protected or exploited. Value management thus requires genuine and complex assessment of the competitive environment, operational options and their financial impact.

Although SVA has done much to address the shortcomings of traditional financial analyses, it does not remove many of the inherent uncertainties surrounding strategy evaluation. The exponents of SVA have been criticised for being heavily prescriptive in selling the virtues of SVA without necessarily highlighting the required changes in decision making, control systems and implementation. Nevertheless, the idea of valuing a strategy may serve to give greater realism and clarity to otherwise vague strategies, as shown in Illustration 8.6.

8.3.2 Analysing Risk

The likely return from a particular strategy is an important measure of the acceptability of that strategy. However, another measure of acceptability is the *risk* which the organisation faces in pursuing a particular strategy. This risk can be particularly high for organisations with major long-term programmes of innovation or where high levels of uncertainty exist about key issues in the environment. This section outlines some ways in which this risk can be assessed as part of an evaluation of specific options.

Financial Ratio Projections[12]

The projection of how key financial ratios would change if a specific option were adopted can provide useful insights into risk. At the broadest level, an assessment of how the *capital structure* of the company would change is a good general measure of risk. For example, options which would require the extension of long-term loans will increase the gearing of the company and increase its financial risk. The level of financial risk created by funding a proposed strategy from long-term loans can be tested out by examining the likelihood of the company reaching the *break-even point*, and the consequences of falling short of that volume of business while interest on loans continues to be paid.

At a more detailed level, a consideration of the likely impact on an organisation's *liquidity* is important in evaluating options. For example, a small retailer eager to grow quickly may be tempted to fund the required shopfitting costs by delaying payments to suppliers and increasing bank overdraft. This reduced liquidity increases the financial risk of the business. The extent to which this increased risk threatens survival depends on the likelihood of either creditors or the bank demanding payments from the company – an issue which clearly requires judgement.

STRATEGY IN ACTION
Illustration 8.6

Strategy Evaluation at BP and Rolls-Royce

Companies need to find a use for financial analysis which reflects their specific circumstances and provides information to managers when choosing new strategies.

Shareholder Value at British Petroleum (BP)

Between 1986 and 1991, the BP Group shifted its corporate decision-making processes towards *value-based management* with the aim of enhancing BP's shareholder value. This change occurred because BP top management were dissatisfied with measuring performance through return on capital employed (ROCE), which was based on financial accounting measures and was backward-looking. BP looked to value-based management to:

- Align all of its financial decision-making processes with its corporate financial objective of creating value for its shareholders.
- Give management a top-down check on where BP was adding to shareholder value and also where it might be dissipating value among its business portfolio.
- Enable managers within the businesses to evaluate strategies in detail using economic bases of appraisal (looking at SBUs as projects or bundles of projects).
- Set business performance targets and indicators in a way consistent with these strategies.

Over the five-year period, many major benefits had been secured. However, the process of implementation and of learning was still continuing. An important factor was that from the start the process had the firm commitment of top BP management, who refused to allow any sacred cows to dilute the changes needed.

Strategic Project Appraisal at Rolls-Royce Aeroengines

As a major player in a high-technology international market, Rolls-Royce Aeroengines had invested substantial sums in product development. Typically, it would take many years to recoup the value of these investments. Rapid growth in the past had resulted from airline deregulation, economic growth and changes in consumers' leisure patterns. However, this growth proved vulnerable to a variety of factors: for instance, recession, overcapacity of the airline industry and cutbacks in defence spending. In addition, aerospace companies competed fiercely to win orders for major new projects to ensure that (a) the requirement of a single major customer could be met, (b) there would be some winners so that manufacturing capacity would be well utilised, and (c) synergies were gained in development spend where possible.

The evaluation of individual projects was thus clouded by external uncertainty and by interdependency within the product range. Financial measures of project value were therefore seen as indicative rather than precise and definitive.

Rolls-Royce had also experimented with mapping the value-creating profiles of all its major projects in order to explore the interdependency effects and key vulnerables.

Questions

1. Are the analytical challenges described in the illustration confined to these kinds of businesses?
2. Are these the only ways of mitigating risk and improving return to shareholders?

Source Research undertaken by Tony Grundy, Cranfield School of Management. Reproduced with permission. Also published in A.N. Grundy, *Corporate Strategy and Financial Decisions*, Kogan Page, 1992.

Sensitivity Analysis[13]

Sensitivity analysis is a useful technique for incorporating the assessment of risk during strategy evaluation. It is sometimes referred to as *what if?* analysis. Its use grew with the availability of computer spreadsheet packages, which are ideally suited to this type of analysis.

The technique allows each of the important assumptions underlying a particular strategy to be questioned and changed. In particular, it seeks to test how sensitive the predicted performance or outcome (e.g. profit) is to each of these assumptions. For example, the key assumptions underlying a strategy might be that market demand will grow by 5 per cent p.a., or that the company will stay strike-free, or that certain expensive machines will operate at 90 per cent loading. Sensitivity analysis asks: what would be the effect on performance (in this case, profitability) if, for example, market demand grew at only 1 per cent, or by as much as 10 per cent? Would either of these extremes alter the decision to pursue that particular strategy? A similar process might be repeated for the other key assumptions. This process helps management develop a clearer picture of the risks of making particular strategic decisions and the degree of confidence it might have in a given decision. In turn this helps determine the way in which resourcing should be planned and controlled for the key elements of strategy. For example, the management of the funding of major programmes of innovation should be influenced by the outcomes of sensitivity analysis. (Illustration 8.7 shows how sensitivity analysis can be used in strategy evaluation.)

Simulation Modelling

Strategic simulation models attempt to encompass all the factors considered by the separate analyses discussed in this chapter into one quantitative simulation model of the company and its environment. It should be no surprise that such global models have been virtually impossible to build. Nevertheless, the principle of *simulation modelling*[14] is a useful one in strategy evaluation, in those aspects which lend themselves to this quantitative view.

Financial models are often used to assess strategic options. *Risk analysis*[15] is a technique which seeks to assess the overall degree of uncertainty in a particular option by mathematically combining the uncertainties in each of the elements of the option. For example, the likelihood of a particular profit projection is governed by the uncertainties surrounding costs, prices and volume forecasts.

One of the limitations on the use of strategic modelling is the need for large amounts of high-quality data concerning the relationship between environmental factors and company performance. In this respect, the work of the Strategic Planning Institute (SPI) using the Profit Impact of Market Strategy (PIMS) database[16] has been interesting (see Chapter 7). Research at SPI has tried to build a number of quantitative causal models

STRATEGY IN ACTION
Illustration 8.7

Sensitivity Analysis

Sensitivity analysis is a useful technique for assessing the extent to which the success of a preferred strategy is dependent on the key assumptions which underlie that strategy.

In 1997 the Dunsmore Chemical Company was a single-product company trading in a mature and relatively stable market. It was intended to use this established situation as a cash cow to generate funds for a new venture with a related product. Estimates had shown that the company would need to generate some £4m cash (at 1997 values) between 1998 and 2003 for this new venture to be possible.

Although the expected performance of the company was for a cash flow of £9.5m over that period (the *base case*), management was concerned to assess the likely impact of three key factors:

- Possible increases in *production costs* (labour, overheads and materials), which might be as much as 3 per cent p.a. in real terms.
- *Capacity fill*, which might be reduced by as much as 25 per cent owing to ageing plant and uncertain labour relations.
- *Price levels*, which might be affected by the threatened entry of a new major competitor. This could squeeze prices by as much as 3 per cent p.a. in real terms.

It was decided to use sensitivity analysis to assess the possible impact of each of these factors on the company's ability to generate £4m. The results are shown in the graphs.

From this analysis, the management concluded that its target of £4m would be achieved with *capacity utilisation* as low as 60 per cent, which was certainly going to be achieved. Increased *production costs* of 3 per cent p.a. would still allow the company to achieve the £4m target over the period. In contrast, *price* squeezes of 3 per cent p.a. would result in a shortfall of £2m.

The management concluded from this analysis that the key factor which should affect their thinking on this matter was the likely impact of new competition and the extent to which they could protect price

(using multiple regression) which explain how companies' performance has been influenced by up to two dozen different factors – such as those seen in business profiling, discussed in section 8.2.1 above and in Illustration 8.2.

In general, the use of modelling in strategy evaluation is limited to well structured problems. Particular care needs to be taken for the following reasons:

- There is a danger that the model will become a gross oversimplification of reality, and fail to encompass the most important uncertainties and risks.

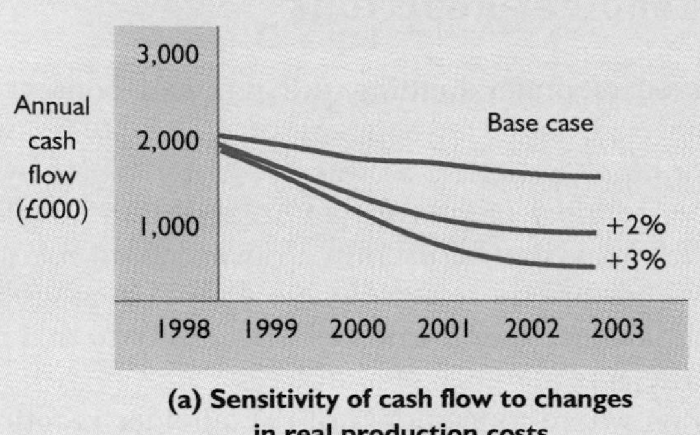

(a) Sensitivity of cash flow to changes in real production costs

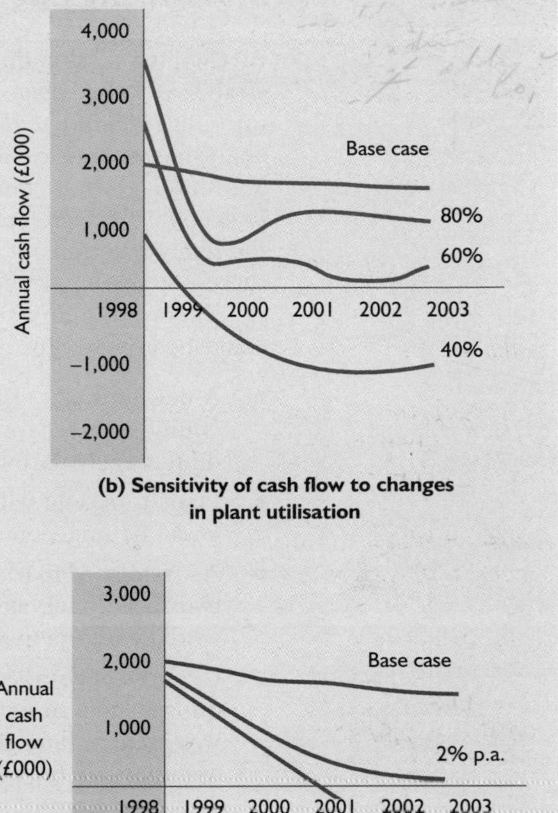

(b) Sensitivity of cash flow to changes in plant utilisation

levels if such competition emerged. They therefore developed an aggressive marketing strategy to deter potential entrants.

Question

What should the company do if its marketing campaigns fail to stop real price erosion

(a) Push to achieve more sales volume/capacity fill?
(b) Reduce unit costs of production?
(c) Something else?

Source The calculations for the sensitivity test utilise computer programs employed in the Doman case study by P.H. Jones (Sheffield Business School).

Annual cash flow (£000)
3,000
2,000
1,000
−1,000
Base case
2% p.a.
3% p.a.
1998 1999 2000 2001 2002 2003

(c) Sensitivity of cash flow to reductions in real price

- Attempts to incorporate a very large number of variables make the model highly complex, and all the critical interrelationships need to be included, which is in practice very difficult, if not impossible.
- Some key data, such as competitor reactions, are difficult to assess or incorporate into the model. The overriding danger with models of all types is that they can result in less insight for managers or decision-makers than much simpler techniques (such as sensitivity analysis), as they hide the analysis away in a 'black box' which managers do not feel they can open. The model-builders create a level of detail which starts to conceal the important strategic questions and issues.

8.3.3 Analysing Stakeholder Reactions

In Chapter 5, the importance of understanding the political context of strategic change was emphasised, and the concept of *stakeholders* was introduced. *Stakeholder mapping* (Exhibit 5.5) was presented as a way of analysing and prioritising the 'political agenda' for an organisation. Readers are reminded that stakeholder maps can be usefully drawn only in relation to specific strategic options. They are therefore a valuable tool in assessing the likely reactions of stakeholders to new strategies, the ability to manage these reactions, and hence the acceptability of a strategy.

There are many situations where judgements of stakeholder reactions could be crucial. For example:

- A new strategy might require a substantial issue of *new shares*, which could be unacceptable to powerful groups of shareholders, since it dilutes their voting power.
- Plans to *merge* with other companies or to *trade* with new countries could be unacceptable to unions, government or some customers.
- A strategy of market development might require the cutting out of *channels* (such as wholesalers), hence running the risk of a backlash which could jeopardise the success of the strategy.
- **Changes in competitive strategy in static markets might upset the status quo to such an extent that competitors will be forced to retaliate in a way that is damaging to all parties, but which would undermine the assumptions on which the strategy's acceptability had been assessed. The most common example of this would be a price war.**

Stakeholder mapping is a useful technique for encouraging managers to predict both the degree of interest that stakeholders are likely to exhibit for or against a strategy, and whether they have the power to help or hinder the adoption of that strategy.

Since an important issue may be the likely reactions of competitors to particular strategic changes, *game theory*[17] should, in principle, have some use as an evaluation technique. This is an approach to decision analysis which assumes that competitors are likely to react to any moves which the company makes (or that the company will need to react to their moves). The technique lays out and quantifies the costs and benefits of the various combinations of the company moves and competitor reactions. For example, a product modification option has four possible outcomes or combinations, ranging from neither the company nor the competitor modifying the product to *both* companies modifying the product. This helps in comparing these various strategies or courses of action. However, the difficulties of coping with the complexity of the strategic situation have limited the use of game theory to largely qualitative applications. The biggest difficulty lies in the assumption that the strategic competitive behaviour of companies can be predicted and categorised into a small number of clearly defined categories – this is rarely true in practice.

8.4 ANALYSING FEASIBILITY

Feasibility is concerned with whether an organisation has the resources and competences to deliver a strategy. A number of analytical approaches can be used to assess feasibility.

feasibility *is concerned with whether an organisation has the resources and competences to deliver a strategy*

8.4.1 Funds Flow Analysis[18]

The assessment of financial feasibility should normally be an important part of any strategy evaluation. A valuable piece of analysis is a *funds flow forecast*, which seeks to identify the funds which would be required for any strategy and the likely sources of those funds, as shown in Illustration 8.8.

It should be remembered that funds flow analysis is a forecasting technique, and is subject to the difficulties and errors of any method of forecasting. Such an analysis should quickly highlight whether the proposed strategy is likely to be feasible in financial terms, and it could normally be programmed onto a computer spreadsheet should the model be repeatedly required during evaluation. This would also assist in identifying the *timing* of new funding requirements.

8.4.2 Break-even Analysis[19]

Break-even analysis is a simple and widely used technique which is helpful in exploring some key aspects of feasibility. It can be used to assess the feasibility of meeting targets of return (e.g. profit) and, as such, combines a parallel assessment of acceptability. As shown in Illustration 8.9, it also provides an assessment of the risk of various strategies, particularly where different strategic options require markedly different cost structures.

8.4.3 Resource Deployment Analysis[20]

The previous two methods have concentrated on the assessment of feasibility in *financial* terms. It is often helpful to make a wider assessment of the resources and competences of the organisation in relation to *specific* strategies. This can be done through a *resource deployment analysis*, which is a way of comparing options with each other using the kind of framework already shown in Exhibit 8.4.

The requirements of alternative future strategies should be laid out, indicating the key resources and competences for each strategy. For example, a strategy of geographical expansion in the home market might be critically dependent on marketing and distribution expertise, together with the availability of cash to fund increased stocks. In contrast, a different strategy of developing new products to sell to current customers is

STRATEGY IN ACTION
Illustration 8.8

Funds Flow Analysis: A Worked Example

A funds flow analysis can be used to assess whether a proposed strategy is likely to be feasible in financial terms. It does this by forecasting the funds which would be required for the strategy and the likely sources of those funds.

Kentex plc (a UK electrical goods retailer) was considering pursuing a strategy of expansion which in the immediate future would involve opening new stores in the Irish Republic. To evaluate the financial feasibility of this proposal and establish what funds would be required and how these funds may be sourced, the company decided to undertake a funds flow analysis.

Stage 1: Identification of Sources

Opening of the new stores was estimated to increase the sales revenue from the current £30m to £31.65m per annum over the following three years. This was expected to generate funds from operations totalling £15m over the three years. This was the estimate of future profits corrected for non-fund items such as depreciation and represents real flow of funds into the company for a three-year period.

Stage 2: Identification of Uses

There would be a number of costs associated with the new stores. First, Kentex decided to purchase rather than lease property so there would be the direct costs of the capital investment required for purchasing and fitting out the stores. This was forecast to be £13.25m. Also there will be additional working capital costs to cover stock, etc. This was not calculated by separate consideration of each element, e.g. stock increases, increased creditors; instead the forecasts were based on a simple pro rata adjustment. On the previous sales level of £30m a working capital level of £10m was required, so the expected increase in sales of £1.65m would require an additional £0.55m in working capital. Tax liability and expected dividend payments were estimated at £1.2m and £0.5m respectively.

Stage 3: Identification and Funding of Shortfall

These calculations show a shortfall in funds of £0.5m. The company then finalised the forecast by looking at alternative ways of funding the shortfall. Whilst it could raise funds through the issue of new share capital, it chose to seek a short-term loan of £0.65m. It should be noted that this in turn would incur interest payments of £0.15m over the three-year period assuming simple interest at 7.5% per annum, hence leaving a net income of £0.5m.

Questions

1. Which parts of this assessment are likely to have the greatest probability of error?
2. What are the implications of your answer to question 1 to how the analysis should be presented to the decision-makers?
3. How might this uncertainty influence the management of the implementation phase if approval is given?

Prepared by Sara Martin, Cranfield School of Management.

SOURCES	£	USES	£
Funds from operations	15,000,000	New fixed assets	13,250,000
		Working capital	550,000
		Tax	1,200,000
		Dividends	500,000
Subtotal	15,000,000	Subtotal	15,500,000

Note: Shortfall between sources and uses amounting to £500,000.

STRATEGY IN ACTION
Illustration 8.9

Using Break-Even Analysis to Examine Strategic Options

Break-even analysis can be a simple way of quantifying some of the key factors which would determine the success or failure of a strategy.

A manufacturing company was considering the launch of a new consumer durable product into a market where most products were sold to wholesalers which supplied the retail trade. The total market was worth about £4.4m (at manufacturers' prices) – about 630,000 units. The market leader had about 30 per cent market share in a competitive market where retailers were increasing their buying power. The company wished to evaluate the relative merits of a high-price/high-quality product sold to wholesalers (strategy A) or an own-brand product sold directly to retailers (strategy B). The table summarises the market and cost structure for the market leader and these alternative strategies.

The table shows that the company would require about 22 per cent and 13 per cent market share respectively for strategies A and B to break even.

Questions

1. Which option would you choose? Why?
2. What would be the main risks attached to that option and how would you attempt to minimise these risks?
3. Create another option (strategy C) and explain the kind of break-even profile which would be needed to make it more attractive than either strategy A or strategy B.

MARKET AND COST STRUCTURE	MARKET LEADER	STRATEGY A	STRATEGY B
Price to retailer	£10.00	£12.00	£8.00
Price to wholesaler	£7.00	£8.40	—
Total variable costs (TVC)	£3.50	£4.00	£3.10
Contribution to profit per unit sold (= Price sold – TVC)	£3.50	£4.40	£4.90
Fixed costs (FC)	£500,000	£500,000	£500,000
Break-even point: no. of units to sell (= FC/Contribution to profit)	**142,857**	**136,363**	**81,633**
Total market size (units)	630,000	630,000	630,000
Break-even point: market share (= Break-even point units/Mkt size)	**22.6%**	**21.6%**	**13.0%**
Actual market share	30.0%	—	—

Exhibit 8.9 Resource deployment analysis – some important questions

Staying in the business	• Do we lack and necessary resources? • Are we performing below threshold on any activity?
Competing successfully	• Which unique resources already exist? • Which core competences already exist? • Could better performance create a core competence? • What new resources or activities could be unique or core competences?

dependent on engineering skills, the capability of machinery and the company's reputation for quality in new products.

The 'scoring' system described for Exhibit 8.4 can be used to compare various strategic options against the current resources and competences of the organisation in order to judge two things: first, the extent to which the current resources and competences would need to change to reach or maintain the threshold requirements for each strategy, and second, the unique resources and core competences required to sustain competitive advantage. These two aspects can be assessed by addressing the questions in Exhibit 8.9.

There is a danger that resource deployment analysis will simply result in organisations choosing strategies which most closely fit the configuration of their present resources and competences. It should be remembered that the real benefit of such an analysis is the identification of those necessary changes in resources and competences which are implied by any strategy, and an analysis of whether these changes are *feasible* in terms of scale, quality of resource or timescale of change. Ambitious stretching of resources and competences in innovative ways is the hallmark of a robust competitive strategy as it will be difficult to imitate.

It will be seen in Chapter 10 that this broad process of assessing the resource requirements of specific strategies provides a link to a detailed assessment of the critical factors for success of any strategy and the kind of resource configuration which will be necessary to ensure success. Chapter 11 will look at how a remapping of an organisation's cultural web can be used to assess the need for cultural change and the extent to which such changes are likely to be feasible.

8.5 SELECTION OF STRATEGIES

Chapters 6, 7 and 8 have so far explored, described and provided a critique of the literature, research evidence and managerial 'wisdoms' regarding the

Exhibit 8.10 Processes for selecting strategies

APPROACH	DOMINANT PROCESSES	ELEMENTS OF GOOD PRACTICE	DANGERS
Planning	Analytical techniques Tested against objectives Quantified where possible	Involve line managers Analyse 'holistic' picture Build in flexibility Communication between analysts and decision-makers	No ownership Fragmented analysis Rigidity – lost opportunities Decision-makers disown analysis
Enforced choice	Bend to environmental 'pressure'	Assess risk Prepare contingencies	'Victims of circumstances' Evaluation not done
Learning from experience	Reactive moves in separate parts of organisation Cultural/political context important	Processes need credibility Avenues of challenge Promote inter-unit learning	Fragmented/inefficient Pragmatism Risk of strategic drift
Command	Dominant stakeholder selects strategies	Inform/educate decision-maker Need 'completeness' Challenge the paradigm	Incomplete vision Vision institutionalised

merits of a range of strategic options for organisations. This has been done in terms of the broad bases of an organisation's strategies as well as the more detailed choice of directions and methods of development.

This final section is concerned not so much with *what* those choices are, but with *how* the *process* of strategic choice and *selection* of strategies are and can be undertaken within organisations. This relates back to the discussions of strategic development processes in Chapter 2, which will be used as the framework against which to look at these process issues. This section reviews how strategic choice and selection are likely to occur within different processes of strategic development. The important question is: what role will be played by the types of analytical approach covered in Chapters 6, 7 and 8? Exhibit 8.10 provides a summary of the following discussions.

8.5.1 The Planned Approach: Formal Evaluation

This could be a view of how a 'rational' selection of future strategies should occur. Here the organisation's objectives, quantified where possible, are used as direct yardsticks by which options are assessed (for example, whether strategies are likely to meet target for return on capital or market share). The types of evaluation technique discussed above are therefore central to the decision-making process, and are expected to provide quantified 'answers' regarding the relative merits of different courses of action and to come up with the 'right' strategies. Such an approach might avoid too much of the 'gut feeling' which other approaches can represent.

The view taken throughout this book is that formal planning and evaluation can be valuable tools for strategic managers, but they should not be regarded as an exclusive process through which strategies are selected. So the critical issue for strategic managers is to ensure that the organisation's formal planning and evaluation activities assist whichever is the dominant approach to strategy selection. For example, *sensitivity analysis* (section 8.3.2 above) is a useful technique for allowing decision-makers to understand the risks and uncertainties surrounding specific strategies, but it does not select strategies for those decision-makers. Formal planning and evaluation are useful means of *raising the level of debate* among the decision-makers during the selection process. Strategy workshops or future search conferences[21] can fulfil a similar purpose and allow many more people in the organisation to contribute to the quality of thinking about future strategies.

8.5.2 Enforced Choice

It was stated in Chapter 2 that there are some circumstances where the strategic development of the organisation is largely imposed from outside. This may be because major changes in the environment overshadow other considerations – as with a major technological breakthrough. Imposition may occur because of the dominant influence of an external stakeholder – say, in the case of small companies and their dependency on a few major customers, such as Ford or Marks and Spencer. It may be that a particular set of circumstances – perhaps a crisis – dictates the immediate priorities for strategic choice (e.g. the loss of a customer or a major product failure).

It could be concluded that in these situations the organisation is largely a victim of circumstance, so there is no role for strategy evaluation by managers. However, this is not the conclusion which should be drawn for two reasons. First, a danger of enforced choice is that the risk profile of the organisation becomes too great. Strategy evaluation should reveal this in the ways described earlier in the chapter, and should perhaps lead to a medium/longer-term strategic reorientation with the specific purpose of reducing this risk – for example, through spreading the customer base, repositioning the product, or even withdrawing from some products or markets. Second, techniques of evaluation, such as *scenario planning* (section 8.2.2 above), can be helpful in reminding strategic managers of the need for *contingency plans* if enforced choices are likely to lead to unacceptably poor performance. They help managers prepare for a change in direction.

Exhibit 8.11 Organisational learning in a multinational

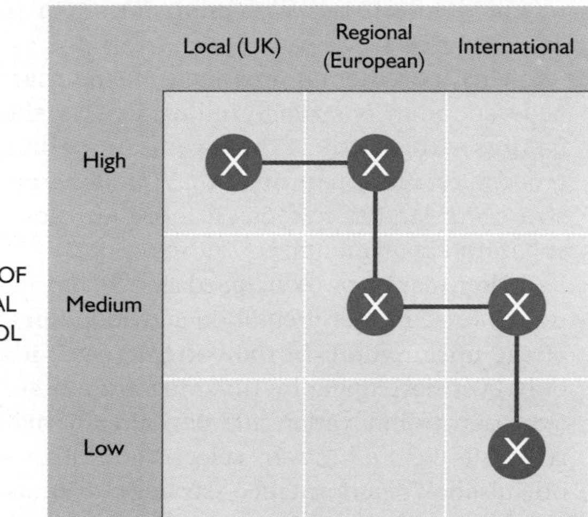

8.5.3 Learning From Experience

An incremental view of strategic development might see strategy evaluation and selection as a fragmented process occurring within the 'operating units' of the organisation as they reactively adapt to a changing environment. It was suggested in Chapter 2 that such a view of an organisation's development has much to commend it, providing the process is 'managed' in the organisation. Otherwise it is likely to lead to inefficiency, to different parts of the organisation pulling in different directions and a lack of a coherent approach to innovation. Together these factors tend to lead to *strategic drift*.

The strategy evaluation and selection processes need to counteract these dangers. For example, it is important to ensure that organisational *learning* occurs between various parts of the organisation and that innovatory processes are working in a way which meets ambitious targets for improvement and change. An example of how this would occur in a large multinational is shown in Exhibit 8.11. New developments are encouraged within local (national) divisions and this is where most evaluation of strategic options occurs and innovative solutions are designed and tested. However, the corporate centre is monitoring these local initiatives for ones which might be potential winners internationally. So the corporate centre's parenting skills must include good market knowledge and the capability to foster and monitor innovation programmes and to disseminate the outcomes. This could then be followed by two or more divisions regionally (e.g. Europe) being encouraged to test the wider acceptability of the innovation or any modifications or variants which might be required for different local circumstances. If this proves successful, the innovation could then be adopted by all European divisions. The same process can then be repeated internationally, culminating in a formal acceptance of a new international strategy.

This incremental approach means that selection of new strategies for wide adoption is strongly influenced by the experiences of successes and failures within parts of the organisation. Illustration 8.10 shows how Asda, a grocery retailer operating in fast-moving markets, changed its approach to strategy selection to focus it more on the experience of those running the separate departments.

There are, of course, dangers in allowing too much freedom for unauthorised experimentation and adoption of new strategies within the parts of the organisation. In the extreme case, it could result in the organisation only ever developing by tinkering around at the edges through a fragmented approach to innovation and never really making fundamental evaluations or reappraisals, and never selecting strategies which would *transform* the organisation's performance (strategic drift, as discussed in Chapter 2).

Therefore, formal planning and evaluation processes can play an important part in organisations which are developing and selecting strategies through these fragmented, incremental processes. They can be an important device to ensure that best practice is communicated through the various parts of the organisation, and that managers are aware of the wider organisational context when making their 'local' decisions. Planning can be about changing minds, not just making plans.[22] This would be close to the stereotype of *logical incrementalism*, discussed in Chapter 2, where managerial intentions guide and steer the fragmented processes of evaluation and selection.

8.5.4 Command

In some organisations, the dominant process for the selection of strategies is *command*, since the decision is taken at the highest level with involvement and advice from inside (and outside) the organisation to varying degrees. The efforts of those involved in formal evaluation are concerned to ensure that selections made through this command process are *well informed*. The discussion in Chapter 2 emphasised that there are many circumstances in which this command process is essential in counterbalancing the risk of strategic drift, which is likely to occur because of the power of the *paradigm* of the organisation. This is particularly evident where command is of the visionary type, providing 'shock' and impetus to the organisation by pursuing transformational strategies – or great leaps forward.

It is important that, if strategies are selected in this way, they have some *completeness* and are workable in practice. For example, it may be helpful for a CEO to declare his or her *intentions* that the organisation

STRATEGY IN ACTION
Illustration 8.10

Asda's Open Plan

In fast-moving businesses, a 'command and control' approach to strategy selection may be too inflexible. There may be a need to focus selection of strategies much more at the business unit (or departmental) level.

In 1991, when Archie Norman became CEO of Asda (the UK grocery retailer), he inherited dwindling customers and mounting debts, and the company looked ready to close its doors. However, by 1996 it had become a much more open business with a management team that claimed to listen to both customers and staff. Performance had been transformed – with the company back in the black and a 30 per cent rise in customers.

The new approach was nurtured by de-layering management to shorten the line between stores and head office, but also by changing the way that departments were organised. For example, each in-store department, such as bakery or fishmongery, had its own profit and loss account. Head office functions were also split into business units (e.g. for meat, drink, clothing), each of which, in turn, was split into smaller categories (e.g. spirits, wines, soft drinks). In each category, the buyers and the head of marketing work with category (product) managers to develop their category business.

The overall aim had been to move away from a 'command and control' (by senior management) approach to what they called an 'inform and involve' culture. This took several forms. There were 'listening groups' on current issues and listening surveys of staff and customer opinion. Instead of the old-style weekly managers' meetings, they had twice-daily 'huddles' between managers and their work teams to plan ahead. There was a 'tell Archie' suggestions scheme which attracted 14,000 ideas in the first 18 months.

The style of senior management combined a high degree of approachability with the readiness to take (informed) decisions. Colleagues were expected to challenge management decisions and to take decisions of their own. Communication had also been improved in many small ways from newsletters to customer compliments, and an ample number of open and inviting meeting rooms.

The working environment was open, with plenty of opportunity for informal meetings, stimulating creativity and sparking off ideas. It was all part of 'getting rid of the treacle' of the old approach.

Questions

1. Use Exhibit 8.10 to critique Archie Norman's new approach to strategic decision-making at Asda.
2. What changes would you make to his approach? Why? (You may also find it useful to refer back to sections 2.3–2.6 in Chapter 2.)

Source *Management Today*, December 1995.

should develop as a centre of excellence (i.e. focused differentiation). But without some detailed substance in terms of specific strategic choices of development directions and methods (as discussed in Chapter 7), the vision and intentions are not a basis on which strategy selection can proceed. A dangerous combination can be powerful visionary stakeholders who are able to dominate the processes of strategic choice, but who are badly informed about the practicalities of making strategies work. This is a situation familiar to many public sector managers in their relationship with politicians, and raises the critically important issue of how the formal evaluation processes ensure good *policy advice* to politicians from their executive advisers (officers or civil servants).

SUMMARY

- Strategies can be assessed against three criteria: suitability, acceptability and feasibility.
- Suitability is a broad assessment of whether a strategy addresses the circumstances in which the organisation is operating. It is often a qualitative assessment of the *rationale* of a strategy. This can be done in a number of ways, several of which should be used to 'test' a strategy. These include life cycle, value chain, portfolio, positioning and business profile analyses.
- Suitability tests can be used to compare the relative merits of various strategies before more detailed analysis. This is a process of *screening* and can involve different techniques such as ranking, decision trees or scenario planning.
- The acceptability of a strategy relates to three issues: the expected *return* from a strategy, the level of *risk* and the likely *reaction of stakeholders*. There are many specific techniques available to assess these three factors.
- Feasibility is concerned with whether an organisation has the resources and competences to deliver a strategy. Again there are several techniques which can assist this evaluation.
- Strategies are selected in different ways, not just through a formal analytical (planned) approach. It is important to understand the role which formal evaluation will play in different processes of selection.
- If new strategies are *enforced* upon an organisation, evaluation still has a place – for example, in assessing the risks of the new strategy and preparing contingencies.
- Organisations that develop incrementally are likely to suffer from strategic drift. Formal evaluation is one way of attempting to minimise this danger whilst acknowledging the preference for incremental or reactive change. It can help to promote learning and communication within the organisation.
- Many strategic choices are ultimately made by one individual or a small group who have the authority to make such decisions. So the role of the 'analysis' is to 'raise the level of debate' amongst decision-makers.

RECOMMENDED KEY READINGS

- A companion book which explores techniques more fully is V. Ambrosini with G. Johnson and K. Scholes (eds), *Exploring Techniques of Analysis and Evaluation in Strategic Management*, Prentice Hall, 1998. See, for example, the chapters on SWOT analyses by T. Jacobs, J. Shepherd and G. Johnson, and gap analysis by J. Billsberry.
- Useful texts on financial analyses for both strategic analysis and strategy evaluation are: A.N. Grundy with G. Johnson and K. Scholes, *Exploring Strategic Financial Management*, Prentice Hall, 1998; J. Ellis and D. Williams, *Corporate Strategy and Financial Analysis*, Pitman, 1993; and A.N. Grundy, *Corporate Strategy and Financial Decisions*, Kogan Page, 1992.

REFERENCES

1. For a companion book which explores techniques more fully see V. Ambrosini with G. Johnson and K. Scholes (eds), *Exploring Techniques of Analysis and Evaluation in Strategic Management*, Prentice Hall, 1998.
2. The techniques built around the life cycle concept have been developed and explained by the consultants Arthur D. Little in a series of booklets, the first of which was R. Wright, *A System of Managing Diversity*, 1974. Life cycle analyses are also covered in A. Hax and N. Majluf, *Strategic Management: An integrative approach*, Prentice Hall, 1984. Some of the limitations of this and other portfolio analyses are discussed by Faulkner (see reference 4 below).
3. See A. Campbell and K. Luchs, *Strategic Synergy*, Butterworth/Heinemann, 1992.
4. Portfolio analyses are discussed in a number of books. See, for example, D. Faulkner's chapter on portfolio matrices, in Ambrosini with Johnson and Scholes (see reference 1); A. Hax and N. Majluf, in R. Dyson (ed.), *Strategic Planning: Models and analytical techniques*, Wiley, 1990; C. Bowman and D. Asch, *Managing Strategy*, Macmillan, 1996, chapter 8.
5. This example is taken from T. Clayton, *An Introduction to Benchmarking*, PIMS Europe Ltd, 1996.
6. See Billsberry's chapter in V. Ambrosini with G. Johnson and K. Scholes (eds), see reference 1.
7. Decision trees are discussed in many books on management science and operational research. See, for example, W. Stevenson, *Introduction to Management Science*, 2nd edition, Irwin, 1992, chapter 10; S. French, *Readings in Decision Analysis*, Chapman and Hall, 1989.
8. The use of scenarios by Shell is described in G. Ringland, *Scenario Planning*, Wiley, 1998.
9. Useful texts on financial analyses for both strategic analysis and strategy evaluation are: A.N. Grundy with G. Johnson and K. Scholes, *Exploring Strategic Financial Management*, Prentice Hall (1998); J. Ellis and D. Williams, *Corporate Strategy and Financial Analysis*, Pitman, 1993; and A.N. Grundy, *Corporate Strategy and Financial Decisions*, Kogan Page, 1992. R. Butler, L. Davies, R. Pike and J. Sharp, *Strategic Investment Decisions*, Routledge, 1993, looks at several financial aspects of strategy development.
10. Cost–benefit analysis is discussed in A. Williams and E. Giardina, *Efficiency in the Public Sector: The theory and practice of cost–benefit analysis*, Edward Elgar, 1993. (Despite the title, the book covers the private sector too.) See also G. Owen's chapter, 'Cost/benefit analysis' in V. Ambrosini with G. Johnson and K. Scholes (see reference 1).
11. The main proponent of shareholder value analysis was A. Rappaport, *Creating Shareholder Value: The new standard for business performance*, Free Press, 1986. See also J. Kay, *Foundations of Corporate Success*, Oxford University Press, 1993, chapter 13, and A. Grundy, *Breakthrough Strategies via Growth*, Pitman, 1995. See also R. Mill's chapter, 'Understanding and using shareholder value analysis', in V. Ambrosini with G. Johnson and K. Scholes (see reference 1). An interesting article is H. Kay, 'More power to the shareholders', *Management Today*, May 1991.
12. See Ellis and Williams (reference 9 above), part III.
13. B. Taylor and J.R. Sparkes, *Corporate Strategy and Planning*, Heinemann, 1977, discusses the use of sensitivity analysis. Computer spreadsheet packages are ideally suited for simple sensitivity analysis. Ellis and Williams (reference 9 above) give an example on pp. 348–9 in relation to share price.
14. T.H. Naylor, 'A conceptual framework for corporate modeling', *Operational Research Quarterly*, vol. 27, no. 3 (1976), pp. 671–82; reprinted in Dyson (reference 4 above).
15. See D. Hertz, 'Risk analysis in capital investment', *Harvard Business Review*, vol. 57, no. 5 (1979), p. 169; reprinted in Dyson (reference 4 above).

16. The PIMS database is discussed more fully in Chapter 7. Their approach is explained in R.D. Buzzell and B.T. Gale, *The PIMS Principles*, Free Press, 1987.
17. G. Saloner, 'Modeling, game theory and strategic management', *Strategic Management Journal*, vol. 12 (Winter 1991), pp. 119–36, discusses the uses and limitations of game theory in strategic evaluation. See also A. Brandenburger and B. Nalebuff, 'The right game: use game theory to shape strategy', *Harvard Business Review*, vol. 73, no. 4 (1995), pp. 57–71.
18. See Ellis and Williams (reference 9 above), pp. 188–93, for a discussion of the funding of strategies.
19. Break-even analysis is covered in most standard accountancy texts. See, for example, M. Broadbent and J. Cullen, *Managing Financial Resources*, Butterworth/Heinemann, 1993, chapter 7.
20. This relates to the idea of 'resource-based strategies' discussed in Chapter 4. Useful references are B. Wernerfelt, 'A resource-based view of the firm', *Strategic Management Journal*, vol. 5, no. 2 (1984), pp. 171–80, and D. Collis and C. Montgomery, 'Competing on resources: strategy in the 1990s', *Harvard Business Review*, vol. 73, no. 4 (1995), pp. 118–28.
21. Future search conferences are discussed by M. Weisbord, *Productive Workplaces*, Jossey-Bass, 1987, p. 285.
22. A. De Geus, 'Planning as learning', *Harvard Business Review*, vol. 66, no. 2 (1988), pp. 70–4.

WORK ASSIGNMENTS

8.1 Referring to Exhibit 8.2, explain how any of the broad approaches to assessing suitability might assist in establishing the rationale for particular strategies in the case of PSA Peugeot Citroën* or an organisation of your choice.

8.2 Explain how the life cycle/portfolio matrix (Exhibit 8.3) might assist an organisation of your choice in mapping out its preferred strategic direction for the next few years. Are there any dangers with this approach?

8.3 Undertake a ranking analysis of the choices available to Coopers Creek,* PSA Peugeot Citroën* or an organisation of your choice similar to that shown in Illustration 8.3.

8.4 Choose a specific strategy for PSA Peugeot Citroën,* Kronenbourg,* Coopers Creek* or an organisation of your choice, and explain which financial measures you would regard as most appropriate in assessing the anticipated return.

8.5 Bearing in mind your answers to the questions in Illustration 8.5:
(a) What is your feeling about the overall 'validity' of cost–benefit analysis?
(b) How could it be improved?

8.6 ● Using Illustration 8.7 as an example, what would you propose as the most important parameters to include in a sensitivity analysis in the case of each of the following organisations?
(a) The News Corporation*
(b) Sheffield Theatres*
(c) Kronenbourg*
(d) PSA Peugeot Citroën*
(e) An organisation of your choice

What general conclusion can you draw about the use of sensitivity analysis by comparing your answer for each organisation?

8.7 For an organisation of your choice, describe the dominant processes by which strategies are selected in the organisation. Now look at Exhibit 8.10 and make your own assessment of whether you would wish to change these processes. Justify your proposals.

8.8 ● Using examples from your answer to previous assignments, make a critical appraisal of the statement that 'Strategic choice is, in the end, a highly subjective matter. It is dangerous to believe that analytical techniques will ever change in reality.' Refer back to the recommended key readings by Johnson and Stacey (Chapter 2), who between them conclude that strategic decision making neither is, nor should be, driven by analysis.

---

* refers to a case study in the Text and Cases edition.
● denotes more advanced work assignments.

CASE EXAMPLE

The Benefits of Multi-utility?

A common feature of public sector restructuring in many countries was the privatisation and deregulation of utilities – particularly telecommunications, electricity supply, gas and water. The rationale was that private ownership and a deregulated market would improve the value for money provided in these services. As this programme of change proceeded, issues and opportunities arose for 'cross-ownership' between hitherto separate utility companies, for foreign ownership and diversification away from 'single-strand' utilities (such as electricity) into what became known as 'multi-utility' providers. The arguments for this latter change were typified by an article written by Ian Robinson, the chief executive of Scottish Power, in *Management Today*, October 1997.

> The rate of change in the utility industry since privatisation has been very fast. Customers have, in general, seen significant improvement in service and price reductions in power, telecoms and gas, while shareholders have seen returns beyond their original expectations. Rationalisation in the industry has produced further change, some overseas ownership and the birth of multi-utility companies selling electricity, gas, telecoms and water. There is no doubt that the change process will continue at a high pace, though the direction will be somewhat different from the last five years. The full deregulation of the gas and electricity industry in 1998, which involves the opening up of the domestic consumer market to full competition, will produce change on a scale not seen anywhere else in the world and I believe both the customer and shareholder will benefit.
>
> Utilities in Scotland have been different since privatisation, with electricity companies being vertically integrated and the water industry still in the control of local authorities. In Scottish Power, the early thrust of post-privatisation produced a tremendous effort to bring each element of the business to the highest efficiency point through benchmarking against those companies that were the best in the world. Today it is interesting to note that many international companies want to benchmark against us. The other major thrust in Scotland of both 'sweating the asset' and working with our customer base resulted in the birth of Scottish Power as a multi-utility. By taking the telecoms infrastructure that controlled our power network, upgrading it and extending it using our transmission system, we have created a state-of-the-art telecoms network. Similarly, as we are already in the gas business, it was a small step to supply the deregulated industrial customer. The major deregulation of domestic customers in our regions, many of whom we already supply with power, will be an exciting yet demanding step forward.
>
> Multi-utility is still in its embryonic stage in the UK, though few recognise it as being commonplace and, in fact, the 'norm' in many European countries. Few people predicted the major improvements that have occurred in utilities following privatisation. In most utilities, the strong focus from both commercial and technical aspects has resulted in a higher quality product, reduced prices for customers and good shareholder returns. Further focus on the customer, coupled with major investments, led to a number of utility companies striding forward in terms of reputation. The developments in information technology gave companies the opportunity to enhance their knowledge of both customers and assets. The change process in both organisation and attitude picked up in tempo to create a number of high-quality, customer-responsive companies. The emergence of the competitive markets in industrial electricity and gas focused the mind strongly and, by 1995, most UK utility companies were in the position of being advanced by global standards in terms of efficiency and competitiveness.
>
> In late 1994, Trafalgar House, through their bid for Northern Electric, started a process that would have a far-reaching impact on the UK utility industry. In the hot summer of 1995, there were ten bids for regional electricity companies of which seven were successful.

Three US companies established themselves in the UK, two water companies bought their local electricity companies and there was one electricity/electricity takeover. Most of these companies were able to make significant efficiency improvements, however, the latter two groupings also moving to focus on their customer base and its growing needs.

Research shows that customers focus on utility companies from several different viewpoints. Price, quality of supply and safety are major issues, but there is also a strong and growing trend for convenience. The desire for convenience in meter reading, billing, payment, common utility installation and energy management is a factor that is attractive to the customer and efficient for the modern utility company.

The development of the employees within the utility industry, together with advances in IT, has produced management and staff who are much more focused on customers, efficiency and cost. An influx of new management from outside the industry brought step changes in practice. Today's focus is on enhancing employee and management development with a strong emphasis on the young, high-potential employees, so the leaders of tomorrow can, in future, come from within.

Full deregulation of the domestic electricity and gas market will produce opportunities for both customers and utility companies. It will be on a scale not seen or tried before anywhere in the world. The efficient and customer-responsive utility company will be able to provide the customer with a quality bundle of products at competitive prices. Clearly, economy of scale will be a critical factor in provision of such a service.

The multi-utility industry will need satisfied customers to progress. Therefore the equation is well balanced between the customer and the shareholder. Within the customer focus lies the community which brings both local responsibilities and potential market advantages. The environment features significantly in most utilities' thought processes, and local communities benefit from this focus.

Today multi-utility is defined as power, gas, telecoms and water, and only a handful of companies have this portfolio available. Others will undoubtedly stick to their core solo product but in a world where quality of service, timing, convenience and price dominate, where will that leave them? Much greater forces are with us today or on the horizon: the Internet, home-shopping and other information services that will change our views on lifestyle. Lifestyle in the 21st century will demand more and more innovative convenience products and multi-utility will just be one of them. The modern utility company will need to understand these products and will have an unique advantage to serve this growing customer need.

Today's emergence of bundling utilities to customers is in its early days, but tremendous opportunity lies ahead for both the companies and their customers.

It was, indeed, early days for such radical changes in the way that utilities were 'bundled' and marketed. It was important to remember that consumers, in general, were unclear about what deregulation meant to them in practical terms. After all, they had known nothing other than highly regulated supply from single utility companies. There had also been some 'scare stories' in the press about dubious marketing practices as deregulation approached and there was 'poaching' of customers by utility companies. The press was also keen to remind readers that they would be free to buy their gas and electricity from other providers such as these local supermarkets. Exactly what this meant was a mystery to most consumers. For the utility companies themselves there were some difficult choices to make as deregulation moved forwards in many countries. Should they remain a single-utility specialist – after all this is where all their experience lay? Should they join the multi-utility bandwagon – but were not companies in other industries retreating from diversification? Or perhaps the best way forward was through international expansion by acquisition of their counterparts in other countries?

QUESTIONS

1. From the case example, describe four or five different strategies which Scottish Power could pursue, in terms of both development direction and method (e.g. 'Develop into a multi-utility company by internal development and not by alliances or acquisitions'). For each strategy:
   (a) try to summarise in one or two sentences why you feel it is a good strategy (or not)
   (b) undertake an assessment of suitability by applying the various 'tests' summarised in Exhibit 8.2.
2. Screen the options by using one or more of the methods described in section 8.2.2 (ranking, decision-trees, scenarios). Illustrations 8.3 and 8.4 should help.
3. Choose your preferred strategy and explain how you would assess its acceptability. (Refer to Exhibit 8.7 for guidance.)
4. How would you assess feasibility? (Refer to section 8.4.)

Source *Management Today*, October 1997. With permission.

IV
STRATEGY IMPLEMENTATION

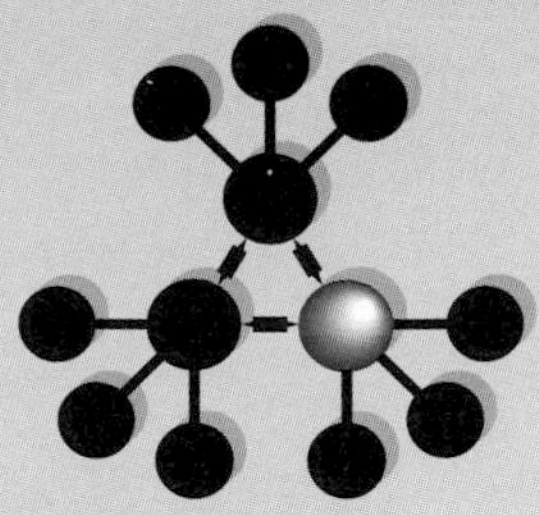

Strategic analysis and choice are of little value to an organisation unless the strategies are capable of being implemented. Strategic change does not take place simply because it is considered to be desirable; it takes place if it can be made to work and put into effect by members of the organisation. Part IV deals with the vital issues of implementing strategy, the planning of that implementation, and the difficulties and methods of managing strategic change. Chapter 1 made it clear that one of the main characteristics of strategic decisions is that they are likely to give rise to important changes. It is therefore vital to consider the types of change required, how they can be managed, and the strategic architecture which needs to be in place to ensure success. This discussion of architecture includes a range of related issues:

- Chapter 9 is about organisation design at various levels of detail. It looks at various types of organisation structure and the circumstances in which they might sensibly be adopted. However, the important issue of organisation design from a strategic viewpoint is where within this structure strategic and operational decisions will be made. This is the issue of centralisation and devolution, which will include a discussion of the 'parenting' role of the corporate centre in relation to divisions, as introduced in Chapter 6. The most detailed issues of organisation design are concerned with the configuration of the organisation – its building blocks and co-ordinating mechanisms – and how these need to vary from one organisation to another depending upon its circumstances.
- Chapter 10 discusses resource allocation and control within organisations as critical issues of implementation. The discussion includes the impact of improvements in information technology on these processes and business process re-engineering and internal market mechanisms. Overall, an important theme of the chapter is the need for managers to steer strategy through the way in which they influence the context in which other people work, rather than simply being the masterplanners of the organisation. Resource allocation and control is one of the most important ways in which this 'shaping of context' can be achieved.
- Chapter 11 examines more specifically how strategic change might be managed. This is done by considering different explanatory models of change; means of diagnosing blockages to change; and

THIS PART EXPLAINS

1. The strengths and weaknesses of different organisation structures.
2. The elements of organisational design.
3. Choices about centralisation vs. devolution.
4. Organisational configurations.
5. Resource allocation and control.
6. The importance of information.
7. Different types of strategic change.
8. How to manage strategic change – tools, styles and change roles.

different approaches to managing change, including the styles of management and techniques which can be employed in managing change. These include the management of political and symbolic issues, the importance of communication, changes to organisational routines and other specific tactics of managing change. The chapter concludes by linking its contents to other issues raised in the rest of the book.

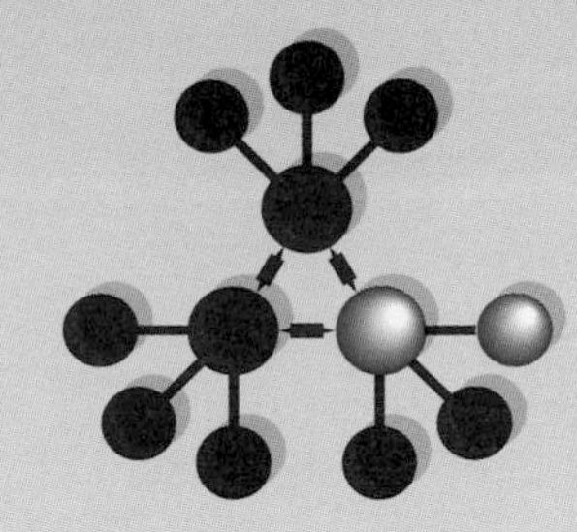

9 ORGANISATION STRUCTURE AND DESIGN

LEARNING OUTCOMES

After reading this chapter you should be able to:

- Describe the main structural types of organisations.
- Compare the different structural forms in multinational organisations.
- Define devolution.
- Describe strategic planning, financial control and strategic control.
- Define organisation configuration, building blocks and co-ordinating mechanisms.
- Describe Mintzberg's six organisational configurations.

9.1 INTRODUCTION

Perhaps the most important resource of an organisation is its *people*, so how people are organised is crucial to the effectiveness of strategy. Traditional views about regulation through organisation can be traced back to early twentieth-century management scientists and beyond.[1] These approaches are commensurate with a view of strategy making which is essentially top-down. Strategy is formed at the top and the rest of the organisation is seen as a means of implementation, so organisation design becomes a means of top-down control. Such principles of control are known as *bureaucratic* or *mechanistic*.[2] However, as was seen in Chapter 2, the idea that strategy is formulated in a top-down way is questionable, and the extension of this, that mechanistic structures and controls are necessarily appropriate, is therefore also questionable.

This chapter considers organisational structure/design in the context of the strategic management of organisations. It is accepted that there is a need to regulate the implementation of strategy, but this needs to take account of many influences. For example, what are the *types* of problem that the organisation faces in constructing strategy? How important is innovation? Is the organisation in a highly *complex* or *changing* environment, or in a fairly stable environment? How *diverse* is the organisation? For example, the needs of a multinational company are different from those of a small local firm. To what extent is the organisation reliant on simple or complex technologies? How answerable are the top executives to *external stakeholders*: for example, is the organisation a public body, perhaps answerable to a government minister; is it a privately owned firm; or is it perhaps a charity or a co-operative? It has already been seen in Chapter 6 that all these different influences have a bearing on strategic choices made by organisations. In turn, they also impact on the way the organisation needs to be designed. It is not possible to have a simple set of rules which can prescribe organisational structures and systems.

This chapter examines these issues, first by reviewing *basic structural forms*, and second by looking at how the authority to make strategic and operational decisions is mapped on to the structure – the issue of *centralisation vs. devolution*. Finally, the chapter looks at how the detailed design – or *configuration* – of an organisation needs to match its circumstances. Chapter 10 will complete the discussion of organisation design by exploring how the processes of *resource allocation and control* relate to the circumstances and structural arrangements of the organisation.

9.2 STRUCTURAL TYPES

Managers asked to describe their organisation usually respond by drawing an organisation chart, in an attempt to map out its structure. These structures are like skeletons: they define the general shape and facilitate or constrain certain activities. This chapter begins with a review of these basic structural types, and their advantages and disadvantages. It should be remembered that an organisation's performance will be mainly influenced by how the 'flesh' is built onto this skeleton. This is the area of organisational design which will be discussed in sections 9.3 to 9.5 and in Chapter 10.

9.2.1 The Simple Structure

in a **simple structure** *the organisation is run by the personal control of an individual*

A simple structure can be thought of as no formal structure at all. In a **simple structure** the organisation is run by the personal control of an individual. It is the type of organisation common in many very small businesses. There may be an owner who undertakes most of the responsibilities of management, perhaps with a partner or an assistant. However, there is little division of management responsibility, and probably little clear definition of who is responsible for what if there is more than one person involved.

The main problem here is that the organisation can operate effectively only up to a certain size, beyond which it becomes too cumbersome for one person to control alone. This threshold size will depend on the nature of the business: an insurance broker may personally handle a very large turnover, whereas a similarly sized business (in terms of turnover) in manufacturing and selling goods may be much more diverse in its operations and therefore more difficult to control personally because of the wider range of competences needed within the business.

9.2.2 The Functional Structure

A **functional structure** is based on the primary activities that have to be carried out, such as production, finance and accounting, marketing and personnel. Exhibit 9.1 represents a typical organisation chart for such a business, and Illustration 9.1 shows the importance of the functional structure in a multinational company. This structure is typically found in smaller companies, or those with narrow, rather than diverse, product ranges. However, within a multidivisional structure, the divisions themselves are likely to be split up into functional management areas.

a **functional structure** *is based on the primary activities that have to be carried out, such as production, finance and accounting, marketing and personnel*

Exhibit 9.1 also summarises the advantages and disadvantages of a functional structure.[3] There are advantages, mainly in so far as it allows greater operational control at a senior level in an organisation; and linked to this is the clear definition of roles and tasks. However, there are disadvantages, particularly as organisations become larger or more diverse. In such circumstances, senior managers might be burdened with everyday operational issues, or rely on their specialist skills rather than taking a strategic perspective on problems.

In previous chapters there have been a number of discussions about *strategic business units* (SBUs) as the level at which an organisation should construct its product and market strategies, in terms of the choice of *generic competitive strategy* and the *positioning* in its markets. In organisations of any size, there is likely to be a diversity of product/service and market/client groups, which may lead to a diversity of positioning decisions for the different SBUs: for example, an airline or a hotel wishing to differentiate between its business and 'family' customers. A functional structure can be very problematic in coping with this diversity, since the structure is built around *business processes* which cut across the various SBUs, and there is often an attempt to impose an unhelpful uniformity of approach between the SBUs. So lead times in production, debt control in finance, advertising expenditure in marketing, bonus systems in personnel, are too rigid to reflect the diversity which the organisation faces. The work of individuals is planned around a specialist business process and no one (other than the most senior managers) has any real ownership of the whole product or client group.

Exhibit 9.1 A functional structure

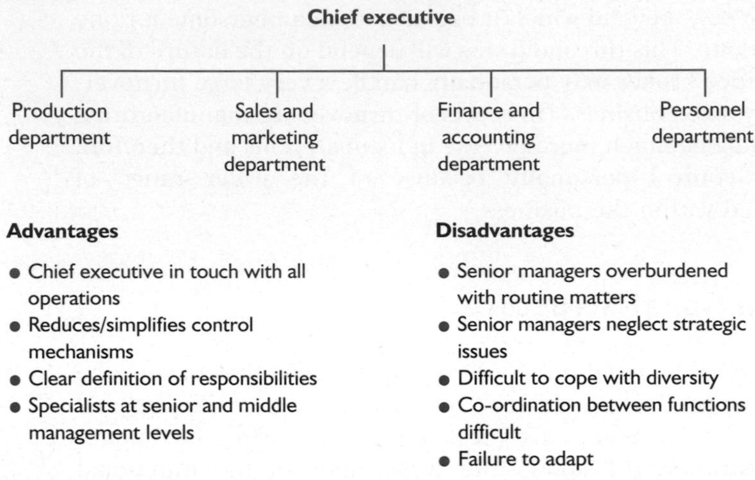

Advantages

- Chief executive in touch with all operations
- Reduces/simplifies control mechanisms
- Clear definition of responsibilities
- Specialists at senior and middle management levels

Disadvantages

- Senior managers overburdened with routine matters
- Senior managers neglect strategic issues
- Difficult to cope with diversity
- Co-ordination between functions difficult
- Failure to adapt

Of course, there are ways of minimising these problems with the functional structure, and they will be discussed more fully below (section 9.2.6). They are of two broad types: first, improving *co-ordination* between functions; and second, creation of a *substructure* within a business function which brings ownership of product or client group. For example, within sales and marketing, there might be roles such as product managers or key account sales staff.

9.2.3 The Multidivisional Structure

a **multidivisional structure** *is subdivided into units (divisions) on the basis of products, services, geographical areas or the processes of the enterprise*

A **multidivisional structure** is subdivided into units (divisions) on the basis of products, services, geographical areas or the processes of the enterprise (see Exhibit 9.2).

Divisionalisation often comes about in an attempt to overcome the problems that functional structures have in dealing with the diversity mentioned above.[4] Its main advantage is that each division is able to concentrate on the problems and opportunities of its particular business environment. The products and markets in which the company operates may be so diverse that it would be impractical to bring the tasks together in a single body. So divisions can be created which relate closely to the SBUs, allowing a tailoring of the product/market strategy to the requirements of that SBU and improving the ownership of the strategy by divisional staff. A similar situation exists in many public services, where the organisation is structured around *service departments* such as recreation, social services and education.

STRATEGY IN ACTION
Illustration 9.1

Scandinavian Airlines System

Even when ownership and governance are split across three countries, the operational effectiveness of the company may require a single functional structure.

Scandinavian Airlines System (SAS) was formed in 1946 as a consortium of three national airlines – Denmark's DDL, Norway's DNL and Sweden's SILA. However, over the years the pressure from competition required SAS to operate as a single uniform company – at least in terms of the customer perception and experience. This dominant need for integration led to a functional structure for the company as a whole, despite the separate ownership of the three member companies.

The 1995 annual report explained how this functional structure worked across the three countries:

> SAS's central organisation has five operational line functions and five staff functions.
>
> The line functions are Business Systems (routes/products, SAS trading and cargo), Marketing and Sales, Station Services, Production (service on board, technical and flight operations), and Information Systems.
>
> The five staff functions are Corporate Finance and Control, Human Resources, Public Relations and Government Affairs, Safety and Quality Control, and Information Systems Strategies.
>
> This functional organisation was refined in 1995, among other things in order to guarantee good local support in the three parent countries. In the SAS Management Team (SMT), which comprises nine people, Vagn Sørensen is responsible for strategically important Danish issues and Gunnar Reitan has a similar responsibility for Norway. Since SAS has its head office in Sweden, it was not considered necessary to appoint someone to be responsible for Swedish issues.

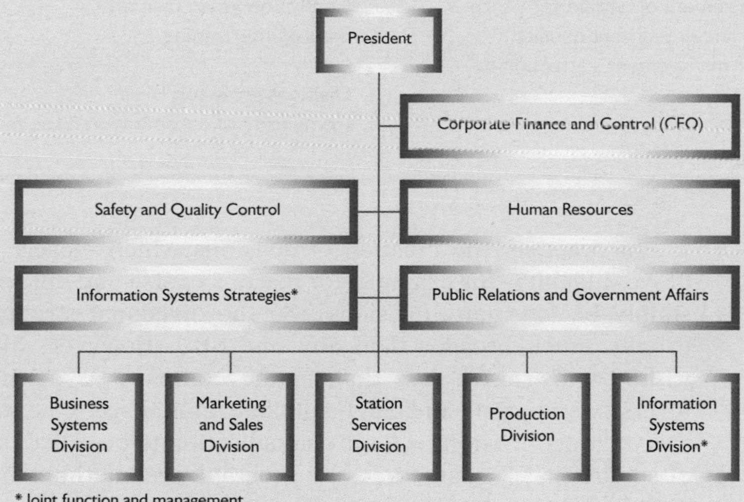

SAS organisation, 1996

Questions

1. Draw up other structures that could be adopted by SAS, for example country-based divisions or subsidiaries, a matrix structure, etc.
2. Create a table that lists the strengths and weaknesses of each structure (including the current structure). Remember to do this in the light of an industry that is becoming less regulated and where global competition is increasing rapidly.

Source Company annual report, 1995.

Exhibit 9.2 A multidivisional structure

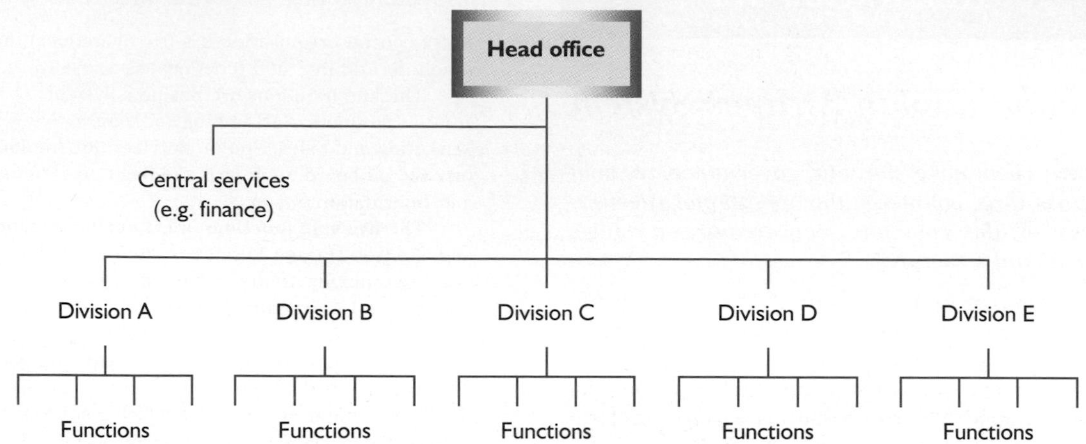

Advantages

- Concentration on business area (e.g. product/market)
- Facilitates measurement of unit performance
- Ease of addition and divestment of units
- Facilitates senior management's attention to strategy
- Encourages general management development

Disadvantages

- Possible confusion over locus of responsibility (centralisation/devolution confusion)
- Conflict between divisions
- Basis of intertrading
- Costly
- Divisions grow too large
- Complexity of co-operation if too many divisions

In practice, the creation of divisions which closely match SBUs can prove difficult – for example, for reasons of size and efficiency (there would simply be too many divisions). So the divisional structure, in reality, is usually much broader than any one SBU. However, while the diversity within a division is less than in the company as a whole, nevertheless diversity still exists and can be difficult to manage. One way of coping with this in larger divisions is for divisionalisation to be rolled down to a next tier of subdivisions – sometimes by geography, sometimes by client group. A police force usually has territorial divisions. An education department often has subdivisions for primary, secondary and tertiary education.

A common problem in creating divisions is in deciding the *basis* of divisionalisation – should it be based on products or markets or technologies? The result can, of course, be a complex organisation: for example, a company may decide that it needs a number of levels of divisions in order to break up business activities sensibly. Exhibit 9.3 shows this. The company might be broken into a first level of divisions based on broad product groups. Within each of these divisions, there may be separate businesses which in turn have their own divisional structure.

Exhibit 9.3 Levels of divisions

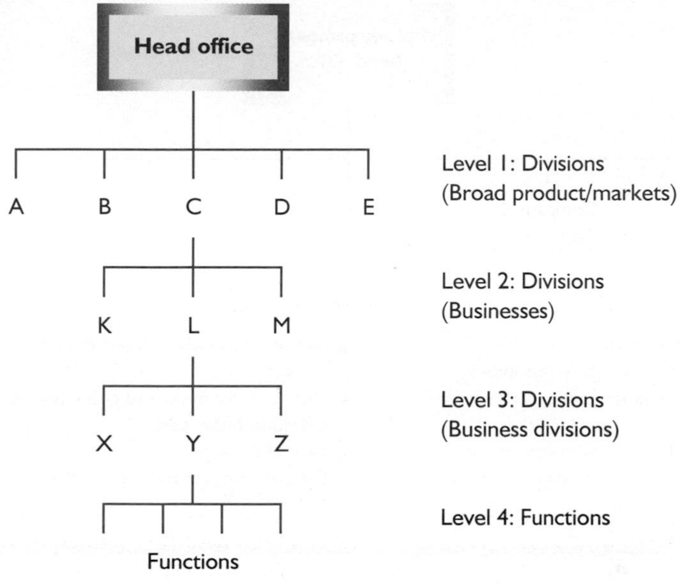

At some level in the organisation, a division will then be split into functionally based departments dealing with the specialist tasks of that business.

This raises the problems of which businesses should be in each division, which functions are to be included at each level of divisionalisation, and which functions are properly placed within the corporate head office rather than within any one of the divisions. For example, in Exhibit 9.3, where should a function such as financial planning be placed? Presumably, this is required both at a corporate level and at some level within an operating business; but should this be at level 1, 2 or 3? This issue will be discussed more fully in section 9.4 below, and is the aspect of organisational design concerned with choices about centralisation or devolution.

The advantages of divisional structures mainly centre on the virtues of specialisation within a division whereby the competences and the processes of innovation can be focused on a particular product group, technology, customer or market need. It can also make it easier to monitor the activities of a division as a separate business (or business unit). There are disadvantages and difficulties, however, since the operation and control of multidivisional organisations is often far from straightforward. These issues are discussed more fully in section 9.4 below. Exhibit 9.2 also summarises the advantages and disadvantages of a multidivisional structure.

Exhibit 9.4 A holding company structure

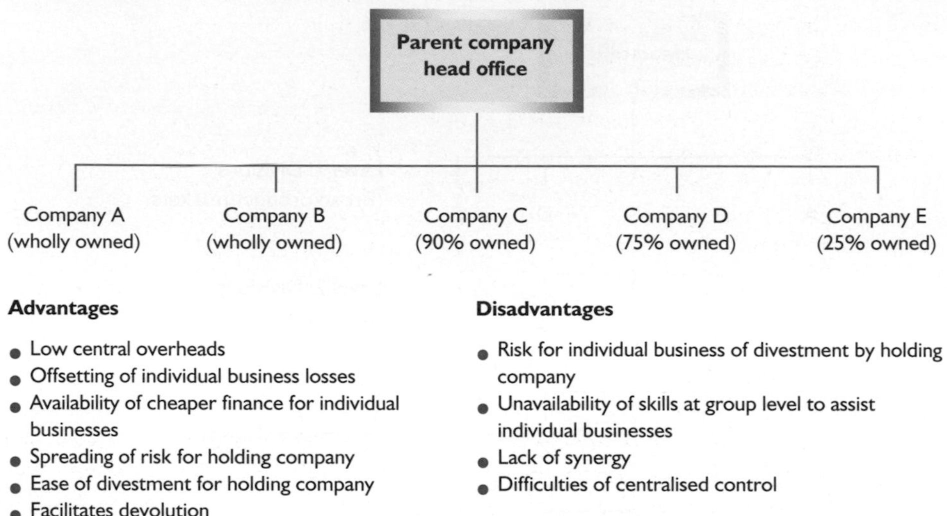

Advantages

- Low central overheads
- Offsetting of individual business losses
- Availability of cheaper finance for individual businesses
- Spreading of risk for holding company
- Ease of divestment for holding company
- Facilitates devolution

Disadvantages

- Risk for individual business of divestment by holding company
- Unavailability of skills at group level to assist individual businesses
- Lack of synergy
- Difficulties of centralised control

9.2.4 The Holding Company Structure

a **holding company** *is an investment company consisting of shareholdings in a variety of separate business operations, over which the corporate centre exercises simple control*

A **holding company** is an investment company consisting of shareholdings in a variety of separate business operations, over which the corporate centre exercises simple control. Although part of a parent company, these business units operate independently and probably retain their original company names. As mentioned in Chapter 6, the role that the parent company takes may be limited to decisions about the buying and selling of such companies with little involvement in their product or market strategy. Arguably, this is the situation as far as Lonrho or BTR is concerned.

An example of a holding company structure is given in Exhibit 9.4. The business interests of the parent company are likely to be varied: some of them may be wholly owned and some not, and there may be many business units within the group.

The advantages that a holding company can offer are based on the idea that the constituent businesses will operate their product/market strategy to their best potential if left alone, particularly as business environments become more turbulent. The management of innovation in both products and markets is the sole responsibility of the separate businesses. They should not have to carry the burden of a high central overhead, since the head office staff of the parent is likely to be small. However, the business units can benefit from their membership of the group in such ways as the offsetting of profits against others' losses and the benefits of cheaper finance for investment from the parent company. The holding company itself may also claim benefits, such as the spreading of risk across many business ventures and the ease of divestment of individual companies.

Perhaps the greatest weaknesses of this structure are the risk of lack of internal strategic cohesion, duplication of effort between business units or a failure to manage innovation within the separate businesses because of lack of skill or through short-term pressures to deliver. It is one thing to say that business units operate better if they are given the profit responsibility to do so on their own; but in a large, perhaps multinational, operation there may be very considerable payoffs from having some sort of overall product or market logic to the activities and some central capacity to sponsor innovation and change. These issues will be discussed more fully in section 9.4 below.

9.2.5 The Matrix Structure[5]

A **matrix structure** is a combination of structures which often takes the form of product and geographical divisions or functional and divisional structures operating in tandem. Exhibit 9.5 gives examples of such a structure.

a **matrix structure** *is a combination of structures which often takes the form of product and geographical divisions or functional and divisional structures operating in tandem*

Matrix structures may be adopted because there is more than one factor around which a structure could be built, so that pure divisional or functional structures would be inappropriate. For example, if a company extends its operations on a multinational scale and also develops new product lines, it may regard geographically defined divisions as the operating units for the purpose of local marketing, and product divisions as responsible for the worldwide co-ordination of product development, manufacturing and distribution to these geographical divisions.

Matrix structures do not occur only in large, complex organisations; they are sometimes found in quite small organisations and are very common in professional service organisations (both public and private sector).

It is claimed that matrix structures improve the quality of decision making in situations where there is a risk of one vital interest of the enterprise (e.g. a geographical area) dominating strategy at the expense of others (e.g. worldwide co-ordination of manufacturing). Formal bureaucracy is replaced by direct contact between individuals. The matrix structure is also supposed to increase managerial motivation and development because of the wider involvement in strategies.

However, matrix structures also have problems associated with them:

- There is a high risk of a *dilution of priorities*, whereby the message to those in the organisation is that everything matters equally and deserves equal debate.
- The *time* taken for decisions to be made may be much longer than in more conventional structures.
- It can be unclear who is *responsible* for what; while the idea of joint responsibility may conceptually be laudable, it can give rise to problems.

Exhibit 9.5 Two examples of matrix structures

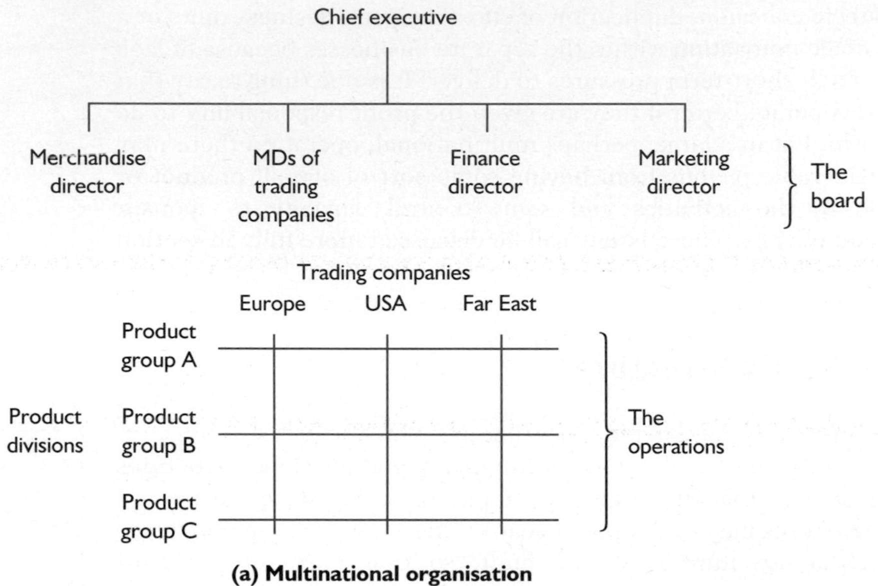

(a) Multinational organisation

Head teacher

Subject leadership

		Head of languages	Head of science	Head of social studies	etc.
Pupil groups	Head of lower school				
	Head of upper school				
	Head of sixth form				

(b) School

Advantages

- Quality of decision making where interests conflict
- Direct contact replaces bureaucracy
- Increases managerial motivation
- Development of managers through increased involvement in decisions

Disadvantages

- Length of time to take decisions
- Unclear job and task responsibilities
- Unclear cost and profit responsibilities
- High degrees of conflict
- Dilution of priorities
- 'Creeping bureaucracy'

- Organisations with matrix structures may have to cope with a good deal of *conflict* because of the lack of clarity of role definition and responsibility.

A summary of advantages and disadvantages is provided in Exhibit 9.5. The critical issue with any organisation structure in practice is the way in which it is operated. This is particularly important in the case of matrix structures, and the following guidelines should be considered:

- In practice, one arm of the matrix needs to *lead* in order to minimise the risk of paralysis. For example, the key issue for many major global manufacturing companies is the development and production of products in volumes which achieve financial viability. Although local 'tailoring' of products and marketing is also important, it is not the leading edge of the company's global strategy.
- The allocation of workloads and duties for individuals should not normally be spread evenly across the matrix. So, for example, within a central personnel function there will be some degree of matching of individuals with the separate divisions to provide the *ownership* which can be lost in a matrix structure. In the extreme form, the matrix structure will shade through into project teams of dedicated individuals from central functions seconded to divisions.
- Senior managers must be capable of *collaborating* across the matrix. It does not suit managers who are fiercely competitive (internally) and who cannot cope with *ambiguity*.
- There should be a clear means of breaking stalemate. Usually, this is through referral to the chief executive. If this mechanism needs to be used too frequently, it is a sign that the matrix structure is not working sufficiently well.

9.2.6 Intermediate Structures and Structural Variations

In reality, few organisations operate entirely like one of the pure structural types discussed above. The skill is in blending structure to the organisation's circumstances. There exists a whole range of 'shades of grey' between these pure types of structure, through which an organisation's structures might emerge and change over time in an attempt to reflect its changing circumstances. For example, a company may move from a functional structure to a divisional structure by a series of smaller incremental changes, and through changes in the approach to resource allocations and control (discussed in Chapter 10). Problems first arise within the functional structure as new products or markets compete for resources. Initially, these conflicts might be resolved by pushing the decision upwards until a sufficiently *senior executive* makes the decisions. When too many conflicts need to be resolved in this way, new *rules*, guidelines and procedures may develop to guide how resources are to be shared between products. The next step may be to *formalise* these procedures in the planning process by, for example, allocating a budget to the new products or markets. Up to this stage the problem has been dealt with by manipulating methods of control and operation rather than by structural changes.

As the new products or markets become more important and create competition for resources, it may be necessary to create *interdepartmental liaison roles*: for example, a committee or a temporary taskforce may be set up to advise on priorities. This may lead either to permanent teams of co-ordinators or special *co-ordinating jobs* (the product manager is a good example). Another step which may prove necessary to maintain the functional structure is the creation of departments with the sole function of co-ordination: *centralised planning departments*, for example. Ultimately, as the diversity increases, the organisation will divisionalise because the 'costs' of maintaining the functional structure will be unacceptably high. Or alternatively, the 'new venture' is created as a new division or even subsidiary, and the functional structure in the 'parent' reverts to its previous *modus operandi* as the 'problem' of diversity is removed. There may be issues about how the subsidiary relates to, and is supported by the corporate centre. For example, will it have access to central activities of product and market innovation? If not, how will the processes of innovation be managed in the new subsidiary?

9.2.7 Network and Virtual Organisations

The various intermediate structures discussed above are essentially an illustration of the importance of *horizontal integration* between the various activities within an organisation. In Chapter 4, it was emphasised that sustainable competitive advantage is likely to be gained by organisations which are able to 'manage' *linkages* between the separate activities in the organisation and, importantly, into the supply and distribution chains too.

Recent dramatic improvements in the cost and effectiveness of telecommunications and the convergence with computer technology have opened up possibilities for many organisations to improve their management of these linkages. So the issue is how they might restructure the organisation (internally) to reflect and exploit these developments, and how they might relate (externally) to other organisations within their value chain. This has been of particular concern to many international organisations.[6] Some of the more detailed implications for organisation design will be discussed in later parts of this chapter and in Chapter 10 (for example, business process re-engineering). At this stage it is important to note some important trends in restructuring.

1. The drive to make organisation structures *flatter* through *de-layering* – although also driven by other factors like slowness in response of multitiered hierarchies – is now a real possibility for more

organisations. Improvement in the speed and quality of management information allows for *spans of control* wider than was hitherto regarded as desirable.

2. The nature of work in many organisations has now changed such that it is less dependent on a particular place of work. The result is that many more people are able to carry out their work *independently*, but remain connected to key corporate resources (such as databases and specialist advice) and to colleagues, suppliers and clients through the telecommunications and computing infrastructure. The exploitation of the Internet is a major strategic issue for many organisations and will be discussed more fully in Chapter 10. It allows formal structures to be dismantled and replaced with well-functioning networks, supported by this information infrastructure. An example of a network organisation is given in Illustration 9.2.

3. Many organisations are debating and implementing (to a greater or lesser extent) concepts of **virtual organisations**,[7] which are organisations held together not through formal structure and physical proximity of people, but by partnership, collaboration and networking. The important issue is that this organisation feels 'real' to clients and meets their needs at least as adequately as other organisations which are 'real' in the sense described here. Of course, this is *not* essentially a new issue about structures – as mentioned in Chapter 4, it is *normal* for organisations to decide to *specialise* by undertaking only some of the value activities in-house and to rely on other organisations to perform other tasks (in the supply or distribution chain). A major concern is the extent to which activities can be subcontracted or outsourced. It has been argued[8] that extreme forms of subcontracting are likely to result in serious strategic weakness in the long run, as the organisation becomes devoid of core competences (see Chapter 4) and cut off from the learning which can exist through undertaking these activities in-house. This is now an important consideration in many industries such as civil engineering, publishing and specialist travel companies, all of which are highly dependent on outsourcing aspects of their business which hitherto were considered as core. This issue is in essence concerned with whether short-term improvements are being achieved at the expense of securing a capacity for innovation. If all the knowledge needed to run the business exists outside the company there are some critical questions to answer about the management and control of innovation. Section 4.3.7 in Chapter 4 outlined the ingredients of a well managed process of innovation linked to the interplay between explicit and tacit knowledge. An organisation must be confident that it can still foster and control these knowledge creation processes if it is operating with vertical structures. For example, is sufficient time spent in two-way dialogue with the major 'partners'? Is knowledge from one partner's activities used to rethink how the business processes of another partner could be improved? The danger of 'virtuality' is that innovation only

virtual organisations *are held together not through formal structure and physical proximity of people, but by partnership, collaboration and networking*

STRATEGY IN ACTION
Illustration 9.2

The Network Organisation: Asea Brown Boveri

Network organisations need to have a well developed and effective communications infrastructure to promote sharing and organisational learning.

With 215,000 employees in 1997 and operations worldwide, Asea Brown Boveri (ABB) was a vigorous and successful company in the electrotechnical business. Between 1988 and 1996 revenues grew from US$17bn to US$35bn, with return on assets simultaneously improving from 12 per cent to almost 21 per cent.

ABB was organised as a federation of 1,300 companies. Each company, employing an average of 200 people, and generating annual revenues of $25m, was structured as a separate and distinct business and, to the extent possible, as a free-standing legal entity. In addition, each company had responsibility for its complete balance sheet, and it was company policy to permit each unit to retain one-third of its net profits. This gave managers substantial financial independence by limiting their need to rely on corporate management for funding. Only one intermediate level of management existed between these front-line companies and the corporate executive committee. The entire headquarters of this $35bn company, including the CEO and group executives who comprise the executive committee, and the various corporate staff groups together numbered less than 150 people.

In ABB there was a clear recognition that those with the specialised knowledge and expertise most vital to the company's competitiveness were usually located far away from the corporate headquarters – in the front-line research laboratories, marketing groups or engineering departments. By decentralising assets and resources into these small specialised operating units, ABB was trying to create an environment in which this scarce knowledge could be developed and applied most appropriately. However, this decentralised structure had itself created a need for a powerful horizontal integration process to ensure that the entire organisation benefited from the specialised resources and expertise developed in its entrepreneurial units. This co-ordination was needed both between the 65 'Business Areas' (in turn grouped into six 'Business Segments') and geographically in the major regions of operation. Indeed, ABB's own 'Mission, Values and Policies' document stated that 'a decentralised organisation will only work effectively with a good reporting system that gives higher level managers the opportunity to react in good time'.

The centrepiece to ABB's commitment to this information sharing approach was ABACUS (Asea Brown Boveri Accounting and CommUnication System), a sophisticated fully automated information system. Governed by strict rules concerning definition, format and timing, this democratic system provided accurate and timely data to the field operations, ensured that managers around the company received the same information at the same time regardless of their hierarchical level, and helped the group executives evaluate performance. As such, it allowed the company to co-ordinate and control its diverse operations, keeping managers at all levels equally well informed.

Questions

1. Refer forwards to Exhibit 9.8 and assess the ways in which the corporate centre at ABB both does and could add value to its 1,300 separate businesses.
2. Could the network operate without a centre (or a hub) at all?
3. Do you feel that this networking approach could be adopted by other organisations? What are the circumstances in which it would be most and least useful?

Sources C. Bartlett and S. Ghoshal, 'Beyond the M-form: toward a managerial theory of the firm', *Strategic Management Journal* (1993) pp. 23–46; Cranfield MBA projects 1996/97.

Prepared by Sara Martin, Cranfield School of Management.

occurs within the narrow 'boxes' represented by the activities of separate partners. There is no one who has the competence or authority to manage innovation and change for the value system *as a whole*.

4. Networks can be organised in different ways, particularly in relation to how the interface with customers is structured (see Exhibit 9.6):
   - A *one-stop shop* is where a 'real' and physical presence is created through which all client enquiries are channelled. The function of the one-stop shop is to put together a complete package of services by co-ordinating the various services provided. A 'turn-key' contractor (say, in civil engineering) might operate in this way – using its own expertise in project management and managing a network of suppliers, but not actually undertaking any of the detailed work itself.
   - A second option is a *one-start shop*, again involving a real and physical presence dealing with client enquiries. However, the role here is essentially one of *diagnosing* the client's needs and *referring* them to the most appropriate provider. This is often referred to as 'pigeon-holing'. The role of primary health care practitioners (GPs) has traditionally been concerned with this process. Many advice services for small businesses have been established in this way – whether it be by banks or by government-sponsored agencies (e.g. Business Link in the UK).
   - The *service network* is where there is no single starting point for clients in the network. The customer may access all of the services of the network through any of the constituent members of the network. A well-functioning network may not be easy to achieve, since it requires all members of the network to be fully informed, capable and willing to 'cross-sell' other people's products and to act collaboratively. Some service networks also have a one-start shop facility. For example, Best Western is an international network of independent hotels, where customers can receive information or make bookings at any hotel in the network or through central booking points. This facility has the clear advantage of encouraging travellers to 'book on' their next destination with Best Western.

9.2.8 Structural Types in Multinational Companies[9]

The growth in the size and importance of multinational businesses warrants some special mention, since the structural implications can be significant. A basic form of structure for a multinational is the retention of the 'home' structure and the creation of overseas subsidiaries which are managed through *direct contact* between the top manager of the subsidiary and the chief executive of the parent company. This is most common in single-product companies or where the overseas interests are relatively minor. Beyond this simple structure, the critical issue is the extent to which local independence and responsiveness should take precedence over global co-

Exhibit 9.6 **Linking services: three approaches**

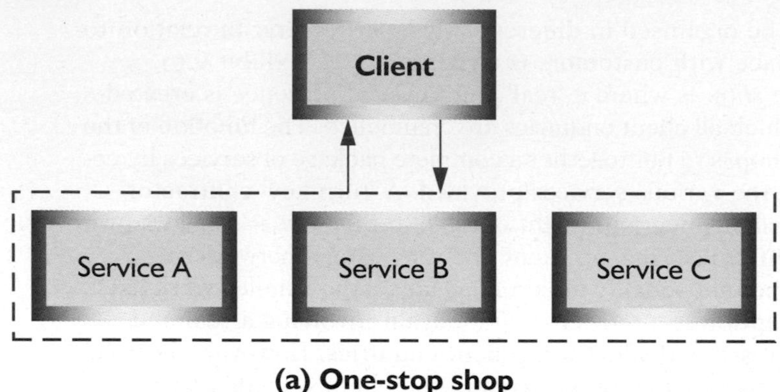

(a) One-stop shop

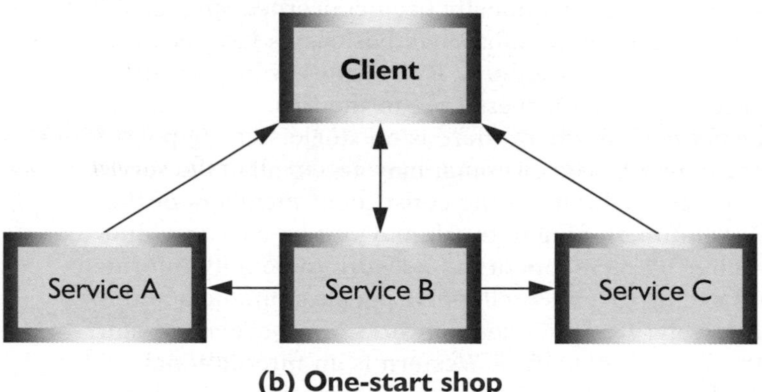

(b) One-start shop

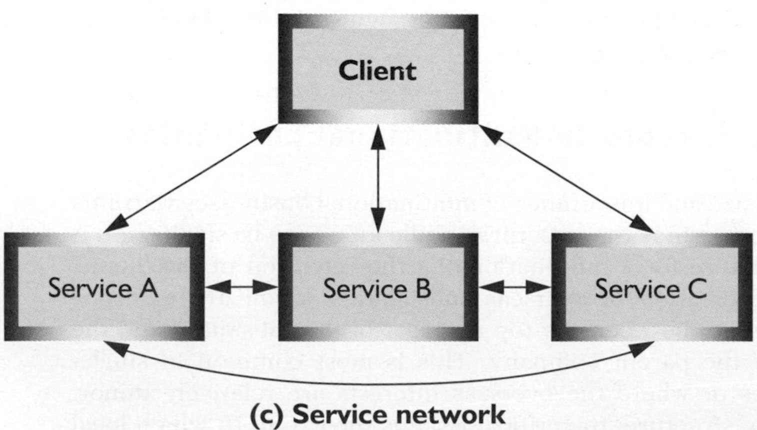

(c) Service network

Exhibit 9.7 Structural types in multinational companies

LOCAL INDEPENDENCE AND RESPONSIVENESS \ GLOBAL CO-ORDINATION	Low	High
Low	International divisions	Global product companies
High	International subsidiaries	Transnational corporations

Source Based on C. Bartlett and S. Ghoshal, *Managing across Borders: The transnational corporation*, Harvard Business School Press, 1989.

ordination (see Exhibit 9.7). In other words, it is an example on a global scale of the more general problems of co-ordination discussed in the previous three subsections. How this co-ordination is achieved will vary with circumstances and over time.

1. A common form of multinational structure is the *international division*. Here the home-based structure may be retained at first – whether functional or divisional – and the overseas interests managed through a separate international division. This draws on the products of the home company with the disadvantage of lack of local tailoring of services. Such structures tend to work best where there is a wide geographical spread and a portfolio of closely related products.
2. Geographically based *international subsidiaries* often evolve from the previous structure (as seen in the case of 3M in Illustration 9.3). These subsidiaries are part of a multinational whole, but operate independently by country. In these companies, virtually all the management functions are nationally based, allowing for higher degrees of local responsiveness. Many of the multinationals founded in colonial days operated this way, such as Inchcape, Shell or Burmah. In such circumstances, the control of the parent company is likely to be dependent on some form of planning and reporting system, and perhaps

STRATEGY IN ACTION
Illustration 9.3

3M's Structures for Europe

Changing circumstances – both inside and outside companies – may require structural changes. Often, these changes will occur incrementally over time.

The Minnesota Mining and Manufacturing Company (3M) is based at St Paul, Minnesota, USA. Over an 80-year history (from 1914), it had diversified into leadership positions in seemingly unrelated fields such as adhesive tape, medical supplies, traffic signs and electrical equipment. In the mid 1990s, its turnover was about US$14bn and it employed 87,000 people worldwide. The growth and development of the company had required many changes in structure, as shown by its approach in Europe. Some of the most significant changes were as follows:

- 3M originally formed international divisions to exploit US products overseas.
- By the 1950s, as 3M expanded its international presence, it created country subsidiary organisations (CSOs) in Europe with their own managing directors. The approach and product range of each CSO varied considerably, and the local language and culture prevailed in each CSO.
- Although CSOs were very autonomous, strong links to headquarters were encouraged by not appointing a country national as the head of a CSO.
- Once sales volumes justified investment, European manufacturing was allowed to substitute for imports from the USA. These plants were owned by one CSO and products sold to other CSOs in Europe.
- By the early 1970s, 3M was experiencing fierce competition from the Japanese and needing to strengthen its technical and management capabilities. The status of the MD of a CSO was raised considerably, becoming a role through which high flyers were expected to progress.
- A 3M Europe office was established. Although this had no direct authority over CSOs, it was expected to co-ordinate activities between CSOs.
- By the late 1970s, the need for European-designed and developed products had increased and technical directors were appointed to CSOs to achieve this.
- In the early 1980s, the need to co-ordinate the efforts of CSO-based laboratories for the benefit of all European CSOs was reinforced by creating a reporting relationship of the technical directors to the appropriate laboratory head in the USA. Global potential of products started to dominate local considerations.
- To foster European/US exchange further, a whole series of informal and formal

the ultimate veto over national strategies; but the level of global co-ordination is likely to be low.

3. In many industries there has been a move away from the international division or subsidiary structure to what has become known as a *global product* or integrated structure. Here the multinational is split into product divisions which are then managed across the world. The logic of

networks and relationships were developed between technical teams, including annual (global) technical planning meetings.

- In 1982 the European management team in Brussels was extended to include a European director for each product group. They functioned in an advisory capacity to CSOs.
- European management action teams (EMATs) were formed by pulling together sales and marketing managers from the larger CSOs. The heads of EMATs became product managers for 3M Europe.
- Conflict emerged for these heads of EMAT if the MDs of CSOs refused to implement the European product strategy in their division.
- As a result of these tensions, in 1986 a taskforce recommended that a formal pan-European structure based on product lines should be adopted, while keeping CSOs to support the local needs of business. The US parent decided not to accept the recommendations.
- By the end of the 1980s, many large customers (e.g. Ford Europe) were demanding a single access point to service their pan-European operations. It was also clear that the EMAT structure was not powerful enough to solve inefficiencies in CSOs.
- In 1990, another taskforce looked at the European organisation of 3M and its recommendations were similar to the 1986 report.
- Over the next two years, the company went through a major change process to adopt the new structure. They created European business centres (EBCs) which were product divisions reporting back to the US group vice-president; the 17 CSOs were reshaped to become ten regional subsidiaries (RSOs – most covering more than one country) and reported to the vice-president (Europe). Finally, a European operating committee was created as a forum to oversee the new European organisation. This included the heads of both EBCs and RSOs.

Questions

1. By refering to section 9.2.8 of the text, make a detailed critique of the organisational design of 3M, to include:
   (a) whether the historical changes in design can be explained by changing circumstances
   (b) whether its current design takes note of 'best practice' for global companies
   (c) whether it fits the particular stategies which 3M is pursuing – particularly its commitment to constant innovation.
2. Do you feel that other global organisations have lessons to learn about organisational design from 3M?

Source M. Ackenhusen, D. Muzyka and N. Churchill, 'Restructuring 3M for an integrated Europe, part one: initiating the change', *European Management Journal*, vol. 14, no. 1 (1996), pp. 21–36.

such an approach is that it should promote cost efficiency (particularly of production) on an international basis, and provide enhanced transfer of resources and competences (particularly technology and innovation) between geographical regions. The network of plants, each one in a separate country, may be making parts of cars, for example, which are assembled in yet another country: this manufacturing network may be supported by an international research and development network. The international development of many Japanese companies – for example, in electronics – has been managed in this way. A key requirement to support this structure is planning mechanisms to co-ordinate the various operations, and it is in these organisations that the planning and control systems are likely to be most sophisticated.

The obvious danger with a global product strategy is that local needs and differences may be ignored. Also, it is likely that the multinational will have several companies or divisions selling into the same country and these may be uncoordinated – perhaps creating inefficiencies through duplication of effort and confusing customers.

transnational corporations *combine the local responsiveness of the international subsidiary with the advantages available from co-ordination found in global product companies by creating an integrated network of interdependent resources and competences*

4. More recently, some organisations have become **transnational corporations** which combine the local responsiveness of the international subsidiary with the advantages available from co-ordination found in global product companies by creating an integrated *network* of interdependent resources and competences.[10] Specifically, the transnational exhibits the following features:
   - Each national unit operates independently, but is a source of ideas and capabilities for the whole corporation.
   - National units achieve global scale through specialisation on behalf of the whole corporation.
   - The corporate centre manages a global network by first establishing the role of each subsidiary, then sustaining the culture and systems to make the network operate effectively.

   The success of a transnational corporation is dependent on the ability *simultaneously* to achieve global competences, local responsiveness and organisation-wide innovation and learning. This requires some degree of clarity as to the roles which the various global managers need to perform.[11] For example:
   - Those responsible for *global products or businesses* have the overriding responsibility to further the company's global competitiveness, which will cross both national and functional boundaries. They must be the *product/market strategist*, the *architect* of the business resources and competences, the driver of product innovation and the *co-ordinator* of transnational transactions.
   - Managers of *countries or territories* must act as a *sensor* of local needs. They must be able to *build* unique competences: that is, become a centre of excellence which allows them to be a *contributor* to the company as a whole.
   - Managers of *functions* such as finance or IT have a major responsibility for ensuring worldwide innovation and learning across the various parts of the organisation. This requires the skill to recognise and spread best practice across the organisation – a form of *internal benchmarking*. So they must be able to *scan* the organisation for best practice, *cross-pollinate* this best practice and

STRATEGY IN ACTION
Illustration 9.4

Nestlé's Global Challenge

Even organisations with a long history of global sales may need to consider how they will face the period ahead.

Nestlé's first 130 years were ones of spectacular growth and development – from being the first European condensed milk factory in Switzerland in 1866 to a company selling £30bn of food products to more than 100 countries in all five continents and only 2 per cent of its sales originating from Switzerland. An important part of this growth had been acquisition of companies that had leading brands in the fields in which Nestlé was operating – few of its acquisitions were diversifications, the exception being pharmaceuticals (Alcon) and cosmetics (through partnership with L'Oréal).

The group's main activities in food were beverages (coffee, mineral water and fruit juices), milk products/ice cream, chocolate/confectionery, and prepared dishes/cooking aids (frozen foods, sauces, condiments). Broadly, its strategy was wide geographical coverage with heavily marketed leading brands. Manufacturing was mainly local with 489 factories in more than 60 countries.

This history of development through local subsidiaries raised some important issues for the future. In developed economies, in most food sectors, there was room for only two or three branded products on a supermarket's shelves – this increased the pressure to invest heavily in brand image and reduced the number of potential targets for further acquisitions. Market share became increasingly important to maintain profitability. In these circumstances the question arose as to whether production and distribution efficiency and product quality were best supported by the localisation of production (in the 489 factories) or whether rationalisation would improve competitive performance. There were also issues of the relationship between the corporate brand – Nestlé – the brands inherited through acquisition and still used, such as Maggi, Perrier and Buitoni, and the individual product brands such as those acquired from Rowntree (Kit-Kat, Smarties and Crunchie).

The central question was whether this hybrid approach to global organisation – the production localised in subsidiaries and global product brand management – was the best way forward.

Questions

1. List the main advantages and disadvantages of rationalising manufacturing onto a regional or even global basis.
2. Compare the current approach of Nestlé to managing global strategy with that of Unilever (the case example at the end of this chapter).

Sources Nestlé management report 1996; Cranfield MBA reports 1996.

be the *champion* of innovations, for example in re-engineering business processes.

- The critical issue is the role played by the *corporate managers*, which is vital in the transnational corporation in integrating these other roles and responsibilities. Not only are they the *leaders*, but they are also the *talent spotters* among business, country and functional managers, facilitating the interplay between them. For example, they must foster the processes of innovation and knowledge creation discussed in section 4.3.7 of Chapter 4. They are responsible for the *development* of a strong management centre in the organisation.

These issues about the role of the corporate centre and the way in which it adds value to the activities of the various parts of the organisation are issues about organisational design which will now be discussed (sections 9.3 to 9.5). It will be seen in Chapter 10 that there are also responsibilities concerned with ensuring that the processes of resource allocation and control of the organisation are adequate for the challenges of the future.

5. There are interesting differences between countries in the way that global strategies have tended to develop.[12] Companies which originated in many European countries (such as Unilever or Nestlé) needed to internationalise their activities at an early stage, owing to the small size of their home markets. This typically took the form of international subsidiaries (see Exhibit 9.7 and Illustration 9.4). Their challenge now is to reduce local autonomy and increase global integration.

   In contrast, US companies with a large domestic market tended to favour international divisions. They now face two challenges in globalisation: first, the issues of local autonomy; and second, the barriers between their separate strategic views of the domestic and international business. Japanese companies had traditionally been strongly domestically focused, and their international activities first developed through exporting. This resulted in strong global product strategies, and the subsequent need to relocate some production facilities overseas strengthened this position. The challenge is currently one of increasing local autonomy without losing the benefits of the global product strategies.

9.3 THE ELEMENTS OF ORGANISATIONAL DESIGN

It should be clear from the previous sections that structure in itself will not ensure the success of strategy, although an inappropriate choice of structure could impede success. The successful implementation of strategies will be influenced strongly by how the 'flesh' is hung on the structure. This is the province of organisational design and consists of three elements:

- *Centralisation vs. devolution* – deciding where within the structure the responsibility for operational and strategic decision making should lie. This has also been referred to as *management styles*.[13]
- *Organisational configurations* – the need to match the *detailed* structure with the context within which the organisation is operating.

- *Resource allocation and control processes*, and how they influence the behaviour of people and assist or impede strategic developments.

The first two elements will be discussed in the following sections. Resource allocation and control is the subject of Chapter 10.

9.4 CENTRALISATION VS. DEVOLUTION

One of the most important debates since the late 1980s in both public and private sector organisations has been concerned with *devolution*.[14] **Devolution** is the extent to which the centre of an organisation delegates decision making to units and managers lower down in the hierarchy.

devolution *is the extent to which the centre of an organisation delegates decision making to units and managers lower down in the hierarchy*

It is probably no accident that this interest in the importance of devolution coincided with a sustained period of market and financial pressure for most large organisations. Public services in many countries had seen their budgets significantly curtailed, while large private sector companies felt the bite of the market brought about by an extended recession in many parts of the world. This triggered senior managers to take action to address a number of issues which they were, perhaps, avoiding:

- Top managers were becoming out of touch with the 'sharp-end' action in the markets and operations of the business. In fast-moving markets, or during periods of significant change in the public services, there was a feeling that more authority was needed *close to the action* in order to improve corporate performance.
- Overcentralisation had resulted in organisations losing their way and becoming too concerned with internal matters at the expense of serving the customer or client.
- Some would say that the drive towards greater devolution was largely a reaction to the previous era of overcentralisation. The issue of centralisation vs. devolution is best discussed as a *continuum* from highly centralised to highly devolved and not as a black or white choice.

9.4.1 The Role of the Centre

In large organisations, most of the managerial activity which occurs between the centre of the organisation and its parts – departments, divisions or subsidiaries – has tended to be concerned with targeting and controlling the activities of those managing the parts. If organisations are to benefit from increased devolution, these activities of assessing the performance and value added by each part of the organisation remain important. However, a critical question which also needs to be answered is: what value does the centre of the organisation add to the activities of these separate parts? So asking the radical question, 'Do we need a centre at all?' can be a valuable discipline in understanding the role of the centre of the organisation and the centre/parts relationships. This is now referred to as the *parenting* role, as introduced in Chapter 6, particularly in organisations structured into divisions or operating a holding company model.[15] It should be remembered that, in most organisations, the concept of 'the centre' will be relevant at several levels. The head of a division sees head office as the centre, but, in turn, the head of division is the centre for the constituent parts of the division, and so on. Therefore, for many managers the discussion that follows will need to be viewed from both directions – which should lead to a balanced appraisal of how 'the centre' adds value. There are many different ways in which the centre (as a good parent) can add value (see Exhibit 9.8):

- Improving *efficiency* – perhaps through scale advantages from resource sharing, particularly in the use of infrastructure, support services and other overhead items. The corporate centre may have more *leverage* in either purchasing or market access.
- Providing *expertise* and *services* not available within smaller units – for example, personnel and financial services, estates management and IT infrastructure. Some of the most successful corporate parents have competences in market analysis, or cost analysis, which help fundamentally to reassess the role and future of divisions or subsidiaries. Human resource and management developments and succession planning may be important ways in which the centre adds value.
- Providing *investment*, particularly during the early days of new ventures. This investment could be in resources and infrastructure, but also could be concerned with developing or changing the core competences within divisions. This could be linked to structural decisions – for example, the need to develop different specialist competences in the different divisions of a transnational corporation, as discussed in section 9.2.8 above.
- *Fostering innovation* through the management of the knowledge creation processes. This will involve *coaching* of people and managers in divisions and the important role of providing a larger *peer group* through which individuals improve their own knowledge and skills, and where organisational *learning* occurs.
- *Mitigating risk* which smaller units inevitably run, and easing the problems created by the variety and variability of demands from customers. Bigger units can smooth out these problems more easily.
- Providing a strong *external image* from which smaller units can benefit, and accessing *external networks* better than any separate unit.
- Encouraging *collaboration* and *co-ordination* of effort – in the ways discussed in sections 9.2.6 to 9.2.8 above – but not at the expense of diluting the core competences which are essential to separate strategic business units. This can often result in products or services which a single unit could not deliver. The corporate centre may also be able to

Exhibit 9.8 **The role of the centre**

Increasing value for money through

- Efficiency/leverage
- Expertise
- Investment and competence building
- Fostering innovation – coaching/learning
- Mitigating risk
- Image/networks
- Collaboration/co-ordination/brokerage
- Standards/performance assessment
- Intervention (e.g. acquisition, disposal, change agency)

broker external linkages or collaborations which may be essential to the processes of innovation.

- Setting *standards*, assessing *performance* of individuals and units, and *intervening* to improve performance (for example, by replacing managers, selling off businesses or ensuring turnaround of poorly performing divisions or businesses).

9.4.2 Dividing Responsibilities

It has already been mentioned that the critical issue is a proper definition of the role of the centre of the organisation and its various parts. This is essentially concerned with how responsibilities for decision making are *divided* between the centre and the divisions or departments. Goold and Campbell provide three valuable *stereotypes* (or management styles) of different ways of dividing these responsibilities (see Exhibit 9.9). The parenting approach is very different in each case and requires very different competences at the corporate centre.

Strategic Planning

Strategic planning (Exhibit 9.10) is the most centralised of the three approaches. In **strategic planning style**, the centre of the organisation operates as a parent who is the *masterplanner* and prescribes detailed roles for divisions and departments. The latter are seen as *agencies* which *implement* part of the organisation's plan. Their role is confined to the operational delivery of the plan. In the extreme form of strategic planning, the centre is expected to add value in *all* the ways outlined above. The centre orchestrates, co-ordinates and controls all of the activities of the departments and divisions, resulting in the extensive use of the management devices shown

in a **strategic planning style** *the centre of the organisation operates as a parent who is the masterplanner and prescribes detailed roles for divisions and departments*

Exhibit 9.9 Centre – division relationships

APPROACH	KEY FEATURES	ADVANTAGES	DANGERS	EXAMPLES
Strategic planning	'Masterplanner' Top-down Highly prescribed Detailed controls	Co-ordination	Centre out of touch Divisions tactical	BOC Cadbury Lex STC Public sector pre-1990s
Financial control	'Shareholder/banker' Financial targets Control of investment Bottom-up	Responsiveness	Lose direction Centre does not add value	BTR Hanson plc Tarmac
Strategic control	'Strategic shaper' Strategic and financial targets Bottom-up Less detailed controls	Centre/divisions complementary Ability to co-ordinate Motivation	Too much bargaining Culture change needed New bureaucracies	ICI Courtaulds Public sector post-1990

Source Based on M. Goold and A. Campbell, *Strategies and Styles*, Blackwell, 1987.

in Exhibit 9.10. The centre also directly manages the infrastructure and provides many corporate services. This would include the management of innovation, which is seen as a key corporate responsibility. This is the classic bureaucracy familiar to many managers in large public and private sector organisations. Many of the multinational fast-food chains, such as McDonald's, would arguably come closest to this stereotype.

A follow-up study by Goold, Campbell and Luchs[16] of organisations categorised as strategic planning in the original study concluded that strategic planning can be a useful approach and one in which corporate managers add value, but only if they are able to have a detailed working knowledge of each 'core business'. Where attempts are made to extend beyond this arena, strategic planning as a management style becomes difficult to operate and often dysfunctional. Essentially, corporate managers run the risk of holding back the development of business areas which they do not understand or, even worse, steering them in inappropriate directions. The potential costs of bureaucracy are also dangers with this style, both in money and in lost opportunities.

The problems experienced with this approach have encouraged many organisations to devolve further (as seen in the case of IBM UK – Illustration 9.5). In particular, the relationship between the centre and divisions or departments tends to become entirely tactical and characterised by a 'special pleadings' mentality in the divisions and departments.

Exhibit 9.10 Strategic planning

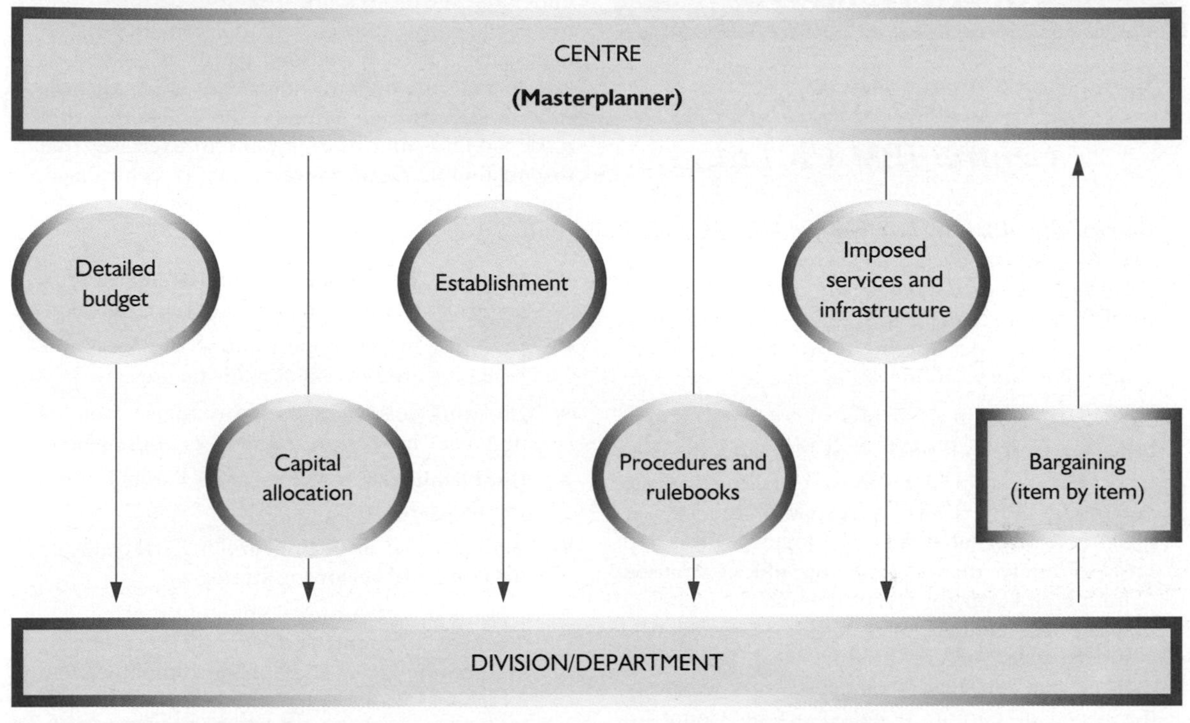

Financial Control

Financial control (Exhibit 9.11) is the most extreme form of devolved structure – short of complete dissolution of the organisation. The centre behaves as a parent who is like a *shareholder or banker* for divisions. There is little concern for the detailed product/market strategy of divisions – even to the extent that they can compete openly with each other. They might even have authority to raise funds from outside the company.

In **financial control** the role of the centre is confined to allocating capital (against bids), setting financial targets, appraising performance and intervening to avert or correct poor performance (e.g. by replacing divisional managers). The centre is attempting to add value in only a few of the ways listed earlier – in particular, through its corporate image and leverage (particularly in money markets) and mitigating the risk of individual divisions through the management of a portfolio of activities. Importantly, the centre is bringing managerial core competences (say, in turnround of poor performance) which add value to the various businesses, by setting standards and reviewing performance.

in **financial control** *the role of the centre is confined to allocating capital (against bids), setting financial targets, appraising performance and intervening to avert or correct poor performance*

STRATEGY IN ACTION
Illustration 9.5

A Change of Role for the Centre: IBM UK Ltd

Historically, IBM had a centralised command and control structure supported by a strategic planning style at the corporate centre. However, as the structure has changed to a federation of individual businesses, the strategic style of the centre has also changed to one of strategic control.

Between 1991 and 1993, IBM UK was forced to take radical action in response to falling revenue and profitability levels. A review of the market place revealed that it was developing so fast and into so many niches that the old centralised planning and control structure was incapable of reacting fast enough. Within this structure, the company was largely product and technology driven, and product strategies were primarily developed at corporate headquarters. Countries were responsible for short- and medium-term targets, and for managing their resources and skills to achieve these targets. Within the country, sales branches had no strategic flexibility. They were given annual revenue, headcount and expense targets, with the main focus being on the achievement of revenue.

Under increasing pressure, a decision was taken to restructure the organisation into a federation of businesses, so devolving decision making closer to the customer to get the responsiveness needed. Further actions included changing the management system and substantially increasing the focus on quality. In this new environment, where there was considerable interdependence between the businesses, retaining the strategic planning style would have damaged the federal concept and a pure financial control style would have suboptimised the interdependencies between businesses. The adoption of a strategic control style was the optimal choice.

The adopted strategic control style means the individual businesses are free to experiment and to display the entrepreneurial characteristics necessary for rejuvenation. Power is placed as low down in the organisation as practical, with the sales branches and functions having both profit responsibility and the power to exercise that responsibility. Some power remains centralised, but only where there is good reason to do so. The centre's role has thus changed to:

- Deciding the allocation of limited financial resources between members of the federation.
- Investing in new opportunities and areas not being covered by existing businesses.
- Divesting those markets and systems which are no longer integral to the success of the whole.
- Establishing shared values and a style to bind the federation.
- Adding value through provoking strategic thinking and reviewing strategies.
- Optimising performance by not granting 'licences' for unattractive markets. Licences are obtained from the holding company when a business wants to operate in a specific area. Normally this will be an exclusive licence, although in some cases it may be appropriate for more than one business to be licensed.

Questions

1. Critique the role of the new IBM against the checklist provided in Exhibit 9.8.
2. *In your opinion* is this the best form of strategic control given the nature of IBM strategies in the late 1990s?
3. What would have been the practical difficulties of moving IBM from a style of 'strategic planning' to one of 'strategic control'?

Source G. Lloyd and M. Phillips, 'Inside IBM: strategic management in a federation of businesses', *Long Range Planning*, vol. 27, no. 5 (1994), pp. 52–63.

Prepared by Sara Martin, Cranfield School of Management.

Exhibit 9.11 Financial control

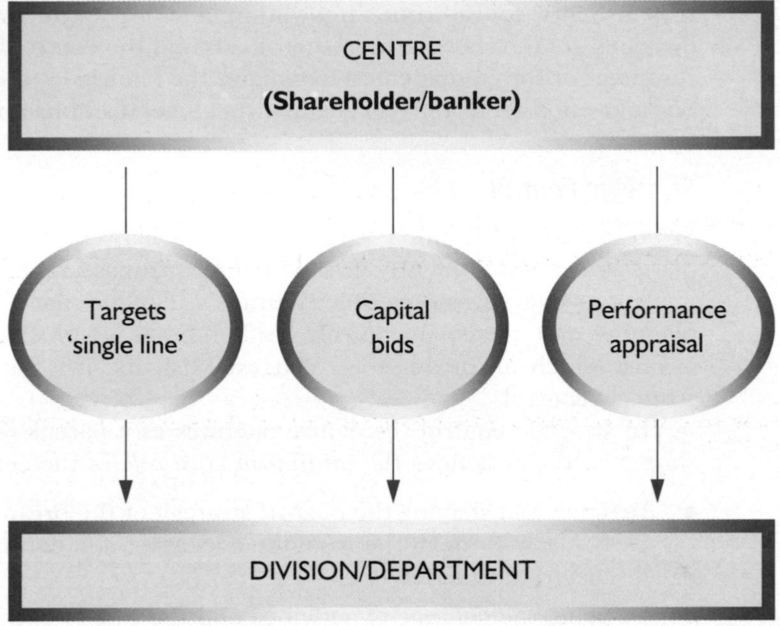

This extreme is rarely found – even in the private sector. Some public sector managers appear to hold this as their ideal of what devolution means, but in reality, such extreme devolution is likely to remain unacceptable within the public sector for reasons of political accountability. Some countries (e.g. New Zealand) have created state-owned enterprises (SOEs) with considerable commercial freedom but one step short of privatisation.

The follow-up study led to some interesting further observations about this style. First, it seems most appropriate to organisations operating in stable markets with mature technologies, and where the decision-making cycle (cause and effect) is short term: for example, organisations dealing with basic products. Second, there needs to be sufficient similarity between the divisions or subsidiaries for the core management competences to apply in similar ways to all divisions/subsidiaries. Otherwise, the parent may not have the competence to cope with a widely diverse set of subsidiaries. In terms of discussions earlier in the book, the management paradigm needs to be genuinely transferable from one organisation to another. Third, the target-setting and performance-appraisal regime needs to be applied consistently and tightly – an issue which proved difficult for some companies in the recession. Finally, the issue was raised of whether this style runs out of steam after a period of time, and is therefore most applicable to organisations which take a shortish-term view of their ownership of subsidiaries – where financial control is used to turn around companies which are divested once in good shape. A major concern with financial control can be the dominance of short-termism. No one has responsibility for fostering innovation and organisational learning. The divisions are too short term in their focus and the centre does not have the resources or the competences to manage the knowledge creation processes. So innovation tends only to occur through acquisitions and disposals.

Strategic Control

Strategic control (Exhibit 9.12), which lies between these two extremes, necessarily defines the way in which most organisations operate. In a sense it is not a single stereotype, since it bridges all of the space between strategic planning and financial control. So Exhibit 9.12 provides the *checklist* against which an organisation can establish its own particular brand of strategic control.

In strategic control the centre operates as a parent who is a *strategic shaper*, and this defines the *minimum core role* of the centre as follows:

- Defining and shaping the *overall* strategy of the organisation – particularly through the resource allocation and control regime (to be discussed in Chapter 10).
- Deciding the *balance* of activities and the role of each division or department.
- Defining and controlling organisational *policies* (on employment, market coverage, etc.).
- Fostering innovation and organisational learning.
- Defining standards and assessing the *performance* of the separate divisions and departments and intervening to improve performance.

However, the centre does not fulfil these roles through an imposed master-plan. Rather, strategic control is built through the process of agreeing business plans produced by divisions – but within central guidelines. **Strategic control** is where the corporate centre is less concerned with developing strategy through structuring the *tasks* of its various departments or divisions. Rather, it is concerned with shaping the *behaviour* in departments and divisions[17] and with shaping the *context* within which managers are operating. So, referring back to the earlier discussion and Exhibit 9.8, the centre would expect to add value through facilitating links and collaborations between divisions and departments – for example, through internal suppliers or collaborative product developments. Gaining advantage through *synergy* would often be an important objective in organisations. It would be concerned with promoting organisational learning by benchmarking and disseminating best practice. Central services may be optional rather than imposed.

strategic control *is where the corporate centre is concerned with shaping the behaviour in departments and divisions and with shaping the context within which managers are operating*

Goold, Campbell and Luchs' follow-up study[18] concluded that fulfilling this particular type of parenting role is difficult unless the

Exhibit 9.12 Strategic control

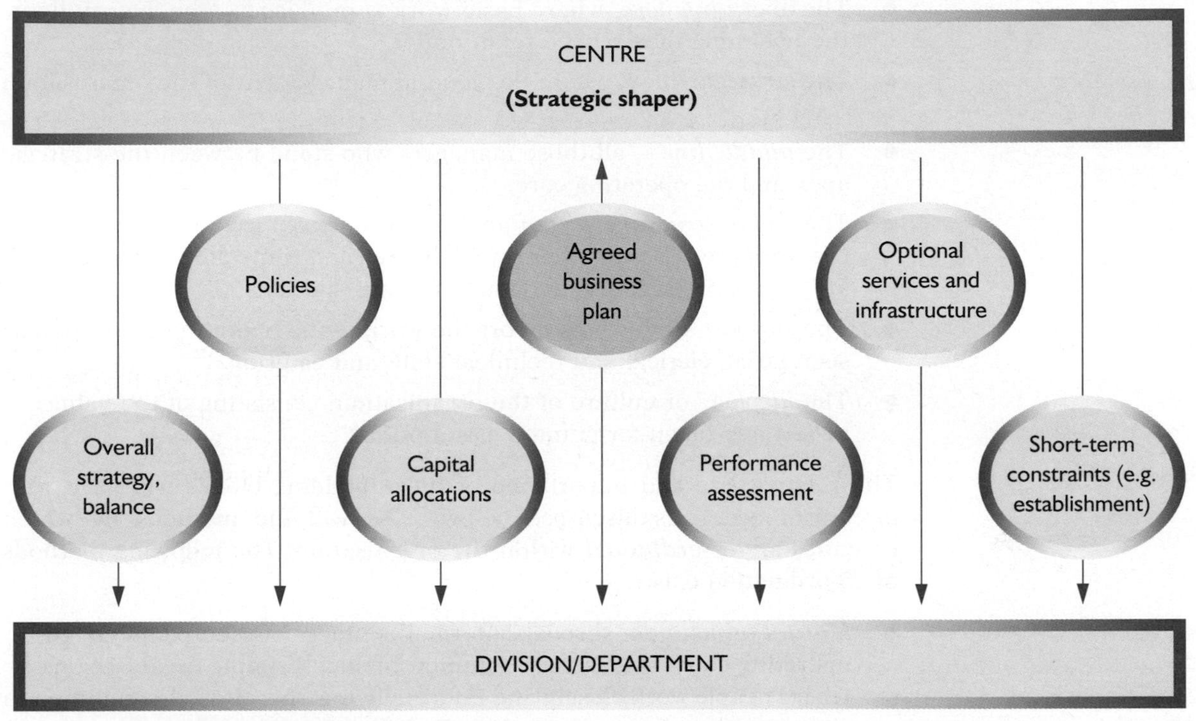

various divisions show similar characteristics. They cite the 1990s demergers in Courtaulds and ICI as examples of the difficulties of coping with too much diversity.

9.5 ORGANISATIONAL CONFIGURATIONS

The discussions in section 9.2 presented structure as essentially synonymous with levels in a hierarchy. The discussions in the previous section have shown that organisational design is in practice more complex than this. The *configuration* of an organisation is the detailed design consisting of a number of *building blocks* and *co-ordinating mechanisms*.

Mintzberg[19] has suggested that there are in essence six pure configurations which can be adopted (or emerge) to fit the context which different types of organisation face. Before considering these configurations, it is necessary to describe the building blocks which make up each of them.

Exhibit 9.13 shows Mintzberg's six basic building blocks of organisational design:

- The *operating core*, where basic work is produced – the factory floor, the operating theatre, the retail outlet.
- The *strategic apex*, where the general management of the organisation occurs.
- The *middle line* – all those managers who stand between the strategic apex and the operating core.
- The *technostructure* – staff analysts who design the systems whereby the work processes of others are delivered and controlled. Included here are engineers, accountants and computer specialists.
- The *support staff*, who support the work of the operating core, such as secretarial, clerical and technical staff, and catering.
- The *ideology* or culture of the organisation, consisting of the values, beliefs and taken-for-granted assumptions.

The relative size and importance of these building blocks will vary with circumstances – as discussed below – as will the methods by which activities are *co-ordinated* within the organisation. The following methods of co-ordination exist:

- *Mutual adjustment* through informal contact between people in the operating core. This is very common in small, simple organisations where people work closely and informally together. It is also common in very complex situations, such as R&D projects.
- *Direct supervision* through the hierarchy. Work is supervised by instruction from the strategic apex, through the middle line to the operating core.
- *Standardisation of work processes* through systems which specify how work should be undertaken. It is usually the job of the analysts in the technostructure to design and develop these systems of work standardisation.
- *Standardisation of outputs*: for example, through product or service specifications. This is particularly important where responsibility for separate activities is divided within the organisation. Many organisations are now developing *service-level agreements* between departments in order to clarify the parameters of service expected from, say, computer services, credit control, etc. The corporate centre may also specify levels of output performance which are expected of divisions or subsidiaries – particularly in devolved organisations, as discussed above.
- *Standardisation of skills*, including knowledge and competences. This is an important co-ordinating mechanism in many professional service organisations (private and public sector). So the operating core of a professional service such as a hospital or an architect's practice

Exhibit 9.13 **The six building blocks of organisations**

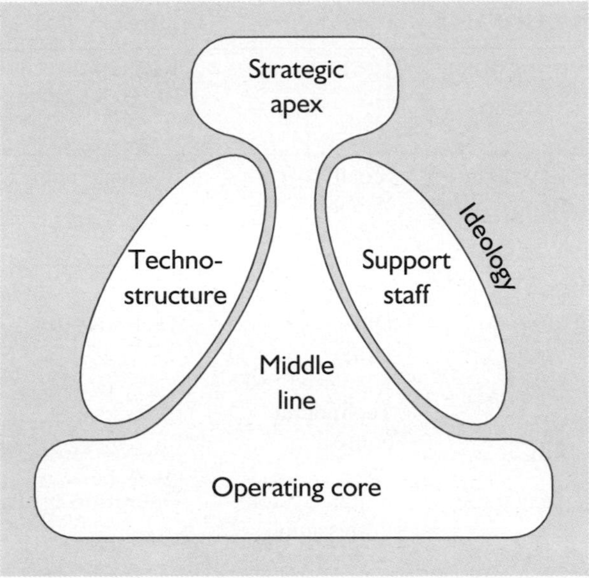

Source H. Mintzberg, *The Structuring of Organizations*, Prentice Hall, 1979.

functions smoothly because the operators share the same core knowledge and competences through their professional training.

- *Standardisation of norms*, where employees share the same core beliefs. This is particularly powerful in many voluntary organisations.

9.5.1 Configurations in Practice

The choice of configuration to support an organisation's strategies can best be thought of in terms of matching the organisation's configuration to its strategic situation through the choice of the two design parameters discussed above: the *building blocks* and *co-ordinating mechanisms*. It should be clear from previous discussions in this book that this match is likely to *emerge* over time as an organisation finds ways of adjusting to the context in which it is operating. So it is unlikely to be a carefully considered choice as such. Nonetheless, it is useful for managers to reflect on the extent to which they see a match or mismatch between their organisational configurations and the context in which they are operating.[20]

Exhibit 9.14 summarises the key features of Mintzberg's six configurations, in terms of the circumstances or situations to which each is best

Exhibit 9.14 Mintzberg's six organisational configurations

	Situational Factors		Design Parameters	
Configuration	Environment	Internal	Key Part of Organisation	Key Co-ordinating Mechanism
Simple structure	Simple/dynamic Hostile	Small Young Simple tasks CEO control	Strategic apex	Direct supervision
Machine bureaucracy	Simple/static	Old Large Regulated tasks Technocrat control	Technostructure	Standardisation of work
Professional bureaucracy	Complex/static	Simple systems Professional control	Operating core	Standardisation of skills
Divisionalised	Simple/static Diversity	Old Very large Divisible tasks Middle-line control	Middle line	Standardisation of outputs
Adhocracy	Complex/dynamic	Often young Complex tasks Expert control	Operating core Support staff	Mutual adjustment
Missionary	Simple/static	Middle-aged Often 'enclaves' Simple systems Ideological control	Ideology	Standardisation of norms

Source H. Mintzberg, *The Structuring of Organizations*, Prentice Hall, 1979.

suited and also the 'shape' and *modus operandi* of the organisation – its building blocks and co-ordinating mechanisms.

- The *simple structure* is in many senses a 'non-structure'. Few of the activities are formalised, and it makes minimal use of planning. It has a small management hierarchy, dominated by the chief executive (often the owner) and a loose division of work. The organisation is driven forward by the vision and personality of the chief executive. This configuration can prove highly effective in small entrepreneurial organisations where flexibility to changing circumstances is critical to success.

- The *machine bureaucracy* is often found in mature organisations operating in markets where rates of change are low. It is characterised by a large staff function – or *technostructure* – which develops systems and work routines to standardise work. The major improvements in cost efficiency in manufacturing industries early in the twentieth century were largely achieved through machine bureaucracies. This configuration is still very appropriate for organisations producing commodity products or services where cost leadership is critical to the organisation's competitive performance (mail services would be an example).
- The *professional bureaucracy* is bureaucratic without the centralisation found in the machine bureaucracy. Professional work is complex, but it can be standardised through ensuring that the professionals operating in the core have the same core knowledge and competences. An emphasis on training and peer group interaction and learning is important to sustaining this standardisation.
- The *divisionalised* configuration is often found as a response to diversity in the products and markets of the organisation, as discussed earlier in the chapter. The important organisation design issues are concerned with centre/division relationships, as discussed in section 9.4. In particular, the corporate centre will specify levels of performance output expected from divisions or subsidiaries. These might be generic, such as overall profit performance, and might be found when *financial control* is the management style. In contrast, in organisations closer to *strategic control*, this specification of outputs is more likely to be expressed as a series of *performance indicators*, such as market share, efficiency ratios and a 'league table' position.
- The *adhocracy* is found in organisations whose competitive strategy is largely concerned with innovation and change. This configuration is highly organic, relying on direct interaction between workers in the operating core and a management style which assists and promotes this 'mutual adjustment'. Many professional service organisations (when providing tailor-made services rather than standard or routine services) may configure themselves in this way. The 'style' of the corporate centre in fostering knowledge creation and innovation is of particular importance in an adhocracy. It is important to avoid a bureaucratised approach and to allow knowledge creation to occur in the natural 'communities' within the organisation and between these communities (both internally and externally). An adhocracy needs to be seen as a 'community of communities'[21] if innovation is to thrive.

Exhibit 9.15 Changing configuration: some examples

FROM	TO	REASON	EXAMPLE
Simple	Machine bureaucracy	Growth	Manufacturing companies
Machine bureaucracy	Divisionalised	Growth and diversity	Many companies
Professional bureaucracy	Adhocracy	Changing environment	Many service organisations
Missionary	Professional	Growth	Not-for-profit organisations
Professional bureaucracy	Network organisation	Dynamic environment	Professional service organisations
Single configuration	More than one type	Dynamic/complex environment	Many

- *Missionary* organisations are dominated by cultural issues which are clear, focused, inspiring and distinctive. These ideals dominate the organisation's purposes and its *modus operandi*. Many voluntary organisations operate in this way: they attract like-minded individuals who share the missionary vision, and as such rely little on structures and systems to drive the organisation along.

Although few organisations will fit neatly into just one of these stereotypes, they can be used to think through some important issues concerning the structure/strategy fit in an organisation. Managers can check out in Exhibit 9.14 which stereotype their organisation currently most resembles. More importantly, they can describe the situational factors (both external and internal) for their organisation and see how closely these match the situation for which that particular configuration is best suited. For example, the simple structure is particularly appropriate for small companies in simple but dynamic environments.

9.5.2 Changing Configuration

It is quite possible that changing circumstances will have created a mismatch between the configuration and the situation. This is where many difficulties occur in practice, not least for cultural reasons, as will be seen in Chapter 11. For example, the small company may have grown and diversified so that the simple structure can no longer cope. Many public

STRATEGY IN ACTION
Illustration 9.6

The Service Factory as Regulator

Changing situations require a rethink about an organisation's configuration and flexibility. This has been a major challenge for many service organisations.

In the early twentieth century the introduction of the conveyor belt represented a fundamental change in the running of manufacturing companies. Its introduction brought a new mode of work tied to machinery and to fixed places. The logistic chain of supply within and between firms has since replaced the conveyor belt. The mutual dependency of people and businesses has increased still further.

Service industries were historically regarded as more flexible and less standardised than manufacturing. However, this classical distinction between the sectors has become blurred. Many organisations in both sectors now work in a standardised fashion with a strong customer orientation. They provide a standard 'package' around which the needs of the individual customer can be 'assembled' according to the production or service philosophy of the organisation.

They have become what could be called a 'service factory'. A Dutch bank director summed it up as follows: 'It takes only 100 seconds to service a client in a call centre and they get satisfaction – that is the norm.' Speed combined with service has been made possible by the standardisation of work procedures, protocols, reports, results assessment, instructions and regulations. In such a 'mechanised' world the organisation actually has more time to respond to the 'unusual' – the request that deviates from the norm. The skill is in finding a proper balance between the routine and the non-routine. Employees are expected to convert the customised to the standard and vice versa. They have become the regulators – they have more control.

On the other hand, control has become more centralised. For example, in a hospital, the nurse or doctor is given more information than ever about the patient, while being directed by information from elsewhere. In general, it can be said that the logistic 'process-tied' nature of work is on the increase so that employees are, as it were, 'condemned' to each other on the modern-day conveyor belt of business process interdependence. In this context the regulatory functioning of the 'service factory' determines flexibility rather than the 'flexible employee' bargaining over his or her flexibility. Flexibility means being equal to the demands that the service factory imposes.

Questions

Refer to Mintzberg's six organisational configurations (Exhibit 9.14) and consider the following.

1. What are the main situational factors that have driven the changes in service organisations?
2. Classify the 'service factory' into Mintzberg's stereotypes.
3. Does the service factory configuration match the situational factors from your answer to question 1?

Source Professor W. Buitelaar, University of Amsterdam.

services took on features of professional bureaucracies during a period of little change, and then experienced considerable difficulty in adjusting parts of their organisation towards an adhocracy as a necessary response to a dynamic environment which required more flexibility and customisation of services. Exhibit 9.15 shows some of the situations which create the need to change an organisation's configuration.

An issue which most large organisations face – because of their diversity in product or market positioning – is the need for different configurations to support different SBUs or areas of the organisation's work. So the machine bureaucracy may be ideal for delivery of the commodity products or services, while the specialist product division positioned in a niche market may well need to operate like an adhocracy. For example, in a legal practice, for the *routine* legal work – say, wills or house conveyancing – the legal experts can design standard systems of delivery and the day-to-day work can be undertaken by other staff (or even partly by computer-based systems). *Standard* services require the experts to perform 'pigeon-holing' or diagnostic work (referred to in section 9.2.7 above) with clients to decide which standard services best suit their needs and circumstances – this can then be progressed by other staff. For *tailor-made* legal work, the legal expert needs to work with the client all the way through, since the work is genuinely unique to that client. The organisational configuration therefore needs to be a mix or a hybrid of the pure stereotypes, since the legal experts have different roles and contributions to make to these different types of service. These issues are of central importance to many service organisations as the full impact of IT systems becomes apparent, as seen in Illustration 9.6

SUMMARY

- Structure is a means to an end (improved performance). All too often it is seen as an end in itself. An inappropriate choice of structure can impede an organisation's strategies. However, the reverse is not true – structural change will not guarantee success.
- There are many stereotypical structures (such as functional, divisional, matrix). It is important to be familiar with the strengths and weaknesses of each structural type and to understand that real organisation structures are usually a blend of these pure stereotypes.
- *Globalisation* presents a special problem for organisations in trying to balance the competing forces of global uniformity and local responsiveness. There are several different 'solutions' to this problem depending on circumstances.
- A key issue of organisational design is the *centralisation/devolution* decision. Where, within the structure, will authority for strategic decisions reside?

- There are three stereotypes for devolution: *strategic planning*, *financial control* and *strategic control*. These should be used to determine the role of the centre of the organisation and the management tools that should tie the centre to its departments, divisions or subsidiaries. The key issue is to have a consistent model of devolution that suits the purposes and circumstances of the particular organisation.
- Organisation design also needs to be understood at a more detailed level. Here Mintzberg's organisational configurations are useful as they show the relationship between the organisation's circumstances, the 'building blocks' and the co-ordinating mechanisms.
- Difficulties often arise as circumstances change and organisations need to change configuration. This is difficult as the relative importance of each building block and co-ordinating mechanism needs to change.

RECOMMENDED KEY READINGS

- The centralisation/devolution considerations are discussed in M. Goold and A. Campbell, *Strategies and Styles*, Blackwell, 1987.
- Parenting is discussed fully in M. Goold, A. Campbell and M. Alexander, *Corporate Level Strategy: Creating value in the multibusiness company*, Wiley, 1994.
- Organisational configurations are covered comprehensively in H. Mintzberg, *The Structuring of Organizations*, Prentice Hall, 1979, and H. Mintzberg and J.B. Quinn, *The Strategy Process: Concepts and cases*, 3rd edition, Prentice Hall, 1995.
- Organisational design issues in multinational corporations are covered in C. Bartlett and S. Ghoshal, *Managing Across Borders: The transnational corporation*, Harvard Business School Press, 1989, and G. Yip, *Total Global Strategy*, Prentice Hall, 1995.

REFERENCES

1. Some of these early writings are to be found in D. Pugh, *Organisation Theory*, Penguin, 1984.
2. These definitions come from T. Burns and G. Stalker, *The Management of Innovation*, Tavistock, 1968.
3. The advantages and disadvantages of functional structures are discussed in H. Mintzberg, *The Structuring of Organizations*, Prentice Hall, 1979.
4. This view of divisionalisation as a response to diversity was put forward by A.D. Chandler, *Strategy and Structure*, MIT Press, 1962, and supported by others, such as D. Channon, *The Strategy and Structure of British Enterprise*, Macmillan, 1973.
5. Matrix structures are discussed by C. Bartlett and S. Ghoshal, 'Matrix management not a structure, a frame of mind', *Harvard Business Review*, vol. 68, no. 4 (1990), pp. 138–45.
6. Network organisations are discussed in: J.C. Jarillo, *Strategic Networks: Creating the borderless organisation*, Butterworth/Heinemann, 1993; R.E. Miles, C. Snow and H. Coleman, 'Managing 21st century network organisations', *Organisational Dynamics*, vol. 20, no. 3 (1992), pp. 5–20; R. Miles and C. Snow, 'Causes of failure in network organisations', *California Management Review*, vol. 34, no. 4 (1992), pp. 53–72; H.H. Hinterhuber and B.M. Levin, 'Strategic networks – the organisation of the future', *Long Range Planning*, vol. 27, no. 3 (1994), pp. 43–53; W. Ketelhohn, *International Business Strategy*, Butterworth/Heinemann, 1993, chapter 4; D. Cravens and N. Piercy, 'Relationship marketing and collaborative networks in service organisations', *International Journal of Service Industry Management*, vol. 5, no. 5 (1994),

pp. 39–53. Also interesting is G. Redding, 'Overseas Chinese networks: understanding the enigma', *Long Range Planning*, vol. 28, no. 1 (1995), pp. 61–9.

7. Virtual organisations and the extensive use of subcontracting have been widely discussed. For example, W. Davidow and M. Malone, *The Virtual Corporation*, Harper Business, 1992; T. Peters, 'Get innovative or get dead', *California Management Review* (Fall 1990), p. 13; Jarillo (reference 6 above).
8. Jarillo (reference 6 above).
9. Good general texts on multinational corporations are G. Yip, *Total Global Strategy*, Prentice Hall, 1995; J. Ellis and D. Williams, *International Business Strategy*, Pitman, 1995.
10. C. Bartlett and S. Ghoshal, *Managing Across Borders: The transnational solution*, Harvard Business School Press, 1989; and 'Tap your subsidiaries for global reach', *Harvard Business Review*, vol. 64, no. 6 (1986), pp. 87–94.
11. C. Bartlett and S. Ghoshal, 'What is a global manager?', *Harvard Business Review*, vol. 70, no. 5 (1992), pp. 124–32.
12. Yip (reference 9 above), chapter 8.
13. M. Goold and A. Campbell, *Strategies and Styles*, Blackwell, 1987.
14. K. Scholes, 'Making the most of devolution', Sheffield Business School Occasional Paper No. 11, 1994. This issue of the centre/division relationship has also had a good deal of debate in the public sector context of the 1990s. See, for example, M. Clarke and J. Stewart, *The Enabling Council*, Local Government Management Board, 1988, and *The Role of the Centre*, Local Government Management Board, 1991.
15. Parenting has been discussed in Chapter 6. The key references are: M. Goold, A. Campbell and M. Alexander, *Corporate-level Strategy: Creating value in the multibusiness company*, Wiley, 1994; A. Campbell, M. Goold and M. Alexander, 'Corporate strategy: the quest for parenting advantage', *Harvard Business Review*, vol. 73, no. 2 (1995), pp. 120–32. S. Ghoshal and H. Mintzberg, 'Diversification and diversifact', *California Management Review*, vol. 37, no. 1 (1994), pp. 8–27, discusses the implications of diversification on organisation design and the role of the corporate centre.
16. M. Goold, A. Campbell and K. Luchs, 'Strategies and styles revisited: strategic planning and financial control', *Long Range Planning*, vol. 26, no. 5 (1993), pp. 49–60.
17. C. Bartlett and S. Ghoshal, 'Changing the role of top management: beyond strategy to purpose', *Harvard Business Review*, vol. 72, no. 6 (1994), pp. 79–88; S. Ghoshal and C. Bartlett, 'Changing the role of top management', *Harvard Business Review*, vol. 73, no. 1 (1995), pp. 86–96.
18. M. Goold, A. Campbell and K. Luchs, 'Strategies and styles revisited: strategic control – is it tenable?', *Long Range Planning*, vol. 26, no. 6 (1993), pp. 54–61.
19. H. Mintzberg, *The Structuring of Organizations*, Prentice Hall, 1979. These configurations are also discussed fully in H. Mintzberg and J.B. Quinn, *The Strategy Process: Concepts, contexts and cases*, 3rd edition, Prentice Hall, 1995.
20. For further reading on the relationship between configuration and organisational context, see D. Miller, 'The genesis of configuration', *Academy of Management Review*, vol. 12, no. 4 (1987), pp. 686–701, and 'Organisational configurations: cohesion, change and prediction', *Human Relations*, vol. 43, no. 8 (1990), pp. 771–89; D. Jennings and S. Seaman, 'High and low levels of organisational adaptation: an empirical analysis of strategy, structure and performance', *Strategic Management Journal*, vol. 15, no. 6 (1994), pp. 459–75. In addition, a collection of research papers on configuration and strategy is included in the *Academy of Management Journal*, vol. 36, no. 6 (1993), pp. 1175–361.
21. J.S. Brown and P. Duguid, 'Organisational learning and communities of practice: towards a unified view of working, learning and innovation', *Organisational Science*, vol. 2, no. 1 (1991), pp. 40–57.

WORK ASSIGNMENTS

9.1 Draw up organisation charts for a number of organisations with which you are familiar and/or any of the case studies in the book. Why are the organisations structured in this way?

9.2 Do you feel that the networking approach of ABB (Illustration 9.2) could be adopted by other organisations? What are the circumstances in which it would be most and least useful?

9.3 Compare the structure of 3M (Illustration 9.3) and Nestlé (Illustration 9.4). To what extent do you think they are in line with current thinking on organisational structure for multinational corporations (see Exhibit 9.7)? Would you recommend any changes in approach?

9.4 ● Make a critical appraisal of the importance of the centre/division relationship in underpinning the strategic development of organisations (see Exhibits 9.9 to 9.12). Illustrate your answer by describing (with justification) the relationships which you feel would be most appropriate for the following organisations:
(a) The News Corporation*
(b) Burmah Castrol*
(c) PSA Peugeot Citroën*
(d) IBM (Illustration 9.5)
(e) an organisation of your choice.

9.5 ● Referring to Exhibit 9.8, choose an organisation with which you are familiar and discuss the following two situations: (i) increasing centralisation, (ii) increasing devolution. In each case, explain and justify:
(a) examples of the circumstances in which you would recommend each change
(b) which specific items in Exhibit 9.8 you would centralise or devolve further
(c) how the change would assist the organisation to improve its performance
(d) any potential dangers of the change and how these might be avoided.

9.6 By referring to Exhibits 9.13 and 9.14, explain which of Mintzberg's organisational configurations best fits the situation of each of the organisations in assignment 9.4. To what extent is the actual configuration of the organisation in line with this expectation, and what are the implications of any mismatches?

9.7 ● By using specific examples from your answers to the previous assignments, explain how the various aspects of organisational design need to fit together to support an organisation's strategies. How close are theory and practice? Refer to Mintzberg and Quinn in the recommended key readings to assist with your answer.

* refers to a case study in the Text and Cases edition.
● denotes more advanced work assignments.

CASE EXAMPLE

Unilever

> Our strategy is to focus resources on a portfolio of product categories and geographic regions which together offer good prospects for the creation of value through profitable growth.
>
> The scale and scope of our core product categories require corporate strategic direction ... Active portfolio management is the key to long-term value creation. We should concentrate our efforts on fast moving consumer goods which represent over 90 per cent of Unilever's sales.

This was the vision of the way forward for Unilever outlined in the 1996 annual report by the newly appointed joint chairman Niall FitzGerald and his longer-standing partner Maurice Tabaksblat.

As one of the world's largest consumer goods businesses (turnover in the year was £33bn), 1996 marked an important turning point for Unilever. It was the year in which the first major corporate restructuring for almost thirty years took place in order to support its efforts to remain a leading global player in its industry. The company had been unusual in its corporate governance since the formation of the Unilever Group in 1930 which merged the interests of the Dutch and British companies, whilst maintaining them as separate legal entities (Unilever plc and Unilever NV) with headquarters in both Rotterdam and London. However, since 1930 the two companies operated as nearly as possible as a single entity with the same directors and a series of 'equalisation' agreements which ensured that all shareholders, whether NV or PLC, shared in the companies' success.

The day-to-day running of the business across the world had always been in the hands of the operating companies. Initially these were international subsidiaries but for many years a three-man special committee (joint chairmen and chairman designate) determined their direction, priorities, resources and targets. There was also a large head office which included worldwide product management groups (foods, detergents, personal products, speciality chemicals); regional management groups (to co-ordinate activities in regions of the world) and corporate functions and services (accountancy, research, personnel, etc.). It was in essence a global matrix structure.

The catalyst for change and restructuring was a marketing calamity, which rocked the company to its foundations. The company had launched a new detergent, Persil Power, which proved to have an ingredient that could ruin garments. Its biggest rival Procter & Gamble ruthlessly exploited the situation – resulting in hitherto unknown tensions between the British and Dutch companies and significant loss of market share in most European countries. But it was an event that brought impetus for change. The roots of its structural problems really went back to the late 1980s following a spectacular period of growth. By the mid 1990s the organisation was underperforming against its main rivals and showing signs of fatigue – lack of dynamism and excess bureaucracy. The already convoluted structure had become a labyrinth for those running operating companies who needed decisions from above. Too many decisions were being referred to head office for resolution.

In 1996 the company decided to call a halt to the drift and, through an initiative called 'shaping for outstanding performance', it restructured its operations. The three-person special committee was replaced with a seven-person executive council. The system of worldwide product co-ordinators was abolished, as was the network of regional co-ordinators. The 1996 annual report explained the new top-management structure:

> The core building blocks in the Unilever organisation remain the individual companies

> operating in their particular markets. These are now organised into 14 Business Groups, each with a President as chief executive who is accountable, with full profit responsibility, for the operational companies within his group.
>
> This grouping is essentially based on geographical markets. In the consumer businesses, Unilever operates in eight regions. In the majority of these regions, all Unilever companies form one Business Group. However, some regional operations are too large to be managed as a single group. Companies in Europe and North America are therefore organised in two or three Business Groups, each focusing on specific product areas. The three industrial Business Groups, on the other hand, are organised globally. Between them they cover Unilever's operations in *industrial cleaning and hygiene*, in *speciality chemicals* and *flavours and fragrances*.
>
> The Chairmen of NV and PLC are the principal executive officers of Unilever. They lead the seven-member Executive Committee, which is now Unilever's top decision making body, having replaced the Special Committee from September 1996. The Executive Committee is responsible for corporate strategic leadership. Other members of the Executive Committee are: the two Category Directors [who had 'strategic oversight' of the company's products and brands] for Foods and for Home & Personal Care; the Strategy & Technology Director who is also the Industrial Category Director; the Financial Director; and the Personnel Director. In the early phase of the new organisation there has been an additional member responsible for the transition from regional management groups to the new Business Groups.
>
> The Executive Committee comes together with the 14 Business Group Presidents within the Executive Council, which is led by the Chairmen.

There was considerable interest and comment on these structural changes from observers. For example, in *Management Today* (July 1996):

> Apart from streamlining and crystallising Unilever's decision-making processes, the new structure represents an attempt ... to globalise by devolution, not centralisation. While giving its executive committee total responsibility for overall strategic leadership, it is taking pains to devolve full operational responsibility, including regional strategy development, to the business group presidents.
>
> As such, the new organisation signals the end, so far as the group is concerned, of centrally driven expansion. The new Unilever will grow as much by local pull as by global push. It is setting out to turn its variegation, its innate diversity, into a source of competitive advantage. 'We used to think of ourselves as a European business with interests in North America and outside', says one executive. 'In the new organisation, Europe is just another region and it has to justify its existence along with all the rest'. With so much of world economic growth coming from Asia, that new equality should play a decisive part in restoring Unilever's flagging momentum.
>
> The obvious danger in devolving so much freedom of action, however, is that the new centrifugal Unilever will spawn a number of regional baronies which create duplicate bureaucracies, wasting resources instead of liberating them. The end result would be fragmentation.
>
> But powerful mechanisms are in place to prevent this and ensure that the regional groups use rather than abuse their new freedom. Each president will report directly to Tabaksblat and FitzGerald, the joint chairmen. The executive committee will be responsible for agreeing business plans with the 14 groups, monitoring their implementation and intervening if the plans are not met. The key interface between committee and presidents, between strategic direction and operating freedom, will be a new annual plan contract, with four components: strategic, investment, and human resource matters, and operational targets.

In the annual report the joint chairmen also explained other things that needed to happen to ensure maximum benefit from the restructuring:

> Last year important work was undertaken to enhance the effectiveness of our organisation

> and systems. We have been particularly concerned to share not only goals and strategy across the Unilever worlds, but also a clearly expressed common sense of purpose, with which all our people can identify. We have prepared a statement of corporate purpose and have begun discussing its implications widely within Unilever. It is an aspiration that expresses what we believe in and are committed to achieving, now and in the future. Sharing it throughout the business should make an important contribution to our success.
>
> We have also made good progress during the year on enhancing and extending our international information network. This helps individuals and project teams from all over the world to work together, enabling the rapid spread of best practice and new ideas. The possibilities opened up by the increasing speed and ease of communication for a company like Unilever are an exciting challenge, allowing us to bring the best of international know-how to the service of local consumers and customers.

Niall FitzGerald was also interviewed for *Management Today* in November 1997. He argued that his main concern was 'to send a clear set of objectives from the centre and give maximum freedom within that framework for people to operate in.' When asked whether that was not the way the company had always operated, his reply was:

> The thing we didn't realise was that we had a management style that purported to be like that, but we interfered a great deal. In short, senior executives spent too much time sorting out other people's decisions, local managers had too many bosses to report to and bureaucratic sloth was leaching any dynamism out of the organisation. Whereas what we needed to do was say very clearly what were the principles by which we do things, reinforce the principles, apply them consistently, and then say 'you go and do it, we won't interfere unless you move outside that framework or you are not meeting your plans.'

It was still early days for the new structure and the old saying that 'the proof of the pudding is in the eating' was particularly apt in this case.

Questions

1. Refer to section 9.2.8 and Exhibit 9.7 and describe how the global structure of the company had been changed over the years – including the 1996 change. Why had these changes been necessary?
2. Refer to section 9.4 and Exhibits 9.10–9.12 and explain which 'styles' of devolution existed prior to 1996 and after 1996. Why had the changes occurred?
3. What management systems and tools are needed between the centre and the operating companies to make this new style of devolution work? (You may wish to refer to Illustration 6.9 in Chapter 6 to give a little more background to this issue.)
4. How would the chairmen ensure that 'active portfolio management' actually did occur in the new structure?

Sources Company annual report 1996; *Management Today*, July 1996, pp. 46–8, and November 1997, pp. 50–4. With the permission of the copyright owner, Haymarket Business Publications Ltd.

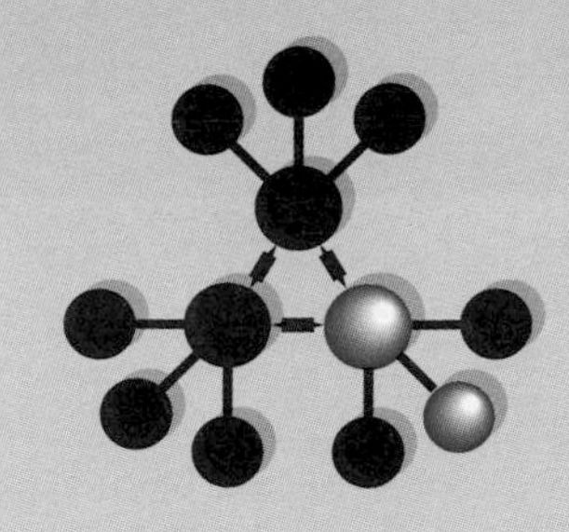

10
RESOURCE ALLOCATION AND CONTROL

LEARNING OUTCOMES

After reading this chapter you should be able to:

- Define business process re-engineering.
- Undertake a critical success factor analysis.
- Define administrative, social and self controls.
- Describe different control processes.
- Create a balanced scorecard for an organisation.
- Explain the different ways in which information management can underpin competitive advantage.
- Analyse how an organisation's strategy can best be supported by the various elements of organisation design.
- Define reinforcing cycles and explain why they occur.

10.1 INTRODUCTION

The previous chapter looked at how people and other resources of an organisation might be organised, first in terms of the basic *structure* of the organisation; and second in terms of where within this structure operational and strategic *decisions* are made. Finally, the detailed way in which organisations might be *configured* in order to support their strategies was discussed in terms of the *building blocks* and *co-ordinating mechanisms* which make organisations work in practice. These are all important aspects of the *architecture*[1] of the organisation, as discussed in the introduction to Part IV.

This chapter is concerned with pushing the discussion of architecture to a further level of detail by looking at the ways in which resources are *allocated* to create and sustain the competences needed to succeed. There is an important link back to the framework and discussions in Chapter 4, which was concerned with analysing and understanding strategic capability. In this chapter, the emphasis is on ensuring that the resources and competences are in place to deliver the particular strategies that the organisation is wishing to pursue. The chapter will also be concerned with the processes of *control* and information management which sustain the resources and competences of the organisation.

It is also important to emphasise again that, in thinking through how strategy will be put into effect, detailed thought is, in fact, being given to the *feasibility* of its implementation. As such, the planning of resource allocation and competence development is also part of the evaluation of strategy. Since much of strategic management is concerned with how an organisation will survive and prosper in a changing world, there is also an important link to the issues in Chapter 11, which is concerned with *management of change*.

Exhibit 10.1 illustrates how the planning and control of resources influence the success or failure of the organisation's strategies, and provides a framework for this chapter:

- The *resource configuration* of the organisation is concerned with both the *identification* of resource requirements and how those resources will be deployed to create the *competences* needed to underpin particular strategies. These competences are usually created through allocating a *mixture of resources* to a particular activity, as discussed in Chapter 4, and the *processes* which link these activities together. Referring back to Exhibit 4.2, the resource configuration will define the broad mix of resources and competences – both necessary, threshold requirements, and also the unique resources and core competences on which competitive advantage will be built. It needs to be remembered that this will include the way in which the separate activities of the organisation are linked together and the management of linkages in the wider value system in which the organisation is operating. Since few strategies are developed in a 'greenfield site' situation, there are usually important practical issues about how existing resources are redeployed and how new competences are developed.
- The resource configuration will define the broad shape of requirements for the future resources and competences of the organisation. There will also need to be specific *resource plans* for new developments (or strategic projects) which identify the critical success factors, priorities, schedules and budgets: in other words, how the resource configuration will be operationalised.
- *Control* of these aspects of strategy implementation can be achieved in a variety of ways, depending on how the organisation is designed and the situation which it faces. This could range from an emphasis on *systems* of planning and co-ordination, through *performance targets* and *rewards*, to looser *'market' forces*, *cultural control* or *personal motivation*. These various mechanisms for sustaining the necessary competences for the future will be discussed in relation both to the

Exhibit 10.1 Resource allocation and control – to support successful strategies

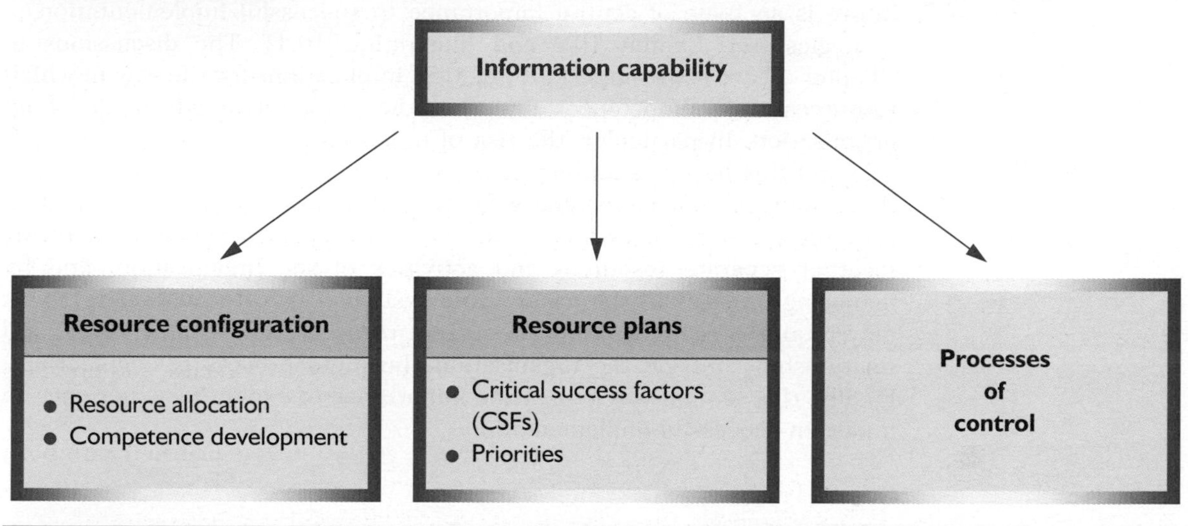

internal activities of the organisation and also to linkages *outside* the organisation into the wider value system.

- The *information capability* of the organisation will have a considerable influence on each of these previous aspects, and in that sense should be regarded as a key resource. For some organisations, information in the form of knowledge or intellectual property may be central to the organisation's competitive strength. New information technologies may also have been exploited to improve competences in, for example, purchasing or selling processes. This could be especially important as organisations globalise and face more complex situations. Similarly, the processes through which control of strategy is exercised can change if the information capability changes. For example, the rapid development of the Internet means that high-quality information is becoming increasingly available at the level of the 'operator', and does not need to be accessed, analysed and interpreted by specialist planning departments or managers. The importance of these changes will be discussed in section 10.5.

The chapter concludes with a short section which looks at how the circumstances of an organisation might determine or influence the structure and organisational design issues described in both Chapters 9 and 10. It will also consider the difficulties of changing organisations (as a precursor to a fuller discussion in Chapter 11).

10.2 RESOURCE CONFIGURATION[2]

The deployment of resources and development of competences for the future is an issue of central importance to successful implementation of strategies (see Exhibit 10.2 and Illustration 10.1). The discussions in Chapter 4 have some important practical implications for the way in which resources and competences underpin the competitive advantage of an organisation. In particular, the risk of imitation was stressed (see Exhibit 4.2) and this becomes an important consideration when thinking through the resources and competences for the future. In addition to protecting resources, competences for the future will need to be created by fitting together separate resources and activities of the organisation, and by managing linkages in the wider value system (e.g. with customers). This may require a reconfiguration of current resources and competences, and relationships outside the organisation (business process re-engineering). Finally, this section will look at the importance of exploiting experience to underpin successful implementation.

10.2.1 Protecting Unique Resources

Where a strategy is dependent on the *uniqueness* of a particular resource, it is important to ensure that this uniqueness is protected. This may be possible through the legal or *regulatory framework* (such as the patenting of products). It may involve *lobbying* to secure protection from competitors who may undermine the uniqueness (for example, import restrictions). It may involve plans for *continued investment* – for example, in R&D – which should be a high priority in terms of using the improved margins that the uniqueness should be creating (for example, through price premiums, as discussed in Chapter 6, or higher budgets for 'centres of excellence').

For some organisations, their uniqueness is difficult to imitate because it lies in the tacit knowledge[3] of a number of individuals or groups. In other words, the capability of the organisation is found in *personal competence* and is not formally owned by the organisation, as discussed in Chapter 4. This is true in many knowledge-based organisations,[4] such as software houses and biomedical companies, particularly where technology and product life cycles are short. Although the organisation may have ensured ownership of current products and developments (through patents or copyright), it is impossible to own the tacit knowledge which underpins the next generation of developments. So the retention of those individuals or groups with this knowledge becomes a key implementation issue: for example, through the development of suitable policies on pay, promotion and working conditions. Also, the management of knowledge creation and the processes of innovation (see Chapter 4, section 4.3.7) should concentrate on ensuring that there is a proper interplay between explicit and tacit knowledge.

Exhibit 10.2 **Resource configuration: creating capabilities for the future**

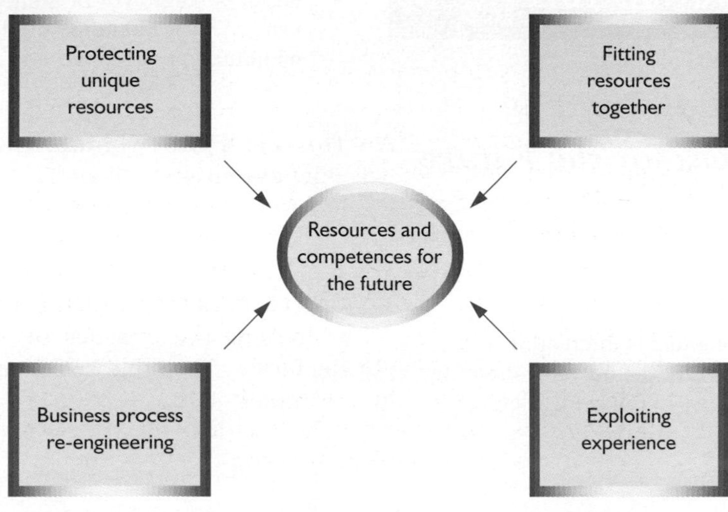

10.2.2 Fitting Resources Together

The organisation must be able to bring together an appropriate *mix* of resources to create competences. This can be a complex matter in many situations. For example, Exhibit 10.3 shows some of the resources and activities which need to be integrated by an organisation hoping to gain competitive advantage through its competence in bringing new products to the market more quickly than competitors. A competence in new product launches results from an ability to integrate and co-ordinate the separate activities of R&D, manufacture, etc. – each of which, in turn, involves bringing together a complex mixture of resources. It is not sufficient simply to own these resources or to be competent in these separate activities. It is the ability to link these together effectively and quickly which determines the success or failure of the strategy and could be a source of real competitive advantage.

10.2.3 Business Process Re-engineering

Few strategic changes are introduced in a greenfield site situation, and therefore a central question in resource allocation is how the *existing* resources and competences of the organisation can be adapted to fit new strategies. **Business process re-engineering** (BPR) is the process of reconfiguring activities to create a dramatic improvement in performance.[5] It will be seen in section 10.5.2 that increased capabilities in information

business process re-engineering *(BPR) is the process of reconfiguring activities to create a dramatic improvement in performance*

STRATEGY IN ACTION
Illustration 10.1

Skandia: Creating Competences for the Future

Competences for the future must relate to value-creating processes.

> The future of Skandia is in creating new work methods, competences and value-creating processes, not just in following the beaten path ... Through these processes emerges an accelerated growth of hidden, intangible, value. This is Skandia's intellectual capital – a combination of human and structural capital.

This was Bjorn Wolrath, the president and chief executive of Skandia – one of Europe's largest insurance groups – in a supplement to the company's annual report in 1995. The supplement was designed to demonstrate the variety of ways in which business units were addressing these issues of competences for the future. The table below summarises some examples.

BUSINESS UNIT	VALUE-CREATING PROCESSES	ORGANISATIONAL CAPITAL	BUSINESS EFFECTS
Vesta Processes for profitable customer relationships	• Systematised risk assessment and selection • Development of distribution channels to extend the duration of customer relationships • Development of IT-based support systems	• Database with overview of customer categories, so-called observation risks, no-risks, authorisation system • Routine manuals and systems for sales, customer care, customer renewal, operations, claims handling • Offer handling and analysis system	• Risk level (claims ratio) better than average • Improved distribution effectiveness • Growing market share • Increasing customer loyalty • Decreasing overhead ratio • Growing sales via alliances
Mexico Processes for risk management	• Risk assessment management and selection • Relationship development, customer care • Competence co-operation	• Guidelines, manuals for risk management • Work procedures for relationship development and customer care • Packaged, communicated strategy	• Greater customer loyalty • Higher contract renewal rate • Greater number of offers handled • Falling administrative expense ratio

Questions

For each of the business units undertake the following analysis.

1. Ensure you are clear about the focus for competence building: for example, Vesta is focusing on the business processes which underpin profitable customer relationships.
2. Consider the 'shortlist' of value-creating processes. Decide whether you would add to or delete from this list.
3. Do a similar critique for the *organisational capital* (in effect, firm-wide systems and infrastructure).
4. Do you feel that the claimed benefits (*business effects*) are likely to result from these competence improvements?

Source 'Intellectual capital – value-creating processes', a supplement to Skandia's annual report 1995.

Business Unit	Value-creating Processes	Organisational Capital	Business Effects
Industry Division Competence centres	● Development of IT-based support systems ● Customer care and customer development teams ● Knowledge sharing, competence co-operation	● INDRA, computer systems ● Customer team manual ● Competence centres ● Network of global competence through co-operation agreements	● Streamlined, more effective work methods ● Decreasing expense ratio ● More satisfied customers ● Doubling in premium volume through added and new sales
SkandiaLink Learning processes	● Automated fund-switching ● Transaction processing and telephone accessibility ● Staff reward system ● Augmentation of customer care	● SkandiaLink Investment Analysis (SIA) ● Value development process ● Automatic fund-switching service, Telelink ● FLINK index (administrative routines for business handling) ● Routine handbook for transaction processing ● Customer centres ● Customer care groups	● Shorter processing times ● Decreasing expense ratio ● Growing volume of assignments/ representative ● Increased number if automatic fund switches ● Greater staff commitment

Exhibit 10.3 Resource integration in a new product launch

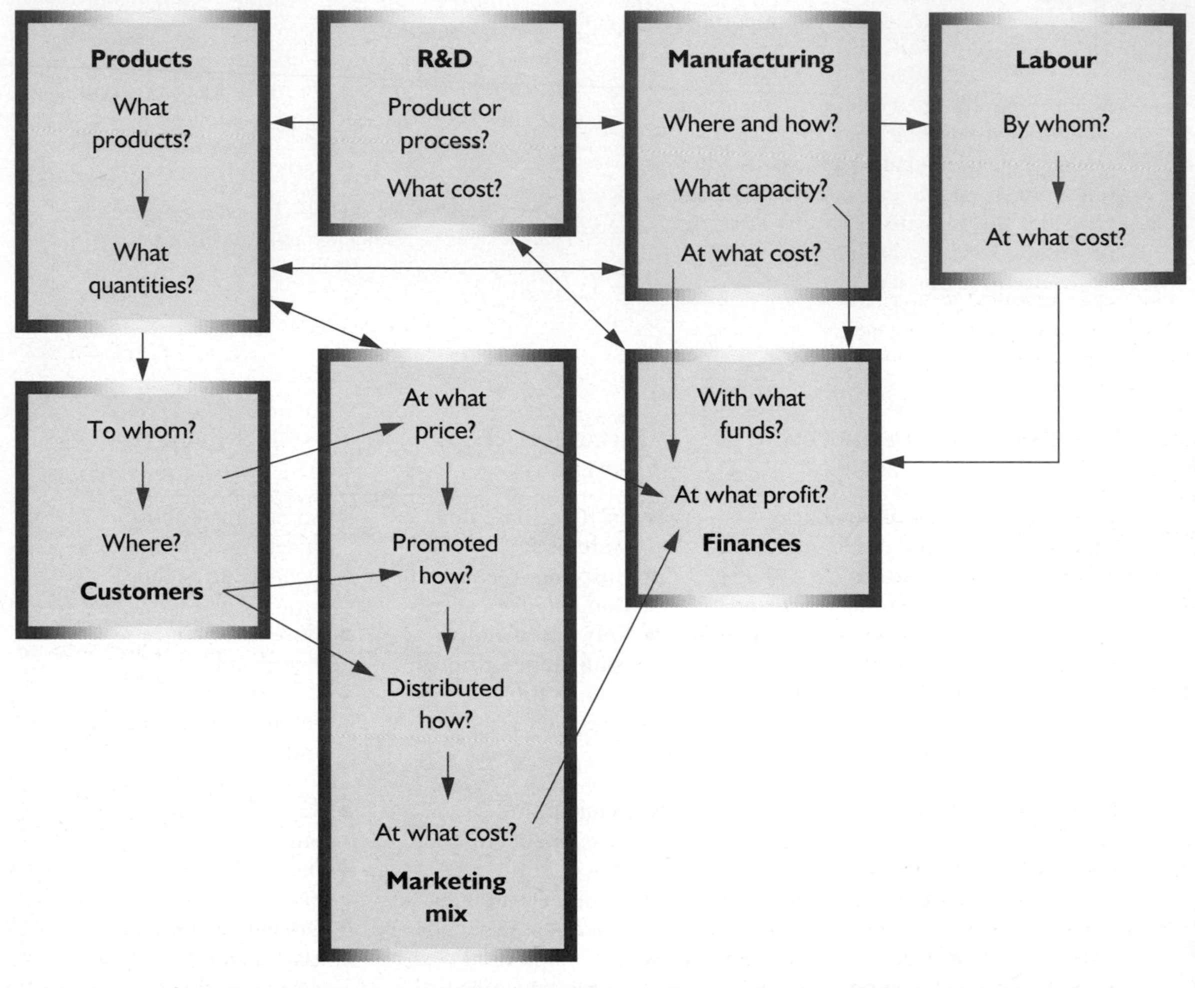

technology have been an important driving force behind BPR (and examples are given in Illustration 10.2).

Sometimes a company will choose to manufacture and market a new product range through a new division or even a new company to avoid problems of conflict or incompatibility with existing operations. So the planning of resources also leads back into structural considerations (Chapter 9) and into issues of managing change which will be discussed more fully in the next chapter. An assessment of this fit between the strategy and the existing resources and competences begins to establish the extent to which implementation is likely to require major changes within

STRATEGY IN ACTION
Illustration 10.2

Business Process Re-engineering at Ford and MBL

Business process re-engineering is concerned with reconfiguring resources and business activities to achieve dramatic improvements in performance.

Ford

In the early 1980s, Ford put its accounts payable sections under scrutiny in order to save costs. Management aimed to reduce the existing headcount of 500 by 20 per cent. This seemed a reasonable goal until they looked across at Mazda, which operated with only five people rather than the 400 Ford planned, implying that Ford's accounts payable section was five times the size it should be. Nothing to do with Japanese culture either!

Analysis of the existing system showed that the major problem was with the work required on purchase order/receipt document/invoice mismatches. Rather than *dealing* with these mismatches, Ford *stopped* them happening. It did this by initiating and storing orders on an on-line database, with no *physical* copies going to anyone. When the goods come in, someone checks the database; if they match, okay, if not they are simply sent back.

The old process required the accounting department to match fourteen data items; the new process needed only three, a part number, the unit of measure and a supplier code, and all of this matching is done automatically by the computer system, whereupon it automatically prepares the cheque, which accounts payable sends to the vendor. There are *no* invoices in the new system, since Ford told vendors not to send them. Ford gained two major benefits, a 75 per cent reduction in headcount and financial information that is significantly more accurate. Ford had completely *re-engineered* its accounts payable.

Mutual Benefit Life (MBL)

Mutual Benefit Life completely *re-engineered* its insurance applications processing by taking a radical approach that was enabled by IS [information systems]. This meant moving from a situation where 5 departments, 19 specialists, 30 internal checks, 7 different computer systems, 225 administrative staff and many months of elapsed time were required to issue a life insurance policy, to a situation that only required 1 case manager, 1 computer system, only 100 administrative staff and 1 day of elapsed time to issue a policy (and more being issued at that). This was done by sweeping *away* specialisation and the fragmentation of the task, and replacing it with IS-empowered single-person decision making. Since this redesign crossed many department boundaries, senior management resolution of disputes was vital to the success of the redesign process.

Questions

What are the general lessons from these two examples of business process re-engineering (BPR) in relation to the following?

1. How value for money can be improved.
2. Whether quality improvement and cost reduction can be achieved simultaneously (many managers see them as either/or).
3. How service organisations (and the service departments of all organisations) should be evaluating their IT strategy.
4. The limitations of BPR as a means of improving strategic performance.

Source Wendy Robson, *Strategic Management and Information Systems*, Pitman, 1994. Reproduced with permission.

the organisation, or is achievable by an adjustment of the current resource base and competences.

An important consideration about an organisation's resource configuration for the future is which activities it continues to undertake in-house and which should be bought in or subcontracted. This would include a review of *strategic alliances* (Chapter 7) and the *external networks* of the organisation (Chapter 9, section 9.2.7). Readers are also reminded of the discussions in Chapter 4 (section 4.3.6) about the dangers of subcontracting activities which are core competences, and this should be a guiding principle in reshaping these external relationships. It is essential that the organisation should be able to manage and influence knowledge creation and the processes of innovation even if some of them occur outside the organisation. So a global fast-food company like KFC is happy to franchise the operation of outlets, but maintains its core competences of product development and marketing in-house. These are the cornerstones of the business' success.

10.2.4 Exploiting Experience

An important way in which organisations improve their competences is through the experience of undertaking activities repeatedly and learning how to do them better (i.e. with lower cost and/or better value). The concept of the *experience curve*, introduced in Chapter 4 (section 4.3.3), underlines this point. There are some important implications for strategy implementation. First, other organisations are likely to imitate the leaders and catch up through their own learning. So learning and improvement need to be permanent features of successful implementation. This is the Japanese philosophy of *Kaizen*,[6] and is fundamental to the idea of gaining competitive advantage by stretching resources and competences to achieve levels of performance which others cannot match.[7] It is about designing a misfit between aspirations and current resources in order to create this stretching.[8] Ensuring that learning does occur and translating through to improvement in products or services are important aspects of the management of innovation in organisations. The processes of knowledge creation discussed in section 4.3.7 of Chapter 4 need to operate in a way which creates a healthy interplay between tacit and explicit knowledge, as shown in Illustration 4.5. This also means that resources will need to be available to sustain this continued improvement, so investment for the future is a permanent feature of successful organisations. One important part of this investment is in peoples' time to gain experience – through training, observation or exposure to new ideas through networking with suppliers, customers or competitors.

Another implication is that resource allocation decisions for the future should be driven by the expectation that efficiency gains (within limits) can be achieved without loss of quality (value); or alternatively, that value improvements can be achieved with the same 'unit of resource' (again

Exhibit 10.4 Competences and management styles to support different strategies

LOW-PRICE STRATEGY	DIFFERENTIATION STRATEGY
Underlying competences	**Underlying competences**
'Process' design	'Product' design
Labour supervision	Marketing
Easily produced 'products'	Creative flair
Low-cost distribution	Research capability
	Corporate image
Requiring	**Requiring**
Tight cost control	Looser control
Detailed reporting	Simpler reporting
Highly structured tasks	Strong co-ordination
Quantitative targets	Market-based incentives

within limits). Where organisations do not face free market situations (for example, many public services), the issue of efficiency gains tends to be a central issue for debate (and friction) during the resource allocation (budget-setting) process. The justification for year-on-year efficiency gains is that such gains through experience are essential to the survival of organisations in a free market situation, so this should be the benchmark against which continuous improvement in the public services is judged.

10.2.5 Sustaining Competitive Advantage

The discussion so far in this section has looked at a range of ways in which organisations might create the resources and competences for successful implementation of strategy. However, the relative importance of these resources and competences will vary depending on the type of strategy being implemented. For example, Exhibit 10.4 shows how the competences needed by an organisation will vary depending on whether the generic competitive strategy is one of low-price positioning or differentiation.

- A *low-price positioning* will need to be underpinned by real cost advantages on one or more of the items listed in Exhibit 10.4.[9] For example, a business purchasing large quantities of a given material from a supplier is likely to obtain better prices, have greater negotiating power to ensure that deliveries are on time (and therefore reduce stocks), and build up knowledge and experience among its buyers that leads to greater internal efficiencies. The same

STRATEGY IN ACTION
Illustration 10.3

Marks and Spencer

Differentiation through added-value products and customer service is difficult to imitate if sustained through the management of linkages in the value chain.

Marks and Spencer had built its reputation through consistency in product quality and levels of customer service. This differentiated M&S from many of its competitors in both food and clothing retailing (its two main areas of activity). The value chain opposite shows the importance of managing linkages to sustain this competitive advantage:

- All aspects of the 'customer experience' worked well together. So the quality of the products themselves was reinforced by the premier location of shops, in-store display, spacious shopping environment, and consistency of store layouts and business practices (e.g. environmentally responsible practices).
- The relationship with suppliers was a model of a genuine long-term partnership, involving a commitment to assisting suppliers to improve.
- This supply chain management was supported by tight systems for inventory control and the development of high standards of specification.
- Customer service standards in the stores required considerable efforts in systems development, exploitation of available technologies and the development of staff.
- There was commitment to improving access for customers – both physical access and ordering systems.

Questions

1. If you were a competitor of M&S, how might your competitive strategy 'respond' to an organisation which has such tight control and consistency over the management of its value chain?
2. If you started to achieve success, what kind of competitive reaction might M&S make?
3. Would this nullify the impact of your strategies (i.e. would they be a robust response to M&S)?

business might be able to identify other activities in which it can also gain cost advantage. Further, it may be possible to identify where competitors are vulnerable because they have a lower market share and therefore higher unit cost (e.g. in distribution). It may then be possible for the business to drive down its costs in these areas as a further means of gaining competitive advantage. All of this requires a mind-set where innovation (in cost reduction) is regarded as essential to survival.

- Crucial to a strategy of *differentiation* is the understanding of customers' needs[10] and the ability to build appropriate product or service features. Competitive advantage through differentiation is likely to be achieved not by one element of the value chain, but by multiple linkages within the value chain. It may be relatively easy for a competitor to imitate a product, or an aspect of technology. It is more

	IL	O	OL	M/S	S
FI	International Network				
TO	Advances in natural fibres owing to partnerships with technologists Best flavours identified by M&S technologists and suppliers together Piece-dyeing techniques	Precise monitoring of store energy consumption Quick response to over-usage	Fast till procedures Sophisticated rapid response network of computers IT system gives nationwide distribution operation	Customer ordering system	Sophisticated dyeing system enables mix and match
HRD			Staff secondments to voluntary organisation	Specialist advisers in key departments	Staff service initiatives
P	Unique supply base High specification standards	Tight inventory control Environmentally responsible practices			
	Partnerships with suppliers Long-term relationships Agreements also with suppliers' suppliers 'Most responsive, shortest supply chains in world'	Take control of whole process Machinery and hand checks of all raw materials Match individual store requirements – not fixed size ratios Store operating and business practices consistent across all franchises 100+ quality checks during production process Fast turnround centres	Premier locations – stores Network of excellent stores Franchise agreements overseas Foods loaded on trucks in combinations to match in-store display counters	Spacious/comfortable shopping environment Bold, attractive, colour co-ordinated displays 'Consistent quality on attractive price'	Easy care, easy wear garments. Improved access and facilities for shoppers

Source Company annual report, 1994.

difficult for a competitor to imitate differentiation based on a multitude of compatible linkages and processes throughout a value chain, as seen in the case of Marks and Spencer (Illustration 10.3). So, creativity and the management of product and process innovations are essential to competitive advantage.

- Businesses may also improve their competitive standing by building *switching costs*[11] into their products or services. Switching costs are the actual or perceived cost for a buyer of changing the source of supply of a product or service. This might be because the buyer is dependent on the supplier for particular components, services or skills. The business which can create significant switching costs is therefore achieving a differentiated position in the market.

It is important to identify bases of such switching costs. Managers might do this by considering how their own value chain might link into the value chain of buyers – a point made in Chapter 4 (section 4.3.5). For example, it could be that a manufacturing company is following a low-price strategy and therefore that low stock levels are of significant strategic importance. A supplier might choose to work closely with the manufacturer to ensure speed of delivery and information on availability of components. The supplier is seeking to build linkages between different parts of the value chain, to gain experience in so doing, and therefore to build switching costs into the service provided. This strategy is being followed by Unipart, the UK-based automobile component manufacturer.

- Difficulties tend to occur when there is a need for SBUs to *reposition*, requiring the development of new competences while the old competences become either redundant or of less importance. Exhibit 10.4 also shows that the approach to management control may need to vary for different types of strategy. A low-price strategy may be well supported by a centralised bureaucratic approach, while differentiation usually requires a more flexible style. This will be discussed more fully in section 10.4 below.

10.3 PREPARING RESOURCE PLANS

The discussion so far should help with defining, in broad terms, the resourcing and competence requirements for the future. However, it does not identify in detail the requirements of specific strategic developments. For this more detailed purpose, an organisation needs resource plans. The importance of these resource plans is to identify the critical factors for success of a particular strategy, and therefore the consequent priorities, schedules and budgets.

10.3.1 Critical Success Factors[12]

One of the major shortcomings of strategy implementation in organisations is a failure to translate statements of strategic purpose, such as gaining market share, into an identification of those factors which are critical to achieving these objectives, and the resources and competences which will ensure success. Chapter 4 introduced the idea of **critical success factors** (CSFs) as those components of strategy where the organisation must excel to outperform competition. These need to be underpinned by core competences which ensure this success. A critical success factor analysis can be used as a basis for preparing resource plans.

critical success factors *(CSFs) are those components of strategy where the organisation must excel to outperform competition*

Illustration 10.4 is an example of how a critical success factor analysis can be undertaken for an information systems company planning to improve its competitive position in a part of the market which requires complete 'turn-key' systems of hardware, standard software and customised information systems applications. It can be seen that the steps in a CSF analysis are usually as follows:

- Identify the critical success factors for the specific strategy, keeping these to a manageable list (preferably fewer than six). These might be factors such as 'global market access', 'quality/reliability' or 'product features' (as previously seen in Exhibit 4.6 of Chapter 4).
- Identify the underpinning core competences which are essential to gaining competitive advantage through each of these CSFs. These may be related to *separate activities* (e.g. lifestyle niche marketing), support activities (e.g. training and development) or the management of *linkages between activities* (e.g. supply chain management).
- Scrutinise the list to ensure that it is *sufficient* to give competitive advantage.
- Identify *performance standards* which need to be achieved to outperform competition: in Illustration 10.4, 24-hour turnround of enquiries, or 5 per cent royalty 'premium'. It is important to remember that competitors are likely to attempt to match or beat these standards and erode competitive advantage. Therefore, these performance standards need to be constantly reviewed (and changed). The use of performance standards to control strategy implementation will be discussed more generally in section 10.4.1 below.
- Assess the extent to which competitors can *imitate* each of the underpinning core competences. As discussed in Chapter 4, this is a critical question in determining the robustness of the core competences of an organisation.
- Decide on the impact of potential competitive moves and how these might need to be *counteracted*. Continual review of performance standards has already been mentioned. In Illustration 10.4, the company took the view that there were certain possible moves which they would *not* attempt to counter (providing global coverage for multinationals).

It is important when implementing strategies that the responsibility for each of the activities relating to the CSF are properly identified. In the illustration, the area where this could go badly wrong is database maintenance. Although this responsibility is assigned to the customer service department, the linkages with both the sales and software systems departments are crucial in ensuring accurate information.

10.3.2 Planning Priorities[13]

A resource plan sets out what resources and competences need to be created and which disposed of. This may well be in the form of a *budget*, but

STRATEGY IN ACTION
Illustration 10.4

Critical Success Factors for an Information Systems Supplier

Success depends on identifying those components of strategy in which the organisation must excel in order to outperform competition. This also requires a clear understanding of the competences which will be needed to underpin these critical success factors (CSFs).

An information systems supplier was planning to improve its competitive position in the part of the market which required 'turnkey' systems (hardware, standard software and customised information systems applications). The approach of most companies currently supplying this market was typified by an overemphasis on 'supplier-led applications' and very poor after-sales support of customers, particularly in the crucial three months after installation. It was also felt that many current customers had now 'matured' in their understanding of their information systems needs and were ready to 'trade up' to more sophisticated applications with a much greater level of customisation to their own particular circumstances.

In order to prepare for this new strategy, the company undertook a critical success factor analysis using the value chain to identify the underpinning core competences needed for each CSF.

Its analysis proceeded as follows:

- It identified three CSFs where it felt it would need to outperform competition. These were *customised software features*, *customer care* and *identification of new business opportunities*.
- The *underpinning core competences* which were essential to gaining competitive advantage through each of these CSFs were identified. So the CSF of *customer care* needed to be underpinned by two competences: responding to *enquiries* and the speed of breakdown *maintenance service*. In turn, these were dependent on competences in key support activities, particularly the *database* on customer installations. Some of these competences related to managing external linkages: for example, the highly developed system for customer feedback (both directly and via salesforce reports) and its use in informing both software feature developments and new business opportunities.
- It scrutinised the list to ensure that it was *sufficient* to give competitive advantage.
- It identified *performance standards* which needed to be achieved in each of the underpinning competences to outperform competition: for example, 24-hour turnaround of enquiries and 5 per cent royalty 'premium'. It knew that competitors were likely to attempt to match or beat these standards and erode competitive advantage. Therefore, these performance standards needed to be constantly reviewed (and changed).

might also be usefully expressed as a sequence of actions or a timetable of *priorities* in a written plan. For example, an organisation introducing a new product line would need a plan of action to co-ordinate the sequencing of the various aspects of its resource plan. On-the-job production line retraining cannot begin until a production facility exists. Until the company

CRITICAL SUCCESS FACTORS	UNDERPINNING CORE COMPETENCES AND PERFORMANCE TARGETS						
	INBOUND LOGISTICS	OPERATIONS	OUTBOUND LOGISTICS	MARKETING AND SALES	SERVICE	SUPPORT ACTIVITIES	MANAGING LINKAGES
Software features	Royalty payments (5% premium)						Customer feedback (monthly)
Customer care		Responding to enquiries (24 hours)			Speed of response (3 hours)	Installations database	Customer feedback (monthly)
New business opportunities				Salesforce reports (monthly)		Competitor profiling (top 10)	Customer feedback (monthly)

- It assessed the extent to which competitors could *imitate* each underpinning competence and any actions needed to counteract this imitation (continual improvement and revision of standards was one approach – it also considered whether to offer longer-term exclusive contracts to a few selected freelance writers).
- Competitors could, of course, also try to shift the competitive ground by identifying different critical success factors which were valued by (at least some) customers and developing their own core competences to underpin these CSFs. For example, they might identify that *global coverage* was of special importance to multinational companies and build a network of support (through strategic alliances) to provide this and gain competitive advantage with that particular group of customers.
- The company took the view that *at this stage* it would not attempt to counteract such a move, since it would overstretch the resources and competences of the organisation. Instead, it would concentrate its efforts on the parts of the market where this CSF analysis showed it could gain real competitive advantage.

Questions

This is a fast-moving industry and the company is conscious of the need to continually change and improve:

1. List the different ways in which the strategy could be changed and improved to stay ahead.
   (a) What *new* critical success factors relate to each new strategy?
   (b) What new competences will be needed to achieve these CSFs?
2. Prioritise the new strategies (giving your reasons), bearing in mind the practicalities of resourcing change.
3. Will the company survive the next ten years?

has examined in detail the timing of development, installation, commissioning and completion of the plant, it is not possible to examine fully the flow of funds required to finance the venture. Until it is known at what rate production is to be geared, a sensible view cannot be taken about the extent of the product launch; that in turn means that there will not be a clear idea

Exhibit 10.5 Network analysis for a customer survey project

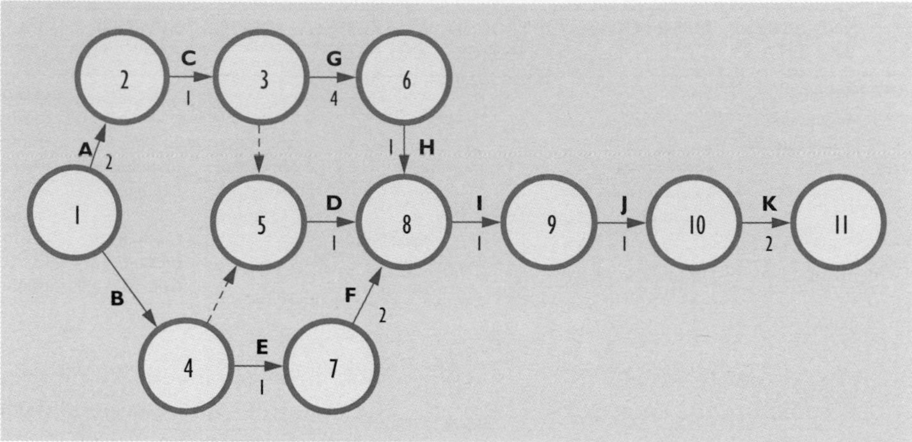

	Activity	Preceding activity	Duration (weeks)
A	Pilot survey	~	2
B	Investigation of computer requirements	~	1
C	Preliminary data analysis	A	1
D	Write initial report	B, C	1
E	Program design	B	1
F	Program testing and debugging	E	2
G	Main data collection	C	4
H	Data collation	G	1
I	Run program on collated data	F, D, H	1
J	Discussion and analysis of results	I	1
K	Final report	J	2

Source G. Worsdale, Sheffield Business School. Reproduced with permission.

of expected revenue flow, making it difficult to think sensibly about the requirement for funds.

The circularity of the problem is quite usual in developing a plan of action, and raises the question of where to start – with a market forecast, an available level of funds, a production-level constraint, or what? The answer is that it may not matter too much where the starting point is, since the plan will have to be reworked and readjusted several times. A useful guideline is to enter the problem through what appears to be the major change area. An organisation planning new strategies of growth may well start with an assessment of market opportunity. Someone starting a new business may well begin with a realistic assessment of how much capital they might have available.

Network analysis,[14] also known as *critical path analysis*, can be useful in this detailed planning of implementation. It is a technique for planning projects by breaking them down into their component activities and showing these activities and their interrelationships in the form of a network. By considering the times and resources required to complete each of the activities, it is possible to locate the critical path of activities which determines the minimum time for the project. The network can also be used for scheduling materials and other resources, and for examining the impact of changes in one sub-area of the project on others. The technique is particularly relevant to projects which have a reasonably definite start and finish, and where completion in the shortest possible time might gain competitive advantage.

It has been used very effectively in new product or service launches, construction of plant, acquisitions and mergers, relocation and R&D projects – all the sorts of activity relevant to strategy implementation. Exhibit 10.5 is an outline network analysis diagram for a customer survey project, which was of major importance in underpinning a drive for improved customer service standards.

10.4 PROCESSES OF ALLOCATION AND CONTROL

Identifying the appropriate resources and competences to support strategy implementation is important, but it will not result in successful implementation unless the organisation is also able to allocate resources and control performance in line with the strategy. There are three broad **types of control**: *administrative control*, through systems, rules and procedures; *social control*, through the impact of culture on the behaviour of individuals and groups; and *self-control*, which people exert over their own behaviour.[15] These can be related to the six co-ordinating mechanisms suggested by Mintzberg (see Chapter 9, section 9.5). Direct *supervision* and the *standardisation of work processes, outputs or skills* are essentially administrative controls. *Standardisation of norms* and *mutual adjustment* are social controls, although the latter invariably involves a measure of self-control in the way that individuals choose to interact with others in and around the organisation.

there are three broad **types of control***: administrative control, through systems, rules and procedures; social control, through the impact of culture on the behaviour of individuals and groups; and self-control, which people exert over their own behaviour*

This section looks at how the circumstances of an organisation might determine the most suitable approach to allocating and controlling resources. Although these circumstances are complex and varied, there are one or two broad issues which should most influence the approach to resource allocation and control: first, the extent of the *perceived need for innovation and change*, whether future strategies will be incremental developments from the past or more transformational in the sense discussed in Chapter 2; and second, the extent to which the organisational design is *centralised or devolved*, as discussed in section 9.4 of Chapter 9.

Exhibit 10.6 is a framework for this section and can be used as a checklist against which readers can assess whether the dominant processes in any organisation (perhaps your own) actually fit the circumstances of the organisation in relation to these two parameters. It may be that strategy

Exhibit 10.6 Approaches to resource allocation and control

PERCEIVED NEED FOR INNOVATION AND CHANGE

EXTENT OF DEVOLUTION	Low	High
Low 'Strategic planning'	'Top-down' planning Formula allocations Direct supervision	Direct supervision Imposed targets
'Strategic control' 'Financial control' High	'Bottom-up' planning Bargaining Performance targets Social/cultural control	Market mechanisms Self-controls

implementation is being impeded by a mismatch such as a continuation of a 'strategic planning' style (top-down plans and formula allocations) in circumstances where the organisation is facing a real need for innovation and change and has committed itself to increased devolution as part of the change process (i.e. a move to 'strategic control').

10.4.1 Control through Planning Systems

This is the archetypal administrative control, where implementation is achieved through *systems* which plan and control the allocation of resources and monitor the actual utilisation against this plan. Many of the major strides forward in manufacturing efficiency and reliability in the early parts of the twentieth century were achieved through this 'scientific management', which is still a dominant approach in many such organisations. Control through planning is particularly useful where the degree of change is low, but will need to operate differently in centralised as against devolved regimes.

Centralised Regimes

In centralised regimes ('strategic planning'), planning is usually 'top-down' and accompanied by *standardisation of work processes* or *outputs* and an organisational configuration similar to Mintzberg's *machine* or *professional bureaucracies* (see Chapter 9, section 9.5). Even in service organisations, such 'routinisation' has been achieved (e.g. in insurance work and some legal services), leading to de-skilling of service delivery and significant reductions in cost. This can give competitive advantage where organisations are positioning on low price with commodity-like products or services. Further advantage can be gained if these systems of allocation and control can stretch more widely in the value-system beyond the boundaries of the organisation into the supply and distribution chains. Fully integrated IT systems for inventory control into suppliers or the use of EPOS (electronic point of sale) systems into outlets are good examples.

Centrally planned systems often use a *formula* approach to resource allocation. For example, the advertising budget might be 5 per cent of sales, or in the public services revenue might be allocated on a per-capita basis (e.g. doctors' patients). There may then be some room for *bargaining* and fine tuning around this formula position – for example, in *redefining* the formula – by weightings or introducing additional factors. The danger is that the need for change is underestimated by the corporate centre and consequently the processes of innovation are under-funded. It could be hard for managers of divisions or departments to counterbalance this weakness as they would need to fund innovation from their current budgets. This is in particular a problem if these divisions or departments are small.

Devolved Regimes

In devolved regimes ('strategic control' or 'financial control'), planning systems can still be used as a primary mechanism for resource allocation and control. However, it is more likely to be centred around 'bottom-up' plans from divisions being developed within central guidelines, as discussed in section 9.4.2. It is important that the corporate centre and the divisions are clear on their respective responsibilities for planning and implementation. It is also essential that there are processes of *reconciliation* between the divisions and the corporate centre to ensure that the sum total of divisional plans can be resourced. This may be resolved through processes of *bargaining* between the corporate centre and each division, and hopefully a revisiting of some of the central policies and guidelines, which should be regarded as movable (to a greater or lesser extent) through these planning processes. There may need to be several iterations of this process, as shown in Exhibit 10.7. The danger of bottom-up planning is that key aspects of strategy are not addressed in the plans of divisions. For example, the failure to invest in innovation. This is where the corporate centre must add value through the way in which it establishes the boundaries and reconciles plans. In turn, this requires the centre to understand best practice (benchmarking) and to have a view on the resources which a division should be allocating to innovation.

Exhibit 10.7 Resource allocation through the strategic planning process

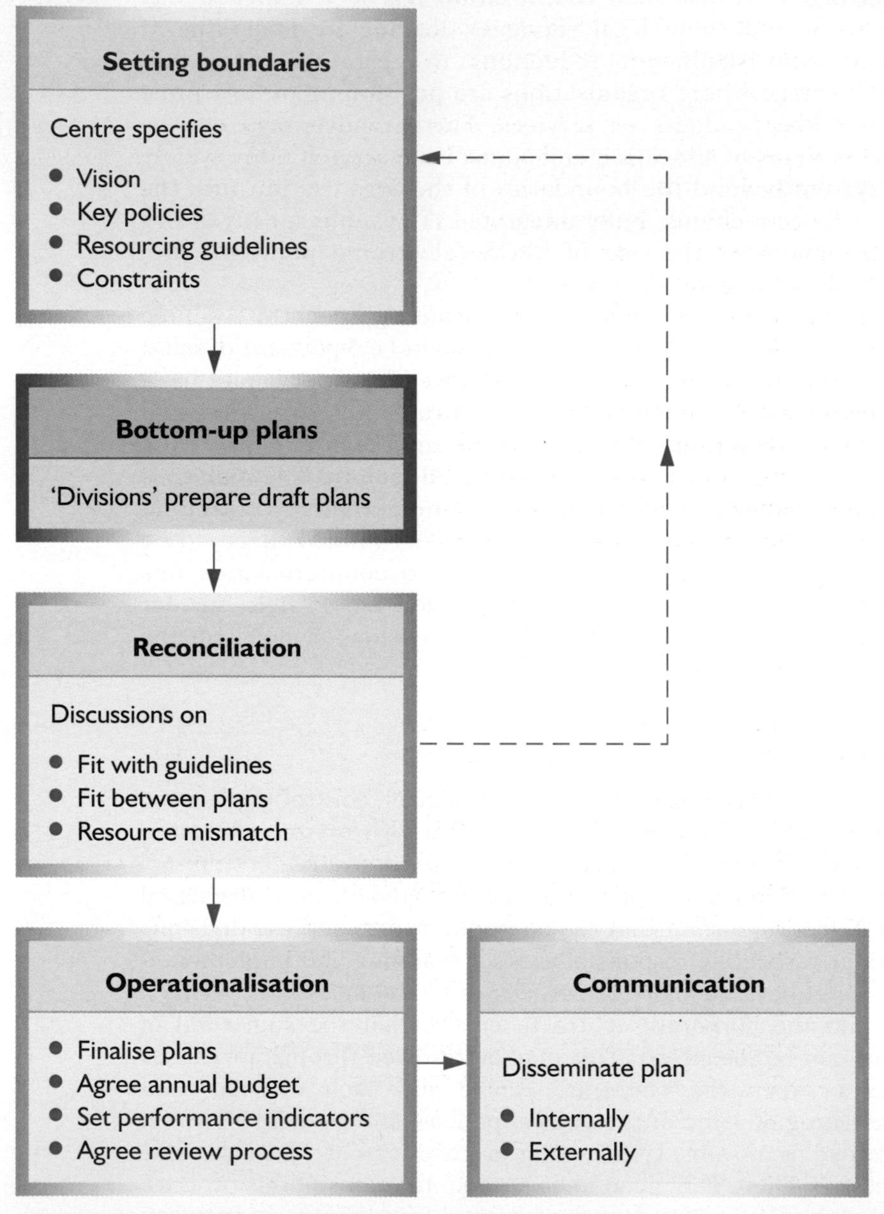

10.4.2 Control through Direct Supervision

Direct supervision is the direct control of resource allocation by one or more individuals. It is a common form of control in small organisations. It can also exist in larger organisations where little change is occurring and if the complexity of the business is not too great for one or a small number of managers to control the organisation *in detail* from the centre. This is often found in family businesses and in parts of the public sector with a history of 'hands-on' political involvement (often where a single political party has dominated for a long period). This situation also prevailed in many parts of the centrally planned economies of eastern Europe prior to 1990.

direct supervision *is the direct control of resource allocation by one or more individuals*

Direct supervision may also be appropriate during major change – for example, an organisational *crisis*. Here the survival of the organisation may be threatened and autocratic control through direct supervision may be necessary. The appointment of receivers to companies in financial difficulty by their creditors is a good example. In devolved regimes a critical issue is which aspects of strategy are supervised centrally and which are devolved. For example, the management and resourcing of innovation, or of development and training, may remain centralised on the grounds that they could become the casualties of short-termism in divisions.

10.4.3 Control through Performance Targets

Another response to high levels of change – whether this is rapid growth, decline or simply reshaping of the organisation's business – is control through *centrally imposed targets*. For example, in the absence of a genuine market, many of the recently privatised utilities in the UK and elsewhere are controlled through the appointment of regulators.[16] These regulators control the organisations through a mechanism of *price-capping*[17] (the so-called K-factors), which imposes a ceiling on prices related to the retail price index (RPI). For example, in the UK, British Telecom in 1995 was subject to a K-factor of RPI – 7.5 per cent imposed by its regulator, Oftel.

However, control through performance targets is not confined to situations of major change or crisis. It is becoming increasingly used in organisations which are wishing to gain some of the benefits of devolution and not necessarily experiencing high degrees of change. Illustration 10.4 (critical success factors) has already shown the importance of understanding the level of performance needed to outperform competition. A common first step is to move to a system of measurement of *outputs* through a series of agreed *performance indicators* (PIs).[18] This may be accompanied by *incentives and rewards* which relate to the achievement of targets – either for groups or individuals. Readers are reminded of the discussion in Chapter 4 about the importance of establishing PIs which relate to *benchmarks* of best performance – even if these are outside the industry or public service.

Exhibit 10.8 The balanced scorecard: an example

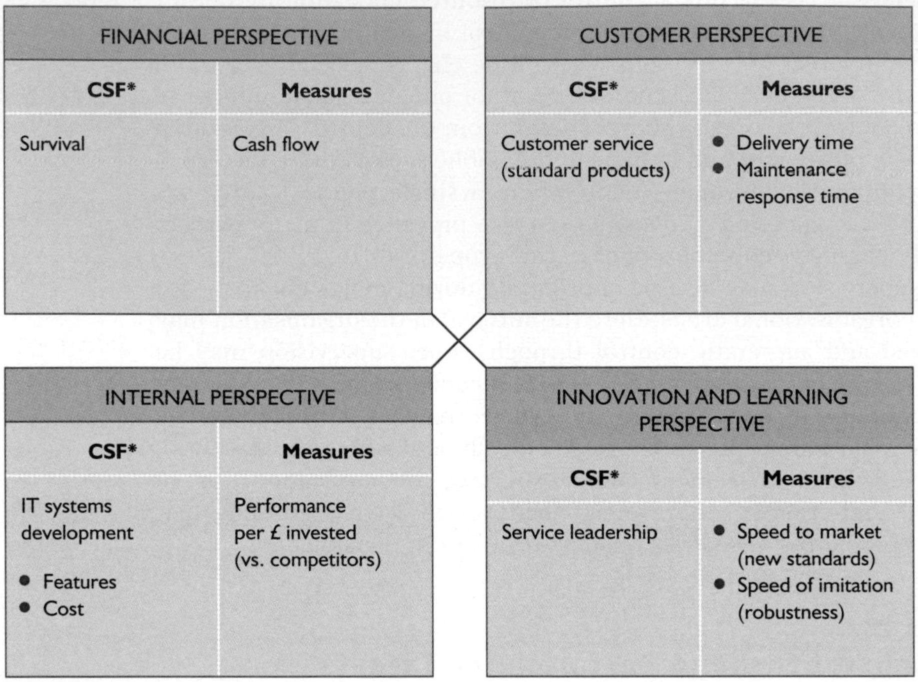

FINANCIAL PERSPECTIVE	
CSF*	**Measures**
Survival	Cash flow

CUSTOMER PERSPECTIVE	
CSF*	**Measures**
Customer service (standard products)	• Delivery time • Maintenance response time

INTERNAL PERSPECTIVE	
CSF*	**Measures**
IT systems development • Features • Cost	Performance per £ invested (vs. competitors)

INNOVATION AND LEARNING PERSPECTIVE	
CSF*	**Measures**
Service leadership	• Speed to market (new standards) • Speed of imitation (robustness)

*CSF=critical success factor

balanced scorecards *combine both qualitative and quantitative measures, acknowledge the expectations of different stakeholders and relate an assessment of performance to choice of strategy*

Many managers find the process of developing a useful set of PIs for their organisations difficult. One reason for this is that many indicators give a useful but only partial view of the overall picture. Also, some indicators are qualitative in nature, while the hard, quantitative end of assessing performance has been dominated by financial analysis. In an attempt to cope with this very heterogeneous situation, *balanced scorecards*[19] have been proposed as a way of identifying a useful, but varied, set of key measures. **Balanced scorecards** combine both qualitative and quantitative measures, acknowledge the expectations of different stakeholders and relate an assessment of performance to choice of strategy (as shown in Exhibit 10.8 and Illustration 10.5). Importantly, performance is linked not only to short-term outputs but also to the way in which processes are managed – for example, the processes of innovation and learning which are crucial to long-term success.

Exhibit 10.8 is an example of a balanced scorecard for a small start-up company supplying standard tools and light equipment into the engineering industry. The owner-manager's financial perspective was simply one of survival during this start-up period, requiring a positive cash flow (after the initial investments in plant and stock premises). The strategy was to compete in customer service both on initial delivery and

STRATEGY IN ACTION
Illustration 10.5

The Balanced Scorecard: Rockwater

Balanced scorecards attempt to reflect the interdependence of different performance factors – which together will determine success or failure.

Rockwater, a wholly owned subsidiary of Brown and Root/Halliburton, a global engineering and construction company, is a worldwide leader in underwater engineering and construction. The table below shows how the company transformed its vision and strategy into a balanced scorecard with four sets of performance measures. The ultimate aim of this exercise was to create value for the whole organisation.

Questions

1. Imagine yourself as the chief executive of Rockwater and draw up a table that shows:
   (a) the various ways in which you would plan to use the balanced scorecard (e.g. establishing targets, assessing individual performance, bonuses, etc.)
   (b) the ways in which the balanced scorecard will assist you
   (c) any shortcomings of the scorecard approach.
2. Give other examples of how a scorecard approach, in general, could build both positive and dysfunctional behaviours in organisations.

Source R.S. Kaplan and D.P. Norton, 'Putting the balanced scorecard to work', *Harvard Business Review*, vol. 71, no. 5 (1993), pp. 134–47.

THE VISION	STRATEGY	OBJECTIVES	BALANCED SCORECARD
'As our customers' preferred provider, we shall be the industry leader. This is our mission.'	Services that surpass needs Customer satisfaction Continuous improvement Quality of employees Shareholder expectations	**Financial** Return on capital Cash flow Project profitability Reliability of performance	**Financial perspective** Return on capital employed Cash flow Project profitability Profit forecast reliability Sales backlog
		Customer Value for money Competitive price Hassle-free relationship High-performance professional Innovation satisfaction	**Customer perspective** Customer ranking survey Customer satisfaction index Market share Pricing index
		Internal Shape customer requirement Quality service Safety/loss control Superior project management Tender effectiveness	**Internal business perspective** Hours with customers on new work Tender success rate Rework Safety incident index Project performance index Project closeout cycle
		Growth Product and service innovation Empowered workforce Continuous improvement	**Innovation and learning perspective** Revenue per employee % revenue from new services Rate of improvement index Staff attitude survey No. of employee suggestions

Exhibit 10.9 Different types of responsibility centre

TYPE	EXAMPLES	CONTROL EXERTED OVER	TYPICAL CONTROLS
Revenue	Sales dept	Income	Sales targets
Cost centre			
● Standard cost centres	Production dept (manufacturing) R&D	Cost of labour, materials, services, etc.	Detailed budgeting Standard product costing
● Discretionary expense centres	Administrative dept	Total expenditure	Budget
Profit centre	Internal services (e.g. design) Product or market division Subsidiary company	Profit	P&L accounts
Investment centre	Subsidiary company	Return on capital	Complete financial accounts

on maintenance back-up. This required core competences in order processing and maintenance scheduling underpinned by the company's IT system. These core competences were open to imitation, so, in turn, the ability to improve these service standards continuously was critical to success.

If performance targets are to be a useful form of control, it is important to decide the *basis* on which each part of the organisation will be assessed. This must relate to the degree of devolution in the organisation and can be achieved through establishing divisions or departments as *responsibility centres* of one or more of the types shown in Exhibit 10.9. Which type of responsibility centre is used should be determined by the other issues of organisational design. So a *financial control* organisation (see section 9.4.2) is likely to establish divisions or subsidiaries as profit or investment centres, since the responsibility for product/market strategy will be substantially devolved to divisions or subsidiaries. In contrast, *strategic planning* organisations are likely to use cost or revenue centres, since the responsibility for many aspects of product/market strategy will be at the corporate centre. Divisions or departments will have devolved responsibility only for particular aspects of strategy, such as production costs or sales revenue.

10.4.4 Social/Cultural Control[20]

Historically, too much emphasis may have been placed on administrative controls as ways of delivering the co-ordination needed to implement successful strategies. In reality, the performance of an organisation will also be determined by the 'softer' controls within organisations – the social controls and self-controls. This section will look at how social controls can play an important part in the resource allocation and control processes in an organisation. **Social controls** are concerned with the *standardisation of norms* (see section 9.5). It is important that social controls are working well in organisations with highly devolved structures ('financial control' or 'strategic control'), since they may be the primary mechanism for co-ordination in the organisation.

social controls *are concerned with the standardisation of norms*

Social controls are of central importance in organisations facing complex and dynamic environments, where the organisational configuration is likely to be that of the *adhocracy* (see section 9.5.1 in Chapter 9). The fostering of innovation is crucial to survival and success in these circumstances – but not in bureaucratised ways. It must be allowed to flourish through the social controls which exist within and between the 'community of communities'.[21]

Social controls can also be important between organisations in their approach to competition and collaboration. Illustration 10.6 shows how important this can be in craft industries and how other forces – globalisation and new technologies – can undermine these controls.

Social controls can also create *rigidities* if the organisation is needing to change.[22] Resistance to change may be 'legitimised' by the cultural norms. For example, plans to de-skill service delivery through routinisation and the use of 'non-professional' staff may be a logical strategy to pursue in terms of increasing value for money, but it is likely to be resisted by the professional staff. The social controls may work against such a change. However, this need not be the case. Since the professionals are likely to be strongly influenced by the behaviour of their peer group in other organisations, they may accept the need to change if they see it working successfully elsewhere. It is for these sorts of reasons that many organisations commit significant resources to maintaining *professional social networks*, both inside and between organisations, as a method of keeping in touch with best practice.

Training and development is another way in which organisations invest in maintaining the social controls within the organisation. It provides a common set of reference points to which people can relate their own work and priorities, and a common language with which to communicate with other parts of the organisation.

control by market mechanisms *involves some formalised system of bidding or 'contracting' for resources*

10.4.5 Control through Market Mechanisms[23]

Control by market mechanisms involves some formalised system of bidding or 'contracting' for resources. Increasing levels of devolution have

STRATEGY IN ACTION
Illustration 10.6

Italy's Craftsmanship Faces a Global Challenge

Well functioning social controls between separate small companies have been a source of competitive advantage for many craft industries – but can they survive and adapt to globalisation and new technologies?

Industrial commentators, of a variety of nationalities, looking for a key to success among small and medium-sized companies (SMEs), have often portrayed 'Third Italy' (in the centre and north east of the country) as a model. It is an area where the environment nurtured an apparently magical network of clusters of smaller firms, a web of subsuppliers providing success and producing the best of Italian craftsmanship in specialist manufacturing sectors such as textiles, footwear or production of kitchen equipment. Relying on an atmosphere of loyalty and trust, they formed an integrated system based on a mixture of competition and co-operation and involving informal agreements on pricing. Overall they believed this helped to obviate some of the hazards which often face small firms, such as exploitation by large customers or suppliers, 'stealing' of good ideas or excessive financial risk.

The real secret of the success of Third Italy was the much-vaunted factor of flexibility. A good example was to be seen in the craft of goldworking. In this specialist sector, ancient traditions and personalised designs were coupled with collective information on new techniques. The result was products that gave satisfaction to a sophisticated market.

Technological advances could provide further flexibility for the small firms of Third Italy by improving manufacturing efficiency without loss of quality. Production cycles could be shortened, and small firms were able to produce a much larger range of products. This was particularly seen in districts like Prato (textiles) or Sassuolo (ceramics), or Mirandola (with a niche in the design and production of biomedical instruments).

That was the picture until a few years ago. Then a change occurred as the forces of globalisation began to take effect. The challenge was now for the local, integrated community of each district to compete with large organisations which enjoyed the benefits of a different kind of integration – international organisations which could site their various activities in different countries and overcome geographical separation with the aid of modern information technology. Also, the IT revolution means that best-practice information that used to be guarded within the local community is now freely available around the world. Big players today are able to impose their will on what used to be local decision making.

Meanwhile, small, specialist firms' sense of 'belonging' (to a geographically defined district) clearly does not work in the way it once did. Small groups of firms compete for global success separately from the district as a whole. This change from local to global networking is difficult and dangerous. Small manufacturing enterprises can no longer rely, as they once did, on a form of social control that defended them against the opportunism of stronger organisations. The emergence of important new players, with a much greater capacity for aggregation and control, changed the stereotyped image of Third Italy but it has strengthened the impact of Italian manufacturing on the global scene.

Questions

1. How did the social controls *between* small firms help in providing value-for-money products for customers?
2. What are the dangers in this type of control?
3. What do you think are the key changes in controls which must be made to make a successful transition from local to global networks?

Source P.A. Vipraio, 'Italy's craftsmanship faces a global challenge', *QED*, September 1997, pp. 14–17.

been accompanied in many large organisations by the introduction of *quasi* market mechanisms for the allocation and control of some or all of the organisation's resources. This has been particularly useful for those parts of the business that are needing to change substantially.

It might start in small ways with *competitive bidding* – perhaps through the creation of an *investment bank* or 'top-sliced' resources from which divisions or departments can bid for additional resources to support particular projects or developments. This can be a particularly successful way of supporting innovative ventures in their early phase, where otherwise they may be starved of resources.

Over the recent past, many organisations have introduced some form of *internal market* as a mechanism for 'regulating' the allocation of resources between the various parts of the organisation, and encouraging improvement in the value for money of the organisation's products or services. For example, a customer–supplier relationship may be established between a central service department, such as personnel, and the operating divisions or departments. It then becomes an important management task to regulate and manage this internal market.

However, an internal market is not the same as an external market. A key difference is that an internal market will always be subject to some degree of *constraint*. The extent of these constraints clearly depends on the degree of devolution. Organisations operating close to the stereotype of *financial control* may limit the constraints to issues of the internal availability of capital, and closely approach the external market situation. However, for many organisations, *strategic control* will require policies, rules and guidelines which constrain the internal market. For example, a pharmaceutical manufacturer which owned its own supplier of a strategically crucial ingredient naturally disallowed any third-party sales of the ingredient to competitive companies.

An important feature of internal markets is the 'right' of the internal customer to specify its requirements (in terms of the value for money it expects from the services or products it is receiving). This may be done in the form of a *service-level agreement* with the internal supplier. It can be particularly helpful if the agreement reflects the best performance which would be achieved from third-party suppliers outside the organisation.

At a practical level, there are some problems which can be created by internal markets and which are to be discouraged. First is the escalation in *bargaining* between units, which can consume important management time. Second is the creation of a new bureaucracy monitoring all of the *internal transfers* of resources between units. An overzealous use of market mechanisms can also have a profound impact on the dominant culture of an organisation, shifting it from one of collaboration and relational processes to competition and contractual relationships, which may prove dysfunctional.

It was for a number of these reasons that the new Labour government in the UK made changes to the operation of the internal market in health care in 1997. There were particular concerns about the effects of over-competitive behaviour and the emergence of a two-tier standard of provision. Symbolically, the language was also changed, for example 'purchasers' became 'commissioners' of health care.

10.4.6 Self-control and Personal Motivation

With the increased devolution and de-layering of organisations, the self-control and motivation of individuals is becoming critically important to the performance of organisations, and raises some important issues about resource allocation and control:[24]

in **self-control**, *resource allocation and control are exercised by the direct interaction of individuals without supervision*

- In **self-control**, resource allocation and control are exercised by the direct interaction of individuals without supervision. This is closely related to the co-ordinating mechanism of mutual adjustment (see section 9.5 in Chapter 9). The contribution of senior managers to this process is to ensure that individuals have the *channels* to interact (perhaps by improving the IT and communications infrastructure), and that the social and cultural controls which this process of interaction creates are properly *regulated* to avoid the rigidities mentioned in section 10.4.4 above. So senior managers are concerned with shaping the *context*[25] in which others are working. This includes the need to create the right context for knowledge creation and innovation, as discussed in section 10.4.4.
- If individuals are to have a greater say in how they perform their work and achieve the organisation's goals, they need to be properly *supported* in the way in which resources are made available to them. One of these key resources is likely to be information, and it will be seen below that the organisation's IT strategy is a critical ingredient in this process of supporting individuals.
- There are important implications for how the credibility of managers and leaders is maintained. For example, credibility may arise from being a member of the peer group – this is why so many seniors in professional service departments or organisations are professional themselves. So the head of the design department undertakes assignments personally as well as overseeing the work of others.

10.5 INFORMATION: A KEY RESOURCE

The previous sections have discussed in detail how the resource configuration and the processes for allocating and controlling resources might sustain the ability of an organisation to implement its strategies successfully. Often, managers are disappointed by the results of their changes in organisational structure, design and control processes because they fail to realise that another key ingredient of implementation is information. If information is not available in the right format at the right time, the potential gains of other changes may be lost. This is increasingly important as many organisations become more complex and geographically dispersed through processes of globalisation.

This section looks at the information requirements of the various aspects of resource allocation and control discussed in this chapter, and at how the management of information might provide competitive advantage.[26]

10.5.1 Information on Individual Resources

It was argued earlier in the chapter (section 10.2) that, if competitive advantage is built on individual resources, it is important to ensure that these resources cannot be imitated. If a key resource is knowledge, the 'intellectual property' needs to be protected. Although legal protection has increased, particularly for knowledge stored on electronic media, it is clearly a concern that the vastly increased capability and reducing cost of IT networks is likely to erode this protection. This may occur in legal ways simply by competitors knowing about new developments more quickly, and hence being able to bring out alternatives or plan a defensive strategy.

IT developments may also erode competitive advantage in other ways by undermining the importance of *tacit knowledge*. IT vastly improves the way in which data can be searched, sifted, sorted and packaged to increase the pace of learning of potential competitors. The improved sophistication of software packages in some arenas is partly able to replace professional skill – for example, in currency trading and medical diagnosis. This software can also include fully programmed controls and limits over the freedom of action of the operators (e.g. by limiting the size of financial deal, or excluding certain medical conditions in the two examples above).

10.5.2 Creating Competences through Information

Improved availability and quality of information can improve an organisation's competences in several ways:

- By reducing the cost of processes – for example, the telecommunications costs of the selling activities of international companies.
- By improving their quality – for example, the speed and accuracy of real-time booking systems.
- In retailing, the recording of sales by electronic point of sale (EPOS) scanning has not only improved efficiency and service in the store, but also provided high-quality information on which to plan stocking, purchasing and sales promotions.

Since the wider availability of information can accelerate the learning of competitors, advantages gained through experience may be shorter lived than hitherto. This will inevitably mean that more organisations will need to revisit and redefine the *positioning* of their products/services in the market place more often, which in turn will put different information demands on the organisation. Managers need to be clear about how these improvements in IT should influence the way in which they manage the processes of innovation and knowledge creation, in particular, the balance and interplay of explicit and tacit knowledge, as discussed in section 4.3.7 of Chapter 4.

As mentioned in section 10.2.3, this reshaping of business processes to create new and better-matched competences has generated a great deal of interest and effort since the early 1990s under the banner of *business process re-engineering (BPR)*.[27] It has become a central plank of IT strategy in many organisations, and has been derived via a philosophy that business processes which suited centrally driven bureaucratic organisations are no longer adequate for organisations competing on quality and service delivered at the 'sharp end' of the organisation. Illustration 10.2 showed how BPR can require quite radical changes in both outlook and resource deployment.

10.5.3 Information, Performance Targets and Market Mechanisms

The recent advances in the speed and lower cost of information processing should – in principle – improve the capability of control systems to measure performance against targets. Therefore, in exploiting this potential, it is important not to lose sight of some principles of good practice for performance measurement already discussed in sections 10.4.3 and 10.4.5. It has already been mentioned that market mechanisms are often introduced into organisations in order to encourage a new emphasis on value for money and increasing performance against the best external standards. However, internal markets are 'information hungry' if they function effectively, and therein lie dangers which need to be avoided when planning management control and information systems. In particular, the cost of monitoring and effecting all the new transactions (cross-charging) can be prohibitive, or the organisation may simply not have the systems to achieve this without a considerable capital investment.

10.5.4 Information, Cultural and Self Controls

Many believe that the 'IT revolution' will genuinely transform the balance of the various processes of resource allocation and control discussed in this chapter.[28] They paint a picture of de-layered organisations, with IT taking the place of middle management, and cultural and self control being the dominant control processes in organisations populated by innovative and motivated 'knowledge workers', whose performance is vastly improved by their direct, personal and on-line access to information (section 10.4.6 above).

The Internet will not respect many of the boundaries which are currently taken for granted, and will increase the ability of individuals low down in the hierarchy to communicate directly without having to go through the *information gatekeepers* and the corporate centre. This gatekeeping role has been a key source of power for managers in steering coherent strategies and allocating resources in organisations. Importantly, this means that social controls, including those provided by key external frames of reference, will need to take on a heightened importance. For example, the need for ethical standards and codes of practice as key regulators of behaviour among professions and industry bodies could prove more crucial.

10.6 INFLUENCES ON ORGANISATIONAL DESIGN AND CONTROL

Together, Chapters 9 and 10 have discussed the various elements of organisational design and control: namely, centralisation versus devolution, organisational configurations and the various processes of resource allocation and control. These elements need to work well together to support the successful implementation of an organisation's strategies. The important issue is how this 'package' will be influenced by the organisation's circumstances. In other words, the 'best' package is contingent on a number of different factors, and these are discussed below. Readers can use this section to assess the degree of 'match' between the circumstances of an organisation and the approach to organisational design and control. Exhibit 10.10 provides a checklist for this purpose.

10.6.1 Type of Strategy

The discussion of organisational configurations in Chapter 9 acknowledged the importance of matching organisational design to the types of strategy that the organisation was pursuing. It also pointed out that this is a two-way process: organisational configuration also influences preferences for particular types of strategy. So different product or market strategies may require different forms of organisational design, as previously summarised in Exhibit 10.4.

The organisation following a low-price strategy will need to find a means of ensuring a cost-efficient operation with an emphasis on cost control, whereas the organisation following a differentiation strategy may need higher degrees of creativity to develop and sustain the aspects of the

Exhibit 10.10 Influences on organisational design and control

		MANAGEMENT STYLE		CONFIGURATION				ALLOCATION AND CONTROL		
		Centralised	Devolved	Simple	Bureaucratic	Divisionalised	Adhocracy/ missionary	Administrative	Social/cultural	Self-control
STRATEGIES/ POSITIONING	Low price	X			X			X		
	Differentiation		X			X	X		X	X
TECHNOLOGY AND INNOVATION	Mass production	X		X	X			X		
	Complex technology		X				X		X	X
TYPE OF ORGANISATION	External accountability	X			X			X		
	Owner control	X		X					X	
	Defenders	X			X			X		
	Prospectors		X				X		X	X
NATURE OF ENVIRONMENT	Simple/static	X			X			X		
	Complex		X			X	X		X	X
	Dynamic		X				X		X	X

product or service which provide competitive advantage. The likelihood is that the low-price strategy will require a more *mechanistic* system of control, with clear job responsibilities, frequent and detailed reports on organisational efficiency and cost, and a clear delineation of responsibility for budgets and expenditure: in other words, a strong emphasis on administrative controls.

An organisation following a differentiation strategy, on the other hand, might need to have looser controls, a greater encouragement of informality and creativity within a more devolved structure, but a good deal of co-ordination between its various activities. The emphasis may be more on groups relating to problems and opportunities than on individual departments being concerned with specific job functions. So cultural and self control processes are of greater importance. An organisation that seeks to follow differentiation and low-price strategies for different parts of its business may experience conflicts in terms of organisational design and the need to have different types of control system.

the public services), requiring standardised work processes which, in turn, are well supported by a defender culture. This culture seeks out stable parts of the environment and the whole cycle is self-perpetuating. A similar reinforcing cycle can occur with the *adhocracy*, as seen in the same exhibit.

None of this may be a problem for the organisation – in fact, the matching of these various organisational issues to each other may prove to be a source of great strength to the organisation. However, it should be remembered from Chapter 2 that this is also likely to be an explanation of why *strategic drift* is so common. The organisation may need the capability to 'break out' of these reinforcing cycles if it is to survive and succeed in the long term. This will be discussed fully in Chapter 11, which is concerned with managing change.

SUMMARY

- New strategies invariably require a reconfiguration of resources. Indeed, radical reshaping of resources and business processes (*business process re-engineering*) has provided the basis of new strategies and organisational regeneration for many organisations.
- It is important to be clear about the relationship between resource deployment and the success of a strategy. This could involve ensuring that unique resources are protected, that the processes of bringing together a variety of resources to create a product are improved, or that the organisation's experience is properly exploited for competitive advantage. It is particularly important to understand that any changes in strategy will require these issues to be rethought and changed.
- Identifying *critical success factors* (CSFs) can be a useful way of ensuring that resource plans and priorities are in line with the requirements to gain competitive advantage (or sustain excellence).
- *Resource allocation and control* can be undertaken in a number of different ways. The choice of approach should be determined by two main factors. First, the perceived need for innovation and change, and second, the 'brand' of devolution – whether decisions are centralised or devolved.
- Within these broad guidelines, the practical choices on how resources should be allocated and controlled consist of planning (top-down or bottom-up), direct supervision, performance targets, social and cultural control, market mechanisms, and self-control (motivation).
- *Information* is a key resource that can determine the success or failure of strategies. The information requirements depend on how resources are to be allocated or controlled. The reverse is also true: improved information capability allows a reappraisal of traditional methods of management control.

- The various elements of *organisational design* (devolution, configuration and management control) need to work together and to suit the circumstances in which the organisation is operating.
- These factors are also connected in *reinforcing cycles* to issues of culture, organisation routines and the nature of the environment. These reinforcing cycles not only help in matching these various elements but can also create rigidities to change that can be detrimental to organisations needing to adopt new strategies.

RECOMMENDED KEY READINGS

- C.K. Prahalad, *Competing for the Future*, Harvard Business School Press, 1994, chapter 10, and J. Kay, *Foundations of Corporate Success*, Oxford University Press, 1993, chapter 5, for a discussion of strategic architecture.
- M. Hardaker and B.K. Ward, 'Getting things done', *Harvard Business Review*, (1987), is an excellent guide to how critical success factors can be identified and used.
- Business process re-engineering and the relationship between information systems management and strategic management are discussed in W. Robson, *Strategic Management and Information Systems: An integrated approach*, Pitman, 1994, pp. 203–14; M. Hammer and S. Stanton, *The Re-engineering Revolution*, HarperCollins, 1995, and D. Francis and P. Alley's chapter, 'Business process re-engineering', in V. Ambrosini with G. Johnson and K. Scholes (eds), *Exploring Techniques of Analysis and Evaluation in Strategic Management*, Prentice Hall, 1998.
- A good general reference for issues of control is P. Johnson and J. Gill, *Management Control and Organisational Behaviour*, Paul Chapman Publishing, 1993.
- P. Jackson and C. Price, *Privatisation and Regulation: A review of the issues*, Longman, 1994, is useful for readers interested in how approaches to resource allocation and control have changed in the public sector.

REFERENCES

1. Strategic architecture is discussed by G. Hamel and C.K. Prahalad, *Competing for the Future*, Harvard Business School Press, 1994, chapter 10, and J. Kay, *Foundations of Corporate Success*, Oxford University Press, 1993, chapter 5.
2. Detailed resource identification is often started by looking at the implications of each functional area of the business. G.A. Steiner, *Strategic Planning*, Free Press, 1979, is a useful guide. Readers who are unfamiliar with resource analysis in any functional area may wish to consult one of the following standard texts: P. Kotler, *Marketing Management: Analysis, planning, implementation and control*, 8th edition, Prentice Hall, 1994; N. Slack and S. Chambers, *Operations Management*, Pitman, 1995; R. Wild, *Production and Operations Management*, 5th edition, Nelson, 1995; M.W.E. Glautier and B. Underdown, *Accounting Theory and Practice*, 5th edition, Pitman, 1994; D. Torrington and L. Hall, *Personnel Management: A new approach*, 3rd edition, Prentice Hall, 1995; C. Fombrun, N. Tichy and M. Devanna, *Strategic Human Resource Management*, Wiley, 1990.
3. Tacit knowledge is discussed in T. Nonaka and H. Takeuchi, *The Knowledge Creating Company*, Oxford University Press, 1995. The importance of people as a unique strategic resource is also argued in: P. Boxall, 'Strategic human resource management: beginnings of a new theoretical sophistication?', *Human Resource Management Journal*, vol. 2, no. 3 (1992), pp. 60–79, and 'Placing HR strategy at the heart of business success', *Personnel Management*, vol. 26, no. 7 (1994), pp. 32–4.

4. For examples, see J.B. Quinn, 'Managing the intelligent enterprise: knowledge and service-based strategies', *Planning Review (USA)*, vol. 21, no. 5 (1993), pp. 13–16; S. Davis and J. Botkin, 'The coming of knowledge-based business', *Harvard Business Review*, vol. 72, no. 5 (1994), pp. 165–70.
5. Business process re-engineering has been of considerable interest to both practitioners and academics. For example, see W. Robson, *Strategic Management and Information Systems: An integrated approach*, Pitman, 1994, pp. 203–14; M. Hammer and S. Stanton, *The Re-engineering Revolution*, HarperCollins, 1995, D. Francis and P. Alley's chapter, 'Business process re-engineering', in V. Ambrosini with G. Johnson and K. Scholes (eds), *Exploring Techniques of Analysis and Evaluation in Strategic Management*, Prentice Hall, 1998. The *Business Process Re-engineering and Management Journal* was launched in 1995.
6. See I. Masaaki, *Kaizen: The key to Japan's competitive success*, Random House, 1986; R. Hannam, *Kaizen for Europe: Customising Japanese strategies for success*, IFS Publications, 1993. The Europe–Japan Centre staff have also published a series of books on the application of *Kaizen* (through the National Book Network).
7. G. Hamel and C. Prahalad, 'Strategy as stretch and leverage', *Harvard Business Review*, vol. 71, no. 2 (1993), pp. 75–84.
8. G. Hamel and C. Prahalad, *Competing for the Future*, Harvard Business School Press, 1994.
9. Cost advantage is discussed in R. Grant, *Contemporary Strategy Analysis*, 2nd edition, Blackwell, 1995, chapter 7, and B. Karlof, *Strategic Precision*, Wiley, 1993, chapter 3.
10. See S. Prokesch, 'Competing on customer service: an interview with British Airways' Sir Colin Marshall', *Harvard Business Review*, vol. 73, no. 6 (1995), pp. 101–12.
11. The importance of switching costs is explained in M.E. Porter, *Competitive Strategy*, Free Press, 1980, p.19.
12. See M. Hardaker and B.K. Ward, 'Getting things done', *Harvard Business Review*, vol. 65, no. 6 (1987), pp. 112–20, for a fuller discussion of how critical success factors can be identified and used.
13. For a fuller discussion of the planning of priorities, see K. Scholes and M. Klemm, *An Introduction to Business Planning*, Macmillan, 1987, chapter 5.
14. Network analysis is explained in Wild (reference 2 above) and K. Howard, *Quantitative Analyses for Planning Decisions*, McDonald and Evans, 1975.
15. A good general reference for issues of control is P. Johnson and J. Gill, *Management Control and Organisational Behaviour*, Paul Chapman Publishing, 1993. Also of interest are R. Simons, 'Strategic orientation and top management attention to control systems', *Strategic Management Journal*, vol. 12, no. 1 (1991), pp. 49–62, and 'How new top managers use control systems as levers of strategic renewal', *Strategic Management Journal*, vol. 15, no. 3 (1994), pp. 169–89.
16. See P. Jackson and C. Price, *Privatisation and Regulation: A review of the issues*, Longman, 1994, chapter 3. M. Bishop, J. Kay and C. Mayer, *Privatisation and Economic Performance*, Oxford University Press, 1994, provides a number of in-depth case studies of deregulation.
17. Price-capping as a regulatory mechanism is discussed in R. Rees and J. Vickers, 'RPI – X. Price-cap Regulation' in M. Bishop, J. Kay and C. Mayer (eds) *The Regulatory Challenge*, Oxford University Press, 1995, chapter 15.
18. Performance indicators are discussed in several different contexts in Jackson and Price (reference 16 above), e.g. pp. 17–18. See also N. Carter, in D. McKevitt and A. Lawton (eds), *Public Sector Management: Theory, critique and practice*, Sage, 1994.
19. See R. Kaplan and D. Norton, 'The balanced scorecard: measures that drive performance', *Harvard Business Review*, vol. 70, no. 1 (1992), pp. 71–9, and 'Putting the balanced scorecard to work', *Harvard Business Review*, vol. 71, no. 5 (1993), pp. 134–47.
20. See Johnson and Gill (reference 15 above), chapter 5.
21. J.S. Brown and P. Duguid, 'Organisational learning and communities of practice: towards a unified view of working, learning and innovation', *Organisational Science*, vol. 2, no. 1 (1991), pp. 40–57.
22. For example, D. Leonard-Barton, 'Core capabilities and core rigidities: a paradox in managing new product development', *Strategic Management Journal*, vol. 13 (Summer 1992), pp. 111–25.
23. Market mechanisms of several types have been introduced into previously administered monopolies in the public sector in many countries. See Jackson and Price (reference 16 above), chapters 5 and 8.
24. G. Morgan, *Imaginization*, Sage, 1993, advocates an approach to strategic management which uses the creativity of people more.
25. The idea of top managers as 'shapers of context' is discussed in S. Ghoshal and C. Bartlett, 'Linking organisational context and managerial action: the dimensions of the quality of management', *Strategic Management Journal*, vol. 15, (1994), pp. 91–112; C. Bartlett and S. Ghoshal, 'Changing the role of top management: beyond strategy to purpose', *Harvard Business Review*, vol. 72, no. 6 (1994), pp. 79–88; S. Ghoshal and C. Bartlett, 'Changing the role of top management', *Harvard Business Review*, vol. 73, no. 1 (1995), pp. 86–96.
26. The important relationship between information strategy and competitive advantage is discussed in W. Robson, *Strategic Management and Information Systems: An integrated approach*, Pitman, 1994, chapter 7.

27. See reference 5 above.
28. A special edition of *Organisation Science*, vol. 6, no. 4 (1995), is devoted to how new electronic communications are changing organisational design. M. Morton, 'Emerging organisational forms: work and organisation in the 21st century', *European Management Journal*, vol. 13, no. 4 (1995), pp. 339–45, looks at how IT and other environmental influences are changing organisational design.
29. R.M. Kanter, *The Changemakers*, Unwin, 1985.
30. This idea of configurations being cohesive is discussed in D. Miller, 'Organisational configurations: cohesion, change and prediction', *Human Relations*, vol. 43, no. 8 (1990), pp. 771–89. There is also a collection of research on configurational approaches to organisation in the *Academy of Management Journal*, vol. 36, no. 6 (1993), pp. 1175–361.

WORK ASSIGNMENTS

10.1 Choose two strategic developments for an organisation with which you are familiar and compare the resource configuration implications (Exhibit 10.2). How would this analysis influence your choice of strategy?

10.2 By referring to Illustration 10.4, undertake an analysis of the critical success factors and the associated underpinning competences for an important strategic development in an organisation of your choice.

10.3 (a) Choose an organisation which is shifting its generic competitive strategy from low price to differentiation (or supplementing the former with the latter). Describe any resource planning difficulties which are occurring as a result of these changes and how they are being tackled (refer to Exhibit 10.4).
(b) Choose an organisation which is attempting the opposite shift (differentiation to low price) and undertake the same analysis.

10.4 Draw up a network analysis for a strategic development in an organisation of your choice (refer to Exhibit 10.5). How could the 'time to completion' be shortened, and what risks would the organisation be taking?

10.5 By referring to Exhibit 10.6, characterise how corporate allocation of resources works in an organisation of your choice. Assess whether or not you would regard the current approach as appropriate.

10.6 ● Referring to Exhibit 10.6 and Illustration 10.5, write a short executive brief to the CEO of a multidivisional organisation explaining how balanced scorecards could be used to monitor and control the performance of divisions. Be sure you present your critique of both the advantages and pitfalls of this approach.

10.7 Referring to Exhibit 10.9 and using an organisation with which you are familiar, identify the various responsibility centres within the organisation and make your own assessment of whether the organisation is controlled in the best way. What changes would you recommend? Why? What might be some of the dangers of these changes, and how could they be avoided?

10.8 ● By referring to the key readings (Robson; Hammer and Stanton), argue the case for and against the contention that: 'The IT revolution will fundamentally transform the way that all organisations go about their business. Those who deny the self-evident truth will not survive!' Use examples to illustrate your answer.

10.9 ● By referring to the issues of organisation design in Chapter 9, and resource allocation and control in this chapter, compare the key difference you would expect to find between the approach of an organisation operating in a relatively simple/static environment and the approach of another organisation operating in a complex/dynamic environment (see Exhibit 10.10 and Illustration 10.7).

10.10 ● By using specific examples from your answers to the previous assignments, explain how the various aspects of organisational design and control need to fit together to support an organisation's strategies. How close are theory and practice? Refer to Mintzberg and Quinn in the recommended key readings (Chapter 9) to assist with your answer.

---

* refers to a case study in the Text and Cases edition.
● denotes more advanced work assignments.

CASE EXAMPLE

Justice Sector Information Strategy in New Zealand

As with many justice systems built on the 'Anglo-Saxon' model, the New Zealand system was made up of a series of separate independent public sector departments or agencies, each with its own role. The overarching responsibility for policy and resource allocation lay with the Ministry of Justice. However, the operation of the system was through the separate agencies – New Zealand Police, Department of Courts, Department of Corrections* and the Department of Social Welfare. Other departments also held information which was essential to the justice process, in particular the Ministry of Transport (motor vehicle registrations) and the Land Transport Safety Authority (drivers' licences).

Like other parts of the public service in New Zealand, there had been significant development and change since the late 1980s with the purpose of improving both the quality and efficiency of services. This was not an easy issue within the justice sector given the history of the fierce independence of the separate agencies – with their own priorities, professional values and ways of working. For example, critical policy issues in policing – such as an increase in cautioning as against charging people – had a profound impact on the workload of the courts. Similarly, changing attitudes towards sentencing in the courts affected both the prisons and probation services. Despite these strong links and connections, it was an important principle of the sector that separation of power in this way was a good thing: it ensured the necessary checks and balances to prevent a corrupt and politically dominated justice system. Nonetheless there was wide agreement across all the agencies that there was much that needed to be done within and between agencies to improve the value-for-money performance of the sector as a whole.

By the mid 1990s the debate about strategy for the sector as a whole had focused on a major resource planning issue for the sector – the upgrading and improvement of information systems. This resource issue was high on the agenda of most of the separate agencies. They were all concerned that the planning of both capital and revenue spend on information systems should demonstrably underpin their strategies of both improving the quality of service and reducing the costs of their agency. This was needed to meet the stringent performance targets for the public sector set by government. The issue for the government (through the Ministry of Justice) was to ensure that the expenditure on IT systems and the ways of working between agencies would ensure that the sector *as a whole* (and not just a few separate agencies) delivered better value for money.

High-quality information was essential in all parts of the justice system. For example, it was needed for crime prevention planning, police investigations, decisions on prosecution, preparing prosecutions, decisions on sentencing, care and probation priorities and planning in the corrections service (prisons, probation and community service). Information was used in two ways: first, to ensure that individual citizens were dealt with fairly and appropriately, and second, to assist in resource allocation between agencies (the Ministry of Justice advised government on these issues) and within the separate agencies. Since 1976 the major source of 'core' information for the sector had been a centralised computer system at Wanganui which was commissioned by the police, the Department of Justice and the Ministry of Transport. However, this system had outlived its usefulness and the advent of modern IT systems and networks was

*Courts and Corrections had been part of an integrated Department of Justice until 1995.

leading individual agencies to develop their own separate systems. This prompted the government, in 1995, to establish an interagency committee to produce recommendations for a justice sector information strategy. The committee's recommendations were approved in July 1996. The overall conclusion was that investment in improved information collection, analysis and communication was the most important strategic resource planning issue for most agencies. In the absence of an overall information strategy for the sector it was likely that sub-optimisation of IT resources would occur as each agency made local decisions which precluded the ability of the information systems to work between agencies. Therefore, the report dealt with the objectives of the information strategy and what was needed to ensure that it fulfilled the broader purposes of improving quality of service and efficiency within the justice sector as a whole. Some of the proposals are outlined below.

Objectives of the Information Strategy

The committee's report highlighted four main objectives for the information strategy that it felt must guide the resource planning decisions in the separate agencies:

- To provide information to all agencies in the justice sector and their customers.
- To ensure that individual agency investments in IT took into account the wider needs of the sector.
- To improve the cost-effectiveness by the sharing of and improving access to information that was currently 'owned' by separate agencies.
- To ensure that the quality and accuracy of information met world-class standards.

Critical Success Factors

The key principle behind the strategy was a move away from a centralised information resource to a situation where information was held separately by the individual agencies but in a way which made information available to others in the sector. If this approach was to be successful it was recognised that the following must be achieved:

- The use of agreed principles and protocols for the creation and handling of common datasets and information.
- Consistent standards for IT – including communications and networking.
- The respecting of the sensitive nature of the information in the justice system – particularly the issue of the privacy of individual citizens.

The report was also keen to underline the following:

- Individual agencies should not be told how to run their business or what information systems to purchase. Responsibility for resource planning must remain 'local'.
- The information strategy should not be a justification for additional 'windfall from the government' investments in the IT systems of agencies. Development should be achieved from current and projected budgets. As the life cycle of IT investments was about three years, this should be possible as new systems were acquired within the guidelines of the report.

Key Deliverables

The report concluded by identifying specific elements of the strategy that should be a priority for the sector as a whole and for the individual agencies:

- A shared and common *information directory* (a 'high-level' guide to where and how common information could be accessed).
- An *information management policies guidebook* which would deal with all the

protocols needed to ensure that information was collected, analysed, stored and communicated in ways which achieved the overall purpose.

- A *data dictionary and an information resource roadmap* (to contain all agreed definitions, data formats and a detailed guide to all the information available within the justice sector).
- *Communications standards and technology framework* – technology standards for secure interchange of (often sensitive) information.

Implementation

The devolved philosophy of systems development and operation created some potential problems of implementation. However, sector agencies had agreed to commit expertise (staff time) and to earmark some of their IT budgets to the priorities in the report (see above). A number of the 'key deliverables' (such as the development of the data dictionary and information roadmap) required the Ministry of Justice to take the lead co-ordinating role. However, it was crucial that all agencies committed staff time to ensuring that these elements of the strategy were put into place quickly and efficiently and were comprehensive in their coverage. The central issue which would determine the success or failure of the strategy was the next round of resource planning decisions within the separate agencies on their capital and revenue IT spending. Unless these local decisions were made strictly within the overall vision and detailed framework for the justice sector information strategy, the collective improvement would fail.

Although in the long run the report anticipated improved quality of service and cost reductions for all agencies, there were some difficult short-term problems for many agencies. Perhaps the most sensitive issue was the uneven impact on the separate agencies in terms of short-term costs and benefits. For example, a single agency – such as the police – may have to increase its information systems spend by some 20–30 per cent to acquire and manage a system that gave faster and easier access to information for other agencies. This could reduce the need for a duplicate system elsewhere which, from the viewpoint of the Ministry of Justice was a good overall solution. However, as far as the individual agency (police) was concerned, these investments would need to be found from current budgets. Resource allocation to individual agencies and the assessment of their 'business performance' was carried out separately for each agency.

There was another concern too. The ultimate success – in terms of improved quality of service and increased efficiency – was likely to be determined by the 'weakest link' in the system. So agencies that committed themselves to 're-engineering' their information systems in line with the guidelines may well incur costs without gaining any benefits if other agencies did not follow suit. These were difficult resource planning decisions for managers who were already feeling the pressure of year-on-year squeezes on their resources. In practice, it was found that some agencies that started slowly had by 1998 overtaken the early leaders.

In his foreword to the report, the Minister of Justice in 1996, The Honourable Douglas Graham, summed up the government's expectations of the justice sector as follows:

> This strategy document is the product of a major co-operative effort [between the agencies]. I am delighted to see the commitment to working together [on a strategy for the sector]. The next stages will be challenging but I believe that together we will ensure that the New Zealand justice sector moves with confidence into the 21st century.

Questions

1. The government was clearly expecting major improvements in value for money within the justice system by re-engineering the way in which information was collected, analysed and communicated in the sector. List some of the *specific* ways in which the proposed changes will (a) improve quality of service and (b) increase efficiency.
2. The proposed improvements required all agencies to replan their IT resources in a consistent way. Imagine yourself as a member of the Ministry of Justice responsible for the implementation of the strategy. Refer to section 10.4 of the text and list the advantages and disadvantages of each of the six different forms of control in ensuring that the strategy is successful.
3. Do you think that improved information would result in the government making significant changes to the relative size of the budgets for the individual agencies?
4. Systems improvement and resource redeployment are two ways of improving performance. To what extent could/should other methods be used (for example, restructuring the sector or changing the values and attitudes within the separate agencies)? Refer to Chapters 9 and 11 in considering your answers.

Source *Justice Sector Information Strategy*, New Zealand Ministry of Justice, August 1996.

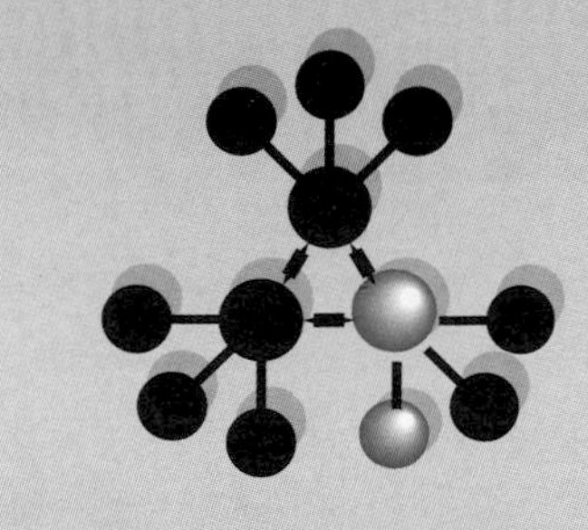

11
MANAGING STRATEGIC CHANGE

LEARNING OUTCOMES

After reading this chapter you should be able to:

- Describe the main types of strategic change processes.
- Define a learning organisation.
- Undertake a forcefield analysis based on cultural web mapping.
- Describe the main styles of managing change.
- Explain how symbols can be managed to facilitate change.
- Describe how political processes and change tactics might facilitate change.
- Understand the role of a change agent and the roles of others in managing strategic change.
- Understand how effective strategic change relates to wider aspects of strategic management.

11.1 INTRODUCTION

Throughout this book there has been an attempt to explain strategic management both in terms of tools and techniques of analysis and planning, and in terms of the behaviours and assumptions associated with organisational cultures. In considering the management of strategic change, the subject of this chapter, these two approaches are also important. Some writers, and some practitioners, approach strategic change as an extension of the planning process. The emphasis is on getting the *logic* of the strategy right and then *persuading* people of that logic; designing *structures and control systems* appropriate to the strategy and using them as mechanisms of change; putting in place the *resources* required; and planning *timing and sequencing* of change in detail. Much of this has already been discussed in Chapters 9 and 10.

However, ultimately the success of strategic change in an organisation depends on the extent to which people change the *beliefs and assumptions* that they hold and their behaviour in their organisational lives, for example towards customers or each other. Those who emphasise a *process* view of strategy tend to highlight these aspects of the change process. While not dismissing the need for planning, they stress the importance of achieving the *commitment* of people in the organisation to change and the need for *behavioural* change not only in terms of that which is formally controlled, but also in terms of *everyday aspects* of organisational life. Indeed, there are those who argue that in a rapidly changing environment, organisations cannot rely on formal planning of change, but rather need to become *learning organisations*, continually sensitive to changes in the environment and able to adapt continually to those changes.

These organisational processes are the main focus of this chapter, which builds on four underlying premises:

- It is important that there is a clear view within an organisation of the strategy to be followed. This issue has been emphasised in much of the book, and will be re-emphasised in parts of this chapter.
- However, this is not enough. Change will not occur unless there is *commitment* to change in the organisation. It is vital that managers consider how such commitment can be achieved.
- The approach taken to managing strategic change is likely to be *context dependent*. It will not be the same for all situations in all types of organisation. Managers need to consider how to balance the different approaches to managing strategic change according to the circumstances they face. Some guidelines are given on this as the chapter progresses.
- Whatever the emphasis and approach, it must address the powerful influence of the *paradigm* and the *cultural web* on the strategy being followed by the organisation. As explained in Chapters 2 and 5, these can result in strategic inertia and resistance to change.

Exhibit 11.1 provides a structure for the chapter. The chapter begins by providing some explanatory frameworks of strategic change and linking these to the explanations of strategy development provided in Chapter 2. A framework of *types of strategic change* is provided, which shows that change events may differ in scale. Next, different explanations are provided of how change might occur in organisations: one which is more suited to explaining *managed change*; one which is more to do with the notion of the *learning organisation*; and one which acknowledges that *imposed* or *forced* change does occur.

Section 11.3 then moves on to discuss more specifically the management of change. First, some important points about the formulation of strategy are re-emphasised. This is followed by a discussion of the *diagnosis* of strategic change *needs*, considering the signs and symptoms of *strategic drift*, how *forces blocking and facilitating change can* be identified, and how the *cultural web* can be used to map the sorts of change that might be needed.

Exhibit 11.1 A framework for managing strategic change

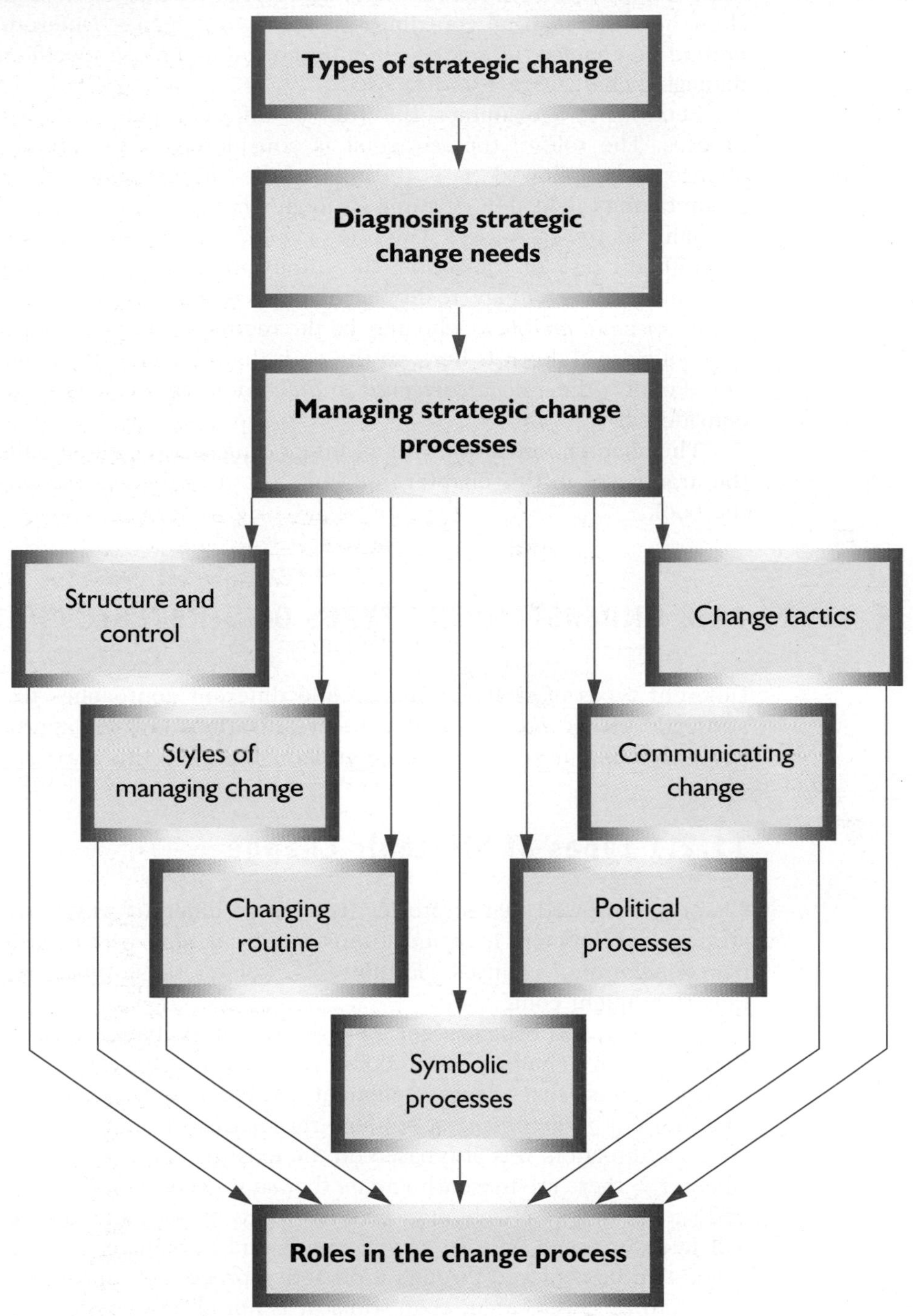

Section 11.4 considers the *processes* which can be employed *for managing change*. Elements of the cultural web including organisational *routines*, *symbols*, *political activity* and *structure and control* are used to show how they can all contribute to achieving change. Different *styles of managing* change, the role of *communication* and more specific *tactics* for managing change are also discussed.

Section 11.5 examines the role of different players in the change process. The role of the *strategist* is considered as the architect of the change to be followed, as is the role of the *change agent*, the person or group taking the lead in effecting strategic change (who may or may not be the same as the strategist). The role of *middle managers*, often faced with the difficult task of translating the intentions of change by top management into the everyday reality of change, is also discussed. The role of *organisational members* who may be the recipients of the change process is also considered, for it is here, in the end, that change will be successful or not. Finally, the role of *external stakeholders* in the change process is considered.

The chapter concludes with an integrating section which pulls together the arguments in this chapter and links them to themes running through the book.

11.2 UNDERSTANDING TYPES OF STRATEGIC CHANGE

Different types of strategic change and different approaches to managing strategic change are observable in organisations. Which approaches are likely to make more or less sense are considered in this section.

11.2.1 Types of Strategic Change

Chapter 2 showed that strategies develop in different ways. In the main, strategy development in organisations is *incremental*, with occasional more *transformational* changes.[1] Exhibit 11.2 relates these types of change to how they might come about.

Arguably, it is beneficial for an organisation to change incrementally. In this way it will build on the skills, routines and beliefs of those in the organisation, so that change is efficient and likely to win their commitment. The aim is a *realignment* of strategy rather than a fundamental change of strategic direction; it is also based on the existing paradigm. As explained in Chapter 2, there are those who argue that such incremental realignment can and should be proactively managed, and that, by so doing, the organisation will keep in touch with its environment and anticipate needs for change which can be achieved through a proactive process of *tuning* current ways of operating. Others argue that, whilst it is not always possible to anticipate the need for change, organisations do *react* to external competitive or

Exhibit 11.2 Types of strategic change

NATURE OF CHANGE

MANAGEMENT ROLE	Incremental change	Transformational change
Proactive	Tuning	Planned transformational
Reactive	Adaptation	Forced transformational

environmental pressures. Managers may not see the need for major strategic changes, but rather may *adapt* the existing paradigm and current ways of operating within the existing paradigm. Both proactive tuning and reactive adaptation may therefore take form in incremental change.

One way in which incremental change is explained is by conceiving of organisations as 'learning systems', continually adjusting their strategies as their environment changes. This has given rise to the idea of the *learning organisation*, which has been discussed elsewhere in the book and is revisited in section 11.2.2 below.

However, Chapter 2 also points out that within incremental change may lie the dangers of strategic drift because change is based on, or bounded by, the existing paradigm and routines of the organisation, even when environmental or competitive pressures might suggest the need for more fundamental change. There are, then, circumstances when more fundamental or *transformational change* is needed, either because incremental change has been inadequate or because the external pressures for change are extreme – for example, if profits decline or takeover threatens the continued existence of a firm.

Transformational change is change which cannot be handled within the existing paradigm and organisational routines; it entails a change in the taken-for-granted assumptions and 'the way of doing things around here'. Such transformational change may also come about as a result of either reactive or proactive processes. If strategic drift has occurred and has led to deteriorating performance or an uncompetitive position in its markets, or if external stakeholders (e.g. major shareholders) are not happy with the current strategy, management may be in a *forced transformational* position. Such a position may also be reached if other changes in the organisation's environment are so evidently significant or severe that the

transformational change *is change which cannot be handled within the existing paradigm and organisational routines* organisation is forced into such transformational change. It may, however, be that managers anticipate the need for transformational change, perhaps through the sorts of analytical technique described earlier in the book. They may then be in a position of *planned transformational* change, which may provide them with more time in which to achieve it. However, implementing such change may be difficult to achieve if others in the organisation are resistant to it.[2]

There are, then, different explanations of how strategic change occurs in organisations. In this book, however, we are mainly concerned with exploring how the process can be managed. In doing this, it is helpful to consider different views about the role of management in change processes (see sections 11.2.2 and 11.2.3 below); then in the rest of the chapter we will consider the means whereby change might be managed.

11.2.2 Change and the Learning Organisation

a **learning organisation** *is capable of benefiting from the variety of knowledge, experience and skills of individuals through a culture which encourages mutual questioning and challenge around a shared purpose or vision*

Traditionally, organisations have been seen as hierarchies and bureaucracies set up to achieve order and maintain control; as structures built for stability rather than change. Arguably, this conception of the organisation is not suited to the dynamic conditions and often global forces for change of the late twentieth century (see Chapter 2, section 2.8.3, and Chapter 8, section 8.5.3). The organisation needs to be seen not as a stable hierarchy, but as an adaptive, continually changing **learning organisation**, capable of benefiting from the variety of knowledge, experience and skills of individuals through a culture which encourages mutual questioning and challenge around a shared purpose or vision.

Advocates of the learning organisation point out that the collective knowledge of all the individuals in an organisation usually exceeds what the organisation itself 'knows' and is capable of doing; the formal structures of organisations typically stifle organisational knowledge and creativity. As suggested in Chapter 10 (section 10.4.6), in certain contexts the aim of management should be to encourage processes which unlock the knowledge of individuals, and encourage the sharing of information and knowledge, so that each individual becomes sensitive to changes occurring around them and contributes to the identification of opportunities and required changes. The organisation then becomes capable of taking an holistic view of its environment rather than being reliant on partial, filtered information from its various functions. There is an absence of power plays and blocking routines, so that a shared vision of the future can be created and reinforced by mutual support by organisational members. Such an organisation, it is argued, will be creative and continually changing, and be able to cope with the ambiguity and contradictions it faces. These will be seen not as threats, but as opportunities.[3]

Arguably, some of the organisational forms (e.g. adhocracy) explained in Chapter 9, section 9.5.1, aspire to this rather than to the more traditional notions of stability and control. Clearly, if such organisations exist, they are well positioned to manage strategic change through continual *tuning*, such that proactive incremental change – or logical incrementalism – might come about. As an aim for managers, this is commendable. However, perhaps regrettably, there is little evidence of the common existence of such organisations. One reason for this, as shown in Chapter 2, is the forces for compliance with current ways of doing things and the current paradigm exerted by the cultural web.

11.2.3 Managed Change

While a learning organisation is, then, a worthy aspiration, managers are typically faced, not with a continually changing learning organisation, but with resistance to change. How can managers overcome such resistance and manage change?

If resistance to change and organisational inertia are the result of the organisation becoming trapped in its own paradigm and routines, there is a need for an 'unfreezing' of the paradigm. Exhibit 11.3 describes how such change might take place.[4] However, it needs to be recognised that at the different stages described in Exhibit 11.3, there is a likelihood that the powerful effect of the paradigm may act to promote conformity around the existing strategy and counter the proactive management of change.

- A significant change in the environment of the organisation – for example, new technology, changes in customer tastes, or the entry of new competitors leading to a deteriorating market position – may act over time as an *unfreezing mechanism* and lead to an increasingly *felt need for change*. It is often said that 'a crisis is an opportunity' when it comes to managing change because it can provide a catalyst for unfreezing. However, in its absence, or in the absence of a clear and dramatic external force for change, there is likely to be a need to *manage the unfreezing process*.

  Managing the unfreezing process is not easy. Managers may seek to persuade people of the need for change (see section 11.4.6 below), emphasise – even exaggerate – external signs of problems or threats, make internal changes such as the removal of long-established management, or find ways of signalling symbolically the need for change (see section 11.4.4 below). Nonetheless, there is a tendency for signals of change to be made sense of within the paradigm even when they appear undeniable to the observer. For example, one senior executive in a retail business commented, after five years of changing customer tastes had led to the decline of his company: 'We must be patient: when the market comes back to its senses, we will be in a good position.'
- There may develop a situation of *flux* in the organisation, in which competing views surface about causes of, and remedies for, the problems. It is likely to be a time of high political activity (see section

Exhibit 11.3 'Unfreezing' and the management of change

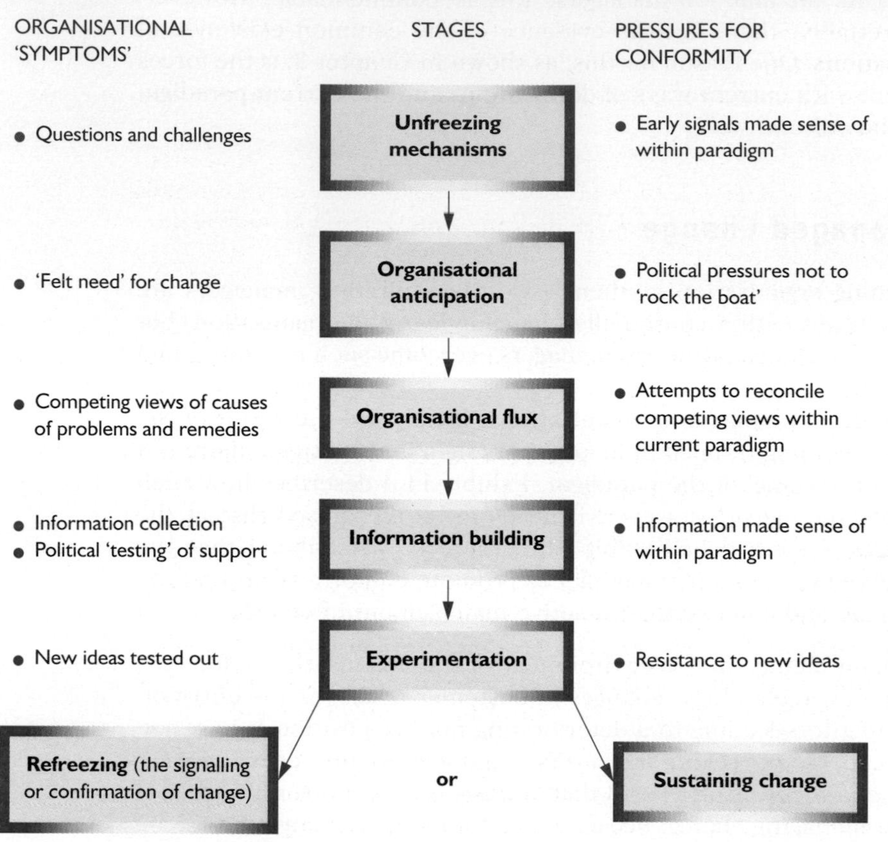

11.4.5 below) and rumour spreading. While such processes give rise to conflict and appear to be disruptive, they can actually be useful in managing change because they can facilitate the debate of different points of view and help surface and challenge what is taken for granted.[5]

- This debate may give rise to and be fed by *information building*, as executives attempt to check, test or find means of supporting their position – a stage which is likely to be a lengthy, iterative process. Again, however, it may be that this information building is constrained by the organisational paradigm – that information is deemed meaningful when it 'makes sense' and overlooked when it is outside the experience of people in the organisation. Market research information might be interpreted very selectively, for example.

  It may therefore be especially important to manage this stage of information building. For example, *strategy workshops* could be useful, in which groups of managers debate needs and options for change. Or project teams may be set up to gather information and consider options. In such ways, the taken for granted may be questioned and challenged, advocates of new ideas provided with a platform, and those resistant to change exposed to arguments and pressures to change.

- Conflict and new information may contribute to individuals or groups arguing for different strategic ideas. These may then be tried out in practice – a process of *experimentation*. If successful, this could lead to the emergence of a change in strategy and changes in the organisation's paradigm and accompanying ways of doing things. Change managers may therefore deliberately try to involve key individuals in the organisation in such experiments (see section 11.4.2 below).
- Members of the organisation, faced with such disruption, may require a 'safety net' for the future. It may be that they will be ready to relate to the emerging new paradigm, although there are still dangers that they will revert to the old. *Refreezing* processes may be needed to confirm the organisational validity of the changed paradigm, so managers may need to consider ways of signalling this: for example, by changing organisational structures, by finding symbols of change (see section 11.4.4 below) or by changing everyday routines (section 11.4.3 below). The implication of the 'learning organisation' is, however, that change will be continual. The challenge is to move, not to a new 'steady state' but to an organisation that continually challenges the status quo. The aim here, then, would be to *sustain* change within the organisation by trying to establish the sort of situation described in section 11.2.2 above.

In practice, change programmes often adopt approaches to managing strategic change which utilise similar concepts and may recognise the need to build a learning organisation. Illustration 11.1 shows the approach taken by Gemini Consulting in the 1990s.

11.2.4 Imposed (Or Forced) Change

There are, of course, situations where change is imposed on the organisation (see Chapter 2, section 2.5, and Chapter 8, section 8.5.2). This could either be because changes in the industry environment are so marked that the organisation has no choice, or because some external agency forces change. For example, many of the changes that have occurred in public sector organisations throughout the world, either in the form of deregulation or privatisation, have been forced on them. An external agency, perhaps government, may impose different structures of organisation or different regulatory devices to effect change. In such circumstances, an individual or group of managers will need to carry through such changes;[6] and again, the frameworks for managing change and the concepts and techniques discussed in this chapter will be useful in considering how this might be achieved.

STRATEGY IN ACTION Illustration 11.1

Gemini's Framework for Planned Strategic Change

Business transformation is seen as a four-dimensional process: reframe, restructure, revitalise and renew.

Reframing

Reframing is about questioning what the organisation is and what it can achieve so as to open up new possibilities and challenges. The first stage of the process is to *achieve mobilisation*; to create the will and the desire of individuals within the organisation to change. Next is to *create the vision* of a shared mental framework of where the organisation is going and then to *build a measurement system* which sets targets and defines the actions needed to achieve them.

Restructuring

Restructuring deals with the organisation's structure and is usually associated with cultural change. Their first stage is to *construct an economic model* of the organisation's processes, to give a detailed view of where and how value is created, and to ensure that resources can be provided to different parts of the organisation as and when required. Next is the *alignment of the physical infrastructure* of the organisation, to ensure that it fits with the strategic direction of the company, and then to *redesign of the work architecture* or processes of the organisation so that they add value by interacting together in a seamless way.

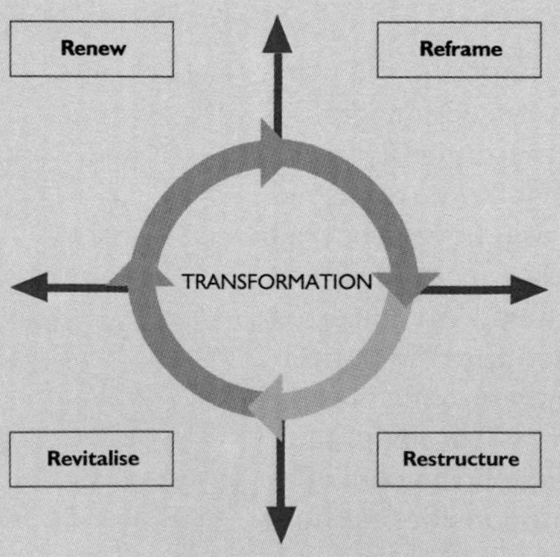

Gemini's four R's of transformation

Revitalising

Revitalising seeks to achieve a good match between the organisation and its environment; a 'good fit' will allow the company to grow and prosper. The first stage is to *achieve market focus*. A customer focus will enable the organisation to *invent new businesses* – the next stage. This enables the organisation to use existing capabilities in new or enhanced ways. The third stage is to *change the rules* of competition through technology. Information technology, in particular, can provide new bases for competition, perhaps through product or process differentiation.

Renewal

Renewal seeks to ensure that individuals acquire the necessary skills to take the company forwards and that a culture of acceptance of change is present. The first stage is to *create a reward structure* to provide a powerful motivating force and then to *build individual learning* – the encouragement for individuals to acquire the new skills necessary for the success of the transformed company. The final stage is to *develop the organisation*, in particular its learning capacity, to adapt constantly to changed circumstances.

Questions

Read sections 11.2.1 and 11.2.3 of the text and refer to Exhibits 11.2 and 11.3.

1. Does the Gemini approach take into account all the stages explained in sections 11.2.3 and Exhibit 11.3? Which does it emphasise and which does it not emphasise?
2. Is Gemini's approach to strategic change suited to all the different types of change described in Exhibit 11.2 and section 11.2.1?

Source F.J. Gouillart and J.N. Kelly, *Transforming the Organisation*, McGraw-Hill, 1995.

Prepared by Tony Jacobs, Bristol Business School.

In the rest of this chapter, the emphasis is on the role of managed change processes, both tuning and transformational. The question posed is: what can the manager do when faced with managing strategic change? Section 11.3 commences by looking at ways of diagnosing strategic change needs, and section 11.4 moves on to consider mechanisms for change.

11.3 DIAGNOSING STRATEGIC CHANGE NEEDS

It is important to remember that, in managing strategic change, much of what has been written in previous chapters in this book is an essential precursor in identifying the need for and direction of strategic change. It will not be repeated in any detail here, but it is important to remember the need for clarity on the following points:

- Why strategic change is needed (discussed in Part II of the book).
- The basis of the strategy in terms of strategic purpose, perhaps encapsulated in the form of a clear statement of strategic intent and bases of competitive advantage (discussed in Chapter 6).
- The more specific directions and methods of strategy development (discussed in Chapter 7).
- The changes in strategic architecture required (discussed in Chapters 9 and 10).

However, there is also a need to understand the magnitude of the challenge faced in trying to effect strategic change. It can be useful to assess the extent to which *strategic drift* (see Chapter 2, section 2.8.2) has occurred and therefore the extent to which incremental or transformational change is required. It is also helpful to identify the specific *blockages* to change that exist and what forces might exist to *facilitate* the change process. It can then be useful to map the sorts of change that might be required.

11.3.1 Detecting Strategic Drift

Incremental strategic change is more typical within an organisation, and much less disruptive, than transformational strategic change. However, it is important to gauge when incremental change has given rise to strategic drift and therefore in what circumstances more fundamental change may be required. Determining this is problematic because there is no absolute set of conditions which describe a state of strategic drift – this is a matter of managerial judgement. However, there are a number of symptoms:

- A highly homogeneous organisational culture and paradigm: where there are few differences of beliefs and assumptions about the organisation and its place in the external world; established routines which are not deviated from; powerful symbols and stories of an historical and conservative nature, and so on.

- Little toleration of questioning or challenge in the organisation and a readiness to dismiss new ideas with 'we've tried this before and it didn't work', together with an avoidance of debate of really difficult or sensitive issues and few avenues for challenging existing norms (see section 11.3.3 below).
- Major power blockages to change, either because of resistant dominant leaders or because a group or layer of management is resistant to change. As one chief executive put it in a manufacturing company: 'Our problem is our senior managers: they've been there years and most of them are going nowhere and know it; but they can block anything if they choose. They are our "concrete ceiling".'
- An organisation with little focus on its external environment, particularly its markets. This might take the form of a lack of market information in a company; a reliance on price or cost control as a basis of competing, rather than delivering added value to customers; or a bias towards 'selling what we make' rather than responding to market and customer requirements. Such organisations are likely to be building their strategy on internalised views of the world and skill bases. This might be checked by means of research comparing managerial and customer perceptions of the organisation.
- Deteriorating relative performance: for example, is the performance of a business unit keeping pace with or outstripping its rivals, or has there been a gradual decline in relative performance? This may be detected, for example, by benchmarking, discussed in Chapter 4 (section 4.4.3).

11.3.2 Identifying Forces Blocking and Facilitating Change

Given that the overall strategic direction of the organisation has been identified, it is helpful to consider the forces within the organisation that could help or hinder change. Chapters 2 and 5 have already shown how the many aspects of the culture of the organisation work to shape and guide strategy, and how its influence can result in strategic drift. The *cultural web* is therefore a useful way of considering forces for and against change.[7] Illustration 11.2 shows how this exercise was undertaken in Hay Management Consultants, the international human resources consultancy firm.[8]

Although operating near to full capacity, by 1994 Hay realised that it would have to grow considerably just to meet demand and would need to become better at co-ordinating a range of services, rather than concentrating on its historical strength of job evaluation. Its executives used the framework of the cultural web to map out the existing culture (shown in Illustration 11.2(a)). While this confirmed that the firm had a focus on clients, it flagged up a number of concerns. The dominance of job evaluation as the 'core business' was very strong and potentially worked against the development of a greater range of services. The autonomy and individualism of consultants – the 'lone rangers' of the organisation – worked against co-ordination: these consultants tended to see themselves as generalists, which worked against the development of depth expertise. Change had become institutionalised to the point where people in the organisation tended not to take the latest change seriously. Indeed, there was a perception that, although decisions were taken, not much changed.

It can also be useful to consider the sort of culture that would exist if the required strategy were being followed effectively. This amounts to drawing a picture of an ideal. Again, the cultural web can be used because it not only provides a basis upon which the formal structures and systems of the organisation can be considered, but also requires managers to consider the day-to-day aspects of the organisation represented by routines, symbols and so on. Moreover, some of these aspects of culture – for example, organisational rituals and routines – can be managed and provide powerful messages of change (see sections 11.4.3 and 11.4.4 below).

Illustration 11.2(b) also shows how Hay managers redrew their cultural web. Here is an organisation much more integrated not only in terms of structures, but also in terms of systems and routines, and one in which the stories and symbols of the organisation represent that integration successfully. The core business is HR consultancy not just job evaluation; it is more team oriented as an approach, with group rather than individual bonuses, better information flows across departments, stories of successful teams and a lot of informal interaction. Many aspects of the existing web remain and can be built on, but the redrawn web can provide clues as to how change might be managed.

A **forcefield analysis** can be used to identify forces for and against change (see Exhibit 11.4). This is a representation of the sorts of forces for and against change discussed above, and which may have been identified in the web. A forcefield analysis can provide an initial view of the problems that need to be tackled, by building on the forces that might work for change and reducing the forces against change. For example, in Hay the existing culture raised problems – the embeddedness of job evaluation, the individuality, autonomy and power of individual consultants, complacency about change and so on – but it also highlighted existing forces for change: in particular, the client orientation of the firm and the fact that consultants spent a lot of time with clients, the flexible structure and approach to work in the firm, the fact that change was 'normal' in the organisation, the informal interaction that existed between people, and the fact that it was a fun place to work.

a **forcefield analysis** *identifies forces for and against change*

What emerges is that the routines, control systems, structures, symbols and power or dependency relationships can be both important blockages and facilitators to change. Changes in the structure, design and control systems of organisations have already been reviewed in Chapter 9. In the

STRATEGY IN ACTION
Illustration 11.2

Forces Blocking and Facilitating Change in Hay Management Consulting

The cultural web can be used as a means of identifying blockages to and facilitators of change, and required changes in culture.

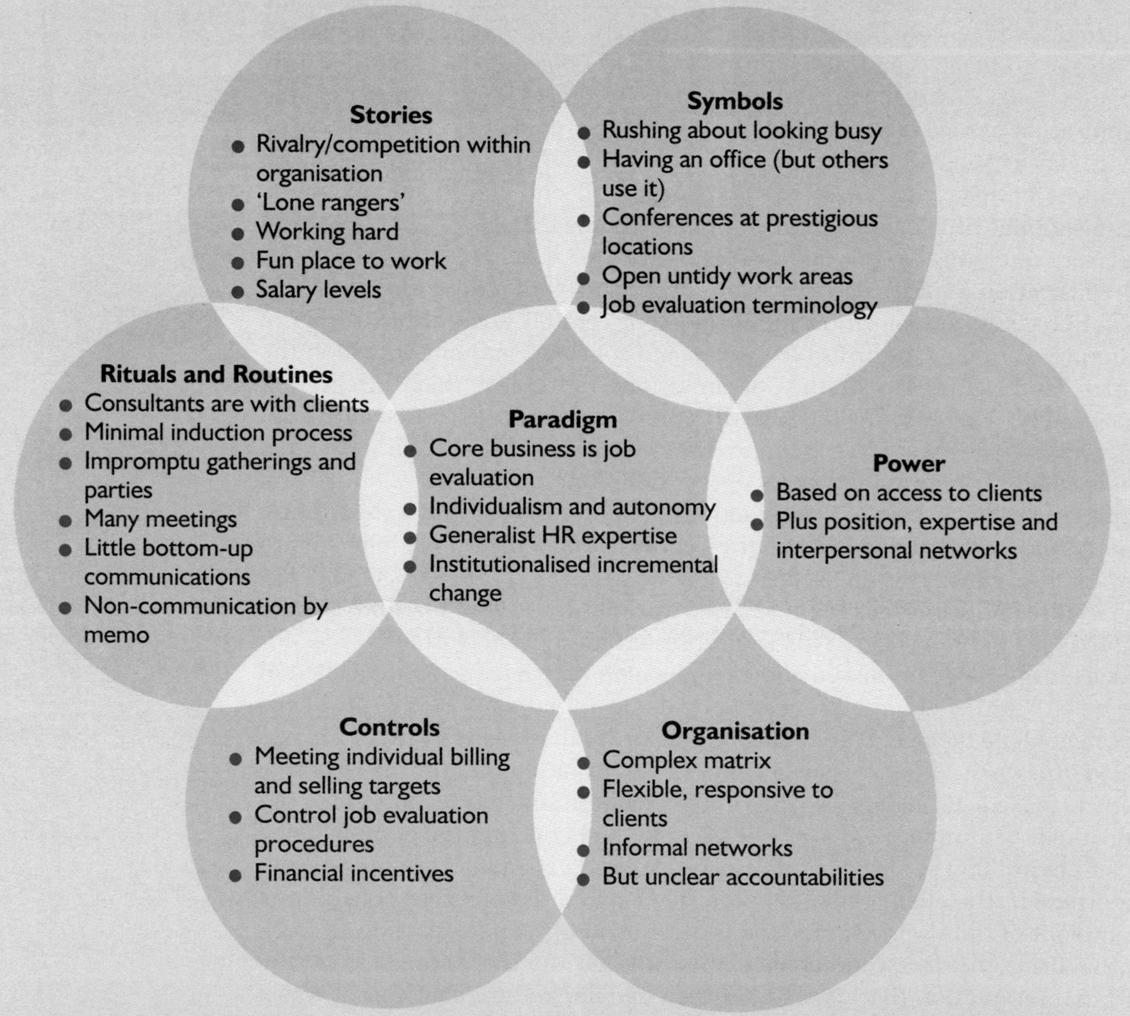

Stories
- Rivalry/competition within organisation
- 'Lone rangers'
- Working hard
- Fun place to work
- Salary levels

Symbols
- Rushing about looking busy
- Having an office (but others use it)
- Conferences at prestigious locations
- Open untidy work areas
- Job evaluation terminology

Rituals and Routines
- Consultants are with clients
- Minimal induction process
- Impromptu gatherings and parties
- Many meetings
- Little bottom-up communications
- Non-communication by memo

Paradigm
- Core business is job evaluation
- Individualism and autonomy
- Generalist HR expertise
- Institutionalised incremental change

Power
- Based on access to clients
- Plus position, expertise and interpersonal networks

Controls
- Meeting individual billing and selling targets
- Control job evaluation procedures
- Financial incentives

Organisation
- Complex matrix
- Flexible, responsive to clients
- Informal networks
- But unclear accountabilities

(a) The cultural web in 1994

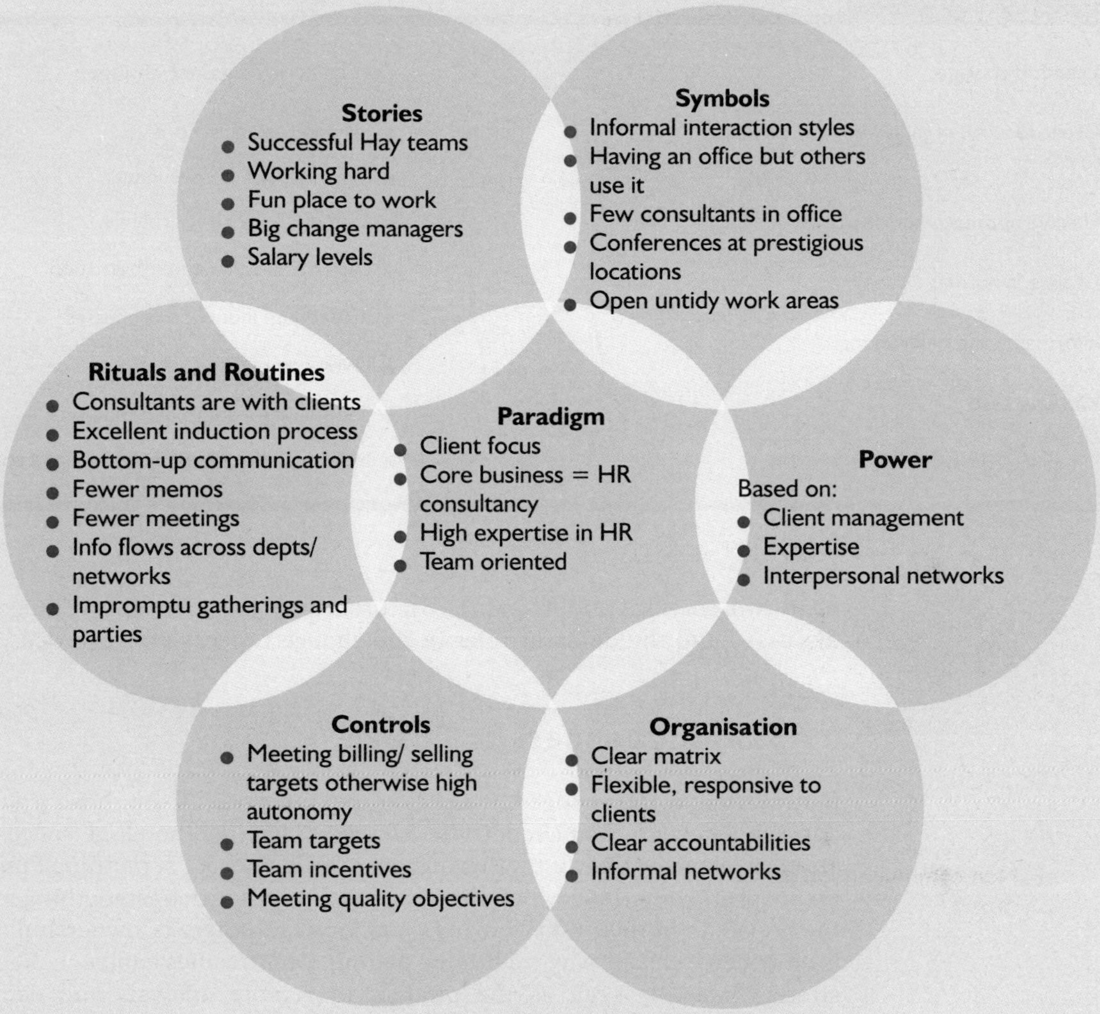

Stories
- Successful Hay teams
- Working hard
- Fun place to work
- Big change managers
- Salary levels

Symbols
- Informal interaction styles
- Having an office but others use it
- Few consultants in office
- Conferences at prestigious locations
- Open untidy work areas

Rituals and Routines
- Consultants are with clients
- Excellent induction process
- Bottom-up communication
- Fewer memos
- Fewer meetings
- Info flows across depts/ networks
- Impromptu gatherings and parties

Paradigm
- Client focus
- Core business = HR consultancy
- High expertise in HR
- Team oriented

Power
Based on:
- Client management
- Expertise
- Interpersonal networks

Controls
- Meeting billing/ selling targets otherwise high autonomy
- Team targets
- Team incentives
- Meeting quality objectives

Organisation
- Clear matrix
- Flexible, responsive to clients
- Clear accountabilities
- Informal networks

(b) The cultural web aspired to

Questions

With reference to the two culture webs in the illustration and the forcefield analysis in Exhibit 11.4:

1. What might Hay prioritise for change?
2. What problems might management find in doing so?
3. Undertake a similar analysis for another organisation (or for the KPMG (A) case study at the end of chapter 2).

Exhibit 11.4 An example of forcefield analysis (based on the Hay cultural web)

Forces for change	Forces acting against change
• Client-focused organisation and closeness to clients	• Job evaluation as 'core'
• Flexible approach and structure	• Individualism of consultants
• Change is normal	• Complacency about change
• Informality and networking	• Lack of co-ordinated information
• Working hard	• Inadequate induction processes
• Fun place to work	• Over-complicated structure
	• Too many meetings and memos
	• Individual, not team, incentives and controls

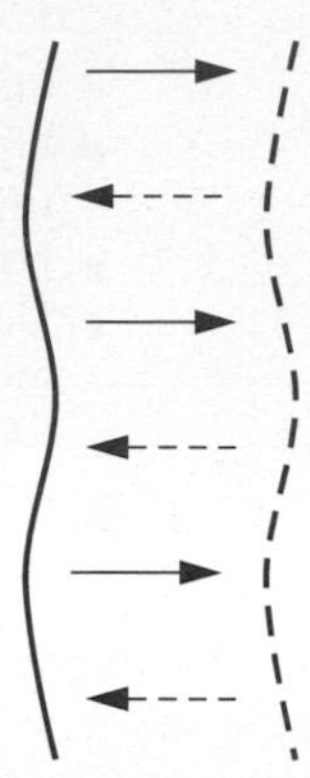

next two sections (11.4 and 11.5), processes for managing change are discussed and the different roles in the change process are reviewed.

11.3.3 An Openness to Change

If strategy is to be changed, it needs to be 'internalised' by those it affects and who have to implement the change. The likelihood of success in strategic change is low if the strategy is regarded as just something imposed on people – something which they have to do, rather than something which they relate to in their everyday lives and for which there is 'ownership'. This is one of the reasons why traditional planning approaches can be ineffective: strategy may be seen as the product of remote analysis and decision making, not the concern of those who have to put it into effect. Involvement in the change process beyond just the most senior executives could therefore be important.

the **zone of uncomfortable debate** *encompasses sensitive aspects of the organisation and managerial attitudes and beliefs which tend to be avoided in open discussion*

A further problem arises because the analysis of strategic issues and formulation of strategy may challenge the vested interest of managers, so there may be an unwillingness to tackle really difficult questions. Bowman[9] refers to *zones of comfortable and uncomfortable debate* (see Exhibit 11.5). Managers readily debate strategy in what he calls the *zone of comfortable debate*. Here they may well employ the techniques of strategic analysis and formulation, perhaps in formal corporate planning procedures or by hiring consultants to address strategic issues. However, the **zone of uncomfortable debate** encompasses sensitive aspects of the organisation and managerial attitudes and beliefs which tend to be avoided in open

Exhibit 11.5 The zone of uncomfortable debate (ZOUD)

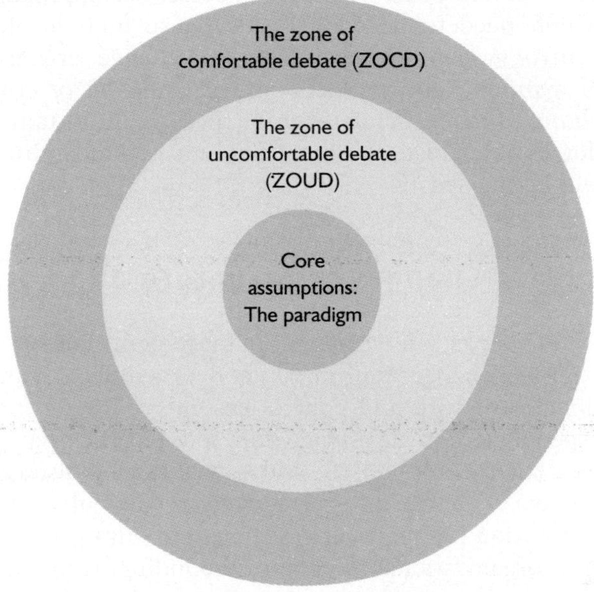

Source Adapted from C. Bowman, 'Strategy workshops and top team commitment to strategic change', *Journal of Managerial Psychology*, vol. 10 (1995), pp. 42–50.

discussion. They may be talked about informally, but not raised in formal meetings, planning reviews and the like. They are areas of organisational life which touch on vested interest, bases of power, reputation and so on. If real strategic change is to be effective, managers have to enter this zone of uncomfortable debate and be prepared to discuss and challenge such issues. Given the defence mechanisms they can employ, this can be difficult to achieve.

There are, however, ways in which this may happen. Managers may perceive the risk of avoiding uncomfortable debate to be greater than that of pursuing it. For example, this may be the case if the organisation is in crisis. Managing entry into the uncomfortable is more problematic. It may be possible to enter through accessing a discussion about the core assumptions of the organisation – the paradigm. Mapping out the cultural web of the organisation may provide a visual image of the very aspects of the organisation which are typically not discussed – the underlying power structures, the day-to-day routines and the taken-for-granted assumptions which guide everyday life – and therefore facilitate debate about that which is rarely brought out into the open. Without such an openness of debate about the really significant blockages to change, it is unlikely that they will be tackled.

11.4 MANAGING STRATEGIC CHANGE PROCESSES

This section deals with the processes, or approaches, to managing change which need to be considered. These include changes in *structure and control systems*, *styles* of managing change, organisational *routines*, the use of *symbolic* and *political* activity, means of *communication* and other *change tactics*. While each of these is important in itself, the greater the degree of change, the more likely it is that multiple approaches to change will be needed.

11.4.1 Changes in Structure and Control Systems

Many books on strategic management regard the implementation of strategic change as primarily concerned with changing aspects of organisational structure and control systems.[10] These are regarded as important aspects of strategic change here too, but they have been covered elsewhere (see Chapters 9 and 10) and so will not be discussed in detail here. These aspects of change may have received particular attention because they tend to position top managers as the paramount agents or controllers of change, with organisational members responding to the systems imposed by them. It is a top management, top-down, view of change. The danger is that changes in structure and control systems may not affect the everyday existence of members of the organisation, that there will be a conformity towards such structures and systems, but that people will just carry on doing what they previously did on a day-to-day basis. Top management may think they have set up systems to implement strategy, but behaviour and assumptions may not have changed.

11.4.2 Styles of Managing Change

There are more or less appropriate styles of management for those faced with managing change.[11] These styles are summarised in Exhibit 11.6.

education and communication *involves the explanation of the reasons for and means of strategic change*

- **Education and communication** involves the explanation of the reasons for and means of strategic change. It might be appropriate if there is a problem in managing change based on misinformation or lack of information. However, there are problems here. If large numbers of people are involved in the change, managers may try to communicate by mass briefings. But they are likely to find this ineffective, not least because those being briefed may not get a chance to assimilate the information, or because there is a lack of mutual trust and respect between managers and employees. Relying on processes of communication in a top-down fashion may be problematic: involvement of those affected by changes in strategy development and planning change processes may therefore be important.

Exhibit 11.6 **Styles of managing strategic change**

STYLE	MEANS/CONTEXT	BENEFITS	PROBLEMS	CIRCUMSTANCES OF EFFECTIVENESS
Education and communication	Group briefings assume internalisation of strategic logic and trust of top management	Overcoming lack of (or mis)information	Time consuming Direction or progress may be unclear	Incremental change or long-time horizontal transformational change
Collaboration/ participation	Involvement in setting the strategy agenda and/or resolving strategic issues by taskforces or groups	Increasing ownership of a decision or process May improve quality of decisions	Time consuming Solutions/outcome within existing paradigm	
Intervention	Change agent retains co-ordination/control: delegates elements of change	Process is guided/controlled but involvement takes place	Risk of perceived manipulation	Incremental or non-crisis transformational change
Direction	Use of authority to set direction and means of change	Clarity and speed	Risk of lack of acceptance and ill-conceived strategy	Transformational change
Coercion/edict	Explicit use of power through edict	May be successful in crises or state of confusion	Least successful unless crisis	Crisis, rapid transformational change or change in established autocratic cultures

collaboration *or participation in the change process is the involvement of those who will be affected by strategic change in the identification of strategic issues, the setting of the strategic agenda, the strategic decision making process or the planning of strategic change*

- **Collaboration** or *participation* in the change process is the involvement of those who will be affected by strategic change in the identification of strategic issues, the setting of the strategic agenda, the strategic decision making process or the planning of strategic change. This can be helpful in increasing ownership of a decision or change process, and in increasing commitment to it. It may entail the setting up of project teams or taskforces. The outcome may be of higher quality than decisions taken without such an approach. In the late 1980s, when British Airways effected major and successful change, there was widespread involvement across levels of management and staff in the critique of current practices and in workshops proposing new ideas and appraising proposed solutions.

  Strategy workshops can also usefully cross levels of management to work on particular strategic problems, provide proposed solutions within a broad strategic framework, and drive change mechanisms down to routine aspects of organisational life. However, there is the inevitable risk that solutions will be found from within the existing paradigm. Anyone who sets up such a process, therefore, may need to retain the ability to intervene in the process.

intervention *is the co-ordination of and authority over processes of change by a change agent who delegates elements of the change process*

- By **intervention** is meant the co-ordination of and authority over processes of change by a change agent who delegates elements of the change process. For example, it might be that particular stages of change, such as idea generation, data collection, detailed planning, the development of rationales for change and the identification of critical success factors, are delegated to project teams or taskforces. Such teams do not take full responsibility for the change process, but they do become involved in it and see their work building towards it. The sponsor of the change ensures the monitoring of progress and that change is seen to occur.[12] An advantage here is that it involves members of the organisation not only in originating ideas, but also in the *partial implementation* of solutions. For example, those who originate ideas might be given responsibility for co-ordinating or overseeing the implementation of such aspects of the strategic change. This involvement is likely to give rise to greater commitment to the change.

direction *involves the use of personal managerial authority to establish a clear future strategy and how change will occur*

- **Direction** involves the use of personal managerial authority to establish a clear future strategy and how change will occur. It is essentially top-down management of strategic change. It may be associated with a clear vision or strategic intent developed by someone seen as a leader in the organisation; but it may also be accompanied by similar clarity about the sorts of critical success factors and priorities discussed in Chapter 10.

coercion *is the imposition of change or the issuing of edicts about change*

- In its most extreme form, a directive style becomes **coercion**, involving the imposition of change or the issuing of edicts about change. This is the explicit use of power and may be necessary if the organisation is facing a crisis, for example.

There are some overall observations that can be made about the appropriateness of these different styles:

- Different styles are likely to be suited to different contexts and circumstances. For example, strategic change for an organisation has implications for different stakeholders. Education and communication may be highly appropriate for some stakeholders, such as city institutions in the case of a public corporation. However, at the same time other styles may be more appropriate to galvanise change internally within the organisation. Styles of managing change are not, then, mutually exclusive in a change programme.
- Different stages in the change process should, perhaps, also be regarded in different contexts. Clear direction may be vital in the unfreezing and refreezing stages, whereas participation or intervention may be especially helpful in information building and experimentation.
- The evidence is that participative styles are most appropriate for incremental change within organisations, but that where transformational change is required directive approaches are more common. It is also worth noting that even where top management see themselves adopting participative styles, their subordinates may perceive this as directive and, indeed, may welcome such direction.[13]

Illustration 11.3 shows how chief executives use different styles in different contexts.

11.4.3 Changes in Organisational Routines

routines *are the organisationally specific 'ways we do things around here' which tend to persist over time and guide people's behaviour*

Routines are the organisationally specific 'ways we do things around here'[14] which tend to persist over time and guide people's behaviour. As has been seen in the discussion on the value chain in Chapters 4 and 10, it may be that an organisation which becomes especially good at carrying out its operations in particular ways achieves real competitive advantages. However, there is also the risk that the same routines act to block change and lead to strategic drift (see Chapter 2, section 2.8.2).

The power of such routines is clear enough when they need changing in order to accommodate a new strategy. Managers can make the mistake of assuming that because they have specified a strategy which requires operational changes in work practices, and explained to more junior management what such changes are, the changes will necessarily take place. They may find that the reasons which emerge as to why such changes should be delayed or cannot occur have to do with the persistent influence of long-standing organisational routines.

A manager in a hospital trust in the UK, determined to make the hospital services more 'client friendly', tried to persuade a medical consultant both to adhere to appointment times so as to cut down waiting time and not to require patients to change into the white gowns traditional

STRATEGY IN ACTION
Illustration 11.3

Styles of Managing Change

Executives use different styles of managing change.

Education, Communication and Participation in the Electrical Industry

In the early 1990s, Jan Timmer, the chief executive of Philips NV, was seeking to move the company from its cumbersome technologically focused, organisationally complex past to a more market-, customer-focused future. A 'customer day' was organised in January 1992 on which Timmer communicated by satellite with 80,000 Philips employees throughout Europe. He spoke to every employee in their local workplace for an hour. This was followed by groups of employees locally identifying what a customer-oriented organisation and a customer-responsive employee should be like. Views on these local deliberations, together with questions for Timmer, were sent to the Eindhoven head office that same day. In the afternoon, Timmer again spoke to employees by satellite, answering the questions, commenting on the views and taking live questions from an audience in Eindhoven.

Intervention in the Oil Industry

A Dutch executive of an oil company was appointed as chief executive in a national subsidiary in southern Europe which had long been subject to government regulation on prices. 'I faced a sleepy management team which had simply managed the distribution of oil products; there was no thought about competition. Within a year we had to face a free market and all that meant in competitive terms. It was tempting to try to tell them what to do, but it would not have worked. They knew they had to change, but they did not know what it meant or how to do it. I set up project teams to tackle some of the major issues. I gave them the questions; they had to come up with the answers. I made it clear that the questions were based around the performance levels achieved in other businesses in the group, so they knew they could be achieved. For example, how do we reduce costs by 30 per cent. How do we increase share by 50 per cent. Members of the project team visited companies in other countries to see what they were doing; they came to me and asked questions, and I offered some suggestions; consultants I brought in argued with them and challenged them. Their task was to come up with recommendations for the future within a six-month period. This they did and we debated them. I then led a team to pull it all together and identify specific plans of action to make it happen.'

Central Direction in the British Labour Party

Following its defeat by the Conservatives in 1979, the British Labour Party became factionalised and, some commentators said, unelectable. When Tony Blair took over as leader, he made it clear that his aim was electoral victory. His challenge to his party colleagues was whether they wanted this or a role of perpetual opposition; and his strategy was to shift 'New Labour' to the centre of British politics. Although some complained that a lack of democracy had developed in the party, there was general agreement that 'something had to be done' and a desire for clear direction, even though differences in policy remained. By the time of the election in 1997, the Labour Party was seen by the voters as unified around a strong leader; and won by its biggest ever majority

Questions

Read section 11.4.2 of the text and Exhibit 11.6 then answer the following questions separately in relation to each of the three examples above.

1. Does the style match the circumstances?
2. Might a different *individual* choose a different style even in the same circumstances?
3. Only some stakeholders are specifically mentioned in the examples. Does this mean that the style should be the same towards all stakeholders? (Reading section 5.3 in Chapter 5 might help here.)

in that hospital: 'People could be sitting or lying around for an hour in very scanty gowns; it was embarrassing for them.' After much debate the consultant agreed to more diligent appointment timing, but insisted the gowns were imperative. The manager instructed the white gowns to be removed from the consulting room. The following week, the consultant had purchased his own gowns and was bringing them into the hospital every morning.

Chapter 10 (see section 10.3.1) argued that it is important to drive the planning of strategic change down to the identification of critical success factors and competences underpinning these factors. In so doing, the planning of the implementation of the intended strategy is being driven down to operational levels, and it is likely this will require changes in the routines of the organisation. It is at this level that changes in strategy become really meaningful for most people in their everyday organisational lives. Moreover, as mentioned above, routines are closely linked to the taken-for-grantedness of the paradigm, so changing routines may have the effect of questioning and challenging deep-rooted beliefs and assumptions in the organisation. It is vital that managers who are trying to effect strategic changes take personal responsibility not only for identifying such changes in routines, but also for monitoring that they actually occur. The changes may appear to be mundane, but they can have significant impact. Illustration 11.4 gives some examples.

11.4.4 Symbolic Processes in Managing Change[15]

Change processes are not always of an overt, formal nature: they may also be symbolic in nature. Chapter 2 explained how symbolic acts and artefacts of an organisation help preserve the paradigm, and Chapter 5 explained how their relationship to culture and strategy can be analysed. Here the concern is how they can be managed to signal change.

symbols *are objects, events, acts or people which express more than their intrinsic content*

Symbols are objects, events, acts or people which express more than their intrinsic content. They may be everyday things which are nevertheless especially meaningful in the context of a particular situation or organisation. It is argued that the creation or manipulation of symbols has impact to the extent that changing symbols can reshape beliefs and expectations[16] because meaning becomes apparent in day-to-day experience in the organisation. This is one reason why changes in routines (discussed above) are important, but other such everyday or 'mundane' aspects include the stories that people tell, the status symbols such as cars and sizes of office, the type of language and technology used, and organisational rituals.

- Many of the *rituals* of organisations are implicitly concerned with effecting or consolidating change. Exhibit 11.7 identifies such rituals.[17] They are capable of being managed proactively: new rituals can be introduced or old rituals done away with. Using the terminology of Exhibit 11.7, change agents can consider the rituals which may be

STRATEGY IN ACTION
Illustration 11.4

Changes in Organisational Routines

Changes in organisational routines can be a powerful signal and stimulus of change.

- The management of a transport and distribution firm, seeking to emphasise rapid response to customer needs, established a routine of telephone answering in the head office. No phone was allowed to ring more than twice before being picked up by someone; and no one was allowed to ignore a ringing phone – 'it might be a customer'.
- Public sector organisations have been obsessed with the stewardship of public funds, often resulting in very risk-averse cultures. Some have tried to break this by setting up internal 'investment banks' so that staff can 'bid' for the funding of new ventures.
- The activities of branch personnel in many UK banks were dominated by manual form-filling procedures. The effect was that these procedures were often seen as more significant than dealing with customers. In the late 1980s, the banks moved to computerised systems: this was not just to reduce staff costs, but also to remove the paperwork from remaining staff. As one manager put it: 'If you haven't got a form to fill in, you have to attend to customers, and that is at the heart of our strategy.'
- The chief executive of a long-established Danish company manufacturing hearing aids, sought to transform the organisation into a 'knowledge-based' company. He introduced an open-plan office with mobile seating arrangements, and put everyone to work in project-based teams. Traditional job responsibilities were broken down and all head office staff were required to do up to five jobs, deciding themselves what they should prioritise and working in frequently changing project teams. The new office had no walls, but only workbenches with computer terminals. People moved between desks according to the projects they were working on, taking a set of drawers with them. Incoming mail was scanned onto the computer; if someone wanted to view something on paper, they went to the mail room, and it was then shredded.
- The members of an operating board of a subsidiary of a major multinational had offices in different sites of its operation in the UK. They had a tendency to blame each other for the problems of the firm. The result was over-defensiveness and low-quality decision making. Eventually the board members relocated to one site with offices in the same building. The day-to-day contact with each other resulted in more open personal relationships, a greater readiness to sort out day-to-day problems and, eventually, a greater understanding of strategic issues.

Questions

1. For each of these examples, why did the change agents wish to change the routines?
2. Extend the list of examples in the illustration by suggesting routines that might be changed in order to effect change in some organisations with which you are familiar.

useful. *Rites of enhancement* might include the spreading of 'good news' of transformation and the rewarding of those contributing to it. Corporate newsletters are often used for this purpose. There could be *rites of integration*, such as conferences which applaud change and 'change heroes', or which involve or associate members of the organisation with new approaches, activities or belief systems. *Rites of conflict reduction* to minimise or contain disunity may take the form of structural change or personnel appointments that demonstrate which executive groups have significant influence and which have been marginalised. *Rites of passage* can signal change from one stage of the organisation's development to another: for example, the departure of the old and introduction of new management, perhaps the replacement of senior board members or even a whole board, can signify much more than individual personnel changes as an indication of the passing from one era to another.

- Symbolic significance is also embedded in the *systems* discussed elsewhere in this chapter and in Chapters 9 and 10. For example, reward systems, information and control systems, and the very organisational structures that represent reporting relationships and often status are also symbolic in nature. Even budgeting and planning systems come to take on symbolic significance in so far as they represent to individuals the everyday reality of organisational life.

  To take an example of such systems; the way selection interviews are conducted is likely to signal to those being interviewed the nature of the organisation, and what is expected of them. A highly formal interview procedure may signal a mechanistic, rather hierarchical organisation, whereas a more informal dialogue, perhaps preceded by open questioning of potential colleagues, is likely to signal an environment and expectation of challenge and questioning. If selection processes are changed, different types of manager are appointed, and visible encouragement to challenge and questioning is given, this can signal within the organisation the commitment to strategic change. In this sense, selection processes are symbolic in nature.
- Changes in *physical aspects* of the work environment are powerful symbols of change. Typical here is a change of location for the head office, relocation of personnel, changes in dress or uniforms, and alterations to offices or office space.
- The most powerful symbol of all in relation to change is the *behaviour of change agents* themselves. The behaviour, language and stories associated with such executives can signal powerfully the need for change and appropriate behaviour relating to the management of change. Too few senior executives understand that, having made pronouncements about the need for change, it is vital that their visible behaviour is in line with such change because, for most people in an organisation, their organisational world is one of deeds and actions, not of abstractions. In a retail business with an espoused strategy of

Exhibit 11.7 Organisational rituals and culture change

Types of Ritual	Role	Examples
Rites of passage	Consolidate and promote social roles and interaction	Induction programmes Training programmes
Rites of enhancement	Recognise effort benefiting organisation Similarly motivate others	Awards ceremonies Promotions
Rites of renewal	Reassure that something is being done Focus attention on issues	Appointment of consultants Project teams
Rites of integration	Encourage shared commitment Reassert rightness of norms	Christmas parties
Rites of conflict reduction	Reduce conflict and aggression	Negotiating committees
Rites of degradation	Publicly acknowledge problems Dissolve/weaken social or political roles	Firing top executives Demotion or 'passing over'
Rites of sense making	Sharing of interpretations and sense making	Rumours Surveys to evaluate new practices
Rites of challenge	'Throwing down the gauntlet'	New CEO's different behaviour
Rites of counter-challenge	Resistance to new ways of doing things	Grumbling Working to rule

customer care, the chief executive, on visiting stores, tended to ignore staff and customers alike: he seemed to be interested only in the financial information in the store manager's office. He was unaware of this until it was pointed out; and his change in behaviour afterwards, insisting on talking to staff and customers on his visits, became a 'story' which spread around the company, substantially supporting the strategic direction of the firm.

- *Stories* themselves can be managed to some extent. The use of corporate newsletters and newspapers is an example. There are, however, more subtle examples. One chief executive claimed that the most effective way of spreading a story in his business was to get his secretary to leave a memo from him marked 'strictly confidential' by the photocopier for ten minutes: 'Its contents would be all over the office in half an hour and round the regions by the end of the day.'
- Also important in effecting change is the *language* used by change agents.[18] Either consciously or unconsciously, change agents may

employ language and metaphor to galvanise change. Some examples are included in Illustration 11.5. In this context, language is not simply concerned with communicating facts and information; language is also powerful because it is symbolic and is able to carry several meanings at once. For example, it may link the past to the future: it may attack or undermine an image of the past, and therefore carry a very serious message, yet do so in a playful way; and it may evoke emotional feelings more strongly than rational understanding. Of course, there is also the danger that change agents do not realise the power of language and, while espousing change, use language that signals adherence to the status quo, or personal reluctance to change. Those involved in change need to think carefully about the language they use, and the symbolic significance of their actions.

Illustration 11.5 gives other examples of such symbolic signalling of change.

11.4.5 Power and Political Processes in Managing Change[19]

It is likely that there will be a need for the reconfiguration of *power structures* in the organisation, especially if transformational change is required. In order to effect this reconfiguration of power, it is likely that the momentum for change will need *powerful advocacy* within the organisation, typically from the chief executive, a powerful member of the board or an influential outsider: indeed, an individual or group combining both power and interest, as described in Chapter 5 (see section 5.3.2 and Exhibit 5.5).

However, political activity is not relevant only at the chief executive or senior executive level. Any manager faced with managing change needs to consider how it might be effected from a political perspective. Managers also need to realise that analysis and planning may themselves take on political dimensions. A new marketing director of a company commissioned market research on customer perceptions of service, and the results were highly critical. However, he found that the presentation of the findings to the board gave rise not to analytical debate, but to systematic 'rubbishing' of the research report. He failed to realise that his work had been seen 'not so much as an analytical statement, as a statement of political threat': it had threatened the very bases of the business upon which many on the board had built their authority and power in the organisation. So managers need to be sensitive to the political dimensions of their activities, both because there might be blockages to apparently rational behaviour and because political activity might, itself, help effect change.

Chapter 5 discussed the importance of understanding the political context in and around the organisation. Having established this understanding, there is also a need to consider the implementation of strategy within this political context. The approach developed here draws on the

STRATEGY IN ACTION
Illustration 11.5

Symbolic Activity and Strategic Change

Symbolic aspects of management can aid the change process in organisations.

Language which Challenges and Questions

The chief executive of a retailing firm facing a crisis addressed his board: 'I suggest we think of ourselves like bulls facing a choice: the abattoir or the bull ring. I've made up my mind: what about you?'

In another company, the chief executive described the threat of a takeover in terms of pending warfare: 'We've been targeted: they've got the hired guns [merchant bankers, consultants, etc.] on board. Don't expect chivalry: don't look for white knights; this is a shoot-out situation.'

Physical Objects such as Clothing which Signal Change

The head nurse of a recovery unit for patients who had been severely ill decided that, if nurses wore everyday clothes rather than nurses' uniforms, it would signal to patients that they were on the road to recovery and a normal life; and to nurses that they were concerned with rehabilitation.

However, the decision had other implications for the nurses too. It blurred the status distinction between nurses and other non-professional members of staff. Nurses preferred to wear their uniforms. While they recognised that uniforms signalled a medically fragile role of patients, they reinforced their separate and professional status as acute care workers.[1]

Confirmatory Action Signalling Change

In a textile firm in Scotland, equipment associated with the 'old ways of doing things' was taken into the yard at the rear of the factory and physically dismantled in front of the workforce.

When the new president of Asaki Breweries in Japan introduced Koku-Kire beer, he signalled a fundamental shift in product policy and required commitment to the new product, not only with a high-publicity launch and a change in company logo, but also by dumping all stocks of the old product and recalling it from 130,000 stores.[2]

Questions

Refer back to page 77 in Chapter 2 which gives some general examples of symbols. Then, for an organisation with which you are familiar (or for the KPMG (A) case study at the end of chapter 2):

1. Identify at least five important symbols in the organisation.
2. In what way could they be changed to support a different strategy? Be explicit as to how the symbols might relate to the new strategy.
3. Why are these potential levers for change often ignored?

Sources

1. M.G. Pratt and E. Rafaeli, 'The role of symbols in fragmented organizations: an illustration from organizational dress', presented at the Academy of Management Meeting, Atlanta, GA, 1993.
2. T. Nakajo and T. Kono, 'Success through culture change in a Japanese brewery', *Long Range Planning*, vol. 22, no. 6 (1989), pp. 29–37.

content of Chapter 5 and also some of this chapter to provide a framework. Exhibit 5.6 in Chapter 5 lists sources of power in organisations. These also provide indicators of some of the mechanisms associated with power which can be used for change. Summarised in Exhibit 11.8, these include the manipulation of *organisational resources*; the relationship with powerful groupings and *élites*; activity with regard to *subsystems* in the organisation; and again, *symbolic activity*. All of these may be used to: (1) build a power base; (2) encourage support or overcome resistance; and (3) achieve commitment to a strategy or course of action.

- Acquiring additional *resources* or being identified with important resource areas or areas of expertise, and the ability to withdraw or allocate such resources, can be a valuable tool in overcoming resistance or persuading others to accept change.
- Powerful groupings in the organisation are of crucial importance and may, of course, correspond to powerful *stakeholder groups*. Association with such groupings, or their support, can help build a power base, and this may be necessary for the change agent who does not have a strong personal power base from which to work. Similarly, association with a change agent who is respected or visibly successful can help a manager overcome resistance to change.
- It may be necessary to remove individuals or groups resistant to change. Who these are can vary – from powerful individuals in senior positions, to loose networks within the organisation and sometimes including external stakeholders with powerful influence, to whole layers of resistance perhaps in the form of senior executives in a threatened function or service – the 'concrete ceiling' referred to earlier in the chapter.
- Building up *alliances* and a *network* of contacts and sympathisers, even though they may not be powerful themselves, may be important in overcoming the resistance of more powerful groups. Attempting to convert the whole organisation to an acceptance of change is difficult – it is likely that there will be parts of the organisation or individuals in it more sympathetic to that change than others. The change agent might sensibly concentrate on these to develop momentum, building a team strongly supportive of the activities and beliefs of the change agent. He or she may also seek to marginalise those who are resistant to change.

  The danger is that powerful groups in the organisation may regard the building of such a team, or acts of marginalisation, as a threat to their own power, and that this may lead to further resistance to change. An analysis of power and interest similar to the stakeholder mapping described in Chapter 5 might, therefore, be especially useful to identify bases of alliance and likely political resistance.
- As has been seen, the employment of *symbolic mechanisms* of change can be useful. From a political point of view, this may take several forms. To build power the manager may initially seek to identify with

Exhibit 11.8 Political mechanisms in organisations

Activity Areas	Mechanisms: Resources	Élites	Subsystems	Symbolic	Key Problems
Building the power base	Control of resources Acquisition of/identification with expertise Acquisition of additional resources	Sponsorship by an élite Association with an élite	Alliance building Team building	Building on legitimation	Time required for building Perceived duality of ideals Perceived as threat by existing élites
Overcoming resistance	Withdrawal of resources Use of 'counter-intelligence'	Breakdown or division of élites Association with change agent Association with respected outsider	Foster momentum for change Sponsorship/reward of change agents	Attack or remove legitimation Foster confusion, conflict and questioning	Striking from too low a power base Potentially destructive: need for rapid rebuilding
Achieving compliance	Giving resources	Removal of resistant élites Need for visible 'change hero'	Partial implementation and collaboration Implantation of 'disciples' Support for 'Young Turks'	Applause/reward Reassurance Symbolic confirmation	Converting the body of the organisation Slipping back

the very symbols which preserve and reinforce the paradigm – to work within the committee structures, become identified with the organisational rituals or stories that exist and so on. On the other hand, in breaking resistance to change, removing, challenging or changing rituals and symbols may be a very powerful means of achieving the questioning of what is taken for granted. Symbolic activity can also be used to consolidate change by concentrating attention or 'applause' and rewards on those who most accept change, its wider adoption is more likely; and there may be means of confirming change through symbolic devices such as new structures, titles, office allocation and so on, so that the change is to be regarded as important and not reversible.

- Change agents also have to cope with the tactical political manoeuvring of other managers resistant to change. The sorts of tactic typically employed to counter change are identified in Exhibit 11.9. The exhibit also identifies some of the actions that might be taken in countering such countermoves: many of these build on the discussion in this chapter of styles of managing and symbolic and political aspects of management.

Political aspects of management in general, and change specifically, are unavoidable; and the lessons of organisational life are as important for the manager as they are, and always have been, for the politician (see Illustration 11.6). However, the political aspects of management are also difficult, and potentially hazardous. Exhibit 11.8 summarises some of the problems.

One problem in building a power base is that the manager may have to become so identified with existing power groupings that he or she either actually comes to accept their views or is perceived by others to have done so, thus losing support among potential supporters of change. Building a power base is a delicate path to tread.

In overcoming resistance, the major problem may simply be the lack of power to be able to undertake such activity. Attempting to overcome resistance from a lower power base is probably doomed to failure. There is a second major danger: in the breaking down of the status quo, the process becomes so destructive and takes so long that the organisation cannot recover from it. If the process needs to take place, its replacement by some new set of beliefs and the implementation of a new strategy is vital and needs to be speedy. Further, as already identified, in implementing change the main problem is likely to be carrying the body of the organisation with the change. It is one thing to change the commitment of a few senior executives at the top of an organisation; it is quite another to convert the body of the organisation to an acceptance of significant change. The danger is that individuals are likely to regard change as temporary: something which they need to comply with only until the next change comes along.

Exhibit 11.9 Political manoeuvres and change

COUNTERMOVES TO CHANGE

- Divert resources. Split budget across other projects, give key staff other priorities/other assignments.
- Exploit inertia. Request everyone to wait until a key player takes action, reads a report, or makes an appropriate response; suggest the results from another project should be assessed first.
- Keep goals vague and complex. It is harder to initiate appropriate action if aims are multidimensional and specified in generalised, grandiose or abstract terms.
- Encourage and exploit lack of organisational awareness. Insist that 'we can deal with the people issues later', knowing these will delay or kill the project.
- 'Great idea – let's do it properly'. Involve so many representatives or experts that there will be so many different views and conflicting interests it will delay decisions or require meaningless compromise.
- Dissipate energies. Conduct surveys, collect data, prepare analyses, write reports, make overseas trips, hold special meetings ...
- Reduce the change agent's influence and credibility. Spread damaging rumours, particularly among the change agent's friends and supporters.
- Keep a low profile. Do not openly declare resistance to change because that gives those driving change a clear target to aim for.

COUNTERING COUNTERMOVES TO CHANGE

- Establish clear direction and objectives. Goal clarity enables action to proceed more effectively than ambiguity and complexity, which can slow down action.
- Establish simple, phased programming. For the same reasons as having clear goals.
- Adopt a fixer–facilitator–negotiator role. Resistance to change can rarely be overcome by reason alone, and the exercise of these interpersonal skills is required.
- Seek and respond to resistance. Take a proactive approach to resistance in order to overcome, mitigate or block it: appeal/refer to high values/standards or powerful authorities; warn them off; use influential intermediaries; infiltrate meetings and supporters; wait them out or wear them down.
- Rely on face to face. Personal influence and persuasion is usually more effective in winning and sustaining support than the impersonal memo or report.
- Exploit a crisis. People will often respond more positively to a crisis which they understand and face collectively than to personal attempts to change behaviour.
- Co-opt support early. Build coalitions and recruit backers, of prior importance to the building of teams; co-opting opponents may also be tactically useful.
- The meaningful steering committee/taskforce/project team. Include in its membership key players in the organisation who carry 'weight', authority and respect.

Source Adapted from D. Buchanan and D. Boddy, *The Expertise of the Change Agent: Public performance and backstage activity*, Prentice Hall, 1992, pp. 78–9.

STRATEGY IN ACTION
Illustration 11.6

Machiavelli on Political Processes

'It should be borne in mind that there is nothing more difficult to handle, more doubtful of success, and more dangerous to carry through, than initiating changes in a state's constitution.'

> The innovator makes enemies of all those who prospered under the old order, and only lukewarm support is forthcoming from those who would prosper under the new. Their support is lukewarm partly from fear of their adversaries, who have the existing laws on their side, and partly because men are generally incredulous, never really trusting new things unless they have tested them by experience. In consequence, whenever those who oppose the changes can do so, they attack vigorously, and the defence made by the others is only lukewarm. So both the innovator and his friends come to grief.
>
> (Niccolò Machiavelli, *The Prince*, 1513)

Machiavelli's prince is precariously balanced between four interest groups: the army, the nobility, the populace and the state. Gauging the relative power of these and devising strategies which take this into account become crucial, as Machiavelli illustrates.

Scipio's *army* rebelled against him in Spain for allowing too much licence. Commodus and Maximinus (two Roman emperors) both exhibited excess cruelty, and both were killed by their armies.

The *nobility*'s desire is to command and oppress the people. Bentivogli, Prince of Bologna, was killed by the Canneschi (nobility) who conspired against him. However, after the murder, the people rose up and killed the Canneschi. The Canneschi misjudged the goodwill of the people towards Bentivogli.

It is necessary for a prince to possess the friendship of the *populace*, particularly in times of adversity. Nabis, prince of the Spartans, sustained a siege by the rest of Greece and a victorious Roman army, defended his country against them, and maintained his own position through unifying the populace.

Machiavelli commends three principles:

- Establish whether you are in the position, in case of need, to maintain yourself alone, or whether you need the protection of others.
- Esteem your nobles, but do not make yourself hated by the populace.
- Follow the example of Ferdinand, King of Aragon and Spain, who 'continually contrived great things which have kept his subjects' minds uncertain and astonished, and occupied in watching their result'.

Questions

1. Do you agree that Machiavelli's three principles apply to effecting strategic change in organisations? Discuss this in relation to the power/interest matrix (Exhibit 5.5).
2. How might the political mechanisms outlined in Exhibit 11.8 be used to put the three principles into effect?

Prepared by Roger Lazenby, Middlesex University.

11.4.6 Communicating Change

Managers faced with effecting change typically underestimate substantially the extent to which members of the organisation understand the need for change, what it is intended to achieve, or what is involved in the changes. Some important points to emphasise are as follows.

- The reasons for a change in strategic direction may be complex, and the strategy itself may therefore embrace complex ideas. However, to be effective it is important that it is communicated in such a way that complexity has a meaning and vitality which can be assimilated across the organisation. This message has already been discussed elsewhere in the book, when considering the importance of *vision* and *strategic intent* in Chapters 5 and 6. These should not be banal statements of strategy, but rather should encapsulate the significance and challenge of that strategy.
- It may be important to clarify and simplify further the priorities of the strategy. Some writers argue[20] that a *three themes* approach is useful, emphasising a limited number of key aspects of the strategy, rather than expecting to be able to communicate overall complexity and ramifications.
- There are *choices of media* by which to communicate the strategy and the elements of the strategic change programme.[21] Exhibit 11.10 summarises some of the choices and the likely effectiveness of these in different circumstances. Choices of media richness vary from face-to-face, one-to-one communication through to routine bulletins on noticeboards and circulars sent round the organisation.

  The extent to which these different forms of media are likely to be effective depends on the extent to which the nature of the change is routine or complex. To communicate a highly complex set of changes, it would be inappropriate to use standardised bulletins and circulars with no chance of any feedback or interaction. In situations of strategic change, members of the organisation not involved in the development of the strategy may see the effects of change as non-routine even when senior executives regard them as routine. So communication which provides interaction and involvement is likely to be desirable.
- The *involvement* of members of the organisation in the strategy development process or the planning of strategic change is also, in itself, a means of communication and can be very effective. Those who are involved might be used to cascade information about the change programme into the organisation, in effect becoming part of the change agency process themselves. This is an important element of the *intervention* style described in section 11.4.2.
- Communication needs to be seen as a two-way process. *Feedback* on communication is important, particularly if the changes to be introduced are difficult to understand or threatening or if it is critically

Exhibit 11.10 Effective and ineffective communication of change

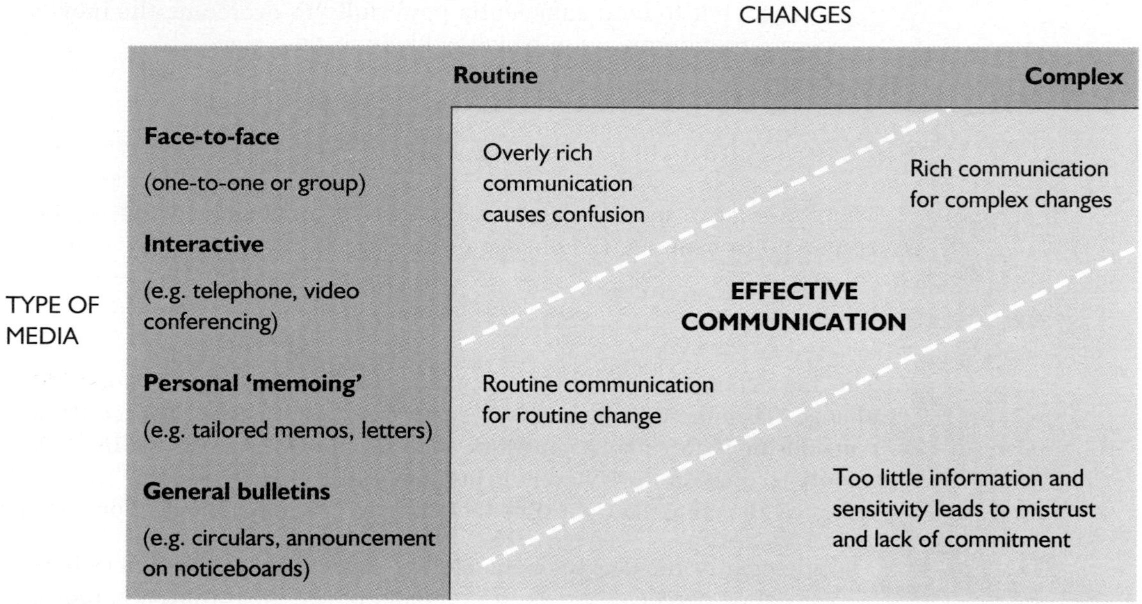

Source Based on R.H. Lengel and R.L. Daft, 'The selection of communication media as an effective skill', *Academy of Management Executive*, vol. 2, no. 3 (1988), pp. 225–32.

important to get the changes right. It is rare that changes have been thought through in ways which have meaning to or can be put into effect at lower levels in the organisation. In addition, the purpose of the changes may be misunderstood or misconstrued at such levels.

These problems can be tackled in various ways. If there has been a cascading process in the organisation, this can also be used to obtain feedback. It may be useful to set up 'focus groups' which give feedback to senior executives on the implementation and acceptance of change. Some organisations employ survey techniques to check the extent to which change processes are being followed, understood or welcomed. In other organisations, senior executives invite feedback by 'walking the talk', ensuring that they meet with those responsible for implementing change, perhaps on an informal basis in their workplace.

- There is, however, another reason why communication is very important. Communication occurs in organisations not simply because managers trying to effect change wish to communicate, but because members of the organisation need to make sense of what is happening for themselves. They therefore communicate with each other. This takes the form of *rumours*, *gossip* and *storytelling*. Indeed, it has been noted that at times of threat and change, such storytelling increases in importance.[22] In managing change, the task is not only to communicate change, but to do it sufficiently powerfully to overcome the inevitable *countercommunication* which is likely to take place.

11.4.7 Change Tactics

There are also some more specific tactics of change which might be employed to facilitate the change process.

Timing

The importance of timing is often neglected in thinking about strategic change. To some extent this has already been covered in Chapter 10, when considering issues such as network analysis. However, network analysis has mainly to do with the scheduling tasks within a change project. Timing also refers to choosing the right time tactically to promote change. For example:

- The greater the degree of change, the more it may be useful to build on actual or perceived *crisis*. If members of the organisation perceive a higher risk in maintaining the status quo than in changing, they are more likely to change. For example, the management of a company threatened by takeover may be able to use this as a catalyst for transformational strategic change. Indeed, it is said that some chief executives seek to elevate problems to achieve perceived crisis in order to galvanise change.
- There may also be *windows of opportunity* in change processes. For example, the period following the takeover of a company may allow new owners to make more significant changes than might normally be possible. The arrival of a new chief executive, the introduction of a new highly successful product, or the arrival of a major competitive threat on the scene may also provide such opportunities. These windows of opportunity may, however, be brief; and the change agent may need to take decisive action during these periods.
- It is also important that those responsible for change do not provide conflicting messages about the timing of change. For example, if they see that rapid change is required, they should avoid the maintenance of procedures and signals which suggest long time horizons. For example, managers may exhort others to change while maintaining the same control and reward procedures or work practices that have been in place for many years. So the *symbolic signalling of time frames* becomes important (see section 11.4.4 above).
- Since change will be regarded nervously, it may be important to choose the time for promoting such change to avoid unnecessary fear and

nervousness. For example, if there is a need for reduction in personnel or the removal of executives (see below), it may make sense to do this before rather than during the change programme. In such a way, the change programme can be seen as a potential improvement for the future rather than as the cause of such losses.

Job Losses and De-layering

Change programmes are often associated with job losses, from the closure of units of the organisation, with hundreds or thousands of job losses, to the removal of a few senior executives. In the 1990s, in some countries change was associated with de-layering: the removal of whole layers of management. As indicated above, the timing of such job losses in relation to the change programme can be important. There are other considerations which can affect a change programme:

- The tactical choice of where job losses should take place related to the change programme may be important. For example, it could be that there is a layer of management or particular individuals who are widely recognised in the organisation as *blockers* of change. Their removal may indicate powerfully the serious nature and intent of the change. The removal of one layer of management may also provide perceived opportunities to management below. As one chief executive commented: 'If I have to lose people, then I will choose the most senior levels possible: they're the ones most usually resistant to change; and it provides a wonderful incentive for those below.'
- It may also be important to avoid 'creeping' job losses. If the change programme is continually associated with a threat to security, it is less likely to be successful. The same chief executive continued: 'It is better to cut deeply and quickly than hack away remorselessly over time.'
- It is also important, however, that if job losses are to take place, there is a visible, responsible and caring approach to those who lose their jobs. Not only are there ethical reasons for this, but tactically it signals to those who remain that the organisation cares. There are now many examples of companies which have successful redeployment, counselling services, outplacement arrangements, retraining facilities and so on. Indeed, British Coal Enterprise was set up with this purpose and was very successful in helping past employees in the coal-mining industry in all these respects.

Visible Short-term Wins

Strategy may be conceived of as having to do with long-term direction and major decisions. However, the implementation of strategy within a change programme will require many quite detailed actions and tasks. It is important that some of these tasks are seen to be put into place and to be successful quickly. This could take the form, for example, of a retail chain quickly developing a new store concept and demonstrating its success in the market; the effective breaking down of old ways of working and the demonstration of better ways; the speeding up of decisions by doing away with committees and introducing clearly defined job responsibilities; and so on.

In themselves, these may not be especially significant aspects of a new strategy, but they may be visible indicators of a new approach associated with that strategy. The demonstration of such wins will therefore galvanise commitment to the strategy.

11.5 ROLES IN THE CHANGE PROCESS

While it is very important to identify blockages to change and understand mechanisms of change, it is also necessary to consider the roles that individuals or groups of individuals play in the change process, and the sorts of skill they require. A good deal of the literature on leadership emphasises the personal, individualistic aspects of change management in organisations. Such literature sometimes suggests that strategic change is heavily dependent on the activities of charismatic leaders.[23] These views can be misleading because they fail to identify the context in which change agency occurs, the fact that change usually depends on more than one individual, and the extent to which skills in managing change can be developed.

In the sections below, a number of roles in the management of strategic change are reviewed. However, it should be emphasised that this is not meant to suggest that these roles are mutually exclusive. For example, the creator of a strategy may, or may not, also be the change agent; and it may be that a middle manager is also a recipient or indeed a change agent in a different context. So these are roles that different people in organisations may find themselves in at different times and in different contexts.

11.5.1 The Change Agent

the **change agent** *is the individual or group that effects strategic change in an organisation*

The person or people who develop a strategy may or may not be the same as those who take a lead in actually managing strategic change. By '**change agent**' is meant the individual or group that effects strategic change in an organisation. Some strategists may be especially good at creating a vision for the future, but may need to rely on others to take a lead in effecting the changes. It may be that there is a group of change agents from within the organisation or perhaps from outside, such as consultants, who have a whole team working on a project, together with managers from within the organisation. So change agency does not necessarily correspond to one individual, though it may.

Those faced with effecting change need to consider the extent to which the various components of change agency discussed in this chapter are in place or can be developed, and how these components match the context of change. The successful change agent will therefore:

- Be sensitive to the *external context* of change – for example, the triggers in the environment giving rise to change, or the pressure from external stakeholders.
- Be sensitive to *organisational context*, building on or relating to the values and beliefs of those in or around the organisation who advocate or feel sympathy towards the need for change and the history of the organisation.[24]
- Understand the overall strategy in terms of required *strategic architecture* (see Chapter 10) and therefore the magnitude and *type of change* necessary (see section 11.2).
- Employ an appropriate *style* of managing change, adapting that style to the circumstances rather than imposing his or her style without regard for the specific context of change.

In a study carried out on the perceived effectiveness of change agents, many of these aspects of managing change were shown to be important. They are reflected in fifteen key competences identified from that study (see Exhibit 11.11).

Personal traits of change agents may, however, be relevant. To what extent do successful change agents demonstrate special or different personal traits from others, and are the personal traits of the change agent appropriate to the context of change? The literature on *leadership* typically argues that they have visionary capacity, are good at team building and team playing, are self-analytical and good at self-learning, have mental agility and 'constructive restlessness' while also being able to concentrate for long periods, and are also self-directed and self-confident.[25]

There is a tendency here to overemphasise such personal attributes. However, managing the complexity of strategy development and strategic change certainly places special demands on change agents. One of the more telling commentaries on change agency arises from Peters and Waterman's[26] argument that the successful manager of change in organisations is a 'master of two ends of the spectrum'. By this they mean that the change agent is simultaneously able to cope with potentially conflicting ways of managing.

- In strategy creation, they have an ability to undertake or understand detailed analysis, and at the same time to be visionary about the future. In achieving organisational credibility for a strategy, they need to be seen as having insight about the future, and yet action oriented about making things happen.

Exhibit 11.11 Fifteen key competences of change agents

Goals

1. Sensitivity to changes in key personnel, top management perceptions and market conditions, and to the way in which these impact the goals of the project in hand.
2. Clarity in specifying goals, in defining the achievable.
3. Flexibility in responding to changes without the control of the project manager, perhaps requiring major shifts in project goals and management style, and risk taking.

Roles

4. Team-building abilities, to bring together key stakeholders and establish effective working groups, and to define and delegate respective responsibilities clearly.
5. Networking skills in establishing and maintaining appropriate contacts within and outside the organisation.
6. Tolerance of ambiguity, to be able to function comfortably, patiently and effectively in an uncertain environment.

Communication

7. Communication skills to transmit effectively to colleagues and subordinates the need for changes in project goals and in individual tasks and responsibilities.
8. Interpersonal skills, across the range, including selection, listening, collecting appropriate information, identifying the concerns of others, and managing meetings.
9. Personal enthusiasm in expressing plans and ideas.
10. Stimulating motivation and commitment in others involved.

Negotiation

11. Selling plans and ideas to others by creating a desirable and challenging vision of the future.
12. Negotiating with key players for resources, or for changes in procedures, and to resolve conflict.

Managing up

13. Political awareness in identifying potential coalitions, and in balancing conflicting goals and perceptions.
14. Influencing skills, to gain commitment to project plans and ideas from potential sceptics and resisters.
15. Helicopter perspectives, to stand back from the immediate project and take a broader view of priorities.

Source From D. Buchanan and D. Boddy, *The Expertise of the Change Agent: Public performance and backstage activity*, Prentice Hall, 1992, pp. 92–3.

- In challenging the status quo in an organisation, they need an ability to maintain credibility and carry people with the change, while attacking the taken-for-granted and current ways of doing things.
- In communicating strategic intent, they need an ability to encapsulate often quite complex issues of strategy in everyday ways which people can understand.

- In consolidating a strategy, and making it happen, they need an ability to maintain performance of the organisation while breaking down old assumptions and old ways of doing things, which potentially could jeopardise the efficiency of the organisation.

It is a challenging task, demanding the abilities to cope with ambiguity, to demonstrate flexibility, insight and sensitivity to strategic context, and to relate to others.

However, not all change agents are the same. Their personal traits and orientations lead to different approaches to strategic change. It is therefore important for them to understand that such personal orientations may or may not be appropriate to the context in which they are working. The change agent might, for example, have a personal inclination towards a *planning* view of strategic change, with a bias towards analysis, expert knowledge, control and persuasive logic; or a reliance on a *directive* style, having worked through his or her own logic for change.

Other change agents may, in processes of change, emphasise *collaboration* and feedback systems, so that people in the organisation can contribute to and develop the change process. Here, then, the change agent may be more sympathetic to the notion of the *learning organisation*, trying to improve relationships between organisational members and the environment in which they work, such that learning can take place and change be adaptive. Others may lean towards a more *interventionist* or manipulative approach, seeking to identify signals and symbols of change by which taken-for-granted assumptions can be challenged and questioned, and routines changed so as to require changes in behaviour.[27]

The important point is that the perspective that the change agent brings to the situation may not always be the same as the organisational context in which he or she is operating. For example, the change agent who takes a planning approach may find that members of the organisation are adept at using the systems associated with this to avoid tackling the really difficult questions or issues that may be necessary (see section 11.3.3 above). Or the change agent who leans towards a learning perspective may find it is necessary to move towards this gradually, within a context which emphasises formal planning systems and is not used to questioning, challenging and open debate. Sensitivity to context is therefore important.[28]

11.5.2 Middle Managers

A top-down approach to managing strategy and strategic change sees middle managers as implementors of strategy: their role is to put into effect the direction established by top management by making sure that resources are allocated and controlled appropriately, monitoring performance and behaviour of staff and, where necessary, explaining the strategy to those reporting to them. Those who take such an approach view middle managers not as facilitators of the strategy, but as blockages to its success. Indeed, this is sometimes seen as one reason for reducing the numbers and layers of management, so as to speed up communication between top management and organisational members, and to reduce potential blockages and filters.

However, there is evidence that middle managers can and do provide a real benefit in both the development and the implementation of strategy.[29] Their involvement in strategy development is important first because in their role they are likely to be intimately associated with the processes which represent the competences of the organisation (see Chapter 4); and also because they are likely to be in day-to-day contact with aspects of the business environment (see Chapter 3). If they are committed to helping develop effective strategy, they can help to interpret the extent to which such processes can provide advantages, and help to identify strategic opportunities.

Such involvement is also likely to mean that they have both a greater understanding of strategy and a greater commitment to it. This is important in effecting strategic change because they can play three vital roles. The first is the systematic role of implementation and control. The second is the reinterpretation and adjustment of strategic responses as events unfold (e.g. in terms of relationships with customers, suppliers, the workforce and so on). The third is as the crucial bridge between top management and members of the organisation at lower levels.

Middle managers are likely to contribute substantially either to galvanising commitment to strategy and the change process, or to blocking it. Commitment through involvement is likely to result in a positive role here. Lack of commitment can result in serious blockages and resistance. As suggested earlier, then, the involvement of middle management in strategy development, the planning of strategic change programmes and feedback on strategic change can be vitally important (see Illustration 11.7).

11.5.3 Other Organisational Members

The critical measure of the effectiveness of a strategy is the extent to which it affects the behaviour of those who interact with the organisation – for example, by customers buying more products, becoming more aware of a firm's benefits or using the services of a hospital or library more. If this is to happen, people perhaps in very junior roles in organisations play a crucial role because they are usually the interface between the organisation and those affected by the strategy outside the organisation. A critical question is how their commitment and understanding can best be gained at that level.

The point has already been made that relying on intellectual persuasion or assuming that changes in structure and control procedures are enough to effect strategic change may be a mistake. A senior executive in a bank, who understood the powerful blockages within the bank's culture built up over decades, had just heard the chief executive present the new strategy to 200 employees. The presentation had included a careful explanation of the strategy and the new structure demonstrated with videos, slides and glossy

STRATEGY IN ACTION
Illustration 11.7

Middle Management Contribution to Competitive Success at Pepperidge Farms

Middle managers' exposure to daily operating problems can create awareness of important technical or marketing trends before such issues surface at the top of the organisation.

Pepperidge Farms is a baked goods unit of Campbell Foods based in Wilton, Connecticut. Among other things, the company bakes and distributes premium-priced gourmet cookies with which it established a national reputation as the ultimate answer for late night 'munchies'. These cookies were sold in packs of eight or ten at prices equal to what competitors were only able to charge for dozen.

In the mid 1990s the firm began to feel the competitive pinch from a host of smaller bakeries selling fresh gourmet cookies in single servings through convenience stores. Whilst these outlets were attractive and lucrative to Pepperidge, packaging and distributing the product in quantities of one or two posed a major problem. Existing packages were hand filled, and the firm was already coping with complaints by employees of carpel-tunnel syndrome, a chronic condition from overuse of the hand. Smaller packs seemed unimaginable.

In response to employee complaints, a production manager in one of the bakeries had already been investigating automated packaging systems. The stress injuries had also taught him that smaller packages were not feasible, and he understood the industry well enough to know that the firm would eventually be forced to respond to competition. He had begun working with an equipment supplier without any explicit direction from above and had even contracted for a mock-up of a new, customised, assembly process. His interest had also spread to other members of the production team who had begun to work with him on the project.

When word surfaced that top management wanted to study automated assembly, his plant was identified as the place to start. In six months the pilot project was up and running and managers from other plants were brought in to learn about the new approach to packaging, helping to create a knowledge base and level of acceptance that quickened the pace of response and change. Within the year, the company had a video-activated robotic packaging line in two plants. Not only had the source and design of the technology been developed, but also management and employees in the pilot plant had begun to build the necessary competences and willingness to change.

The middle-level production manager who began thinking about automation did so because he was first to appreciate the significance of the capability barrier facing the company. The stress injuries had taught him that smaller packages were impossible, and he understood the industry well enough to know that the firm would eventually be forced to respond to the competition.

Questions

Suggest ways in which a middle manager might influence

1. the strategy development of an organisation
2. strategic change in an organisation.

Source Adapted by Steve Floyd from S.W. Floyd and W. Wooldridge, *The Strategic Middle Manager: How to create and sustain competitive advantage*, Jossey-Bass, 1996, pp. 16–17.

handouts. The presentation was heard in respectful silence, but as the audience left for lunch, he remarked: 'There really is no contest between a 35 mm slide show and 100 years of culture. This is a bank; no matter how well intentioned, that talk will not change things.' The point he was making is that the day-to-day procedures and routines operating in the bank would persist. So how can change be effected at junior levels in the organisation?

Running through this chapter, indeed through the whole book, has been the theme that changing strategy requires making changes in the taken-for-granted assumptions and the taken-for-granted routines and ways of doing things that are the elements of culture. Richard Pascale argues: 'It is easier to act your way into a better way of thinking than to think your way into a better way of acting',[30] easier to change behaviours and thus change taken-for-granted assumptions than to try to change taken-for-grated assumptions and therefore change behaviour. This is the distinction between what is known as programmatic change, by which is meant the attempt to convince people by persuasion and logic of the need for change; and task alignment, by which is meant changes in behaviour and routines.[31] The argument is that task alignment is a more powerful way of achieving change than the programmatic. Those who take this view would argue that the style of the change agent (see section 11.5.1 above) needs to take this into account.

As explained earlier (see section 11.2.2), others argue that long-term change is best achieved by trying to create a *learning organisation*, in which, in effect, all its members need to become strategic thinkers, aware of the strategic impacts of the environment around them, questioning and challenging their colleagues and contributing to the development of strategy. Clearly, this is a challenging task, requiring a major commitment and investment in intellectual resources and, for most organisations, a significant change in organisational culture. Few organisations have succeeded in this, but some take it seriously. For example, organisations such as Motorola and Unipart have set up organisational 'universities' which are serious attempts to develop such a capacity.

11.5.4 External Stakeholders

Just as it is important to tailor approaches to change according to different organisational contexts, the same may be required for different stakeholders. Exhibit 5.5 in Chapter 5 shows how different stakeholders can be identified according to their level of interest and political influence. It also suggests that the approach to managing change with regard to these different stakeholders will differ. For example, those with a high level of interest in the organisation but low power may simply need to be kept informed of change requirements and processes, so careful thought needs to be given to means of communication here. Others, with a low level of interest, but high actual or potential political influence, need to be kept satisfied. They may not be so concerned about understanding the details of the change process or wanting to be involved in it, but serious attention needs to be paid to convincing them of its effectiveness and its benefits for them.

The key players are those with high power and high interest. These may differ by organisational context. Indeed, as shown in Illustration 11.3, there may be different stakeholder groups requiring different approaches within the same organisation. For example, it may make sense to deal with fund managers representing key investments in an organisation by adopting an essentially logical approach and a style of education and communication. The approach taken towards managers or other organisational members may need to vary according to existing culture or time available for the change process. Others – for example, in the public sector – may find more explicit uses of political influence necessary: for instance, if the chief executive of a local government authority has to deal with different political parties or, indeed, central government.

11.5.5 Outsiders

The use of outsiders in the change process can be productive.

- A new chief executive from outside the organisation may be introduced into a business to effect change. He or she brings a fresh perspective on the organisation, not bound by the constraints of the past, or the everyday routines and ways of doing things which can prevent strategic change. *Hybrid* new chief executives seem to be especially successful. These are chief executives who are not part of the mainline culture of the organisation, but who have experience and visible success from within the same industry or even the same company. For example, they might have been a successful change agent with a competitor or some other part of a conglomerate.
- The success of introducing outsiders in middle and senior executive positions is likely to depend on how much explicit, *visible backing* they have from the chief executive. Without such backing they are likely to be seen as lacking authority and influence. With such backing, however, they can help galvanise change in the organisation.
- *Consultants* are often used in change processes. This may be to help formulate the strategy or plan the change process. However, consultants are increasingly used as facilitators of change processes: for example, in a co-ordinating capacity, as facilitators of project teams working on change, or of strategy workshops used to develop strategy and plan the means of strategic change.

  The value of consultants is twofold: first, they too do not inherit the cultural baggage of the organisation and can therefore bring a dispassionate view to the process; and second, they signal symbolically the importance of the change process, not least because their fees may be of a very high order. For example, a consultancy project undertaken by some of the major strategy consultancy firms might involve large numbers of consultants on a worldwide basis and fees running into millions of pounds.

11.6 MANAGING STRATEGIC CHANGE AND STRATEGIC MANAGEMENT

In their study of firms which had managed change successfully, Pettigrew and Whipp[32] summarised their findings in a way which usefully integrates much of the material in this chapter with other chapters in this book. They argue that organisations which manage change successfully demonstrate five important characteristics.

11.6.1 Environmental Assessment

Chapter 3 explained the importance of understanding the business environment. However, this does not mean simply employing techniques of analysis, or hiring analysts to do this. Organisations which manage change effectively are more like open learning systems: the sensitivity to the environment is organisation-wide; it is not dependent on a set of techniques or specialists. Managers and staff in the organisation see their role as keeping close to, being sensitive to, and responding to signals in the environment. The external orientation is, therefore, part of the culture of the organisation; it is 'taken for granted' that this is an important orientation, and it is championed visibly by senior management. Further, the structural characteristics of the organisation are such that there is an emphasis on external rather than internal orientation (see Chapter 10).

11.6.2 Leading Change

It is a mistake to think of the management of change as a prescribed set of activities. The way in which change is led by change agents must depend on contexts which will differ by organisations, or perhaps by market. However, the ability of the change agent to establish, or develop, a context for change is crucial, both in cultural terms and also in terms of the capabilities of the organisation. It is also necessary to tailor the agenda for change specifically in terms of the organisational context and the values and beliefs of those in the organisation. This chapter has emphasised this point, discussed methods of managing strategic change and indicated that these need to be drawn upon in ways which are specific and relevant to context.

11.6.3 Linking Strategic and Operational Change

Organisations which have successfully managed change have been able to link strategic change with operational change and the everyday aspects of the organisation. This emphasises the importance not only of translating strategic change into detailed resource plans, critical success factors and key tasks, and the way the organisation is managed through control processes (Chapter 10), but also of how change is communicated through the mundane and symbolic aspects of the organisation discussed in this chapter. This is more likely to be effective if change can be continual and incremental, occurring in the everyday aspects of the organisation, rather than being implemented in major one-off steps.

So successful change may not be as dramatically observable as transformational change. The problem arises, of course, when an organisation has not been changing continually and arrives at a point where more transformational change is necessary. Then the bridging of strategic change and operational and mundane aspects of the organisation is much more difficult.

11.6.4 Strategic Human Resource Management

Organisations which successfully manage change are those which have integrated their human resource management policies with their strategies and the strategic change process. As discussed in this final part of the book, training, employee relations, compensation packages and so on are not merely operational issues for the personnel department; they are crucially concerned with the way in which employees relate to the nature and direction of the firm, and as such they can both block strategic change and also be significant facilitators of strategic change.

11.6.5 Coherence in Managing Change

The final point that needs emphasising in a sense summarises the whole thrust of this book. Strategic change is much more likely to work if it is coherent across all aspects of the organisation. By this we mean the following:

- There is a consistency between the intended strategy, the stated strategic objectives, their expression in operational terms and, very important, the behaviour of executives to reinforce the strategy.
- The direction of strategic change is consistent with what is happening in the environment, and the way in which this is understood in the organisation. It is also managed with due regard to stakeholders, including suppliers and customers, on whom the organisation is critically reliant.

- The strategy is feasible in terms of the resources it requires, the structuring of the organisation, and the changes that need to occur in organisational culture and operational routines.
- The strategic direction is clearly related to achieving competitive advantage or excellent performance; and internally it is understood how this is so.

Overall, such coherence means that there needs to be an ability to hold the organisation together as an efficient, successful entity, while simultaneously changing it.

There are a growing number of studies on the reasons why some organisations are more successful than others. All make it clear that the clarity of strategy direction and its relevance to a changing environment are crucial. The wiser researchers and writers realise, however, that it is not possible to reduce the explanations of how this is done to simple do's and don'ts. This book has aimed to provide an insight into some of the ways in which managers might contribute to this. It has done so by describing research which tries to explain success, and by explaining techniques of analysis, evaluation and planning which can help organisations understand bases of success and plan for the future. But most of all, it has stressed that it is the processes of management, the skills of managers and the ability of managers to relate to their external environment, their internal culture and the people around them, that will ensure success.

SUMMARY

This chapter has emphasised a number of key points in the management of strategic change:

- There are different *types of strategic change* observable in organisations, varying from incremental change which is reactive (adaptation) or proactive (tuning), to transformational change which also can be reactive (forced) or proactive (planned). Different approaches may be required for different types of change, and these are discussed in the chapter.
- There are also different views about the management of change. At the beginning of this chapter, the distinction was made between change processes which are intentionally *planned change*, changes resulting from *learning*, and *imposed change*. Later sections in the chapter focused on ways in which the intended change might be managed.
- Diagnosing the need for and means of change might include the identification of symptoms of *strategic drift* and the use of the *cultural web* and *forcefield analysis* as means of identifying blockages of change and potential levers for change.

- Processes for managing strategic change include the importance of changes in *structure and control*, appropriate *styles of managing change*, the need to change organisational *routines* and *symbols*, and the importance of *political processes*, *communication* and other change *tactics*.
- There different *roles in the change* process, including those of change agent, middle managers, other members of the organisation, different stakeholder groups and outsiders. Different approaches to change are likely to be necessary according to different contexts and in relation to the involvement and interest of different groups.
- The management of strategic change cannot be thought of or put into effect in isolation. Effective strategic change is built on effective overall strategic management.

RECOMMENDED KEY READINGS

- J. Balogun, V. Hope-Hailey (with G. Johnson and K. Scholes), *Exploring Strategic Change*, Prentice Hall, 1999, builds on and extends many of the ideas in this chapter. In particular it emphasises the importance of tailoring change programmes to organisational context.
- For a discussion of styles of managing strategic change, see D. Dunphy and D. Stace, 'The strategic management of corporate change', *Human Relations*, vol. 46, no. 8 (1993), pp. 905–20.
- The task alignment view of strategic change argues for concentrating on changes in routines and tasks so as to promote behaviour change. This is explained by M. Beer, R.A. Eisenstat and B. Spector, 'Why change programmes don't produce change', *Harvard Business Review*, vol. 68, no. 6 (1990), pp. 158–66.
- For a fuller discussion of symbolic aspects of change management, see G. Johnson, 'Managing strategic change: the role of symbolic action', *British Journal of Management*, vol. 1, no. 4 (1990) pp. 183–200.
- G. Johnson, 'Mapping and re-mapping organisational culture', in V. Ambrosini with G. Johnson and K. Scholes (eds), *Exploring Techniques of Analysis and Evaluation in Strategic Management*, Prentice Hall, 1998.
- There are surprisingly few readings which focus on aspects of political management. The best book remains Machiavelli's sixteenth-century work *The Prince*.

REFERENCES

1. See E. Romanelli and M.L. Tushman, 'Organisational transformation as punctuated equilibrium: an empirical test', *Academy of Management Journal*, vol. 37, no. 5 (1994), pp. 1141–61.
2. This discussion is based on an adaptation of the framework used by D.A. Nadler and M.L. Tushman in their paper 'Organisational frame bending: principles for managing reorientation', *Academy of Management Executive*, vol. 3, no. 3 (1989), pp. 194–204.
3. See P. Senge, *The Fifth Discipline: The art and practice of the learning organisation*, Century Business, 1992.
4. This framework of 'organisational learning' builds on the work of K. Lewin, *Field Theory in Social Science*, Tavistock, 1952. The framework is used by a number of writers to discuss strategic change. See, for example, L.A. Isabella, 'Evolving interpretations as a change unfolds: how managers construe key

organisational events', *Academy of Management Journal*, vol. 33, no. 1 (1985), pp. 7–41; and E.H. Schein, *Organisational Culture and Leadership*, Jossey-Bass, 1985. A number of other writers on strategic change employ similar models: for example, F. Gouillart and J. Kelly describe Gemini Consulting's approach in *Transforming the Organisation*, McGraw-Hill, 1995.

5. The argument that conflict can bring about useful debate is developed by J.M. Bartunek, D. Kolb and R. Lewicki, 'Bringing conflict out from behind the scenes: private informal and non-rational dimensions of conflict in organisations', in D. Kolb and J. Bartunek (eds), *Hidden Conflict in Organisations: Uncovering behind the scenes disputes*, Sage, 1992.
6. For an account which shows the role of managers in such circumstances, see A. Pettigrew, E. Ferlie and L. McKee, *Shaping Strategic Change*, Sage, 1992.
7. See G. Johnson, 'Managing strategic change: strategy culture and action', *Long Range Planning*, vol. 25, no. 1 (1992), pp. 28–36. See also the chapter, 'Mapping and re-mapping organisational culture', in V. Ambrosini with G. Johnson and K. Scholes (eds), *Exploring Techniques of Analysis and Evaluation in Strategic Management*, Prentice Hall, 1998.
8. The illustration is based on a description of the use of the cultural web by L. Heracleous and B. Langham, 'Strategic change and organisational culture at Hay Management Consultants', *Long Range Planning*, vol. 29, no. 4 (1996), pp. 485–94.
9. See C. Bowman, *Strategy in Practice*, Prentice Hall, 1998.
10. For example, see L. Hrebinrak and W. Joyce, *Implementing Strategy*, Macmillan, 1984, and the chapters on implementation in G. Greenley, *Strategic Management*, Prentice Hall, 1989.
11. See, for example, J.P. Kotter and L.A. Schlesinger, 'Choosing strategies for change', *Harvard Business Review*, vol. 57, no. 2 (1979), pp. 106–14.
12. The intervention style is discussed more fully in P.C. Nutt, 'Identifying and appraising how managers install strategy', *Strategic Management Journal*, vol. 8, no. 1 (1987), pp. 1–14.
13. Evidence for this, as well as a discussion of different styles, is provided by D. Dunphy and D. Stace, 'The strategic management of corporate change', *Human Relations*, vol. 46, no. 8 (1993), pp. 905–20.
14. T. Deal and A. Kennedy refer to 'the way we do things around here', in *Corporate Cultures: The rights and rituals of corporate life*, Addison-Wesley, 1982.
15. For a fuller discussion of this theme, see G. Johnson, 'Managing strategic change: the role of symbolic action', *British Journal of Management*, vol. 1, no. 4 (1990), pp. 183–200.
16. This reference is taken from one of Tom Peters's early papers, 'Symbols, patterns and settings: an optimistic case for getting things done', *Organisational Dynamics*, vol. 7, no. 2 (1978), pp. 3–23.
17. See H.M. Trice and J.M. Beyer, 'Studying organisational cultures through rites and ceremonials', *Academy of Management Review*, vol. 9, no. 4 (1984), pp. 653–69; H.M. Trice and J.M. Beyer, 'Using six organisational rites to change culture', in R.H. Kilman, M.J. Saxton, R. Serpa and associates (eds), *Gaining Control of the Corporate Culture*, Jossey-Bass, 1985.
18. The importance of the language used by corporate leaders has been noted by a number of writers, but particularly L.R. Pondy, 'Leadership is a language game', in M.W. McCall, Jr and M.M. Lombardo (eds), *Leadership: Where else can we go?*, Duke University Press, Durham, NC. See also J.A. Conger and R. Kanungo, 'Toward a behavioural theory of charismatic leadership in organizational settings', *Academy of Management Review*, vol. 12, no. 4 (1987), pp. 637–47.
19. This discussion is based on observations of the role of political activities in organisations by, in particular, H. Mintzberg, *Power in and around Organisations*, Prentice Hall, 1983, and J. Pfeffer, *Power in Organisations*, Pitman, 1981.
20. See reference 2 above.
21. See R.H. Lengel and R.L. Daft, 'The selection of communication media as an executive skill', *Academy of Management Executive*, vol. 2, no. 3 (1988), pp. 225–32.
22. Both Isabella (see reference 4) and Johnson (reference 15) note this.
23. For example, see W.G. Bennis and B. Nanus, *Leaders: The strategies for taking charge*, Harper and Row, 1985; and Conger and Kanungo (see reference 18).
24. The importance of context in relation to the leadership of change is a theme running through B. Leavy and D. Wilson, *Strategy and Leadership*, Routledge, 1994.
25. For a review of the support characteristics and traits of successful corporate leaders, see C. Garfield, *Peak Performers: New heroes in business*, Hutchison Business, 1986.
26. Peters and Waterman argue that 'An effective leader must be the master of two ends of the spectrum: ideas at the highest level of abstraction and actions at the most mundane level of detail.' See *In Search of Excellence*, Harper and Row, 1982, p.287.
27. For a fuller discussion of these observations, see P. Felkas, B. Chakiris and K. Chartres, *Change Management: A model for effective organisational performance*, Quality Resources, 1993.
28. See reference 24 above.
29. See S. Floyd and W. Wooldridge, *The Strategic Middle Manager: How to create and sustain competitive advantage*, Jossey-Bass, 1996.
30. This quote is taken from R. Pascale, *Managing on the Edge*, Viking, 1990.

31. The argument for a task alignment approach is given by M. Beer, R.A. Eisenstat and B. Spector, 'Why change programmes don't produce change', *Harvard Business Review*, vol. 68, no. 6 (1990), pp. 158–66.

32. This integrating framework is from the research on strategic change undertaken by Andrew Pettigrew and Richard Whipp: see *Managing Change for Competitive Success*, Blackwell, 1991.

WORK ASSIGNMENTS

11.1 Based on cultural webs you have drawn up (e.g. for assignment 5.8 in Chapter 5), or on the basis of the cultural web in Illustration 2.7, identify the main blockages to change in an organisation.

11.2 ● Draw up a cultural web and use forcefield analysis to identify blockages and facilitators of change for an organisation (e.g. one for which you have considered the need for a change in strategic direction in a previous assignment). Redraw the web to represent what the organisation should aspire to given the new strategy. Using the cultural webs and forcefield analysis, identify what aspects of the changes can be managed by a change agent and how.

11.3 With reference to section 11.4.2 and Exhibit 11.6, identify and explain the styles of managing change employed by different change agents (e.g. Colin Sharman in KPMG* or the three CEOs described in the Burton* series of case studies).

11.4 Using Exhibit 11.7, give examples of rituals which signal (or could be used to signal) change in an organisation with which you are familiar.

11.5 ● Consider a process of strategic change that you have been involved in or have observed. Map out the steps in the change process in the following terms:

(a) new rituals introduced or old rituals done away with, and the impact of these changes
(b) the means of communication employed by change agents, and how effective they were.

11.6 ● In the context of managing strategic change in a large corporation or public sector organisation, to what extent, and why, do you agree with Richard Pascale's argument that it is easier to act ourselves into a better way of thinking than it is to think ourselves into a better way of acting? (References 29 and 30, and also 15 and 17 will be useful here.)

11.7 ● Might the levers and tactics for change employed by change agents need to differ according to different stakeholders? Give examples for an organisation of your choice.

11.8 ● There are a number of books by renowned senior executives who have managed major changes in their organisation. Read one of these and note the levers and mechanisms for change employed by the change agent, using the approaches outlined in this chapter as a checklist. How effective do you think these were in the context that the change agent faced, and could other mechanisms have been used?

* refers to a case study in the Text and Cases edition.
● denotes more advanced work assignments.

CASE EXAMPLE

South African Fabrication (SAF)

In 1996 Peter Connor, a South African management consultant, organised a series of strategy workshops for South African Fabrication (SAF), one of his clients. Peter had worked with the company over many years and knew the chief executive, Alan Tait, well. SAF was an engineering company with services and products as diverse as heavy engineering and steel fabrication to the manufacture of armaments. It had prospered in South Africa from government contracts during apartheid. During this time the trade embargoes on South Africa had prevented free trade on an international basis; the result was that indigenous firms like SAF had faced little competition. However, with the end of apartheid and the freeing up of the South African market, by the late 1990s the company was facing competition on an international scale. An international holding company had also recently acquired the business; so there was an issue of corporate-level expectations to be dealt with too.

Alan Tait and his board recognised that they needed to rethink company strategy and how strategic change might be managed. The workshops explored competitive strategy and organisational culture as a basis for considering strategic change.

The underlying problem was that most of the company's activities were production oriented rather than customer focused. For example, during the apartheid era, managers had busily acquired all manner of secondhand engineering plant so that they could service virtually any engineering contract for the government. The style of management was also more attuned to a protected market than the situation it now faced: it tended to be autocratic, highly directive and at times impulsive. The workshops concluded that there was a need to focus much more on who customers were, what their needs were, and how SAF's various businesses could meet those needs.

Following the workshops, Peter Connor had been asked to help the managers implement the conclusions which emerged. Peter had known Gerry Johnson for some years and had discussed with him the plans for the workshops and the issues raised by them. He asked Gerry to note down his thoughts following these discussions. What follows are some of the points from Gerry's letter to Peter.

Dear Peter,
I hope questions I raise below are helpful to you in thinking through the priorities for attention in SAF.

Clarity of Corporate Strategy

Is it clear what the parent company expects of SAF? From what you say, the managers on the workshops are unclear where the firm is going or what is expected of the SBUs. If this is not made clear they have to deduce future direction from where the firm has come from. There also seem to be important portfolio issues and links to corporate structure and control. It does not seem to be clear what the logic of the SAF portfolio is. There are questions as to why some of the SBUs are in the portfolio at all, what corporate control styles are appropriate, and whether or not the group should be restructured. It does not seem that much thinking of this sort has been going on; and I imagine the new parent will want it addressed sooner rather than later. In its absence it seems inevitable that there will be a corporate centre which is too cumbersome and too involved in issues not central to the main purpose of the corporation; the businesses will carry too much overhead; and managers will be distracted both at the centre and in the businesses from focusing on the strategic priorities.

Communicating Strategy

From what you say, some thought needs to be given to how both corporate strategy and SBU strategies are communicated. The outcome of board views on corporate expectations and strategy needs to be made clear. It is difficult to communicate complex messages down the line. At one level there is a need to reduce the complexity, perhaps in terms of some clear statement of intent; don't try to overcomplicate messages, and make sure that they are presented in a way which people can remember and relate to. If more complex explanation of strategy is needed, remember the more it affects individuals, the more it needs to be seen as personal to them. Currently, communication seems to be very formal and impersonal.

What is the Trigger for Change?

I'm not sure what the trigger for change in SAF is. The demise of apartheid and the opening up of markets does not seem to have achieved this. You say people may know there are problems but do not seem to *feel* the need for change. There may be a need to create a trigger; not necessarily a crisis but something which clearly signals that things have to be done. I wonder, for example, whether the changed ownership structure could be used; a parent requiring changes, perhaps even a time period for those changes, might be useful. It would not surprise me if the new parent required some management changes at the top; and this could also be a helpful trigger. One other thought: I think you said the most senior black employee was a supervisor. Taking seriously the sorts of change taking place in South Africa, actively developing and advancing black management and avoiding tokenism in this regard might signal that transformational change is being taken seriously. It might be a signal, if not a trigger for change.

Human Resource Systems Need to Support the Strategy

I'm not sure what HR systems are in place but if, as you say, a key requirement is to create a more customer-focused organisation, do the HR systems support this? You say that the feeling in the organisation currently is that it is an old boys' network when it comes to appointments, promotions and rewards; that more is achieved by who you know than what you do and how good you are at doing it. If so, it is not surprising that more attention is given to playing that system and avoiding blame, or passing blame, than it is to delivering customer value.

The Role of Top Management

The CEO needs to recognise that he has a personal role to play which he cannot delegate. I have no doubt he sees the need for change for the firm, but that is not enough; it has to be visible, personal commitment and consistently so. If the future of SAF depends on change, it needs to be very clear that that is at the top of his priorities. There also has to be open debate and discussion about the changes. That doesn't mean to say that the chief executive needs to agree with everything, but people should feel that they are not constrained in putting forward their views. You say that currently they feel very constrained in stating their views to Alan. His manner is threatening, even bullying. I recall we initially thought it would be good to have him launching the workshops and taking feedback. Had that occurred and open discussion had been encouraged, that would probably have been a very positive sign of change. It is a pity you feel that, had he attended, it would have stifled discussion.

Top management doesn't need to do much out of line with the intended strategy for its behaviour to backfire badly. You say a good deal surfaced at the workshops about top management behaviour. The managers spend their time protecting their backs, defending their empires, 'fire fighting' and, as others see it, interfering. They need to be clear what their priorities are and ensure they 'walk the talk'. If they don't think they have managers down the line that can take responsibility, then they need to replace them, not resort to doing their jobs for them.

The Wider Culture

The culture webs the managers did on the workshops seem to suggest that it is, however, not just at top management level that the problem lies. They describe a wider culture of defensiveness, harking back to the 'good old days', a lack of praise and what you describe as a 'blame culture'. If a problem occurs, the tendency is to find someone to blame for it; so the natural behaviour is to expect a question or challenge to be followed up not with a sound argument but by an excuse or opportunity to blame someone for something going wrong. If this is so, I agree, it will not lead to improvements or change. Top managers are role models, so changes in their behaviour would greatly help here. However, thought could also be given to some rituals which applaud success, reduce conflict and help create more sharing of responsibility. The workshops themselves have surfaced the problems, got people talking and started to move towards some solutions; maybe you could build on their evident success.

Everyday and Symbolic Action Needs to be in Line with Strategic Intent

It's not enough to say what is required and intended; it needs to be acted out daily and converted into organisational routines. For example, there is a need to translate what is meant by customer focus into the day-to-day activities of all those who can influence it. How does the service engineer or, indeed, telephonist deal with customers? How much time is spent by whom sharing ideas about meeting customer needs? Symbolic action is also needed to support and signal change. What are the offices like? Are they welcoming to customers and, indeed, to staff? Do the offices have pictures of customer applications on their walls or examples of SAF's own technology? You say the annual golf day is for suppliers and the friends of top management; why not customers? Also remember that one of the biggest symbols of all is senior executive behaviour and action in line with the strategy. From what you say, I am not sure Alan understands this.

Short-term Wins but No Quick Fix

Whilst I agree that it would be very useful to be able to demonstrate some quick 'wins', for example in benefits from a greater market focus, there are also dangers in a short-term focus. My impression is that Alan and some of his managers think that change can be achieved quickly. Change of this sort takes time. There also has to be an understanding that change does not mean changing from one steady state to another; rather continual change is likely to be needed. Do Alan and his senior team recognise the magnitude of the task of change they face? It will require a great deal of attention, persistence and resilience; it is not a quick fix.

Your Position

Have you given thought to your position in all this? Might you find yourself being regarded as responsible for making change happen rather than Alan and his top team? I suppose there is a political element to this that you cannot avoid. Presumably you need to try to ensure that there are powerful sponsors of what you are trying to do and that they are seen as the change agents. Who might these people be? Do they have the required influence and, if not, how might they gain it?

One final observation. These principles go hand in hand; they are not independent. SAF cannot expect to change its culture without getting the strategy sorted out; and both relate to structure, the systems employed, the style of management and so on.

Questions

1. If you were Peter Connor what would you concentrate on first? Would this differ from what you would concentrate on if you were a new CEO of SAF?
2. Are any of the issues described in the letter more important than others in the management of change? Why?
3. Consider the points made in the letter in relation to another change situation with which you are familiar (e.g. KPMG). Do they hold good for that situation? Which others would you add based on the lessons from that situation?
4. Suggest some specific examples of:
   (a) symbolic signals and changes in routines to help achieve greater customer focus
   (b) top management behaviour to encourage questioning and challenge.

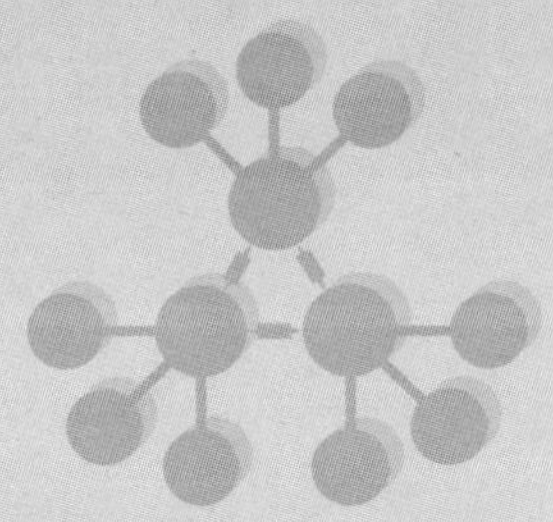

CASE STUDIES

A GUIDE TO USING THE CASE STUDIES

The main text of this book includes 82 short illustrations and 11 case examples which have been chosen to enlarge specific issues in the text and/or provide practical examples of how business and public sector organisations are managing strategic issues. The case studies which follow allow the reader to extend this linking of theory and practice further by analysing the strategic issues of specific organisations in much greater depth – and often providing 'solutions' to some of the problems or difficulties identified in the case.

The case studies are intended to serve as a basis for class discussion and not as an illustration of either good or bad management practice. They are not intended to be a comprehensive collection of teaching material. They have been chosen (or specifically written) to provide readers with a core of cases which together cover most of the main issues in the text. As such, they should provide a useful backbone to a programme of study but could sensibly be supplemented by other material. In the 5th edition we have provided a mixture of longer and shorter cases to increase the flexibility for teachers. Additionally there is now a short *case example* at the end of each chapter (in both versions of the book). This increases the reader's and tutor's choice. For example, when deciding on material for chapter 3 the case example, *Irish Ports*, helps a reader's understanding of the range of environmental issues influencing an organisation. Those wishing to undertake a comprehensive industry analysis can use *The European Brewing Industry*. However, if the purpose is more focused – illustrating the use of '5-forces' analysis for example – the *Pharmaceuticals Industry* should be used.

Some cases are written entirely from published sources but most have been prepared in co-operation with and approval of the management of the organisation concerned. The *video* provides supplementary material for four of the case studies.

Case studies can never fully capture the richness and complexity of real life management situations and we would encourage readers and tutors to take every possible opportunity to explore the *live* strategic issues of organisations – both their own and others.

The following brief points of guidance should prove useful in selecting and using the case studies provided:

- The summary table which follows indicates the main focus of each of the chosen case studies – together with important subsidiary foci (where appropriate). In general, the sequence of cases is intended to mirror the chapter sequence. However, this should not be taken too literally because, of course, many of these cases cover a variety of issues. The 'classification' provided is therefore guidance only. We expect readers to seek their own lessons from cases, and tutors to use cases in whichever way and sequence best fits the purpose of their programmes.
- Where cases have been chosen to illustrate the issues of strategic choice and implementation covered later in the book, it will normally be a prerequisite that some type of strategic analysis of the case material is undertaken. When planning the use of these cases within programmes, care needs to be taken to balance the time taken on strategic analysis so as to allow the time required to analyse the main issues for which the case has been chosen.
- Where the text and cases are being used as the framework for a strategy programme (as we hope they will), it is essential that students are required to undertake additional reading from other sources and that their 'practical' work is supplemented by other material as mentioned above.

A Guide to the Main Focus of Cases

Case	Introduction to strategy	Strategic management process	Business environment	Five forces	Resource and competence analysis	Stakeholder expectations/purposes	Culture	Overall strategic analysis	Corporate strategy/parenting	Competitive strategy	Strategic options	Diversification	Acquisitions	Strategy evaluation	Global management	Structure, organisation design	Resource planning and control	Managing change	Strategic leadership	Public sector management
British Steel, p. 551(U)	●●																			
New Town, p. 559		●●				●														●●
Castle Press, p. 567		●●																		
Pharmaceuticals, p. 574			●	●●																
European Brewing, p. 582(U)			●●	●									●		●					
Kronenbourg, p. 607				●			●	●	●		●			●●						
Brewery Group Denmark, p. 622		●			●						●●			●	●●					
Stewart Grand Prix, p. 633(N)					●●												●			
Laura Ashley, p. 641					●●	●									●					
Iona, p. 656						●●	●													
Sheffield Theatres, p. 670					●	●●											●			
Fisons, p. 685						●●								●						
World Automobile Industry, p. 691			●●																	
Peugeot, p. 709(U)								●		●●	●				●	●				
Rover/Honda, p. 725										●	●●				●					
BMW, p. 738										●	●●		●●	●	●					
Barclaycard, p. 746(N)								●			●●			●						
Coopers Creek, p. 756					●										●●	●				
Dutch PTT Telecom, p. 768(N)											●●				●●					●
News Corporation, p. 779		●			●	●			●●			●●			●	●	●		●	
Nokia, p. 807					●					●		●●	●●		●					
Bord Gais Eireann (BGE), p. 827(N)																●●	●●			●
Doman, p. 838														●●			●●			
Royal Alexandra Hospital, p. 852(U)		●				●	●									●		●●	●	●
Burton Group A, p. 868(N)		●					●		●			●	●	●		●●		●	●●	
Burton Group B, p. 874(N)		●					●			●								●●	●●	
Burton Group C, p. 882(N)		●					●			●						●			●●	
KPMG (B): Strategic Change, p. 891(U)						●	●									●	●	●●	●	
KPMG (C): Global Firm, p. 909(N)			●												●●	●				
UNHCR, p. 918(N)		●				●●	●											●●	●	●
Burmah Castrol, p. 935		●			●●				●●			●●			●	●				

Note: ●● = Major focus
● = Important subsidiary focus

U = Updated
N = New

BRITISH STEEL

Kevan Scholes

This case study concerns one of the UK's largest and best-known manufacturing companies – British Steel. It covers the period before and after privatisation in 1989 and through to 1997. In reviewing the history of the company during its period of nationalisation (1967–89) it highlights many of the reasons for good or poor performance. The period from 1989 to 1992 was the time when British Steel became an internationally competitive company. Indeed, in 1990/1 it was the world's most profitable steel company. The case follows the company through the next recession (1991–3), underlining the importance of a strong balance sheet in a cyclical industry. The main issues for the company by 1997 were its plans to become a truly global steel company in the face of difficult issues in its business environment – particularly the dramatic rise in the value of sterling against the Deutschmark during 1997. There is also the possibility that mergers between competitors within Europe will weaken the company's position.

• • •

In the past, excess steel-making capacity in Europe has been sustained by a high level of exports to regions where local capacity was either insufficient or inefficient. This source of demand cannot be relied upon in the longer term. In areas where there is insufficient capacity, such as Asia, new competitive capacity is being installed locally, while the efficiency of capacity in the United States, for example, has improved dramatically. At the same time, import pressures in western European markets are intensifying, most notably from eastern Europe.

While I believe that the western European industry can continue to compete successfully in key markets, it is very likely that over time net exports will diminish. Thus, the pressures on European Union companies to restructure will continue. The changes in the industry structure relate to both ownership and concentration. In the past, the western European steel industry has been

---

This case study was prepared by Professor Kevan Scholes, Sheffield Business School, from published sources. It incorporates information from the British Steel case studies published in previous editions of this book. It is intended as a basis for class discussion and not as an illustration of either good or bad management practice.

> very fragmented and has had a high level of state ownership. The process of privatisation is reducing state ownership, and there are signs that mergers and joint ventures, some of them across national boundaries, are accelerating.
>
> In this environment, British Steel is well placed. The company's UK assets are in good shape and we have no major capital expenditure requirements in the near term. We are strongly placed in the European market, with very low costs, high quality of product and service and a very competitive range of products.
>
> We expect this region to provide the profitable core of our business for many years to come. However, for the company to grow, we are looking to reduce dependence on the UK and European markets and we are seeking to shift the balance of our assets into other regions.

This was Ted Denham, British Steel's director of corporate planning, speaking in September 1995 about the future challenges for a company which over the previous decade had achieved one of the most remarkable turnrounds in corporate history.[1] From being a near-bankrupt state-owned corporation (BSC) with cumulative losses of some £7bn between 1975 and 1984, the company had been transformed into the super-fit privatised British Steel.

At the time of privatisation in 1989, the ingredients of the transformation could be clearly seen. For example, labour costs had fallen from 31 per cent to 20 per cent of total costs since 1980 as the workforce was reduced from 140,000 to 51,000 (this had declined to 41,000 by 1995); and in terms of productivity, by 1987 the UK steel industry produced around 320 tonnes per man-year against West Germany's 279 – a remarkable change from 1981 when Germany led the UK by 227 tonnes to 167. These improvements in performance were dependent on a number of important changes and management decisions made during that period:

- An investment programme of £985m for modernisation and re-equipping was undertaken. For example, by early 1989, the company produced about 80 per cent of its output by the efficient continuous casting method rather than by the ingot method. This represented savings of about £14–18 per tonne. However, the French, Italian and West German industries were all nearly 90 per cent committed to continuous casting by 1988. The company itself believed that it needed about £250m annually to maintain the necessary investment programme.
- British Steel had completely revamped its management structure, reducing central overheads considerably and devolving responsibility for operations and profit to a substantial degree.
- There was a revolution in working practices. Up to 18 per cent of pay became bonus related, giving British Steel room to curb its wage bill during fluctuating demand (by 1995 this variable element of pay had risen to 25–30 per cent).

[1] *American Market Metal*, vol. 103, no. 182 (1995), p. 14.

The period immediately prior to and following privatisation was one of the growing international demand and impressive financial performance from British Steel, as shown in Appendix 1. However, by 1991 the recession and overcapacity in Europe had forced both prices and volumes down by more than 10 per cent. The economics of British Steel's position were harsh. A 10 per cent reduction in price took some £300m off profits; and a 10 per cent off volumes reduced profits by a further £500m, transforming a healthy profit of £773m in 1989/90 to losses in both 1991/2 and 1992/3.

In 1993/4, although turnover continued to decline marginally, the company made a small (but rare among steel-makers) profit. The company's market share in the UK was still declining to between 50 and 65 per cent (depending on sector). However, its spread of sales had also increased with only 53 per cent of turnover being from the UK; 30 per cent came from Continental Europe, 10 per cent from North America and the reminder from elsewhere. The year 1994/5 showed a strong recovery in both sales and profits as the general economic climate improved. This once again underlined the harsh economic equation in such a cyclical industry. The £330m rise in half-year profits from the same time in the previous year could be traced to £130m from increased volumes, £130m from increased prices and £70m from efficiency gains.

By 1996, under the leadership of chairman Brian Moffat, the company had an ambitious and well communicated vision to be a genuinely internationally-based steel company – which did not exist anywhere in the world at that time. Its formula for achieving this vision was also spelled out:[2]

- To continue to achieve efficiency gains and remain one of the most cost-efficient producers globally.
- To build the business in a market-led way rather than simply increasing capacity and trying to fill it.
- To target capital investment carefully – for example, with a strong emphasis on flexible 'mini-mills' – and to reuse or relocate assets where possible, as it was doing in the construction of a joint venture mini-mill in Tuscaloosa (USA) using 'mothballed' production units from the UK.
- To use a range of different approaches to global development, such as joint ventures (western Europe and USA); overseas transplants (USA, eastern Europe and possibly Asia and South America); and continued exports of high added-value products.
- Above all, to keep a strong balance sheet (good cash management and low gearing) to ride out the fierce cycles in demand.

This globalisation of the company's activities was the culmination of many years of recognising and adjusting to a changing business environment. Exchange rates were of critical importance to international businesses, and

[2] *Management Today*, June 1995, pp. 42–6.

the combination of a strong pound against the US dollar and weakness against the Deutschmark was almost an ideal situation for British Steel (as an exporter to Continental Europe and an 'offshore' manufacturer in the USA). Although process technologies in steel-making were long established, there were still important competitive advantages to be gained by both product development and the management of the logistics of the supply and distribution chains. The 'steel intensity' in many products (e.g. motor cars) had declined remarkably over 20–30 years, with average steel thickness (for the same performance) reducing from 2 mm to 0.8 mm. In the reverse direction, improvements in cost and metallurgical properties were allowing steel beams to make major inroads into the construction market at the expense of concrete.

Perhaps the greatest problem for British Steel in the UK had been the poor international performance of the UK-based manufacturing industries using steel – particularly the automobile industry. As they lost out in world markets, their need for steel declined. The advent of Japanese transplants in the UK had reversed this trend. The most encouraging aspect of the mid-1990s was the new willingness – at least in Europe – of national governments to remove their subsidy of state-owned steel firms and to move towards privatisation. Over the previous decade, British Steel had cited this as a major problem – the unwillingness to tackle the 20 per cent excess capacity in Europe.

Following acquisitions in the late 1980s, British Steel was also a major player in the distribution (stockholding) of steel in the UK, with over 30 per cent market share. Here the exploitation of information technology to reduce costs and increase customer service was critical to success. By 1996 the vision was clear as to how British Steel would take on the might of its international competitors. This was fighting talk for a company that was only one-half the size of the market leader (Nippon Steel) by volume or one-quarter by value (see Appendix 2). There were many rumours about proposed mergers within Europe, which could affect British Steel. Indeed, the company itself had agreed in principle to purchase Preussag Steel (Germany) but were thwarted when Gerhard Schroder, the prime minister of Lower Saxony and candidate for the German Chancellorship job, vetoed the sale and nationalised Preussag. The company's best view on this issue in 1997 is shown in Appendix 3. There were rumours in 1998 that British Steel might rival Usinor in its bid for Cockerill Sambre the Belgian steel producer. It was well placed financially to support such a bid, with a forecast net cash position of more than £450m by year-end (March 1998).

But the uncertainties of international trade turned against the company.[3] In January 1996, the pound sterling stood at 2.22 DM. The company economists were modelling the future with pessimistic assumptions of 2.4 DM. By January 1997 the exchange rate rose to 2.7 DM – and peaked at 3.07 DM in July 1997. Although the company's policy of hedging exchange

[3] *Management Today*, August 1997, pp. 34–7.

rates reduced the impact, this was a serious challenge since 82 per cent of sales were still in Europe (including the UK) where Germany was the biggest producer. The impact was also likely to be felt indirectly, as British Steel's UK-based customers also came under competitive pressure in their own industries. The wage cost advantage over French and German producers was also eroded, as shown in Appendix 4. A further worry was that the social costs of employment in the UK would rise following the election victory of the Labour party in May 1997.

Profits for 1996/7 fell to £451m – partly affected by the strength of sterling but more by destocking by customers across Europe, which drove down prices. Financial year 1997/8 saw a further fall in profits to £315m. The chairman's report stated that the strong pound had cost the company an estimated £500m. Nevertheless, exchange rates were not a factor that the company could control and its future plans must assume a continuing strong pound.

The response of senior management to these new circumstances was to accelerate its programme of strategic change within British Steel – using a three pronged attack: productivity gains, exploitation of information technology (IT), and significant reduction in costs of supplies.

Productivity gains were not to be of the old style – reductions in blue-collar workers – but to consist of management de-layering to achieve overhead ratios more in line with the best mini-mills in the world. Secondly, a move towards a multi-skilled technician as the model of the shopfloor worker was seen as essential to cost improvement by exploiting IT. Without investments in IT these productivity improvements could not be achieved.

IT was also essential to the third strand of reducing supply costs. Seven hundred of British Steel's major UK suppliers had been invited to a series of seminars on how they could both reduce prices and improve service. There was a feeling amongst the British Steel board that too many UK suppliers to major globalising companies such as British Steel were shielded from the harsh realities of the global market place – such as exchange rate shifts – and needed to bear some of the burden. Brian Moffat, the chief executive, felt that the likely outcome of reviewing supply chain management would be a substantial reduction in the number of suppliers as some suppliers reduced prices for guaranteed volumes and long-term contracts.

This was certainly a rapidly changing world where the profits would go to those steel manufacturers who could adapt and change successfully. Would British Steel succeed?

APPENDIX 1

Turnover and pre-tax profits (m)

	REVENUE	PRE-TAX PROFIT(LOSS)
1980/1	2,954	(1,800)
1981/2	3,443	(492)
1982/3	3,231	(866)
1983/4	3,358	(253)
1984/5	3,736	(378)
1985/6	3,735	(42)
1986/7	3,461	177
1987/8	4,116	419
1988/9	4,906	593
1989/90	5,113	733
1990/1	5,000	254
1991/2	4,600	(55)
1992/3	4,300	(149)
1993/4	4,190	80
1994/5	4,780	578
1995/6	7,050*	1,100
1996/7	7,224	451
1997/8	6,947	315

*This figure includes about £1,800m as a result of the reincorporation of United Engineering Steels (UES) and 51 per cent ownership of Avesta Sheffield.

APPENDIX 2

Major steel producing companies by crude steel output, 1996

	COMPANY	COUNTRY	OUTPUT*
1	Nippon Steel	Japan	26.4
2	POSCO	Korea	23.4
3	British Steel	UK	16.1
4	Usinor Sacilor	France	15.0
5	Riva	Italy	13.1 (est.)
6	Arbed	Luxembourg	11.8
7	USX	USA	11.3
8	NKK	Japan	11.3
9	SAIL	India	11.0
10	Kawasaki	Japan	10.6
11	Sumitomo	Japan	9.9
12	Thyssen	Germany	9.3

*Million metric tons.

Source *World Steel in Figures 1997*, International Iron and Steel Institute.

APPENDIX 3

Possible mergers within Europe

Company	Production (metric tonnes)*	Share of European production (%)
British Steel	15.2	17.4
Usinor Sacilor	14.5	16.6
Arbed	9.9	11.3
Thyssen	9.3	10.6
ILP	7.7	8.8
Krupp Hoesch	6.5	7.4
Cockerill Sambre	6.2	7.1
Hoogovens	6.2	7.1
CSI	4.2	4.8
Preussag	4.1	4.7
Saarstahl	2.1	2.4
Dillinger	1.7	1.9
Total	**87.6**	

Company	Production (metric tonnes)*	Share of European production (%)
Usinor/Cockerill-Sambre	20.7	23.3
Thyssen Krupp Stahl	15.8	17.8
British Steel	15.2	17.1
Arbed/CSI	14.1	15.9
ILP	7.7	8.7
Hoogovens/Boel (est.)	7.4	8.3
Preussag	4.1	4.6
Saarstahl	2.1	2.7
Dillinger	1.7	1.9
Total	**88.8**	

* Based on 1995 output.

Source Company.

APPENDIX 4

Relative labour costs in Europe

	BRITISH STEEL	GERMANY	FRANCE
Wages	85	84	75
Other employment costs	15	40	40
Total	**100**	**124**	**115**

Note Index based on British Steel = 100; exchange rates £1 = DM2.8 and FF9.5.

Source Company.

STRATEGY DEVELOPMENT AT NEW TOWN COUNCIL

Andy Bailey and Julie Verity

The two cases, New Town Council and Castle Press, illustrate the process of strategy development within different organisational contexts. Both cases are based on the views of the strategy development process as seen by members of the respective top management teams. The New Town case describes how four members of the top management team view their strategy process. Both cases are constructed around two general themes. The process of strategy development and the organisational context in which it takes place.

The two cases illustrate differences in the strategy development process, demonstrating that the process of managing strategy development in one organisation may not be the same as, or necessarily appropriate to, managing strategy development in another organisation.

• • •

> I'm not really comfortable with the way we develop strategy here, but I'm not sure I know how to manage the process to make it more coherent either.
>
> CHIEF EXECUTIVE, NEW TOWN COUNCIL, 1995

New Town Council formed one part of a two-tier system of local government responsible for the provision of services within a geographical area of the UK; the other part was the county council. Both authorities operated under Acts of Parliament, with specific duties laid down by these Acts and with central government controlling many of the activities of local authorities. The county council had responsibility for school education, fire and police services, highways and social care, while the council had responsibility for environmental health, housing, planning, recreational facilities and refuse collection.

This case study was prepared by A. Bailey and J. Verity, Cranfield School of Management. It is intended as a basis for class discussion and not as an illustration of either good or bad management practice.

Local authorities consist of councillors (Members) and paid employees. The councillors are elected representatives and decide the council's policy and priorities. The paid employees are responsible for implementing policy, with the role of senior officers (the senior ranks of the paid employees) being to advise the councillors on policy and to implement the policy decided.

New Town Council grew up alongside New Town as it was built on its greenfield site in the 1970s. Central government decreed that New Town would exist and the Development Corporation designed, planned and built it. As the bricks, mortar and amenities were developed, the council 'followed on behind, picking-up the litter, literally. I mean the Corporation built it and we provided the refuse collection systems for the people when they arrived to live here. When the Corporation was wound up and we had to take over, it was a lot to cope with. I think we are still learning to cope in some respects,' explained a senior officer at the council.

When the Development Corporation ceased activities in the early 1990s, New Town Council took responsibility for housing, environment, recreation, economic development and community development services. It did not assume control of education or social services, which remained with the county council, an arrangement which by 1995 was under review. From 1979 to 1997, the Conservative Party had been in central government and had made frequent and significant changes to local government legislation.

It was against this backdrop that some of the top management team of New Town Council described how they thought strategy came about in their organisation.

MAKING SENSE OF STRATEGY

The chief executive had been in his role for ten years:

> For the majority of my time here we have had a hung council.[1] My 'management board', therefore, is a group of elected representatives who are generally interested in a common aim – the greater good of the community – but who are totally split about the way to achieve it. They also rarely make a clear decision; they simply delegate, and when they don't like the proposed solution, they block implementation. Hence, my role is to act as an interface between the party political processes of the Members of Council and my management organisation [the officers]. I have to seek to understand the party political process, interpret it and help manage things via that process. At the same time, I have to understand the strengths and weaknesses of my management organisation [the officers], repair the weaknesses and build on the strengths.

Two senior officers had been recruited to the organisation within the last five years. One was head of personnel services:

> Our focus is the local community. Our strategy is based on the combined expectations of these people. Being a new town, taking over from the

[1] No political party in overall control.

> Development Corporation, you would expect us to have a defined vision to do with the social and physical development of New Town. The vision we have is not our own vision, we have inherited it. It is the vision of the government who decided to build New Town 30 years ago.

The other was commercial director of the direct services directorate. This was one of six main directorates within the council with responsibility for those services which the government had decreed should be subject to compulsory competitive tendering (CCT).[2] This included services such as landscape, highways, building, vehicle maintenance and leisure management, and accounted for about a fifth of the council's workforce:

> From my perspective, strategy develops in fits and starts. Since I've been here we have had a hung council, which has meant that no one political party has been able to stamp its views firmly on the whole organisation. In strategy terms, that has left us floundering because it has been very unclear whether an initiative will get approval or not.
>
> As a group of officers, we have had to say that, regardless of the party political situation, there are certain things we are going to have to cope with: one is the extension of CCT, another is the Local Government Review[3] and lastly is our struggle with the budget, whereby the money that we get from government has been held at the current level or reduced, year-on-year, while they have mandated we provide extra services!

Finally, there was the central services director, with responsibility for 200 people who largely provided services internally, to council departments. This directorate included computer services, estates management, the law division and central administration:

> In 1987 we held a conference to think about the future. We coupled that with a large public consultation exercise and as a result, the elected Members were asked to approve a strategic plan which had six main objectives in it. The process since then has been yearly reviews conducted by a small team within the policy directorate, which has reported back to the management team on the changes that have occurred in the environment and sought endorsement from Members. As a result of this review process, this year there are some fairly significant changes to the strategy document.
>
> Strategies also arise through the various council directorates: for example, Housing or Environment. Directorates produce their service plans each year, reviewing the external and internal influences and reacting to changed circumstances, revising their objectives for the current year in line with these changes.
>
> Therefore, the council's strategy is a series of very broadly based objectives which express the aspirations of the community. This is meant to be

---

[2] Central government legislation which compelled local authorities to invite competitive tenders for the provision of certain types of work, with in-house teams bidding against private sector competitors for a specified task.

[3] A review of local government structure from which recommendations are made for either the retention of the present two-tier system or the creation of a single unitary authority to provide services within a geographical area.

supplemented by the council's short-term objectives, its policies and the directorates' service plans. It is an interaction between these two sets of objectives that determines the way we go.

PLANNING IS DESIRABLE, BUT...

> Traditionally the organisation has not been focused on planning or developing policy. There was actually an anti-policy line. Instead, strategy developed in an ad-hoc manner, with the council being able to do as it wanted because it was well resourced. In the late eighties, we developed a community strategy – New Town 2000. This was perhaps a first for a local authority: that is, to try and devise a corporate strategy. After that, I think we got blown off course by events of the time: massive inflation, couldn't find staff or keep staff, so I spent a lot of time reorganising and looking internally. When we did find time, we tried to get the individual businesses of the council (because we are a series of services) to project their own services into the future and formulate their own plans.
>
> Now we are back to trying to realise the community strategy. So strategy to us is about determining where we are principally in our community, the key influences which are pushing us around within this, and trying to make sense of the steps we are taking, knowing that we are going to falter on some and going to be accelerated on others.
>
> CHIEF EXECUTIVE

The chief executive went on to conclude that planning was desirable and something he had tried to introduce into the organisation by bringing in facilitators and training his people to become skilled in planning processes and techniques. He admitted, however, that the organisation was still struggling to plan effectively. Some issues were easier to plan for than others. The Local Government Review, for example, 'had encouraged officers to come together and realise that, despite the political differences, you can have planning for the future'.

Others in his team, however, stressed that strategies had to be built around a theme of flexibility. With strategies liable to change at any point, there were doubts about the value of planning in this sort of organisation.

> What strategic objectives we have do not emerge from inside the organisation, they emerge from outside the organisation [from central government].
>
> HEAD OF PERSONNEL SERVICES

> The strategic objectives and priorities of New Town do not really come out of planning. Whatever is particularly powerful at the time will get attention first, and then next week it could be something different. This creates cynicism in the organisation because this week something is important and the week after it is something else entirely, and all the time we are required to keep picking up the bits and pieces and delivering them.
>
> COMMERCIAL DIRECTOR, DIRECT SERVICES

NEW TOWN COUNCIL IS ACTION ORIENTED

> The culture is not about restricting actions. Even in times of severe financial constraint – which we have at the moment – the culture about this place is always to develop and try something new.
>
> CENTRAL SERVICES DIRECTOR

The chief executive believed that, in the past, the council would have grasped every opportunity, a situation influenced by Members who saw everything as a priority. Things were changing. Now it was not realistic to try and put everything first on the priority list; budgets were shrinking and central government's list of demands was growing. However, despite an environment apparently littered with obstacles, there were opportunities to get things done and his council did deliver. After all, local authorities were essentially independent. There was a choice:

> You have to look at what you want to achieve, understand what is limiting and what is possible. A classic example is how we were capped[4] on capital projects in every area except for housing. Despite this we have just built a £6m recycling facility which we persuaded the government was in line with their ideas about the environment. There is no doubt that we have to accommodate ourselves to deliver what central government want, but there are ways and means of getting what you want as well. Another example is to get your community supporting you. If you can stand together, you can be vastly influential – if you ignore them, you are dead!
>
> CHIEF EXECUTIVE

POWER IS NOT EVENLY DISTRIBUTED

While all the officers agreed that political behaviour was common at New Town Council, there were differing views on how this influenced the development of strategy. The chief executive said:

> No one individual has dominated New Town. Individuals and groups do, however, determine the nature of the organisation and the way it does its business, and heavily impact on strategy.

Power was held in certain directorates because of the size of their budgets, the nature of the service or the strength of the director's personality:

> There is some internal competition where one director is more powerful than another. These people tend to get more resources and perhaps develop their services at a faster pace. That often goes along with having more party political support. For example, housing is traditionally a strong department. It is an important concern of the council, and strong Members have chaired that committee. So resources do tend to move in that direction.
>
> HEAD OF PERSONNEL SERVICES

---

[4] Limits placed on the amount which can be spent.

> We had an extremely powerful finance director, for example, because he was a very powerful individual. But, finance was also a key issue for us, so the function was important. Now, since this particular director left, finance is still an important issue, but the department does not have the same amount of power. By definition, the directorate structure tends to isolate us; communication does not happen across directorates. It is only through corporate working groups that we have been able to get people together.
>
> COMMERCIAL DIRECTOR, DIRECT SERVICES

> From my position, we are divided into two camps. Those who provide a central service (in a co-ordinating corporate role) and those who provide specific services like housing and recreation. In effect, we at the centre think we always compromise in favour of the direct services. Those in direct services always say that they find themselves compromising in favour of the centre. But I don't think this has a big impact on strategy.
>
> CENTRAL SERVICES DIRECTOR

The way to win the game of influence in this organisation was described by officers and chief executive alike as being close to members. However, only the chief executive thought he was good at bridging the divide between members' ideas and the organisation's ability to deliver. The central services director knew that, on the rare occasions that he had been particularly close to members, he had been very effective at influencing decisions. Influencing fellow officers was a matter of being 'in on the network' or leading a working group on a specific issue.

The head of personnel did not like 'politicking' with members, but realised that while she resisted indulging in this behaviour she was liable to remain less effective at getting her view heard. Talking with people was how the commercial director of direct services tried to get her ideas adopted – talking with colleagues on the top management team who might be sympathetic to her cause, or influential members and other senior managers. This took the form of informal preparation before the formal process. By the time the formal process was in action, she would have a good idea of the likelihood of her initiative being successful.

A DEMOCRATIC CHIEF EXECUTIVE

New Town officers were in agreement about the chief executive's style. He was a leader, but not a domineering one. He sensed the issues and hot spots: he was very conscious of what members were thinking; he was a facilitator and someone who moderated the power of different interest groups.

> He is not the most powerful person in the organisation. There are others with more outright power. He doesn't lay down the law or anything like that. But he is very good at making sure all interests are met, and when you look back, you can see what he has achieved even though it was difficult to appreciate at the time.
>
> COMMERCIAL DIRECTOR, DIRECT SERVICES

> The previous CE was an extreme autocrat, in complete contrast with our current CE, who is a democrat. The power is not institutionalised in the position.
>
> HEAD OF PERSONNEL SERVICES

> He is the counterbalance between the power of two or three of the service chiefs and their committees on the one hand and, the members of the council as a whole. He is a facilitator who uses his personality to manage the process.
>
> CENTRAL SERVICES DIRECTOR

A CLARITY OF PURPOSE?

> If you asked people working here if they had a good understanding of what this organisation was trying to achieve, then I predict their answer would be 'no'. This is partly because we are very poor at communicating about these issues.
>
> CHIEF EXECUTIVE

Other members of his team agreed. The commercial director of direct services said:

> I don't think there is a strong shared assumption about what New Town Council is here for – other than to provide services. I doubt if you would even get people to agree on what those services should be on a priority list. When the Development Corporation was dissolved, New Town Council was suddenly responsible for everything and it struggled to cope and is still not taking a lead. Members in particular have found it quite difficult to become strategic thinkers and develop long-term plans, particularly given that none of them have overall responsibility anyway.

The head of personnel disagreed, believing that there was a unifying theme:

> We have managed to hold on to being something other than what the government requires us to be. That is the over-riding *raison d'être* of the organisation. This makes organisational life difficult, because we are fighting against the government's direction and trying to set a strategic direction of our own.

IN PURSUIT OF THE IDEAL

How would members of the top management team like to improve the strategy process?

> I don't think strategy is about forecasting the future. I think strategy is about setting out to say what do I want to do, what are we seeking to do, what are the guidelines that are going to take us in this direction. It's like playing football; you need to know if the strategy is to attack or defend.
>
> Also, because we are all rational, well most of us are, we want a strategy to be rationally based on some sort of hard evidence. What we have not done in

organisations like this is develop a very rational basis of thinking. Our thinking is based partly on principle, partly on political philosophy and partly on the way you interpret what your local community might want in the future. The rationality comes when we try and bring these three together. Then something changes, as it always does, and we have to be prepared for that change as well.

If we could forecast it rationally, it would be ideal. That is what we should strive for.

CHIEF EXECUTIVE

My criticism is that we spread ourselves too thin, that if we focused our strategy and concentrated on two or three very important goals then we might make more impact. On the other hand, by spreading ourselves thinly we have achieved an amazing amount. Maybe the downside of that though is that we have not all been pulling in the same direction, which means there could be room for improvement.

CENTRAL SERVICES DIRECTOR

There is scope for improvement. We need to develop strategic skills and redefine the Members' role. We need to prevent the debate from slipping into the nitty gritty, operational details and move it into the arena of developing policy and the strategic direction of the council.

HEAD OF PERSONNEL SERVICES

In the top management team, we spend a lot of time talking about strategy, but we don't talk much about the implications of the strategy. So, we all may leave the room, having spent three hours together, with different interpretations of what the strategy means. Therefore, how we implement it may actually vary.

What we need is general agreement as to what our purpose is. Some people might call it a vision. Something which says this is what we are trying to achieve and this is the direction we are trying to pursue.

I don't believe we have this, but we need it. Why? Because we have lots of conflicting demands that we can't meet. A lot of our time therefore, is spent fire-fighting. I don't know if there is an alternative. Fire fighting might not be a bad thing if there is no clear system to direct you otherwise. You just try and keep as many balls in the air as is possible until it becomes clearer. It's just that we seem to have been doing that for such a long time now!

COMMERCIAL DIRECTOR, DIRECT SERVICES

One view was that they should make a virtue of their system, given the hostile and volatile environment:

In a way it works. It is very flexible and we may be doing exactly the wrong thing in trying to fit a rigid framework on to something that is inherently unstable. In which case we need to try and get this message over to staff, who see the process as it currently is as a mess and difficult to work in.

STRATEGY DEVELOPMENT AT CASTLE PRESS

Andy Bailey and Julie Verity

The two cases, New Town Council and Castle Press, illustrate the process of strategy development within different organisational contexts. Both cases are based on the views of the strategy development process as seen by members of the respective top management teams. The Castle Press case describes how five members of the top management team view the process. Both cases are constructed around two general themes. The process of strategy development and the organisational context in which it takes place.

The two cases illustrate differences in the strategy development process, demonstrating that the process of managing strategy development in one organisation may not be the same as, or necessarily appropriate to, managing strategy development in another organisation.

• • •

> I am not a commanding manager. I seek consensus, I am methodological, I'm a planning type of manager.
>
> MANAGING DIRECTOR

Castle Press is a specialist publisher of educational materials and the largest subsidiary of a significant, UK-based publishing and media group. Despite the company's long history in the UK and a strong tradition in its specialist field, it markets its products and related services to an increasingly global audience. Castle Press is the largest company of those in the corporate group, with 200 people working from the UK office creating an annual turnover of £30m in 1995 and accounting for more than 40 per cent of total group revenue.

This case study was prepared by A. Bailey and J. Verity, Cranfield School of Management. It is intended as a basis for class discussion and not as an illustration of either good or bad management practice.

CHANGING TIMES

For more than a decade, prior to 1995, Castle Press was the market leader in its field, but it had slipped into second place. This change in market status provided a new incentive for organisational change, after a long period of relative internal stability (some now say, complacency). Internal determination to regain market dominance was supported by a new strong message from corporate headquarters to 'go for growth', with the stated objective of doubling turnover by the year 2000.

> Because we didn't change in the past, now we are having to make major changes. We were locked into the past and into the way we did things before. If an area had a certain level of resources one year, it would get more of the same next year. That was the business approach, more of the same and building on what we already had.
>
> PUBLISHING DIRECTOR

> We have been too conservative, too slow to respond to the market, too conservative in the way we progress careers, too slow to embrace new technology.
>
> MANAGING DIRECTOR

CHANGING MARKETS

Castle Press found the global market place to be increasingly challenging. Since the late 1980s the company had been exposed to recession-bound Europe, the growth prospects of the Pacific Rim and newly opened communist countries, and the highly volatile and regulation-prone South American markets. Overall, demand for its products was growing, but competition was strong and the competitive map was also changing.

> From an international perspective the market is becoming more competitive as the result of smaller companies being bought-up by (mainly) UK and American groups whose aspirations are to become truly global. As far as the local perspective is concerned, we're getting ferocious competition, as we have done for many years, but it is now in our core markets from local publishers who are becoming experts in producing this material, and they are becoming more effective because they're learning the tricks.
>
> MARKETING DIRECTOR

CHANGES IN THE TOP MANAGEMENT TEAM

The top management team (TMT) consisted of five executive directors (the managing director, finance director, publishing director, marketing director and production director) and one non-executive director from the corporate group. With the exception of the finance director (who was relatively new to the organisation), all TMT members were promoted from the business, either from within the subsidiary or from the group. Only two years before, however, the team was much bigger:

> Two years ago, I inherited a TMT of twelve people. It was impossible to discuss strategy with that number of people. Six months later, three key people and myself 'retreated' for a few days and thought about what we needed rather than what we had. The outcome was implemented about eighteen months ago. We now have a TMT of six people and the focus of our meetings is higher level discussions and strategic planning.
>
> MANAGING DIRECTOR

As a group, the TMT thought that they were compatible and rarely in conflict with each other. The collective criticism of team meetings was the danger that discussions gravitated towards the operational rather than the strategic, since this was the one time that team members found themselves together in one place at one time. The finance director (only two years with Castle Press) noted that he could bring a different contribution to the team's discussion:

> I think we were very internally focused. It is easier when you come from outside the organisation and from this position I can be constructive. I'm the only person on the Team who hasn't been with Castle Press for the past twenty years, so I do have some useful external benchmarks.
>
> FINANCE DIRECTOR

A TRADITION OF PLANNING

Planning had a long history at Castle Press and was an established part of the yearly routines of the TMT. The five-year planning horizon did, however, have its critics, as did the emphasis and reliance on the planning process:

> We have a five-year business plan. We revise it every year, so it's ongoing. It is continuous, changing annually as we progress.
>
> PRODUCTION DIRECTOR

> The strategy process is mainly planning. But because we are dealing with global markets and there are always things happening, like economic changes in various parts of the world, we have to react to these rather than plan for them! We might be able to plan that something could happen, but to predict when and where is not so easy – we have to react to these external influences.
>
> PUBLISHING DIRECTOR

> We are commissioning new books now that will reach a peak of sales in the year 2000. So I think there is too much emphasis on the short term. We need to force ourselves to think longer term, not just five years down the line.
>
> MARKETING DIRECTOR

> In my view, the information for strategy development tends to be more informal than formal. We are not very good at collating centrally what is key information about the external environment. It tends to be much more in people's heads rather than having a resource that can be consulted and information taken from there.
>
> PUBLISHING DIRECTOR

A PARENTAL DRIVE FOR PLANNING

The strong emphasis on planning, while driven from within Castle Press, was reinforced by the corporate group. At this group level, a recent change in TMT make-up had changed the style of downward communication to Castle senior management. New planning formats were being imposed with clearer monitoring and review systems. In general, the Castle top team looked on these changes favourably, but also felt that strategy was a very 'downward' (rather than upward) process and that there was a lot of time spent making plans.

> The group require each of their Strategic Business Units [SBUs] to prepare a strategic planning document, once every two years. Derived from that is the operating plan, and from that the budgets. The group have actually imposed a new strategic planning and implementation structure, which we think is going to work very well. For once we agree with what our parent company has said.
>
> What is good about the new planning system is that it provides us with a clear evaluation document that we can use in the future to measure whether we've done what we said we would do, whether it's been successful or not.
>
> MANAGING DIRECTOR

However, despite a clear requirement for planning from corporate headquarters, what was planned was largely down to the Castle Press team. Where parental constraint was obvious, it was in the financial demands made by the parent and in agreeing budgets and profit expectations.

> Apart from the 'go for growth' message, no one limits what we can do, anything can be considered.
>
> One of the key things is that our part of the business is very profitable and cash generative. We are also big relative to the other parts of the group. These factors allow us a lot of freedom.
>
> FINANCE DIRECTOR

> The group do constrain us in the level of profit they demand. They have the power to tell us to make 5% or 15% profit this year; this limits what we can do.
>
> The divisional structure does mean we operate in a fairly well-defined area of operation. When we have suggested operating outside these areas, we have been told it is not our responsibility. So while there is a lot of discussion about going for growth and being entrepreneurial, there are constraints placed on individual business units which perhaps go against that.
>
> MARKETING DIRECTOR

A CONSENSUAL APPROACH

Formal planning activities were associated with more informal team needs, such as the need to arrive at a consensus, coupled with a strong sense of community, respect and belonging. Once agreed at this level, the strategy was cascaded down through the organisation and more consensus was sought from employees. Without this, the TMT argued, little of the plan would be implemented.

> I think there is an element of tradition. We have our plans every year, we continue to do them every year, and I think it's also a reflection of the function of doing everything by consensus, and the planning approach we take here is very much about developing a consensus view.
>
> PUBLISHING DIRECTOR

> We are very consensual and we like to debate everything and then reach an agreement. If somebody is in disagreement with something, it is unlikely that it will proceed very far.
>
> PRODUCTION DIRECTOR

> Because we employ people who are intellectual and academic, we take into account that they will have strong opinions on how the business is run and ignoring them will mean trouble. It is the nature of the people we employ that means that we have to have a more consensual and sensitive approach to management.
>
> At the beginning of this year we decided within our management board what our key objectives were. We took twenty of our senior managers away for two days and spent time explaining our key strategies. Then we asked them to work out action plans for how they would implement those strategies within the units. This is important because we have had problems with implementation before. We assumed that senior managers understood what we were trying to do after a short briefing! Now we are involving the senior guys more. This is a very traditional and conservative division and people are resistant to change, so we spend a lot of time trying to get people thinking in a different way.
>
> MANAGING DIRECTOR

POLITICS AND POWER

Because of the drive towards consensus, the issues of power and politics were not seen as very strong, although they were not absent:

> I don't think there is really any conflict. I think there are differences – we all know where we're trying to get, but the difference is about how we should get there.
>
> PUBLISHING DIRECTOR

> At board level I think we are quite well balanced power wise; people respect each other. I don't see that there is any one dominant player. However, influence comes about because of the business we're in – publishing and selling your product. So it is these groups who have influence ... at the end of the day decisions come down in their favour rather than on the processing side like my

> department. My area is only here on sufferance, because they need the product to be produced.
>
> PRODUCTION DIRECTOR

CULTURAL INFLUENCES

Employees at Castle Press were proudly professional and passionate about publishing quality books – the best in their specialist area. These commonly shared values about their trade directed strategy by keeping Castle Press away from certain areas of business and certain markets.

> There is a strong feeling here and within the group of 'we have always done things this way'. It is an even stronger culture in Castle Press where, in its specialist area of publishing, it is very much in a world of its own. I think people in this area of publishing around the world are just a family apart from the rest. They are very committed to this area rather than to publishing. I think people have this work in their blood and that is one of the things that gives it a very strong culture. Wherever you go worldwide, we get sucked into that culture.
>
> PRODUCTION DIRECTOR

Long service among the workforce was common in Castle Press. This helped to reinforce the common culture of the organisation. Even when new people were recruited from outside the organisation, the tendency was that these were selected from the publishing arena and publishing houses which were very similar to Castle Press.

> In the top management team and more generally, we are limited [in terms of experience] to Castle and then to a slightly wider level of publishing. We have deliberately recruited people who don't have any experience in either, but there aren't many of them at the moment.
>
> PUBLISHING DIRECTOR

> I think our strategy is principally historical, to some extent dictated by our wish to be the number one and our assumption that we can be that. In order to be number one, we have got to have fairly high objectives and to some extent that assumption dictates the overall strategy that we've got to be a major player wherever we operate.
>
> There are accepted industry ways of producing, selling and promoting materials in our business. There are common strategies, and following these is only restrained by size – the bigger and closer in size the competitors are to us, the more similar the strategies are.
>
> MARKETING DIRECTOR

REACTING TO A CHANGING ENVIRONMENT

While there had been a strong focus on strategy development through planning processes, the changing nature of the operating environment, changes in economic conditions and the speed of environmental change were dictating a different response from the organisation.

> This incremental approach – that's what we're getting more of now and it's because the environment is changing. New opportunities are arising. Before, we never really took them. Over the last couple of years we have started to take more risks in the hope that they will work. We try to set things up in a way where we can keep it low key and we can withdraw if it doesn't work, but if it looks as if it's a success, we can build on it.
>
> PUBLISHING DIRECTOR

> I think that we should experiment more and when there's an opportunity we should take it. This has happened on a small scale and I think there will be more of it. But there will always be pressure on us not to waste the money, so having a flutter will always be a bit of a problem.
>
> PRODUCTION DIRECTOR

PARTICIPATING AT THE TOP AND THE IDEAL FUTURE

> One reason the process is as it is, is that it is the way I like to do it. I suppose in that sense, that is power and that is what I have done. Also the business we are in is quite straight forward in the materials we produce, and in other respects it's a big, global, complex business. Therefore, we need a whole variety of inputs from people in order to agree our strategic goals and implement actions. The other reason is of course we are required to plan by the group.
>
> MANAGING DIRECTOR

> The managing director is very much a member of the team rather than a leader of the team.
>
> PUBLISHING DIRECTOR

The TMT at Castle Press envisaged the future of the strategy process to be more of the same, with some different emphases: more involvement, for example, of people who will deliver the strategy. Their role was seen not necessarily as a direct contribution to the strategy debate, but as greater ownership and commitment to making it work. There was also recognition that the TMT would have to be swifter-of-foot, to counter new competition and unpredictable environmental changes. A new focus on formal information gathering would be essential to try and read future trends and be sensitive to external changes sooner. The planning process itself needed to be pushed further into the future, five years being too short a time frame to promote informed, creative strategic thinking. Finally, there was a voice of challenge against the consensual approach:

> There is a strong argument for less of the consensual, democratic approach. At times we should say 'let's do it' and actually just go and do it!

THE PHARMACEUTICAL INDUSTRY

Gerry Johnson

The case looks at the development of the modern pharmaceutical industry since the early 1950s. The various forces affecting the competitive environment of the industry are discussed in terms of the past and the immediate future. The most important change has been the move from competition based around brand names and 'muscle marketing' to the provision of low cost drugs to large institutional buyers who are increasingly price sensitive and no longer brand loyal. As such, the case study allows readers to gain a greater understanding of how to assess the competitive environment of an industry. It provides an opportunity to conduct a Five Forces Analysis and shows that forces change over time and how they can pose serious threats or open up opportunities for companies in the development of competitive strategy.

• • •

The origins of the pharmaceutical industry are primarily post war and during that time it has been driven greatly by technological innovation. For example, if we go back to the early 1950s, the discovery of tetracycline by such companies as Pfizer and Lederle led to them becoming numbers one and two in the market. You can then see a progression of drugs that have made or broken companies over time. For example, the betablockers were largely discovered by ICI, who formed major franchises out of the treatment of cardiovascular diseases. Companies such as Syntex and Boots were based primarily on the discovery of the non-steroidal inflammatory drugs. Smith-Kline was based on the success of Tagamet, and Zantac formed the base for the global success of Glaxo, going on to be the world's number one product with sales in excess of £2 billion per annum. Technological new product success has therefore fuelled the growth of the industry.

In 1996 Graham Leask of Astra Pharmaceuticals was engaged in a review of the firm's strategy. This case study is based on extracts from his briefing to consultants on the background to developments in the pharmaceutical industry. The comments made represent the views of Graham Leask and not necessarily those of Astra Pharmaceuticals.

This case study is intended as a basis for class discussion and not as an illustration of either good or bad management practice.

In the UK, the general practitioner (GP) – the local doctor – did not really know the price of products, so pharmaceutical companies tended to make their money out of minor adjustments or 'me-too' adjustments to existing products or a copy of a competitor's product, traditionally priced at a premium to the existing market on the back of 'muscle marketing'. The doctors would accept a premium price for a new product because it was a new product, offering a minor advantage. For example, it might be a less frequent dosage or it might have a slightly improved side-effect profile; but with regards to its therapeutic outcome, it was very similar to the product which it was competing with. The doctors really acted as gatekeepers. The patients consumed the product, the health authorities paid for the product. All the doctors did was diagnose the problem and prescribe the product. The industry therefore was one which achieved its profitability through constant production of minor product improvements, strong marketing and selling which financed the breakthrough R&D discoveries.

It used to be said that to develop a world-class capability R&D cost in excess of $100 million a year. Now the cost of bringing a new drug to market is approximately $300 million. Every day lost in bringing a new drug to market probably loses you approximately $1 million in sales, if the product is successful. If we go back to the early 1960s the time from discovery to launch was probably only 3–5 years, whereas now because of increased safety standards and the requirements of clinical testing brought about by such disasters as thalidomide, it takes approximately 12 years from patent of drug to bringing that drug on the market. In the past you probably had 6–7 years' lead on your nearest competitor. Now because of improved chemistry and computer generation of analogues, you see the lead times down to about 18 months. So the time you have to establish a viable market position prior to meeting your first competitor is much reduced. It takes 12 years to develop a drug, but when you have got it on the market there is likely to be a competitor in 18 months. Patents only relate to your own process and the discovery of the drug. What people are doing very cleverly now is coming up with similar products. However, overall the chances of success of a new product are very low. Approximately 1–4 per cent see the market, and of those that reach the market, approximately 60 per cent fail to achieve sufficient sales to justify their R&D expenditure.

One of the other things that the industry has had to watch out for is substitute products. This could be an alternative at a much lower cost: a generic product, for example, or a new way of gaining a better clinical outcome, for example with surgery, which makes intervention by drugs unnecessary.

Going back to the industry in the early 1980s, success in the market place was driven by having good product supply, but also by having a successful sales and marketing operation. This meant achieving an optimal visit frequency of about 6 visits a year to each general practitioner and gaining sufficient coverage or seeing sufficient GPs. Over time, salesforces have increased very sharply in size. In 1985, there were approximately 3,000 representatives in the UK, calling on approximately 30,000 doctors.

By 1992 there were 36,000 GPs being called on by 7,000 representatives. So the ratio had changed from 1–10 down to nearer 1–5, a trend which has been mirrored in a lot of other countries, notably Germany, Italy and France.

THREATS AND CHANGES IN THE UK

The industry of the early 1980s was driven by premium-priced product improvement, strong sales and marketing, calling on a customer group which was not responsible for purchasing drugs and did not have a high awareness of drug prices. It was an industry which traditionally produced returns in excess of 20 per cent on investment. The National Health Service in the UK was established in 1948, and for a long time very little happened to change the original statement, which was quality health care as required, free at point of need, irrespective of status. There have been marked changes. In the 1980s there was a realisation that patients' expectations were increasing, the cost of health care was increasing and at the same time the capability of the country to sustain such spending was not increasing. That has been common worldwide, with the highest problem occurring in countries like the United States. In fact, it is said that in America, General Motors spends more on health care for its employees than it does on steel to make its cars. But it is the same for all the larger pharmaceutical markets in Europe too.

For some time within the UK there had been an agreement with government, the pharmaceutical price regulation scheme, which limited the level of profit which pharmaceutical companies were allowed to make in the UK. From the mid-1980s, though, government started to take more direct intervention. Prescription prices were raised, though bear in mind that the majority of the population was exempt, being under 16, elderly or unemployed. Then in 1985, the UK government introduced its blacklist. This delisted certain groups of products, some anti-hypnotics, such as valium, and some cough syrups. This had a tremendous differential effect on the industry. For example, Roche, which was in the top ten within the pharmaceutical industry, very rapidly fell to the 40s or even 50s within the industry as its two major products were delisted.

The next significant change was signalled in 1989 when the Conservative government introduced a white paper entitled *Working for Patients. Working for Patients* was put together on the premise that, through competition, patients would gain better services and value for money would be increased. There were four main changes within *Working for Patients.* The first was that for the first time the cost of drugs and other services on both the GP side in the community and on the hospital side were brought under control of the local regional health authority (of which there were then fourteen in England and Wales). The second change was that for the first time responsibility was linked with accountability within the management of the NHS, and NHS managers were recruited from outside on short-term performance contracts. The third change was the splitting of the so-called purchaser, who bought the service, from the provider, who provided it, with the result that competition among providers for money held by purchasers was encouraged. An internal market was thus created. The fourth main change was that all hospitals were no longer part of the district health authority. If they were sufficiently large and had the right managerial resources, they could become NHS trust hospitals, which meant that they were able to raise their own independent sources of finance and operate more independently. This affected competition because hospitals for the first time could specialise. They didn't have to provide all the services to the community which they had traditionally. In the past, hospitals were paid on the basis of their resident population, now they were being paid on the basis of the amount of work they did, as money followed the patient.

The government was also very worried about the cost of prescribing drugs and the fact that their cost was steadily increasing year on year, at a rate greater than the rise in GDP. Two key measures were introduced: the first was the introduction of indicative prescribing amounts which rapidly became changed to prescribing budgets, which produced a ceiling beyond which GPs were not supposed to go. The second change was the introduction of a new type of GP, a fund-holding GP, who was given a fund to cover staff, prescribing and certain specified hospital procedures: for example, hip replacements and cataracts. The advantage to the fund-holder was that they could move money from one budget to another and, if they saved money on the budget, could keep 50 per cent of those savings towards improvements in their own practices. Concomitant with this and as a requirement of fund-holding was that the GP practice installed an approved computer system, which had two benefits. The first one was that it held all the patients' records, but the second was that it often allowed the computer to set a formary, a limited list of drugs, that they used routinely. At the same time it also allowed the practice, if it wished, to print all prescriptions in their generic form, rather than a branded form, which meant that if an alternative cheaper generic drug was available, the pharmacist could prescribe it and hence save the practice money. The result was that the old brand loyalty, which the pharmaceutical industry had spent so much time and money developing, disappeared. Within the UK this fund-holding scheme has been very marked in its success in controlling prescribing costs. For example, in the first year of operation, fund-holders were 0.7 per cent below their expected budget, whereas non-fund-holding GPs had exceeded their budget.

By 1996, given the far more price-sensitive market, GPs were far more aware of the cost of drugs and they have a number of reminders from medical advisers, pharmaceutical advisers and their local PACT data which detail exactly what they have spent and where they have spent the money. Competition has also increased because it is no longer viable to introduce me-too products at a premium price because they simply won't sell; so new products are, for the first time, being introduced at a price discount and hence becoming early generics. This further increases the pressure on the industry's profitability, while as access to GPs declines, the viability of large salesforces becomes increasingly called into question.

CHANGES IN EUROPE

In other European countries, companies faced the same fundamental issues: a rise in patient expectation, increasing costs of healthcare and the fact that GDP is not increasing at a rate sufficient to offset rises in costs. In other European countries, therefore, there have been similar changes. For example, in Germany in 1993, the government introduced a system called 'reference pricing'. Government took a series of products and said that the price that they were willing to reimburse for those was the mid-point. As a result, patients had to pay extra in order to obtain a product listed above the cost of the reference price. The result of this was that the value of the pharmaceutical market fell by 25 per cent in three months. In Germany, in common with the UK and several other European countries, there was also a price freeze. For example, in the UK pharmaceutical companies had to reduce prices by $2\frac{1}{2}$ per cent. In Germany similar price freezes were put in place alongside reference pricing. However, what worried the Germans most was the imposition of 'global budgets'. A global budget was introduced for doctors. If it was exceeded, the excess would be paid half by the pharmaceutical industry and half by the doctors. Doctors reacted very quickly by using cheaper products because they didn't know how much they would be charged and feared high costs being passed on to them. The result was that in Germany a number of pharmaceutical companies reacted quickly by cutting the size of their salesforces and looking for ways to decrease their costs.

In Sweden reference pricing was also introduced, and by 1996 it was rumoured that the county councils, who administer health care, had been given budgets for drugs and were starting to set up drugs and therapeutics committees to evaluate which products they would endorse within their local community.

In Italy they have imposed a number of price freezes, followed by a banding system for drug reimbursement in 1994. Drugs in band A are classified as being essential and fully reimbursed, drugs in band B are 50 per cent reimbursed and drugs in band C are not reimbursed at all. There is also band H which is hospital drugs, which tend to be reimbursed at 50 per cent of the cost. The interesting thing here is that a drug can move from band A to band C without a pharmaceutical company being given prior warning. Price changes are sometimes imposed with such rapidity that you don't have time to change the printing on your packaging, so you have to do it with labels. The Italian government has tried to set the price fairly. They have taken an average of two high-cost markets – for example, the UK and Germany – and two low-cost markets, Spain and France. Unfortunately they have not set exchange rates which are realistic.

There are, then, a number of different cost containment measures and most governments have tried some or all of them to some degree with some success. We've had negative lists, we've had positive lists, we've had price freezes, we've had price reductions, we've had reference pricing, we've had price banding, we've had patient co-payments; and all these factors have made the environment more difficult.

On top of all this, distribution, which in the past used to be seen as very much a given within the pharmaceutical industry, is now becoming more important. As large distribution companies begin to become pan-European in their operation, they can source products from the lowest point of supply in Europe through the medium of parallel imports. These are products which are available at a cheaper price in lower fixed cost countries. Within Europe the higher-priced markets are Germany, the UK, Sweden and Holland; and the lower-priced markets, Spain, Portugal, France, Italy and Greece; and it's from the lower-priced markets that parallel imports are coming. The price differences can be significant.

Another difficulty has been the growth of a strong generic industry, particularly in the UK and Germany. In Germany the market has become far more price driven because of 'branded generics'. A generic product is a product manufactured after patent expiry by another manufacturer, normally at a cheaper price. These are normally at the bottom of the market. It is not developed and manufactured by the original manufacturer and is not backed by the manufacturer's quality control and medical information department. To a lot of GPs that makes little difference. Between these two price points there is an opportunity to have branded generics; these are generic products which offer a small advantage and which are sold at a price above the lowest-priced generics. In Germany you have original branded products at the top of the market, high-priced high-quality generics, middle-priced generics and low-priced generics.

It is often said that the pharmaceutical industry is a global industry. I'm not sure I would agree with that. In Europe, production facilities tend to be strategically placed and hence are often not present in each country. With respect to advertising and methods of marketing, however, it can differ from country to country. For example, a colleague of mine in Germany asked me why in the UK the industry holds so many doctors' meetings. The answer became obvious when I spent some time in Germany; going out with a German representative for a day, you might see ten doctors for face-to-face conversations. In the UK access is declining and the average now is probably about 3.3 calls per day; so to see sufficient customers, it's important to find other ways in which to see them – for example, through postgraduate education meetings. In Sweden, on the other hand, access to doctors is again difficult, but unlike the UK, where the average conversation is five to ten minutes, in Sweden you make appointments to see the doctor and they expect to spend half an hour with you. So whereas you don't see them so easily or so frequently, you do get a decent length of time in which to discuss your product. One of the major differences which the NHS changes in the UK have brought about is that the demands on doctors' time have become much more severe. Five years ago a doctor planned on a five-minute patient consultation on average. Now that patient consultation is 8–10 minutes, hence to see the same number of patients takes almost twice as long. In the UK there is also a larger requirement for paperwork from the health authority, which has meant that GPs have to spend more time on administration. Fund-holding has also meant that GPs have to become more professional in terms of buying goods and services and running their surgeries more like a business. In the rest of Europe they don't face quite the same pressures, but access to doctors is starting to decline. Certainly in Sweden getting satisfactory access to doctors at a reasonable frequency is difficult, especially bearing in mind that it may take 3–6 calls a year to convince a doctor of the benefits of a product, depending upon its complexity and the perceived risks.

The result of all this is that, whereas operating costs have remained the same, sales growth of products has slowed, and increasingly you can no longer cover the costs of innovative R&D through incremental me-too product modifications. Profitability is starting to fall quite sharply, and in some cases it is reaching 10 per cent or lower and is predicted to fall to between 3 and 5 per cent by the end of the century. A change would put pharmaceuticals very much in line with the average profitability of many other manufacturing industries who do not face such risks in new product discovery and development.

THE CORPORATE RESPONSE

There are increasingly three types of company: those that make things happen, those that watch things happen and those that wonder what the hell happened! Within the pharmaceutical industry there have been several major trends. The first has been towards mergers and acquisitions, as companies have sought to merge with other companies in order to become larger to leverage economies of scale, and exercise the benefits of critical mass in exploiting more efficient R&D and better sales and marketing practices; and at the same time hopefully gain improved geographical reach. Examples here are Glaxo Wellcome, Smith-Kline Beecham, Hoechst and Marion Rousse. Other strategies have included the building of distribution systems to gain information on product usage, parallel imports and generics such as the Glaxo distribution initiative. Another strategy aimed at gaining better control of distribution and getting closer to customers is the purchasing of pharmacy benefit managers[1] in the USA, led by Merck who purchased Medco for $6 billion, followed by Smith-Kline who purchased

[1]Pharmacy benefit managers arose when managed core organisations in the USA developed. In principle they 'carve out' the prescription benefit from the health care maintenance organisations and manage it. Mechanisms such as drug utilisation review, start formularies and direct telephone intervention to both prescriber and patient in order to encourage switching to lower-cost alternatives are commonly employed.

DPS and Eli Lilly who purchased PCS. So this is vertical integration. Another approach has been that taken by Rhône Poulenc, who have started to form alliances with several small R&D companies and biotechnology companies on the basis that by funding research in a number of companies, which are small and innovative, chances of coming up with a new product lead are improved. Other strategies have been very much to stick to the knitting, as with Astra, while some other companies have moved to disease management, such as Zeneca, with Salick for cancer.

There are of course other changes that could happen which are much less certain. Perhaps it is surprising that some of the large Japanese pharmaceutical companies have not made more inroads into Europe and the USA. They have not; but that is not to say that they will not. After all, they have in many other industries. And if they did, the further increase in competition could very well prompt even more mergers and acquisitions. We should also remember that most of the major pharmaceutical markets are currently in the West and Japan. There are other potentially huge markets for pharmaceuticals that are, as yet, underdeveloped – China, India, South America to name but a few. Who knows the extent to which they might develop as market opportunities? And then there are the advances in biotechnology: the media hype this up as a major development for the future. I suspect that that is an exaggeration, but we just do not know at the moment.

THE EUROPEAN BREWING INDUSTRY

Tony Jacobs and Murray Steele

This case study reviews the brewing industry up to 1996. Information is presented at the European industry level, individual country level and major competitor level, and offers the opportunity to analyse the industry and some of the competitors. It is particularly useful in examining differences in industry structure throughout the region, factors affecting globalisation in the industry and the influence of this on the competitive situation of different types of player. It is also a useful background to the later case studies on Kronenbourg and Brewery Group Denmark.

• • •

Europe is the major centre of beer consumption and production in the world. As a production entity, European output is more than 50 per cent greater than that of the USA, the world's largest beer-producing country. However, significant differences exist from country to country, in terms of both industry structure and market characteristics.

This case study is in three parts:

- A general description of the European brewing industry.
- Characteristics of the principal brewing countries.
- A description of major European brewers.

A GENERAL DESCRIPTION OF THE EUROPEAN BREWING INDUSTRY

In terms of value, the European alcohol market is dominated by beer, which accounts for over 50 per cent of the total alcohol market.

This case study was prepared by Tony Jacobs, Bristol Business School and Murray Steele, Cranfield School of Management. They are grateful to the MODEM Research Group who provided the quotations from their book, *The Business of Europe: Managing change*, which punctuate this case study. It is intended to be used as a basis for class discussion and not as an illustration of either good or bad management practice.

Exhibit 1 Top fourteen brewers in Europe, 1994

	Estimated European beer sales	Estimated market share (%)	Estimated rest of world sales	Estimated total sales
1. Heineken (Holland)	30.0	10.1	30.4	60.4
2. Carlsberg (Denmark)	24.4	8.2	5.8	30.2
3. Danone (France)	20.9	7.0	5.8	26.7
4. Guinness (Eire)	13.7	4.6	11.9	25.6
5. Bass (UK)	15.9	5.3	0.5	16.4
6. Interbrew (Belgium)	14.3	4.8	0.4	14.7
7. Courage (UK)	12.2	5.3	—	12.2
8. Oetker (Germany)	9.4	3.2	0.2	9.6
9. Bräu & Brunnen (Germany)	9.4	3.2	0.1	9.4
10. Maerz (Germany)	8.9	3.0	0.4	9.3
=11. Whitbread (UK)	7.8	2.6	—	7.8
=11. Holsten (Germany)	7.3	2.5	0.5	7.8
13. S & N (UK)	6.8	2.3	0.1	6.9
14. Grolsch (Holland)	2.0	0.7	0.1	2.1

Notes
1. All figures are in millions of hectolitres.
2. Volumes include those companies in which the relevant brewer has a financial interest.

Source Annual reports and trade sources.

Industry Structure

Exhibit 1 shows the top fourteen European brewing companies by their output in 1994. The European market, taken as a whole, is not very concentrated; the top five brewers have a combined market share of 35.2 per cent. The European brewers are also relatively insular. Only four of the top fourteen have sales of any significance outside Europe (i.e. over one million hectolitres per annum) and for the majority of them, the bulk of their output is produced in their country of origin.

On a global comparison, only two of the brewers listed in Exhibit 1 are in the top ten brewers of the world (1994 figures). Heineken is the second largest, and Carlsberg is the eighth. To put this further in context, Anheuser-Busch of the USA, the largest brewing company in the world, had an annual output of nearly 107 million hectolitres in 1994, and Heineken, Europe's largest brewing group, produced just over 60 million hectolitres in the same year.

Exhibit 2 **Estimated industry concentration by country, 1994**

Country	Industry situation	Number of competitors	Degree of concentration (%)
Denmark	Monopoly	1	71
Holland	Monopoly	1	74
Italy	Monopoly	2	61
Belgium	Monopoly	2	86
France	Monopoly	2	71
United Kingdom	Concentrated	5	84
Spain	Concentrated	5	87
Germany	Fragmented	5	26

Notes

1. The degree of concentration relates to the combined market share held by the number of competitors indicated.
2. Estimates for 1994. Mergers and acquisitions within the industry have led to further concentration in several key markets.

Industry Concentration

Individual European countries have substantially different industry structures. They vary from the highly concentrated to the highly fragmented. Some countries, such as the United Kingdom, have regulations which limit the degree of concentration allowed in industries. Other countries do not have these rules, and in fact may encourage concentration to help the creation and development of significant international competitors. Exhibit 2 shows the varying degrees of concentration in the principal European brewing countries.

Ownership

There is little ownership of breweries by other European companies in Germany and none in Denmark. However, significant proportions of the Italian and Spanish industries are owned by foreign brewers as a result of cross-border acquisitions since the 1970s, driven by small domestic markets causing ambitious brewers to seek international expansion. Exhibit 3 shows the major European cross-border ownership stakes.

There is little ownership in Europe by non-European brewers. There are, however, licensing arrangements whereby brewers in one country brew a brand from another country. This principally takes place in the United Kingdom. A good example is Whitbread, which brews and sells both Stella Artois and Heineken under licence in the UK. This provides them with an expanded portfolio of brands with which to compete.

Exhibit 3 Cross-European ownership stakes

	HEINEKEN	DANONE	CARLSBERG	INTERBREW
France	*	**		*
Germany			*	
Belgium		*		**
Holland	**			
Denmark			**	
Spain	*	*	*	
Italy	*	*	*	*
Greece	*	*		
United Kingdom			*	
Ireland	*			

** Denotes country of origin. * Denotes an ownership presence.

Consumption

Exhibit 4 shows the consumption per capita in litres per annum for the major European markets for the years 1989–96.

Brands

With low growth, or declines, in consumption in the European markets, branding has become increasingly important. Brewers have intensified their brand development policies and a very high brand awareness exists among consumers, principally due to high-profile (and high-cost) advertising. As one British brewing manager put it:

> You have got to own your own brands, and they have got to be good brands, or else you are going to be dead in the water.

Exhibit 5 shows the top ten selling beer brands in millions of hectolitres in Europe. Not surprisingly, the top three brands are marketed by the three largest companies which have the most extensive operations across Europe. Heineken has two of the top five brands – Heineken and Amstel – and Carlsberg has two of the top ten brands – Carlsberg and Tuborg.

Market Segmentation

> In a saturated market there is segmentation. In a growing market beer is beer, in a segmented market this is not the case.
>
> DUTCH BREWING MANAGER

Exhibit 4 Consumption (litres) per capita

	1996	1995	1994	1993	1992	1991	1990	1989
Germany	132	138	140	138	144	143	143	143
Czech Republic	160	159	161	155	167	131	135	132
Slovakia	92	94	93	56	72			
Denmark	121	124	127	126	128	126	127	127
Belgium/Luxembourg	101	104	106	108	113	112	121	115
Austria	114	116	117	117	123	124	121	119
United Kingdom	102	101	102	101	105	109	113	114
Hungary	75	83	81	77	98	101	107	103
Ireland	118	113	113	123	124	123	124	118
Holland	85	86	86	85	90	91	90	88
Spain	65	67	67	67	71	71	72	71
Portugal	62	65	62	64	65	67	65	64
Greece	39	40	42	42	42	37	41	39
France	40	39	39	39	41	41	42	41
Italy	24	25	26	25	24	23	23	22

Sources BLRA and CBMC.

Exhibit 5 Top ten European brands in the early 1990s

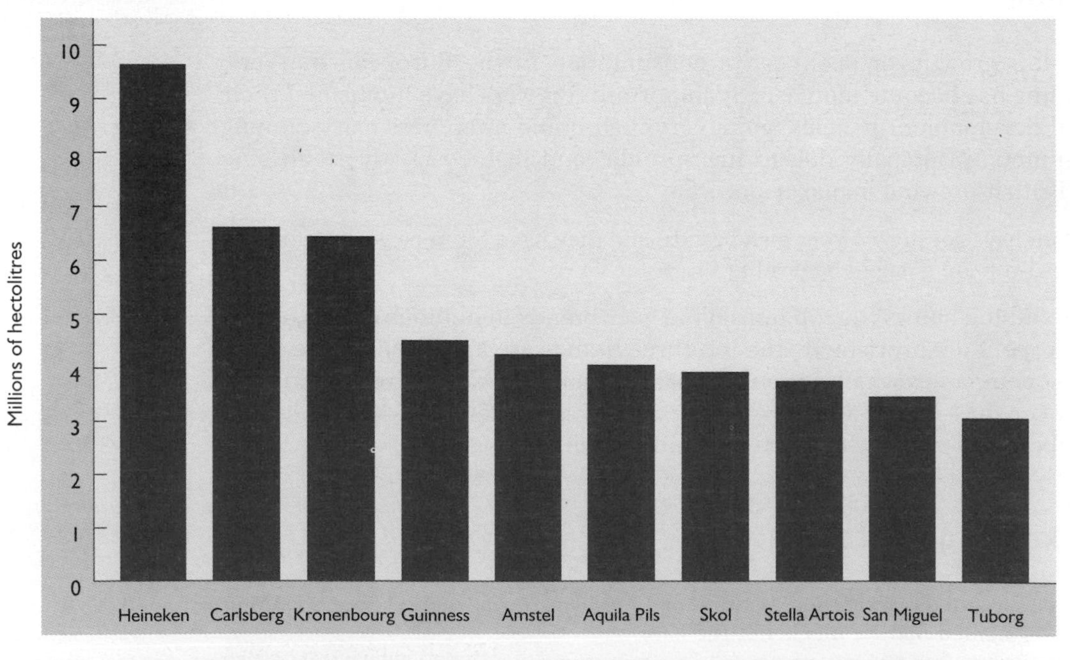

Exhibit 6 European market segments in the early 1990s

Segment	Estimated market share (%)
Low and no alcohol	7
Premium or strong	25
Speciality – aperitif or special occasion beers	5
Ordinary – the major volume sector	63
of which:	
Branded products	50
Supermarket chain low-price, own-label beers	13

An example of a growing segment in a mature market is the increase in lager sales in the United Kingdom. Since the 1970s the total volume of beer sold in the UK has not fluctuated substantially, but in the same period lager's share of the market has increased from 7.5 to 55 per cent, before falling back to 50 per cent in 1993. Distinct segments of the European market appear to be developing. These are shown in Exhibit 6.

The segments which have been growing and are expected to continue to grow are at either end of the market: the low- and no-alcohol beers and particularly the premium and speciality beers. Also seen as growing are the supermarket chain own-label beers as a result of their low price and the distribution power of the supermarket chains.

Different brands in their segments are viewed differently from country to country. Brands which do not have their origin in a country, i.e. which are 'foreign', are often viewed as premium segment products. A good example of this is Danone's Kronenbourg 1664, which is sold in France as an ordinary beer, but is viewed in almost all other markets as a premium product. However, potential hazards exist for brewers in pursuing this policy.

> In Great Britain, Stella Artois is a premium beer, one of the most expensive beers you can get there, and people buy it because it is expensive. It is marketed and promoted that way. The British are travelling people, now when they come to Belgium, they discover that Stella Artois is a cheap beer, so they ask themselves if it is justified to pay so much for it in Great Britain.
>
> FRENCH BREWING MANAGER

Another diversity exists in price relationships between premium and ordinary beers and by region:

> In southern Europe the price differential is high between the premium/speciality segment and the ordinary segment – of the order of 40%. In northern Europe the difference is much lower, only 15%.
>
> FRENCH BREWING MANAGER

A possible source of explanation for this wide discrepancy could be the widely differing duty and taxation rates on beer across Europe.

Duty

The duty levied on beer in Europe is calculated by one of two methods – the wort system and at the brewery gate (BG). The latter, as its name implies, means that tax is levied at the 'brewery gate' on point of shipment to the next stage in the distribution channel. The wort system is more complex and dates from the last century. Duty is calculated during the brewing process, at the point of fermentation.

Rates of duty vary dramatically across Europe from the equivalent of 2.8 pence per pint of beer in Luxembourg to 71 pence per pint in Finland. Tax rates vary between 15 and 25 per cent. This variation in duty rates impacts on the economics of brewing. In the UK, for example, raw materials, salaries, packaging, etc. are one-third of total manufacturing costs, the other two-thirds is duty.

The anticipated harmonisation of rates of duty throughout the EU member countries since the introduction of the single market has, so far, yet to materialise. One British manager summed up the present duty situation:

> The harmonisation of duty is a mess in Europe, frankly. There are very wide duty differences across Europe. You have the situation where there is a potential price difference between France and the UK of 25 per cent in a very saleable commodity. The UK government are saying that there won't be any need to harmonise duty, because they will be able to control it one way or the other, they will capture it at the border. I really don't think that is realistic, because if you can make £25,000 profit bringing a tanker of beer across the Channel, you will bring a tanker of beer across the channel, whether it is legal or illegal, and if you get caught once or twice it is probably still worth it.

Distribution

European consumers purchase their beer in two main ways. They either purchase beer in stores to drink at home (known as the 'off trade') or they purchase it, principally on draught, in an outlet such as a bar, pub, café, restaurant or hotel to be consumed immediately. Exhibit 7 shows the percentage of beer purchased in draught form in recent years in the major European markets.

The type of container in which beer is purchased also varies significantly from country to country. The four principal types are: draught, where the beer is served in a glass and drunk immediately, normally in a bar; returnable bottles, where the bottle is returned to the point of sale or some other point after the beer has been drunk; non-returnable bottles, where the bottle is discarded after consumption of the beer; and cans, which are also normally discarded after consumption of their contents.

Exhibit 7 **Percentage of beer consumed on draught by country**

	1994	1992	1989	1988	1987	1985
Germany	22	22	28	28	29	29
Denmark	7	6	5	4	4	3
Belgium	40	40	44	45	40	40
United Kingdom	67	70	72	73	75	77
Ireland	82	83	86	86	88	88
Holland	31	30	29	30	31	31
Spain	37	37	40	40	n/a	35
Portugal	32	34	25	25	24	19
Greece	4	4	3	3	n/a	n/a
France	24	25	25	25	24	22
Italy	16	14	16	16	16	16

Source CBMC.

Exhibit 8 shows the percentages of consumption by the different types of container for the major European countries in 1994. With the exception of the United Kingdom and Greece, beer sold in cans is not a significant feature of the European market, and for environmental reasons beer cannot be purchased in cans in Denmark by law.

There is a growing tendency throughout Europe for premium beers to be sold by the bottle rather than by the can, as bottles are perceived to be of higher quality by many consumers.

Channels of distribution also vary, which is to be expected given the different consumption characteristics of each market. The channels of distribution which exist in France, Holland, Spain, Italy, Belgium and Denmark are similar. What does vary from country to country is the proportion of beer sales which flows through each channel.

In the aforementioned countries, the brewers do not own many of the retail outlets and tend to distribute through wholesalers, which may or may not be owned by the brewers. The supermarket chains have substantial power in the distribution channels and offer the brewing companies attractive economies of scale. Brewers can deliver large volumes to a central point in the supermarket chain distribution system. This power is growing across Europe as more beer is sold through supermarkets.

In the UK and to a lesser extent Germany, the brewing companies owned a significant proportion of the retail outlets – 44 per cent in the United Kingdom and 22 per cent in Germany – distributed direct to the pubs and bars. However, since the Monopolies and Mergers Commission report into the UK brewing industry in 1989, there has been a substantial change in ownership patterns and some estimates suggest that the number of retail outlets owned by brewers will drop to around 19 per cent by the

Exhibit 8 Consumption patterns by country, 1994 (%)

	Draught beer	Returnable bottles	Non-returnable bottles	Cans
Germany	22	78*	0	0
Denmark	7	93	0	0
Belgium	40	53	4	3
United Kingdom	67	4	6	23
Ireland	82	4	4	10
Holland	31	64	6	0
Spain	36	38	19	7
Portugal	32	55	9	4
Greece	4	76	4	16
France	24	16	55	5
Italy	16	15	58	11

* Includes all bottles and cans.

Source CBMC.

Exhibit 9 Brewing output (millions of hectolitres) by country

	1996	1995	1994	1993	1992	1991	1990	1989
Germany	114.2	117.4	118.6	115.8	120.2	118.0	104.3	93.0
Czech Republic	18.2	17.8	18.1	17.8	19.5 }	22.3	23.5	22.8
Slovakia	4.5	4.4	4.5	3.0	3.8 }			
Denmark	9.6	10.1	9.4	9.4	9.8	9.7	9.0	8.8
Belgium	14.7	15.4	14.7	14.2	14.2	13.8	14.1	13.2
Austria	9.5	9.7	10.1	9.8	10.0	10.2	9.6	9.2
United Kingdom	58.1	56.8	58.3	56.7	57.6	59.6	61.8	62.1
Hungary	7.3	7.8	8.3	7.9	9.9	9.6	9.5	9.7
Ireland	7.8	7.4	7.2	6.9	6.7	6.4	6.4	6.1
Holland	23.5	23.1	22.2	20.4	20.7	19.9	20.0	18.8
Spain	24.7	25.3	25.0	24.3	26.1	26.4	27.3	27.3
Portugal	6.7	6.9	6.6	6.6	6.9	6.9	7.0	6.8
Greece	3.9	4.0	4.3	3.9	3.9	3.7	4.1	3.9
France	20.4	20.6	20.4	20.8	21.3	21.0	21.4	20.9
Italy	11.1	12.0	12.1	11.7	10.9	10.7	11.1	10.4
Total	334.2	338.7	339.8	329.2	341.5	338.2	329.1	313.0

Sources BLRA and CBMC.

Exhibit 10 Imports as a percentage of consumption

	1996	1995	1994	1993	1992	1991	1990	1989
Germany	2.0	2.3	2.4	2.4	2.6	2.5	1.8	1.7
Denmark	1.5	1.8	0.7	0.3	0.3	0.3	0.4	0.3
Belgium/Luxembourg	5.7	5.1	5.1	4.4	4.3	4.3	5.2	5.8
United Kingdom	9.3	8.8	8.7	7.9	9.3	8.8	8.0	7.2
Ireland	13.0	12.1	9.8	13.4	17.0	15.0	11.7	10.2
Holland	4.6	4.6	4.1	4.3	3.9	5.7	4.5	4.5
Spain	7.0	7.4	7.7	6.2	6.6	5.0	4.2	3.3
Portugal	3.2	3.6	2.7	2.2	1.8	2.0	1.6	1.5
Greece	5.9	5.6	4.7	5.4	5.6	4.6	3.8	2.3
France	19.4	15.4	17.3	13.3	12.0	12.7	13.0	12.0
Italy	22.3	20.5	21.0	19.7	20.3	19.0	18.2	16.7

Source BLRA and CBMC.

Exhibit 11 Exports as a percentage of production

	1996	1994	1993	1992	1991	1990	1989	1988
Germany	7.5	6.7	6.3	5.4	5.2	5.6	5.7	5.7
Denmark	29.6	28.4	26.8	28.0	26.5	25.8	23.7	23.8
Belgium/Luxembourg	31.2	31.2	26.1	23.6	23.1	18.5	17.8	18.3
United Kingdom	6.3	5.3	3.8	3.7	3.2	2.7	2.2	2.1
Ireland	41.2	45.3	45.3	42.9	40.9	39.2	37.7	38.8
Holland	44.6	42.2	38.2	35.6	34.6	36.0	33.3	33.1
Spain	1.5	1.4	1.2	1.2	1.0	0.8	0.7	0.5
Portugal	10.4	9.2	6.5	7.0	4.3	4.4	2.8	2.2
Greece	7.6	5.9	3.4	3.3	1.6	0.7	1.8	1.0
France	8.8	6.3	4.8	4.8	4.8	5.1	4.0	3.6
Italy	3.8	2.0	1.8	1.3	1.4	1.7	0.8	0.5

Source BLRA and CBMC (1995 data unavailable).

year 2000. In both the UK and Germany, supermarket chains are increasingly becoming important channels for distribution.

Production

Exhibit 9 shows the production output of the major European beer-producing countries during recent years in millions of hectolitres.

Imports and Exports

Exhibits 10 and 11 show imports as a percentage of consumption and exports as a percentage of production respectively for the major European brewing countries.

CHARACTERISTICS OF THE PRINCIPAL BREWING COUNTRIES

The characteristics of some of the major markets are now reviewed briefly.

Denmark

The Danish brewing industry is dominated by Carlsberg, which has a 71 per cent share of its home market and is a major global competitor, being, in 1994, the eighth largest brewer in the world. Its brand is the second most popular beer in Europe, selling almost 7 million hectolitres annually. Carlsberg's majority shareholder is a charitable trust.

There are 15 breweries in Denmark divided among 9 brewers. In 1989 a merger created the Brewery Group Denmark (BGD), making it the second largest brewer in Denmark, supplying roughly 15 per cent of the beer consumed there. However, a significant amount of their production is exported.

Danish brewers are also the largest producers of soft drinks in Denmark, with Carlsberg having a 50 per cent market share. This has been useful in gaining access, for beer, to channels of distribution.

Danish beer drinkers are by nature conservative. Most of the beer sold in Denmark is brewed domestically, and attempts to introduce foreign beer, even when brewed under licence in Denmark, have been unsuccessful.

A particular feature of the Danish beer market is the 'border trade' on the German–Danish border, where Danes cross to buy cheap beer. The price differential is principally due to differences in the rates of duty on alcohol between the two countries. The 'border trade' beer is likely to be supplied by Danish breweries to German retailers.

Border trade sales once contributed significantly to total sales and caused the Danish government to lose tax revenue. However, since Denmark joined the EU in 1993, the Danes have dramatically reduced duty on beers – by about 46 per cent – which has led to a reduction in the border trade in beer.

Roughly 70 per cent of beer is sold through retailers such as the supermarket chains. These are therefore extremely important customers of the brewing companies. The big supermarket chains have introduced their own beer brands, which are sold as cheap discount beers. These beers are also brewed by Danish brewers and are estimated to have 10–20 per cent of the market.

An important feature of the Danish beer market is the bottle reuse system. Beer and soft drinks must be sold in reusable bottles; cans are banned. It has been claimed that the bottle reuse system is a major barrier to foreign brewers entering the Danish market. With these barriers in mind, the ban on the use of cans was up for reconsideration in 1996, with the EU trying to balance environmental considerations with fair trade.

Holland

Holland is one of the world's largest producers of beer and has increasingly concentrated on exporting to overcome the lack of growth opportunities in its home market. Indeed, Holland is one of the largest exporting countries in the world for beer and the most international, exporting to 170 countries, principal of which is the USA, taking 37 per cent of Holland's beer exports in 1994. The proportion of its production exported has grown from 23.7 per cent in 1980 to 42.2 per cent in 1994, while imports remain relatively static at 4.1 per cent in 1994. Some 93 per cent of beer imports come from Belgium.

Like Denmark the brewing industry in Holland is dominated by one brewer, in this case Heineken, which is the largest brewer in Europe and the second largest in the world. Although Heineken only produces 6.7 million hectolitres of beer in Holland, it produces over 60 million hectolitres (1994 figures) worldwide.

Heineken also has ownership stakes in brewing companies in Spain, France, Italy, Greece, Holland, Hungary, Poland, Switzerland and Ireland, and has a licensing agreement with Whitbread in the UK to brew Heineken for sale there. Heineken is the largest imported beer brand in the USA, with 1.5–2 per cent of the total market.

Approximately 70 per cent of beer purchased in Holland is from the supermarket chains for consumption at home, making these retailers an important part of the distribution channel in Holland.

There are three mid-size Dutch brewing companies: Bavaria, Interbrew Netherland and Grolsch. Their sales, in millions of hectolitres, for 1993 were 3.4, 2.0 and 1.5 respectively. Grolsch, despite its relatively small output, has carved out a strong niche market position in many of the world's major beer markets.

Belgium

The Belgian brewing industry produces a large number of beers: 420 different brands of 18 different types. Belgian brewers claim that no other country offers such a wide variety.

Belgium is one of the world's leading exporters of beer. In 1994 it exported over 31 per cent of its production, almost all to other EU countries. The biggest export market was France, which took 63 per cent of Belgian exports. Imports account for less than 5 per cent of consumption and are in slow decline.

The Belgian beer industry is dominated by Interbrew and Alken-Maes. Between them they have approximately 85 per cent of the Belgian market. Interbrew was formed in 1986 by a merger between Artois and Piedboeuf, and now incorporates Lamot. The company is also a significant producer of soft drinks, owns production and bottling units in France, Italy and a number of African countries, and has licensing agreements in the UK and Canada and distribution companies in Holland, France, Italy and the USA.

Alken-Maes is 85 per cent owned by the French brewer Danone, having been created in 1988 by a merger of Alken Kronenbourg and Maes. It has subsidiaries in France, Italy, Spain and Holland, and a presence in many other markets. It has 20 per cent of the Belgian market.

Principal among the distribution channels in Belgium is the specialist dealer or *negociant*, who provides home delivery of beverages, operates beverage discount outlets, delivers to the hotels, restaurants, cafés and bars and deals as a wholesaler.

The home delivery system is a typically Belgian approach to distribution and highlights the importance of drinking to the Belgian consumer. The growth in supermarkets which offer a wider range of beers at lower prices, and changes in lifestyle such as increased car ownership, rising real disposable income and more working women (who are therefore not available to take deliveries at home during the day) have led to the decline of the home delivery system in recent years.

By the 1990s there were around 1,000 discount outlets for beverages. These combined a large choice of products with a fast service and lower than average prices. The hotels, restaurants, cafés and bars sector also represents a large part of the market. In this sector the *negociant* still plays a large role. It is estimated that 49 per cent of beer sales are distributed through *negociants*, 27 per cent through supermarkets and 6 per cent through direct sales in cafés and bars.

Italy

In Italy, beer became a popular drink only recently and Italy still has the lowest consumption per capita of all European countries. This consumption is concentrated in the north of the country. Traditionally, beer was produced with a low alcohol content and was seen as a refreshing drink, frequently accompanied by snacks, pizzas or fast food.

Because of their comparatively high alcohol content, imported beers were almost always classified as 'special' beers. However, recent EU legislation (a decree passed in 1992 defined what might constitute a beer)

Exhibit 12 Domestic output of main Italian beer producers, 1993 (million hectolitres)

Peroni	4.5
Dreher-Heineken	3.5
Poretti	1.4
Moretti	1.1

Source BLRA.

has led Italian brewers to raise the level of alcohol to the EU average, and this might change consumers' perceptions over time.

Beer imports have increased steadily for a number of years, reaching 20 per cent in 1992. This figure rises significantly when foreign beers brewed under licence in Italy are included. Principally imports come from Germany, Holland, Belgium and Denmark. Their products are seen as being of higher quality and constitute the upmarket segment of the market. Exports are negligible.

The main competitors and their domestic output in 1993 are shown in Exhibit 12. Peroni is the largest brewery group in Italy and is 75 per cent owned by the Peroni family; the remaining 25 per cent is owned by Danone, the French brewer. It produces a wide range of beers and has a strong sales network, giving it national coverage. Dreher-Heineken is the second largest brewer in the country and is fully owned by the Heineken Group. Poretti is half owned by Carlsberg and half by Bassetti, an Italian group of companies. Moretti was formed when it and Prinz, another brewer, were bought and merged together by Labatts of Canada, which has now itself been bought by Interbrew of Belgium.

Distribution is similar to other European countries, with roughly 40–50 per cent being through hotels, restaurants, cafés and bars. Supermarkets and hypermarkets take a further 20 per cent and traditional grocery outlets about 16 per cent. Door-to-door distribution is a small but growing channel. Traditionally used by wholesalers of soft drinks, in recent years this channel has extended its service to include beer. Only the supermarkets buy directly from the breweries.

France

Wine is the French national drink and, of the major European countries, consumption of beer is only lower in Italy. Despite this, Danone is the second largest brewing company in Europe and eighth largest in the world.

At the end of the Second World War, there were 1,000 breweries in France. Since then there has been considerable concentration. By the mid-

Exhibit 13 Domestic output of main French beer producers, 1993 (million hectolitres)

Danone (Kronenbourg)	9.8
Brasserie Heineken	5.2
Interbrew France	2.2
Brasserie Fischer	1.3
Brasserie St Omer	1.3

1990s there were three main breweries and another two brewers which had production of around 1.3 million hectolitres. Additionally, France has approximately twenty smaller, specialist breweries. The main competitors and their domestic output in 1993 are shown in Exhibit 13.

France is not a major exporter of beer. In 1994 it exported 6.3 per cent of its output, principally to its neighbours, Italy and Spain. In the same year, 17.3 per cent of its consumption was imported, principally from Belgium.

The brewing and drinking of beer in France is essentially a northern activity. Average consumption in the north is 80 litres per capita compared with the French national average of 41 litres.

Distribution patterns have remained static throughout the 1980s. Supermarkets and hypermarkets account for over 63 per cent, with hotels, restaurants and cafés accounting for roughly 36 per cent. Breweries do not own bars or cafés but will provide them with cheap finance deals in return for a contract to sell their beers for a fixed period of time, typically 5–10 years.

The market is segmented similarly to other European countries, with light or low-alcohol beers, ordinary beers and stronger speciality beers. The low-alcohol and strong/speciality beers are the fastest-growing market segments in the 1990s.

The five countries already discussed, i.e. Denmark, Holland, Belgium, Italy and France have much in common in their brewing industries. They have similar degrees of industry concentration and distribution systems. Spain, the United Kingdom and Germany exhibit considerably different characteristics from the first five.

Spain

The brewing industry in Spain is not dominated by any one company. The major brewing companies with their domestic output in 1993 and their ownership are shown in Exhibit 14. There are three other small breweries with a local focus and small production outputs.

Exhibit 14 **Domestic output of main Spanish beer producers, 1993 (million hectolitres) and their ownership**

Cruzcampo	6.5	89% Guinness 11% Carlsberg
El Aguila	4.2	65% Heineken
Mahou	4.2	33% Danone
Damm	4.0	16% Oetker 5% San Miguel
San Miguel	3.5	Affiliated to San Miguel in the Philippines and 25% Danone

The Spanish market is regionally oriented with three very strong regional groups which have been able to develop strong production economies of scale and distribution power. These three are Cruzcampo, Mahou and Damm. Only San Miguel markets its brand successfully on a national scale at the moment, although this is expected to change as the international brewers take more interest in the Spanish market.

An interesting feature of the Spanish industry is the high degree of foreign ownership compared with other European countries (see Exhibit 14), and there are also many licensing agreements to produce beer locally. For example, in 1995 Damm announced that it had signed an agreement with Anheuser-Busch to produce Budweiser beer for the national market. One explanation for this is that importation from any country other than France is difficult due to the distances involved. The Spanish market is not as well developed as other European markets, and Spanish consumption is almost entirely satisfied by domestic production. In 1994 Spain exported 1.4 per cent of its output and imported 7.7 per cent of its consumption.

It is only in recent years that the market segments well established in other European countries have begun to develop in Spain. There are three basic market segments – ordinary, special and strong beers. However, the consumers' perception of these segments can vary from region to region, so strong are the three regional brewers. The market is developing rapidly, forced mainly by the foreign brewers such as Carlsberg and Heineken through strong advertising and brand development campaigns. The 'new' market segments, i.e. special, strong and a small non-alcoholic segment, are the fastest growing.

Distribution in Spain is currently split 25 per cent through supermarkets and 75 per cent in cafés, bars, hotels and restaurants. However, there is a definite move towards increased sales through supermarket grocery chains, as in the rest of Europe. This development has to do with the changing lifestyles of the Spanish. More of them are now buying beer in supermarkets for consumption at home. Packaging trends are also changing, from returnable bottles to non-returnable bottles and cans.

United Kingdom

In the UK there are three principal types of beer – lagers, ales and stouts. Lagers are served chilled, ales are brown in colour and are drunk at an ambient temperature, and stouts are heavy, dark-coloured beers, principal among which is Guinness. Most of the beer drunk in the UK is produced domestically, with imports standing at 8.7 per cent of consumption in 1994. In the same year, 5.3 per cent of output was exported.

In 1970, ales dominated the beer market, having an 85 per cent share. However, in the following two decades, lagers became increasingly popular, accounting for 55 per cent of the market in 1990. By 1993 their market share had declined to about 50 per cent as ales regained some of their popularity.

A growing trend is the increased sale of beer from grocery supermarket chains. Their share grew from 12 to 18 per cent during the 1980s and is predicted to be 25 per cent by the year 2000. Personal imports of beer from France are also increasing since the removal of trade barriers in 1993. The popularity of this cross-border trade is due to beer duty being seven times higher in the UK than in France. In 1994 personal imports of beer, principally from France, accounted for 16.5 per cent of the off-trade (take-home) market – approximately 4 per cent of total beer sales in that year.

In 1994 over two-thirds of beer sold was through on-trade licensed outlets, principal of which are the pubs. This figure shows a decline of about 5 per cent since 1989, due in part to off-trade prices being reduced and changing consumer lifestyles. Traditionally, the British brewing industry was highly vertically integrated, with brewers owning production and retailing facilities and even, in some cases, the sources of raw materials. In many independent pubs a supply agreement, known as a 'tie', existed. This meant that, in return for preferential loans, they would only sell beer provided by the brewer they were 'tied' to.

This level of integration changed dramatically after the Monopolies and Mergers Commission report into the industry in 1989. It concluded that a complex monopoly existed which restricted competition at all levels of the industry, and its findings led to brewers being restricted to owning no more than 2,000 pubs plus 50 per cent of their original holdings, the elimination of the loan tie arrangement and the enabling of pubs to buy at least one brand of beer from a brewer other than its usual supplier.

The report effectively forced brewers to decide between brewing or retailing activities, and the takeovers and asset swaps that followed have led to the UK brewing industry becoming increasingly concentrated in the 1990s. In 1990 Courage and Grand Metropolitan merged their brewing interests. Courage acquired Grand Met's breweries and concentrated on brewing. Grand Met focused on retailing and property management, acquiring Courage's pubs. In 1995 Courage was bought by Scottish and Newcastle, whose brewing division, now known as Scottish Courage, became the largest brewer in the UK. Another example of consolidation occurred in 1991 when Carlsberg (UK) combined with Allied Lyons in a

Exhibit 15 **Market share of the largest UK brewers, 1995**

BREWER	MARKET SHARE (%)
Scottish Courage	25
Bass	23
Carlsberg-Tetley	15
Whitbread	14

50/50 joint venture to form Carlsberg-Tetley, then the third largest UK brewer.

Despite a growing number of small regional breweries, which sell beer on a local basis, four large brewing companies had the majority of the market in 1995 (see Exhibit 15).

In the UK, beer consumption is in long-term decline. Some 25 per cent of brewing capacity is in excess of demand. This has left some companies as uncertain holders of brewing or pub assets and the potential for further concentration within the industry. Allied Lyons, now known as Allied Domecq following the 1994 takeover of the world's biggest producer of sherry, Pedro Domecq, decided to focus on spirits and in 1996 entered into negotiations with Bass concerning the sale of its 50 per cent share of Carlsberg-Tetley, a deal which would give Bass around 38 per cent of the UK market. The proposed merger was not allowed by the Monopolies and Mergers Commission on the grounds that it was anti-competitive.

Germany

Germany is the largest beer-producing nation in Europe and has not experienced concentration of its brewing industry on the same scale as the rest of Europe. There are approximately 1,200 breweries in Germany, with 800 in Bavaria alone. The German brewing industry produces 5,000 different brands of beer, accounting for nearly half the world's total.

German drinkers are very conservative and loyal to their favourite beer, normally a beer brewed locally. Ninety per cent of breweries sell their products within a 30-mile radius. This is encouraged by the *Reinheitsgebot* or 'purity laws', which were first introduced in 1516. The law states that only malted cereals, hops, yeast and water can be used in the brewing process. Artificial additives are not allowed to improve quality or extend shelf life, thus clearly inhibiting imports or the transportation of local products over any significant distances.

In 1987 the European Court of Justice ruled that the *Reinheitsgebot* could not be used to prevent the sale of imported beers. Germany compromised, allowing beers with additives to be sold, but they had to be clearly labelled and could not be called beer. Despite this ruling, only a few foreign companies have entered the German market and imports are negligible, standing at 2.4 per cent of total consumption in 1994.

The proportion of beer production exported grew during the 1980s from 3.2 to 6.7 per cent. The principal countries exported to were the UK, France, Italy, Spain, Austria and Switzerland.

Another feature of the German brewing industry is the low profitability of the brewing companies. The margin is about 1 per cent, compared to approximately 10 per cent in the UK. This is another factor contributing to the low importation of beer brands.

Distribution channels have some similarities to the rest of Europe, but also some differences. The major similarity is that 60 per cent of beer sales are made through supermarkets for consumption in the home. The German brewers sell and deliver direct to the supermarket chains. It is estimated that 60 per cent of all beer sales across Europe are now made through supermarkets. The remaining 40 per cent of German beer sales are sold through cafés, bars, hotels and restaurants.

Where Germany differs from the rest of Europe, with the exception of the UK, is that about 22 per cent of cafés and bars are owned by the breweries. In addition, many cafés and bars that are not owned directly by the breweries have agreements with breweries to sell only their products in return for cheap loans. It is a strategy which helps breweries to maintain a strong hold in their local market place.

A DESCRIPTION OF MAJOR EUROPEAN BREWERS

Heineken

The Dutch brewer Heineken is essentially a family controlled business, with the family holding 51 per cent of its shares. With more than 90 breweries worldwide, Heineken is the second largest brewer in the world and the most international, with activities in every continent. It is possible to buy Heineken in 150 countries.

The main area of activity is Europe, where Heineken is the leading beer brand. It is also the biggest import beer brand in the United States – its biggest market outside Europe. Current estimates suggest that the USA accounts for 6 per cent of total production and 30 per cent of profits. In 1993 Heineken sold over 60 million hectolitres of beer worldwide.

Due to the small size of its home market, Heineken began international operations as early as 1928, although the major move towards internationalisation took place in the 1980s with a series of acquisitions in France, Spain, Italy and Greece. In the UK, Whitbread brews 2.6 million hectolitres of Heineken beer under licence. In 1996 Heineken owned 1 per

Exhibit 16 **Financial history of Heineken, 1990–5 (millions of guilders)**

	1995	1994	1993	1992	1991	1990
Turnover	10,443	9,974	9,049	8,944	8,696	8,210
Operating profit	1,006	895	798	733	730	613
Net profit	664	662	519	463	410	366
Total assets	9,641	8,919	8,132	7,834	7,925	7,484

Note Exchange rate, August 1996: £1 = 2.55 guilders.

Source Company annual reports.

cent of Whitbread and had a seat on the board. The company's international brands are Heineken, Amstel, Buckler and Murphy's Irish Stout. They play a central role in the brand policy and are supported by a large number of national brands.

In eastern Europe, Heineken is developing activities to increase brand awareness and the distribution of Heineken beer. Despite the difficult economic situation during the early 1990s, Heineken exports show a sizeable growth, though the volumes are still modest. In 1994 Heineken bought a 25 per cent stake in the Polish brewer, Zywiec Brewing, to facilitate the introduction of Heineken in Poland, and increased its stake in the Hungarian brewer, Komaromi Sorgyar, from 55 to 100 per cent following considerable rises in its sales. Also in 1994, Heineken boosted its stake in El Aguila, the Spanish brewer, from 51 to 65 per cent. In 1995 Heineken bought Interbrew Italia, a subsidiary of the Belgian brewer Interbrew, which raised its share of the Italian beer market to 30 per cent. Heineken is also looking to expand its operations in the Far East and South America.

The financial history of Heineken between 1990 and 1996 is summarised in Exhibit 16.

Carlsberg

Carlsberg is the second most international brewer in the world after Heineken, with operations in 38 countries selling more than 80 per cent of its beer outside its home market of Denmark.

Carlsberg sought international expansion for the same reasons as Heineken, i.e. the small size of its domestic market. In the UK Carlsberg-Tetley, the 50/50 joint venture with Allied Lyons, became operative at the turn of 1992/3 after a lengthy approval process by the British authorities and the European Commission. Carlsberg has a 5.6 per cent share of the UK market.

Exhibit 17 **Financial history of Carlsberg, 1990–5 (millions of kroner)**

	1994/5	1993/4	1992/3	1991/2	1990/1
Turnover	17,072	16,919	15,595	14,957	14,462
Operating profit	1,203	1,153	1,086	1,161	957
Net profit*	1,003	802	910	854	802
Total assets	18,599	18,018	17,798	14,921	13,108

*After minority shareholders' share of profit in subsidiaries.
Note Exchange rate, August 1996: £1 = 8.88 kroner.

Source Company annual reports.

Carlsberg's most significant businesses outside Europe are in Hong Kong, where it has 15–17 per cent of the market, and Malaysia, where its share exceeds 50 per cent. Exposure is also strong in the remainder of the Far East, with further breweries soon to open in Thailand and China. Carlsberg brews about 0.5 million hectolitres in Africa.

The largest shareholder in the company is the Carlsberg Foundation, which is pledged to possess a minimum of 51 per cent of the shares. The Danish Labour Market Supplementary Pension Scheme accounts for more than 10 per cent of the shares and the Tuborg Foundation has 6 per cent.

The Carlsberg Foundation was established by Carlsberg's founder in 1876 and its income goes to support Danish natural and social sciences as well as the humanities. In 1991 the Carlsberg and Tuborg Foundations merged in order to improve Carlsberg's ability to raise new capital.

Carlsberg derives approximately 30 per cent of sales from non-beer-related activities. These include wines and spirits, soft drinks, supplying complete processing plants to the beverage and food industries, and Royal Copenhagen, which manufactures and sells porcelain, glassware, silverware and plastic and glass packaging.

The financial history of Carlsberg between 1990 and 1995 is summarised in Exhibit 17.

Grolsch

Grolsch is a 'super premium' niche brewer, selling its Grolsch product in draught and in the very distinctive and identifiable swing-top resealable bottles in its primary market of north-west Europe. Grolsch is one of the leading brewing groups in Holland, where it has a market share of 17 per cent. In 1994 it was estimated to have produced 2.1 million hectolitres of beer. Its reputation for product differentiation was enhanced by the recent introduction of Grolsch Special Malt and Grolsch Meibok.

Exhibit 18 **Financial history of Grolsch, 1990–5 (millions of guilders)**

	1995	1994	1993	1992	1991	1990
Turnover	630.5	554.1	793.5	866.7	791.5	793.5
Operating profit	88.4	80.2	65.6	64.3	55.7	48.9
Net profit	58.8	52.4	43.5	43.4	41.9	37.9
Total assets	545.4	523.7	675.6	635.4	704.1	430.4

Note Exchange rate, August 1996: £1 = 2.55 guilders.

Source Company annual reports.

Grolsch began exporting in the mid-1970s for two reasons – the small size of the Dutch market and its dominance by Heineken. Exports increased from 14 per cent in 1985 to 31 per cent in 1989. However, export sales represent only 20 per cent of Grolsch's volume, showing the higher-price premium it can command in overseas markets.

Its principal foreign markets are the USA and the UK, estimated at 25 and 40 per cent of its export volume respectively, but it is available in a total of 35 markets worldwide. Duty-free sales are estimated to account for another 25 per cent of sales by volume.

In 1991 Grolsch acquired Germany's Rheinisch-Bergischen Brauerei, doubling its sales. However, this was sold on to the German brewer Bräu und Brunnen AG in 1994, which then signed a distribution agreement for Grolsch's products, giving Grolsch entry to 6,000 cafés across Germany.

In 1992 Grolsch purchased the Ruddles real ale brand and brewery from Courage for £40 million. The move was part of a strategy to create a 'Europe of Brands', as opposed to one pan-European brand, and to develop a strong north-west European brewing group.

In 1994 Grolsch set up a distribution joint venture with Bass, then the UK's largest brewer, to boost sales in Britain and Ireland. This gave Bass the right to produce Grolsch beer locally, although not in Grolsch's trademark swing-top bottles. The move was a departure for Grolsch, which had previously been keen to set itself apart in the UK by being a foreign-brewed beer. This venture, coupled with the Bräu und Brunnen distribution deal in Germany, was predicted to lead to significant improvement in the company's results. Its next marketing thrust will be to further its market penetration in southern and eastern Europe.

The first three brewing companies we have considered have beer as their principal activity. For the next two – Bass and Danone – beer is only a constituent part of a range of diverse activities. However, the brewing activities are significant on a European scale.

The financial history of Grolsch between 1990 and 1995 is summarised in Exhibit 18.

Exhibit 19 **Financial history of Bass, 1990–5 (£m)**

	1995	1994	1993	1992	1991	1990
Turnover	4,541	4,452	4,451	4,307	4,383	4,461
of which:						
Brewing	1,251	1,295	1,202	1,191	1,056	929
Pub retailing	1,121	1,079	1,024	1,100	1,173	1,089
Operating profit	672	633	603	602	616	673
of which:						
Brewing	144	140	154	173	148	177
Pub retailing	240	220	205	218	238	245
Net profit	396	364	329	318	263	216
Total assets	3,697	3,582	3,413	3,343	3,622	2,935

Source Company annual reports.

Bass

Bass is one of the leading brewing companies in Europe, and in 1994 had a market share of 23 per cent in the UK. Bass reorganised in 1989 to a divisional structure separating brewing and pub retailing, primarily to comply with the UK's Monopolies and Mergers Commission directives. In 1996 there were five divisions:

- Bass Brewers – which owns and markets a portfolio of brands of beer.
- Bass Taverns – the leading UK pub retailer with 4,200 outlets.
- Britvic Soft Drinks – a soft drinks company with brands such as Pepsi, Tango and 7-Up.
- Holiday Inn – the single largest hotel brand in the world, with more than 1,770 hotels and 338,000 guest rooms.
- Bass Leisure – one of the UK's leading leisure retailers, with bingo, betting and bowling operations.

Bass Brewers has strengthened its market share by targeting the fast-growing take-home sector in the UK, and by increasing sales to the free on-trade, including the emerging chains of pub multiples. In 1993 Bass successfully launched a number of new brands, including premium lagers such as TAG, Zeiss and Carling XD, an extra-dry bottled lager.

In the same year, Bass Brewers acquired a 34 per cent share in Prague Breweries, the second largest brewer in the Czech Republic, and increased its shareholding further in 1995 – a year which also saw the company take a majority stake in two further Czech brewers and the setting up of a brewing joint venture in northern China. Bass also took up its option to brew Grolsch in the UK, although the flip-top bottled version was still to be imported from Holland.

In early 1996, Bass entered into negotiations with Allied Domecq concerning the possible acquisition of the latter's 50 per cent stake in Carlsberg-Tetley. This deal which would give Bass around 38 per cent of the UK beer market and make it the largest brewer in the UK – a position lost when Scottish and Newcastle bought Courage in 1995.

The financial history of Bass between 1990 and 1995 is summarised in Exhibit 19.

Danone Group

Danone changed its name from BSN in 1994 and is France's largest consumer product company and Europe's largest mineral water, dairy products, glass bottle and biscuit company, with significant positions in beer, pasta and champagne.

Danone's beer division accounted for only 9 per cent of the group's total sales in 1993. Total production was 26.7 million hectolitres in that year, placing it third in Europe after Heineken and Carlsberg and making it the eleventh largest brewer in the world.

Its principal brands are Kronenbourg, Kanterbräu, 1664 and Tourtel, a no-alcohol beer. Since the mid-1980s it has promoted these brands as pan-European. However, France remains the main area of operations, accounting for 46 per cent of group sales. Danone has almost a 50 per cent market share, double that of Heineken, its nearest rival. Its Kronenbourg and 1664 brands have benefited significantly from the trend towards premium beers. It has also been successful with its light beer, Kronenbourg Light, and Tourtel, its no-alcohol beer, which together now account for 400,000 hectolitres of production. In 1990 it introduced 1664 Brune, a dark beer to complement the traditional 'blond' 1664. The end of 1993 brought a string of new product launches, which included Kronenbourg Tradition Allemande, Kronenbourg Tradition Anglaise and Wel Scotch, the last based on whisky malt.

Danone brews approximately 16.5 million hectolitres outside France, principally in Italy, Spain, Belgium and Greece. In Italy it merged its interests with Peroni, giving it a share in 4.9 million hectolitres of production or nearly 40 per cent of the market. In Spain the company owns one-third of Mahou, which produced 4.2 million hectolitres in 1993 and has an efficient distribution system concentrating on the Madrid area. In Belgium it has an 85 per cent stake in Alken-Maes, which sells 1.2 million hectolitres. This is equivalent to a 17 per cent market share, in a market which is dominated by Interbrew with a 60 per cent share.

In 1989 Danone entered the Greek market with the acquisition of a 19 per cent stake in Northern Breweries, formerly known as Henninger Hellas.

Exhibit 20 **Financial history of Danone, 1990–5 (millions of FF)**

	1996	1995	1994	1993	1992	1991	1990
Turnover	83,940	79,450	76,820	70,108	70,840	66,069	52,897
of which:							
Brewing	7,543	7,423	7,222	6,395	6,552	6,599	6,598
Operating profit	7,478	7,018	6,832	6,351	7,117	6,701	5,675
of which:							
Brewing	885	973	912	808	899	806	843
Net profit	3,382	2,133	3,527	3,422	3,638	3,445	3,091
Total assets	100,871	93,233	87,181	78,777	71,712	70,188	59,303

Note Exchange rate, August 1996: $1 = FF7.74.

Source Company annual reports.

With 1.1 million hectolitres of production or a 27 per cent market share, Danone is well behind Heineken's share of 65 per cent. Northern has three breweries and some rationalisation may be needed. Danone's other major brewing business in Europe is the licence of the Kronenbourg brand to Courage in the UK, which in 1994 accounted for 700,000 hectolitres of production.

The financial history of Danone between 1990 and 1996 is summarised in Exhibit 20.

BRASSERIES KRONENBOURG

Roland Calori and Philippe Monin

This case study describes the strategy of Brasseries Kronenbourg, the main company in the Beer Division of the French group Danone. Brasseries Kronenbourg and the other breweries where Danone had dominant stakes were the second largest in Europe, behind Heineken. The case focuses on the international strategy and the organisation of Kronenbourg. This includes international acquisitions and expansion in the context of a fragmented multi-domestic industry. The case also gives an illustration of the complex nature of international operations in the company.

• • •

THE COMPANY

In 1994 Kronenbourg SA was number two in the European beer market. Kronenbourg SA was the holding company of the beer division of the Groupe Danone, and Brasseries Kronenbourg was the main department of the beer division based in Alsace, a region with a strong brewing tradition.

Brasseries Kronenbourg had been formed from the merger of Kronenbourg and Kanterbräu, two companies acquired by the BSN Group (the former name of Danone) in the 1970s. By 1986 the two firms shared their production units, functional departments (human resources, administration and finance) and top management. In 1994 the two marketing departments and sales forces were merged, and Brasseries Kronenbourg produced and marketed a unified set of 28 brands.

By 1994 Brasseries Kronenbourg had a strong leadership position in the French market, with over 40 per cent market share. The number two was Brasseries Heineken with 23.1 per cent; third was the Belgian Interbrew-Stella with 8.3 per cent; and number four was Fischer (a French

---

This case study was prepared by Roland Calori and Philippe Monin, professors at the Groupe ESC Lyon. The authors would like to thank the Brasseries Kronenbourg for their assistance in the writing of this case study. It is intended as a basis for class discussion and not as an illustration of either good or bad management practice.

Exhibit 1 Kronenbourg SA: balance sheets and statements of income (simplified)

(SIMPLIFIED) balance sheets (FF000)

	1994	1993	1992
Assets			
Net property plant, equipment and intangible assets	1,885,533	1,899,148	1,971,609
Financial assets	2,727,774	2,632,093	2,350,600
Current assets	1,795,484	1,689,190	1,677,479
Miscellaneous	7,568	12,131	15,422
Total assets	6,416,359	6,232,562	6,015,110
Liabilities			
Equity	2,103,721	2,126,514	2,085,827
Provisions	101,982	136,690	199,031
Debts	4,087,379	3,856,620	3,627,541
Miscellaneous	123,277	112,738	102,711
Total liabilities	6,416,359	6,232,562	6,015,110

(SIMPLIFIED) statements of income (FF000)

	1994	1993	1992
Net sales	5,709,108	5,838,607	5,926,784
Operating costs and expenses	4,814,146	5,029,719	5,111,258
Operating profit*	894,962	808,888	815,526
Net profits	496,038	456,898	428,942

*Before financial revenues and expenses, before extraordinary items and before income tax.

Source Annual reports, 1993, 1994.

independent firm) with 7.7 per cent of the market (19 other brewers shared the rest of the market).

In 1994 the French market represented 22.7 million hectolitres, including 1.5 million hectolitres bought by British citizens crossing the Channel to buy cheaper beer in France and on the cross-Channel ferries (due to lower taxation). According to the Nielsen panel, such cross-border trade was increasing (it was estimated at around 0.8 million hectolitres in 1993), while French consumption was decreasing (21.9 million hectolitres in 1993, 21.2 million hectolitres in 1994).

Kronenbourg beer was also produced under licence in the UK and in Ireland, although production under licence in Africa (about 1 million hectolitres in Congo and Nigeria) ceased in 1994. Through Kronenbourg SA, Danone was also represented in several other European markets and its beer brands were distributed in 80 countries in the world. In 1994, the

Exhibit 2 **Volumes sold by Brasseries Kronenbourg and other companies under control of Kronenbourg SA (hectolitres, beer)**

	1994	1993	1990
Brasseries Kronenbourg			
France	9,733,000	9,838,000	10,698,000
(incl. Kronenbourg)		(6,400,000)	(6,769,000)
(incl. Kanterbraü)		(3,438,000)	(3,929,000)
Direct export sales*	541,000	510,000	873,541
Total	10,274,000	10,348,000	11,571,541
Production under licence abroad	766,000 (UK and Ireland)	1,095,000 (UK, Ireland and Nigeria)	1,030,000 (UK and Nigeria)
Subsidiaries and companies in which Kronenbourg was a significant stakeholder			
Alken-Maes (Belgium)	2,167,000	2,010,000	2,377,000
Peroni (Italy)	4,549,000	4,522,000	5,369,000
Mahou (Spain)	4,366,000	4,196,000	4,316,000
San Miguel (Spain)	3,516,000	3,527,000	–
Northern Breweries (Greece)	520,000	491,000	617,000
Congolaise de Brasseries		577,000	368,000
Total	15,118,000	15,323,000	13,047,000

* Including Switzerland: 110,000 hl; Spain: 10,000 hl; Germany: 6,000 hl; Belgium: 5,000 hl; USA: 5,000 hl, etc.

Source Annual reports, 1990, 1993, 1994.

volume sold by the breweries in which Danone had dominant or significant stakes was around 26 million hectolitres.

The turnover and sales volumes of Brasseries Kronenbourg itself are shown in Exhibits 1 and 2. In France the original brands from Kronenbourg represented about two-thirds of sales and those from Kanterbräu about one-third.

At the beginning of the 1990s, some of the foreign breweries controlled by Danone started to brew locally the international brands of Brasseries Kronenbourg: for instance, Tourtel and Kronenbourg were brewed in Italy and in Spain (by San Miguel) and 1664 was brewed locally in Italy. (This evolution explains the decrease of direct export sales as compared to 1990.) The Kronenbourg 1664 upmarket beer and Tourtel (a non-alcoholic beer) were particularly successful. However, during this period, the market share of Kronenbourg SA in France decreased slightly (from 43.5 per cent to 42.9 per cent), whereas the share of private labels increased, particularly in the mass market. Indeed, all the major beer brands suffered from the growing power of food retail chains.

In 1994 Brasseries Kronenbourg invested FF292 million in industrial plant and equipment to modernise production sites, improve productivity and launch new packaging. Financial investment amounted to FF292.6 million in 1993, in order to increase the shares of the group in the companies under its control and to take over wholesalers. In 1994 the holding company of the beer division started to increase its shares in the Spanish brewery San Miguel, so as to hold 100 per cent of the equity by the end of 1997 (i.e. a financial investment of FF2 billion in four years 1994–7). By completing this acquisition, Danone (which already had a minority stake in Mahou) will become the leader on the Spanish beer market. At the end of 1994 some important commercial investments were made in order to merge the sales forces of Kanterbräu and Kronenbourg and sell a unified product range.

KRONENBOURG, THE BEER DIVISION AND THE DANONE GROUP

BSN (the former name of the Danone Group) was primarily a glass manufacturer when it acquired Kronenbourg in 1970. The BSN Group then began a radical diversification from glass making to the food and drinks industries. In 1973 it acquired Gervais Danone, a major dairy products business, followed by other food companies. From FF300 million in 1966, the turnover of the group went up to about FF53 billion in 1990, and FF76.82 billion in 1994 (packaging representing 8.1 per cent). Exhibit 3 breaks down the sales turnover and the operating income of the Danone Group by division and geographical zone.

The goal of Antoine Riboud, président directeur général of the group, was to become the leader or the number two in each area of business, first at the European level, then at the world level. The stated strategy of Danone was:

- to strengthen the leadership in Europe in growth business (such as *plats cuisinés)*;
- to accelerate international extension;
- to innovate and strengthen the corporate image.

At the end of 1990, Danone sold its champagne business, Lanson and Pommery, to LVMH for FF3.1 billion in order to focus on the businesses in which leadership or number two positions could be reached. By 1995 Danone was the third leading food marketer in Europe, challenging Nestlé and Unilever. It was also the world's largest seller of dairy products (under

Exhibit 3 **Sales turnover and operating income, Danone Group (1992–4), by division and by geographical zone (FF000,000)**

	Sales turnover			Operating profits		
	1994	1993	1992	1994	1993	1992
Europe						
• Dairy products	22,624	22,067	23,041	2,181	2,123	2,412
• Epicerie, pasta	14,689	13,142	13,081	940	970	1,027
• Biscuits	12,837	12,949	13,457	807	862	1,126
• Beer	7,222	6,395	6,552	912	808	899
• Mineral waters	7,000	5,898	5,716	1,060	955	898
• Packaging	6,368	6,663	7,046	624	556	730
Total Europe	70,740	67,114	68,893	6,524	6,224	7,092
International	7,804	4,608	3,605	387	180	111
Internal sales	(1,724)	(1,614)	(1,658)			
Other profits				(79)	(103)	(86)
Group total	76,820	70,108	70,840	6,832	6,351	7,117

the Danone brand and with Galbani Italian cheeses); the second in the world for mineral waters (Evian, Volvic, Badoit, Lanjaron), pasta sales (Panzani) and biscuits (Lu, Jacob's, leader in Europe and in Asia); the leader in Europe in sauces and condiments (Amora, Maille); the number two in Europe in the beer industry and in the glass packaging business (bottles and pots); and the number three in Europe in *plats cuisinés* (Vivagel).

Danone was the biggest food marketer in France, in Italy and in Spain, and the number six worldwide. The international division (i.e. outside Europe, cf. Exhibit 3) included businesses and exports in Asia, Oceania, America and Africa which represented about 10 per cent of the total sales turnover in 1994 and showed high growth potential.

Between January 1993 and June 1995, Danone acquired a number of food and drink concerns worldwide. The most significant acquisitions included: Bagley (biscuits, Argentina), Campineira de Alimentos (biscuits, Brazil), Vivagel (*plats cuisinés*, France), Serdika (joint venture, dairy products, Bulgaria), Keletpest BTV (dairy products, Hungary), Bolshevik (biscuits, Russia), Britannia Group (biscuits, Asia), Aquaterra (mineral waters, Canada), Bonafont (mineral waters, Mexico), San Miguel (beer, Spain), Aguas de Lanjaron (mineral waters, Spain), Volvic (mineral waters, France), Deslile (dairy products, Canada) and Jiangmen (biscuits, China). Franchise agreements were also signed in Malaysia and Singapore in order to develop the Danone brand locally.

The year was 1994 when the group changed its name to Danone: 'Our image will benefit from the influence of our most global brand, a symbol of quality, innovation, taste and health' (Antoine Riboud, Assemblée Génralée Ordinaire, July 1994).

Belonging to a large, diversified group meant shared responsibilities between the headquarters and the companies. Antoine Riboud explained the relationships in *Le Figaro* (9 September 1991):

> You have to limit the number of hierarchical levels, avoid complicated procedures, avoid barriers to the free circulation of information, cash flow and people. You have to delegate operational decisions. At BSN [Danone] the managers of divisions and departments are free with regard to the management of operations, but each one knows his limits. On the other hand, strategy must be centralised, it is the responsibility of the 'Premier Rond' of BSN [Danone].

The 'Premier Rond' of Danone consisted of Antoine Riboud (président), the vice-president and chief executive (Franck Riboud) and three vice-chief executives. The 'Deuxième Rond' consisted of the managers of the product divisions (among whom was the manager of the beer division), three regional managers (Asia, America-Africa-Oceania and exportation), and two functional managers (finance and human relations). The 'Troisième Rond' included 86 general managers of the departments and of the subsidiaries of the group, among them the managing director of Brasseries Kronenbourg.

Each year, the managing director of each department/company in the group presented the previous year's results and the future scenarios for the company to the Premier Rond. The Premier Rond responded with general objectives for the coming year. It was then the responsibility of the manager of the corresponding division to monitor the achievement of the objectives of the department. The headquarters left the managing directors of departments/companies free to manage their businesses, as long as the objectives were achieved. In the beer division, Brasseries Kronenbourg in France, Alken-Maes in Belgium, and Mahou and San Miguel in Spain were four departments. The participations in Peroni (Italy) and Northern Breweries (Greece) were managed directly by the director of the beer division.

Even the companies in which Danone did not have a dominant financial stake participated in the Danone planning system. The division level helped in restructuring companies joining the group when needed, and was also in charge of transferring skills between the departments.

In 1994 Danone employed 68,181 persons. The management style of the group, personified by Antoine Riboud, also influenced Kronenbourg. The cornerstone of this philosophy was a double economic and social intent: *Pas d'économie sans social, pas de social sans économie*. Indeed, the group won the Palme d'Or for the best corporate institutional image among managers in an Ipsos-L'Expansion study conducted in 1990 in France. 'Dialogue' at work and with strong unions, 'participation of the personnel in the profits of the firm' and 'mutual support' were the key characteristics of the management at Danone.

THE STRATEGY OF BRASSERIES KRONENBOURG

The top management of Brasseries Kronenbourg saw brewing as a 'heavy industry' with the emphasis on the capacity of production units and increasing capital intensity due to the development of automatic processing. They therefore believed that there were three key success factors for the business:

- Managing the high level of investments with a tight control of the debt/equity ratio.
- The achievements of economies of scale – the high level of fixed costs required a focus on lower production costs through larger units to cover bigger geographical areas (up to 1,000 km for mass-market beer).
- Improvements in productivity and quality through effective human resource management to keep up with new techniques (e.g. automation and quality control).

The management of inventories and production planning were also seen as critical functions, as beer consumption was seasonal, especially in southern Europe.

Compared to many other food-processing businesses, the beer industry dealt with two distinct distribution channels: cafés and restaurants; and food retailing for home consumption. Each distribution channel required a specific approach.

The food channel was taking an increasing share of the market: 58 per cent in 1990 and 62.8 per cent in 1994, 70 per cent of which was through the major retail chains. Dealing with the food channel, especially with large retail chains, demanded both high expenditure and management skills in advertising and merchandising. Brasseries Kronenbourg had strengthened partnerships by developing a merchandising system, called 'Pluton', that improved the presentation of beers and adapted it to each retail chain, each region and each season.

Selling to cafés, hotels and restaurants (37.2 per cent of the French market in 1994) required investment in the place of consumption, and long-term contracts were concluded with cafés. This channel offered higher margins and an opportunity to advertise beer brands – the main opportunity in France since the Loi Evin forbade advertising of alcoholic drinks in most other places. The distribution to the 150,000 sales points was done by wholesalers (*entrepositaires*), a profession which had undergone a high concentration (about 1,000 wholesalers in 1994 compared to 2,000 in 1985). In order to strengthen their positions and increase their market share, Kronenbourg and other brewers had started to develop downstream activities in wholesaling. For instance, in its division France Boissons, Heineken had a particularly strong distribution network of 35 wholesaling subsidiaries and 70 warehouses. Merging the sales forces and commercial assets of Kronenbourg and Kanterbräu contributed to a better positioning of brands and a more effective distribution in the traditional channel. Since 1993, through a wholly owned subsidiary, Elidis, Brasseries Kronenbourg had acquired 60 warehouses (half of which were wholly owned). In 1994 Elidis distributed about 20 per cent of the volumes sold to cafés and restaurants. Elidis and France Boissons had a reciprocal distribution agreement of their respective ranges of bottled beer, in order to complement their coverage of the French territory.

In both channels the image of the product and the brand name were viewed as key success factors, and marketing skills and financial support were seen as critical to strengthen and expand the brand image. Finally, in order to grow in a mature market and to cover the company's high fixed costs, international development was considered crucial.

PRODUCTIVITY, QUALITY AND HUMAN RESOURCE DEVELOPMENT

One of the objectives of Brasseries Kronenbourg was to be among the best brewers in the world in terms of productivity; this was vital given overcapacity of around 30 per cent in the industry. High investments in automation were made during the 1980s. Between 1989 and 1991 a *restructuration* plan was implemented to improve productivity. Staffing levels were reduced by 570 jobs during this period,[1] mostly by voluntary departures (an agreement was signed between the top management and the unions to organise the re-employment of the workers).

The number of hierarchical levels was also reduced. At the same time, professional development was strengthened, and Brasseries Kronenbourg became involved in an extensive qualification and apprenticeship programme for young people. Personnel training represented 3.5 per cent of the wages, and the company distributed FF130 million to the personnel *au titre de la participation des salariés aux fruits de l'expansion* (shares) in 1994.

MARKETING, INNOVATION AND IMAGE

The company strategy was to develop several brands, to address all the market segments according to quality and alcohol levels.

[1] In 1994 Brasseries Kronenbourg employed 2,127 persons (53 per cent in production; 30 per cent technicians, supervisors and administrative staff; and 17 per cent managers).

1. *Bières de luxe* for the mass market represented 64 per cent of the total French market (branded beers 39 per cent and lower-priced products and beer sold under retailers' names about 25 per cent).[2] Brasseries Kronenbourg dominated this segment in France, with two labels: Kronenbourg and Kanterbräu (which amounted to 70.9 per cent of the sales turnover of the company in 1994). The main competitor was the 33 Export from Heineken. However, the competition from lower-priced retail private labels at one end and from upmarket *bières spéciales* at the other end was increasing. Brasseries Kronenbourg responded by launching new products and labels such as Kronenbourg Tradition Allemande, Kronenbourg Tradition Anglaise, 'K' and new packaging. Brasseries Kronenbourg also brewed beer for a major French retail chain (about 600,000 hectolitres a year) selling under private label.

    According to the top management of Brasseries Kronenbourg, there was a particular phenomenon in the brewing industry: a beer positioned in the mass market in its country of origin tended to become an upmarket beer in the foreign countries to which it was exported. For instance, Heineken was seen as a *bière spéciale* in France (competing with Kronenbourg's 1664), and Kronenbourg was seen as an upmarket beer in several foreign countries. Actually the differences between the two products (in terms of taste and quality) were minimal.
2. Upmarket beers, *spéciales* and *spécialités*, together represented 21 per cent of the French market (of which about two-thirds were *spéciales* and one-third *spécialités*), and 21.7 per cent of the sales turnover of Brasseries Kronenbourg in 1994. The company had two *bières spéciales* – 1664 from Kronenbourg and Gold from Kanterbräu – and imported Carlsberg in France. *Spécialités*, even further upmarket, included beers with higher levels of alcohol and premium imported foreign beers. The demand for *spécialités* was growing rapidly. Brasseries Kronenbourg distributed some Belgian beers produced by Alken-Maes – Blanche de Bruges, Mort Subite and Grimbergen. It also imported Guinness stouts and Kilkenny, and launched a new product in 1994: Wel Scotch (a whisky malt beer). Kronenbourg 1664 was seen as a premium beer in foreign countries.
3. Non-alcoholic beer had developed rapidly in Europe in the late 1980s, but by 1994 it had reached maturity, representing 5 per cent of the market. Brasseries Kronenbourg was the leader in France, Belgium and Italy with its brands Tourtel (originally from Kanterbräu, with sales of around 1 million hectolitres) and Silver (originally from Kronenbourg, launched in 1991). This segment was characterised by being more international or pan-European, and Brasseries Kronenbourg competed with the Buckler brand from Heineken.
4. Low-alcoholic beer or 'light beer' represented about 5 per cent of the market. Brasseries Kronenbourg had two brands: Kronenbourg Light and Obernai.

---

[2] Percentages are estimations of volumes sold.

Exhibit 4 Main product lines and brands of the Brasseries Kronenbourg

SEGMENTS	BRANDS	
Main product lines and brands sold on the French market		
Bières de luxe	Kronenbourg	Kanterbräu
(mass market)	K	
	Kronenbourg Tradition Anglaise	
	Kronenbourg Tradition Allemande	
Bières spéciales	1664 Blond	Gold
	1664 Brune	
Spécialités	Blanche de Bruges	Grimbergen
		Mort Subite
		Wel Scotch
Non-alcoholic beer	Silver	Tourtel
Light beer	Kronenbourg Light	
	Obernai	
Panachés	Force 4	Chopp
	Force 4 lemon	
Other imported beers	Carlsberg (*spéciale*)	
	Guinness (*spécialité*)	
	Kilkenny (*spécialité*)	
Main products/brands sold on foreign markets by direct exportation or through the foreign companies controlled by the group		
Spéciale	Kronenbourg	
Spécialité	(Kronenbourg) 1664	
Non-alcoholic beer	Tourtel	

5. *Panachés* were a mix of beer and lemonade, and they represented about 5 per cent of the French market. Brasseries Kronenbourg had two brands – Force 4 and Chopp, competing with Panach from Heineken.

Non-alcoholic beer, light beer and *panachés* amounted to 7.4 per cent of the sales turnover of Brasseries Kronenbourg in 1994. Exhibit 4 summarises the main products and brands of the company.

Product innovation was seen as important in Brasseries Kronenbourg. Tourtel was the first non-alcoholic beer launched in the European market, and Kanterbräu was the first to expand the range of non-alcoholic beers to dark beer with Tourtel Brune (1989), Tourtel Ambrée (1990) and Tourtel 100% pure malt (1994). In 1993 and 1994 Brasseries Kronenbourg launched several new products in order to 'de-banalise' beer in the French mass market: Kronenbourg brewed in the German tradition, Kronenbourg brewed in the English tradition, and Christmas beer. These were followed in 1995 by a non-bitter beer called 'K' (Mexican style).

Innovations in packaging were also seen as important. For instance, Kronenbourg had won an award for packaging with its 'prestige' bottle for cafés and restaurants – thin, with angles and an encrusted label, and preserving the brilliance of the glass after several uses. It had also equipped its bottles of 1664 with a label that changed colour when the optimal consumption temperature was reached. Moreover, it adopted a variety of presentations (bottles and packaging) for the French market and for the international market. This policy was supported by the links with the packaging division of the Danone Group.

From 1993 in France, the *Loi Evin* limited advertising of alcoholic drinks, TV advertising was forbidden, radio advertising was restricted to a few hours a day, press advertising was only permitted in magazines for adults, and street advertising was forbidden in many areas. Most of the other markets in Europe had less strict limitations. As a consequence, Brasseries Kronenbourg strengthened the promotion of its products in the cafés, and developed sponsoring to support its non-alcoholic brands (Tourtel and Force 4) with two main partners, the Paris Saint Germain and the Strasbourg football teams. The advertising campaigns for these products were based on conviviality. The concern for ecological issues also contributed to the company's image: 80 per cent of the bottles were made of recycled glass and Kronenbourg had the world record for low water consumption.

THE INTERNATIONAL STRATEGY OF BRASSERIES KRONENBOURG AND THE BEER DIVISION OF DANONE

Given high relative costs of transportation and logistics and high marketing expenses, the geographical scope of the market was seen as limited around a production unit. The case of upmarket beers (at the top of the pyramid) was different: the higher margins of the premium products would cover the costs of distribution logistics and marketing. So Brasseries Kronenbourg started to export its premium products in the 1960s, selling to local importers and distributors, complementing their range of drinks to be sold mainly in the cafés, hotels and restaurants. This export mode was still employed in 1990 in the case of more distant foreign countries such as Japan, Hong Kong, Australia, Canada and Sweden.

However, this strategy would not lead to high volume, and volume sales required a significant position in a foreign market, a broader range of products, including lower-priced beers, and therefore higher costs of distribution and marketing. Given the overcapacity in the beer industry, the executives from Brasseries Kronenbourg believed that partnerships and acquisitions were the best way quickly to achieve a significant position in a foreign market.

As far as licences were concerned, Brasseries Kronenbourg had established a position in the United Kingdom by entering into a production agreement with Courage when the British market started to consume more and more Continental/international lagers and reduce its consumption of traditional ale. The volumes of Kro 1664, a specific beer for the British market, increased to 766,000 hectolitres in 1994.

This strategy of entering into partnerships with other strong local breweries was also employed in Italy, Belgium, Spain and Greece. Several criteria were considered to select the priority countries for international development:

- A permeable upmarket segment.
- Growing demand for beer.
- Signs that the competitive structure of the industry might be beginning to concentrate.

The Mediterranean countries were typically in this situation at the end of the 1970s, and it was regarded as a priority to establish a position in these countries before international competitors did so.

The selection of the brands that Brasseries Kronenbourg would make international was based on the success of the brand in its home market. The leading brands in France were selected: namely, Kronenbourg (including 1664) and Tourtel. Selectivity was crucial because it was recognised that developing an international brand would require very high marketing investments. The formula applied to dealing with the product range overseas was to keep the strongest local brands of the partner (or the acquired company), but to add the Kronenbourg, 1664 and Tourtel brands from Brasseries Kronenbourg to the product range of the local partner, positioning them as upmarket beers.

In Italy, Kronenbourg SA first took control of Wührer, which had a 10 per cent market share and was particularly well established in the north of Italy. However, Peroni was the market leader and well established in the south. BSN arranged the merger of Wührer and Peroni, Kronenbourg SA having a 25 per cent stake in the company. Between 1991 and 1994 the Italian market stagnated (with good years and bad years). Peroni maintained its leadership position with a 40 per cent market share, sales around 4.5 million hectolitres a year, and a turnover around 470 billion lire. In 1994 Peroni sold four main brands: Peroni (mass-market), Nastro Azzuro (an Italian premium beer), Kronenbourg (with increasing sales) and Tourtel (the leading brand among non-alcoholic beers). By 1995 the Italian market had become very competitive, and large European brewers were involved in negotiations to strengthen their positions. For instance, Heineken increased its market share from 23 per cent to 30 per cent by taking over the Italian subsidiary of Interbrew.

The market in Belgium was nearly as big as the Italian market, due to a high consumption of beer per capita, but it was slowly decreasing. Kronenbourg SA first took control of Alken and of Anglo Belge, which together held 10 per cent of the market. Then, in 1988, a joint venture with Maes gave a 25 per cent share of the market to Alken-Maes, in which Kronenbourg SA had 50 per cent of the capital. In 1993 Kronenbourg SA increased its participation to 84.7 per cent. Interbrew (created after the merger of Stella Artois and Jupiter) was the leader in Belgium with a 50 per cent market share. Alken-Maes was number two with sales of 2.2 million hectolitres and a turnover of BF6,086 million in 1994. The company had a broad portfolio of brands: Maes on the mass market, Tourtel, and many Belgian specialities such as Blanche de Bruges, Grimbergen, Gueuze and Krick Mort Subite, Cristal, and Cuvée l'Ermitage. Exports of these *spécialités* were rapidly growing (18 per cent in 1994).

Spanish consumption had regularly increased by 3–4 per cent a year in the 1980s. From 72 litres per person per year in 1989, experts forecasted consumption of 100 litres per person per year by the end of the century. Actually, the consumption stopped growing at the beginning of the 1990s. Several major European competitors had taken over Spanish breweries and brands. Heineken was number three with its subsidiary El Aguila (17.3 per cent market share in 1993). Guinness was number two with its wholly owned subsidiary, Cruzcampo, acquired in 1991 (25.1 per cent market share in 1993). Kronenbourg SA first acquired 33 per cent of the capital of Mahou in 1988. As Mahou did not accept distribution of the international brands of Brasseries Kronenbourg in Spain, the company had to continue parallel distribution through a sales subsidiary. In 1992 Kronenbourg SA acquired 24.6 per cent of the capital of San Miguel, and started to distribute Kronenbourg and Tourtel with this partner. In 1994 the Danone Group announced that San Miguel would become a wholly owned subsidiary by 1997. Mahou had an 18 per cent market share in 1994, a brand new brewery and growing sales: 4.4 million hectolitres, 46 billion pesetas (a 10 per cent increase compared to 1993). San Miguel produced 3.5 million hectolitres in 1994 and its sales turnover amounted to 33.5 billion pesetas. With Mahou and San Miguel, Danone became the leader on the Spanish market with a 33 per cent share.

In 1989 Kronenbourg SA acquired 80.3 per cent of the equity of Henninger Hellas, the number two Greek brewery. Sales decreased during the commercial and industrial restructuring of the company, but started to grow when the Kronenbourg and Tourtel brands were introduced beside the Henninger. In 1992 Kronenbourg SA reduced its participation to 19.6 per cent of the capital when the Greek Boutari Group (involved in wholesaling) became a partner and acquired 67 per cent of Henninger Hellas. The company sold 520,000 hectolitres in 1994 (about 12 per cent of the Greek market) and started to export to Albania. In 1995 its name was changed to Northern Breweries. In Greece the leader was Heineken with its subsidiary, Athenian Brewery, having a 77 per cent market share.

With strong bases in southern Europe, Kronenbourg therefore planned to develop both local brands and the international brands of Brasseries Kronenbourg.

ACQUISITIONS STRATEGY

Acquisitions were prepared and implemented at the level of the beer division. The decision was shared between the Premier Rond and the Deuxième Rond of the Danone Group.

A constant effort was made to rationalise the industrial process. Before each acquisition, the specialists from Danone analysed the commercial value of the potential acquisition (brands, market shares, distribution network); but they also analysed the potential productivity gains after integration into the Danone industrial network.

The beer division would transfer skills in R&D, production and marketing, and if necessary help the restructuring of the company. Brasseries Kronenbourg could also play a role in the process of international acquisitions and joint developments: by signalling opportunities to the beer division, by providing cash and by transferring its distinctive skills.

Brasseries Kronenbourg also retained marketing control over its international brands which were distributed by Alken-Maes, Peroni, San Miguel and Henninger. European marketing co-ordination functions were established at Brasseries Kronenbourg – one for Kronenbourg and one for Tourtel – in order to support the international development of these brands. However, the packaging of Kronenbourg, 1664 and Tourtel on foreign markets was slightly different from the packaging of these products in France, and pricing policy was different between countries for a given product.

THE FUTURE

It was the view of the top management of Kronenbourg that, considering the positions taken by major brewers such as Heineken, Kronenbourg and to a lesser degree Interbrew and Carlsberg, and considering the constraints of anti-monopoly institutions, it would be hard for any major brewer to achieve any new significant acquisition in the EU. The major uncertainties concerned the British and German brewing industries, the latter still highly fragmented and with customers having a preference for local German brands.

The executives of Brasseries Kronenbourg believed that it was too early to try to move into the German market. It was impossible then to find a partner at a national level. In order to take a significant share, a foreign brewer would have had to take over several breweries, manage the diversity of the resulting product range and probably close some of the breweries. The idea was to let the Germans first restructure their industry. However, the German market was so large (about 119 million hectolitres in 1994) that several competitors had reached a significant scale. Bräu und Brunnen produced 14 million hectolitres a year (with the following brands: Brinkoff,

Schlösser, Küppers, Henninger, Jever and Eichbaum), Binding produced 8.8 million hectolitres a year (DAB, Berliner, Kindl and Radebergen) and Holsten produced 6.6 million hectolitres.

The 57 million hectolitre British market was slowly declining. The British brewing industry was in the process of restructuring, with a vertical split between brewing and retailing (imposed by the Monopolies and Mergers Commission in the early 1990s) and large-scale takeovers followed by capacity reductions.

Kronenbourg believed that the European single market would not bring radical changes, especially for the major brewers already established in several countries. However, the pricing policy would probably have to change between countries. The level of taxes (excise duties and VAT) were very different across Europe (for instance, high in the UK and low in France), and the same brand was often positioned differently in different countries. With customers travelling more and more across borders and comparing prices and quality, with the expected progressive harmonisation of taxes and duties across European countries, and with the free circulation of goods, international breweries were pushed to harmonise their prices across Europe, generally at a lower level. International logistics and co-ordination of marketing across Europe seemed to become crucial.

At the beginning of 1995 some major competitors increased their worldwide ambitions. Miller, the US-based number three brewer in the world (part of the Philip Morris Group) showed interest in an alliance with Heineken. Heineken preferred independence and continued to push its global product and spend fortunes on advertising (about three times as much as their competitors). Interbrew (previously number four in Europe) acquired the Canadian brewer Labatt for US$2 billion, to create the world's fourth largest brewing group.

When presenting the annual report of the Danone Group in June 1995, Antoine Riboud declared:

> Danone is now based on three main activities: dairy products, mineral waters and biscuits ... In the future the expansion of beer will be decided step by step. (*Les Echos*, 8 June 1995)

THE BREWERY GROUP DENMARK: FAXE, CERES AND THOR

Flemming Agersnap

The case study explains the strategic moves of Brewery Group Denmark (BGD), a small Danish brewery fighting for a position in a world market. The case shows how small companies can co-exist with giant competitors in an international context and how a coherent international strategy can be built whilst allowing for different local strategies. BGD is an example of a firm which has achieved a distinctive position in a highly competitive industry by focusing on importing Danish beer into selected markets, through a network of alliances. The case provides an opportunity to consider the strengths and weaknesses of the company's strategy and options for future development.

• • •

> It is better to be dominant in a small niche than to be a marginal supplier in a big market.
>
> CLAUS NIELSEN, INTERNATIONAL SALES DIRECTOR, BGD

Denmark is a beer-drinking country with a long tradition of brewing beer. The Danish brewing industry is dominated by the Carlsberg Group, holding a market share of 70–75 per cent and a worldwide position with sales and production in many countries.

In the Danish market there are four mid-size breweries and a number of smaller ones competing with Carlsberg. In 1989 two of the mid-size breweries merged their brewing activities into a joint venture 'Bryggerigruppen', The Brewery Group Denmark (BGD). This made it the second largest brewer in Denmark and was the background to significant international expansion.

This case study was prepared by Flemming Agersnap, Copenhagen Business School. It is intended as a basis for class discussion and not as an illustration of either good or bad management practice.

Exhibit 1 Financial statistics for BGD, 1989–95

	1995	1994	1992	1990	1989
Turnover (mill. DKK)	2.274	2.204	1.977	1.607	1.624
Export share (%)	59	59	52	51	43
Profit before tax (mill. DKK)	103	93	46	16	−19
Return on equity (after tax) (%)	18	18	12	7	−8
Number of employees	1,089	1,005	1,039	824	930

BREWERY GROUP DENMARK (BGD), FAXE, CERES AND THOR

Together BGD supplies about 15 per cent of the beer consumed in Denmark, although its share varies within the various Danish regions. Located in Aarhus, Jutland, Ceres has had a strong market position there for many years and over the last 30 years it has merged with breweries in neighbouring towns. One of these breweries was the Thor brewery in Randers. In 1996, Thor had a strong position in the northern part of Jutland. Located on Zealand, Faxe has only a small local market, but it had long been an important supplier to restaurants and retailers in Copenhagen.

At an early stage, both Ceres and Faxe felt a need for growth in order to obtain sufficient volume gains in production and subsequent reductions in costs. They first expanded in the domestic market to become national distributors, but any substantial growth could be obtained only through exports.

Exhibit 1 shows the financial data for the years after the establishment of the joint venture.

Organisation and Management

Exhibit 2 shows the organisation structure of BGD. After the merger in 1989, the positions of chief executive officer and of international sales director were filled with people without previous experience of breweries. Claus Nielsen came with a background from the international pharmaceutical industry. Hiring a manager from outside also solved the problem of choosing a candidate from one of the two existing sales organisations.

BGD was formed as a limited company, where the Faxe and the Ceres companies each owned 49 per cent and their common bank 2 per cent.

Exhibit 2 Organisation diagram (simplified)

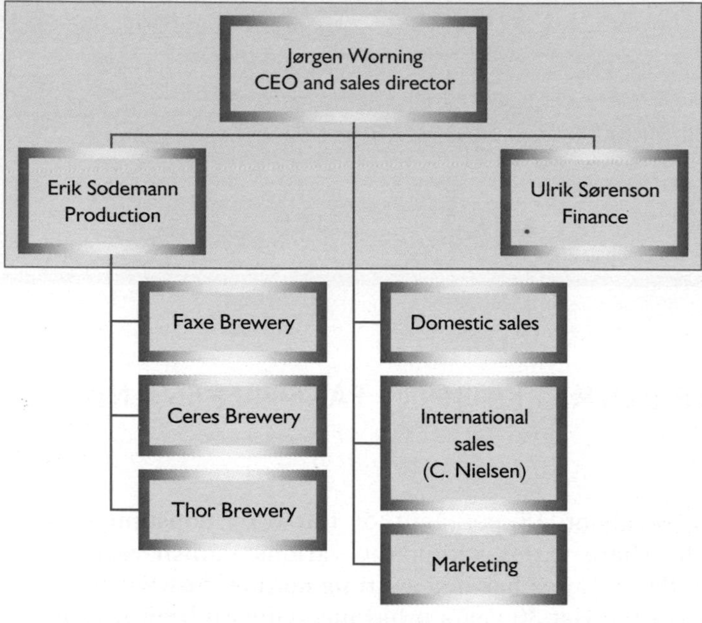

All beer and soft drinks activities were transferred to BGD. The parent companies also had a few other small activities besides BGD. Both companies were listed separately on the Copenhagen Stock Exchange. The Faxe brewery had a controlling capital owned by the founding family, whereas the Ceres company had no such controlling shareholder group. Carlsberg owned 38 per cent of the predominantly non-voting B-shares of Ceres, but without a seat on the board of the company. Carlsberg declared that it had no wish for a more active role in the management of Ceres or BGD, rather its involvement was said to be an investment for financial reasons. Others argued that the investment could be seen as a defensive investment guarding against a foreign acquisition of Ceres.

INTERNATIONAL DEVELOPMENT

Despite the dominance of Carlsberg, in its annual report BGD could lay claim to being the largest Scandinavian beer exporter. This was because Carlsberg placed emphasis on licensing agreements or local production for its foreign markets, while BGD's strategy was export led: 'Eighty-three out of every hundred bottles of beer that we produce are sold in foreign markets.' By 1995 the percentage of export sales by region of the world was as follows: western Europe 63 per cent, the Americas 10 per cent, eastern Europe 22 per cent, others 5 per cent. The development of BGD's operations in some of these markets is now reviewed.

Italy

More than 30 years ago, Ceres entered into co-operation with a slaughterhouse for pork (Tulip) in a neighbouring Jutland town. This slaughterhouse specialised in select meat cuts and canned meat for different markets. The co-operation led to export to Italy based on the transportation of meat and beers in refrigerated vans. Ceres joined this co-operative venture at the invitation of the slaughterhouse, but in 1996 beer export accounted for 75 per cent of turnover and more than 95 per cent of profit – and the joint sales company in Italy had been bought fully by BGD, though still acting as agent for the slaughterhouse.

Claus Nielsen commented:

> We are the largest exporter of beer to Italy and dominate the 'duplomolto' [strong beer] segment. Our success has been largely due to our marketing strategy. For the last 30 years we have been concentrating on the on-licence trade – restaurants, discos, bars and so on. We have achieved a very strong position in such outlets, which has given us a strong brand presence in Italy. In these outlets we have strongly promoted our bottled Ceres brand at point of sale. We would prefer people who go to restaurants and discos to be holding our bottle with our brand name on than drinking draught beer out of a glass without a brand name on it. In the last ten years we have also started to develop our presence in the off-licence retail trade – the shops selling beer. As in so many markets, the retailers have become more powerful, but a good indication of our brand strength is that we are able to resist the pressure they put on us for increased discounts. If they want to press us for such discounts, we simply refuse. They can delist us if they like, but they have to come back again because of the strength of the brand.
>
> The Italian culture also helps us. Most young men do not get married until they are about 30 and live at home until then. This means that there is a great deal of disposable income for men in their early 20s; and they spend a lot of money in restaurants, discos and bars, where we are strongly represented. They also prefer our brand, which is a premium, strong beer. The trend in Italy away from wine drinking has also helped us. It has become less common to drink wine heavily at lunch, for example. But Italians do like to have a drink and our beer is a good deal stronger than Italian beer. So they can feel good about not drinking wine, but drink a couple of Ceres instead. It looks better, but has much the same effect.

The Ceres concept in export markets such as Italy has been to emphasise the origin of the beer, that the beer is imported, and to emphasise premium and strong lager beers.

The Caribbean

Ceres also found and developed a market in the Caribbean islands for malt beer. A Ceres manager on vacation in the Caribbean observed that some of the locals were drinking a rather distinct type of beer, dark and sweet. When it was analysed back at the brewery, it turned out that the beer was very much like Danish malt beer, an almost non-alcoholic beer. Exports started and a market niche was developed in that region.

The product, Vitamalt, is rich in vitamins B and D and proteins. Claus Nielsen explained:

> In the Caribbean you have two markets for beer: those who drink alcoholic beer and those who do not drink alcohol at all. Our market is for the non-alcoholic market people who do not drink because of their religious beliefs, as well as a significant percentage of women and children too. The product is also believed by some to have aphrodisiac properties.

In a few markets in the Caribbean, local production is beneficial because of high import duties, and Heineken produce Vitamalt in the Bahamas under licence. However, Vitamalt became so successful that both Heineken and Guinness approached BGD with a view to licensing the product for production elsewhere in the Caribbean.

In fact, Vitamalt has a market not only in the Caribbean, but also in many other parts of the world where there are people of Caribbean origin. Sales are high in London, Amsterdam and Paris, for example.

Germany

On the border between Germany and Denmark, a special border trade has developed, since Danes can avoid paying the high Danish duty on beer by purchasing it in Germany. At times this trade has accounted for approximately 10 per cent of Danish beer consumption. Ceres has dominated the border market.

Before the joint venture, Faxe also developed a market in the wider Germany for canned beer. In the 1970s Faxe bought tapping equipment for canned beer; for environmental reasons, canned beer was not allowed to be sold in Denmark, but it is accepted in Germany. And canned beer is especially suitable for supermarket chains. This development (plus bottled beers) created a comparatively strong position for Faxe in the German market – considering the low level of German imports of beer. Its beers were sold partly in ordinary retail shops and supermarkets, but increasingly also in restaurants.

The Baltic States

The changed political and economic situation in the former Communist bloc has opened up many sales opportunities. Following the break-up of the

Soviet bloc, the Baltic states of Estonia, Latvia and Lithuania wished to become more closely linked to other Nordic states, a move encouraged by the governments of the Nordic countries. Trade delegations were organised from Denmark, and BGD took part in the first of these. 'We realised all the breweries were worn out and the quality of the beer was poor, but the population liked beer.' As a result, BGD appointed two distributors in Lithuania.

> We often appoint two distributors when we start up in a country to see which will be most successful. Here we agreed that both could import the Faxe brand and compete in Lithuania; one would also export to Latvia and the other to Estonia. It has been very successful. Unfortunately we also found that a good deal of the product was crossing the border into Russia, and we got complaints from our Russian distributors about this. We have to change the contract with our distributors in the Baltic states to prevent exporting Faxe to Russia. What we did was to provide them with another brand each, providing they did not export Faxe to Russia. They also have the right to export the other brand to Russia.

Elsewhere in Western Europe

In 1993 BGD bought a small British brewery, Cain's, located in Liverpool, England, and with an established local market. Besides involving a transfer of brewing technology, the acquisition of Cain's brewery opened up more possibilities for pub sales of BGD beers in that region, though still as imported beer. Similarly, Cain's traditional English beer was introduced into Denmark and other European countries as a supplement to the BGD range.

There are also markets for beers in Holland, Belgium, Austria and Switzerland. Yet, as Claus Nielsen said, 'Why bother when we know we won't get any result?' These beer markets are very competitive, but also stagnating. He continued:

> We were about to move into Spain, but I said: Stop, Stop. Look how much the others have invested. Carlsberg has lost 500 mill. DKK. Heineken and all the other big ones are there. Why enter that fight? Why not look to the nice neighbouring country, Portugal, where imported beers account for less than 1 per cent of beer consumption? They are an extraordinarily kind and pleasant people to work with. Let us focus on these 10 million people and try to gain a foothold there. So we were established there before anybody else with imported beer.

Brazil

A fast-growing market for BGD is Brazil. Traditionally, the Brazilian market has been protected by high import duty, varying from 8 to 60 per cent depending on the economic situation of the country. Furthermore, the

Brazilian government has been very restrictive and avoided foreign capital. Big Brazilian breweries took advantage of the situation and set very high prices. But partly as a consequence of the GATT negotiations and partly to counteract inflation, the Brazilian government planned to open the country for imports. The entrance of American and European breweries into the market led to a price reduction of about 80 per cent. Claus Nielsen explained:

> There was an opening coming up and I could see there was an under supply. We took the step with imported beer before anybody else and were successful. It was a combination of timing, of finding the right partner and of the change in regulations.
>
> We thought of using our Caribbean concept, malt beers, since the northern parts of Brazil resemble the Caribbean climate and population. However, a closer study and an awareness of the culture of Brazilian society led us to act differently.
>
> Brazil is a multiethnic country, although many Brazilians get angry and agitated when one wants to distinguish between the European and African parts of the population. Such distinctions do not exist for the Brazilians. Now I have been there several times and differences do exist. For me it was like walking around in Africa and in the ethnic parts of London and Paris. Those who understand and adapt to the differences will obtain benefits in this market. And that is what we have done. So in the end we have emphasised a European approach – also because of the partner we found.
>
> We were very lucky with the partner we found. Cafe Bom Dia is a company with a distribution network covering all relevant segments of the market. It is a modern coffee roaster with ISO 9000 certification of quality; the biggest in Brazil. They have a distribution network covering coffee shops and supermarkets and delivery to 90,000 restaurants. And today our beers are placed on their vans.
>
> They know – or we tell them – that if they choose Heineken or Carlsberg, these breweries in a few years' time will start local production and take over the distribution. The big ones enter as 'big brothers'. They chose us – we have been very lucky and the sales volume is growing rapidly.
>
> There is also a benefit with regard to the cost of distribution. They are one of Brazil's biggest coffee exporters and we have arranged to use their empty containers to ship product into Brazil at a lower cost than we would normally incur.
>
> I have never – like other breweries – entered a market together with other breweries, not even local ones, in a joint operation. It may give an easy start if the partner has the set-up, knows how to distribute the beer – and has the same target group. But one only gets the share of the market the partner allows one to get. I want to find a partner where we complement each other instead of competing. It can be a soft drinks distributor – or a coffee distributor. In India we will enter a contract with the biggest tea distributor.

Russia

By 1996 BGD was also operating in Russia.

> The Russian market is huge and the demand for beer very high; but there had been no investment in the breweries and they produced very low-quality beer. In 1993 we began with a number of distributors in order to handle the problems

> of distribution. However, eventually it became clear there were two performing really well and we were approached by both of them for sole distribution rights. Given the way in which business is done in Russia, this is not a straightforward matter. We eventually decided on one distributor who is also a major distributor of other food products to cash 'n' carries and small shops in the cities. It also has associates who can handle distribution elsewhere in Russia; and it is a very sophisticated operation in terms of the education of their management and their computer and distribution systems. It is proving to be immensely successful: for example, we have 80 per cent retail penetration in Moscow. Russia is now our biggest export market, in terms of volume.
>
> Initially we found problems because of transport costs to Russia. There was one major container distributor from Denmark who quoted extremely high costs of distribution. We overcame this in a rather novel way. We decided in the summer to ship our products direct to Moscow by river using barges with loads of 2 to 6 million bottles. Keeping transport costs down in beer distribution is extremely important.

China

The Chinese market for beer is growing at around 10–20 per cent per annum, and Claus Nielsen sees it as one of the most attractive markets for the future.

> It is of course a huge market, but we had to be very clear about our positioning. Most of the people in China are not that wealthy, but there is a percentage of the population which is. China has become one of the largest markets for Rolex watches, Mercedes cars and French XO Cognac. We decided to position Faxe as a premium product and target geographic regions where there was high disposable income. Our distribution strategy was also important. Most western companies have tended to go through Hong Kong, where they can find English-speaking distributors. But of course it adds to costs of distribution. We wanted to export to China direct. Most organisations we contacted wanted a joint venture arrangement for manufacturing and the building of a brewery. This is of course not our strategy; we only deal with export beer, so we were not prepared to do this. We spent three years finding the right distributor and eventually did so. It is a government-owned organisation, regionally structured, selling mainly liquor and tobacco, but not beer until now, to tax-free shops throughout China. We began in September 1995 and we are doing well. We also distribute Ceres through the more traditional route via a Hong Kong distributor.

THE MARKETING CONCEPT

BGD did not intend to compete directly with the big international breweries on their major markets, with standard-type beers. It looked for niches for special forms of distribution or special products. The core of BGD's international marketing concept has been to emphasise that its beers are *imported*. There was no local production of its brands outside Denmark and its beers are alike in all countries. As Claus Nielsen says: 'The big breweries adapt their brands to the various markets. Let them have these markets. If we are to get any distinction, it must be tied to the fact that our beer is always the same Danish beer.'

So BGD emphasised the development of its sales organisation in the various markets more than price and production costs. In this way, its beers could be seen as competing more with beers like the Dutch Grolsch beer than with widely sold beers from, for example, Heineken or Carlsberg. The consumer might think of the beer as something to be chosen for a special occasion and not as a daily standard product.

The types of customer and the consumption patterns of the standard beers and of special beers were quite different. Although in a specific country the market for expensive imported beer might be small, it could be an attractive size for BGD. Furthermore, imported beers were acquiring an increasing market share worldwide, even though by 1996 they exceeded 10 per cent of the total market in only a few countries.

BGD IN DENMARK

Like Carlsberg (and Tuborg), BGD had a wide assortment of beers, ranging from non-alcoholic beers and ordinary beers to premium beers and strong beers. Alongside their traditional beers the two breweries introduced a number of specialities, such as Dortmunder beer (Ceres), draught beer in cans or special bottles (Faxe), and Christmas and Easter beers. BGD had not produced and sold discount beers to the big retail chains.

In the Danish market, Faxe had intended to launch draft beer in cans. When distribution in cans was banned, Faxe launched draft beer in special dark bottles with a different shape than ordinary beers. The dark brown colour of the bottles was necessary because the draft beer was more sensitive to sunlight than ordinary beers. It was a success at the time, since many smaller restaurants and bars did not have beer-tapping equipment. Gradually the price on this equipment has fallen and many restaurants and bars have got beer taps, so this special market has almost vanished.

In 1996 the ban on canned beer was up for reconsideration. The EU understood the environmental reasons behind the ban. However, in Sweden, canned beer has been allowed provided there is a 'pawn' on each can which is refunded when the empty can is returned. This system, which is similar to the present Danish one for bottles, ensures that the cans are recycled. It is actively debated whether, by such a system, cans represent a heavier burden on the environment than bottles. The cans have a high return rate (to cash the pawn) and are reused through a melting process. The bottles are directly reused, but the washing of the bottles requires many chemicals and considerable amounts of water.

The major reason that the EU wanted the ban lifted was that it is seen as a trade barrier. It is difficult for a foreign brewery to tap beer in the special Danish bottles and to handle the bottle return system. If the ban is lifted, canned beers are expected to account for only about 10 per cent of the market. But it would be far easier for a German brewery to enter this market niche.

In the Danish market, BGD also sells a number of soft drinks, some under its own brands and others under licence to tap and sell, such as Pepsi Cola and 7-Up.

INTERNATIONAL MANAGEMENT

With so many international opportunities to consider, Claus Nielsen commented:

> I have a well-functioning organisation with seven regional managers and their staff and the most efficient shipping/transportation department in Denmark, exporting more than 15,000 containers a year. I only want to expand at the pace of adding a new colleague each year. He or she has a chance really to get versed in the job and to get attention from the organisation. Then soon they may get their own independent area of responsibility. So physically we cannot enter all the potential markets, not even all the promising ones. We must focus on some and leave the others till we have the organisation to enter them. We aim at structured and well-studied approaches, but sometimes it is incidental information that tells us where the best potentials surface.
>
> I like to run a very flat structure. The regional executives have total operating control over their regions. It is my job to set up new businesses around the world – I spent a lot of time in China in 1995, for example – and deal with overall strategy, price setting and yearly budgets. They then run the businesses. It does mean a lot of travel; I try to visit all major markets at least once a year. In 1995 I spent 150 days out of Denmark.

MANAGING THE BGD JOINT VENTURE

The joint venture mainly had an impact on the organisation of sales and distribution, but not on production. In the domestic market, a number of depots were merged and considerable cost savings achieved. In the international markets where Faxe had a significant export market Ceres was virtually absent and vice versa. Faxe was positioned in one way and Ceres in another, so they complemented each other without overlap. The success was evident. In 1989 exports were DKK 514m and in 1995 DKK 1,522m.

Although the sales organisation became fully merged, the production units remained separate according to the old company structures, with breweries in the towns of Faxe, Ceres and Thor, and brands exclusively brewed where they were first introduced. This was said to be necessary due to special requirements as to water and yeast as well as local knowledge of the brewing processes.

> Just for fun we have tried to let the Ceres people brew some Faxe beer. It didn't taste the same. Similarly, Faxe people have tried to make Ceres Dortmunder. It didn't work either. We do not want any risk of mixing of the yeasts, so they are kept apart. The water supply is also very different. Carlsberg has a brewery in Copenhagen and one in Fredericia, Jutland, where they brew the same beer brands, but experienced brewers can tell where one of these beers is brewed.

The absence of merged activity in production was also attributed to the existing cultures and loyalties among managers and workers. Traditionally, the two breweries have been staffed at the top levels by 'brewers' – people with a pharmaceutical, chemical or engineering background at university and later trained within the trade and with formal education from the special advanced Scandinavian Brewing High School. This tradition had created a high professional standard and intimate knowledge of the trade, but had also meant a certain level of closure to other forms of training and experience from other consumer goods industries. Similarly, the experienced brewery workers had developed a competence in, for example, adjusting the beer taste and a strong attachment to the specific brewery.

This has meant that the brewers have emphasised their wish to have full discretion in running a brewery and have been reluctant to consider more integrated operations. However, the expansion in sales volume required the full use of capacity, utilising established production patterns.

STEWART GRAND PRIX

Mark Jenkins

The case study focuses on the period from 1995 to 1997 when Stewart Grand Prix was created to take part in the highly competitive world of Formula One motor sport. Whilst Paul Stewart Racing had been highly successful in the less powerful formulas such as Formula 3 and Formula 3000, Formula One presented a quite different challenge. The case illustrates the different resources and competences which are required to enter a new, although related, area of activity. It shows that the management task is a question not just of acquiring the needed resources and competences but also of ensuring that these are integrated to create a coherent organisation.

• • •

In an article on new entrants to Formula One (F1) motor racing, a journalist likened their situation to that of a football team moving from the first into the premier division. However, this analogy belies the huge barriers to entering motor sport's most prestigious category. In 1996, Pacific became the seventeenth team to withdraw from F1 since 1989. In 1997, Lola, a manufacturer of successful race-cars collapsed in financial chaos after only one race. The rewards for success in F1 are huge, but so are the odds against staying to enjoy them.

PAUL STEWART RACING

Paul Stewart Racing (PSR) was formed in 1988 by Paul Stewart, son of three times world champion Jackie Stewart. Paul, a successful driver in his own right, decided to start his own team competing in Formula Ford, Formula 3

This case study was prepared by Mark Jenkins, Cranfield School of Management. The case is based on published materials and an interview with Paul Stewart, managing director of Stewart Grand Prix, whose co-operation and input to this case is gratefully acknowledged. The case is intended as a basis for class discussion and not as an illustration of good or bad management practice.

Exhibit 1 **The staircase to Formula One – estimated cost of two cars per season**

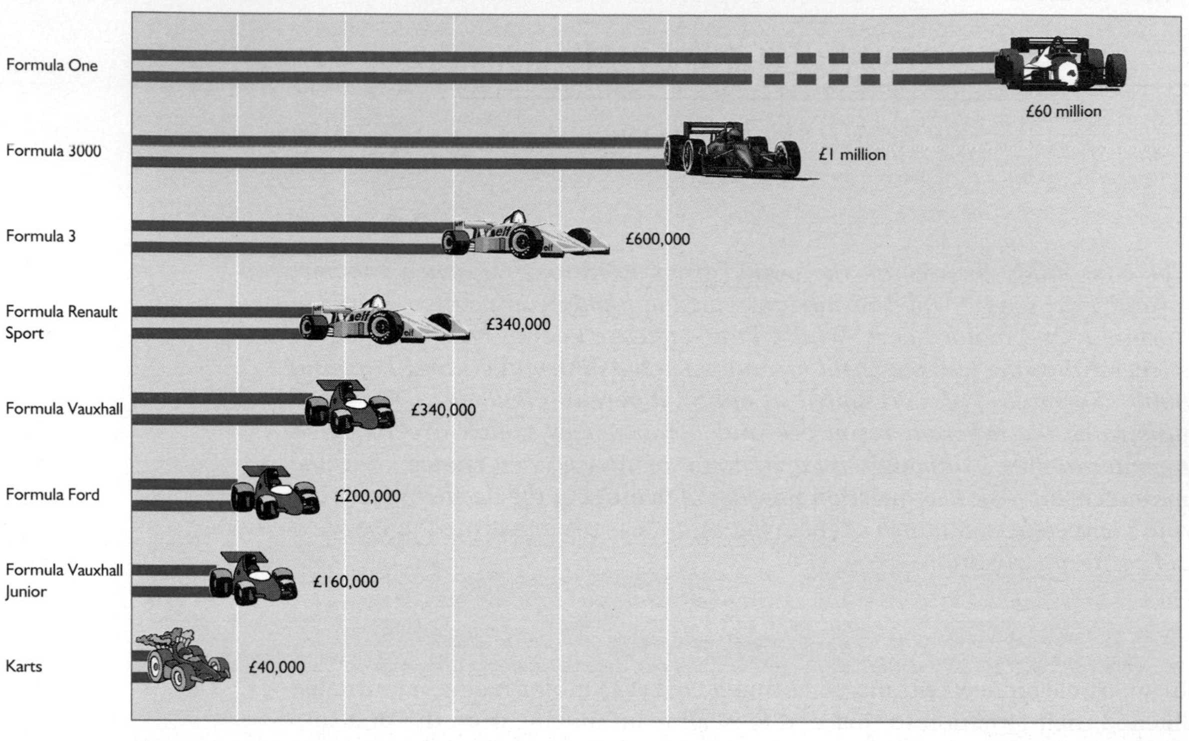

and also moving into Formula Vauxhall and Formula 3000 (Exhibit 1). Whilst Jackie Stewart was appointed chairman of PSR, the business was very much Paul's responsibility. By 1997 PSR had grown into a highly successful and efficient operation having won the ultra-competitive Formula 3 championship for the past six years; a category in which a number of F1 teams have tried their luck but failed to become established. To run a team in these lower categories requires some of the competences needed to compete in F1, such as the ability to prepare and set up cars, to define and implement a race strategy, to raise funding through developing relationships with sponsors, and to identify and recruit talented drivers.

However, there are also significant differences. In F1 the scale of operations is global rather than national, requiring a sophisticated logistics operation to move cars, equipment and people around the world on a regular basis. The yearly costs for the sixteen to seventeen grand prix are immense: the annual budget of running a top F1 team is around £60 million, sixty times the cost of a Formula 3000 team. But the most significant difference is that the F1 teams design and construct their own cars. In the other categories cars are purchased from specialist manufacturers such as Lola, Van Diemen and Reynard. Even Indycar, the US equivalent to F1, uses bought-in cars, most of which are manufactured in the UK.

PSR had become a well established business with a reputation for high standards of presentation and strength in acquiring and managing corporate sponsors. With a fleet of immaculate transporters and a modern factory in Milton Keynes, PSR was one of the most impressive race teams not competing in F1. Paul's ambitions for the team went well beyond Formula 3000 and the like. In 1994, an attempt to pull together an entry into F1 ended abruptly when the consortium of backers unexpectedly withdrew. Other options such as Indycar and saloon car racing (where cars are also bought in from specialist manufacturers such as Reynard) were given serious consideration; however, F1 was soon back on the agenda.

STEWART GRAND PRIX

On 29 June 1995, Jackie Stewart was returning from commentating duties at the Canadian Grand Prix in the Ford executive jet. Ever since his days as world champion he had maintained a close link with the Ford Motor Company as an adviser and occasional test driver. The highest placed Ford-powered car had been eighth in Canada, a pale imitation of the early 1970s when they dominated the sport, a Ford engine having powered every championship-winning car between 1968 and 1974. Second in size only to General Motors, the Ford Motor Company has a huge presence in the world automotive market. In addition to its size, Ford has shown a unique and consistent commitment to a wide variety of motor sports. This enduring priority has led to a strong sporting association in terms of both Ford's automotive consumers and the worldwide network of distributors and dealers. With most of the Ford Motorsport senior management present, the discussion in the plane centred around Ford's future in F1. Jackie Stewart offered the opinion that it should either withdraw completely or do the job properly. The Ford management responded by asking him to come up with a proposal as to how it could be done properly and present this to them on 30 October 1995.

This was the first challenge in a dramatic sequence of events which culminated in the official launch of Stewart Grand Prix (SGP) and the SF-1 car at the Marriott Hotel in London on 10 December 1996. Almost exactly a year had elapsed between the point when Ford finally agreed to proceed with the Stewart proposal on 6 December 1995. Once Ford had given the go-ahead, the race was on to get all the elements of a F1 team in place. The existing PSR operation was able to provide the basis for the organisation. The two major challenges were concerned with raising finance and with creating and building a competitive F1 car.

Whilst the project would not have got off the ground without a five-year commitment from Ford, this was only the beginning. Ford and SGP were very clear that whilst the Ford relationship was central, it was not underwriting the whole project and SGP would have to raise the additional funds to create a workable annual budget. The task of raising the financial support fell naturally to a man who was recognised worldwide as an ambassador for motor racing and someone with acute business sense – Jackie Stewart. Having played a relatively low-key role in the development of PSR, SGP was to place new demands on the time and energy of the triple world champion. Since retiring from motor racing in 1973, Jackie Stewart had become a successful consultant and spokesman for companies such as Goodyear, Elf and the Ford Motor Company. His approach was characterised by professionalism, an eye for detail, and boundless energy and enthusiasm. His activities in the sporting and charity worlds had brought him into contact with many personalities, business people and royalty. These were contacts which would prove invaluable to the task which Jackie Stewart now faced – one he was later to refer to as his most difficult challenge ever.

CREATING THE BUDGET

Contacts alone would not secure the funding needed to support the team, particularly as the strategy was to focus on long-term funding rather than relying on a series of one-off deals. Contacts may open doors, but only a well argued business case would secure the commitments needed. One example of this was the five-year deal for $25m which was secured from HSBC (in 1997 the largest bank in the world). Sir William Purves, a fellow Scot and chairman of HSBC, was contacted by Stewart. Purves's immediate response was that if it was about sponsorship, HSBC would not be interested. Stewart argued that he should at least hear him out before he said no. Purves agreed, and a series of meetings took place culminating in a well rehearsed SGP presentation to the board of HSBC. This finally secured the agreement. If SGP could strike this kind of deal with a group of hard-headed bankers, surely anything was possible. But the task was still an uphill one. The following weeks saw a further £60m agreed and then withdrawn; this was a major blow, not just to the balance sheet but also to Stewart's faith in the business world. However, bit by bit a substantial package was built up, with Ford and HSBC as the major sponsors.

Stewart's approach was characterised by creating opportunities in areas hitherto unconnected with F1. He also spent a lot of time generating potential in the Far East, culminating in an agreement with the Malaysian government to promote Malaysia. Other sectors were represented by the Lear Corporation (automotive interiors) and MCI (telecommunications). All this activity came at a time when the Formula One constructors, as a whole, were heavily reliant on tobacco sponsorship. However, in March 1998 Max

Moseley, president of FIA (the regulatory body for world motor sport), surprised many by suggesting that tobacco advertising could be banned by 2002 if there was clear evidence that carrying adverts on cars encouraged individuals to take up smoking. If such a ban occurred, established teams such as McLaren, Williams, Ferrari and Benetton would find themselves having to fill huge holes in their budgets through non-tobacco sources.

CREATING THE CAR AND THE TEAM

Whilst the search for funding was gathering pace for SGP, the other major challenge was the design and construction of the F1 car. As an organisation, PSR had a great deal of experience in racing cars, but it was starting from zero when it came to designing and building them. The central element of this part of the strategy was the recruitment of a first rate technical director who could create the team and the systems necessary to build the first Stewart-Ford F1 car. Alan Jenkins was a designer who had experienced the pains of a scratch launch into F1 with the Onyx team. He had also worked with established F1 teams such as McLaren and Williams and had experienced the American version of F1 – Indycar with the Penske team. He was currently with the Arrows F1 team and was Paul Stewart's first choice as technical director for SGP, a position which he accepted at the end of December 1995, despite advances from two leading F1 teams. With Alan Jenkins signed up, the process of recruiting could begin in earnest. PSR had already attracted many talented people who would occupy key positions within SGP. In addition to a range of mechanics and technicians these included individuals such as David Stubbs, manager of the F3000 team who became F1 team manager, Nigel Newton, financial controller of PSR who became finance director of SGP, Andy Miller, operations director of PSR who moved to the same position in SGP, as did commercial director Rob Armstrong. However, it was also important to bring as much F1 experience as possible into the team. SGP put a series of modest quarter-page adverts into *Autosport* and were deluged with applications from many experienced F1 people who were excited at the prospect of the SGP project.

With Alan Jenkins released from his Arrows contract at the end of February 1996, the first computers were installed in March to allow the design process to begin. Using an EDS-Unigraphics system with Hewlett Packard hardware, SGP became the first team to design a car from scratch with a full CAD system. This was in stark contrast to the major teams who still relied heavily on draughtsman's drawings and which often had to be digitised in order to manufacture finished components. A key element in the design of an F1 car is the aerodynamics. Whilst computer simulation is an option, the only way to do this properly is to use a wind tunnel with a half-sized model of the car. In F1, only teams like Williams and Ferrari went to these lengths. SGP had the model constructed and in July it was tested in the Swift wind tunnel in San Clemente, California.

A lot of press speculation surrounded the drivers which SGP would hire for its entry to F1. During 1996, the world champion elect, Damon Hill, had acrimoniously ended his relationship with the Williams team and was considering his options for 1997. SGP had a number of choices. One was to go for top drivers such as Hill who would bring a lot of publicity for the sponsors, but would make a sizeable hole in the budget and increase the pressure on the new team. Another possibility was to bring in a 'pay driver' who, whilst perhaps not the most talented, could bring a sizeable purse of sponsorship – this was often owing to support for a driver of a particular nationality or because of family connections to wealthy organisations. Whilst such an option would be financially attractive, Paul Stewart's view was that to bring in drivers on the basis of finance rather than talent could compromise the spirit and commitment of the new team.

The option taken was to recruit a combination of F1 experience in Rubens Barrichello, a talented Brazilian who was unhappy with his current position in the Jordan team, and Jan Magnussen, a rising star from F3, who had been British champion in 1994 with PSR. One of the reasons for PSR being involved in a number of different formulas was that it provided a 'staircase of talent' for both drivers and team personnel, enabling the Stewarts to spot and develop potential future stars at an early stage. It is for this reason that F1 teams such as McLaren have become involved in the lower formulas, even down to the level of karting. At 24 and 23 years respectively, Barrichello and Magnussen presented a positively youthful profile. Both were hired on unusually long contracts, Barrichello for three years and Magnussen for four. Whilst it could be argued that SGP should have used more experienced (and therefore more expensive) drivers, the racing experience of Jackie and Paul Stewart provided a wealth of knowledge to complement their new enthusiastic drivers.

1997: THE FIRST SEASON

SGP's first season in F1 was an undoubted success, particularly considering that it had built in a year what many teams took decades to develop. There were highs and lows to the season. The high came at the Monaco Grand Prix when Barrichello took second place at a rain-soaked Monte Carlo. It was an emotional moment and one where the real significance of their achievements was brought home to those both inside and outside SGP. But the lows were also there. At the British Grand Prix in July 1997, both cars retired after starting from lowly grid positions. This had been due to engine problems which were to revisit SGP repeatedly throughout the year. Whilst Ford was the major backer for SGP, the engines themselves were built by Cosworth Racing near Northampton, UK. Cosworth was a name to be reckoned with in the world of motor sport. In 1967 it had revolutionised F1 with the DFV engine which was not only powerful and reliable, but also formed an integral part of the structure of the car, keeping the weight down to an absolute minimum. Whilst the names Cosworth and Ford were synonymous to many, Cosworth was owned by the Vickers group which had a wide portfolio of manufacturing businesses involved mostly with the defence sector. The need to generate cash for its core businesses of tanks and ships had necessitated the sale of Rolls-Royce cars, and there was some speculation about the future of Cosworth and whether Ford would step into the frame as a potential buyer.

As part of their five-year agreement with Ford, SGP would be the sole recipient of the most highly developed version of the Cosworth engine. Whilst Cosworth would also supply Ford engines to other teams such as Tyrrell, SGP had an important advantage in that its chassis could be developed in parallel with the engine and modifications to the engine could be made to benefit the SF-1 design. For example, the oil tank was moved from the gearbox to in front of the engine to improve the oil flow around the engine. But questions were being asked as to how far behind Cosworth were the likes of Mercedes, Ferrari, Mecachrome (supplying Renault engines in 1998), Peugeot and Mugen-Honda. F1 was becoming a battle of engines, a clear contrast to the 1970s when most of the teams used the same engine/gearbox configuration. These concerns led the Stewarts to lobby urgently, not just the senior management at Cosworth, but also Ford and Vickers to make sure that everything possible was being done to improve the performance and reliability of the engines. In addition to its relationship with Ford and Cosworth, SGP worked with Texaco, to develop fuel and lubricants for the car, and, significantly, a new entrant to F1, Bridgestone tyres. Over the past decade, Goodyear had dominated the supply of tyres to F1, but in 1997 Bridgestone launched its bid to become a major force in F1. Initial tests had suggested that the Bridgestone tyres were more durable, meaning that the Bridgestone cars may need fewer pitstops than those using Goodyear. For 1997, only a few of the middle- to lower-ranking teams would use Bridgestone tyres, one of which would be SGP.

MAKING THE DIFFERENCE

Whilst most commentators would point to a team having a better engine, driver or just more finance, Paul Stewart's view was that no single factor makes the difference when you are competing at this level:

> If you haven't got the money, none of it is possible, so money is one key to success – but what makes a difference is how the money is used. It's not down to any one thing like a driver or an engine, but the interaction that matters. If you look at the Williams team, they rely on a solid framework: their organisation, their engine, their car design is all amalgamated into something that gives a platform for everyone to work on. They don't believe putting millions into a driver is going to make all the difference.

The issue for SGP was the development of its own 'solid framework'. Whilst it seems incongruous to refer to any F1 organisation as a family business, Stewart Grand Prix has the style and commitment of exactly that. Paul and Jackie bring complementary knowledge and skills to the project. Their working relationship is a close one; whilst Jackie's commitments mean that he is rarely in one country for any length of time, he and Paul speak on a daily basis. Their commitment to SGP and its employees manifests itself in many ways. At the end of their first season in 1997, Jackie and Paul sat down to sign 200 framed photographs of the SF-1 car to each of their employees; every photograph was personally dedicated. At the launch of the SF-2 car for the 1998 season, it was the designers who unveiled the car rather than Jackie or Paul Stewart. SGP adopted a style where the employees themselves were able to play a major role in the creation of the new team. The key challenge which SGP faced in 1998 was to maintain the momentum and energy which had brought it into one of the most competitive industries in the world. No one knew this better than Paul Stewart:

> The excitement and energy that comes from creating something new is something that you should never take for granted. Very few times in your life do you have the privilege of being in that sort of fresh, new, exciting environment. But it doesn't go on for ever. A lot of people say it's great working for Stewart, but one day they may say it's boring – and we will be the old boys on the block one day, but hopefully not too soon.

LAURA ASHLEY HOLDINGS PLC

John L. Heath

The case describes the growth, development and varied fortunes of a leading clothing, home furnishings and related products group from its origins in the early 1950s until 1995. Over this period the business grew from a home-based husband and wife concern to an international group whose brand name Laura Ashley was recognised around the world and regarded by many as the group's major asset. The case illustrates how competitive advantage may be eroded as the management problems of coping with organic and acquisitive growth, expanding international operations, and environmental change of various kinds, all increase in complexity. As a result, mismatches arise between the organisation's strategic capability and its competitive environment that are difficult to correct.

• • •

INTRODUCTION

In the spring of 1996 Laura Ashley's shareholders began to believe, at long last, that better times really were on the way. The group had paid only nominal dividends since 1989 and had survived a cash crisis in 1990 and several years of indifferent performance and recovery attempts since then. Shareholders looked back on the company's heady successes of the 1980s and wondered what had gone wrong. How was it that the distinctive strengths on which the group's fortunes had been built were unable to sustain it in the 1990s?

Now, however, there were encouraging signs. Since Ann Iverson's appointment as chief executive in June 1995 the share price had doubled, and when results for the year to January 1996 were released in April it was clear that the turnaround she had instituted was already bearing fruit. The group announced a return to profit and the first dividend payment for six

---

This case was prepared by John L. Heath as a basis for class discussion rather than to illustrate either effective or ineffective handling of management issues.

years. Pre-tax profit of £10.3m was the highest since 1989 and a strong turnaround from the £30.6m loss in the previous year.

EARLY HISTORY

In 1953 Bernard and Laura Ashley started printing tea towels and scarves to their own design in their flat in Pimlico, London. The success of these designs led the Ashleys to form their first company, Ashley, Mountney Ltd in 1954.

In 1960 the Ashleys decided to move their expanding business to Wales, where Laura Ashley was born and where in 1966 Laura Ashley designed her first clothing items, two apron dresses. These were not originally intended as fashion items but proved to be of profound significance to the subsequent development of the group. Encouraged by their success the Ashleys opened the first Laura Ashley retail shop in London, in 1968, and the subsequent growth and development of the group stems from this move into direct retailing. Within two years the group was concentrating primarily on producing goods for sale in its own shops. The basic structure of Laura Ashley as a vertically integrated business embracing design, fabric printing, clothing manufacture and retailing was thus established.

Laura Ashley's design philosophy, deeply rooted in traditional English country values, was the foundation for the group's designs. She created and trained teams of designers to develop her work. Laura Ashley died following an accident in September 1985, and although her death was a severe blow to the company, her design concepts had been thoroughly absorbed and understood throughout the group.

By 1985 the group's product range embraced both clothing and home furnishings, and as a vertically integrated group Laura Ashley manufactured around 85 per cent by value of these products itself. Clothing and home furnishing products were supplied directly to each shop in the United Kingdom, principally by the group's own vehicles, supplemented in Continental Europe by arrangements with local carriers. Clothing for North America was dispatched weekly by airfreight to each shop.

A vital element in the group's organisation was its major commitment to information technology in all areas of its operations. By 1985 its three main computer centres – in Carno (Wales), Helmond (Netherlands) and Mahwah (New Jersey, USA) – were all linked through a communications network. Its IT capability was regarded by management as a crucial element in the effectiveness of the group's vertically integrated structure.

Laura Ashley shops were designed to create the same look and atmosphere throughout the world and played an important part in projecting the image of Laura Ashley. In its shops the group was an early adopter of electronic point of sale (EPOS) systems, whereby sales figures from each shop were analysed daily by product line.

The complementary talents of the Ashleys – Laura's design flair and Bernard's business acumen and interest in fabrics printing – had by 1985 transformed a cottage industry into an international group with 219 shops in Europe, the United States and the Pacific Basin, and worldwide sales exceeded £100m. Laura Ashley became a public company in November 1985. It was floated on the stock market to a rapturous City, and such was the enthusiasm for the company that the offer was oversubscribed 34 times. The flotation valued the Ashley family's 70 per cent stake at £292m.

Although the share offer was widely endorsed by the business press as an attractive investment, there were some notes of caution amid the general euphoria:

> Although storming ahead in the USA, European performance is at best lukewarm. Mrs Ashley's death will be a severe loss.
>
> Expansion in Europe, notably France, has not been a success.
>
> Does a mish-mash of designing, manufacturing and retailing warrant a premium store rating?

INTERNATIONAL DEVELOPMENT

Acquisitions

In 1986 the group began a series of acquisitions with the purchase of Sandringham Leather Goods Ltd of Llanidloes and Bryant of Scotland Ltd, a high-quality knitwear company. In August 1987, Willis and Geiger, a traditional outdoor clothing specialist with both wholesale and retail businesses in the USA, was acquired for $3m. In November, Penhaligons Ltd, an old established perfumery business offering an exclusive range of gentlemen's fragrances from five distinctive shops in London, was acquired for £1m. It was intended to develop the Penhaligon range of products and extend its business internationally. Since 1979 the group had also produced its own unique range of women's fragrances through its Swiss-based subsidiary, Parfums Laura Ashley. The group intended to extend the product ranges and shop openings of its acquisitions in their base countries and later internationally.

In March 1989 the purchase of Revman Industries Inc., a US home furnishings marketing company, was announced. The company was established as an important source of quality designer bedlinen selling to major department stores, specialist chains and catalogue houses across the United States.

Manufacturing Investment

In August 1985 work commenced on a new 135,000 sq. ft textile factory in Wales. The following year work began on a new vinyl wallpaper plant on an adjacent site. These facilities represented an investment of some £7.5m, a significant part of the cost of which was offset by a grant from the Development Board of Rural Wales.

In 1987 a £1.3m computer-aided design system was installed in the textile design studios at Newtown, and in the following year a computerised garment-cutting room was opened at Carno at a cost of £1.7m. Other investments in manufacturing included a £670,000 computerised handling system for the Newtown garment factory. This was designed to reduce garment throughput times from several days to a few hours, and thereby allow more rapid response to retail demand.

1988 Reorganisation

Early in 1988 the group was restructured into seven divisions in order to facilitate its growth over the next five years. Each division had a managing director separately accountable to the main board for his division's profit performance. The reorganisation was reported to reflect, in part, the group's decision to break away from the vertically integrated structure that had been a distinctive feature of the Laura Ashley organisation almost since its inception.

The new divisions were as follows:

- *Laura Ashley Group Services*, responsible for finance, legal work, informatics and strategic planning.
- *Laura Ashley Brand Management Group*, responsible for design, sourcing, image protection and licensing.
- *Laura Ashley Industries*, responsible for textile, wallpaper, and garment manufacture and distribution, together with leather goods and knitwear subsidiaries.
- *Laura Ashley UK Retail*, responsible for retail operations in the UK.
- *Laura Ashley BV*, responsible for retail operations in Continental Europe.
- *Laura Ashley Inc.*, responsible for retail operations in the USA and Canada.
- *Laura Ashley Pacific Basin*, responsible for retail operations in Australia and Japan.

Major cost-cutting, restructuring and quality improvement initiatives were introduced within Industries Division as the group gradually reduced its dependence on its own manufacturing activities. Whereas around 85 per cent of products sold in 1985 were manufactured in-house, by 1988 this was down to 60 per cent and falling.

Retail Developments

In 1987 the group took a 'major step towards segmentation' with the opening of six Laura Ashley Mother & Child shops in the USA. These sold a co-ordinated range of clothes and bedroom furnishing products for babies and children up to 12, and dresses for their mothers. Mother & Child collections were also launched in the UK and Continental Europe the following year.

In 1989, 'Laura Ashley Home' shops were launched to sell a wider range of home furnishings than was available in existing Laura Ashley outlets. The range featured Laura Ashley designed furniture carrying the Laura Ashley brand name, but manufactured outside the group. This, together with the home furnishing range, offered customers a complete Laura Ashley lifestyle package.

Also in 1989 Laura Ashley opened the first of 50 'Units' shops it planned to open in the UK by 1992. These stores were operated under licence from a subsidiary of the J.C. Penney retailing group, and offered a range of unsophisticated women's knitted clothing items which could be co-ordinated into several different garments.

In the UK and Ireland, the number of Laura Ashley outlets increased from 87 in 1986 to 182 by early 1991. UK turnover over this period rose from £56.4m to £143.6m. An enlarged Mail Order Centre was opened in Newtown in December 1987. Mail order sales grew steadily over the period, increasing by 50 per cent in 1988, 45 per cent in 1989 and 40 per cent in 1990 to overtake the turnover performance of Laura Ashley's most successful UK store.

Laura Ashley's international expansion continued and by early 1991 there were over 500 outlets worldwide. Expansion in Continental Europe, primarily through shop-in-shops, was slow at first but gathered pace towards the end of the period. In North America, garments and home furnishing sales accounted for 70 and 30 per cent respectively of 1990/1 turnover of £136.2m. In the Pacific Basin, Laura Ashley's principal markets were Australia and Japan. The number of outlets in Japan doubled from 12 to 24 in the year to January 1990, a further 13 were opened by January 1991 and 12 more were planned for the following year.

RETRENCHMENT

By the end of the 1980s, Britain's economy was causing increasing concern in government and business circles alike. British business was bracing itself for a difficult start to the 1990s. High interest rates, combined with new restrictions on mortgage interest tax relief, brought a virtual standstill in the housing market. There were serious knock-on effects in the construction industry, and in home furnishing and home improvements markets. Sterling was under almost constant attack on foreign exchanges.

Among the casualties of the recession were a number of well-known competitors of Laura Ashley. At Next, the retail group that George Davies had made a high street star, many of the group's acquisitions were sold to reduce its debts and in December 1988 Davies was ousted. At Coloroll profits slumped and in March 1990 chairman John Ashcroft resigned. November saw Sir Ralph Halpern's departure from the Burton Group after a 39 per cent fall in profits.

Difficult Times at Laura Ashley

In the year to January 1989, Laura Ashley reported its first fall in profits, down to £20.26m from the previous year's figure of £23.08m. This was blamed on a 1m start-up loss at Willis & Geiger, higher interest charges, and the strength of sterling. Chief executive John James said that, in spite of the exchange rate problems, the company had adopted an expansionist policy in the USA, which it saw as its biggest potential market.

For the year to January 1990, the group reported a net loss of £4.7m before tax, despite sales increases across all divisions. Sir Bernard Ashley acknowledged the need to reduce the group's high borrowing levels and in response a major rationalisation programme was set in motion. This, he warned, might include disposals of businesses and restrictions on new shop openings. Among the exceptional costs for the year were management consultants' fees of £1.5m. Press comment on the group's losses highlighted a series of problems: in particular, severe production difficulties, especially over supplies to the USA. 'The 1989 autumn range arrived three months late in the shops long after everyone's thoughts had turned to spring.'[1]

Some commentators wondered whether Laura Ashley was becoming dated. 'What has happened is that the typical buyer has simply grown up. Laura Ashley has failed to provide for the more discerning sophisticated 30-plus consumers – who don't want their homes or their clothes to evoke the design team of a chain store.'[2]

In June 1990 difficult refinancing negotiations were concluded and the company agreed to recruit two new non-executive directors and strengthen its top management. John James acknowledged that the company had been overstretching its executive talent. For more than a year, to May 1990, the group had been without a finance director, and Mr James had covered this responsibility in addition to his role as chief executive. His long association with the group ended with his resignation on 1 September 1990. Press reports suggested that John James's attempts to reorganise the group had been hindered by the company's somewhat insular family culture and a very conservative board. The Ashley family's 70 per cent stake in the company led one writer to comment, 'the upheavals at Laura Ashley must make investors wonder whether companies should ever be floated with such dominant shareholdings'.[3]

At the end of August 1990 the Aeon Group, Laura Ashley's partner in Japan, acquired a 15 per cent stake in the group in return for a cash

[1] *Sunday Times*, 4 February 1990.
[2] Quoted in the *Sunday Times*, 4 February 1990.
[3] *Independent*, 25 August 1990.

injection of £39m. As part of the deal, Aeon secured exclusive rights to both sales and manufacture of Laura Ashley goods throughout Asia. The Aeon deal reduced Laura Ashley's gearing from 100 per cent plus to 30 per cent and Ashley family holdings fell to 59.2 per cent. Sir Bernard said he would allow his stake to fall below 50 per cent in the future as the company expanded. In September closure of seven UK factories was announced. 'It is no longer viable to source current levels of garments worldwide from our British factories when products of a similar quality can be bought at significantly lower cost from suppliers abroad,' said Sir Bernard.

The 1991 Report and Accounts highlighted actions taken to strengthen the group's financial position. Central controls over profit and cash management were implemented and new policies were introduced on capital expenditure and investment appraisal. A stringent stock control programme was implemented to reduce lead times, eliminate buffer stock and dispose of slow-selling lines. During the year net borrowings were reduced from £87m to £23m, and stocks from £105m to £40m.

Businesses that were not core to the Laura Ashley brand were closed or divested, including Penhaligon's, Bryant of Scotland and Sandringham Leather Goods. A programme to improve relations with the City, investors and the financial press was instigated to develop a better understanding of the company's plans and actions.

1991 Reorganisation

In his 1991 report, Sir Bernard highlighted the international brand name 'Laura Ashley' as the company's most valuable asset, and in order to develop and exploit the brand more effectively worldwide, a new corporate structure was put into place with effect from February 1991.

> The Group Marketing Division is responsible for all aspects of marketing the brand, and for designing and sourcing products to satisfy consumer expectations.
>
> The UK and Continental Europe Retail Divisions have been amalgamated with the objective of obtaining synergies from shared marketing and a reduction of overheads. The intention is to retain regional marketing focus. The retail divisions use their knowledge and experience of their own markets to maximise opportunities for Laura Ashley branded products.
>
> The Group Operations Division is responsible for co-ordinating the logistical aspects of the business, moving product from the suppliers into retail and other distribution outlets. It accommodates the in-house manufacturing

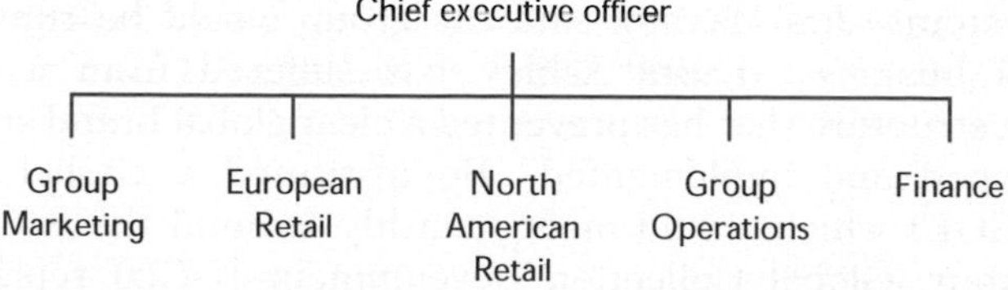

facilities which now comprise the print factories in Newtown, the Welsh-based garment operation (4 factories) and one home furnishing factory.

New Leadership

In July 1991 the company announced the appointment of a new group chief executive, Dr Jim Maxmin aged 48, to take effect from 16 September 1991.

Jim Maxmin was born in the United States and lived in the UK from 1964 to 1988. After completing a PhD in Philosophy at King's College, London, he joined Unilever plc, working primarily in marketing roles. In 1971 he joined Lex Service Group plc, rising to chief executive and joint chairman of Volvo Concessionaires UK by 1979. In 1983 he moved to Thorn-EMI as chief executive of television rentals. In 1988 he moved to Boston to oversee the acquisition of Rent-a-Center Inc. and was also appointed president of Thorn-EMI Inc.

Taking Stock

The new CEO's first few weeks were spent visiting Laura Ashley stores, manufacturing units and offices around the world. This confirmed to Jim Maxmin that the question of Laura Ashley's core identity had not been resolved. No one seemed to know whether its key strengths were in design, manufacturing or retailing, or resided primarily in the brand. The result was a lack of coherent strategy and operational and organisational confusion.

In Jim Maxmin's discussions with staff a common theme emerged – one of complexity, bureaucracy and people feeling impotent to act. They felt trapped within the group's 22 strategic business units, which forced them to think parochially rather than in global terms. Business units were managed vertically as profit centres with no integration of such key functions as warehousing, distribution, stock management and financial control.

Simplify, Focus and Act

Under the heading 'Simplify, Focus and Act', Jim Maxmin announced a major management reorganisation programme designed to refocus group activities. The changes would remove 100 management jobs and cost more than £5m. This included capital spending of £3m to upgrade and unify computer systems. Jim Maxmin said the group would be run as a single international business. 'Laura Ashley has suffered from a fragmented management structure that has prevented a clear global brand strategy from being developed and implemented.' He instituted a Global Operations Executive (GOE) which would meet monthly 'around the world'. On the marketing front, Global Collection Development (GCD) replaced Group

Marketing. Its mission was 'single global image marketing', rather than five or six separate campaigns.

Prior to Jim Maxmin's appointment, Glenne Gibson, senior retail consultant with Coopers Lybrand & Deloitte, had been recruited to develop Laura Ashley's marketing strategy. She set up a programme of quantitative and qualitative market research, the first comprehensive survey of its customers that Laura Ashley had undertaken. This elicited a huge response from some 57,000 customers in the UK and USA. The overriding message of the research was the very strong customer loyalty that the brand continued to enjoy. Other aspects of the research were fed back into the design process and the marketing of goods in shops. Commented Jim Maxmin:

> To my way of thinking Laura Ashley is a brand. It is not a retailing company. It is not a fashion company. It is not a production or manufacturing company. I see the management task as simply unleashing the intrinsic strength of that fantastic brand.[4]

One of the chief executive's main aims was to implement and explain the change programme to staff quickly, in order to avoid as much speculation and worry as possible. He ran a week of roadshows for senior managers throughout the world, making presentations in the UK and at the group's overseas locations in Holland, the USA and Japan. Senior managers then briefed staff using a video of the roadshow to support the communication process. The message was further reinforced by a special edition of the staff newspaper, *LA News*, distributed to every Laura Ashley employee around the world. Jim Maxmin said:

> This isn't a one-off thing. Our business is all about communication – talking with each other, talking to our customers and listening to what people have to say. All staff will be kept fully in touch with the decisions being made which will affect the operations and future of the company.

Described variously as an effusive, highly active manager with a ready line in marketing jargon and an obsessive concentration on target customers, and a man guided by market research, financial disciplines and management consistency, Jim Maxmin's management style came as something of a shock to Laura Ashley staff. Maxmin was an 'enabling manager' who believed in empowering employees in order to enhance customer service. Incentive schemes were introduced to encourage employee suggestions for improving customer service. To encourage corporate staff to make contact with customers and better understand the demands on shop staff, Maxmin asked all managers to spend at least one day each month working in a Laura Ashley shop.

In January 1992 Andrew Higginson, group finance director, announced a new five-year, £50m finance facility agreed with Laura Ashley's banks. This would replace the shorter three-year arrangement signed in

[4] *Financial Times*, 31 July 1991.

November 1990 and was seen as 'a strong vote of confidence from our banks ... and reflects our success in putting the business on a sound financial footing'.

Later that month Laura Ashley announced the appointment of Denise Lincoln as global human resources director. Recruited from Grand Metropolitan plc, where she had been group management development director, she was the first woman to join Laura Ashley's main board and her appointment reflected the importance attached by Jim Maxmin to 'the development of people in building a world class business'. A management development programme was put in place, designed to improve integration and understanding among the senior team. Significant changes were also made in the way in which the company recruited, trained and managed its shop staff. Older store managers were recruited to better match the age profile of Laura Ashley customers.

Logistics: A Strategic Alliance

On 19 March 1992 Laura Ashley and Federal Express Business Logistics announced a global alliance – reported as the first of its kind. The accompanying press release acknowledged that Laura Ashley's existing logistics were 'complex, costly and inefficient'. The agreement was seen as a critical step in Laura Ashley's 'Simplify, Focus and Act' programme. The benefits to Laura Ashley of the alliance were listed as follows:

- Savings from the simplification of the existing supply chain amounting to 10–12 per cent of total distribution costs (based on like-for-like service levels) as well as substantial reductions in working capital.
- Access to the global systems of Federal Express. This will provide Laura Ashley with leading-edge distribution systems within a short timeframe. At a minimum this will save Laura Ashley 3m in planned system development costs.
- The ability to improve customer service, with the objective of being able to deliver anywhere in the world within 24 to 48 hours if required, by September 1993.
- Enable Laura Ashley management to focus on areas of core competence.
- The key systems infrastructure to enable flexible response and the opportunity for new initiatives such as worldwide mail order.

The alliance was intended to be of indefinite duration, but had a minimum contract period of ten years. Over this period the estimated value to Federal Express was £150m. Commenting on the alliance, Jim Maxmin said:

> This alliance gives us access to management systems and logistics capacity that we could not dream of developing ourselves. It represents a quantum leap in our strategy of simplifying and focusing operations. We now have a unique

opportunity to break new ground in developing a global mail order business with the objective of 48-hour delivery anywhere in the world. The alliance opens the door to lower costs, enhanced delivery performance, higher stock turn and improved customer service. It also enables us to focus our own resources where we can add value to the core business.

Back From the Brink

Results for the year to 25 January 1992, released in April, showed a recovery from a £6.7m loss to a profit of £2.7m before exceptional items. 'The extraordinary thing about Laura Ashley is not that it has been dragged back from the financial brink', commented the *Daily Telegraph*, 'it is that it was ever pushed there in the first place. It took a rare combination of management failure, over-ambition and bad luck to bring such a business to its knees.'[5]

Pre-tax profits for the year to 30 January 1993 were £1.8m, but the group continued to suffer badly in the USA where stock problems produced a £6.9m loss. 'We are rebuilding the business, but that takes time,' said Jim Maxmin.

In February 1993 it was announced that the Ashley family had reduced its stake in the business with the sale of 10 million shares. This reduced the family's holding to about 50 per cent and followed the sale of a similar amount fourteen months earlier, when Sir Bernard had relinquished his executive duties. A further 30 million shares were sold in May and Sir Bernard retired as chairman of the company.

Headaches in the USA

Laura Ashley's difficulties in the USA had been hidden to some extent by the rapid growth of sales through new shop openings. However, analysis showed that no store had produced year-on-year growth after the second year. The group's problems in the USA had persisted for more than two years despite the efforts of Jim Maxmin and others to turn the operation around. He found that there were no standard shop operating systems, and that the managers of US shops were not as capable as their UK counterparts. In the fiscal year 1993/4, 53 per cent of US shop managers were replaced.

To add to the US problems, heavy snowstorms in March 1993 led to a loss of 800 store days as the spring and summer collection was being introduced, which led to yet more discounting. Since 40 per cent of Laura Ashley turnover was in the USA, losses there were jeopardising the group's development elsewhere.

---

[5] *Daily Telegraph*, 7 April 1992.

On 13 April 1994 Jim Maxmin abruptly announced his departure from Laura Ashley after a row over the group's American operations. The *Financial Times* commented:

> His departure, accompanied only by a brief statement, is unsatisfactory. The appointment of Mr Hugh Blakeway Webb as executive chairman looks like a victory for the old guard, who have let down shareholders before.[6]

The group made an operating loss of £100,000 for the half-year to 30 July 1994, after a £3.3m first tranche of restructuring costs. This figure included a £1.2m pay-off to Jim Maxmin.

BACK TO BASICS

More Restructuring

In marked contrast to the previous management, whose priority had been to invest in the Laura Ashley brand, the new management team emphasised its determination to tackle costs in every area of the business. It believed that substantial savings could be made by cutting jobs and rationalising offices and stock levels.

For the year to 28 January 1995, the group made a loss of £30.6m after absorbing £34.4m of exceptional charges. Hugh Blakeway Webb acknowledged that the action being taken was hurting, but said that it was necessary to return Laura Ashley to acceptable levels of profitability. The restructuring measures were aimed at tackling the group's £44m central overhead costs. Laura Ashley's ratio of sales to overheads stood at 14 per cent, whereas the average figure for comparable retailers was 10 per cent. The group's product range was also being rationalised to allow Laura Ashley to return to its core products and drive up margins. Ranges such as food, swimwear and furniture were to be scrapped.

With its share price languishing at around 75p, Laura Ashley was seen as vulnerable to predators seeking what, despite a decade of problems, remained a strong international brand.

A New Chief Executive

On 15 June 1995 it was announced that Ann Iverson had been persuaded to join Laura Ashley as chief executive after the top job had been left vacant

---

[6] *Financial Times*, 13 April 1994. Hugh Blakeway Webb was appointed a non-executive director and deputy chairman in January 1991. A partner at accountants Coopers & Lybrand Deloitte from 1983, Mr Blakeway Webb was known to be close to Sir Bernard Ashley and had advised him on tax matters since the early 1980s. He resigned his partnership prior to joining the Laura Ashley board.

for almost a year. Ann Iverson came to Britain in 1990 from Bloomingdales, the American retail group, to join Storehouse as BHS stores director. Two years later she became managing director of Mothercare and revitalised the ailing company. Mrs Iverson's appointment eased rumours that a bid for Laura Ashley was in the offing, but also had a less welcome effect. Lazards, Laura Ashley's merchant bank, terminated its relationship with the company because it had not been consulted over Ann Iverson's appointment.

In September 1995 Ann Iverson presented her first review of the business and announced that she was bringing the design, buying and merchandising functions under one roof, reducing the product range by a quarter, and introducing a common look across the group.

> By re-establishing a 'retail culture' and a strong unified look in the product ranges, the Laura Ashley brand still has scope for significant expansion. It is a brilliant brand, it is resilient; we haven't killed it. It is fixable, and we have positioned it at the end of three years for double-digit operating margins.

Previous restructuring attempts had concentrated on cutting costs, without considering how to develop the brand, and improve sales and gross margins. 'You never heard anything about how we were going to grow the business,' commented Mrs Iverson.

Her review of the company had shown that its clothing and furnishing products and its marketing lacked a 'single point of view'. The range was too broad, the supply chain was inefficient, and many shops – particularly in the USA – were too small. The group also lacked 'clear lines of accountability'. After tackling these problems, the next stage would be to make the supply chain more efficient. This would include a review of the role of manufacturing operations, which still supplied 25 per cent of Laura Ashley products. The store portfolio in the USA and UK would also be reviewed.[7]

Ann Iverson's observations came as the company reported a fall in pre-tax profits from £5.1m to £3m for the six months to 29 July 1995. As the group embarked on its targeted turnaround by the end of the decade, the company's shareholders kept their fingers firmly crossed.

Back to the Brink

In announcing a return to profit in April 1996, the company said that its turnaround would take another two to three years to complete. Ann Iverson said the group was embarking on an expansion programme in the USA and UK, but not in Continental Europe. 'We are going after real estate and growth relative to our opportunities right now, which are in the US and the UK,' said Mrs Iverson. She planned to expand the group's sales in home furnishings to two-thirds of total sales and reduce the garment element

---

[7] *Financial Times*, 22 September 1995.

accordingly. The store portfolio was being reshaped, with smaller stores being closed and replaced by larger outlets which could show a wider range of the home furnishings.

To the surprise of some commentators the group had decided to retain its manufacturing plant, but this was being radically overhauled. Finance director Jim Walsh said that the group's manufacturing plant in Wales had 'lost touch with economic reality'. Press reports spoke of 'horrific levels of seconds and utilisation running at a lowly 70 per cent'.[8] The 1,100 jobs in the Welsh operation would fall to around 700 over the next three years. Cost savings of £2m to £3m were expected.

The company also intended to cut costs in its distribution network, consolidating its use of Federal Express. Selling prices, which Ann Iverson said were too high, were also being scrutinised. The mail order business, which was reined back sharply in 1995 after a disastrous year, was to be relaunched.

'Analysts now believe the company has fallen into good retail hands,' commented the *Financial Times*.

> Mrs Iverson has already shown the light at the end of the tunnel by proving she can achieve cost savings, and has shrewdly latched on to the growth prospects of the home furnishings market in the US. It is possible the group will not even sell garments in 10 years' time.[9]

By 1998 the optimism of 1995 had proven to be ill-founded. Iverson was dismissed in November 1997 after a series of events reported in the press, including:

- issuing three profit warnings within a year;
- extremely high stock levels, resulting in huge discounts on surplus stock;
- halting the US expansion programme after too many shops were opened in wrong locations, and concentrating too heavily on home furnishings;
- giving shareholders unrealistic recovery expectations;
- the unsuccessful re-launch of the Laura Ashley brand.

The company was left with a weak financial position, resulting in the closure of the Welsh factories. In May 1998, Laura Ashley was saved from bankruptcy by a £44 million cash injection from a Malaysian tycoon who obtained a 40 per cent share of the business. The departure of Sir Bernard Ashley as a director followed the Malaysian backing. In August 1998 David Hoare, who had taken over as Chief Executive when Iverson left, was also replaced.

(For more detailed developments of Laura Ashley's activities between 1995 and 1998 see WWW.)

---

[8]*Independent*, 19 April 1996.
[9]*Financial Times*, 19 April 1996.

APPENDIX 1 GROUP FINANCIAL RECORD, 1991–6

	1996 (m)	1995 (m)	1994 (m)	1993 (m)	1992 (m)	1991 (m)
Profit and loss account						
Turnover	336.6	322.6	300.4	247.8	262.8	328.1
Operating profit/loss before exceptional operating costs	9.1	4.1	2.3	1.1	–0.6	3.4
Exceptional operating costs	0.1	–33.4	–	–	–	–
Operating profit/loss	9.2	–29.3	2.3	1.1	–0.6	3.4
Profit from associated undertakings	2.0	1.5	1.8	1.5	1.9	0.1
Exceptional items	–	–1.0	–	–	–8.1	–2.6
Net interest payable	–0.9	–1.8	–1.1	–0.8	–2.3	–12.4
Profit/(loss) on ordinary activities before taxation	10.3	–30.6	3.0	1.8	–9.1	–11.5
Taxation	–3.3	–0.9	–1.9	–1.0	–	2.5
Profit/(loss) on ordinary activities after taxation	7.0	–31.5	1.1	0.8	–9.1	–9.0
Dividends	–1.2	–	–0.2	–0.1	–0.1	–0.1
Retained profit/(loss) for the year	5.8	–31.5	0.9	0.7	–9.2	–9.1
Balance sheets						
Fixed assets	45.2	48.3	71.7	66.3	60.5	67.1
Net current assets	27.0	43.7	50.2	53.9	52.8	66.9
Long-term creditors	–0.9	–15.0	–35.1	–34.4	–28.0	–41.4
Provisions for liabilities and charges	–8.3	–21.3	–0.7	–0.3	–0.5	–0.4
Net assets	63.0	55.7	86.1	85.5	84.8	92.2
Issued capital	11.8	11.7	11.7	11.7	11.7	11.7
Reserves	51.2	44.0	74.4	73.8	73.1	80.5
Equity shareholders' funds	63.0	55.7	86.1	85.5	84.8	92.2
Statistics						
Earnings/(loss) per share (p)	2.97	–13.41	0.45	0.34	–3.86	–4.39
Dividends per share (p)	0.50	–	0.10	0.10	0.10	0.10
Operating profit as a percentage of sales (%)	2.7	1.3	0.8	0.4	0.2	1.0
Profit/(loss) on ordinary activities before taxation as a percentage of net assets (%)	16.3	–54.9	3.5	2.1	–10.7	–12.5
Net asset value per ordinary share (p)	26.6	23.7	36.6	36.4	36.1	39.3
Gearing (%)	–	–1	19	19	5	25

THE IONA COMMUNITY

Peter H. Jones

The Iona Community is a voluntary group centred in Scotland but having a widespread reputation. The case illustrates the role of values and history in the management and decisions of an organisation. It shows how, as time moves on, an organisation needs to redefine its role. But there are difficulties in doing this when there are strong values underpinning the organisation and a need to take organisation members along with any changes. It is made especially difficult when members' adherence to the organisation is largely emotional rather than monetary. The case also shows that there may well be conflicts between the espoused aims of an organisation and the practicalities of implementing those aims.

• • •

The Iona Community is an association of some 200 members committed to work out together a particular expression of their Christian beliefs. The movement, started in the 1930s, is popularly associated with the Abbey on Iona, a small island off the west coast of Scotland. Its leader, Norman Shanks, indicated the difficulties of giving concrete shape to its purpose as the early vision of its founder ceased to be so obviously relevant 60 years on.

> It was easy to see the Community's purpose being fulfilled when we were re-building the Abbey. Now it is less tangible; it is building the Church in the world; it is building lives of service and celebration in God's Kingdom. We still need to be linked to our centres in Iona, but we must be more than an agency which runs a spiritual conference centre.

AN HISTORICAL REVIEW OF DEVELOPMENTS

The Iona Community was founded in 1938 by George MacLeod, a Church of Scotland minister. In the 1930s he had a parish in the shipbuilding area of

---

This case study was written by Peter H. Jones, Sheffield Business School. The co-operation of the Iona Community is gratefully acknowledged. The study is for educational use and is not designed to portray either good or poor management practices.

Govan in Glasgow, but though preaching to a large congregation of middle- and upper-class people, he made little impact on the working-class men of Govan. He felt that his training had been irrelevant to the concerns and language of the industrial working class of his parish.

His vision to change this was to put ministers and craftsmen alongside each other in a long-term building project where they could work together and learn from each other. An opportunity to do just this arose on the tiny island of Iona, lying off the west coast of Scotland.

Why Iona? To understand this one must travel back 1,400 years, to AD 563, when Saint Columba with twelve followers landed from Ireland on Iona. Columba used Iona as a base for the establishment of Christianity and Christian colonies all over Scotland and as far afield as the east coast of England. During the following 1,400 years several monasteries were built, destroyed and rebuilt on the site. In 1899 the Duke of Argyll, who owns the land and the monastery, made a gift of the Abbey remains to the Iona Cathedral Trust, an independent trust body representing the established Church of Scotland. An appeal was launched and the Abbey cathedral was restored by the Trust between 1902 and 1910 through public subscription money. The monastery, however, remained in ruins.

In MacLeod's vision, rebuilding the monastery was fused with his passionate desire to find a way to renew the corporate life of the church in industrial settings. He resigned as parish minister of Govan. The Iona Community was born: 1938 saw it start with George MacLeod and twelve others. On Iona in the summer months, the pattern of living was simple, austere and communal: worship led by MacLeod himself – morning and evening – was part of the pattern; eight hours of manual labour rebuilding the monastery; communal sleeping accommodation; shared chores. At the end of the summer, the twelve returned to mainland Scotland – ministers to their work in their churches, craftsmen to seek scarce work.

Those first minister-members wished to remain as a community, and a pattern emerged in which the 'member' was the man who had been through an initial two years' training experience; the man still serving those two years was to be regarded as a novice. Even though the rebuilding of the Abbey was completed in 1967, those embarking upon a two-year initiation programme still attend a 'Work Week' when manual work of maintaining or improving a centre is done. Thus elements of the original concept of creating community through shared work is maintained.

As new members joined in the rebuilding work, the Iona Community began to grow. But what does community mean for members on the mainland of Scotland living apart from each other? The answer that evolved is embodied in five personal disciplines to which members commit themselves. It forms the 'five-fold rule of the Iona Community' or, more simply, 'The Rule'.

The five-fold rule calls each member to:

1. Daily Bible reading, and prayer for each other, common concerns, and the wider work of the church.

2. Share and account for the use of their money – the economic discipline. Members donate a tenth of their disposable income to the work of the Community and the wider work of the church.
3. Account for the use of their time to their 'Family group'.
4. Act for justice and peace in society. A full statement of the commitment in this area is given in Appendix 1.
5. Meet with and account to each other. Each member belongs to one of 28 geographically-based Family groups which meet monthly, and is also expected to attend some of the four annual Plenary meetings.

Up to the mid-1960s members were almost exclusively male ordained ministers of the Church of Scotland, but that is no longer so. By 1995 there were 201 members; 95 were ordained, 120 were domiciled in Scotland, and 90 were women.

But if the Rule defines the Community, what does the Community do? There are three strands which have developed over the years. They are the Island Centres, the mainland work, and the Wild Goose Publishing arm of the Community. Each is described in turn.

THE ISLAND CENTRES

The *Abbey*, finished in 1967, can accommodate 44 guests, mostly in bunk-bedded rooms. During 1995 just over 1,500 people stayed, as is customary, for a week's programme, being charged £150 per adult for a week's full board. However, the Community did not see the Abbey as a holiday hotel. As early as 1939 lecturers had been invited to lead discussion with the new minister-members on topics concerning how spiritual and secular matters should relate. A programme on these broad lines has continued ever since. A week on Iona is thus focused on the experience of sharing 'the common life' through a combination of relaxation, worship, discussion and daily chores.

Young people's camps have also been a feature of the Community's work on Iona. However, by the mid-1980s the accommodation for these was becoming inadequate and inappropriate. With increasing numbers also coming to the Abbey, a decision was taken to celebrate the 90th birthday of the founder with the establishment of the *MacLeod Centre*. Opened in 1988, at a cost of £1 million, it has accommodation for 52 guests. The Mac, as it is known, is particularly geared to young people and families, and has residential facilities for the disabled (lacking in the Abbey). It is close to the Abbey and many events are shared. Charges are the same as at the Abbey. In 1995 just over 1,300 people stayed.

The centres are staffed by 24 full-time staff who look after the running of the Abbey, the Mac, a shop and a coffee house shop. About half are on one-year appointments, though some, including the warden of the Abbey and the director of the MacLeod Centre are three-year appointments. In addition some 30 extra volunteer staff are paid 'pocket money', and over

100 volunteers work on Iona over the season for periods of 6–12 weeks. There is a policy that the Abbey warden should be a member of the Community, so that the key leadership position should be filled by a person committed to the vision and purposes of the Community.

The centres are open from March to December, though there is minimal use in November and December. In the other eight months the Abbey has an occupancy of 99 per cent and the Mac just under 80 per cent. Though full details of potential bookings turned away were not kept, it was believed that the Abbey accommodation was oversubscribed three or four times over. It was hoped to increase total guests to 3,500 for 1996.

In 1994 just under half the guests came as part of a group, the remainder being individual bookings. Twelve groups (out of 90 group bookings) were brought by Community members, and there was a desire for this to be a higher proportion. However, fewer members were working in jobs where they had opportunities to take groups away for residential experiences. Thus increasingly guests came by word-of-mouth recommendations. No post was primarily responsible for publicity or marketing the centres.

A third much smaller residential centre operated by the Community was not on Iona, but on the adjacent larger island of Mull. The *Camas Adventure Centre* provides accommodation for sixteen. Its emphasis is on outdoor activities for young people.

Financial data for the centres are included in Appendix 2.

THE MAINLAND WORK

The work and initiatives of the Community on the mainland of Britain are many and varied. They arise from the concern of members to see their Christian beliefs and commitment to the purposes and ideals of the Community worked out in the wider society. Seven working groups seek to raise awareness of particular issues within the Iona Community, to influence outside agencies (including churches and government), and to network with other similarly concerned groups. In 1995 two of the working groups were supported by full-time paid workers.

The *Justice and Peace Planning* group aimed to create practical expressions of all members' general commitment to this area. There were a variety of initiatives: an exhibition on Iona on fair trade between nations; the promotion of a video 'The Invisible Wall', exploring how trade and debt are used to exploit the world's poorest people; a resources centre and a Peace House, with a full-time peace and justice worker, supported jointly with the Quakers.

The *Youth Work Planning* group supported and advised the Community's Youth Development worker, including the mounting of a Youth Programme on Iona and Camas. Some of the programme weeks had specific themes (e.g. exploring prejudice and reconciliation); others were open weeks attracting school parties. Both types sought to give a flavour of the

'Iona Experience'. Additionally, the group organised a range of opportunities in which young people who have been to Iona can maintain contact with each other.

The main purpose of the *Interfaith and Racism* working group was to raise awareness of the perceived need for change in the nationality and immigration laws of the UK.

The *Cause of the Poor* group acted to support and lobby for legislation on social and disability issues.

The *Rediscovery of Spirituality* group sought to refocus the Community's energy towards 'reflective activism'. Work included reviewing the training of new members, and encouraging members in their prayer discipline to fulfil item 1 of the Rule.

The *Sharing Communion by the year 2000* group aimed to encourage and support members in ecumenical activity.

The *Constitutional Matters* group dealt mainly with issues concerning Scotland's constitutional relationship within the United Kingdom.

Groups met on an *ad hoc* basis. Few members belonged to more than one group. Each group had a budget principally to cover travelling expenses of members on group matters. There was no fixed measure of a group's success, though most groups provided themes and leaders for Iona weeks. If a particular topic emerged, a new group could be created and a budget sanctioned, subject to the approval of Council. In 1995 there was the possibility of groups forming to deal with interfaith issues (as it was felt the existing group concentrated on race issues), and unemployment and work issues.

In addition to the working groups there was the *Wild Goose Resource and Worship* group. This comprised four full-time workers and sixteen volunteer young adults involved in developments in worship which 'capture the imagination and enable the participation of young people'. By 1995 funding for the group was mainly self-generated (70 per cent), with the Church of Scotland (20 per cent) and the Iona Community (10 per cent) making up the balance, although historically the self-generated funding proportion had been significantly lower.

Norman Shanks, the leader of the Community, summed up this aspect of the Community's work:

> Our primary emphasis is not what any full time staff can do, but what members do in their daily lives of work, worship and service. We are not out to build an Iona empire but to be a gift to the Church.

WILD GOOSE PUBLICATIONS

The publishing arm of the Community, Wild Goose Publications, sold books of Christian songs and associated cassettes, meditations and prayers, and collections of short drama pieces for use in worship. In 1994 it had sales of £112,000, making a loss of £6,000. Of those sales, 81 per cent were accounted for by material generated by the Wild Goose resource group. The main reason for the loss was a slowdown in new titles published, arising from several changes of personnel. Since 1995 there had been a move to broaden the scope of material published by Wild Goose to include more works dealing with the wider work of the Community.

A 'BIAS TO THE POOR'?

In maintaining and running the centres on Iona, Community members wanted there to be a policy of a 'bias to the poor' in their use. This was felt to be consistent with one founding purpose of the Community, to blend together people from all walks of life. Thus in both centres there were special discounts for families, groups and young people. Those on benefit or low income could apply for special subsidised rates which were funded from the Subsidy Fund: £15,000 was available in 1994 for this purpose. This had enabled 204 guests to be subsidised at the two centres. The sum of £8,500 was used to allow four groups to come to the Mac at virtually no cost. The remainder was spread fairly evenly across all weeks at both centres. There was a general feeling among Community members that more subsidies should be given. Otherwise a fear expressed was that the centres would become 'middle-class spiritual Butlins offering a dose of quick fix spirituality'. Money for the Subsidy Fund came from the interest on the Islands Access Fund. This was a typical way in which charities turned capital gifts and legacies into income. The Fund had been set up in 1989 when interest rates were high and interest income was expected to provide a healthy amount for the purpose. But as interest rates fell in the 1990s, so had the Subsidy Fund. The Community had committed itself to increase the Access Fund from its 1994 level of £160,000 to £500,000. In 1994 applications to the Subsidy Fund were significantly oversubscribed.

However, there was considerable debate over the effectiveness of the mechanisms to achieve the aim of getting mixed socioeconomic groups at the centres. Of the £15,000 subsidy given in 1994, only £3,200 was to guests at the Abbey, the rest was to those going to the Mac. In members' eyes this reinforced the stereotypes that the Abbey catered mainly for 'middle-class English women', while 'younger Scottish males' went to the Mac centre. But according to Peter Macdonald, the convener of the Islands Committee:

> We don't want to perpetuate this situation. I hope we can move towards a greater mix of people at the Abbey. If we then have to say 'no' to repeat bookings from, for example, English middle-class areas I'd not worry. But I'm not happy about our procedures to make this greater mix happen through subsidy payments. Some may be put off by the high cost and by the impression this could give that the Abbey was not the place for folk like them. That 'cultural shift in guests' occurred at the Mac when we went from a youth camp charging £20 per week to a purpose-built centre charging nearer £150; and then some people wondered why our client group changed!

Another convener echoed this thought.

> We need to make the Mac centre much more of a youth centre – not a carbon copy of the Abbey. Unfortunately fewer of our members now work with the poor, or in churches in poor areas. There has been a shift in our members' jobs. Perhaps as a Community we are no longer seen as being on the cutting edge of new forms of church life; not seen as so relevant to younger church ministers. We need to be more proactive in seeking out what I call the 'multipliers'; those such as teachers, social workers, and youth workers who can bring groups of the disadvantaged to Iona. The state has taken over more responsibility in this area compared to 40 years ago, so we need to capture such people's interest. We have written a job description to appoint someone to market the centres to these groups – but not made an appointment yet.

The 'Robin Hood' mechanism of charging guests more than costs and using the excess to offer more subsidies drew mixed reactions.

> I'd be happy with it, as long as it wasn't too blatant, especially in the Abbey. It would be a tragedy if we only got wealthy guests. It would be great to get more mixed groups.

> I'd be reluctant to do this. I don't think you can mix people if they know they are paying different rates. I feel the younger Scots would end up saying 'they are not my kind of people'.

> If the price went up too much, guests would expect a higher level of service – we'd end up just running a hotel.

There was a two-stage booking procedure. Draft brochures for the following year were sent in August to groups who had previously booked. Confirmed brochures were not sent to individual members and friends until December. Group bookings were accepted from November, but individuals could not apply until January. It was rare for people from poorer areas to apply as individuals. Thus the 'bias to the poor' was largely driven by groups that applied.

ISLAND CENTRES OWNERSHIP

Surprisingly, perhaps, the Community only owned one of the three centres it used: the Mac.

The Abbey was owned by the Iona Cathedral trustees. This body was set up in 1899 by the then Duke of Argyll to look after the Abbey, but had no endowment money. Since 1938 when the Community commenced the completion of the monastic buildings, the Community have effectively both occupied and looked after the buildings. Only since the early 1980s have the Trustees become active again in terms of both fundraising and buildings maintenance. It had become increasingly clear to them that some full-time management was needed to administer their responsibilities, and that any large donors or funding bodies would need to see a properly constituted management structure in place to administer moneys donated for the preservation or development of the Abbey. Thus in 1993 Iona Abbey Limited was formed.

The split of responsibilities was that the maintenance of the Abbey Cathedral, and of the exterior of all the Abbey buildings, grounds and monuments, was the responsibility of Iona Abbey Ltd, while the Community undertook the internal maintenance of the Abbey buildings. The Community had an agreement to use and occupy the Abbey buildings at zero cost. This agreement is due for renewal in 1999.

The chief executive of Iona Abbey Ltd was a successful architect and property developer. He maintained that the Community had assumed responsibilities for running activities such as the bookshop and coffee shop in a situation where the legal lease position was not clearly specified. The Cathedral trustees had not really been interested in such matters. He pointed out that the Community:

- Paid no realistic rent for use of the Abbey buildings.
- Repaired the interior of the Abbey buildings, but had no obligation to do so, other than a need to operate the accommodation.
- Paid only 20 per cent of their heating bills.
- Paid no rent on the coffee shop and bookshop, yet took the profits and used the shops as a 'shop window' where the Community's concerns were publicised.
- Took on responsibility for showing visitors round the Abbey cathedral.

He believed that this situation needed to be put on a 'proper footing' and wished to create an understood partnership between the Community and Iona Abbey Ltd.

Asked why the current 'murky situation' should not continue, he feared a renewal of what he called a 'giving-barrel war' as the financial needs of maintaining the Abbey increased. In such a 'war', visitors to the island could be confused and antagonised by separate requests for money from two bodies, each claiming jurisdiction over different parts of the Abbey.

> With over 120,000 visitors to Iona each year, this could be a real bone of contention. In 1997, it will be 1,400 years since the death of Columba. This can be a national tourist event, an opportunity not to be missed. Visitors from all over the world will be coming to Scotland and Iona. I have plans for several major events. There must not be open war between the Community and the Abbey during this period.
>
> I can see various undesirable outcomes which neither party wants unless we develop a realistic partnership. If the lease is not renewed, it could split the Church of Scotland. There is a lot of goodwill towards the Community in Scotland as a whole. Besides, I personally don't want to see the Abbey becoming a luxury hotel only for wealthy guests. I support what the Community is doing, but not all the Trustees are sympathetic to the radical stances of the Community, especially on the nuclear issue. If we cannot come to some agreement, we could pull out of the monastery altogether, forcing the

> Community to take over all the exterior maintenance as well. I very much doubt they would be set up to or want to do that.

Community members, in general, saw a responsibility to co-operate with Iona Abbey Ltd. As one member said, 'We must not be confrontational, but on the other hand we must not let them walk all over us.'

Detailed discussions had not taken place over the issue of the lease renewal, but representative views included:

> If the rent went up so high that we had to charge, say, £300 per week, I'd rather pull out.
>
> There are very stringent rules on what one can do in such a historic building, but we have to live here. You cannot live in a monument; there needs to be a greater degree of sympathy to us.
>
> Keeping up the monastery interior is a form of rent anyway. Normally landlords would do that for you.

Faced with the question of what would happen to the Community if the lease on the Abbey were not renewed at a satisfactory rent, reaction was fairly uniform. One said:

> Losing it would be tragic, but not a death blow. We'd have the Mac centre on the island, and we could still worship in the Abbey itself. We might well develop a mainland base. Our Community is a community of the heart, whereas often the Church is a community of the mind. Losing Iona would be a blow to our heart, but I hope members see the Community as more than Iona – it is a movement of like-minded people.

Another commented:

> Iona holds the key to vivid experiences in which we have encountered one another and God. I had a personal crisis just recently. To sort myself out I went 'home' – to Iona. It's my spiritual home, although I know God is not restricted to Iona.

The buildings used by the Camas Camp on Mull were owned by the Duke of Argyll and leased at a rent of £400 p.a. This lease was renegotiated in 1995 without difficulty.

ORGANISATION AND DECISION MAKING IN THE COMMUNITY

Legally the Iona Community was a company limited by guarantee, but the diverse set of activities undertaken by the members and full-time staff of the Community was co-ordinated by a structure of leader, Council and committees. The ultimate authority was a Plenary meeting.

The *Publishing* committee acted as an editorial board and gave policy direction to Wild Goose Publications.

The *Mainland* committee oversaw the working groups and outreach projects, including the Wild Goose resource group.

The *Islands* committee set policy for the three centres on Iona and Mull.

The *Finance and Staffing* committee acted in a co-ordinating role for matters relating to central administration and finance. It comprised the conveners (chairs) of the above three committees, six elected members, the Iona warden and four members of staff (the leader and three heads of department) from the Glasgow office of the Community. It met seven times a year in the afternoon, when in the evening the Council met.

The *Council* was the main executive body of the Community. It consisted of six elected members of the Community, the four conveners of the above committees – all as voting members – together with the leader, Iona warden and three heads of departments, who did not have voting rights.

The committees and Council involved just over 30 members of the Community. All positions were elected for a three-year term, and there was usually not too much difficulty filling vacancies, although ensuring knowledge levels adequate to the tasks was sometimes problematic. On occasions there had been the need to hold elections (particularly for the Islands committee) when more than one nomination was received, but this was not frequent.

The Community met in *Plenary* four times a year:

- Twice a year for a day to discuss a current topic of interest. There was an attempt to move these around the country, but geography and British Rail meant they were usually in central Scotland.
- Once (in Glasgow) for the AGM and the transaction of business formalities.
- For a week on Iona during Community Week.

Members shared their concerns at Plenary meetings, which provided a focus for opinion sounding and communal decision taking.

Although formally the Community's ultimate decision body, the Plenary meetings usually discussed only general strategy issues, setting down a policy framework within which Council worked out detailed decision making. Attendance at Plenaries varied. At the Community Week on Iona there were usually about 100–120 members; meetings in central Scotland attracted about 80, while a meeting in Newcastle in 1994 attracted only 40. One English member explained:

> There is a real barrier at the England/Scotland border. Few Scottish members travel south when we hold Plenaries in England, and English members feel put out by this. We're expected to travel to Scotland, but it doesn't work the other way round.

The various committees wrestled with the extent to which they should be involved in day-to-day matters. The senior full-time administrator saw a distinction between the Community as a 'movement' and as an 'organisation'. He wanted a clear distinction between setting policy (the purpose of committees) and operational management (the remit of full-time staff). However, he acknowledged that longer-standing committee members found it difficult to let go of minor matters.

Among some committee conveners there was a wish to focus the energy of the Community.

> Some working groups do too little. We should be prepared to close down working groups or give them a limited life. We need to be clear what added value we give to activities as the Iona Community. For me that is the Iona experience of community, and our ability to link faith and spirituality with a concern for social justice.

In a Strategic Plan Review, the convener of Council wrote:

> Review of strategy is not first and foremost an opportunity to refine a structure, nor to oil the wheels of an organisation. It is rather the attempt to allow ourselves to be disturbed and challenged – even goaded – into new things to stay faithful to the same God.

The leader of the Community was elected by and from the membership, and had a seven-year term of office. Norman Shanks became leader in August 1995, having served on all four committees and Council since he became a member in 1980. He saw a variety of roles for the leader: as the public relations face of the Community, as a pastor to members, offering support and encouragement, and as the clarifier and embodiment of the purpose and direction of the Community. Looking out from what he saw as a basically healthy Community, he said:

> We must not lose our nerve or sense of direction. We must continue with a sense of adventure, faith and hope that God is at work in the world through us, as in so many other ways. We must also not lose our sense of togetherness. A Community of many more than the present 200 could easily become too fragmented, lacking cohesion and togetherness. Larger scale would change our character.

RELATING TO THE WIDER WORLD

The Community, through its members, had many informal contacts with the outside world. It was not a closed Community, a sect or a cult. The great majority of individual members were members of local churches.

As an entity, there was a formal link to mainstream churches through the Iona Community Board of the Church of Scotland. This board, appointed by the Church of Scotland, also contained representatives of other denominations to which Community members belonged (such as the Church of England, Roman Catholic, United Reformed, Methodist and Society of Friends). It received an annual report on the activities of the Community and acted as a formal channel of communication regarding the Community's concerns and activities.

The Community was affiliated to several other organisations, including the following:

- Church Action on Poverty.
- Christian CND.
- The Scottish Environmental Forum.
- The Ecumenical Association of Laity Centres.
- The Scottish Council for Voluntary Organisations.
- Strathclyde Community Relations Council.
- Action for Southern Africa.
- Ecumenical Committee for Corporate Responsibility.

Such affiliations provided networking possibilities for members, in addition to their own personal links to a whole range of bodies. This provided immense networking potential to the Community as a whole.

Iona was a popular place for visitors and pilgrims. This was a combination of the Abbey Church, its Benedictine and Columban antecedents, and the Community itself. On summer days there could be upwards of 1,000 visitors and over 120,000 per year. Visitors to the Abbey were asked by Iona Abbey Ltd to make a donation of £2 towards its upkeep and most did. This money went to the Abbey trustees. The Community operated both the coffee house and Abbey shop, which catered for day visitors as well as residents. In both these shops the work and concerns of the Community were publicised.

Over the years many people who had visited Iona, who had stayed at the Abbey or Mac centres, or who just wished to keep in contact with what the Iona Community stood for, had expressed a wish to be linked to the Community and support its work. There was an active network of just over 1,600 Friends of the Community, who received its bi-monthly magazine, *The Coracle*. Additionally there were around 1,400 Associates who were bound by the Prayer discipline of the Rule, and who could follow the other disciplines voluntarily. They were encouraged to participate in the economic discipline by donating 2 per cent of their disposable income to a 'Common Fund' whose disposition was decided by a sub-group of Associates.

A SUCCESSFUL COMMUNITY?

Musing about success over a cup of coffee, the Islands convener said:

> Over the last 10 years we've grown considerably. We've been scrambling to keep pace. Turnover has gone from tens of thousands to a million pounds. We've just started to get a grip on our finances and budgets. I suppose only now are we starting to answer the 'success' question. Up to now our answers have been anecdotal. We do believe lives have been changed; people tell us so. They tell us that in their struggles, they have found peace. Quantitatively, however, I don't think we have many measures. I sometimes wonder if we should?

APPENDIX 1 STATEMENT ON 'JUSTICE AND PEACE COMMITMENT'

We believe:

1 that the Gospel commands us to seek peace founded on justice and that costly reconciliation is at the heart of the Gospel.
2 that work for justice, peace and an equitable society is a matter of extreme urgency.
3 that God has given us partnership as stewards of creation and that we have a responsibility to live in a right relationship with the whole of God's creation.
4 that, handled with integrity, creation can provide for the needs of all, but not for the greed which leads to injustice and inequality, and endangers life on earth.
5 that everyone should have the quality and dignity of a full life that requires adequate physical, social and political opportunity, without the oppression of poverty, injustice and fear.
6 that social and political action leading to justice for all people and encouraged by prayer and discussion, is a vital work of the Church at all levels.
7 that the use or threatened use of nuclear and other weapons of mass destruction is theologically and morally indefensible and that opposition to their existence is an imperative of the Christian faith.

As members and family groups we will:

8 engage in forms of political witness and action, prayerfully and thoughtfully, to promote just and peaceful social, political and economic structures.
9 work for a British policy of renunciation of all weapons of mass destruction and for the encouragement of other nations, individually or collectively, to do the same.
10 work for the establishment of the United Nations Organisation as the principal organ of international reconciliation and security, in place of military alliances.
11 support and promote research and education into non-violent ways of achieving justice, peace and a sustainable global society.
12 work for the reconciliation within and among nations by international sharing and exchange of experience and people, with particular concern for politically and economically oppressed nations.

APPENDIX 2 FINANCIAL PERFORMANCE: PROFIT AND LOSS BY ACTIVITY (£000)

	1991	1992	1993	1994
Shops on Iona	75	74	107	115
The Abbey	13	48	49	65
Mac centre	−13	12	−7	21
Camas	−7	−2	−3	−5
Islands admin.	n/a[1]	−65	−91	−99
Outreach projects	−9	−14	−29	−15
Wild Goose Publications	−16	−8	27	−6
Net HQ staffing[2]	−35	−53	−65	−86
Total	9	−8	−12	−10

[1]In 1992 the basis of accounting was changed. Islands Admin. is the cost of central administration of all the activities of the centres and shops, i.e. the four account categories above it.

[2]Donations from members are included in this category.

SHEFFIELD THEATRES TRUST

Gareth Morgan and Kevan Scholes

The case study concerns a charitable trust which is responsible for two of the UK's leading provincial theatres – the Crucible and Lyceum Theatres in Sheffield (plus a third stage – the Studio). It covers the period from 1971 (when the Crucible Theatre opened) to 1996. During the 25-year period the theatres saw many new developments and significant changes in the environment, particularly regarding funding. The case study shows that strategy formulation is not a simple process of matching capabilities to environmental 'requirements'. It is crucial to analyse the political context within which strategies are formulated. Stakeholder analysis is a useful method of analysing this political dimension. The fact that the theatre has both commercial and public service objectives to pursue illustrates that strategy formulation usually proceeds through a process of compromise and the balancing of different stakeholder interests and not through optimisation of the needs of just one group.

• • •

> Theatres face survival fight – subsidies in danger as audiences dwindle ... But Sheffield Theatres chief executive Stephen Barry and Board chairman John Cornwell said they welcomed Sheffield Council's call for a three year survival plan to ensure the future of live drama in the city.
>
> *SHEFFIELD STAR*, MAY 1996

Sheffield has two distinct theatrical traditions: a profile of high-quality production theatre (represented by the Playhouse and subsequently by the Crucible) and a strong history of touring theatre (for which the main venue is the Lyceum). This distinction is fundamental: a producing theatre, through its artistic director, commissions and finances its own productions and employs its own artistes. By contrast, a touring theatre enters into

---

This case study was prepared by Dr Gareth G. Morgan and Professor Kevan Scholes, Sheffield Business School, with the assistance of theatre management, external bodies and press reports. It incorporates information from the previous Crucible Theatre case studies (1976, 1988, 1992). It is intended as a basis for class discussion and not as an illustration of either good or bad management practice. Please note: Sheffield Theatres regrets that it *cannot* respond to further enquiries related to this case study.

contracts with touring companies, which bring their productions (and their own artistes) to the theatre concerned.

Today, these traditions are brought together in a charitable company known as the Sheffield Theatres Trust, which is unique in the UK in running a producing house and a touring house in one complex. By 1995, Sheffield Theatres was hosting total attendances of over 350,000 per year across its three stages. Serving the population of the fourth largest English city outside London, it had almost £4.5m overall income, making it one of the largest 350 charities in the UK.

THEATRE BUILDINGS IN SHEFFIELD

The Lyceum Theatre opened in 1897; it was designed by the leading theatre architect of the day, and is now a grade II listed building. It has the rare advantages among traditional theatres of having no pillars obstructing audience views and of having one of the deepest stages in the country. By the early part of the twentieth century it had established itself as one of the UK's leading touring venues, a reputation which grew further in the 1940s. In the 1950s and 1960s it was especially famous for pantomime. But lack of investment and modern amenities forced the Lyceum to close as a venue for music and drama in 1968; demolition was considered, but it subsequently became a bingo hall.

Modern producing theatre in Sheffield dates from the foundation of the Sheffield Repertory Company around 1923, which was renamed 'The Playhouse' in 1938. Initially its work was purely commercial, but it received an Arts Council of Great Britain grant (£5,000) in the 1960/1 season: 'to allow the Playhouse to undertake more prestigious productions than their own resources allow'. This grant marked the change from commercial to subsidised theatre, a transition completed in 1963 when the Playhouse became one of only eight theatres outside London to be taken into formal association with the Arts Council.

In 1966 Sheffield Council announced its intention to sponsor the building of a new theatre of 800–900 seats, and a board of trustees was appointed with representatives from Sheffield Council, the University of Sheffield, the Trades and Labour Council, and the Playhouse itself. This board was responsible for organising the public appeal and other decisions about building the new theatre. This would be mainly a producing house, although with the demise of the Lyceum, it would also host some touring productions.

The result was the Crucible Theatre, completed in 1971 at a total cost of £884,000, on a site next door to the old Lyceum. The 'Crucible' name was chosen to reflect the design of the building and Sheffield's historically famous steel industry. After some controversy, the final building comprised a main auditorium with 1,000 seats around three sides of a thrust stage (which critics complained limited its use for large-scale opera and ballet), and a smaller Studio Theatre with 250 seats (now increased to 400). Sheffield Corporation agreed to lease the site (valued at £250,000) and in addition agreed to contribute £350,000 to the capital cost. The Arts Council granted a further £300,000 from its 'Housing the Arts' fund. A further £150,000 was raised from the public appeal and £50,000 from the Gulbenkian Foundation.

The Playhouse completed its last season in 1970/1 and the Crucible opened in a blaze of local publicity. One of the most notable differences between the Crucible and the old Playhouse was the range of activities which were undertaken. Apart from the two stages, there was a restaurant, coffee bar, shop and licensed bar. Most of these services were operated throughout the day on the principle that the more people who could be enticed through the doors for whatever purpose, the stronger the theatre-going community would be. The foyer/bar was exceptionally large by most standards and was also used for exhibitions and for *ad hoc* folk music performances.

However, as early as 1981 there was a major local campaign to reopen the Lyceum as a theatre, and in 1987 Sheffield City Council agreed to redevelop it as part of the decision to build a number of first-class sporting and leisure facilities for the 1991 World Student Games. The building was by this time derelict and the renovation cost £12.4m. On completion in 1990, the restored Lyceum Theatre provided a superb example of a historic theatre, thoroughly refurbished to modern standards, and with seating for 1,100.

The Crucible and Lyceum stand physically together overlooking a paved square, and for reasons of economy of scale it was decided to form a new company, Sheffield Theatres, to run both venues. The distinctive role of each theatre was, however, to be retained with the Crucible as a producing house, and the Lyceum now hosting a new range of touring companies for the 1990s. The Studio theatre hosts a mixed programme of chamber music and drama, and is the resident home of the Lindsay String Quartet.

CONTROVERSIES

The Crucible Theatre, and more recently Sheffield Theatres as a whole, have been no strangers to controversy. In September 1972, less than a year after the Crucible opened, it found itself heading for unprecedented losses and the centre of a public storm. Leaks from a confidential report by the city treasurer claimed that the theatre should slash costs and attract bigger audiences to improve its financial position. It was criticised for not staging enough popular shows, for inadequate use of the building, and for 'having too many chiefs and not enough Indians'. Sheffield Corporation was offering to bail out the Crucible provided it put its house in order on these lines, but the theatre administrator claimed that the vital artistic standards would be endangered.

At that time the theatre was run jointly by an administrator and an artistic director, but by 1975 the former had resigned and the latter had retired, and a new post of 'the Director' was created, filled initially by Peter James. However, this first season was a classical one with attendances below 50 per cent of capacity. Speaking to the *Sheffield Star* he said: 'There is a wealth of difference between what an audience thinks they want and what contemporary writers want to write about. The problem is trying to strike a balance.' In 1981 he was succeeded by Clare Venables, who said in an interview shortly after her arrival in the city: 'A theatre that isn't controversial is dead. If people aren't talking about it and getting excited about the theatre, even if it includes criticism, then you are having no impact.'

A further financial crisis in 1982 led to an investigation by the Arts Council and Sheffield City Council. According to the *Sheffield Star*, the subsequent report criticised the board for only meeting twice a year, not even enough to fit in with Arts Council rules for theatres they subsidise. The Management Committee was accused of failing to manage, and scathing comments were made about the 'ill-defined and ineffective' role of the Finance Committee.

Following this, structures were changed. The chair of the board resigned, and the board membership was widened to give greater representation of external and internal interests. For example, in 1986 Sheffield City Polytechnic (now Sheffield Hallam University) was represented on the board for the first time, and observers attended the board representing theatre staff and Yorkshire Arts Association. The board was by then meeting bi-monthly and the Finance and Management Committees were replaced by a new Executive Committee. Changes were made to budgets, to plan on an average of 50 per cent fill capacity instead of 70 per cent – the figure which had been used since the early 1970s despite the fact that 70 per cent had only been achieved once (in 1974). More recently this has been further refined, as even 50 per cent has been found over-optimistic for many Crucible productions, particularly with three theatres operational, and capacity fill is now estimated individually for each production.

However, such changes were not easily received. Clare Venables came close to resignation over the reduction in artistic freedom which arose from the more stringent financial policies. By the mid-1980s a new national climate of public finance had emerged, with no guarantees against loss from the Arts Council, and no scope for local authorities to advance substantial sums to bail the theatre out of difficulties.

Under Clare Venables the theatre enjoyed a considerable reputation – at least among its regular audiences – with productions that were both controversial and challenging artistically. By 1987 the Crucible reached a capacity fill of 74 per cent. But then, as the *Sheffield Telegraph* subsequently noted, 'attention began to focus on the Lyceum, and suddenly the Crucible started to take a back seat'.

With the reopening of the Lyceum, a new post of chief executive of Sheffield Theatres was advertised. In January 1990, Stephen Barry (previously with the Theatre Royal, Bath) was appointed to manage the overall Crucible/Lyceum complex. Clare Venables completed her final season as artistic director the same year, and a number of other staff changes took place.

The Lyceum brought big name touring productions and popular drama and musicals to Sheffield for much of the year. Previously the Crucible had hosted some touring productions (for up to 30 per cent of the year), but it was now able to concentrate almost entirely on its own work. Seats at the Lyceum sold well with average fill at over 60 per cent of capacity, and up to 80–90 per cent for some shows.

By 1991, a new crisis was emerging. In October, the *Sheffield Weekly Gazette* reported: 'The artistic director has resigned, attendances are down by 50 per cent, productions planned for the new year are cancelled, the company is heading for a £250,000 deficit.' This came after an emergency meeting of the directors of Sheffield Theatres Ltd to discuss the drastic fall in Crucible box office receipts following the opening of the Lyceum. However, Stephen Barry insisted that the situation could be managed. 'We are not asking for more money, nor are we trying to take audiences away from the Lyceum,' he said. 'There are different types of audiences out there and we must look at ways of attracting them to the Crucible.'

Two years later he reflected:

> In retrospect we were too defensive about the Crucible – narrowing our market appeal and attempting an over-specialist role. We did not capitalise on the single site thinking brought about by the management structure. We knew the Lyceum would inevitably have an initial effect on the Crucible audiences – which was no doubt deepened by the recession. However, by 1991/2 a balance between the two theatres' programmes had begun to emerge and the box-office turned upwards again.

Some relaxation of the split between the role of the two theatres was agreed, with a few touring productions being accommodated in the Crucible, and one local production (the annual pantomime) being staged at the Lyceum.

However, a new financial crisis emerged in 1993, this time unrelated to box office sales or grants, but caused entirely from within. It emerged that the assistant head of the accounts department had, over a period of two years, embezzled nearly £0.5m of funds from the various companies under the Sheffield Theatres umbrella. The person responsible was charged and convicted by the courts, and around a third of the money was subsequently recovered. But the events of the fraud created a major trauma for everyone involved, and produced a large overdraft in the theatre accounts, with consequent ongoing interest charges.

STRUCTURES

Until the opening of the Lyceum, all the work of the Crucible was handled by one Trust Board. But from 1987 a separate Lyceum Trust was established, and until 1995, Sheffield Theatres actually comprised four separate companies, each with their own boards, under common management:

- Crucible Theatre Trust Ltd, which leased the Crucible site from the City Council and which had responsibility for the Crucible productions.
- Sheffield Lyceum Theatre Trust Ltd, which had responsibility for the Lyceum site.
- Sheffield Theatres Ltd (a management company owned equally by the boards of the two theatres, which employed most of the non-artistic staff).
- Offstage Ltd (a trading subsidiary company responsible for the bars, catering and commercial sponsorship).

Stephen Barry described this as 'an extraordinary structure based on a shotgun marriage of two charitable trusts, requiring in total no less than 22 board meetings per year'. The complexity was largely due to the separate charitable status of each building. This structure meant that few board members had a full picture of the overall financial situation, and grant aid might be increased to one company while being withdrawn from another.

In 1995, after extensive debate, the boards collectively agreed, and it was subsequently approved by Sheffield City Council, to transfer overall legal responsibility for the work of *both* theatres to one body, the Sheffield Theatres Trust. This took over the former responsibilities of the Crucible Trust and Sheffield Theatres Ltd, and assumed all responsibility for managing the Lyceum as a theatre.

Sheffield Theatres Trust is a registered charity and a company limited by guarantee (with permission to omit the word 'Limited' from its title). Its charitable objects, as stated in its Memorandum of Association, are:

- 'To promote, maintain, improve and advance education, particularly by the production of educational plays and the encouragement of the arts of drama, mime, dance, singing and music ...'
- 'To receive, educate and train students in drama, dancing, music, and other arts, and to promote the recognition and encouragement of special merit in students ...'.

The Lyceum Trust continues to exist, but it employs no staff and its role is simply as custodian of the Lyceum building. It leases the building to Sheffield Theatres Trust for use as a theatre for a payment of £90,000 per year – most of this money goes into a long-term building fund to cover future repairs and maintenance.

As with most charitable organisations of any size, it is necessary to have a trading subsidiary company to undertake non-charitable activities such as the sale of food and drink, and this role continues to be met by Offstage Ltd. Offstage is wholly owned by Sheffield Theatres Trust, and at the end of each year, Offstage undertakes a gift aid payment to transfer all its profits to Sheffield Theatres Trust. This means that no corporation tax is paid, and the theatres get the full benefit of all associated activities undertaken on their premises.

Thus, from April 1995, the Board of Sheffield Theatres was able to operate in effect as one organisation, with overall responsibility for management of professional theatre in Sheffield. The board membership is shown in Appendix 2. The board members are both directors of the company and trustees of the charity; as such they are unpaid. The full board takes responsibility for the entire work; the only subcommittee is an Audit Committee. Staff of the two theatres, from the chief executive downwards, are employees of the board: they are not actually directors of the company, even if the job title 'director' is used.

The change to a single board meant that many long-standing members on one or other of the original boards had to be asked to retire in order to reduce the overall numbers to a workable size. However, a separate Advisory Council was formed, comprising most of those who stepped down. This meets two to three times per year to offer general guidance on the work of the two theatres.

GRANT FUNDING

Since the beginning of subsidised theatre in Sheffield in 1960/1, income had shifted from purely commercial sources towards a heavy dependence on grants, primarily from the Arts Council of Great Britain and the local authorities. By 1977 some 63 per cent of the income was in the form of grants; this declined to about 55 per cent by the 1980s, to 40 per cent in 1989, and to 27 per cent by 1995 (this last figure being calculated on both theatres together) – see Appendix 3. It should be noted that the Arts Council does not give grants to touring theatres, but instead gives grants to certain touring companies towards the cost of their productions. However, Sheffield City Council makes grants towards both theatres (in the case of the Lyceum, the bulk of the grant is simply to cover lease payments back to the Council).

The policy on public funding of the arts had changed substantially over the period of this case. In 1985 there was an attempt to build up genuine 'centres of excellence' in the regions, and the Crucible was one of thirteen regional theatres selected as a major beneficiary. The Crucible thus received significant increases in its Arts Council grant – for example, in 1986/7 the grant increased by £100,000, allowing the theatre to move to genuine 52-week operating, and to relaunch its 'Theatre in Education' programme, which organises extensive work with schools.

Another important policy change in the late 1980s was the introduction of 'parity funding', by which the Arts Council aimed that the total public funding of any theatre should be shared equally between the Arts Council and the local authority. However, Sheffield City Council was unable to reach agreement with the Arts Council on this issue as capping of local authority expenditure forced the council to make cuts. David Patmore, director of arts for Sheffield City Council, explained in 1992 that much of the problem was due to the internal structures of the Arts Council, which treated production theatre and touring companies completely separately. As a result, the substantial money which the city council was contributing to the Lyceum project was not recognised by the Arts Council in calculations of overall parity. 'From our point of view,' he stated, 'we'd prefer to talk to the Arts Council about our theatre policy as a whole – but their structure gets in the way of this.' The net effect was that the Crucible lost out substantially in the overall 'pecking order' of Arts Council grants, compared to other large provincial repertory theatres.

In the early 1990s, the Arts Council moved to a regional structure, which meant that the grant to Sheffield Theatres came from Yorkshire and Humberside Arts Board rather than direct from the Arts Council of Great Britain. This meant the Crucible was no longer in direct competition for funds with as many other theatres as previously (there being only one other production theatre in Yorkshire and Humberside of comparable size), but it also meant that the scope for Arts Council grants was influenced heavily by the initial split of the 'cake' into regional 'slices', over which the theatre had relatively little influence. The result was that in the years 1994–6, the Arts Council grant remained static in cash terms at around £650,000 – effectively a cut each year after allowing for inflation.

In 1991, Sheffield City Council commissioned a consultant's report on its funding of Sheffield Theatres. This recommended that the council should reaffirm its commitment to the vital roles which the theatres played in the city in relation to the strategy for regeneration, based on a growth in leisure facilities and increases in tourism. The theatres were seen as a primary focus for the city centre, and a contribution to the new image of the city.

The resultant recommendation was that the council's funding support should be directed to certain key *target investments* – funding only those aspects of the theatres' operations which were of key importance to the city, such as building maintenance, production support and audience development. (The city council was particularly concerned to widen the range of people attending the theatres, as surveys in the past had shown that some 70 per cent of all seats were sold to a core of around 20,000 regular theatre attenders, drawn largely from the professional classes.) At the same time, the theatres were encouraged to become more entrepreneurial, generating a wider range of commercial income.

These recommendations were accepted in general terms: the city council funding became focused on certain areas of the theatres' work, with a service-level agreement which specifies standards that the theatres were expected to achieve. However, the overall restrictions on the city council's budget made it difficult to develop this further, and in any case it was almost impossible to cost things like 'audience development' as a separate activity. The total funding from the city council (excluding grants related purely to the lease of the site) was some £732,000 in 1995, a figure which was actually reduced by £12,000 in 1996. A small amount of grant aid was also received from two neighbouring local authorities (Rotherham and Barnsley), but financial pressures meant that Rotherham entirely withdrew its £11,000 grant in 1996.

The static grant from the Arts Council, and the direct cut in local council funding, meant that in real terms the theatres lost some £66,000 of income from public sources between 1995 and 1996 – a trend which was likely to continue.

ATTENDANCES AND PRICING

The largest part of Sheffield Theatres' revenue is dependent on tickets sold at the box office, and this money must meet all the remaining costs not met by grants or ancillary income. Budgeting for this is dependent upon the three issues of: how seats are priced, what proportion of seats for any production are sold, and to what extent seats are sold at concessionary prices.

In 1995/6, seats in the Crucible ranged from £7 to £13.50 including VAT (with two slightly different scales for different productions). In the Lyceum prices varied widely according to the production, but could be as high as £34 for prime seats at opera performances. The Studio theatre prices were £5 to £10 when used for the theatre's own productions, but it also hosts many musical concerts and smaller outside production companies. In each theatre a wide range of discounts are offered for regular theatre-goers who belong to certain membership schemes which the theatres run; concessions are also available to those over 60, children, students, registered unemployed, disabled people and members of certain unions. Standby seats (£3 to £4 in 1996) were also offered in certain cases.

In the case of the Lyceum, the revenue from ticket sales is distributed between Sheffield Theatres and the touring company according to a contract which is negotiated individually for each production. In some cases quite complex formulae can be used, but a typical split is for 70 per cent of revenue to go to the touring company and 30 per cent to be retained by the theatre. The revenue figures in Appendix 3 show total box office receipts, which increased substantially when the Lyceum opened, but payments to touring companies form a very substantial cost to be met.

Although most performances at the Lyceum are well attended, many of the Crucible productions since 1994 failed to sell as well as hoped, and Sheffield Theatres as a whole had two very poor trading years in 1994/5 and 1995/6. Stephen Barry attributed this partly to the state of economy and partly to the fact that 'people are spending their leisure money on other things, such as the National Lottery'. The theatre has made many attempts over the years to widen its audience, but despite a high profile (a 1990 study found 95 per cent of the local population were aware of the Crucible) many people simply did not see themselves as theatre-goers. This situation – which was typical of theatres in general – was often referred to as 'threshold fear'. Other difficulties in the 1995/6 financial year included a very hot summer (which makes theatre less attractive in the main tourist season), a Christmas pantomime which lacked a well-known television actor, and a difficulty in finding 'touring productions of the required quality' to fill the entire 40–45 weeks needed at the Lyceum.

OTHER INCOME

In addition to the grant and box office income, Sheffield Theatres worked hard, particularly after 1990, to generate other forms of income.

The most long-standing source of external income has been from hosting the World Snooker Championships. To many people in the UK, the Crucible became synonymous with the championships, which have been held there over three weeks in April/May every year from 1977, under the sponsorship of a tobacco company (which itself caused some controversy in the early days). Although the snooker brought in substantial revenue (around £160,000 in 1995, including extra catering profits), this decision was not without its critics. As the chair of the Advisory Council said in 1996: 'I don't like snooker. I really object to my theatre being used as a snooker hall and it breaks up the theatre season. But it does mean that five or six times a day the *Crucible, Sheffield* is mentioned on prime-time TV. And we do need the money!' The overall view of the board has been that the Crucible needed the revenue, and in 1996 the theatre was negotiating to continue hosting the championships.

The profits of the restaurant, bars and gift shop form an important source of additional income, which is generated via the trading subsidiary Offstage Ltd. By the mid-1990s, Sheffield Theatres became increasingly successful in attracting sponsors for many Crucible productions (and for some at the Lyceum, too, if not already sponsored through the touring company), although after a recession this income was harder to obtain, as sponsorship of the arts is an obvious area for companies to reduce in times of difficulty. The total profits of such commercial activities contributed about £250,000 to theatre funds in 1995/6, although the theatre does not charge Offstage any rental for the space used by bars, etc.

In addition, as a charity, Sheffield Theatres has been active in various forms of fundraising over the years. A Programme Development Fund launched in 1994 was due to generate around £100,000 over four years, from individuals who took out four-year covenants to support the development of new Crucible productions. The Friends of the Lyceum also made a small contribution to the costs of that building.

Certain capital projects have also been supported by fundraising – in particular, in 1994 the £400,000 enlargement of the Studio theatre from 250 to 400 seats and improved access for disabled people were funded by money raised from the European Regional Development Fund, from a local trust committed to the arts, and from the Foundation for Sport and the Arts.

In 1996 the theatre was seeking further funds from the arts distribution of the National Lottery in order to upgrade the Crucible with improved access to the main theatre and consequent better use of foyer space.

EMPLOYEES

In 1996, Sheffield Theatres employed 161 staff on on-going contracts: 70 in selling and front of house, 53 technical (stage crews, etc.), 25 in maintenance and security, and 13 administrative and secretarial. A further 53 were employed by Offstage Ltd in catering and retailing. Actors and production staff are taken on individually for each production – the most recent average was 29.

ISSUES FOR THE LATE 1990s

For Sheffield Theatres, the principal challenge as the Crucible approached its 25th birthday in 1996 was the on-going requirement to maintain the quality of output on the three stages, while attracting sufficient revenue to make this possible. In May 1996 this came to a head with Sheffield City Council calling for a three-year business plan to reverse the decline in Crucible attendances, as a condition of further grants.

Two very difficult years in 1994/5 and 1995/6 had led to major concerns that went beyond the board to outside funders. There was no doubt that, while attendances as a whole had increased dramatically since the opening of the Lyceum, numbers at the Crucible had fallen by roughly a third.

The declining external grants situation meant that the Crucible production budget is 'carved up into ever smaller slices', as Stephen Barry explained it. This had forced the artistic director into offering smaller productions: choosing plays with fewer actors and opting for simpler sets and costume design. Over a seven-year period, the theatre had seen a substantial reduction in the size of productions – at a time when it desperately needed big high-profile productions to win back audiences and influence critics.

But all those involved agree there is a limit to this: it is impossible to promote a 1,000-seat major regional theatre on the basis of small, underfunded productions, particularly when there is the Lyceum and Studio to fill as well. Some local commentators felt that Sheffield was simply unable to support 2,500 seats of professional theatre (although there was no attempt to use all three stages for productions for 52 weeks per year). In addition, attitudes take many years to change, and the city lacks the strong tradition of arts and commerce which is enjoyed by many regional theatres elsewhere in the UK.

On the income side, for many years the theatre had employed a development officer to attract further funding, as well as having a marketing department responsible for promoting productions to the public. In early 1996 a decision had already been taken to recruit for a new post of sales and marketing director to assume overall responsibility for marketing and for the box office. This led to a reorganisation of internal structures (see Appendix 1) following the extensive reorganisation of governance the previous year.

By 1996 the board was equipped with a unified structure to direct the three stages as one financial operation, and had established a new management structure to carry it out. The fraud which had caused so much anguish was moving into history. Yet public sector grants were falling, and fundamentally the future of the theatres would depend on their own marketing efforts, with funders even making this a condition of their support.

The ultimate challenge facing the new marketing director on appointment was to generate sufficient revenue (through ticket sales and other income) not just to enable Sheffield Theatres to survive, but to allow the Trust to maintain the quality and diversity of artistic output for which the Crucible, in particular, had always been known. The management were confident that it could be done – as the *Sheffield Star* reported:

> Stephen Barry and John Cornwell insisted that it was possible to reverse the downward trend: 'Trading last year declined in both theatres, mainly due to the failure of both Christmas shows, but the recently-announced programme for 1996 has the fastest-booking Christmas show ever.'

APPENDIX 1 MANAGEMENT STRUCTURE AS AT MAY 1996

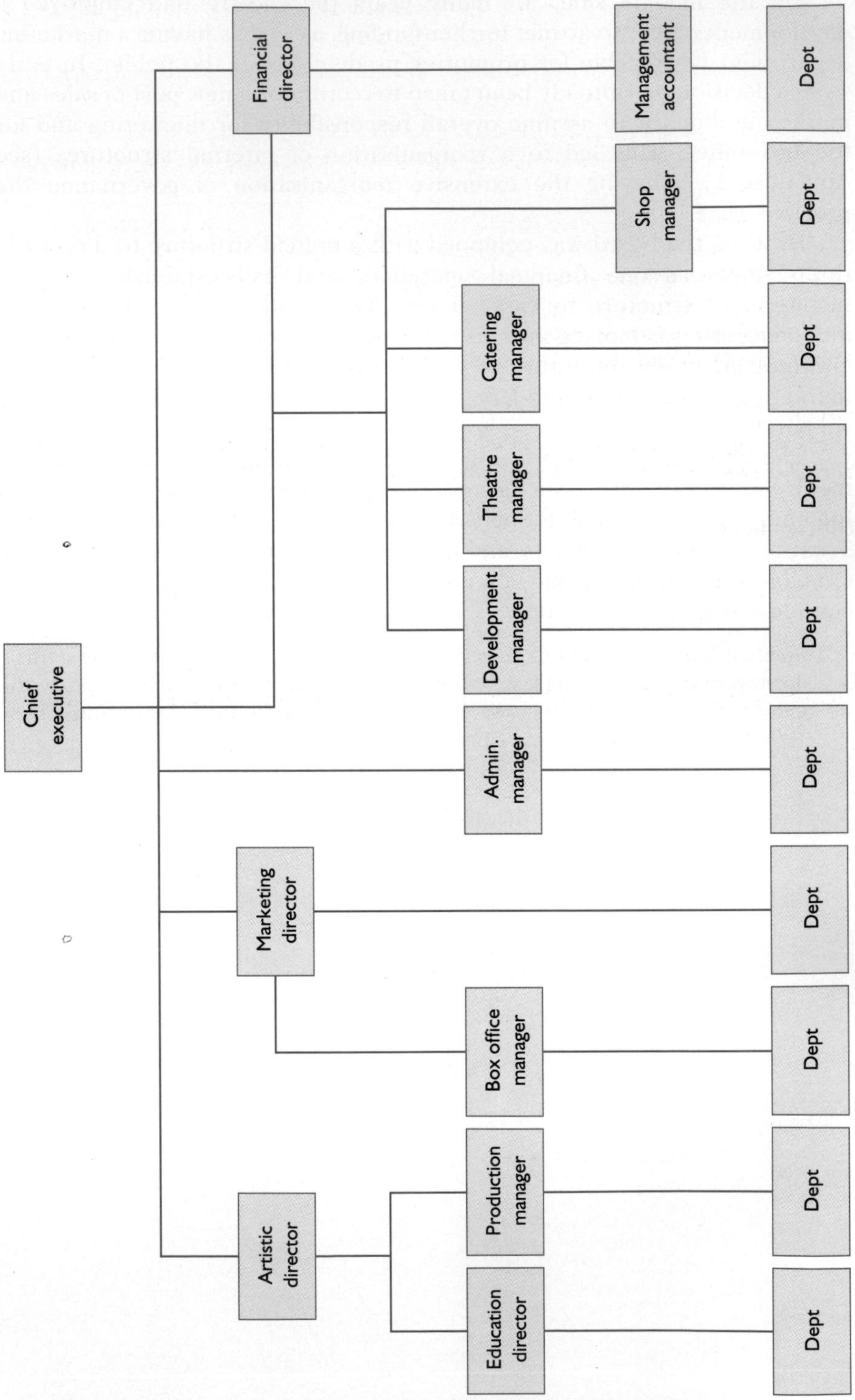

Chief executive
Artistic director
Marketing director
Financial director
Education director
Production manager
Box office manager
Admin. manager
Development manager
Theatre manager
Catering manager
Shop manager
Management accountant
Dept
Dept
Dept
Dept
Dept
Dept
Dept
Dept
Dept
Dept

APPENDIX 2 SUMMARY OF SHEFFIELD THEATRES TRUST BOARD MEMBERSHIP, MAY 1996

Directors/Trustees (15 persons)
Nominated by Sheffield City Council – three members, including the deputy chair of the board.
Elected – ten members, including the chair (John Cornwell) and company secretary. These members serve for periods of three years after which they may be re-elected for one further three-year period. The board elects its own successors.
Nominated by the Lyceum Trust – one member.
Nominated by the Advisory Council – one member.

Observers
Sheffield City Council Arts Department – two observers (officers of the council).
Yorkshire and Humberside Arts Board – one observer.

Officers in attendance
Chief executive
Artistic director
Finance director
Marketing director

Full papers for board meetings are also circulated to all members of the Advisory Council.

APPENDIX 3 PERFORMANCE FIGURES AND SUMMARY REVENUE ACCOUNTS (1972–95)

MEASURE	1972	1973	1974	1975	1976	1977	1978	1979	1980	1981	1982	1983	1984	1985	1986	1987	1988	1989	1990	1991	1992	1993	1994	1995
Attendances																								
Crucible total (000s)	190	221	246	215	227	197	183	174	201	193	176	182	176	186	232	222	192	173	180	110	139	131	92	84
Crucible – capacity fill (%)	52	69	77	49	51	62	61	49	66	55	59	71	58	63	74	74	65	58	65	41	64	63	49	40
Studio total (000s)	13	15	20	32	22	18	21	15	13	19	17	13	8	18	21	15	17	13	5	10	9	15	28	22
Lyceum total (000s)	—	—	—	—	—	—	—	—	—	—	—	—	—	—	—	—	—	—	51*	316	288	299	253	219
Financial																								
Box office (£000s)	89	119	142	152	209	226	256	343	380	399	389	454	486	1145[1]	1306[1]	1330	1446	1596	2274[2]	4051	3929	4599	3789	3017
Grants (% of income)	64	58	56	60	63	58	58	53	53	53	53	55	55	45	45	44	43	40	36[2]	25	27[3]	23	27	30
Surplus/(deficit) (£000s)	(12)	(12)	(8)	(43)	(53)	(5)	(80)	(38)	(111)	(170)	40	(8)	(22)	54	82	(19)	40	(170)	98[2]	(31)	(36)	(115[4])	(228)	(318)
No. of productions																								
Crucible/Studio[5]	73	78	46	44	64	48	52	59	60	64	42	32	37	37	46	37	34	39	21	37	43	44	34	45
Lyceum	—	—	—	—	—	—	—	—	—	—	—	—	—	—	—	—	—	—	4*	50	52	41	40	41

Note Years shown relate to the financial year *commencing* with the season indicated: e.g. the column '1995' refers to the year Apr. 1995–Mar. 1996.

[1] Catering revenue accounted differently from 1985.

[2] Accounting principles again changed in 1990 (to a basis similar to that used in 1985). Also from 1990 the figures include box office sales and grants for the Lyceum (i.e. the figures from the Crucible Trust and Lyceum Trust have been amalgamated for this table).

[3] From 1992 the Lyceum site was the subject of a lease-back arrangement with the City Council – grants relating to lease payments are excluded from the calculation.

[4] The final surplus or deficit for each of the years 1990–3 is affected to some extent by the fraud referred to in the text.

[5] Figures for numbers of Crucible/Studio productions include: home productions, tours and concerts. However, concerts at the Lyceum (being generally one day events) are not included in the numbers of Lyceum productions.

* Part year only.

Source Theatre records and published accounts.

FISONS: THE FALL FROM GRACE

Helen Peck

The case study covers the period from 1990 to 1995 which saw the spectacular decline of Fisons through a series of events triggered by the environmental impact of the peat digging activities of the company's smallest division (Horticultural). From a position of great strength in the late 1980s – when Fisons was generally regarded as very well managed – by 1995 the company was reduced to a pharmaceutical division turning in losses. The other two divisions had been sold and rumours of a takeover persisted. The case study illustrates the importance of understanding and managing stakeholder expectations and relationships.

• • •

During the early 1980s, John Kerridge, chairman and chief executive of Fisons, achieved one of the most remarkable business turnarounds in recent times. After selling off the company's loss-making core fertiliser business, he went on to create a highly profitable mini-conglomerate with three distinct areas of business. The Pharmaceutical Division, with its small portfolio of specialist asthma and anti-allergy drugs, was by far the most profitable part of the business. The Scientific Equipment Division was the largest non-American supplier of scientific equipment anywhere in the world. It occasionally outperformed Pharmaceuticals in terms of turnover, but never profits. The very nature of the Scientific Equipment business meant that it was vulnerable to recession. Then there was the tiny, reliable and modestly profitable Horticulture Division, specialising in lawn fertilisers and an array of value-added peat products.

By 1984, Kerridge's transformation of the business was complete. In January 1986, a poll conducted by stockbrokers James Capel had identified Fisons as the best managed company in its sector.[1]

As the 1990s dawned, Fisons was generally regarded as a superbly managed company; highly skilled in the art of mergers and acquisitions, and

---

This case was prepared from published sources by Helen Peck, Cranfield School of Management, as a basis for class discussion rather than to illustrate effective or ineffective handling of administrative situations.

[1] The *Financial Times* Health and Household sector.

very efficiently run. Fisons' senior management saw, therefore, no need to give regular presentations to analysts (unlike its pharmaceutical competitors who communicated assiduously with the City), and field trips to view the company's sites and facilities were not permitted. Despite this tendency towards secrecy, the majority of analysts slept soundly in their beds at night, confident that Fisons' remarkable financial performance could be relied upon for the foreseeable future. But while the City fêted Kerridge and his management team, the company's reputation was declining fast in other quarters. It seemed that the Horticulture Division's peat-cutting activities were rapidly developing into a *cause célèbre*.

Fisons was by far the largest cutter of peat in the UK. According to the conservationists, 90 per cent of its cutting was on land which had been designated at Sites of Special Scientific Interest (SSSIs). Fisons was legally entitled to continue working the sites where planning permission predated the award of SSSI status. It was, however, clearly sensitive about outside interest in its peat-cutting activities, and was rapidly acquiring a very bad reputation among sections of the local and national press. In 1989, a *Sunday Times* photographer had had to be rescued by police after being held against his will by Fisons' employees, who blocked in his car for 45 minutes, demanding that he hand over his film. But in March 1990, Fisons overstepped the mark when it illegally drained and severely damaged a 65 acre peat bog on the edge of Thorne Moor, a South Yorkshire nature reserve. The company admitted destroying the Thorne Moor bog, but claimed that it had been a 'genuine mistake'. Environmentalists were not convinced. Similar incursions had been made before when the company 'accidentally' cut peat from important conservation sites on neighbouring Snaith and Cowick Moor.

The Thorne Moor incident prompted ten highly influential conservation groups – including Friends of the Earth, the Royal Society for Nature Conservation, the Royal Society for the Protection of Birds and the Worldwide Fund for Nature – to take up the cause, banding together to form the Peatlands Campaign. The campaigners, led by the Prince of Wales, called for gardeners to boycott peat products and save the remaining peat bogs from total destruction. The Peatlands Campaign did not stop there. In May 1990, it contacted 50 investment managers controlling over £870m worth of Fisons' shares (around 42 per cent of the total) in advance of the company's forthcoming annual meeting. Institutional shareholder, the Borough of Lewisham, supported by the South Yorkshire Pensions Authority (SYPA) and the Pearl Assurance Pension Fund, agreed to press the company to end its peat-cutting operations, urging it to invest instead in the development of peat substitutes. Fisons refused, but its vocal opponents were rallying support from other quarters. The issue was debated in the House of Lords and in the House of Commons, where an early day motion in support of the Peatlands Campaign was signed by 25 Members of Parliament. Fisons remained firm, but 34 local authorities joined the Prince of Wales in banning the use of peat products on their properties. More worryingly for Fisons' shareholders, B&Q – Britain's largest DIY and gardening chain – announced that, 'on conservation grounds', it had decided to ban all peat cut from SSSIs from its stores. Its leading competitors quickly followed suit.

The row rumbled on, but the overall impact on the group's bottom line was negligible. The entire Horticulture Division accounted for only 7 per cent of the company's turnover and 5 per cent of its profits. However, the SYPA – holder of £1m worth of Fisons' shares – continued to demonstrate concern for its local bogs, requesting that it be allowed to visit the SSSIs in its own area where peat cutting was taking place. The SYPA received a letter from head of corporate affairs, Peter Woods, informing it that 'Relations between Fisons and major customers are operational and confidential and as such we would not comment on these to shareholders or any other third party.' Permission for the visit was refused. In the meantime, investors' attention focused on the forthcoming announcement of Fisons' results for the half-year to June 1991.

On 16 September, the eve of the announcement, analysts were still gleefully predicting an 11 per cent rise in interim profits. Little growth was expected from the Scientific Equipment or Horticulture businesses, but hopes were high for the seemingly recession-proof Pharmaceuticals Division. Sales of the anti-asthma drug 'Tilade' – Fisons' most important new drug for many years – were expected to have gathered momentum, and analysts were hopeful that the US Food and Drugs Administration (FDA) was about to approve the drug, granting it access to the world's most lucrative pharmaceutical market.

However, the results announced by Kerridge the following day were not quite as everyone had expected. For the first time in over a decade, Fisons' profits – while up by 6 per cent – had failed to meet expectations. The reason, explained Kerridge, was that £10m had been wiped off profits following supply problems with two of the company's older drugs – Imferon (a blood product) and Opticrom (an anti-allergy eye treatment). Kerridge went on to explain that the disruption to supplies was caused by the 'extremely pedantic' FDA. The City was stunned, and Fisons' share price took a 35p downward leap, closing at 464p on the day (see Exhibit 1).

The analysts had rarely complained about Fisons' non-communicative manner while profits soared, but the company's continued reluctance to discuss key areas of the business now made them suspicious that the US problems were more serious than the interim statement had implied. Their worst fears were confirmed – and exceeded – on 11 December 1991, when Fisons announced that the drugs would not be reinstated as quickly as was originally thought, and that the result would be a £65m reduction in profits for 1991. Fisons stressed that the impact on profits would be short term in nature, and that US sales and market share of both drugs would be quickly recaptured, once full supply was resumed the following year. Fisons was nevertheless reportedly furious with the FDA, blaming the delay in clearing Imferon and Opticrom on a dispute between the FDA's Washington and Buffalo offices. Within minutes of the announcement, a further £340m was sliced off the value of the company. The affair had by now reduced the price

Exhibit 1 **Fisons' share price, 30 December 1988 to 31 December 1993**

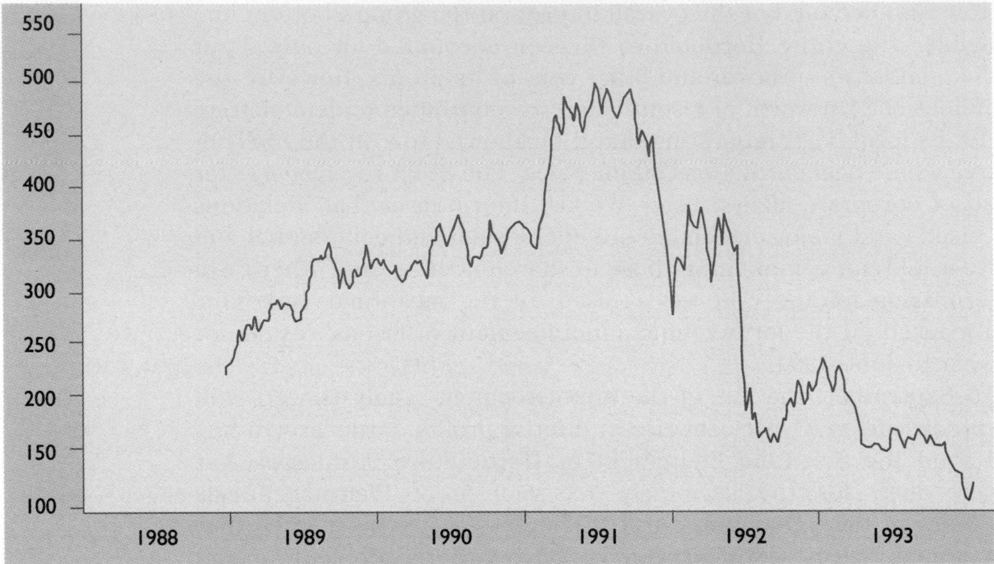

High 510.00 21/6/91 Low 112.00 17/12/93

Source Datastream.

of the company's stock by a third, wiping over £1bn off its stock market value. Fisons' longer-term growth prospects were now in doubt. As one analyst observed: 'They've been growing through acquisitions based on the strength of their shares, and with the shares so weak, they won't be able to keep it up.'

Two weeks later, as the stock markets reopened from the Christmas break, Fisons' share price nose-dived again, as further revelations about its difficulties with the FDA swept the City. According to an article published in *FDC Reports* – an American technical magazine with close links to the FDA – there were long-standing leakage problems with the inhalers used to dispense the anti-asthma drug Intal – Fisons' best-selling pharmaceutical product. The article claimed that the company had switched to an alternative design of valve without FDA approval, and that the company had allegedly produced deceptive test results on the new equipment. According to the magazine, Intal had been allowed to remain on the market only because of 'the medical necessity of the product'. The report went on to reveal that the FDA inspectors had also uncovered significant deviations from best practice at Fisons' Holmes Chapel manufacturing plant, including the practice of storing drug solutions for the manufacture of Imferon in what the inspector identified as 'beer kegs'.

The company's immediate reaction was to dismiss the allegations as 'scaremongering' and 'nonsense'. The City was unimpressed. Three days later, on 30 December, a detailed press statement was issued by the company. It stated that 'At no time did Fisons use "beer kegs" in the manufacture of Imferon', and refuted or explained in detail the background to each of the allegations made by the *FDC Reports*. The statement steadied the stock market, but for at least one institutional investor – the SYPA – this was one mishap too many. On 6 January 1992, in a letter to the *Financial Times*, the institution's clerk and financial officer expressed his concern over 'the board's failure to manage effectively both its business and its investor relations'. The SYPA was looking for institutional support for a motion to challenge the board at the forthcoming annual meeting. Fisons' shares were widely held, with the six largest shareholders controlling around 15 per cent of the equity. The following day, an article in London's *Evening Standard* revealed that the SYPA's letter had drawn a 'positive response'. Kerridge's resignation – with immediate effect – was announced one week later.

The man who stepped into Kerridge's shoes to become executive chairman was Patrick Egan, a non-executive director of the company since 1985. Egan stressed that, once a new chief executive had been appointed, he would be concentrating his energies on the company's strategic direction and on improving relations with the City and the company's shareholders. Promising a more open style of management, Egan acknowledged that Fisons' relationships with institutional investors and City opinion-formers had not always been well handled in the past. 'But if you think there are any further skeletons to come out of the cupboard, then you are wrong,' he said.

The respite was short-lived. On 16 January, the full report of the FDA's latest visit to the Fisons' Holmes Chapel plant became available under US freedom of information legislation. The report revealed that the FDA had identified a catalogue of faults during an inspection of the site in 1990. Several months later, a reinspection by the regulators had found that some of its recommendations had still not been put into practice. A spokesman for Fisons had dismissed the FDA's findings as 'not significant', adding that 'All drug companies get these reports. The FDA is ever increasing its quality standards.'

The FDA was incensed. The following day, Peter Smith, associate director of the FDA's International Programmes and Technical Support Branch – the department responsible for overseas inspections – made plain his views on the matter. In a statement in the *Guardian* newspaper, Smith insisted that 'The points in the inspection report were very significant from the FDA standpoint ... We have invested more time and money in Fisons than any other company ever and [they] keep failing inspections.' Smith went on to explain that an inspection usually takes two to five days, but visits to Fisons could take up to three weeks. 'And this is all at the expense of the FDA. There are always problems there.'

At the company's annual meeting on 12 May 1992, it became apparent that Opticrom was unlikely to be readmitted to the USA in time for the all important hay fever season. Worse still, it came to light that its US patent would expire early the following year. With sales of Opticrom disrupted, its market would quickly disappear as rival versions of the relatively simple drug entered the market. The company also confirmed that, due to the long absence of Imferon, the American drugs group Starius had just received FDA approval to market a similar product.

Fisons was at this point still awaiting final approval from the FDA for its new drug, Tilade. The shares took their now customary skip downwards. A profits warning was issued one month later, indicating that profits for the half-year to June 1992 would be only around half those for the same period last year. The shares crashed 77p on the day, wiping off almost a quarter off the company's value. Only speculation that a bid must now be imminent prevented them from falling further.

Fisons struggled through the next year, under a new chief executive, former head of the Scientific Equipment Division, Cedric Scroggs. The company continued its negotiations with the FDA, finally securing approval for Tilade on 31 December 1992. The difficulties surrounding Intal's dispensers were resolved, but discussions regarding the relicensing of Opticrom continued, in the hope that it might yet win back some of its market share. Imferon was formally abandoned. Scroggs' tenure as chief executive was short-lived. He was effectively sacked in December 1993, after recessionary pressures had plunged the Scientific Equipment Division deep into the red, and some dubious (though not illegal) accounting practices were revealed in the Pharmaceutical Division.

Under a new chief executive, Stuart Wallis, Fisons sold off its Scientific Equipment and Horticulture interests, disposing of the troublesome peat bogs. By early 1995, all that remained of the mini-conglomerate was a cash-rich pharmaceutical shell which continued to turn in operating losses. The company was negotiating a possible merger with Medeva, a small and dynamic pharmaceutical company, and in the meantime speculation persisted that Fisons was a takeover target for a much larger player, Zenica.

A NOTE ON THE WORLD AUTOMOBILE INDUSTRY, 1996

Ranjit Das

This note briefly highlights the market trends facing the automobile industry in the different regions of the world. The case discusses five main geographic regions: the traditional trading regions (western Europe, NAFTA and Japan) and the developing regions of eastern Europe and Asia Pacific. The automobile industry was undergoing rapid changes not least because of competition from the producers based in the Asia Pacific region. It also represented a very important part of European economies in terms of GNP and employment and illustrates the process of globalisation of an industry. The case can be used separately as a basis for industry analysis or as a first stage before working on the PSA Peugeot Citroën, Rover Honda or BMW/Rover case studies.

• • •

INTRODUCTION

The automobile industry is dependent on the state of the economy, and the early 1990s witnessed an economic depression in the three traditional vehicle markets: Japan, western Europe and North America. Between 1990 and 1993 new registrations of passenger cars across the three regions fell from 28.87m to 25.30m. In the same period, production dropped from 31.28m units to 27.6m. See Exhibit 1 for a regional breakdown.

In comparison, during 1990–3, sales and production grew in the rest of the world – particularly in Asia, eastern Europe and Latin America. Sales of passenger cars in the rest of the world increased from 5.72m in 1990 to 6.85m in 1993, and production rose from 4.72m to 6.42m in the same

This case study was prepared from published sources by R. Das, Sheffield Business School. It is intended as a basis for class discussion and not as an illustration of either good or bad management practice.

Exhibit 1 **Registrations and production of passenger cars, in Japan, western Europe and North America, 1990–3 (000s)**

	REGISTRATIONS		PRODUCTION	
	1990	1993	1990	1993
Japan	5,100	4,200	9,950	8,500
Western Europe	12,230	11,450	13,580	11,300
NAFTA*	10,530	9,650	7,750	8,170

*NAFTA is the North American Free Trade Association and comprises Canada, Mexico and the USA.

Source Industry journals.

period. However, the economic triad of NAFTA, Japan and the EU accounted for three-quarters of the world's vehicle sales, so while the newly developing Asian vehicle markets offered a higher growth rate, their volume sales were comparatively small. Also, many of the markets were closed to foreign producers: for example, South Korea and Taiwan and certain car-makers had established close links with some governments, so creating a barrier to entry for other car manufacturers, such as Volkswagen and Peugeot in China. Manufacturers also had to take into account the increased risk of entering Asian markets.

The worldwide demand for passenger cars grew in 1995 to 33.26m units and was predicted to reach 38.68m units by 2000 (see Exhibit 2). Similarly, production had increased slowly from the low of 1993 and was predicted to increase by about 2 per cent a year (see Exhibit 3). The world automobile industry was forecast to grow at about 3 per cent per year between 1995 and 2000. The largest growth rate was expected in Asia, where a 7–8 per cent growth rate was predicted between 1995 and 2000. However, during that period, growth in western Europe and the NAFTA region was forecast at less than 3 per cent a year, and in Japan sales were predicted to stagnate while production was expected to decrease as Japanese companies began to develop overseas production. The growing shift of production from Japan to overseas facilities had a major impact on exports from Japan, which in turn put pressure on domestic production, where most Japanese car-makers suffered from overcapacity.

In every market in the world, competition among the car manufacturers intensified during the 1990s. Although the Japanese trade barriers were being lifted, the nationalistic buying habits of the Japanese meant that that market would be very hard for US and European car-makers to enter. The US market was dominated by the American manufacturers, General Motors (GM), Chrysler and Ford, as well as by Toyota, Nissan and Honda. Between them they accounted for 87.5 per cent of car sales. This oligopoly was not

Exhibit 2 Actual and predicted new registrations of passenger cars by region, 1994–2000 (000s)

	1994	1995	1996	1997	1998	1999	2000
Western Europe*	11,838	12,018	12,475	12,770	13,110	13,470	13,705
NAFTA**	10,155	9,420	9,380	9,435	9,600	9,875	10,250
South America	1,600	1,720	1,900	2,100	2,250	2,400	2,575
Japan	4,210	4,443	4,600	4,700	4,625	4,575	4,525
Asia exc. Japan	3,072	3,179	3,425	3,665	3,915	4,220	4,615
Eastern Europe	1,456	1,488	1,580	1,627	1,738	1,814	1,904
Other	970	990	1,015	1,035	1,055	1,075	1,110
Total world	33,301	33,258	34,375	35,332	36,293	37,429	38,684
% change	n/a	−0.1	3.4	2.8	2.7	3.1	3.3

Note Figures for 1994–5 are actual; figures for 1996–2000 are forecasts.
*Western European countries are Austria, Belgium, Denmark, Finland, France, Germany, Greece, Ireland, Italy, Luxembourg, Netherlands, Norway, Portugal, Spain, Sweden, Switzerland, UK.
**NAFTA countries are Canada, USA and Mexico.

Sources Trade journals; author's forecasts.

Exhibit 3 Actual and predicted production of passenger cars by region, 1994–2000 (000s)

	1994	1995	1996	1997	1998	1999	2000
Western Europe*	12,798	13,129	13,490	13,670	13,825	14,100	14,360
NAFTA**	8,672	8,370	8,030	8,315	8,475	8,670	8,895
South America	1,556	1,510	1,700	1,850	2,000	2,100	2,200
Japan	7,801	7,610	7,600	7,800	7,725	7,625	7,500
Asia exc. Japan	3,118	3,596	3,970	4,270	4,590	4,845	5,190
Eastern Europe	1,637	1,736	1,829	1,924	2,024	2,093	2,161
Other markets	90	92	94	96	99	102	105
Total world	35,672	36,043	36,713	37,925	38,738	39,535	40,411
% change	n/a	1.0	1.9	3.3	2.1	2.1	2.2

Note Figures for 1994–5 are actual; figures for 1996–2000 are forecasts.
*Western European countries are Austria, Belgium, Denmark, Finland, France, Germany, Greece, Ireland, Italy, Luxembourg, Netherlands, Norway, Portugal, Spain, Sweden, Switzerland, UK.
**NAFTA countries are Canada, USA and Mexico.

Sources Trade journals; author's forecasts.

expected to change throughout the 1990s. The western European market was more balanced. Toyota, Nissan, Honda, Ford and GM had 32 per cent of sales in 1995 and the European manufacturers – Volkswagen, Renault, Peugeot and Fiat – had 50 per cent of the market. However, the government protection enjoyed by Renault, Peugeot and Fiat was predicted to disappear, leading to a more level playing field by 2000.

For ease of discussion the case has been divided into five sections. The first three sections consider the automobile business in the traditional trading regions of western Europe, NAFTA and Japan respectively. The final two sections review the developments in the regions of Asia-Pacific (excluding Japan) and eastern and central Europe.

WESTERN EUROPE

In western Europe the passenger car market had reached maturity in about 1990/1. The expected downturn in the region was delayed by German unification in 1991, the former East Germans being responsible for an unpredicted 1.1m extra car sales. The boom was unsustainable and 1993 saw the overdue downturn with a 15.2 per cent drop in car sales.

Registrations in western Europe rose by just 1.5 per cent in 1995 (see Exhibit 4). This slight increase was achieved by using expensive market-boosting measures, such as cheap finance and one-off special offers. Incentives were the crutch of the European car industry, with registrations in France and Spain almost all due to such schemes. The only significant sales rises in 1995 came in Germany, Europe's biggest car market, and the UK, the second biggest. In both cases, the increases had been driven by discounting and incentives. With the integration of Austria, Finland and Sweden into the European Union (EU) and the cyclical upturn in the region, a slight improvement in the economy was expected between 1995 and 2000.

As Exhibit 5 indicates, there was an increase in supply in western Europe, due mainly to the establishment of Japanese factories in the UK. Nissan, Toyota and Honda had a joint capacity of more than 500,000 units a year in 1995, and further planned expansion would increase production to 650,000 by 1999. European car-makers also expanded. Fiat's southern Italian factory produced up to 450,000 cars a year; Ford and Volkswagen set up a new plant in Portugal; and Volvo and Mitsubishi expanded a factory in the Netherlands as part of their Nedcar joint venture.

The problem of oversupply worsened because of foreign imports into the region: for example, Hyundai and Daewoo of Korea, Proton of Malaysia and Tata of India. Oversupply was forecast to increase in 1996 with Chrysler's strategy to expand into Europe. The increase in supply had been partly mitigated by more sales outside western Europe. The Japanese, for example, shipped limited numbers of cars to Japan. Exports to eastern Europe were also increasing, and were estimated to increase further with the removal of local tariffs on imported cars.

Exhibit 4

Actual and predicted new registrations of passenger cars in western Europe by country, 1994–2000 (000s)

	1994	1995	1996	1997	1998	1999	2000
Germany	3,209	3,316	3,430	3,490	3,590	3,700	3,800
France	1,973	1,930	1,970	2,000	2,100	2,150	2,200
Italy	1,610	1,704	1,740	1,810	1,925	2,100	2,150
UK	1,911	1,945	1,995	2,070	2,100	2,125	2,150
Spain	879	834	900	940	960	980	1,000
Netherlands	434	451	460	480	470	465	460
Belgium	387	360	380	400	390	380	375
Others	1,435	1,478	1,600	1,580	1,575	1,570	1,570
Total	11,838	12,018	12,475	12,770	13,110	13,470	13,705
% change	n/a	1.5	3.8	2.4	2.7	2.7	2.7

Note Figures for 1994–5 are actual; figures for 1996–2000 are forecasts.

Sources Society of Motor Manufacturers and Traders; trade journals; author's forecasts.

Exhibit 5

Actual and predicted production of passenger cars in western Europe by country, 1994–2000 (000s)

	1994	1995	1996	1997	1998	1999	2000
Germany	4,094	4,320	4,360	4,460	4,560	4,650	4,725
France	3,175	3,050	3,130	3,160	3,190	3,250	3,300
Italy	1,341	1,422	1,510	1,570	1,550	1,560	1,575
UK	1,467	1,532	1,650	1,720	1,825	1,925	2,000
Spain	1,822	1,865	1,850	1,755	1,725	1,750	1,800
Netherlands	92	95	150	165	160	155	155
Belgium	408	390	375	360	350	340	340
Others	399	455	465	480	465	470	465
Total	12,798	13,129	13,490	13,670	13,825	14,100	14,360
% change	n/a	2.6	2.7	1.3	1.1	2.0	1.8

Note Figures for 1994–5 are actual; figures for 1996–2000 are forecasts.

Sources Society of Motor Manufacturers and Traders; trade journals; author's forecasts.

Exhibit 6 Market shares of passenger cars in western Europe by manufacturer, 1991–7 (%)

MANUFACTURER	1991	1992	1993	1994	1995	1996	1997
Volkswagen Group (Volkswagen, Audi, Seat, Skoda)	16.4	17.5	15.9	16.7	16.8	16.3	16.2
General Motors (Opel/Vauxhall, Saab)*	12.0	12.4	12.9	13.1	13.0	13.0	13.1
Ford Group (Ford, Jaguar)*	11.8	11.2	12.0	12.1	11.9	11.0	10.9
PSA Peugeot Citroën	12.1	12.2	12.8	12.0	12.0	12.4	12.1
Fiat Group (Fiat, Lancia, Alfa Romeo, Maserati)	12.7	11.8	10.8	10.9	11.1	10.6	10.4
Renault	9.9	10.6	10.8	10.4	10.4	10.6	10.7
BMW Group (BMW, Rover)	3.1	3.3	6.5	6.2	6.3	6.7	6.7
Mercedes-Benz	3.4	3.1	3.6	3.4	3.3	3.3	3.1
Volvo	1.5	1.5	1.7	1.8	1.8	1.7	1.7
Nissan	3.2	3.2	3.3	3.1	3.1	3.4	3.5
Toyota	2.7	2.5	2.6	2.6	2.5	2.6	2.7
Honda	1.2	1.3	1.4	1.5	1.5	1.6	1.7
Mazda	1.3	1.4	1.5	1.4	1.4	1.5	1.5
Mitsubishi	1.4	1.2	1.0	1.1	1.1	1.2	1.3
Others	7.3	6.8	3.2	3.7	3.8	4.1	4.4
Total sales in western Europe (000s)	13,500	13,498	11,250	11,838	12,018	12,475	12,770

Note Figures for 1991–5 are actual; figures for 1996–7 are forecasts.
* Includes cars imported from USA and sold in western Europe.

Sources European Automobile Manufacturers Association; author's forecasts.

With supply outstripping demand, manufacturers had to spend heavily on marketing and new product development. Niche buyers were targeted, such as four-wheel-drive sports utilities, convertibles and multipurpose vehicles (people-carriers). But the risk was that the strategy of targeting niches would be self-defeating as the niches became overcrowded. For example, Fiat and its Alfa Romeo subsidiary already had two models competing with Rover's MGF for the two-seater sports car sector, and in 1996 BMW, Mercedes-Benz, Porsche and Renault also introduced two-seaters. The same was happening with multipurpose vehicles: Renault's Espace was competing with two models from the Fiat Group and from Peugeot Citroën. Ford and VW also launched products in 1995, and in 1996 Mercedes-Benz, Opel and Chrysler were all to produce their own models for this sector.

An alternative strategy to stimulate demand was through price cuts, but this would require rationalisation, meaning plant closures and possible mergers.

Exhibit 6 gives a breakdown of manufacturers' market shares in the region. The top six manufacturers held 75 per cent of the market, but with the threat of entry of the US producer Chrysler, a rationalisation within the industry via mergers and acquisitions was a likely strategy: BMW had acquired Rover in 1995 and there had been a failed merger attempt between Renault and Volvo in 1993.[1]

We will now examine specific western European markets.

France

A dramatic drop of 18.3 per cent in the French car market in 1993, from 2.11m units to 1.72m, forced the government to introduce a temporary incentive scheme to boost registrations. Owners of cars over ten years old were given a cash incentive ($800) towards the cost of a new car in return for scrapping their old car. This incentive was matched by the car manufacturers. New car registrations rose sharply in 1994, but levelled out in 1995 as most of the potential buyers had bought replacement cars in 1994. Increases in new registrations were forecast for the late 1990s due to the natural replacement cycle.

Germany

German unification in 1991 boosted the German market, with a 37 per cent increase in new registrations between 1990 and 1991, from 3.04m cars to 4.16m. The demand for cars in former East Germany had never been met under Communist control, and the favourable exchange rates given to the East Germans following reunification led to a flood of new registrations. Demand for cars in the former West Germany was dictated by the economic conditions and the replacement cycle. The former West Germany had been entering a downturn in demand just as unification occurred, and this resulted in an unpredicted boost in demand. Thus, when the downturn came in 1992/3 a sharp fall was seen, from 3.93m in 1992 to 3.19m in 1993.

Demand grew in 1995, but predicted increases in taxes to pay for higher welfare spending and a levy to cover car recycling costs meant that the demand for cars was expected to grow only gradually between 1995 and 2000.

---

[1] During 1997 and 1998, the industry was restructured due to several prominent mergers and acquisitions. The main focus of this activity was the merger of Daimler-Benz and Chrysler, and the complicated acquisition of Rolls Royce, whereby BMW bought its brand name, and Volkswagen purchased the remainder of the company.

Italy

The Italian market fell sharply during 1992–4, from 2.38m cars to 1.61m, but a slight growth in new registrations was expected up to 2000. Low consumer confidence due to an expected rise in taxes, poor economic conditions and political instability meant that growth in the late 1990s would be due principally to the replacement cycle.

Spain

The underlying decline in the Spanish car market between 1991 and 1993 was only temporarily halted in 1992 because the government reduced the VAT rate on cars and many suppliers took that opportunity to cut prices. This boosted sales from 0.87m units in 1991 to 0.98m in 1992, but sales fell to 0.74m in 1993. The rise in sales between 1993 and 1994 was again due to government cash incentives towards the cost of a new car in return for scrapping an old car. New car registrations were expected to grow slightly up to the year 2000 due to an economic upturn, lower income taxes and the normal replacement cycle.

UK

UK car sales peaked in the late 1980s with the registration of 2.35m vehicles in 1989. The 1990–2 recession caused a 30 per cent reduction in car sales, which fell to 1.59m in 1992. The rate of recovery in the mid-1990s was lower than expected, and growth was forecast to be low throughout the 1990s.

Some 45 per cent of the UK car market was made up of the company fleet car sector. As part of their remuneration package, most senior and middle managers received a company car leased from a fleet car operator. Companies had been able to negotiate favourable deals on the leasing of luxury cars and so distorted the registration figures of such cars in the UK. Government taxes on company cars meant that many employees had opted to take a financial payment in lieu of a company car, and then buy their own, typically smaller, vehicles directly. This trend was forecast to continue, so the demand for smaller cars was expected to rise.

The shift away from company cars may have been expected to increase private car sales. However, due to the large depreciation suffered by new cars, private buyers were buying low-mileage, used cars. Thus, it was forecast that the demand for new cars would be low, but that the market for used cars would grow.

Other Western European Markets

Austria's membership of the EU meant a fall in car prices. That, together with a peak in the cyclical replacement cycle in the mid-1990s, led to an increase in registrations in 1995, which were forecast to reach 300,000 cars a year in 1996. Demand was expected to fall beyond 1996 as the market was mature, the replacement cycle was expected to wane and expected new taxes on cars would make car ownership less appealing.

Due to steady economic growth, the car market in *Belgium* was predicted to grow, peaking at 0.4m cars a year in 1997, after which demand was expected to fall gradually. The market was saturated, the population was stable and the possibility of new fuel and vehicle taxes meant that new registrations were predicted to reduce in the years leading up to the year 2000.

New registrations in the *Netherlands* were expected to rise to 0.48m by 1997, due to a peak in the replacement cycle and an improvement in the economy. Growth beyond 1997 was expected to be driven only by the replacement demand, since the population was stable and alternative forms of transport were fully developed.

THE NAFTA REGION

In 1995 performance of the North America Free Trade Association region (NAFTA), comprising the USA, Canada and Mexico, was let down by Mexico. The USA and Canada had mature markets, but their growth rates during the late 1990s were expected to improve and their inflation was under control. Mexico, however, was thrown into an economic downturn when the currency was devalued by 40 per cent in 1994. Consumer confidence, buying power and savings were lost, and it was expected to take many years before consumer confidence and growth rates recovered and inflation fell. Car sales in Mexico had shown a dramatic drop in 1995 (see Exhibit 7). Mexico's economic difficulties meant that the country's vehicle sales were expected to fall sharply in the mid-1990s and then recover by 2000.

Due to a combination of the General Agreement on Trade and Tariffs (GATT), the initiation of the North American Free Trade Agreement, the economic recovery and an upturn in the replacement cycle, the demand for passenger cars was forecast to grow steadily in Canada and the USA from the mid-1990s, but new registrations in 1995 were lower than in 1994. The industry was paying for price rises in 1994 and a flood of two-year-old cars on to the used car market – the product of the promotion of cheap short-term leases. Also, discounts and lease deals used to sell new vehicles in the early 1990s had encouraged customers to resist higher prices.

In the USA six manufacturers dominated the market in 1995: General Motors (33.9 per cent), Ford (20.7 per cent), Chrysler (9.1 per cent), Toyota/Lexus (9.2 per cent), Honda/Acura (8.6 per cent) and Nissan/Infiniti (6.0 per cent). There was a similar scenario in Canada, where the respective market shares of the main firms were: GM (33.9 per cent),

Exhibit 7 Actual and predicted new registrations of passenger cars in the NAFTA region, 1994–2000 (000s)

	1994	1995	1996	1997	1998	1999	2000
Canada	749	670	690	750	790	900	1,100
Mexico	414	110	115	160	200	275	350
USA	8,992	8,640	8,575	8,525	8,610	8,700	8,800
Total NAFTA	10,155	9,420	9,380	9,435	9,600	9,875	10,250
% change	n/a	−7.2	0.4	0.6	1.7	2.9	3.8

Note Figures for 1994–5 are actual; figures for 1996–2000 are forecasts.

Sources AMIA; author's forecasts.

Exhibit 8 Actual and predicted production of passenger cars in NAFTA, 1994–2000 (000s)

	1994	1995	1996	1997	1998	1999	2000
Canada	1,211	1,340	1,365	1,420	1,455	1,470	1,495
Mexico	856	700	665	720	770	850	950
USA	6,605	6,330	6,000	6,175	6,250	6,350	6,450
Total NAFTA	8,672	8,370	8,030	8,315	8,475	8,670	8,895
% change	n/a	−3.5	−4.1	3.5	1.9	2.3	2.6

Note Figures for 1994–5 are actual; figures for 1996–2000 are forecasts.

Sources AMIA; author's forecasts.

Ford (16.9 per cent), Chrysler (14.5 per cent), Honda (9.9 per cent) and Toyota (8.5 per cent). The balance between the main manufacturers was not forecast to shift dramatically in the 1990s unless takeover or joint venture strategies were followed.

Passenger car production was forecast to dip in 1996, but then to grow steadily in the following years (Exhibit 8). It was predicted that US growth would be due to the local US producers meeting the increased demand and the Japanese transplants coming on-line, and growth in Mexico due to the manufacturers developing their capacity.

JAPAN

Political scandals, the strength of the yen and concerns about interest rates and taxes had left consumer confidence in Japan weak at the start of the 1990s. A slowing down of the growth of GNP induced a rise in interest rates in the early 1990s, leading to a slowing of the economic boom. This was reflected in a 13.8 per cent fall in new registrations between 1991 and 1993, from 4.87m to 4.20m cars.

Although the economic prospects were improving in the mid-1990s, recovery was predicted to be slow. Aided by a cut in sales tax for cars in 1994, the following few years were predicted to show an increase in new car registrations. The stringent and expensive vehicle testing regime on older vehicles also acted to create an upturn in the replacement cycle in the mid-1990s. The 1995 sales figures showed that Toyota was the market leader with 33.6 per cent market share, with Nissan's 18 per cent share placing it second. These two manufacturers dominated sales, with Mitsubishi (9.2 per cent), Honda (8.5 per cent), Suzuki (7.4 per cent) and Mazda (6.3 per cent) trailing behind.

Sales of foreign-produced cars, excluding models made by Japanese manufacturers overseas, accounted for only about 7 per cent of the market in 1995. For years US and European car-makers had complained about the barriers to entering the Japanese car market, ranging from high tariffs to superfluous safety checks. But trade negotiations have removed such barriers and as a result the big three US manufacturers forecast a sixfold increase in sales to 100,000 cars each by the year 2000. European car-makers also believed they could take a substantial share of the world's second largest market, with imports predicted to reach between 20 and 30 per cent of the market.

A key factor for the predicted surge in imports into Japan had been the strong yen, which allowed foreign manufacturers to reduce prices and offer additional features at no extra cost. Even prestige marques, such as Mercedes-Benz and Audi, were able to cut the differential between their prices in Japan and those in their domestic market. The year 1995 saw an increased demand for the less prestigious brands: almost half of Rover's sales were for the Mini and the Rover 100, and VW enjoyed a similar upturn. But some big European manufacturers, such as Fiat, Peugeot Citroën and Renault, found Japan a hard market.

The Japanese government was becoming increasingly protective of the environment, with expectations that the use of alternative fuels and more environmentally friendly vehicles would be needed in the longer term. These were likely to be more expensive than the 1995 models. By 1995 the market for passenger cars in Japan was saturated. Although the number of cars per person remained low by world standards, congestion and parking restrictions made ownership of a car unattractive. Thus, sales were expected to flatten out in the late 1990s and then fall slightly by the end of the decade, due to the predicted tightening of environmental laws, parking restrictions and increases in sales tax (see Exhibit 9).

Exhibit 9 **Actual and predicted new registrations of passenger cars in Japan, 1994–2000 (000s)**

	1994	1995	1996	1997	1998	1999	2000
Japan	4,210	4,443	4,600	4,700	4,625	4,575	4,525
% change	n/a	5.5	3.5	2.2	−1.6	−1.1	−1.1

Note Figures for 1994–5 are actual; figures for 1996–2000 are forecasts.

Exhibit 10 **Actual and predicted production of passenger cars in Japan, 1994–2000 (000s)**

	1994	1995	1996	1997	1998	1999	2000
Japan	7,801	7,610	7,600	7,800	7,725	7,625	7,500
% change	n/a	−2.5	−0.1	2.6	−1.0	−1.3	−1.6

Note Figures for 1994–5 are actual; figures for 1996–2000 are forecasts.

Sources DRI; author's forecasts.

Motor vehicles were Japan's largest export business. Although in the first half of the decade, exports to Malaysia and Indonesia had dropped sharply, shipments to China had increased. There was also a growth in exports to the Middle East and South America. In total, however, the volume of exports had fallen. Thus, vehicle production fell sharply in the first half of the decade.

Apart from falling exports, other factors like a shrinking home market, self-imposed cutbacks by the Ministry of International Trade and Industry (MITI), the appreciation of the yen and growth of overseas operations all led to a drop in local production in the early 1990s. Labour shortages and increasing production costs also gave manufacturers serious problems.

Production had fallen from 9.75m to 8.50m cars between 1991 and 1993, and further decreases were expected by the end of the decade due to a predicted fall in local demand and the further development of overseas transplant operations (Exhibit 10). There had been an increase in such operations in order to avoid the impact of exchange rate fluctuations, which undermined the competitiveness of direct exports. Overseas production also helped allay trade frictions and allowed car-makers to respond more flexibly to local market needs.

The three largest Japanese companies, Toyota, Nissan and Honda, focused on the USA and the UK as their bases for overseas development. In the UK, Japanese car companies produced more than 500,000 units in 1995, and this was forecast to reach 650,000 units by 1999. Honda remained the most international of Japan's three leading car-makers. Honda expanded overseas output more rapidly than Toyota and Nissan because its home sales were smaller, and the company predicted that by 1996 it would make more cars overseas than in Japan. The company expected to build 996,000 vehicles overseas in 1996, compared with 975,000 units at home. Toyota increased overseas production by 20 per cent in 1995 and expected a 9 per cent rise in 1996 to 1.37m units. By contrast, Nissan, one of the first Japanese car-makers to shift production abroad, did not plan significant increases in overseas output.

ASIA PACIFIC EXCLUDING JAPAN

Asia Pacific had one of the fastest growing economies in the mid-1990s and this was predicted to continue if the countries in Asia could keep inflation under control. The political uncertainty of many of the governments in the area and the risk of cross-border wars remained the key potential stumbling blocks in the region's growth.

Vehicle sales were predicted to grow by 7 per cent annually for the region (see Exhibit 11). Vietnam, China, Indonesia, India, Thailand and the Philippines were all predicted high growth rates. However, slower growth was predicted in South Korea (5 per cent a year) and Taiwan (2 per cent a year), and demand in Australia was expected to fall by 0.2 per cent a year.

In 1995, South Korea was the largest producer of passenger vehicles in the region, with a 55.6 per cent share of production (see Exhibit 12). With a rapid development of production operations in India and China predicted during the latter part of the decade, South Korea's share of the production market was expected to fall to 48.2 per cent of all the region's output. Australia's importance as a producer in the region was expected to decline.

China's automotive policy, announced in 1994, froze new car manufacturing ventures until 1997 and demanded that companies wanting to produce vehicles in China showed a commitment by investing in the components sector. China was clearly the biggest potential new market for the automobile industry, and Volkswagen of Germany led the early entry of European manufacturers into China: the company established its first manufacturing joint venture facility in 1985. The dominance of German companies was reinforced when the Chinese government selected Mercedes-Benz and Porsche in preference to Chrysler and Ford for two important industry projects. Mercedes-Benz explored the possibility of building 60,000 multipurpose vehicles (also known as people-carriers) and 100,000 engines, and Porsche agreed to set up a technical and research centre for new car lines.

Exhibit 11 Actual and predicted new registrations of passenger cars in Asia (excluding Japan), 1994–2000 (000s)

	1994	1995	1996	1997	1998	1999	2000
China	376	330	400	500	600	725	850
India	282	390	440	510	550	600	720
South Korea	1,140	1,150	1,220	1,250	1,320	1,400	1,490
Taiwan	435	455	465	475	485	495	505
Others	839	854	900	930	960	1,000	1,050
Total	3,072	3,179	3,425	3,665	3,915	4,220	4,615
% annual change	n/a	3.5	7.7	7.0	6.8	7.8	9.4

Note Figures for 1994–5 are actual; figures for 1996–2000 are forecasts.

Sources DRI; author's forecasts.

Exhibit 12 Actual and predicted production of passenger cars in Asia (excluding Japan), 1994–2000 (000s)

	1994	1995	1996	1997	1998	1999	2000
China	250	321	400	500	600	700	850
India	298	390	430	500	580	640	740
South Korea	1,760	2,000	2,220	2,300	2,390	2,450	2,500
Taiwan	283	308	320	340	360	375	390
Others	527	577	600	630	660	680	710
Total	3,118	3,596	3,970	4,270	4,590	4,845	5,190
% change	n/a	15.3	10.4	7.6	7.5	5.6	7.1

Note Figures for 1994–5 are actual; figures for 1995–2000 are forecasts.

Sources DRI; author's forecasts.

Japanese car-makers remained wary of the relatively undeveloped Chinese market and were cautious about large investments there. Japanese ventures in China included the Jinbel/Toyota joint venture and the General Motors/Daihatsu joint venture to produce the minibus model. Isuzu was also involved in a venture to produce vehicle bodies.

General Motors beat Ford to one of China's largest car manufacturing projects involving a foreign partner. General Motors planned to invest $1bn in a plant in Shanghai to produce a new company car for Chinese corporations. The joint venture with state-owned Shanghai Automobile Industry Corp. will build 100,000 vehicles a year by the end of the decade.

Ford had a clear strategy of establishing vehicle manufacturing in China, although it was not well represented there. The company had four joint venture agreements to produce automotive components with Chinese companies, and took a 20 per cent share of Jiangling Motors, a small company based in the southern province of Jiangxi, producing 120,000 light trucks a year.

In sharp contrast to China, Vietnam opened its doors and gave licences to twelve foreign car manufacturers ranging from Chrysler and Ford of the USA and Toyota of Japan to smaller, less experienced players such as Hyundai. The government seemed to have taken the philosophy of free-market economy to extremes. Fierce competition as well as neighbouring Thailand's ambitions of producing 1m cars by the year 2000 could force some car-makers out of Vietnam.

Japanese car-makers were well positioned to take advantage of growth in the Far East region; they were geographically close to the market and some companies had been in some of these markets for as long as 30–40 years. For example, in Thailand, Japanese brand names had a market share of more than 90 per cent. Japanese brands also dominated the markets in Indonesia, the Philippines and Malaysia: for example, Mitsubishi Motors had a 58 per cent share of the Malaysian car market. Mitsubishi planned annual car sales in the Asia Pacific region of 900,000 units by the year 2000.

Japanese car-makers strengthened their position in the region with vehicles tailored specifically to regional needs. The companies took cars developed in Japan and modified them to suit local needs. Referred to as 'Asia cars', such models were viewed almost as 'national cars' by local consumers.

India was a very attractive market for foreign investment in the 1990s when the government abolished industrial licensing in the passenger car sector in 1993. For decades two companies had dominated the Indian car market: Hindustan Motors and Premier Automobiles. In 1983 a Suzuki–Indian government joint venture formed a third manufacturer, Maruti. Targeting the small-engined 'people's car', Maruti gained 71 per cent of the car market. However, numerous joint ventures (JVs) indicated a potential explosion in car sales and production in the years leading up to the end of the decade:

- Daewoo and DCM, an Indian heavy goods vehicle (HGV) maker, entered a JV to produce a small car called the Cielo.
- Mercedes and Telco, another HGV maker, entered a JV to make the Mercedes E220 saloons.
- A 50/50 JV between Hindustan Motors and General Motors planned to produce the Opel/Vauxhall Astra.
- Hindustan also had a licensing agreement with Mitsubishi to produce the Lancer.

- Premier Automobiles and Peugeot had a JV to build the 309 saloon.
- Premier also had a separate JV with Fiat to produce the Uno.
- Mahindra & Mahindra, the Indian utility vehicle-maker, had a JV with Ford to produce the Escort and Fiesta.
- Siel, the Indian engineering group, had a JV with Honda to make the latter's Civic.
- Volkswagen and Eicher, the Indian commercial farm vehicle group, planned to produce the Gold.

None of the new joint ventures aimed directly to challenge the low-price, high-volume sector of the market dominated by Maruti, but instead aimed to create a new upmarket sector.

EASTERN AND CENTRAL EUROPE

Apart from an ailing Russian economy, in 1995 most of the economies of the countries in this region were growing, albeit at a slow rate. Poland's economy had grown every year since 1992, and Hungary, Romania, Bulgaria and the Czech Republic all showed signs of being over their economic decline. Russia's social and political instability meant that the trend of a declining economy since 1989 was not expected to change during the 1990s.

Following the collapse of the region's command economy, the low currency value in eastern Europe meant that, although many people aspired to own a new car, few could actually afford one. Between 1990 and 1995 demand had fallen from 1.1 million units to 0.69m units in the region's largest market, Russia and the Ukraine, which accounted for 65 per cent of the region's vehicle sales in 1990 (see Exhibit 13). There was a similar trend in the other countries of eastern Europe, with the region's sales falling from 2.0m cars to 1.49m units between 1990 and 1995.

Production levels were on the decline in the early 1990s. In Russia and the Ukraine production had fallen from 1.1m units to 0.81m between 1990 and 1995. In the rest of eastern Europe production fell from 0.72m units to 0.68m between 1990 and 1992, but then recovered to 0.92m units by 1995. Foreign investment had boosted production: for example, Fiat in Poland and Volkswagen in the Czech Republic. The increase in production was predicted to continue between 1995 and 2000 (see Exhibit 14).

Hungary led the way in market-led reforms in the former Communist bloc and was rewarded by attracting foreign investment. Between 1990 and 1994, the country attracted $8.49bn in foreign investment, more than was invested in all other eastern European countries combined. Hungary's geographic location between the European Union and the huge former Soviet market meant that the country was the natural route for western companies into eastern Europe, Ukraine, Russia and Romania. Ford moved

Exhibit 13 Actual and predicted registrations of passenger cars in eastern and central Europe, 1994–2000 (000s)

	1994	1995	1996	1997	1998	1999	2000
Russia and Ukraine	690	675	700	750	800	850	900
Czech Republic	95	110	115	120	125	132	140
Slovakia	15	25	28	33	38	42	50
Hungary	91	56	70	65	62	60	60
Poland	250	260	267	277	287	300	320
Others	315	362	400	382	426	430	434
Total	1,456	1,488	1,580	1,627	1,738	1,814	1,904
% change	n/a	2.2	6.2	3.0	6.8	4.4	5.0

Note Figures for 1994–5 are actual; figures for 1996–2000 are forecasts.

Sources Industry journals; author's forecasts.

Exhibit 14 Actual and predicted production of passenger cars in eastern and central Europe, 1994–2000 (000s)

	1994	1995	1996	1997	1998	1999	2000
Russia and Ukraine	798	805	835	890	950	980	1,030
Czech Republic	174	195	205	215	220	225	230
Slovakia	8	22	26	28	32	40	46
Hungary	32	51	58	66	72	78	85
Poland	338	364	375	385	400	410	420
Others	287	299	330	340	350	360	350
Total	1,637	1,736	1,829	1,924	2,024	2,093	2,161
% change	n/a	6.0	5.4	5.2	5.2	3.4	3.2

Note Figures for 1994–5 are actual; figures for 1996–2000 are forecasts.

Sources Industry journals; author's forecasts.

its central European headquarters from Vienna to Budapest in order to give its executives a better understanding of market conditions in eastern Europe.

Hungary also had an agreement with the EU which abolished or provided for the phasing out of tariffs on goods produced in Hungary. Thus, western European companies could produce in Hungary and then sell the goods on the EU markets without incurring heavy import taxes. This reduction in production costs more than offset the cost of moving production to Hungary. Audi, for example, shipped components overnight to its engine plant at Gyor in western Hungary, and following assembly they were sent back via a train link which came directly on to the factory floor. Manufacturers from the USA and Asia, such as Ford and Suzuki, also moved production to Hungary because it was a low-cost base from which to export to the EU.

However, Poland and the Czech Republic were also competing for such investment. General Motors planned to invest $359.7m in a new east European car plant site in southern Poland, with a possible further $250m expansion to raise production capacity from 72,000 cars to 150,000. The Polish government offered corporate tax relief and customs duty incentives to encourage the investment in Poland. In some designated economic development zones, the Polish government offered complete relief from corporation tax for up to ten years, a further ten years in which corporation tax would be paid at half the normal rate, and relief on customs duty for imported plant and equipment.

PSA PEUGEOT CITROËN

Roland Calori, Philippe Very and Michel Berthelier

The case describes the strategy of PSA Peugeot Citroën in the automobile industry. The group includes two general car manufacturing companies: Automobiles Peugeot and Automobiles Citroën. In 1995 it was the third largest car manufacturer in Europe with a 12 per cent market share, and the largest French exporter. The case examines the strategy of a company facing intense rivalry in the context of industry globalisation. It provides the opportunity to evaluate current strategies and consider the relevance of different competitive strategy options in an international context. An important issue is the need to understand the political aspects of international strategies, the role of governments and the EU and the debate on protectionist or liberal trade policies.

• • •

The PSA Group included two general car manufacturing companies: Automobiles Peugeot and Automobiles Citroën. The two were linked by strong technological, industrial and financial synergies, although each marque kept its identity, and its own marketing and sales. In 1994 the PSA Group was the third largest car manufacturer in Europe, with a 12.8 per cent market share.

The year 1994 showed improved performance of PSA, after difficulties in 1993: profitability rose from a FF1 billion loss to profits of FF3.1 billion, and the sales turnover increased from FF145.4 billion to FF166.2 billion (95 per cent of which was in car manufacturing). PSA employed 139,800 people and manufactured 1,989,000 vehicles, of which two-thirds were sold outside France in 150 countries and 22,000 sales locations. With export sales of FF74.9 billion, the group was the main French exporter.

This case was prepared by Roland Calori, Philippe Very and Michel Berthelier, professors at the Group ESC Lyon. The authors would like to thank the PSA Group for its support in writing the case study. It is intended as a basis for class discussion and not as an illustration of either good or bad management practice.

Exhibit 1 PSA Group: main consolidated financial data

	1996	1995	1994	1993	1992
Net sales	172.9	164.2	166.2	145.4	155.4
Cash flow	11.2	12.8	15.2	8.3	13.7
Investments (tangible assets)	10.3	11.0	10.5	11.3	13.8
Net profit	0.7	1.7	3.1	(−1.4)	3.4
Shareholders' equity	55.5	54.6	53.5	50.5	53.1
Net financial debts	8.9	9.8	7.6	16.7	14.3
Earnings per share (FF)	16	34	62	(−28)	67

Note Figures in billions of French francs unless stated.

Source Adapted from annual report, 1994.

THE PSA GROUP

In 1976 Peugeot, a family owned company, took over Citroën. Then in 1978 it took over the European subsidiaries of Chrysler. At the beginning of the 1990s, the group (Peugeot and Citroën) was controlled by the Peugeot family, who owned 22.7 per cent of the equity, the largest other shareholder being Michelin. The rest of the equity was held by financial institutions and individual stockholders.

From 1980 to 1984 the PSA Group went through financial difficulties, its net debts rising to FF33.1 billion and its equity dropping to FF5.3 billion in 1984. In 1983 the group lost FF2.6 billion. The renaissance of PSA came with the hiring of a new top manager, Jacques Calvet, and with the growth in the European market (+4 per cent per year on average) between 1985 and 1989. Jacques Calvet became président directeur général of Peugeot, then président directeur général of Citroën in 1983 and président du directoire of the holding company in 1984. Formerly he had been directeur du trésor at the French Ministry of Finance and president of the Banque Nationale de Paris. Experts believed that his skills and the rigour of his management were at the centre of the recovery of the PSA Group. Losses were cut as early as 1984, and debts were reduced starting from 1987. At the end of 1989, the company announced net profits of FF10.3 billion (a net margin of 6.7 per cent of turnover); the sales turnover was about FF153 billion and debts had been reduced to FF1.9 billion.

Substantial progress in production methods was also achieved: productivity improvements were about 72 per cent between 1982 and 1987 (the best European performance according to the consulting company Luvigsen Associates), and 50 per cent during the period 1985–9. High investments were made to rationalise manufacturing and to develop the company's range of products.

In 1986 Jacques Calvet announced an ambitious goal for PSA: to become the leading car manufacturer in the European market in terms of number of vehicles sold. However, the aim of dominant market share was postponed with the recession of the western European market and the unexpected opening of the eastern European market, which was more favourable to competitors based in Germany (Volkswagen and GM-Opel). Indeed, from 1990 to 1993, with the economic recession, the European car market decreased and sales and profits of the PSA Group slowly declined before the 1994 revival.

Exhibit 1 gives the main financial indicators of PSA between 1992 and 1996, and Exhibit 2 gives information on the two main companies of the group, Automobiles Peugeot and Automobiles Citroën.

MARKETS

Western European market shares fluctuated depending on two main factors: significant changes in relative prices and the success of new models. The top management of the PSA Group was preoccupied with the price war that had been taking place since 1990. They were also concerned with monetary fluctuations within Europe, particularly with the competitive devaluations of sterling, the peseta and the Italian lira (about 38 per cent since 1992), which had upset sales at the beginning of the 1990s. PSA and several other car manufacturers were looking forward to the possibility of a single European currency. As Jacques Calvet remarked in the annual stockholders' meeting in June 1995:

> For Europe, which is now truly a single market, the worst wounds have come from within, with the breakdown of the European Monetary System and competitive devaluations, notably of the Italian lira. Europe will not hold up long if there is not a rapid solution to this problem.

Moreover, new competitors were emerging. The market share of Korean car manufacturers in Europe (about 3 per cent in 1994) was growing, particularly in the low-priced segment.

The eastern European markets had stagnated at around 1 million vehicles a year and experts forecast a maximum of 1.5 million vehicles by the year 2000. The Russian market was estimated around 2 million vehicles and moderate growth was expected.

The North American market grew in 1992 (5 per cent) and in 1993 (7.3 per cent), and it represented 16.5 million vehicles in 1994. 'Light trucks' (mini-vans, pick-ups, four-wheel-drives) represented 40 per cent of sales, with a high growth. General Motors, Ford and Chrysler had a 73 per cent market share, compared to the Japanese 23 per cent, and the European car manufacturers' 2.7 per cent. PSA had left the US market in 1985, since it could not establish a significant position in this highly competitive

Exhibit 2 The two main companies of the PSA Group: Automobiles Peugeot and Automobiles Citroën

AUTOMOBILES PEUGEOT				AUTOMOBILES CITROËN			
Group's holding: 100% (fully by Peugeot SA) Plants in: Sochaux-Montbéliard, Mulhouse, Poissy, Ryton (UK) and Villaverde (Spain). Plants in: Dijon, Lille, Saint-Etienne, Sept-Fons, Vesoul, Valenciennes and Villers la Montagne.				**Group's holding: 100% (fully by Peugeot SA)** Production sites in: Aulnay, Rennes, Vigo (Spain) and Mangualde (Portugal). Plants in: Asnières, Caen and Charleville.			
	1996	1995	1994		1996	1995	1994
Economic data				*Economic data*			
Production (in number of vehicles)	1,146,500	1,142,300	1,202,000	Production (in number of vehicles)	832,500	745,600	787,800
Sales (in number of vehicles)	1,170,100	1,118,800	1,209,200	Sales (in number of vehicles)	836,000	746,300	779,600
Employees				*Employees*			
Company	49,600	50,800	41,900	Company	28,400	28,900	28,900
Group	67,400	68,600	69,200	Group	45,700	45,600	45,700
Consolidated financial data (FF m)				*Consolidated financial data (FF m)*			
Net sales	107,052	99,581	101,778	Net sales	76,858	73,912	70,653
Working capital provided from operations	6,171	6,216	7,545	Working capital provided from operations	2,375	4,169	4,416
Net income	830	1,102	1,394	Net income	(2,693)	(1,324)	184
Capital expenditures	4,963	5,857	6,047	Capital expenditures	4,588	4,439	3,240

Source Annual report, 1994

Exhibit 3 European sales of the PSA Group: share of passenger car registrations (%)

	1996	1995	1994
France	29.4	30.2	31.1
Austria	7.0	7.6	7.8
Belgium–Luxembourg	14.3	13.5	13.7
Denmark	13.7	13.1	14.8
Finland	8.1	8.3	8.4
Germany	3.7	4.1	4.5
Greece	8.8	10.0	11.3
Ireland	6.2	6.3	7.0
Italy	6.7	6.8	7.0
Netherlands	9.8	10.6	12.1
Norway	7.2	7.5	8.9
Portugal	12.5	12.3	13.3
Spain	20.6	19.0	19.9
Sweden	3.7	3.8	4.6
Switzerland	8.0	8.4	7.9
United Kingdom	11.3	11.5	12.1
Total Europe	11.9	12.0	12.8
Europe outside France	8.5	8.5	9.2

Note Does not include light commercial vehicles registrations.

Source Annual report, 1994 and 1996.

environment (on average the price of cars in the United States was 30 per cent lower than in Europe).

The Japanese market showed signs of revival in 1994 (an increase of 1 per cent) after three years of decline. It represented 6.5 million vehicles. In this market, dominated by Toyota (with a 41 per cent market share), imports from foreign OECD countries were marginal. German manufacturers together exported 121,000 vehicles in 1994, Americans exported 37,000 vehicles, and the French sold 6,800 units.

The African and Middle East markets remained marginal (stable at around a total of 1 million vehicles a year). Two other zones experienced high growth: South America (2.8 million vehicles a year, with a 6 per cent annual growth) and Asia (apart from Japan), which represented annual sales of 4.8 million vehicles (with a 9 per cent annual growth).

Exhibit 3 gives the breakdown of market share for the group in Europe and Exhibit 4 shows the breakdown of the sales of the PSA Group in the world.

Exhibit 4 Worldwide sales of the PSA Group (passenger cars and light commercial vehicles, 000s)

	1996	1995	1994
Western Europe			
France			
Peugeot	417	396	430
Citroën	321	305	304
PSA Peugeot Citroën	738	701	734
Other western European countries			
Peugeot	576	552	585
Citroën	430	385	416
PSA Peugeot Citroën	1,006	937	1,001
Outside Western Europe			
Eastern Europe			
Peugeot	28	18	14
Citroën	23	10	8
PSA Peugeot Citroën	51	28	22
Africa			
Peugeot	21	26	24
Citroën	10	9	9
PSA Peugeot Citroën	31	35	33
America			
Peugeot	70	68	99
Citroën	13	13	11
PSA Peugeot Citroën	83	81	110
Asia Pacific area			
Peugeot	38	41	40
Citroën	35	23	21
PSA Peugeot Citroën	73	64	61
Special registrations			
Peugeot	19	17	19
Citroën	3	2	10
PSA Peugeot Citroën	22	19	29
Total worldwide			
Peugeot	1,170	1,119	1,209
(including small collections)	(23)	(32)	(40)
Citroën	836	746	780
PSA Peugeot Citroën	2,006	1,865	1,989

Source Annual report, 1994 and 1996.

At the annual stockholders' meeting in June 1995, Jacques Calvet commented on the 1994 performance of PSA as follows:

> The market-share of Peugeot and Citroën in western Europe, 12.8 per cent, as compared to 12.1 per cent in 1992 and 12.4 per cent in 1993, has grown significantly. This commercial dynamism results both from the deployment of our ranges of vehicles ... and from the favourable evolution of European markets: those where Peugeot and Citroën have a high share have evolved more favourably than the European average.

THE STRATEGY OF PSA

Jacques Calvet chose to be chairman of Automobiles Peugeot and chairman of Automobiles Citroën in order to stimulate synergies between the two companies, which had kept their own culture for several years after the merger. Peugeot and Citroën were both involved in the main segments of the market and adopted parallel market positioning (see Exhibit 5). Automobiles Peugeot had a 7.7 per cent market share in western Europe (18.7 per cent in France) and Automobiles Citroën had a 5.1 per cent market share in western Europe (12.4 per cent in France).

Some other competitors also had more than one marque. The Volkswagen Group had several, with Seat and Skoda at the low end of the market, Volkswagen as a generalist and Audi at the top end of the market. The Fiat Group had Ferrari at the very top of the market, Alfa Romeo, Fiat itself and Lancia. Other car manufacturers such as Renault had only one marque.

At PSA, the standardisation of vehicles was relatively high between the two product lines, about 50 per cent of the components being common. These were the non-visible components – engines, gearboxes, etc. – while the elements of the car that could be seen were different. Joint purchasing of components through Sogedac, a group company (with an annual sales turnover of FF80 billion), was seen as a source of competitive benefit by the company.

Part of the R&D expenses were also shared: thanks to the two parallel model ranges, synergies in R&D had increased, particularly in the early phases of new product development. For instance, the Citroën XM and the Peugeot 605 were developed by a single 'technical platform' (multi-functional project team). Innovations concerning new materials and new methods were shared. Industrial teams also worked together on international operations.

Differences and separation between the two marques were apparent in product design and style, the development of production processes, and marketing and sales, with two distinct dealer networks competing with each other. There was no intention to merge the two distribution networks, since executives believed the weaker marque could be disadvantaged (a problem which occurred when Peugeot took over Chrysler-Simca in 1979). Besides, the view was that merging the two independent distribution networks could give an opportunity for foreign competitors to take over dealer networks.

Exhibit 5 Group production of Peugeot and Citroën models (number of vehicles)

	Peugeot		Citroën	
Sector	Model	1996	Model	1996
Mini	106	350,500	AX	116,400
Super mini	205	76,900	Saxo	201,500
Lower medium	306	350,200	ZX	197,800
	309	2,300		
Upper medium	405	35,700	Xantia	157,300
	406	196,100		
	504 Paykan	22,600		
	505	3,100		
Executive	605	9,600	XM	12,500
'Monospace'	806	20,700	Evasion	12,200
	Expert	14,200	Jumpy	14,000
	Partner	24,600		
Utility and miscellaneous	J5, J9, Boxer	40,000	C15, Berlingo, Jumper	120,800
Total		1,146,500	Total	832,500

Source Annual report, 1996.

Such a strategy required a significant effort to renew the range of models of the two companies. In order to renew eight basic models (four Peugeot and four Citroën) every six years, PSA would have to launch one or two new models every year. On average the investment to launch a new model was estimated at around FF10 billion.

The PSA Group was the world leader in diesel cars with 957,400 vehicles in 1994, and had a significant competitive advantage in this domain. It sold diesel engines to Rover and Ford. In general, French car manufacturers PSA and Renault had a particularly strong position in diesel cars, with a 38 per cent market share in western Europe. The top management of PSA argued that diesel engines consumed less and cheaper fuel, produced less pollution, and were more reliable and long lasting than petrol engines. The proportion of diesel cars was very low in Japan and in the United States, but it was significant and growing in Europe, particularly where the taxation of fuel was not unfavourable (see Exhibit 6).

Renewal

Since the beginning of the 1990s, a particular effort was made to launch new models and renew existing models. In 1994 PSA launched the 806

Exhibit 6 Percentages of diesel cars in the main EEC countries

	1990	1994
France	33.0	47.6
Germany	9.8	16.6
Italy	7.3	8.7
United Kingdom	6.4	21.7
Netherlands	10.9	12.0
Belgium–Luxembourg	31.8	41.4
Spain	14.7	28.2
European Union (12 countries)	14.2	23.1

Source PSA.

monospace (Peugeot) and its brother, the Evasion (Citroën). At Peugeot the 605 was restyled and re-engined, and new versions of the 306 (a cabriolet and a 'tri-corps'), and new utility vehicles (Boxer and 205 van) were launched. At Citroën the XM was restyled and re-engined, new versions of the ZX (Break) and the Xantia (Activa) were produced, and a new utility vehicle (Jumper) was launched. Advertising and promotional budgets were increased so as to rejuvenate the image: warm and relaxed for Citroën, humorous and lively for Peugeot. Peugeot reinvested in the Formula 1 Grand Prix and won eight podiums in 1994 with the McLaren team; they also won 'super tourism' competitions with the 405. Citroën won the world rally championship for the second time with its ZX. The co-operation between Peugeot and Citroën was crucial in order to share the efforts in renewing products. For years PSA also co-operated with Renault in the development and manufacture of components as well as in research on environmentally friendly cars. At the beginning of the 1990s, the co-operation with Fiat was strengthened in order to share the development and manufacturing of a monospace. In 1994 the Sevelnord plant at Valenciennes (France) started to manufacture the monospace for the four companies: Peugeot 806, Citroën Evasion, Fiat Ulysse and Lancia Zeta. Sevelnord, a 50/50 joint venture between PSA and Fiat, required a FF6 billion investment and was to produce 130,000 vehicles a year. The same type of co-operation was set up in Italy in order to share the manufacturing of small utility vehicles: Peugeot Boxer, Citrëon Jumper and Fiat Ducat. Sevelsud was to manufacture 190,000 vehicles a year. The top management of PSA viewed such focused alliances at the best way to compete in new market niches.

From 1988 to 1990 PSA spent 3.5 per cent of its turnover on R&D. In 1994 the budget for R&D was FF7.2 billion, representing 3.8 per cent of the consolidated turnover, a high percentage compared to other European competitors, but lower than the Japanese Toyota and Honda (both around 5 per cent). Most of the 9,200 persons employed in R&D worked for the two marques: on the development of new models, on market-driven technological innovations or on manufacturing technologies and methods. For instance, PSA participated in a joint European programme, Prometheus, to improve road traffic in Europe with the help of electronic systems. The group was also active in joint European programmes for the recycling of vehicles. The improvement of subsystems such as diesel engines and suspensions was also seen as a priority: for instance, the launch of the Xantia Activa in 1994 was based on a new system of active suspensions.

The electric car was one of the top research priorities for PSA. In 1991, PSA was the first car manufacturer to sell electric vehicles for urban use (to Electricité de France and to local government authorities and public institutions). The market was estimated by executives to be around 250,000 vehicles in Europe by 1995. The large-scale manufacturing and sale of the electric Peugeot 106 and Citrëon AX was planned to start in 1996. The electric car was to become the second family car, for driving short distances mainly in towns. The PSA executives believed they were three years ahead of competition in this domain. The group co-operated with several townships so as to implant the necessary infrastructure to provide power for recharging batteries. PSA also launched the 'Tulip' project, a system of electric car rental for the town. Small two-seater Tulip cars would be rented by subscribers in several places in a town, and batteries would be recharged in a number of parking places with an electric terminal. The system was experimented with in Tours at the end of 1995, and PSA decided to continue its further development.

Productivity and Effectiveness

Investment was particularly high at the beginning of the 1990s, about FF15 billion a year in 1990 and 1991. It represented about 9.5 per cent of the sales turnover, one of the highest ratios of the industry, and was financed internally rather than through borrowing. 'Investments are aimed at renewing the product range. They are also aimed at continuing the modernisation of the industrial assets of the group, in order to improve productivity, flexibility, efficiency and the quality of the products' (annual report, 1990). With the crisis in 1993, investment was reduced; however, in 1994 it still represented FF10.5 billion.

On average, productivity was improved by 10 per cent a year during this period, with a 12 per cent improvement in 1994 compared to 1993. Reductions in costs were vital. Jacques Calvet stated that the market reversals in 1990 and 1991 and the price war made them even more so.

Purchases represented 58 per cent of production costs in 1994. Cost cutting on procurement was a priority for the Sogedac, and productivity plans were implemented with suppliers. On average, suppliers increased their added value ratio by 5 per cent a year.

In PSA's plants the number of hierarchical levels was reduced and a price controller was named for each model. His or her role was to validate suggestions for technical simplifications and cost cutting, many of which came from the workers (128,765 suggestions were in 1994 compared with 78,434 in 1991). Progress was also made in logistics and manufacturing; and delivery times were reduced to a total of 25 days in 1994. Inventories were reduced by FF2,000 million in 1993 and FF759 million in 1994. When investments were made, the group tended to choose simple, reliable, less costly solutions. Cost cutting was seen as a priority, productivity improvement targets for the period 1995–2000 remained very ambitious, and the simplification of product ranges and assembly lines was seen as the way to achieve these goals and improve the quality of vehicles.

In order to improve the effectiveness of R&D, after 1994 every development process (subsystem or new model) was organised in a 'project team' based on a 'technical platform'. This form of organisation was begun in the 1980s by the Japanese in order to reduce the development time of new models and to improve the simplicity of manufacturing. A project leader was in charge of quality, cost, scheduling and specific performance targets (for a new model, he or she reported directly to the top management of PSA). All the professions and functions were represented within a 'technical platform': designers, process engineers, the manufacturing, quality and procurement functions as well as some key suppliers. Typically, the technical platform for a new model would include 20–30 permanent members and a total of 200–300 people working temporarily on particular phases of the project. In 1994 the new model development time had been reduced to 196 weeks at PSA (compared to 250 weeks in 1990); the objective was to reduce it further to 156 weeks by the year 2000. The Japanese car manufacturers and General Motors Europe (Opel Vauxhall) had the shortest new product development times in the industry (between 160 and 180 weeks). The only problem with independent project teams and technical platforms was the risk of overlooking potential synergies between models, creating new components and increasing their unit costs. At PSA the early phases of development of new models were shared between Peugeot and Citroën. The role of Sogedac (the group company in charge of components and procurement) also helped achieve such synergies. It was in the latter stages of product development, when design and the development of production processes dominated, that the two technical platforms for Peugeot and Citroën became more apparent.

Given the limited growth opportunities, productivity improvements led to a regular reduction in staff, particularly in France: 139,800 employees in 1994 compared to 143,900 in 1993 and 150,800 in 1992. The forecasts for the period 1995–2000 showed a continuation of this trend. Careful personnel planning and forecasts at PSA reduced the risk of crises in the long term. Indeed, work patterns were changing: between 1984 and 1994 the percentage of highly skilled workers rose from 10 to 25 per cent, the percentage of technicians from 9 to 13 per cent, and the percentage of supervisors and managers from 4 to 8 per cent. The group had developed an ambitious training programme, representing more than 4 per cent of the wages in 1994 (as compared to 2 per cent in 1984).

THE INTERNATIONAL STRATEGY OF PSA

Europe

PSA had industrial units in several countries in Europe. In 1994, about 80 per cent of manufacturing was done in France. Indeed, France was considered a competitive country in terms of production costs. Peugeot Talbot España (with 205 and 306 manufactured at Villaverde) and Citroën España (with AX, ZX and C15 manufactured at Vigo) represented about 16 per cent of the production. Peugeot Talbot Motors, based at Ryton (United Kingdom), manufactured the 405 until 1993 and the 306 after 1993 (75,300 vehicles in 1994, representing about 3 per cent of the total). The Mangualde plant in Portugal manufactured 14,000 AXs. The Sevelsud joint venture with Fiat in Italy manufactured small utility vehicles. Automobiles Peugeot and Automobiles Citroën made 87 per cent of their sales in Europe; and the European market was seen as a priority for the PSA Group, particularly the large countries (see Exhibit 4). In the German market, seen as particularly attractive, PSA had tried to strengthen its position and had developed its network of dealers. Since Peugeot had taken over the chronically loss-making UK operations of Chrysler, production had risen from about 20,000 units in 1985 to 116,500 in 1990. It then started to decrease with the decline of the British market. However, PSA aimed at improving its UK market share for Peugeot and Citroën as the main export market of the group.

The relationships between the corporate centre in France and the foreign subsidiaries were becoming more complex as the international strategy developed. Research and development was centralised in France; product marketing, pricing and communication policies were also decided in France; but some adaptations to particular important foreign markets were negotiated between the headquarters and its subsidiaries.

Peugeot Talbot Motor Company Ltd (UK) also had a higher degree of autonomy than most of the Peugeot operating businesses. From 1982 onwards, PSA took over the marketing and design decisions for the UK, and disbanded the Ryton design centre. However, PSA Centre did realise the differences in the UK market, especially because of the importance of the fleet market (cars purchased centrally by companies for company personnel). There was therefore a marketing director in the UK, but with a strong functional reporting link through to marketing and design in PSA Centre. The degree of autonomy was less than had been expected by George Turnbull, the chief executive from 1978 to 1985, and he left. The increasing autonomy of the later 1980s had been 'earned' not only by the UK company delivering against its business objectives and the improvements made in industrial relations and productivity, but also by the 'diplomatic' style of the chief executive at that time, Geoffrey Whalen, towards the corporate centre.

Europe was seen as the domestic market of European car manufacturers, and Jacques Calvet was known for his defensive strategy against Japanese competitors. In *European Motor Business* (November 1989) he stated:

> We must develop a common foreign policy towards Japan. We must limit the imports of Japanese cars as long as we do not sell a significant number of cars in Japan, that is to say a ratio of at least one [European car sold to Japan] for two [Japanese cars sold in Europe]. We must also have a common policy concerning the Japanese transplants in Europe ... We need a significant proportion of local content [in Japanese transplants in Europe] – namely 80 per cent – because this relates to the problem of employment and to sustaining technological capabilities in Europe ... We should examine the suggestion made by Gianni Agnelli [president of the Fiat Group] who says that there should be an overall quota on the importations of Japanese cars – wherever they come from – and a limitation to the manufacturing of Japanese cars in Europe.

As far as the strategy of the PSA Group was concerned, Calvet also stated, in *Le Figaro Economie* (April 1991): 'As long as I am President of the Group, I will never accept an agreement with the Japanese.' It was a view he retained in 1995.

The PSA Group was actively lobbying at the EC level to defend the argument of protection against the Japanese, as stated in the annual report of the group in 1990:

> The group will continue its efforts of persuasion in order to avoid dangerous drifts in building Europe and in the negotiations, which are badly opened, between the twelve states of the EC and Japan ... Do we make Europe for the Europeans, for employment, for technology, for European wealth and power or do we abandon ourselves to a competition which is not truly based on free trade and which would lead to a weaker Europe?

With the exception (to some extent) of the Fiat Group, the other European car manufacturers had less intransigent positions towards Japanese competition. However, the attitude of the German companies and of the subsidiaries of the North American companies in Europe evolved towards more protectionism between 1989 and 1991. The attitude of the EC Commission also changed in this direction during the same period. The result was the EEC–Japan agreement of 1991. Japanese imports into Europe would be limited to their 1990 level – that is, to about 1.23 million vehicles a year – during a transitory period until the end of 1999. More precisely, the quotas limiting Japanese imports in some European countries (mainly France, Italy and Spain) would be increased progressively. With regard to Japanese transplants in Europe (not subject to the above limitations), both parties had agreed to limit the production of Japanese transplants to under 1.2 million vehicles until the end of 1999. Actually a complicated system of monitoring was put in place, taking into account the annual evolution of the European market in order to define limits to Japanese growth.

As far as eastern Europe was concerned by 1990 the group had established a distribution network in most of the countries, but exports represented fewer than 22,000 vehicles in 1994.

New Continents

In the 1990s PSA started to look for growth in other continents. As stated in the annual report (1990):

> The industrial projects target countries with a real potential of development for the group, considering the situation of the economy of the country, its industrial base, and the perspective of growth of the automobile market.

In his address to the annual stockholders' meeting in June 1995, Jacques Calvet declared:

> We have made great strides in extending our international presence. Our ambitious goal in this area is for Peugeot and Citroën to progressively make 25 per cent of their sales outside western Europe. Advances in this area include the new phase in Citroën's manufacturing operations in China, Peugeot's recent co-operation agreement in India, our plans to begin production of the 306 in Argentina, and Citroën's negotiations with Proton in Malaysia, which may soon come to a conclusion.

Peugeot had a good reputation in Africa, but this continent offered limited growth opportunities. Morocco and Egypt were the only exceptions (the 405 and AX were assembled in Egypt). The further aim was to complete the group's representation around the Mediterranean basin (including Turkey and Tunisia). Iran was the main base of the group in the Middle East, but local assembly was limited to 8,400 vehicles in 1994.

In Asia, the Japanese market was too competitive to expect significant growth for PSA: 6,600 vehicles were sold in 1994. The Korean market was attractive (900,000 vehicles and 1.2 million expected in the year 2000), but it was tightly protected and dominated by local manufacturers (Daewoo, Hyundai). On the other hand, the sales of the group were growing in Malaysia (3,400 units in 1994), in Taiwan (4,500) and in Thailand. In most of these countries, Japanese car manufacturers already had dominant market shares and strong positions with their networks of local suppliers (for instance, Toyota produced diesel engines and electrical equipment in Thailand, gearboxes and transmissions in the Philippines, petrol engines in Indonesia, steering systems in Malaysia, and co-ordinated activities in Singapore). The Chinese market was less structured and experts forecast annual sales of 1.2 million vehicles in the year 2000 to be manufactured locally. In this market European competitors were more active, particularly Volkswagen and PSA. Peugeot had a joint venture with the Canton township. Guangzhou Peugeot Automobile had the capacity to produce

45,000 vehicles a year (505, pick-up 504). Actual production was around 20,000 units a year; however, there was a project to extend capacity and to manufacture the 405 (150,000 units in the year 2000). Dongfeng Citroën Automobile Company manufactured 8,000 Citroën ZXs in 1994 (compared to 5,000 in 1993), and new plants were being built in Wuhan and in Xiangfan in order to produce 37,000 ZXs and extend the capacity to 150,000 vehicles in the year 2000.

There were about 200 million individuals belonging to the middle and upper classes in India, and the 300,000 vehicle market was expected to become a 600,000 units annual market by the year 2000. The Indian car industry was dominated by Maruti, a joint venture between Suzuki and the Indian state which had a 70 per cent market share (particularly with the small Maruti 800). A number of international competitors were making agreements with local partners: Mercedes with the local Telco, Daewoo with the local DCM, Opel with Hindustan (objective: 12,000 vehicles) and Volkswagen with Eicher Motors (objective: 30,000 vehicles of the Golf 4 and Audi). At the end of 1993, PSA had signed an agreement with Premier Automobile Ltd (the number two in India) to manufacture the Peugeot 309 in Kalyan, starting from 1995. After a FF1 billion investment, the objective of the joint venture PAL Peugeot Ltd was to produce 60,000 vehicles a year.

In the South American continent, Peugeot and Citroën had significant positions in Argentina (with a 15 per cent market share) and in Chile (8,000 vehicles in 1994). The industrial presence of Peugeot in Argentina through the Sevel joint venture was a key success factor in the context of the new Mercosur free-trade agreement in this zone. Peugeot and Citroën had just established sales subsidiaries in Brazil and sales grew from 3,000 vehicles in 1993 up to 10,300 in 1994.

Finally the top management of PSA was studying the opportunity of a 'come back' in the North American market. Like several other European car manufacturers, PSA had been pushed out of the US market in the late 1980s. At the time, it distributed the 505 and the 405 through a limited number of megadealers, in the east coast, the west coast and the south-east. A study conducted in 1994 recommended the following:

- Specific vehicles were needed (given the local norms and preferences).
- A complete sales network was needed (because cars travel all around the country).
- At least two and up to four models were needed in order to feed the sales network.
- It was necessary to have local production (given the evolution of the US dollar and the relatively low cost of manpower in this zone); plants could be located in the USA, in Canada or in Mexico (Volkswagen had plants in Mexico; BMW and Mercedes had plants in South Carolina).
- Such an investment was estimated around FF20 billion in four years, and the next 'high cycle' of the US market was expected in the year 2000 (after the 1994–5 high cycle).

A New Era

By 1995 the top management of PSA was concerned with the possibility of a decrease in consumption. Price differentials between European countries, mainly due to competitive devaluations, stimulated the development of parallel distribution channels (for instance, the price of French cars in Italy was 30 per cent lower than in France for some models). This situation, combined with increased competition in a mature market, was driving down prices. Moreover, according to the EEC–Japan agreement, the competition with the Japanese would be free in Europe starting from the year 2000, and Korean competitors were expected to sell about 1 million vehicles in Europe by the end of the century.

In June 1995 Jacques Calvet concluded his address to the annual stockholders' meeting as follows:

> The challenges facing us are clear. The economic and monetary environment and the intense competition in our markets are serious threats. On the other hand, the Group's forward looking attitude and our employees' strong commitment to achieving our objectives – which I greatly appreciate – are precious, even crucial strengths. As a result we can face the future with confidence.

In October 1997, Jacques Calvet's chairmanship ended and Jean-Martin Folz became the new chairman. Folz had previously worked with French industrial groups such as Rhone-Poulenc and Pechiney and was formally the Chief Executive of Eridania-Beghin Say, the Italo-French foods group. At the beginning of 1998 Folz announced reorganisation plans, which would cut PSA's cost base, and revitalise and help differentiate the Peugeot and Citroën brands.

The main enphasis of the plans was the merger of the manufacturing sites. Peugeot and Citroën cars of a similar production type were grouped together and built at the same factory with the aim of achieving synergies and common areas for savings. However Peugeot and Citroën remained distinct as brands, keeping the customer facing attributes of the cars, such as branding, marketing and sales separate. The intent of the restructuring was to facilitate new product development, innovation, and growth, while significantly reducing costs, and increasing sales and profitability.

In July 1998, Folz was able to report a rise in sales of 15 percent, almost double the growth of the market as a whole. This was coupled with geographic expansion plans. PSA moved into several new markets through joint ventres or direct investment; it became established in Iran, Brazil, and Argentina and was in discussion to enter Malaysia. By being based in these markets, PSA hoped to lessen the effects of overcapacity in Europe, when the EEC-Japan agreement ends.

THE ROVER/HONDA ALLIANCE

David Faulkner

The case study demonstrates some of the key characteristics found in international strategic alliances and the role that alliances can play in helping companies to implement their chosen competitive strategy. This alliance was a key element of Rover's strategy during the period covered in the study. The case illustrates the benefits of strategic alliances to competitors with limited resources in industries facing globalisation of markets. It shows the conditions, both external and internal, likely to lead to alliances. It also illustrates the main factors involved in making alliances successful and the importance of organisational learning to the evolution of alliances. The case also raises questions about the overall strategy of Rover and Honda and can be used in conjunction with 'A note on the world automobile industry' and 'The BMW acquisition of the Rover Group'. It can also be used with the PSA Peugeot Citroën case to compare different strategies in the automobile industry.

• • •

The strategic alliance between the Rover Group and Honda was embarked upon after a meeting between the two companies at the Fairmont Hotel, San Francisco, in September 1978. From that time it evolved from a limited licensing agreement into a multifunctional relationship including joint development and production and a 20 per cent share exchange between the two companies.

BACKGROUND

At the time of the approach to Honda, Rover was an ailing car manufacturer owned reluctantly by the British government, and still making large losses despite attempts by its then chief executive, Michael Edwardes, to

---

This case was prepared by David Faulkner of Oxford University School of Management Studies and is intended for class discussion and not to illustrate either correct or incorrect handling of an administrative situation.

modernise it through a major rationalisation plan, and a determination to curb the trade union power that had contributed in a major way to making BL an example of failing British industry.

By 1979, despite the rationalisation plan, the company was still losing money (£46 million in 1979), and was facing the prospect of a Conservative government less likely to continue to finance unprofitable development. The world automobile market, after a number of years of growth, had shown signs of becoming less attractive. Rover had been pinning its hopes on the Metro, the Maestro and the Montego, but none of these models was reaching its targeted sales figures. The major problem seemed to be Rover's poor reputation for quality.

At the very least Rover needed a new product in the 'lower-medium' sector to plug a gap in its product range, but it lacked both the time and the finance to do this unaided. Still named the British Leyland Motor Corporation (BLMC), the company was facing a declining market share and had poor financial results. The world automobile industry was dominated by the multinational giants, and entry to this exclusive club did not seem to be available to Rover.

Furthermore, the Japanese were beginning to make their presence felt on the world automobile stage with their emphasis on quality, reliability, robotic methods of manufacture and fuel economy.

Among the Japanese car-makers, Honda was something of a maverick. Having started its international life as predominantly a motor-cycle manufacturer, it did not develop a presence in the car market until 1963. In automobile company terms Honda was a medium-sized organisation, with a very high reputation for sound engineering, high quality and high productivity. It had a philosophy based on customer satisfaction and customer improvement, and aspired to be a global player.

Honda was a successful company, but in world automotive industry terms it was still regarded as principally a motor-cycle manufacturer. Honda's image was not sufficient at the time of the alliance formation for it to take its place naturally among the General Motors or even, in its own country, the Toyotas.

Honda had established itself well in the USA, but of the three legs of the Triad, the European leg was to Honda almost entirely undeveloped in 1979. Also Honda felt insecure in this area as it knew European tastes differed from American ones, but it did not trust its understanding of them. Furthermore, Honda did not believe it had the time to set up in Europe, and develop its own European arm from scratch. The development costs of new European models would be too great at that stage of Honda's development, and the time scale too long to be acceptable. As Mr Hayashi, managing director of Honda UK commented:

> At that time there were restrictions on exports to Europe, therefore there was no way to increase our exports there ... Europe was suffering from over-capacity, so we had no chance to build our own factory there ... We thought the Rover approach might help in Europe. It was company policy to be flexible with

> people who approached us, and to have international collaboration, so we agreed to license Rover to manufacture Honda products from knock-down kits.

However, they covered any reservations they might have had by limiting the first deal to an arm's length licensing arrangement, and some time later embarked on the building of the Honda Swindon factory to maintain their flexibility.

In 1978 Rover and Honda were approximately the same size, in terms of world sales, at about £4 billion turnover. Honda was profitable and growing fast, however, and Rover was loss making and possessed factories operating at a level substantially below capacity.

DEVELOPMENT OF THE ALLIANCE

The 1978 meeting in San Francisco came about because BLMC had recognised that, if it wanted a successful future in the world automobile industry, it needed a partner. Roland Bertodo, Rover's strategic planning director, described how the BLMC top management tackled the problem:

> We consciously sat down and wrote down all the automotive companies and listed the pluses and minuses against each one. Honda was the one that came out top purely because it was a similar size to us, it had growth ambitions, and a reputation for high quality at a time when quality for us was the biggest problem. It was renowned for its management at a time when we were struggling for management know-how. We were therefore attracted to Honda.

Rover lacked the financial resources and the time to produce market-acceptable new models after the lack-lustre performance of the Maestro and the Montego. It also lacked a self-confident company culture after years of loss making, union restrictive practices disputes, and poor press. It knew that it was regarded as one of the major 'lame ducks' of British industry.

Rover had access to an acceptable UK and European network of component suppliers and subcontractors. It had ample spare capacity in its factories, and could manufacture as many cars for Honda as the Japanese company could manage to sell. Rover also had an understanding of European tastes, and it could contribute to the development costs of new models to make this necessary factor come within the financial reach of both companies.

Rover was a little concerned at the outset that Honda would absorb its know-how and then walk away. As Bertodo noted:

> We took steps to limit transparency and minimise informal transfer of knowledge by circumscribing a partner's opportunity to learn in an uncontrolled manner ... The challenge is sharing sufficient skill to create a competitive advantage for both partners while avoiding wholesale transfer of core ability.

The risk from Rover's viewpoint was at shopfloor level, where close discipline in relation to information transfer was unlikely to prevail. Honda faced little risk in this area since, as John Bacchus, Rover's director of collaborative strategy, commented, the Japanese are traditionally secretive and do not seem to feel the need to demonstrate their knowledge to show their abilities.

Rover was the driving force in bringing about the alliance, and was subsequently the active partner in proposing new avenues for collaboration.

Honda responded positively to Rover's initiative, and the first deal was signed in December 1979, which was a limited licensing arrangement for BLMC to manufacture the Triumph Acclaim from Honda 'knocked-down' kits at the BLMC factory in Longbridge in Birmingham. The Triumph Acclaim was based on the Honda Accord and filled the vacant position in Rover's product range. There were 130,000 Acclaims manufactured at Longbridge, and the brand achieved a regular position in the top ten UK sellers list, although it was in reality no more than a rebadged Honda.

The next phase of the partnership was the Rover 200 launched in 1984, of which 175,000 were built. This was the 'sister' model to the Honda Ballade. The 200 was a Japanese-designed car, but with Rover wheels, bumpers and interiors. Both the 200 and the Ballade were produced at Longbridge and equipped with different badges. The agreement was more than a simple licence this time. Rover had the right to change the basic design if it wished to do so for its version of the car, and there was also a manufacturing agreement to make cars for Honda. For the Ballade, Rover provided the missing European values in terms of styling that Honda needed.

In 1985, however, Honda announced its intention to build a factory in Swindon. This concerned the British press; *The Times* warned of a possible Rover takeover by stealth, and questions were asked in the House of Commons on the issue of whether this move heralded the decline of the alliance with Rover. This proved not to be the case. Honda proposed only to make engines in Swindon at first, and subsequently to make both Rovers and Hondas there. On the question of whether Honda might be in the market to buy Rover, Honda's president Mr Tadashi Kume claimed it lacked the resources. *The Times* concluded also that this was not generally how Japanese companies behaved. Organic development was much more the rule than acquisition. By 1985 Honda was still a very small player on the British market. It sold 19,000 cars in the UK that year for 1 per cent market share.

In 1986 the partnership evolved further with the launch of the Rover 800 and the Honda Legend. This was the first car that was the product of a joint development effort. The experience of working closely together on design made the relationship between the two companies much closer, and led to a substantial improvement in Rover's understanding of quality standards. At this time Rover and Honda signed a statement of understanding to extend the partnership, which dealt with the principles of the relationship. However, it was felt that the mutual trust that had developed

Exhibit 1 **Progressive shortening of Rover product life cycle**

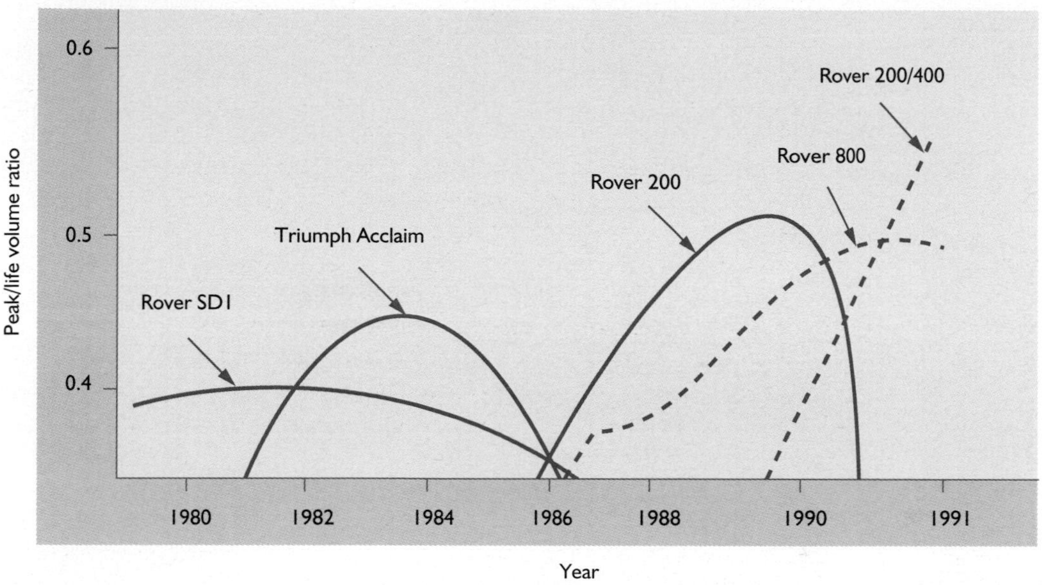

during the work on Project XX, as the 800 was called, was much more important than any legal document.

By this time Rover's product life cycle for new models had become considerably shorter than it had traditionally been. Exhibit 1 illustrates this reduction from about seven years to nearer five. Rover's productivity was also on a steeply improving curve (see Exhibit 2), with average costs moving rapidly towards Japanese levels. These improvements followed from absorbing the Honda philosophy that it was not in the business of making excellent cars. Its aim was to make *perfect* cars!

A further maturing of the relationship occurred in 1988. Rover and Honda agreed to stop making the Rover 800 and the Honda Legend for each other at their respective factories. It was claimed by both companies that this was because both parties wanted to make refinements that could not be easily carried out at each other's factories. However, Honda had built only 1,600 Rover 800s at its Suyama works in Japan, and Rover only 3,500 Legends in Cowley, and these low volumes were probably a major factor behind the move. The decision did not appear to damage the relationship in any way.

The year 1989 saw the next project, the Rover 200/400 with its twin the Honda Concerto. This heralded a further development, in that it was the product of joint development and co-production plus the cross-sourcing of components. In 1990 Rover built more than 40,000 Concertos for Honda for sale in the UK and EC to a quality standard acceptable to the Japanese.

Exhibit 2 Comparative productivity experience

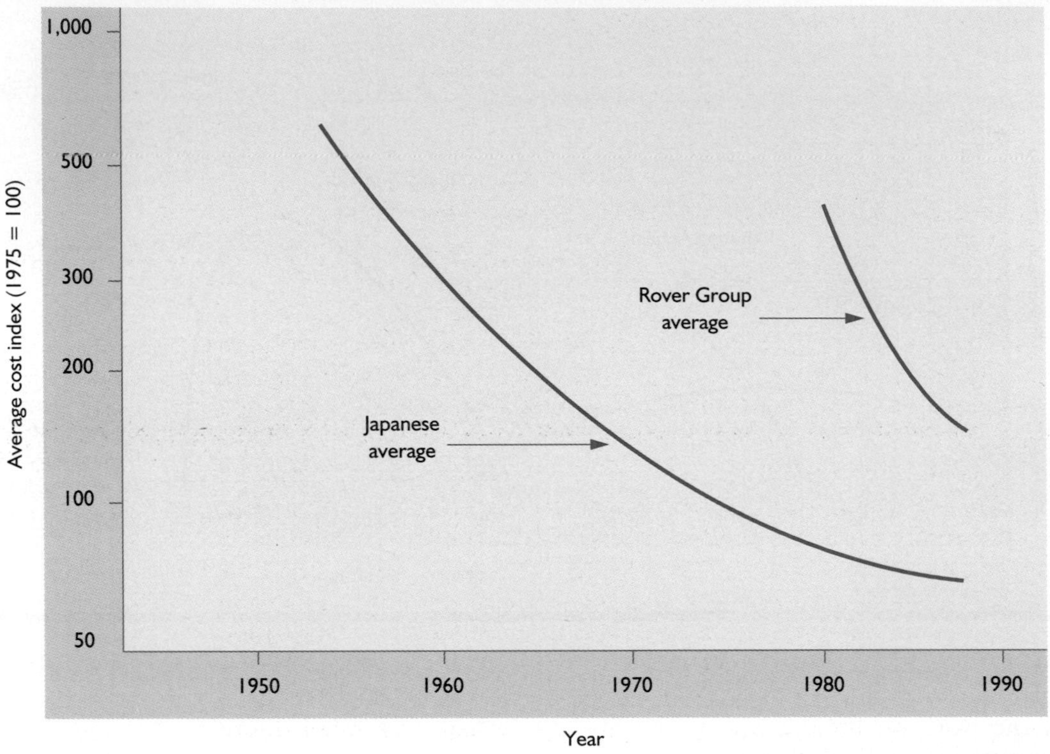

By 1990 Rover and Honda were engaged on a further collaborative venture involving integrated development and production, and demonstrated their further confidence in the future potential longevity of the alliance by concluding a 20 per cent share exchange between Rover and Honda Manufacturing (UK) Limited.

Thus from an arm's length licensing agreement in 1979 the alliance had progressed a long way in terms of mutual development and production, and had even reached the point of minority share exchange. However, there was no attempt to collaborate in merging marketing identity, or in management off the shop floor.

Honda was still clearly a Japanese company with its own aims and ambitions. Its objectives were wider than Rover's. It sought to provide a range of cars to meet all quality segments save the top and bottom, and to become a true global player. It had a distinct strategy and Rover featured in this only as a European partner. At the time the alliance was concluded, Honda was strong in the USA and a medium-sized player in Japan. Its European presence was negligible.

Rover was fairly strong in the UK, had 2.9 per cent share of the European market and had little presence anywhere else. In fact 95 per cent of its production in 1980 was for Europe, including the UK. Similarly, Rover had its distinct identity and showed no sign of losing it.

THE COMPANIES BY 1990

Despite trebling its size in turnover terms during the 1980s, Honda was still not among the giants of the motor world by 1990. In Europe its sales accounted for only 1.2 per cent of the European market, and Rover's accounted for 3.1 per cent against Volkswagen's 15 per cent and Ford of Europe's 14 per cent. However, much progress had been made in performance terms for both companies since 1979. Rover was back in profit and with a coherent strategy, and Honda had an established foothold in Europe.

Honda grew from a medium-sized player in 1978 with a turnover of around £4 billion to one with a worldwide sales level of more than £12 billion, of which 66 per cent was earned outside Japan, and a net profit after tax of more than £500 million in 1990. Honda was already large in the USA at the time of the alliance formation, and motor cycles, power products and parts accounted for a quarter of total revenue, as was still the case in 1990 (see Exhibit 3). However, in Europe, Honda's sales of cars increased from a negligible amount in 1978 to £700 million of 191,00 units in 1990 (see Exhibit 4). Not only had Honda raised its European direct sales, but it also benefited from part of Rover's sales of approximately 450,000 units.

Honda had the characteristic Japanese total quality control attitude to manufacturing, which by lengthy tuition had been able to elevate Rover into a quality performer. It had a pragmatic attitude to design that facilitated the creation of reliable marketable cars. It had the robotics-dominated methods of manufacture that could gain the necessary cost economies in unit terms. Also it had sufficient finance to collaborate with Rover in the production of new models and this was an important attraction.

Rover aimed to become an upmarket quality executive marque with a high reputation for style, quality and reliability; and priced at a level to make the senior management fleet buyer its natural customer. It now became unashamedly a niche marketeer under its chairman Sir Graham Day, and was no longer the largest UK car producer, coming third behind Ford and Vauxhall.

However, from its position as a regular loss-maker, Rover moved steadily into profit from 1986 onwards, and in 1990, as a subsidiary of British Aerospace plc, it contributed an annual profit in excess of £50 million to its parent. But that was not the whole of the picture. Rover's overall financial performance through most of the 1980s was pretty dismal. It only became profitable with financial restructuring after its acquisition by British Aerospace (Exhibit 5).

Exhibit 3 Percentage of total Honda sales by volume (1990)

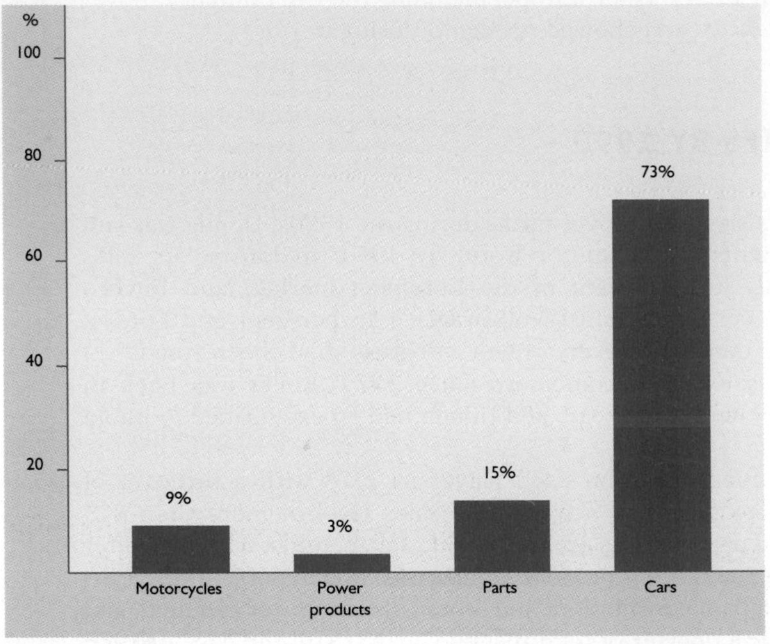

Exhibit 4 Honda car sales by geographical area

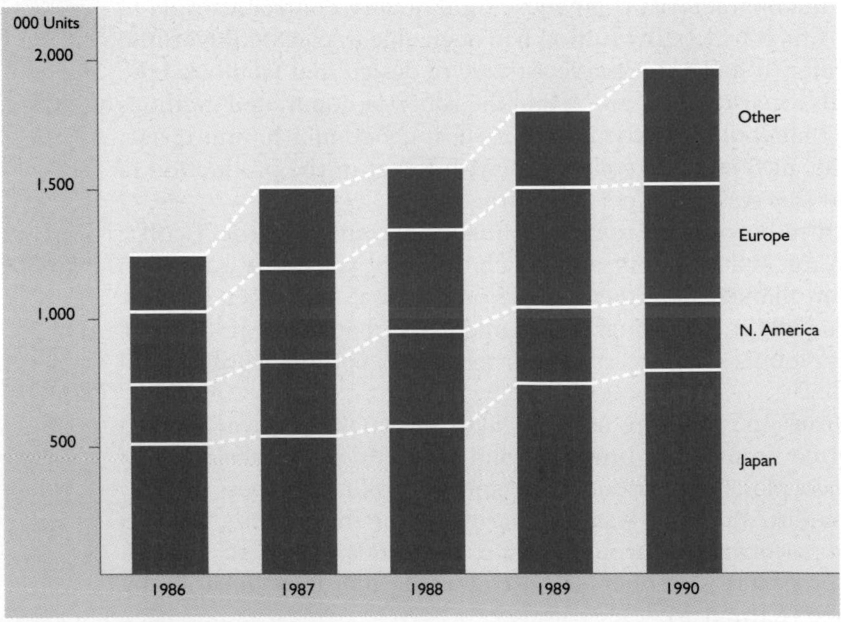

Exhibit 5 Summary of Rover Group results, 1983–7

	1983	1984	1985	1986	1987
Turnover (m)					
UK	1,935	1,987	2,353	2,228	1,827
Overseas	1,486	1,415	1,062	1,184	1,269
Total	3,421	3,402	3,415	3,412	3,096
Exports from UK (including above)	917	827	764	768	1,042
Profits and losses **(£m)**					
Operating profit (loss)	4.1	(11.7)	(34.6)	(246.4)	16.8
Exceptional losses	—	—	(15.0)	(109.2)	
Share of profits of associated companies, formerly subsidiaries	—	—	—	—	11.1
Profit (loss) before interest and taxation	4.1	(11.7)	(49.6)	(355.6)	27.9
Interest	(71.2)	(61.6)	(75.7)	(100.0)	(49.5)
Loss on ordinary activities before taxation	(67.1)	(73.3)	(125.3)	(455.6)	(21.6)
Taxation on ordinary activities	(7.2)	(7.7)	(4.1)	(6.5)	(5.2)
Loss on ordinary activities after taxation	(74.3)	(81.0)	(129.4)	(462.1)	(26.8)
Minority share of profits of subsidiaries	(3.8)	(1.8)	(1.4)	—	—
Loss before extraordinary items	(78.1)	(82.8)	(130.8)	(462.1)	(26.8)
Extraordinary profits (losses)	(64.8)	163.4	(7.2)	(430.0)	—
Profit (loss) after extraordinary items	(142.9)	80.8	(138.0)	(892.1)	(26.8)
Loss on translation and other movements	(8.6)	(6.7)	(25.8)	(6.9)	(0.1)
Transfer to (from) reserves	(151.5)	73.9	(163.8)	(899.0)	(26.9)
Balance sheets					
Fixed assets	1,014.6	908.5	939.2	772.8	703.7
Other net assets	500.2	434.7	447.1	26.3	190.2
Total	1,514.8	1,343.2	1,386.3	799.1	893.9
Net borrowings	(796.5)	(571.9)	(790.5)	(1,108.7)	(560.2)
	718.3	771.3	585.8	(309.6)	333.7
Called-up share capital	2,139.5	2,139.5	2,139.5	2,139.5	2,762.2
Reserves	(1,463.2)	(1,389.3)	(1,553.1)	(2,452.1)	(2,428.5)
	676.3	750.2	588.4	(312.6)	333.7
Minority interests in subsidiaries	42.0	21.1	9.4	3.0	—
	718.3	771.3	595.8	(309.6)	333.7
Net asset value per share (pence)	15.8	17.5	13.7	—	6.0
Capital expenditure including tooling (£m)	247.7	234.2	231.5	172.8	119.8
Depreciation and amortisation (£m)	177.9	147.2	154.5	160.3	135.7
Vehicle unit sales (000s)	564	511	542	494	513
Weekly average number of employees (000s)	103	96	78	73	49
Ordinary shareholders (year-end) (000s)	67	65	63	62	60

Note These Exhibits include all divested businesses up to their effective date of leaving the group, including Jaguar to July 1984, and Unipart, Leyland Vehicles and Freight Rover to December 1986.

Source Rover Group.

Sales turnover remained on a plateau at £3–4 billion and not growing, and in terms of assets Rover contracted dramatically from its bloated 1970s size. Rover's export sales were pretty stable in the late 1980s, and its UK sales showed little growth either (Exhibits 6 and 7).

But if quality and a regenerated reputation were prime objectives, these seemed to be established. The 800, the 200 and the 400 series were all generally acknowledged to be first-class cars from a quality viewpoint, and Rover's reputation was reflected in its profit figures. It was estimated also that the business between the two companies at that time was currently worth in the region of £500,000 annually. However, the Honda-related models accounted for only about a quarter of total Rover production (see Exhibit 8). The much maligned Metro, Maestro and Montego were still responsible for a substantial tranche of Rover's sales.

The 20 per cent share exchange between the companies was intended as a positive demonstration of commitment. On the issue Hayashi commented that the share exchange was most important for the manufacturing and development staff, since it engendered trust, in that it showed that the partnership was for the long term. Of course, the trust had not been naive. Rover only released information on a 'need to know' basis; the Japanese likewise, and the two teams did not fraternise greatly at a social or shopfloor level. However, trust did develop as the two sides grew used to working together. Matters moved on successfully and as Hayashi said:

> The Legend, the joint Honda–Rover product, cleared the way for Honda to enter into the executive car sector of the market. Rover's interior design and European taste contributed to the success of the Legend ... Now Rover is a truly integral part of Honda's strategy in Europe.

Thus the alliance with Honda had had a dramatic effect on Rover's quality performance, and as John Bacchus said, it no longer saw itself as a 'loser'.

THE ALLIANCE IN 1990

It was one thing to form an alliance; quite another to make it work. Two separate studies, one by McKinsey, and one by Coopers and Lybrand, showed that more than 50 per cent of alliances foundered within five years. Rover also had some experience of disappointing alliances. As Bertodo recounted, they had been in fifteen previous alliances since 1921 with, among others, Isuzu, BMW, Ferguson, Hindustani, AMC, Perkins and, at the time of the Honda negotiations, Nissan. Only seven could be judged successful, he commented, and only four outstandingly so.

In Bacchus's view if Honda were to exit the alliance, Rover would be unlikely to maintain the quality standards it had learned to achieve under Honda's discipline. Furthermore, Rover was still small in global terms, and

Exhibit 6 Total Austin Rover retail export sales, 1982–9 (units)

	1982	1983	1984	1985	1986	1987	1988	1989*
Passenger cars	110,328	100,165	89,709	101,821	117,963	139,289	132,720	130,500
Car derived vans	1,582	856	412	566	388	388	1,312	1,500
Total	111,910	101,021	90,121	102,387	118,351	139,677	134,032	132,000

* EIU estimates.

Source Rover Group.

Exhibit 7 Development of the Rover Group's car sales in the UK, 1980–9

		Change on previous year		Market share (%)	Change on previous year (%)
	Units	Units	%		
1980	275,798	−61,186	−18.2	18.2	−1.4
1981	285,071	9,273	3.4	19.2	1.0
1982	277,260	−7,811	−2.7	17.8	−1.4
1983	332,725	55,465	20.0	18.6	0.8
1984	312,054*	−20,671	−6.2	17.8	−0.8
1985	327,955	15,901	5.1	17.9	0.1
1986	297,466	−30,489	−9.3	15.8	−2.1
1987	301,811	4,345	1.5	15.0	−9.8
1988	332,607	30,796	10.2	15.0	—
1989	312,306	−20,301	−6.1	13.6	−1.4

* Excludes Jaguar.

Source SMMT.

its only hope would be to find another partner or establish a defendable niche. Also, some major issues appeared in 1990: Rover was losing market share in Europe and even in the UK, and the technological and financial power of Honda threatened to turn the alliance into one dominated by the Japanese company.

Hayashi saw it differently: 'If we broke apart, we would be in competition with the same technology, the same components, the same suppliers, and the same products: a duplicate of ourselves.' But an EIU article in *European Motor Business* in 1990 suggested that:

> Model development in the car programme has been shifted over largely to Honda, with Rover manipulating the available hardware to encompass its

Exhibit 8 Production of the Rover Group by model, 1985–9 (units)

	1985	1986	1987	1988	Jan.–Nov. 1989
Mini	34,974	33,720	37,210	34,574	37,193
Metro	174,466	158,546	161,285	144,701	128,930
Rover 200/Honda Ballade	65,844	63,167	80,263	95,859	84,355
New Rover 200 series	—	—	—	—	8,105
Maestro	88,848	63,722	58,280	67,406	56,032
Montego	95,874	70,623	73,447	79,316	71,221
Rover SDI	15,916	2,870	—	—	—
Rover 800 Series/Honda Legend	—	16,029	57,111	49,894	36,787
Land Rover	23,772	19,195	20,475	22,229	17,160
Range Rover	13,314	14,494	20,815	24,021	25,962
Discovery	—	—	—	—	2,632
Total	513,008	442,366	508,886	520,000	468,377

Source Rover Group.

upmarket and niche model ambitions. This compromise will permit a more rapid updating of the model range than Rover could otherwise contemplate, but this attachment to Honda has also given rise to uninspired styling and uncompetitively bland designs.

If there were any validity to this criticism, the joint enterprise would need some rejuvenation to succeed in the next round of competition. Hayashi was confident, however:

> We have strong commitment to the alliance. Even when we start production in Swindon we will still benefit from the joint supply network, and Rover is still in need of Honda's capability in product development, and quality standards. In that sense both companies have a management policy of strong commitment, because competition in Europe is very keen, and since we are already established in the UK with suppliers and co-operation with Rover this confirms our commitment.

The inevitable early problems with contrasting cultures seemed to have been largely successfully handled, as Hayashi commented:

> Much endeavour and patience were needed to overcome many barriers ... in language, culture, ways of thinking and sense of value to name just a few. By overcoming these barriers, the people of Honda and Rover were able to generate mutual understanding and trust, which eventually led to close friendship.

Bertodo confirmed his belief in the future of the alliance similarly: 'Honda have compressed our learning curve and given us better value for money by sharing resources on R and D.'

There were joint design teams working on new models. Both companies' factories produced for the other partner. There was joint sourcing of components, and many compromises were made to accommodate the respective manufacturing needs of the two partners. However, from the outset the marketing arms of the two companies remained separate. Entry into Europe by Honda did not mean the use of Rover's sales network.

Bertodo saw the alliance as requiring constant refreshing, by both sides being ready with something extra to trade at each crucial point in what he called the 'collaboration vortex' to prevent the alliance flying off centrifugally into independence, or centripetally into one-sided dependency. He saw a key part of his job as preventing Rover, in particular, from doing the latter.

Some key issues remained, however: How would the parties to the alliance deal with the increasingly likely prospect of Rover being sold by its parent company? In the existing world automobile industry, was a strategic alliance a secure way to achieve competitive advantage that could be sustained in the face of keen competition by integrated corporations? And finally, do the undoubted costs involved in co-ordinating alliances lead to a competitive cost advantage in relation to the major world players in the global market place? Only the future would answer these questions.

THE BMW ACQUISITION OF THE ROVER GROUP

Nick S. Potter

The case covers the BMW acquisition of Rover Group and includes the rationale and events leading to the purchase. It shows the position and options for BMW in 1993 and the position of both Rover and Honda before and after the takeover. It can be used to consider the way in which the merged company could and should develop and the issues facing BMW after acquiring Rover Group.

• • •

BACKGROUND

The strategic alliance between Rover and Honda had developed into a wide-ranging relationship by the early 1990s. British Aerospace (BAe) had acquired the Rover Group from the British government in 1988 and, under the terms of sale, Honda had the right to be informed of any intent to sell and offered first refusal over the balance of equity. BAe further undertook not to sell Rover until August 1993 at the earliest.

The recession in many parts of the world continued to be the dominant industry factor affecting both Rover and Honda during 1992 and 1993. Rover announced losses of £83 million in February 1992, including a £45 million write-off as a result of withdrawing from the US market. Honda's profits during 1992 fell by 32 per cent.

George Simpson, managing director of Rover, knew that although the company had gained immeasurably from its collaboration with Honda, there were still many problems to overcome if he was to create a business with sustainable profits. Although break-even was down from 530,000 to 450,000

This case was prepared by Nick Potter of Birmingham Business School and is intended as a basis for classroom discussion rather than to illustrate correct or incorrect handling of an administrative situation.

units per year, sales were still running at fewer than 420,000. Simpson knew that international sales had to play an even greater role in the future.

A major restructuring of the business occurred early in 1992, and as a consequence the internal objectives regarding overseas sales were raised from 45 to 60 per cent of total turnover. Rover also signed Japanese-style agreements with its workforce which included a radical 'Jobs for life' guarantee. The restructuring split the company into three new trading divisions:

- Rover Europe – managing director, Graham Morris.
- Rover International – managing director, Chris Woodwark.
- Rover Marketing – managing director, Kevin Morley.

During this period, Rover continued to learn an enormous amount about quality and manufacturing techniques through the Honda alliance, and was even training BAe staff in lean manufacturing techniques. Other Japanese car manufacturers were, however, setting up operations in the UK, and Simpson felt that the restructuring and working agreements were necessary to compete with them on level terms.

THE PROCESS BEGINS

The first indication of what lay ahead came in March 1992. Volkswagen shocked the entire car industry by announcing that it would like to buy Rover in order to gain a foothold in certain markets. In reality, the company was impressed with the outcomes of the Rover/Honda agreement and extremely interested in an alliance with Honda. Ford also let it be known that it was interested in the possibility of acquiring Rover. BAe responded to these informal advances by simply restating that, under its agreement with the British government, Rover could not be sold until at least August 1993.

By late 1992, however, speculation about Rover's future was rife. BAe chairman John Cahill still repeated that he had no intention of selling Rover, although earlier in the year he had talked of a long-term strategy based around core businesses in aircraft and defence.

Volkswagen had bought both Seat and Skoda in the meantime and was no longer thought to be in a financial position to bid. Fiat and Peugeot were interested, although Jacques Calvet, chairman of Peugeot, was known to display an almost legendary hostility towards Japanese companies.

Honda had only purchased its 20 per cent stake in Rover as a sign of good faith. As far as it was concerned, the relationship was a complete success and had become the envy of the motor industry. It was based on trust, reciprocal need and mutual benefits. Honda's chief executive officer, Nobuhiko Kawamoto, was convinced that there were important political factors ruling out any increased shareholding, and Honda was, in any case, short of money.

COLLABORATION INTENSIFIES AS COMPETITION INCREASES

George Simpson continued to demonstrate his belief in collaborative deals by increasing Rover's stake in its joint venture with Lombard Finance, and entering into talks with the Bulgarian government about a 49.9 per cent stake in a joint venture to assemble and sell the Maestro range of medium-size 'hatchback' cars when UK production ceased.

Honda was by now building its own manufacturing facility in Swindon, and Rover had opened a new £200 million factory at Cowley. The collaborative agreement with Honda had played a significant part in the planning process for the new facility as the futures of the two companies became steadily more linked and interdependent.

At around the same time, the Economist Intelligence Unit published a report which concluded that Rover was too small to survive as an independent manufacturer and had insufficient volume to service such a wide model range. The report also stated that, by the year 2000, the car industry would be dominated by a group of only five global manufacturers: General Motors, Ford, Toyota, Volkswagen and Nissan.

In late 1993, the Rover 600 was jointly launched with the new Honda Accord. Engines and gearboxes were the same in both ranges and most other components were also shared. George Simpson restated Rover's joint strategy of co-operation with Honda and a continued move upmarket – Roverisation as he called it. He estimated that Rover had saved around 150 million in development costs on the 600 due to the alliance, and that this had further contributed to lower break-even volumes. Significantly, in the light of later developments, Nobuhiko Kawamoto was reported as saying that it would be difficult for Honda to continue the sharing of technology and designs if Rover were sold to another manufacturer.

In June 1993, the two companies reached an agreement to rebadge the Land Rover Discovery as the Honda Crossroad for sale in Japan. Honda was becoming increasingly interested in further alliance possibilities based on Rover's four-wheel-drive expertise, as it lacked the finance to develop the technology alone.

In July 1993, George Simpson explained in an interview why Honda would not increase its stake from the current level of 20 per cent. He repeated that the success of the alliance was based on mutual trust, and the creation and nurturing of relationships which facilitated synergies, and that this would not necessarily be enhanced by a larger shareholding. Simpson knew that Honda already considered Rover part of its 'empire' and did not therefore consider it necessary to use scarce resources to obtain full control. He felt the alliance would continue to expand along the value chain from process technology and product development into areas such as shared distribution.

Exhibit 1 European car sales, 1993

MANUFACTURER	VOLUME (000s)	% CHANGE	MARKET SHARE (%)
Volkwagen	1,886	−20.1	16.4
General Motors	1,489	−11.8	13.0
Peugeot/Citroën	1,405	−14.4	12.3
Japanese manufacturers	1,396	−12.8	12.2
Renault/Volvo	1,373	−16.0	12.0
Ford	1,316	−13.3	11.5
Fiat	1,272	−20.6	11.1
BMW	371	−15.0	3.2
Rover	363	+9.7	3.2
Mercedes	334	−14.0	2.9

Notes Japanese category includes Nissan, Toyota, Mazda, Honda and Mitsubishi. The market for the year was down 15.1 per cent in total.

Source Society of Motor Manufacturers and Traders.

ROVER BY MID-1993

The company had by this time successfully exploited the alliance to create a chic image combining British styling and Japanese reliability. Quality had improved to such an extent that Rover dealers complained they had insufficient work to carry out under warranty.

Rover's performance had even been instrumental in raising the share price of BAe. However, in March 1993, BAe was forced to repay £110 million to the British government after the European Commission ruled that the state aid or 'sweeteners' granted by the British government to BAe at the time of the original purchase was an illegal subsidy under EC law.

Sales performance continued to strengthen, with unit volumes up 20 per cent on the previous year. Sales of Rover cars in Japan were up 40 per cent for the same period, due to the penetration of middle and upper segments of the market, and the break-even point was falling to around 400,000 units per year as cost savings continued to accrue from the alliance. Sales of the Land Rover four-wheel-drive range were also running ahead of production capacity. Rover's gains compared favourably with the reductions in volume being experienced by the other car manufacturers (see Exhibit 1).

Around this time, there was talk of a management buy-out (MBO), but with BAe maintaining an equity stake prior to eventual flotation. However, the dynamics of the car industry had moved on – Volkswagen was now thought to be in financial trouble and Ford was trying to digest its acquisition of Jaguar. The biggest question centred around whether BAe should sell Rover at all, particularly in the short term. Rover was poised to widen its joint venture policy even further by entering a development project with Kia of Korea to produce a new V6 engine for top-of-the-range models (this would also have the effect of slightly reducing Rover's dependency on Honda's engines).

BMW – THE NEED FOR STRATEGIC CHANGE

BMW was less troubled by the recession of the early 1990s than most European car companies. It had not only avoided short-time working, but remained in profit throughout the period. The company had monitored Rover's progress for a period of years, as the two companies were of similar size in terms of unit volume and increasingly competed in certain market segments.

On 13 May 1993, Bernd Pischetsrieder succeeded Dr Eberhard Kuenheim as chairman of BMW, and his first task was to carry out a strategic audit of the whole business. The conclusion he reached was inescapable. Like Rover, BMW was too small to survive on its own as a manufacturer into the twenty-first century. The company needed to extend its range and achieve economies of scale in sourcing, production, distribution and R&D. By a process of eliminating alternatives, it appeared that Rover was of potential interest in this regard. On direct instructions from Pischetsrieder, BMW's R&D director visited all of Rover's facilities during September 1993 and drove every model in its entire range. Senior management of BMW then spent the period until Christmas digesting every piece of financial, marketing and strategic information available on Rover.

Rover had already been in discussions with BMW for some time about the possibility of using a BMW diesel engine in the new Range Rover, as Honda lacked diesel engine expertise. As this relationship and the investigations developed, Pischetsrieder began to realise that with Rover they could 'offer a comprehensive range of cars in virtually every category'.

In fact, as BMW's senior management studied future market trends and the joint capabilities, they realised that the two companies were a perfect fit. The Rover brands, in particular Land Rover, had considerable value. Having observed the efforts of Mercedes to develop four-wheel-drive during the 1980s, Pischetsrieder could see the synergies emanating from selling a range of off-road vehicles through BMW showrooms, with the added benefit of applying Land Rover's four-wheel-drive expertise across the BMW car range. The development and brand promotional costs involved in achieving these objectives organically would almost certainly be more than Rover's market value.

BMW made an informal approach to BAe in October 1993 about the possibility of acquiring Rover Group. It also contacted Honda in order to gauge reaction – but received no response at all. Honda was concerned at the prospect of a third party having open access to joint secrets, and was anxious not to lose its grip on Rover. However, under the cross-shareholding agreement, Honda had to be formally told that Rover was potentially for sale and was given first option to buy the remaining equity. Nobuhiko Kawamoto felt this afforded Honda a high degree of protection. Privately, he was prepared to raise the stake to 40 per cent, but could see little benefit in going further. He had his own problems, as Honda was stuck halfway between mass market volumes and being a niche manufacturer. Moreover, pressure caused by the strong yen had seen Honda's profits fall by 32 per cent, and financially Honda was in no real position to bid for the whole of Rover.

On 6 November 1993, the first press speculation appeared linking BMW with Rover. Comment centred around similarities in size and the complementarity of product range, as well as the difficulties both would face in trying to stand alone. BAe responded by saying that Rover was now part of its core business and this, together with the announcement of George Simpson's departure to head Lucas Industries, seemed to indicate that no sale or flotation of Rover was imminent.

On 19 January 1994, however, at the first extraordinary meeting of the supervisory board in the history of the company, BMW made the decision to bid for Rover. The formal offer was made on Wednesday 26 January and, on the following day, after a meeting lasting five hours, the BAe board decided to accept the offer in principle. BMW would pay 800 million and take on around £900 million in net debt and off-balance-sheet finance.

Honda had raised its previous offer to £165 million for a further 27.5 per cent of Rover. George Simpson was told by BAe management, however, to take the next flight to Tokyo and to inform Honda that this latest offer had been refused. He was to offer Honda the opportunity to increase its shareholding to 51 per cent. BAe would continue to hold 49 per cent as long as agreement was reached on a market flotation within five years. But Honda refused to increase its offer and the meeting between Simpson and Kawamoto was described as 'extremely tense'.

THE ALLIANCE – IMPLICATIONS OF THE ACQUISITION

John Towers, managing director of Rover Cars, did not find out about the bid until the day after the BAe board meeting. He was immediately concerned about the reaction of his Japanese partners and the possible implications for the company. On Saturday, however, in a meeting with Tim Sainsbury MP, a minister at the Department of Trade and Industry, BMW reassured the British government that its fears over job security and the impact on Anglo-Japanese relations were unfounded.

Following this meeting, and approval from the British government, the deal was concluded ten days after the formal offer. Honda was said to be 'surprised and humiliated', and threatened to sever all links with Rover, privately saying that it would never do business with BMW, its fiercest rival in the USA. Honda immediately set up a taskforce to assess the benefits of continuing the alliance, which, it was realised, would also allow a 'cooling off' period. John Towers attempted to explain to Honda that in the end it was BAe's problems that had set the agenda, regardless of the relationship built up during the alliance.

Neither BAe nor Honda had wanted ownership of Rover, and so BMW had won. By this move, it was to become the largest 'specialist maker' of cars in the world, with a range of potential synergies with its new subsidiary, including range extension, economies of scale across the board, access to front-wheel and four-wheel-drive technology, one of the best small car engines in Europe, and a selection of valuable and, in some cases, underdeveloped brands.

Although shaken by the acquisition, the reaction of Honda's senior management underlined the cultural differences involved in the original alliance. BAe had clearly been discharging its obligations to its shareholders. Even so, the behaviour shown in breaking trust was absolutely inexplicable to the management team within Honda.

On 17 February, a delegation from BMW and Rover, including both MDs, flew into Tokyo for talks with Honda. BMW wanted Honda to swallow its pride and to work along with both companies. The only response was a statement from Nobuhiko Kawamoto: 'We will accelerate our policy of establishing independent and self-reliant operations in Europe.' On existing relations with Rover, he went on to say:

> We will continue those that are beneficial from a business standpoint such as mutual sourcing of parts and components – although our relationship with Rover Group will continue, the acquisition by BMW has caused a fundamental review of our European strategy.

On 17 February, the cross-shareholding was formally dissolved with a net payment from BMW to Honda of £116 million. Toshio Ishino, head of Honda UK, said that the company would continue to honour its agreement to supply components to Rover, but hinted that there would be no further major collaborative projects. This conflicted with claims by John Towers that the alliance would continue beyond 2006.

Bernd Pischetsrieder made clear his intention to transform Rover into an exclusive upmarket producer, involving development of new models. The implication is that this leaves little scope for future collaboration with Honda. His plan was to turn Rover into a brand as strong and exclusive as BMW, and at the same time to double or even treble world sales. As part of this strategy, Pischetsrieder realised that BMW's logistics technology had to be transferred to Rover in order to build cars to individual customer specifications, as opposed to the Honda system of batch production of 30 identical cars.

BMW AND ROVER – FACING THE TWENTY-FIRST CENTURY

Bernd Pischetsrieder always viewed the transformation of Rover as a long haul. By 1996, BMW was committed to an investment programme of £500 million per year in the UK until the year 2000, in order to counteract the effects of decades of low investment, and Rover was not expected to make a net contribution to the group until early in the next century. BMW had a target margin of 6–7 per cent pre-tax, and this was regarded as the minimum necessary to fund long-term growth in the industry.

BMW was positioned to appeal to successful, affluent buyers. However, companies such as Toyota and even Honda continued to attack this exclusive segment with some success. Questions inevitably arose regarding BMW's ability to withstand this sustained competition, while simultaneously funding Rover's future development.

In May 1996, the structure of Rover was totally reorganised. Emphasis was placed on design, by separating the engineering and manufacturing functions. Much of Rover's future design work would emanate from Munich, and sales and marketing were directly controlled by Tom Purves, head of BMW in the UK.

BMW attempted to reduce costs further by the standardisation of non-visible components where possible between both the Rover and BMW model ranges. Marketing objectives concentrated on the globalisation and focusing of the Rover brands.

Pischetsrieder argued that the core of BMW's thinking was not about brand names, but about brand identity. He went on to add: 'The first task is to build a Rover brand identity and a solid presence in the market. You cannot do this in a hurry, you must be properly prepared, because in this industry you only get one shot.' He also stated: 'Either you become a global player or you will be out of business in twenty years' time.'

BMW made a series of changes to Rover, the first of which was the redeployment of senior BMW staff to top Rover positions. This was shortly followed by the appointment of BMW's Walter Hasselkus as Rover's Chief Executive.

By 1998, BMW was, however, still facing difficulties in getting Rover on course. The financial press argued that BMW's decision to build an engine plant in Britain rather than Austria, was strongly influenced by the Government's promise of regional assistance, rather than Rover's competitiveness: its cars were 30 per cent more expensive than comparable non-UK based competitors. In July 1998 Bernd Pischetrieder announced that Rover remained unprofitable; shortly afterwards Rover introduced a 4 day week at the Birmingham and Oxford plants, and began to use overseas suppliers to reduce costs. A week later BMW cut 1,500 jobs from Rover's UK workforce.

In September 1998, the press reported BMW's relationship with Rover, hinting that Rover could be the downfall of BMW. There was speculation that because Rover continued to have major problems, BMW might be forced to freeze its £600m investment programme, and close another Rover plant.

BARCLAYCARD

Kevan Scholes

The case study is concerned with how a long-standing market leader maintains leadership and develops its business in a fast-moving industry undergoing significant change. There are many different strategic options open to Barclaycard, but which will be most suitable? Will all the options be acceptable not only in terms of the likely risk and returns but also to the major stakeholders? Will the options be feasible? The case invites readers to evaluate and compare a range of strategic options and to choose the best way forward for Barclaycard.

• • •

Barclays Bank decided on Christmas Eve 1965 to go ahead and launch the UK's first credit card. The decision followed an evaluation of how the scheme had operated in the USA. A team of only seven Barclays Bank staff were given just six months to prepare for the launch of what was still, in 1998, the UK's most used credit card. One of their first acts was to set up camp in a disused shoe factory in Northampton.

Before the official launch 30,000 retailers had been signed up to take the card, and by the end of the year there were 1 million cardholders. Early promises to retailers to publish the name and address of every shop accepting Barclaycard led to what is still believed to be one of the largest ever press advertisements. It appeared in the *Daily Mail* on 29 June 1966 and extended over eight pages and carried 30,000 names and addresses. By 1998 Barclaycard had over 9 million cards issued and employed over 5,000 people at three locations around the country and its Northampton headquarters. Barclaycard was accepted at over 400,000 places in the UK and more than 12 million worldwide.

This case study was prepared by Professor Kevan Scholes, Sheffield Business School from published sources and the work of the following Cranfield MBA students: Mark O'Brian, Steve Randall, Beat Meyer, Jason Gong, Ann Jones and Hamish Williams. It is intended as a basis for class discussion and not as an illustration of either good or bad management practice.

THE PLASTIC CARD MARKET

By 1998 Barclaycard was operating in a sophisticated and highly competitive industry – the question was whether and how it could stay ahead. Barclaycard Services provided the plastic card infrastructure for Barclays Bank and was responsible for producing, issuing and replacing all Barclay's plastic cards. It also managed directly all customer relationships for Barclay's plastic card services (the full range of services is described below).

By the late 1990s the UK market for plastic card services was large and growing. There were almost 60 million credit or debit cards in circulation, supporting nearly £85 billion of consumer purchases. At any one time, more than £12 billion in credit was extended to cardholders. Appendix 1 describes the different kinds of plastic payment card and Appendix 2 summarises the market shares held by the major credit card issuing companies. With more than 9 million cards issued and capturing some 27 per cent of the total value of bank issued credit card transactions, Barclaycard was the dominant card issuer.

Credit cards were one part of a wider consumer payment system shown in Appendix 3 – and one of three main types of plastic card. Collectively, card payments continued to grow in popularity at the expense of cash or paper transactions (e.g. cheques) – which together accounted for some 43 per cent of retail sales by value (cash still accounted for some two-thirds of the number of payment transactions). Within the card sector, credit cards accounted for about 50 per cent of the value of consumer transactions.

Appendix 4 describes the five main players in the credit card industry. Individual *cardholders* use their cards for purchases in *retail outlets*. These outlets are reimbursed by an intermediary called a *merchant acquirer* who, in turn, is reimbursed by the *card issuer* (e.g. Barclaycard). The loop is closed when the individual cardholders receive their monthly statement from the card issuer. *Payment associations* (e.g. Visa and MasterCard for credit cards, Switch and Delta for debit cards) provided card issuers and merchant acquirers with an acceptable 'marque', technical specifications, standards and IT services. Brand shares in combined UK credit and debit cards issued (1995) were: Visa (29 per cent), MasterCard (21 per cent), Switch (27 per cent), Delta (23 per cent).

COVERAGE AND DISTRIBUTION

Plastic cards were an essential shopping 'tool' for some 54 per cent of UK adults. There were significant differences between retail sectors in the usage of credit and debit cards – largely resulting from the choices made by retailers (see Appendix 5). The most strikingly different sector was food and drink purchases where supermarkets had traditionally avoided credit card transactions – leading consumers to use debit cards as a substitute for cash or cheques.

Another important usage of credit cards was to obtain cash from automatic teller machines (ATMs). The use of plastic cards in ATMs was growing in importance as the banking industry went through a period of major change resulting in the closure of many branches and a move to ATMs and telephone banking. It was essential that plastic card users had ready access to ATMs and the major financial service organisations had formed alliances to allow 'cross-usage' of ATMs.

THE INTERNATIONAL PICTURE

With more than 1 billion cards issued worldwide, credit cards were becoming an increasingly important form of payment in many countries. The usage of debit cards was also growing. Appendix 6 shows the difference in credit cards issued between North America and Europe. It also shows differences within Europe. The USA accounted for about 40 per cent (400 million) of the cards issued and a massive £340bn credit card spending in 1995. This compared with the UK's £44bn and Italy's £6bn. In some countries, such as France, debit cards and charge cards were dominant and the credit card market was underdeveloped.

BARCLAYCARD PRODUCTS AND SERVICES

By 1998 Barclaycard had a wide portfolio of services covering many of the types of card in Appendix 1 – as well as additional (non-card) services:

- **Credit cards**

  Standard credit cards: Visa and MasterCard

  Special privilege cards: Barclaycard Gold, Barclaycard Premier

  Company Barclaycard

  Barclaycard Sense: For consumers new to credit cards
- **Free user benefits**

  Barclaycard purchase cover: 100 days of free insurance

  Barclaycard holiday club: Discounts for over 80 tour operators; free travel accident insurance

  Barclaycard Profiles: 'Reward points' to be collected for gifts or cash
- **Advice**

  International rescue: Cash advances, advice or local doctors, etc.

  Barclaycard assist: advice on legal, home or roadside assistance

- **On-line services**
  Barclaycard Call Service: Direct debiting for phone calls worldwide
  Barclaycard Netlink: On-line banking services (internet)

BARCLAYCARD'S STRATEGY

Barclaycard's strategy was to develop and maintain market leadership by differentiating its product using the comprehensive benefits package described above. As it operated semi-autonomously from Barclays Bank it could also market its products as a unique service. This differentiated Barclaycard from other high street bank credit cards that were sold as another feature of the bank's service.

Barclaycard did not compete on price – its interest charges (APR) were not the lowest on offer. It had invested heavily in an energetic and sustained promotion/advertising campaign. Barclaycard's investment in advertising exceeded that of all other companies in the industry. For example, in 1995/6 it spent over £12m compared with NatWest's £1.5m and American Express's £3m. Few in the UK will not be conversant with the long-running television advertisement series featuring Rowan Atkinson. The message in the advertising encapsulated the essence of Barclaycard's strategy and how it planned to differentiate itself from competitors. The advertisements emphasised peace of mind – in case of an emergency such as losing your card or passport; medical problems on holiday or losing goods purchased with Barclaycard. It underlined the benefits package of support provided by Barclaycard.

It also capitalised on its strong customer base by relationship marketing alliances with leading organisations in other service industries such as BT and Cellnet (telecommunications) and Marks and Spencer and J. Sainsbury (retailing).

In 1998 Barclaycard was the subject of an MBA student project at Cranfield School of Management in the UK. The student groups produced detailed analyses of Barclaycard's strategic position, summarised as a SWOT analysis. The results are described below.

The *strengths* of Barclaycard were:

- Market leadership with a market share of 34 per cent in terms of credit cards issued, and 27 per cent in terms of transaction value (see Appendix 2 for further details). This provided the company with a strong financial base.
- Low-cost production, resulting from accumulated experience as the first credit card issuer in the UK and economies of scale derived from its high market share. However, this was being rapidly eroded and in September 1998 the company announced its intention to shed 1100 jobs (about 25% of its workforce).

- Brand status, the Barclaycard name was almost a generic term for a credit card and was widely recognised by consumers.
- A well established distribution network, through Barclays Bank, other financial institutions and large retail organisations which made its product available to a wide range of potential customers.
- Information technology capability, which allowed Barclaycard to develop improved products through alliances with companies such as British Telecom and Cellnet.

However, Barclaycard had two *weaknesses*:

- The annual transaction value per card of £1,719 was low in comparison to NatWest's figure of £2,121.
- Barclaycard as a credit card issuer was not international, it was limited to the UK market.

In the late 1990s there appeared to be a number of possible *opportunities* for Barclaycard:

- Spending on credit and debit cards amounted to 43 per cent of total retail sales, leaving scope for further development.
- Only 54 per cent of UK adults owned credit cards, leaving room for increased market penetration.
- Technological developments and new products would improve security and flexibility of payment by plastic systems.
- Company branded cards and store cards provided access to a base of new users and the opportunity to develop loyalty based ties. This could enable further marketing of discounts, bonuses, new products, etc. Company cards also provided an opportunity to expand into the charge card market for business customers.
- The short-term macroeconomic situation in the UK was encouraging, with real income increasing, low inflation and strong economic growth. The expansion in the credit card industry was expected to continue in the foreseeable future.

However there appeared to be a number of *threats*:

- New entrants such as building societies offering similar products.
- Low APR cards were being offered by some new entrants. This included some American banks that were used to operating in a home market where APR had been driven down by 'no frills' operators who had continued to gain market share. In 1996, MBNA International Bank (which claimed to be the world's second largest bank credit card lender with 16 million cardholders) launched a new Advantage card with an APR of 16.9 per cent, no annual fee and credit limits up to £25,000. Barclaycard's APR was about 22 per cent at the time.

- The cannibalisation of the credit card market by debit cards and electronic purse (smart) cards.
- Increased availability of other forms of credit, e.g. point-of-sale interest-free credit schemes.
- Increased opportunities for potential card fraud.
- Reliance on electronic communications – the effect of a major breakdown in national communications (e.g. a strike at British Telecom) could be catastrophic.

STRATEGIC OPTIONS

In such a fast-moving and competitive industry there were many opportunities for all competitors to develop. It was important that Barclaycard was clear which of the various options it should itself pursue.

Sources ***The 1997 Guide to Barclays Merchant Services; Credit and Other Finance Cards*****, Key Note Ltd, September 1996; Credit Card Research Group; Cranfield MBA student projects 1997/8.**

APPENDIX 1 TYPES OF CARD AVAILABLE

Bank-issued credit cards (e.g. Barclaycard)	Holders are set a credit limit – depending on financial status. Statements are issued monthly.
Charge cards (e.g. American Express)	Initially called travel and entertainment cards, these were the first credit cards (Diners Club – 1951). Cardholders are given up to 45 days to settle their account.
Special privilege cards (e.g. Gold Card)	For those with above-average incomes – they allow more cash to be withdrawn from dispensing machines and guarantee a higher value when used as a cheque guarantee card. Higher credit limits also are available.
Company branded cards (e.g. General Motors card)	Allow special credits against particular items of merchandise (e.g. motor vehicle products).
Retailers' store cards	These operate with a credit limit or a set monthly payment for purchases in a particular store. Many are run by banks on behalf of the store.
Debit cards (e.g. Switch, Delta)	Were rapidly replacing cheques – and were the fastest growing method of payment. Payments are charged to the consumer's bank account within about 24 hours.
Electronic purse (e.g. Mondex, Visacash, Proton)	These were expensive to produce and contained smartcard technology – a computer chip. Cards are preloaded with credit and used to make payments in retail outlets and then reloaded with credit. Initially they were used for special applications but by 1998 they were being trialled for general shopping use. Their major potential attraction was the curbing of fraud[1] – particularly the growing incidence of counterfeit cards. It was claimed that smartcards were virtually impossible to counterfeit. Also they allowed for the use of PIN numbers for purchases in shops – protecting against improper use of stolen cards.
Other cards (e.g. Oxfam, AA)	*Affinity cards* can be used to make contributions to charities with each transaction. *Facility cards* are issued exclusively to members of a particular organisation (which receives income from user transactions).

[1] Fraud losses on plastic cards in the UK were about £83m in 1995 (this was about half that in 1991). Lost or stolen cards accounted for 72 per cent with counterfeiting at about 10 per cent but growing. APACS reported a 27 per cent increase in fraud in 1997.

APPENDIX 2 MARKET SHARES OF BANK-ISSUED CREDIT CARDS*, 1995

ISSUER	CARDS ISSUED (%)	TURNOVER (%)
Barclaycard	34	27
Lloyds/TSB	19	9
NatWest	16	13
Midland	12	8
Bank of Scotland	5	4
Others	14	39

Source Based on figures produced by the British Bankers Association.

*This table relates to bank-issued credit cards only.

APPENDIX 3 POSITIONING OF CREDIT CARDS WITHIN CONSUMER PAYMENT SYSTEMS

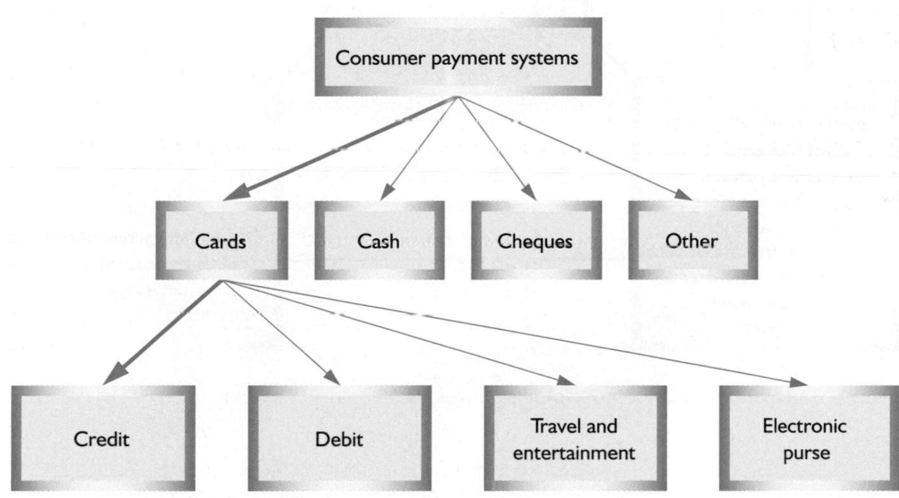

The market shares of the different types of cards were, in 1996:

	% OF CARDS ISSUED	% OF TRANSACTION VALUE
Credit cards	37	51
Debit cards	38	33
Charge cards and store cards	25	16
Electronic purse	small	small

Source Based on figures produced by the British Bankers Association.

APPENDIX 4 THE FIVE PLAYERS IN THE PLASTIC CARD GAME

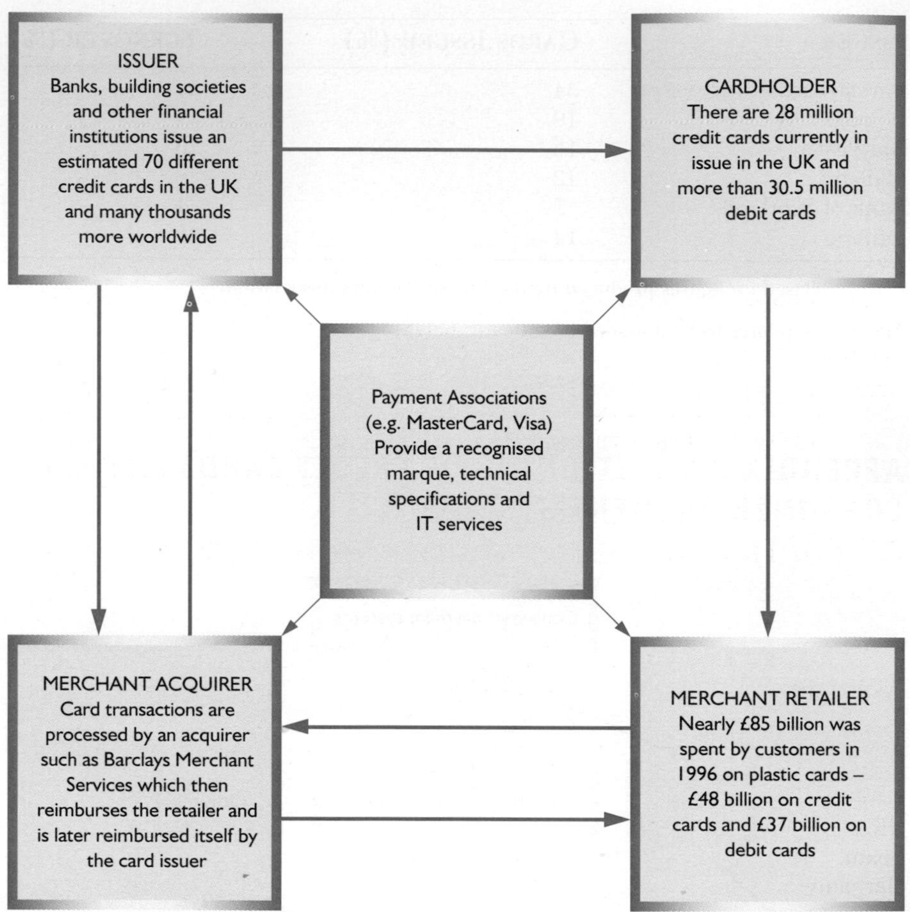

Source Adapted from *The 1997 Guide to Barclays Merchant Services*.

APPENDIX 5 PERCENTAGE OF CARD SPENDING BY RETAIL SECTOR (BY VALUE), 1995

Retail Sector	Credit Cards (%)	Debit Cards (%)
Travel	14	5
Food/drink	13	43
Motoring	13	12
Services	10	4
Household	10	6
Entertainment	7	3
Mixed business	7	10
Hotels	6	1
Clothing	6	9
Other	14	9

Source Credit Card Research Group.

APPENDIX 6 INTERNATIONAL COMPARISONS – CREDIT CARDS, 1995

Country	No. of Cards Per Capita of Adults	Turnover Per Card (£p.a.)
USA	1.4	950
Canada	1.0	1,100
UK	0.5	1,500
Spain	0.23	1,200
Germany	0.11	1,700
Italy	0.09	1,100
France	0.075	3,900

Sources Visa; Europay.

COOPERS CREEK AND THE NEW ZEALAND WINE INDUSTRY

Heather Wilson and Maureen Benson-Rea

The case study examines the international growth of a new, small, New Zealand winery – Coopers Creek. The case highlights the international strategies employed by Coopers Creek and the future aspirations of Andrew Hendry, its managing director. This is set against the background of a small, rapidly internationalising economy within a global market environment and the effect upon the New Zealand wine industry. It is against this scenario that Andrew Hendry needs to consider the future strategic options for the company. A crucial issue is how a small company in a small economy can compete globally. A key ingredient of success is the capability to gain leverage through the management of linkages and networks both inside New Zealand and internationally.

• • •

Coopers Creek, established in 1982, was one of New Zealand's more successful medium-sized wineries by 1996 in terms of sales of quality, award-winning wines. Andrew Hendry, the managing director, consciously managed the growth of the company in order to attempt to retain the benefits of small size. He did this by leveraging resources and managing networks of co-operative relationships with other New Zealand wine-makers better to serve both local and export markets. As a result of this greater experience and success in domestic and international operations, Hendry was faced with questions of whether to pursue growth and, if so, how, given his lifestyle aspirations; and whether to maintain his commitment to network-based strategies and, if so, how to maintain and develop them.

This case study was prepared by Heather Wilson and Maureen Benson-Rea of the University of Auckland Business School, and is intended as a basis for class discussion and not as an illustration of either good or bad management practice.

BACKGROUND

Andrew Hendry, an accountant by training, considered himself a good salesperson. Indeed, he had always been a bit of a trader, having dealt in jewellery and gold from the Middle East before setting up a small business producing home-made pâtés with his wife, Cyndy. Andrew maintained that his overall approach to business was seeing a good deal, while balancing this with the cautious, measured approach of an accountant. His aim has been to take advantage of opportunities without overextending himself or his financial situation. Andrew's first encounter with the wine industry was when he worked on behalf of a syndicate as a buyer at the auction houses of Sotheby and Christie in London. When he returned to New Zealand, he took a position with a finance company until he was headhunted to join the Penfolds Wine Group, which became part of Montana Wines, as financial director/general manager.

According to Andrew Hendry, he was essentially a sole trader and he operated best by himself. Hence the desire to run his own company. When he first established the company, he was determined to keep it small and not to get to the stage where his time was occupied by management tasks. He wanted the operation of the company to be a pleasurable experience which did not involve sitting behind a desk most of the time. By 1996, Andrew found that the company was a lot bigger than he ever thought it would be. From the production of 2,500 cases of wine in 1982, the company produced 57,500 cases in 1995. When Andrew first set up the business, he envisaged producing 30,000 cases, with 90 per cent of that comprising domestic sales by year 10.

The land for the Coopers Creek vineyard west of Auckland was purchased by the Hendrys in 1980 with seed capital from the home-made pâté business. Coopers Creek winery was established with 40 per cent loan capital from a local bank and 60 per cent equity capital (20 per cent from Andrew Hendry and 40 per cent from other shareholders). Andrew Hendry fostered relationships with grape growers to encourage them to invest as shareholders in the business. In addition, he fostered contacts with colleagues of his former life, partners in Coopers and Lybrand, and involved them in the partnership.

Finally, the most important relationship at start-up was with the winemaker, and Andrew arranged the ownership structure so that the winemaker owned one-third, he owned one-third and the other shareholders owned the final third of the company. A partnership was formed which enabled the company to enjoy tax write-offs, and the participants essentially earned a tax holiday until the company returned a profit.

Like most small businesses, Coopers Creek relied heavily on borrowed capital during the early years. This also coincided with rising interest rates from 1985 onwards, resulting in the interest bill being the second major disbursement after the grape bill. Later on, as profits were generated, Andrew Hendry bought out the partnership, and by 1996 he owned just under 75 per cent of the shares of the business, and the ratio of debt to equity was 1 : 3.3. The original winemaker partner left the business, sold his shareholding to Andrew and returned to the USA. He has since been replaced by a New Zealander. Andrew maintained that the winemaker was key to the success of the various wines' labels. He recognised this contribution by paying one of the highest salaries for a winemaker in the New Zealand industry. The new winemaker, Kim Crawford, was offered shares in the company, but chose to operate on a contract basis rather than defer current earnings until some future dividend date. Only one grower has retained a shareholding in the Coopers Creek business, although all of the shareholder growers experienced capital gain. Essentially, the growers decided they could no longer operate on both sides of the fence: as growers they wanted to negotiate the highest price, but as shareholders they wanted to bargain for the lowest price.

When Hendry set up the winery in the early 1980s, the New Zealand environment was highly regulated. For example, the early development of Coopers Creek was severely limited by the local council's refusal to permit the new winery to press grapes from outside the region. However, this restriction did not apply to older wineries in the area. By 1984, the New Zealand government had initiated a programme of deregulation, which included devaluation of the New Zealand currency, exchange rate flotation and general anti-inflationary initiatives, with the aim of maximising sustainable medium-term growth within a framework of price stability. As a result, the small, protected and debt-burdened New Zealand economy was transformed into one of the most competitive in the OECD, ranking seventh in 1995.

The opening up of New Zealand's domestic market meant that businesses had to improve their efficiency substantially over a short period. Both industry and agriculture sought out new products and markets to replace the loss of their traditional dependence on the European market. While this dependence has declined, from 65 per cent of all New Zealand exports in 1965 to 15 per cent in 1994, exports to Australia, Japan and the rest of Asia increased over the same period. The make-up of these exports also changed considerably, from predominantly sheepmeat and dairy products to more fresh fruit, venison and wine. A further response to fiercer competition at home and in overseas markets was the increasingly strong focus on quality – of the product itself and of service responsiveness in support of the product. This had been the main thrust of strategies in the New Zealand wine industry since the beginning of its phenomenal growth in the 1980s and 1990s.

THE NEW ZEALAND WINE INDUSTRY

The New Zealand wine industry accepted the consequences of the liberalisation of the domestic economy and, faced with the strength of the

New Zealand dollar against sterling (an appreciation of 35 per cent during the two years to 1994), also recognised the need to understand how on-going changes in the international economic environment affected its prosperity and how to plan accordingly. Building from a low international base in the 1980s ($4.5 million in exports in 1987), New Zealand wine exports achieved phenomenal growth and accounted for $41 million in 1995. This was down slightly from $48 million in 1992/3 due to poor grape harvests. The industry has a target of $100 million in export earnings by the year 2000.

In 1995, the UK market was the most important export market for the industry, accounting for 64 per cent of New Zealand wine exports by value and 70 per cent by volume. This amounted to some $27 million in 1995 (see Exhibit 1). Since 1985, exports to the UK increased by almost 700 per cent, although since 1993, export dollar values had been disadvantaged by the appreciation of the New Zealand dollar.

The wine industry in 1996 was dominated by four large firms: namely, Corbans, Montana, Villa Maria and Nobilo. Between them, these four firms accounted for around 65 per cent of all exports, with another twelve medium-sized companies handling 25 per cent in combination. For the most part, industry participants exported between 10 and 25 per cent of their production, but a few producers had a much higher export intensity.

In 1996, the New Zealand wine industry was still considered to be young, and this was the key characteristic of its products and strategies. The main features of the industry were its small scale, its distinctive 'clean and green' growing conditions, high-cost structures and a focus on premium wines. This last point was in keeping with the trend for New Zealand producers to move away from the commodity mentality to more value-added, quality products. New Zealand's range of international-quality products included New Zealand Sauvignon Blanc, Chardonnay and Riesling, red wines based on Cabernet Sauvignon, Merlot and Pinot Noir, and sparkling wines. Quality was maintained by high competitive standards domestically, protection of prime viticultural land, the fostering of close relationships between wineries and quality grape growers, improvement in winemaking standards, and certification of export wine quality. New Zealand wines competed with other 'new world' wines from Australia, California, Chile and South America primarily in advanced economies.

Investment in plantings had been important for the industry as a whole – rising grape prices followed poor yields in the 1992 and 1993 seasons. Some wine producers diversified away from high-priced contract grapes and invested extensively in their own vineyard plantings. After two relatively small harvests, the 1995 vintage produced a bountiful crop, the second largest ever for the New Zealand wine industry. However, the New Zealand wine industry was expecting to face an oversupply situation in 1996, given the stock of grapes in the ground and the winemakers' predictions. There was a concern among existing wine companies that the growers would form a co-operative to utilise the excess grapes and produce their own wine. This could be bought as supermarket own-label wine, and/or could be introduced into

Exhibit 1 **New Zealand wine exports, 1995**

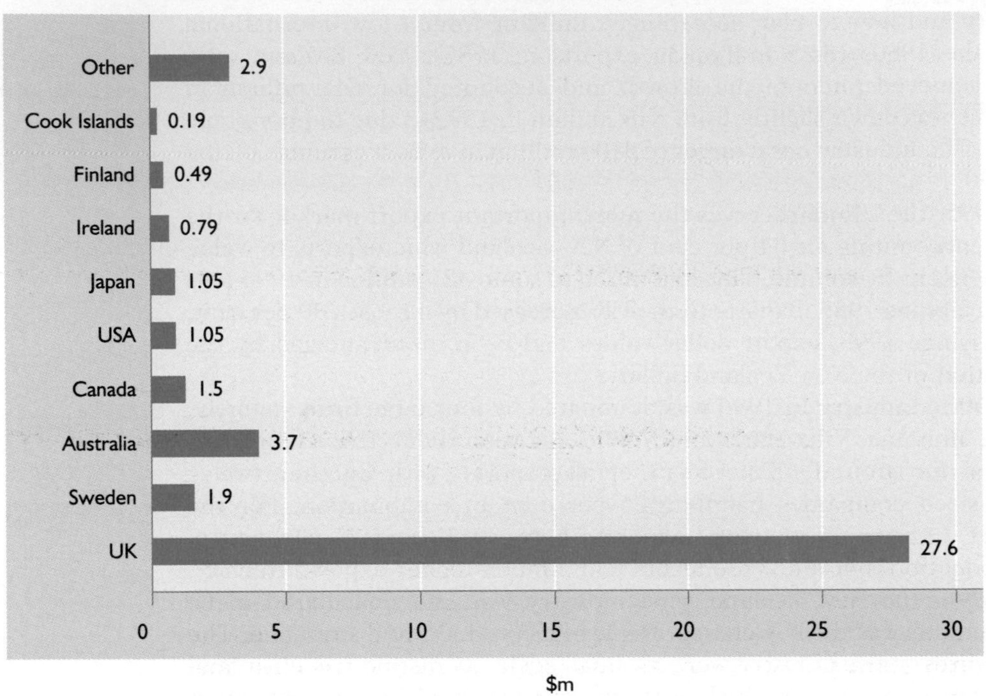

Source Statistics New Zealand (1995).

the New Zealand market place as a low-cost competitor. The introduction of a low-cost competitor would affect the export market more than the domestic market, because domestic customers value particular vineyard labels in the local market, while export customers were considered to be more price sensitive because they lacked this local knowledge. However, it should be borne in mind that, in the past, the liabilities of a small economic base and the vagaries of the New Zealand climate had left the industry without sufficient product to tackle the task of export market diversification, and an oversupply situation could be a temporary phenomenon.

THE NEW ZEALAND WINE INSTITUTE, THE WINE GUILD AND COUNTRY ACTION GROUPS

All New Zealand winemakers had to belong to the New Zealand Wine Institute. In order to sell wine, companies were legally obliged to acquire a licence and take out membership of the Institute. The Institute acted as a self-regulatory body for the wine industry. Among its regulatory activities, the Institute administered the Ministry of Health's export certification procedures, which involved chemical testing and blind tastings. Andrew Hendry was elected to the board in 1986 as a representative of small producers (the wineries were categorised according to size by annual litre sales). By 1993, however, Coopers Creek was categorised as a medium-sized company. In 1995, there were 204 members of the Wine Institute comprising 4 large producers, 12 medium-sized companies and 188 small, 'boutique' wineries.

Some Institute members with export interests in specific markets had established special interest groups: the Wine Guild was formed by those wineries either already established in the UK export market or interested in entering this market; and another four groups, termed Country Action Groups, were established to share information, experiences and promotional activities relating to Germany, the USA, Canada and Australia.

By 1996, the Wine Guild involved around 53 full members and about 25 associate members. Generally, the associate members were very small producers not currently exporting, but intending to at some stage. It is important to note that, of all the potential members of the Wine Guild, around 15 could be termed active participants of the network targeting the UK. The Guild, originally organised on an informal basis, was expected to become more formalised in future as government funding ran out. Tradenz (the New Zealand government body concerned with promoting overseas trade) provided a third of the Wine Guild's funds in order to facilitate New Zealand wine exports. This government funding would be available until 1997. After that, the Guild was expected to continue with Wine Guild membership funding only. Meanwhile, members of the Wine Guild provided the additional two-thirds funding, which was calculated as a percentage levy on sales (a 1 per cent levy on free-on-board sales). Thus, members felt that they paid in proportion to the individual company benefits. However, some increases in sales were not always a direct result of the Guild's initiatives; rather, they were due to single company marketing efforts. Individual firms paid for any additional exporting costs and extra promotion they wished to undertake beyond that provided by the Guild.

The overall Wine Guild administration, based in the offices of the Wine Institute in Auckland, was controlled by a board of directors, of which Andrew Hendry was deputy chairperson in 1996. At that time there were also two Tradenz representatives (one based in Auckland, the other in Wellington), as well as a rotating chairperson. Another director on the board of the Guild was the executive officer of the Wine Institute. In addition, the Wine Institute had seconded a part-time employee to work on behalf of the Wine Guild. These links with the Wine Institute facilitated information sharing, although the Institute had no voting rights in how the Wine Guild operated. Essentially, the board provided financial and marketing expertise for the successful operation of the Guild, as well as ideas for future developments. Although a voting system was in place, decisions were usually made by consensus.

The four Country Action Groups developed marketing plans to explore and, ultimately, exploit export opportunities within the chosen markets. The marketing plan was implemented through a semi-formal funding arrangement whereby individual companies contributed to costs on a project-by-project basis. For example, only those companies which were interested in a particular promotion contributed to the costs of mounting it. Coopers Creek was actively involved in the Canadian and US Country Action Groups in terms of joint promotional efforts.

COOPERS CREEK – EXPORT MARKETS

In 1987, less than 1 per cent of Coopers Creek produce was exported (mainly to Australia). Indeed, Andrew Hendry's approach to exports was to delay efforts until the company had secured enough long-term commitments from suppliers of the grape and had established a firm foothold in the New Zealand market. Also, the aim was to consolidate, build the value of the label and establish wine styles before export commitments were made.

The first export market was Australia, which, according to Hendry, was a hard market in which to sell. This opportunity arrived almost by chance, or certainly ahead of Hendry's original export schedule. Entry to the market place was facilitated by the company's relationship with the Wine Institute of New Zealand, which co-ordinated a Wine Expo in Sydney in 1984. At the time, the opportunity to venture into this market proved irresistible because it coincided with the devaluation of the New Zealand currency and the resulting value for money prices in the Australian market place. Despite some initial difficulties associated with new market entry, this exporting experience proved to be invaluable in overcoming problems associated with selling New Zealand wines abroad.

Coopers Creek initiated a serious export strategy in 1989, having delayed for one year because 1988 was a bad season for the production of grapes. The UK was the next market targeted by the company, again in partnership with the Wine Institute (from which the UK Wine Guild evolved). This was followed two years later by excursions into other European countries (Holland, Belgium and Switzerland) and North America, principally because Andrew Hendry did not want to become too reliant on the UK market. In terms of volume in 1995, 65 per cent of exports were sold in the UK market, with around 5 per cent each for Australia, Canada, Holland and the USA (east coast states). Smaller markets where, according to Hendry, decent quantities of Coopers Creek wine were sold comprised Fiji, Belgium, Switzerland, Ireland, Hong Kong and Singapore. For the future, Coopers Creek was looking to expand in Hong Kong, Switzerland and the USA, and develop new export markets in Denmark, France, Germany, Norway and Sweden.

Coopers Creek's focused export strategy involved considerable collaborative and individual efforts. Collaboratively, Coopers Creek entered the

Australian, UK, US and Canadian markets, although considerable individual effort was also expended in the process. For example, it took Andrew Hendry six months of negotiations with the Ontario Liquor Control Board to gain their agreement to distribute his wines to all of the Board's 630 stores throughout Ontario. Special labels and cartons had to be developed to meet local requirements; and, because the wine could be shipped in the depths of the Canadian winter, when temperatures can be as low as minus 20°C, the wine was transported in heated containers. This effort was recognised by the award of a Tradenz Export Commendation on the recommendation of the New Zealand Trade Commissioner in Canada. Markets which Coopers Creek has essentially developed on its own include Holland, Belgium, Ireland, Hong Kong, Singapore and Switzerland.

In those markets where collaborative efforts had been employed, the principal aim had been jointly and effectively to sell the New Zealand label ahead of individual wine company labels. Promoting the generic New Zealand brand in this way was seen as a way of benefiting all New Zealand exporters. For example, the network of wineries involved in the UK Wine Guild comprised 15 active participants in 1996. This Wine Guild, set up on the initiative of the Wine Institute in 1992, established an office in London with two full-time employees to promote and support sales of New Zealand wines. Basically, the agents of this Guild provided organised tastings of New Zealand wines, an information bureau, placement of advertisements, and travel arrangements for local wine writers and trade buyers to visit New Zealand.

In the UK market, sales and distribution remained the responsibility of the exporting firms and, typically, they used exclusive agreements with established agents and distribution networks. However, these relationships evolved from more co-operative structures. For example, in the UK, one firm was agent for several New Zealand wine companies initially until the volume of business became too large for the agent to handle. Subsequently, the wineries had to find agents able to handle increasing volumes, and the agency/distributor relationships began to fragment. In the German and US markets, where growth was at an early stage, the New Zealand companies tended to share the same agents. The Wine Institute and the Guild played a role in facilitating distribution processes by hosting visits by groups of agents.

Despite the fragmented distribution structure in the UK, Andrew Hendry was still able to develop a collaborative relationship with one major UK customer, the supermarket chain Tesco's. Both Andrew Hendry and Kim Crawford visited Tesco's, Coopers Creek was actively involved in the promotion of new vintage releases through the chain, and agents of the supermarket were invited to visit New Zealand and provide input into the development of wine styles. This relationship resulted from Hendry's basic inclination to conduct some personal selling in export markets in addition to his appointed agents. This approach also provided an opportunity to ensure that export customers were very clear about the amount of product they could expect from Coopers Creek in the coming years.

A new development for the company targeted the US market place. Coopers Creek and eight other members of the Wine Institute (not through the US Country Action Group) planned to take a joint New Zealand stand at the Boston Wine and Food Show in 1996. Wine would be promoted alongside seafood, venison and other produce. Hendry was actively seeking New Zealand government funding to support this initiative.

Andrew Hendry maintained that it was the export market which provided the major impetus to the growth experienced by his company and the wine industry in general. Coopers Creek had been experiencing around 25 per cent growth per year, compared with an industry average of 5–10 per cent growth. In 1995, exports comprised around 40 per cent of Coopers Creek's production level. So, instead of the company operating in the small New Zealand market as first envisaged, the developed economies of the world were presenting new and exciting opportunities. Nevertheless, the domestic market place was still important to the company. Indeed, the domestic market place alone was in 1995 accounting for more business than Hendry ever envisaged for the company (35,000 cases sold recently in the domestic market).

Domestically, Coopers Creek had established collaborative relationships with a group of local competitors in the West Auckland area. These competitors comprised Selaks, Kumeu River, Matua Valley and Nobilo. The relationships were established on the initiative of Andrew Hendry, who, on a visit to Australia, observed some local Australian winemakers collaborating locally. The group initially came together for joint advertising and promotions. For example, over Easter weekends, three of the companies arranged tours, special wines, meals and music, with the aim that visitors should sample a different food course at each vineyard. This initiative promoted custom, getting a larger proportion of people to visit the wineries than on normal weekends. This event had been operating since 1990. The grouping had also collaborated on trade tastings in Wellington, when they emphasised current releases and invited retailers, restaurant owners and wine vendors to sample the wine.

These companies regularly gathered as a group in an informal committee to decide on their next collaborative efforts. The situation had arisen where only two or three companies in the group had gone ahead with a particular promotion. Other times, all five companies had been involved. Beyond this committee, there had been co-operation on the production side of the companies' operations. For example, at key times, equipment had been shared and some key processes, like grape crushing during peak periods, had been performed on the competitors' sites. On the level of key inputs, the grouping had recently considered collaborating to negotiate discounts on purchases from bottle producers.

A feature of all the networks in which Coopers Creek was involved was horizontal or competitor-based co-operation. Competition in the domestic market place was considered to be intense. However, this did not impede collaborative efforts where these were deemed more efficient or beneficial (while paying heed to the need to avoid anti-competitive behaviour). In the international market place, once the customer had decided to purchase New Zealand wine, Coopers Creek considered itself to be in competition with all New Zealand wineries present, whether large or medium sized. The exception was the Canadian market place, where, because the company had been particularly successful, competition was centred around only the larger New Zealand wineries. Regardless of size, according to Andrew Hendry, the overseas perception of New Zealand wine was based on the development of personal relationships, and the quality and price of the wine.

In international markets, before the decision to purchase the New Zealand brand, the competition for sales and market share was seen by New Zealand wine companies to be from other countries rather than from individual firms. The newer producing countries, such as Chile, were perceived to be the bigger threat due to rapid advancements in production quality. However, even within the international market place there was co-operation, with industries across countries sharing information and learning about new techniques and processes. This international learning was achieved through informal means, such as exchange visits by producers and by New Zealand-based winemakers spending the off-season in northern hemisphere wineries to build connections and to benefit from low-level technology exchange.

In order to keep up with the growth, principally driven by exports, Coopers Creek had to increase its supply of grapes from the original 4 hectares west of Auckland. This was achieved by acquiring additional land for its own plantings in Hawkes Bay and West Auckland, as well as buying grapes from independent growers in Marlborough and Gisborne. This strategy enabled the company to spread the risk of adverse weather conditions in any of the four growing regions. By 1996 Coopers Creek sourced 90 per cent of its grape supplies from eighteen independent growers, basing the purchase decision entirely on the quality of the harvest. The company would have liked to have grown more of its own supplies, but decided to wait until prices stabilised before purchasing more land.

In addition, the company invested in plant to the extent that, by 1996, it was in a position to double production without further investment. This development meant that Coopers Creek was able to do all of its own crushing, processing, bottling and packaging. The company still intended to use local trucking companies as well as sourcing grapes, bottles, labels and corks from independent suppliers.

Andrew Hendry also recruited a marketing director in 1996 to free himself for some of the more pleasurable tasks he first envisaged when establishing the company, such as building direct relationships with top-class restaurants. The new marketing director was responsible for promotions, liaison with customers and agents, co-ordination of label design and point-of-sale material, and direct marketing. To a certain extent, Hendry felt that this step went against the grain of maintaining a controlled, rather than monolithic, lifestyle operation. However, his company at the time was operating with generally fewer staff than some winemaking companies of equivalent size. Filling this position enabled Andrew to pursue and cultivate relationships by doing more personal selling, spending one day a week on this task. For example, Andrew found that a particularly effective personal selling strategy was to visit restaurants in the domestic market place in order to encourage them to include the Coopers Creek label on their wine list. However, he avoided going down the route of supplying the wine directly to these customers and continued to utilise distributors.

Andrew Hendry's future strategy for the company was not to grow, but to become more effective. He wanted to protect the $3\frac{1}{2}$ million dollar turnover achieved in 1995, considering this to be sufficient for his purposes. However, Andrew recognised that, given the previous momentum, the company was likely to continue to grow by about 5 per cent each year, and that in ten years' time the company could be three and a half times the size he first imagined. This would pose some dilemmas for him personally. Although Andrew and Cyndy had four daughters, none of them had shown an interest in taking over the business in the future.

In terms of the further pursuit of network-based strategies, Andrew Hendry looked less than favourably on the links with other organisations which Coopers Creek was obliged to maintain, believing that relationships based on compulsion were difficult to assess in terms of outcomes. Even if the relationship with the Wine Institute was not a successful or beneficial one, Coopers Creek could not legally relinquish membership. The general benefits for the involvement of Coopers Creek were considered to be information from technical sub-committees, industry-level participation and lobbying. For example, the Institute has been a supporter of the New Zealand government's membership of the International Wine Office (Office International de la Vigne et du Vin) and the negotiating leverage that can bring in international trade.

The benefits of Coopers Creek's relationship with the UK Wine Guild were easier to gauge. From the time of inception to 1996, New Zealand wine sales to the UK had risen by around 200 per cent. The direct outcome for Coopers Creek was increased profitable sales, as the UK Guild helped to raise the number of case sales while also raising the perception of the quality of New Zealand wines, enabling Coopers Creek to command higher prices. The critical issue for the future was to ensure that the Guild efforts were maintained and, possibly, the momentum raised in terms of both the Guild and the Country Action Groups.

One possible impediment to this future momentum was the need to consider the individual company contributions to Guild operations as a result of a financial shortfall in 1994. A suggestion was on the table in 1996 that there should be a tiered flat fee structure (with larger exporters paying the higher fees). The potential danger was that these larger exporters would take the position that they were essentially supporting competitors' sales, and would refuse to accept the flat fee structure. At a more extreme level, they could even decide to initiate their own marketing efforts, thus endangering the viability of the Guild partnership.

The local network was considered to be 'very neighbourly considering we're all in competition'. Andrew Hendry had been involved in so many local network activities that assessment of mutual benefit for the networked wineries was an important consideration when developing his own company strategy. The overall benefit of the local network was the critical mass that a number of wine companies working together were able to achieve – basically being able to act big while retaining the benefits of small size.

Thus, in 1996, Andrew Hendry was faced with the potential dilemma of enforced growth resulting from continuing participation in networks. His strategic options were broad, but the key issue seemed to be how to balance sustaining and consolidating existing markets with developing new ones. The question was whether both approaches were sustainable and whether he should develop independently or in collaboration with other firms (by establishing either vertical or horizontal linkages). In addition, he had to consider whether he could balance his desire to stay small with the opportunities for growth which seemed to present themselves.

Bibliography

M. Cooper, *The Wines and Vineyards of New Zealand*, Hodder and Stoughton, 1994.

G.T. Crocombe, M.J. Enright and M.E. Porter, *Upgrading New Zealand's Competitive Advantage*, Oxford University Press, 1991.

New Zealand Trade Development Board, *Export News*, 30 January 1992 and 2 May 1994.

Wine Institute of New Zealand, *Annual Report 1995*.

World Economic Forum, *World Competitiveness Report*, 1995.

DUTCH PTT TELECOM

Jan Eppink

The case explores the impact of deregulation in the globalising world of telecommunications. This raises both threats and opportunities for the previously state-owned monopoly companies. Dutch PTT Telecom finds itself moving from being a dominant player in a protected market to a small player in a globalising industry. How should it position itself? How should it develop new strategies – alone or through alliances and/or acquisitions? What are the implications to the way the company is organised and managed? These are some of the challenging questions facing the company in 1998.

• • •

In mid-December 1997 Joop Drechsel had been a director of PTT Telecom, one of the two major divisions (the other being Post) of KPN, for ten months. Before February 1997, he had worked as a regional co-ordinator for Shell, lastly in East Asia. As a director, his main responsibility was to guide the international activities. After a period of getting to know the company and its markets he had set out to further refine the strategy and the organisation of its international activities. These were challenging times. Deregulation of national markets was moving ahead in many parts of the world, threatening the dominant status of telecom companies in their home markets but opening up international opportunities for the ambitious. It was particularly important that telecom operators with relatively small home markets (by international comparisons) were clear about where they might 'fit' in this new world of international telecommunications. So Joop Dreschel's shaping of PTT Telecom's international strategy was of major importance to the company's long-term survival and success.

This case study was prepared by D. Jan Eppink, Professor of Strategy at Vrije University, Amsterdam, and partner, Felix & Co. Strategic Management Consultants, Amsterdam and Budapest. It is intended as a basis for class discussion and not as an illustration of either good or bad management practice.

BACKGROUND

On 1 January 1989, the legal form of the PTT was changed from a department of the Ministry of Transportation and Public Works into a plc – initially wholly government owned. From the early 1980s, various committees had studied the needs for and possibilities of liberalising mail and telecommunications. In the mid-1980s the Steenbergen committee proposed that the date for the privatisation be set at the first day of 1989. The mission of the new company, called KPN (Koninklijke PTT Netherlands), was stated as:

> Royal PTT Netherlands is a company that within and outside of the concession it has been granted will deliver to the business and private market a complete set of high quality products and services, concentrated around the national and international transportation of information, goods, and valuables.

The concession described the products and services that would be the exclusive domain of KPN and the 'terms of trade'. The annual report for 1989 mentioned that the progressive deregulation of markets would erode the concession. For PTT Telecom this would mean, for instance, that it would lose its monopoly on the sales of hardware, ranging from telephones for private homes, costing a few hundred guilders (1 guilder $\simeq$ 30 pence), to telecom infrastructures for big companies, costing several millions. Further in the future, new entrants in the home market would compete for existing business as well as for new growth opportunities. But deregulation would provide new opportunities also.

The change from government department into government-owned company was not just a legal one. Government decided that in view of the liberalisation of the markets and the expected increase in competition, a change of management style was also required. Furthermore, flotation of the stock on the Amsterdam Stock Exchange was anticipated. After a short transition period the whole executive board consisted of newcomers. The new CEO of KPN came from Unilever and another director was lured away from IBM. Also, top managers for the two divisions (Mail and Telecom) were attracted from outside. The new CEO of PTT Telecom, Ben Verwaayen, was recruited from the Dutch subsidiary of Alcatel, a French company supplying to the telecom industry. One of his main challenges was to change the culture from a bureaucratic one into an entrepreneurial one. The annual 1989 report stated:

> External conditions change at high speed. Because of this, our company is continually confronting new challenges.

Rather than seeing these changes as threats, the company applauded them:

> PTT Telecom is in favour of this deregulation, provided it is based on international reciprocity and on equal terms for all suppliers of telecom services.
>
> Annual report 1994

OBJECTIVES AND STRATEGY

The objectives and strategy of the company were stated as follows in the 1993 annual report:

> KPN has the following objectives for the coming years:
>
> - maintain market leadership on the national markets for mail delivery and telecommunications;
> - in the year 2000 be one of the ten largest international providers in the field of mail delivery and telecommunications;
> - increase turnover whilst at the same time achieving a good level of profitability;
> - continuous improvement of price/quality performance.

In order to achieve these objectives the company had formulated the following strategy:

> - introduction of new services and stimulation of the use of existing ones. Customers' choice will be increased;
> - improvement of the quality of service while at the same time controlling costs;
> - from a solid position in the home market to increase internationalisation, often in co-operation with others;
> - attention to the quality of our staff through a tailor-made human resources policy. That does not exclusively mean the recruitment of new talent, but also for the internal and external mobility of our staff.

DEREGULATION

Until the early 1990s, international calls were handled on the basis of bilateral agreements between countries. A call from Holland to Germany would cost a certain amount per minute and the revenue would be split between the German and Dutch operator on an agreed basis. A call from Holland to Italy would involve four national operators. There was a clearing system for making these payments. Deregulation meant that the exclusive rights of the national operators would soon disappear. It was even expected there would be possibilities to start trading in 'traffic minutes' and to route traffic in other ways than through the traditional fixed bilateral arrangements. In this respect it is important to note that the capacity of the telecom infrastructure was determined by the level of demand during business hours, usually not more that eight per day. This meant that telecom lines, for instance between Holland and the USA, are considerably underutilised for large parts of the week. In the historical situation, a telecom company had no other choice than to increase capacity if it wished to grow. In the new, deregulated situation, telecom companies could make use of the unused capacity of other companies, which could considerably lower investments and thus costs per call. In some instances it could be cheaper to route a call from the USA to Canada through a country in western Europe than to route it directly. Dramatic changes in technology made reroutings of this type possible.

So deregulation of national markets meant that competition would no longer be national, but on a European and even worldwide scale. Deregulation would mean new entrants to the home market, but also new opportunities abroad.

CUSTOMERS

Historically, PTT Telecom had two groups of customers: private individuals and small businesses that did not spend large amounts on telecommunications, and big companies whose telecommunication bills would run into millions of guilders. The latter group was especially important for future success for two reasons. First, it was expected that because of the ongoing internationalisation of business, telecommunications needs would increase. Secondly, developments such as just-in-time deliveries, enterprise resource planning systems, the Internet, and increasing size of companies (through mergers and acquisitions) were expected to have an impact on the demand for telecommunication and the competitive situation.

UNISOURCE AND OTHER STRATEGIC ALLIANCES

One of the pillars for internationalisation was the formation of strategic alliances. Initially these were relatively small-scale. In 1991, the alliance with Televerket from Sweden (now Telia) was announced just before the international Telecommunication Exhibition in Geneva. Both companies would eventually join their international activities in a new company called Unisource. Unisource would offer network and advanced fax services for larger international companies worldwide. Depending on the area and the service, Unisource would seek appropriate additional partners. In 1992, Swiss PTT Telecom announced it would join Unisource. In that year, an agreement also was signed between Unisource and Sprint for the distribution of worldwide network services.

The formation of Unisource was calculated to fulfil two aims for the parents. The first was to achieve economies of scale. To give an idea of the relative size of the companies in the international arena: PTT Telecom was the sixth largest company in the field of international telecommunications, but only one-tenth of the size of the fifth largest. The other aim was to make possible one-stop shopping for international businesses.

In 1993 Unisource had the following subsidiaries:

- Unisource Business networks, delivering services in the fields of data communication, company networks and management of telecommunication systems for third parties.

- Unisource Satellite Services.
- Unisource Mobile Services.

Later introductions were:

- Unisource Card Services.
- Unisource Carrier Services, which aimed at developing a pan-European network.

In 1993, Unisource made deals with SITA, the worldwide telecommunications systems of the airlines. An agreement was signed with KDD, a Japanese telecom company for the distribution of services. In 1993, Telefonica, a Spanish operator, signed an agreement for mutual support for international clients. It was agreed that in 1995 Telefonica would become the fourth equal partner in Unisource: this was effected as per 31 May 1996.

In December 1994 the European perspective was enlarged when AT&T and Unisource decided to start a joint venture under the name of Uniworld. The new entity targeted large, internationally operating companies with an integrated package of worldwide data and voice services. The company offered its services via its own offices or through local providers. Uniworld also represented in Europe World Partners (the alliance of Unisource, AT&T, KDD from Japan and Singapore Telecom). In 1996 the name Uniworld was changed into AT&T–Unisource Communication Services, in which Unisource had a 60 per cent share and AT&T 40 per cent. This company was one of the market activities of Unisource, the others being:

- Unisource Carrier Services, which operated a pan-European network and supplied wholesale services to the owners of Unisource, but also other telecommunication companies and suppliers of telecom services.
- International Business Development through which Unisource expanded its position in various national markets of the European Union.

Examples of the latter's activities were a 7.5 per cent stake of Arcor, the German telecommunications company of a consortium of Mannesmann (a conglomerate) and Deutsche Bundesbahn, the national railway company. Arcor would compete directly with Deutsche Telekom with a complete package of telecommunication services for German customers. In France, Unisource took over the shares in Siris from Compagnie Générale des Eaux; Siris provided national telecommunication services to businesses. Siris also was the distributor of services provided by AT&T–Unisource to large companies. Similar activities were reported in Belgium and Italy.

In the course of 1997 it was planned that Unisource Satellite Services would be integrated into AT&T–Unisource Communication Services. Two other new activities were in preparation:

- Electronic commerce, for the provision of Internet-based services.

- Solutions for managing third parties' networks and provision of consulting services.

The alliance between Unisource and AT&T was not the only worldwide telecom alliance aiming at international companies. Global One had been formed early 1996 by US-based Sprint and Europe's Atlas, which was formed by Deutsche Telekom and France Telecom (each 50 per cent). Another big alliance was Concert, formed in 1994 by British Telecom and MCI from the USA. On 3 November 1996, BT and MCI announced that they had entered into a merger agreement. BT would offer $20bn for the shares of MCI.

On 18 April 1997, Telefonica, BT and MCI announced they had formed a new strategic alliance. To compensate for the damage this caused to Unisource, Telefonica had to pay several hundreds of millions of dollars to the three other Unisource partners. When finally Worldcom made a far higher bid ($37bn) in October 1997 for MCI's shares and won the contest with BT, Telefonica was, for the time being, left without a partner. At the end of 1997 there were rumours in the financial press that, because of a possible link with Norwegian Telecom, Telia might also leave Unisource. At around the same time it was disclosed that Unisource and Telecom Italia were negotiating a deal that would tie the Italian company to the Unisource group, either as owner or as strategic partner.

PARTICIPATIONS AND JOINT VENTURES

The internationalisation of Dutch PTT Telecom also was pursued in another way – through direct equity participation in existing or newly formed telecom operators in other countries. The political changes in central and eastern Europe of the late 1980s was a trigger to explore the market possibilities in that area.

The 1990 annual report mentions the start-up of joint ventures with the Czech and Slovak operators Telecomspol SRO and Isysspol SRO. A consultancy agreement was signed with the Czech partner in 1993, whereas with the Slovak partner further possibilities were under investigation. The Slovak national operator SPT Telecom was privatised in 1995. Together with Swiss Telecom, PTT Telecom bought a 27 per cent stake in the SPT. At the time of purchase SPT was profitable, with growth opportunities: the number of telephones per 100 inhabitants was 20, a total of 2 million. In 1996, 400,000 new telephones were installed, with a similar expansion expected for 1997. SPT share prices showed a satisfactory increase.

In 1992, PTT Telecom participated in two joint ventures in the Ukraine. One was with Utel, with the aim of modernising the national and international infrastructure. The other was with UMC, a company that had to build and manage the infrastructure for mobile telecommunications in the Ukraine. As a result the first big international gateway was opened in L'vov in 1993.

In 1993 a concession for mobile communication in Hungary was granted to a consortium called Pannon GSM. PTT Telecom was one of the partners in this consortium. In the course of 1994 the mobile network became operational. In the same year a licence for a regional fixed network was obtained in co-operation with Swiss Telecom and the Hungarian partner Jasz-Com.

Besides central and eastern Europe the focus was also on other areas. Some ventures were in small markets such as Antillean Telematics that was established in 1991 to provide telematic services in the Caribbean area. Other targets were large and fast-developing markets such as Indonesia where, in 1993, an umbrella agreement was signed with PT Telkom for joint activities and projects in Indonesia and Southeast Asia. The two initial projects were a trial with GSM mobile telephony in Indonesia and the building of infrastructure for companies in the Jakarta area. The next year PTT Telecom took a 30 per cent stake in PT Bakrie Electronics Company (BEC). Through this participation PTT Telecom co-operated with the national Indonesian telephone company in Ratelindo to build and manage fixed networks in Jakarta and Western Java. BEC held 87.14 per cent of the shares in Ratelindo.

Participation in a mobile operator was obtained in 1996 when 17 per cent of the shares of PT Telekomunikasi Selular (Telkomsel) were acquired. The company provided services on the main islands Sumatra, Java, Bali, Lombok, Kalimantan and Sulawesi. The number of mobile phones increased beyond expectations: by the end of 1996 there were 188,000 – 54,000 more than anticipated.

In 1996 PTT Telecom formed a consortium, Comsource, with its Swedish Unisource partner Telia to acquire a 20 per cent stake in Telecom Eireann costing DF500m. The agreement with the Irish government included an option to increase participation by a further 15 per cent not later than 1999. For the Irish partner, Comsource could make an important contribution to cost reductions and thus increase financial and commercial performance. These could be achieved not only by better management of existing operations but also by means of joint purchasing, and software and systems developments. For PTT Telecom the attractiveness of Ireland as a new market was the international orientation of Irish industry: the Irish partner could be a powerful distributor of Unisource products and services. Also the relatively low penetration of telephones in Irish households provided opportunities for growth. In Holland there were 54 telephone connections for every 100 persons, whereas in Ireland there were only 36.

By the end of 1997 PTT Telecom discussed internally a link with the Chinese People's Liberation Army to set up a telecom company in the biggest markets in the world. It was anticipated that the initial investment would be modest, but that in future the build-up of infrastructure would run into billions of dollars. The critical issues were not commercial or technical, but political: particularly the role of the army in the Tianenmen square massacre of 1989.

On these participations Joop Drechsel commented:

> They all have in common that as a minority partner we do not have much influence. Moreover the initial capital outlays are very high with value creation expected on the longer term.

ORGANISATION

In 1997 the responsibility for the international activities of PTT Telecom were concentrated in the Business Development department. But its origin was the department that since 1989 took care of the administration of international calls, then called Business Unit International Telecommunications. This accounting-oriented department had to be turned around to become the initiator of acquisitions and international co-operation as well as the 'manager' of investments in foreign telecom companies.

In 1994 it was decided that the central organisation of PTT Telecom would be reorganised to become more market oriented. The changes brought with it, amongst other things, the shaping of the Business Development department (BD), which was given responsibility for the international activities of PTT telecom. To be included in BD was the former Business Unit International Telecommunications, which took care of the administration of international calls. There were two options for redesigning BD. One was to set it up along functional lines; another was to create geographical divisions. The latter had the disadvantage that there would be some duplication of groups such as finance and support, acquisition, etc. Initially a functional form was chosen because of the scarcity of people and the need for efficiency. The following managers reported to the director for Business Development: international acquisitions, international operations, and finance and support. Later a manager for human resources (HR) joined the management team. The BD department saw its role as orchestrator and co-ordinator of all the activities that were necessary to grow the business internationally. For this, it had to get the co-operation of many other departments and business lines within PTT Telecom. If, for instance, in a foreign project there was a need for certain types of specialist then the HR part of Business Development had to seek them out in other parts of the company and persuade them to work abroad for a while.

APPENDIX 1 SOME DATA ABOUT PTT TELECOM

	1996	1995	1994	1993	1992	1991	1990	1989
Turnover (DF million)	14,276	13,623	12,686	11,831	11,122	10,345	9,649	8,953
Gross profit	3,456	3,179	2,862	2,676	2,789	2,634	2,622	2,444
Net profit after tax	1,774	1,579	1,389	1,366	1,330	1,311	1,290	1,251
Investment in P&E	2,425	2,629	2,665	2,728	2,854	3,046	2,714	3,007
% of total assets	10.4	12.0	12.6	12.4	12.7	14.1	13.1	N/A
Investment in other companies (KPN) (excl. goodwill)	1,304	862	105	149	69	24	22	21
Of which in telecom companies	620*	724†	N/A	N/A	N/A	N/A	N/A	N/A
% of total assets of PTT Telecom	2.7	3.3	N/A	N/A	N/A	N/A	N/A	N/A
Turnover international calls (DF million)	2,188	2,467	2,459	2,410	2,704	2,539	2,338	2,088
% of total turnover	15.3	18.1	19.4	20.4	24.3	26.15	25.6	23.3
No. of international calls (million)	492	434	405	372	334	294	259	222
No. of full-time employees	29,690	30,548	31,671	31,981	32,327	30,819	29,262	28,977

* Includes investments in Telecom Eireann and Telkomsel (Indonesia).

† Includes investments in SPT Telecom (Czech Republic, DF624 million) and Unisource (DF100 million).

Source KPN annual reports.

APPENDIX 2 TURNOVER OF TELECOMMUNICATION COMPANIES AND ALLIANCES

In most cases it is difficult or impossible to get reliable information about turnover of alliances. Many of them are based on agreements, but do not form a legal entity that is obliged to publish data. Nevertheless the following information could be collected from annual reports and Internet sites.

Unisource

	1996	1995	1994	1993
Turnover (DF million)	2,432	1,315	932	293
Net result	(375)	(319)	(41)	(49)

The company expects to break even by the year 2000.

AT&T

	1996	1995
Turnover (US$m)	50,546	48,445
Net profit (US$m)	5,908	5,492

Worldcom MCI
The combination of Worldcom and MCI expect to have a turnover in 1998 of US$30 billion. The total global telecommunications market is expected to reach US$670 billion (press release of 10 November 1997).

Deutsche Telekom

	1996	1995
Turnover (DM million)	66,529	69,455
Net profit (DM million)	1,647	1,291

France Telecom
Turnover in 1997 was expected to reach FF156.7 billion (US$25.5) with profits of FF14.9 billion (US$2.4 million).

Sprint
Turnover in 1995 was US$13.6 billion, net profit US$395 million.
A press release from Global One, dated 25 July 1996, states that operational results exceed expectations, but does not give any figures about revenues, profit, etc.

APPENDIX 3 MAJOR EVENTS

Unisource

1991	Telia of Sweden and PTT Telecom of the Netherlands decide to form Unisource as the first pan-European company for cross-border telecommunications (effective 1992).
1992	Agreement between Unisource and Sprint for the distribution of worldwide network services.
1993	Swiss Telecom joins the partnership.
	Strategic alliance between AT&T (USA) and Unisource: Uniworld.
	Unisource joins AT&T, KDD of Japan, and Singapore Telecom as an equity partner in World Partners, an association of 16 leading telecom operators in 32 countries.
1994	Announcement that Telefonica will later join Unisource.
1995	Name Uniworld changed into AT&T–Unisource Communication Services.
	Telefonica (Spain) joins Unisource as an equal partner (May).
1996	Telefonica leaves Unisource and joins BT and MCI in worldwide strategic alliance.
	Unisource and AT&T discuss possible partnership with Telecom Italia.

PTT Telecom participations

		FIXED	MOBILE
1990	Joint venture Telecomspol, Czech Republic	x	
	Joint venture Isysspol, Slovakia	x	
1991	Start Antillean Telematics		
1992	Joint venture (Utel) in Ukraine	x	
	Joint venture (UMC) in Ukraine		x
1993	Participation in Pannon GSM		x
	Participation in Hungary (with Swiss) in Jasztel	x	
	Umbrella agreement with PT Telkom in Indonesia	x	x
1994	30 per cent stake in Bakrie Electronics Company (Ratelindo)	x	
1995	Participation (with Swiss Telecom) in SPT Telecom	x	
1996	17% stake in Telkomsel Indonesia		x
	20% stake in Telecom Eireann (with Telia)	x	x
1997	Discussions about link with PLA in China		

Sources Annual reports of KPN and Unisource, and internet sites.

THE NEWS CORPORATION

Julie E. Norton and Leslie P. Willcocks

The case examines how the financial and business logic of an organisation's strategic development may be reinterpreted through the attitudes, values and resulting strategies of the key management officers of the business. It illustrates the importance of analysing the financial basis of an organisation's strategies and the development of a diversified group in terms of business and financial logic. It shows how the values, aspirations and style of a dominant personality, Rupert Murdoch, influenced this development.

• • •

For the year ending 30 June 1995, turnover at The News Corporation (TNC) reached over £5bn. This made TNC the fourth largest media business in the world, eclipsed only by America's Time Warner and Disney/Capital Cities, and Germany's Bertelsmann. Yet there was no doubting who was the leader in the media industry. What was breathtaking about TNC was its global reach, its sweeping ambition and the extent to which it was the creation of one man. Rupert Murdoch has been the chief executive since 1953.

EARLY YEARS AND GROWTH TO 1980

The company was established in Australia in 1923 by Rupert Murdoch's father, Sir Keith, with the founding of *The News* in Adelaide. By 1980 the company was publishing that country's only national newspaper, *The Australian*, two national magazines and over twenty provincial newspapers. Interests in book publishing and television had also been acquired, along with film making, record production, farming and transport interests. The

---

This case was written by Julie E. Norton, University of Reading, and Leslie P. Willcocks, Oxford University. It is intended as a basis for class discussion and not as an illustration of either good or bad management practice.

Murdoch family interest in the company, however, remained strong, through an equity holding of nearly 45 per cent.

The profitability of this Australian base was the springboard to multinational status. It provided the financial backing for the 1968 purchase of the UK-based News of the World Organisation, publishers of the *News of the World* (*NOTW*) Sunday newspaper. By 1980 News International Ltd, the UK subsidiary, was publishing not only the *News of the World*, but also the *Sun*, both newspapers with consistently the largest circulation in the UK, and had interests in magazine and book publishing, printing, warehousing and transport. During the early 1980s this subsidiary was the major contributor to TNC's profits.

From 1973, with the purchase of the Express Publishing Company of San Antonio, Texas, the company also operated in the United States. During the 1970s, expansion in the USA occurred in the areas of local newspaper publishing (the *New York Post* was acquired in 1976) and in magazine publishing (the *Star*, a national magazine, was founded in 1974, and the *Village Voice* and *New York Magazine* were acquired in 1977).

In TNC's annual report for 1980, Rupert Murdoch outlined the company's approach to its early growth and development:

> Over the years expansion has been both by original start-up and acquisition. Typically, acquisition has been followed by a mobilisation of energies and talents to transform both the professional quality and the market performance of old or failing publications ... In virtually every market where [TNC] operates, it has achieved its position by first purchasing the weakest existing publication and slowly restoring its viability.

TELEVISION AND FILM MAKING

The 1980s saw TNC accelerate its real growth and development, with expansion continuing to focus on traditional product areas. Major acquisitions included Times Newspapers Limited in the UK and, in the USA, the *Boston Herald* and *Chicago Sun-Times* newspapers, *New Woman*, a general interest magazine, and a group of technical and travel magazines. By 1984, turnover had reached nearly £1.2bn. The financial results for the period of the case are summarised in Appendix 1, and Appendix 2 details the major acquisitions and disposals.

However, 1984 saw the beginnings of a major geographical and product shift. This expansion was US based. It aimed to transform TNC into an integrated global media group, with a place in all parts of that industry from newspapers to television, from magazines to film.

In 1984, TNC acquired the film company Twentieth Century Fox. This company was in a poor financial position. In 1984 it had lost £60m on revenues of £520m and was heavily indebted, and its net worth had fallen from £260m to just over £35m. A successful future would require large injections of cash. On the plus side, the purchase created an integrated entertainment company and provided access to studios for making films and television programmes, and to a film library valued at £700m.

In 1985, six television stations in the USA were acquired from the Metromedia broadcasting group. Though operationally very profitable, this company suffered from high interest charges on debt incurred from an earlier leveraged buy-out. Rupert Murdoch's purchase involved paying only £160m in cash, but taking over £1bn in high-interest debt.

These US acquisitions were restructured into three principal operating groups:

- Twentieth Century Fox Film financed, produced and distributed television programmes and theatrical motion pictures throughout the world. The company had a film library of more than 2,000 titles, including such classics as *Star Wars* and *Butch Cassidy and the Sundance Kid*, plus syndicated TV series such as *M*A*S*H* and *Dynasty*.
- Fox Television Stations owned and operated seven independent television stations, all within the top ten US television markets (and including the first three).
- Fox Broadcasting Company (FBC) provided first-run original entertainment programming by satellite to independent affiliated television stations.

For Rupert Murdoch, this consolidation confirmed that:

> The News Corporation is now a multi-national, multi-media, company ... at the forefront of global marketing, ready to encourage the cross-fertilisation of ideas between continents, and the different media within them ... The News Corporation is a citizen of the global village.

However, these purchases had two further significant implications for TNC. Revenues and operating profits increased, but so too did debt levels. Rupert Murdoch had to be careful that his acquisitions, and the debt associated with them, did not breach bank loan agreements, which required total borrowings not to exceed net assets by more than 10 per cent. Furthermore, as US law prevented foreign citizens from holding more than 25 per cent of any company with a broadcasting licence, in 1985 Rupert Murdoch became a US citizen.

THE STRATEGY OF GLOBALISATION

In a speech to the International Institute of Communications in September 1988, Rupert Murdoch confessed that he did not have a very detailed strategic plan:

> If in 1980 we had attempted to chart on paper the destiny of our company, we would never have anticipated the 30 very diverse acquisitions we made on four

> continents, almost all of which arose from unique and unanticipated events. Business situations and business opportunities simply change too quickly for there to be much point in loading ourselves down with piles of strategic speculation.

He has, however, asked himself three questions about the globalisation of the media:

> Is a global communications network a reality? Yes. Are there really going to be world-wide media networks? Yes. Is it really going to be possible for an advertiser to achieve, in practice, a single order with the media of his choice across the world? Yes.

Other media groups had come to similar conclusions. For example, in its 1988 annual report, Time Inc. stated that 'by the mid-1990s, the media and entertainment industry will consist of a handful of vertically integrated, worldwide giants'. In this period the media were seen as tremendous growth industries, with long-term growth encouraged by rising real incomes and new technologies, which, for example, saw US communications spending growing half as fast again as GNP between 1960 and 1990.

The attraction of globalisation was based on the belief that tastes, income levels, technologies and even political philosophies around the world were converging on the American model, producing strong demand for American-style films and television programmes. In 1988, for the first time in history, foreign television stations spent more on American movies than stations in the USA itself.

Combining globalisation with integration was expected to increase profits through economies of scale. For example, a group's publishing house could gain preferential access to authors for potential movie subjects. Through its cable or satellite television network, it would have a ready market for its film output and could pay more to attract best-selling authors or star directors by putting them to work on numerous related books, films or television projects under one roof.

RUPERT MURDOCH – THE WIZARD OF OZ

> He's an expansion minded person, he's wanted to buy assets, he's wanted to take over, to move around the world, to build his media empire. But he also wants to retain control.
>
> AUSTRALIAN FINANCIAL ANALYST

What was unique about TNC was that it was not a faceless multinational, but an organisation keenly linked to its chief executive – as a 1990 UK television programme commented, it was Murdoch's 'Empire', built on his 'vision, ruthlessness and daring'.

Rupert Murdoch himself managed the various businesses through the 'formulae' that he had for their products. As a former newspaper editor explained: 'He talks in formulae terms. He has formulae for newspapers.

There is the broadsheet formula, the popular formula. There is the downmarket tabloid formula, and so on.'

The implementation of these 'formulae' was achieved through the appointment of known and trusted lieutenants to run key products or business segments. However, the whole management structure was very informal with no defined responsibilities. One aide suggested that TNC was 'an emotionally driven and bonded company, where executives don't spend time guarding territories because nobody has one nailed down'. Another suggested that Rupert Murdoch's idea of management was to put in a manager and put in someone beside him, and not quite tell either of them what they were doing. A News International executive confirmed: 'I think he does do that. I don't think he does it to undermine the original person. I think he thinks that if the two can work off each other things will improve.'

Rupert Murdoch disliked committees, bureaucracy and red tape. In the late 1980s, the worldwide headquarters in midtown Manhattan, USA, employed barely 60 people, with hardly a memo in sight and communications kept to a bare necessity.

At the same time, this management style was supplemented by an extremely efficient reporting system. This focused on a weekly document known as the 'Flash', for which each operating unit had to provide a summary of its operating results. These had to include the budgeted figures for every aspect of its affairs set against the actual figures for the week, and then compared with the same week in the previous year. Each Thursday it was passed to headquarters, with Rupert Murdoch studying it over the weekend. He might then casually ring to query a figure. The call might come only once in the year, but it kept everyone on their toes for the other fifty-one weeks. Control was also achieved by unannounced 'parachuting-in' trips to check in person on the details of a business's activities and management, or to take personal control at key moments. As a News International financial manager confirmed:

> He really is the driving force and most major decisions are made by him ... even relatively minor decisions – like whether we start our TV burst of advertising now or do we put it back three weeks. Those are the sort of things that would be discussed with him before the final timings are decided. He does like leading from the front and where there's likely to be a bit of excitement he'll wade in ... I think his biggest advantage is understanding the businesses that he's in. He can get down to the core of the business and has a lot of vision as to where that business ought to be going.

Maintaining control also required that Rupert Murdoch looked outside of the business to the regulatory environment that might constrain his activities. Most governments believed that the media was an industry whose importance required regulation, particularly regarding foreign ownership, cross-ownership and concentration. Controlling a business with a global reach, with several media products, Rupert Murdoch was likely to find himself affected by national regulatory systems. Many commentators have suggested that his political friendships have bought him influence in this area.

For example, in 1979 the Australian government amended the rules regarding the ownership of television stations, from a requirement that an owner be resident in Australia to one requiring only that an owner be an Australian citizen. This enabled Rupert Murdoch to acquire Channel 10 in Melbourne, even though he was no longer resident in Australia. These amendments were christened by the Australian press as 'the Murdoch amendments'. Again, it was suggested that the support of Murdoch's newspapers for Margaret Thatcher in the 1979 UK general election helped to ensure that his acquisition of Times Newspapers in 1981 was not referred to the Monopolies and Mergers Commission, and certainly the government called a three-line whip to stop any referral.

However, as one commentator has put it: 'His personal politics are right-wing ... but he's opportunistic in his business dealings. He doesn't support only right-wing leaders – he supports winners. And he supports people who are going to promote his business interests.'

PROGRESS AND CONFLICT IN FLEET STREET

It is useful to return to the UK to examine in more detail the developments during the 1980s at the subsidiary that was the major contributor to TNC's profits.

Times Newspapers Ltd (TNL), in the UK, was acquired for £25m in 1981. The previous year, the company had reported losses in excess of £10m. Over the next four years, however, *The Times*'s circulation more than doubled to over 485,000 copies, and advertising revenues increased by over 30 per cent in both 1984 and 1985. This improvement was achieved on the basis of a traditionally loyal market, the appointment of new people in management and editorial, savings from economies of scale, some reduction in manpower, and aggressive selling of the paper. Profitability, however, required cutting production costs further, and maintaining uninterrupted production to make inroads into competitors' markets and to maintain advertising revenue.

The *Sun*, following earlier price-cutting campaigns and the introduction of 'Bingo' cards, increased circulation in 1985 to 4.165 million, and the *NOTW*, having introduced a free colour Sunday magazine and having been relaunched in tabloid format, increased to 5.2 million. These two papers were the dominant contributors from the UK to multinational profitability. The *Sun*'s production, however, was stuck at around 4 million due to limited printing press capacity.

In terms of increasing revenue and profits from increased circulation and advertising, Rupert Murdoch's strategies at News International had been fairly successful. The major problem in 1985 seemed to be how to secure continued stable growth for all of these titles. News International had invested nearly £100m in new plants at Wapping in Tower Hamlets, London, and at Kinning Park, Glasgow. However, both remained idle due to the nature of industrial relations within the national newspaper industry.

In particular, over the years, Fleet Street management had shown a repeated failure to resist local union claims. This resulted from the weak position of supervisors and middle management, the short-term irrationality of resistance (suspension of production meant the loss of revenue from what was essentially a 'perishable' good – news) and the predominance of editorial, rather than financial, goals among senior management.

Management failure was coupled with strong union bargaining power due to the integratedness of the production system, and the fact that a point of maximum bargaining strength occurred nightly throughout most of the production shift and at each stage in the production cycle. The managing director of News International at the time, Bruce Matthews, indicated his frustration by saying that the company could 'no longer tolerate being bled to death by unnecessary industrial action' by employees who 'have the advantage of industrial blackmail each night'.

Given the opportunity, management would not wish to import into Wapping the same customs and practices that operated in Fleet Street. However, to bypass the old unions successfully required the introduction of a new computerised production system, a new workforce to run the machinery and journalists to write the copy, a new method of distribution and a means of neutralising the effect of any industrial action by the old unions. The assessment of such a project kept management away from negotiations during much of 1985.

Feasibility studies to determine the profitability of a new London evening paper masked the installation at Wapping of new technology and a new workforce, and the establishment of a new distribution system. This allowed management to put forward proposals for moving to Wapping that were so restrictive (as far as the unions were concerned) that acceptance was extremely unlikely, and a resort to industrial action the only likely response. On 24 January 1986, the unions declared strikes across News International's four titles. All production was transferred to Wapping and, although the dispute was a bitter one, the unions were unable to bring pressure to bear to disrupt production or distribution.

The accounts of News International to June 1986 included an exceptional item of £66m as the cost of moving to Wapping. However, operating profit at the subsidiary had nearly doubled to £81m during that year, and it increased again the following year by a further 65 per cent to £133m.

TOWARDS THE 1990s – THE SKY IS THE LIMIT?

During the second half of the 1980s, TNC continued to expand and develop in its traditional product and market areas. The US book publishers Harper

& Row were acquired for £194m (outbidding rivals Harcourt Brace Jovanovich by £65m). More significant, however, were the acquisitions of the Australian *Herald and Weekly Times* (*HWT*) in 1987 and the American Triangle Publications in 1988. Although the acquisition of *HWT* was largely funded by the issue of convertible notes (classified as equity finance), the increased debt involved with the acquisition of Triangle Publications was of such magnitude that Rupert Murdoch was obliged, in 1988, to commit TNC to a significant debt reduction programme. This commitment, however, did not restrain the company from the launch in the UK on 5 February 1989 of Sky Television, a direct broadcasting by satellite European television network, offering four (initially) free-to-air, advertiser-supported channels.

The UK had regulations regarding the cross-ownership of media interests, including a requirement that no national newspaper proprietor may own more than 20 per cent of a television company. However, as Sky Television was beamed on channels rented from the Luxembourg-controlled Astra satellite, it fell outside the UK government's jurisdiction, even though its programmes were aimed almost exclusively at a UK audience. Rupert Murdoch, a non-UK national, was therefore able to own newspapers with 25 per cent of the national UK market, as well as his four television channels.

There were fewer subscribers than expected, resulting in lower subscription and advertising revenues. Although stringent cost reductions were implemented (one of Rupert Murdoch's maxims being that it was always easier to take a million off costs than add a million to revenues), the performance of Sky Television had marked financial consequences for TNC. In the year to 30 June 1990, £134m had been invested in the venture, yet losses of nearly £10m per month were being incurred, and it was estimated that £400m of investment would still be required through to the end of 1991.

RUPERT BEARS THE DEBT BURDEN

In March 1989, Rupert Murdoch announced plans to launch a new investment company – Media Partners International (MPI). The aim was to raise approximately £850m in equity funds, which would then give the company access to £2.6bn when borrowings were included. This was to be spent on buying media and communications companies all over the world. The News Corporation was to hold only a minority (20 per cent) stake, but would have a ten-year management contract to run the company. The venture's first acquisition was to be HarperCollins, TNC's publishing interest.

By January 1990, however, MPI had been abandoned. There were reports of considerable resistance by potential investors to the idea of effectively making a 'blind bet' on Rupert Murdoch. HarperCollins was, therefore, put into a joint venture company established by TNC and its investment bankers, Credit Suisse First Boston. Effectively, the bank agreed to purchase, on a short-term basis, half of HarperCollins. The News Corporation was then able to equity account for this investment and so move the debt associated with it 'off' its balance sheet.

In November 1990, Rupert Murdoch announced the merger of Sky Television with its UK rival, British Satellite Broadcasting (BSB). BSB had begun broadcasting in March 1990. Start-up costs here had also been higher than expected and the purchase of satellite dishes lower than expected. The News Corporation and BSB each owned 50 per cent of the equity of the newly-created company, BSkyB (although, because BSB was a consortium, the next largest individual shareholder held only 11 per cent). However, the new company came to be dominated by Sky Television. The Astra satellite channels and the technology used by Sky Television were adopted, redundancies following the merger occurred mainly among the BSB staff, and Sky executives came to dominate senior management, giving it operational and editorial control of the new company.

These moves could not disguise the severe problems that had materialised for the company in 1990. These included a protracted strike at the 50 per cent owned Ansett Airlines and a poor year at Fox Film Studios. The News Corporation was also investing £500m in new printing presses in the UK. This was a heavy cash drain at a time when there was a slowing of the economies of each of TNC's three main markets. These problems resulted in a gap in working capital of £1.3bn, financed by highly expensive short-term borrowing. At the same time, banks worldwide experienced a liquidity crisis which resulted in TNC facing difficulty in refinancing maturing bank debt and in meeting working capital requirements.

By January 1991, in response to these problems, TNC's shares fell to a low of 156p – way below their peak of 850p, touched ahead of the stock market crash of 1987. Even during 1990 the shares had traded as high as 680p. The group's bonds were trading on yields of nearly 50 per cent and its debt had been downgraded by Moody's Investor Services, the US ratings agency, to near default levels. The News Corporation's market value of nearly £800m was a fraction of the £5bn net asset value of the 1990 accounts, and its borrowings of over £4.5bn were five times this stock market capitalisation. It became clear that, without some form of restructuring, the company would default on loans due for repayment in 1991.

OPERATION DOLPHIN

In October 1990, TNC called in Citibank of New York and began negotiations (codenamed Operation Dolphin) for the refinancing of its debt. At the time it was the largest and geographically most diverse corporate restructuring sought from international banks. For Rupert

Murdoch it was a very different banking relationship to the one he was used to. As one commentator suggested, during the 1980s TNC had dominated the relationship:

> Sarazan [then chief financial officer] liked to use only banks who understood News Corp well ... The bank also had to accept Sarazan's clever global accounting practices, and the fact that News Corp would not secure loans with its own holdings and would brook very few restrictive covenants. In the end it seemed as if News Corp were doing the bank a favour by agreeing to borrow money.

Now Murdoch was flying between New York, Sydney and London, being grilled on TNC's figures, trying to sell himself and convince the bankers that he was a long-term survivor.

The banks faced a dilemma. Theoretically, they could push TNC to repay all its debts. However, with the exception of a small amount in Australia, none of the company's loans was secured on individual assets. The banks would be forced to liquidate the company to sell its assets and, although TNC was a strong business as a going concern, £6bn of assets were revalued intangibles. It was not clear how such values would hold up in a forced sale situation.

Many bankers discounted the possibility of calling in the company's loans from the start. They liked and respected Murdoch, he had a reputation among his business peers for honouring his commitments, he was also seen as a winner – if they pulled the plug on him, they did not believe that anyone else could run the business as well, in which case they could again wave goodbye to their money.

However, agreement to the restructuring was not automatic. The majority of problems developed following the discovery that original lenders had, quite legally, passed on some of their exposure to TNC to other banks, without TNC's knowledge. The result was that the company had to obtain unanimous agreement to the restructuring from a total of 146 banks. Some, particularly those with much less to lose, were not always supportive – on 6 December 1990, the £4bn (US$7.6bn) restructuring plan nearly collapsed and the company almost went into receivership when a modest US bank, Pittsburgh National, wanted to call in a US$10m loan.

In February 1991, TNC finally entered into a three-year, £3.8bn debt restructuring agreement and a £300m bridging loan agreement. Apart from the increased financial cost to TNC of these agreements, several strict financial covenants were introduced. Rupert Murdoch had to agree to quarterly meetings with the banks to discuss progress and to monitor the new covenants, and to guarantee to reduce debt levels by £1bn. He was also tied to the deal. One of the events of default related to a change in control of TNC, which would occur if Murdoch ceased to be chief executive or if the Murdoch family shareholding in the company fell below 20 per cent.

In explaining TNC's problems, Rupert Murdoch admitted: 'I had taken my eye off the financial side.' In retrospect, he concluded that the decision to modernise printing plants in Australia and the UK should have been delayed by three to four years, that the purchase of Triangle 'could have been a deal of US$1bn too much' and that he 'wasted time' with the MPI initiative.

ON THE REBOUND

By October 1991, TNC had raised £900m through asset sales, and had announced plans for the flotation of 55 per cent of its Australian printing and magazine interests to raise a further £314m. By the end of 1991, most of the £470m debt repayment due in February 1992 had been paid, and it appeared that further obligations could be met from existing cash flows without raising new money.

The important issues again lay with business directions. The perception of brokers Potter Warburg was that the company's profits in the 1990s would come from BSkyB, Twentieth Century Fox and Fox Broadcasting. Other market analysts saw consumers turning increasingly to film and television, perhaps reflecting the fact that newspaper circulation was in long-term decline. According to the UK's *Sunday Telegraph* newspaper, 'Murdoch's watchers say that while his heart is always in newspapers his head is increasingly in television.'

Rupert Murdoch himself set out his view of TNC's longer-term future in his chief executive's review of 1992. This involved 'steering a growth course' according to the following principles:

- Further strengthening the company's balance sheet.
- Improving and expanding existing businesses.
- Building new businesses.
- Nurturing and guiding the creative process as the foundation of the company's products.
- Strategic planning, involving examining opportunities for owning and operating media and entertainment ventures around the world. Particularly:

> We believe that our future is to be the pre-eminent supplier of first-rate creative and editorial product. The more we think about our businesses, and the more we look at the whole communications industry in all its facets, the more we define ourselves as a global supplier of what is now called 'software'. For us, the hardware developments that attract so much attention are secondary to our real business.

Elements of the implementation of Murdoch's five principles can be seen in the progress of the company through to early 1996.

A major refinancing of all borrowing took place. This resulted in short-term bank debt as a proportion of total debt falling from 80 to 8 per cent, and the average maturity of public debt being extended from less than three years to over ten years. Debt repayments due in 1994 under the agreement were paid early. In 1993, Standard and Poor's and Fitch Investors Service re-rated TNC's public debt securities investment grade.

In August 1995, MCI Communications Corporation, the second largest US long-distance telecommunications operator, agreed to pay £1.2bn in return for a 13.5 per cent stake in TNC. This, and other share issues, reduced the Murdoch family holding to just over 30 per cent (over which MCI was given first refusal should it be offered for sale). The terms of the alliance, however, limited MCI to a maximum 20 per cent investment in TNC and, although having voting rights, MCI was obliged to vote with the majority.

Existing newspaper businesses in Australia and the UK benefited from the reduced production costs resulting from the completion of capital investment programmes upgrading printing facilities. British newspapers added new sections which offered better-targeted advertising, and initiated aggressive price competition. In Australia, the company was at the forefront of the introduction of colour printing.

In 1995, the printed word of newspapers and magazines still provided over half of TNC's profits. But increasingly, profits were coming from the screen, from films and television.

ON THE BOX

Sky and BSB (and the subsequent merged company, BSkyB) were first marketed primarily as movie channels, for films receiving their first-time television screening. This was still seen as important, with BSkyB securing exclusive pay-television rights to all major Hollywood films until the year 2002, which increased subscribers to 1.7 million. In September 1992, BSkyB launched Sky Sports channel, having secured exclusive rights to broadcast English football Premier League matches for five years. In under six weeks, a million new subscribers were added. A gap in the market had been identified that was to revolutionise the nature of sport and the finances of BSkyB.

By 1996, BSkyB dominated the televising of English club football. It also had a stranglehold on international golfing championships, and live rights to all English overseas cricket and domestic one-day internationals. The company had also bought the rights to rugby union's Pilkington Cup and Courage Clubs Championship, and had offered £175m for five years' coverage of the Five Nations Championship. In contrast, the BBC's total sports budget stood at £100m.

The strategy was exported to other areas. In 1994 in the USA, Fox obtained the broadcast rights to the National Football League's NFC games for four years and the 1997 Super Bowl. A ten-year television deal was also made with the rugby unions of South Africa, New Zealand and Australia. In Australia, TNC even went so far as to create its own rugby Super League of ten teams, whose games would be shown exclusively on TNC-owned channels.

While advantages from increased payments have accrued to many sports, TNC's moves have not been without criticism. There were concerns that limiting sport to pay-television would have a detrimental effect on participation levels. Furthermore, when BSkyB's target was one of the sporting calendar's traditional highlights, or when the players involved were amateurs, arguments concerning sport as part of a 'national birthright' were evoked. These were influential enough to force an amendment to the UK's 1990 Broadcasting Act, ensuring that eight high-profile events were broadcast on terrestrial television. These were the Wimbledon finals weekend, the FA Cup Final, the Scottish Cup Final, the football World Cup Finals, domestic cricket Test Matches, the Olympics and the Derby.

The success of BSkyB's sports strategy increased subscribers to 3.6 million by September 1994. BSkyB was easily the most profitable television station in the UK. In December of that year, the company made a public offering of 20 per cent of its shares for over £4bn. This reduced TNC's interest in the company from 50 to 40 per cent, but its share of the flotation funds was a useful £600m.

In September 1998 BSkyB shocked the sporting world by a spectacular £623 million takeover of Manchester United – England's most successful and profitable football club.

By 1996, BSkyB was providing 28 channels, compared with the four it offered on launch and the four available on terrestrial television. Yet while the tenth-rated programme on Sky One, the most popular satellite channel, might win an audience of 350,000, the tenth-rated programme on ITV pulled in over 12 million. What provided the value in BSkyB was the fact that 80 per cent of revenues came from subscription. For the future, analysts believed that the company's exclusive rights to key programmes – films and sport – would drive the subscriber base forward:

> As critical mass is achieved and additional advertising revenues obtained, the strong cash flow generated will put the group in pole position to secure further sports rights and renegotiate the movie contract, which will in turn further stimulate subscriber interest.
>
> BARCLAY DE ZOOTE WEBB

With subscription television, it was important to have in place a system that allowed for the correct collection of revenue. This required secure 'scrambling' and 'decoding' of the satellite signal. In the UK, the only established technology was controlled by News Datacom, a subsidiary of TNC. Using News Datacom's proprietary encryption code, BSkyB sent viewers a card which, when inserted into the decoder box connected to the television set, allowed programmes to be viewed.

Not only has this ensured full and appropriate payment for services provided by BSkyB, but, as one industry executive pointed out, for the future the company 'is in a position to skim off money from anyone who wants to start a satellite channel'. Control of encryption technology made BSkyB a channel 'gatekeeper'. For any channel operator, getting through the gate would require the payment of significant fees. However, by-passing the BSkyB 'gatekeeper' would require any new channel establishing its own encryption and marketing systems. Apart from the high investment and running costs, this would require viewers to buy a new decoder box to sit on top of their television sets.

In 1993, TNC moved into Asia with the acquisition of the Hong Kong-based company Star TV, which broadcast over China, India and 51 other countries containing approximately two-thirds of the world's population.

Murdoch's strategy in Asia was a variant of the 'be global, act local' philosophy that had come to dominate much thinking about international business. With the media, this was reflected in the realisation that, with the possible exception of Hollywood feature films, regional programmes in local languages were needed to make any impact outside English-speaking élites. To that effect, Star Television acquired Media Assets, which had a film library of approximately 550 Chinese-language motion pictures, and took a 50 per cent stake in Zee TV, a Hindi television channel in India. It was also clear that Star would not be profitable remaining as a free-to-air, advertiser-supported channel. While Sky moved from a free-to-air service to a pay-for-view network with surprisingly little difficulty, the cost of developing such a network in the immature Asian market was one reason Star was losing so much money.

Other problems stemmed from having to find a *modus vivendi* with Asia's political leaders. In September 1993, addressing an audience in London, Rupert Murdoch had claimed that 'advances in the technology of telecommunications have proved an unambiguous threat to totalitarian regimes everywhere'. Expansion in Asia by TNC was hindered by the authorities there, many of which were opposed to the free flow of information and the expansion of American cultural influence, recognising the truth of this statement. In response, Murdoch sold the embarrassingly anglophile *South China Morning Post* and Star removed the BBC World Service from its northern Asia channel. Murdoch also offered authorities the opportunity of controlling satellite programming through TNC's decoding technology. This would effectively allow censors to filter programmes to be broadcast.

In 1995 in Australia, TNC established a pay cable television joint venture, Foxtel, with Telstra, the country's national telephone company, utilising newly laid fibre-optic networks. In the USA, Fox Television, which had created a name for itself with youthful and irreverent programmes such as *The Simpsons* and *Married with Children*, repeated its success with *The X-Files*, a detective-and-conspiracy series which attracted huge audiences of young males all over the world. By 1995, Fox Broadcasting had signed up nearly 200 independent stations as affiliates. Together with Fox television stations, this gave Fox Broadcasting the ability to deliver its programmes to 98 per cent of the total US network. A 24-hour general entertainment cable programming service and a cable movie channel were also launched in the USA. Murdoch then announced that TNC would set up a 24-hour global television news service and combine most of its sports interests with those of Tele-Communications Inc., the biggest cable TV group in the USA, to create a global sports network. In January 1996, TNC and MCI paid US$682m for the last unclaimed frequency slot for American satellite television.

In November 1995, TNC closed one of the last significant holes in its global TV coverage by joining with three other television, programming and distribution groups to create a satellite service covering Latin America. These partners were Globo, Brazil's biggest media group; the Mexico-based Grupo Televisa, the biggest Spanish-language programming provider in the world; and TCI International, a subsidiary of Tele-Communications Inc.

THE SUPERHIGHWAY

Traditionally, television, film, printing and publishing companies were considered independent entities, even if part of large national or multinational organisations. The 1980s, however, saw the emergence of a trend towards integration and globalisation, centred around television. The News Corporation was at the forefront of this with its acquisition of 20th Century Fox and Metromedia in the USA, and the development of Sky TV in the UK.

The 1990s saw the convergence and globalisation of media and entertainment industries with the information industry (creating the 'info-tainment' industry), and of companies involved in content production and packaging with those involved with distribution. This convergence of media, information and computing, of electronics, satellite, cable and telecommunications, laid the foundations for the development of the 'superhighway' of interactive services to be accessed from every office and living room.

These moves were further fuelled by the arrival of digital compression technology, which allowed many more television programmes or channels to be broadcast and cut the cost of a broadcasting channel significantly. By the end of 1997, most parts of the world would have the opportunity to tune into at least 150 channels of digital television; in Europe, the total could easily be more than 500. Importantly, this digital technology could be utilised by all the differing methods of distribution – satellite, cable, terrestrial land-based transmission and the telecommunications network. Sir Iain Vallance, chairman of the UK telecommunications company British Telecom, spoke for all such distributors when he said: 'We are becoming retailers of anything that can be converted into digital form.'

The development of the superhighway initiated a string of strategic alliances, acquisitions, mergers and investments between media content providers and packagers, telecommunications operators, cable television companies and computer makers.

For example, in 1989 Time created the first fully-fledged 'supergroup' by merging its publishing and cable interests with Warner's film and music business, and in 1995 Time Warner also acquired Turner Broadcasting. In 1993, the regional telephone operator US West paid US$2.5bn for 25.5 per cent of Time Warner, and in 1995 Time Warner, US West and Toshiba of Japan announced a US$400m joint venture to develop cable television in Japan.

In 1995, Walt Disney paid US$19bn (£12bn) to acquire Capital Cities/NBC and formed a joint venture with three US regional telephone companies to create interactive videos. In the same year, Bill Gates's software group, Microsoft, announced plans to add to its Internet package with the launch of a 24-hour news channel in conjunction with the US television network NBC. The company also invested US$500m in Dreamworks, the entertainment group founded by the film director Steven Spielberg.

It is in this context that one should view MCI's investment in TNC, and both companies' subsequent commitment to joint ventures exploiting TNC's media resources and MCI's ability to distribute electronic information over its telecoms network.

MCI, like other telecoms operators at this time, was a significant cash generator, but was also under pressure to increase volume on its network and to add value to the traffic being transmitted, as increased competition would erode profitability by the end of the century. MCI needed a way to differentiate its version of what was quickly becoming a commodity service – long-distance transport of telephone traffic – from those of competitors, if it was to maintain profitability. Rupert Murdoch detailed the possibilities:

> Imagine being able to access the innovative Internet, MCI, and Delphi Internet shopping and on-line information over the same service that brings you first-rate original entertainment. Imagine being able to retrieve computerised information stored in the MCI network wherever you are, whenever you want, without limitation. That's the power of this relationship.

Having said that, however, Murdoch is also convinced that the superhighway, and the brave new world of interactive television, will take longer to develop than most people expect: 'That's 15 to 20 years away in the US and Europe – and 50 years in the rest of the world.' Furthermore, 'we don't know where technology is taking us in the delivery of content'. However, the MCI link 'opens up all these options as technology develops'.

AND INTO THE MILLENNIUM

In July 1996 TNC purchased New World Communications Group of America. Murduch combined this acquisition with Fox Broadcasting to create America's largest television company. In 1998 TNC merged its TV Guide interests with United Video, providers of electronic television programming information, to produce a global platform of television guide services. Murdoch's sporting purchases continued in 1998 with the acquisition of National League baseball team Los Angeles Dodgers for US$315m, and the £623m bid by BSkyB for Manchester United.

The possibility of Rupert Murdoch's retirement, with all its implications for TNC's future, seemed remote. This was perhaps fortunate, as the company had no senior, experienced executives capable of filling his shoes.

Murdoch had repeatedly quarrelled with potential successors. He appeared to prefer the hereditary principle. Asked which of his two daughters and two sons he would like to succeed him, Murdoch, aged 65 in 1996, was quoted as saying: 'I hope we can work it out between us'; adding, however, that he would probably make a judgement about his successor in about twenty years. For the future, the activities of TNC will continue to be linked with the motivations, personality and perceptions of Murdoch himself. It is appropriate, therefore, that he should have the last word:

> News Corporation is institutionally committed to the proposition that fortune favours the brave. We believe it, and we act on it, and it works for us. It requires more intense management discipline and a more penetrating creative insight [but] I believe we have shown these qualities since our start against large odds in Australia forty years ago.
>
> News Corporation has helped to define the new world of media: our own internal evolution from primarily a newspaper publisher to an electronic media powerhouse is evidence of this shift ... Today, we are working to shape the media products of tomorrow.

APPENDIX 1 THE NEWS CORPORATION LTD: FINANCIAL DATA

CONSOLIDATED PROFIT AND LOSS ACCOUNTS, 1982–95 (SUMMARISED)

	For year ending 30 June (£m)[1]					
	1982	1983	1984	1985	1986	1987
Turnover						
USA	136	198	319	525	909	1,233
UK	351	378	433	501	551	587
Australia	266	300	410	525	396	481
	753	876	1,162	1,551	1,856	2,301
Operating profit[2]						
USA	2	12	17	16	132	154
UK	7	39	39	48	83	145
Australia	30	25	40	40	33	49
	39	76	96	104	248	348
Interest charges	31	33	66	47	108	172
Profit after tax	22	51	60	61	118	159
Extraordinary items[3]	(2)	(25)	(38)	32	1	199
Profit after extraordinary items	20	26	22	93	119	358

[1] Trading results have been converted at the average exchange rates for the year.
[2] Operating profit is shown before interest payments.
[3] Extraordinary items include the following:

1982–4	Foreign exchange losses totalling £100m
1986	Costs of relocating production facilities £66m
1987	Profit on the sale of non-current assets £255m
1988	Write-off of new business start-up and termination costs £57m
1989	Profit on the sale of non-current assets £400m
1990	Profit on the sale of non-current assets £209m
	Previously capitalised start-up and development costs of Sky Television written off £134m

1988	1989	1990	1991	1992	1993	1994	1995
1,050	1,780	2,321	3,105	2,831	3,128	3,404	3,590
698	808	819	1,064	860	841	835	893
740	1,140	986	1,023	763	656	664	655
2,488	3,728	4,126	5,192	4,454	4,625	4,903	5,138
155	288	376	487	385	417	455	493
153	191	62	93	167	174	125	137
100	208	200	157	144	146	94	71
408	687	638	737	696	737	674	701
245	448	474	577	431	357	281	251
192	235	133	152	232	424	419	446
3	316	29	(338)	(13)	(50)	37	24
195	551	162	(186)	219	374	456	470

[3] *(continued)*

1991	Losses on the sale of non-current assets £82m Refinancing costs £91m
1992	Profit on sale of non-current assets £96m Refinancing costs £12m
1993	Profit on sale of non-current assets £27m Refinancing costs £18m
1994	Profit on sale of non-current assets £61m
1995	Profit on sale of non-current assets £314m Provisions £213m

CONSOLIDATED BALANCE SHEETS, 1982–95 (SUMMARISED)

	As at 30 June (£m)[4]					
	1982	1983	1984	1985	1986	1987
Current assets						
Cash	3	11	12	74	29	95
Receivables, inventories and other items	206	248	336	394	746	887
Total current assets	209	259	354	468	775	982
Non-current assets						
Investments	110	136	255	300	213	1,156
Property, plant and equip.[5]	164	196	266	305	459	550
Publishing rights, titles and TV licences[6]	49	52	437	673	1,480	2,160
Goodwill					331	343
Other	12	21	37	44	447	434
Total non-current assets	335	405	995	1,322	2,930	4,643
Total assets	544	664	1,349	1,790	3,705	5,625
Current liabilities						
Borrowings	20	40	33	8	84	346
Creditors and accruals	143	202	359	382	637	800
Total current liabilities	163	242	392	390	721	1,146
Non-current liabilities						
Borrowings	162	154	266	607	1,068	1,626
Creditors and accruals	16	37	57	91	275	367
Total non-current liabilities	178	191	323	698	1,343	1,993
Total liabilities	341	433	715	1,088	2,064	3,139
Net assets	203	231	634	702	1,641	2,486
Shareholders' equity						
Share capital						
Ordinary[7]	16	16	16	32	32	70
Other[8]						600
Revaluation reserve			381	249	210	561
Other reserves	170	173	194	333	413	945
Minority interests[9]	17	42	43	88	986	310
Total shareholders' equity	203	231	634	702	1,641	2,486

[4–9] See page 800.

1988	1989	1990	1991	1992	1993	1994	1995
60	78	72	96	161	294	204	582
876	1,188	1,478	1,454	1,057	1,400	1,563	2,006
936	1,266	1,550	1,550	1,218	1,694	1,767	2,588
1,600	1,616	1,556	1,419	1,389	1,458	1,603	1,808
744	932	1,561	1,538	1,427	1,647	1,674	1,821
2,320	4,290	6,017	5,867	5,072	5,943	6,214	6,493
294	298	258	237	184	235	216	210
609	840	848	1,149	1,010	1,194	1,248	1,346
5,567	7,976	10,240	10,210	9,082	10,477	10,955	11,678
6,503	9,242	11,790	11,760	10,300	12,171	12,722	14,266
278	246	1,332	354	139	8	53	67
874	1,059	1,395	1,499	1,202	1,448	1,671	1,754
1,152	1,305	2,727	1,853	1,341	1,456	1,724	1,821
2,296	3,568	3,419	4,698	3,882	4,535	3,679	3,848
341	475	531	614	482	479	491	863
2,637	4,043	3,950	5,312	4,364	5,014	4,170	4,711
3,789	5,348	6,677	7,165	5,705	6,470	5,894	6,532
2,714	3,894	5,113	4,595	4,595	5,701	6,828	7,734
70	70	70	70	86	428	456	718
600	600	600	600			187	250
606	595	1,961	2,017	1,620	1,756	1,797	1,844
1,101	1,744	1,697	1,564	2,571	3,215	4,158	4,681
337	885	785	344	318	302	230	241
2,714	3,894	5,113	4,595	4,595	5,701	6,828	7,734

[4] The financial position has been converted at the exchange rate at balance sheet date.
[5] Including capitalised interest: £162m 1995.
[6] Assets are stated at cost or, from 30 June 1984, at valuation. Where at valuation, assets are revalued triennially and are recorded at 70% of revaluation figure. Changes in value from the 1993 revaluation exercise have not been reflected in the financial accounts. No amortisation is provided since, in the opinion of the directors, they do not have a finite economic life.
[7] Changes include the following:

1985	1 for 1 bonus issue
1987	1 for 1 bonus issue
1993	3 for 1 bonus issue
1995	£232m preferred limited voting ordinary shares

[8] Convertible notes (1987–92) pay 5% semi-annually, and are convertible at any time at the option of the holder into ordinary shares. All notes not converted by 31 January 1992 were converted into ordinary shares. The difference between the face value and the market value of these shares was credited to the share premium account.

1994 includes issue of £172m $8\frac{5}{8}\%$ guaranteed perpetual preference shares only redeemable at the option of TNC.

1995 includes issue of £63m of adjustable rate cumulative preference shares only redeemable at the option of TNC.
[9] 1986 includes issue of preference shares by a subsidiary as a swap for Metromedia debt.

CONSOLIDATED SOURCE AND APPLICATION OF FUNDS, 1982–8 (SUMMARISED) (£M)[1]

	1982	1983	1984	1985	1986	1987	1988
Source of funds							
From operations	23	62	83	95	207	279	292
Issue of shares:							
Ordinary					3	167	
Preference		31		93			244
Convertible						545	
Sales of assets	14	8	79	145	55	99	212
Gain on sale of businesses					39	240	5
Increase in liabilities:							
Current	23	91	94	38	380	436	48
Non-current	17	(2)	120	443	801	693	661
Increase in minority interest					1,007		
Other	8	7	56	40	140	21	181
	85	197	432	854	2,632	2,480	1,643
Application of funds							
Increase in assets							
Current	28	60	77	175	385	225	(22)
Property, plant and equipment	23	53	81	97	281	171	250
Investments	1	25	95	156	41	868	603
Publishing rights, etc.			37	321	992	404	210
Increase in goodwill					391		
Tax paid	18	8	4	31	20	20	28
Dividends paid	6	6	7	10	45	57	16
Redemption of preference shares		4		26		608	234
Other	9	41	131	38	477	127	324
	85	197	432	854	2,632	2,480	1,643

[1] See page 796.

CONSOLIDATED STATEMENT OF CASH FLOWS, 1988–95 (SUMMARISED)

	For the year ended 30 June (£m)[1]		
	1988	1989	1990
Interest payments	(241)	(444)	(484)
Income tax payments	(28)	(24)	(17)
Cash provided/(used) by operating activity	0	(22)	441
Investing and other activity			
Property, plant and equipment	(138)	(295)	(835)
Investments	(747)	(2,348)	(572)
Proceeds from sale of non-current assets (incl. business entities)	255	1,233	505
Other	(38)	(26)	(16)
Cash provided/(used) in investing activity	(668)	(1,436)	(918)
Financing activity			
Issuance of debt	961	1,220	1,114
Repayment of debt	(323)	(264)	(405)
Issue of ordinary shares	—	—	—
Issue of other stock	244	575	188
Preference capital redeemed	(234)	(41)	(400)
Dividends paid	(10)	(14)	(14)
Other	(5)	—	(6)
Cash (used)/provided by financing activity	633	1,476	477
Net (decrease)/increase in cash	(35)	18	0
Opening cash balance	89	60	78
Exchange movement	6	0	(6)
Closing cash balance	60	78	72

[1] See page 796.

1991	1992	1993	1994	1995
(529)	(337)	(324)	(266)	(210)
(20)	(28)	(39)	(10)	(33)
222	170	505	583	474
(306)	(147)	(247)	(187)	(199)
(134)	(69)	(73)	(484)	(499)
461	275	168	439	423
(6)	—	—	—	—
15	59	(152)	(232)	(275)
418	361	3,753	595	509
(369)	(717)	(4,190)	(1,342)	(360)
—	175	408	4	59
—	80	—	361	—
(151)	(1)	(98)	—	—
(21)	(15)	(26)	(28)	(56)
(97)	(41)	(106)	(19)	(29)
(220)	(158)	(259)	(429)	123
17	71	94	(78)	322
72	96	161	294	204
7	(6)	39	(12)	56
96	161	294	204	582

INDUSTRY SECTOR ANALYSIS, 1984–95

(£M)	1984	1985	1986	1987	1988
Revenues[1]					
Newspapers	781	1,014	953	875	1,062
Magazines	141	216	222	247	252
Television	84	22	170	297	233
Filmed entertainment	—	—	267	601	490
Commercial printing	70	77	72	77	107
Book publishing	—	—	—	—	—
Other	86	122	172	204	344
	1,162	1,551	1,856	2,301	2,488
Operating income[1]					
Newspapers	47	50	74	150	198
Magazines	25	35	47	44	44
Television	5	6	26	50	34
Filmed entertainment	—	—	37	74	34
Commercial printing	4	4	8	8	9
Book publishing	—	—	—	—	—
Other	15	9	56	22	89
	96	104	248	348	408
Identifiable assets[4]					
Newspapers	619	686	647	1,367	1,754
Magazines	132	448	400	372	375
Television	169	133	1,332	1,324	1,249
Filmed entertainment	—	—	853	757	684
Commercial printing	28	36	35	56	141
Book publishing	—	—	—	—	—
Other	147	187	227	592	700
Corporate items	254	300	211	1,157	1,600
	1,349	1,790	3,705	5,625	6,503
USA	276	660	2,649	2,621	2,440
UK	348	442	463	911	989
Australia and Pacific Basin	471	388	382	936	1,474
Corporate items	254	300	211	1,157	1,600
	1,349	1,790	3,705	5,625	6,503
Capital expenditures[4]					
Newspapers	20	70	63	50	115
Magazines	3	10	3	10	4
Television	1	4	6	9	8
Filmed entertainment	—	—	3	6	5
Commercial printing	4	6	3	7	6
Book publishing	—	—	—	—	—
Other	6	8	12	9	18
	34	98	90	91	156
USA	6	15	20	25	23
UK	9	58	44	33	90
Australia and Pacific Basin	19	25	26	33	43
	34	98	90	91	156

[1] See page 796.
[4] See page 800.

1989	1990	1991	1992	1993	1994	1995
1,374	1,420	1,461	1,291	1,329	1,216	1,200
554	680	619	719	717	695	705
352	552	630	540	699	884	1,095
572	596	1,041	1,059	1,135	1,300	1,322
224	243	234	—	—	—	—
—	—	—	635	655	671	642
652	635	1,207	210	90	137	174
3,728	4,126	5,192	4,454	4,625	4,903	5,138
325	306	247	258	290	183	206
131	150	133	167	174	142	150
47	3	58	114	161	196	216
57	50	100	56	23	59	64
23	27	26	—	—	—	—
—	—	—	89	87	87	77
104	102	173	12	2	7	(12)
687	638	737	696	737	674	701
2,345	3,596	3,612	3,392	3,720	3,447	3,594
1,820	1,745	1,615	1,362	1,744	1,686	1,789
1,696	2,222	2,003	1,692	2,236	2,867	3,135
725	751	1,075	947	1,065	1,256	1,522
171	164	145	—	—	—	—
—	—	—	1,141	1,410	1,429	1,579
869	1,757	1,890	417	538	434	258
1,616	1,555	1,420	1,349	1,458	1,603	2,389
9,242	11,790	11,760	10,300	12,171	12,722	14,266
4,736	5,519	5,920	5,074	6,479	6,558	6,924
1,420	2,804	2,448	2,383	2,414	2,452	2,692
1,470	1,912	1,972	1,494	1,820	2,109	2,261
1,616	1,555	1,426	1,349	1,458	1,603	2,389
9,242	11,790	11,760	10,300	12,171	12,722	14,266
179	536	248	152	216	120	67
5	5	4	5	3	5	8
81	206	48	3	20	48	68
6	10	14	7	6	7	40
12	21	9	—	—	—	—
—	—	—	2	4	4	3
18	19	20	4	7	28	45
301	797	343	173	256	212	231
24	32	33	19	39	81	135
220	634	207	57	33	37	24
57	131	103	97	184	94	72
301	797	343	173	256	212	231

APPENDIX 2 THE NEWS CORPORATION LTD: MAJOR ACQUISITIONS AND DISPOSALS, 1984–95

Year	Acquisitions			Disposals		
1984	***Chicago Sun-Times***	(USA)	£16m			
	New Woman	(USA)				
	Ziff Davies Magazines	(USA)	£287m			
	Twentieth Century Fox	(USA)	£400m			
1985	Metromedia	(USA)	£160m			
1986	***South China Morning Post***	(Hong Kong)	£115m	***Chicago Sun-Times***[1]	(USA)	£101m
				Houston Community Papers	(USA)	
1987	***Herald & Weekly Times***	(Australia)	£1bn	Newspaper interests and television stations[2]	(Australia)	£535m
1988	Harper & Row	(USA)	£194m	***New York Post***[1]	(USA)	£41m
	Triangle Publications	(USA)	£1.7bn	Aviation Trade Publications	(USA)	
1989	William Collins	(UK)	£400m[3]	***Elle Magazine***	(USA)	£110m
				Travel Trade Publications	(USA)	£480m
1990				***Star***	(USA)	£243m
				Medical journals	(USA)	£140m
				South China Morning Post (49%)	(Hong Kong)	£160m
1991				Magazine interests	(USA/UK)	£520m
1992				Magazine and printing interests (55%)	(Australia)	£208m
1993	Star Television (63.6%)	(Hong Kong)	£323m	San Antonio Express News	(USA)	£114m
	Delphi Internet Services					
1994				***South China Morning Post*** (51%)	(Hong Kong)	£323m
1995	Star Television (36.4%)	(Hong Kong)	£194m			

[1] Disposed of in compliance of the USA Federal Communication Commission's general rule that joint ownership of a newspaper and television station in the same market is not permissible.
[2] Disposed of to comply with Australian Trade Practices Law.
[3] Acquisition of the outstanding 58% not already owned. Subsequently merged with Harper & Row to create HarperCollins.

Source Annual reports, 1984–95.

NOKIA: THE CONSUMER ELECTRONICS BUSINESS

Martin Lindell and Leif Melin

The case describes the entry of the Finnish company, Nokia, into the consumer electronics market – resulting in a significant reorientation of the company. It describes the internationalisation of the Nokia Group from a Finnish company, to a Nordic company, to a European company and finally to a global player in world markets. The case raises three main questions. Why and how did Nokia acquire consumer electronics businesses? Why was the integration process of acquisitions so difficult? And why, after a decade of investment, did Nokia divest its consumer electronics businesses in 1996? The case can be used to explore the difficulties of integration in terms of management, culture and strategy.

• • •

INTRODUCTION

Nokia, the large Finnish industrial group, was founded in 1966 through a merger of three companies. The main business units at that time were pulp and paper, tyres and cables, with paper manufacturing as the oldest business, established 130 years ago. During the 1970s Nokia started to diversify through expansion in different electronic product areas. In 1995, after twenty years of acquisitions, divestments, internationalisation and rapid growth, 99 per cent of the turnover (FIM36,810 million)[1] was

---

This case study was prepared by M. Lindell of the Swedish School of Economics and Business Administration and L. Melin of Jønkøping University in Sweden. It is intended as a basis for class discussion and not as an illustration of good or bad management practice.

[1] The exchange rates in June 1996:

1 British pound (£)	= 7.27 FIM
1 Swedish krona (SEK)	= 0.70 FIM
1 German mark (DM)	= 3.07 FIM
1 US dollar ($)	= 4.70 FIM

Exhibit 1 The acquisitions made by Nokia in consumer electronics

1983	Salora (Finland), Luxor (Sweden)
1987	Oceanic (France)
1988	Standard Electric Lorenz (Germany) Main plants: Bochum (Germany) and Ibervisao (Portugal), with six other plants supporting the manufacturing of TV sets
1992	Finlux (Finland)

represented by three business units in electronics: mobile phones, telecommunications and consumer electronics. The three original businesses had been divested and 91 per cent of the turnover was derived from exports. Nokia had become one of the leading global producers of mobile phones and telecommunication systems, and the third biggest in Europe in consumer electronics, with 34,000 employees, 14,000 of them working outside Finland in 45 different countries.

The Nokia case is a remarkable corporate transformation, achieved through focusing the company's strategic activities in the consumer electronics industry, where Nokia attained its position after a series of rapid acquisitions of five different European companies between 1983 and 1992 (Exhibit 1). Colour TV was the dominant product group in the consumer electronics business, with audio systems and satellite receivers as other product groups.

The radical changes in Nokia can be seen from the division of the turnover into various business areas for four fiscal years (Exhibit 2). The main products in these different business areas have been as follows:

- *Paper industry* – soft tissues, consumer products, power.
- *Tyres fabric* – tyres, industrial rubber, footwear.
- *Telecommunications* – telecommunication systems used in mobile and fixed networks.
- *Mobile phones* – products for all major digital and analogue systems.
- *Consumer electronics* – colour TV sets, satellite receivers, VCRs and audio equipment.
- *Cable* – cables, accessories and systems for use in the construction industry, and the telecommunications and power-transmission sectors.

Furthermore, for more than a decade from the mid-1970s, computers/information systems also formed a business area within electronics.

Exhibit 2 **Nokia's turnover by business groups (%)**

	1972	1983	1988	1995
Paper industry	19.9	22.7	10.0	0
Tyres fabric	24.5	11.1	6.0	0
Electronics	8.0	19.1	60.0	99.0
Telecommunications				27.0
Mobile phones				43.0
Consumer electronics				29.0
Cable fabric	47.6	22.0	9.0	—
Others	—	25.1	15.0	1.0

FORMULATION OF A NEW LONG-TERM VISION FOR NOKIA

During the mid-1970s, after the oil crisis in 1973, Nokia experienced strategic problems. The original core businesses, representing the main part of the corporation, were expected to have limited growth in the future. Top management felt that the company could get into serious trouble if no strategic changes were initiated. The change process began with the formulation of a growth vision, which implied new strategic directions for Nokia. The ambition was to enter industrial sectors with growth potential, so as to increase the share of products with growth potential in Nokia's product portfolio. The top management set out the following strategic goals for future development:

- Internationalisation.
- Increased share of high-tech products.
- Maintain the competitiveness of the original businesses (paper, tyres and cables).

The chief executive officer of Nokia at that time, Kari Kairamo, was the strategist behind the vision. His belief was that growth could not be achieved by remaining in Finland. Nokia had been too dependent on its domestic market. He also made a strong point of the need for strategic flexibility and a readiness to take opportunities.

In order to increase the share of high-tech products, Nokia soon started to diversify. Entering the consumer electronics market was one of the main moves towards the vision of diversification and internationalisation. All in all, five major acquisitions created the bridge into consumer electronics. The manufacture of televisions was to prove an important element in this.

At the beginning of the 1980s, the total annual sales of TV sets in Europe were almost 20 million, about the same as in both the USA and Japan. However, the European market was much more fragmented, with several technical standards and local protectionism. The consequence was more local producers in Europe, each with a rather small production volume. The two biggest European competitors were Philips and Thompson (France), but even these firms had fairly local strategies. Large production volume was at this time not regarded as a major critical factor for success. Instead, the flexibility to change production rapidly from one type of TV set to another brand, model or size was a critical factor for competitiveness. Eventually, the non-European competition from the Japanese and other Far East companies led to an increased focus on price competition in Europe. With more focus on price, the small-scale orientation created vulnerability for several European companies.

NOKIA ENTERS THE CONSUMER ELECTRONICS INDUSTRY: THE ACQUISITIONS OF SALORA AND LUXOR

In the mid-1970s Nokia moved into computers, with the importation and distribution of Honeywell Bull computers, following which the then small electronic business area was divided into professional electronics and computers. At the same time, another opportunity to expand in electronics appeared when the Finnish army wanted a new type of portable radio telephone. It invited most domestic firms in the electronics industry to develop them, and nearly all Finnish electronics firms started to construct mobile radio telephones. The military order was eventually placed with three different companies, Salora, Televa and Nokia. The top management in Nokia thought that three domestic companies in this area were too many. As Salora was regarded as slightly ahead in its R&D activities, Nokia made an initial contact with that company. A co-operation agreement was soon signed between Nokia and Salora regarding their radio telephone businesses, and in 1980 the co-operation was extended. A joint venture on a fifty-fifty basis was formed – Mobira, a mobile telephone business unit.

Salora was also the biggest manufacturer of TV sets in Finland, but in the late 1970s it had problems with its TV business because of a decline in the Scandinavian market. At the same time, the company's owners were accused of selling on the black market and were forced to relinquish their ownership. The Union bank looked for new owners and Nokia was invited to acquire Salora. But the head of Nokia's electronics division, Kurt Wikstedt, was only interested in Salora's mobile telephone business and not at all in consumer electronics, which were not seen as high-tech

Exhibit 3 **Turnover and profit of Luxor, 1975–82 (in millions of SEK)**

YEAR	1975/6	1976/7	1977/8	1978/9	1979/80	1980/1 (16 MONTHS)	1982
Turnover	484	523	611	700	745	1,010	730
Profit/loss	12	15	−104	−69	−50	−117	−45

Source: *Affärsvärlden*, 1983, no. 48, p. 33.

products. He saw no competitive advantages for Nokia in the consumer electronics sector:

> In Finland we cannot produce on such a scale in this product area that we could be successful. The production scale of Salora is too small. We should concentrate on products where the production costs are high, as in professional electronics.

Nokia's group chief executive officer and his corporate planner were in favour of an acquisition, as they regarded consumer electronics as a growth industry. But Wikstedt's arguments were stronger, and instead Salora was taken over by the shipbuilding company Hollming.

The difficulties in Salora continued and the company made huge losses: FIM18 million in 1980 and FIM25 million in 1981. The president of Salora was forced to resign after only a few years in office and Salora was put up for sale again. But Nokia did not show any interest in the consumer electronics part of Salora. It just wanted Mobira. In this situation the owners of Salora, the Hollming Group, linked the possible sale of their share of Mobira to the sale of the rest of Salora. The result was a compromise – Nokia acquired 18 per cent of the shares in Salora in order to be allowed to acquire the remaining 50 per cent of Mobira from Salora. In 1982 Mobira became a subsidiary of Nokia, and Nokia became represented in the Salora board. Nokia later acquired Televa as well and eventually became a global leader in mobile phones.

The new president of Salora, Antti Lagerroos, succeeded in improving the company's performance in consumer electronics: 1982 was a good year and 1983 was expected to be even more successful. Markets were growing rapidly. Salora obtained two big orders for colour TV sets which gave rise to capacity problems. Lagerroos looked for more production capacity and became interested in Luxor, a Swedish competitor, which itself had survival problems in the late 1970s (Exhibit 3). In 1979 the Swedish state saved Luxor from bankruptcy, acquiring it from the family owners for the symbolic sum of one Swedish krona, and put fresh capital into the company in an attempt to improve its fortunes. In 1983 the Swedish Minister of Industry wanted a new solution for Luxor, after having subsidised a financial reconstruction of the company. The minister looked for a large corporation as a partner, but held the opinion that Salora was not large or strong enough. Other firms showed an interest in acquiring Luxor, but none found favour with the Swedish governmental officials.

In this situation, Antti Lagerroos introduced a new idea to Nokia's top managers. Although Nokia's previous interest in Salora was lukewarm, a Salora–Luxor combination put the matter in a quite different light; after all, internationalisation was an important ingredient in the Nokia corporate vision and Finnish firms had traditionally made their initial foreign expansion in the Swedish market. Nokia had also become more interested in know-how in mass production and marketing. The production knowledge in consumer electronics was quite different from that in the production of computers, for instance. At the beginning of the 1980s, computers were still mostly tailor-made. Marketing too was different. Brands and distribution channels were important success factors in consumer electronics, where a good product was not enough in order to obtain a large market share. An acquisition of both Salora and Luxor could give Nokia the possibility of supplementing the competences in R&D and small-scale production with mass production and market orientation.

Relations between the group chief executive officer of Nokia, Kari Kairamo, and ministers in the Swedish government were good, and Sweden was motivated to accept the successful Nokia Group as the acquiring company. The production capacity of a combined Salora and Luxor was expected to make it a strong unit. The acquisition took place in January 1984 and Kari Kairamo stated:

> Nokia's acquisition of Salora and Luxor means that the company's position in Sweden is now much stronger. The Luxor, Salora and Nokia venture means that Scandinavian co-operation in this important area has improved.

Kairamo saw Luxor as a first step in further international co-operation, and expected that the clear boundary between consumer electronics and professional electronics would disappear in the future. Kurt Wikstedt strongly stressed the international side of the acquisition:

> Now we enter Europe. We begin with Scandinavia. We try with Luxor to see if we can be successful in this business, and then continue with Europe. That is the strategy.

After many twists and turns, Nokia had entered the consumer electronics business and taken a serious step into the international market. The initial result of the acquisitions was that Nokia got 58 per cent of the shares in Salora and 51 per cent of the shares in Luxor. Later in 1984, Nokia increased its share to 70 per cent of the capital stock in Luxor. In 1983 the turnover for Luxor was FIM590 million and for Salora FIM737 million. The staff of Luxor was 1,500 and of Salora 1,700. All in all, Nokia now had 8,000 employees in its electronics businesses. Nokia's acquired market share in the TV sector was 36 per cent in the Finnish market and over 20 per cent in the Swedish market.

Exhibit 4 **Production of TV sets in Luxor**

1983	120,000
1984	184,000
1985	240,000
1987	380,000

THE INTEGRATION OF SALORA AND LUXOR

The new consumer electronics business was organised as a separate division in Nokia, partly because of the doubt over consumer electronics expressed by the head of the electronics division, Kurt Wikstedt. The president of Salora, Antti Lagerroos, was selected as the new president for consumer electronics (Salora–Luxor), and Kurt Wikstedt stayed as president for the remaining businesses in electronics, relabelled 'industrial electronics'.

The integration of Luxor and Salora was arduous, and made no real progress until the Swedish president of Luxor was forced to leave the company in May 1985. Besides the declining consumer electronics business, Luxor also had a successful personal computer division. Nokia closed this computer division, which of course aroused a lot of criticism. Several managers in Nokia were of the opinion that the co-ordination of activities in Salora and Luxor was not sufficient and that the potential synergy advantages had not been fully realised. In 1985 Salora–Luxor got a new president, Heikki Koskinen, when Antti Lagerroos was appointed director in charge of consumer electronics in the top management team of the Nokia Group. Koskinen was a spokesman for decentralisation and local autonomy. Salora and Luxor kept their own sales subsidiaries; only logistics and R&D were integrated. Still, the development of Salora–Luxor was very favourable and quite profitable in the mid-1980s. The production of TV sets in Luxor increased rapidly, although small (14-inch) TV sets represented almost 50 per cent of all production (see Exhibit 4).

In 1987, the Salora–Luxor TV brands had a market share of 35 per cent in the Nordic markets. In Finland the market share was about 45 per cent. According to Heikki Koskinen, Salora–Luxor was the only profitable significant consumer electronics producer in Europe in 1987. Gradually, Nokia increased its ownership share in both Luxor and Salora to 100 per cent. The aim of the continued integration was to arrange production in a more optimal way, and to utilise more effectively all the possibilities of synergy, including integrating production plants in a total product planning and production system, in order to decide more efficiently which products should be produced where and in what quantities.

NOKIA ENTERS MAJOR EUROPEAN MARKETS

In 1986, when the Luxor–Salora integration was considered to be under control, Nokia began to think of the future. Market share was already about 40 per cent in the Nordic markets, which implied that further expansion for Salora–Luxor in Scandinavia was not possible. An alternative growth and product brand strategy, to turn to western Europe, was decided during the strategic planning process in spring 1986. Heikki Koskinen explained the plans:

> We had plans to acquire two major brands in Europe, of which we intended to build a local net of brands. One of the brands was going to be more extensive to be sold in all European countries where Nokia was active in consumer electronics.

There were several reasons for entering the western European markets. It was thought to be important to be in the home markets of major competitors, in order to prevent them from dumping their products on Nokia's domestic markets. European co-operation might also prevent the Japanese and American firms taking over the European TV markets. The major European competitors Philips and Thompson started to co-operate within the Eureka framework (European Research Co-ordinating Agency)[2] in order to develop the European HDTV (high-definition TV) concept. This joint development was a threat to smaller European producers, which were afraid of not getting the key technology when needed. In order to become a partner in the development process of the HDTV concept, the opinion was that Nokia had to grow bigger.

At this time the situation in consumer electronics in Europe had also changed. Competition had become more intensive. Philips, the biggest TV manufacturer in Europe, with a market share of 25 per cent, acquired an American firm and began to think more globally. Thompson, the second biggest TV manufacturer in Europe, with a market share of 20 per cent, acquired two main competitors in the USA and England. Economies of scale through mass production were now considered as very important. The Salora and Luxor factories had a capacity of only 400,000 TV sets each. Nokia was number three in Europe, but still had only 5 per cent market share. The opinion within Nokia was that a volume of 2 million TV sets per year was needed to be competitive with both Philips and Thompson, and the Japanese and Korean competitors. In the late 1980s, the price competition became tougher in the European consumer electronics markets because of a more aggressive penetration from Far Eastern competitors. It was also

---

[2] Originally, the Eureka programme was launched to serve as a European complement to the Strategic Defense Initiative launched by the Reagan administration in the United States. Another reason was that previously launched European technology development programmes were considered too bureaucratic, too slow or too narrowly defined.

expected that the fixed R&D costs would rise, which implied that there was going to be a volume advantage regarding R&D too.

The Acquisition of Oceanic

Nokia's profitability in consumer electronics was good, especially in 1987, and it had passed Philips in market shares in all Nordic markets. In April 1987 the Nokia board of directors approved the strategic plan to acquire European TV brands. The plan was to acquire a French and a German brand, and a factory in either of these two countries. There were negotiations with different sellers, including the French company Oceanic which was for sale. Personal relationships between Nokia top management and the owner of Oceanic, the Swedish Electrolux Group, resulted in a rapid acquisition of Oceanic. Electrolux wanted to divest this business, which had no synergy with its core know-how. Through the acquisition of Oceanic, Nokia got inside the EC with the production of TV sets. Furthermore, Nokia acquired a significant market share in the French market, which was rather closed and difficult for an outsider to penetrate.

The pre-acquisition phase took less than three months and only four meetings were needed. Immediately after the acquisition, the integration process between Salora, Luxor and Oceanic was started. Oceanic had a turnover of 600 million FIM, mainly in colour TVs, and 800 employees. Oceanic's market share of consumer electronics in France was just below 10 per cent, with the Oceanic and Sonolor brands. The strategy was to keep the French production unit apart from the other factories because of differences in standards, while accounting systems, logistics and marketing should be integrated. The French local managers were trusted by the Finnish management and retained.

The next step in the conquest of European markets was to look for other brands. Nokia was interested in Thompson's German brands Saba, Nordwede and Telefunken. According to Heikki Koskinen, who headed the negotiations, an agreement was close for one of the brands, when the Standard Electric Lorenz possibility emerged.

Nokia Doubles its TV Production: The Acquisition of Standard Electric Lorenz

At this time, an internal struggle for power was going on between future candidates for the top position in the Nokia corporation. Top managers were traditionally recruited internally, and in 1985 a new manager for industrial electronics was appointed, Timo Koski, after close internal competition. He was seen as the probable next chief executive officer of Nokia. However, the earlier successful president of Salora, Antti Lagerroos, now heading the consumer electronics businesses in Nokia, had strong personal ambitions to advance to the very top of Nokia. This thirst for power became a driving force behind the next acquisition.

Parallel to Heikki Koskinen's negotiations with Thompson, Antti Lagerroos made the initial analysis that resulted in his suggestion to acquire a very big competitor, Standard Electric Lorenz (SEL) in the former West Germany. Lagerroos then used the freedom of action given to him by Kari Kairamo, and started to negotiate with SEL and its owners on his own, partly assisted by the director of technology in Nokia. Almost at the same time, Timo Koski acquired the whole personal computer and information systems business of the Ericsson Group in Sweden – an acquisition of the same size as SEL. Nokia became the largest information technology company in Scandinavia. Ericsson's large-scale production of terminal systems and established position in systems for commercial, industrial and banking sectors, together with Nokia's intelligent workstations and retail systems, were expected to enhance the Nokia Group's competitiveness in the information technology sector. The significantly enlarged division led by Timo Koski was named Nokia Data. Both Antti Lagerroos and Timo Koski had now extended their internal domains significantly in the struggle for further power in Nokia. However, in 1987 Timo Koski suddenly died of a heart attack.

The acquisition of SEL from the US conglomerate ITT was made early in 1988, just a couple of months after the Oceanic acquisition. The production capacity increased from 1 million TV sets annually to almost 2.5 million. The chief executive officer, Kari Kairamo, attached great importance to this acquisition. The opinion was that SEL completed Nokia's consumer electronics business both technically and regionally. SEL was ahead of Nokia in digital TV technology. And regionally Nokia now became strong not only in France, but also in German-speaking Europe (15 per cent market share) and even in southern Europe as SEL exported to Italy, France, Spain and Portugal. The net sales of SEL were FIM4.9 billion in 1988, with an annual production of 1.2 million colour TVs, 1.7 million picture tubes and 350,000 video recorders. The main production facilities for SEL's colour TV sets and video recorders were located near Bochum in the Ruhr region. The picture tube factory was located near Stuttgart, and the loudspeaker factory was in Bavaria. SEL also had four other smaller production facilities in West Germany. The SEL acquisition included assembly plants in Spain and Portugal as well, and shares in joint ventures in Hungary, Malaysia and Italy.

With the incorporation of SEL, Nokia's position as Europe's third largest colour TV manufacturer was strengthened. Nokia was now the ninth largest colour TV manufacturer in the world, and the market share in Europe was estimated to be about 15 per cent, with the new brand names ITT, Schaub–Lorenz and Graetz.

In 1992 Nokia acquired the only remaining Finnish competitor, Finlux, which was in good shape and profitable. The production capacity of Finlux was just over 200,000 TV sets. The turnover was about FIM600 million and the personnel 770.

POST-ACQUISITION INTEGRATION BECOMES PROBLEMATIC

In January 1988, Simo Vuorilehto, the chief operations officer of Nokia, was of the opinion that all Nokia's consumer electronics units should be consolidated within a wholly new division with its headquarters in Continental Europe. Significant investments in upgrading and modernisation of production technology and logistics were needed in the new division that was formed, which was named Nokia Consumer Electronics. The integration and co-ordination of Salora–Luxor, Oceanic and SEL started in February 1988 with the appointment of an integration group led by Antti Lagerroos. The group was working hard during spring 1988 with the aim of integrating administration and production in all four acquired consumer electronic units, a total of ten factories, within six months. The purpose was to be able to present an integrated structure for the new division in the summer of 1988. But the timetable could not be met entirely.

The chief executive officer, Kari Kairamo, was worried that Nokia did not have enough internationally experienced personnel, and believed that many new managers were needed, especially in the consumer electronics business. This opinion was further strengthened by some analysis carried out by external consultants in early 1988. Furthermore, Antti Lagerroos could not implement the necessary changes fast enough and lost Kari Kairamo's confidence to lead Nokia Consumer Electronics into Europe. Instead, he was appointed president of Nokia's Mobile Phones (previously Mobira). He soon wanted to merge Nokia Consumer Electronics and Nokia Mobile Phones, but did not get any support for that. Antti Lagerroos eventually left the Nokia Group in February 1990.

In June 1988 a new president, Jacques Noels, was appointed for Nokia Consumer Electronics. Head hunters found him in France at Thompson – one of Nokia's large competitors in consumer electronics. Before that he had been working for many years in European units of large US companies in the electronics industry. Jacques Noels had to start to organise the consumer electronics division from scratch, and at least half a year of integration was totally lost. Furthermore, ten senior managers in SEL had left the company. Initially, Noels rented an office in Paris for three months and brought his secretary with him from Thompson. The first task was to build a new management team with the right mixture of competence. A new head office for Nokia Consumer Electronics was established in Geneva (regarded as 'neutral ground') in order to facilitate further recruitment and the establishment of a truly international division.

In 1989, Jacques Noels presented a new organisation structure for Nokia Consumer Electronics, more than one year after the latest acquisition. During that time Nokia's market share of TV sets had declined from 14 to 11 per cent in the European markets. Not only the consumer electronics business but the whole group showed weak results. The relations between the chairman of the Nokia board and the chief executive officer, Kari

Kairamo, became more and more strained. The external directors were expected to suggest some changes in the top management structure of Nokia. In this situation, Kari Kairamo suddenly died (suicide, according to the media) in December 1989.

After Kari Kairamo's tragic death, Simo Vuorilehto became the new chief executive officer. According to him, the key factors in the consumer electronics strategy were marketing, design and production:

> We are not at all the kind of company that could develop semiconductors or picture tubes in the future. But we can be competitive and ahead of other competitors in marketing, design and production. In production we perhaps cannot be superior to our competitors, but we can at least be at the same level. We cannot develop everything ourselves, which was a mistake in the first integration plans.

Heikki Koskinen, responsible for strategic planning in Jacques Noels' new management team, emphasised similar competitive advantages of Nokia Consumer Electronics:

> Our strength is in rapid application of new technology. When technologies shift you have to forecast the trends and minimise the investment costs. Our competitive advantage is in the brain of the engineers. That is especially true in application issues.

He had never fully understood the volume thinking behind the acquisition of SEL:

> The only advantage you reach by large-scale production is that you can control the material costs. On the other hand, you have less flexibility and you have to be global. In 1987 we manufactured 900,000 TV sets in Salora–Luxor, and we were very profitable. In Europe there are other profitable but small companies. It is a question of the overall strategy. A small company making half a million TV sets can be profitable. That firm has to co-operate with manufacturers of components and in that way reduce the cost for necessary R&D activities. With small R&D costs, a clear market focus and a strong product range there are good possibilities to be successful.

The manager in charge of export sales also held the opinion that too much emphasis had been put on production costs:

> I cannot understand that acquisitions are made based on production advantages. In our acquisitions there were no synergies between the brands. When you combine factories and brands you take away a large part of the turnover. I am astonished that Nokia had not made clear the future brand policy before the acquisitions. That was the greatest problem.

Jacques Noels' strategy was to become big in some niches, not in the whole market. Nokia should concentrate in high-quality and high-technology TV sets, with good profit margins. According to him, the market share of the total market was therefore not as important. Still, the most profitable markets were the Nordic ones, with a total demand of 1.5 million TV sets, and in these markets Nokia was strong.

Exhibit 5 **Turnover in the production units of Nokia Consumer Electronics, 1988**

PRODUCTION UNIT	TURNOVER (IN MILLIONS OF FIM)
Germany	3,000
Finland, Salora	1,500
Sweden, Luxor	900
France, Oceanic	500
Portugal, Ibervisao	100

Jacques Noels saw Nokia's portfolio of different electronics businesses as a future strength. The group had telecommunication, mobile phones, information systems, computers and consumer electronics, and more and more synergies were expected to emerge between these different business areas. The border between professional and consumer electronics was expected to disappear. According to Jacques Noels, Nokia already had a strong technological capacity and good management resources. But he saw some disadvantages compared with the main competitors:

> I think they have a different position, because they have very strong brands. Telefunken is a much stronger brand than, for example, Graetz [an SEL brand]. They have also much stronger corporate brands, e.g. Philips compared to Nokia. Their strategy can be very different; they can let almost every brand have its own life. Grundig can have its own strategy, nobody has to know that it is owned by Philips. But at the same time Philips is not putting the same efforts in Grundig as in the Philips brand. Their positioning is very different from ours.

The magnitude of the integration task is illustrated by Exhibit 5, which shows the turnover of the acquired Nokia Consumer Electronics units in five European countries. A FIM6,000 million division had to be integrated. In order to integrate the acquisitions, Jacques Noels had two possibilities. The first was to continue as before and integrate the different units over a long period. The second was to try to merge the different units into one organisation more rapidly. The latter alternative was chosen despite the fact that the president thought that, in the short run, this approach would lead to bigger difficulties because the units were used to working on their own. In the long term, after a few hard years of integration, the profits were expected to be considerable.

A New Organisation Structure and Culture

Jacques Noels wanted strong functional centralisation and stressed the importance of a competent and powerful management team. This was the first priority because the management team was seen as the motor of the organisation. But it took time to put together the new team. Both old and new managers were tested by external consultants. Eventually, about 35 people were working at the head office in Geneva. All decisions concerning production, R&D and marketing were made there. Finance and strategic planning were centralised as well. All acquired companies became pure production plants, separated from the sales and marketing activities, but with some R&D activities decentralised to these plants.

Jacques Noels especially emphasised the connection and co-operation between R&D and marketing:

> We have regrouped the marketing and R&D centres so that the head of marketing and the head of R&D work side by side in Geneva, because we believe that they have to work closely together on new models. Production is only how to manufacture as cheap as possible, when the products have been developed.

He highlighted the cultural difficulties in integrating the different units and nationalities. A new integrated culture for Nokia Consumer Electronics needed to be built on new management principles, but it had to emerge over several years. The tools for cultural integration were an international management group, circulation of leaders between countries, and a 'Euro-manager' programme. Young and recently employed graduates from all countries involved were taken into this Euro-manager programme, developed in 1989–90. The creation of this new pan-European culture was planned to continue after 1990 for another three to five years. But Jacques Noels did not have an easy task in seeking to create a 'Europeanised' business unit out of Nokia Consumer Electronics:

> If you make two major acquisitions in three months, you get many problems regarding product strategy; sales channels; general management, etc. There is nothing that works by itself. You have to struggle and that is what we did. First we worked out a product strategy in order to concentrate our R&D efforts. Then, from the middle of 1989, we put a lot of efforts in new brand, sales and marketing policies.

Marketing and Production Strategies Within Nokia Consumer Electronics

In 1989 Nokia Consumer Electronics launched a universal brand, ITT–Nokia, that would be positioned as a middle-range product. The ITT–Nokia brand would then be combined with one or two other and more local Nokia brands in each local market, including a 'high-end' brand representing higher quality and/or more exclusive design. For the integration of product development and manufacturing, a 'Euro-line-concept' was launched. Nokia Consumer Electronics reduced the number of chassis from 25 to 10, and the goal was to come down to three or four product chassis. All R&D centres were supporting this product concept, but it was modified in accordance with the country and the brand characteristics. The different centres were concentrated on different levels in the product range, from low-end to high-end chassis.

The marketing strategy was to be achieved through an integrated sales, product and distribution strategy. Marketing of the brands was the most important part. All acquired brands were local brands, and Nokia as a brand was unknown within the distribution channels. The problem after the acquisition of SEL was to convince the distribution channels that the brand ITT–Nokia had a future. The solution was to combine the innovation image of ITT and resource image of Nokia[3] in this new brand ITT–Nokia, with the intention of later dropping ITT. There were many discussions and different opinions about the wisdom of using the Nokia name. Many managers were sceptical about the possibilities of transferring the ITT image to the Nokia name. However, ITT–Nokia was introduced as the pan-European brand in the medium range; a modern brand with modern technology, which was going to compete with Philips. Salora was marketed as high-range brand, while the other brands were used as local brands. Jacques Noels stated:

> Our strategy is to have three brands per country. The major brand, in the beginning, has to be the established local brand. But this is short term. Gradually we are introducing Nokia as the major European brand. But we want to do that gradually, not brutally. In all countries we are also supporting the original brand. That is why we support Luxor in Sweden, Salora in Finland, ITT–Nokia in Germany and Oceanic in France, and then gradually introduce Nokia as a complementary brand.
>
> A brand strategy with three brands means three different channels. The specialised independent retailers are very important. They want to have their local brands. Then we have the large specialised channels that are only selling electronics. Finally we have the supermarkets, big stores, they want to have one brand, one styling, easy to recognise.

Some managers were critical of using acquisition as a means of growth and also sceptical of the possibility of transferring the image of one brand to another. The brand Salora had a quite good image. Investigations by Nokia showed that Salora had some recognition in England, Italy, France, Netherlands, Belgium, Austria and Switzerland, and much more recognition than the new brand Nokia.

Finally, Jacques Noels distinguished between three different production strategies:

> Today we have two or three complementary strategies. One is volume; it is clear that the volume in TV assembling is important. We are working with that in Germany, where our Bochum plant is one of the largest in Europe; one million TV sets. The second strategy is to specialise, when a plant only produces one product and we can extend that product line. We are doing that in Salo where we are producing our high-end chassis. In Luxor we are producing all our

[3] The Nokia Group had a very strong financial position in 1987. The use of Nokia as a brand name indicated that the top management of the group was serious about the business and also acted as a signal to the distribution channels.

> decoders and satellites, and there we also have the technical expertise for these products. In those products the technical expertise is what makes the cost, not so much the production volume, but also how well and quickly we can introduce our products. We have a factory in Portugal, where labour cost is an important factor. We are trying to rationalise our production by stage of the product life, labour cost, volume and engineering. Those are the four criteria and they give different answers for different products.

THE DIVESTMENT OF CONSUMER ELECTRONICS

However, the integration of the units in Nokia Consumer Electronics proved to be much more difficult than expected and the profitability much lower than predicted. The development of Nokia Consumer Electronics was problematic after the acquisition of SEL. In 1990, the director of corporate finance, Jorma Ollila, described the German acquisition as a big disappointment. The chief executive officer, Simo Vuorilehto, stressed the importance of a new strategy so that the company could take control of the situation. The first step in this turnround of Nokia Consumer Electronics was to close down both the Oceanic plant in France and the plant in Portugal.

A New Chief Executive Officer makes Radical Changes

Simo Vuorilehto (chief executive officer) and Kalle Isokallio (chief operations officer) did not agree on many issues and did not work well together. Competing proposals were often brought to the board. Early in 1992 the board of the Nokia Group made the radical decision to replace both men. Simo Vuorilehto retired earlier than originally planned and Kalle Isokallio was asked to look for a new job externally.

Jorma Ollila became the new chief executive officer for Nokia in 1992, after two very successful years as the president of Nokia Mobile Phones. He started to reconstruct the group immediately. Only two weeks after Ollila's arrival, Jacques Noels had to leave Nokia Consumer Electronics. The group controller of Nokia, Hannu Bergholm, was appointed the new president for Consumer Electronics and Heikki Koskinen re-entered the top management team of Consumer Electronics after having left the Noels team in 1990. Later in 1992, production of TV sets in Sweden at the Luxor plant was ceased. All production of TV sets was concentrated on Bochum in Germany and Turku in Finland (at the recently acquired Finlux plant). The aim was to decrease the costs of logistics and to make production more efficient in the remaining two plants.

The basic goals for the Nokia Group in 1992 were still the same as two decades previously: that is, growth through products with growth potential and internationalisation. But there were additions. Central values were formulated in a slogan, 'the Nokia way'. The values common to all businesses were customer satisfaction, respect for the individual, achievement and continuous learning. New key words were telecommunications, global, focus and value added. It was decided that telecommunications (including mobile phones) should be the future core business area. Jorma Ollila stated in the annual report of 1992 that the fastest growth, the most productive investments and the best results were in Nokia's telecommunication sector. Europe remained Nokia's largest market, but growth was concentrated outside Europe: in North America and the Far East. The strategic focus on telecommunications was confirmed in a statement by the board of directors:

> Nokia's strategy is to invest in telecommunications and closely associated business operations. It focuses on industry segments and geographic regions that have good opportunities for growth and profitability.

But what was to be done with the still unprofitable Nokia Consumer Electronics? One internally discussed possibility was to develop an alliance with another company in the industry. A corporate analyst at Morgan Stanley in London was of the same opinion: 'Nokia has to co-operate with another European or a Japanese firm in order to be competitive.' However, the Nokia Group acted more radically. A decision was made to concentrate more and more on telecommunications. Digital signal processing became the key concept in most of Nokia's operations and in the group's future strategy. This direction was further strengthened in 1993 when part of the cables and machinery businesses was divested. Telecommunications increased its share of net sales to 52 per cent. By this time Nokia had become a global leader in the manufacture and supply of telecommunication systems and mobile phones.

The divestments continued. In 1995 Nokia divested all its remaining tyres and cable businesses. Finally, in February 1996 Nokia announced its total withdrawal from the consumer electronics business and its main product, colour TV sets. In April 1996 Nokia made a provision of FIM 2,000 million in order to close the consumer electronics plants in Germany. The only TV plant left after that was the Finnish Finlux. But in June 1996 Nokia announced that the Hong Kong-based group Semi-Tech Ltd had acquired the remaining TV business. After these moves Nokia has almost 100 per cent of its operations in the telecommunications and mobile phones industry. Jorma Ollila stressed in the annual report:

> This is an important milestone since we shall now have the structure in place to concentrate on the growth segments of the telecommunications industry, thereby improving our shareholder return. This strategy has already helped us to grow faster than the overall market during the past few years. With operations in 120 countries, manufacturing on four continents and with improved brand-recognition worldwide, we are now a truly global player.

The internally much debated journey of Nokia into consumer electronics had come to an end.

APPENDIX 1

Turnover and personnel of the Nokia Group, 1990–5

	TURNOVER (FIM MILLIONS)	PERSONNEL
1990	22,130	37,336
1991	15,500	29,100
1992	18,168	26,700
1993	23,697	25,800
1994	30,177	28,000
1995	36,810	31,900

Net sales as a percentage of total sales and number of personnel in each business group, 1991–5

	1991		1992		1993		1994		1995	
	%	No.	%	No.	%	No.	%	No.	%	No.
CE	33	10,854	31	9,386	29	8,268	22	6,611	29	9,937
CM	20	7,766	25	6,307	20	5,070	16	4,560		
MP	12	3,545	20	3,164	26	4,223	35	7,554	44	11,821
NT	16	4,474	17	5,219	19	6,365	22	8,082	28	11,297
OO	9	1,874	7	1,606	6	1,597	5	1,786	1	729

CE = Nokia Consumer Electronics
MP = Nokia Mobile Phones
NT = Nokia Telecommunications
CM = Cables and Machinery
OO = Other Operations

Net sales by market area of the Nokia Group (%)

	1990	1991	1992	1993
1. Scandinavia	45	38	32	25
2. Other western European countries	39	44	44	47
3. Other countries	16	18	24	28

	1994	1995
1. Finland	11	9
2. Other EU countries	50	48
3. Other European countries	9	8
4. Other countries	30	35

APPENDIX 2

Nokia 1992–5 according to International Accounting Standards (IAS)

	1992	1993	1994	1995
Profit and loss account (in millions of FIM)				
Net sales	18,168	23,697	30,177	36,810
Cost of sales	(17,880)	(22,232)	(20,808)	(25,518)
Operating profits	288	1,465	3,596	5,012
Share of results of associated companies	(5)	28	22	85
Net interest and other financial expenses	(441)	(347)	384	(164)
Profit before tax and minority interests	(158)	1,146	4,933	4,002
Tax	(167)	(299)	(932)	(769)
Minority interests	(88)	(80)	(75)	(77)
Profit before extraordinary items	(413)	767	2,995	2,232
Extraordinary items	(310)	(1,917)	944	—
Net profit	(723)	(1,159)	3,939	2,232
Balance sheet items (in millions of FIM)				
Fixed assets and other non-current assets	7,630	7,930	7,943	9,047
Current assets	13,608	14,653	19,906	23,714
Inventories and work in progress	3,840	5,129	6,803	9,982
Accounts receivable and pre-paid expenses	6,650	6,227	7,835	9,518
Liquid funds	3,118	3,297	5,268	4,214
Current liabilities	10,111	11,520	11,319	15,955
Accounts payable and accrued liabilities	4,314	5,976	8,086	9,388
Restructuring provision	342	1,436	—	1,652
Advance payments	399	534	502	396
Current portion of long-term loans	1,221	139	278	187
Bank overdrafts and short-term loans	3,835	3,435	2,453	4,332
Net current assets	3,497	3,133	19,906	23,714
Shareholders' funds	6,727	6,511	12,418	13,806
Minority shareholders' interests	695	536	555	422
Long-term liabilities	3,705	4,080	3,557	2,578
Long-term loans	3,124	3,397	3,071	2,121
Other long-term liabilities	581	683	486	457
Total assets	21,238	22,647	27,849	32,761
Key ratios				
Earnings per share (FIM)	neg.	13.7	10.97	14.36
Dividend per share (FIM)	2.00	3.2	2.50	3.00
Shareholders' fund per share	113		43.65	48.55
Return on capital employed (%)	5.9	12.5	25.4	29.1
Return on shareholders' funds (%)	neg.	12.4	31.6	31.2

APPENDIX 3 KEY MANAGERS: APPROXIMATE PERIODS AT TOP POSITIONS

Kari Kairamo	Chief executive officer	1976–88
Simo Vuorilehto	Chief operations officer	1986–8
	Chief executive officer	1989–91
Kalle Isokallio	President of Cable Machinery	1983–5
	Head of Nokia Information Systems	1986–7
	President of Nokia Data	1988–9
	Chief operations officer	1990–1
Jorma Ollila	Corporate finance	1986–9
	President of Mobile Phones	1986–9
	Chief executive officer	1992–
Kurt Wikstedt	Head of professional electronics (industrial electronics)	–1986
Antti Lagerroos	President of Salora	1982–3
	President of Salora–Luxor	1984
	Executive board member (in charge of consumer electronics)	1985–8
	President of Mobile Phones	1989
Heikki Koskinen	President of Salora–Luxor	1985–7
	Nokia Consumer Electronics, strategic planning	1988–9
	Technology manager in Nokia	1990–1
	General manager, Nokia Consumer Electronics	1992
	Head Office positions	1993–6
Timo Koski	President of Nokia Data	1985–7
Jacques Noels	President of Nokia Consumer Electronics	1988–91
Hannu Bergholm	Controller of Nokia	1987–91
	President of Nokia Consumer Electronics	1992–5

BORD GÁIS EIREANN

Eleanor Doyle and Frederic Adam

Bord Gáis Eireann is a semi-state body in Ireland responsible for providing natural gas services for domestic, industrial and commercial purposes. The company's monopoly status as a gas provider ended in 1996, following the Irish government's application of the European Union directive. Top management at BGE recognised that success in the future lay in the organisation's ability to become more competitive and more customer-oriented. The case study focuses on the implications of this new strategy and the role of the information technology department of BGE in re-engineering the organisation's activities to meet this overall aim.

> It is fair to say that these are very exciting and dynamic times for the natural gas industry, not just for Ireland, but for Europe as a whole.
>
> EMMET STAGG, IRISH MINISTER OF STATE FOR TRANSPORT, ENERGY AND COMMUNICATIONS

• • •

Bord Gáis Eireann (BGE) was a state-owned body responsible for providing natural gas services in Ireland for domestic, industrial and commercial purposes. Its turnover for 1996 (at IR£271m) was 14 per cent higher than in 1995 and pre-tax profits of IR£82m represented a 22 per cent increase on 1995. Sales rose by 13 per cent, compared with the 1995 volume, owing largely to increased residential sales, which enjoyed sustained growth of 88 per cent between 1991 and 1996. Ongoing extension of the pipeline network meant that by 1996 some 285,000 homes were BGE customers.

> These figures tell a story of a vibrant energy company, competing with alternative fuels in an increasingly competitive market and creating a growing demand for its product.
>
> M.N. CONLON, CHAIRMAN

This case study was prepared by E. Doyle and F. Adam, University College Cork. It is intended as a basis for class discussion and not as an illustration of either good or bad management practice.

Such enthusiasm by the chairman was justified by the prospect of further development in the Irish gas network; however, deregulation of the Irish gas market was set to open the door to 'gas-to-gas' competition. As long as BGE enjoyed a monopoly on the distribution of gas in Ireland it faced competition only from other fuels, but following the EU directive dealing with third party access (TPA) in Europe, BGE had to persuade customers not only that gas was the best fuel to use but also that they should purchase it from BGE.

BGE faced the prospect of major changes in the nature of its traditionally captive national market and was forced to deal with competition in almost 80 per cent of its market. Up to 1996, BGE was purely a utility company responsible for developing an infrastructure of pipelines in Ireland and distributing the gas supplied by a single supplier Marathon. According to one senior manager at BGE, this monopolistic situation had meant that 'BGE was essentially an engineering company' where managers perceived that the main purpose of the company was to extend and maintain the gas distribution architecture of the country as opposed to any other, more customer-oriented activity.

GOODBYE MONOPOLY

BGE's monopoly position ceased, slowly but surely, following the application by the Irish government of the EU directive dealing with third party access (TPA) in Europe. The Energy Act 1995 meant that certain categories of customers could buy their gas abroad and import it through the Bord Gáis Interconnector: BGE's major corporate customers (representing 30 per cent of turnover) could purchase their supplies abroad. Other suppliers would be able to sell their gas to any customer in Ireland by paying a transportation fee in order to purchase capacity on the BGE infrastructure. To deal with its changing competitive environment, BGE decided to develop a separate branch of activity to serve customers who wanted only to buy capacity but not gas from BGE. This required the creation of 'Chinese walls' in order to prevent sensitive customer information passing between the transportation and the trading sections of the company. It was suggested that this should be achieved under the watchful eye of an independent regulator to ensure that there was no sharing of information between the sales departments of the two separate activities.

Top management at BGE recognised that the only guarantee for continuous success lay in its ability to become more competitive and to turn its focus from technology towards customers, requiring the elaboration and implementation of a new strategy for the organisation with major implications for all functional areas. One area compelled to radically rethink its role within the overall structure was the Information Systems department which had to proactively plan for the systems and services required to successfully deal with 'new' Bord Gáis Eireann.

TRANSFORMING BORD GÁIS THROUGH INFORMATION TECHNOLOGY

As part of its customer-orientation strategy, BGE set about altering the structure that had consisted of a number of regional offices in each of which all functional areas were replicated. This situation was the product of the evolution of BGE over the past twenty years whereby separate local companies had been purchased and integrated into one single organisation with its headquarters based in Cork under the name BGE. Up to 1997, regional offices had maintained their original procedures and processes which resulted in customers in different locations receiving a different service. More importantly, this resulted in the management information relayed to headquarters being different, depending on its provenance. Thus, the transformation involved a move towards the standardisation of procedures and processes to turn BGE into a truly national organisation. This move was paralleled by another change from a focus on functional areas to a focus on processes, e.g. customers would deal with only one process manager, the sales manager, who would distribute the work required in dealing with the customer towards the relevant functions. Once the company had identified the key processes required to provide a quality service to its customers, internal staff restructuring was initiated to ensure the success of the customer focus strategy.

Naturally, information technologies (IT) and the information systems (IS) departments were instrumental in accomplishing such a move by linking all offices to the same network and providing an organisation-wide set of computer applications. Through the computerisation of the revised processes, standardisation occurred naturally. In addition, the standardisation of the reporting of the regional offices increased the visibility to top managers of the performance of all units, and an executive information system was intended to support the implementation of a 'performance management culture'.

According to the chief information officer (CIO), IT had to enable, support and facilitate change by proactively redesigning information systems as required by the re-engineering of key business processes. For the first time, an analysis of the role of information systems was carried out at the level of the overall corporation as opposed to within functional areas or within regional offices. A new information infrastructure was required to support the emerging two-way information flows between headquarters and regional agencies:

- Top management at headquarters needed reliable information channels and procedures in order to disseminate the new strategy.
- Reporting mechanisms needed to be standardised to improve the monitoring of the company's progress to provide top management at headquarters with seamless access to feedback from the market and to local managers themselves.

Failure to implement such an information infrastructure could have meant that potential gains from the structural changes would be diminished.

A range of processes were created or altered in implementing the strategy, in particular, those that provided services to BGE's customers (as emphasised in BGE's customer care charter). For example, as BGE attempted to become a customer-focused organisation, its transaction processing systems needed to cater for both existing and new services. These included a comprehensive national integrated telephone network to handle customer complaints and a gas-card metering system providing an easy payment option for householders who preferred to budget for fuel on a weekly basis. Another aspect of the strategy was the introduction of a customer package which consisted of free connection and a single, highly competitive gas price, especially attractive to low volume users.

The success of the strategy also required close monitoring, which was achieved through the instigation of customer satisfaction ratings that measured progress made and identified where future improvements might be made, while also highlighting those areas of business that required further attention. Better management and organisation of the data contained in the transaction processing systems made it possible for managers to learn much more about their customers and their needs – vital for an organisation whose mission is to provide 'excellent value to customers'. The exploitation of this invaluable source of information was envisaged through the hiring of a business analyst charged specifically with meeting management information needs and managing BGE's information resource.

MANAGERIAL MECHANISMS AT BGE

The main managerial mechanism at Bord Gáis revolved around the management committee (see Exhibit 1) which met three times a month for at least half a day, plus some special *ad hoc* meetings. This committee was chaired by the chief executive officer and it was customary that all top managers would attend although deputies were called in to report on special issues where technical or other types of expertise was required.

Typically, heads of functions prepared reports on their respective areas and presented them in session to the entire group. Questions were asked and answered on the spot or noted in the minutes to be addressed in a following meeting once information had been prepared. These minutes were the central document guiding the tactical efforts of the firm, and to reflect this importance they were prepared with great care and classified under a number of headings such as 'Action point', 'Report', 'Opinions'. The set of minutes arising from one meeting was used to structure the next, for which an agenda was prepared and circulated in advance. The organisational effort was thus steered in certain directions and the attention of top managers was focused on the items listed for the next meeting.

As in any commercial company, board members had a supervisory role in the adoption of the strategic orientation of the organisation. Board

Exhibit 1 **Formal managerial structure at Bord Gáis Eireann, 1996**

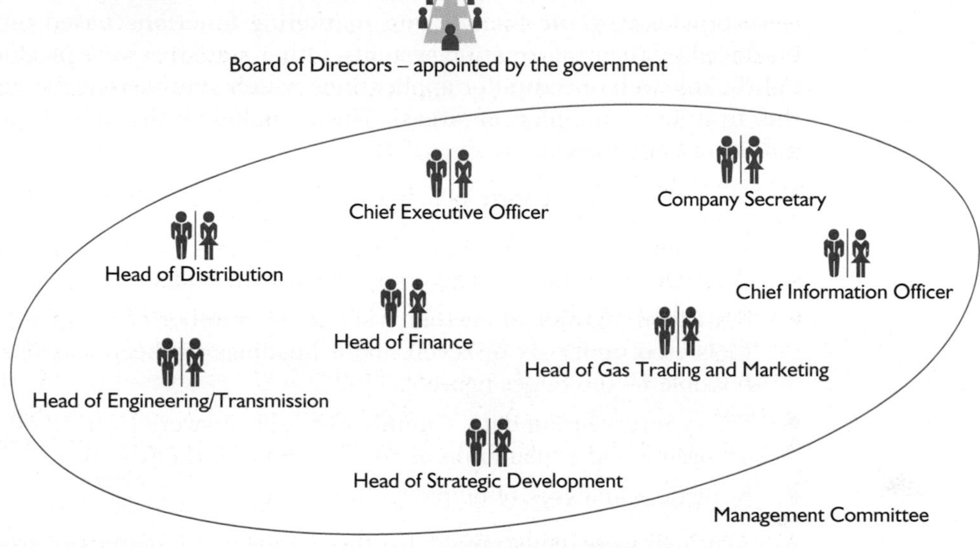

members were not normally full time in their capacity, but the chairman revealed that he worked in BGE's headquarters at least three days per week. This can be explained by the frequency of meetings involving board members. Full meetings took place once a month and were the occasion to monitor critical indicators; but other board committees existed such as the audit committee (that dealt with supervision of the quarterly accounts), the human resources committee (that considered managerial structure, ethics and organisational culture) and the strategic planning committee.

According to the chairman, the role of the board was not just hands-on, but also included 'setting the tone'. In the list of tasks that the board carried out, he ranked the adoption of the long-term strategy first, followed by setting the tone, the elaboration of the budget, the monitoring of business targets and finally, the proper implementation of decisions. Thus, setting the tone was an important matter which 'nobody else can or will do in an organisation'. Contacts were much more frequent than the twice yearly full meetings that were required by the statutes of BGE and there was a certain level of co-operation between the board and the management committee outside the reporting/monitoring relationship that the monthly reviews revealed.

Monthly special review meetings were held to monitor the performance of the various areas during the period elapsed. Each head of function had to be able to explain the performance of his or her area based on monthly accounting statements (balance sheet and profit and loss account) set against the budget for this period and the same period of the previous year and, more specifically, against the backdrop of key indicators which had been identified through experience over the years. Variances were noted and explanations were proposed to account for them. These financial data were provided by the finance and marketing functions based on reports produced by their information systems. Other statistics were produced by a tightly knit web of computer applications which synthesised the activity of the firm in a number of areas. These included the following closely monitored analyses:

- Statistical sales reports per division on the five main markets.
- Evolution of the number of customers.
- Weather analysis report in comparison with budget.[1]
- Statistical analysis of customer service – number of complaints registered under six or seven major headings (to keep as close as possible to the target figures).
- Safety intervention data – number of calls answered within 60 minutes of logging and explanation as to why some of them were not.[2]
- Statistical analyses of employee turnover.

As meetings were constrained by time, individual managers were often required to take the reports away to study them in detail to enable the group to keep abreast of the latest progress.

As noted by the finance director, the functional areas of BGE were relatively independent and they operated from different budgets for which they were accountable. They had control of the costs in their areas and were responsible for the monitoring of their variances. The departments could, therefore, be viewed as the responsibility centres of BGE and each head of department was aware of the basis for evaluation of the performance of his or her area. Some interdependencies did exist, though, as overall sales depended upon the public perception of gas as a resource, which could only be changed through corporate advertising (which has developed significantly over recent years, promoting gas as a user-friendly, cheap and low maintenance resource). Increasing customer numbers depended upon the extension of the network of pipelines delivering the gas to new areas of the country, which was the responsibility of the engineers. This gave rise to the often-used phrase 'no pipes no sales' to which marketing staff routinely referred in order to explain below-target performance. At the centre of this conventional architecture of interdependencies, the finance department would arbitrate the discussions between the different departments, flagging when budgets were overspent or when expected returns failed to materialise.

---

[1] Weather reports were strongly correlated to the consumption of gas of BGE's customers. Thus, they were useful in explaining some of the variances between actual and budget figures.

[2] Public safety was always a critical topic. Explanations had to be given when delays occurred in answering calls involving suspected gas leaks. Increased traffic in Dublin aggravated this problem.

In addition, special studies and projects were carried out by the top managers in the management committee. These projects normally fell neatly within the individual areas, but a proportion of them involved more than one manager, in which case the managers involved arranged a special meeting to plan and co-ordinate their efforts. Ultimately, all reports were submitted to the management committee.

THE SIGNIFICANCE OF IT IN TRANSFORMING BGE

Following the restructuring of the IT functions, the IS department was led by a chief information officer (CIO) who reported directly to the CEO and participated in the management committee. Before the restructuring, the IS department had been headed by an IS manager reporting to the head of finance. The intention was to transform the IS department from a reactive service department in charge of developing and maintaining the IT infrastructure into a department engaged in proactively developing and implementing the systems required to accomplish BGE's metamorphosis. This modification was the only major change initially envisaged at senior executive level at BGE and the overall structure of the company is represented in Exhibit 1. The structure was, however, likely to evolve further as the reports of consultants who had examined the organisation in 1996 awaited compilation into a detailed future plan by the head of strategic developments (see Exhibit 1).

The increased pressure on the IS department to enable the change process had led to considerable analysis of the role and missions of the department and the interaction between it and its users. The focus of attention on the IS department was justified by its size – 22 full-time staff plus a number of contract developers (or approximately 5 per cent of the total workforce) – and the importance of its contribution to BGE as the service department for a user population of 450 PC users and an even larger minicomputer user population (2 DEC alpha on a wide area network) largely dependent on electronic mail for its communication. The sizeable IT budget of several million Irish pounds indicated the significance of the IT effort at BGE.

The favoured solution to accomplish the change from IT as a service department to a more proactive contributory function involved the addition of one level to the reporting structure of the department, and job descriptions were rewritten to achieve better defined and broader individual responsibilities. The extensive departmental redesign required significant negotiations with the trades unions. The goals of the changes were obvious: to create an environment where responsibilities, objectives, targets and critical success factors were clearer at both individual and department levels. An overall increase in the flexibility of the department was also sought.

Despite the additional hierarchical level, it was planned that reporting lines would become simpler within the department. Every member would report directly to either the technical systems manager, the project manager or the support manager. In turn, these three managers would report directly to the CIO allowing for a faster transmission of information and requests. The creation of the position of business analyst (at project leader level) was aimed at developing within IT the ability to deal with and investigate the information needs of executives. As noted by the CIO, these types of needs had not been addressed specifically and they were best dealt with separately, especially in the context of the new strategy. Another related function of the analyst consisted of developing an awareness and a sufficient knowledge of all the systems used in BGE to become the 'information expert' of the organisation. This was regarded as paving the way for the development of a data warehousing project which would involve the creation of a central database with highly flexible data retrieval mechanisms, the aim of which is to integrate all the information available in the organisation so that it can be accessed and used by all staff. Such an information 'warehouse' would serve to support the proactive IT plan and to provide the centralised storage and retrieval infrastructure required to enable the move to a more market-oriented and customer-oriented approach.

PRIORITISATION OF IT DEVELOPMENTS

The CIO wanted to share the responsibility of prioritising and allocating resources to IT projects with the functional areas as opposed to trying to evaluate their merit solely from an IT perspective. This was attempted through the development of a two-level structure based on an IT steering committee and a number of 'manager IT groups' as shown in Exhibit 2. This revolution in the way IT expenditure was prioritised was also reflected in the fact that IT projects would be assessed on the same basis as any other investment project. It involved the introduction of the notion of *contribution* for evaluating IT projects, mostly in the form of cost–benefit analysis. Thus, systems would have to show their potential for reducing costs, increasing turnover and/or improving the quality of service. In effect, a new kind of competition was introduced whereby IT projects were measured against non-IT projects and a business case was to be made for them as opposed to a solely technical case.

The emergent committee structure was a cross-functional group from the user and manager population reflecting the various systems and information problems that the organisation had to address. The steering committee was made up of all function heads, including the CEO who would also act as chairman. Under this restructuring, the manager IT groups consisted of four to seven members from different departments and the IT project manager who was a member of all groups. For example, the

Exhibit 2 **Manager IT committee structure**

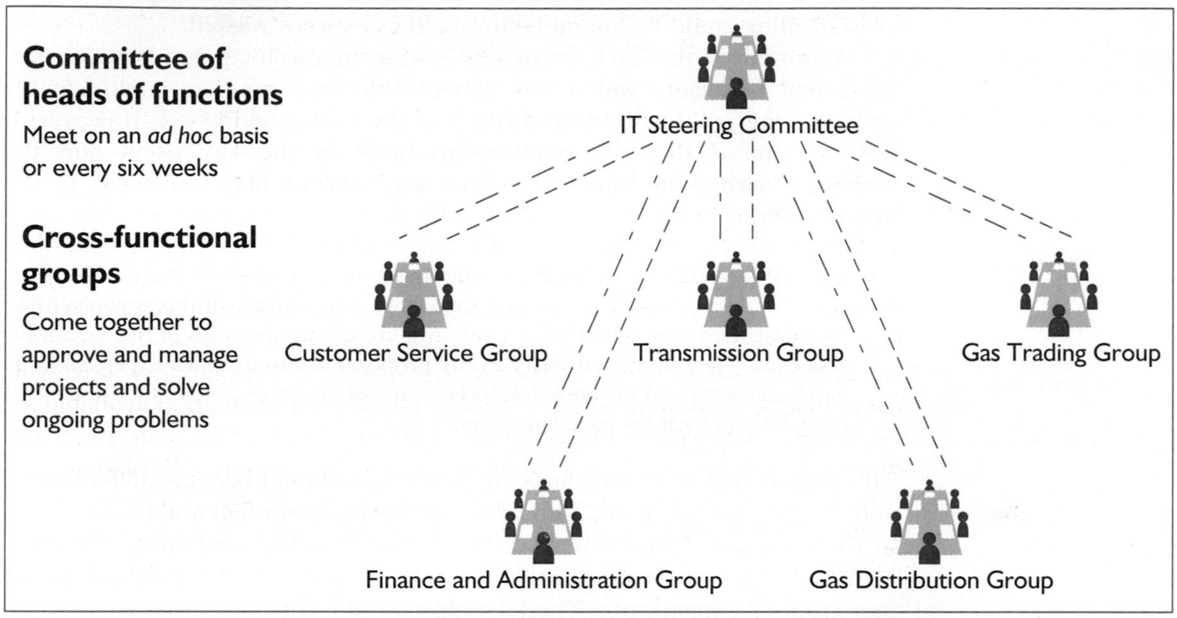

customer service group consisted of representatives from the distribution function (as gas suppliers), the finance function (as functional area in charge of billing) and the marketing functions (as area in charge of gas trading, promotion of BGE and search for new customers). The groups initially set out to clear the backlog of systems development requests that had accumulated. The previous lack of formal procedures to assess the merit of information systems proposals had meant that decisions were often postponed. Users had often refused to make decisions that would solve recurrent problems and IT staff had to spend substantial time trying to work out overly complex compromise solutions.

The new procedures attempted to address these problems by relying on a network of 'key users' from different departments, who had been trained in order to develop their abilities to

- specify IT requests
- specify bug fixing/maintenance requests
- assess the relative merits of IT proposals.

It was planned that key users would become sponsors for the new projects and act as an underlying network of IT expertise, supporting managers in their attempts to develop the use of IT. This increased the visibility of the flow of requests for systems development and allowed a more global approach to the management of the portfolio of corporate applications. When system requests were out of line with the strategic change under way at BGE, they could be halted before resources were wasted.

As noted by the CIO, there was a wide hierarchical gap between key users and managers and it was conceivable that conflicts could emerge owing to the political nature of some of the issues addressed. However, it was recognised that the relationship between the key users and the managers within the functional areas was vital to BGE's success. In the opinion of the CIO,

> I regard key users as 'facilitators' who 'must' be consulted by their colleagues and 'should' be consulted by their managers. The culture of this organisation would make it very difficult for a subordinate to put obstacles in the way of his superior. A key user's authority in my proposal is based on his expertise in a particular area and his potential to keep his manager out of conflict both with the CIO and with his peer managers.

This meant that the procedures implemented should become self-adjusted and IT/user groups should find a balance between conflict and co-operation in their actions. Ultimately, the CIO hoped that the committee structure would evolve into both a conflict-reduction and a lobby mechanism for increased IT expenditure. The IT budget would, thus, eventually reach the level required to implement the new strategy successfully.

As BGE moved to a process-focus organisation and from being regionally differentiated to being nationally standardised, the task of the IS department became much simpler. When regional idiosyncrasies still existed, company IT users had become frustrated with the lack of progress in certain areas, as systems that required a solution of cross-functional problems were not dealt with. In addition, the lack of reliable resident IT expertise within the functional areas had prevented a meaningful increase in user participation in this crucial aspect of IT development. The results were many unfounded requests that wasted time and energy. More importantly, there was no possibility to align the IT strategy with the business strategy.

CHALLENGES FOR BGE

The main challenge for BGE was to ensure that its internal response to changes in its environment allowed it to provide the quality service to customers that they desired and they recognised that

> A culture change is necessary to convert any state-owned organisation into a commercial, market-driven, customer-focused company, ... this can only be achieved by the active co-operation of the staff at all levels.
>
> M.N. Conlon, Chairman

The development of corporate-wide information systems would switch the burden of work from information preparation tasks towards information analysis tasks. It was hoped that this would lead to better decision making at all managerial levels of the organisation and, thus, provide a sound basis for BGE's future competitive position.

A crucial aspect in implementing the new strategy was managing the changes in the balance of power that the increased reliance on information systems brought about. The difficulty in managing these fundamental changes stemmed from the redundance of some positions as a result of the standardisation of procedures, the increased preparation of information and reports by systems, and from the greater efficiency and effectiveness of information systems in pinpointing areas of below-target performance. These factors, while contributing to enhancing BGE's productivity, were not perceived positively by all staff. Thus, the need to have many information providers in the local offices could be reduced as top management sought the information they needed directly on the central servers of the organisation. A significant challenge also existed in managing the organisational impacts inherent in firm-wide electronic communication systems such as e-mail that provided bypasses in the interaction between individuals by creating new and alternative channels of communication. This could reduce the power of middle managers who previously were important bridges between employees in BGE. The opposition of people who used to be in these powerful positions and their resistance to the change programme cannot be underestimated.

According to Dr Conlon in 1997, BGE was half way in its change programme. More planning was required in attempting to make up for the business lost in TPA (third party access), for example by developing commercial operations in Northern Ireland and the UK (where TPA will also operate). The real challenge for BGE resides in facing up to these realities and attempting to implement the vision of managers in unbundling the organisation's accounts to allow for the dual focus of BGE's future business: selling gas and managing its gas distribution function.

DOMAN SYNTHETIC FIBRES PLC

Peter H. Jones

The case study describes a company that has drifted strategically, letting an established and profitable product move into being marginally profitable. The product is in a niche market at the interface of the chemical and synthetic textile market. The company has developed a replacement product and the case is concerned with the resource planning issues required to progressively replace their existing product with the new one. The case presents three strategic options for the future which can be analysed by using the evaluation criteria in the text. This will require assumptions about capacity planning, company culture, market size, market share and many other issues. The nature of these assumptions and their 'robustness' is a focal issue in the evaluation. The case also allows readers to develop a detailed resource plan to implement their chosen strategy.

• • •

> Over the past few years, as the results of major companies continue to show, textiles and fibres in particular have continued to be a difficult market and, although last year's results were up on the previous year, they were still very poor compared to other industries.
>
> FROM AN ARTICLE IN THE TEXTILE TRADE PRESS, JULY 1995

It was against this gloomy scene that Doman Synthetic Fibres (DSF) had been trading. Appendices 1 and 2 give details of its financial results for 1993–5. DSF was a small but technically successful company by the standards of the man-made fibre industry. Founded in 1936 by Wilfred Doman, grandfather of the present managing director, Wendy Doman, the company was heavily dependent on the sales of Britlene, which accounted in 1995 for some 95 per cent of total sales. This heavy dependence on a single product had been a familiar characteristic of the company for nearly twenty years, first with Decalene and then since the late 1980s with

---

This material was compiled from general experience. It was prepared by Peter H. Jones with the assistance of other members of Sheffield Business School, Sheffield Hallam University, as a basis for class discussion and is not intended as an illustration of good or bad management practice.

Britlene. It was only the patent protection on Britlene which had enabled DSF to survive the turbulent and difficult situation of recent years.

Synthetic fibres as a whole represented some 40 per cent of the total UK textile production, but within that, Teklatite fibres, of which Britlene was the leading commercial type, accounted for only 3 per cent of total synthetic fibre production. Britlene was used mainly in the manufacture of heavy-duty clothing, although small quantities were used to produce industrial goods such as tyre cord and industrial belting.

In 1994, however, the R&D department had developed a new product, Britlon, which like Britlene was a Teklatite fibre. Britlon had all the properties of Britlene but was superior in its heat-resistant qualities. It was hoped that this additional property would open up new clothing uses (e.g. a substitute for asbestos clothing, adding to night wear to improve its flame resistance), and new industrial uses in thermal and electrical insulation.

Wendy Doman expressed her attitude to Britlon:

> For too long we've relied on Britlene as our only product. It's been a faithful friend to us, but with patent protection running out in 1997, we must expand into something else and Britlon is the obvious candidate. We've got the technical experience in this area; it'll use our existing sales outlets; we could even convert some Britlene capacity to cut down on our capital costs and our agent has drawn up a watertight patent.

By late 1995, the major technical and engineering problems associated with bulk production of Britlon seemed to have been solved, but two years of the patent had already expired. Wendy Doman had set up a Capital Investment Working Party to put forward proposals on how the new product should be phased into the company's activities.

PRODUCTION

The basic production method of Britlene and Britlon is similar to that of most man-made fibres. To make a man-made fibre, an oil-based organic chemical is polymerised (a process of joining several molecules into a long chain) in conditions of intense pressure and heat, often by the addition of a suitable catalyst. This polymerisation takes place in large autoclaves (an industrial pressure-cooker). The polymer is then extruded (similar to being forced through the rose of a garden watering can), rapidly cooled and then either spun on to cones and bobbins or collected in bales. The spun material is known as filament yarn; the bales are called staple fibre.

For Britlene, DSF had bought the polymer Polymutastine 15 as its raw material, which it chemically processed before the extrusion stage. However, for Britlon, it would be buying Hexatitanone and polymerising this organic chemical itself. The raw materials for Britlene and Britlon were produced at Teesside by ICI. For both raw materials, DSF took a low percentage of ICI's production and ICI was not a direct competitor of DSF in the fibre market.

Britlene Facilities

Britlene was produced at three factories: Teesside, Bradford and Dumfries. The largest site was Teesside with three plants. There was one plant at each of the other two sites. The Teesside plant was next door to the raw material supplier and was not too far from the main markets in Lancashire and Yorkshire. Bradford was close to the main customers, and as such proved a help for sorting out customer liaison on matters such as quality and rush orders. The factory at Dumfries dated back to the Second World War.

All five production plants, purchased over the last eight years, had a design capacity of 5.5 million lbs per annum of Britlene, independent of whether filament or staple was produced. However, after allowing for maintenance and an annual shutdown, expected output was 5 million lbs pa. Each plant was still in excellent order. Production was done on a 5 days per week, 24 hours per day (3 shifts) basis. There was no weekend production, although Saturday had been worked occasionally in times of high demand and the trade unions had agreed to allow members to work one Saturday per month at overtime rates.

Each plant employed about 72 people on production and 11 on maintenance. There was no difference in plant labour levels for the three shifts, but maintenance workers were mainly attached to the day shift.

Proposed Britlon Facilities

The distinctive features of Britlon were created in the new polymerisation process. When asked to explain the differences between the two products, the research director, Roger Tillotson, used to draw the diagram shown in Exhibit 1.

> The key to Britlon is in the dotted boxes. What we'll need is a new polymerisation-cum-autoclave unit to replace the old autoclave-only unit. The extrusion unit for Britlon is basically the same as we are using for Britlene. By the time we've reached the molten polymer state, we've done the chemistry. Extrusion is just to get a storable and saleable product.

Together with a major construction company, DSF had produced an acceptable plant design. A pilot plant was working very satisfactorily. This had provided valuable cost information. Jim Lewis explained:

> Our self-produced Britlon polymer should be about 10 per cent cheaper than Polymutastine 15, despite the extra costs of about 15 men on the new polymer plant and its extra depreciation. Of course, these are only estimated from our pilot plant experience.

Exhibit 1 **Production processes for Britlene and Britlon**

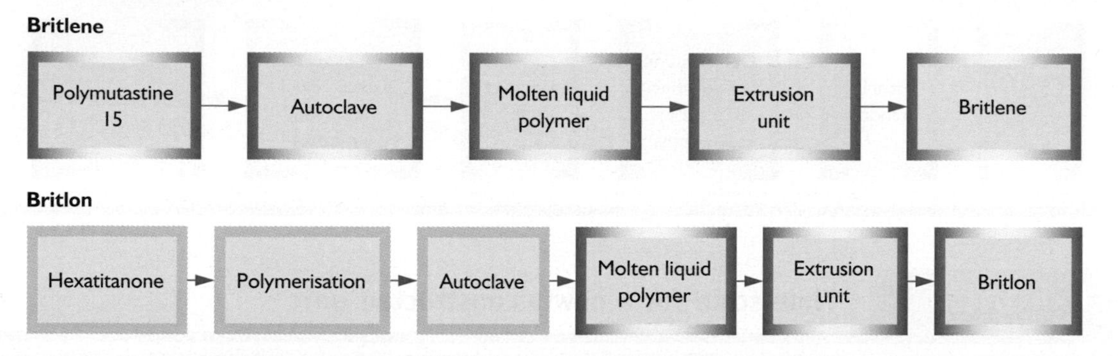

Acquiring Britlon Capacity

There were two ways of acquiring Britlon capacity. DSF could convert a Britlene plant, or it could construct an entirely new plant.

For a *conversion*, a new polymer unit would need to be constructed first; when complete it would be connected to the extrusion unit, which would require minor conversion taking three months. Instrumentation and start-up checks would then be performed for a further three months, during which time there could be roughly half capacity. This meant that from the completion of the new polymer unit, the whole plant would not be at full capacity for about six months. At least six months' planning and technical work was required by Alpens before construction could start.

Exhibit 2 sets out Alpens's estimated time scale for conversion of a Britlene unit to make Britlon.

A newly constructed plant would mean building both a polymerisation and an extrusion unit. Although no conversion was involved, such a plant could only operate at roughly half capacity for three months after start-up, while testing took place. Alpens's estimated time scale for a newly constructed unit is shown in Exhibit 3.

Preliminary market estimates for the new product made in 1995 indicated that an increase in the total number of plants might well be needed, especially if the predicted new industrial uses materialised. Wendy Doman, however, had gone on record saying:

> The creation of an entirely new site for operations would increase the complexities of multisite operation to an unacceptable level. Conversely, the complete closure of one of the three existing sites is, I consider, a waste of the human and physical resources that we have invested in that location. I believe expansion could take place at one, two or all of the existing sites.

Exhibit 2 Time scale for conversion of a Britlene unit

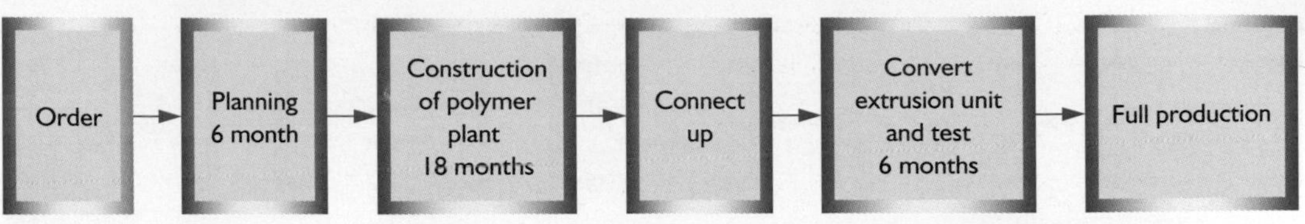

Exhibit 3 Time scale for a newly constructed unit

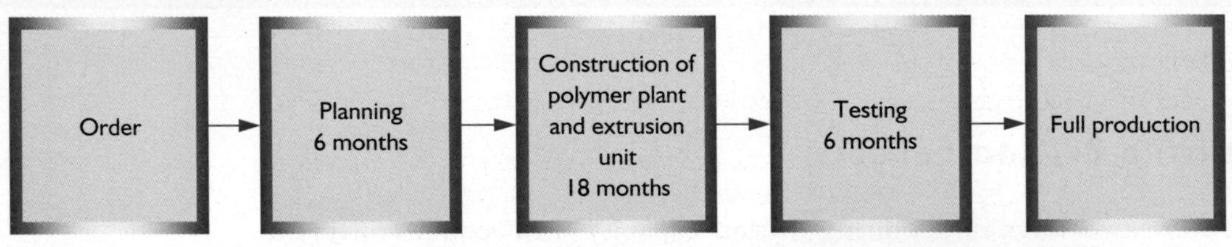

Estimated Britlon Capital Costs

The estimated costs and stage payments required by Alpens for Britlon polymer plant and extrusion unit construction were as follows:

For a Britlon polymer plant	£3,000,000
For a new Britlon extrusion unit	£1,800,000
For conversion of a Britlene extrusion unit to Britlon	£600,000

Thus, the total cost of a new Britlon plant would be £4.8m and that of a conversion £3.6m.

The cost of the polymer plant was payable in three 6-monthly instalments of £1,000,000, the first being due one year after ordering. The cost of new extrusion units or conversions was due on completion.

Land for two more plants was already available at Teesside and for one more at Bradford, but any other developments would require an additional purchase.

MARKETING

Since the mid-1970s, DSF had been a one-product company. Prior to the introduction of Britlene in 1987, the company had relied on the patent-protected product Decalene before moving into Teklatite fibres with Britlene. Experience with Decalene suggested that the new monopoly position held by Britlene could be eroded fairly rapidly once patent rights were removed at the end of 1997. One other UK manufacturer was producing Teklatite fibres and was thought to have plans to produce Britlene after that date.

Supply and Demand Britlene – Britlene

Britlene had carved out a secure niche in the man-made fibre market. Sluggish world trade in textiles and fibres had curtailed growth since 1992, but DSF had been able to produce and sell at virtually full capacity during 1992–5. They had not needed, nor had they tried, to penetrate foreign markets, with the exception of a small effort in 1990.

Peter Moore, DSF's marketing director, was confident that Britlon would enable DSF to regain a 90 per cent share in the UK of Teklatite fibres within three years of its introduction. He felt confident in the future of Britlon:

> With the right kind of effort, I believe we can also generate sales of 5–10 million lbs of Britlon for use in thermal and electrical insulation. This is a mere flea-bite in comparison to sales of asbestos, glass and mica for this purpose.

Pricing

Since 1993, prices for Britlene had moved only marginally. DSF had not really tried to pass on cost increases, as in the depressed textile market Peter Moore felt that this would have been resisted by customers. DSF had opted to keep running at full capacity with lower sales margins rather than risk a drop in sales at higher prices. In 1995, the list price for Britlene was 98 pence/lb.

There was considerable uncertainty about the price which could be obtained for Britlon. For textile uses it might command a premium (estimated at 10–20 per cent) over Britlene due to its improved qualities, but Peter Moore felt that this premium could well be used up in trying to shift customers on to the new product. Additionally, the increased competition anticipated once Britlene patents expired was expected to depress Teklatite prices.

The industrial market was a great unknown. Rough-and-ready calculations suggested that a price between 100p and 120p/lb ought to put it on a competitive basis with existing materials. However, the conservative nature of manufacturers which would be taking a totally new material threw doubt on these estimates.

Selling and Promotion

In 1995, promotion expenditure was £50,000, spent on sales literature (£13,000) and limited advertising in newspapers and trade journals

(£37,000). This expenditure level was typical of the previous few years. For the launch of Britlene in 1987–9, the company had 'gone to town' by industry standards, spending £250,000, on press advertising (£80,000) and a joint promotion with selected customers (£170,000). This was equivalent to £550,000 at 1995 prices. This had enabled the rapid acceptance of Britlene by the textile industry.

Peter Moore felt that, once Britlon was established in the textile market, its promotional needs would be similar to those for Britlene, but to break into the new industrial markets would require a much greater promotional effort.

PERSONNEL

In December 1995, DSF employed 556 people. Of these, weekly payroll employees, concerned mainly with production and maintenance, numbered 415. There were approximately 83 payroll employees at each of the five plants. The remaining 141 employees were monthly paid staff. Apart from supervisory production staff and commercial staff at the sales offices, all staff worked at the Teesside headquarters. Nearly all payroll employees in DSF were unionised. John Williams described the company's relationship with the union as 'good', although there was unease about possible plant closures. He was also concerned about poor labour relations in the construction industry, which he feared could delay building programmes and increase costs.

Unemployment

At all locations there was higher than average general unemployment, but the unemployment rate for skilled workers was lower at all sites. Supply of the particular skills DSF wanted was low, and only at Teesside would extra demand for skilled labour be readily met.

FINANCE

Financial Performance

The financial performance of the company during 1993–5 had been a cause of real concern (see Appendix 1). Up to the early 1990s, the profit figures had been steady and a return on capital employed before tax of over 25 per cent was considered to be most satisfactory. As Mr Greenhaugh put it:

> In the late 1980s this company was considered a good investment by most analysts. We have always been financed solely by the share capital and retained

earnings, and this, coupled with our patent protection, made us a safe bet. In the last two or three years, however, things haven't looked so good. Our share price has dropped to a disturbing level, despite our continuing policy of maintaining the level of dividends. Our P/E ratio is now 7 and this is very disappointing. Investors are not sure where we are going as a company, but I hope the introduction of Britlon, if it comes through in time, will restore some of that confidence.

Raising Finance

Mr Greenhaugh compared the 1995 situation to the similar position in 1987 when Britlene had been introduced to the market. Then, the initial development costs had been financed internally out of previous profits, as had about half the capital investment. Another £2.5m had been required from external sources. This was a substantial quantity for a company the size of DSF, but confidence had been high and a 1 for 1 rights issue at 62.5p had been fully subscribed. (The share price at the time had been standing at 68p.) Mr Greenhaugh wished that confidence in DSF was as buoyant in 1995 and the share price as strong.

Investment grants were part of the measures taken by successive governments to increase the level of investment undertaken in the economy, and also to direct this investment to areas of particular concern. As far as DSF was concerned, the latest measures might enable grants of up to about 20 per cent of the capital cost to be obtained at Teesside and Dumfries. The Bradford site was unlikely to attract a grant.

THE FIRST WORKING PARTY MEETING

In setting up the working party to consider the Britlon case, Wendy Doman had picked one up-and-coming manager from each major function. It was clear that she considered this exercise as part of their development, and success could easily mean rapid advancement on the back of Britlon expansion. As they sat down for their first meeting, the members of the working party realised that they all had a personal as well as a professional interest in how the study progressed. They did, however, differ in their initial views on the pace of expansion into Britlon and on whether a price premium could be commanded for Britlon.

Les Hill, the most cautious of the team, was not convinced that there was a need to replace Britlene with Britlon at all. He argued that they ought to be able to ward off major potential inroads into their market share by reducing prices slightly, given that all their capital plant would be fully depreciated and any new entrants' capital would have to bear a depreciation cost.

Chris Henson disagreed, arguing that the new product would give benefits to most customers and that they knew about it anyway from samples available from the pilot plant built in 1994. She did, however, agree with Les's view that not all customers would transfer to Britlon, so she wanted to retain some Britlene capacity. She believed that it would be appropriate to enter the industrial market with Britlon in a small way.

Trevor Bryant's initial views were considerably more optimistic about Britlon. He could see no point in 'hanging on to a dying product', as he put it. He felt that nearly all customers would be forced to move to Britlon once the majority had. He also wanted to tackle the industrial market vigorously.

A computer simulation model had been commissioned to help the team forecast the future, given varying assumptions about future price levels, demand, etc. Key assumptions and corresponding results for the main protagonists' views are given in Appendix 3. In these results, it was assumed that a government grant of 20 per cent towards capital purchase would be available.

APPENDIX 1 PROFIT AND LOSS SUMMARY, 1993–5 (£000s)

	1993		1994		1995	
Sales						
Products	23,602		23,840		24,042	
Licences	951		976		1,050	
		24,553		24,816		25,092
Cost of goods sold						
Raw materials	6,086		6,592		7,230	
Direct labour	6,391		6,940		7,521	
Prod. overheads	2,177		2,602		2,869	
Depreciation	700		700		700	
		15,354		16,834		18,320
Gross profit		9,199		7,982		6,772
Other overheads						
Promotion and sales		374		395		402
Distribution		905		986		1,030
General admin.		2,738		3,009		3,320
R&D		890		1,250		950
		4,907		5,640		5,702
Operating profit		4,292		2,342		1,070
Interest payable		(189)		(231)		(240)
Net profit before tax		4,481		2,573		1,310
Corporation tax		1,814		1,146		704
Net profit after tax		2,667		1,427		606
Dividend declared		750		750		750
Retained earnings		1,917		677		(144)

Source Company annual reports.

APPENDIX 2 BALANCE SHEET AT 31 DECEMBER 1995 (£000s)

	COST	DEPRECIATION	NET
Fixed assets			
Freehold land and buildings	8,010	(150)	7,860
Teesside 5,210			
Bradford 1,605			
Dumfries 1,195			
Plant and machinery	8,790	(7,000)	1,790
Teesside 4,780			
Bradford 2,050			
Dumfries 1,960			
			9,650
Trade investments at cost			4,152
Working capital			
Current assets			
Work in progress and stock	2,720		
Debtors	2,980		
Cash	868		
		6,568	
Less current liabilities			
Creditors	2,307		
Taxation	436		
Dividend	510		
		3,253	
Net working capital			3,315
			17,117
Financed by:			
Share capital			5,000
Capital reserves			
Share premium		500	
Revaluation reserve		4,500	
			5,000
Retained earnings			
Balance at 31.12.94		7,261	
Retained profit 1995		(144)	
			7,117
			17,117

Source Company annual report.

APPENDIX 3 ALTERNATIVE STRATEGIES

Table A Les Hill – consolidation strategy

	1996	1997	1998	1999	2000	2001
Assumptions						
Volume of Britlene (m lb)	25	25	24	22	22	22
Price of Britlene (£/lb)	1.00	1.00	0.95	0.95	0.95	0.95
Key results						
Net profit before tax (£m)	2.0	2.3	1.6	0.6	0.5	0.5
Annual trading cash flow (£m)	1.6	1.6	0.3	−0.3	0.1	0.2
Investment capital (£m)	–	–	–	–	–	–
Net cash flow (£m)	1.6	1.6	0.3	−0.3	0.1	0.2
Cumulative cash flow (£m, inc. trade investments)	6.6	8.2	8.5	8.2	8.3	8.5

Table B1 Chris Henson – 'two-horse strategy' – no price premium

	1996	1997	1998	1999	2000	2001
Assumptions						
Volume of Britlene (m lb)	25	25	20	15	10	10
Volume of Britlon (m lb)	–	–	5	11	17	20
Price of Britlene (£/lb)	1.00	1.00	0.95	0.95	0.95	0.95
Price of Britlon (£/lb)	–	–	0.95	0.95	1.00	1.00
Key results						
Net profit before tax (£m)	2.0	2.3	−1.3	−1.8	−0.4	1.9
Annual trading cash flow (£m)	1.6	0.6	−2.0	−0.9	0.6	3.2
Investment capital (£m)	–	1.6	4.5	5.1	1.3	–
Net cash flow (£m)	1.6	−1.0	−6.5	6.5	−0.7	3.2
Cumulative cash flow (£m, inc. trade investments)*	6.6	5.5	−1.0	−7.0	−7.7	−4.5

*The lowest negative figure indicates the maximum cash injection needed by DSF to fund the strategy, in addition to selling its trade investments of £4.2m.

Table B2 Chris Henson – 'two-horse strategy' – with price premium

	1996	1997	1998	1999	2000	2001
Assumptions						
Volume of Britlene (m lb)	25	25	20	15	10	10
Volume of Britlon (m lb)	–	–	3	11	17	20
Price of Britlene (£/lb)	1.00	1.00	0.95	0.95	0.95	0.95
Price of Britlon (£/lb)	–	–	1.15	1.15	1.20	1.20
Key results						
Net profit before tax (£m)	4.5	5.0	−0.5	0.6	3.4	7.5
Annual trading cash flow (£m)	3.8	2.6	−2.7	1.3	4.0	6.9
Investment capital (£m)	–	1.6	4.5	5.1	1.3	–
Net cash flow (£m)	3.8	1.0	−7.2	−3.8	2.7	6.9
Cumulative cash flow (£m, inc. trade investments)*	8.8	9.8	2.6	−1.2	1.5	8.4

*The lowest negative figure indicates the maximum cash injection needed by DSF to fund the strategy, in addition to selling its trade investments of £4.2m.

Table C1 Trevor Bryant – 'go for it' – no price premium

	1996	1997	1998	1999	2000	2001
Assumptions						
Volume of Britlene (m lb)	25	25	16	5	–	–
Volume of Britlon (m lb)	–	–	9	22	33	40
Price of Britlene (£/lb)	1.00	1.00	0.95	0.95	0.90	0.90
Price of Britlon (£/lb)	–	–	0.95	0.95	1.00	1.00
Key results						
Net profit before tax (£m)	2.0	1.7	−3.8	−5.3	−1.8	1.7
Annual trading cash flow (£m)	1.6	1.0	−1.9	−2.9	−1.1	4.4
Investment capital (£m)	–	4.8	9.6	8.0	3.5	–
Net cash flow (£m)	1.6	−3.8	−11.5	−10.9	−4.6	4.4
Cumulative cash flow (£m, inc. trade investments)*	6.6	2.8	−8.7	−19.6	−24.3	−19.9

*The lowest negative figure indicates the maximum cash injection needed by DSF to fund the strategy, in addition to selling its trade investments of £4.2m.

Table C2 Trevor Bryant – 'go for it' – no price premium

	1996	1997	1998	1999	2000	2001
Assumptions						
Volume of Britlene (m lb)	25	25	16	5	–	–
Volume of Britlon (m lb)	–	–	9	22	33	40
Price of Britlene (£/lb)	1.1	1.1	0.95	0.95	0.9	0.9
Price of Britlon (£/lb)	–	–	1.15	1.15	1.2	1.25
Key results						
Net profit before tax (£m)	4.4	4.4	−1.8	−0.6	5.5	12.9
Annual trading cash flow (£m)	3.8	2.0	−1.5	1.5	5.8	12.5
Investment capital (£m)	–	4.8	9.6	8.0	3.5	–
Net cash flow (£m)	3.8	−2.8	−11.1	−6.5	2.3	12.5
Cumulative cash flow (£m, inc. trade investments)*	8.8	6.0	−5.1	−11.6	−9.3	3.2

*The lowest negative figure indicates the maximum cash injection needed by DSF to fund the strategy, in addition to selling its trade investments of £4.2m.

ROYAL ALEXANDRA HOSPITAL

Sandra Hill

The case study examines the changes faced by a general hospital, the Royal Alexandra (RAH), as it moved to Trust status in 1993. It covers the period immediately before Trust status was granted on 1 April 1993 until March 1998. Staff and managers were needing to come to terms with the notion of increased accountability, tighter control on the use of resources, greater involvement of clinicians in management and the introduction of non-executive directors. These factors, coupled with emerging relationships with new purchasing bodies in health care meant that challenges in the management of the National Health Service had never been greater. The case ends with new challenges following the election of a Labour government in 1997.

The case is concerned with the process of managing these changes in a turbulent environment. It illustrates the need for changing management styles, strategies and structures to ensure survival of the hospital as it faced increasing competition from other acute health care providers and an increasingly tight financial regime throughout the health service. There was a crucial role for the leaders of the organisation in ensuring that strategic change was linked to operational change and that the changes were communicated to key internal and external stakeholders of RAH clearly and effectively.

• • •

BACKGROUND

The Royal Alexandra Hospital (RAH), a district general hospital in Paisley, Scotland, opened to its first patients in October 1986 and, after a period of six months, 880 of its 950 beds were being utilised. In line with the Griffiths Enquiry into the management and organisation of the National Health

---

This case study was prepared by Sandra Hill, Glasgow Caledonian University, with the assistance of Martin Hill, chief executive of the Royal Alexandra Hospital. It is intended as a basis for class discussion and not as an illustration of either good or bad management practice.

Service (NHS) in 1983, the concept of general management was introduced to the hospital and, as a result, Martin Hill was appointed as the first general manager of the General Acute and Maternity Services Unit at the hospital in 1987. This post was accountable to the health board and, unlike previous administrator posts, was responsible for the management of all of the services including doctors and other professional and clinical staff.

The concept of the district general hospital had been largely born out of an NHS which gave priority to hospital provision accessible to local people. The RAH came on stream towards the end of a 25-year period of development of such hospitals throughout Britain. Long before its opening, however, concerns were being raised throughout the country about the cost of the public sector and, from its beginning, the RAH had to fight hard for resources to operate in competition with the more established and politically stronger institutions in the west of Scotland. It did, however, benefit from being a new institution less burdened with restrictive trade practices, which allowed industrial relations within the hospital to be conducted with fewer problems than might otherwise have been the case.

In order to address concerns over the organisation of the health service, the Conservative government of the day focused attention initially on the management of the service in the form of the Griffiths Enquiry of 1983. The most fundamental impact of government policy affecting the hospital in its early years came in the wake of the Thatcher government reforms heralded in its white paper *Working For Patients* published in January 1989.

The Conservative government's reforms brought about three major changes for the RAH:

- The creation of an internal market and the distancing of the health board through the separation of the purchaser and provider functions.
- The contracting process, resulting in hospitals no longer receiving budgets based on what was spent, but contract income in return for the delivery of specified patient services.
- The opportunity for the RAH to become a self-governing trust.

Closer scrutiny of public services, to ensure value for money, has shown up significant differentiation in the resourcing of different parts of the NHS. As community and primary care services were seen to be in need of development, the general acute hospital sector came under increasing pressure to shift resources to facilitate the process. As demand for hospital care continued to grow and the resources available began to reduce in real terms, the policy of 'more for less' provided a new challenge for the RAH. Coping successfully with the pressures which arose out of the inexorable drive for efficiency year after year highlighted the need for particularly effective management and a different form of partnership between clinicians and managers. The introduction of the Patients' Charter and the growing recognition of consumerism also led the health service to view the involvement of the local community in the design and delivery of its services as essential to bringing about the culture changes seen as vital in the NHS of the 1990s.

The RAH was granted trust status in shadow form from 1 January 1993 with full effect from 1 April 1993. The changes that this move brought were complex and had to be introduced within a climate which was certainly not fully supportive of the move with some staff being philosophically opposed to the government's reforms. In addition, some staff feared that this would lead to privatisation and reduction or loss of nationally negotiated terms and conditions of service since the trust would be able to determine pay and conditions locally.

THE TRUST BOARD

As the Royal Alexandra Hospital NHS Trust came into shadow form the first part-time non-executive chairman was appointed, closely followed by the appointment of five non-executive directors. These appointments were made by the Secretary of State for Scotland following a nomination process which included widespread public advertisement. Nevertheless, the process was to engender fierce political opposition a few years later in the war against quangos.[1]

The first task of the new shadow board was to appoint a chief executive. The board had the option of interviewing and appointing the incumbent unit general manager or to market the post publicly. In this case Martin Hill, the incumbent general manager, was appointed after internal interview, without the post being advertised externally.

The next task was for the chief executive and shadow board to appoint the other four executive directors. In the event, the existing director of nursing was confirmed, both the directors of finance and human resources were external appointments from industry in England and the medical director was headhunted from the post of director of health promotion at a neighbouring health board. Also in attendance at board meetings (although not a voting member) was the board secretary/director of services who, along with the director of nursing and chief executive were the only members of an eleven-strong board with any experience of knowledge of the RAH.

The cost of the trust boards was a new cost to the NHS representing an expensive overhead which clearly had to demonstrate its value in the face of mounting attacks by the government on public spending.

While the non-executive directors, including the chairman, were additional to the previous management structure, the executive directors replaced previous senior managers. It was clear that the director posts would need to function at a higher strategic level than the posts which they replaced and the significant change at the top of the management structure was thereby justified. Martin Hill was clear when he explained, 'this was

[1] Quango stands for quasi-autonomous non-governmental organisation.

about creating leadership out of structures previously focused on operational management'.

Roles and Responsibilities

For the first time, the RAH was to be directly responsible to the Secretary of State through the Scottish Office and accountable for its own future, albeit within a framework of powers for trusts which were subsequently diluted, and constraints which increased, as time went by.

The new trust had three distinct areas of responsibility:

- Shaping the strategic direction of the organisation and overseeing its management.
- Developing relationships with professionals whilst bringing lay challenge to their advice.
- Building a partnership with the community.

Although the chief executive and the director of nursing had, to a limited extent, the advantage of development geared specifically towards preparation for trust status, training for the other directors was superficial and occurred after the event. The national preparation of chairmen and non-executives was particularly poor, representing little more than single-day induction programmes arranged by the management executive (ME) for the National Health Service in Scotland (NHSIS). The RAH had the added challenge of having two directors from industries unrelated to hospitals or the health service (brewing and confectionery) but felt confident that the experience of these individuals in commercial accounting and industrial relations would be highly beneficial to the trust in its formative years.

IDENTIFYING STRATEGIC CHANGE NEEDS

Creating an Autonomous Organisation

From January 1993, in preparation for full trust status, the RAH needed to be seen to be independent of the health boards' command and control and *demonstrate its capability in terms of making strategic decisions* that would strengthen its services for patients. Initially there were two approaches. A campaign of staff education, aimed at encouraging staff to stop looking to the health board for support, reassurance and direction was embarked upon. Also, the commitment to creating an autonomous organisation was further strengthened by the significant structural change which had occurred as a result of the formation of the new trust board consisting of executive and non-executive directors which would act in a monitoring and governance role that had previously been expected of a health board. In order to support the new independent organisation, certain functions were decentralised from the area health board service to become trust-specific functions. These included finance, audit (clinical and financial) statutory reporting to the Scottish Office, human resource management, information services, occupational health and safety management, holding senior staff contracts including consultant medical staff, and press handling and public relation. Significant change was also to come through the empowerment of the trust to develop its own local policies and terms and conditions of service and the fact that it was now to operate under guidance from the Scottish Office rather than dictates from the health board.

Creating a Competitive Organisation

The government reforms introduced the notion of an internal market, with trusts competing with one another through the provision of patient services to win contracts from health boards and GP fundholders who were now acting as purchasers. It was founded on the principle that money would follow the patient and that if the main hospital of referral changed to a significant degree then the income of the losing hospitals should reduce and that of the gaining hospital should increase. Since the new system encouraged purchasers to demand a greater amount of information on the outputs of the service both in terms of quality and quantity, trusts would be required to concentrate on output and to become conscious for the first time of what was being delivered by the way of health care for the income received. This meant that the relationship between income and output was becoming more direct and, given the increasingly demanding requirements of purchasers, the specification and information which trusts required to generate were considerably greater than had existed before. To support this new role as a competitor, new functions of marketing and contracting were established and information services were significantly enhanced. Martin Hill said of these changes that, 'it was this requirement which was primarily responsible for the oft-quoted criticism that the new NHS had been invaded by an army of bureaucrats'.

The development of a marketing strategy, instigated and led by the chief executive was devised by the executive team, many members of which had no experience of working in an overly competitive environment. This involved *various stages of attempts at analysing the external and internal environment* by senior managers within the RAH and the commissioning of consultants to undertake market research which included identifying the perception of users of the service of the trust. At the same time it was clear that traditional exchange of information between neighbouring hospitals was becoming more and more difficult as they now acted in their new guise of competing trusts. This behaviour began amongst managers but was soon adopted by clinicians, many of whom operated within region-wide clinical networks.

The contracting function came under control of the finance director who co-ordinated the development of contractual relationships between the trust and its purchasers and figured prominently in the process of negotiation of contracts. These contracts ranged in value from a few thousand pounds per annum with distant GP fundholders, to over £40m with the trust's main purchaser, the local health board. Explicit quality requirements were specified for the first time and a trust-wide quality monitoring function was established under the director of nursing.

The minimum datasets describing treatment which underpinned these contracts were largely constrained by the capacity of existing information systems and little capital investment of any significance was made to any trusts to enable these to become more sophisticated. Nonetheless, a number of systems were introduced designed to facilitate the capture and transmission of patient data to purchasers. Initially these purchasers of patient services, particularly the new GP fundholders, had unrealistic expectations of the trust's information systems and withheld payment of invoices causing cash flow problems to differing degrees. A negative feature resulting from the creation of these autonomous organisations was that the central information function of the Scottish Office information services department, which previously received information from health boards to publish in annual statistical tables, no longer required some of these data from individual trusts. This threatened the continuation of some very important statistical data which was essential for epidemiological studies.

Responding to Patients, GPs and Health Boards

The data requirements underpinning contracts were one example of the trusts' responses to purchasers. It soon became clear, however, that the internal market required national publication of comparative data on such things as waiting times and waiting lists and of clinical performance indicators such as the number of patients in each hospital surviving thirty days following a heart attack. The publication of this comparative data created concern across Scotland by professionals who feared that the quality of services that their patients received would be misunderstood by patients who, with limited information, were concerned that they may not be receiving the best services locally.

In a more dynamic and locally relevant sense, the RAH established a dialogue with GPs and patients in order to confirm that it was designing and delivering the services that these bodies wanted. As far as the 129 local GPs were concerned, a regular satisfaction survey was instituted and various individual hospital departments initiated their own specific surveys and used the results to inform their business plans.

A new range of information leaflets for patients was developed telling them what they could expect when they came into hospital for treatment. These covered both general and procedure-specific information. At the same time, suggestion boxes were introduced to encourage feedback, and wider publicity was given to the complaints procedure which was also made more user friendly. An example of another initiative was to invite an ex patient, who had complained about the range of food, to join the hospital's catering group to look at improving patient menus.

Improving the Efficiency of the Trust

In making explicit the relationship between income and output, *the concept of efficiency became more meaningful*. Staff were encouraged, right from the point of induction, to accept some responsibility for resource management and were reminded that the money which paid their salaries and for the material they used in going about their daily work came out of their own pockets in the form of income tax and National Insurance contributions. Huge gains in efficiency were achieved primarily by increasing output by a greater proportion than the growth in income, but efficiency was also gained by the achievement of targeted cash releasing savings and redeployment. However, after a few years, efficiency savings became exhausted and financial cuts were beginning to lead to cuts in the quality of service. Example of this were to be found in various departments where patients were having to wait longer for treatment in accident and emergency, laboratory results were taking longer to report and some patients were waiting longer for X-rays and related examinations. These were only subsequently rectified through additional investment.

The market required some way of comparing efficiency between organisations and this should have been relatively simple since price was meant to equal cost. Thus, a straightforward comparison of trusts' price lists should have been one way of measuring relative efficiency, particularly given the lack of sophistication around quality measures. For various reasons, the main driver of efficiency did not become the market, as might have been anticipated, but turned out to be the management approach of health boards in trying to fasten down expenditure – in some staff's opinion, to an unrealistic degree. This was not helped by funding levels to health boards from the Scottish Office which were inequitable in certain respects and meant that some health boards had a greater level of resources and were able to spend more than others on acute hospital services per head of population.

As far as the RAH was concerned, although in a health board which was less affluent than its much larger neighbour in the city of Glasgow, the RAH's considerably lower prices and, in some cases, shorter waiting times for patients still did not encourage market behaviour. It soon became clear that money was not following patients. Despite considerable growth in admissions, the RAH received very little real increase in income.

Exhibits 1–3 give comparative information relating to in-patient costs per case (representing the areas consuming the largest part of the trust resources), average length of stay, and in-patient activity and income for the RAH.

Exhibit 1 In-patient costs per case (£)

	General Medicine		General Surgery		Orthopaedic Surgery		Ophthalmology		Gynaecology	
	92/3	96/7	92/3	96/7	92/3	96/7	92/3	96/7	92/3	96/7
RAH	779	905	1,206	1,116	1,786	1,901	873	1,231	845	989
Inverclyde	1,086	1,137	1,267	1,693	1,449	2,402	926	1,685	1,029	1,563
Vale of Leven	1,127	1,276	1,349	1,279	1,224	1,987	–	–	979	1,000
Southern General	1,697	1,030	1,732	1,400	1,880	1,916	1,038	1,409	659	1,076
Western Infirmary	1,823	1,290	1,222	1,283	2,623	2,180	1,743	1,700	740	971
Crosshouse	1,043	1,089	1,035	1,189	1,801	1,826	–	–	901	986

Notes 1992/3 general surgery costs included urology, which featured as a separate speciality in 1996/7. 1992/3 was the year immediately before trust status.

Source Scottish Health Service Costs 1992/3 and 1996/7.

Exhibit 2 In-patient average duration of stay (days)

	General Medicine		General Surgery		Orthopaedic Surgery		Ophthalmology		Gynaecology	
	92/3	96/7	92/3	96/7	92/3	96/7	92/3	96/7	92/3	96/7
RAH	6.6	6.5	6.0	5.0	9.4	9.0	4.4	1.9	3.8	3.5
Inverclyde	7.1	6.5	5.4	5.3	9.0	7.9	2.7	2.2	3.1	3.3
Vale of Leven	8.6	7.0	4.8	4.0	4.0[1]	10.7	–	–	3.6	3.2
Southern General	8.4	6.5	6.1	5.9	10.5	6.3	4.4	2.5	3.7	3.0
Western Infirmary	5.9	5.1	4.7	4.7	9.9	7.3	3.5	2.4	2.5	2.9
Crosshouse	7.0	5.6	5.2	5.2	8.7	7.2	–	–	3.3	3.7

Note Restricted range of service.

Source Scottish Health Service Costs 1992/3 and 1996/7

Exhibit 3 **Numbers of patients admitted and annual income (£000s)**

	1993/4	1994/5	1995/6	1996/7
In-patient	28,521	28,050	28,884	28,608
Day cases	11,285	13,262	15,607	15,430
Total	**39,806**	**41,312**	**44,491**	**44,038**
Income	**48,827**	**50,653**	**50,887**	**51,653**

Source RAH annual reports 1993/4 and 1996/7.

STRATEGIC CHANGE PROCESSES

Organisation and Communication

To secure the orientation of staff and activity related to the priorities of the trust rather than the National Health Service as a whole or individual professional aspirations, great emphasis was placed on developing the teamwork approach to the delivery of services to patients. This meant not just multidisciplinary working but a restructuring of management and the channels of communication to encourage more of matrix organisation. Instead of doctors, nurses, technicians and support staff acting in isolation or in functional groups and directed vertically, service developments required individuals from different professions to work together and to some extent to ignore traditional lines of demarcation. For example, when services were developed for diabetic patients they were designed with reference to the skills of different individuals working together with the responsibility of patient care shared across a team including doctors, specialist nurses, chiropodists, dietitians and others.

As part of the culture change process, a continuous improvement programme was established around developing problem-solving approaches and skills within multidisciplinary teams. Each of these teams focused on a single aim of solving a particular problem with the outcome of improved quality or efficiency of service delivery. The teams were non-hierarchical and were led by a variety of staff members.

The changes were welcomed by the majority of staff, although as doctors felt more and more constrained by shortage of resources and competing organisational priorities, they, in particular, reverted to tribal behaviour to protect their position as key influencers and protectors of the patients' interest. This behaviour was also believed to be a reaction against the perceived threat of managerial power within the organisation. This was probably wise as a balance against the behaviour of some managers who were less inclined to see their role as facilitating the delivery of health care and enabling clinicians to do so in a supportive environment, and who were beginning to adopt the very command and control style of management which had proven to be inappropriate when practised by the health board, pre-trust status. The style developed as a result of extremely tight financial regimes imposed upon the trust and insufficient acceptance of these regimes by clinical staff. It was also the case that managers were expected to take responsibility for delivering change, but without the authority over senior medical staff that was required to deliver the managerial objectives. Thus a mismatch between managers' accountability and their real authority existed.

NEW STRUCTURES

The Trust Board

By early 1996, several changes had occurred in the personnel of the RAH board. Promotions and retirements meant that the finance, nursing and medical directors had all been replaced in the first three years of the trust. Whilst this could have had a destabilising effect on the organisation, the new postholders were viewed as bringing new approaches and were welcomed and valued. The new medical director was promoted from within the existing consultants and so was familiar with the medical issues affecting the RAH.

Operational Reorganisation

In the summer of 1996, a major restructuring of the clinical and support service directorates was undertaken. The number of clinical directorates was reduced from nine to five, creating dissatisfaction amongst many doctors who feared a lessening of both their influence and their involvement with management. In fact, opportunities for them to participate were greater since, within each directorate, 'lead' consultants were identified for each speciality. By reducing the number of directorates the new organisations commanded larger budgets and justified higher-paid directorate managers with extended roles and responsibilities who were able to address change issues in ways that previous service managers had been unable to do (Exhibits 4(a) and 4(b)).

One of the strategic aims of the trust was to develop and extend the specialist role of key staff, particularly that of nurses. It was therefore decided to introduce at directorate level a nursing manager to replace H grade nurses (middle managers), and to establish a Nursing and Midwifery Development Group under the leadership of the director of nursing to strengthen the role and contribution of nursing and midwifery across the trust's services.

There was a significant reduction in the number of middle management posts within the support services directorate and one innovative feature was

Exhibit 4(a) **Royal Alexandra Hospital management structure: (a) 1993–6**

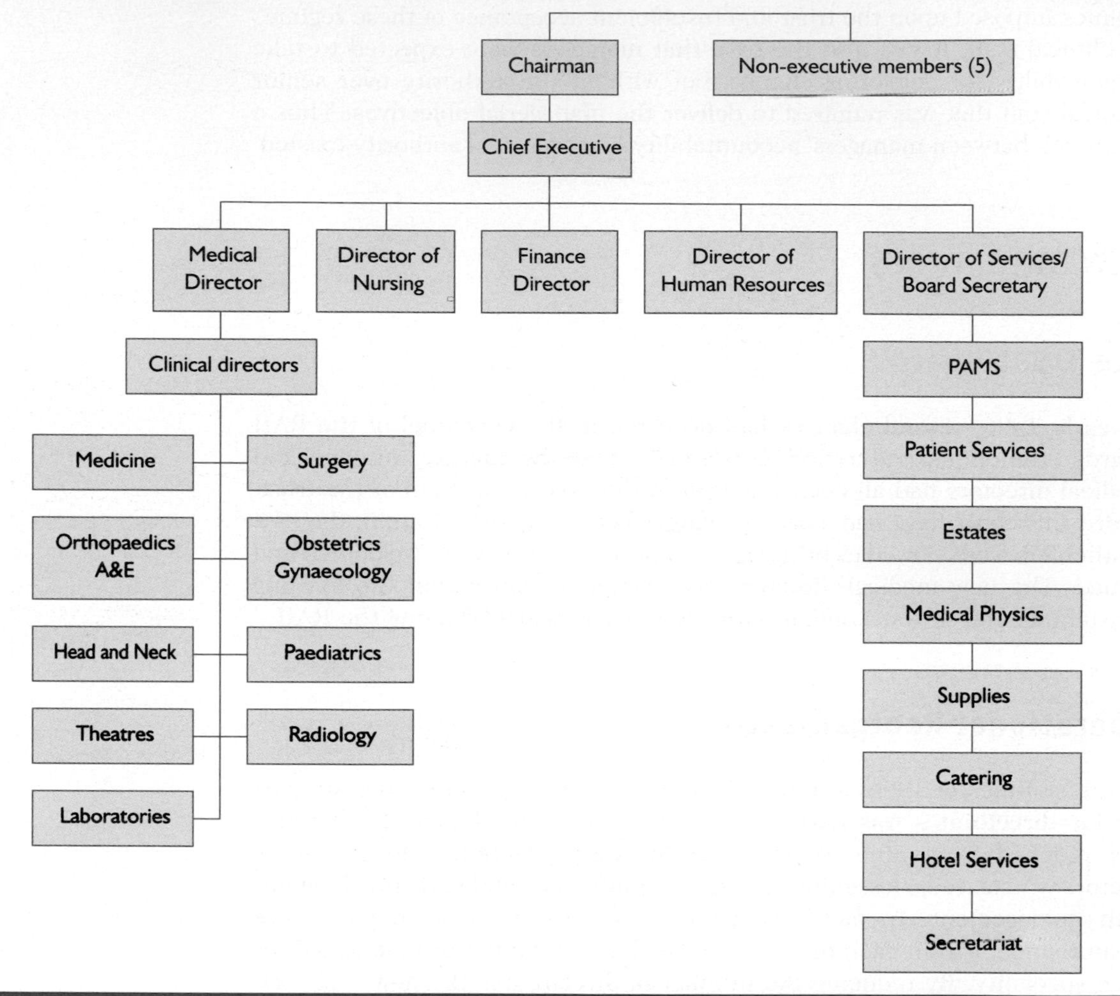

the amalgamation of medical physics and estates. This was intended to recognise the potential of the common engineering functions and also, by heading up the new department with the chief physicist, it was believed that more of a clinical focus would be brought to the priorities of the estates function. In addition, both catering and supplies management were combined and were managed within a much flatter structure along with hotel services.

The results of the new structure were not only more focused management, but also a reduction in management costs of around £200,000 per year. The resultant job losses were felt throughout the

Exhibit 4(b) **Royal Alexandra Hospital management structure: (b) 1996**

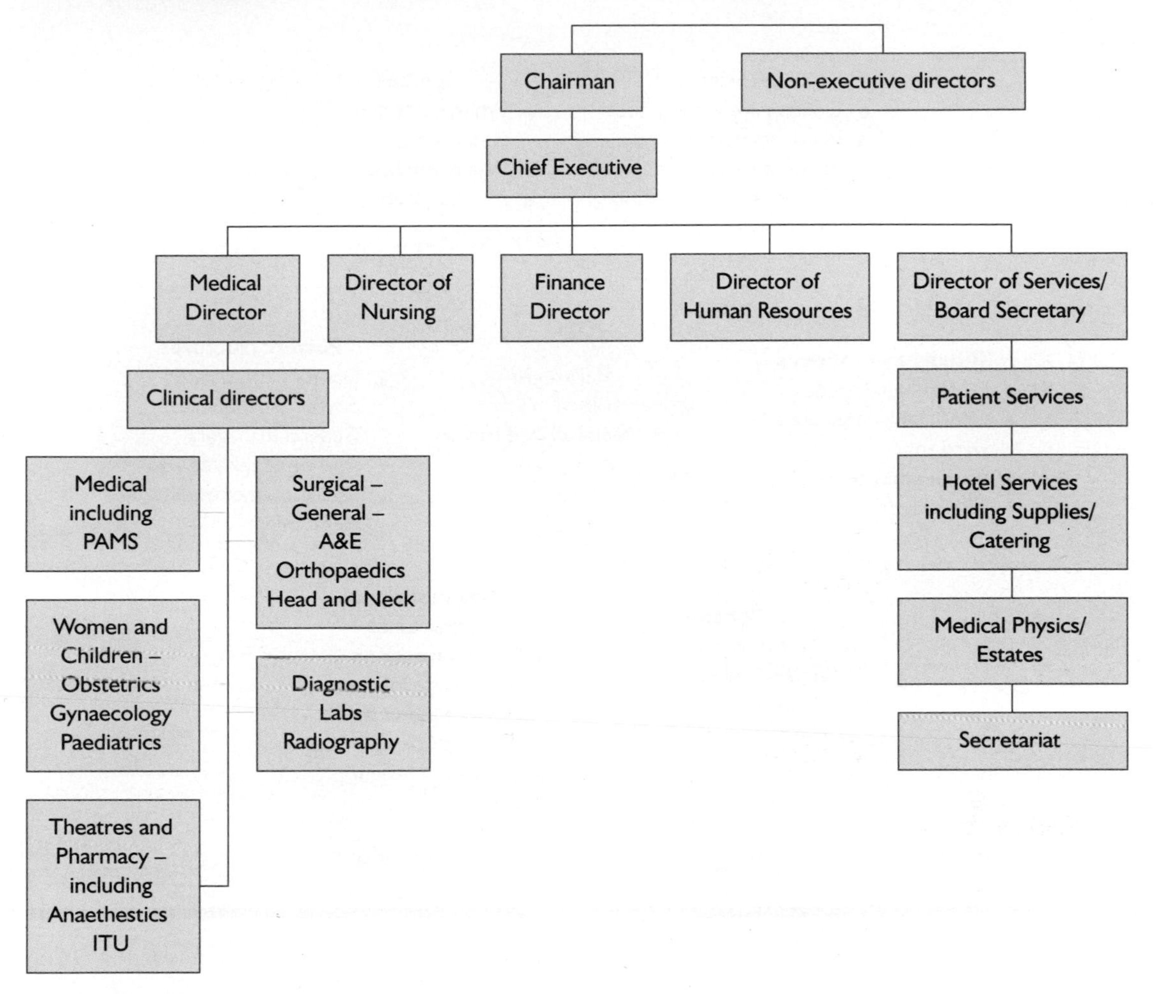

organisation, with some long-serving staff either choosing to take redundancy or early retirement and many remaining staff seeing their traditional job promotion prospects disappear.

DEVELOPING EVIDENCE-BASED PRACTICE

In order to address clinical efficiency, a number of initiatives relating to the improvement of patient care were introduced. The national movement

Exhibit 5(a) Cultural web of the Royal Alexandra Hospital: (a) pre-trust

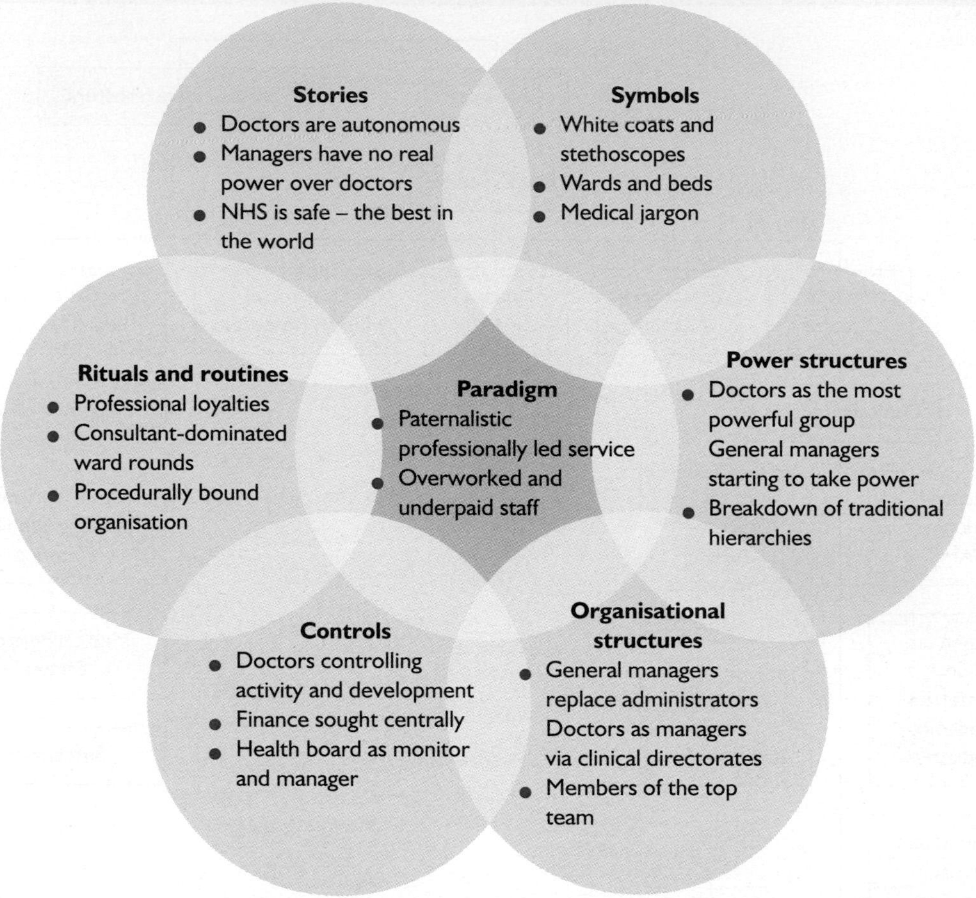

Stories
- Doctors are autonomous
- Managers have no real power over doctors
- NHS is safe – the best in the world

Symbols
- White coats and stethoscopes
- Wards and beds
- Medical jargon

Rituals and routines
- Professional loyalties
- Consultant-dominated ward rounds
- Procedurally bound organisation

Paradigm
- Paternalistic professionally led service
- Overworked and underpaid staff

Power structures
- Doctors as the most powerful group General managers starting to take power
- Breakdown of traditional hierarchies

Controls
- Doctors controlling activity and development
- Finance sought centrally
- Health board as monitor and manager

Organisational structures
- General managers replace administrators Doctors as managers via clinical directorates
- Members of the top team

towards the development and prioritisation of clinical practice in patient services according to evidence as to their effectiveness was mirrored locally by the establishment of clinical effectiveness groups. These encouraged clinical audit, which more and more became a multidisciplinary activity involving not only hospital doctors, nurses and other professional groups but also GPs through interface audits. It has taken many years for a culture of audit to become the norm, and even now many patient services are not as regularly reviewed as they might be. The importance of this in the hospital context is to see and review future change according to objective rather that the latest medical fashion. This focus has not always been welcomed by staff, some of whom view it as either another management 'fad' or as an infringement of their individual clinical freedom.

Exhibit 5(b) **Cultural web of the Royal Alexandra Hospital: (b) post-trust**

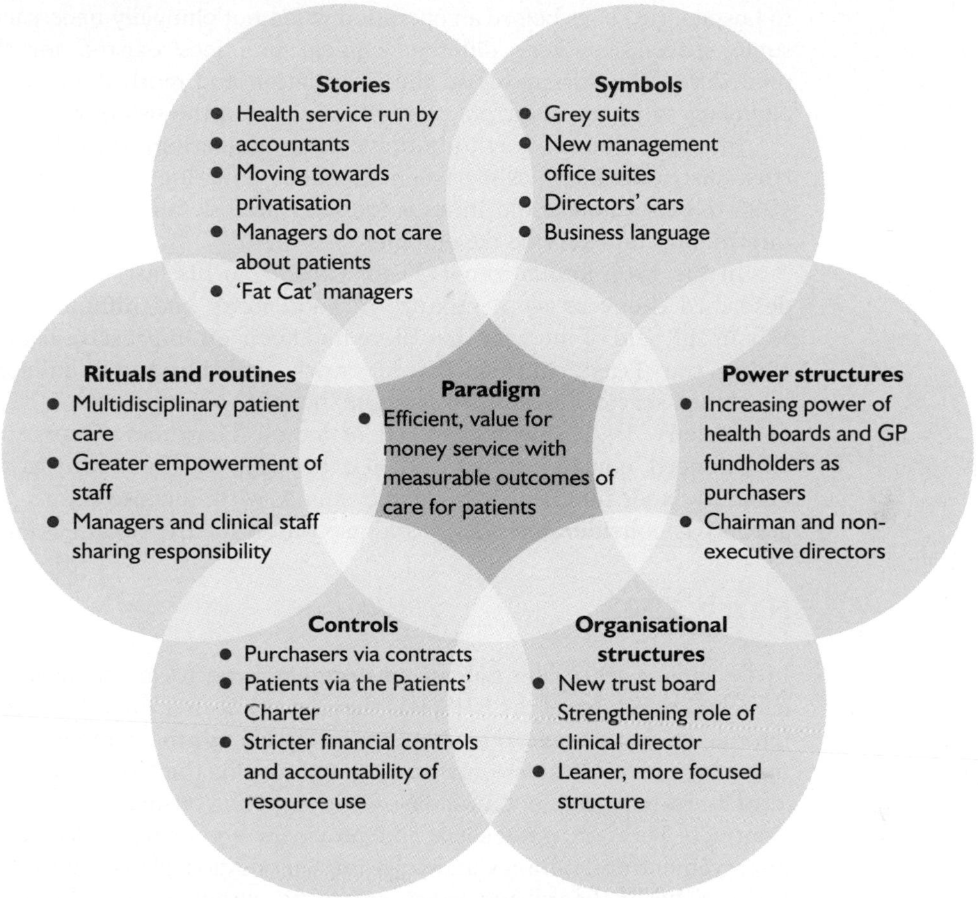

RESPONSES TO CHANGE

The RAH has undergone constant change since its opening in 1986. The impact of trust status was that it had become an autonomous organisation, responsible for its own success and future direction. Many clinical staff and, indeed, the public were concerned by the emphasis within the trust movement on management and that it detracted from patient care, with scarce resources being diverted away to pay for new managerial structures and what were perceived as 'fat cat' salaries and perks. Significant changes had occurred in all aspects of the cultural web (see Exhibits 5(a) and 5(b)).

Managers faced some resistance from staff when trying to implement the changes that had been instigated, first by the internal market and secondly from the need to live within continuing financial restraints. Clinicians had been used to having the freedom to organise their services without regard to the use of resources. Examples of this included consultants admitting a patient to hospital two days before an operation when not clinically necessary, and, in some specialities, very different clinical practices existed for the same procedure. Managers now had the information and motivation to encourage clinicians to review their practice with an eye on the use of resources.

In a continuous effort to improve communications with the public, the trust distributed an eight-page news-sheet covering its annual report in 1996 to every household in its catchment area detailing activity, financial information and service development.

In the 1996 annual report, Tom Gibson, in his last year as chairman, described the year as 'a mixture of good news and difficult challenges'. Martin Hill said of the year that there had been 'an impressive list of ways in which the Trust, through harder work and improved efficiency, has developed services further to patients' benefit...'.

January 1997 saw the arrival of a new chairman. George Gibb, an experienced consultant with KPMG, brought to the board a wealth of business and financial experience along with, according to the chief executive 'considerable energy and aspiration for the organisation'.

March 1998

In December 1997, the Labour government, true to its manifesto promise, launched its reform of the NHS, less that ten years after the introduction of the internal market. *Designed to Care* sets out to change the competitive nature of trusts by removing the internal market and turning the NHS in Scotland into a 'firm' to be managed, not an industry of competing businesses to be regulated. Contracts between purchasers and providers are being replaced by health improvement programmes and trust implementation plans. The relationships between health board and trusts are to be within a strategic management process rather than the purchaser/provider divide which existed. Collaboration and partnership will replace competition and GP fundholding will no longer exist. A major change in the design and delivery of health care will be the formation of new primary health care trusts which will see greater involvement of GPs and their ability to influence the future design and delivery of services.

Designed to Care aims to deliver a 'modern designed health service which puts patients first', providing seamless care, centred on the primary care setting and which ensures that patients receive care quickly and with certainty, where they want it, when they want it. It sets, as a priority, the development of clinical networks of health care professionals, working in teams to provide integrated care.

The supplementary paper, which focused on supporting staff through the changes, recognises that:

- Changes in service delivery and new care skills need to be underpinned by investment in education, training and development.

- As change impacts on employment and jobs, an employee relations framework is required to give staff the opportunity of real consultation, involvement and the ability to influence decision making.
- Workforce planning needs to support the development of a flexible, responsive workforce.
- The approach needs to be underpinned by set of core values which are applied consistently across the whole service.

Like other trusts, the RAH will not exist in its present form. The merger and subsequent reduction of trusts from 47 to around 25 will bring about major change in terms of their role, relationships, organisation and management. The consultation process suggests that the RAH will merge with two neighbouring acute trusts – Inverclyde and the Vale of Leven – to form a new Renfrewshire Acute Trust. The trust board will not exist in its present form and executive directors will need to apply for suitable posts within the reformed Scottish health service. Chairman and non-executive directors will also be reviewed.

THE BURTON GROUP 1969–97

This series of three case studies describes the different strategies and changing fortunes of the Burton Group over three decades. In that time the influence of three chief executives was pronounced: Ladislas Rice, who in the early 1970s attempted to refocus the menswear business whilst pursuing a strategy of retail diversification by acquisition; Ralph Halpern whose 'lifestyle retailing' approach took form in the development of men's and women's fashion shops focused on different market segments; and John Hoerner who sought to bring a disciplined approach to the retailing of the Group. This series of cases provides a basis for considering the fortunes of the Group in terms of the management styles of those CEOs, their strategies and their consequences.

BURTON GROUP (A): LADISLAS RICE, 1969–75

Gerry Johnson

At the beginning of the 1970s Burton had an annual turnover of around £80m, 15 factories manufacturing mainly made-to-measure suits and over 600 menswear shops. The company employed 27,000 workers, 10,000 of whom were employed at the Leeds Hudson Mills manufacturing base. Burton was essentially a manufacturer of made-to-measure garments with retail outlets as order points. Ready-to-wear merchandise was considered to be of secondary importance and was normally unavailable or low in stock. Yet by the late 1960s the company was operating in a retail environment undergoing rapid change. The 1960s was the era of the Beatles and the fashion conscience young male who wore imported ready-to-wear Italian suits and colourful clothes. Market growth came from men aged under 25 who were increasingly purchasing ready-to-wear clothes, which they could buy at similar or better quality for less money at the increasing number of more fashionable shops which were a growing competitive threat to Burton.

From 1967 to 1969 the company had attempted to recruit a new senior management team. By 1970 this was in place under the direction of Ladislas

---

This case study was prepared by Professor Gerry Johnson, Cranfield School of Management. It is intended as a basis for class discussion and not as an illustration of either good or bad management practice.

Rice, a Harvard-trained executive who had worked for a prestigious management consultancy and became the first CEO of any of the major UK clothing multiples to come from outside the industry.

1969–73: REORGANISATION AND RESTRUCTURING

At a corporate level, Rice sought to develop Burtons as a group of separate profit-responsible retail divisions, each with experienced senior executives heading them up.

For menswear, the central problem, his aim was to switch from a manufacturing focus to a retailing focus by 'building a team of managers capable of buying and selling ready made men's suits and outerwear, and in controlling the purchasing, sales and stocks of ready-to-wear garments'. This was to be done by splitting off manufacturing from retailing as separate divisions with the dual purpose of releasing the menswear buyers from internal buying obligations, and also requiring the manufacturing division to produce to the needs of retailing – be it Burton retailing or any other customers they might deal with. It was not an easy task to move towards ready-to-wear because made-to-measure entailed low stock commitment compared with higher stock levels and better stock control necessary for a ready-to-wear business. However, the new retail buying director was given the job of widening the product range to include ready-to-wear suits and, on the manufacturing side, attempts were made to switch production from made-to-measure to ready-to-wear.

At group level, other major steps were the tightening of controls on costs, increased mechanisation of manufacturing, the recruitment of fifty new senior executives, a new remuneration scheme including profit sharing and the establishment of a training centre. Planning systems were also put in place. The group executive set annual goals to divisions which were required to demonstrate how they could contribute to these goals. The result was divisional plans, revised every six months and reported against monthly. Such plans also provided the basis for a system of management by objectives, so that all managers to middle management level could know how they were expected to contribute to the company's performance.

In an attempt to utilise the asset base of the company and to move away from over-reliance on the clothing retail sector, Burton also diversified. Already involved in department stores with Peter Robinson, mail order and the French menswear operation, the years 1969 to 1973 saw a flurry of acquisitions. Rice summarised his policy of diversification as 'to seek well managed retail businesses, in any field, capable of expansion but needing, for real growth, the kind of property and financial strength which we can offer'. This meant using the property base both as a means of raising capital and as a yardstick against which to measure the viability of the store's operation. If properties could not be used by group retail businesses, they were to be let to other retail companies to gain income. Where properties could not generate adequate income or find outside users, they were to be

Exhibit 1 The Burton Group management structure in the early 1970s

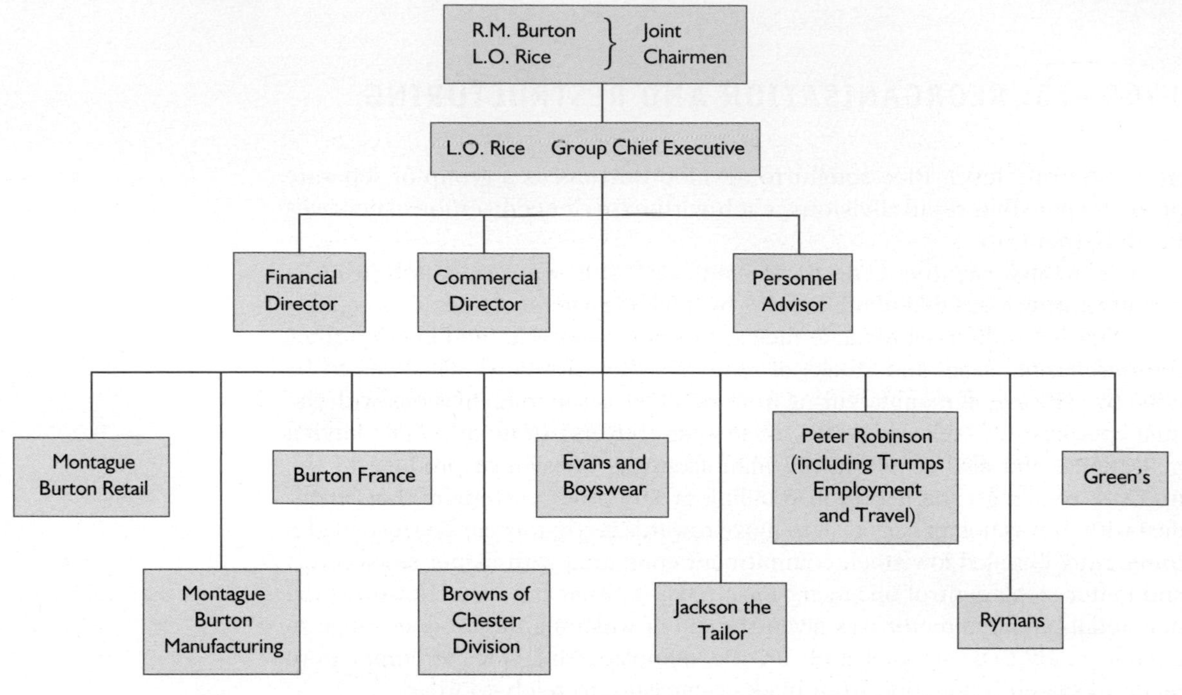

disposed of. In 1972, a separate property company, Montague Burton Property Investment Limited, was established.

The mail order operation, never a significant profit earner, was sold. However, in the six months from autumn 1970 to spring 1971, acquisitions followed. First, St Remy, a French operation which retailed men's and women's clothing through 35 shops across France. The reason behind this acquisition was the need to provide additional volume to the Burtons factory which was running at 50 per cent capacity: in France the made-to-measure market was also holding up better than elsewhere.

The next acquisition was Evans Outsize. Burtons not only acquired its 76 shops but also its computerised stock control systems, highly regarded at the time, and the retail skills of Cyril Spencer, its chief executive. Evans was a profitable business which had been growing and could be seen as a potential beneficiary of the properties available through Burtons. Ryman Conran, an office supply company was then acquired. Rymans had 75 retail outlets selling office stationery, furniture and machines, and had four manufacturing units. The same year, 1971, also saw the internal development of a new retail venture, 'Orange Hand', which was aimed at the 5–15-year-old boy and designed to exploit the growing fashion awareness of the young. Finally, in 1973, the group acquired Green's, retailer of consumer and electrical goods, then at the beginning of its growth in the consumer market. The resulting divisionalised structure is shown in Exhibit 1.

CONSEQUENCES

The initial results of all this activity were not encouraging. An initial profit increase in 1971 hid a decline in menswear profits and a less than convincing trading performance, almost one-third of the group profits coming from its property division. The capital spent on its acquisitions was also leading to increased borrowings, and the market and internal shift away from made-to-measure suits were giving rise to underutilised factory capacity.

Efforts were made to improve performance, including the refurbishment of some one hundred shops and the rationalisation of the production capacity including redundancy programmes in three factories: but change was simply taking too long. Managers with buying or computer skills took time to recruit; and the shops needed converting to present a more up-to-date image. One executive recalled:

> I remember there were window models that looked like something out of Joe Stalin's secret service. We needed to replace them but there wasn't the capacity to do it in less than five years. We had to change the heads in one year and so on down the body.

The production focus was switching to ready-to-wear – the problem was that capacity far outstripped demand, despite a voluntary redundancies programme and manufacturing cut-backs. Efforts were made to sell outside the group but with little success. Shop managers could also see they were losing sales to ready-to-wear. The problems were the time it took to refit shops, the failure of new ideas in merchandise to appeal to customers in shops that were out of date, and the 'learning curve' of the new merchandisers which 'was much longer than expected'.

By 1973, group sales were rising but largely because of the acquisition of new businesses. Yet these other retailing interests barely showed a profit. The French operation was also giving rise to concern; management admitted that it was trying to 'buck the trend' on made-to-measure, even in France. The overcapacity in menswear manufacturing was getting worse and stocks remained stubbornly high.

1974–5: ATTEMPTED READJUSTMENT

In 1974 the strategy was changed. In the annual report, Rice stated:

> Having achieved a better balance of retailing businesses we decided that the right course of action was to concentrate on their improvement rather than to continue to broaden our retailing base.

There followed the disposal of a factory in Boulogne, further cutbacks in UK manufacturing capacity and the contraction of Peter Robinson, the department store operation. Menswear entered a period in 1974 of what amounted to a continual sale, in an effort to move stock. In addition, new ranges were introduced. However, as one retail manager of the time explained, having attended a merchandising strategy presentation:

> Most of the new merchandise we were shown was imported stuff, casual wear and cheaper ready-to-wear suits ... But when we got back out in the field not much changed. They put in some new merchandise, but it was added onto, rather than instead of the bespoke tailoring ... we were still bespoke tailors ... We had a lot of cloth to sell.

Orange Hand the fashion shop for boys was closed down. The only area of investment in expansion was Top Shop run by Ralph Halpern, then part of Peter Robinson. This was one of only two profitable businesses in 1974, the other being Evans with Cyril Spencer as chief executive.

EXTERNAL INTERVENTION

It was clear by the end of 1974 that the costs of consolidation and rationalisation were high; the stock clearance policies depressed margins; the Boulogne closure incurred costs of £900,000 and the contraction of Peter Robinson £1.6m. The 1974 results were called an 'unmitigated disaster' in the *Financial Times*. Although turnover had increased by 16 per cent, trading profits had declined by 44 per cent. By 1975, return on capital employed had slumped to just 4 per cent; and it was only positive because of the property interests.

All of this had to be seen in the light of the reluctance of the Burton family to implement closures. The share structure of the company ensured that Burtons had remained under the control of the family who had also long prided themselves on their responsibility to their employees and were reluctant to enforce redundancy by major factory closures.

In 1975, a stockbroking firm with a special interest in retailing issued a report on Burtons to the company's shareholders. It was leaked to the *Sunday Telegraph*, which published extracts from it. Its comments were damning:

- The splitting of retailing and manufacturing had created 'competition between rather than co-ordination between the divisions'.
- 'We estimate that over the period [1969 to 1974] these [sales of made-to-measure] have fallen from approximately £1 million to approximately £550,000, a decline of 45 per cent. Nationally we believe the decline in made-to-measure suits over this period has been closer to 30 per cent.'

- The attempts by the company to move to more fashionable merchandise had not been successful because the 'trendy' clothes were not trendy enough to attract new customers, whilst being too trendy for their traditional customers.
- The attempted rationalisation of manufacturing was too slow, particularly at Leeds. This was made worse by inadequate stock control and distribution.
- It was a mistake to diversify. It would have been wiser to concentrate on the central problem of menswear. Many of the acquisitions placed strains on management resources because they had problems inherent within them 'at a time when the major priority was the rejuvenating and restructuring of the "guts" of the business'.

The report concluded by saying that 'the present situation ... rewards neither the shareholders nor the public and should not be allowed to continue'. The stockbrokers called on the institutions and the non-executive directors to put pressure on the company to replace Rice and his senior management team, and felt that Burtons needed someone with more retail experience to head it.

BURTON GROUP (B): RALPH HALPERN, 1976–90

Gerry Johnson

HALPERN JOINS THE BOARD

In 1976 the Burton Group went into a trading loss for the first time. Despite the imposition of tighter controls and many disposals, more drastic action was needed. Cyril Spencer took over from Ladislas Rice and Ralph Halpern joined the board. The Halpern team, which was already running Peter Robinson and Top Shop, the speciality younger women's fashion boutique, also assumed responsibility for Burton Retailing. Halpern moved the merchandising team to London, and manufacturing was cut by one-third and reorganised to become a service to the retail operation.

The Hudson Mills factory closure was seen by Ralph Halpern as more than just trying to resolve a problem of manufacturing overcapacity; it was also a symbol of the past:

> People used to go to work in Hudson Road, Leeds, and feel protected; it was a feudal castle. They had their lunch in the feudal canteen, the feudal barons called Burton turning up and administrating the rites and allowing employment to be granted and there would be a medical man on the premises and a bit of billiards and a bowling green. So the whole of the village set-up was really to show that we could protect you there; protect you from society.

Halpern believed that within Burtons there was scope for several different types of retailer, each appealing to different market segments. The strategy became more focused on fashion retailing of both men's and women's clothing. The other interests of Burtons were either disposed of or rationalised. One executive who was a field manager at the time commented: 'This was not like the early seventies: shops were completely refitted – gutted. There was real money spent on them. We were in retailing at last.' For example, Halpern promised that for Burton Menswear, 'The

---

This case study was prepared by Professor Gerry Johnson, Cranfield School of Management. It is intended as a basis for class discussion and not as an illustration of either good or bad management practice.

future store will have the most beautiful shop fittings, the best deep-pile carpets, the best windows, but relatively good value, keenly priced merchandise.'

By the end of 1979 the group's turnround looked impressive. From the heavy losses of 1976 and 1977, the group returned to profitability in 1978 and, in 1979, was able to show all retailing divisions as profitable. Interest payments had been brought down by half in the four years and the high costs of closure and redundancy appeared to be behind them. By 1980 the emphasis was on investment in the men's and women's retail chains and the pruning of loss-making peripheral ventures. A total of £36million was spent on the shops, £12million on new sites and £20million on modernisation. Other activities were cut; the Evans mail order operation was disposed of and the number of Evans shops reduced; and two more of the remaining four factories were also closed. In 1981 both the French operation and Rymans were sold.

HALPERN TAKES CHARGE

In 1979 the decision was taken to enfranchise the non-voting shareholders. Burton, then, ceased to be in essence a family-controlled business. Next came the reorganisation of the board. At the end of 1979, Rice stepped down as chairman to become non-executive deputy chairman and Spencer was appointed chairman and joint managing director, with Halpern as the other joint managing director. But dramatic changes were to occur in 1981. Prior to Burtons' annual general meeting in 1981, the *Observer* newspaper carried the story of why Spencer would not be seeking re-election as chairman. It was revealed that Spencer had held discussions with Gerald Ronson of the Heron Corporation for the sale of Burton shares.

> Spencer and Ronson were old friends. The deal which Ronson is reliably understood to have discussed involved a buy-out by Heron of the Burton family's interests accounting for some 15 per cent of the equity ... At the time the Burton Group was valued on the stock market at a little under £100 million although its rich property assets were estimated to be worth around £240 million or 300p a share ... Ronson's plan was clearly to buy Burton's at a discount to assets.
>
> *OBSERVER*, 24 JANUARY 1982

Ralph Halpern was invited by Spencer to attend his meeting with Ronson. *The Observer* continued:

> Unknown to Ronson and Spencer, a recording system was hidden in his [Halpern's] bespoke Burton suit ... Halpern's view of the ... whispering was that it was improper for the deals to be discussed without the rest of the board's knowledge.

At the board meeting on 2 July 1981, Spencer was asked to stand down. Ralph Halpern was appointed chairman and chief executive of Burtons.

'You have to understand, he has immeasurable ego and immeasurable confidence – perhaps they are the same thing. The guy just exudes confidence.' As a description of Ralph Halpern by one of his management team of the early 1980s, it is typical of what colleagues and competitors said of him.

Halpern operated by centralising what he considered to be the major policy decisions on his top team, making such decisions explicit and then delegating their implementation to other teams in each of the operating divisions. Since the shops were fashion shops, Halpern also believed they had to change as fashion changed. By 1980, Top Shop was already going through its third refitting programme. Indeed, Halpern talked about 'institutionalising change':

> Change is always on the agenda: we don't just expect our executives to run the show, we expect them to change the show as well ... We are positioned as the lifestyle clothing experts of the high street and it's a tough position to maintain. Hence our management philosophy is that people are trained and motivated to plan for change ... No store is allowed to go more than 4–5 years without complete modernisation ... only the most visionary retailers recognise the need to change a successful formula while it is still working.

His view was that a positive attitude to risk taking should be encouraged too,

> But within a tight framework. We maintain very tight controls on areas that matter, but seek a balance between control and flexibility, each company must evolve its own solution to this conflict.

The rewards were very high on this basis.

> We believe in high pay and incentives and we stress promotion from within for those who succeed ... For all our management and staff, substantial bonuses are linked to target plan ... A senior executive member of a divisional board can double his salary for outstanding performance.

Demanding targets were seen by Ralph Halpern as essential if change was to be achieved and maintained. His view was that, given demanding targets, executives could not be content with running businesses the way they always had.

Similarly, Halpern believed that the expectations for change needed to be built into the financial plans and measures of the business: for example, in rates of depreciation which were adjusted to faster replacement of fixtures and fittings.

A unique organisation structure was also introduced. By the early 1980s each division had functional senior executives reporting directly to functional managing directors on the main board. These functional areas were shop operations, merchandising, concessions, finance, personnel and systems. There were no divisional managing directors. Halpern explained:

> If you have a series of managing directors in the divisions and you sit on top of that you are more likely to get out of touch. If you filter all knowledge through an individual it's very much filtered, so you only hear. It's really an explanation of his good performance or poor performance as filtered by him. I know because

> I've done it myself. What we wanted to happen was that central management should keep in touch with every facet of the business. They can see what's happening down to the market place.

As one executive explained, 'It's a very open system, it has to be: you can't hide anything.' It was also an approach to management that bred mutual challenge within management teams: indeed, outsiders to the Burton system of management commented on how aggressive Burtons' managers were.

1982–5: A SUCCESS STORY

By 1983, the portfolio of retail businesses included:

- Top Shop specialising in fashion clothes for young women aged 15–25.
- Top Man for 15–30-year-old men.
- Dorothy Perkins 'providing colourful, and good value fashion for women of 20–30'.
- Evans, which had been a specialist store concentrating on clothes for 'larger' ladies, was restyled to 'Evans Collection' to improve the fashionable image of the business.
- Burtons itself remained and concentrated on mens clothing but less and less on formal suits and more on casual wear.
- Principles was launched in 1984 to cater for 25–45-year-old, more sophisticated women.

The 1983 results showed sales of about £300m, pre-tax profits up to £39m and a return on capital employment of 16 per cent, after a total of £29m had been spent on the store openings and 79 shop modernisations, all of which expenditure had come from internal cash flow.

Halpern no longer regarded Burtons as competing as a mens and womenswear multiple with other such multiples. The aim was to take share from those dominating the market and that meant competing with market leaders such as Marks & Spencer. Such expansion would require growth backed by larger financial resources than even the new cash-rich Burtons could draw upon. Consequently, in 1983, Halpern announced the intention to increase share capital from the current £55m to £125m; the shareholding of the family and directors was thus reduced to just 8 per cent.

THE ACQUISITION OF THE DEBENHAMS GROUP AND GROUP RESTRUCTURING

In 1985 the Burton Group made its largest acquisition, the Debenham Group, one of the largest retailers in the UK, with 68 department stores.

Traditionally, department stores offered a wide range of products on a single site. However, the appeal of a wide range under one roof suffered with the growth of specialist retailers, particularly in the fashion goods sector. This trend accelerated with the increased popularity of shopping precincts and covered shopping areas.

The size of Debenhams meant there had to be a restructuring of the Burton Group itself. The new structure was based on three divisions: Retailing, Consumer Financial Services, and Property, Design and Construction. Each had a managing director and operating board. By 1986 there were 345 senior executives in the organisation.

To fuel future expansion plans and provide sites for new outlets, Burtons embarked on three years of property development and major financial deals. The acquisition of Debenhams had provided 63 new properties for its portfolio, but had left the group with a £300m debt and 70 per cent gearing. Burtons set up a new holding company, jointly (50 per cent) owned with the banks. It then sold £100m of property to the holding company, using £30m of Burton Group cash with the £70m difference being met by the banks. This £70m was then used to pay off some of the Debenhams acquisition debt. With some sale and lease back deals, this left gearing at 30 per cent and debt at £130m by the end of 1986. In addition, Burtons went twice to the banks for £900m multi-option loans to replace all previous lines of credit.

Personally, Ralph Halpern was at the pinnacle of his reputation. Cited as an example of British business acumen and talent by Prime Minister Mrs Thatcher, he was rewarded with a knighthood. His personal standing seemed unassailable; even when the newspapers reported his dalliance with a young model, Fiona Wright, the shareholders and the City acknowledged few tremors of doubt. In 1986 profits rose to £146m. For Sir Ralph, success was reflected in his annual income, up 35 per cent to £1.359m. This was, at least in part, the result of the controversial share option scheme introduced at the beginning of the year. The scheme gave 80 senior executives bonuses after five years of up to eight times their salary, and could have meant £8m for Sir Ralph himself. Shareholders approved the scheme, though protests from City investors later in the year saw the package cut significantly.

GROWING CONCERNS

Though continuing to show growth and profits, by the end of 1988 City analysts began to complain that there was a lack of clarity as to the performance of the different parts of the Group; for example, the Debenhams figures were consolidated into retailing profits, with only portions declared. They were also concerned that the gearing, at 47 per cent, whilst not particularly high for the level of profits, showed a continuing upward trend.

A Department of Trade and Industry (DTI) investigation into the bitterly contested takeover of Debenhams was also initiated in 1987.

Although Halpern insisted that the group's tactics and behaviour throughout the process was correct in all respects, inquiries centred around the business relationships entered into by Burton Group with those who helped it gain control of Debenhams. Inevitably the inquiry took up the time of management for over a year, from January 1988 to May 1989, when it was finally concluded and it became clear that no action was to be taken. However, during that time it provided a focus of media attention,

The move by Burtons into property development had been typical of the mid-1980s when many businesses expanded via property-based deals. However, by 1989 the property slump had reached the balance sheet. Profits were up again for the ninth successive year but by only 5.7 per cent. By March 1990 the impact of the recession was leading to a reduction in property development. There was also a sharp rise in debt to over 125 per cent of shareholders funds, chiefly because of the cost of shopping centres that had been opened, aggravated by the low rental income that was not covering running costs.

Halpern had been one of the first retail chief executives to highlight the descent into retail recession. In company reports from 1987, despite ever-growing profits, he was warning that each subsequent year would be harder, and margins tighter. After the credit boom of the mid-1980s, consumer confidence was low as high interest rates and high unemployment discouraged both spending and borrowing. By mid-1990 the recession had surpassed even the gloomiest forecasts in the retailing sector and was even affecting the market for young women's clothing, usually resilient even when other sectors were suffering.

Meanwhile the financial press continued to talk Burtons down. Sir Ralph Halpern's share option scheme that in 1989 brought him an income of £1.53m, became increasingly unpopular. Attacks ranged from the questioning of the validity of combining the role of chairman and chief executive, to articles on his private life. Headlines such as 'Burton in Bimbo Limbo' appeared even in serious newspapers such as the *Telegraph*, harking back to 1986 and the Fiona Wright affair. Executives were also accused of being defensive, in contrast to the openness, even razzmatazz, that had accompanied Burton announcements in the mid-1980s.

DIVESTMENT AND DEPARTURE

In mid-1990, analysts were revising Burton's profit forecasts for 1990 downwards to £150m as compared to the £223m of 1989. Faced with the declining profit performance and mounting debt, in July 1990 Burton Group announced its sale of Burton Group Financial Services Division (BGFS). The main business of BGFS was the provision of consumer credit finance, and it was the largest retail credit card operator in the UK with over 3 million cards in issue. This was regarded as a sensible action by the City as it substantially reduced Burton's debt, but it was clouded by the simultaneous announcement that the property division was to be sold. Although this had been mooted by analysts, it provoked gloomy forecasts that it could take two years to sell; and in the meantime drag down profits into the 'black hole of property'.

By September 1990, Burton's share price was sliding from a 1990 high of 226p to 55p before recovering to 71p. Explanations varied for this. One analyst, John Richards of County NatWest, complained, 'It is a credibility problem. The reason people are worried is that the company is not telling us what is happening, so people are running around and worrying ...' And given the importance of the declining value of property assets at that time, he was also concerned that, 'We simply can't quantify the value of the company's assets.' Others pointed to the poor trading conditions and faltering profits or to the financial structure of the Group. Some analysts were forecasting profits for 1990 as low as £65m with Group debts of £400m. In fact, profits before tax were declared at £133m, certainly a dramatic reversal in Burton's fortunes. Moreover, the withdrawal from property development cost the group some £169m and resulted in a loss after tax and dividends for the first time in over a decade.

The trend in the previous decade was to link closely the success of a corporation to the figure of its chairman and there was increasing pressure from the City to remove Sir Ralph from the role of chief executive, leaving him as chairman. In fact, in November 1990 he stepped down from both his roles as chairman and chief executive under a golden parachute of £2 million plus a £456,000 a year pension. There followed a flurry of press discussions on his years at Burtons and their success or failure:

> Halpern provided Burton with outstanding leadership throughout the 1980s. He brought style and panache. He cared about the ambience in which people bought clothes and improved it out of all recognition. He catered brilliantly in clothes design and range for the career girl aged between 18 and 30. His skill was to focus on an idea and squeeze it for all it was worth ... His belief was that large and successful companies were not just created to provide an income for shareholders, and that everybody, from the chief executive down to the teenage shop assistants, deserved a spoonful of the gravy as a reward for hard selling ... At one east London branch yesterday the assistant manager of a Burton store was right on cue: 'We all did well from Sir Ralph. He may have got millions, but we got the regular 50 to 100 quid extra in our pay-packets, right down to the trainee on the floor. He was good news in this industry' ... At the top, Halpern lived out the fantasies of sales assistants the country over with a £1 million a year salary, the gold Rolex and cuff links, sessions in the gym and playing on his organ (a Yamaha synthesizer in the basement). Staff did not despise the style, they envied it.
>
> *SUNDAY TELEGRAPH*, 18 NOVEMBER 1990

Halpern's own views were also stated:

> My wealth is minute to what I have created. Look at what the company has earned and what it is worth, and then look at my salary and my perks. And also look at the incentive bonuses that are paid right down the line, to every employee in the company, all 35,000 of them.

The article went on to say that there were many in the City, including his enemies, who grudgingly admitted that his sexual indiscretion and its accompanying lifestyle had been the ruination of what could have been an extraordinary business career. They could see the tragic element in the tale. His boast that he alone had been responsible, helped by a small group of hand-picked executives, for the astonishing success of the Burton empire was not disputed by many. A merchant banker suggested that Halpern was a much more complicated character than many of the comments made about him would suggest.

> There is no doubt that he is an absolute megalomaniac, ... but he is a listener and was able to put together a strong team around him and right down through the organisation. A lot of the credit for that can be given to the remuneration package and generous option scheme. Two years ago he had the strongest and best retailing scheme in the whole industry.
>
> *Sunday Times*, 18 November 1990

BURTON GROUP (C): JOHN HOERNER, 1991–7

Jacqui Gush

THE LEGACY OF THE 1980S

As it entered the 1990s, Burtons was grappling with the effects of overstimulated growth in the previous decade. Bold expansionism and a quest for market share and domination had resulted in a legacy of middle to downmarket retail chains, occupying too much space, whose tired fascias were showing an increasing mismatch between trading format and target market. As the brands focused on broadly defined markets, they competed against each other, and in the process margins were sacrificed and brand values were rapidly eroded as customers became bargain hunters. The quest to maintain market share had led to lower mark-ups and had reduced gross profit to 9 per cent of sales in 1991. The costs of supporting the property portfolio resulted in high operational gearing, sensitive to changes in sales volumes; the company therefore suffered from a higher cost base than its rivals. Half of the company's debt was due to unsaleable property. All of this was at a time when the UK was moving into recession. 'Its problems go deeper than the vagaries of consumer confidence' (*Sunday Times*, 16 February 1992.)

THE SITUATION IN 1991

With Halpern's resignation in November 1990, the roles of chairman and chief executive officer were split: Laurence Cooklin became chief executive officer and Sir John Hoskyns non-executive chairman. Altogether, seven

---

This case study was prepared by Jacqui Gush, Bournemouth University. It is intended as a basis for class discussion and not as an illustration of either good or bad management practice.

directors had stepped down by the end of 1990. By March 1991 three more had resigned. Laurence Cooklin had held the role of joint managing director for the past year and at that stage had a twenty-year record with the company, having joined Burtons soon after graduation.

Cooklin set in motion plans to consolidate the business and to strengthen core areas whilst initiating major cost-cutting exercises. At that stage the group managed 2,056 stores with 1 million square metres of floor space. He initiated 'Blueprint' and 'Heartland' operations which went some way towards rationalising space, distribution and buying. In the words of one fund manager, 'he was shy, awkward and evasive' (*Sunday Times*, 16 February 1992), contrasting with Halpern's confidence and aggression. With a collapse in consumer confidence, substantial reduction in property values and a sharp rise in unemployment, by the end of the following year Burtons was plunged into the red for the first time since 1977. Cooklin resigned after 15 months with a £773,000 payoff.

It was recognised that the benefits the group had were not producing the results. In the 1992 annual report, the chairman believed 'the recession is only partly to blame for Burtons downturn ... The task ahead was not a matter of fine tuning but implementing deep seated change.'

INTRODUCING JOHN HOERNER

In February 1992, 'The Suit' as Laurence Cooklin had been known (*Retail Week*, 26 May 1995) was replaced by the chief executive of Debenhams, John Hoerner. Debenhams had been the one jewel in the Burtons crown since 1990, contributing 52 per cent of the Group's profits in 1990 and 83 per cent by 1992.

Hoerner had demonstrated a record of achievement within the Group in the same way that Halpern had done with Top Shop in 1974. An American, with over 30 years of retailing experience, he was appointed by Halpern and joined the group as chief executive of Debenhams in 1987 from the position of chairman and chief executive with the Ayres chain in Indianapolis. In 1991 he was appointed to the Group board. The move was set to demonstrate a break with the past and the start of a positive strategic direction and new energy for the group. His reputation was as a 'feet on the ground' retailer; one of his directors described him as 'a practitioner with good experience from both sides of the traditional divide', being very customer- and market-focused while understanding the back-of-house systems. He had been described in *Retail Week* (26 May 1995) as a 'lateral thinker who retains an exasperating eye for detail'. Where Halpern had been labelled 'The inspired despot', Hoerner was 'the serious hands on retailer'. As such, he was the antidote to the excesses of Halpern. Where Halpern had been newsworthy, Hoerner was a private man, shunning the cult of personality and steering a 'puritanical' reign.

THE PROCESS FOR CHANGE

Hoerner faced the short-term challenge of returning the group to profit, whilst at the same time establishing a strategy for the 1990s. With an eye for detail and a reputation for extreme thoroughness and high standards, Hoerner set about rationalising the costly structure. As he said in the 1993 annual report, the programme of change was approached 'methodically, logically and analytically ... Many of the changes we've made have been radical, but they've all been based on highly disciplined thinking and planning'. He also stressed his long-term approach to reviving the business: 'We're in this business for the long haul, so we looked ahead and began the task of refurbishing the group's entire fabric.' A year earlier, the 1992 annual report wrote candidly on his initial approach to the process of change:

> The first step to achieving change was to create an environment in which change was not only possible but actively encouraged. Making this shift in culture was Hoerner's first priority. It meant introducing a far more open way of exchanging views and reaching decisions. It called for managers right across the Company to share and support common goals ... The meeting which took place ... three days after Hoerner's appointment, was a unique event. It marked the first gathering of The Burton Group management board, a newly formed team of 16 senior managers. The assembly, chaired by Hoerner, represented the full spread of the Group's activities by including the managing directors of all the retail Divisions and the top management from central services functions ... This sense of co-operation and mutual support had been missing for several years. In the rush for expansion, the Divisions had widened their specialist niches and gone for all the business they could get.

This was emphasised independently by the managing director of Evans:

> As autonomous businesses we'd become possessive of our information. Now, the aim is to share knowledge, because it's in everyone's interest to know what's going on throughout the group.

The Group management board answered to a board of directors of seven executive directors and six non-executive directors. Broad strategic directions were mapped out by senior executives, while at the same time the managing directors of the divisions formulated their annual business plans from analysis of markets and products. As Keith Cameron, Group Personnel and Stores Director, said: 'hopefully the two meet somewhere in the middle, a bit like the Channel Tunnel'. The intention was that 'strategy development and process was itself a collective effort, a pooling of experience and expertise, with everyone committing themselves to the final proposal' (1992 annual report).

THE CHANGES FROM 1992–7

Organisational Structure

To support this Group mentality and to take initial action to simplify the top heavy, multi-level structure that had characterised Halpern's regime, early structural rationalisation resulted in increased integration of the Group's activities.

The first move was to integrate previously independent service functions, bringing together the back office processes whilst maintaining brand differentiation in the stores. The aim was for all divisions to utilise the services of common group functions. Layers of management were eliminated. Where Halpern had had two directors in each function, by the end of 1992, managing directors of the retail divisions were reporting direct to Hoerner instead of through divisional CEOs. The rationale for the structural changes was stated in the 1992 annual report: 'The Burton Group has no *raison d'être* unless it can create synergy and get more out of the Divisions than would be possible if they ran as stand alone businesses.'

Under Halpern, Central Services constituted a separate strategic business unit (SBU) for the Burton Group and operated as a profit centre. Each SBU supported layers of management and directorships. Hoerner disposed of the peripheral business units of Financial Services and Property and Central Services to focus on the retail divisions. The climax of a lengthy process of integration was in 1997. Each retail division remained responsible for its own buying and marketing but store operations management was reorganised and area managers became responsible for all retail brands within one geographical area. Seven retail directors oversaw the new regionally organised structure, reporting to Group Operations, one of five Central Service functions responsible for supporting the retail divisions (see Exhibit 1). The resulting group management board brought together sixteen senior managers from both the retail divisions and Central Service functions. (In 1997 new service functions representing international development, home shopping and design and development were added.)

A reappraisal of target markets was undertaken, with the aim of narrowing the focus and gaining clearer definition. Each target market would represent a definable 'taste range'. In turn this would allow the group to use marketing as a longer-term strategic tool instead of a short-term tactical weapon. The Blueprint programme started in 1991 was strengthened, and in 1993 it was renamed Townprint. It became a major component of group strategy, with the objective of reviewing the space allocation between the branded fascias, rationalising and disposing of space where possible. This ensured that the space was allocated in a way that matched the market demands of each particular town and the ever-shifting consumer demand patterns. Linked to this was an extensive programme of modernisation using money from a £163m rights issue that year to support the refocused and clearly defined brand values of the different fascias.

Exhibit 1 Organisational chart for the Burton Group, 1997

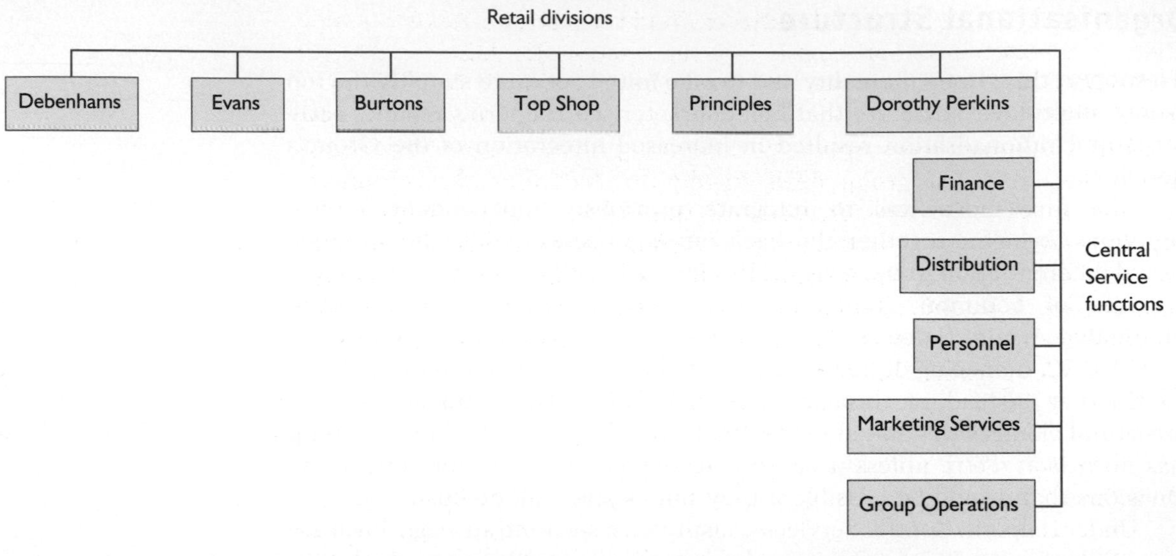

Any proposal to spend capital on the estate beyond an inexpensive visual update now triggered a community analysis that treated each trading locality as a single market and analysed the potential it held for each division. Burton Group 'town councils' were established in 1995 to enhance divisional co-operation within a locality.

Human Resource Management

The need to streamline operations to reduce overheads and implement better ways of working led to the introduction of the 'Best Practice' initiative in 1993. This involved a cross-divisional, cross-functional taskforce approach, to rethink fundamentally company procedures, structures and systems across all functions of the business. Incompatible divisional practices were replaced with streamlined, standardised group-wide systems based on current best practice within the group. As a result, two thousand jobs were lost across the group and a wholesale switch to part-time working was introduced with three thousand 'key time' jobs created. Head office staff was reduced by 25 per cent. Linked to this overhaul of jobs, new standardised personnel practices were introduced, including universal terms and conditions, staffing methods, job evaluation and grading based on competence assessment, salary structures and training requirements. The severe and rapid action caused much media attention: 'the treatment of staff appears almost cruel and could prove to be disruptive in the long term' (*Menswear*, 21 January 1993).

Supply Chain Management

The same approach was taken to the management of the supply chain in 1995. 'Fastflow' carried the objective to build a fast and flexible supply chain to ensure product quality, better supply flexibility and stock availability. As a result, the supplier base was rationalised by half in four years, as effective long-term relationships were sought. A group supplier handbook enforced conformity to common procedures and standards. This stated that the group deals firmly with suppliers breaching the conditions. The *Drapers Record* (9 December 1995) reported that suppliers commented that 'the terms and conditions are terribly onerous', and that several put the manual in the hands of their lawyers. An analyst commented, 'It sounds a bit harsh ... how is this going to help them build a relationship with suppliers? But it will help the bottom line.' In 1995–6 gross margins rose 2.3 per cent.

Rewarding Performance

The 1996 annual report cited performance-related bonuses as an important factor in the group's recovery. The key performance indicators were quantitative, based on a series of models or templates which were applied to measure and control staff performance in all areas of the business. Staff were rewarded solely on numerical outcomes. These objective and personal measures were highly visible to all employees.

Performance-related bonus schemes for staff had remained in force since the 1980s and the majority of staff were eligible for bonuses based on individual and team performance. In addition, staff were encouraged through different schemes to become shareholders, and at the end of 1996 more than half were. Working with American consultants, in 1996 changes were made to the bonus scheme, employing the concept of economic value added. In addition, to encourage sustained performance, part of the bonus was held back, dependent on performance the following year. Both of these initiatives served to reduce the potential bonus each year and met with staff dissatisfaction.

Executive performance was similarly incentivised. Performance-related bonus involved a sophisticated scheme linking reward to annual profit targets, following an escalating structure of measures and based partly on divisional and partly on group performance. In exchange for demanding targets, bonuses of between 30 and 70 per cent of salary could be realised. Only in 1992 was a cap of 100 per cent of salary imposed on executive directors. The 1987 executive share option scheme was replaced in 1996 by one which linked executive reward more closely to long-term corporate performance.

When the losses of the previous year were reversed in 1993, Hoerner benefited from a 60 per cent pay increase to £624,000. By 1996 his pay had risen to £1.12m with the benefit of increased performance-related bonus of nearly £500,000.

MANAGEMENT STYLE AND ORGANISATIONAL BEHAVIOUR[1]

Burton executives typically described the organisation as temperamentally impatient, direct and forceful, intolerant of negativity and resistance. Keith Cameron saw resistance 'being flushed out by others'. He claimed that staff had a 'succeed at all odds' mentality, and were used to managing change. All the time John Hoerner was 'driving and directing from the front'. Hoerner's style has been described as 'collegiate ... but he never shied away from taking the final decision' (*Retail Week*, 26 May 1995). A former director reported, 'He would seek ideas from everyone and then make his own mind up. If you didn't follow this decision through you were in big trouble' (*Retail Week*, 26 May 1995). Another recollects that at board meetings, 'John would sit down and tell me what my opinion was. He rejected anyone he perceives is not 100% with him' (*Financial Times*, 17 May 1997).

Despite management's endeavours towards greater collaboration across the Group, there was evidence that the old culture of a defensive, competitive, power-based culture endured. The Top Shop and Top Man divisions merged in 1992 as part of the rationalisation and since then had shared floorspace at head office. However, in 1997, according to employees, it was still rare for staff from the buying team of one division to cross the floor to the other. Information was closely guarded and those leaving the division were treated as outcasts.

New recruits were inducted with stories of a flat structure, flexible culture, with co-operative teamwork, yet in reality one reported finding an intensely competitive atmosphere where nothing was shared, and where everyone looked after number one. 'It's not really a group, they're all competing ... There's a battle for information, it's like individual companies in the same building.'

There was a quick reaction to sales with 'best and worst' meetings being held weekly where, according to an employee, failure was quickly and publicly criticised: 'performance counts for everything'. Yet a senior executive believed 'the company is more forgiving than people think'.

Executives talked of an informal culture, where communication and access up and down as well as across the Group was made easy and encouraged, with John Hoerner making himself available and cutting across hierarchy for a direct one-to-one. Yet some staff at head office remember 'seeing him once in the last year'. 'Everyone is very status driven and differentials are maintained and protected. The only informal aspect of working for Burtons is the dress code.'

However, staff from Debenhams talked of good motivation and being 'one big team', with high visibility from top management. A senior executive believed 'culture makes all the difference ... we need people with the right approach and attitude'.

---

[1] Unreferenced quotes in this section are from interviews with graduate employees and with Keith Cameron, Group Director of Stores and Personnel.

In an article on ex-financial director, Andrew Higginson in *Retail Week* (5 December 1997), he was described by industry experts as 'a genuinely nice guy when most people at The Burton Group are not'. However, Higginson rejected such views: 'The Burton Group is wonderful. It is a tough environment ... success in recent years is the result of a team effort ... it is a strong management team that has delivered.'

In 1992 the average length of service of executive directors was under three years compared to Marks & Spencer where it was nine years. During 1992 and 1993, one-third of the Group management board departed, and between 1993 and 1995, 41 per cent departed. By 1996/7 the company was still suffering a high turnover of senior executives, with two more executive directors leaving in 1997. However, there was widespread respect for Hoerner and faith in his leadership, and stories circulating in 1996 recalled how the company had turned itself around under his leadership.

COMPANY PERFORMANCE

In 1996, Burton Group turnover topped £2bn for the first time. Profits stood at £161m, an increase of 58 per cent over 1995. All divisions traded profitably for the first time, although Debenhams still contributed 64 per cent of total group profits. Gearing stood at 11.7 per cent, and gross profit at 14 per cent. Between 1992 and 1996, 98 new stores had been acquired, 293 disposed of and 340 transferred between fascias. New sites were being secured in airports, factory outlets and shopping centres. During 1996 Burtons purchased two home shopping retail businesses, Innovations and Racing Green. As a result some of the existing brands moved rapidly to introduce catalogue shopping and, with the development of leading edge Internet retail sites for each division, future alternative channels of distribution for the group's merchandise were in place. The group made initial incursions into international markets, and established an international division in 1996.

Despite these developments the share price remained stubbornly low over a long period. The board made an attempt in April 1997 to woo City analysts by hosting visits to new developments in Leeds Whiterose Centre and Ireland. After announcing a 23 per cent increase in interim profit in May 1997, the shares fell by 6 per cent. By the middle of 1997 there were signs of a slowdown in trading.

On the 9 July 1997, the company announced that Debenhams would demerge from the group and seek its own stock market listing as an independent company. The reason given for this significant move was the different characteristics of the multiples and Debenhams and the benefits to be gained from separate management teams focusing wholly on their respective businesses. Management was now confident that the multiples were strong enough to establish themselves as an independent business. The 1997 annual report gives the following explanation:

> The Board now believes that the multiples and Debenhams form two quite separate businesses. This, and other factors, have convinced us the demerger is the best way forward for the brands under the Burton Group umbrella, brands which have come a long way in recent years.

'Arcadia' was chosen as the name for the Multiples business as a result of nationwide competition launched by the company to find a suitable corporate name.

KPMG (B)*: MANAGING STRATEGIC CHANGE

Gerry Johnson

KPMG is one of the major accounting firms worldwide. In the 1990s it was trying to change its strategy from a discipline-based firm to a market-focused firm. The case is primarily concerned with the management of strategic change processes to achieve this. This case study chronicles the processes of change that took place between 1992 and 1997 and includes verbatim explanations of the problems. The case provides a context in which to evaluate the extent to which structural and systems changes in the UK firm in the 1990s succeeded in effecting strategic change.

• • •

BACKGROUND TO KPMG

KPMG is a large international firm of accountants and consultants. By 1997 the fee income of KPMG International was over US$9bn, of which Europe accounted for $4.1bn and North America $3.6bn. The UK accounted for $1.1bn (or 13 per cent of world fee income). In the UK, KPMG was in the lead in terms of fee income in several of its market sectors, and where not in the lead was generally second or third (see Exhibit 1). Within the UK, KPMG employed 9,400 staff and partners; nearly 5,300 in the south-east region – and the rest spread over five other regions.

Colin Sharman, KPMG's UK senior partner, explained the competitive position of the firm:

> The accountancy profession has been in a period of turbulence and change for some time. It is threatened by litigation, subject to 'low-balling', increasingly governed by rules and regulations and lacking a recognised market leader. The

This case study was prepared by Professor Gerry Johnson, Cranfield School of Management. It is intended as a basis for class discussion and not as an illustration of either good or bad management practice.

* The KPMG (A) case can be found at the end of chapter 2.

Exhibit 1 The fee split for leading UK accounting firms

Firm	Audit and accounting	Tax	Consulting	Other
KPMG (Dec. 1997)	41	21	17	21
Arthur Andersen (Dec. 1996)	23	19	52	6
Coopers & Lybrand (Dec. 1997)	33	21	27	19
Ernst & Young (Dec. 1997)	34	30	21	15
Deloitte & Touche (Nov. 1996)	34	25	28	13
Price Waterhouse (June 1995)	43	28	22	7

Sources *International Accounting Bulletin*, 21 December 1995; KPMG annual report.

market is dominated by six large firms though this will change in 1998 as Price Waterhouse and Coopers & Lybrand will merge whilst Andersen's looks certain to split into Arthur Andersen and Andersen Consulting. These large firms have clearly distinguished themselves from smaller players and have built up barriers to entry due to the range of services and skills the major firms now have.

In the 1980s the leading firms underwent a series of international mergers and diversified into a range of professional services – corporate finance, consulting, investigations and forensic accounting. There are portfolio differences – for example, KPMG is clearly a leader in corporate finance and the only player in career consulting, but the similarities are far greater than the differences.

The players are broadly similar in size and in their range of resources, consequently there is no natural leader to direct and structure the market. Even where the professional offerings are similar, effective relationships can provide a competitive edge through understanding the business and client needs.

The ability to co-ordinate and integrate people to create a real benefit for the client can also be a distinguishing factor since this is the area that accountancy firms have been notoriously bad at. The result is that teamwork, relationship management and integration are the competences that may distinguish one firm from the pack given their equivalence in many technical aspects. One of the fascinating aspects of this struggle of the giants is that success lies not necessarily in the originality of the idea or strategy but in the ability to implement the idea effectively.

KPMG faced changed market circumstances in the 1990s. The expectations of clients were changing: they expected their advisers to understand the problems they faced, and to be able to provide a range of services to meet their needs. The issue for KPMG was, therefore, to ensure that partners were seen as, and performed the role of, business advisers. Whilst this was a challenge understood by some in the firm, including Colin Sharman, there were many who saw little need for change at that time. After all, the firm had experienced years of growth and was, clearly, very successful.

THE IMPETUS FOR CHANGE AT KPMG

Sharman had become senior partner of the south-east region in 1992. It was in this role that he had begun the programme for change that would characterise KPMG in the 1990s.

> In 1992, we organised a series of eight strategy workshops for the region's partners; around one-third went through them. Quite deliberately, those who attended the workshops, particularly the early ones, were partners with a desire for change and views about what those changes might be; and they were not necessarily my views. What those workshops did was to work through the strategic position of the firm, what the competitive strategy should be, what the blockages to change were, what the critical success factors were and crucially what actions needed to be put in place.

In fact the workshops achieved some 'ownership' of the problems the firm was likely to face if it did not change. The partners, working together in groups, came to see the extent to which the services offered by the main firms were largely undifferentiated; and the consequent likelihood of eventual 'price-based' competition leading to reduced fees was a powerful stimulus for change. Colin Sharman explained the outcome of the workshops:

> I personally attended a debriefing session at the end of each of the workshops. The messages that came out of them were remarkably consistent. They confirmed the need for increased client focus. Major issues of specialism and integrating our service delivery also emerged.
>
> At the end of the series of workshops I arranged for some more detailed feedback sessions for all of the partners. I held ten evening sessions with all but a small handful of partners coming to one of the sessions. There we took the main messages from the workshops, discussed the main directions of the firm and tried to surface any real concerns. Those proved a very useful way of building the consensus that we needed and also reinforcing the fact the change was definitely coming. I also used the senior management conference, which was an annual ritual for our senior managers to complain about the firm, as a way of getting them into strategic issues. The managers worked through much the same process as the partners had done on the workshops. At the end of that, the senior managers produced a serious analysis of the issues facing the firm and the kinds of action that were needed.
>
> I tried to capture that enthusiasm, that commitment, that sense of change by holding a series of briefing sessions for partners and senior managers together to spread some of the messages. The messages I wanted to get across

Exhibit 2 Visuals for the presentation

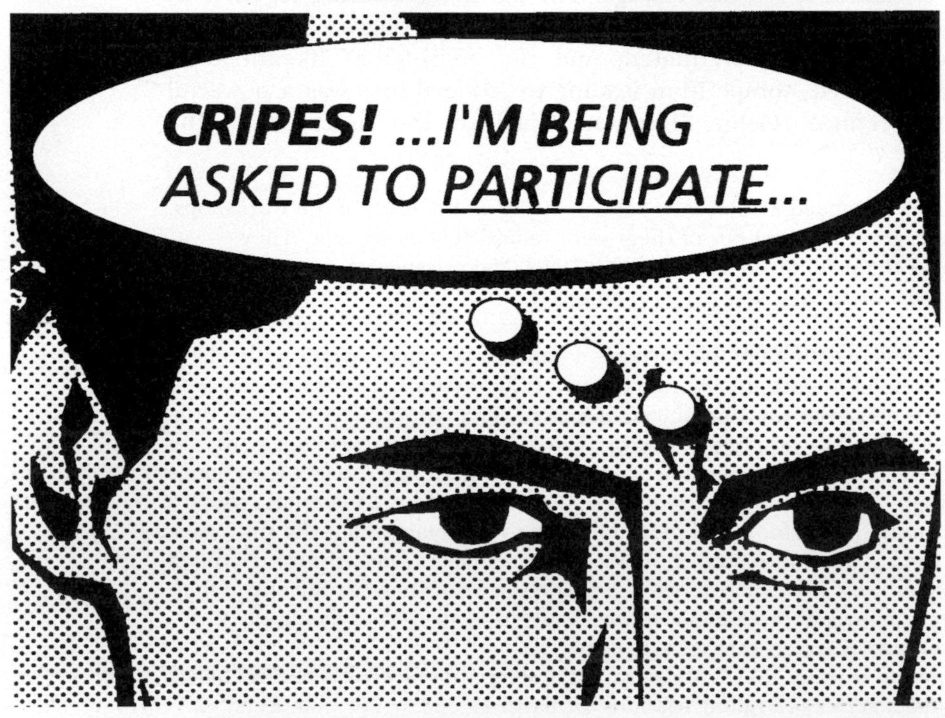

> were that we were serious about change; that we needed to become a much more open organisation; that we needed to involve people at all levels in the development in the organisation and that we needed to communicate very much better than we had done in the past. To make them have a real impact I had the sessions designed to reinforce the underlying message, which was that we are going to do things very differently in future. For example, you might think that the visuals [see Exhibit 2] we used were pretty ordinary but my KPMG audience was accustomed to nothing more exciting than slides with a KPMG-blue background and logo. So if nothing else, my pop art images made an impact. People started talking openly about wanting to change, wanting to try new things and wanting to succeed.

The workshops had, then, helped identify the main elements of the strategy. Colin Sharman had also developed his views about the required approach to change:

> The key was to get client focus into our organisation. Initially I thought that I could operate successfully by changing only the behaviour and skill sets of our people, in particular our partners. But I came to the conclusion that was not going to work. If we changed the behaviour of partners and staff to become more client focused, more market sector focused, more knowledgeable about the market place, that would rapidly fall apart. We would need to reinforce it by measurement systems to ensure that our people were measured by these new ways of doing things; and by a structure which aligned with what people were being asked to do. If people, accountable in one direction, were told to focus their efforts in another, it was likely that one or other would lose out; and if our measurement systems and reward systems measure something other than the new behaviour we are asking for, it is fairly clear what would happen. So I concluded that we needed what I call a virtuous circle of change consisting of three interlinking elements – structure, measurement and behaviour – all needing to operate on each other.
>
> The most important change to achieve, however, was in the behaviour and skills of our people. We also had to have a proper identification of accountabilities and responsibilities for individuals. I was also clear that our communication systems – which were primitive – had to be very much better. Communications needed to be used in a positive way to ensure that partners and staff understood and were committed to the new direction.

THE LAUNCH OF 20 : 20 VISION

Following the strategy workshops in 1992, many partners within KPMG had become impatient for action. Colin Sharman was rather more cautious: 'What some of the partners did not understand was that to get from strategic concepts to implementation you had to do some work.' He believed it might take three to four years to put proposed changes into effect. However, a plan which set out structural changes had been put together by the end of April 1992. This plan was central to the guiding vision of the future and became known as '20 : 20 Vision'.

Exhibit 3 KPMG structure in 1992

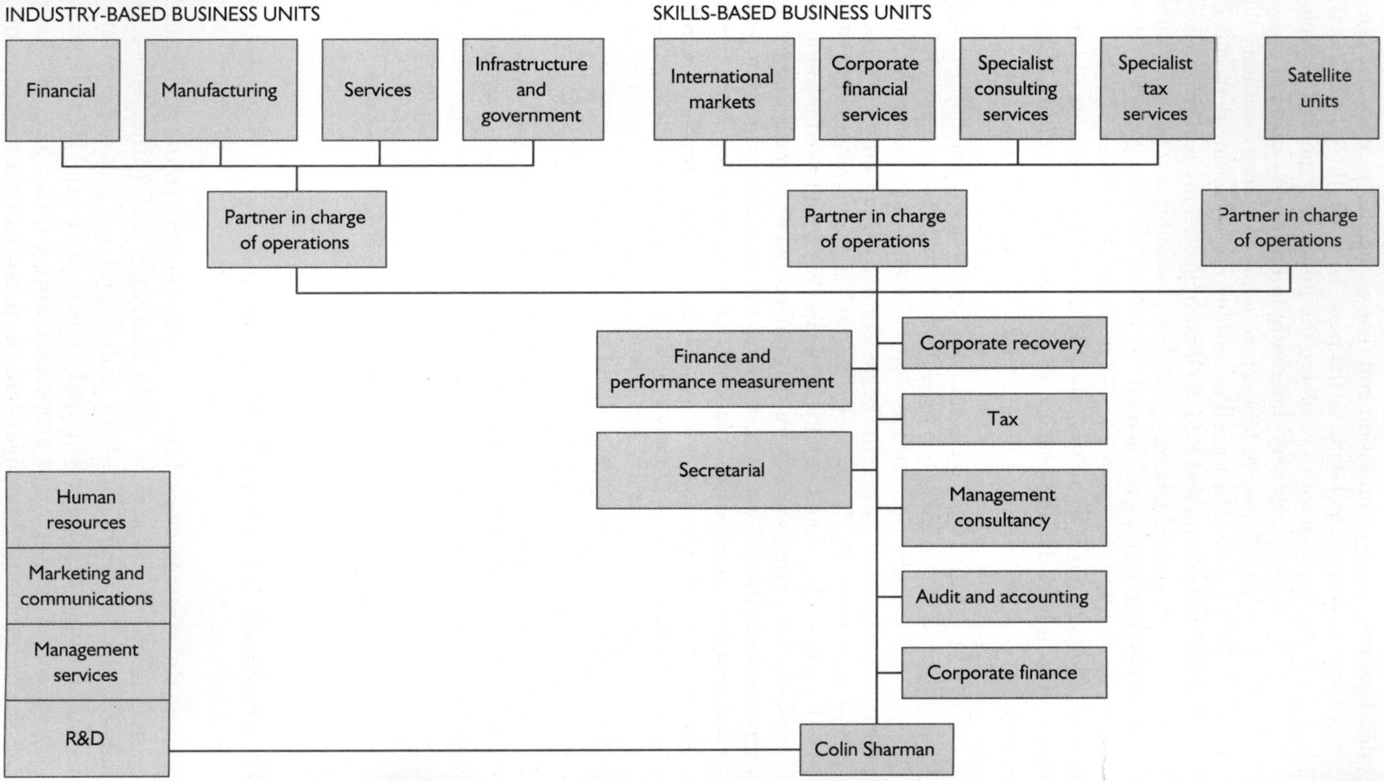

INDUSTRY-BASED BUSINESS UNITS

- Financial
- Manufacturing
- Services
- Infrastructure and government

Partner in charge of operations

SKILLS-BASED BUSINESS UNITS

- International markets
- Corporate financial services
- Specialist consulting services
- Specialist tax services

Partner in charge of operations

- Satellite units

Partner in charge of operations

- Finance and performance measurement
- Secretarial

- Corporate recovery
- Tax
- Management consultancy
- Audit and accounting
- Corporate finance

Colin Sharman

- Human resources
- Marketing and communications
- Management services
- R&D

In an innovative move for KPMG, a special partners' conference was called in which 20 : 20 Vision was presented together with details of the key players. Colin Sharman recognised that 'the culture at the time meant that partners were frightened to ask questions', so to overcome this, Jonathan Dimbleby, the British TV current affairs commentator, was invited to field questions from the floor to the panel. Two similar events were then held to inform senior managers and junior managers of the plan, and it was then cascaded throughout the whole organisation through company press releases.

The underlying strategic thrust of 20 : 20 Vision was to move to an industry-based focus for service delivery to clients; to develop teams of auditors, consultants, tax specialists and so on who were experts by industry sector, not just by discipline. To do this a new structure for the firm was introduced made up of four industry-based business units and four skills-based business units, headed by senior partners reporting to two partners in charge of operations, Mike Rake (Industry Units) and Alan Reid (Skills Units). These were directly accountable to Colin Sharman (see Exhibit 3).

The initial aim was to start with 60 per cent of staff in industry-based units and move over time towards 80 per cent. The timetable of events prepared in April 1992 envisaged that this structure would begin with one business unit in October 1992, with the others introduced a year later. Colin Sharman initially considered this cautious approach appropriate because he 'was desperately worried about maintaining control of the business, with the existing steam-cranked information systems not capable of being changed quickly enough'. However, by mid-June the initial timescale had been dismissed as being too cautious. Three weeks later that decision was taken and on 1 October the south-east region of KPMG undertook the most significant restructuring in the firm's history, involving physically moving 2,500 people to achieve co-location of partners and managers in the new industry units.

A MIXED RESPONSE

There was a mixed response to these moves initially. Some parts of the firm were enthusiastic; others were not. As Alan Reid explained:

> It was audit that went hell for leather into it, led by Michael Fowle; it was a way of getting the audit practice managed. I don't think they recognised that 20 : 20 Vision was for the whole firm. However, on the tax side 49 out of 50 partners did not want it because they had been going through 3 years of change themselves, had only just come to the end of it and felt well poised to drive forward. What they thought they could do was to co-locate rather than merge. They accepted they had to work together but there was a question of whether they were managed by tax people. They had come out of subservience to the audit practice

> and they thought that this was a magnificent ruse to get them back into that position. Consultancy never really debated it.
>
> In the initial stages the staff were probably the most supportive and that's perhaps worth learning from. We were much more concerned with partners' reactions and developing it than with staff. The staff saw the reality of the vision quicker than partners. In fact, as staff became more excited the whole thing accelerated, but quite a few partners lingered behind. The ratio of staff to partners was much greater in the industry business units. I think some partners thought that all this might cancel itself out in due course.

By 1993 the structure was in place and co-location had occurred. However, the extent to which the new strategy had become accepted and put into effect was mixed. In some industry units it was being pursued energetically. One of the heads of the industry-based units established a co-located multidisciplinary team, with team briefings, tailored training in the strategic analysis of clients for all partners and managers, whether consultants, auditors or tax specialists; and was able to demonstrate the effective working of the unit in half the time initially planned. In others it was little more than co-location at that time. As one audit manager put it: 'I had moved my office but nothing else had changed. As far as I was concerned, I was dealing with the same clients in the same way.'

Although the new structure had set up a management team for running the region, its early effectiveness was sometimes unclear, especially in sorting out 'turf disputes' which arose, for example, between industry-based and skills-based units. Changes to established control procedures were also slow. For example, it was unclear who would be allocated fee income for an assignment between business units and skills-based units, where joint teams were operating. This lack of clarity was exacerbated by the concentration of some of the senior partners on the traditional monitoring of chargeable hours on client business.

In 1993 Colin Sharman was appointed to UK senior partner and Mike Fowle, previously a senior audit partner was appointed as senior partner of the south-east region. Colin Sharman readily admitted that Mike Fowle was seen to be 'driven by technical excellence' and that 'the chat in the office was that Mike would undo it all'. However, 'that has not happened. He has been committed and has driven 20 : 20 harder that I would have done. Certainly in Tax it was seen as "Oh, Michael will stop all this nonsense" but in fact he hasn't and the Tax people have had a much harder time under Michael than they would have had under me.'

THE LEADERSHIP PROJECT

At the time Colin Sharman became UK senior partner there were other developments taking place. At an international level in KPMG there were the beginnings of an international strategy to position KPMG as the leading 'advisory firm' rather than an audit firm. This took shape in the UK in what became known as the 'Leadership Project'.

In his address to the UK partners meeting in October 1994, Colin Sharman announced KPMG's aim 'to become the leading accountancy firm in the UK'. Research with clients showed that they expected their accountancy firm to be able to offer a full range of advisory services.

> The very fact that KPMG has more long-standing and enduring client relationships than any other firm gives us a superb opportunity to build our business. If we can develop these relationships and win more business from our clients then we have the potential to achieve clear leadership across the whole range of our client services ... Our research shows that clients are saying: 'know me, know my business. Give me advice, help me to compete. I want frequent contact, robust and independent opinions, proactive advice and fast reactions to changes in my business. I want value for money.' ... They want a trusted and valued relationship. If KPMG can succeed in genuinely making the transition from audit firm to business adviser, it can pull ahead of its competitors rather than being just one among the leaders ... I want us to be indispensable to our clients because we give robust opinions, offer advice and provide business solutions that they simply could not get for themselves. I want us to attract the best people and to be the best firm to work for. The best firm because we have the most interesting clients, and the most attractive careers, the most demanding assignments. I want us to employ people who will make a real difference to their clients' business. I want us to be the firm that other leading advisers want to work with. We want the merchant banks, the lawyers, the specialist consultants to be alongside us. I want us to be the leading firm in the new markets – business transformation, forensic accounting – right at the cutting edge. I want us to foster a culture that sees opportunities and not problems, strengths not weaknesses, teamwork and not just individuals.

He explained how this would be put into effect:

> The concept of having a leader on a client account – the lead partner – is not new. However, in KPMG, the role historically adopted has been that of a senior audit partner with the key relationship at the finance director level. It is now much more than this. The role is defined as an account management role that carries the ultimate responsibility for management of the client relationship, particularly at the chairman/chief executive level. The aim is to allow a single individual to be the integrator of all the firm's services to a client and of the people supplying those services. There is also a leadership aspect to the role as it includes responsibility for effective teamwork and managing internal relationships.
>
> A lead partner is identified for every client and potential client of the firm. Selection is based on client needs, personal chemistry and relationships, ability to perform the role and industry knowledge. It is not related to the original skill set or technical background of the partner. It is widely recognised within the firm that this is not the role that all the partners should aspire to since specialist partners and engagement partners are essential to ensuring that the service delivery and advice are first class and this is the 'must have' of any professional service firm. It would not be commercially sensible to use the time of leading edge specialists in what is essentially a generalist role.

> Each project or piece of work performed for the client will be led by an engagement partner whose role is to deliver that specific piece of work. Take an audit, for example; the audit engagement partner retains responsibility for the independent opinion. However, all services and relationships are co-ordinated through the lead partner.

The Leadership Project also provided a vehicle to roll out some of the changes already made in the south-east to the rest of the UK and develop human resource practices and policies in line with the changing strategy.

Competences

It was acknowledged that the new strategic focus would not be achieved successfully by structural means alone; other changes would be needed to reinforce it. The idea of a competence framework was established and developed in 1993. David Westcott, HR Partner, explained that:

> The starting point for this framework was the question, what are the characteristics we need in our future partners? External consultants conducted a whole series of interviews which asked clients, partners in key positions together with younger partners what they thought the behavioural characteristics should be for the future success of the company.

From this, six categories of competence emerged (see Exhibit 4).

Rewards

Reward systems were also revised. David Westcott:

> Pay had been largely a matter of how long anyone had been in a particular grade ... We set out to introduce a pay structure and review system which sought to reward improvement and achievement rather than time in grade.

Colin Sharman explained the basis of the system:

> We changed all our systems to move everybody into just five bands so that instead of having everybody promoted every year, which was the old system, we had a situation where promotion meant something ... Promotion would only be between the bands, on the basis of performance in terms of the competences. Eventually, we completely restructured the reward system for partners, right the way across the UK.

There were problems on these changes, as David Westcott explained:

> A language problem existed because we were talking about performance, which had never really featured before. Time was no longer an issue. Disquiet around this was driven by the uncertainty many people were feeling – they knew where they were under the old system and so did their managers and senior managers and partners because it had been going for years. Suddenly the whole thing was turned upside down. As far as many people were concerned, there were inadequate answers on what would happen in the future.

Exhibit 4 The competence framework

Client responsiveness	● Relationship building – establishes rapport and builds long-term relationships with key decision makers ● Professional judgement – knows who the 'real' client is at all times and uses this knowledge to operate effectively for KPMG
Business skills	● Commerciality – relates all aspects of KPMG's service to client's business perspective and commercial drivers ● Business development – is seen by existing clients to market effectively and appropriately
Management	● Task management skills – controls the process of delivery to the client ● Team skills – encourages openness and co-operative working ● People development – gives staff responsibility and autonomy appropriate to their level of competence
Personal effectiveness	● Drive and commitment to results – goes beyond clients' expressed requirements and meets their real need ● Resilience – recovers crisis situations; is resourceful at times of pressure and stress
Social skills	● Communication skills – speaks clearly and with impact ● Social confidence – is perceived to enjoy the company of a wide range of people
Thinking skills	● Analytical thinking – analyses large amounts of complex data, extracts essentials ● Proactive thinking – comes forward with ideas unprompted by clients

Another issue was the introduction of discretionary bonuses:

> The principle had been decided that we would have a discretionary bonus for those at the senior manager level. It would be for good performance over and above that which was expected and it would be a one off – not recurring. This produced a tremendous amount of heat and no light. There was a lot of concern expressed and rumours were around before the thing was even debated. The alternative would have been to spend two years sorting this out, the normal KPMG practice, and we probably would never have achieved it.

Development Centres and Assessment Centres

Development centres were established to which newly promoted senior managers were sent to identify personal development plans to prepare them for the role of partner. David Westcott explained the purpose of these senior manager development centres:

> There had been some concern within the practice that the role of the senior manager, which is a very important one within KPMG but is largely a production and operational job, did not prepare people for partnership, which is more about relationships and social skills. So we ran a development centre as people were promoted to senior manager. It was initially seen as being to do with judgement, assessment and appraisal rather than development; but they have now been accepted and people find them very valuable.

In the past, appointment to partner was seen by many in the firm as dependent on a senior manager being seen by existing partners as 'the right sort of chap'. However, in 1994, Partner Assessment Centres were introduced:

> Before anyone is admitted to partnership in any of the regions of the firm they have to have the approval of the UK board. The UK board had for some time expressed concern that their job had become one of a rubber stamp. Another concern was that a number of partners around the UK had been asked to leave the partnership within five years of their becoming a partner. The combination of those two concerns led to the conclusion that we needed something more rigorous in the way partners were admitted into the firm. We needed to ensure that the competences we had defined for future partners were those in evidence or they had the potential to be. So in 1994 the board agreed to establish nationally two processes for partner admission. One was an assessment centre and the other was an interview panel which represented the board. It's much clearer now what it takes to become a senior manager and to become a partner because there is a greater openness in terms of the sort of behaviour expected of people. There are those who are upset that the patronage system has gone ... but by and large there is a general belief that it is a better way of doing things.

Colin Sharman commented:

> It was the most unfair thing we've done really. What we were saying was the old system finishes here. Very justifiably a lot of the guys said 'until today I knew how to become a partner: you attach yourself to a powerful guy, keep your head down and you don't make mistakes; and he will see you all right'. That was the problem, there was enormous patronage in the system and at a stroke we took that away. In 1994 we had about ten that were rejected by the panel. Of the ten, seven were withdrawn by their senior regional partners. Three of these were put forward to the board for admission even though they did not have the support of the panel and those three were rejected by the board. For the first time the board was not going to accept someone bullying through his boy – and that had never happened before. In 1995 we had a large number, but of the people rejected by the panel 100 per cent were withdrawn by their senior partners. Down the line people are saying 'OK the rules have changed but I know what I have to do and I can still make it even if I don't have a patron'. It is one of the key things helping us get behavioural changes.

Assessment centres were also adopted for recruitment. David Wescott:

> We asked if we were happy about the quality of the graduates that we were getting? So we introduced a new selection process, which incorporated a mini assessment centre whereas previously we, like all other firms of accounts, had relied exclusively on interviews. By introducing a new and very much more rigorous selection process for the 600 graduates that we take on we are getting a much higher acceptance rate of people we offered positions to. Our feedback from them is, (a) we seem to know what we want from a new recruit, and (b) we have made it difficult to join – and that has an attraction.

COMMUNICATIONS AND FEEDBACK

Colin Sharman believed that one of the most significant means of change was communications:

> For example, internally we now do a report on the partners conference. In the past it would have been a paragraph in the house magazine saying we had a partners conference. What we now do is take a video of it, interview the partners as to what they think and then we roll that right out immediately after the partners conference to tell everyone about it. I exercise very little editorial control over that.
>
> Then there is the UK-wide staff opinion survey. Some people say 'we shouldn't ask because they will tell us we are not very good'. Interestingly enough, the survey work I have seen shows that an awful lot of them identify with what we are trying to do, but that they think some of the partners need to change their behaviour. One of the things we are doing for this year's partners conference is to give some feedback from the staff to the partners about partner behaviour and about what the partners are doing. The other thing that is being developed is upward appraisal. That's becoming accepted throughout the organisation.

In addition to internal communication, Colin Sharman became very visible in the national press explaining KPMG's new strategy and the changes in the firm. As one manager put it:

> You can hardly pick up a paper these days without seeing Colin in it. It's good for the firm and, of course, we all read it in here.

INTEGRATION INTO INDUSTRY-BASED UNITS

Colin Sharman believed that:

> Where we have been able to integrate things into the industry-based business units we have had unparalleled success. Consulting volumes delivered through the industry groups are growing like topsy. Where we have failed is in those bits we left in the skills groups.

There were certainly problems in integrating the consultancy practice. Alan Reid explained:

> There were very few consultants put into the industry business units originally. Two consultants headed up industry units because it was important that not all the business units were headed by auditors. But I would say maybe 70–80 consultants went into industry business units and 600 were left in the skills unit. So there was a very strong force of consultants left. I don't think that they wanted to be submerged below auditors. Our auditors are very suspicious of our consultants. If you actually assess them as separate business units, some of our most talented people are in our consultancy, but audit has performed better than consultancy. It is a lot to do with their market place and the nature of their work. We have to win £2 million of new work every week for our consultancy – our audit practice has a more recurring base of work. There is a lot of concern that they just don't understand each other. We had also grown consultancy by just adding on services: little cottage industries and boutiques here and there. They went in and sold the service they had to a client, worked hard in doing it, then came away again and left it instead of nurturing the relationship and trying to sell other services. They acted as 35 cottage industries.

By 1997, however, consultants had been integrated into industry units more extensively with the exception of Business Transformation, concerned with strategic change work for major corporate clients (approximately sixty people) and the Implementation Consulting business unit with about three hundred consultants specialising in IT implementation.

INCORPORATION

In 1995, KPMG announced that it planned to incorporate that part of its audit practice dealing with companies listed on the UK stock exchange or in the regulated financial services industry. One reason for this was the need to protect the personal assets of partners from increasing threats of litigation affecting the profession as a whole, especially in the USA. However, as the *Financial Times* reported early in 1996, KPMG believed the move would provide competitive advantages:

> KPMG felt that a stronger corporate management structure would give it an edge in competing with the looser partnerships of the other Big Six firms. With incorporation comes disclosure. Accounts will have to be published for the audit company but KPMG has pledged that it will go further – it will produce full financial results for the whole firm. This has wrong-footed the competition, most of which are still pondering a response ... KPMG's focus on auditing is a strategy which sets it apart from many of the other big firms. While some firms have boosted volumes by entering markets such as outsourcing and information technology – and the implementation of services – KPMG is seeking to preserve the pre-eminence of auditing.
>
> *Financial Times*, 25 January 1996

The FT reported the publishing of 50,000 copies of KPMG's annual report for the UK – the first major accountancy firm to do so:

> Why has KPMG become the first to disclose so much about what is still, legally, a private business? Whatever the truth, the firm's chutzpah is admired by most – albeit privately. The firm admits that it would have had to publish full results for the audit plc, but that its decision to open all the books was prompted by a desire to present a transparent business to clients and the general public. It feels the public has a legitimate interest in an organisation which audits 400 listed companies.

REFLECTIONS ON THE CHANGES

In 1995, an internal KPMG attitude survey on the progress of the Leadership Project showed that staff and partners saw KPMG as above average compared with the rest of the Big Six, as a firm with a successful future and that job satisfaction was above average for a professional firm. However, it confirmed some concerns. KPMG was not seen as a people-oriented firm and development and career opportunities were still not clear. The Leadership Project had not yet impacted in a practical way on the way most staff worked day to day. Teamwork was not yet fully effective. And whilst relationships between partners and staff were seen as good locally, barriers still existed: there was still a sense of 'us and them'. This was borne out in a survey of the consultancy operation reported in *Accountancy Age* in February 1995:

> Over half of the 74 staff questioned said they would not recommend KPMG 'as a good place to work', nor did they 'expect to be with this organisation two years from now' ... And well over 60% said they only knew what was expected of them to a 'slight' or 'moderate' extent ... A huge 82% of staff named 'avoidance' as a key feature, involving 'shifting responsibility, procrastinating and avoiding issues'. Power was another dominant characteristic with 'empire-building' at the fore. And while 90% said that 'winning is valued and staff feel they have to outperform each other', just 20% believed there was any 'value placed on constructive interpersonal relationships, friendliness and openness' within the KPMG culture. Similarly, just 16% felt that any regard was given to 'coaching and developing people, being supportive and constructive'.

Colin Sharman commented on the strengths and weaknesses of the change programme:

> Everyone has heard the key messages about leadership and change and there is strong support for the concepts. What we have to achieve next is to translate the concepts into everyday actions everywhere in the business. I'd say we're where I thought we'd be at this stage of the change process. The next stage will be even more challenging because it's not just about changing systems and structures – which we've done – it's about really changing people's everyday actions and decisions at every level in the business.

Looking back on the developments since 1992, David Westcott reflected:

> Perhaps we did too much in too much of a hurry but it is now actually working, so there will be others that say that we did it at the right speed. In the past there would have been great debate, it would have been decided by committees of partners and then dropped on an unsuspecting world. Suddenly Colin opened it all up, said we were going to do this, here are the principles, here is what we are going to achieve, asked people for their views and then the infrastructure followed on.
>
> We have got some superb HR practices and procedures, but we have variable quality in the nature of our people management. No amount of procedures or policies can necessarily affect this. There are those people around who will say we've seen all this before if we keep our heads down it will go away and we will carry on as usual; so its business as usual: and there are those who capture the vision and say yes we see the need for change and we will pursue it energetically. All that HR were able to do was to provide the framework to support and effect that change. But change can only come about when the management of the units want it to happen, and visibly demonstrate that.

Colin Sharman believed that, overall, the changes had been a success.

> Individuals very clearly identify with the new units. And we've been able to capture the imagination of the troops with what we are doing with a lot of the newer initiatives. They will now say 'well we don't care what you middle ranking partners say – you don't matter'. Our managers are now more confident. In the old days it was keep your mouth shut, keep your head down and patronage will take care of you. Now it is we don't care, we have been told what is going to happen and you guys had better change, because if you don't you're going to get squeezed from the top.
>
> Clients love it. We asked them what they wanted and then we were able to sell it to them and they bought more of it. We've gone back and said, 'do you like what you're getting?', and by and large our clients are very positive about what we have done. We have put 6 points on our market share in the last four years.

LOOKING FORWARD

The attitude and culture survey at the end of 1995 emphasised the need to develop the leadership project further into a culture and behaviour change programme. The need for change was understood, but it was behaviour, not understanding that remained a problem.

In spring 1996 there was a 'leadership awayday' attended by the UK operations committee, in effect the management board of the UK firm. A 'core team' was also established to take forward key issues identified on the day. This team, reporting direct to Colin Sharman, was charged with three key tasks: to identify the issues for the future firm in 2005; to reconsider and design a continuing change programme for the organisation; and to develop the first national HR strategy of the firm. It was intended as Colin Sharman's think-tank for future development until a new UK board could be set up.

Exhibit 5 **UK structure of KPMG, 1997**

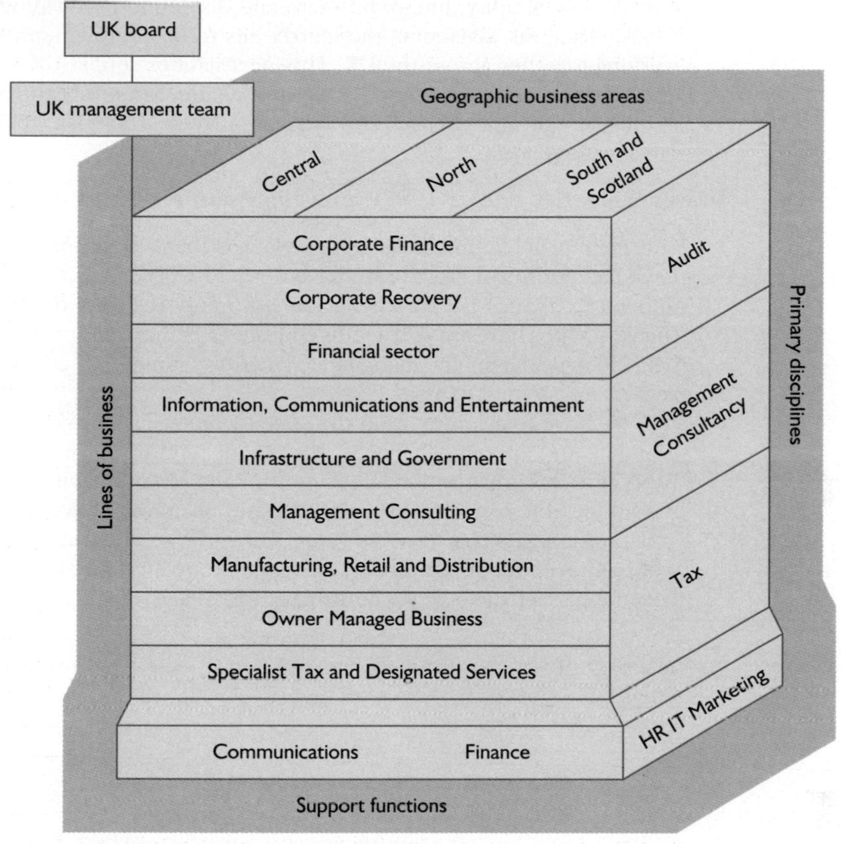

In October 1996 the new UK board was established. Its brief was strategic rather than operational, with board members selected for their ability to contribute to the strategy of the firm. It was non-representational, in that it did not consist of the heads of parts of the organisation; and it institutionalised the separate role of chairman and chief executive. Colin Sharman moved to the role of chairman, while Mike Rake took over as chief executive. Following the establishment of this board, reconsideration of the structure of the firm took place with the intent of bringing the UK firm together more. The result was the structure for the UK as a whole shown in Exhibit 5. Under the UK board was established a UK management team with operational responsibilities for running the KPMG UK. This structure was explained in the firm as follows:

> KPMG's move to becoming an advisory firm is about creating a clear leading position in the market. The old regional structure provided a strong presence in

> local geographic markets, but insufficient UK investment and focus on the industry and specialist needs of clients (our lines of business) and strong but not always consistent processes or disciplines. The challenge is to balance the matrix of geography, line of business and discipline in a way which builds on KPMG strengths. Balancing the matrix has to be complemented by better working together across the UK. This necessitates robust UK support functions and effective reward systems. Structural change is merely the most visible sign of change; cultural changes and business-driven strategies will help us achieve our business goals.

However, by the end of 1997 Colin Sharman reflected that:

> Our main problem in changing behaviour is that we do not have a problem. We have had continual growth; we have not had a poor year for some time; so it is difficult to change people's behaviour. In many respects the problem starts at the very top. There are still senior colleagues of mine who believe they can solve behaviour problems by changing a structure, going on a course or sending someone else on a course.
>
> We have to get away from the idea of change as a project, with a beginning, a middle and an end. Change is continuous, and my prime objective is to turn KPMG into an organisation which continually renews itself. That's the only way we will be able to maintain our leadership position. I have just provided the 'push' which gets that process going. Once the momentum gets going, change will be independent of me, and unstoppable by anyone else: it will simply become part of the way we do things in KPMG.

KPMG (C): DEVELOPING A GLOBAL FIRM

Gerry Johnson

KPMG, as a worldwide partnership, also provides an interesting context in which to consider the problems of globalisation. In the late 1990s expectations of global clients and international opportunities for development were prompting greater global co-ordination and the need for a clearer global strategy in KPMG. The case allows these developments to be considered in the light of the context of KPMG as a worldwide partnership but with a history of localised service delivery.

• • •

In January 1997 Colin Sharman received a telephone call from Jon Madonna, international chairman of KPMG, asking if they could get together for an urgent meeting. They met for breakfast the next morning in London. At this meeting Madonna announced that he was leaving KPMG within the next two weeks and was nominating Colin Sharman as the next international chairman. Sharman took over on 1 February 1997.

THE CHALLENGE OF THE GLOBAL FIRM

In 1997, KPMG had practices in 156 countries throughout the world; more than their competitors. However, the USA, UK, Netherlands, Germany, France, Canada and Australia accounted for 80 per cent of fee income (see Appendix 1 for further descriptive statistics of KPMG worldwide).

The main challenges for KPMG's international strategy into the millennium were twofold. The first was how to develop a coherent strategic approach to service delivery across the world, given the globalistion of so many existing and potential clients. The second was that most of the major opportunities for

---

This case study was prepared by Professor Gerry Johnson, Cranfield School of Management, as a basis for class discussion and not as an illustration of either good or bad management practice.

growth were in areas of the world in which neither KPMG nor their competitors had well established practices – eastern Europe in particular.

There were the beginnings of a global approach expressed in Madonna's 'Advisory Firm Strategy' which Sharman inherited.

> It was really a summary of the ten key thrusts for future development (see Exhibit 1). I remember at my first meeting I wrote them on my fingers to make sure I remembered them ... The notion of the Advisory Firm was liked, but it needed better articulation; and we needed to capture people's imagination. It was about trying to build a global business, but not through structure because this would have meant going back to the fundamentals of ownership.
>
> What we want to build is a McDonalds of our service industry. Like them, we have to get three things right. We have to get some uniformity of product but with local variations; we have to have a process which is similar across the world; and we have to get a recognised brand across the world.

By the end of 1997 a mission statement had emerged:

KPMG is the Global Advisory Firm whose aim is to turn knowledge into value for the benefit of its clients, its people and its communities.

Sharman explained that:

> The fundamental purpose is to turn knowledge into value. We then need to consider what this means in terms of the values, product range, processes and infrastructure in the firm. To be honest, we have done very little on any of these so far. We have set up project teams to look at them. Some points are clear. As far as the product range is concerned, it means we have to be clear about what we don't do as well as what we do. We shouldn't be into health systems in Manchester or car leasing in Puerto Rico or architecture in Switzerland for example. They do not help provide a uniform image of what KPMG is about in line with our mission.

In an address to the international board in May 1997, Colin Sharman made this quite clear:

> We need clear, agreed criteria by which we judge whether a service should be core to all KPMG practices worldwide, optional according to local markets, or forbidden to all practices.

As far as the infrastructure was concerned, Sharman believed it was necessary to develop quickly a more common international approach to IT, HR and marketing.

> That means that some of the bigger firms have got to have a bit of give and take. And I include the UK firm in that. We are not going to be able to have it all our own way; neither is anybody else. We've got to come to common approaches and then we've got to manage them sensibly from the centre. I don't think it's a structural issue. I think this is about behaviour. We need common processes across disciplines, because we need to get people to work the same way wherever we are. It doesn't matter whether you are a consultant in Ecuador, a registered accountant in the Netherlands, a chartered accountant in the UK, and IT specialist in Malaysia or a tax lawyer in Nigeria, you need to approach client

Exhibit 1 The advisory firm strategy 'Key Thrusts'

- Attitude/mindset
- Specialisation by market, industry, service
- New services
- Risk management
- Geographical markets (emerging)
- Technology
- Human resources
- Productivity
- Marketing image
- Profitability and growth

> work through a set of common processes. That melds us together as one firm. The fact that your ownership structure is different is not terribly relevant.

However, the realities of a successful federated partnership structure of KPMG had to be recognised. His view at that time was that:

> The easiest way to waste our time and energy would be to attempt to reorganise the international firm. We have seen some of our major competitors fall into this trap. We will clarify the role and responsibilities and sharpen the focus of our committees and other bodies – including the board, executive committee and international HQ. We will strengthen and centralise the support functions. But we will not spend the next three years wrestling with the structure of the international firm. This would not be successful. We will aim to become a 'virtual global entity in the knowledge business'. This means we will look and act like one organisation while retaining our individual member firm structure.

This was to be achieved by concentrating on operationalising what Sharman referred to as the four building blocks of KPMG's values:

> *Why* we are doing what we are doing: our product range; *what* to do and what not to do: our business processes; *how* we should do things: and our global infrastructure.

Project teams had been established to make these more explicit. However, this also had implications for the leadership style that Sharman saw as necessary:

> One thing I've learned about leadership style is that you can't direct and you can't instruct. A leadership style within our type of business has to be one of persuasion, of cajoling, of encouraging and leading by example. That's how I intend to lead the international firm as well.

THE CHALLENGE OF GLOBAL GROWTH

The development of a global firm had to be achieved within a requirement for increased growth. 'Standing still' was not seen as an option because, as competitors sought growth internationally, this would in effect mean losing share and market standing in the eyes of international clients. A lack of growth would also, very likely, affect the ability to attract the best people into the firm; slow growth would mean diminishing opportunities – or at least perceived opportunities – to advance in the firm. In an interview in June 1997, Sharman admitted that the growth rate of KPMG worldwide was not good enough. He explained:

> Growth will come in the developing world: in Asia Pacific, eastern Europe and Latin America. But even if we are growing at 40 per cent in those regions, the impact on our overall growth rate can be only marginal because of the composition of KPMG. If the US, the UK, the Netherlands, Germany and France are growing rapidly, that will put our growth rate right. So first and foremost, the task is to get the big practices growing quickly; especially the US where our position is not as strong competitively as it needs to be. That means that we've got to diversify into the faster-growing services in those countries.

There were already some global initiatives underway to try to address this. Project Globe was about trying to achieve a consistent international approach in management consulting and speed up the international development of higher added-value consulting projects. Audit 2000 was seeking to develop a risk-focused audit by building elements of strategic analysis into auditing. The Global Tax Vision was, again, attempting to provide a consistent international dimension on the tax practice. As far as the USA was concerned, it was concentrating on organic growth and looked set to achieve a 25 per cent growth rate in 1997 (50 per cent in consultancy).

> We've then got to look at the developing areas of the world – Asia Pacific's tiger economies, the restructured economies in eastern Europe – and achieve very, very dynamic growth there.

There was also the question of the required investment internationally. Despite KPMG's size, Sharman believed that the biggest challenge was finding the money to spend for international development and information systems infrastructure. This included the development of a global knowledge management system, automation of audit systems and up to $100m on India and eastern Europe alone. KPMG knew that at least one other firm had spent a similar sum developing their global consulting business.

A GLOBAL MERGER?

KPMG was aware that two of their main rivals, Coopers & Lybrand and Price Waterhouse were talking about merging; and KPMG had also been approached other competitors – both Deloitte & Touche and Ernst & Young. In fact, Coopers & Lybrand and Price Waterhouse announced their intentions to merge in September 1997, earlier than expected, and this prompted KPMG to consider its own options. In considering the possibility of KPMG merging, Colin Sharman explained:

> In terms of our global development, the option of doing nothing was really not acceptable. In the US, for example, bigness matters. You don't get into major companies if you are not in the top four; and following merger we would have been fifth out of five; and we could not get back into a top four position through organic growth in the US. You also have to be one of the biggest to operate in eastern Europe, China and Russia. Anderson and a combined Coopers and Price Waterhouse operation would be bigger there too and with more to invest. So we would be disadvantaged in developing markets too. So the driver for us to consider a merger too was nothing to do with the UK but to do with international markets.

By the end of 1997, KPMG and Ernst & Young were in merger negotiations:

> A merger with Ernst & Young seemed most sensible, particularly in the US. Ernst & Young are strong in the US; KPMG are strong in Europe. Moreover, we are both industry focused firms. I believe we will be able to work together well with them. There are differences. They are more centrally managed than we are at KPMG, for example. They focus more on the short term than we do. Had we moved down the route of integration further, there would have been problems. But I believe that if we ensure that the two practices are mixed up well and we do not leave pockets of separate activities, it will work.

Not everyone saw the proposed merger in the same way. In December 1997, the FT Lex column warned:

> If the mega mergers proceed, shrinking choice, customers may be less keen to have all their eggs in the same few baskets.

The European Commission also expressed concern about both the KPMG/Ernst & Young and Coopers/Price Waterhouse mergers. Karel Van Miert, the EU competition commissioner, said his office 'had been overwhelmed by the amount of concern generated by the announcement'. Regulatory authorities elsewhere, particularly in the USA, were also concerned, especially about the KPMG/Ernst & Young merger which, it was argued, would give too great a share of key markets to the merged firm.

As negotiations proceeded in the first few months of 1998, it also became clear that the operationalisation of this merger was giving rise to doubt amongst partners in both firms. In March it was announced that the merger would not proceed.

THE SITUATION IN 1998

The fact that the merger was not to proceed magnified rather than diminished the need for the global development of KPMG; indeed Sharman's belief was that there was a massive momentum for change resulting from the idea of the merger. KPMG had also seen Ernst & Young at close quarters. It faced similar challenges and it too had been through significant changes; but it was much more centralized than KPMG. As one partner said, 'It was rather like holding a mirror up to ourselves.' Sharman was quick to re-emphasise the priorities to the partners and by Spring 1998 was sketching out what he believed had to be done:

> I believe we have learned a lot over the last few months in these merger negotiations. We have realised that we have quality in depth throughout the firm and probably more cohesion than we thought. What we need is more focus on what we do well across the world, better alignment with global strategies and greater investment in global infrastructure. We need to give attention to a number of priorities.
>
> The first is our international structure. This needs to be clearer in order to manage a global strategy more effectively. In particular we need to focus our management activities on a number of regions, with people responsible for implementing global policy, especially the development of emerging markets and identifying investment opportunities. I am also proposing we have managing partners responsible for the key services we provide. Again they will be responsible for ensuring the implementation of global strategy, but from a service point of view. They should determine and manage our portfolio of services to be offered by member firms and make sure there are common business process methodologies. I believe we need full-time, international, senior-level executives for these roles. These appointments will be senior people who might be located anywhere but who will report into a central worldwide office in Amsterdam. This international executive team will report to an international board, responsible for reviewing and endorsing the vision and policy for the global firm and monitoring the implementation of strategy. The council will be the firm's ultimate governing body.

Exhibit 2 shows the proposed structure. An international executive team, with a CEO would be responsible for managing the global strategy. This team would report to Sharman and his international board, which would have on it senior partners from the major country based partnerships around the world.

> We also need to clarify the agreements and arrangements we have across the world with our various partnerships and licensees. They need to have a stronger alignment to our goals, a clearer definition of their rights and responsibilities; and we need to develop their commitment to the important role they play in providing a coherent range of services internationally. I think there needs to be clarity, for example, on the use of the KPMG name and brand; the acceptance of lead partner authority for international assignments; the mandatory acceptance and delivery of core services; and we need to ensure their acceptance of global policies on investment, technology, knowledge sharing, human resource development and our business processes. Not least, we need globally enforced standards in quality, risk management and management information; and I believe we need the approval by the international board of national senior partner appointments.

Exhibit 2 The proposed international structure

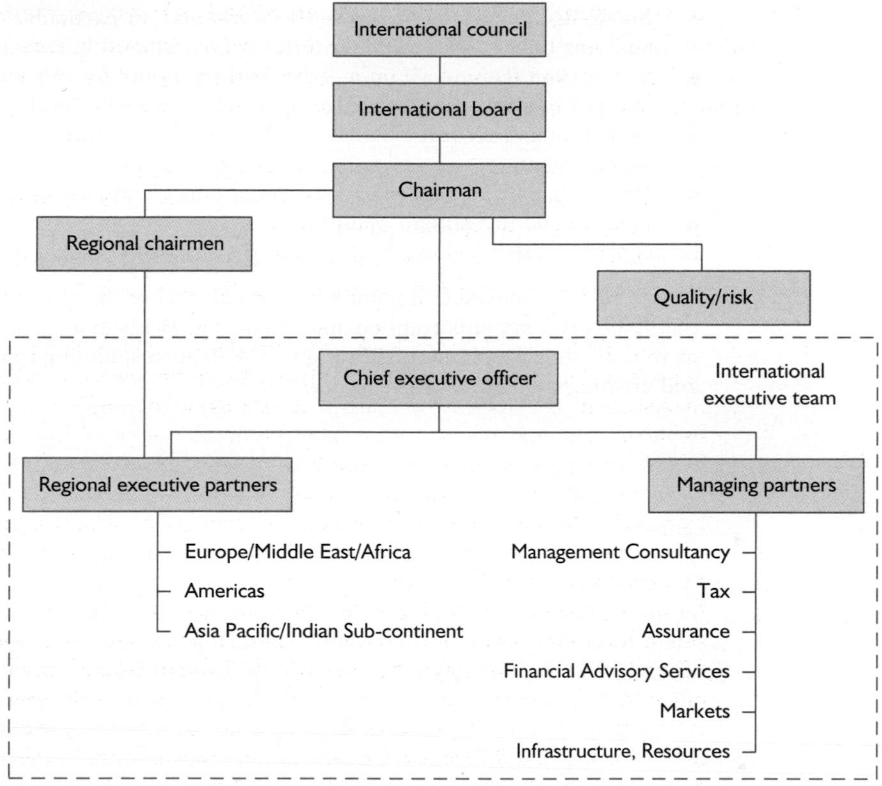

We have already started work on developing a clearer statement of our values. This has shown that, although we have moved a long way towards putting our clients first, rather than ourselves – and partners in particular – and there is a great value put upon technical excellence and professional standards and integrity, there remains a culture of individualism and a lack of openness and trust. If we are to put our mission into effect, we need to put a great deal more emphasis on further valuing our clients but also valuing our people and a sharing of knowledge across the firm. We need to pay much more attention to how we are to achieve this in the next year or so.

As far as business processes are concerned, we have been working hard on what this means; project teams have developed process maps for the ten key areas of our business [see Exhibit 1]. Briefing packs have been completed for all of these process areas and should be available by June this year. Process workshops will be conducted to explain these and generate buy in, followed by regional board discussions which should be completed by the end of April this year. We need visible top-level commitment to these priorities and some quick wins in these areas to demonstrate success across the firm.

None of this will be possible without making quite clear what the international centre of KPMG is responsible for. I believe the priorities of the centre are:

- Knowledge management across the world and, in particular, means of ensuring that we extend the frontiers of our shared knowledge.
- Information technology on a global basis not only for purposes of control but also to share the knowledge upon which we will develop.
- Global human resource policies and, in particular, international partner development.
- Marketing and, in particular, our global image and positioning.
- Finance and investment planning.
- Global communications both within the firm and outside.

I think we have moved to a point where we all accept the global challenge, and that it means some important changes to how KPMG is managed. The next year or so is all about working this through; it is about responding to the challenges and creating the KPMG of the future.

APPENDIX 1 KPMG STATISTICS

KPMG Revenue and Personnel, 1997

REGIONS*	REVENUE (US$M)	PARTNERS	PROFESSIONALS	ADMINISTRATIVE	PERSONNEL (TOTAL)
Africa	100	231	2,320	766	3,317
Asia Pacific	858	841	10,052	2,324	13,217
Europe	4,181	2,769	26,674	8,594	38,037
Latin America	203	268	3,088	1,137	4,493
Middle East	34	71	767	222	1,060
North America	3,624	2,381	16,762	6,024	25,167
Total	**9,000**	**6,561**	**59 663**	**19,067**	**85,291**

Note All international revenue and growth figures are measured in US dollars and are affected by fluctuations in exchange rates.

*Countries 155; cities 844.

Total fees for leading accounting firms

FIRM	USA 1997 $m	UK 1997 £m	GERMANY 1996 DM m	FRANCE 1996 FF m	NETHERLANDS 1966 DF m	CANADA 1997 C$m
KPMG	3,000.0	575.2	1,151.5	3,483	878.8	607.0
Andersen Worldwide	5,445.0	694.6[1]	379.0	2,563	204.0	321.0[2]
Coopers & Lybrand	2,500.0	766.0	1,170.0	1,430	748.8	368.2
Deloitte & Touche	3,600.0	440.9	367.0	1,050	496.9	570.0
Ernst & Young	4,416.0	525.1	681.0	1,384	826.4	418.0
Price Waterhouse	2,340.0	520.0[1]	277.0	1,040	123.7	372.9[1]

Notes [1]Estimated by IAB.
[2]Estimated by IAB as Andersen Consulting declined to disclose 1997 figures.

Sources USA IAB, 17 February 1998; UK IAB, 1 December 1997; Germany IAB, 14 May 1997; France IAB, 12 June 1997; Netherlands IAB, 12 September 1997; Canada IAB, 25 March 1998.

International fee split for leading accounting firms (%)

FIRM	AUDIT AND ACCOUNTING	TAX	CONSULTING	OTHER
KPMG (Sept. 1997)	48	22	22	8
Andersen Worldwide (Dec. 1997)	24	14	81	54
Coopers & Lybrand (Dec. 1996)	53	19	17	11
Ernst & Young (Dec. 1997)	44	23	33	0
Price Waterhouse (Dec. 1997)	46	22	26	6

UNHCR – ACHIEVING THE IMPOSSIBLE

Ian Sayers and Gerry Johnson

UNHCR (United Nations High Commission for Refugees) is one of the best-known United Nations agencies. In the late 1990s hardly a day passed without it being mentioned in television news articles covering the refugee crises in Africa and the former Yugoslavia. During this time the organisation had not only to manage the largest and most complex refugee crises in its history but, at the same time, to face the internal challenges of demands for radical strategic reform. UNHCR faced two conflicting pressures: the nations that provided funding for its operations were demanding a reduction in administrative overhead and better accountability; whilst the organisation's 4,500-strong field workforce needed greater decision-making latitude to respond more rapidly to local needs. The inevitable conflict between the centre and field operations was exacerbated by a need to reduce costs overall and improve operational efficiency. The case explains these conflicts and the innovative programme for change that was introduced to try to satisfy the internal and external demands for reform.

• • •

INTRODUCTION

In the first few weeks of July 1994 more than 1.3 million sick and destitute people joined an exodus from Rwanda to a remote and inhospitable volcanic region in Zaire. Thousands died from disease and ended their journey in

---

This case study was prepared by Ian Sayers, formerly of UNHCR, with Gerry Johnson, Cranfield School of Management, as a basis for class discussion rather than to illustrate effective or ineffective handling of an administrative situation. The views expressed are those of the authors and do not necessarily represent those of their organisations.

mass graves. The impact on the environment was so great that it was clearly visible to astronauts orbiting the earth in the space shuttle 180 nautical miles up. Harrowing pictures broadcast across the world's television networks liberated common sentiments of grief and sympathy. Millions of dollars in donations poured into relief organisations from governments and individuals. Within days of the arrival of the first refugees in Zaire the United Nations High Commissioner for Refugees (UNHCR) had international staff in Goma co-ordinating the arrival and distribution of relief items. Water and medical equipment, food and shelter materials were airlifted into Goma from all over the world on more than forty flights a day co-ordinated through the Air Operations Unit in Geneva. Staff on the ground worked day and night planning camps and resource requirements, integrating the work of the many agencies and NGOs,[1] and relaying information to the outside world to support fundraising activities.

Five years earlier, UNHCR would have found it almost impossible to manage such an operation. The crisis in the Great Lakes region of Africa and the situation in the Former Yugoslavia are reminders of the challenges of the 'new world disorder'[2] and the changing shape of refugee problems since the demise in power of the Communist bloc. This is the story of how the organisation tried to meet those challenges and reinvented itself to avoid marginalisation on the world stage.

THE BIRTH OF UNHCR

UNHCR began its work on 1 January 1951 with a five-year mandate and a 'statutory responsibility for seeking permanent solutions for the problems of refugees'.[3] For many years it worked primarily within its mandate for protection, concentrating efforts in countries of asylum. Its extraordinary growth started with the Gulf War crisis, marked by the exodus of Kurds from Iraq in 1991. Then came the former Yugoslavia with more than 3.5 million beneficiaries – and, in 1992, UNHCR's budget topped the billion dollar mark for the first time. Its staff had doubled in size in each of the previous years and stood at just over 4,000 in total (Exhibit 1). By the end of 1995, UNHCR had more than 5,300 staff of 185 different nationalities, 83 per cent of whom were employed outside of headquarters in some 255 field offices located in 118 countries. The organisation could provide worldwide exposure to refugee problems that might otherwise go unnoticed, a global protection mandate and the expert delivery of neutral and independent humanitarian aid.

---

[1] A glossary of abbreviations can be found in Appendix 1.

[2] *The State of the World's Refugees: In search of solutions*, Oxford University Press, 1995.

[3] A short history of UNHCR can be found in Appendix 2.

Exhibit 1 UNHCR funding, 1987–96

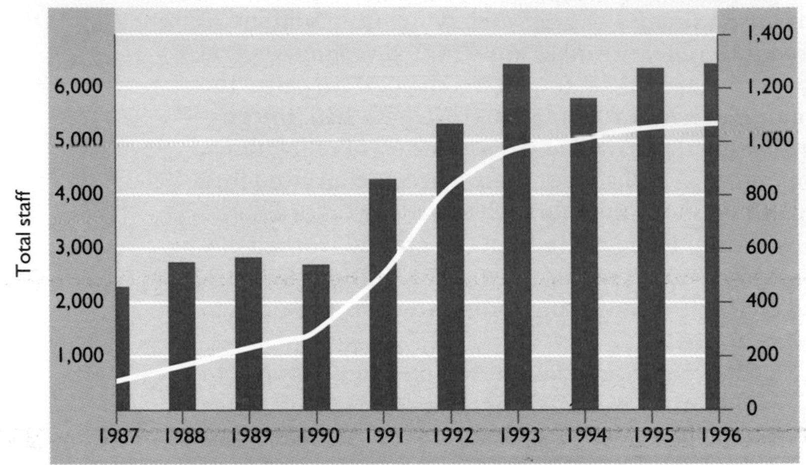

Total staff is represented by the white line

MORE IS NOT ALWAYS BETTER

In the five years to 1995 the number of 'persons of concern to UNHCR' jumped from 17 million to 27 million worldwide. Expenditures increased accordingly from $544m in 1990 to $1.3bn in 1995. 'We are at a maximum level,' said Ernest Chipman, head of UNHCR's Fund Raising Service in relation to the 1995 figure. 'It is difficult to imagine that donor countries will agree to increase contributions any further in future.'

Less than 2 per cent of UNHCR's $1.3bn total funding in 1996 came from UN sources. It was one of the few UN organs whose revenue depends on discretionary donations from governments and private individuals. Since 1992 the level of worldwide resources available for funding relief programmes had remained largely static whilst the number of humanitarian organisations had exploded, plunging agencies into head-on competition for the first time. Despite the overall rise in UNHCR's funding at the field level the problem was increasingly becoming one of how to do more with less.

At the same time, external pressures from public opinion and donor-country governments were forcing the organisation to become proactive rather than merely reactive to crises. There was a new emphasis on prevention, containment and seeking solutions to the root causes of refugee crises. Whilst scrupulously respecting the right to seek asylum, UNHCR also became concerned with finding ways to improve conditions in countries of origin. Governments and humanitarian organisations had become increasingly aware that refugee problems could not be resolved by means of uncoordinated activities in separate countries. Since 1994, regional approaches to refugee questions had combined the efforts of countries of origin and asylum, as well as other governments, development agencies, human rights organisations, peacekeeping forces, international financial institutions and regional bodies such as ECHO, NATO and the OSCE. What were once considered to be the domestic affairs of nation states had become the subject of legitimate international concern. Whilst establishing a local solution, UNHCR had to broker diplomatic accords at an international level: for example, a relief operation cannot be started until the organisation receives either an invitation from the host country government, all governments responsible for the region in crisis, or the UN secretary-general.

Externally, UNHCR was recognised as one of the most effective UN agencies in a crisis, but frustrations were growing amongst its field staff over the inefficiency of its centralised rule-based bureaucracy and the inflexibility of headquarters support. Enormous growth in the number and complexity of operations was straining the administrative and financial systems. The following comment from a senior field officer from an African refugee camp illustrates the situation:

> We have more than 300,000 refugees in 23 camps spread over a very bad road area. About 40 local and international staff need to be in those camps on a daily basis. Nine vehicles are down, so we have only eleven left to deliver these staff people and supplies to the camps. We can't get spare parts. Three months ago the front shock absorbers came, but not the back ones – typical! So nine vehicles are stuck in a garage tent. Then the HQ security people turn up, walk in, and write a report that says we don't have any security in the camps due to lack of vehicles. When I call headquarters to ask for extra vehicles, they ask whether I have malaria.[4]

These frustrations were echoed by donor states in the organisation's governing executive committee's (EXCOM) specialist sessions, although their concerns related to the high cost of UNHCR's administration and the risk of the organisation suffering a major operational embarrassment. 'To maintain the support of the donor community the organisation must be seen to be efficient, well managed and effective. If it fails to deliver on any one of these points it will cease to exist in its current form. That would be a great loss to the millions of unfortunate people that the organisation assists,' said Lynn Wallis, UNHCR's former controller, in a statement to the 1993 EXCOM session.

UNHCR had a delicate balancing act to perform: it had to maintain control and accountability in the eyes of the donors yet give its regional and local staff the information, authority, resources and flexibility they required in order to respond rapidly to crises as they arose under the full attention of the world's media. Inconsistencies in delivery from one crisis to another would be clearly visible to the donor community. 'The intrusion of networked television cameras into our work has meant that people all

[4] *Delphi News*, February 1996.

around the world are instantly taking a global view of our operations: a view that the situation manager on the ground, wrapped up in the local crisis, has, until now, been unable to share,' said Filipo Grandi, from UNHCR's Fund Raising Service. 'The organisation sees the media as an ally in the struggle to carry out its mandate. Transparency is fine if we all clearly understand what the organisation is about and speak with the same voice.'[5]

UNHCR'S ADMINISTRATION

Uppermost in the criticisms of donors and implementing partners was the cost and inefficiency of the cumbersome centralised administration. Until 1993 the internal structure resembled the 'functional silos' of the traditional UN bureaucracy. Terms of reference, instruction manuals and regulations governed the responsibilities and scope of each functional entity. The objectives and performance measures for each division related more to the control of their own area of responsibility rather than to the support of the operations that the organisation was mandated to carry out. This resulted in a constant battle between headquarters, regional bureaux and field-based representatives whose responsibility was to deliver practical solutions, and administrative support divisions whose responsibility was to count the dollars and cents. Exhibit 2 illustrates the internal structure as it was in 1995, before changes were made. An urgent request from a field camp for supplies would first be evaluated by the regional office administrator and the local representative's office before being sent on by fax or telex to a country desk in a regional bureau at headquarters. There it would be vetted before being passed up the hierarchy to the regional director's office. Requests involving expenditure of more than $1,000 required approval from the budget section before they could be actioned by the relevant support division. The whole process required some eleven authorising signatures and could take more than ten days to complete.

Some management practices were considered by the Senior Management Committee (SMC) to be inviolate: UNHCR had a policy of rotating management staff to different functions and locations every 2–4 years, depending on the severity of living conditions at the duty station. This policy was designed to maintain uniformity of implementation, a high level of field management skills and practical experience.

The organisation suffered from the legacy of a number of ineffective support division driven change projects as staff rotated into headquarters tried to make their 'mark'. Delivery was usually attempted through inter-office memoranda, or 'IOM', that were printed in the same pica typeface and format used in the days of typewriters. These documents hardly inspired enthusiasm and were difficult to read as the rules demanded that they

[5] *Refugees Magazine, IV: The high cost of caring*, 1995.

Exhibit 2 UNHCR internal structure (principal units in 1995)

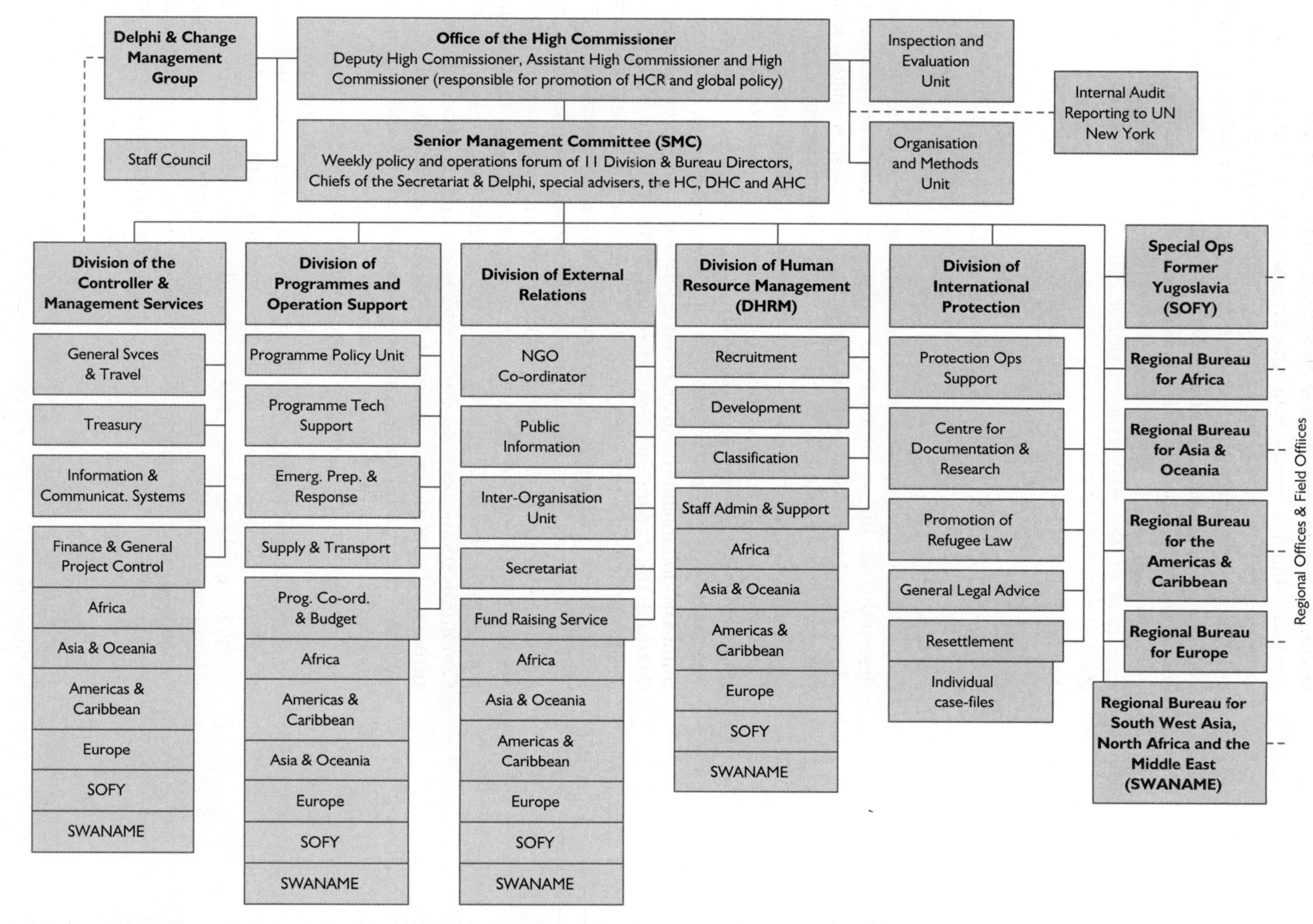

contain references in the text to any previous memoranda related to their contents. In most cases staff quickly reverted to their old familiar ways, sceptical and reluctant to follow any new initiatives. To survive in the emerging competitive environment it was clear that UNHCR would have to change its management procedures. The problem was how to achieve change without destroying the incredible dedication to duty of the front-line workforce on which the organisation relied. This responsibility fell on the shoulders of the high commissioner, Mrs Sadako Ogata, who was first elected to office in 1991.

FIRST MOVES

After receiving support for a second term of office from the General Assembly, the high commissioner embarked on a series of moves to bring about the changes she desired. First, she appointed a change agent in the position of controller: Lynn Wallis, the first female appointment to the previously all-male Senior Management Committee joined UNHCR in 1993. Later that year, in a speech to EXCOM, the high commissioner made it clear that her intention was to make UNHCR 'a slimmer, trimmer organisation'. She said, 'We must restructure the way in which we work, so as to improve our delivery, accountability and performance and build the capacity to contract and expand in response to operational demands.'[6]

Immediately, the new controller set a different style from her predecessors. Streamlining procedures in her own division (Controller and Management Services), reducing paperwork to a minimum, eradicating surplus personnel and championing improvements in accountability and productivity. Chiefs of sections were encouraged to delegate work to their staff and to visit field offices and other organisations whenever possible. Communications became direct and horizontal instead of up and down through the structural hierarchy. Major investment was approved to overhaul the existing radio communications facilities and provide electronic mail links to and throughout all offices.

Throughout 1993 and 1994, buoyed up by the success of programmes covering the introduction of a global electronic communications network, asset management and records management systems, the controller's team developed plans for how the high commissioner's 'new and streamlined UNHCR' would look in the future. The plans included devolution of administration and support resources to the field to give representatives the capacity to take more strategic decisions locally, and a complete revamp of systems to provide them with the management information they required to do their job. In September 1993 a three-year strategic plan for UNHCR, was

[6] Rupert Colville, Press release, UNHCR Division of External Relations, November 1995.

presented to the SMC by the controller. It was rejected despite extensive lobbying, not because of any disagreement about its content, but because the members did not like to have any one division dictating the future of the others. 'We had all put a lot of time and effort into that plan. The SMC decision seemed like a major blow at the time but, in hindsight, it was for the best. It taught us a salutary lesson about how not to implement a change programme in an organisation like ours,' said the director of human resources.

The high commissioner, meanwhile, coming under renewed pressure to limit demands for increased funding, called her senior management team together for a two-day 'retreat' away from the office. At the retreat, senior management finally agreed that centralised control was limiting the effectiveness of the organisation's proactive role in the field. Devolution was seen as a necessary but painful surgery to be performed, like the amputation of a deseased limb. Two far-reaching pronouncements came out of that meeting: UNHCR's prime role in field operations should be that of co-ordinator and disseminator of expertise, and the entire chain of delivery and support operations should be reviewed using internal resources under the direction of the controller. Wallis explained:

> Ownership of solutions had always been a problem for UNHCR – hence the proliferation of committees. No one liked having someone else's personal opinion forced upon them. We asked for nine volunteers from field offices and the bureaux to work together in a preliminary study team called the Change Management Group [CMG]. Their first task was to look at the information and communications systems strategy but it soon occurred to us all that a step-by-step approach would take too long. There were too many interactions to cover at once, and the changes required were too fundamental. Finally, with the help of some outside government consultants we hit on the idea of 'Project Delphi'. We had to change the way people thought and there was only one way to do it. They had to find the answers for themselves.

GETTING THE MESSAGE ACROSS

January 1996 saw the birth of the *Delphi News*. 'We experimented with different types of communication media using video, group training, mass meetings and an informal high-print-quality, "snappy" newsletter with photographs and cartoons. Everyone read it.' Submissions from staff, editorial articles and comments were published anonymously. Using humour and cartoons to get the message across, the *Delphi News* juxtaposed stories about the old procedures typed in the IOM pica font against new ideas from the CMG depicted in attractive, clear fonts. Through the *Delphi News* readers were also reminded of the basic concepts underpinning the Delphi process, as the following example shows:

Delphi – the Basics: a joint effort and a common commitment

- Eliminate redundancy, strive for efficiency and effectiveness.
- Review, redesign, or scrap existing systems, procedures as needed; rebuild.
- Never hesitate to go back to the drawing board.
- Be user-friendly.
- Field thinking is primary in shaping systems design; HQ/field consultations are crucial to determine capacity for delegation.
- Field management should be enabled to solve problems autonomously.
- Information technology must be widely available, shared, adaptable.
- Answer the following questions: WHAT is it that needs to be done? WHY does it need to be done? (perhaps it doesn't!) and HOW might it be done better?

DELPHI NEWS, ISSUE 8, AUGUST 1996, TAKEN FROM A MEMORANDUM CIRCULATED TO ALL STAFF IN ALL OFFICES IN JANUARY 1996

Confirmation that staff were ready for change came from an anonymous staff attitude survey conducted in March 1996 by a firm of independent specialists. In the support staff and lower management grades, more than 50 per cent of all respondents wanted fundamental change to the system but, in the higher management grades, the percentage dropped to less than 30 per cent.

Staff everywhere were exhorted to set aside a 'Delphi day' to brainstorm in small independent groups, called Delphi cells, about how any aspect of their work could be changed to make UNHCR more effective. Instructions were clear. 'Begin with a blank page, don't get bogged down in policy, personalities or organigrams but concentrate on processes.' There was to be no framework or format to follow except that freewheeling considerations should take place under three headings: People, Money and Operations. Results had to be sent to the Change Management Group anonymously and by a variety of routes before 1 March 1996. For two days, all but essential work stopped as staff left their desks to 'think'.

Delphi day in UNHCR Washington Office

This process was the best briefing I could have hoped for. The discussions threw everything out in the open. We talked about areas where there was duplication; we looked at how people could share the administrative work more equitably. Now, in the office, we have a calendar for everybody, so we can keep track of each other's commitments. Everybody has access to my calendar, so if they feel I should meet with someone they can just make the appointment. There are many more important changes too. This has been a wonderful training for me.

ANNE-WILLEM BIJLEVELD, UNHCR REPRESENTATIVE IN WASHINGTON, APRIL 1996

The result was astounding: 2,220 ideas were collected on a database from more than 100 Delphi cells and over 118 country offices. Printed, it amounted to more than 550 pages. A bound copy was sent to each office and made available on the intranet. 'It was important for the credibility of the project that all contributors could see that their ideas and comments had been taken seriously and not altered or suppressed. As editor, I was told to print it all, except the names. Delphi wasn't going to boost anyone's ego or promote a witch-hunt.'

Exhibit 3 Examples of the Needs and Actions Contained in the CMG Report

Operations Group

- There was a need for an organisational centre to provide vision and strategic policy, maintain standards, provide guidance, collect and disseminate information.
- Core and non-core functions should be identified, core functions should be resourced from UNHCR staff and non-core functions from implementing partners – supporting 'the accordion principle' (the rapid expansion and contraction of implementation staff).
- An exit strategy should be programmed at the start of every operation.
- An up-rated operations management system with global logistics management capability was required to improve the response to major crises like Rwanda.

People Group

- Reduce the number of different types of staff contract.
- Improve manpower planning, personal development, performance review, promotion and rewards by implementing the new career management system (CMS) piloted in Asia.
- Rotation should be needs-based and within a limited geographical region to allow families a greater degree of stability.
- Staff recruited for non-rotating specialist functions should undertake a three-month hardship post deployment as part of their induction into UNHCR.
- Phase out contracts of predetermined duration and replace with service contract for an undetermined period.
- UNHCR staff recognised the need for, and indeed welcomed, change in both the organisation's processes and its culture.

Money Group

- The whole budgeting process needs to be completely reviewed and focused on field situation planning.
- Objectives and benefits should be clearly identified before financial commitments are made.

Several themes and definitions arose out of the exercise and were incorporated into the phase 2 of Project Delphi: functional assistance had to replace functional control; headquarters should be responsible for policy co-ordination – with a maximum of three substantive levels between the beneficiaries and the high commissioner; some members of the headquarters senior management committee should become field-based mobile 'situation directors', physically close to the operation but without adding another layer of permanent 'regional' offices.

'It was clear that the whole focus of the organisation's administration had to swing round to actively support operational situations in the field,' said one of the CMG members. 'Any refugee crisis always involves at least two countries – the country of origin and the country of asylum.' From this observation the 'situational approach' was born.

Deciding what to do with this outpouring of conscience was the next problem. 'As in any commercial film production, success could be won or lost on the cutting-room floor; yet we had to reduce 550 pages to a set of manageable issues for further review.' The CMG split into three focus groups (Operations, People and Money) and worked hard with staff all over the world to define the 'needs and actions' for Delphi (see Exhibit 3). Completion of the definition stage marked the end of the planning phase and the CMG was disbanded.

The next phase of the Delphi Project handed over to a project management-oriented Change Management Support and Co-ordination Group (CMSCG), composed of a core of 4–5 competent project managers under the direct supervision of the high commissioner. It was recognised that this group would have to work closely with field units in order to ensure ownership of projects at the field level and to assess the impact and results of changes outside of headquarters.

SQUEEZED IN THE MIDDLE

Lacking the protection of a permanent appointment, many managers were forced to choose between the new and the old ways, whilst maintaining the crucial support of their general service staff team members. Life as a middle manager in the change process was not easy, as the following comment illustrates:

> In the beginning it was not so easy to get things done. I had no direct authority, no terms of reference memorandum, conflicting priorities and I couldn't 'fire' anybody. Coercion and discussion were the order of the day, it seemed to take forever; building bridges and networks, finding champions and supporting them until some success was evident and critical mass was achieved. It was a real 'hearts and minds' operation: you had to believe! In the end this approach carried us through some incredibly difficult moments when problems did arise and politically inclined forces tried to exploit our temporary weakness to derail the project. If things had gone wrong though, it was easy to see whose head would have been on the chopping block!

MAINTAINING THE MOMENTUM

'During phase 2 of Delphi, staff didn't "see" the same level of progress they had become accustomed to in phase 1. They began to feel let down and some openly voiced concern that Delphi would never really go anywhere,' said Lynn Wallis. Again, communications were the key to maintaining contact with the now vociferous workforce. Open meetings called 'Lunchtime learning', and 'In the hot seat' were held in the main headquarters auditorium at midday. In the latter, prominent directors were invited to deliver an address and then withstand questions from the floor for up to 30 minutes. 'Too much detailed planning doesn't work in a public organisation.

In the end a lot of people do just what they want to unless they are put in the spotlight and shown up in front of their peers,' commented the organiser of the 'In the hot seat' sessions. SMC directors spent one week at a UK business school together with directors from commercial enterprises learning about leading change and avoiding micro-management. A global representatives conference was also arranged at headquarters, creating the 'organisation's most experienced Delphi cell'.

Still, progress through the planning stages in early 1997 was slow, with little happening on the surface for almost four months. By this time almost all of the original leaders of the Delphi process, including Lynn Wallis, had been rotated to other posts outside of headquarters. 'In the resulting vacuum some small, informal project "development" cells had started up. They were mainly composed of junior managers, but no one knew what they were really up to,' said one new member of the CMSCG. It had also been some weeks since the last *Delphi News* publication, and rumours of imminent 'bad news' were rife. Staff felt apprehensive that change would not continue. 'There were many rumours about possible staff reductions. *Delphi* almost stalled at that time and we had to resort to a number of measures to keep it going.' Delphi instruction sessions were held twice each week to remind everyone what it was all about, and staff visiting the field were encouraged to take along a newsreel-type slide presentation briefing pack.

DIFFICULT NEWS

As crisis operations around the world stabilised and media interest subsided, there was a notable fall in pledges for future funding from donor governments. Despite a recruitment freeze, by late 1996 it was obvious that more than 20 per cent of headquarters posts would have to be cut by the end of 1997. Higher than the figure suggested by the Delphi process, achieving this cut was to be the toughest test of the organisation's resolve. The high commissioner was adamant that senior management should bear an equal burden, and two directors immediately took early retirement. Many long-serving 'specialist' staff were encouraged to move to the field to support the new situational approach. A programme was created to train and promote any HQ general service staff that wanted to work in the field to professional grade. Many took up the offer. But as reality struck home and more familiar faces departed, there was a noticeable drop in morale at headquarters. The timely announcement by the secretary-general of 1,000 post cuts in the UN in New York and the launch of a similar reform project modelled on that of UNHCR did a lot to share the burden, but the mood of staff at headquarters remained sombre.

The situation was made worse by the lack of new emergencies; the familiar saviour of UNHCR in times of financial or organisational hardship. People had too much time to dwell on the uncertainties of their own future. The deputy high commissioner summed up this sentiment in a statement to the standing committee in the General Assembly: 'It surely would be unrealistic, even incorrect, to state that we are not experiencing difficulties, bottlenecks or setbacks ... but there is a sense among us that the change process has taken hold, that we maintain a healthy momentum and that we are moving forward.'

GETTING BOGGED DOWN

Despite momentous progress in the way that the organisation thought about itself and its work, by early 1998 there had been eight months without any great visible change. The staff at headquarters had expected much more. In September 1997 the finance, budget and fundraising administrative staff openly protested their dissatisfaction at the way their Delphi projects were being led. What had gone wrong? The new chairman of the CMSCG:

> One thing has changed for good. Once staff got used to tackling problems themselves, they developed into a highly critical, integrated and demanding body. If some process doesn't work too well, they just wanted to get on and fix it themselves. The problem is that we allowed small groups to get too far down the development path. Some chiefs, keen to rush through their own pet project, built up a clan following before looking to see which other units would be affected by what they were doing. When they did finally talk to their counterparts it became a battle over whose system was better and who would back down. Scarce resources were being squandered on incompatible developments. We did achieve our goal of having only three substantive layers between the high commissioner and the beneficiaries but other support service projects designed to back up field empowerment lacked top management commitment. It was exasperating. We had also become a task-oriented leadership. Several directors were still looking inwards and were not aware how much the behaviour of their staff had changed. Even some of the old SMC animosities were back. Management had forgotten that they were now 'on stage' and transparent to the watchful eyes of an enlightened staff.
>
> In a Delphi-type change process, implementation, control and management of expectations are vital. Freedom of thought can be exhilarating, but the actions that ensue still have to be co-ordinated – someone still has to lead. Losing momentum is the beginning of the end for any high-level change project. You can never get it back. It is like letting the steam out of the locomotive half way up a long incline.

By the end of 1997, Project Delphi had a lot of accomplishments to be proud of: field representatives had better decision-making flexibility than before within more broadly defined budgetary categories; administrative staff at headquarters were no longer 'second guessing' demands from the field, and open collaboration between administrative staff at all levels had improved response time. Still, many of the most important structural issues that Delphi had put before the SMC had not been resolved. Project Delphi had been launched as much in an effort to remove necessary reforms from the political arena as an attempt to achieve ownership of change by the staff affected. Ownership of change and long-lasting changes in staff behaviour had occurred, but mass enthusiasm was in danger of turning into mass indifference without confident and open leadership. The problem facing the high commissioner in 1998 was how to regenerate the original trust and enthusiasm in senior management that existed in the early days of Delphi and how to achieve the major constitutional changes that the workforce and external partners continued to demand.

APPENDIX 1 GLOSSARY OF ABBREVIATIONS

CMG	Change Management Group
CMSCG	Change Management Support and Co-ordination Group (successor to the CMG)
ECHO	European Community Humanitarian Organisation
EXCOM	Executive Committee of the High Commissioner's Programme (UNHCR's governing body)
FAO	United Nations Food and Agricultural Organisation
IRC&RC	International Red Cross and Red Crescent
NATO	North Atlantic Treaty Organisation
NGO	Non-governmental Organisation
OSCE	Organisation for Security and Co-operation in Europe
SMC	Senior Management Committee of UNHCR
SOFY	UNHCR's Special Operation in the Former Yugoslavia
UNDP	United Nations Development Programme
UNICEF	United Nations Children's Fund
UNOPS	United Nations Office for Project Services
WFP	World Food Programme
WHO	World Health Organisation

APPENDIX 2 UNHCR IN BRIEF

The creation of UNHCR

The Office of the United Nations High Commissioner for Refugees – UNHCR – was created by the UN General Assembly and began its work on 1 January 1951. Since that time, the organisation has been responsible for protecting refugees and promoting lasting solutions to their plight. Although the organisation was initially established as a temporary one, with a life-span of three years, the General Assembly has renewed UNHCR's mandate for successive five-year periods, the most recent of which expires at the end of 1998.

The high commissioner

The High Commissioner for Refugees is elected by the General Assembly, on the nomination of the secretary-general. There have been eight high commissioners since the organisation was established. The current high commissioner, Mrs Sadako Ogata of Japan, took up office on 1 January 1991. An executive committee, a body composed of 50 governments and donor states, oversees UNHCR's budget and advises on refugee protection issues.

The organisation's mandate

According to its statute, UNHCR is competent to provide protection and assistance to any person who, 'owing to well-founded fear of being persecuted for reasons of race, religion, nationality or political opinion, is outside the country of his nationality and is unable or, owing to such fear or for reasons other than personal convenience, is unwilling to avail himself of the protection of that country ...'

While this definition still forms the core of UNHCR's mandate, the organisation often works on behalf of people who are fleeing from armed conflict and generalised human rights violations. When refugees go home, UNHCR also helps them to reintegrate in their countries of origin. In recent years, the UN secretary-general, the General Assembly and the member states of the United Nations have also regularly called upon the organisation to extend its services to people who have been displaced within their own country, to war-affected populations and to programmes aimed at creating an environment for prolonging peace and stability.

Protection activities

The protection of refugees remains UNHCR's primary function. Protection lies at the heart of the organisation's efforts to find lasting solutions to the plight of refugees, and provides the context in which UNHCR carries out its relief activities.

Assistance programmes

Most of the world's refugees and displaced people are to be found in the least developed countries and in other states which cannot be expected to bear the cost of large-scale humanitarian relief efforts. In such cases, UNHCR, in consultation with the relevant government authorities, provides assistance to the affected population in the form of food, shelter and health services, as well as education, social welfare and income-generating activities.

Over the years, UNHCR has developed four principal types of assistance programme: emergency relief operations; longer-term 'care and maintenance' programmes for refugees who are awaiting a solution to their plight; local settlement programmes, intended to help refugees become self-sufficient in their country of asylum; and repatriation and reintegration operations, established to help refugees who wish to go home and resume a productive life in their own community.

Partnerships

Many of UNHCR's assistance activities are undertaken jointly with other organisations, such as government departments, other UN agencies, non-governmental organisations, and even, in recent years, with military and peacekeeping forces. UNHCR is also committed to the active participation of beneficiaries in its assistance programmes, and therefore encourages the creation of refugee committees and other structures that enable this objective to be achieved.

More than ever before, the prevention and resolution of refugee problems depends upon effective co-ordination amongst the various organisations concerned. This has sometimes been achieved by designating a 'lead agency', responsible for the co-ordination of a specific operation – a role that UNHCR has played, for example, in former Yugoslavia. In 1992, the UN's Department of Humanitarian Affairs was established, with a mandate to co-ordinate a worldwide response to complex emergencies.

Funding

With the exception of a very limited subsidy from the UN regular budget, which is used exclusively for administrative expenditures, UNHCR's activities are funded by voluntary contributions from governments, intergovernmental and non-governmental organisations, as well as individuals. The organisation's provisional budget for 1995 stands at some US$ 1.3 billion. This budget is divided into two parts: general programmes, which consist of ongoing protection and assistance activities, planned and approved in advance; and special programmes, which consist primarily of refugee emergency operations and voluntary repatriation programmes.

Source UNHCR, *The State of the World's Refugees: In search of solutions*, Oxford University Press, 1995.

BURMAH CASTROL CHEMICALS GROUP

Gerry Johnson

The Chemicals Group of Burmah Castrol grew throughout the 1980s and early 1990s largely by acquisition. This case study is based on the deliberations that followed a new chief executive taking over the Chemicals Group in 1995. The case provides the opportunity to consider the strategic logic of the Chemicals Group in the context of the parent company's expectations and the 'parenting needs' of the businesses identified by their managers in considering competitive strategy. This, in turn, raises questions about the 'added value' which the Group brings to the separate businesses and the way it should be organised to do so.

• • •

BACKGROUND

With its head office in the UK, Burmah Castrol is a manufacturer of specialised lubricants and chemicals, marketing to consumers and industrial customers in over 150 countries. In 1995 its worldwide turnover exceeded £3 billion with profit before tax of £253 million. The lubricants business is centred on the Castrol brand automotive, industrial and marine products.

The Chemicals Group had been formed by Burmah Castrol in 1981 by bringing together two of its businesses, Dussek Campbell (waxes) and Expandite (operating in the construction market); and this was followed by a series of acquisitions including Foseco plc in 1990 (see Exhibit 1), with the intention of bringing together chemicals businesses of a speciality, rather than commodity nature, based on formulatory skills. By 1995 its turnover was £810 million with profits of £62.4 million. On taking over as chief executive in 1995, Mike Dearden was determined to develop a clear strategy for the group, and by the end of that year this process had begun.

This case study was prepared by Professor Gerry Johnson, Cranfield School of Management. It is intended as a basis for class discussion and not as an illustration of either good or bad management practice.

Exhibit 1 Chemicals Group acquisitions

YEAR	ACQUISITION	SBU
1982	Industrial Adhesives Ltd, UK	Adhesives
1983	Sericol, UK	Printing Inks
1985	Yates Manufacturing, USA	Coatings
1986	National Wax, USA	Coatings
1986	Columbia Cement, USA	Adhesives
1987	Midwest Coatings, USA	Printing Inks
1990	Fragival, Spain	Printing Inks
1990	Foseco plc, UK	Metallurgical, Construction and Timber Treatment
1991	Dysons, UK	Metallurgical
1992	Tri-Union, Hong Kong	Printing Inks
1993	Kerax, UK	Coatings

THE DIVISIONS AND THE BUSINESSES

Exhibit 2 shows the structure of Burmah Castrol in 1995, and in particular the businesses in the Chemicals Group. The group included five divisions, Metallurgical Chemicals (Foseco), Construction and Mining Chemicals (Fosroc), Printing Inks (Sericol), Coatings (Dussek Campbell and Protim Solignum) and Adhesives (IAL, Columbia). These in turn included fourteen business units (SBUs), brief summaries of which are provided in Appendix 1. An indication of the 1995 performance of these business units is shown in Exhibit 3.

The main business activities of the divisions of the Chemicals Group were described by the divisional chief executives as follows. John Briggs of the Printing Inks division:

> Sericol sells printing inks to screen printers around the world. It is market leader in many of its markets and shares are growing. Success comes from the strong customer orientation of the whole company and the value that the customer has then placed on our product offering. We offer reliability and a commitment to outstanding product availability and speed of delivery. In effect, we encourage customers to expect more than competitors can achieve. This offering has particular value to our market – one which is highly fragmented with a large number of small players. One of our main advantages is our knowledge of where the customers are and we have achieved this through a very sophisticated IT system. Given that we keep innovating in the areas of reliability, consistency, delivery, IT and so on, competitors are always trying to catch up, but they are one or two steps behind. We do all this by working as a team, not individuals. Really, it's getting a lot of things right in detail in relatively small markets. You can see why it's not that attractive to competitors.

Exhibit 2 Burmah Castrol and Chemicals Group structure, 1995

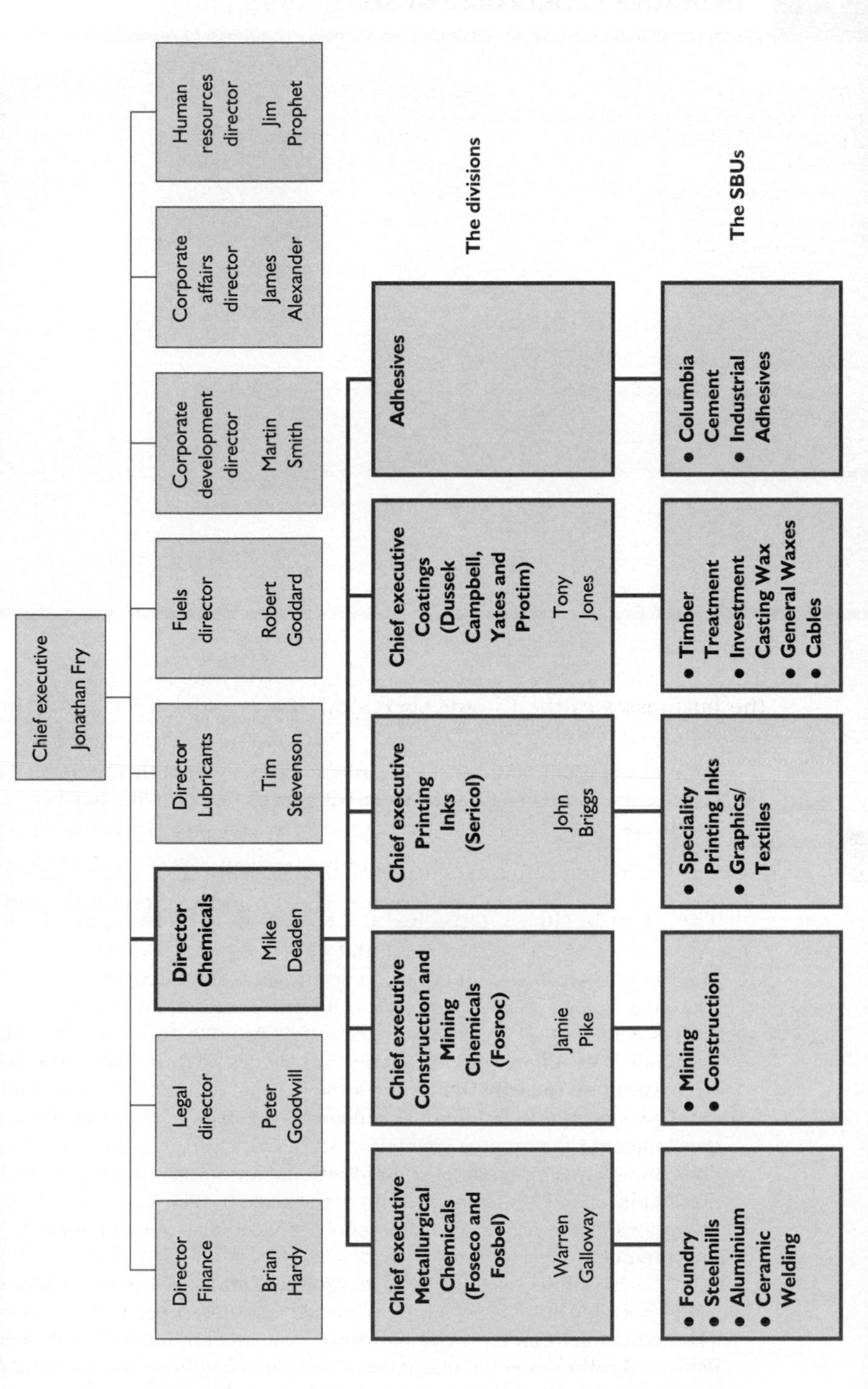

Exhibit 3 Indicative performance of SBUs, 1995

	Sales (£m)	Gross Margin
Foundry	100+	M
Construction		H
Printing Inks		H
Graphics/Textiles		
Speciality		
Steelmills		M
General Waxes	30–100	L
Adhesives		L
Aluminium		M
Mining		M
Ceramic Welding (Fosbel)	Below 30	H
Timber Treatment		H
Cable Products		L
Casting Waxes		L

Note Gross margin key: H, 40%; M, 30–40%; L, below 30%.

For many of them, screen printing inks is a small part of their portfolio; and they have to try and compete with us in very small markets. It's not very attractive for them.

Warren Galloway, chief executive of the Metallurgical Chemicals division, summarised the differences between the Foundry, Steelmills and Aluminium businesses:

The Foundry business addresses a very large, fragmented and international customer base. The ability to offer solutions based on an intimate understanding of all areas of the customer's process and product application skills is key to differential advantage and success. Whilst still dependent to a large extent on the experience and knowledge of its technical sales and product management people, Foseco has enhanced its skills in this area through the development of computer simulation software. Customer needs and buyer behaviour varies from complex multinational automotive foundries such as Fiat, Ford and General Motors at one end of the scale to relatively small, local jobbing operations at the other, where, in effect, Foseco also act as technical consultants.

The Steelmills business sells its products and services to a small number (300+) of large but mainly nationally-based customers spread around the world. The main target market is the slab and bloom steel producers, and these clients have many common characteristics and Foseco has been good at spotting niche opportunities within the operations of these large customers.

> The main Foseco products are consumed in the continuous casting area, which is at the heart of the steel plant and critically important to its successful operation. The products are all used in, or close to, the tundish,[1] and Foseco steelmills engineers are specialists in controlling steel flow through the tundish and mould. This operation is extremely complex and Foseco offers to take responsibility, through its Tundish Management Services, for lining the tundishes with refractory. Though critical, this is peripheral to the process of making steel.
>
> In this way Foseco Steelmills become partners with their clients in jointly controlling the successful management of the steel casting process.

As for Fosbel, he saw this as rather different from the other businesses within the division: 'There are differences with Fosbel. This is a business heavily reliant still on patent technology across the world.'

Jamie Pike, chief executive of the Construction and Mining Chemicals division, reviewed the Fosroc businesses:

> Construction in particular is an applications business; applications in complex and difficult circumstances. The applications are very often customer specific and the key issue is how teams of sales people and technical people working together in different parts of the world can work effectively. To do this they have to do things differently in different markets sometimes with very localised needs. It's difficult to put your finger on why we are successful where we are, but in some markets we have 80 per cent share and competitors are less than 5 per cent. There are many reasons, primarily about teams of people interfacing very closely with local customer needs.
>
> I suppose Mining is more structured in the way we operate. The provision of powders to the mining industry requires, again, a close understanding of customer needs and high-quality teams to do it; but the market is more concentrated than in construction. We are successful in our resin capsules indeed, probably the largest in the world – and if I have to explain why, I suppose it is because we are good at bringing new products to market in ways which reduce cost to customers.

Tony Jones, chief executive of the Coatings division:

> As far as Cables is concerned you need type approvals to get into the market, so there are not that many competitors. There are also usually large, often global, buyers and they regard as important long-term relationships and a proven track record in those relationships. When you have got in, the key to success is therefore customer relations and, again, between teams rather than individuals and the customers. You then have to offer good reliable supply with a global back-up in product development. The Yates Investment Casting business serves a highly fragmented and geographically widespread market, but one in which technical service is important.
>
> The market for general waxes is fairly concentrated in packaging and very fragmented in candles, but in both cases success comes down to intimate knowledge of customer applications again, and tailoring products to their needs.

---

[1] Tundishes are 5–10 metre refractory troughs that feed molten metal to continuous casters. As well as lining tundishes, Foseco provides comprehensive on-site monitoring in the Steelmills and Aluminium Businesses.

> The same success factors apply to the Protim Solignum treatment business, where, due to the complications of handling environmentally sensitive products, a thorough knowledge of customers' processes is vital.

Finally, the Adhesives division:

> The market for Adhesives is very fragmented. Products are becoming more commodity-oriented, with increasing competitor consolidation in the industry. A large part of our business is in pressure-sensitive adhesives, where tailoring products to customer needs is important. But here again, cost is a key driver, with raw material supplies starting to move downstream to supplying customers directly.

THE NEED FOR A GROUP STRATEGY

Mike Dearden held the view that the key questions to be asked by the Group Executive were how, and to what extent, the group or the divisional levels within the group could be of benefit to the business units; and to what extent the businesses gained by being part of the same portfolio.

> If the centre doesn't or can't add value, then we are just a cost and may destroy value. The businesses would be better off on their own, or with someone else. If we can add value, how: and how should we be organised to do it?

The Burmah Castrol Board had made clear it was seeking to develop a chemicals business with global dimensions and investment potential for growth. However, Mike Dearden believed that, in order to be clear about the role of the group centre, it was necessary to begin by considering the bases of strategy at the business level; and then ask how the centre could or should help the businesses. This process began with workshops for representatives of most of the business units so that they could contribute to the debate in two ways:

- To consider and identify bases of SBU competitive strategy in terms of competitive position and the core competences of the SBUs.
- On these bases, to consider how, if at all, they thought structures above SBU level – for example, the Chemicals Group itself – could add value to the SBUs.

These workshops were completed by January 1996. Each was attended by David Hughes and Mark Rowley, who worked with Mike Dearden on strategy development.

In January 1996 the Chemical Group executive met to consider the outcome of the workshops and asked David and Mark to produce a report drawing together the findings from the workshops and summarising the key issues which arose. The report is summarised in Appendix 2.

THE EXECUTIVE DEBATE

The executive of the Chemicals Group met to consider the report from the workshop at a two-day meeting in March 1996. After dinner the night before the meeting, Mike Dearden outlined the issues:

> The Chemicals Group has been through a number of phases in its development. There was the creation of the portfolio in the 1980s; this was followed by the acquisition of Foseco plc; and our emphasis has been on improving performance in each of the businesses in the last few years. The question now is: what next? I think we have got two or three years more of improvement – efficiency growth, if you wish – but where do we go from there? It seems to me in answering that we have to take into consideration three very important issues. The first is that the investment community is not yet convinced of what Burmah Castrol really brings to running a chemicals business. We have to be much clearer about that. The second is that we ourselves have to be clear what we add to the businesses. If we as a Chemicals Group bring no benefits to them, then presumably we are just a cost. They would be better off on their own or with someone else. The third issue is just what the synergy is between the businesses. It seems to me the workshops didn't show much 'hard' synergy. We have to ask if there is anything else and what this says about how we, as a group, can help the businesses.
>
> Within all this I think it is clear that Burmah Castrol is looking for investment opportunities and they are as likely, perhaps more likely, to be in our area than in Lubricants. However, we cannot expect that sort of investment unless we are very clear as to where we are going. They also expect us to be developing, if not a truly global, then a clear international strategy.

ADDING VALUE TO THE BUSINESSES

The executive meeting discussed the views of the SBUs on how the centre had and could add value. They began by considering what the centre's role had been traditionally. Using the same checklist as the workshops had used, they concluded that in their view the main skills had been in managing people, internationalisation, strategic planning, intervention and central financial services, although there was some discussion of whether the way they were delivered was in line with SBU needs.

> I think the central personnel function has been good when it comes to recruitment, management succession, training and the provision of central services. Certainly, historically we have been active in acquisitions and disposals; and in the last few years businesses have seen us intervening quite a lot to get better efficiencies; but the emphasis has been on cost efficiency. I think our strategic planning is rather formalised and that the businesses see it as much more to do with us or Burmah Castrol than to do with them. I am also not sure that they would be very clear about what the corporate strategy is – but then that is what we are meeting about.

There was a good deal of debate about skills and needs in internationalisation. One view was:

> It surprises me that the report says we are not so good at internationalisation. I cannot think of many firms that would give as much encouragement to local management to set up local manufacturing plants or invest locally. In some companies the suggestion to invest in somewhere like Thailand might raise all sorts of difficulties. We tend to regard that sort of thing as relatively normal. I would have thought we are very encouraging in the internationalisation process.

Another:

> But I think we are less good when it comes to proactive internationalisation. Everyone ends up 'inventing the wheel'. One business does something and a year later someone else is doing the same sort of thing without any knowledge of what the other business has done. We make difficulties for ourselves rather than helping businesses on internationalisation. We don't build on our experience.

Many of the businesses had been established either as UK firms which had developed international divisions or export businesses, or as widely scattered and largely independent subsidiaries. Over the past few years, some of these had developed more coherent global strategies, but the extent to which this was happening was variable. To get a picture of this, they used a matrix of global co-ordination versus local independence and responsiveness (see Exhibits 4a–d) to map the historic position and the future direction of the businesses in terms of international structures. The exhibits below show these for each of the main businesses.

> It seems to me that many of our businesses are developing clearer global strategies; but many of them need to retain a great deal of local flexibility. How we deal with that is problematic. How we do that within the businesses and what role the centre plays in that needs to be thought about very carefully. From what we have been discussing so far, it seems we have some different views about that.

THE ROLE OF THE CENTRE

The meeting went on to discuss the role of the group centre in the future. The first view was this:

> Whatever the criteria for the acquisitions of the businesses in the group, the fact of the matter is there are very few linkages between them. It is not enough to say that they are all chemicals businesses. They use chemicals as raw materials, but that is all. There are really no linkages technologically between many of the businesses. There are not many market linkages either. To the outsider, a steel-mill and foundry may sound very similar, but they are very different indeed; and what relationship they have to screen printers is very difficult to see. I tried drawing out what linkages I could see and couldn't find many [see Exhibits 5a and b]. There are rather more on technology than markets, but not so many you could build a group rationale around them.

Exhibit 4

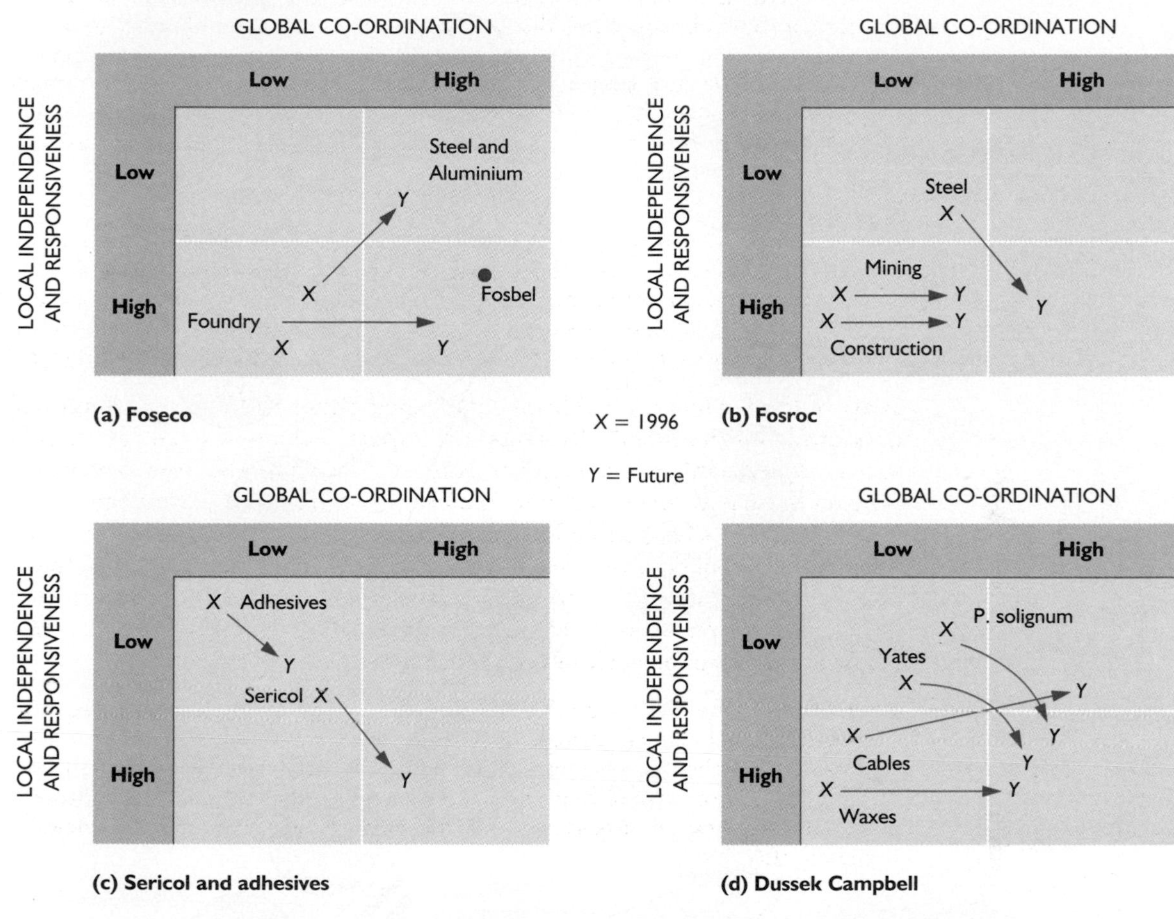

My recommendation is that we should regard the businesses as a set of discrete units, each with their own technology and their own markets, and each perfectly capable of making good returns for the group. But they should be left alone to get on with it. We should recognise that the group really cannot add value to these businesses because there are not substantial linkages between them. The centre should recognise that it is at real risk of simply adding costs without value, and should therefore seek to reduce cost to a minimum and simply exercise financial control. It should set clear targets about what returns are expected, provide investment if returns are being met, change the management if they are not or, at the extreme, dispose of the business. If we follow this route, we can manage the portfolio we have more efficiently and cost effectively than we are doing currently. We could probably also get rid of some of the intermediate divisional structures because we would not require the degree of co-ordination that we currently try to achieve.

Exhibit 5 Linkages

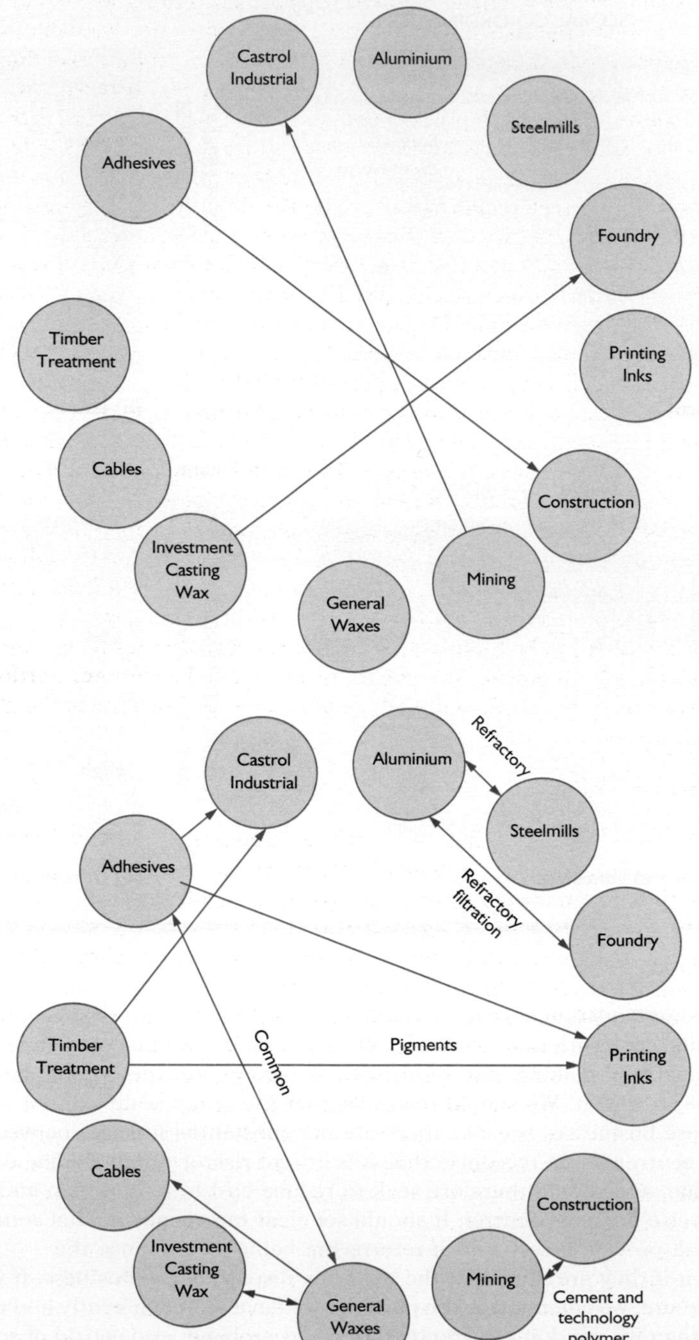

There was a second view:

> Burmah Castrol has chosen to set up a chemicals business and has acquired or developed business units in chemicals over two decades. I think we should start by asking what Burmah Castrol wants of these businesses, not just what these businesses happen to be doing now. The fact is that a main aspiration of Burmah Castrol is to become a much more global organisation than currently; in particular, to grow in the developing economies of the East. We should therefore be aiming to create a chemicals business which is much more global than it is now. I do not necessarily mean we should be in all parts of the world, but at least multidomestic with a very real presence in the Far East. We already have some businesses that do this, but we do not have a co-ordinated strategy to achieve it.
>
> The role of the centre should be to develop a global strategy for chemicals. First, we should identify which businesses are, or can be, more global. They are the businesses in which we should invest, and the centre should take a proactive line in developing them. If businesses cannot be developed in this way, then we should review whether they should be part of the portfolio.
>
> Secondly, we cannot leave it to the individual businesses to develop global strategies in a haphazard way. The centre has to be much more proactive in the strategic development of these businesses. The centre should be identifying the market opportunities, the product requirements and the market entry strategies.
>
> The centre also has a role to play in implementing this strategy. Suppose we see China as a major opportunity – and we do. We should have a co-ordinated, planned entry into China across the group. If we do not, we will have any number of businesses entering markets in all sorts of different ways.
>
> If we truly intend to be a global firm, then the centre has a role in planning it and developing it. Of course, this might mean we need a slimmer portfolio than we have currently; but then not all of our businesses might meet the global criteria that we set.

A third view was as follows:

> I agree that, unless we believe that the centre can add something to enhance the value of the business, then we should simply try to cut the costs at the centre and reduce the burden on the businesses. The question is: just what can and should we be doing? The interesting conclusion the workshop report comes to is the businesses themselves think they need help. They may not always think we do it that well; but they do think they need help.
>
> One of our problems is the very title of Chemicals Group. We are not a chemicals business in the sense ICI is. We don't make profits out of selling chemicals. We make profits out of mixing and blending basic materials in ways which are useful to customers. We are particularly successful where those formulated products account for a low percentage of cost to customers, but are really important to them. Many of our products may not cost much; but if they go wrong or fail in their purpose, the risk is high. If you are filling a crack in a dam, the actual cost is low, but the risk is enormous if it goes wrong. If we get that right, then we can sell at premium prices.
>
> There is another way we are different from basic chemicals. We make our money out of knowing our customers well enough to spot the sorts of opportunities that solve their problems and make us money. It's knowing our customers intimately that matters; not being good as chemists. It tends to point us to niche markets; sometimes quite small niche markets. It is not technologies

> as such, but application skills which give us real advantages. It isn't a question of market or technology linkages; it's about know-how, teamwork and applying that to the benefit of customers by knowing their businesses intimately.
>
> We should also recognise that we are most successful at managing certain sorts of businesses. They are businesses which have relatively low capital intensity; they are not based on rocket science, and they are where service requirements are high, so people matter.
>
> What we should be doing is focusing on such businesses; businesses where marketing expertise can be leveraged and where we can add value to customers' processes. In particular, businesses where the cost of our products to the customer is low, but where there is high potential risk for the customers.
>
> Virtually all of our businesses are like this or ought to be. I suppose Steelmills and Aluminium are more dependent on basic technology; and Cables relies heavily on type approvals and large global buyers. I am not sure we really capitalise on all this in the Aluminium and Construction and Waxes businesses, but I think we ought to be able to. Of course, Fosbel is different. The role of the centre is therefore to build a portfolio of the sort of business in which we can add value in these ways and make sure they learn from one another.

Mike Dearden summed up the discussions:

> I did not expect us to reach clear and absolute conclusions today. We started off the workshops some months ago with ideas of the questions we needed to ask. I think we have added a lot of information and discussion about those questions. What we need to do between now and at the next meeting is think about this, pull our thoughts together and start moving to some decisions. I think the questions we posed at the beginning of the workshops should form the agenda for the next meeting. What is the fit of businesses within the group; do they all fit equally well? Whatever the fit, is the current structure within the group sensible? And just how should we manage all this from the centre? I think we have thought a good deal about all this over the last day or so, but we need to move forward to some decisions.

APPENDIX 1 CHEMICALS GROUP DIVISIONS AND SBUs IN 1996

Metallurgical Division – Foseco

Foseco Metallurgical is the leading supplier of metallurgical chemicals to the world's metals industries, serving the vehicle manufacturing, construction, engineering and aerospace sectors. A truly international company, with operations in some 34 countries, Foseco has a particularly strong position in the important markets of Germany, Japan, the USA and the UK.

Foundry

The Foundry business unit comprises sales to ferrous and non-ferrous foundries. Ferrous foundry products include a complete range of feeding systems, fluxes, filters, molten metal transfer materials, binders and coatings that offer significant benefits in the production of high-quality castings.

The non-ferrous business supplies filters, direct pouring units, degassing systems and granulated fluxes. Ceramic foam filters and direct pour filtration systems raise yield and productivity, and remove inclusions through purpose-built engineering equipment, such as the degassing systems.

Foseco understands the requirements of Foundries and is committed to proactive research and development to further increase customers' productivity and competitiveness.

Steelmills

Foseco products allow steelmills to produce steels capable of meeting the most demanding specifications, quickly and cost effectively. Foseco supplies tundish lining systems, where a tundish can be lined in around one hour using either Tuncast (a spray system) or Garnex (insulating refractory boards).

As well as tundish lining systems, Foseco also offers an extensive range of products for the tundish area, including black refractories (ladle shrouds, stopper rods, submerged entry shrouds and nozzles), pre-cast and castable refractories, and continuous casting mould fluxes. Foseco offers extensive technical advice and support, including on-site assistance.

Foseco's strategy is to focus resources globally on the tundish and near tundish area in the key market segments of slab and bloom continuous casting.

Aluminium

Foseco products and services are used in the production of light metals and their alloys, principally aluminium.

Products offered include degassing equipment, special ceramic and refractory materials, filters and filtration systems, grain refiners, modifying and alloy additions, and refractory coatings.

The products represent a comprehensive range for the cast house and are supported by a proactive technical service.

Foseco is in the process of separating the Aluminium and Steelmills businesses from the Foundry business to form distinct global business units.

Fosbel

Ceramic Welding

Fosbel provides customers in the glass, coke and iron/steel industries with a specialised furnace lining repair service, based on advanced ceramic welding technology.

Construction and Mining Division – Fosroc

Mining

Fosroc's products to the mining industry include resin and cement-based anchors, which ensure reliable roof anchoring and side wall strata control; and high-yield grouts for roof supports and tunnel stoppings.

Fosroc's chemical-based products and services for strata control are recognised as being leaders in the international mining field. Customers are served across five continents, ranging from global conglomerates and state-owned organisations to small public and private companies.

The Fosroc name is established in each of the world's mining markets, most notably in the UK, the USA, Australia, India, South Africa and eastern Europe.

Construction

Fosroc is a leading world supplier of construction chemicals, focusing on the civil engineering and repair and protection sectors. It has close working relationships with international contractors, specifiers and operators, with a strong emphasis on after-sales service.

For the civil engineering sector, Fosroc provides concrete admixtures, surface treatments, precision grouts, chemical anchors, sealants and ancillary products. Products are used extensively in brick and concrete structures, including reservoirs, dams and tunnels, as well as commercial and residential developments.

In concrete repair and protection, Fosroc has built an international reputation for protecting new concrete and extending the life of old structures. It provides a wide variety of repair mortars, fluid micro-concretes and modified liquid polymers, together with protective coatings and sealants.

Fosroc recently acquired Norwegian Concrete Technologies (NCT), an Oslo-based company offering electrochemical methods for concrete repair.

Printing Inks Division – Sericol

Speciality

Sericol is the world leader in screen printing inks, a specialised niche in the printing industry. To retain its market focus on screen printing applications, Sericol does not supply printing inks for other printing processes, such as gravure and lithography.

Sericol's major market sectors are graphic printing (traditional posters and point-of-sale displays), textiles (leisure and sports wear) and packaging (labelling, bottle printing and box cartons).

The major markets are the graphic and textile markets, where customers are generally independent screen printers. Speciality markets have been earmarked for strategic growth, principally by acquisition. Speciality customers are those where screen printing is part of the process (e.g. compact discs and rub removable applications).

Sericol has operations in the UK, the USA, France, Germany, Hong Kong, Spain, Switzerland and India. Sericol products are supplied worldwide to over 80 countries through a network of distributors and licensees.

Graphics/Textiles

Sericol is the world leader in screen printing inks and chemicals. Sericol's major markets are in graphics and textile printing, with its market position in graphics being particularly strong.

Graphic printing includes traditional posters and point-of-sale displays. Textile printing covers leisure and sports wear, but excludes the commodity reel-to-reel textile market for printing curtain materials, furnishings, etc.

Sericol supplies water-based, solvent-based and ultraviolet (UV) curable inks. Both water-based and UV curable inks have substantial environmental benefits.

Strong service support is a particular feature of Sericol's marketing approach. Its customer service centre networks provide rapid delivery, backed by technical support and colour-matching service. Sericol also has an International Training Facility for customers, distributors, licensees and staff.

Coatings Division

Timber Treatment

Protim Solignum (PS) is a leading UK supplier of wood treatment chemicals, with companies in the UK, Eire, New Zealand and Australia. A range of decorative stains is also supplied under the Solignum brand.

PS supplies mainly solvent-based wood preservatives, where it has a dominant market share. However, the worldwide wood preservative market is predominantly water-based, in which PS has a minor market position. Environmental pressures are being placed on the use of solvent-based preservatives. Decorative stains are supplied principally to timber and builders merchants, so avoiding direct competition in the retail 'shed' with Cuprinol, Saddolins and Sikkens.

Investment Casting Wax

Dussek Campbell-Yates supplies investment casting wax from operations in the USA and the UK. Recently, the two businesses were restructured into a single entity managed from the USA, with a European manager based in the UK.

Investment casting wax is supplied to the aerospace/defence and commercial markets for the precision engineering of high-performance alloys.

General Waxes

Dussek Campbell supplies waxes for a wide range of applications, including packaging, construction, rubber tyres, candles, pharmaceuticals and cosmetics, histology, paint and ink additives, PVC lubricants, additives for plastic processing, anti-corrosives, cheese coatings and adhesives.

The largest market for wax application is in paper and board lamination. In construction, wax emulsions are used in board sizing. Candles are a substantial market, with the more specialised segments being craft and pressed candles. In packaging, Dussek Campbell has developed water-based barrier coatings, with the environmental bonus of being recyclable.

Following the acquisition of the UK-based Kerax company in 1993, Dussek Campbell's European wax business and Kerax were integrated into a single European wax business. In North America, waxes are supplied by National Wax.

Cables

Dussek Campbell is the world leader in the supply of cable compounds and application machinery. It supplies two market segments in the cable industry – power cables and telephone cable compounds, with the latter further divided into copper and fibre optic cable compounds.

In the power cable market, Dussek Campbell has a long-established presence in the supply of resin-based insulants. It markets a range of void-filling gels for copper and fibre optic telephone cables, backed by a comprehensive engineering service, which designs and installs the equipment with which the products are applied.

In 1995 cable compounds were organised into a global business unit within the Coatings division.

Adhesives division

The Adhesives division comprises two companies, Columbia Cement in the USA and Industrial Adhesives Limited (IAL) in the UK.

Columbia Cement is the leading supplier of contact adhesives for decorative laminates in the USA. The product range is primarily solvent-based, although water-based adhesives have been developed to meet the technical demands of the high-pressure decorative laminate market and the environmental regulations in the USA.

IAL is the leading UK supplier of pressure-sensitive adhesives. The company offers a wide range of adhesive technologies, including solvent-based, water-based, hot melt and reactives. Markets served include converting, which covers packaging and pressure sensitives, and industrial. The industrial markets include construction, insulation, fire protection and laminating.

IAL exports to Europe, the Middle East and Asia, principally with pressure-sensitive adhesives and insulation products.

APPENDIX 2 SUMMARY OF THE REPORT ON STRATEGY WORKSHOPS TO THE CHEMICALS GROUP EXECUTIVE

As a means of considering:

1. The fit of the different SBUs within the Chemicals Group.
2. The role of the parent (or centre) in managing the businesses.

Each SBU in the group undertook the following exercise:

- A consideration of its competitive strategy and the competences underpinning that strategy.
- The parenting skills required of the centre by the business units.

Competitive Strategies

All the SBUs saw the need to develop competitive strategies on the basis of differentiation or focused differentiation. Whilst there was an acknowledgement of the need to reduce costs or keep costs low, it was recognised that this was not a basis for achieving competitive advantage.

Competences

Exhibit A summarises the competences identified by each SBU (together with competences they identified as likely to be needed to pursue the strategies they wished to follow). There is a considerable degree of commonality of competences between the businesses which can, in generic terms, be summarised as:

> Close customer relationships, intimate understanding of customers' processes, ability to 'package' the businesses' product/service in innovative ways on the basis of customer need, focus on particular types of businesses, ability to work internationally and teamwork between business functions based on the delivery of customer need.

There were, however, some qualifications to this: in particular, the Adhesives division recognised that a difficulty they face is that they buy in processed materials, whereas their competitors are raw material processors with adhesives as a by-product.

Parenting Skills

Exhibit B summarises the parenting opportunities/skills identified by the SBUs. In aggregate, these are summarised in Exhibit C, which also shows how required parenting skills differ from that which the SBUs currently perceive being provided by the group.

The most important parenting skills, as seen by the businesses, are to do with the development of people required for strategy development, the facilitation of international development, group intervention to sort out problems, and the questioning and challenging of SBU strategy through 'coaching' and shared learning.

Questions raised

There are questions which arise from the workshops which the executive might consider.

- Managing international businesses is seen as a key parenting characteristic. However, SBUs vary in the degree to which they are, or have the potential to be, internationalised. Should the SBU potential and quality, over the next ten years, for international growth – and the likely ease of implementation – be determined and taken as a measure of fit within the Chemicals Group?
- Traditionally, SBUs have been grouped principally by technology linkage. Recently, the divisions have created distinct SBUs to improve market focus. However, few major market linkages seem to exist between SBUs. What are the linkages – if any – between SBUs?
- Should SBUs be separately managed by the group, without the divisional layer, and with technology linkages facilitated by some other means?
- Should SBUs be grouped by market linkage, rather than technology linkage, whenever appropriate, e.g. Investment Casting Wax and Foundry?
- Should SBUs with similar multinational styles, particularly global businesses, be grouped together due to common parenting skills being required to manage those businesses?
- SBUs consider the parent (or centre) to be anything above SBU level. There is duplication at the divisional, Chemicals Group and overall Burmah Castrol centres in providing parenting skills, e.g. financial and strategic planning. Where should the central (or parental) services be located – at divisional, group or SBU level?
- Certain key parenting skills are not provided sufficiently well to the SBUs, particularly skills to internationalise SBUs in emerging markets. How can key parenting skills, particularly internationalisation skills, be better provided to the SBUs?

Exhibit A SBU perceived competences

SBU	Perceived competences	Perceived missing competences
Foundry	● Customer relationships – understanding customers' processes and costs	● Professional marketing ● Manufacturing/engineering – lowest-cost producer experience ● Purchasing – international leverage/partnership ● Internal communications/teamwork ● Product costing systems
Construction	● Customer responsiveness – but not good in UK, Australia	● Operational effectiveness ● Supply chain management ● Creative/innovative approach
Printing Inks	*Graphics/Textiles* ● Reputation/relationships – customers/suppliers ● Application skills ● Supply chain management	● Digital printing expertise ● Environmental solutions
	Speciality ● Package of services ● International skills ● R&D expertise/innovation ● Market focus	● Brand/name ● Industry alliances – with machinery manufacturers ● Independent assessments – of product performance
Steelmills	● Customer relationships – knowledge of customer needs/processes ● Full system application engineering ● Team culture – local/global ● Strategic global marketing	● Strategic marketing and teamwork introduced by Burmah Castrol to overcome missing competences
General Waxes	● Purchasing relationships ● Customer relationships ● Blending, formulating, engineering skills ● Innovative development	● Attitude to quality

Exhibit A (continued)

SBU	Perceived competences	Perceived missing competences
Adhesives	● Supplier relationship ● Customer relationship – marketing assistance partnership ● Market focus ● Supply chain management	● Geographic spread – increasing internationalisation of customer base ● Being basic in raw materials ● Synergy between IAL and Columbia Cement ● Lack of critical mass
Aluminium	● Customer knowledge/relationships Ceramic/metallurgy/engineering know-how ● International organisation plus local presence ● Guro culture	● Management/team culture ● Marketing skills ● Customer-driven R&D
Mining	● Technical leadership ● Material-linked technology – backfill, anchoring, coatings ● Complete system engineering – with a focus on strata control ● Personal customer relationships	● Supply chain management ● Geographic covering in emerging markets – India, China, Indonesia, Vietnam, Russia
Timber Treatment	● Collective industry experience ● Reputation ● Quality of advice/support (consultancy) ● Engineering/environmental service	
Cables	● Complete product/service package – including bespoke service ● International business ● Image/reputation ● Attitude – 'can do, will do'	● Product innovation
Investment Casting Waxes	● Global international network – through BC/Foseco Foundry ● Executive experience – dependence on a few individuals ● Innovative capability	● International market development resources ● Lack of critical mass ● Lack of central product development

Exhibit B Comments on parenting opportunities/skills by SBUs

These are comments made by SBUs about required parenting opportunities and skills, from the parent.

Intervention
Timber Treatment. Assistance required in acquisition for internationalisation.
Adhesives. The adhesive business in its key sectors does not have critical mass or sufficient multinational presence to meet future key objectives. Acquisitions are an important area for intervention.
Construction. Need assistance with acquisitions to support strategic objectives. Group needs greater turnaround skills.

Coaching
Foundry. General transfer of knowledge, both technical and marketing.
Aluminium. Marketing practice, brand management, best practice transfer. More best practice/benchmarking identification and transfer is needed.
Construction. Transfer of knowledge is possibly where group can add greatest value.
General Waxes. Transferring knowledge is not effective, but centre dictatorial in coaching approach.
Adhesives. The SBU requires some intellectual 'beefing up' – no change since takeover. The main players are industry specialists rather than general managers with associated problems of succession and envisaging a move from a small to large business culture.

Specialist expertise
Timber Treatment. Legal requirements are often urgent, but due to SBU size, we do not always get acceptable response from the corporate legal department.
Aluminium. Legal services should be bought in as needed; present set-up cannot provide an effective service across the businesses. An IT strategy is also needed.

Developing linkages
Cables. Transferring best practice, i.e. supply/purchasing information.
General Waxes. There is a lack of focus on integrating the international units. To ensure complete flow of information, this has to be addressed within the centre and the units in a co-ordinated way. The centre is not structured to transfer experience.

Brokering relationships **(outside portfolio)**
Timber Treatment. No specific mechanisms exist (for encouraging alliances/facilitating networks) other than the Chemicals Industry Association.
Adhesives. As the SBU has no (significant) multinational position, assistance in alliances, networks, joint venturing is crucial.

Sharing experiences/resources
Aluminium. Financial management/administrating sharing. Resource sharing to develop economies. More sharing of basic business services and functions.

Exhibit B (continued)

Leveraging

Foundry. Marketing power in the automotive industry with Castrol Industrial.
Adhesives. The centre makes very little use of its corporate clout in areas of purchasing, best business practice, marketing skills.

People

Aluminium. Setting standards, training, appraisal, rewards, organisation development.
Construction. A key potential area to add value, with added benefit of spreading BC culture.
General Waxes. Essential to provide people with career path and training of people. Even short-term 'Expert' transfer of value.
Mining. Culture is the greatest asset. Invested in relatively few people, therefore needs protection.
Steelmills. Clearly, divisional interchange is good for all staff. A better understanding of each other's business is key. This will create opportunities for everybody. Cross-divisional management succession is crucial to the strength of Chemicals in the future.

Strategic planning

Construction. Need a Burmah Castrol process for strategic planning. A joint exercise would be valuable. Burmah Castrol need to share strategy more openly.
Aluminium. Provide more leadership. Train/coach to improve quality of strategy.
Foundry. Clear strategic objectives/definition.
Steelmills. A clear SBU strategy needs to be defined and discussed with the parent. This is key now and differs from financial targets. Unaware of Chemicals strategy and hence how SBU fits into the overall plan.
General Waxes. Facilitating corporate strategy to allow SBUs to 'dovetail' into it.
Adhesives. There is a lack of clear corporate strategy.

Internationalisation

Timber Treatment. Support level is limited.
Printing Inks. Assisting geographic expansion and future international structuring.
Aluminium. Pooling group resources to develop economies and reduce cost/risk, particularly in emerging markets such as China, eastern Europe, etc.
Cables. New start-ups may require looking after by local group company. Important to use overseas offices when and where required.
General Waxes. Co-ordination around the world is vital to take advantage of the wealth of knowledge.
Adhesives. Chemicals Group needs to take a view on decentralisation versus corporate. Setting up of corporate facilities (as opposed to SBU facilities) in strategic markets would be a start.
Mining. Assistance required in Russia, China and South America.
Steelmills. We are a small voice that may gain strength from cross-divisional support, i.e. Chemicals China. The use of corporate offices may allow us to grow into areas that each SBU cannot afford.

Exhibit C SBU provision rating of parenting skills: summary table

RANKING OF RATING IMPORTANCE BY SBUs	PARENTING SKILL		RATING OF CURRENT PARENTING SKILLS OF PARENT*
1	People	Seen as particularly important	−1
2	Internationalisation		−3
3	Strategic planning		−1
4	Intervention		+1
5	Financial		+2
6	Coaching		A
7	Sharing		+1
8	Brokering		A
9	Specialist expertise		+1
10	Leveraging		+1
11	Linkages		+1
12	External relations		+3

* This rating indicates SBU perceptions of how valuable the centre has been to SBUs in terms of specific parenting skills. The ratings indicate:

+3	Much more than needed
+2, +1	More than needed
A	Appropriate
−1, −2	Less than needed
−3	Much less than needed

GLOSSARY

acceptability is concerned with the expected performance outcomes, such as risk or return, if a strategy is implemented *(p. 370)*

acquisition is where an organisation develops its resources and competences by taking over another organisation *(p. 337)*

balanced scorecards combine both qualitative and quantitative measures, acknowledge the expectations of different stakeholders and relate an assessment of performance to choice of strategy *(p. 468)*

benchmarking seeks to assess the competences of an organisation against 'best in class' wherever that is to be found *(p. 181)*

business process re-engineering (BPR) is the process of reconfiguring activities to create a dramatic improvement in performance *(p. 449)*

a **business profile analysis** shows the extent to which a strategy matches the favourable performance parameters from PIMS analyses *(p. 362)*

business unit strategy is about how to compete successfully in a particular market *(p. 12)*

the **change agent** is the individual or group that effects strategic change in an organisation *(p. 530)*

coercion is the imposition of change or the issuing of edicts about change *(p. 512)*

collaboration or participation in the change process is the involvement of those who will be affected by strategic change in the identification of strategic issues, the setting of the strategic agenda, the strategic decision making process of the planning of strategic change *(p. 512)*

a **command view** is where strategy develops through the direction of an individual or group *(p. 54)*

competitive strategy is the basis on which a SBU might achieve competitive advantage in its market *(p. 270)*

consolidation is concerned with protecting and strenghtening the organisation's position in its current markets through its current products *(p. 312)*

control by market mechanisms involves some formalised system of bidding or 'contracting' for resources *(p. 471)*

core competences are those competences which critically underpin the organisation's competitive advantage *(p. 160)*

corporate parenting is the search for a fit between the skills of the corporate centre and the strategies of SBUs so as to add value to those SBUs *(p. 290)*

corporate social responsibility are the issues on which an organisation exceeds its minimum required obligations to stakeholders *(p. 230)*

corporate strategy is concerned with the overall purpose and scope of the organisation to meet the expectations of owners or major stakeholders and add value to the different parts of the enterprise *(p. 11)*

cost efficiency is a measure of the level of resources needed to create a given level of value *(p. 165)*

critical success factors (CSFs) are those components of strategy where the organisation must excel to outperform competition *(pp. 192, 458)*

cultural view: strategies are the outcome of the taken-for-granted assumptions and routines of organisations *(p. 58)*

the **cultural web** is a representation of the taken-for-granted assumptions, or paradigm, of an organisation and the physical manifestations of the organisation culture *(pp. 73, 231)*

a **decision tree** ranks options by progressively eliminating others *(p. 367)*

devolution is the extent to which the centre of an organisation delegates decision making to units and managers lower down in the hierarchy *(p. 423)*

a **differentiation strategy** seeks to provide products or services unique or different from those of competitors in terms of dimensions widely valued by buyers *(p. 276)*

direct supervision is the direct control of resource allocation by one or more individuals *(p. 467)*

direction involves the use of personal managerial authority to establish a clear future strategy and how change will occur *(p. 512)*

the **directional policy matrix** positions SBUs according to (a) how attractive the relevant market is in which they are operating, and (b) the competitive strength of the SBU in that market *(p. 135)*

diversification involves directions of development which take the organisation away from its present markets and its present products at the same time *(p. 323)*

the **'do nothing' situation** represents the likely outcome if the organisation were to continue with current strategies, disregarding any changes occurring in the environment or the resource position of the organisation *(p. 365)*

an **education and communication** change style involves the explanation of the reasons for and means of strategic change *(p. 510)*

effectiveness is a measure of the level of value which can be created from a given level of resources *(p. 169)*

an **enforced choice** is the imposition of strategy by agencies or forces external to the organisation *(p. 66)*

environmental drivers of change are forces likely to affect the structure of an industry or market *(p. 104)*

environmental uncertainty increases the more that environmental conditions are dynamic or the more they are complex *(p. 100)*

the **ethical stance** is the extent to which an organisation will exceed its minimum obligations to stakeholders *(p. 225)*

feasibility is concerned with whether an organisation has the resources and competences to deliver a strategy *(p. 383)*

in **financial control** the role of the centre is confined to allocating capital (against bids), setting financial targets, appraising performance and intervening to avert or correct poor performance *(p. 427)*

five forces analysis is a means of identifying the forces which affect the level of competition in an industry *(p. 115)*

a **focused differentiation** strategy seeks to provide high perceived value justifying a substantial price premium usually to a selected market segment *(p. 282)*

a **forcefield analysis** identifies forces for and against change *(p. 505)*

a **functional structure** is based on the primary activities that have to be carried out, such as production, finance and accounting, marketing and personnel *(p. 403)*

the **governance framework** determines whom the organisation is there to serve and how the purposes and priorities of the organisation should be decided *(p. 203)*

historical analysis looks at the deployment of the resources and performance measures of an organisation by comparison with previous years in order to identify any significant changes *(p. 179)*

a **holding company** is an investment company consisting of shareholdings in a variety of separate business operations, over which the corporate centre exercises simple control *(p. 408)*

a **hybrid strategy** seeks simultaneously to achieve differentiation and a price lower than that of competitors *(p. 281)* an **industry norm analysis** compares the relative performance of organisations in the same industry (or public service) against an agreed set of performance indicators *(p. 181)*

an **industry recipe** is a set of assumptions held in common within an industry or public service about organisational purposes and a 'shared wisdom' on how to manage organisations *(p. 235)*

intended strategy is an expression of desired strategic direction deliberately formulated or planned by managers *(p. 49)*

internal development is where strategies are developed by building up the organisation's own resource base and competences *(p. 336)*

intervention is the co-ordination of and authority over processes of change by a change agent who delegates elements of the change process *(p. 512)*

a **joint development** is where two or more organisations share resources and activities to pursue a strategy *(p. 340)*

key rigidities are activities which are deeply embedded and difficult to change *(p. 174)*

a **learning organisation** is capable of benefitting from the variety of knowledge, experience and skills of individuals through a culture which encourages mutual questioning and challenge around a shared purpose or vision *(pp. 83, 498)*

leverage is a measure of the improvement in performance achieved through the management of linkages between separate resources and activities *(p. 171)*

a **life cycle analysis** assesses whether a strategy is likely to be appropriate given the stage of the product life cycle *(p. 356)*

logical incrementalism is the deliberate development of strategy by 'learning through doing' *(p. 55)*

a **low price strategy**, seeks to achieve a lower price than competitors whilst trying to maintain similar value of product or service to that offered by competitors *(p. 271)*

market segmentation analysis seeks to identify similarities and differences between groups of customers or users *(p. 129)*

a **matrix structure** is a combination of structures which often takes the form of product and geographical divisions or functional and divisional structures operating in tandem *(p. 409)*

the **mission statement** is a generalised statement of the overriding purpose of the organisation *(pp. 241, 264)*

a **multidivisional structure** is subdivided into units (divisions) on the basis of products, services, geographical areas or the processes of the enterprise *(p. 404)*

networks are arrangements whereby two or more organisations work in collaboration without formal relationships *(p. 341)*

a **'no frills' strategy** combines a low price, low perceived added value and a focus on a price-sensitive market segment *(p. 271)*

operational strategies are concerned with how the component parts of the organisation in terms of resources, processes, people and their skills effectively deliver the corporate- and business-level strategic direction *(p. 13)*

a **paradigm** is the set of assumptions held relatively in common and taken for granted in an organisation *(p. 59)*

PEST analysis involves identifying the political, economic, social and technological influences on an organisation *(p. 104)*

a **political view** is that strategies develop as the outcome of processes of bargaining and negotiation among powerful internal or external interest groups (or stakeholders) *(p. 61)*

Porter's diamond suggests that there are inherent reasons why some nations are more competitive than others, and why some industries within nations are more competitive than others *(p. 108)*

portfolio analysis analyses the balance of an organisation's strategic business units *(pp. 186, 362)*

power is the extent to which individuals or groups are able to persuade, induce or coerce others into following certain courses of action *(p. 221)*

primary activities are *directly* concerned with the creation or delivery of a product service *(p. 157)*

punctuated equilibrium is the tendency of strategies to develop incrementally with periodic transformational change *(p. 46)*

ranking is a systematic way of analysing specific options for their suitability or fit with the factors arising from strategic analysis *(p. 367)*

realised strategy is the strategy actually being followed in practice *(p. 49)*

reinforcing cycles are created by the dynamic interaction between the various factors of environment, configuration and systems *(p. 480)*

related diversification is development beyond the present product and market, but still within the broad confines of the 'industry' *(p. 323)*

a **resource audit** identifies and classifies the resources that an organisation owns or can access to support its strategies *(p. 153)*

routines are the organisationally specific 'ways we do things around here' which tend to persist over time and guide people's behaviour *(p. 513)*

scenario planning builds plausible views of different possible futures for an organisation based on groupings of key environmental influences and drivers of change about which there is a high level of uncertainty *(p. 111)*

screening is the process of comparing the relative merits of different strategies *(p. 364)*

selective attention is the selection from total understanding the parts of knowledge which seem most relevant *(p. 140)*

self-control, resource allocation and control is exercised by the direct interaction of individuals without supervision *(p. 474)*

in a **simple structure** the organisation is run by the personal control of an individual *(p. 402)*

social controls are concerned with the standardisation of norms *(p. 471)*

stakeholder mapping identifies stakeholder expectations and power and helps in establishing political priorities *(p. 215)*

stakeholders are those individuals or groups who depend on the organisation to fulfil their own goals and on whom, in turn, the organisation depends *(p. 213)*

strategic analysis is concerned with understanding the strategic position of the organisation in terms of its external environment, internal resources and competences, and the expectations and influence of stakeholders *(p. 17)*

a **strategic business unit** (SBU) is a part of the organisation for which there is a distinct external market for goods and services *(p. 12)*

strategic choice involves understanding the underlying bases guiding future strategy, generating strategic options for evaluation and selecting from among them *(p. 20)*

strategic control is where the corporate centre is concerned with shaping the *behaviour* in departments and divisions and with shaping the *context* within which other managers are operating *(p. 430)*

strategic drift occurs when the organisation's strategy gradually moves away from relevance to the forces at work in its environment *(p. 79)*

strategic fit sees managers trying to develop strategy by identifying opportunities arising from an understanding of the environmental forces acting upon the organisation, and adapting resources so as to take advantage of these *(p. 23)*

strategic group analysis aims to identify organisations with similar strategic characteristics, following similar strategies or competing on similar bases *(p. 127)*

strategic intent is the desired future state or aspiration of the organisation *(pp. 243, 264)*

strategic management includes strategic analysis, strategic choice and strategy implementation *(p. 17)*

strategic planning is a sequence of analytical and evaluative procedures to formulate an intended strategy and the means of implementing it *(p. 51)* in a **strategic planning style** the centre of the organisation operates as a parent who is the *masterplanner* and prescribes detailed roles for divisions and departments *(p. 425)*

strategic scope is concerned with the boundaries that managers conceive for their organisation in terms of geography, product (or service) diversity or the way in which business is conducted *(p. 266)*

strategy is the direction and scope of an organisation over the long term: which achieves advantage for the organisation through its configuration of resources within a changing environment, to meet the needs of markets and to fulfil stakeholder expectations *(p. 10)*

strategy development by 'stretch' is the identification and leverage of the resources and competences of the organisation which yield new opportunities or provide competitive advantage *(p. 25)*

strategy implementation is concerned with the translation of strategy into organisational action through organisational structure and design, resource planning and the management of strategic change *(p. 22)*

suitability concerns whether a strategy addresses the circumstances in which the organisation is operating *(p. 355)*

support activities help to improve the effectiveness or efficiency of primary activities *(p. 158)*

a **SWOT analysis** summarises the key issues from an analysis of the business environment and the strategic capability of an organisation *(p. 190)*

symbols are objects, events, acts or people which express more than their intrinsic content *(p. 515)*

synergy can occur in situations where two or more activities or processes complement each other, to the extent that their combined effect is greater than the sum of the parts *(p. 331)*

transformational change in change which cannot be handled within the existing paradigm and organisational routines *(p. 497)*

transnational corporations combine the local responsiveness of the international subsidiary with the advantages available from co-ordination found in global product companies by creating an integrated *network* of interdependent resources and competences *(p. 420)*

there are three broad **types of control**: administrative control, through systems, rules and procedures; social control, through the impact of culture on the behaviour of individuals and groups; and self-control, which people exert over their own behaviour *(p. 463)*

unique resources are those which create competitive advantage and are difficult to imitate *(p. 155)*

unrelated diversification is where the organisation moves beyond the confines of its current industry *(p. 330)*

value chain analysis describes the activities within and around an organisation and relates them to an analysis of the competitive strength of the organisation *(pp. 156, 360)*

vertical integration describes either backward or forward integration into adjacent activities in the value chain *(p. 326)*

virtual organisations are held together not through formal structure and physical proximity of people, but by partnership, collaboration and networking *(p. 413)*

the **zone of uncomfortable debate** encompasses sensitive aspects of the organisation and managerial attitudes and beliefs which tend to be avoided in open discussion *(p. 508)*

INDEX OF COMPANIES AND ORGANISATIONS

GENERAL INDEX